CANADIAN POLITICAL PARTIES, 1867–1968

A Historical Bibliography

CANADIAN POLITICAL PARTIES 1867-1968

A HISTORICAL BIBLIOGRAPHY

COMPILED AND EDITED BY

GRACE F. HEGGIE

MACMILLAN OF CANADA

Canadian Cataloguing in Publication Data

Heggie, Grace F., 1933–
Canadian political parties

Includes index.
ISBN 0-7705-1341-7

1. Political parties—Canada—Bibliography.
2. Canada—Politics and government—1867—
Bibliography. * I. Title.
Z7165.C2H34   016.3299′71   C77-001119-5

DESIGN / RICHARD MILLER

COMPOSITION & TYPOGRAPHY / JULIUS TOTH

This book has been published with the
help of a grant from the Social Science Research
Council of Canada, using funds provided
by the Canada Council.

Printed in Canada for
The Macmillan Company of
Canada Limited

CONTENTS

PART I
THE FEDERAL POLITICAL PARTIES
OF CANADA

PART II

GOVERNMENT AND POLITICAL INSTITUTIONS

* *See* Note to the Reader *pg. xvi.*

This book
is dedicated
to
MY PARENTS
and to
W. W. PIEPENBURG

FOREWORD

ORTUNATELY THERE ARE AMONG US those whose imagination, curiosity, energy, or ambition refuse to be bounded by the conventional limits of a job. Grace Heggie found that even the callenging task of helping to build the history and geography collection of a major university library was not enough to keep her fully absorbed. Some years ago she walked into my office to talk about the possibility of preparing a bibliography on Canadian politics, largely as an adjunct to the teaching and research in the York University history department. My own enthusiasm for such a project was tempered by the realization that the task was formidable, particularly as a part-time, largely leisure-time, avocation. But her enthusiasm and determination were nourished, not diminished, by a realism on my part that she interpreted as scepticism, and ultimately led to a project that, while more tightly defined, was even more ambitious than her original idea because the bibliography was not to be a departmental resource but a truly academic and professional book.

While Ramsay Cook and I helped Grace formulate the general conception and broad structure of the bibliography, in every sense the book is hers and hers alone. It seems to me that Grace Heggie represents that ideal professional in a university library, where technical expertise is matched by a deep interest in the subject matter and where professor and librarian-bibliographer enjoy a symbolic relationship. Her bibliography will be an essential companion not only for academic researchers and the reference librarian, but for everyone interested in modern Canadian politics.

JOHN T. SAYWELL

PREFACE

THIS WORK is an annotated historical bibliography devoted to federal Canadian politics spanning the period from July 1867 to April 1968. The bibliography begins, therefore, with the years of Macdonald and concludes with the Pearson years.

There are approximately 8,850 items recorded. The bibliography includes books published to 1970; relevant articles in books of collected essays published to 1970; publications of Canadian historical and political societies published to 1970; theses accepted at Canadian, American, and British universities to 1970; and articles appearing in historical and political journals and in a selection of general periodicals and magazines published in Canada to the year 1969.

Periodicals were excluded, with some exceptions, that represent specific groups or interests, for example, publications of trade unions, church groups, professional associations, and farm organizations. Appendix B gives a listing of the 190 periodical titles examined. Further exclusions include newspapers, manuscript material, and political party publications, e.g., newsletters, handbooks, and propaganda literature. There is no systematic inclusion of government publications and pamphlet material.

Most of the material was examined at first hand. A systematic search was made of countless published bibliographies: reference sources consulted are listed in Appendix A. Locations for the material have not been supplied. The National Library of Canada will give location information to any person working through library facilities. Most of the items described in this bibliography were seen at the Metropolitan Toronto Central Library, the National Library of Canada in Ottawa, and the John P. Robarts Library at the University of Toronto. The inter-library loan facilities in the Scott Library at York University located items throughout Canada.

Material compiled for this work is identified and described according to the bibliographic standards set out in the *Anglo-American cataloging rules* published in 1967. Those using this bibliography as a reference source should be able to locate the material cited when checking the catalogues of libraries and other institutions.

Each item that appears in the bibliography is given full bibliographic description. The main author statement is recorded or supplied as accurately as possible. The title page is transcribed exactly; paging is given precisely and annotations, in the form of brief explanatory or background notes, are provided wherever there is a need to clarify the content or the nature of the item cited. Essays in books of collected works are retrieved and listed as separate entries. Articles in journals and periodicals are included with distinctive titles or with an author's signature or initials. Unsigned articles and brief editorial comments have, as a rule, been excluded. Detailed cataloguing has been used to accommodate precise detail and, at the same time, to give the bibliography a quality of readability.

The organization of the bibliography rests on a chronological/topical arrangement. The structure is designed to allow a natural flow and a candid reflection of the works contained in each section of the bibliography.

The book is divided into two parts. Part one is concerned with the central theme of the bibliography and follows the events and issues that constitute national political history. It is sub-divided into categories that follow a chronological sequence. This sequence provides for the inclusion of material both by date of publication and content, for example, material dealing with the Second World War period includes items written during that time, as well as those written at a later time, about that period. This method enhances the contemporary flavour of the categories and smooths out some of the rigidities that accompany categorization.

The organization is not without its problems, as some of the material defies categorization or is open to varied interpretations. Arbitrary decisions were often made for purposes of expediency. The breakdown for political parties is grounded on a pragmatic as well as on an ideological basis. The period divisions for any given political party represent its policies and its time in office or in opposition. This procedure is devised as an attempt to deal with countless problems; one particular difficulty is to accommodate those political figures with varied careers. These arbitrary arrangements, for example, assign Joseph Howe, a life-long Reformer and Liberal, to the Conservative party category because the material concerning him involves his post-Confederation activities as a minister in the Macdonald administration; Israel Tarte is to be found listed as a Conservative as he ran for parliament while a member of the Conservative party and as a Liberal when he served under Laurier; N. W. Rowell, a Liberal Unionist, is listed under the Conservative-party umbrella as a member of Sir Robert Borden's cabinet; Donald Gordon, a non-partisan, is located in Liberal party categories because he served actively and is identified closely with the government of Mackenzie King during the Second World War. When books and articles cover a career in its entirety and that career is varied, the work cited is usually located in the general political history sections or, in a section that seems to coincide with the time when the subject was most prominent, or served as a federal MP, or held a federal cabinet position. If a book or article deals with an aspect of a career, or was written about that person at any given time, the material is placed in the relevant category.

Part two is based on a topical arrangement. The works cited in this part of the bibliography gravitate towards constitutional history and political science. The inclusion of related material should contribute to an understanding of the political process as it has developed, often as a result of the decisions taken by particular administrations and through the legislation initiated or enacted by particular governments. Active politicians sometimes took time to reflect and analyse the political system and institutions through which they had to work. The written comments and opinions of politicians, as well as of academics, journalists, civil servants, and others, are to be found in this section of the bibliography.

The reference sources checked and consulted for the purpose of verifying the information contained in this bibliography are listed and described in Appendix A. Every title listed has been used for one reason or another: it was decided, in view of the fact that each item was seen, to provide full bibliographic treatment. This listing of reference sources is not a comprehensive bibliography of bibliographies in Canadian history, but it is a contribution toward such a work.

Appendix B is a compilation of all 190 periodicals examined for this work. The information identifies the periodical title, traces change of title, records the life-span of a publication, and indicates, wherever it seems necessary, the nature or policy of a particular periodical. Editors are often noted because of their political influence or association. It is hoped that the detailed listing of these periodicals provides a substantial contribution to a union list of Canadian serial publications.

It is hoped that this bibliography proves to be of service to scholars, students, teachers, librarians, booksellers, and the interested general reader. The aim of this work is to provide selective objective information of historical significance. It seeks to search out and identify sources to further historical research, while at the same time, presenting a contemporary record, through an organized presentation, of the political literature of post-Confederation Canada.

G.F.H.

York University, Toronto   June, 1977

ACKNOWLEDGEMENTS

IT IS, INDEED, a great pleasure to take the opportunity to express my warmest thanks and appreciation to those who contributed their support and assistance to the final realization of this nine-year endeavour.

Vida (Jurgulis) Mockus prepared the final bibliographic description for this work. She also did the original descriptive cataloguing for the periodicals listed in Appendix B. Mrs. Mockus was, for ten years, senior cataloguer in the Department of Rare Books and Special Collections of the University of Toronto Library. She is a librarian of noted reputation and I was most fortunate to enlist her as a friend and colleague for this project. Gail Kordyback worked, for three years, as general secretary and research assistant. She undertook the arduous task of reading the microfilm copy of *Maclean's* and *Saturday Night*. She deserves much credit for her endurance and her significant contribution to this work.

John Hardy assisted me for a brief period in the difficult task of searching and verifying bibliographical information. The indispensable author index was prepared, over the period of a year, with patience and thoroughness by Barbara Heggie. The challenging task of typing this manuscript was met, at various stages, by Jill Chess, who typed an early draft, by Nimo Aer, who performed the incredible feat of typing the entire manuscript in an extraordinarily short time, and by Giulia Pincente and Bonnie Monette, who typed the indexes with great accuracy and skill.

John Saywell, professor of history at York University, endorsed the idea of a bibliographic work, suggested its subject matter, and offered general consultation. He lent the moral and material support which made the project possible, and for this I am most grateful. Ramsay Cook assisted the work through his public support and personal interest. Thomas F. O'Connell, former Director of York University Libraries, and the administrative staff of the library allowed me to take the time that was necessary, and on generous terms, to bring this long work to a conclusion.

The Canada Council provided the funds that enabled me to maintain a staff for the project. I would like to acknowledge the efficient administration of my research grant and the cordial attitude on the part of the members of the Humanities and Social Science Division.

The grinding routine that accompanies an extended research project needs patience and kind assistance from those who staff libraries and other research institutions. For three years, I worked mainly in the Canadiana and Manuscripts Section (the Baldwin Room) of the Metropolitan Toronto Central Library, which is headed by Edith G. Firth. The Baldwin Room staff, especially, Christine Mosser, John Crosthwait, William Parker, Christopher Clapp, and Susan McGrath, graciously went far beyond their duty to enable me to use effectively the great Canadiana collection located there. They gave me encouragement, hospitality, and superb service. I should like to express my genuine gratitude to Edith Firth. I frequently benefited from her wisdom, and her professional advice, at a number of crucial points, had significant influence on the subsequent direction of my work. I should like, especially, to mention the valuable advice she gave me in the preparation of the subject index. In a very real sense, this book might have been dedicated to the staff of the Baldwin Room.

Members of the staffs of other research institutions were extremely helpful to me. At the National Library, where I worked in 1972, Jean Higginson, Francine Letellier, and Ruth Tolmie of the Periodicals Division, were most gracious and co-operative. They arranged for me to have complete access to the vast un-catalogued stack area of the library. I am also grateful to the staff of the University of Toronto Library and, in particular, the Department of Rare Books and Special Collections (now the Thomas Fisher Library) who were always helpful and accommodating. I used the library at Maclean-Hunter Limited and was made to feel most welcome by the librarian, Jean MacKay, during my brief stay there. I regularly exploited the services and good nature of the staff in the Scott Library at York University, especially the members of the Reference Department. I wish to thank my colleagues for all the small and large services they rendered to me.

Bernard Merrett, now of Southam Press Ltd., followed the progress of this project and decided to bring my work to the attention of the Macmillan Company of Canada. Mr. Patrick Meany of Macmillan encouraged me to finish the work with a view to publication. The manuscript, in due course, was accepted and Mr. Meany and his colleagues, Virgil Duff and Beverley Beetham, during the production of the book, made my first publishing venture a rewarding and agreeable experience.

The contributions of interested colleagues, close friends, and immediate members of my family were invaluable. I especially should like to acknowledge the understanding and supportive advice of Willard Piepenburg, professor of history at York University, and Olga Gill and Dorothy Templin. My family were, as they always are, my main encouragement and support. I particularly would like to recognize the efforts of my sister Barbara, my mother, who assisted with the author index, and my father, who organized the inventory of all the entries in this book.

Many people contributed to this work, but as its editor I assume full responsibility for any shortcomings it may have.

GRACE HEGGIE
1977

CANADIAN POLITICAL PARTIES, 1867–1968

A Historical Bibliography

NOTE TO THE READER

The Conservative Party of Canada
has held several official titles:
Liberal-Conservative Party, 1867–1917;
Unionist (Party) Government,
Oct. 12, 1917–July 10, 1920; National
Liberal and Conservative Party,
July 1920–Dec. 1921; Liberal-Conservative
Party, 1921–38; National Conservative
Party, July 1938–42 (called the National
Government Party during the 1940
election campaign); and Progressive
Conservative Party, Dec. 1942–.

Réal Caouette led Quebec members from
the Social Credit Party of Canada in 1963 to
form le Ralliement des Créditistes.

The Communist Party of Canada
held two other official titles: Workers' Party
of Canada, 1922–24 (its founding name);
and Labor Progressive Party, 1943–59.

THE FEDERAL POLITICAL PARTIES OF CANADA

COMPREHENSIVE HISTORIES AND GENERAL STUDIES

ADAIR, EDWARD ROBERT The Canadian contribution to historical science. By E. R. Adair. (In *Culture*. Québec. v. 4 (1943), pp. [63]-83.)

ALLEN, RALPH Ordeal by fire; Canada, 1910-1945. [1st ed.] Toronto, Doubleday, 1961. 492 p. [The Canadian history series, v. 5.]

Approaches to Canadian history. Essays by W. A. Mackintosh, A. R. M. Lower, F. H. Underhill, W. L. Morton, D. G. Creighton, J. M. S. Careless, M. Brunet. Introd. by Carl Berger. [Toronto] University of Toronto Press [1970, c1967] x, 98 p. (Canadian historical readings, 1.)

Partial contents: Two ways of life; the primary antithesis of Canadian history, by A. R. M. Lower. – Some reflections on the liberal tradition in Canada, by F. H. Underhill. – Sir John Macdonald and Canadian historians, by D. G. Creighton.

ARNOLD, A. J. Donald Creighton on Canadian history. (In *Viewpoints*. Montreal. v. 3, no. 3 (1968), pp. 3-12.)

AUBERT DE LA RUE, PHILIPPE Canada incertain; un pays à la recherche de son identité. Paris, Editions du Scorpion [1964] 217 p. (Collection Alternance.)

BAUDONCOURT, JACQUES DE Histoire populaire du Canada, d'après les documents français et américains. 2. éd. Paris, Bloud et Barral [1888] iv, 510 p.

Note: Chapter XIX.

BEAUDE, HENRI Nos historiens; cours de critique littéraire professé à Montréal sous les auspices de l'Action française. [Par] Henri d'Arles [pseud.] Montréal, Bibliothèque de l'Action française, 1921. 243 p.

BERGER, CARL CLINTON (ed.) Imperialism and nationalism, 1884-1914; a conflict in Canadian thought. Toronto, Copp Clark [c1969] 119 p. (Issues in Canadian history.)

A selection of readings.

BERGER, CARL CLINTON Race and liberty; the historical ideas of Sir John George Bourinot. By Carl Berger. (In Canadian Historical Association. *Report of the annual meeting*. [Ottawa] (1965), pp. [87]-104.)

—— The sense of power; studies in the ideas of Canadian imperialism 1867-1914. [Toronto] University of Toronto Press [c1970] 277 p.

"This book is a study in Canadian nationalist thought." – Introd. Chapter 8 deals with "Democracy and leadership".

"Notes on sources": pp. [266]-269. Provides a listing of primary source material and periodicals on late nineteenth and early twentieth century Canadian imperialist thought.

BERGERON, GERARD Le Canada-Français après deux siècles de patience. Paris, Editions du Seuil [1967] 280 p. (L'Histoire immédiate.)

BERTRAM, THOMAS The story of Confederation. (In *MacLean's magazine*. Toronto. v. 30, no. 9 (July 1917), pp. [19]-24; 106-111.)

BOISSONNAULT, CHARLES MARIE Genèse de la Confédération. (In *La Revue de l'Université Laval*. Québec. v. 2, no 3 (nov. 1947), pp. [184]-199.)

BONENFANT, JEAN CHARLES Cultural and political implications of French-Canadian nationalism. By Jean-C. Bonenfant and Jean-C. Falardeau. (In Canadian Historical Association. *Report of the annual meeting*. Toronto. (1946), pp. 56-73.)

BOURGEOIS, PHILEAS FREDERIC L'histoire du Canada depuis sa découverte jusqu'à nos jours. Montréal, Beauchemin, 1913. 236 p. (Bibliothèque canadienne. Collection Champlain.)

BOURINOT, SIR JOHN GEORGE Canada. New and rev ed., with additional chapter by William H. Ingram. [3d ed.] London, T. Fisher Unwin [1922] xx, 492 p. (*The Story of the nations*, no. 45.)
Chapter XXVIII by Edward Parritt; chapter XXX written by William H. Ingram.

—— Canada during the Victorian era: a historical review. Illustrated. By J. G. Bourinot. (In Royal Society of Canada. *Proceedings and transactions*. Ottawa. ser. 2, v. 3 (1897), section 2, pp. 3-38. illus., map.)
"Read June 23rd, 1897."

—— Canada under British rule, 1760-1900. Toronto, Copp Clark, 1901. xii, 346 p.

—— Canada under British rule, 1760-1905. Rev. with an additional section by G. M. Wrong. Cambridge, [Eng.] University Press, 1909. xi, 352 p. (Cambridge historical series, v. 19.)

—— The intellectual development of the Canadian people; an historical review. Toronto, Hunter Rose, 1881. xi, 128 p.
"This series of papers has been prepared in accordance with a plan . . . of taking up, from time to time, certain features of the social, political and industrial progress of the Dominion." – Prelim. note.

—— Our intellectual strength and weakness: a short review of literature, education and art in Canada. By J. G. Bourinot. (In Royal Society of Canada. *Proceedings and transactions*. Ottawa. [ser. 1] v. 11 (1893), section 2, pp. 3-54.)
"Read May 22nd, 1893."
"Bibliographical, art and general notes": pp. 37-54.

—— The story of Canada. New York, G. P. Putnam, 1896. xx, 463 p. (The Story of the nations.)

BOVEY, WILFRID Canadien, a study of the French Canadians. London, Dent [1933] xiv, 242 p.

—— Les Canadiens-Français d'aujourd'hui; l'essor d'un peuple. Traduit de l'anglais par Jean-Jacques Lefebvre. Montréal, Editions ACF [i.e. Action canadienne-française] 1940. 417 p. (Documents sociaux.)

—— The French Canadians today; a people on the march. Toronto, Dent. [1938] xii, 362 p.

BRACQ, JEAN CHARLEMAGNE L'évolution du Canada français. Paris, Plon [1927] 457 p.
Also published in English.

—— The evolution of French Canada. New York, Macmillan, 1924. viii, 467 p.
Also published in French.

BRADLEY, ARTHUR GRANVILLE Canada. London, Williams and Norgate [1912] 256 p. (Home university library of modern knowledge, no. 34.)

BRADY, ALEXANDER Canada. New York, C. Scribner, 1932. vii, 374 p. (The Modern world; a survey of historical forces.)
Contents: I. National and political life. – II. Economic developments. – III. Cultural life. – IV. Imperial and external relations.

BREBNER, JOHN BARTLET Canada; a modern history. By J. Bartlet Brebner. New ed., rev. and enl. by Donald C. Masters. Ann Arbor, University of Michigan Press [c1970] xvii, 570, xviii p. (The University of Michigan history of the modern world.)
First published 1960.

BROWN, GEORGE WILLIAMS (ed.) Canada. Chapters by Edgar McInnis . . . D. G. Creighton, C. P. Stacey . . . R. MacGregor Dawson, Hugh McD. Clokie . . . Frank H. Underhill, Alexander Brady [and others] Berkeley, University of California Press; Toronto, University of Toronto Press, 1953 [c1950] xviii, 621 p. (The United Nations series.)
Partial contents: The Dominion, by D. G. Creighton. – The twentieth century, by C. P. Stacey. – The federal constitution, by R. M. Dawson. – The machinery of government, by H. M. Clokie. – Political parties and ideas, by F. H. Underhill. – The state and economic life, by A. Brady.

—— Canada in the making. By George W. Brown. (In Canadian Historical Association. *Report of the annual meeting*. Toronto. (1944), pp. 5-15.)
Presidential address.

—— Canada in the making. Seattle, University of Washington Press [1953] 151 p.

—— Canadian democracy in action. [New ed.] Toronto, Dent [1952] 136 p.

First published 1945. Written, primarily, as a school text book.

BRUCHESI, JEAN Canada; réalités d'hier et d'aujourd'hui. Préf. de Etienne Gilson. [2. éd., rév.] Montréal, Beauchemin, 1957. 364 p.

First published: Montréal, Editions Variétés, 1948.

Partial contents: Chapitre 5. D'un océan à l'autre. L'union des deux Canadas; origine et nature de la Confédération; emancipation politique; Ottawa et les provinces.

—— Histoire du Canada. Nouv. éd. Montréal, Editions Beauchemin, 1959. 2 v. in 1.

—— Histoire du Canada pour tous. Montréal, A. Lévesque, 1933-35. 2 v. (Documents historiques.)

Contents: t. 1. Le régime français. – t. 2. Le régime anglais.

—— History and national life. (In Culture. Québec. v. 7 (1946), pp. [177]-194.)

—— A history of Canada. Translated from the French by R. W. W. Robertson. Toronto, Clarke, Irwin, 1950. xiii, 358 p.

Translation of Canada, réalités d'hier et d'aujourd'hui.

First published in French: Montréal, Editions Variétés, 1948. Based on a series of lectures given at the Sorbonne in the spring of 1948.

BRUNET, MICHEL Canadians et Canadiens; études sur l'histoire et la pensée des deux Canadas. 2. éd. Paris, Montréal, Fides [1960, c1954] 173 p. (Bibliothèque économique et sociale.)

—— French Canadian interpretations of Canadian history. (In The Canadian forum. Toronto. v. 44, no. 519 (Apr. 1964), pp. 5-7.)

"This article was originally a speech delivered at Thornhill Seconday [sic] School on February 12 under the auspices of the York Central District High School Board."

BRUNET, MICHEL (comp.) Histoire du Canada par les textes. Par Michel Brunet, Guy Frégault et Marcel Trudel. Ed. rev. et augm. Montréal, Fides [c1963] 2 v.

First ed., 1952, par M. Brunet, G. Frégault, et M. Trudel; Tome 2: 1855-1960, par M. Brunet.

Collection of historical documents.

BRUNET, MICHEL La présence anglaise et les Canadiens; études sur l'histoire et la pensée des deux Canadas. Montréal, Beauchemin, 1964 [i.e. 1968, c1958] 323 p.

—— Québec-Canada anglais; deux itinéraires, un affrontement. Montréal, Editions HMH, 1968. 309 p. (Collection Constantes, v. 12.)

BRYCE, GEORGE A short history of the Canadian people. New and rev. ed. Toronto, W. Briggs, 1914. xiii, 621 p.

First ed. published: London, S. Low, Marston, Searle & Rivington, 1887.

BRYCE, JAMES BRYCE, VISCOUNT Canada; an actual democracy. Toronto, Macmillan, 1921. 54 p.

BUCK, TIMOTHY Canadian history and Canadian independence. By Tim Buck. (In The Marxist quarterly. Toronto. no. 6 (summer 1963), pp. 73-83.)

BUMSTED, JOHN MICHAEL (ed.) Documentary problems in Canadian history. Edited by J. M. Bumsted. Georgetown, Ont., Irwin-Dorsey, 1969. 2 v.

A collection of readings based on thematic problems designed as a textbook aiding those who teach Canadian history at the university level. Cf. Pref.

Partial contents: v. 2. Post-Confederation.

BURT, ALFRED LE ROY A short history of Canada for Americans. By A. L. Burt. Minneapolis, University of Wisconsin Press [1942]. xvi, 309 p.

CADIEUX, MARCEL Le Dualisme canadien. Par Marcel Cadieux et Paul Tremblay. (In Revue trimestrielle canadienne. Montréal. v. 27 (mars 1941), pp. [63]-75.)

The Cambridge history of the British Empire. General editors: J. Holland Ross, A. P. Newton, E. A. Benians. Cambridge, Eng., The University Press, 1929–1936. 8 v.

Volume 6. Canada and Newfoundland: Advisor for the Dominion of Canada, W. P. M. Kennedy.

Canada and Newfoundland. Cambridge [Eng.] University Press, 1930. xxi, 939 p. (The Cambridge history of the British Empire, v. 6.)

"Advisor for the Dominion of Canada: W. P. M. Kennedy."

Bibliography: pp. [813]-885.

Canada, unité et diversité. Par Paul G. Cornell, Jean Hamelin, Fernand Ouellet, et Marcel Trudel. Avant-propos par Marcel Trudel. Montréal, Holt, Rinehart et Winston [c1968] 578 p.

Canada, unity in diversity. By Paul G. Cornell, Jean Hamelin, Fernand Ouellet, and Marcel Trudel. Introd. by William Kilbourn. Toronto, Holt, Rinehart and Winston [c1967] xiii, 529 p.

A general interpretative history covering the period from 1840 to 1960.

Partial contents: Section 3. The Dominion of Canada to 1931, by J. Hamelin and P. G. Cornell. – Section 4. Canada since 1931, by P. G. Cornell and F. Ouellet.

CARELESS, JAMES MAURICE STOCKFORD Canada; a story of challenge. Cambridge. [Eng.] University Press, 1953. 417 p. (British Commonwealth series, book 2.)

—— Canada; a story of challenge. [Rev. and enl. ed.] Toronto, Macmillan, 1965. xii, 444 p.

—— Canada; a story of challenge. By J. M. S. Careless. [3d ed.] Toronto, Macmillan [1970] xiii, 449 p. illus., maps.

First published 1953.

—— Canadian nationalism—immature or obsolete? By J. M. S. Careless. (In Canadian Historical Association. Report of the annual meeting. [Ottawa] (1954), pp. 12-19.)

CARELESS, JAMES MAURICE STOCKFORD (ed.) The Canadians, 1867-1967. Edited by J. M. S. Careless and R. Craig Brown. With a fine art section of monochrome and colour plates. Toronto, Macmillan, 1967. xix, 856 p.

Part one. "... eleven historians record the life of Canada decade by decade since the 1860s." – Introd.

Contents: the 1860s, by D. Creighton. – The 1870s, by G. F. G. Stanley. – The 1880s, by W. S. MacNutt. – The 1890s, by J. T. Saywell. – The new century, by H. B. Neatby. – Through the First World War, by R. Graham. – The 1920s, by W. L. Morton. – The 1930s, by K. McNaught. – Through the Second World War, by C. P. Stacey. – The 1950s, by W. Kilbourn. – The 1960s, by L. L. La-Pierre.

—— The Canadians, 1867-1967; part one. Edited by J. M. S. Careless and R. Craig Brown. Toronto, Macmillan [1970, c1968]. xii, 412 p.

"This volume is Part One of 'The Canadians, 1867-1967', first published in 1967." – Verso of title page.

CARELESS, JAMES MAURICE STOCKFORD Frontierism, metropolitanism and Canadian history. By J. M. S. Careless. (In The Canadian historical review. Toronto. v. 35 (1954), pp. 1-21.)

—— History and Canadian unity. By J. M. S. Careless. (In Culture. Québec. v. 12 (1951), pp. [117]-124.)

—— "Limited identities" in Canada. By J. M. S. Careless. (In The Canadian historical review. Toronto. v. 50 (1969), pp. 1-10.)

CHAPAIS, SIR THOMAS Discours et conférences. Québec, Garneau, 1897-1943. 4 v.

CLARK, SAMUEL DELBERT The frontier and democratic theory. By S. D. Clark. (In Royal Society of Canada. Proceedings and transactions. Ottawa. ser. 3, v. 48 (1954), section 2, pp. 65-75.)

Argues that "Canada shared in the revolutionary tradition of [the North American] continent". Questions "the assumption that an entirely different set of forces have shaped the development of democratic institutions in this country [i.e. Canada] than in the United States".

CLEMENT, WILLIAM HENRY POPE The history of the Dominion of Canada. By W. H. P. Clement. Toronto, Briggs, 1898. viii, 350 p.

COCKBURN, ALEXANDER PETER Political annals of Canada; a condensed record of governments from the time of Samuel de Champlain in 1608 down to the time of Earl Grey in 1905 ... Toronto, W. Briggs, 1905. 574 p.

Chapter 13: The Dominion of Canada.

CODY, HENRY JOHN The Canadian heritage. By the Rev. Canon H. J. Cody. (In Canadian Club of Toronto. Addresses. Toronto. (1925/26), pp. 90-103.)

Address delivered November 2, 1925.

COLBY, CHARLES WILLIAM The day after confederation. By C. W. Colby. (In The University magazine. Montréal. v. 14 (1915), pp. [446]-460.)

COOK, GEORGE RAMSAY Canada and the French-Canadian question. By Ramsay Cook. Toronto, Macmillan, 1966. 219 p.

—— French Canadian interpretations of Canadian history. By Ramsay Cook. (In Journal of Canadian studies. Peterborough, Ont. v. 2, no. 2 (1967), pp. 3-17.)

—— Le sphinx parle français; un Canadien-Anglais s'interroge sur le problème québécois. Par Ramsay Cook. Traduit par François Rinfret. [Montréal Editions]

HMH. 1968. 187 p. (Collection Aujourd'-hui.)

Translation of *Canada and the French-Canadian question*.

First published in English: Toronto, Macmillan, 1966.

COPP, TERRY The Whig interpretation of Canadian history. (In *Canadian dimension*. Winnipeg. v. 6, no. 1 (Apr./May 1969), pp. 23-24; 33.)

CORY, HARPER Modern Canada. London, Heinemann, 1930. xvi, 289 p.

COYNE, JAMES HENRY The sixty eventful years. By James H. Coyne. (In Royal Society of Canada. *Proceedings and transactions*. Ottawa. ser. 3, v. 21 (1927), pp. [xlv]-lxiii.)

Presidential address delivered on the occasion of the Diamond Jubilee of Canadian confederation.

CREIGHTON, DONALD GRANT Canada's first century, 1867-1967. By Donald Creighton. Toronto, Macmillan [c1970] 378 p.

"Books for further reading": pp. [373]-378.

—— Confederation; the use and abuse of history. By D. G. Creighton. (In *Journal of Canadian studies*. Peterborough, Ont. v. 1, no. 1 (1966), pp. 3-11.)

—— The course of Canadian democracy. By D. G. Creighton. (In *University of Toronto quarterly*. [Toronto] v. 11 (1941/42), pp. 255-268.)

—— The decline and fall of the empire of the St. Lawrence. By D. G. Creighton. (In Canadian Historical Association. *Historical papers*. [Ottawa] 1969, pp. [14]-25.)

—— The Dominion: genesis and integration. (In Brown, G. W. (ed.) *Canada*. Berkeley, 1953. pp. 99-123.)

—— Dominion of the North; a history of Canada. By Donald Creighton. Boston, Houghton Mifflin, 1944. 535 p.

—— Dominion of the North; a history of Canada. By Donald Creighton. New ed. Toronto, Macmillan, 1957. ix, 619 p.

Also published London, Macmillan, 1958 [c1957].

—— A history of Canada, Dominion of the North. Rev. and enl. ed. Boston, Houghton Mifflin, 1958. 619 p.

First ed. published in 1944 under title: *Dominion of the North*.

—— Presidential address [to the Canadian Historical Association ... annual meeting held at Ottawa, June 12-15, 1957] (In Canadian Historical Association. *Report of the annual meeting*. [Ottawa] 1957, pp. 1-12.)

". . . a brief retrospective review of historical writing about Canada, its chief problems and its main tendencies, during the past quarter-century." – p. 1.

—— The story of Canada. By Donald Creighton. Toronto, Macmillan; London, Faber and Faber, 1959. 291 p.

—— Towards the discovery of Canada. By Donald Creighton. (In *University of Toronto quarterly*. [Toronto] v. 25 (1955/56), pp. 269-282.)

Discusses Canadian writing in history and the social sciences.

DAFOE, JOHN WESLEY Canada, an American nation. By John W. Dafoe. New York, Columbia University Press, 1935. 134 p. (Columbia University lectures. Julius Beer Foundation, 1933/34.)

DAVID, LAURENT OLIVIER Histoire du Canada depuis la Confédération, 1867-1887. Montréal, Beauchemin [1909]. 256 p.

—— Mélanges historiques et littéraires. Par L. O. David. Montréal, Beauchemin, 1917. 338 p.

Consists of brief reflections.

DENT, JOHN CHARLES The last forty years; Canada since the union of 1841. Toronto, G. Virtue [1881]. 2 v.

DESROSIERS, ADELARD Histoire du Canada. Par Adélard Desrosiers et Camille Bertrand. Montréal, Beauchemin, 1919. 567 p.

—— La race française en Amérique. [Par A.] Desrosiers & [Pierre Auguste] Fournet. Préf. de Philippe Perrier. Illus. de Henri Julien. Montréal, Beauchemin. 1910. xxiv, 293 p.

EDINBOROUGH, ARNOLD The idea of Canada. (In *Saturday night*. Toronto. v. 83, no. 4 (Apr. 1968), pp. 27-28.)

—— One history for us all. The meaning of a Canadian society. (In *Saturday night*. Toronto. v. 82, no. 1 (Jan. 1967), pp. 32-33.)

Onward to the centennial, 4.

EGERTON, HUGH EDWARD Canada—part II, historical. Oxford, Clarendon Press, 1908. vi, 365 p. maps. (A Historical geography of the British colonies. [By C. P. Lucas] v. 5, pt. 2.)

—— Canada. Part II, the history from 1763-1921. 3d ed. Oxford, Clarendon

Press, 1923. 367 p. maps. (A Historical geography of the British dominions. [By Sir C. P. Lucas] v. 5, pt. 2.)

Published 1908 under the title: Canada - part II, historical.

EWART, JOHN SKIRVING The independence papers. By John S. Ewart. [Ottawa?] 1925-[32]. 2 v.

Vol. 2 without general title page.

Issued in parts. Deals, primarily, with foreign policy.

—— The kingdom of Canada; imperial federation, the colonial conferences, the Alaska boundary, the other essays. Toronto, Morang, 1908. xv, 370 p.

—— The kingdom papers. Ottawa, 1912-14. 2 v.

FALCONER, SIR ROBERT ALEXANDER The individuality of the Canadian people. (In *The University monthly*. Toronto. v. 10, no. 8 (June 1910), pp. 437-448.)

"Address delivered by President Falconer at Johns Hopkins University, February 22, 1910."

—— The individuality of the Canadian people. By R. A. Falconer. (In Canadian Club of Vancouver. *Addresses and proceedings*. [Vancouver] (1912/13), pp. [23]-30.)

Address delivered May 8, 1913.

—— The quality of Canadian life. By R. A. Falconer. (In *The Federation of Canada, 1867-1917*. Toronto, 1917. pp. [109]-138.)

FARLEY, PAUL EMILE Histoire du Canada; cours supérieur. [Par] Paul-Emile Farley et Gustave Lamarche. 3. éd. Montréal, Librairie des clercs de St.-Viateur, 1937 [c1935]. 551 p.

FLENLEY, RALPH (ed.) Essays in Canadian history presented to George MacKinnon Wrong for his eightieth birthday. Edited by R. Flenley. Toronto, Macmillan, 1939. x, 372 p.

Partial contents: Two North American federations: a comparison, by E. McInnis. – The terms of the British North America Act, by W. P. M. Kennedy. – Professor G. M. Wrong and history in Canada, by C. Martin. – Edward Blake and Canadian Liberal nationalism, by F. H. Underhill. – Conservatism and national unity, by D. G. Creighton. – The position of the Lieutenant-Governor in British Columbia in the years following Confederation, by W. N. Sage.

FORSEY, EUGENE ALFRED Canada, one nation or two? (In Congress on Canadian Affairs, 1st, Quebec, 1961, Le Canada, expérience ratée . . . ou réussie? Quebec, 1962. pp. [55]-69.)

—— Canada: two nations or one? By Eugene A. Forsey. (In *The Canadian journal of economics and political science*. [Toronto] v. 28 (1962), pp. 485-501.)

"Presidential address delivered at Hamilton, June 9th, 1962 at the annual meeting of the Canadian Political Science Association."

Discusses the concept of the Canadian nation in terms relating to French-Canadian and Anglo-Canadian relations.

FRASER, BLAIR The search for identity: Canada, 1945-1967. [1st ed.] Garden City, N.Y.; Toronto, Doubleday, 1967. viii, 325 p. (The Canadian history series, v. 6.)

On spine: The search for identity: Canada, postwar to present.

FULLER, BASIL Canada to-day and to-morrow. With thirty-nine half-tone illustrations. Toronto, Ryerson Press, 1935. 288 p.

GAY, FRANCISQUE Canada XXe siècle, aujourd'hui, demain. Montréal, Beauchemin [1949]. xii, 205 p.

GIRAUD, MARCEL Histoire du Canada. [1. éd.] Paris, Presses universitaires de France, 1946. 134 p. (Que sais-je? No 232.)

—— Histoire du Canada. 4. éd. mise à jour. Paris, Presses universitaires de France, 1966. 127 p. (Que sais-je? No 232.)

First ed. 1946; 2d ed. 1950; 3d ed. 1961.

GLAZEBROOK, GEORGE PARKIN DE TWENEBROKES A short history of Canada. By G. P. de T. Glazebrook. Oxford, Clarendon Press [1964] 238 p.

GOODRICH, JOSEPH KING The coming Canada . . . with 40 illustrations from photographs. Chicago, McClurg, 1913. x, 309 p. (His *The world to-day* series.)

GOSNELL, R. EDWARD The story of Confederation, with postscript on Quebec situation. [Foreword by Hugh J. Macdonald. n.p., The Author, c1918] 156 p.

GOSSELIN, DAVID La Confédération, 1867-1920. (In his *Mélanges historiques*. Quebec, 1920. pp. 43-55.)

GRAHAM, GERALD SANDFORD Canada; a short history. London, Hutchinson's University Library, 1950. 187 p. (Hutchinson's university library. British Empire history, no. 52.)

GREENING, WILLIAM EDWARD Canada's slow road to national maturity. By W. E. Greening. (In *Culture*. Québec. v. 17 (1956), pp. [242]-250.)

GRESWELL, WILLIAM HENRY PARR History of the Dominion of Canada. By the Rev. William Parr Greswell. Under the auspices of the Royal Colonial Institute. Oxford, Clarendon Press, 1890. xxxi, 339 p. (Clarendon Press series.)

GRIFFITH, WILLIAM LENNY The Dominion of Canada. London, I. Pitman, 1911. x, 449 p. (The All red series.)
Published also in Toronto, McClelland and Goodchild [1911].

GROULX, LIONEL ADOLPHE La Confédération canadienne; ses origines. Par Lionel Groulx. Montréal, Imprimé au Devoir, 1918. 264 p.
"Conférences prononcées à l'Université Laval (Montréal, 1917-1918)."

—— Histoire du Canada français depuis la découverte. [Montréal] l'Action nationale [1950-52]. 4 v.
Volume 4: 1848 à nos jours.
Based on a series of lectures in history for a radio broadcast.

—— Notre maître; le passé. Première série. 3. éd. [Montréal] Granger frères [1941]. 298 p.

GROVE, FREDERICK PHILIP The meaning of nationhood. (In *The Canadian nation*. Ottawa. v. 2, no. 1 (Mar./Apr. 1929), pp. 8-10; 28-29.)

HARDY, WILLIAM GEORGE From sea unto sea. Canada—1850-1910; the road to nationhood. Garden City, N.Y., Doubleday, 1960. 528 p.

HAWKES, ARTHUR This home of freedom. "Canada's history is the history of a people who craved liberty and ensued it." (In *Maclean's*. Toronto. v. 40, no. 13 (July 1, 1927), pp. 8; 51-55.)

HOPKINS, JOHN CASTELL Canada; the story of the Dominion. A history of Canada from its early discovery and settlement to the present time. New York, Co-operative Publication Society [c1900]. 516 p. (World's best histories.)

—— Canadian life and character. By J. Castell Hopkins. (In *The University magazine*. Montreal. v. 8 (1909), pp. [291]-304.)

—— Histoire populaire du Canada; quatre cents ans des annales de la moitié d'un continent...Traduite par Benjamin Sulte. Philadelphia, Winston [1901]. 698 p.
Translation of *The story of the Dominion*.

—— Progress of Canada in the nineteenth century. Toronto, Progress of Canada Pub. Co. [1900]. xxiv, 592 p. (Progress series.)
Cover title: Canada in the nineteenth century.
Partial contents: Part 3. National development 1867-1900.

—— The story of Canada; a history of four centuries of progress from the earliest settlement to the present time. Toronto, Winston [1922]. 788 p.
Early editions have title: The story of the Dominion (1901), and The story of our country (1912).

KILBOURN, WILLIAM MORLEY (ed.) Canada; a guide to the peaceable kingdom. Edited and with an introd. by William Kilbourn. Toronto, Macmillan [c1970]. xviii, 345 p.
An anthology.
Partial contents: Two styles of historian, by W. Kilbourn. – The northern frontier, by W. L. Morton. – The scrutable Canadian, by J. Eayrs. – The man in the mask, by M. McLuhan. – The Diefenbaker legend will live on, by P. Newman. – Red Tory, by G. Horowitz. – The Canadian solution, by C. Ryan.

KILBOURN, WILLIAM MORLEY Two styles of historian: Donald Creighton and Frank Underhill. By William Kilbourn. (In his *Canada: a guide to the peaceable kingdom*. Toronto, 1970. pp. 274-279.)

LACOUR-GAYET, ROBERT Histoire du Canada. [Paris] Fayard [c1966]. 605 p. (Les Grandes études historiques.)

LANCTOT, GUSTAVE Le Canada d'hier et d'aujourd'hui. 3. éd. Montréal, A. Lévesque, 1935. 315 p. (Documents historiques.)
First published in 1934.
Contents: 1. ptie. L'histoire. – 2. ptie. La géographie. – 3. ptie. L'organisation sociale.

LA PIERRE, LAURIER JOSEPH LUCIEN (ed.) French Canadian thinkers of the nineteenth and twentieth centuries. Edited by Laurier L. LaPierre. Montreal, Published for the French Canada Studies Programme, McGill University, by McGill University Press, 1966. 117 p. (Four o'clock lectures, 1.)
Includes bibliographies.
Partial contents: Sir George-Etienne Car-

tier, by J. C. Bonenfant. – Lionel Adolphe Groulx, by G. F. G. Stanley.

LAURENDEAU, ANDRE Le Canada; une nation ou deux? (In Congress on Canadian Affairs, 1st, Quebec, 1961. Le Canada, expérience ratée . . . ou réussie? Québec, 1962. pp. [71]-87.)

LE BOURDAIS, DONAT MARC Nation of the north; Canada since Confederation. New York, Praeger [1953]. x, 270 p.

LEMIEUX, RODOLPHE L'évolution du Canada. (In Revue de l'Université d'Ottawa. [Ottawa] 1. année (1931), pp. [32]-42.)
Concerns Canadian autonomy.

LE MOINE, SIR JAMES MAC PHERSON Maple leaves: a budget of legendary, historical, critical and sporting intelligence. [1st-7th ser.] Quebec, Printed for the Author by Hunter, Rose, 1863-1906. 7 v.
Note: 7th ser., Maple leaves. History, biography, legend, literature, memoirs, etc.
Author was president of the Royal Society of Canada, 1894.

LEVESQUE, ALBERT La dualité culturelle au Canada; hier, aujourd'hui, demain. Montréal, A. Lévesque [1959]. 225 p.

—— La nation canadienne-française; son existence, ses droits, ses devoirs. Montréal, A. Lévesque, 1934. 172 p. (Documents politiques.)

LIGHTHALL, WILLIAM DOUW Canada; a modern nation. Montreal, Witness Print House, 1904. 78 p.

LIPSET, SEYMOUR MARTIN Revolution and counterrevolution; the United States and Canada. By S. M. Lipset. (In Kruhlak, O. M. (comp.) The Canadian political process. Toronto [c1970] pp. 13-38.)
Reprinted from Ford, Thomas R. (ed.) The revolutionary theme in contemporary America. Lexington, Ky., 1965. (pp. 21-64).

LITVAK, ISAIAH A. Dynamics of the Canadian environment. By Isaiah A. Litvak and Raymond A. Young. (In Litvak, I. A. (ed.) The nation keepers. New York, Toronto [c1967] pp. 3-24.)

LOWER, ARTHUR REGINALD MARSDEN A bright future for a dull subject. By A. R. M. Lower. (In The Manitoba arts review. Winnipeg. v. 3, no. 4 (fall 1943), pp. 10-21.)
Reflections on the significance of Canadian history.

—— Canada, nation and neighbour. Toronto, Ryerson Press [1952]. vii, 202 p.

—— Canadian unity and its conditions. (In Canadian Institute on Economics and Politics. Problems in Canadian unity. Toronto [c1938] pp. 1-21.)

—— Canadians in the making; a social history of Canada. By Arthur R. M. Lower. [Toronto] Longmans, Green, 1958. xxiv, 475 p.

—— Colony to nation; a history of Canada. By Arthur R. M. Lower. With maps by T. W. McLean. Toronto, Longmans, Green [c1946]. xiii, 600 p.
"First Canadian edition, October, 1946."
"Family tree of Canadian parties, 1867-1945" at end.

—— Colony to nation; a history of Canada. By Arthur R. M. Lower. With maps by T. W. McLean. [4th ed., rev. Toronto] Longmans [c1964]. xlv, 600 p.
First ed. 1946; 2d ed. 1949; 3d ed. 1957.

—— National policy—revised version. By A. R. M. Lower. (In The Manitoba arts review. Winnipeg. v. 3, no. 3 (spring 1943), pp. 5-14.)
Argues that "political independence combined with some degree of cultural independence" would provide Canadians with psychological independence.

—— Two nations or two nationalities. By A. R. M. Lower. In Culture. Québec. v. 4 (1943), pp. [479]-481.)
Reflections on French-Canadian and English-Canadian relations as they affect the Canadian nation.

—— Two ways of life; the primary antithesis of Canadian history. By A. R. M. Lower. (In Canadian Historical Association. Report of the annual meeting. Toronto. (1943), pp. 5-18.)

—— Two ways of life; the spirit of our institutions. (In The Canadian historical review. Toronto. v. 28 (1947), pp. 383-400.)
A general statement that reflects upon the French and English cultural traditions that form the basis for Canadian institutions.

LOWER, JOSEPH ARTHUR Canada; an outline history By J. A. Lower. Toronto, Ryerson Press [1966] 248 p. (Ryerson paperbacks, 1.)

MC INNIS, EDGAR WARDWELL Canada; a political and social history. By Edgar McInnis. 3d ed. Toronto, Holt, Rinehart and Winston of Canada [c1969] xxii, 761 p.
First ed. 1947; 2d ed. 1959.

MAC KIRDY, KENNETH A. (ed.) Changing perspectives in Canadian history; selected problems. Edited by K. A. MacKirdy, J. S. Moir and Y. F. Zoltvany. Don Mills, Ont., Dent [c1967]. xxxiii, 373 p.

A selection of readings. "The book is designed primarily for use in discussion groups of introductory survey courses in Canadian history."

MCNAUGHT, KENNETH WILLIAM KIRKPATRICK The history of Canada. By Kenneth McNaught. London, Heinemann; Toronto, Bellhaven House [c1970]. 336 p. (Heinemann educational books.)

—— The Pelican history of Canada. By Kenneth McNaught. [Harmondsworth, Middlesex, Eng.] Penguin Books [c1969]. 336 p. (A Pelican original.)

Published also London, Heinemann, 1970, under title: The history of Canada.

—— Violence in Canadian history. By Kenneth McNaught. (In Moir, J. S. (ed.) Character and circumstance. Toronto, 1970. pp. 66-84.)

MACPHAIL, SIR ANDREW The Dominion and the spirit. (In The University magazine. Montreal. v. 7 (1908), pp. [10]-24.)

MARION, SERAPHIN Canadian unity and Quebec. By Dr. S. Marion. (In Women's Canadian Historical Society of Ottawa. Transactions. [Ottawa] v. 10 (1928), pp. 170-185.)

MARTIN, CHESTER BAILEY (ed.) Canada in peace and war; eight studies in national trends since 1914. Edited by Chester Martin. London, Oxford University Press, 1941. xix, 244 p.

"Issued under the auspices of the Canadian Institute of International Affairs."

Partial contents: Trends in Canadian nationhood, by C. Martin. – Federal relations in Canada since 1914, by D. G. Creighton. – Economic trends, by H. A. Innis. – Population problems and policies, by V. W. Bladen. – Canada and the last war, by F. H. Underhill. – Democracy in the overseas Dominion, by A. Brady.

MASSEY, VINCENT The making of a nation. Boston, Houghton Mifflin, 1928. 44 p.

"A lecture at Milton Academy on the Alumni War Memorial Foundation, November 30, 1927."

MASSICOTTE, EDOUARD ZOTIQUE (comp.) Miettes d'histoire canadienne. Par E. Z. Massicotte. Montréal, Beauchemin, 1924. 123 p. (Bibliothèque canadienne, Collection Dollard.)

MASTERS, DONALD CAMPBELL CHARLES A short history of Canada. By D. C. Masters. Princeton, N.J., Van Nostrand [1958]. 191 p. (An Anvil original, no. 36.)

MEALING, STANLEY ROBERT The concept of social class and the interpretation of Canadian history. By S. R. Mealing. (In The Canadian historical review. Toronto. v. 46 (1965), pp. 201-218.)

MOIR, JOHN SARGENT (ed.) Character and circumstance: essays in honour of Donald Grant Creighton. Edited by John S. Moir. Toronto, Macmillan, 1970. xii, 241 p.

"Donald Grant Creighton: a bibliography of his academic writing": pp. 235-239.

Partial contents: Donald Grant Creighton, by J. S. Moir. – Donald Creighton and Canadian history, by J. M. S. Careless. – Charisma and Canadian politics, by R. Graham. – Violence in Canadian history, by K. McNaught. – Fleming and Tupper, by A. Wilson. – Macdonald's Conservative successors, 1891-1896, by L. C. Clark. – Stephen Leacock and the age of plutocracy, 1903-1921, by R. Cook.

MORCHAIN, JANET KERR Search for a nation: French-English relations in Canada since 1759. [Foreword by Mason Wade] Toronto, Dent [c1967]. vi, 176 p.

Contents: Pt. 1. Search for a nation (pp. 1-82) Pt. 2. Sources and documents (pp. 89-166).

MORTON, WILLIAM LEWIS The bias of Prairie politics. By W. L. Morton, presented by D. G. Creighton. (In Royal Society of Canada. Proceedings and transactions. Ottawa. ser. 3, v. 49 (1955), section 2, pp. 57-66.)

Contends "that the difference between prairie and other Canadian politics is the result of an initial bias".

—— Clio in Canada: the interpretation of Canadian history. (In University of Toronto quarterly. Toronto. v. 15 (1945/46), pp. 227-234.)

Reprinted in Approaches to Canadian History. Toronto, c1967.

—— The Canadian identity. Madison, University of Wisconsin Press, 1961. ix, 125 p.

Comprises three lectures delivered at the University of Wisconsin, 1959-60; and a presidential address to the Canadian Historical Association at Queen's University, Kingston, Ont., June 1960.

—— A fresh look at history. How historians are developing a new concept of Canadian history. By W. L. Morton. (In *Canada month*. Montreal. v. 3, no. 11 (Nov. 1963), p. 13.)

Discusses "the study and writing of history in Canada".

—— The kingdom of Canada; a general history from earliest times. By W. L. Morton. [2d ed. Toronto] McClelland and Stewart [1970, c1969]. 594 p.

First ed. 1963.

"Bibliography": pp. [557]-562.

—— Manitoba; a history. By W. L. Morton. [2d ed. Toronto] University of Toronto Press [1967]. xii, 547 p.

First ed. 1957.

"Notes" (bibliographical): pp. [503]-533.

—— Manitoba's historic role. (In Historical and Scientific Society of Manitoba. *Papers*. Winnipeg. ser. 3, no. 19 (1964), pp. 50-57.)

—— The northern frontier; key to Canadian history. By William Morton. (In Kilbourn, W. M. (ed.) *Canada; a guide to the peaceable kingdom*. Toronto, 1970. pp. 280-284.)

—— The relevance of Canadian history. (In Canadian Historical Association. *Report of the annual meeting*. [Ottawa] 1960, pp. [1]-21.)

Presidential address read before the Canadian Historical Association, Queen's University, Kingston, Ontario, June 11, 1960.

—— The shield of Achilles; aspects of Canada in the Victorian age. Le bouclier d'Achille; regards sur le Canada de l'ère victorienne. Toronto, McClelland and Stewart [c1968]. 333 p.

Text in English or French.

Partial contents: Victorian Canada by W. L. Morton.

—— Victorian Canada. By W. L. Morton. (In Morton, W. L. (ed.) *The shield of Achilles*. Toronto. [c1968] pp. [311]-333.)

NELSON, JOHN The Canadian provinces; their problems and policies. With an introd. by Right Hon. Arthur Meighen. Toronto, Musson Book Co. [c1924]. xix, 219 p.

A collection of articles which appeared originally in *Maclean's magazine* during 1923. Cf. Pref.

Attempts "to relate the various sections of Canada to one another, to explain in popular form the problems with which each is confronted. . . ." – Foreword.

NICHOLSON, PATRICK Vision and indecision. Don Mills, Ont., Longmans [c1968]. xiv, 387 p.

NORRIS, LEONARD Canada's future. By L. Norris. (In Okanagan Historical Society. *Report*. Vernon, B.C. 11th (1945), pp. 80-98.)

Argues the need for national unity and a national spirit in Canada.

OUELLET, FERNAND L'étude du XIXe siècle canadien-français. (In *Recherches sociographiques*. Québec. v. 3, no 1-2 (jan./août 1962) pp. [27]-42.)

"Bibliographie sommaire": pp. 38-42.

—— Nationalisme canadien-français et laïcisme au XIXe siècle. (In *Recherches sociographiques*. Québec. v. 4, no 1 (jan./avril 1963), pp. [47]-70.)

Our living tradition. 1st- series. Toronto, Published in association with Carleton University by University of Toronto Press, 1957-

Some volumes have also a distinctive title: 1st series, Seven Canadians. – 5th series, Canada's past and present; a dialogue.

Editors: 1st series, Claude T. Bissell; 2d series, Robert L. McDougall.

PARK, JULIAN (ed.) The culture of contemporary Canada. Ithaca, N.Y., Cornell University Press [1957]. 404 p.

PARKIN, SIR GEORGE ROBERT The great Dominion; studies of Canada. By George R. Parkin. London, Macmillan, 1895. viii, 251 p.

Chapter X: Labour, education and political tendencies (pp. [209]-243).

PEART, HUGH W. The winds of change; a history of Canada and Canadians in the twentieth century. By Hugh W. Peart and John Schaffter. Toronto, Ryerson Press [1961]. ix, 460 p.

PEAT, LOUISA (WATSON) Canada: new world power. By Louisa W. Peat. New York, R. M. McBride [1945]. 293 p.

"First edition."

PELLERIN, JEAN Le Canada ou l'éternel commencement. [Paris] Casterman, 1967. 226 p. (Années tournantes.)

PIERCE, LORNE ALBERT A Canadian nation. [Designed by Thoreau MacDonald] Toronto, Ryerson Press [1960]. viii, 42 p.

These "chapters were read in part, before Mount Allison University Summer Institute, in August, 1957, and were revised for the Annual Convention of the Canadian

Authors' Association, Windsor, Ontario, June 1959". – Foreword.

—— A Canadian people. [Designed by Thoreau MacDonald] Toronto, Ryerson Press [1945]. viii, 84 p. (His *The Beverley papers*, 9.)

"Chapters II and III first appeared in the Canadian spokesman, April and May, 1941, and were issued as [the author's The armoury in our halls] Beverley paper v, in the same year."

PRANG, MARGARET EVELYN   Nationalism in Canada's first century. (In Canadian Historical Association. *Historical papers*. [Ottawa], (1968), pp. [114]-125.)

QUINN, HERBERT FURLONG   Canadian unity and the need for nationalism. (In *Queen's quarterly*. Kingston. v. 47 (1940), pp. [318]-329.)

Considers the problems, political, economic, social, which obstruct Canadian national unity.

REAMAN, G. ELMORE   A revisionist looks at Canadian history. (In *Waterloo review*. Waterloo, Ont. v. 2, no. 1 (summer 1959), pp. 52-57.)

REVEILLAUD, EUGENE   Histoire du Canada et des Canadiens Français de la découverte jusqu'à nos jours. Par Eug. Réveillaud. Paris, Grassart [1884]. 551 p.

RICHER, LEOPOLD   Le Canada et le bloc anglo-saxon. Montréal, Edition du Devoir, 1940. 155 p.

RIDDELL, WILLIAM RENWICK   Canada. By Hon. Mr. Justice Riddell. (In Canadian Club of Toronto. *Addresses*. Toronto. (1925-26), pp. 315-325.)

Address delivered March 29, 1926.

ROBERTS, SIR CHARLES GEORGE DOUGLAS   A history of Canada. Boston, Page [c1897]. xi, 493 p.

ROBLIN, DUFF   The Canadian experiment. By the Hon. Duff Roblin. (In *The Canadian forum*. Toronto. v. 43, no. 517 (Feb. 1964), pp. 250-252.)

"This is the English version of an address given before the Chambre de commerce du district de Montréal in December, 1963."

—— Confederation in perspective. By Honourable Duff Roblin. (In Historical and Scientific Society of Manitoba. *Papers*. Winnipeg. ser. 3, no. 24 (1967/68), pp. 43-50.)

ROY, PIERRE GEORGES   Les mots qui restent. Québec, Garneau, 1940. 2 v.

ROZ, FIRMIN   Vue générale de l'histoire du Canada 1534-1934. Préf. de Sébastien Charléty. Paris, P. Hartmann, 1934. xii, 337 p.

RULE, JOHN C.   L'historiographie du Canada français. Par John C. Rule. Présenté par Gustave Lanctôt. (In Royal Society of Canada. *Proceedings and transactions*. Ottawa. ser. 4, v. 2 (1964), section 1, pp. 97-103.)

RUMILLY, ROBERT   Histoire du Canada. Paris, La Clé d'Or [c1951]. 592 p.

—— Pages d'histoire politiques. [n.p.] Ligue de l'autonomie des provinces [194-]. 47 p.

RYERSON, STANLEY BREHAUT   French Canada; a study in Canadian democracy. By Stanley Ryerson. With a foreword by Evariste Dubé. Toronto, Progress Books, 1944 [c1943]. 256 p.

—— 1763-1963: In the beginning was the conquest. By Stanley Ryerson. (In *The Marxist quarterly*. Toronto. no. 7 (autumn 1963), pp. 12-20.)

SANDWELL, BERNARD KEBLE   The Canadian peoples. By B. K. Sandwell. London, Oxford University Press, 1941. 128 p. (The World to-day.)

SCHOFIELD, FRANK HOWARD   The story of Manitoba. By F. H. Schofield, Winnipeg, S. J. Clarke Pub. Co., 1913. 3 v. plates, ports., maps.

Vols. 2-3 contain biographical sketches.

SCHOLEFIELD, ETHELBERT OLAF STUART   A history of British Columbia. Part one, being a survey of events from the earliest times down to the Union of the Crown Colony of British Columbia with the Dominion of Canada, by E. O. S. Scholefield. Part two, being a history, mainly political and economic, of the Province since Confederation up to the present time, by R. E. Gosnell. Vancouver, British Columbia Historical Association, 1913. 2 v. in 1. ports.

Half-title: Sixty years of progress, British Columbia.

"This edition . . . is limited to three hundred and fifty signed and numbered copies. . . ."

SHORTT, ADAM   Canada and its provinces; a history of the Canadian people and their institutions, by one hundred associates. Adam Shortt and Arthur G. Doughty, general editors. Author's ed. Toronto, T.

& A. Constable for Publishers' Association of Canada, 1913-17. 23 v.

Contents: v. 1-2. New France. – v. 3-4 British Dominion. – v. 5. United Canada. – v. 6-8. The Dominion: Political development. – v. 9-10. The Dominion: Industrial development. – v. 11-12. The Dominion: Missions; Arts and letters. – v. 13-14. The Atlantic provinces. – v. 15-16. The province of Quebec. – v. 17-18. The province of Ontario. – v. 19-20. The Prairie provinces. – v. 21-22. The Pacific provinces. – v. 23. General index: Manuscript sources, bibliography, chronological outlines, historical tables.

SIEGFRIED, ANDRE Canada. Translated from the French by H. H. Hemming and Doris Hemming. London, J. Cape [1937]. 315 p.

Translation of *Le Canada, puissance internationale.*

—— Canada, an international power. Translated from the French by Doris Hemming. [2d ed.] London, J. Cape [1949]. 283 p.

First published in 1937 under title: *Canada.*

—— Le Canada, les deux races; problèmes politiques contemporains. Paris, A. Colin, 1906. 415 p.

—— Le Canada, puissance internationale. Paris, A. Colin, 1937. 234 p.

—— The race question in Canada. London, E. Nash, 1907. viii, 343 p.

Translation of *Le Canada, les deux races.*

—— The race question in Canada. Edited and with an introd. by Frank H. Underhill. [Toronto] McClelland and Stewart, 1966. 252 p. (The Carleton library, no. 29.)

SIMARD, GEORGES Le Canada d'aujourd'hui et de demain (In his *Etudes canadiennes*. Montréal, 1938. pp. [123]-157.)

—— Etudes canadiennes; education, politique, choses d'Eglise. Montréal, Beauchemin, 1938. 218 p.

Partial contents: Chapt. 6. Principes et faits en histoire; état idéal et état canadien. – Chapt. 7. Le Canada d'aujourd'hui et de demain.

SKELTON, OSCAR DOUGLAS The Canadian Dominion; a chronicle of our northern neighbor, by Oscar D. Skelton. New Haven, Yale University Press, 1921. xi, 296 p. (The Chronicle of America series, 49.)

First published in 1919.

SPRY, GRAHAM "One nation, two cultures". (In *The Canadian nation*. Ottawa. v. 1, no. 4 (Feb. 1929), pp. 14-23.)

"The substance of an address delivered in English and French to the Canadian Club of Quebec on January 17th, 1929."

STACEY, CHARLES PERRY The twentieth century. By C. P. Stacey. (In Brown, G. W. (ed.) *Canada*. Berkeley, 1953. pp. 124-151.)

STANLEY, GEORGE FRANCIS GILMAN Regionalism in Canadian history. By George F. G. Stanley. (In *Ontario history*. Toronto. v. 51, no. 3 (summer 1959), p. [163]-171.)

"Read during a session on Nationalism and regionalism in recent Canadian history which formed part of the programme of the American Historical Association, meeting in Washington, D.C., December 28-30, 1958."

STEWART, HERBERT L. Lord Bryce's estimate of Canada. (In *The Dalhousie review*. Halifax. v. 1. (1921/22), pp. [170]-181.)

SULTE, BENJAMIN Histoire des Canadiens-Français, 1608-1880. Montréal, Wilson, 1882-84. 8 v.

Note: t. 8, chapt. XIV. 1867-1880.

TAYLOR, KENNETH WIFFIN Canada's historical developments and prospects. By K. W. Taylor. (In Royal Society of Canada. *Proceedings and transactions*. Ottawa. ser. 4, v. 5 (1967), section 2, pp. 187-199.)

Presidential address.

TESSIER, ALBERT Histoire du Canada. 2. éd., rev. et illustrée. Québec, Editions du Pélican, 1957-58. 2 v.

Contents: t. 1. Neuve-France, 1542-1763. – t. 2. Québec-Canada, 1763-1958.

THOMSON, CLARA LINKLATER A short history of Canada. London, H. Marshall, 1911. 213 p.

TRACY, FRANK BASIL The tercentenary history of Canada from Champlain to Laurier MDCVIII–MCMVIII. Revised to the present time by Britton B. Cooke. New York, P. F. Collier [c1913]. 3 v.

TROTTER, REGINALD GEORGE Canadian federation; its origin and achievement. A study in nation building. Toronto, Dent, 1924. xiv, 348 p.

—— Charters of our freedom. Toronto, Ginn [1947]. vi, 138 p.

TURCOTTE, EDMOND   The future of unity in Canada: two views. I. As seen by a French-speaking Canadian. By Edmond Turcotte. II. As seen by an English-speaking Canadian. By B. K. Sandwell. (In *University of Toronto quarterly*. Toronto. v. 14 (1944/45), pp. 117-134.)

TUTTLE, CHARLES RICHARD   Short history of the Dominion of Canada, from 1500 to 1878. With the contemporaneous history of England and the United States; together with a brief account of the Turko-Russian War of 1877, and the previous and subsequent complications between England and Russia. By Charles R. Tuttle. Fully illustrated with steel and wood engravings. Boston, Lee and Shepard, 1878. 666 p.

—— Tuttle's popular history of the Dominion of Canada. With art illustrations. From the earliest settlement of the British American colonies to the present time. With biographical sketches of the most distinguished men of the nation. By Charles R. Tuttle. Complete in two volumes. Montreal, D. Downie; Boston, Tuttle & Downie, 1877. 2 v.

Added title page: An illustrated history of the Dominion, 1535-1876.

UHLMAN, HAROLD JOSHUA   Canada, a North American nation, 1914-1947. [Wolfville, N.S. 1948]. 1 v.

Thesis (PH D) – Acadia University.

UNDERHILL, FRANK HAWKINS   A Canadian philosopher-historian. By Frank H. Underhill. (In *The Canadian forum*. Toronto. v. 27, no. 318 (1947), pp. 83-84.)

A review article of *Colony to nation*, by A. R. M. Lower. Toronto, Longmans, Green, 1946.

—— The conception of a national interest. (In *The Canadian journal of economics and political science*. Toronto. v. 1 (1935), pp. 396-408.)

—— The conception of a national interest. (In his *In search of Canadian liberalism*. Toronto, 1961. pp. 172-182.)

A paper read at the annual meeting of the Canadian Political Science Association, 1935, and printed in the *Canadian journal of economics and political science*, August, 1935.

—— The image of Confederation. Toronto, Canadian Broadcasting Corp. [1964]. 84 p. (The Massey lectures, 3d ser.)

—— The radical tradition; a second view of Canadian history. The text of two half-hour programs by Frank H. Underhill and

Paul Fox originally presented on the CBC Television Network in the program "Explorations", June 8th and 15th, 1960. [Toronto, CBC Publications Branch, 1960]. 12 p.

Cover title.

At head of title: Script, Canadian Broadcasting Corporation.

WADE, MASON   Les Canadiens français de 1760 à nos jours. Traduit de l'anglais par Adrien Venne. Avec le concours de Francis Dufau-Labeyrie. 2e éd. rev. et augm. [Ottawa] Cercle du livre de France [c1963]-66. 2 v. (L'Encyclopédie du Canada français, 3-4.)

Translation of *The French Canadians, 1760-1945*. London, Toronto, Macmillan, 1955.

"Epilogue, 1945-1963": t. 2 (pp. [548]-558).

Contents: t. 1. 1760-1914. – t. 2. 1911-1963.

—— The French-Canadian outlook; a brief account of the unknown North Americans. New York, Viking Press, 1946. 192 p.

—— The French-Canadian outlook; a brief account of the unknown North Americans. With a new introd. by the author. [Toronto] McClelland and Stewart [c1964]. xvi, 94 p. (The Carleton library, no. 14.)

First published New York, Viking Press, 1946.

—— The French Canadians, 1760-1967. Rev. ed. in two vols. Toronto, Macmillan, 1968. 2 v. (1128 p.)

First ed. published London [Toronto] Macmillan, 1955, under title: *The French Canadians, 1760-1945*.

Contents: v. 1. 1760-1911. – v. 2. 1911-1967.

—— 100 years of crisis. (In *Canada month*. Montreal. v. 3, no. 4 (Apr. 1963), pp. 17-18.)

A brief historical sketch describing French Canadian attitudes toward confederation.

WAITE, PETER BUSBY   The edge of the forest. By Peter B. Waite. (In Canadian Historical Association. *Historical papers*. [Ottawa] (1969), pp. [1]-13.)

Presidential address read before the Canadian Historical Association, York University, Toronto, June 6, 1969.

WALKER, ALGERNON STANLEY   Canada. By A. Stanley Walker. London, Arrowsmith, 1934. xii, 132 p. (Modern states series, no. 4.)

WALLACE, WILLIAM STEWART The growth of Canadian national feeling. (In *The Canadian historical review*. Toronto. v. 1 (1920), pp. 136-165.)

—— The growth of Canadian national feeling. Toronto, Macmillan, 1927. 85 p.

"This essay was published originally in the Canadian Historical Review in 1920, and was then issued separately . . . as a pamphlet." Its re-issue is a revised and expanded version of the original essay. Cf. Pref.

—— A history of the Canadian people. Authorized by the Minister of Education. Toronto, Copp Clark Co. [c1930]. xiii, 404 p.

WARNER, CLARENCE M. The growth of Canadian national feeling. (In *The Canadian magazine of politics, science, art and literature*. Toronto. v. 45 (1915), pp. 273-281.)

Clarence M. Warner was President of the Ontario Historical Society.

WITTKE, CARL FREDERICK A history of Canada. New York, Knopf, 1928. xiv, 397, xviii p. (The Borzoi historical series.)

—— A history of Canada. 3d ed. New York, Crofts, 1942. 491 p.

WOODCOCK, GEORGE Canada and the Canadians. With photos. by Ingeborg Woodcock. London, Faber and Faber [1970]. 344 p.

WRONG, GEORGE MCKINNON The Canadians; the story of a people. Toronto, Macmillan, 1938. viii, 455 p.

—— Fifty years of federation—a look backward and a look forward. By George M. Wrong. (In Royal Society of Canada. *Proceeding and transactions*. Ottawa. ser. 3, v. 11 (1917), section 2, pp. [61]-70.)

Presidential address delivered at the May meeting, 1917.

—— Should the King of Canada have a "Kingdom"? By George M. Wrong. (In *Saturday night*. Toronto. v. 52, no. 1 (Nov. 7, 1936), p. 2.)

Traces the historical background of how Canada came to be called "Dominion" rather than "Kingdom".

YOUNG, JAMES Public men and public life in Canada; the story of the Canadian confederacy. Being recollections of Parliament and the press and embracing a succinct account of the stirring events which led to the confederation of British North America into the Dominion of Canada. By Hon. James Young. Toronto, W. Briggs, 1912. 2 v.

Vol. 2 has title: Public men and public life in Canada . . . embracing a succinct account of the stirring events which followed the confederation of British North America into the Dominion of Canada.

First ed. of vol. 1, Toronto, 1902.

From 1867 to 1878 the Author represented South Waterloo in the Canadian House of Commons. Cf. Wallace, W. S. (ed.) *The Encyclopedia of Canada*, 1937.

BIOGRAPHY
(COLLECTED AND MISCELLANEOUS)

ADAM, GRAEME MERCER Professor Goldwin Smith. By G. Mercer Adam. (In *The Canadian magazine of politics, science, art and literature*. Toronto. v. 24 (1904/05), pp. 113-119.)

ALDWORTH, D. V. The warlike pacifist. J. A. Macdonald of the Globe, who loves a row for righteousness' sake. (In *Canada monthly*. London, Ont. v. 17, no. 5 (Mar. 1915), pp. 303-304.)

ALLEN, RALPH The princely beggars: Mackenzie—Mann. (In *Maclean's*. Toronto. v. 74, no. 16 (Aug. 12, 1961), pp. 21; 26-30.)

Excerpt from *Ordeal by fire*, by R. Allen. Toronto, 1961.

ANDERSON, HARRY W. J. K. Munro—political pundit. (In *Maclean's*. Toronto. v. 35, no. 9 (May 1, 1922), p. 25.)

BATTEN, JACK A gallery of drones and other press people. (In *Saturday night*. Toronto. v. 83, no. 1 (Jan. 1968), pp. 19-22.)

Canadian papers, 1.

Brief assessments of the reporting of five Press Gallery members: Douglas Fisher, George Bain, Blair Fraser, Charles Lynch, and Peter Newman.

BELANGER, ANDRE J. La pensée politique et économique d'Emmanuel Mounier. Montréal, 1961. 1 v.

Thesis (MA) – McGill University.

BENOIT, JOSEPH PAUL AUGUSTIN Vie de Mgr. Taché, archevêque de St.-Boniface. Par Dom Benoît. Montréal, Beauchemin, 1904. 2v.

Concerns Alexander Antonin Taché who performed an important function in the events relating to the Red River rebellion of 1869-70 and later was involved in the initial stages of the Manitoba schools question.

BERGERON, GERARD Ne bougez plus! Portraits de 40 politiciens de Québec et d'Ottawa. Montréal, Editions du Jour [1968]. 223 p.

BIBAUD, MAXIMILIEN Le panthéon canadien; choix de biographies. Nouv. éd. rev., augm. et complétée jusqu'à ce jour par Adèle et Victoria Bibaud. Montréal, J. M. Valois, 1891. vi, 320 p.

First ed. published in 1858.

BISSELL, CLAUDE THOMAS (ed.) Seven Canadians. Edited by Claude T. Bissell. [Toronto] Published in association with Carleton University by University of Toronto Press [1962, c1957]. x, 149 p. (Our living tradition, ser. 1.)

Partial contents: Edward Blake, by F. H. Underhill. – Goldwin Smith, by M. Ross. – Sir John A. Macdonald, by D. G. Creighton. – Sir Wilfrid Laurier, by M. Wade.

BOWMAN, CHARLES ARTHUR Ottawa editor; the memoirs of Charles A. Bowman. Sidney, B.C., Gray's Pub. [c1966]. 273 [i.e. 278] p. ports.

The Author was editor of the Ottawa Citizen during the years 1913-1946.

BREBNER, JOHN BARTLET Harold Adams Innis as historian. By J. B. Brebner. (In Canadian Historical Association. Report of the annual meeting. [Ottawa] (1953), pp. 14-24.)

BRIDLE, AUGUSTUS The coat of many colours. How the Toronto News has survived the shock of radical changes. (In The Canadian courier. Toronto. v. 20, no. 13 (Aug. 26, 1916), pp. [3]-4; 19.)

Traces the career of Sir John S. Willison.

—— Dafoe, political pivot. By "Domino" (the Make-up man) [pseud.]. (In Maclean's. Toronto. v. 34, no. 17 (Oct. 1, 1921), pp. 16; 50-51.)

Concerns John W. Dafoe.

—— Goldwin Smith—deceased. Born August 23rd, 1823; died June 7th, 1910. Scholar, historian, journalist and litterateur—and fine old English gentleman. (In The Canadian courier. Toronto. v. 8, no. 3 (June 18, 1910), pp. 11-13; 26.)

—— Personalities and problems. No. 20— Sir John Willison. Who by a single ambition and much reading in his youth became one of the most unusual editors in Canada. (In The Canadian courier. Toronto. v. 13, no. 7 (Jan. 18, 1913), pp. [5]-6.)

—— Personalities and problems. No. 21— Honourable S. H. Blake. Eminent counsel, evangelist, autocrat and political critic; one of the most famous Irishmen ever born in Canada. (In The Canadian courier. Toronto. v. 13, no. 8 (Jan. 25, 1913), pp. 8-9.)

S. H. Blake was the brother of Edward Blake.

—— A political Mattawa of the West; John Wesley Dafoe. (In his The masques of Ottawa. Toronto, 1921. pp. 215-224.)

—— A political transformer. John W. Dafoe, managing editor of the Manitoba Free Press, steps down political voltage to Ottawa. (In The [Canadian] courier. Toronto. v. 21, no. 1 (Dec. 2, 1916), pp. [5]-6.)

—— Rev. J. A. Macdonald. (In his Sons of Canada. Toronto, 1916. pp. 275-[280].)

—— Sons of Canada; short studies of characteristic Canadians. Drawings by F. S. Challoner. Toronto, Dent, 1916. viii, 279 [i.e. 280] p.

Partial contents: Sir Robert Borden. – Sir Wilfrid Laurier. – Sir Clifford Sifton. – Henri Bourassa. – Sir Sam Hughes. – Sir William Mulock. – Sir George Foster. – Lord Strathcona. – Rev. J. A. Macdonald.

BRUCHESI, JEAN Oscar Dunn et son temps. (In Revue trimestrielle canadienne. Montréal. v. 14 (juin 1928), pp. [183-204].)

BUTCHART, REUBEN Sheppard: man and journalist. (In Saturday night. Toronto. v. 53, no. 1 (Jan. 1, 1938), pp. 8-9.)

A biographical sketch of Edmund E. Sheppard, founder and editor of Saturday night from 1887 to 1906.

BYNG, EVELYN (MORETON) BYNG, VISCOUNTESS Up the stream of time. By Viscountess Byng of Vimy. Toronto, Macmillan, 1945. 274 p.

"Thumbnail sketches of episodes in my long life." – Foreword.

Canadian celebrities. No. XXXVII. – Lieutenant-Colonel Denison. By E. Q. V. (In *The Canadian magazine of politics, science, art and literature*. Toronto. v. 19 (1902), pp. 398-400.)
Concerns Colonel George T. Denison.

Canadian celebrities. No. XXXIX – Mr. J. S. Willison. By E. Q. V. (In *The Canadian magazine of politics, science, art and literature*. Toronto. v. 20 (1902/03), pp. 222-224.)

CARELESS, JAMES MAURICE STOCKFORD Donald Creighton and Canadian history: some reflections. By J. M. S. Careless. (In Moir, J. S. (ed.) *Character and circumstance*. Toronto, 1970. pp. 8-21.)

CHARLESWORTH, HECTOR WILLOUGHBY Candid chronicles; leaves from the note book of a Canadian journalist. By Hector Charlesworth. Toronto, Macmillan, 1925. xv, 404 p.
Partial contents: Chapt. 8. Two famous figures, Sir John A. Macdonald and Goldwin Smith. – Chapt. 11. Politics of the nineties. – Chapt. 13. Laurier and Tupper.

—— I'm telling you; being the further candid chronicles of Hector Charlesworth. Toronto, Macmillan, 1937. xiv, 344 p.
Essays covering a variety of subjects, with emphasis on the post-World War I period.

—— J. W. Bengough; pioneer cartoonist. Long career of one who satirized many statesmen of by-gone days. By Hector Charlesworth. (In *Saturday night*. Toronto. v. 38, no. 48 (Oct. 13, 1923), p. 2.)

—— More candid chronicles; further leaves from the note book of a Canadian journalist. Toronto, Macmillan, 1928. xv, 429 p.
Partial contents: Chapt. 5. Students in rebellion. – Chapt. 6. An octogenarian's survey of Confederation. – Chapt. 8, When politics was poker. – Chapt. 9. Two rare personalities, Peter Ryan and George H. Ham.

—— Two famous figures: Sir John A. Macdonald and Goldwin Smith. By Hector Charlesworth. (In his *Candid chronicles*. Toronto, 1925. pp. 105-122.)
Consists, primarily, of anecdotes.

CHERRY, P. C. Sir William Mackenzie—individualist. (In *MacLean's magazine*. Toronto. v. 22, no. 2 (June 1911), pp. [33]-37.)

CLARKE, GREGORY "H.F.G." the glorified reporter. Who finds a broad grin in Canadian politics and transfers it to the faces of his readers via his page in the Toronto Saturday night. (In *Canada monthly*. London, Ont. v. 18, no. 3 (July 1915), p. 162.)
Concerns Henry Franklin Gadsby.

CLIPPINGDALE, RICHARD THOMAS GEORGE J. S. Willison and Canadian nationalism, 1886-1902. By R. T. Clippingdale. (In Canadian Historical Association. *Historical papers*. [Ottawa] (1969), pp. [74]-93.)

—— J. S. Willison, political journalist; from liberalism to independence, 1881-1905. [Toronto] c1970. 2 v.
Thesis (PH D) – University of Toronto.

COLE, DOUGLAS LOWELL The better patriot; John S. Ewart and the Canadian nation. [Seattle] 1968. viii, 404 leaves.
Thesis (PH D) – University of Washington.

Colonel George T. Denison. A Canadian patriot and an Imperial statesman. (In *Willisons monthly*. Toronto. v. 1, no. 2 (July 1925), pp. 49-51.)

COLQUHOUN, ARTHUR HUGH URQUHART Goldwin Smith in Canada. By A. H. U. Colquhoun. (In *The Canadian magazine of politics, science, art and literature*. Toronto. v. 35 (1910), pp. 315-323.)

—— Our eight prime ministers. By A. H. U. Colquhoun. (In *The Canadian magazine of politics, science, art and literature*. Toronto. v. 49 (1917), pp. 218-228.)
Ranges from Sir John A. Macdonald to Sir Robert Borden.

—— Press, politics and people; the life and letters of Sir John Willison, journalist and correspondent of the Times. Toronto, Macmillan, 1935. 306 p.

—— Sir John Willison. (In *The Canadian magazine of politics, science, art and literature*. Toronto. v. 51 (1918), pp. 75-78.)

—— Sir John Willison. By A. H. U. Colquhoun. (In *The Dalhousie review*. Halifax. v. 7 (1927/28), pp. [159]-162.)
An obituary.

COOK, GEORGE RAMSAY André Laurendeau: Canadien ou Canadian? By Ramsay Cook. (In *The Canadian forum*. Toronto. v. 42, no. 495 (Apr. 1962), pp. 8-11.)

—— L'historien et le nationalisme; le cas Michel Brunet. Par Ramsay Cook. (In

Cité libre. Montréal. no 73 (jan. 1965), pp. 5-14.)

—— John W. Dafoe; conservative progressive. [In Canadian Historical Association. *Report of the annual meeting.* [Ottawa] (1961), pp. [75]-85.]

—— The political ideas of John W. Dafoe, 1866-1944. [Toronto] 1960. 2 v.
Thesis (PH D) – University of Toronto.

—— The politics of John W. Dafoe and the *Free Press.* [Toronto] University of Toronto Press [c1963]. xii, 305 p.

—— Stephen Leacock and the age of plutocracy, 1903-1921. By Ramsay Cook. [In Moir, J. S. (ed.) *Character and circumstance.* Toronto, 1970. pp. 163-181.]

COOPER, JOHN ALEXANDER   The editors of the leading Canadian dailies. With forty special photographs. By the Secretary of the Canadian Press Association. (In *The Canadian magazine of politics, science, art and literature.* Toronto. v. 12 (1898/99), pp. 336-352.)
Consists of factual biographical information.

COOPER, JOHN ALEXANDER (ed.)   Men of Canada. A portrait gallery of men whose energy, ability, enterprise and public spirit are responsible for the advancement of Canada, the premier colony of Great Britain. Edited by John A. Cooper. Montreal, The Canadian Historical Co., 1901-2. xviii p., 296 p. of ports.

COX, COROLYN   Canadian strength. Biographical sketches by Corolyn Cox. Majority of portraits by Karsh. Foreword by the Right Honourable C. D. Howe. Toronto, Ryerson Press [c1946] 192 p.
Character sketches of personalities who were in the Dept. of Munitions and Supply and served on the Wartime Prices and Trade Board.

—— Name in the news. Dr. Charlotte Whitton shining wherever she chooses to be. (In *Saturday night.* Toronto. v. 60, no. 2 (Sept. 16, 1944), p. 2.)
A biographical sketch.

—— Name in the news. First Lord of the fourth Estate. (In *Saturday night.* Toronto. v. 59, no. 1 (Sept. 11, 1943), p. 2.)
Biographical sketch of Robert Kenneth Carnegie, president of the Press Gallery.

—— Name in the news. Heirs to the Sifton Kingdom headed by Winnipeg's Victor. (In *Saturday night.* Toronto. v. 59, no. 40 (June 10, 1944), p. 2.)

A biographical sketch of Victor Sifton, son of Sir Clifford Sifton, and general manager of the *Winnipeg Free Press.*

—— Name in the news. News makes the newspaper man. (In *Saturday night.* Toronto. v. 58, no. 15 (Dec. 19, 1942), p. 2.)
Biographical sketch of Grant Dexter.

CRAICK, WILLIAM ARNOT   The romance of the Taschereaus. A remarkable French-Canadian family, whose members have been conspicuous in the public life of the country for nearly two centuries. By W. A. Craick. (In *MacLean's magazine.* Toronto. v. 27, no. 6 (Apr. 1914), pp. [17]-20.)

—— The story of the Casgrain family. By W. A. Craick. (In *MacLean's magazine.* Toronto. v. 28, no. 1 (Nov. 1914), pp. [21]-23; 109-112.)

—— William MacKenzie, a constructive genius. By W. A. Craick. (In *The Busy man's magazine.* Montreal, Toronto. v. 13, no. 3 (Jan. 1907), pp. [13]-16.)
The personality of the senior partner in the firm of Mackenzie & Mann.

CREIGHTON, DONALD GRANT   Harold Adams Innis; portrait of a scholar. [Toronto] University of Toronto Press [1957]. 146 p.

CROSS, AUSTIN FLETCHER   Oligarchs at Ottawa. By Austin F. Cross. (In *Public affairs.* Halifax. v. 14, no. 1 (autumn 1951), pp. [16]-24.)
Part 1.
Discusses the personalities and power held by the following senior civil servants: William Clifford Clark, J. W. Pickersgill, Norman Alexander Robertson, Louis Rasminsky, and John Deutsch.

—— Oligarchs at Ottawa. By Austin F. Cross. (In *Public affairs.* Halifax. v. 14, no. 2 (winter 1952), pp. [21]-29.)
Part 2.
Presents character sketches of personalities in the senior civil service, including Ken Eaton, Robert Bryce, Kenneth Taylor, Graham Towers, Arthur MacNamara, Maxwell Weir Mackenzie, Arnold Danford, Patrick Heeney, and Charles Bland.

DAFOE, JOHN WESLEY   Press, politics and people. (In *The Canadian historical review.* Toronto. v. 17 (1936), pp. 59-64.)
A review article of *Press, politics and people: the life and letters of Sir John Willison,* by A. H. U. Colquhoun. Toronto, 1935.

—— The views and influences of John S. Ewart. (In *The Canadian historical review*. Toronto. v. 14 (1933), pp. 136-142.)

DAVID, LAURENT OLIVIER Biographies et portraits. Par L.-O. David. Montréal, Beauchemin & Valois, 1876. 301 p.

Partial contents: M. Joseph Roy. – Monseigneur Plessis. – Messire I. – S. Lesieur-Désaulniers. – Sir George-Etienne Cartier. – Francis Cassidy. – Joseph Papin. – L'Hon. P.-J.-D. Chauveau. – Mgr. Bourget. – Mgr. Charles-Edouard Fabre. – M. Evariste Gélinas. – Mgr. Taché.

—— Mes contemporains. Par L. O. David. Montréal, E. Senécal & fils, imprimeurs, 1894. 288 p.

—— Monseigneur Alexandre-Antonin Taché, archevêque de Saint-Boniface. Par L. O. David. 2. éd., rév., cor. et considérablement augm. Montréal, Cadieux & Derome, 1883. 111 p. (Bibliothèque religieuse et nationale. 1. sér.)

—— Souvenirs et biographies, 1870-1910. Par L. O. David. Montréal, Beauchemin, 1911. 274 p. ports.

Brief character sketches. Includes H. T. Taschereau, L. O. Taillon, H. Mercier, L. Gouin, H. Bourassa, and others.

DEMPSON, PETER Assignment Ottawa; seventeen years in the Press Gallery. Toronto, General Pub. Co. [c1968] 312 p.

DEXTER, GRANT His grey eminence. A portrait sketch of Arthur Beauchesne, untangler extraordinary of parliamentary snarls. (In *Maclean's*. Toronto. v. 44, no. 19 (May 15, 1931), pp. 11; 48.)

Concerns Arthur Beauchesne, Clerk of the House of Commons, appointed January 7, 1925.

—— Oscar Douglas Skelton. (In *Queen's quarterly*. Kingston. v. 48 (1941), pp. 1-6.)

Written on the occasion of the death of O. D. Skelton, January 28, 1941.

DONALD, HEATHER M. Lord Mount Stephen, 1829-1921. [London, Eng., 1952] 1 v.

Thesis (PH D) – University of London.

DONALDSON, GORDON Fifteen men; Canada's prime ministers from Macdonald to Trudeau. Illustrated by Don Morrison. Toronto, Doubleday, Canada, 1969. xii, 265 p.

DONNELLY, MURRAY SAMUEL Dafoe of the *Free Press*. By Murray Donnelly. Toronto, Macmillan, 1968. 207 p.

—— J. W. Dafoe. By M. S. Donnelly. (In McDougall, R. L. (ed.) *Our living tradition*. Fourth series. [Toronto, c1962] pp. 93-118.)

—— The political ideas of J. W. Dafoe. By M. S. Donnelly. (In Aitchison, J. H. (ed.) *The political process in Canada*. [Toronto, c1963] pp. [99]-117.)

DRAPEAU, JEAN "Cette couronne d'épines." (In *L'Action nationale*. Montréal. v. 33 (juin 1949), pp. [441]-450.)

Discusses the ideas of John S. Ewart.

DUNN, OSCAR Dix ans de journalisme; mélanges. Montréal, Duvernay frères & Dansereau, 1876. 278 p.

EDMONDS, WILLIAM LEWIS "Gentlemen, we have with us to-night." Toastmaster, W. L. Edmonds. (In *Saturday night*. Toronto. v. 33, no. 14 (Jan. 17, 1920), pp. 2; 11.)

Concerns Colonel George Taylor Denison. Adopts the form of an introductory speech.

—— Our governors-general since Confederation. (In *The Canadian magazine of politics, science, art and literature*. Toronto. v. 49 (1917), pp. 243-255.)

Includes Lord Monck to the Duke of Devonshire.

EGGLESTON, WILFRID Capital comment. A great public servant. (In *Saturday night*. Toronto. v. 66, no. 27 (Apr. 10, 1951), p. 3.)

A biographical sketch of W. F. A. Turgeon.

—— Reporter to deputy minister. Alex. Johnston as raconteur. (In *Saturday night*. Toronto. v. 67, no. 12 (Dec. 29, 1951), p. 27.)

ELLIOTT, WILLIAM EDMUND Politics is funny. [2d ed.] Toronto, Burns & MacEachern [1952] xi, 170 p.

First published Toronto, Britannia Printers, 1951.

Anecdotes and reminiscences about Canadian politicians by a Canadian journalist.

FARR, DAVID MORICE LEIGH John S. Ewart. By David M. L. Farr. (In McDougall, R. L. (ed.) *Our living tradition*. Second and third series. [Toronto, c1959] pp. 185-214.)

FERGUSON, GEORGE VICTOR John W. Dafoe. Toronto, Ryerson Press [c1948] v, 127 p. (Canadian biography.)

FLEMING, JAMES GRANVILLE The fighting Denisons. A military instinct that runs in the blood of five generations. (In *Mac-Lean's magazine*. Toronto. v. 27, no. 2 (Dec. 1913), pp. [5]-10; 136-137.)

FORD, ARTHUR RUTHERFORD As the world wags on. By Arthur Ford. Foreword by Fred Landon. Toronto, Ryerson Press, 1950. x, 228 p.

The Author was a member of the Press Gallery of the House of Commons. Reviews political personalities and events extending over a period of fifty years.

FRASER, ANNIE ERMATINGER A poet-pioneer in Canada. By A. Ermatinger Fraser. (In *Queen's quarterly*. Kingston. v. 35 (1927/ 28), pp. 440-450.)

Concerns Charles Mair.

FRASER, BLAIR Ottawa champion penny-pincher. (In *Maclean's*. Toronto. v. 68, no. 10 (May 14, 1955), pp. 22-23; 114-117.)

Concerns Robert Watson Sellar, appointed Auditor-General of Canada in 1940.

GAGAN, DAVID PAUL The Queen's champion: the life of George Taylor Denison III, soldier, author, magistrate and Canadian Tory patriot. [Durham, N.C.] 1969 [c1970] viii, 278 leaves.

Thesis (PH D) – Duke University.

GAGNON, MARCEL A. Olivar Asselin. (In *Le Magazine Maclean*. Montréal. v. 2, no. 5 (mai 1962), pp. [30-31]; 48-54.)

GOLDEN, LOU L. L. A distinguished senior civil servant. (In *Saturday night*. Toronto. v. 55, no. 23 (Apr. 6, 1940), p. 5.)

A biographical sketch of Ephraim Herbert Coleman, Under Secretary of State and Deputy Registrar General, and chairman of the Voluntary Service Registration Bureau.

—— Red tape cutter. By L. L. L. Golden. (In *Saturday night*. Toronto. v. 55, no. 32 (June 8, 1940), p. 5.)

A biographical sketch of James Stuart Duncan, the acting Deputy Minister for Air.

GORDON, CHARLES WILLIAM Postscript to adventure; the autobiography of Ralph Connor. New York, Farrar & Rinehart [c1938] xvi, 430 p.

Partial contents: Chapt. 28. War politics in Canada. – Chapt. 32. "Now cracks a noble heart" (Interview with Laurier concerning his membership in the Union Government). – Chapt. 33. "Vale Laurier" (Election of 1917).

GRANATSTEIN, JACK LAWRENCE On Vincent Massey. By J. L. Granatstein. (In *The Canadian forum*. Toronto. v. 47, no. 565 (Feb. 1968), p. 246.)

GRANT, GEORGE MUNRO Sandford Fleming, CE, LL D, CMG. By G. M. Grant. (In *The Week*. Toronto, v. 5, no. 17 (Mar. 22, 1888), pp. 265-266.)

Prominent Canadians – XIV.

GROULX, LIONEL Monseigneur Taché. (In *L'Action française* Montréal. v. 10 (Oct. 1923), pp. [211]-223.)

GUAY, JACQUES André Laurendeau; l'histoire d'un nationaliste. (In *Le Magazine Maclean*. Montréal. v. 8, no 1 (jan. 1968), pp. [9]-11; 34-37; 39.)

HAM, GEORGE HENRY Reminiscences of a raconteur, between the '40's and the '20's. By G. H. Ham. Toronto, Musson [1921] xvi, 330 p.

Relates anecdotes from the 1840s to the 1920s.

HAMILTON, ROSS (ed.) Prominent men of Canada, 1931-32. Edited by Ross Hamilton. Montreal, National Pub. Co. [1932] 640 p.

HAMMOND, MELVIN ORMOND Confederation and its leaders. By M. O. Hammond. With portraits. Toronto, McClelland, Goodchild & Stewart [c1917] x, 333 p. ports.

Consists of brief biographical sketches. Coverage extends beyond 1867.

HANNA, DAVID BLYTHE Trains of recollection. Drawn from fifty years of railway service in Scotland and Canada. And told to Arthur Hawkes. By D. B. Hanna; first president of the Canadian National Railways. Toronto, Macmillan, 1924. x, 340 p.

HARKNESS, ROSS J. E. Atkinson of the Star. [Toronto] University of Toronto Press [c1963] vii, 390 p.

Contains material on the relationship between the *Toronto Daily Star* and the Liberal Party.

HAULTAIN, THEODORE ARNOLD Goldwin Smith; his life and opinions. To which is appended "U.S. Notes", being Goldwin Smith's journal during his first visit to America in 1864. Toronto, McClelland and Goodchild [1913] xi, 304 p.

HENDERSON, MARGARET EADIE The Dufferin family. (In *The Canadian magazine of politics, science, art and literature*. Toronto. v. 29 (1907), pp. 491-500.)

HOLLAND, GEORGE CLARKE My Ottawa memories, 1866-. By George C. Holland. (In *Maclean's*. Toronto. v. 35, no. 10

(May 15, 1922), p. 22-23, 63; v. 35, no. 11 (June 1, 1922), pp. 22, 49.)

In two parts.

Mr. Holland was Senate reporter for almost half a century.

HOPKINS, JOHN CASTELL Hon. John Christian Schultz. By J. Castell Hopkins. (In *The Week*. Toronto. v. 10, no. 48 (Oct. 27, 1893), pp. 1141-1143.)

Prominent Canadians: XIV.

HUGHES, KATHERINE Father Lacombe; the black-robe voyageur. Toronto, McClelland & Stewart [c1920] xxii, 471 p.

"New edition."

A popular account of the life of Albert Lacombe. Relates to the Riel rebellion (1885) and the Manitoba schools question.

HUTCHISON, BRUCE Macdonald to Pearson: the prime ministers of Canada. [Don Mills, Ont.] Longmans Canada [c1967] 233 p.

Condensation of the Author's *Mr. Prime Minister, 1867-1964*, published 1964.

—— Mr. Prime Minister, 1867-1964. [Don Mills, Ont.] Longmans Canada [c1964] 394 p.

Biographical sketches of Canadian prime ministers.

INNIS, HAROLD ADAMS Stephen Butler Leacock, 1869-1944. By H. A. I. (In *The Canadian journal of economics and political science*. Toronto. v. 10 (1944), pp. 216-230.)

Written on the occasion of Leacock's death.

"Select bibliography of Stephen Leacock's contributions to the social sciences": pp. 228-230.

J. G. Bourinot, CMG, DCL, ex-President of the Royal Society of Canada, etc. (In *The Week*. Toronto. v. 11, no. 20 (Apr. 13, 1894), pp. 462-465.)

Prominent Canadians – XLVIII.

KETTLE, JOHN Claude Ryan—a voice to be heard. (In *Canada month*. Montreal. v. 9, no. 3 (Mar. 1969), pp. 13-17.)

A *Canada month* profile.

—— Marcel Faribault. (In *Canada month*. Montreal. v. 8, no. 2 (Feb. 1968), pp. 14-16.)

A *Canada month* profile.

KIPP, V. M. John W. Dafoe. The famous Manitoba editor who is a power in the land. (In *Saturday night*. Toronto. v. 42, no. 23 (Apr. 23, 1927), p. 5.)

KRITZWISER, H. H. Portrait of Dominion Food Controller. (In *Saturday night*. Toronto. v. 57, no. 24 (Feb. 21, 1942), p. 15.)

A biographical sketch of J. Gordon Taggart.

LACOMBE, ALBERT Le père Lacombe, "l'homme au bon coeur", d'après ses mémoires et souvenirs. Recueillis par une soeur de la Providence. Montréal, Imprimé au Devoir, 1916. xv, 547 p.

Includes material on the two Riel insurrections and the Manitoba schools question.

LAPALME, MICHEL Le nouveau chanoine Groulx s'appelle Séguin. Le moins connu et le plus controversé des historiens canadiens-français fabrique des séparatistes... et des défaitistes. (In *Le Magazine Maclean*. Montréal. v. 6, no. 4 (avril 1966), pp. 16; 48; 50; 54.)

Concerns Maurice Séguin.

LEACOCK, STEPHEN BUTLER Andrew Macphail. By Stephen Leacock. (In *Queen's quarterly*. Kingston. v. 45 (1938), pp. [445]-452.)

LEVADIE, MEYER John W. Dafoe and the evolution of Canadian autonomy, 1918-1926. [Winnipeg, 1952] 1 v.

Thesis (MA) – University of Manitoba.

LONGLEY, JAMES WILBERFORCE Great Canadians I have known. By Hon. Justice Longley. (In *The Canadian magazine of politics, science, art and literature*. Toronto. v. 57 (1921), pp. 54-65.)

Includes Howe, Macdonald, Blake, Mackenzie, Laurier, and Sir John Thompson.

—— Mr. Goldwin Smith. Close character study by one who knew him well. A tribute by Justice Longley. (In *The Canadian courier*. Toronto. v. 8, no. 6 (July 9, 1910), pp. 10; 22-23.)

—— Reminiscences political and otherwise. By Hon. Justice Longley. (In *The Canadian magazine of politics, science, art and literature*. Toronto. v. 55 (1920), pp. 443-450; v. 56 (1920/21), pp. 61-67; 147-153.)

Parts 1-3.

LOWER, ARTHUR REGINALD MARSDEN Adam Shortt, founder. By Arthur R. M. Lower. (In *Historic Kingston*. Kingston. no. 17 (1969), pp. [3]-15.)

"An address . . . at a dinner given Nov. 22, 1968, by Queen's University to celebrate the 75th anniversary of the founding in 1893 of the Kingston Historical Society."

—— My first seventy-five years. By Arthur R. M. Lower. Toronto, Macmillan, 1967. 384 p.

MACBETH, MADGE HAMILTON (Lyons) A great Canadian: Sir John Bourinot. By Madge Macbeth. (In *The Dalhousie review*. Halifax. v. 34 (1954/55), pp. [173]-180.)

—— Sir John Bourinot: a great Canadian. By Madge Macbeth. (In *The Atlantic advocate*. Fredericton, N.B. v. 53, no. 12 (Aug. 1963), pp. 73-76.)

MC CREADY, JOHN E. BLAKENY The special correspondent. By J. E. B. McCready. (In *The Canadian magazine of politics, science, art and literature*. Toronto. v. 29 (1907), pp. 548-552.)

"Personal reminiscences of newsgathering at the Capital forty years ago."

The Author was the resident correspondent of the Toronto *Globe* at Ottawa.

MACDONALD, ADRIAN Canadian portraits. Toronto, Ryerson Press [c1925] 230 p.

The treatment is popular in the presentation of the above personalities.

Contents: Wolfe and Montcalm. – Sir Alexander Mackenzie. – Sir Isaac Brock. – Thomas Chandler Haliburton. – Joseph Howe. – Dr. Egerton Ryerson. – Sir James Douglas. – Sir John A. Macdonald. – Lord Strathcona. – Father Lacombe. – Dr. Louis Honoré Fréchette. – Sir Wilfrid Laurier. – Sir William Osler. – Paul Peel. – Archibald Lampman.

MC DOUGALL, ROBERT LAW (ed.) Canada's past and present; a dialogue. Edited by Robert L. McDougall. [Toronto] Published in association with Carleton University with University of Toronto Press [1967, c1965] xii, 179 p. (Our living tradition, ser. 5.)

Partial contents: William Lyon Mackenzie King, by B. Neatby. – Louis Riel, by G. F. G. Stanley. – O. D. Skelton, by W. A. Mackintosh. – Charles Mair, by J. Matthews. – Olivar Asselin, by M. Wade.

—— Our living tradition. Second and third series. Edited by Robert L. McDougall. [Toronto] Published in association with Carleton University by University of Toronto Press [c1959] xvi, 288 p.

Partial contents: [Ser. 2] George Brown, by J. M. S. Careless. – Sir Robert Borden, by J. A. Gibson. [Ser. 3] John S. Ewart, by D. M. L. Farr.

—— Our living tradition. Fourth series. Edited by Robert L. McDougall. [Toronto] Published in association with Carleton University by University of Toronto Press [c1962] x, 158 p.

Partial contents: Joseph Howe, by J. M. Beck. – J. W. Dafoe, by M. S. Donnelly. – Henri Bourassa, by A. Laurendeau.

MC EACHERN, RONALD ALEXANDER Goldwin Smith. Toronto, 1934. 364 leaves.

Thesis (PH D) – University of Toronto.

MAC FARLANE, RONALD OLIVER A law-abiding rebel: John Christian Schultz. By R. O. MacFarlane. (In *The Manitoba arts review*. Winnipeg. v. 1, no. 3 (spring 1939), pp. 21-26.)

MC GRATH, M. HELEN The Grattan O'Leary story. By M. Helen McGrath. (In *The Atlantic advocate*. Fredericton, N.B. v. 49, no. 7 (Mar. 1959), pp. 47-52.)

MC INTOSH, FRANCES ROTHAERMEL Our man in Ottawa. (In Waterloo Historical Society. *Annual volume*. Kitchener, Ont. v. 55 (1967), pp. 63-85.)

Biographical summaries of the ten representatives from Waterloo North, Ont., to the House of Commons since 1867.

"Terms of office of Canadian Prime Ministers and members of Parliament for Waterloo North", a listing: p. 63.

MACKINTOSH, CHARLES HERBERT Ironing a continent. Containing an original story by the late Sir William Van Horne of the building of the CPR. By C. H. Mackintosh. (In *MacLean's magazine*. Toronto. v. 30, no. 9 (July 1917), pp. [30]-32; 111-114.)

MACKINTOSH, WILLIAM ARCHIBALD O. D. Skelton. By W. A. Mackintosh. (In McDougall, R. L. (ed.) *Canada's past and present*. [Toronto, 1967, c1965] pp. 59-77.)

Our living tradition, ser. 5.

MAC TAVISH, NEWTON MC FAUL Goldwin Smith's "Reminiscences". A review, by the Editor. (In *The Canadian magazine of politics, science, art and literature*. Toronto. v. 36 (1910/11), pp. 302-306.)

Review article of *Reminiscences*, by G. Smith, edited by A. Haultain. New York, 1910.

MACWATT, DANIEL FRASER (comp.) Short sketches, with photographs, of wardens, parliamentary representatives, judicial officers and county officials of the county of Lambton from 1852 to 1917. [Sarnia] County Council, 1917. 55 p. illus., ports.

The Makers of Canada series. Anniversary edition. Illustrated under the direction of A. G. Doughty. London and Toronto, Oxford University Press, 1926. 12 v.

Edited by W. L. Grant.

MALCHELOSSE, GERARD Les idées politiques de Benjamin Sulte. (In *Bulletin des recherches historiques*. Lévis. v. 57, no. 1 (jan./mars 1951), pp. 5-7.)

MARQUIS, THOMAS GUTHRIE (ed.) Builders of Canada from Cartier to Laurier. By Agnes Maule Machar, Louis Honoré Fréchette, J. Castell Hopkins, David Creighton, William Buckingham, F. Blake Crofton, J. Lambert Payne, and others. Edited by T. G. Marquis. Embellished with many appropriate engravings. Detroit, Mich., Brantford, Ont. [etc.] Bradley-Garretson Co. [c1903] xvi, 578 p.

Half-title: Makers of Canada.

Published in 1905 under title: *Giants of the Dominion from Cartier to Laurier*.

—— Giants of the Dominion from Cartier to Laurier. By Agnes Maule Machar, Louis Honoré Fréchette, J. Castell Hopkins, David Creighton, William Buckingham, F. Blake Crofton, J. Lambert Payne, and others. Edited by T. G. Marquis. [Philadelphia? c1905] viii, [4], xv-xvi, 578 p.

Published in 1903 under the title: *Builders of Canada from Cartier to Laurier*.

Published in 1903 in Toronto by the John C. Winston Co.

MARSH, D'ARCY The tragedy of Henry Thornton. Toronto, Macmillan, 1935. xv, 293 p.

Includes consideration of the relation between the government and the management of the national railways.

MARTIN, CHESTER BAILEY Professor G. M. Wrong and history in Canada. By Chester Martin. (In Flenley, Ralph (ed.) *Essays in Canadian history*. Toronto, 1939. pp. 1-23.)

MARTIN, W. L. Arthur Hawkes, a character sketch. (In *The Busy man's Canada*. Toronto. v. 2, no. 5 (June 1912), pp. 51-53.)

MASSEY, VINCENT What's past is prologue; the memoirs of the Right Honourable Vincent Massey. Toronto, Macmillan, 1963. 540 p.

MATTHEWS, JOHN Charles Mair. (In McDougall, R. L. (ed.) *Canada's past and*

present. [Toronto, 1967 c1965] pp. 78-191.)

Our living tradition, ser. 5.

MAVOR, JAMES Goldwin Smith. (In *MacLean's magazine*. Toronto. v. 34, no. 5 (Mar. 1, 1921), pp. 12-13; 47-49.)

MOIR, JOHN SARGENT Donald Grant Creighton. By John S. Moir. (In his *Character and circumstance*. Toronto, 1970. pp. 1-7.)

MORGAN, H. R. Dr. Charles Mair. By H. R. Morgan. (In *Willisons monthly*. Toronto. v. 2, no. 3 (Aug. 1926), pp. 110-111.)

MURRAY, PARKYN IAN Edgar G. Burton, national retail administrator. (In *Saturday night*. Toronto. v. 57, no. 32 (Apr. 18, 1942), p. 10.)

O'DONOGHUE, JOHN GEORGE Daniel John O'Donoghue, Father of the Canadian labor movement. By John G. O'Donoghue. (In Canadian Catholic Historical Association. *Report*. [Ottawa] (1942/43), pp. 87-96.)

O'LEARY, MICHAEL GRATTAN Dafoe of the Free Press. By M. Grattan O'Leary. (In *Maclean's*. Toronto. v. 42, no. 2 (Apr. 1, 1929), pp. 5; 79-81.)

—— Ross runs a paper worth quoting. By Grattan O'Leary. (In *Maclean's*. Toronto. v. 37, no. 21 (Nov. 1, 1924), pp. 18; 55-57.)

P. D. Ross, an Ottawa Press Gallery reporter and later owner of the *Ottawa Journal*.

ONDAATJE, CHRISTOPHER The prime ministers of Canada, 1867-1967. By Christopher Ondaatje and Robert Catherwood. Illustrated by C. G. Stephen. Toronto, Canyon Press, 1967. x, 176 p.

Brief biographical sketch. Coverage extends from J. A. Macdonald to L. B. Pearson.

The Ottawa Press Gallery. (In *Canadian illustrated news*. Montreal. v. 12, no. 5 (July 31, 1875), pp. 70-71.)

Lists and gives brief biographical sketches of the members.

OXFORD Lieut.-Colonel George T. Denison. By "Oxford". (In *The Week*. Toronto. v. 7, no. 16 (Mar. 21, 1890), pp. 249-250.)

Prominent Canadians: XXIX.

PAYNE, J. LAMBERT Kilkenny campaigns. Ringside reminiscences concerning some old-time political gladiators. (In *Maclean's*. Toronto. v. 40, no. 24 (Dec. 15, 1927), pp. 17; 46-47.)

Concerns political campaigning in the late nineteenth century.

Personnel of the Senate and House of Commons, eighth parliament of Canada, elected June 23, 1896. Portraits and biographies of the members. Montreal, J. Lovell, 1898. 208 p.

POPE, SIR JOSEPH   Canada finds her own Pepys . . . The diaries of Sir Joseph Pope. (In *Maclean's.* Toronto. v. 73, no. 2 (Jan. 16, 1960), pp. 20; 36-39.)
Excerpts from the diaries of Sir Joseph Pope.

—— Public servant; the memoirs of Sir Joseph Pope. Edited and compiled by Maurice Pope. Toronto, Oxford University Press, 1960. 312 p.

POPE, MAURICE ARTHUR   Soldiers and politicians; the memoirs of Lt.-Gen. Maurice A. Pope. [Toronto] University of Toronto Press [c1962] viii, 462 p.
Refers to the relationship between the Author and W. L. Mackenzie King.

PRESTON, WILLIAM THOMAS ROCHESTER   My generation of politics and politicians. Toronto, D. A. Rose [c1927] 462 p.

PRUD'HOMME, MAURICE   The life and times of Archbishop Taché. (In Historical and Scientific Society of Manitoba. *Papers.* Winnipeg. ser. 3, no. 11 (1956), pp. 4-17.)
Concerns Alexandre Antonin Taché.

RICHER, LEOPOLD   Silhuettes du monde politique. Montréal, Editions du Zodiaque [1940] 264 p. (Collection du Zodiaque '37.)

ROE, J. SYDNEY   The late Sir Joseph Pope. An intimate glimpse of the former dean of the Civil Service and companion of statesmen. By Sydney Roe. (In *Saturday night.* Toronto. v. 42, no. 5 (Dec. 18, 1926), p. 2.)
Written on the occasion of Pope's death Dec. 2, 1926.

—— Political jests of the past. Gems from traditional anecdotage of the House of Commons. By J. Sydney Roe. (In *Saturday night.* Toronto. v. 47, no. 34 (July 2, 1932), p. 3.)
Anecdotes concerning Flood Davin, Fielding, Michael Clark, John Barr, and Sam Barker.

ROSS, MALCOLM   Goldwin Smith. (In Bissell, C. T. (ed.) *Seven Canadians.* [Toronto, 1962, c1957] pp. 29-47.)
Our living tradition, ser. 1.

ROSS, PHILIP DANSKEN   Restrospects of a newspaper person. Toronto, Oxford University Press, 1931. xi, 327 p.
The Author became managing editor of the *Ottawa Journal* in 1886 and president of the Journal Publishing Company in 1891.

RUMILLY, ROBERT   Mgr Laflèche et son temps. Montréal. Editions du Zodiaque [1938] 424 p. (Collection du Zodiaque deuxième.)

RUSSELL, ANNA ALLISON   Goldwin Smith; his life and some of his works. With special reference to his separatism. [New York, 1929] 108 leaves.
Thesis (MA) – Columbia University.

SAINT-PIERRE, ARTHUR   Ce que je pense sur . . . Préf. de N. A. Belcourt. Montréal, Editions de La Bibliothèque canadienne, 1927. 185 p.

SAVARD ANTONIO   Au berceau de la Confédération. (In *Le Pays laurentien.* Montréal. 3. année, no 9 (sept. 1918), pp. 151-157.)
Biographical sketches of Sir John Macdonald, Sir G. E. Cartier, and Sir Wilfrid Laurier.

SCOTT, LESLIE   He wrote the tariffs for six finance ministers. (In *Maclean's.* Toronto. v. 44, no. 13 (July 1, 1931), pp. 19; 30.)
Concerns J. A. Russell.

SHACKLETON, PHIL   "Handyman" for the CCL. (In *Atlantic guardian.* St. John's, Nfld. v. 9, no. 1 (Jan. 1952), pp. 44-46.)
At head of title: Newfoundland abroad.
A brief biographical sketch of Eugene Forsey.

SHANNON, SAMUEL LEONARD   'Twas fifty years ago. (In *The Dalhousie review.* Halifax. v. 10 (1930/31), pp. [353]-357; 535]-540.)
Reminiscences of a civil servant working in the Department of Railways and Canals.

SHORTT, ADAM   A personality in journalism. (In *The Canadian magazine of politics, science, art and literature.* Toronto. v. 29 (1907), pp. 520-524.)
"An appreciation of the editor of the Toronto *Globe,* his independence and forcefulness in public discussion". Concerns J. A. Macdonald.

SHRIVE, NORMAN   Charles Mair; literary nationalist. [Toronto] University of Toronto Press [c1965] xii, 309 p.
Considers the role played by Charles Mair in the Canada First movement and the Red River Insurrection, 1869-70.

—— Poet and politics: Charles Mair at Red River. (In *Canadian literature.* Vancouver. v. 17 (1963), pp. 6-21.)

SIBLEY, C. LINTERN The secret of Van Horne's success. (In *MacLean's magazine.* Toronto. v. 29, no. 1 (Nov. 1915), pp. [45]-48.)

Concerns Sir William Van Horne.

SISSONS, CHARLES BRUCE Nil alienum; the memoirs of C. B. Sissons. [Foreword by Claude Bissell. Toronto] University of Toronto Press [c1964] xii, 260 p.

Partial contents: Chapt. 12. Politicians I have known. Concerns J. S. Woodsworth, E. C. Drury, and others.

SMITH, GOLDWIN Reminiscences. Edited by Arnold Haultain. New York, Macmillan, 1910. xv, 477 p.

—— A selection from Goldwin Smith's correspondence; comprising letters chiefly to and from his English friends, written between the years 1846 and 1910. Collected by his literary executor Arnold Haultain. London, T. Werner Laurie [1913] xxiv, 540 p.

SPRECKLEY, R. O. Statistics expert. (In *Saturday night.* Toronto. v. 51, no. 24 (Apr. 18, 1936), p. 12.)

A biographical sketch of R. H. Coats, Dominion Statistician.

STANLEY, GEORGE FRANCIS GILMAN Lionel-Adolphe Groulx: historian and prophet of French Canada. By George F. G. Stanley. (In La Pierre, L. (ed.) *French Canadian thinkers of the nineteenth and twentieth centuries.* Montreal, 1966. pp. 97-114.)

STEPHENSON, WILLIAM The spritely czar of the CPR. By Bill Stephenson. (In *MacLean's.* Toronto. v. 65, no. 22 (Nov. 15, 1952), pp. 27; 80-86.)

Concerns William Van Horne.

STUBBS, ROY ST. GEORGE John W. Dafoe. (In his *Prairie portraits.* Toronto [c1954] pp. 59-84)

—— Prairie portraits. Toronto, McClelland and Stewart [1954] ix, 176 p.

Partial contents: Lord Bennett. – John W. Dafoe. – E. J. McMurray.

STURSBERG, PETER Ottawa old boys complex. (In *Saturday night.* Toronto. v. 78, no. 11 (Dec. 1963), pp. 9-10.)

Selects four top deputy ministers: Norman Robertson, Robert Bryce, Gordon Robertson, and Louis Rasminsky, and discusses the function of the senior civil service.

SWETTENHAM, JOHN ALEXANDER McNaughton. By John Swettenham. Toronto, Ryerson Press [c1968-69] 3 v.

Concerns Andrew George Latta McNaughton, 1887-1966.

Contents: v. 1. 1887-1939. – v. 2. 1939-1943. – v. 3. 1944-1966.

TACHE, LOUIS JOSEPH CHARLES HYPPOLITE (ed.) Les hommes du jour; galerie de portraits contemporains. Monument érigé à la gloire de la Confédération du Canada. Direction de Louis H. Taché. Montréal, La Cie de moulins à papier de Montréal [1890] 507 p.

At head of title: Ed. populaire.

TACHE, LOUIS JOSEPH CHARLES HYPPOLITE Men of the day; a Canadian portrait gallery. Edited by Louis-H. Taché. [Popular ed.] Montreal, Montreal Paper Mills Co. [1890] 507 p. facsims., ports.

TAYLOR, FENNINGS Portraits of British Americans, by William Notman. With biographical sketches by Fennings Taylor. Montreal, W. Notman, 1865-68. 3 v. 84 ports.

The portraits are mounted photographs.

UNDERHILL, FRANK HAWKINS Canadian writers of today. x. J. W. Dafoe. By Frank H. Underhill. (In *The Canadian forum.* Toronto. v. 13, no. 145 (Oct. 1932), pp. 23-24.)

—— Goldwin Smith. By Frank H. Underhill (In *The University of Toronto quarterly.* [Toronto] v. 2 (1932/33), pp. 285-309.)

—— Goldwin Smith. (In his *In search of Canadian liberalism.* Toronto, 1961. pp. 85-103.)

"This article first appeared in *The University of Toronto quarterly,* April, 1933. I have tacked on to the end of it five paragraphs which formed the conclusion of a talk on Goldwin Smith that I gave over the CBC on 6 December, 1950."

—— J. W. Dafoe. (In his *In search of Canadian liberalism.* Toronto, 1961. pp. 141-147.)

This essay appeared in *The Canadian forum,* October 1932.

—— The political ideas of John S. Ewart. (In Canadian Historical Association. *Report of the annual meeting.* Ottawa. (1933), pp. 23-32.)

URQUHART, HUGH MAC INTYRE Arthur Currie; the biography of a great Canadian. With a foreword by Field Marshal Jan Christian Smuts. Toronto, Dent [1950] xix, 363 p.

VAUGHAN, WALTER The life and work of Sir William Van Horne. Illustrated by photos. New York, Century, 1920. xiii, 388 p.

VINING, CHARLES ARTHUR MC LAREN Mr. Dafoe. By R. T. L. (In *Maclean's*. Toronto. v. 46, no. 19 (Oct. 1, 1933), pp .8; 47.)

Concerns John W. Dafoe.

WADE, MASON Olivar Asselin. [Part] I [-II] (In McDougall, R. L. (ed.) *Canada's past and present.* [Toronto, 1967, c1965] pp. 134-179.)

Our living tradition, ser. 5.

WALDRON, GORDON Goldwin Smith. (In *The University monthly.* Toronto. v. 12, no. 5 (Mar. 1912), pp. 214-222.)

An address delivered at the Modern Language Club, February 12, 1912.

WALLACE, MARY ELISABETH Goldwin Smith: journalist and critic. By Elisabeth Wallace. (In *The Canadian forum.* Toronto. v. 35, no. 422 (Mar. 1956), p. 275.)

—— Goldwin Smith, liberal. By Elisabeth Wallace. (In *University of Toronto quarterly.* [Toronto] v. 23 (1953/54), pp. 155-172.)

—— Goldwin Smith, Victorian liberal. By Elisabeth Wallace. Toronto, University of Toronto Press [1957] 207 p.

WALLACE, WILLIAM STEWART "The Bystander" and Canadian journalism. By W. S. Wallace. (In *The Canadian magazine of politics, science, art and literature.* Toronto. v. 35 (1910), pp. 553-558.)

"The Bystander" was edited by Goldwin Smith.

—— The life and work of George M. Wrong. By W. S. Wallace. (In *The Canadian historical review.* Toronto. v. 29 (1948), pp. 229-237.)

WEIR, WILLIAM Sixty years in Canada. Montreal, J. Lovell, 1903. 268 p.

Author was Secretary of the Tariff Reform Association of 1858 and Government Agent for the exportation of American silver coin in 1870. Cf. Title page.

WHITE, ROBERT SMEATON Parliament and personalities. By R. S. White, MP. (In *The Dalhousie review.* Halifax. v. 16 (1936/37), pp. [5]-15.)

The Author entered the Press Gallery in 1882; his reminiscences concern persons from the late-nineteenth-century Canadian political scene.

WILLISON, SIR JOHN STEPHEN Reminiscences of public life and public men. (In Canadian Club of Hamilton. *Addresses.* Hamilton. (1913/14), pp. 17-21.)

Address delivered October 17, 1913.

The Author proposes "to gossip together on various incidents and various figures in Canadian political history".

Impressions of Edward Blake, John A. Macdonald, and others.

—— Reminiscences, political and personal. By Sir John Willison. (In *The Canadian magazine of politics, science, art and literature.* Toronto. v. 51 (1918), pp. 3-17.)

Part 1.

—— Reminiscences, political and personal. [Pt. 2] Early days in journalism. (In *The Canadian magazine of politics, science, art and literature.* Toronto. v. 51 (1918), pp. 95-104.)

—— Reminiscences, political and personal. [Pt. 5] The press and the press gallery. (In *The Canadian magazine of politics, science, art and literature.* Toronto. v. 51 (1918), pp. 387-397.)

—— Reminiscences, political and personal. [Pt. 12] Office and patronage. (In *The Canadian magazine of politics, science, art and literature.* Toronto. v. 52 (1918-19), pp. 1019-1028.)

—— Reminiscences, political and personal. [Pt. 14] What was left over. (In *The Canadian magazine of politics, science, art and literature.* Toronto. v. 53 (1919), pp. 126-136.)

Verbal portraits of miscellaneous personalities.

—— Reminiscences, political and personal. Toronto, McClelland and Stewart [c1919] 351 p.

—— Sir George Parkin; a biography. By Sir John Willison. London, Macmillan, 1929. 278 p.

YORK Charles Mair, FRSC. By York. (In *The Week.* Toronto. v. 8, no. 3 (Dec. 19, 1890), pp. 39-40.)

Prominent Canadians: XXXII.

POLITICAL HISTORY
(GENERAL WORKS AND STUDIES)

AITCHISON, JAMES HERMISTON (ed.) The political process in Canada; essays in honour of R. MacGregor Dawson. Edited by J. H. Aitchison. [Toronto] University of Toronto Press [c1963] vii, 193 p.

Partial contents: The press and the patronage, by N. Ward. – The democratic process at work in Canadian federal elections, by J. M. Beck. – Group interest in Canadian politics, by S. D. Clark. – Early socialism in Canada, by P. W. Fox. – The political ideas of J. W. Dafoe, by M. S. Donnelly. – The evolution of territorial government in Canada, by R. G. Robertson. – Legislative power to implement treaty obligations in Canada, by W. R. Lederman. – Political retrospect, by R. M. Clokie.

ALFORD, ROBERT R. Class voting in the Anglo-American political systems. (In Lipset, S. M. (ed.) *Party systems and voter alignments; cross-national perspectives.* New York [c1967] pp. 67-93. tables.)

A comparative analysis which includes the Canadian political party system.

—— Party and society; the Anglo-American democracies. Chicago, Rand McNally, 1965 [c1963] xxiii, 396 p. (Rand McNally sociology series.)

"A publication from the research program of the Survey Research Center, University of California, Berkeley, California."

A revised version of a doctoral dissertation submitted to the University of California at Berkeley under title: *Class voting in four Anglo-American countries.*

Partial contents: Chapt. 9. Canada: pure non-class politics? (pp. 250-286).

ALLEN, ALEXANDER RICHARD Salem Bland and the social gospel in Canada. [Saskatoon, Sask., 1961] iv.

Thesis (MA)–University of Saskatchewan.

—— The social gospel and the reform tradition in Canada, 1890-1928. By Richard Allen. (In *The Canadian historical review.* Toronto. v. 49 (1968), pp. 381-399.)

ANDERSON, F. W. Farmers in politics. [Saskatoon, 1949] 1 v.

Thesis (MA)–University of Saskatchewan.

ARES, RICHARD Notre question nationale.

Montréal, Editions de l'action nationale, 1943–v.

Edition varies.

Contents: t. 1. Les faits. – t. 2. Positions de principes. – t. 3. Positions patriotiques et nationales. – t. 4. Positions politiques et constitutionnelles. – t. 5-6. Les sources de l'action. – t. 7. Que faire?

BACCHI-FERRARO, CAROL LEE The ideas of Canadian suffragists, 1890-1920. [Montreal, 1970] 1 v.

Thesis (MA) – McGill University.

Backstage at Ottawa. (In *Maclean's.* Toronto. v. 44, no. 4—v. 81, no. 6 (Feb. 15, 1931—June 1968).)

Column dealing with national politics written by a Politician with a notebook, i.e. Grattan O'Leary (Feb. 15, 1931—Mar. 1, 1941), by the Man with a notebook, i.e. Kenneth Wilson (Apr. 15, 1941—Dec. 1ᶜ 1943), by Blair Fraser (Jan. 1, 1944—June 1, 1950), under the pseudonym of the Man with a notebook; June 15, 1950—Mar. 12, 1960; Nov. 16, 1963—June 1968), and by Peter C. Newman (Mar. 26, 1960—Nov. 2, 1963).

BALLANTYNE, M. G. The relationship between principles and politics. (In *Culture.* Québec. v. 8 (1947), pp. [140]-148.)

BARNES, SAMUEL HENRY The ideologies and politics of Canadian labor organizations. [Durham, N.C. 1957] xii, 304 leaves.

Thesis (PH D) – Duke University.

BASEVI, VINCENT Nebulous politics. (In *The Canadian magazine of politics, science, art and literature.* Toronto. v. 43 (1914), pp. 207-210.)

A general discussion of the political party system drawing upon "Canada and Great Britain when seeking established customs to verify my theory".

BEAUCHESNE, ARTHUR We are stable because of two-party system. (In *Saturday night.* Toronto. v. 60, no. 20 (Jan. 20, 1945), p. 8.)

BECK, JAMES MURRAY The democratic process at work in Canadian general elections. By J. Murray Beck (In Aitchison, J. H. (ed.) *The political process in Canada.* [Toronto, c1963] pp. [36]-63.)

—— The democratic process at work in Canadian general elections. By J. Murray Beck. (In Courtney, J. C. (ed.) *Voting in Canada.* [Scarborough, Ont., c1967] pp. [2]-31.)

Reprinted from *The Political process in Canada,* edited by J. H. Aitchison. Toronto, 1963.

The above has been revised to include the 1963 and 1965 general elections.

—— Party images in Canada. By J. M. Beck and D. J. Dooley. (In *Queen's quarterly.* Kingston. v. 67 (1960), pp. [431]-448.)

—— Party images in Canada. By J. M. Beck and D. J. Dooley (In Thorburn, H. G. (ed.) *Party politics in Canada.* Scarborough, Ont. [c1967] pp. [76]-86.)

"Reprinted from Queen's quarterly, LXVII, no. 3, 1960".

Analyses three types of political party images: the party of economic expansion, the party of national unity, the party led by a leader possessing a commanding personality.

—— Pendulum of power; Canada's federal elections. By J. Murray Beck. Scarborough, Ont., Prentice-Hall [c1968] 442 p.

BELANGER, ANDRE J.   Le nationalisme et les partis politiques. Par André-J. Bélanger et Vincent Lemieux. Marc La Terreur: commentaire. (In *Revue d'histoire de l'Amérique française.* Montréal. v. 22, no. 4 (mars 1969), pp. [539]-566.)

BELL, RICHARD   The political party; its organization, candidates, and finances. By Richard Bell and Richard Stanbury. (In Hawkins, Gordon (ed.) *Order and good government.* [Toronto, c1965] pp. 99-116.)

BENGOUGH, JOHN WILSON   A caricature history of Canadian politics; events from the union of 1841, as illustrated by cartoons from "Grip", and various other sources. By J. W. Bengough, with an introd. by Rev. Principal Grant. Toronto, Grip Print. and Pub. Co., 1886. 2 v. illus.

BENOIT, JOSEPH PAUL AUGUSTIN   Genèse du libéralisme au Canada. Par Dom Benoît. (In *Le Mouvement catholique.* Trois-Rivières. v. 5 (jan./juin 1900), pp. [339]-349.)

BERIAULT, YVON   Les problèmes politiques du nord canadien. [Ottawa] 1941. 251 leaves.

Thesis (PH D) – University of Ottawa.

BERTON, PIERRE FRANCIS DE MARIGNY   The greatest three-cent show on earth. Part one. By Pierre Berton. (In *Maclean's.* Toronto. v. 65, no. 6 (Mar. 15, 1952), pp. 7-9; 57-60.)

An essay on the *Toronto Star.* Includes discussion of political policy.

—— The greatest three-cent show on earth. By Pierre Berton. Conclusion. Hindmarsh of the Star. (In *Maclean's.* Toronto. v. 65, no. 7 (Apr. 1, 1952), pp. 16-17; 37-42.)

BIGGAR, EMERSON BRISTOL   The Canadian railway problem. Toronto, Macmillan, 1917. 258 p.

BJARNASON, EMIL   Class and elite in Canadian society. (In *The Marxist quarterly.* Toronto. no. 16 (winter 1966), pp. 1-10.)

A review article of *The vertical mosaic,* by J. Porter. Toronto, University of Toronto Press, 1965.

BLACK, HAWLEY LISLE   French and English Canadian political journalists; a comparative study. By Hawley L. Black. [Montreal] 1967 [c1969] vi, 378 leaves.

Thesis (MA) – McGill University.

BLAND, SALEM GOLDWORTH   The new Christianity; or, The religion of the new age. By Salem Bland. Toronto, McClelland and Stewart [1920] 168 p.

Exposition of the social gospel reform movement.

BOISSONNAULT, CHARLES MARIE   Histoire politico-militaire des Canadiens-Français (1763-1945) [Trois-Rivières] Editions du Bien public [1967] 310 p.

BONENFANT, JEAN CHARLES   Les études politiques. (In *Recherches sociographiques.* Québec. v. 3, no 1/2 (jan./août 1962), pp. [75]-82.)

BORDEN, SIR ROBERT LAIRD   Political development and relations. (In *Dalhousie review.* Halifax. v. 2 (1922/23), pp. [399]-409.)

"An address delivered at the University of Michigan, Ann Arbor, on the 6th October, 1922. The full title: 'Political development and relations among the English-speaking peoples'." Comparative remarks.

BOURINOT, ARTHUR STANLEY   Politics and letters in Canada. By Arthur S. Bourinot. (In *Willisons monthly.* Toronto. v. 3, no. 11 (Apr. 1928), pp. 430-432.)

Discusses the writings of Joseph Howe,

Thomas D'Arcy McGee, Nicholas Flood Davin, and others.

BOURINOT, SIR JOHN GEORGE The study of political science in Canadian universities. By John George Bourinot. (In Royal Society of Canada. *Proceedings and transactions.* Montreal. [ser. 1] v. 7 (1889), section 2, pp. 3-16.)

"Read May 25, 1889."

BOVEY, JOHN ALEXANDER The attitudes and policies of the federal government towards Canada's northern territories, 1870-1930. [Vancouver] 1967. 1 v.

Thesis (MA) – University of British Columbia.

BRABEK, STANLEY The Tariff Board and the development of tariff policy; a study of Tariff Board references and their influence on the Canadian tariff. [Kingston, Ont., 1965] 1 v.

Thesis (MA) – Queen's University.

BRAULT, FLORENT The fiscal policy of Canada since Confederation. Rochester, N.Y., University of Rochester Press, 1954. ix, 214 p. (University of Rochester Canadian studies series, no. 4.)

Thesis (PH D) – St. Louis University, 1952.

BRECHER, IRVING Monetary and fiscal thought and policy in Canada, 1919-1939. [Toronto] University of Toronto Press, 1957. xii, 337 p. (Canadian studies in economics, no. 8.)

BRIDLE, AUGUSTUS Women are read out of democracy. (In *Canadian courier.* Toronto. v. 25, no. 9 (Jan. 31, 1920), pp. 18-19.)

Presents the views of Sir Andrew Macphail. Cf. Women in democracy, by Sir A. Macphail. (In *The University magazine.* Montreal. v. 19 (1920), pp. [1]-15.)

—— Yea, the great Globe itself. By Augustus Bridle and Britton B. Cooke. (In *The Canadian courier.* Toronto. v. 20, no. 3 (June 17, 1916), pp. 4-5.)

A brief historical survey of the Toronto *Globe.*

BROWN, CLYDE MANNING Evolution of Canadian political parties. [Wolfville, N.S.] 1935. 1 v.

Thesis (MA) – Acadia University.

BROWN, ROBERT CRAIG Canadian nationalism in Western newspapers. By R. Craig Brown. (In *Alberta historical review.* Edmonton. v. 10, no. 3 (summer 1962), pp. 1-7.)

—— Canadian nationalism in Western newspapers. By R. Craig Brown. (In Swainson, Donald (ed.) *Historical essays on the Prairie Provinces.* Toronto [c1970] pp. [89]-98.)

Reprinted from "*Alberta Historical Review,* vol. 10, no. 3 (spring [i.e. summer] 1962), pp. 1-7".

—— The nationalism of the National Policy (In University League for Social Reform. *Nationalism in Canada.* Toronto [1966] pp. 155-163.)

BRUNET, MICHEL Quand un historien se mêle de lire dans la boule de cristal. (In Clarkson, Stephen (ed.) *Visions 2020.* Edmonton [c1970] pp. [123]-127.)

BURWASH, NATHANAEL The evolution and degeneration of party. A study in political history. By N. Burwash. (In Royal Society of Canada. *Proceedings and transactions.* Ottawa. ser. 2, v. 9 (1903), section 2, pp. 3-13.)

"Read May 19th, 1903."

Analyses the form and development of the modern political party.

CAIRNS, ALAN C. The electoral system and the party system in Canada, 1921-1965. (In *Canadian journal of political science.* Toronto. v. 1 (1968), pp. [55]-80.)

". . . a revised version of a paper read at the thirty-ninth annual meeting of the Canadian Political Science Association at Ottawa, 1967."

—— The electoral system and the party system in Canada, 1921-1965. (In Kruhlak, O. M. (comp.) *The Canadian political process.* Toronto [c1970] pp. 139-164.)

Reprinted from *Canadian journal of political science.* v. 1 (1968), pp. 55-80.

—— A reply to J. A. A. Lovink, "On analysing the impact of the electoral system on the party system in Canada". (In *Canadian journal of political science.* Toronto. v. 3 (1970), pp. [517]-521.)

For the original article see Lovink, J. A. A. On analysing the impact of the electoral system on the party system in Canada. (In *Canadian journal of political science.* Toronto. v. 3 (1970), pp. [497]-516.)

CAMERON, JAMES MALCOLM Political Pictorians; the men in the Legislative Council, Senate, House of Commons, House of Assembly, 1767-1967. [Foreword, by

Allan J. MacEachen] Ottawa, The Author [pref. 1966] v, 267 p.

Relates the political history of Pictou County, Nova Scotia.

CAMP, DALTON KINGSLEY   Are political parties obsolete? By Dalton Camp. (In *Saturday night.* Toronto. v. 84, no. 5 (May 1969), pp. 24-25.)

—— The Canadian image. By Dalton K. Camp. (In Litvak, I. A. (ed.) *The nation keepers.* New York, Toronto. [c1967] pp. 105-110.)

CANADA. COMMITTEE ON ELECTION EXPENSES Report of the Committee on Election Expenses, 1966. [Ottawa, R. Duhamel, Queen's Printer, 1966] x, 528 p.

Committee on Election Expenses: Alphonse Barbeau, M. J. Coldwell, Gordon R. Dryden, Arthur R. Smith, Norman Ward.

Contents: pt. 1. Report of the Committee on Election Expenses. - pt. 2. Studies.

—— Studies in Canadian party finance. Contributing authors: Khayyam Z. Paltiel, John Meisel and Richard Van Loon, J. L. Granatstein, Michael Stein. Alphonse Barbeau, chairman. [Ottawa, R. Duhamel, Queen's Printer, 1966. xxviii, 598 p.

Contents: Study 1. Federalism and party finance. - Study 2. Canadian attitudes to election expenses, 1965-66. - Study 3. Financing the Liberal Party, 1867-1965. - Study 4. Conservative Party finances, 1939-1945. - Study 5. The finances of the Co-operative Commonwealth Federation and the New Democratic Party, 1933-1965. - Study 6. The structure and function of the finances of the Ralliement des Créditistes. - Study 7. Candidate attitudes toward the control of election expenses.

Canadian economic policy. By T. N. Brewis, H. E. English, Anthony Scott, Pauline Jewett. With a statistical appendix by J. E. Gander. Rev. ed. Toronto, Macmillan [1965] xv. 463 p.

First ed. published 1961.

Contents: pt. 1. Resource allocation and government policy. - pt. 2. Economic stability and government policy. - pt. 3. Economic welfare and regional aspects of policy. - pt. 4. Policy formation. (Chapt. 15. Political and administrative aspects of policy formation, by P. Jewett).

CANADIAN PRESS ASSOCIATION   A history of Canadian journalism in the several portions of the Dominion. With a sketch of the Canadian Press Association, 1859-1908. Edited by a committee of the Association, [Pref. by J. R. Bone, J. T. Clark, A. H. U. Colquhoun, J. F. Mackay] Toronto, 1908. xv, 242 p.

Canadian society; sociological perspectives. Edited by Bernard R. Blishen, Frank E. Jones, Kaspar D. Naegele, John Porter. 3d ed. Toronto, Macmillan, 1968. xiii, 877 p.

Partial contents: The social bases of political cleavage in 1962, by R. R. Alford. – Voting behaviour and the ethnic-religious variable; a study of a federal election in Hamilton, Ontario, by G. M. Anderson. – Poverty and political movements, by M. Pinard. – Value differences, absolute or relative, by S. M. Lipset. – The religious sect in Canadian politics, by S. D. Clark.

CAPPON, JAMES   The party system of government. (In *Queen's quarterly.* [Kingston] v. 11 (1903/04), pp. 434-436.)

—— The responsibility of political parties. (In *Queen's quarterly.* Kingston, v. 12 (1904/05), pp. [307]-313.)

Discusses the "spoils system" as it relates to the party system of government.

CARRIGAN, DAVID OWEN (comp.)   Canadian party platforms, 1867-1968. Compiled by D. Owen Carrigan. [Toronto] Copp Clark [c1968] xi, 363 p.

CHARTIER, EMILE   Le Canada d'hier et d'aujourd'hui (1840-1914). (In *Revue canadienne.* Montréal. nouv. sér., v. 25 (1920), pp. [401]-426.)

General remarks tracing the political development of Canada to the status of a nation.

CHIRON   The study of politics. By Chiron. (In *The New Dominion monthly.* Montreal. (Aug. 1870), pp. 31-33.)

A theoretical discussion of practical politics.

CHRISTIE, EDWARD ALEXANDER   The Presbyterian Church in Canada and its official attitude toward public affairs and social problems, 1875-1925. [Toronto] 1955. 319 leaves.

Thesis (MA) – University of Toronto.

CLARK, ROBERT MILLS (ed.)   Canadian issues; essays in honour of Henry F. Angus. Edited by Robert M. Clark. [Foreword by Norman MacKenzie. Toronto] Published for the University of British Columbia by

University of Toronto Press [c1961] xx, 371 p.

Partial contents: Administration and democracy, by H. F. Angus. – Constitutional trends and federalism, by J. A. Corry. – The speakership of the Canadian House of Commons, by J. H. Aitchison. – The Senate of Canada – political conundrum, by J. N. Turner. – The Royal Commission on Dominion-Provincial Relations, by R. M. Burns. – Government policy and the public lands, by A. D. Scott. – Bibliography of publications by Henry F. Angus.

CLARK, SAMUEL DELBERT   The Canadian Manufacturers' Association; a political and social study. Toronto, 1938. 217 leaves.

Thesis (PH D) – University of Toronto.

—— The Canadian Manufacturers' Association; a study in collective bargaining and political pressure. By S. D. Clark. Toronto, University of Toronto Press, 1939. xiii, 107 p. (University of Toronto studies. History and economics series, v. 7.)

—— The Canadian Manufacturers' Association and the tariffs. By S. D. Clark. (In The Canadian journal of economics and political science. [Toronto] v. 5 (1939), pp. 19-39.)

Describes the political activities of the Association as a tariff lobbying organization.

—— Group interests in Canadian politics. By S. D. Clark. (In Aitchison, J. H. (ed.) The political process in Canada. [Toronto, c1963] pp. [64]-78.)

—— The religious sect in Canadian politics. By S. D. Clark. (In Canadian society; sociological perspectives. Edited by B. R. Blishen [and others] 3d ed. Toronto, 1968. pp. 384-395.)

"Reprinted in abridged form from American journal of sociology, LI (November 1945), pp. 207-16."

Discussion is confined "to three evangelical groups . . . the Baptists in Nova Scotia, the Methodists in Upper Canada . . . and the followers of William Aberhart in Alberta".

CLARKSON, STEPHEN (ed.)   Visions 2020; fifty Canadians in search of a future. Edited for the Canadian forum by Stephen Clarkson. Edmonton, M. G. Hurtig [c1970] 290 p.

Partial contents: Man and government, by R. Stanfield. – The future politician, by W. L. Gordon. – The shape of government and politics in Canada in 2020, by T. A. Hockin. – The future of the Winnipeg General Strike, by K. McNaught. – A Canadian Utopia; the Cooperative Commonwealth of Edward Partridge, by C. Berger. – Visionaries of the 1930s; the League for Social Reconstruction, by M. Horn.

CLAUSEN, OLIVER   Macpherson: satire to drink beer by. By O. C. [In Canada month. Montreal. v. 2, no. 4 (Apr. 1962), pp. 30-36.]

Discusses the political satire of Duncan Macpherson, Len Norris, Peter Kuch, James Greig Reidford, McNally of Montreal, Robert LaPalme.

CLEVERDON, CATHERINE LYLE   The woman suffrage movement in Canada. [Toronto] University of Toronto Press, 1950. xiii, 324 p.

Thesis (PH D) – Columbia University.

Published also without thesis statement.

"Women in Canadian politics"; pp. 267-283.

CLOKIE, HUGH MCDOWALL   Canadian contributions to political science. (In Culture. Québec. v. 3 (1942), pp. [467]-474.)

—— Parliamentary government in wartime. By H. McD. Clokie. (In The Canadian journal of economics and political science. [Toronto] v. 6 (1940), pp. 359-371.)

Discusses the impact of war-time conditions upon parliamentary procedure and proceedings.

—— The political history of Canada in retrospect. By H. McD. Clokie. (In Culture. Québec. v. 5 (1944), pp. [291]-296.)

—— Political retrospect. By Hugh McD. Clokie. (In Aitchison, J. H. (ed.) The political process in Canada. [Toronto, c1963] pp. [182]-193.)

COHEN, RONALD I.   Quebec votes; the how and why of Quebec voting in every federal election since Confederation. Montreal, Saje Publications [1965] 128 p.

—— Le vote au Québec; les pourquoi et comment du vote fédéral au Québec depuis la Confédération. Montréal, Saje Publications [1965] 128 p.

Translated from the English by Raymond Dionne and Renaude Lapointe.

Translation of Quebec votes.

COLQUHOUN, ARTHUR HUGH URQUHART
The significance of and the reasons for
Confederation. By A. H. U. Colquhoun.
(In *The Canadian magazine*. Toronto. v.
68, no. 1 (July 1927), pp. 5; 32-33.)

CONGRESS ON CANADIAN AFFAIRS, 1ST, QUE-
BEC, 1961 Le Canada, expérience ratée...
ou réussie? The Canadian experiment,
success or failure? Québec, Presses de
l'Université Laval, 1962. 180 p.

Text partly in French, partly in English,
with summaries in the other language.

Congress held Nov. 15-18, 1961, under the
auspices of the Association générale des
étudiants de l'Université Laval.

Contents: La Confédération, par E. D.
Fulton. – Canada, one nation or two? by E.
Forsey. – Le Canada, une nation ou deux?
par A. Laurendeau. – The proper role of the
state, federally and provincially, by J. R.
Mallory. – Le rôle de l'Etat, sur les plans
fédéral et provincial, par R. Lévesque. –
L'avenir du Canada, par M. Chaput. – The
future of Canada, by M. Oliver. – La Confédération en théorie . . . et en pratique,
par J. J. Bertrand.

CONWAY, JOHN Geo-politics and the Canadian union. (In Ontario Advisory Committee on Confederation. *Background
papers and reports*. [Toronto, 1970] v.
2, pp. 28-49.)

COOK, GEORGE RAMSAY Loyalism, technology and Canada's fate. By Ramsay Cook.
(In *Journal of Canadian studies*. Peterborough, Ont. v. 5, no. 3 (1970), pp. 50-
60.)

An analysis of *Lament for a nation*, by
G. Grant. Toronto, McClelland & Stewart,
1965.

An expanded version of this article is
included in the Author's *The maple leaf
forever*. Toronto, 1971 (pp. 46-67).

—— The maple leaf forever; essays on nationalism and politics in Canada. By Ramsay Cook. Toronto, Macmillan [c1971]
253 p.

"Notes" (bibliographical): pp. 215-243.

—— Quebec and Confederation past and
present. By Ramsay Cook. (In *Queen's
quarterly*. Kingston. v. 71 (1964), pp.
468-484.)

"A revised version of a lecture given on
the University of the Air, CBC, May 27,
1964."

COOK, JOHN THOMAS The origin of the

Canadian party system [Saskatoon]
1933. 2 v. (523 leaves)

Thesis (MA)–University of Saskatchewan.

COOKE, BRITTON B. The man without a
party. The growing complaint of the
political orphans of the Dominion. By
Britton B. Cooke. (In *The Canadian courier*. Toronto. v. 20, no. 2 (June 10, 1916),
pp. [5]; 21.)

Concerns the lot of persons committed to
politics, but not affiliated with a political
party.

COOPER, JOHN ALEXANDER Canadian democracy and socialism. (In *The Canadian
magazine of politics, science, art and literature*. Toronto. v. 3 (1894), pp. [332]-
336.)

—— Has the Canadian Club a function,
if so—what? By the Editor. (In *Canadian
courier*. Toronto. v. 25, no. 11 (Feb. 28,
1920), pp. [5]-6.)

CORBETT, DAVID CHARLES The pressure
group and the public interest. By David
C. Corbett. (In Institute of Public Administration of Canada. *Proceedings of
the annual conference*. Toronto. 5th
(1953), pp. 185-195.)

COTE, LOUISE Au nez de l'histoire. (In *Le
Magazine Maclean*. Montréal. v. 3, no. 9
(sept. 1963), pp. [20-23]; 54.)

Concerns political history in cartoons.

COUCHICHING CONFERENCE, 25TH, 1956
Texts of addresses delivered at the 25th
annual Couchiching Conference. A joint
project of the Canadian Institute on Pub-
lic Affairs and the Canadian Broadcasting
Corporation, August 4th–11th, 1956,
Geneva Park, Lake Couchiching, Ontario.
[Toronto, 1956] 119 p.

Cover title.

Partial contents: The condition of Canadian politics, by F. Underhill, J. Marchand,
and R. Graham.

COUCHICHING CONFERENCE, 36TH, 1967 The
image or the issue. [Pref. by Pat Harrison.
Toronto, Canadian Institute on Public
Affairs, 1967] 78 p.

Cover title.

Presented by the Canadian Institute on
Public Affairs and the Canadian Broadcasting Corporation.

Reproduced typescript.

A selection of conference papers dealing
with matters concerning politics and the
press, politics and broadcasting, politics and

public relations, politics and polling, and the future of communications.

COURTNEY, JOHN CHILDS (ed.) Voting in Canada. A selection of papers edited by John C. Courtney. [Scarborough, Ont.] Prentice-Hall of Canada [c1967] 210 p. tables.

Partial contents: The democratic process at work in Canadian general elections, by J. M. Beck. – Our fantastic electoral system, by F. H. Underhill. – By-elections and public opinion in Canada, by H. A. Scarrow. – Voting in the 1960 federal by-elections at Peterborough and Niagara Falls, by P. Jewett. – Canadian political parties, by E. M. Reid. – Federal-provincial voting patterns in Canada, by H. A. Scarrow. – The electoral behaviour of Nova Scotia in 1965, by J. M. Beck. – Patterns of voter turnout in Canada, by H. A. Scarrow. – Questionnaire response, voter turnout and party support, by D. E. Smith. – Voting in Canadian two-member constituencies, by N. Ward. – Ballot behaviour in Halifax revisited, by M. Davis. – Religious affiliation and electoral behaviour, by J. Meisel. – Social structure and Canadian political parties; the Quebec case, by W. O. Filley. – An analysis of voting shifts in Quebec, by W. P. Irvine. – Democracy in Alberta, by S. M. Lipset. – Ethnic and party affiliations of candidates as determinants of voting, by L. J. Kamin. – Appendix A: Voter turnout at Canadian general elections, 1896-1965 (p. [200]-201). – Appendix B: A note on six elections [1953-1965] (p. [202]-205).

COX, BRUCE LORNE A comparison of Canadian and Australian liberalism; its origin and development to 1914. Toronto, 1956. 213 leaves.

Thesis (MA) – University of Toronto.

CREIGHTON, DONALD GRANT The Church: how much political power does it wield? By Donald Creighton. (In Maclean's. Toronto. v. 72, no. 10 (May 9, 1959), pp 28; 62-69.)

Considers, historically, the influence of the Roman Catholic Church on provincial and federal politics, with specific reference to French Canada.

CRERAR, THOMAS ALEXANDER Public order, liberty and nationalism. By Hon. T. A. Crerar. (In Canada month. Montreal. v. 7, no. 8 (Aug. 1967), pp. 14-17.)

CROFT, BARBARA Women's pressure groups

—good or bad? (In Chatelaine. Toronto. v. 38, no. 1 (Jan. 1965), pp. 22; 48; 51.)

CRONIN, FERGUS When voting was a high adventure. (In Maclean's. Toronto. v. 70, no. 11 (May 25, 1957), pp. 28-29; 36; 40-44.)

CROSS, AUSTIN FLETCHER "The other place." By Austin Cross. (In Public affairs. Halifax. v. 15, no. 2 (winter 1953), pp. [39]-45.)

Describes the Château Laurier in Ottawa as a meeting place for politicians.

—— The people's mouths. Toronto, Macmillan Company of Canada, 1943. viii, 171 p.

A popular treatment depicting political personalities in Ottawa. Includes extensive comments on the personality and administration of W. L. Mackenzie King.

CUNNINGHAM, F. J. G. Canada's second century. (In Institute of Public Administration of Canada. Proceedings of the annual conference. Toronto. 10th (1958), pp. 135-146.)

CUNNINGHAM, ROBERT B. The impact of local candidates in Canadian federal elections. [Kingston, 1970] 18 leaves. (In Canadian Political Science Association. Papers presented at the annual meeting. Kingston. 42d (1970), v. 3 [pt.] 40.)

Reproduced typescript.

CURRIE, ARCHIBALD WILLIAM The Grand Trunk Railway of Canada. Toronto, University of Toronto Press, 1957. viii, 556 p.

CURTIS, GEORGE FREDERICK The stresses and strains of Confederation. By George F. Curtis. (In Canadian Institute on Economics and Politics. Problems in Canadian unity. Toronto [c1938] pp. 22-23.)

DAFOE, JOHN WESLEY Canadian problems of government. By J. W. Dafoe. (In The Canadian journal of economics and political science. [Toronto] v. 5 (1939), pp. 285-299.)

"The presidential address delivered at a joint meeting of the Canadian Political Science Association and the Canadian Historical Association on May 26, 1939."

DALES, JOHN HARKNESS Protection, immigration and Canadian nationalism. By John Dales. (In University League for Social Reform. Nationalism in Canada. Toronto [1966] pp. 164-177.)

—— The protective tariff in Canada's development; eight essays on trade and tariffs when factors move with special reference to Canadian protectionism, 1870-1955. By J. H. Dales. [Toronto] University of Toronto Press [c1966] v, 168 p. [Canadian University paper-books, 58.]

——Some historical and theoretical comment on Canada's national policies. By John H. Dales. (In *Queen's quarterly*. Kingston. v. 71 (1964), pp. [297]-316.)

DANESHAZARD, ALI Teenager and politics; a study of political attitudes. [Vancouver] 1968. 1 v.

Thesis (MA) – University of British Columbia.

DAOUST, ROGER Le rose et le noir dans la Presse et le Devoir. Montréal, Editions du Jour [1969] 125 p. [Cahiers de Cité libre, CL-7.]

DAVID, LAURENT OLIVIER La question des drapeaux. Suivi de Noblesse oblige, L'Union nationale, La guerre . . . Croisades nationales, etc. Par L. O. David. Montréal, Beauchemin, 1926. 112 p.

A collection of brief reflective essays.

DAVIN, NICHOLAS FLOOD Great speeches. (In Rose-Belford's *Canadian monthly and national review*. Toronto. v. 5 (1880), pp. 270-285.)

Discusses public speaking, with particular reference to the Canadian Parliament.

DAWSON, HELEN JONES An interest group: the Canadian Federation of Agriculture. (In *Canadian public administration*. Toronto. v. 3 (1960), pp. 134-149.)

A close examination of the various techniques used by the Federation to influence government policies with regards to the specific interests of Canadian farmers.

DAWSON, ROBERT MAC GREGOR (ed.) Constitutional issues in Canada, 1900-1931. Edited by Robert MacGregor Dawson. London, Oxford University Press, 1933. xvi, 482 p.

This book is designed to make "the raw material for a study of Canadian government more accessible – both to the layman and to the university student. . . . The sources used are of two kinds: official documents and newspapers and periodicals."

See, especially, Chapter 8. Political parties. I. Distinguishing features of Canadian political parties. II. The national leader of a party. III. Revolt against the old parties.

DEAN, EDGAR PACKARD How Canada has

voted, 1867 to 1945. (In *The Canadian historical review*. Toronto. v. 30 (1949), pp. 227-248.)

DERBY, ALEXANDER MC INTOSH Politics and Canadian economic development since Confederation. [Hamilton, Ont.] 1924. 39 leaves.

Thesis (MA) – McMaster University.

DESPRES, JEAN PIERRE L'action politique et les syndicats ouvriers. (In his *Le mouvement ouvrier canadien*. Montréal [1946] pp. 81-108.)

—— Le Mouvement ouvrier canadien. Préf. de Edouard Montpetit. Montréal, Fides [1947] 205 p. (Bibliothèque économique et sociale, 3.)

"Publié sous les auspices du Département des relations industrielles de la Faculté des sciences sociales de Laval."

Chapter 4: L'action politique et les syndicats ouvriers (pp. 81-108.)

DESROSIERS, LEO PAUL L'esprit de parti. (In *L'Action française*. Montréal. v. 12 (nov. 1924), pp. [258]-268.)

At head of title: L'ennemi dans la place.

DESSAUER, FREDERICK EMANUEL The party system and the new economic policies. By F. E. Dessauer. (In *The Canadian journal of economics and political science*. [Toronto] v. 9 (1943), pp. 139-149.)

A general comparative discussion considering traditional forms of popular government and the technical approach employed by the modern political administration.

DIAMOND, ROLLAND Les troisième partis et l'esprit de parti dans la province de Québec. [Québec] 1943. 1 v.

Thesis (MA) – Laval University.

DICKS, STEWART KINLOCK The evolution of radicalism in the work of F. H. Underhill [London, Ont.] 1968. ix, 252 leaves.

Thesis (MA) – University of Western Ontario.

DOBBS, KILDARE Canadian heroes? (In *Saturday night*. Toronto. v. 83, no. 2 (Feb. 1968) pp. [21]-23.)

Heroes & villains, 1.

Interpretative remarks on some personalities in Canadian contemporary history, Mackenzie King, John Diefenbaker, René Lévesque, etc.

DOUGLAS, THOMAS CLEMENT The government and the economy. By T. C. Douglas.

(In Litvak, I. A. (ed.) *The nation keepers.* New York, Toronto [c1967] pp. 45-55.)

DRUMMOND, ANDREW THOMAS How far is public ownership wise? By Andrew T. Drummond. (In *Queen's quarterly.* Kingston. v. 25 (1917/18), pp. 17-26.)

Cites, especially, as concrete examples, the construction and operation of canals and railways by the Canadian government.

DUBE, YVES Quelques aspects de la politique des transports au Canada. (In *Canadian public administration.* Toronto. v. 5 (1962), pp. 28-37.)

"Etude d'abord presenté lors du treizième congrès annuel de l'Institut d'administration publique du Canada, du 6 au 9 septembre, 1961, à Ste. Foy, Québec."

DUBUC, ALFRED The decline of Confederation and the new nationalism. (In University League for Social Reform. *Nationalism in Canada.* Toronto [1966] pp. 112-132.)

DUMONT, JACQUES Méditation pour jeunes politiques. (In *L'Action française.* Montréal. v. 17 (jan. 1927), pp. [28]-40; v. 17 (fév. 1927), pp. [100]-110); v. 17 (mars 1927), pp. [170]-178; v. 17 (avr. 1927), pp. [217]-227.)

In four parts.

DYKEMAN, F. A. The genesis of Canada's railway problems. By F. A. Dykeman. (In *The Busy East of Canada.* Sackville, N.B. v. 23, no. 8 (Mar. 1933), pp. 8-13.)

"From a paper read before the Fortnightly Club of Saint John, N.B. on February 20, 1933."

An historical review.

EASTON, DAVID GERALD Social and political aspects of unemployment insurance in Canada; a phase of social security. Toronto, 1943. 250 leaves.

Thesis (MA) – University of Toronto.

Election notes. (In *The Canadian forum.* Toronto. v. 25, no. 293 (June 1945), pp. 57-58.)

A brief historical survey of the six general elections held since 1914.

ENGELMANN, FREDERICK C. Party integration in Canada. By F. C. Engelmann and S. I. Pobihushchy. (In Kruhlak, O. M. (comp.) *The Canadian political process.* Toronto [c1970] pp. 180-197.)

"A translated and slightly revised version of a paper prepared in early 1968 which appeared as 'Parteienintegration in Kanada',

Verfassung und Verfassungswirklichkeit (Jahrbuch, 1969), Koeln und Opladen: Westdeutscher Verlag, 1962 (pp. 137-154)."

ENGELMANN, FREDERICK C. Political parties and the Canadian social structure, by Frederick C. Engelmann and Mildred A. Schwartz. [Scarborough, Ont.] Prentice-Hall [1967] 277 p.

EPSTEIN, LEON D. A comparative study of Canadian parties. (In Kruhlak, O. M. (comp.) *The Canadian political process.* Toronto [c1970] pp. 325-344.)

Reprinted from *American political science review.* v. 58 (1964), pp. 46-59.

EWART, JOHN SKIRVING False political phrases. (In *The Canadian historical review.* Toronto. v. 14 (1933), pp. 123-135.)

FAIRLEY, MARGARET The women's party. (In *The Rebel.* Toronto. v. 3 (1918), pp. 27-29.)

FALARDEAU, JEAN CHARLES Le Canada français politique vu de l'intérieur. Par Jean.-C. Falardeau. (In *Recherches sociographiques.* Québec. v. 2, no. 3-4 (juil./déc. 1961), pp. [295]-340.)

FARTHING, JOHN COLBORNE Freedom wears a crown. Edited by Judith Robinson. Introd. by E. D. Fulton. Toronto, Kingswood House, 1957. xx, 188 p.

Criticizes the Canadian liberal tradition and the policies of the Liberal government under W. L. Mackenzie King.

FAUCHER, ALBERT Pouvoir politique et pouvoir économique dans l'évolution du Canada français. (In *Recherches sociographiques.* Québec. v. 7, no 1-2 (jan./août 1966), pp. [61]-79.)

Federal-provincial integration in Ontario party organizations; the influence of recruitment patterns. By Henry Jaceck, John McDonough, Ronald Shimizu, and Patrick Smith. 28, [11] leaves. (In Canadian Political Science Association. *Papers presented at the annual meeting.* Kingston. 42d (1970), v. 2, [pt.] 24.)

FERGUSON, GEORGE VICTOR Likely trends in Canadian-American political relations. By G. V. Ferguson. (In *The Canadian journal of economics and political science.* [Toronto] v. 22 (1956), pp. 437-448.)

"This paper was presented at the annual meeting of the Canadian Political Science Association in Montreal, June 8, 1956."

This discussion centres on Canadian domestic objectives and interests.

—— Press and party in Canada; issues of freedom [by] George V. Ferguson and F. H. Underhill. Being the seventh series of lectures under the Chancellor Dunning Trust delivered at Queen's University at Kingston, Ont., 1955. Toronto, Ryerson Press [1955] 46 p. (Kingston, Ont. Queen's University. Chancellor Dunning Trust. Lectures. 7th ser., 1955.)

Contents: Freedom of the press, by G. V. Ferguson. – Canadian liberal democracy in 1955, by F. H. Underhill.

FORSEY, EUGENE ALFRED   The problem of "minority" government in Canada. By Eugene Forsey. (In *The Canadian journal of economics and political science*. [Toronto] v. 30 (1964), pp. 1-11.)

An historical and comparative analysis of "minority" government.

—— The problem of "minority" government in Canada. (In Kruhlak, O. M. (comp.) *The Canadian political process.* Toronto [c1970] pp. 487-497.)

Reprinted from *Canadian journal of economics and political science*, v. 30 (1964), pp. 1-11.

—— Too many elections? By Eugene Forsey. (In *Commentator*. Toronto. v. 10, no. 7-8 (July/Aug. 1966), pp. 24-27.)

A general comment on the Canadian electoral system.

—— Unions and co-operatives. By Eugene A. Forsey. (In Careless, J. M. S. (ed.) *The Canadians, 1867-1967*. Toronto, 1967. pp. 487-501.)

FOWKE, VERNON CLIFFORD   Canadian agricultural policy; the historical pattern. By Vernon C. Fowke. Toronto, University of Toronto Press, 1946. xii, 304 p.

—— The national policy and the wheat economy. Toronto, University of Toronto Press, 1957. viii, 312 p. (Social Credit in Alberta; its background and development, 7.)

This background study to the Social Credit movement provides an analysis of the historical development of Canadian agricultural policy, and examines the impact of federal policies on the prairie economy.

——The National Policy—old and new. By V. C. Fowke. (In *The Canadian journal of economics and political science*. [Toronto] v. 18 (1952), pp. 271-286.)

"This paper was presented at the annual meeting of the Canadian Political Science Association in Quebec, June 5, 1952."

An extensive historical discussion of the Canadian protective tariff system termed the "National Policy".

FOX, PAUL WESLEY   Early socialism in Canada. By Paul W. Fox. (In Aitchison, J. H. (ed.) *The political process in Canada.* [Toronto, c1963] pp. [79]-98.)

—— Les partis politiques fédéraux. Par Paul Fox. (In Sabourin, Louis (ed.) *Le système politique du Canada.* Ottawa, 1968. pp. [197]-209.)

FOX, PAUL WESLEY (ed.)   Politics: Canada; recent readings. Edited by Paul Fox. New York, Toronto, McGraw-Hill Co. of Canada [1963, c1962] 344 p.

Includes bibliographies.

"A description and guide to the use of Canadian government publications", by Brian Land (rev. in July 1962): p. [335]-344.

—— Politics: Canada; problems in Canadian government. [Edited by] Paul Fox. 2d ed. Toronto, McGraw-Hill Co. of Canada [c1966] xii, 396 p.

Includes bibliographies.

"A description and guide to the use of Canadian government publications", by Brian Land (rev. in April 1966): pp. 384-396.

—— Politics: Canada; culture and process. By Paul Fox. 3d ed. Toronto, McGraw-Hill Co. of Canada [c1970] xiii, 512 p. (McGraw-Hill series in Canadian politics.)

First ed. 1962 has title: *Politics: Canada; recent readings*; second ed. 1966 has title: *Politics: Canada; problems in Canadian government.*

"A description and guide to the use of Canadian government publications", by Brian Land (rev. in Nov. 1969): pp. 501-512).

FRAPPIER, MONIQUE   Les politiques de sécurité sociale au Canada et la rédistribution des revenus. [Montréal] 1956. 1 v.

Thesis (MA) – University of Montreal.

FRASER, A. M.   The nineteenth-century negotiations for confederation of Newfoundland with Canada. (In Canadian Historical Association. *Report of the annual meeting.* Toronto (1949), pp. 14-21.)

FRASER, BLAIR   Backstage at Ottawa. The facts and myths about lobbies. (In *Mac-*

lean's. Toronto. v. 72, no. 5 (Feb. 28, 1959), p. 2.)

—— Backstage with Backstage. Our terrible-tempered ancestors. (In *Maclean's.* Toronto. v. 68, no. 21 (Oct. 15, 1955), pp. 6; 100.)

Concerns *Maclean's* first Ottawa correspondent, J. K. Munro, and Col. J. B. MacLean, M. Grattan O'Leary and Kenneth R. Wilson. Blair Fraser, Ottawa correspondent, followed K. R. Wilson.

—— "Blair Fraser reports"; selections, 1944-1968. Edited by John Fraser and Graham Fraser. Toronto, Macmillan, 1969. xxiv, 312 p.

Consists mainly of the articles and columns written by the author for *Maclean's* magazine. Cf. Editor's note (p. ix).

—— Our illegal federal elections. (In *Maclean's.* Toronto. v. 66, no. 8 (Apr. 15, 1953), pp. 12; 83-86.)

FRENCH, DORIS CAVELL (MARTIN) Faith, sweat and politics; the early trade union years in Canada. By Doris French. [Toronto] McClelland and Stewart [c1962] 154 p.

FRONSAC, FREDERICK GREGORY FORSYTH, VICOMTE DE Political history of Canada. By the Viscount de Fronsac. St. Johns, P.Q., E. R. Smith [1904?] 68 p.

The Front page. (In *Saturday night.* Toronto v. 19, no. 12—v. 72, no. 7 (Jan. 27, 1906—Mar. 30, 1957.)

Comments on news of the week, including Canadian federal politics.

Title varies: Aug. 28, 1951—Feb. 28, 1953, editorials.

The Function of liberalism. (In *The Statesman.* Toronto. v. 1, no. 22 (Dec. 21, 1918), pp. 3-4.)

Comparative remarks on British and Canadian liberalism.

GADSBY, HENRY FRANKLIN Keeping them in line. By H. F. Gadsby. (In *MacLean's magazine.* Toronto. v. 30, no. 4 (Feb. 1917), pp. [27]-30; 65-66.)

Discusses the disciplining of ministerial cabinets, with special reference to the cabinets of John A. Macdonald and Wilfrid Laurier.

GAGNON, JEAN LOUIS D'où viennent les hommes politiques. (In Institut canadien des affaires publiques, Montreal. *Nos hommes politiques.* Montréal [c1964] pp. [13]-21.)

GARIGUE, PHILIPPE L'option politique du Canada français; une interprétation de la survivance nationale. Montréal, Editions du Lévrier, 1963. 174 p.

GASCON, WILFRID Vers l'indépendance du Canada. (In *L'Action française.* Montréal. v. 8 (août 1922), pp. [100]-116.)

Discusses the political destiny of Canada.

GELLNER, JOHN Need we already lament for Canada? (In *Commentator.* Toronto. v. 9, no. 5 (May 1965), pp. 3-5.)

An editorial review article of *Lament for a nation,* by G. Grant. Toronto, McClelland & Stewart, 1965.

GENEST, JEAN Le Devoir, hier et aujourd'-hui. (In *L'Action nationale.* Montréal. v. 49 (mars 1960), pp. [531]-553.)

GERIN-LAJOIE, PAUL Catéchisme politique. Montréal, Perrault, 1951. 144 p.

GIBBON, JOHN MURRAY The romantic history of the Canadian Pacific; the Northwest Passage of today. New York, Tudor Pub. Co., 1937. 423 p.

First published under title: Steel of empire.

—— Steel of empire; the romantic history of the Canadian Pacific, the Northwest Passage of today. Indianapolis, Bobbs-Merrill [c1935] 423 p.

"First edition".

The narrative relates Canadian political history to the history of the railway.

GIBSON, FREDERICK W. (ed.) Cabinet formation and bicultural relations; seven case studies. Edited by Frederick W. Gibson. [Ottawa, Queen's Printer for Canada, 1970] xiv, 190 p. (Studies of the Royal Commission on Bilingualism and Biculturalism, 6.)

Contents: The Cabinet of 1867, by W. L. Morton. – The Cabinet of 1878, by D. G. Creighton. – The Cabinet of 1896, by J. T. Saywell. – The Cabinet of 1911, by R. Graham – The Cabinet of 1921, by F. W. Gibson. – The Cabinet of 1935, by F. W. Gibson. – The Cabinet of 1948, by D. C. Thomson. – Conclusions, by F. W. Gibson.

GIBSON, JAMES ALEXANDER The Colonial Office view of Canadian federation, 1856-1868. (In *The Canadian historical review.* Toronto. v. 35 (1954), pp. 279-313.)

GIROUX, MAURICE La pyramide de Babel; essai politique sur la crise des deux nations canadiennes. Lettre-préf.: Robert Cliche. Présentation: André Bernard.

Montréal, Editions de Sainte-Marie [1967] 138 p. (Les Cahiers de Sainte-Marie, 6.)

GLAZEBROOK, GEORGE PARKIN DE TWENE-BROKES A history of Canadian political thought. Toronto, McClelland & Stewart [c1966] 360 p.

—— A history of transportation in Canada. By G. P. de T. Glazebrook. Foreword by H. A. Innis. Toronto, Ryerson Press, 1938. xxv, 475 p. (The Relations of Canada and the United States.)

Part 2: The national economy.

Later published Toronto, McClelland and Stewart [c 1964] in 2 v.

GLENN, FERGUS Anatomy of the Liberal. (In The Canadian forum. Toronto. v. 25, no. 299 (Dec. 1945), pp. 205-206.)

". . . subject is really the liberal with a small 'l'."

For a rejoinder to the above, see In defense of Liberalism. by D. Pacey. (In The Canadian forum. Toronto. v. 25, no. 300 (1946), pp. 238-240.)

GOFORTH, WILLIAM WALLACE The Canadian tariff; a political instrument and an economic expedient. [Montreal] 1932. 1 v.

Thesis (MA) – McGill University.

GOOD, WILLIAM CHARLES Farmer citizen; my fifty years in the Canadian Farmers' movement. By W. C. Good. [Introd. by H. H. Hannam] Toronto, Ryerson Press [c1958] xiv, 294 p.

GORDON, WALTER LOCKHART The future politician. By Walter L. Gordon. (In Clarkson, Stephen (ed.) Visions 2020. Edmonton [c1970] pp. [132]-135.)

GRAHAM, WILLIAM ROGER Charisma and Canadian politics. By Roger Graham. (In Moir, J. S. (ed.) Character and circumstance. Toronto, 1970. pp. 22-36.)

GRANATSTEIN, JACK LAWRENCE The armed forces vote in Canadian general elections, 1940-1968. By J. L. Granatstein. (In Journal of Canadian studies. Peterborough, Ont. v. 4, no. 1 (1969), pp. 6-16.)

GRANT, GEORGE PARKIN Lament for a nation; the defeat of Canadian nationalism. By George Grant. Toronto, McClelland and Stewart [c1965] 97 p. (Canada today.)

Considers Canadian politics since 1940, with special emphasis on the policies advocated by John Diefenbaker.

—— Lament for a nation; the defeat of Canadian nationalism. By George Grant. Toronto, McClelland and Stewart [1970, c1965] xii, 97 p. (Carleton library, no. 50.)

First published 1965.

GREEN, S. J. The women's suffrage movement in the Prairies. [Saskatoon, 1950] 1 v.

Thesis (MA)–University of Saskatchewan.

GREENSLADE, JOHN GARETH (ed.) Canadian politics. Speeches by F. M. Watkins, Stanley Knowles, J. R. Mallory and H. D. Hicks. Delivered at Mount Allison Summer Institute, August 13-15, 1959. Edited by J. G. Greenslade. Sackville, N.B. [Mount Allison University, 1959?] 76 p. (Mount Allison University publication, no. 4.)

Partial contents: Democracy and authority, by F. M. Watkins. – The structure of Canadian politics, by J. R. Mallory. – Business, labour and politics, by S. Knowles. – Politicians and the public, by H. D. Hicks. – The Forum: Mackenzie King. Parliament. The character of Canadian politics.

GRIFFIN, MARTIN JOSEPH The history of parliamentary dissolutions in Canada, 1844 to 1891. (In The Canadian magazine of politics, science, art and literature. Toronto. v. 7 (1896), pp. [3]-9.)

HAMELIN, JEAN Aperçu de la politique canadienne au XIXᵉ siècle. [Par] Jean Hamelin, John Huot [et] Marcel Hamelin. Québec [Culture] 1965. 154 p.

—— Aperçu sur la politique canadienne au XIXᵉ siècle. Par Jean Hamelin, John Huot et Marcel Hamelin (In Culture. Québec. v. 26 (1965), pp. [150]-189.)

Contents: L'origine des partis politiques canadiens. – A. Le système Macdonald. – B. Les difficultés de l'opposition. – C. Le rôle du Québec dans le système des partis, 1867-1896.

HARGROVE, ERWIN C. On Canadian and American political culture. (In The Canadian journal of economics and political science. [Toronto] v. 33 (1967), pp. 107-111.)

A comparative discussion in which the Author argues that American politics is utopian and pragmatic, while the political culture of English Canada is strictly pragmatic.

HARVILL, ERNEST EUGENE Money in Canadian politics. By E. E. Harvill. (In Thorburn, H. G. (ed.) *Party politics in Canada*. Toronto [c1963] pp. 60-69.)

Examines the purposes for which national party funds are expended.

—— The structure of organization and power in Canadian political parties; a study in party financing. [Durham, N.C., 1958] 305 leaves.

Thesis – University of North Carolina.

The analysis concludes "that a study of party financing is one of several valid methods of studying the power arrangements of a political party." (Abstracted in *Dissertation abstracts*, v. 19 (1959), no. 8, p. 2126.)

HARRIS, GEORGE Labor's part in the battle for Canadian independence. (In *Horizons*. Toronto. no. 20 (winter 1967), pp. 40-50.)

HARROP, G. GERALD On ruling Canada. (In *Queen's quarterly*. Kingston. v. 71 (1964), pp. [1]-15.)

A review article discussing biographies on Bennett, King, Meighen and Diefenbaker.

HAWKINS, FREDA ELIZABETH Canadian immigration; a study in public policy, 1946-1968. [Toronto, c1969] 518 [i.e. 519] leaves.

Thesis (PH D) – University of Toronto.

HAWKINS, GORDON Reflections of a British parliamentary candidate. By Gordon R. S. Hawkins. (In *The Canadian forum*. Toronto. v. 33, no. 393 (Oct. 1953), pp. 152-153; v. 33, no. 394 (Nov. 1953), pp. 174-176.)

In two parts.

The Author compares the problems of an election campaign first in a British and then in a Canadian setting.

HEDGES, JAMES BLAINE Building the Canadian West; the land and colonization policies of the Canadian Pacific Railway. By James B. Hedges. New York, Macmillan, 1939. vii, 422 p.

—— The federal railway land subsidy policy of Canada. By James B. Hedges. Cambridge, Mass., Harvard University Press, 1934. viii, 151 p. (Harvard historical monographs, 111.)

Covers the period from 1871 to about 1903.

HERBERT, H. F. The political act. (In *Canadian commentator*. Toronto. v. 2, no. 8/9 (Aug./Sept. 1958), p. 2.)

Brief comments on the development of personality grooming for politicians.

HICKS, HENRY DAVIES Politicians and the public. (In Greenslade, J. G. (ed.) *Canadian politics*. Sackville, N.B. [1959?] pp. 49-61.)

Henry D. Hicks became leader of the Liberal party in Nova Scotia during 1956.

HOCKIN, THOMAS ALEXANDER The shape of government and politics in Canada in 2020; some speculations. By Thomas A. Hockin. (In Clarkson, Stephen (ed.) *Visions 2020*. Edmonton [c1970] pp. [136]-140.)

HODGETTS, JOHN EDWIN Regional interests and policy in a federal structure. By J. E. Hodgetts. (In *The Canadian journal of economics and political science*. [Toronto] v. 32 (1966), pp. [3]-14.)

"This paper is a revision of a contribution made to a Symposium on 'Regional Interests and Policy in a Federal Structure' sponsored jointly by the Association of Canadian Law Teachers and the Canadian Political Science Association, University of British Columbia, June, 1965."

The Author invokes the methods devised for systems analysts to arrive at some general conclusions about regionalism in Canada.

HOROWITZ, GAD Conservatism, liberalism, and socialism in Canada: an interpretation. By G. Horowitz. (In *The Canadian journal of economics and political science*. [Toronto] v. 32 (1966), pp. [143]-171.)

—— Conservatism, liberalism and socialism in Canada; an interpretation. By G. Horowitz. (In Thorburn, H. G. (ed.) *Party politics in Canada*. Scarborough, Ont. [c1967] pp. [55]-73.)

"Reprinted from the Canadian journal of economics and political science, XXXII, no. 2, May, 1966."

—— Conservatism, liberalism and socialism in Canada; an interpretation. By G. Horowitz. (In Kruhlak, O. M. (comp.) *The Canadian political process*. Toronto [c1970] pp. 47-74.)

Reprinted from *Canadian journal of economics and political science*. v. 32 (1966), p. 144-171.

—— Red Tory. (In Kilbourn, William (ed.) *Canada: a guide to the peaceable kingdom*. Toronto, 1970. pp. 254-260.)

A comparative analysis considering the common relationship between "socialism" and "toryism" in English-speaking Canada.

—— Toward the democratic class struggle. (In *Journal of Canadian studies*. Peterborough, Ont. v. 1, no. 3 (1966), pp. 3-10.)

For a critical review of the above, refer to the article Class and the Left in Canadian politics, by R. Mathews. (In *Journal of Canadian studies*. Peterborough, Ont. v. 2, no. 2 (1967), pp. 46-50.)

A later version of this article is available in University League for Social Reform. *Agenda 1970*. Edited by Trevor Lloyd and Jack McLeod. [Toronto] University of Toronto Press [c1968] pp. [241]-255.

—— Toward the democratic class struggle. (In University League for Social Reform. *Agenda 1970*. [Toronto, c1968] pp. [241]-255.)

"An earlier version of this paper appeared in the Journal of Canadian studies, November, 1966."

Argues that "our party system must be polarized on a left-right basis, and the main issues raised for discussion in the political arena must be class issues" in order to attain democracy.

HOUGHAM, GEORGE MILLARD The background and development of national parties. (In Thorburn, H. G. (ed.) *Party politics in Canada*. Scarborough, Ont. [c1967] pp. [2]-14.)

—— Minor parties in Canadian national politics, 1867-1940. [Philadelphia] 1954. 314 leaves.

Thesis (PH D) – University of Pennsylvania.

HULL, W. H. N. The public control of broadcasting: the Canadian and Australian experiences. (In *The Canadian journal of economics and political science*. [Toronto] v. 28 (1962), pp. 114-126.)

"This paper was presented at the annual meeting of the Canadian Political Science Association in Montreal, June 10, 1961."

Compares the power held by the two governments over directing the development of radio and television communications.

HUTCHISON, BRUCE Is the two-party system doomed? (In *Maclean's*. Toronto. v. 66, no. 20 (Oct. 15, 1953), pp. [9]; 46; 48; 52.)

—— Ottawa. (In *Maclean's*. Toronto. v. 69, no. 13 (June 23, 1956), pp. 11; 37-47.)

The unknown country, 15.

HUTTON, MAURICE The philosophy of our political parties. (In *The University magazine*. Montreal. v. 8 (1909), pp. [583]-586.)

INNIS, HAROLD ADAMS A history of the Canadian Pacific Railway. By Harold A. Innis. With a foreword by Peter George. [Toronto] University of Toronto Press [c1971] xxii, 365 p.

First published in 1923.

". . . discusses . . . all aspects of CPR construction and operation to 1921." – Foreword.

INSTITUT CANADIEN DES AFFAIRES PUBLIQUES, MONTREAL, 1963 Nos hommes politiques. Travaux présentés à la 10ème conférence annuelle de l'Institut canadien des affaires publiques (ICAP) organisée avec le concours de la Société Radio-Canada et compte rendu des délibérations. Montréal, Editions de Jour [c1964] 119 p. (Collection: Les Idées du jour, D12.)

Partial contents: Le député; législateur ou patroneux, par J. J. Bertrand. – Ce que font les députés, par J. N. Tremblay. – Ce que font les députés, par R. Lévesque. – Mort ou résurrection du député, par J. C. Falardeau. – Nos hommes politiques: Québec 1963, par A. Laurendeau.

JAMIESON, STUART Industrial relations and government policy. (In *The Canadian journal of economics and political science*. [Toronto] v. 17 (1951), pp. 25-38.)

"This paper was presented at the annual meeting of the Canadian Political Science Association, Kingston, June 10, 1950."

Discusses the problems posed in an attempt to define the nature and scope of government regulation over management-employee relations.

JOHNS, HAROLD PERCIVAL British Columbia's campaign for better terms, 1871-1907. [Vancouver] 1935. 207 leaves.

Thesis (MA) – University of British Columbia.

Traces the movement to secure a revision of the terms of union upon which British Columbia joined the Dominion. Cf. Canadian graduate theses in the humanities and social sciences, 1921-1946. Ottawa, 1951 (p. 51).

JULIEN, G. Les élections fédérales et provinciales dans le comté de Portneuf, 1944-1963. [Québec, 1964] 1 v.

Thesis (MA) – Laval University.

KAMIN, LEON J. Ethnic and party affiliations of candidates as determinants of voting. (In Courtney, J. C. (ed.) *Voting in Canada*. [Scarborough, Ont., c1967] pp. [191]-198.)

"Reprinted from the Canadian journal of psychology, XII (December) 1958."

KASTNER, SUSAN   Ottawa report. Ottawa has no lobbyists; that's American style. What Ottawa has is a lot of people who teach other people to be lobbyists. (In *Saturday night*. Toronto. v. 84, no. 9 (Sept. 1969), pp. 17-18; 20.)

Discusses public relations specialists and politics.

KAYE, VLADIMIR JULIAN   Political integration of ethnic groups. The Ukrainians. By V. J. Kaye. (In *Revue de l'Université d'Ottawa*. [Ottawa] 27 année (1957), pp. [460]-477.)

Examines the process of integration into Canadian political life.

KENT, THOMAS WORRALL   Monetary policy; its objectives and methods. By Tom Kent. (In Institute of Public Administration of Canada. *Proceedings of the annual conference*. Toronto. 9th (1957), pp. 5-17.)

KERSELL, JOHN EDGAR (ed.)   Comparative political problems; Britain, United States and Canada. [Edited by] John E. Kersell and Marshall W. Conley. [Scarborough, Ont.] Prentice-Hall [c1968] 261 p.

A selection of readings chosen to illustrate concrete political problems and issues.

KINSEY, GWYN   The possible course for conservatism. (In *Saturday night*. Toronto. v. 68, no. 47 (August 29, 1953), pp. 7-8.)

KITCHIN, P.   Canada; a study in geopolitics. [Kent, 1947] 1 v.

Thesis (MA) – Ohio State University, Kent.

KOERNER, KIRK FINLAYSON   Political alienation. [Vancouver] 1968. 1 v.

Thesis (MA) – University of British Columbia.

KORNBERG, ALLAN   Self-concepts of American and Canadian party officials. By Allan Kornberg and Joel Smith. (In *Polity*. Amherst, Mass. v. 3 (1970), pp. [70]-99.)

"This is a revised version of a paper presented at the annual meeting of the Canadian Political Science Association in 1969." – p. 70.

——   Some differences in role perceptions among Canadian legislators. [Ann Arbor, 1964] x, 274 leaves.

Thesis (PH D) – University of Michigan.

——   Some differences in the political socialization patterns of Canadian and American party officials; a preliminary report. By Allan Kornberg, Joel Smith and David Bromley. (In *Canadian journal of political science*. Toronto. v. 2 (1969), pp. [64]-88.)

"This is a revised version of a paper presented at the annual meeting of the Canadian Political Science Association at Calgary, June 5-7, 1968."

KRUHLAK, OREST M. (comp.)   The Canadian political process; a reader. [Compiled by] Orest M. Kruhlak, Richard Schultz and Sidney I. Pobihushchy. Toronto, Holt, Rinehart and Winston [c1970] vii, 523 p.

Partial contents: Revolution and counter-revolution by S. M. Lipset. – Conservatism, liberalism and socialism in Canada, by G. Horowitz. – The electoral system in Canada, by A. C. Cairns. – One-party dominance and the rise of third parties, by M. Pinard. – Party integration in Canada by F. C. Engelmann and S. I. Pobihushchy. – The national party leadership convention in Canada, by D. Smiley. – The recruitment of candidates for the Canadian House of Commons, by A. Kornberg and H. H. Winsborough. – Politics and social class in Canada, by J. Wilson. – Party identification, stability and change in voting behaviour, by L. McDonald. – The comparative study of Canadian parties, by L. Epstein. – Cabinet-position and personnel, by R. M. Dawson. – President and Parliament, by D. Smith. – The standing committees of Canada's House of Commons since 1966, by T. Hockin. – The Canadian Senate by H. S. Albinski. – Judicial review in Canada, by J. A. C. Grant. – Bibliography (pp. 498-511).

LAMARCHE, PAUL EMILE   Le parti politique; son origine, son évolution, son rôle. (In Revue trimestrielle canadienne. Montréal. v. 3 (nov. 1917), pp. [242]-256.)

A comparative analysis.

——   Le parti politique. (In his *Oeuvres-hommages* [Montréal, 1919] pp. [165]-187.)

"Voici le texte d'une conférence donnée sur le parti politique . . . par Paul-Emile Lamarche . . . à la bibliothèque Saint-Sulpice, à Montréal, le 27 septembre 1917."

LAMONTAGNE, MAURICE   The influence of the cabinet minister. (In Vaughan, Frederick (ed.) *Contemporary issues in Cana-*

dian politics. Scarborough, Ont. [c1970] pp. 159-165.)

Originally appeared under title: The influence of the politician. (In *Canadian public administration.* Toronto. v. 11, no. 3 (1968), pp. [263]-271.)

Discusses the relationship of the cabinet minister to the mass media.

―― The influence of the politician. (In *Canadian public administration.* Toronto. v. 11 (1968), pp. [263]-271.)

"This paper was presented at the 1967 annual conference of the Institute of Public Administration of Canada."

Later reprinted under the title: *The influence of the cabinet minister.* (In Vaughan, Frederick (ed.) *Contemporary issues in Canadian politics.* Scarborough, Ont. [c1970] pp. 159-165.)

―― The influence of the politician. (In Kruhlak, O. M. (comp.) *The Canadian political process.* Toronto [c1970] pp. 479-486.)

Reprinted from *Canadian public administration,* v. 11 (1968), pp. 263-271.

LAMPMAN, ARCHIE What is the separate school question. A setting forth of the essential facts in a century-old issue and of conflicting viewpoints. (In *Maclean's.* Toronto. v. 49, no. 18 (September 15, 1936), pp. 11; 44-47.)

LA PIERRE, LAURIER JOSEPH LUCIEN The apprenticeship; Canada from Confederation to the eve of the first World War. 13 radio scripts by Laurier L. LaPierre. Montreal, Canadian Broadcasting Corp., International Service, 1967. ix, 152 p. (CBC International Service. History of Canada, 3.)

Part 3 of a four-part history of Canada.

LAPONCE, JEAN ANTOINE Canadian party labels. An essay in semantics and anthropology. By J. A. Laponce. (In *Canadian journal of political science.* Toronto. v. 2 (1969), pp. [141]-157.)

LAURENDEAU, ANDRE Nationalisme et séparatisme. (In *L'Action nationale.* Montréal. v. 44 (mars 1955), pp. [572]-580.)

At head of title: Notre enquête 1955 [no] 3.

―― Note sur l'absentéisme politique. Par André L. (In *L'Action nationale.* Montréal. v. 36 (déc. 1950), pp. [315]-320.)

A statistical analysis of some of the facts used in De notre democratie liberale comme expression de la volonté du peuple, par

J. M. Léger. (In *L'Action nationale.* v. 36 (nov. 1950), pp. [186]-212.)

―― Le scandale n'est pas une politique. (In *Le Magazine Maclean.* Montréal. v. 6, no 5 (mai 1966), p. 74.)

Discusses political scandals in Canadian history.

―― A search for balance. (In *The Canadian forum.* Toronto. v. 43, no. 507 (Apr. 1963), pp. 3-4.)

"An editorial in *Le Devoir,* March 9, 1962."

Discusses the idea of bicultural political parties which "is usually manifested by the collaboration of two political leaders within the same party".

LAURENDEAU, ARTHUR Politiciens et éducation nationale. (In *L'Action nationale.* Montréal. v. 5 (avril 1935), pp. [195]-219.)

―― Pour une politique nationale. Conclusions. (In *L'Action nationale.* Montréal. v. 10 (déc. 1937), pp. [243]-250.)

LAXER, JAMES The socialist tradition in Canada. (In *Canadian dimension.* Winnipeg. v. 6, no. 6 (Dec./Jan. 1969/70), pp. 27-33.)

LAZAR, HARVEY Parliamentary control of defence in Canada, 1945-1962. [Vancouver] 1963. 1 v.

Thesis (MA) – University of British Columbia.

LEACH, GEOFFREY C. Economic nationalism; or, why are Canadians afraid of foreigners? (In *Canada month.* Montreal. v. 6, no. 10 (Oct. 1966), pp. 22-23.)

LEACH, RICHARD H. (ed.) Contemporary Canada, by Nathan Keyfitz [and others] Edited by Richard H. Leach. Durham, N.C., Published for the Duke University Commonwealth-Studies Center [by] Duke University Press, 1967 [c1968] xii, 328 p. (Duke University, Durham, N.C. Commonwealth-Studies Center. Publication no. 32.)

Papers presented at the Seminar on Contemporary Canada, 1966, sponsored by the Committee on Commonwealth Studies, Duke University.

Also published: Toronto, University of Toronto Press, 1968.

Partial contents: Canadian parties and politics, by J. Meisel. – Canadian federalism in ferment, by J. M. Beck.

LEACOCK, STEPHEN BUTLER   Essays and literary studies. By Stephen Leacock. Toronto, Gundy, 1916. 310 p.

LEAGUE OF SOCIAL RECONSTRUCTION. RE-
SEARCH COMMITTEE   Democracy needs
socialism. By the Research Committee of
the League for Social Reconstruction. Toronto, T. Nelson [c1938] x, 154 p.
    Appendix: Social Credit theory.

—— Social planning for Canada. By the
Research Committee of the League for
Social Reconstruction. [Foreword] by
J. S. Woodsworth. Pref. signed by Eugene
Forsey, J. King Gordon, Leonard Marsh,
J. F. Parkinson, F. R. Scott, Graham Spry,
Frank H. Underhill. Toronto, T. Nelson
[c1935] xv, 528 p.
    Partial contents: Chapt. 6. Government
intervention and ownership. – Chapt. 9.
National planning in practice. – Chapt. 11.
Administration in a socialized state. –
Chapt. 20. The question of parties, by F. H.
Underhill. – Chapt. 21. Parliament and the
constitution, by F. H. Underhill.

LEDERLE, JOHN WILLIAM   The national organization of the Liberal and Conservative Parties in Canada. [Ann Arbor, 1942]
v, 212 leaves.
    Thesis (PH D) – University of Michigan.

LE DOUX, BURTON   Le problème des cartels.
(In Relations. Montréal. v. 5, no. 53 (mai
1945), pp. 118-121.)
    Considers the mixing of political and eco-
nomic power in a concentrated group as a
tendency in Canada.

LE DUC, LAWRENCE WILLIAM   The leadership selection process in Canadian political parties; a case study. [Ann Arbor,
1970] xii, 255 leaves.
    Thesis (PH D) – University of Michigan.

LEE, DONALD JAMES   The use of aggregate
and survey data in the study of Canadian
voting behaviour; a methodological experiment. [Kingston, 1970] 128 leaves.
    Thesis (MA) – Queen's University.

LEGER, JEAN MARC   De notre démocratie
libérale comme expression de la volonté
du peuple. (In L'Action nationale. Montréal. v. 36 (nov. 1950), pp. [186]-212.)
    For a rejoinder to the above, see Note
sur l'absentéisme politique, par A. Laurendeau. (In L'Action nationale. Montréal. v.
36 (déc. 1950), pp. [315]-320.)

—— Y a-t-il un avenir politique pour le
Canada français? (In L'Action nationale.

Montréal. v. 51 (sept. 1961), pp. [16]-
34.)
    This essay is presented within a national
context.

LEMIEUX, RODOLPHE   Macdonald et Laurier.
Par L'Honorable Rodolphe Lemieux. (In
Royal Society of Canada. Proceedings and
transactions. Ottawa. ser. 3, v. 19 (1925),
section 1, pp. [1]-14.)
    "Lu à la réunion de mai 1925."
    A comparison of their careers.

LEMIEUX, VINCENT   La composition des pré-
férences partisanes. (In Canadian journal
of political science. Toronto. v. 2 (1969),
pp. [397]-418.)

—— Les syndicats et l'action politique.
(In Congrès des relations industrielles de
l'Université Laval, 23d, Québec, 1968. Le
syndicalisme canadien. Québec, 1968. pp.
201-225.)

LESLIE, PETER MALCOLM   The role of constituency party organizations in representing
the interests of ethnic minorities and other
groups; political parties and Canadian unity. [Kingston, 1968] v, 470 leaves.
    Thesis (PH D) – Queen's University, 1967.

—— The role of political parties in pro-
moting the interests of ethnic minorities.
(In Canadian journal of political science.
Toronto. v. 2 (1969), pp. [419]-433.)

LIPSET, SEYMOUR MARTIN   Democracy in
Alberta. (In The Canadian forum. Toronto. v. 34 (Nov. 1954), pp. 175-177; v. 34
(Dec. 1954), pp. 196-198.)
    In two parts.
    A review article of Democracy in Al-
berta, by C. B. Macpherson. Toronto, University of Toronto Press [c1953]
    For a rejoinder see the Reply, by C. B.
Macpherson. (In The Canadian forum. Toronto. v. 34 (Jan. 1955), pp. 223-224.)

—— Democracy in Alberta. (In Courtney,
J. C. (ed.) Voting in Canada. Scarborough,
Ont., [c1967] pp. [182]-185.)
    "Reprinted from The Canadian forum,
XXXIV (November and December) 1954".
    The subject is considered in the broad
context of contemporary Canadian politics.

—— Party systems and voter alignments;
cross-national perspectives. Edited by Seymour M. Lipset and Stein Rokkan. New
York, Free Press [c1967] xvi, 554 p. [In-
ternational yearbook of political behaviour, v. 7.]
    Partial contents: Class voting in the

Anglo-American political systems, by R. R. Alford (pp. 67-93).

The chapter cited above is a comparative analysis that includes the Canadian political party system.

—— Value differences absolute or relative; the English-speaking democracies. (In *Canadian society; sociological perspectives.* Edited by B. R. Blishen [and others] Toronto, 1968. pp. 478-495.)

A comparative study of Canada, Australia and the United States.

LIPTON, CHARLES The trade union movement of Canada, 1827-1959. Montreal, Canadian Social Publications, 1966 [c1967] xiii, 366 p.

The political activities of trade unions are discussed, at various points, throughout the work.

LLOYD, TREVOR OWEN Our ideological tradition; introduction. By Trevor Lloyd. (In University League for Social Reform. *Agenda 1970.* [Toronto, c1968] pp. [1]-14.)

A comparative discussion of Canadian political roots and traditions.

—— The roles of third parties. By Trevor Lloyd. (In *The Canadian forum.* Toronto. v. 43, no. 515 (Dec. 1963), pp. 205-206.)

A comparative study.

LOCKE, GEORGE HERBERT (ed.) Builders of the Canadian commonwealth. By George H. Locke. With an introd. by A. H. U. Colquhoun. Freeport, N.Y., Books for Libraries Press [1967] xiii, 317 p. (Essay index reprint series.)

First published Toronto, Ryerson, 1923.

A selection from the speeches made by Canadian public men from Louis Joseph Papineau to the Hon. Newton W. Rowell. Introduced with brief biographical sketches.

Partial contents: Political liberalism, by W. Laurier. – Canada first, by G. M. Grant. – Death of Sir John A. Macdonald, by W. Laurier. – The evolution of Canadian sentiment, by G. M. Ross. – When Great Britain is at war we are at war, by W. Laurier. – Quebec and Confederation, by L. Gouin. – Liberalism and reconstruction, by W. L. M. King. – From Confederation to the World War, by R. Borden.

LOGAN, HAROLD AMOS Trade unions in Canada, their development and functioning. By H. A. Logan. Toronto, Macmillan, 1948. xvii, 639 p.

Political activities of trade unions are discussed, at various points, throughout the work.

LONG, JOHN ROBERT Canadian politics, with speeches by the leaders of reform and progress in Canadian politics and government. St. Catharines, Ont., Journal of St. Catharines, 1903. vi, 260 p.

Contents: pt. 1. Canadian politics (chapters 1-14). – pt. 2. Speeches by the leaders of reform and progress in Canadian politics and government.

LONGLEY, JAMES WILBERFORCE Politics considered as a fine art. By J. W. Longley. (In Rose-Belford's *Canadian monthly and national review.* Toronto. v. 7 (1881), pp. 418-425.)

LONGSTAFF, STEPHEN ALAN Status politics in English Canada, 1900-1930. [Montreal] 1968 [c1969] vi, 95 leaves.

Thesis (MA) – McGill University.

LOVETT, HENRY ALMON Canada and the Grand Trunk, 1829-1924. The genesis of railway construction in British America and the story of the Grand Trunk Railway Company of Canada from its inception to its acquisition by Canada. [Toronto, 1924] 241 p.

LOVINK, JOHANNES ANTON ALEXANDER On analysing the impact of the electoral system on the party system in Canada. By J. A. A. Lovink. (In *Canadian journal of political science.* Toronto. v. 3 (1970), pp. [497]-516.)

For a rejoinder to the above article, see Cairns, A. C. A reply to J. A. A. Lovink. (In *Canadian journal of political science.* Toronto. v. 3 (1970), pp. [517]-521.)

LOWER, ARTHUR REGINALD MARSDEN Democracy and Parliament. By A. R. M. Lower. (In *The Dalhousie review.* Halifax. v. 14 (1934/35), pp. [5]-15.)

A comparative study.

—— The origins of democracy in Canada. (In Canadian Historical Association. *Report of the annual meeting.* Ottawa. (1930), pp. 65-70.)

—— Political "partyism" in Canada. (In Canadian Historical Association. *Report of the annual meeting.* [Ottawa] (1955), pp. 88-95.)

LUPUL, MANOLY ROBERT Relations in education between the state and the Roman Catholic Church in the Canadian North-West, with special reference to the provisional District of Alberta from 1880 to 1905. [Cambridge, Mass.] 1963. 2 v.

Thesis (PH D) – Harvard University.

LYNCH, CHARLES Order, good government and the press. By Charles Lynch, Norman De Poe and Christopher Young. (In Hawkins, Gordon (ed.) *Order and good government.* [Toronto, c1965] pp. 119-135.)

A discussion on the nature and methods of reporting from Parliament.

LYONS, WILLIAM ELMER One man, one vote. By William E. Lyons. Toronto, McGraw-Hill [1970] xvi, 102 p. (McGraw-Hill series in Canadian politics.)

MC ALLISTER, GEORGE A. Toward a national labour policy. By G. A. McAllister. (In *Public affairs.* Halifax. v. 9, no. 4 (Sept. 1946), pp. [209]-215.)

Relates to the revival of the House of Commons Committee on Industrial Relations.

MACBETH, MADGE HAMILTON (Lyons) Confederation times and heroes. By Madge Macbeth. (In *Canada monthly.* London, Ont. v. 22, no. 3 (July 1917), pp. 111-114.)

—— Running riot through Canada's legislative bodies. By Madge Macbeth. (In *Canada monthly.* London, Ont. v. 19, no. 6 (April 1916), pp. 323-325; 365-368.)

An anecdotal narrative tracing historically the main Parliament Building in Ottawa from its inception in 1859 to its burning in 1916.

MC CARTHY, LILIAN PEARL Patronage in Canadian politics. Toronto, 1919. 1 v. (various pagings).

Thesis (MA) – University of Toronto.

MC CLOSKEY, W. J. The evil of campaign funds. (In *Saturday night.* Toronto. v. 56, no. 30 (April 5, 1941), p. 8.)

Argues that "present methods of obtaining campaign funds for conducting an election are nothing more than a hijacking of industry".

MC CREATH, PETER LEITH The transition in Nova Scotian politics; a study in federal election campaigning, 1945-1965. [Halifax, N.S.] 1968. 1 v.

Thesis (MA) – Dalhousie University.

MC CUTCHEON, MALCOLM WALLACE Canadian businessmen; reluctant politicians. By Sen. M. Wallace McCutcheon. (In Litvak, I. A. (ed.) *The nation keepers.* New York, Toronto [c1967] pp. 144-155.)

MACDONALD, ANGUS LEWIS Out of the historic past; a statement of the principle of liberalism. Made as guest speaker at the Reform Club in 1934 while premier of Nova Scotia. (In his *Speeches.* Toronto, 1960. pp. 1-17.)

MAC DONALD, FLORA The reform of political parties. (In *Queen's quarterly.* Kingston. v. 76 (1969), pp. [707]-709.)

"Based on a paper delivered to the Progressive Conservative Party policy conference, 'Priorities for Canada', Niagara Falls, October, 1969."

MC DOUGALL, JOHN LORNE Canadian Pacific. [Montreal, McGill University Press, 1968] xi, 200 p.

Cover title.

—— Le Canadien pacifique. [Montréal, Presses de l'Université de Montréal, 1968] xi, 207 p.

MC GEE, JEAN CHARLES Histoire politique de Québec-Est. [Par] J. C. McGee. [Préf. de l'hon. Oscar Drouin] Québec, Belisle [c1948] 332 p.

Federal and provincial politics are analyzed in this study.

MC GILL UNIVERSITY. SCHOOL OF COMMERCE Reciprocal and preferential tariffs. [By] the 1925 graduating class in commerce. Toronto, Published by the Macmillan Co. of Canada for the Dept. of Economics and Political Science, McGill University, Montreal [1925] 40 p. (McGill University economics studies, no. 4.)

National problems of Canada.

"Written by Messrs. Glassco, Patton, Mitchell, Potter, Case, Schofield, Mickles, Wait, Fairman, Quinlan, Elliott, and Falls." – Pref.

Contents: Preface, by S. Leacock. – General historical outline of the Canadian tariff. – Preferential treatment under the favoured nation clauses. – Imperial preference. – Reciprocity with the United States of America. – Preference and reciprocity. – Conclusions.

MAC GUIGAN, MARK RUDOLPH Liberalism and socialism. Liberalism, by Mark R. MacGuigan and Socialism, by Trevor O. Lloyd. [Toronto, Exchange for Political Ideas in Canada, 1964] 27 p. (An Exchange pamphlet, no. 1.)

MC INTOSH, G. T. Canadian immigration policy. [Saskatoon, 1949] 1 v.

Thesis (MA) – University of Saskatchewan.

MAC KAY, DOUGLAS   Canada's foremost forum. The single job of the Canadian Clubs is that of producing a sense of national unity. (In *Maclean's*. Toronto. v. 41, no. 5 (March 1, 1928), pp. 13; 74-75.)

MACKAY, LOUIS ALEXANDER   Freedom and authority. By L. A. Mackay. (In *The Canadian forum*. Toronto. v. 22, no. 264 (Jan. 1943), pp. 295-297.)
Analyses the political party system in Canada. Advocates a Senate drawn by lot from the adult citizens of the nation, with three-year terms and compulsory service.

MAC KAY, ROBERT ALEXANDER   The nature of Canadian politics. (In Conference on Canadian-American Affairs. 1st, St. Lawrence University, Canton, N.Y., 1935. *Proceedings*. Boston, 1936. pp. 191-203.)
Followed by discussion by Frank Underhill, J. W. Dafoe [and others] pp. 203-209.

MAC KIRDY, KENNETH A.   Conflict of loyalties: the problem of assimilating the far Wests into the Canadian and Australian federations. By K. A. MacKirdy. (In *The Canadian historical review*. Toronto. v. 32 (1951), pp. 337-355.)

MAC LENNAN, C. PRESCOTT   Reminiscences of parliamentary leaders. (In *The Dalhousie review*. Halifax. v. 26 (1946/47), pp. [75]-84.)
Brief comments on Macdonald, Laurier, the Tuppers, etc.

MC LEOD, JOHN TENNYSON   Party structure and party reform. By John T. McLeod. (In University League for Social Reform. *The prospect of change*. Toronto [c1965] pp. [1]-22.)

MC NAUGHT, KENNETH WILLIAM KIRKPATRICK   National affairs. By Kenneth McNaught. (In *Saturday night*. Toronto. v. 80, no. 8 (Aug. 1965), pp. 7-10.)
An extensive review of *Lament for a nation*, by G. Grant. Toronto, McClelland and Stewart, 1965.

—— The villains! By Kenneth McNaught. (In *Saturday night*. Toronto. v. 83, no. 2 (Feb. 1968), pp. [25]-26.)
Heroes & villains, 2.
Interpretative remarks on some personalities in Canadian history.

MC NEILL, JAMES BAIRD   Political leadership and legislative control under the cabinet system; a critique and some proposals in the light of administrative theory. [Ottawa, 1959] 98 leaves.
Thesis (MA) – Carleton University

MAC NUTT, WILLIAM STEWART   The Fredericton Conference. By W. S. MacNutt. (In *The Atlantic advocate*. Fredericton, N.B. v. 47, no. 1 (Sept. 1956), pp. 11-13.)
Concerns the Conference of the Atlantic Premiers held July 9, 1956, in Fredericton, New Brunswick.
Discusses, historically, the relationship between the Maritime provinces and the federal government in Ottawa.

MACPHAIL, SIR ANDREW   Consequences and penalties. By The Editor. (In *The University magazine*. Montreal. v. 13 (1914), pp. [167]-177.)
"It is not the intention . . . to sketch . . the modern political and economic history of Canada . . . but rather to indicate tendencies, and apply general principles. . . ." – p. 168.

—— Conservative—Liberal—Socialist. (In *The University of Toronto quarterly*. [Toronto] v. 3 (1933/34), pp. 263-285.)
A comparative and historical analysis.

—— Essays in fallacy. New York, Longmans, 1910. 359 p.

—— Essays in politics. London, Longmans, Green, 1909. v, 301 p.
Partial contents: VII. Protection and politics. – VIII. Why the Conservatives failed. – The psychology of Canada.

—— Patriotism and politics. By the Editor. (In *The University magazine*. Montreal. v. 13 (1914), pp. [1]-11.)

—— Theory and practice. (In *The University magazine*. Montreal. v. 12 (1913), pp. [380]-395.)
Contends that "it is not the politicians but the doctrinaires and professional reformers who engender distrust in the institutions of the country". A reflective essay on theory and application in politics.

—— Women in democracy. (In *The University magazine*. Montreal. v. 19 (1920), pp. [1]-15.)

MACPHERSON, CRAWFORD BROUGH   Democracy in Alberta; Social Credit and the party system. By C. B. Macpherson. 2d ed. [Toronto] University of Toronto Press [1962, c1953] xiv, 257 p. (Canadian university paperbooks.)
"While the book deals primarily with the party system in one province, it has something to say about the possible directions and limits of the party system in Canada." – Pref. to the 2d ed. (p. ix).

—— The position of political science. By C. Macpherson. (In *Culture*. Québec. v. 3 (1942), pp. [452]-459.)

MAITLAND, ROYAL   Canada since Confederation. (In Canadian Club of Toronto. *Addresses*. Toronto. (1937/38), pp. 183-192.)
Address delivered on January 31, 1938.

MALLORY, JAMES RUSSELL   The lawyer in politics. By J. R. Mallory. (In *The Dalhousie review*. Halifax. v. 30 (1950/51), pp. [229]-236.)
Discusses reasons for the high proportion of lawyers in Canadian public life.

—— The structure of Canadian politics. By J. R. Mallory (In Greenslade, J. G. (ed.) *Canadian politics*. Sackville, N.B. [1959?] pp. 19-28.)

—— The structure of Canadian politics. By J. R. Mallory. (In Thorburn, H. G. (ed.) *Party politics in Canada*. Scarborough, Ont. [c1967] pp. [24]-32.)
"Reprinted from Canadian politics, Mount Allison University Publication no. 4, Sackville, N.B., 1959."

MANN, WILLIAM EDWARD   For the sake of argument: The Church should meddle in politics. By Rev. W. E. Mann. (In *Maclean's*. Toronto. v. 70, no. 6 (March 16, 1957), pp. 4; 52-54.)

MANNING, ERNEST CHARLES   How a liberty-for-the-citizen government will actually work. By Hon. Ernest C. Manning. (In *Canada month*. Montreal. v. 8, no. 4 (April 1968), pp. 18-20.)
Second of two articles. First article is entitled: Principles for government of free individuals. (In *Canada month*. Montreal. v. 8, no. 2 (Feb. 1968), pp. 18-20.)

—— Liberty, unity and prosperity. By the Hon. E. C. Manning. (In Empire Club of Canada. *Addresses*. [Don Mills, Ont.] (1966/67), pp. [54]-64.)
Address delivered on November 3, 1966.

—— Principles for government of free individuals. By Hon. Ernest C. Manning. (In *Canada month*. Montreal. v. 8, no. 2 (Feb. 1968), pp. 18-20.)
First of two articles. The second article is entitled: How a liberty-for-the-citizen government will actually work. (In *Canada month*. Montreal. v. 8, no. 4 (Apr. 1968), pp. 18-20.)

MARCHAND, JEAN   Nature et sources du socialisme. [Québec] 1942. 1 v.
Thesis (MA) – Laval University.

MARDIROS, ANTHONY   Socialism in Canada: is it relevant? (In *Canadian dimension*. Winnipeg. v. 1, no. 6 (May/June 1964), pp. 4-6.)
Part 1 of Socialism in the 20th century.

MARION, GERALD   La politique canadienne sur les monopoles. [Montréal] 1957. 1 v.
Thesis (MA) – University of Montreal.

MARION, SERAPHIN   Libéralisme canadien-français d'autrefois et d'aujourd'hui. (In *Les Cahiers des dix*. Montréal. no 27 (1962), pp. [9]-45.)

MARKO, ANNE MARIE   Federal representation in the Canadian cabinet, July 1, 1867 to June 29, 1957. [Montréal] 1963. 1 v.
Thesis (MA) – McGill University.

MARTIN, CHESTER BAILEY   The colonial policy of the Dominion. By Chester Martin. (In Royal Society of Canada. *Proceedings and transactions*. Ottawa. ser. 3, v. 16 (1922), section 2, pp. 35-47.)
Read May meeting, 1922.
Discusses the policy of the Canadian government toward the North West Territories and the provinces that emerged from them.

—— The completion of Confederation. By Chester Martin. (In *Queen's quarterly*. Kingston. v. 38 (1931), pp. [197]-210.)
Traces the completion of the Canadian federation in relation to the final settlement of the Natural Resources Question in 1930.

MASSEY, VINCENT   The way of liberalism. An address delivered before the annual meeting of the Ontario Liberal Association, Ottawa, November 18, 1932. Toronto, Ontario Liberal Association [1932?] 15 p.

MASTERS, DONALD CAMPBELL CHARLES   The coming of age. 13 radio scripts, by D. C. Masters. Montreal, Canadian Broadcasting Corp., International Service, 1967. ix, 139 p. (CBC International Service. History of Canada, 4.)
Part 4 of a four-part history of Canada.
Concerns Canada in the period following World War I.

—— Reciprocity, 1846-1911. By D. C. Masters. Ottawa [Canadian Historical Association] 1961. 20 p. (Canadian Historical Association. Historical booklets, no. 12.)

MATHEWS, ROBIN   Class and the Left in Canadian politics; commentary. In *Journal of Canadian studies*. Peterborough, Ont. v. 2, no. 2 (1967), pp. 46-50.)

A critical review of the article Toward the democratic class struggle, by G. Horowitz. (In *Journal of Canadian studies*. Peterborough, Ont. v. 1, no. 3 (1966), pp. 3-10.)

MAYER, LAWRENCE CLARK Federalism and party cohesion in Canada and Australia. A legislative roll call analysis. [Austin, Texas, 1969, c1970] vii, 213 leaves.

Thesis (PH D) – University of Texas at Austin.

MEISEL, JOHN Canadian parties and politics. (In Leach, R. H. (ed.) *Contemporary Canada*. Durham, N.C., 1967 pp. [124]-147.)

—— Party images in Canada. A report on work in progress. [Kingston, 1970] 55 [i.e. 77] leaves. (In Canadian Political Science Association. *Papers presented at the annual meeting*. Kingston, 42d (1970), v. 1, pt. [8].)

At head of title: Draft. Not for publication.

Reproduced typescript.

—— Recent changes in Canadian parties. (In Thorburn. H. G. (ed.) *Party politics in Canada*. Scarborough, Ont. [c1967] pp. [33]-54.)

Deals "primarily with changes dating very roughly from the end of the second World War".

"The basis of a paper delivered to the Association canadienne-française pour l'avancement des sciences, Montréal, November 5, 1965."

—— Le système électoral fédéral. (In Sabourin, Louis (ed.) *Le système politique du Canada*. Ottawa, 1968. pp. [185]-196.)

MELLOS, KOULA Quantitative comparison of party ideology. (In *Canadian journal of political science*. Toronto. v. 3 (1970), pp. [540]-558.)

MELVILLE, THOMAS The land of national leaders. (In *MacLean's magazine*. Toronto. v. 32, no. 7 (July 1919), pp. [30]-31; 75-76.)

Concerns the influence and contributions to national politics made by persons from the Maritime provinces.

MENZIES, MERRILL WARREN The Canadian Wheat Board and the international wheat trade; national and international factors influencing the development of Canadian wheat policy. [London] 1956. 483, xl leaves.

University of London.

Examines the historical relationship between Canadian political parties and economic development in Canada.

MERCER, GEOFFREY The political party organization in a federal riding; a case study of Burnaby-Coquitlam. [Burnaby, B.C.] 1967. 1 v.

Thesis (MA) – Simon Fraser University.

This constituency came into existence in 1953.

MERCIER, C. La politique du Canada envers l'immigration. [Québec, 1957] 1. v.

Thesis (MA) – Laval University.

MERRITT, WILLIAM HAYDEN Government policy and commercial air transportation in Canada. [Toronto, 1948] 230 leaves.

Thesis (MA) – University of Toronto.

Minorities, schools and politics. Essays by D. G. Creighton, W. L. Morton, Ramsay Cook, Manoly R. Lupul, Marilyn Barber and Margaret Prang. Introd. by Craig Brown. [Toronto] University of Toronto Press [c1969] xi, 111 p. (Canadian historical readings, 7.)

MONTPETIT, EDOUARD Considérations sur la politique commerciale du Canada. (In *Revue trimestrielle canadienne*. Montréal. v. 3 (août 1917), pp. [113]-127.)

MOONEY, GEORGE STUART The history of the co-operative movement in Canada. By G. S. Mooney. (In *Public affairs*. Halifax. v. 3, no. 1 (Aug. 1939), pp. 12-16.)

MORTON, DESMOND Democracy and the mass media. (In *The Canadian forum*. Toronto. v. 49, no. 582 (July 1969), pp. 82-84.)

—— French Canada and the Canadian militia, 1868-1914. (In *Histoire sociale*. Ottawa. [no.] 3 (avril 1969), pp. [32]-50.)

MORTON, WILLIAM LEWIS The conservative principle in Confederation. By W. L. Morton. (In *Queen's quarterly*. Kingston. v. 71 (1964), pp. [528]-546.)

"A paper prepared for the National Conference on Canadian Goals, sponsored by the Progressive Conservative Association of Canada, Fredericton, September 9th-12th, 1964."

—— Manitoba schools and Canadian nationality, 1890-1923. (In Canadian Historical Association. *Report of the annual meeting*. [Ottawa] (1951), pp. 51-59.)

—— Manitoba schools and Canadian nationality, 1890-1923. By W. L. Morton.

(In *Minorities, schools and politics.* [Toronto, c1969] pp. [10]-18.)

"Reprinted from Canadian Historical Association, Report, 1951."

—— The progressive tradition in Canadian politics. By W. L. Morton. (In Thorburn, H. G. (ed.) *Party politics in Canada.* Scarborough, Ont. [c1967] pp. [142]-147.)

Reprinted from the author's *The Progressive Party in Canada.* Toronto, University of Toronto Press, 1950.

—— Uncertain nationalism. By W. L. Morton. (In *Journal of Canadian studies.* Peterborough, Ont. v. 2, no. 1 (1967), pp. 28-35.)

A review article of University League for Social Reform. *Nationalism in Canada.* Edited by P. Russell. Toronto, 1966.

MOSHER, RALPH LAMONG   A study of the reciprocity movement in Canada, 1911-1938. [Wolfville, N.S., 1951] 142 leaves.
Thesis (MA) – Acadia University.

MULLER, STEVEN   The Canadian prime ministers, 1867-1948; an essay on democratic leadership. [Ithaca, N.Y.] 1958. 2 v. (vi, 723 leaves)
Thesis (PH D) – Cornell University.
Abstracted in *Dissertation abstracts,* v. 19, no. 1 (1958), pp. 158-159.

MUSOLF, LLOYD D.   Public ownership and accountability; the Canadian experience. Cambridge, Mass., Harvard University Press, 1959. xii, 174 p.
Examines the issue of the accountability of Canadian public corporations. Specific examples used in the study extend to the end of the Liberal Party era in June 1957.

MUTCH, LESLIE ALEXANDER   An history of Canadian fiscal policy. [Winnipeg] 1931. 151 leaves.
Thesis (MA) – University of Manitoba.

NELSON, VIOLET MARGARET   The Orange order in Canadian politics. [Kingston, Ont.] 1950. 232 leaves.
Thesis (MA) – Queen's University.

NEWMAN, CHRISTINA (MC CALL)   Ottawa letter. Meet political man. By Christina Newman. (In *Saturday night.* Toronto. v. 83, no. 3 (Mar. 1968), pp. 15-18.)
Offers a definition of the political personality.

NEWMAN, PETER CHARLES   The lack of Conservative-Liberal differences in Canadian politics. By Peter Newman. (In Hawkins,

Gordon (ed.) *Order and good government.* [Toronto, c1965] pp. 91-98.)

NOEL, S. J. R.   Political parties and elite accomodation: interpretations of Canadian federalism. [Kingston, 1970] 34, [4] leaves. (In Canadian Political Science Association. *Papers presented at the annual meeting.* Kingston. 42d (1970), v. 3. [pt.] 35.)
Reproduced typescript.

NORMAND, EUGENE   Le libéralisme dans la province de Québec. [n.p., n.d.] 95 p.
An obscure pamphlet discussing late-nineteenth-century Canadian liberalism as it relates to Canada as a whole as well as to the province of Quebec.

OBAY, L.   L'esprit de parti et le mal social. (In *Le Mouvement catholique.* Trois-Rivières. v. 3 (jan./juin 1899), pp. [85]-93.)

OBREGON, RAFAEL A.   Changes in Canadian fiscal policy from 1930 to 1948. [Antigonish] 1950. 1. v.
Thesis (MA) – St. Francis Xavier University.

O'LEARY, MICHAEL GRATTAN   Giants of other days. By M. Grattan O'Leary. (In *Maclean's.* Toronto. v. 39, no. 1 (Jan. 1, 1926), pp. 13; 63.)
Sketches of some famed parliamentarians: Laurier, L. P. Pelletier, Dr. Clark, W. Pugsley, etc.

OLIVER, MICHAEL KELWAY   Democratic socialist politics for Canada. By Michael Oliver. (In his *Social purpose for Canada.* [Toronto, c1966] pp. [414]-444.)

—— Quebec and Canadian democracy. By Michael Oliver. (In *The Canadian journal of economics and political science.* [Toronto] v. 23 (1957), pp. 504-515.)
"This paper was presented at the annual meeting of the Canadian Political Science Association in Ottawa, June 13, 1957."
"The main part of this paper examines the hypothesis that French-Canadian political opinion may in the future express itself federally through a variety of channels."

ORR, COLERIDGE WESTERMAN   Pressure group activity; the Canadian Federation of Agriculture. [Ottawa, 1962] 1 v.
Thesis (MA) – Carleton University.

OSLE, BERNARD   War finance in Canada. [Vancouver] 1946. 205 leaves.

Thesis (MA) – University of British Columbia.

The Author endeavours to list and compare the financial measures undertaken by the Dominion government during the two World Wars. Cf. *Canadian graduate theses in the humanities and social sciences, 1921-1946.* Ottawa, 1951 (p. 17).

OXLEY, JAMES MACDONALD   The Canadian Pacific Railway. By J. Macdonald Oxley. (In *The Canadian magazine of politics, science, art and literature.* Toronto. v. 6 (1895/96), pp. [522]-529.)

The political aspects of the construction of the Canadian Pacific Railway are touched upon briefly.

PACEY, DESMOND   In defense of liberalism. (In *The Canadian forum.* Toronto, v. 25, no. 300 (Jan. 1946), pp. 238-240.)

A rejoinder to Anatomy of the Liberal, by F. Glenn. (In *The Canadian forum.* Toronto. v. 25, no. 299 (1945), pp. 205-206.)

PALTIEL, KHAYYAM ZEV   Political party financing in Canada. Toronto, McGraw-Hill [1970] xvi, 200 p. (McGraw-Hill series in Canadian politics.)

PANTING, GERLAND ERNEST   "The people" in politics. By G. Panting. (In *The New Newfoundland quarterly.* St. John's, Nfld. v. 65, no. 4 (June 1967), pp. 15-17.)

Concerns the Fisherman's Protective Union of Newfoundland, founded in 1908 under the leadership of Sir William Ford Coaker. Traces "the similarity between the political ideas expressed by the leadership of the FPU and those thrown up by contemporary political movements in North America".

PAQUET, LOUIS ADOLPHE   Le préjugé sectaire. (In *Le Canada français.* Québec. v. 3 (1919), pp. 81-92.)

An essay on the Society of the Orange Order of Canada and its political influence.

PARE, LORENZO   Les Canadiens Français et l'organisation militaire. [Montréal, Bellarmin, 1951] 16 p. (Oeuvres des tracts, no.382.)

PARIZEAU, JACQUES   Prospects for economic policy in a federal Canada. (In Crépeau, P. A. (ed.) *The future of Canadian federalism.* [Toronto, c1965] pp. [45]-57.)

PATRY, MAURICE   Evolution historique du système politique canadien. (In Sabourin, Louis (éd.) *Le système politique du Canada.* Ottawa, 1968. pp. [21]-34.)

PATTERSON, ANTHONY J.   Three men pushing us all to become wealthy. (In *Canada month.* Montreal. v. 7, no. 5 (May 1967), pp. 16-17.)

Presents the ideas of Louis Kelso and Mortimer Adler, accepted by J. W. Kieran, W. Boyd, and F. S. Capon. Relates their attempt to influence Canadian politicians, especially members of the Liberal Party.

PEERS, FRANK WAYNE   The politics of Canadian broadcasting, 1920-1939. [Toronto] c1966. vi, 633 leaves.

Thesis (PH D) – University of Toronto.

—— The politics of Canadian broadcasting, 1920-1951. By Frank W. Peers. [Toronto] University of Toronto Press [c1969] 466 p.

". . . traces the development of broadcasting policy in Canada up to the inception of television in 1952."

PEPIN, JEAN LUC   Petit dictionnaire politique canadien. Par J. L. Pépin. (In *The Journal of liberal thought.* [Ottawa. v.] 1, no. 1 (summer 1965), pp. 25-51.)

PIGEON, M.   Elections fédérales dans le comté de Lévis de 1940 à l'élection du 5 juin, 1966. [Québec, 1969] 1 v.

Thesis (MA) – Laval University.

PIGGOTT, ELEANORA   Canadian government policy on immigration and colonization. [Vancouver, 1950] 185 leaves.

Thesis (MA) – University of British Columbia.

PINARD, MAURICE   One-party dominance and third parties. (In Kruhlak, O. M. (comp.) *The Canadian political process.* Toronto [c1970] pp. 165-179.)

Reprinted from *Canadian journal of economics and political science.* v. 33 (1967), pp. [358]-373.

—— Poverty and political movements. (In *Canadian society; sociological perspectives.* Edited by B. R. Blishen [and others] Toronto, 1968. pp. 462-477.)

"This essay is a revised version of a paper read at the First Annual Meeting of the Canadian Sociology and Anthropology Association, Sherbrooke, June 1966."

A general hypothetical examination involving the Social Credit Party in Quebec and the CCF Party in Saskatchewan.

PLUMPTRE, ARTHUR FITZWALTER WYNNE   The nature of political and economic development in the British dominion. By A. F. W. Plumptre. (In *The Canadian journal of economics and political science.* [Toronto] v. 3 (1937), pp. 489-507.)

A comparative study of the institutions and problems in Canada, Australia, New Zealand, and South Africa.

The Political ideas of the prime ministers of Canada. Les idées politiques des premiers ministres du Canada. Marcel Hamelin, éditeur. Ottawa, Editions de l'Université d'Ottawa, 1969. 153 p. (Les Conférences Georges P. Vanier. The Georges P. Vanier memorial lectures, 1968.)

Cahiers d'histoire, no 2.

Partial contents: Les idées politiques de George-Etienne Cartier, par J. C. Bonenfant. – The political ideas of John A. Macdonald, by P. B. Waite. – Wilfrid Laurier; politician, by P. Stevens. – The political ideas of Robert Borden, by R. C. Brown. – Some political ideas of Arthur Meighen, by R. Graham. – The political ideas of William Lyon Mackenzie King, by H. B. Neatby. – The political ideas of Louis St. Laurent, by D. C. Thomas.

POLLOCK, JAMES R.   Official costs of Canadian elections. (In *Public affairs*. Halifax. v. 4, no. 3 (Mar. 1941), pp. 123-127.)

PORTER, JOHN A.   The economic elite and political leadership in Canada. (In Thorburn, H. G. (ed.) *Party politics in Canada*. Scarborough, Ont. [c1967] pp. [87]-95.)

Reprinted from the Author's *The vertical mosaic*. Toronto, University of Toronto Press, 1965.

—— Elite groups: a scheme for the study of power in Canada. By John Porter. (In *The Canadian journal of economics and political science*. [Toronto] v. 21 (1955), pp. 498-512.)

"This paper was presented at the annual meeting of the Canadian Political Science Association in Toronto, June 3, 1955."

—— Political parties and the political career. (In *The Canadian forum*. Toronto. v. 38, no. 449 (June 1958), pp. 54-55.)

—— The vertical mosaic; an analysis of social class and power in Canada. [Toronto] University of Toronto Press, 1965. xxi, 626 p. (Studies in the structure of power: decision-making in Canada, 2.)

Part 2. The structure of power. – Chapt. 12. The Canadian political system. – Chapt. 13. The political elite. – Chapt. 14. The federal bureaucracy.

PORTER, ORVILLE REX   The history and development of the Canadian tariff. [Wolfville, N.S.] 1937. 1 v.

Thesis (MA) – Acadia University.

The thesis traces the tariff in Canada from the French regime to the resignation of the Bennett government in 1935. Cf. Canadian graduate theses in the humanities and social sciences, 1921-1946. Ottawa, 1951 (p. [15]).

POTTER, ALEXANDER OBERLANDER   Canada as a political entity. Toronto, Longmans, Green, 1923. viii, 159 p.

Also issued as thesis, Columbia University.

First published: Syracuse, Oberlander Press, 1922.

POWER, CHARLES GAVAN   Quebec nationalism in my time. By Charles G. Power. (In *Queen's quarterly*. Kingston. v. 75 (1968), pp. [1]-20.)

Coverage of nationalist activities extends to the 1930s. Considers the approach of Laurier, Bourassa, King, and others.

—— Wanted: a ceiling on election spending. By Hon. C. G. Power, MP. (In *Maclean's*. Toronto. v. 62, no. 3 (Feb. 1, 1949), pp. 7-8; 48-49.)

—— Wanted: a ceiling on election spending. By Hon. C. G. Power, MP. (In Thorburn, H. G. (ed.) *Party politics in Canada*. Toronto [c1963] pp. 146-150.)

"Reprinted from *Maclean's* magazine, LXII, no. 3, February 1, 1949."

Advocates the need for "urgent reforms in the raising and spending of campaign funds by Canadian political parties."

PRANG, MARGARET EVELYN   Some opinions of political radicalism in Canada between the two World Wars. A study of the views of four Canadian periodicals: *The Canadian forum, Saturday night, The Christian guardian, The New outlook, The Catholic register*. Toronto, 1953. 284 leaves.

Thesis (MA) – University of Toronto.

PRESTON, RICHARD ARTHUR   Canadian defence policy and the development of the Canadian nation, 1867-1917. By Richard A. Preston. Ottawa, Canadian Historical Association, 1970. 22 p. (Canadian Historical Association. Historical booklets, no. 25.)

Translated into French under title: *La politique canadienne du défense et le dé-*

velopment de la nation canadienne, 1867-1917.

QUALTER, TERENCE H. The election process in Canada. Foreword by Paul W. Fox. Toronto, New York, McGraw-Hill [1970] xii, 203 p. (McGraw-Hill series in Canadian politics.)

Deals with the complexities involved in "the requirements and principles of the electoral process at both the federal and provincial levels of government". – Foreword.

—— Representation by population: a comparative study. By T. H. Qualter. (In The Canadian journal of economics and political science. [Toronto] v. 33 (1967), pp. [246]-268.)

Analyses, historically and comparatively, the Electoral Boundaries Readjustment Bill introduced in the House of Commons in 1964 and given further detailed consideration in 1966.

RAINBOTH, MABEL Socialism; its trend in Canada. [Ottawa] 1938. 71 leaves.

Thesis (MA) – University of Ottawa.

RASMUSSEN, JORGEN A research note on Canadian party systems. (In The Canadian journal of economics and political science. [Toronto] v. 33 (1967), pp. 98-106.)

A comparative analysis, applying the method used by Joseph Schlesinger on the American party system, to make an attempt at "clarifying understanding of party competitiveness in Canada".

RAWLYK, GEORGE A. Canada's immigration policy, 1945-1962. By G. A. Rawlyk. (In The Dalhousie review. Halifax. v. 42, no. 3 (autumn 1962), pp. [287]-300.)

REID, ESCOTT MEREDITH Canadian political parties. A study of the economic and racial bases of conservatism and liberalism in 1930. By Escott M. Reid. (In Contritions to Canadian economics. Toronto. v. 6 (1933), pp. 7-39.)

—— Canadian political parties. A study of the economic and racial bases of conservatism and liberalism in 1930. By Escott M. Reid. (In Courtney, J. C. (ed.) Voting in Canada. [Scarborough, Ont., c1967] pp. [72]-81.)

"Reprinted from Contributions to Canadian economics, VI, 1933."

—— Democracy and political leadership in Canada. By Escott M. Reid. (In Thor-

burn, H. G. (ed.) Party politics in Canada. Toronto [c1963] pp. 138-141.)

"Reprinted from University of Toronto quarterly, IV, 1934-1935."

—— The rise of national parties in Canada. By Escott M. Reid. (In Canadian Political Science Association. Papers and proceedings of the annual meeting. Toronto. v. 4 (1932), pp. [187]-200.)

—— The rise of national parties in Canada. By Escott M. Reid. (In Thorburn, H. G. (ed.) Party politics in Canada. Scarborough, Ont. [c1967] pp. [15]-22.)

"Reprinted from Papers and proceedings of the Canadian Political Science Association, IV, 1932."

REILLY, LEONARD M. Compulsory union political check-off—dictatorial. By Leonard M. Reilly. (In Canada month. Montreal. v. 9, no. 8 ([Aug.] 1969), pp. 10-11.)

Concerns the trade unions.

REYNOLDS, R. P. Public policy with respect to the settlement of labour disputes in the Canadian railway industry. [Cambridge, Mass.] 1951. 1 v.

Thesis (PH D) – Massachusetts Institute of Technology.

RHINEWINE, ABRAHAM Looking back a century on the centennial of Jewish political equality in Canada. Rev. and enl. by Isidore Goldstick. Toronto, Kraft Press, 1932. 147 p.

RICHER, LEOPOLD Notre problème politique. Montréal, Editions de l'A.C.F. [1938] 154 p. (Documents politiques.)

ROBIN, MARTIN Determinants of radical labour and socialist politics in English-speaking Canada between 1880 and 1930. (In Journal of Canadian studies. Peterborough, Ont. v. 2, no. 2 (1967), pp. 27-39.)

—— Radical politics and Canadian labour, 1880-1930. Kingston, Ont., Industrial Relations Centre, Queen's University, 1968. xi, 321 p. (Kingston, Ont. Queen's University, Industrial Relations Centre. Research series, 7.)

—— Radical politics and organized labour in Canada, 1880-1930. [Toronto, 1966] 439 leaves.

Thesis (PH D) – University of Toronto.

ROTHNEY, GORDON OLIVER Nationalism in Quebec politics since Laurier. (In Canadian Historical Association. Report of the *annual meeting.* Toronto. (1943), pp. 43-49.)

—— Newfoundland, a history. By G. O. Rothney. [2d ed.] Ottawa [Canadian Historical Association] 1964. 28 p. (Canadian Historical Association. Historical booklets, no. 10.)

—— Quebec, Canada and the world, 1940-1965. By Gordon O. Rothney. (In *Culture.* Québec. v. 26 (1965), pp. [32]-45.)

Describes the political changes that have occurred in Canada since 1940.

RUFF, NORMAN JOHN ROBERT Labour unions and the Canadian political process. [Hamilton, Ont.] 1965. 1 v.

Thesis (MA) – McMaster University.

RUMILLY, ROBERT Histoire de la province de Québec. Montréal, Fides [1940-69] v.

Publisher varies: v. 1-16, B. Valiquette; v. 17-23, Montréal-Editions; v. 24-26, Editions Chantecler; v. 27-41, Fides.

This extensive work is a political history which places the province within a national context. There is a continuing evaluation of federal-provincial reaction to political issues.

RYAN, CLAUDE Ferons-nous de la politique? (In *L'Action nationale.* Montréal. v. 37 (juil. 1951), [451]-477.)

SABOURIN, LOUIS Principaux caractères du système politique canadien; continuité et changements. (In his *Le système politique du Canada.* Ottawa, 1968. pp. [3]-19.)

SABOURIN, LOUIS (éd.) Le système politique du Canada; institutions fédérales et québécoises. Sous la direction de Louis Sabourin. Ottawa, Editions de l'Université d'Ottawa, 1968. xi, 507 p. (Cahiers des sciences sociales de l'Université d'Ottawa, no. 4.)

"Ces textes furent d'abord lus sur les ondes du réseau français de Radio-Canada dans le cadre des Cours universitaires." – Avant-propos.

Partial contents: Principaux caractères du système politique canadien, par L. Sabourin. – Evolution historique du système politique canadien, par M. Patry. – La constitution, par R. Arès. – Le fédéralisme canadien; une nouvelle perspective, par E. R. Black et A. C. Cairns. – Les relations fédérales-provinciales, par J. Y. Morin. – La couronne, par J. R. Mallory. – Le cabinet fédéral, par E. Forsey. – La Chambre des communes, par N. Ward. – Le sénat, par J. C. Bonenfant. – La pro-

cédure parlementaire, par W. F. Dawson. – L'administration fédérale, par E. P. Laberge. – Les sociétés de la couronne, par R. Barbe. – Le système électoral fédéral, par J. Meisel. – Les partis politiques fédéraux, par P. Fox. – Les groupes de pression à l'oeuvre sur la scène, par H. G. Thorburn. – Le Rôle fondamental de la collaboration interprovinciale, par J. Aitchison. – Le système judiciaire canadien, par G. A. Beaudoin. – Les commissions royales d'enquête, par K. Z. Paltiel. – Perspectives d'avenir du système politique canadien, par L. Sabourin.

Bibliography: pp. [475]-502.

SANDERS, WILFRID How good is the Canadian Gallup Poll? (In *Public affairs.* Halifax. v. 6, no. 3 (spring 1943), pp. 136-139.)

SANDWELL, BERNARD KEBLE The convention system in politics. By B. K. Sandwell. (In *Queen's quarterly.* Kingston. v. 55 (1948), pp. [343]-349.)

Compares American and Canadian procedures in the selection of a political party leader.

SCARROW, HOWARD A. By-elections and public opinion in Canada. (In Courtney, J. C. (ed.) *Voting in Canada.* [Scarborough, Ont., c1967] pp. [39]-49.)

"Reprinted from Public opinion quarterly, XXV (Spring) 1961."

—— Federal-provincial voting patterns in Canada. By Howard A. Scarrow. (In *The Canadian journal of economics and political science.* [Toronto] v. 26 (1960), pp. 289-298.)

Investigates the voting phenomenon in Canada which elects to power one political party federally and another provincially. The analysis is based on provincial and federal contests from 1930 to 1957.

—— Federal-provincial voting patterns in Canada. (In Courtney, J. C. (ed.) *Voting in Canada.* [Scarborough, Ont., c1967] pp. [82]-89.)

"Reprinted from The Canadian journal of economics and political science, XXVI (May) 1960."

—— Patterns of voter turnout in Canada. (In Courtney, J. C. (ed.) *Voting in Canada.* [Scarborough, Ont., c1967] pp. [104]-114.)

"Reprinted from Midwest journal of political science, V, no. 4 (November) 1961."

SCHINDELER, FREDERICK FERNAND Theological and political conservatism. Variation in attitudes among clergymen of one denomination. By Fred Schindeler and David Hoffman. (In *Canadian journal of political science*. Toronto. v. 1 (1968), pp. [429]-441.)

Examines "the apparent relationship between religion and voting behaviour in Canada".

SCHUETZ, CHARLES The party system; the fundamental institution of Canadian democracy. [Ottawa] 1961. 1 v.

Thesis (PH D) – University of Ottawa.

SCHWARTZ, MILDRED ANNE Canadian national identity as seen through public opinion polls, 1941-1963. [New York] 1964 [c1966] 2 v. (xxv, 938 leaves)

Thesis (PH D) – Columbia University.

—— Public opinion and Canadian identity. Foreword by Seymour Martin Lipset. Scarborough, Ont., Fitzhenry and Whiteside, 1967. xvii, 263 p.

A revision of the Author's thesis, Columbia University, 1964. [c1966] under title: *Canadian national identity as seen through public opinion polls, 1941-1963*.

SCOTT, FRANCIS REGINALD Areas of conflict in the field of public law and policy. By F. R. Scott. (In Wade, Mason (ed.) *Canadian dualism*. [Toronto, 1969] pp. [81]-105.)

"This paper appeared as an article in 3 McGill law journal (1956-7), pp. 29-50."

—— The efficiency of socialism. By F. R. Scott. (In *Queen's quarterly*. Kingston. v. 42 (1935), pp. [215]-225.)

Considers the effect a socialist system might have on the problems of economic inefficiency and political corruption.

—— New horizons for socialism. Ottawa, Woodsworth House Publishers, [1951] 16 p.

Cover title.

". . . based on the speech made . . . to the 11th CCF National Convention in Vancouver, July 1950. . . ." – Cover p. [2].

—— Political nationalism and Confederation. By F. R. Scott. (In *The Canadian journal of economics and political science*. [Toronto] v. 8 (1942), pp. 386-415.)

SCOTT, JAMES For the sake of argument. Political slush funds corrupt all parties. (In *Maclean's*. Toronto. v. 74, no. 18 (Sept. 9, 1961), pp. 13; 67-70.)

—— Raising funds for a political party. (In *The Journal of liberal thought*. [Ottawa. v.] 1, no. 1 (summer 1965), pp. [61]-67.)

Reproduced typescript.

SCOTT, PETER DALE Alienation and policy. The role of the intellectual. (In *Queen's quarterly*. Kingston. v. 72 (1965), pp. [480]-498.)

A comparative discussion of the modern political process.

SCOTTON, CLIFFORD A. Canadian labour and politics. A short history of the development of the Canadian labour movement and its relationship to and influence on the Canadian political scene. [Ottawa, Political Education Dept., Canadian Labour Congress, 1967] 40 p.

Published also in French.

SEYMOUR-URE, COLIN KNOWLTON An inquiry into the position and workings of the Parliamentary Press Gallery in Ottawa. [Ottawa] 1962. 1 v.

Thesis (MA) – Carleton University.

SHARP, MITCHELL WILLIAM The expert, the politician and the public. By Hon. Mitchell Sharp. (In Hawkins, Gordon (ed.) *Order and good government*. [Toronto, c1965] pp. 78-87.)

SHARP, PAUL FREDERICK The agrarian revolt in western Canada; a survey showing American parallels. Minneapolis, University of Minnesota Press [1948] ix, 204 p.

Examines political unrest in the Canadian West from 1911 to 1930.

SHORTT, ADAM Political corruption. By A. Shortt. (In *Queen's quarterly*. Kingston. v. 12 (1904/05), pp. 324-327.)

Presents a general discussion of political corruption in relation to party politics.

SIMARD, GEORGES Principes et faits en histoire: Etat idéal Etat canadien. (In his *Etudes canadiennes*. Montréal, 1938. pp. [87]-122.)

SISSONS, CHARLES BRUCE Bi-lingual schools in Canada. By C. B. Sissons. [Introd. by J. S. Woodsworth] London, Toronto, Dent, 1917. 242 p.

SKELTON, OSCAR DOUGLAS Railway politics. By O. D. Skelton. (In *Queen's quarterly*. Kingston. v. 21 (1913/14), pp. 507-516.)

Considers the railway question and its historical relationship to Canadian politics.

SMALL, MALCOLM STEWART   The genesis of Canadian parties. Toronto, 1934. 115 leaves.

Thesis (MA) – University of Toronto.

SMILEY, DONALD VICTOR   The alienation of the politician. By Donald V. Smiley. (In *The Canadian forum*. Toronto. v. 39, no. 470 (Mar. 1960), pp. 271-273.)

—— The Canadian political nationality. Toronto, Methuen, 1967. xv, 142 p.

—— Consensus, conflict and the Canadian party system. By Donald V. Smiley. (In *The Canadian forum*. Toronto. v. 40, no. 480 (1961), pp. 223-224.)

—— Contributions to Canadian political science since the Second World War. By Donald V. Smiley. (In *The Canadian journal of economics and political science*. [Toronto] v. 33 (1967), pp. [569]-580.)

"An earlier version of this essay was read to a joint meeting of the Canadian Political Science Association and the Canadian Economics Association in Ottawa in June 1967."

Discusses significant research and work done in the study of Canadian government and politics.

—— The national party leadership convention in Canada; a preliminary analysis. By D. V. Smiley. (In *Canadian journal of political science*. Toronto. v. 1 (1968), pp. [373]-397.)

—— The national party leadership convention in Canada; a preliminary analysis. (In Kruhlak, O. M. (comp.) *The Canadian political process*. Toronto [c1970] pp. 198-223.)

Reprinted from *Canadian journal of political science*, v. 1 (1968), pp. 373-397.

—— One-partyism and Canadian democracy. By Donald V. Smiley (In *The Canadian forum*. Toronto. v. 38, no. 450 (July 1958), pp. 79-80.)

—— The two-party system and one-party dominance in the liberal democratic state. By Donald V. Smiley. (In *The Canadian journal of economics and political science*. [Toronto] v. 24 (1958), pp. 312-322.)

The Author applies his analysis to Canada, Great Britain, and the United States.

SMITH, BRIAN CLIVE   Student political attitudes at McMaster University. [Hamilton, Ont.] 1963. 1 v.

Thesis (MA) – McMaster University.

SMITH, DAVID EDWARD   Questionnaire response; voter turnout and party support. (In Courtney, J. C. (ed.) *Voting in Canada*. [Scarborough, Ont., c1967] pp. [115]-124.)

SMITH, DENIS   Prairie revolt, federalism and the party system. (In Thorburn, H. G. (ed.) *Party politics in Canada*. Scarborough, Ont. [c1967] pp. [189]-200.)

"Based on Politics and the party system in the three prairie provinces, 1917-1958. Thesis (B.Litt) Oxford University, 1959."

Examines the professed national aim of the Progressives, the CCF and the Social Credit parties from 1921 to 1958 to force political realignment in the country.

SMITH, GARY   The politics of youth. A look at political socialization. (In *The Journal of liberal thought*. Ottawa. [v.] 3, no. 1 (winter 1966/67), pp. 120-145.)

Attempts to arrive at generalizations about the Canadian situation through an application of the results of American and British research data.

SMITH, GOLDWIN   The party system of government. (In Canadian Club of Toronto. *Addresses*. Toronto. (1903/04), pp. 63-68.)

Address delivered on February 8, 1904.

SMITH, WILLIAM GEORGE   A study in Canadian immigration. By W. G. Smith. Toronto, Ryerson Press, 1920. 406 p.

The Sources and uses of party funds. (In Thorburn, H. G. (ed.) *Party politics in Canada*. Scarborough, Ont. [c1967] pp. [104]-120.)

"Reprinted from Report of the Committee on Election Expenses. Ottawa, Queen's Printer, 1966."

SQUAIR, JOHN   Statism and individualism. (In *The Onlooker*. Toronto. v. 1, no. 7 (Oct. 1920), pp. 11-15; v. 1, no. 7 (Nov. 1920), pp. 6-10.)

In two parts.

A comparative analysis.

STANFIELD, ROBERT LORNE   Man and government. By Robert Stanfield. (In Clarkson, Stephen (ed.) *Visions 2020*. Edmonton [c1970] pp. [119]-122.)

STEELE, J. L.   Party systems of Canada and the United States. [Boulder, 1968] 1 v.

Thesis (MA) – Colorado University.

STEVENS, GEORGE ROY   Canadian National Railways. With a foreword by Donald Gordon. And an introd. by S. W. Fair-weather. Toronto, Clarke, Irwin, 1960-62. 2 v.

STEVENSON, JOHN A. Ottawa letter. How the Press Gallery works. (In *Saturday night*. Toronto. v. 71, no. 1 (Mar. 17, 1956), pp. 16-18.)

—— Political campaign funds. (In *Queen's quarterly*. Kingston. v. 38 (1931), pp. [635]-647.)

An historical and comparative analysis.

STEWART, ROD Federal elections in Waterloo South (1867-1963). (In Waterloo Historical Society. *Annual volume*. Kitchener, Ont. 51st (1963), pp. 29-34.)

"The source material . . . was derived from the files of the Galt Reporter and the Galt Reformer."

"Waterloo South voting since Confederation", a table: p. 34.

STURSBERG, PETER Ottawa letter. Will conventions become Canadian? (In *Saturday night*. Toronto. v. 75, no. 15 (July 23, 1960), pp. 25-26.)

Compares Canadian and American political party conventions.

SWAINSON, DONALD WAYNE (ed.) Historical essays on the prairie provinces. [Edited by] Donald Swainson. Toronto, McClelland and Stewart [c1970] xiii, 312 [i.e. 319] p. (Carleton library, no. 53.)

Partial contents: John A. Macdonald, Confederation and the Canadian West, by D. Creighton. – Canadian nationalism in Western newspapers, by R. C. Brown. – Liberal politics, federal policies, and the lieutenant-governor: Saskatchewan and Alberta, 1905, by J. T. Saywell. – J. S. Woodsworth and a political party for Labour, 1896 to 1921, by K. McNaught.

TAYLOR, CHARLES L'Etat et les partis politiques. (In Institut canadien des affaires publiques, Montréal. *Le rôle de l'Etat*. Montréal [1963] pp. [111]-121.)

THOMAS, LEWIS HERBERT The North-West Territories, 1870-1905. By Lewis H. Thomas. Ottawa, Canadian Historical Association, 1970. 24 p. map. (Canadian Historical Association. Historical booklets, no. 26.)

Translated into French under title: *Les Territoires du Nord-Ouest, 1870-1905*.

THORBURN, HUGH GARNET Les groupes de pression à l'oeuvre sur la scène fédérale. Par H. G. Thorburn. (In Sabourin, Louis

(éd.) *Le système politique du Canada*. Ottawa, 1968. pp. [211]-226.)

THORBURN, HUGH GARNET (ed.) Party politics in Canada. Edited by Hugh G. Thorburn. Toronto, Prentice-Hall of Canada [c1963] xii, 172 p.

Appendix: Election results, 1878-1962. Data provided by Howard A. Scarrow.

"Readings": pp. 168-172.

Partial contents: The background and development of national parties, by G. M. Hougham. – The rise of national parties in Canada, by E. M. Reid. – The structure of Canadian politics, by J. R. Mallory. – Party images in Canada, by J. M. Beck and D. J. Dooley. – The Liberals in convention, by N. Ward. – Money in Canadian politics, by E. E. Harrill. – Ad-men and scientists run this election, by R. Gwyn. – Mackenzie King as leader, by M. Dawson. – The Progressive tradition in Canadian politics, by W. L. Morton. – The CCF-NDP: membership in a becalmed protest movement, by L. Zakuta. – Prairie revolt, federalism and the party system, by D. Smith. – Democracy and political leadership in Canada, by E. M. Reid. – Political parties and the political career, by J. Porter. – Wanted: a ceiling on election spending, by C. G. Power. – Politics and business in Canada, by H. G. Thorburn.

—— Party politics in Canada. 2d ed. Scarborough, Ont. Prentice-Hall of Canada [c1967] 232. p.

First published 1963.

Appendix: Election results, 1878-1965 (pp. [213]-225).

Partial contents: The background and development of national parties, by G. M. Hougham. – The rise of national parties in Canada, by E. M. Reid. – The structure of Canadian politics, by J. R. Mallory. – Recent changes in Canadian parties, by J. Meisel. – Conservatism, liberalism and socialism in Canada, by G. Horowitz. – Party images in Canada, by J. M. Beck and D. J. Dooley. – The economic elite and political leadership in Canada, by J. Porter. – The Liberals in convention, by N. Ward. – The sources and uses of party funds, issued by Committee on Election Expenses. – Ad-men and scientists run this election, by R. Gwyn. – Mackenzie King as leader, by R. M. Dawson. – Federal strains within a Canadian party, by E. R. Black. – The progressive tradition in Canadian politics, by W. L. Morton. – The New Democratic Party and Canadian politics, by W. Baker. – Prairie revolt, federalism and the party system, by D. Smith.

THORBURN, HUGH GARNET   Politics and business in Canada; some questions. By Hugh G. Thorburn. (In his *Party politics. in Canada*. Toronto [c1963] pp. 151-154.)
"Reprinted from The Commerce journal, Toronto, 1959."
Discusses the influence of business over government policy.

TORRENCE, LOIS EVELYN   The national party system in Canada, 1945-1960. Washington, DC, 1961. xiii, 545 leaves.
Thesis (PH D) – American University.
Abstracted in *Dissertation abstracts*, v. 22 (1961), no. 5, p. 1700.

TROOP, GEORGE ROBERT   Socialism in Canada. [Montreal] 1922. 1 v.
Thesis (MA) – McGill University.

TRUDEAU, PIERRE ELLIOTT   Politique fonctionnelle. (In *Cité libre*. Montréal. v. 1, no 1 (juin 1950), pp. 20-24.)

—— Politique fonctionnelle. (In *Canadian life*. Toronto. v. 2, no. 1 (spring 1951), pp. 2-3; 26.)
English translation of Politique fonctionnelle. (In *Cité libre*. Montréal. v. 1, no 1 (juin 1950), pp. 20-24.)

—— Réflexions sur la politique au Canada français. (In *Cité libre*. Montréal. v. 2, no 3 [i.e. 6] (1952), pp. 53-70.)

UNDERHILL, FRANK HAWKINS   The Canadian party system in transition. By F. H. Underhill. (In *The Canadian journal of economics and political science*. [Toronto] v. 9 (1943), pp. 300-316.)

—— The Canadian party system in transition. [In his *In search of Canadian liberalism*. Toronto, 1961. pp. 192-202.]
A paper read at the annual meeting of the Canadian Political Science Association, 1943, and printed in the *Canadian journal of economics and political science*, August, 1943.

—— Canadian political parties. By F. H. Underhill. Ottawa 1957 [c1956] 19 p. (The Canadian Historical Association booklets, no. 8.)

—— The Canadian version of "The prince". By F. H. Underhill. (In *The Canadian forum*. Toronto. v. 41, no. 1 [i.d. 483] (Apr. 1961), pp. [1]-3.)
A review article of *The Mackenzie King record*, edited by J. W. Pickersgill. Vol. 1. Toronto, University of Toronto Press, 1960,

and of *Arthur Meighen*, by R. Graham, vol. 1. Toronto, Clarke, Irwin, 1960.

—— The conception of a national interest. By Frank H. Underhill. (In *The Canadian journal of economics and political science*. [Toronto] v. 1 (1935), pp. 396-408.)
Discusses the function of the intellectual in formulating policies for the national interest.

—— The development of national political parties in Canada. (In *The Canadian historical review*. Toronto. v. 16 (1935), pp. 367-387.)

—— The development of national political parties in Canada. (In his *In search of Canadian liberalism*. Toronto, 1961. pp. 21-42.)
"This article was first printed in the Canadian historical review, December, 1935."

—— In search of Canadian liberalism. Toronto, Macmillan, 1961 [c1960] xiv, 282 p.
"This volume contains a selection of articles written by me over the last thirty years. They have to do directly or indirectly with the subject of Canadian liberalism. . . ." – Author's introd.
Appendix: A list of some other writings by Frank H. Underhill on various topics (pp. 271-274).

—— On professors and politics. By Frank H. Underhill. (In *The Canadian forum*. Toronto. v. 15, no. 182 (Mar. 1936), pp. 6-7.)

—— On professors and politics. (In his *In Search of Canadian liberalism*. Toronto, 1961. pp. 107-109.)
First printed in *The Canadian forum*, March, 1936.

—— The party system in Canada. By F. H. Underhill. (In Canadian Political Science Association. *Papers and proceedings of the annual meeting*. Toronto. v. 4 (1932), pp. [201]-212.)

—— The party system in Canada. (In his *In search of Canadian liberalism*. Toronto, 1961. pp. 164-171.)
A paper read at the annual meeting of the Canadian Political Science Association, 1932, and printed in its *Proceedings* for 1932.

—— Political parties and ideas. (In Brown, G. W. (ed.) *Canada*. Berkeley, 1953 [c1950] pp. 331-352.)

[UNDERHILL, FRANK HAWKINS] The question of parties. (In League for Social Reconstruction. Research Committee. *Social planning for Canada.* Toronto [c1953] pp. 464-488.)

Author identified in *On Canada; essays in honour of Frank H. Underhill.* Edited by N. Penlington. [Toronto] University of Toronto Press [1971] ("Bibliography": p. 134).

—— Random remarks on socialism and freedom. (In his *In search of Canadian liberalism.* Toronto, 1961. pp. 203-206.)

First printed in *The Canadian forum,* August 1947.

—— Seventy-five years after. By F. H. Underhill. (In *The Canadian forum.*Toronto. v. 22, no. 258 (July 1942), pp. 106-108.)

General comments on the Canadian Confederation.

—— Some observations upon nationalism and provincialism in Canada. By Frank H. Underhill. (In Canadian Institute on Economics and Politics. *Problems in Canadian unity.* Toronto [c1938] pp. 67-68.)

—— Some reflections on the liberal tradition in Canada. (In Canadian Historical Association. *Report of the annual meeting.* Toronto. (1946), pp. 5-17.)

Presidential address.

—— Some reflections on the liberal tradition in Canada. (In his *In search of Canadian liberalism.* Toronto, 1961. pp. 3-20.)

This paper was read at the annual meeting of the Canadian Historical Association in 1946.

—— Some reflections on the liberal tradition in Canada. (In *Approaches to Canadian history.* Toronto [1970, c1967] pp. [29]-41.)

"Reprinted from Canadian Historical Association, Report, 1946."

UNIVERSITY LEAGUE FOR SOCIAL REFORM Agenda. 1970. Proposals for a creative politics. Edited by Trevor Lloyd and Jack McLeod. [Foreword by F. R. Scott. Toronto] University of Toronto Press (c1968)] xii, 292 p.

Essays by the University League for Social Reform.

Partial contents: Our ideological tradition, by T. O. Lloyd. – A new National Policy by M. Watkins. – The flexibility of the BNA Act, by B. Strayer. – What happens to Parliament? by R. Blair. – Toward the democratic class struggle, by G. Horowitz.

– Public power and ivory power, by J. E. Hodgetts. – Government as dialogue, by T. Lloyd.

—— Nationalism in Canada. Edited by Peter Russell. With foreword by Frank Underhill. Toronto, McGraw-Hill [1966] xx, 377 p.

Partial contents: Federalism, nationalism and the scope of public activity in Canada, by D. V. Smiley. – The decline of Confederation and the new nationalism, by A. Dubuc. – Protection, immigration and Canadian nationalism, by John Dales.

—— The prospect of change; proposals for Canada's future. Edited by Abraham Rotstein. With a foreword by Northrop Frye. Toronto, McGraw-Hill [c1965] xx, 361 p.

Papers read and discussed at the League's monthly meetings.

Partial contents: Party structure and party reform, by J. T. McLeod. – The reform of parliamentary proceedings, by T. Lloyd.

VAUGHAN, FREDERICK (ed.) Contemporary issues in Canadian politics. [Edited by Frederick Vaughan, Patrick Kyba and O. P. Dwivedi. Scarborough, Ont., Prentice-Hall [c1970] xi, 286 p.

A selection of articles treating significant features of government and politics in Canada.

Partial contents: The practice and theory of federalism, by P. E. Trudeau. – The limitations of co-operative federalism, by W. R. Lederman. – The possible contents of special status for Quebec, by C. Ryan. – Canadian federalism and the resolution of the federal-provincial conflict, by D. V. Smiley. – Civil liberties and a constitutional bill of rights, by K. Kernaghan. – A democratic approach to civil liberties, by P. H. Russell. – Canadian Charter of Human Rights, by P. E. Trudeau. – The provinces and international agreement, by B. Laskin. – The treaty-making powers of Quebec, by J. Y. Morin. – The monarchy in Canada, by E. Forsey. – The Canadian parliament and cabinet in the face of modern demands, by R. G. Robertson. – The influence of the cabinet minister, by M. Lamontagne. – A century of constituencies, by N. Ward. – The speakership of the Canadian House of Commons, by D. Smith. – The future of the Senate, by the Government of Canada. – The changing nature of the public service, by J. E. Hodgetts. – Political rights of Canada's public servants, by O. P. Dwivedi and J. P. Kyba. – The Canadian Supreme Court and constitutional review, by E. McWhinney. – Quebec and constitutional arbitration, by J. Y. Morin. – Scalogram analysis of the Supreme Court of Canada, by S. R. Peck.

WADE, MASON (ed.) Canadian dualism; studies of French-English relations. Edited by Mason Wade for a Committee of the Social Science Research Council of Canada under the chairmanship of Jean-C. Falardeau. [Toronto] University of Toronto Press; Québec, Presses universitaires Laval 1960 xxv, 427 p.
Added title page in French.
Articles in English or French.
Partial contents: Areas of conflict in the field of public law and policy, by F. R. Scott. – The national political scene, by N. Ward.

WALLACE, WILLIAM STEWART The journalist in Canadian politics; a retrospect. (In The Canadian historical review. Toronto. v. 22 (1941), pp. 14-24.)

WANCZYCKI, JAN K. Union dues and political contributions: Great Britain, United States, Canada; a comparison. (In Relations industrielles. Québec. v. 21 (1966), pp. 143-209.)
Summary in French: Cotisations syndicales et contributions pour fins politiques; comparaison entre la Grande-Bretagne, les Etats-Unis et le Canada (pp. 205-209).
A legalistic discussion as to "how the Legislatures . . . attempted to prevent or regularize the use of union dues, levies or funds for political purposes."

WARD, NORMAN MC QUEEN Electoral corruption and controverted elections. By Norman Ward. (In The Canadian journal of economics and political science. [Toronto] v. 15 (1949), pp. 74-86.)

—— The national political scene. By Norman Ward. (In Wade, Mason (ed.) Canadian dualism. [Toronto, 1960] pp. [260]-276.)
". . . an attempt to appraise some of the important contemporary elements in relations between English and French speaking Canadians in national politics."

—— The press and the patronage; an exploratory operation. By Norman Ward. (In Aitchison, J. H. (ed.) The political process in Canada. [Toronto, c1963] pp. [3]-16.)

Examines the connection between journalism and politics.

—— Why do Canada's elections have to cost so much? By Norman Ward. (In Saturday night. Toronto. v. 64, no. 34 (May 31, 1949), pp. 18-19.)

WATKINS, FREDERICK MUNDELL Democracy and authority. By F. M. Watkins. (In Greenslade, J. G. (ed.) Canadian politics. Sackville, N.B. [1959?] pp. 9-15.)

WEIR, ERNEST AUSTIN The struggle for national broadcasting in Canada. By E. Austin Weir. Toronto, McClelland and Stewart [c1965] xiv, 477 p.

WHITE, W. L. Voting in a single constituency, 1874-1963. By W. L. White. (In Dalhousie review. Halifax. v. 47, no. 4 (winter 1967/68), pp. [513]-525.)
Compares a federal election held in Essex County in January 1874 with one held in Essex West in April 1963, using as contemporary sources the Essex Record and the Windsor Star respectively.

WILLISON, SIR JOHN STEPHEN Journalism and public life in Canada. By J. S. Willison. (In The Canadian magazine of politics, science, art and literature. Toronto. v. 25 (1905), pp. 554-558.)

—— The party system of government. By J. S. Willison. (In Canadian Club of Toronto. Addresses. Toronto. (1903/04), pp. 68-72.)
Address delivered on February 15, 1904.

WILSON, JOHN Towards a society of friends. Some reflections on the meaning of democratic socialism. (In Canadian journal of political science. Toronto. v. 3 (1970), pp. [628]-654.)

WILTON, J. W. Power at any price. By J. W. Wilton. Winnipeg, The Print Shop, 1930. 175 p.
Satirizes political events in Canada from 1896 to the federal election of 1930.

WOOD, LOUIS AUBREY A history of farmers' movements in Canada. By L. A. Wood. Toronto, Ryerson Press [1924] 372 p.

WOOD, SAMUEL THOMAS How an election is won. By S. T. Wood. (In University quarterly review. Toronto. 2d quarter (June 1890), pp. 198-208.)
Explains the routine procedures involved in an election campaign.

WOODLEY, W. J. The influence of Western

farmers on Canadian tariff policy, 1896-1926. [Saskatoon, 1945] 1 v.

Thesis (MA)–University of Saskatchewan.

WOODS, HARRY DOUGLAS Labour policy and labour economics in Canada. By H. D. Woods and Sylvia Ostry. Toronto, Macmillan, 1962. xvii, 534 p.

"Bibliography": pp. 507-524.

—— Trends in public policy in labour relations. By H. D. Woods. (In *Relations industrielles*. Québec. v. 20 (1965), pp. 429-444.)

Summary in French: La politique gouvernementale et les relations de travail (pp. 437-444).

Discusses, in part, the role of government in labour relations.

WOODSWORTH, JAMES SHAVER Political democracy. By J. S. Woodsworth. (In *The University of Toronto quarterly*. [Toronto] v. 4 (1934/35), pp. 296-314.)

WRONG, GEORGE MC KINNON Democracy in Canada. (In *The Canadian historical review*. Toronto. v. 2 (1921), pp. 315-332.)

—— Problems issuing from Confederation. By Prof. George M. Wrong. (In Canadian Club of Toronto. *Addresses*. Toronto. (1927/28), pp. 3-13.)

Address delivered on May 12, 1927.

POLITICAL HISTORY
1867–1896

GENERAL WORKS

BECK, JAMES MURRAY French Catholic problems in Canada from Confederation to the death of Sir John Thompson. [Wolfville, N.S.] 1938. 1 v.

Thesis (MA) – Acadia University.

Reviews in detail each religious and racial issue between 1867 and 1894. Cf. Canadian graduate theses in the humanities and social sciences, 1921-1946. Ottawa, 1951 (p. 49).

BEGG, ALEXANDER History of the North-West. Toronto, Hunter, Rose, 1894-95. 3 v.

Author lived from 1839 to 1897.

Vol. 1, appendix 11: The Manitoba Act; v. 3, appendix 2: Report of the decision of the Judicial Committee on the Manitoba School case.

BERNIER, NOEL Le rôle du gouvernement provisoire. (In *L'Action française*. Montréal. v. 4 (juin 1920), pp. [266-273.)

"A propos du cinquantenaire de l'entrée des Terres de Rupert et du Nord-Ouest dans la Confédération canadienne."

BLAKELEY, PHYLLIS RUTH Party government in Nova Scotia, 1878-1897. [Halifax] 1946. 304 leaves.

Thesis (MA) – Dalhousie University.

The Author considers party government as practised both in the province and at Ottawa. Cf. Canadian graduate theses in the humanities and social sciences, 1921-1946. Ottawa, 1951 (p. 72).

BURKE, TERESA AVILA Canadian cabinets in the making; a study in the problems of a pluralistic society, 1867-1896. Ann Arbor, Mich., University Microfilms [1958] iv, 312 leaves.

Thesis (PH D) – Columbia University.

Abstracted in *Dissertation abstracts*, v. 19 (1958), no. 3, p. 516.

CANADIENNE The national idea in periodicals. By Canadienne. (In *The Canadian courier*. Toronto. v. 1, no. 1 (Dec. 1, 1906), pp. 7-8.)

Reviews the literary and political significance of *The Nation*, first issued April 2, 1874, and *The Week*, first issued December 6, 1883.

COLQUHOUN, ARTHUR HUGH URQUHART The story of eight general elections. By A. H. U. Colquhoun. (In *The Canadian magazine of politics, science, art and literature*. Toronto. v. 16 (1900/01), pp. 17-28.)

Concerns the federal elections held from 1867 to 1896.

COOPER, JOHN IRWIN French-Canadian conservatism, in principle and in practice, 1873-1891. [Montreal] 1929. 1 v.

Thesis (PH D) – McGill University.

DALTON, ROY CLINTON The history of the Jesuits' Estates, 1760-1888. Ann Arbor, University Microfilms [1958] v. 386 leaves.
> Thesis (PH D) – University of Minnesota. Abstracted in *Dissertation abstracts*, v. 18 (1958), no. 1, p. 212.

——— The Jesuits' Estates Question, 1760-1888; a study of the background for the agitation of 1889. By Roy C. Dalton. [Toronto] University of Toronto Press [c1968] ix, 201 p. (Canadian studies in history and government, 11.)

FOSTER, JOAN MARY VASSIE Reciprocity in Canadian politics from the commercial union movement to 1910. [Bryn Mawr, Pa., 1937] 405 leaves.
> Thesis (PH D) – Bryn Mawr, Pennsylvania.

FRUMHARTZ, ESTHER Reciprocity, 1860-1880. Toronto, 1938. 230 leaves.
> Thesis (MA) – University of Toronto.

GOLDENBERG, HYMAN CARL The Canadian budgets, 1867-1896. [Montreal] 1929. 1 v.
> Thesis (MA) – McGill University.

Grip. v. 1-42 (no. 1-1100); May 24, 1873 – December 29, 1894. Toronto. 42 v. illus.
> Publication suspended July 22-Dec. 1893. Edited and illustrated by J. W. Bengough. A humorous weekly consisting mainly of political cartoons.

LESTER, CARL Dominion land surveys. (In *Alberta historical review*. Edmonton. v. 11, no. 3 (summer 1963), pp. 20-28.)
> "This paper was given to the February 1963 meeting of the Edmonton Branch, Historical Society of Alberta."
> Presents background to the Dominion Land Act passed April 14, 1872 and government surveys of public lands in the West to 1887.

MC CREADY, JOHN E. BLAKENY The era of Confederation. By J. E. B. McCready. (In *The Busy East of Canada*. Sackville, N.B. v. 8, no. 9 (Apr. 1918) pp. 5-14; 31.)
> A popular account.

MITCHENER, E. ALYN William Pearce and federal government activity in the West, 1874-1904. (In *Canadian public administration*. Toronto. v. 10 (1967), pp. 235-243.)
> "The biographical material . . . has been taken from the William Pearce papers, University of Alberta Archives, Edmonton, Alberta, file no. 22."

MORTON, WILLIAM LEWIS Confederation, 1870-1896. The end of the Macdonaldian constitution and the return to duality. (In *Journal of Canadian studies*. Peterborough, Ont. v. 1, no. 1 (1966), pp. 11-24.)

ORMSBY, MARGARET ANCHORETTA The relations between British Columbia and the Dominion of Canada, 1871-1885. By Margaret A. Ormsby. [Bryn Mawr, Pa.] 1937. 277 leaves.
> Thesis (PH D) – Bryn Mawr College.

RANNIE, ROBERT JOHN The *Toronto Evening telegram*, 1876-1891; an appreciation of its editorial policy. Toronto, 1948. 348 leaves.
> Thesis (MA) – University of Toronto.

ROBIN, MARTIN The working class and the transition to capitalist democracy in Canada. (In *The Dalhousie review*. Halifax. v. 47, no. 3 (autumn 1967), pp. [326]-343.)
> Concerns the period between 1867 and 1900.

ROSCOE, ALEXANDER ALLAN The Manitoba Act in transition, 1870-1896; the transformation of Manitoba's French-Canadian politico-cultural institutions. [Winnipeg] 1968. xii, 199 leaves.
> Thesis (MA) – University of Manitoba.

SAGE, WALTER NOBLE British Columbia becomes Canadian (1871-1901). By Walter N. Sage. (In *Queen's quarterly*. Kingston. v. 52 (1945), pp. [168]-183.)
> Considers political development, building of the Canadian Pacific Railway and immigration to British Columbia.

——— Federal parties and provincial political groups in British Columbia. 1871-1903. By Walter N. Sage. (In *The British Columbia historical quarterly*. Victoria, B.C. v. 12 (1948), pp. 151-169.)

——— From colony to province. The introduction of responsible government in British Columbia. By W. N. Sage. (In *The British Columbia historical quarterly*. v. 3 (1939), pp. 1-14.)
> "The presidential address to the British Columbia Historical Association, November 18, 1938."
> Considers the historical development of British Columbia as a province and its relationship to the government of Canada.

THOMAS, LEWIS HERBERT The lieutenant governor's proclamation and minutes. (In

Saskatchewan history. Saskatoon. v. 1 (autumn 1948), pp. 9-13.)

Cites the proclamations and minutes of the lieutenant-governor of the North-West Territories, 1876-97.

—— Responsible government in the Canadian North-West Territories, 1870-97. [Minneapolis, 1953] 416 leaves.

Thesis (PH D) – University of Minnesota. Later published under title: *The struggle for responsible government in the North-West Territories, 1870-97.* Toronto, University of Toronto Press [c1956].

—— The struggle for responsible government in the North-West Territories, 1870-97. [Toronto] University of Toronto Press [c1956] viii, 276 p.

"Originally submitted as a doctoral dissertation at the University of Minnesota" under title: *Responsible government in the Canadian North-West Territories, 1870-97.*

TURNER, JOHN PETER   The North-West Mounted Police, 1873-1893. Inclusive of the great transition period in the Canadian West, 1873-1893, when law and order was introduced and established. Ottawa, King's Printer, 1950 [i.e. 1951] 2 v.

Compiled at the request of the Commissioner of the Royal Canadian Mounted Police and represents the official and departmental history of the first 20 years of the Force. Cf. Introd.

WAITE, PETER BUSBY   Canada, 1874-1896; arduous destiny. Toronto, McClelland and Stewart [1971] xii, 340 p. (The Canadian Centenary series, 13.)

"Select bibliography": pp. 318-329.

WARD, NORMAN MC QUEEN   Early electioneering in Canada. By Norman Ward. (In *The Dalhousie review.* Halifax. v. 31 (1951/52), pp. [65]-71.)

Discusses electoral corruption following Confederation to about 1887.

WATT, FRANK WILLIAM   The National Policy, the workingman and proletarian ideas in Victorian Canada. By F. W. Watt. (In *The Canadian historical review.* Toronto. v. 40 (1959), pp. [1]-26.)

WILLISON, SIR JOHN STEPHEN   Reminiscences, political and personal. [Pt. 6] Blake and Thompson in Parliament. (In *The Canadian magazine of politics, science, art and literature.* Toronto. v. 51 (1918), pp. 491-501.)

POST-CONFEDERATION PERIOD, 1867–1878

ACHINTRE, AUGUSTE   Semaine politique. Par A. Achintre. (In *L'Opinion publique.* Montréal. v. 6, no. 6—no. 15 (11 fév.—15 avril, 1875.)

Summarizes proceedings during the second session of the third parliament held February 4 to April 8, 1875.

—— Semaine politique. Les écoles du Nouveau-Brunswick. Par A. Achintre. (In *L'Opinion publique.* Montréal. v. 6, no. 11 (18 mars 1875), pp. 130-131.)

Summarizes proceedings in the federal parliament concerning the school laws of New Brunswick.

ATKINS, B. R.   The first federal election in Yale. (In Okanagan Historical Society. *Report* [n.p.] 15th (1951), pp. 41-43.)

Describes the election held in Yale, B.C., December 19, 1871. C. F. Houghton was elected to the federal Parliament.

AYEARST, MORLEY   The Parti Rouge and the clergy. (In *The Canadian historical review.* Toronto. v. 15 (1934), pp. 390-405.)

BEAUSOLEIL, C.   Réforme du tarif canadien. Montréal. 1871. 61 p.

BENGOUGH, JOHN WILSON   The Grip cartoons, vols. I & II, May, 1873 to May, 1874. With notes and introd., by J. W. Bengough. Toronto, Rogers & Larminie, 1875. [6] p., 52 plates.

A short description precedes each plate.

BERTON, PIERRE FRANCIS DE MARIGNY   The national dream; the great railway, 1871-1881. By Pierre Berton. Toronto, McClelland and Stewart [c1970] xiii, 439 p.

Sequel: *The last spike.*
Bibliography: pp. 415-423.

BESCOBY, ISABEL   A colonial administration; an analysis of administration in British Columbia, 1869-1871. (In *Canadian public administration.* Toronto. v. 10 (1967), pp. 48-104.)

Discusses British Columbia's entry into Confederation.

BLACK, CHARLES E. DRUMMOND   The Marquess of Dufferin and Ava; diplomatist, viceroy, statesman. Toronto, Morang. 1903. xiii, 409 p.

Chapters 5-7: Governor-generalship of Canada (pp. 76-161).

BOLGER, FRANCIS WILLIAM PIUS   Prince Edward Island and Confederation 1863-

1873. (In Canadian Catholic Historical Association. *Report.* [Ottawa] (1961), pp. 25-30.)

—— Prince Edward Island and Confederation, 1863-1873. By Francis W. P. Bolger. [Charlottetown] St. Dunstan's University Press [c1964] viii, 308 p.

BONENFANT, JEAN CHARLES Les Canadiens français et la Confédération. Par J. C. Bonenfant. Ottawa, Canadian Historical Association, 1966. 20 p. (Canadian Historical Association. Historical booklets, no. 21.)

Translated into English under title: *The French Canadians and the birth of Confederation.*

BOURINOT, SIR JOHN GEORGE Notes from Ottawa. By J. G. Bourinot. (In *The Canadian monthly and national review.* Toronto. v. 2 (1872), pp. 170-173.)

BRADFORD, ROBERT ARTHUR Some aspects of the depression of 1873 in Canada. [London, Ont., 1974] 188 leaves.

Thesis (MA) – University of Western Ontario.

A Breach of the constitution. (In *The Nation.* Toronto. v. 2, no. 11 (March 19, 1875), p. 126.)

Refers to the question of repeal by the Dominion government of the New Brunswick school law, passed by the provincial legislature.

British Columbia, and its relations to the Dominion. By F. J. R., Victoria, B.C. (In *The Canadian monthly and national review.* Toronto. v. 10 (1876), pp. [369]-376.)

BROWN, LORNE A. The Macdonald-Cartwright struggle in Lennox, November, 1873. (In *Ontario history.* Toronto. v. 61, no. 1 (Mar. 1969), pp. [33]-50.)

The contestants were Richard Cartwright and Edmund J. G. Hooper.

BRUCHESI, EMILE Les écoles du Nouveau-Brunswick. (In *L'Action française.* Montréal. v. 6 (nov. 1921), pp. [673]-681.)

At head of title: Cinquantenaire.

Refers to the school issue raised in 1871.

BUIES, ARTHUR *La lanterne.* Nouv. éd. Montréal, 1884. 336 p.

Originally published as a periodical, from Sept. 1868 to Mar. 1869. Directed against the clergy of the Catholic Church in Canada.

CAMPBELL, R. H. The repeal agitation in Nova Scotia, 1867-69. (In Nova Scotia

Historical Society. *Collections.* Halifax. v. 25 (1942), pp. [95]-129.)

"Read before the Nova Scotia Historical Society, December 1, 1939."

Concerns the movement to repeal Confederation.

Canada first. (In *The Nation.* Toronto. v. 2, no. 8 (February 26, 1875), pp. 91-92.)

Canadian copyright legislation and the Act of 1875. (In *The Nation.* Toronto. v. 2, no. 18 (May 7, 1875), p. 213.)

Canadian Parliament. (In *Canadian illustrated news.* Montreal. v. 1, no. 17—no. 29 (Feb. 26—May 21, 1870.)

Summarizes proceedings during the third session of the first parliament, held February 15 to May 12, 1870.

Canadian Parliament. (In *Canadian illustrated news.* Montreal. v. 3, no. 8—no. 16 (Feb. 25—Apr. 22, 1871.)

Summarizes proceedings during the fourth session of the first parliament, held February 15 to April 14, 1871.

Canadian Parliament. (In *Canadian illustrated news.* Montreal. v. 3, no. 16 (April 22, 1871), pp. 246-247.)

Summarizes parliamentary activities from April 10 to April 14, 1871. Includes a list of "Bills passed during the session and sanctioned by his Excellency" (p. 247).

Canadian Parliament. (In *Canadian illustrated news.* Montreal. v. 5, no. 16—no. 25 (April 20—June 22, 1872).)

Summarizes proceedings during the fifth session of the first parliament held April 11 to June 14, 1872.

Canadian Parliament. (In *Canadian illustrated news.* Montreal. v. 5, no. 25 (June 22, 1872), pp. 386-387.)

Summarizes parliamentary activities from June 3 to June 14, 1872. Includes a list of the bills accepted by the Crown.

The Canadian question in England. (In *The Nation.* Toronto. v. 2, no. 29 (July 23, 1875), pp. 342-343.)

A full discussion of views on Canadian affairs presented by Lord Dufferin, while Governor-General of Canada, at a dinner speech to the Canada Club in London, England.

CARNARVON, HENRY HOWARD MOLYNEUX, 4TH EARL OF Speeches on Canadian affairs. Edited by Sir Robert Herbert. London, J. Murray, 1902. xvi, 386 p.

CASSELS, CECIL GILLESPIE The Canada First party. Toronto, 1921. 72 leaves.
Thesis (MA) – University of Toronto.

CHALOULT, PIERRE Un an après. Premier anniversaire de la Confédération. (In *Le Magazine Maclean*. Montréal. v. 8, no. 7 (juil. 1968), pp. [20]; 36-40.)
"Un petit bourgeois de Québec raconte le nouveau régime." In the form of a letter.

CHAMPAGNE, J. A. Semaine parlementaire. (In *L'Opinion publique*. Montréal. v. 4, no. 17 (24 avril 1873), p. 201.)
Includes the electoral bill presented by Sir John A. Macdonald, the New Brunswick school law, etc.

—— Semaine parlementaire. (In *L'Opinion publique*. Montréal. v. 4, no. 20 (15 mai 1873), pp. 237-238.)
Covers period from May 6 to May 10, 1873.

Church and State in Quebec. (In *The Nation*. Toronto. v. 2, no. 37 (September 17, 1875), p. 438.)
Relates to the Privy Council decision granting the right of Joseph Guibord to be buried in consecrated ground.

Church and State in Quebec. (In *The Nation*. Toronto. v. 3, no. 14 (April 7, 1876), p. 159.)
Discusses opinions presented in a pamphlet: Church and State, by Sir A. T. Galt. Montreal, Dawson Bros., 1876. 41 p.

COLQUHOUN, ARTHUR HUGH URQUHART Reminiscences of Lord Dufferin. By Arthur H. U. Colquhoun. (In *The Canadian magazine of politics, science, art and literature*. Toronto. v. 18 1901/02), pp. 524-526.)

The Condition of the Dominion. (In *The Nation*. Toronto. v. 3, no. 23 (June 9, 1876), pp. 267-268.)
With reference to an address by Sir Alexander T. Galt surveying Dominion fiscal and commercial policy.

Confederation in Nova Scotia; a crisis past. (In *The Canadian monthly and national review*. Toronto. v. 4 (1873), pp. [361]-375.)
An essay dealing with federal-provincial relations.

CONNER, JAMES MC ARTHUR Canada's first labor paper. (In *Canadian Congress journal*. Montreal. v. 4, no. 12 (Dec. 1925), pp. 9-11.)
Relates the founding, in April 1872, of

The Ontario workman, edited by James Samuel Williams, and his subsequent activities in the federal election campaign of 1872.

Contestation électorale de Charlevoix. Résumé des témoignages. (In Le Réveil. Québec. v. 1, no. 14 (26 août 1876), pp. 214-215; v. 1, no. 15 (2 sept. 1876), pp. 228-230.)
In two parts.
Concerns the disputed by-election held in Charlevoix, Que., January 22, 1876, that resulted in the election of Hector Langevin to the House of Commons. The election was declared void.

COYLE, W. J. Elections in Kingston in 1867. (In *Historic Kingston*. Kingston. no. 16 (1968), pp. [48]-57.)
Concerns the federal election campaign of John A. Macdonald and John Stewart.

CREIGHTON, DONALD GRANT The 1860s. By Donald Creighton. (In Careless, J. M. S. (ed.) *The Canadians, 1867-1967*. Toronto, 1967. pp. 3-36.)

—— George Brown, Sir John Macdonald and the "workingman". An episode in the history of the Canadian labour movement. By D. G. Creighton. (In *The Canadian historical review*. Toronto. v. 24 (1943), pp. 362-376.)
Relates to the strike of the Toronto Typographical Union in March 1872 and its political consequences.

CROPP, ENA AGNES The Canada First Party. [Kingston, Ont.] 1926. 62 leaves.
Thesis (MA) – Queen's University.

Current events. (In *The Canadian monthly and national review*. Toronto. v. 2, no. 6 — v. 13, no. 6 (Dec. 1872 — June 1878.)
Unsigned monthly column which includes comments on Canadian national politics.
Written by Goldwin Smith, December 1872 to December 1874 (except for the period November 1873 to May 1874). Cf. E. Wallace. *Goldwin Smith, Victorian liberal*, p. 72.
Continued in the July and August 1878 issues of Rose-Belford's *Canadian monthly and national review*.

DAVID, LAURENT OLIVIER Affaire Guibord. Par L. O. David. (In *L'Opinion publique*. Montréal. v. 1, no. 14 (9 avril 1870), pp. [105]-106.)

—— Affaire Guibord. Portrait des avocats. Par L. O. David. (In *L'Opinion publique*.

Montréal. v. 1, no. 15 (16 avril 1870), pp. [113]-114.)

—— Canadiens-Anglais et Canadiens-Français. Par L. O. David. (In *L'Opinion publique*. Montréal. v. 1, no. 2 (8 jan., 1870), p. 10.)

—— Canadiens-Français et Canadiens-Anglais. Par L. O. David. (In *L'Opinion publique*. Montréal. v. 1, no. 3 (22 jan., 1870), pp. [17]-18.)

—— Canadiens-Français et Canadiens-Anglais. Par L. O. David. (In *L'Opinion publique*. Montréal. v. 1, no. 5 (5 fév., 1870), p. 34.)

—— Cartier et Dorion. (In his *Au soir de la vie*. Montréal. [1924] pp. [99]-106.)

—— La cause Guibord. Par L. O. David. (In *L'Opinion publique*. Montréal. v. 1, no. 26 (30 juin 1870), p. 206.)

—— Le comité Huntington. Par L. O. David. (In *L'Opinion publique*. Montréal. v. 4, no. 28 (10 juil., 1873), p. 335.)

Refers to the committee, directed by L. S. Huntington, inquiring into affairs relating to the Pacific railway.

—— Echos parlementaires. Par L.-O. David. (In *L'Opinion publique*. Montréal. v. 9, no. 20 (16 mai 1878), pp. [229]-230.)

Comments on a bill against the carrying of arms, proposed by Edward Blake; the independence of Parliament, the Fenians, the question of connecting Quebec's railroads with the Canadian Pacific (via Georgian Bay), etc.

—— Les écoles du Nouveau-Brunswick. Par L. O. David. (In *L'Opinion publique*. Montréal. v. 3, no. 25 (20 juin, 1872), p. 297.)

—— Elections. Par L. O. David. (In *L'Opinion publique*. Montréal. v. 3, no. 30 (25 juil. 1872), p. 357.)

Provides a list of the candidates from Quebec.

—— Elections. Par L. O. David. (In *L'Opinion publique*. Montréal. v. 3, no. 35 (29 août, 1872), p. 147.)

Provides federal election returns for Quebec.

—— Les élections. Par L. O. D. (In *L'Opinion publique*. Montréal. v. 3, no. 36 (5 sept., 1872), p. 429.)

Provides tables showing electoral results for Quebec, Ontario, New Brunswick and Nova Scotia.

—— Galerie parlementaire. Par L. O. David. (In *L'Opinion publique*. Montréal. v. 1, no. 13 (2 avril 1870), p. 101. ports.)

Biographical sketches of Hon. A. A. Dorion, Sir A. T. Galt, Hon. C. Tupper, Hon. L. H. Holton, A. Mackenzie, Hon. L. S. Huntington.

—— Le libéralisme. Par L. O. David. (In *L'Opinion publique*. Montréal. v. 3, no. 22 (30 mai, 1872), p. 262; v. 3, no. 23 (6 juin, 1872), pp. [265]-266.)

In two parts.

—— Lord Dufferin. Par L. O. David. (In *L'Opinion publique*. Montréal. v. 4, no. 7 (13 fév., 1873), p. [73.])

—— Mission des gouvernements. Par L. O. David. (In *L'Opinion publique*. Montréal. v. 1, no. 6 (12 fév., 1870), p. [41]; v. 1, no. 7 (19 fév., 1870), p. [49].)

In two parts.

—— Les prochaines élections. Par L. O. David. (In *L'Opinion publique*. Montréal. v. 3, no. 25 (20 juin, 1872), p. [289.])

—— Noir et blanc. Par L. O. David. (In *L'Opinion publique*. Montréal. v. 3, no. 31 1 août, 1872), p. 369.)

Discusses the general elections held July 20-October 12, 1872. Includes a table listing electoral results from Quebec and Ontario.

—— Nouvelles électorales. Par L. O. D. (In *L'Opinion publique*. Montréal. v. 3, no. 32 (8 août, 1872), p. 381.)

Provides a table listing election results from Quebec, Ontario and New Brunswick.

—— Nouvelles électorales. Par L. O. David. (In *L'Opinion publique*. Montréal. v. 3, no. 34 (22 août, 1872), p. 405.)

Includes a table listing members elected from Quebec, Ontario, New Brunswick and Nova Scotia.

DENISON, GEORGE TAYLOR Sir John Schultz and the "Canada First" party; recollections. By Lt.-Col. George T. Denison. (In *The Canadian magazine of politics, science, art and literature*. Toronto. v. 8 (1896/97), pp. 16-23.)

DESBARATS, GEORGES EDOUARD L'Eglise et l'Etat. Par G. E. D. (In *L'Opinion publique*. Montréal. v. 7, no. 17 (27 avril, 1876), p. [193].)

Discusses the pamphlet "Church and State", by Sir Alexander Galt. Montreal, Dawson, 1876.

DESSAULLES, LOUIS ANTOINE Affaire Guibord. Par L. A. Dessaulles. (In Institut canadien de Montréal. *Annuaire*. Montréal. (1869), pp. [5]-50.)

"Lue le 29 décembre, 1869."

DIANA "Woman's rights": and a woman's view of them. By Diana. (In *Stewart's quarterly*. St. John, N.B. v. 4, no. 1 (Apr. 1870), pp. 70-74.)

Distinguished members of the House of Commons. (In *Canadian illustrated news*. Montreal. v. 1, no. 21 (Mar. 26, 1870), pp. 322-323.)

Brief biographical sketches of A. T. Galt, Charles Tupper, A. A. Dorion, L. H. Holton, Alexander Mackenzie, L. S. Huntington.

Distinguished members of the House of Commons. (In *Canadian illustrated news*. Montreal. v. 1, no. 24 (Apr. 16, 1870), p. 370.)

Brief biographical sketches of J. H. Cameron, A. J. Smith, George Irvine, Joseph Rymal.

Distinguished members of the House of Commons. (In *Canadian illustrated news*. Montreal, v. 1, no. 25 (Apr. 23, 1870), pp. 389-390.)

Our Canadian portrait gallery.

Brief biographical sketches of Walter Shanly, A. G. Archibald, T. N. Gibbs.

Distinguished members of the House of Commons. (In *Canadian illustrated news*. Montreal. v. 1, no. 26 (Apr. 30, 1870), pp. 405-406.)

Our Canadian portrait gallery.

Brief biographical sketches of John Carling, John J. C. Abbott, and Pierre Fortin.

Dominion Parliament. (In *The Nation*. Toronto. v. 1, no. 1-9 (April 2—May 28, 1874.)

Nos. 2, 4, 5 and 6 have title: Dominion Legislature.

Summarizes proceedings during the first session of the third parliament held March 26 to May 26, 1874.

DORGE, LIONEL Bishop Taché and the Confederation of Manitoba, 1969-1970 [i.e. 1869-1870]. (In Historical and Scientific Society of Manitoba. *Papers*. Winnipeg. ser. 3, no. 26 (1969/70), pp. 93-109.)

DRAPEAU BLANC Bleu, Rouge, Blanc. Par Drapeau blanc. (In *L'Opinion publique*. Montréal. v. 5, no. 24 (11 juin 1874), pp. [277]-278.)

Presents ideas for a new political party, "Le Drapeau blanc", concerned with promoting unity of the French-Canadian people.

DRISCOLL, FREDERICK L. Federal politics in Prince Edward Island, 1873-1878. [Ottawa, 1965] 310 leaves.

Thesis (MA) – University of Ottawa.

DUFFERIN AND AVA, FREDERICK TEMPLE HAMILTON-TEMPLE-BLACKWOOD, MARQUIS OF Dufferin-Carnarvon correspondence, 1874-1878. Edited by C. W. de Kiewiet and F. H. Underhill. Toronto, Champlain Society, 1955. lvi, 442, xvi p. (The publications of the Champlain Society, 33.)

—— Speeches of the Earl of Dufferin . . . Governor-General of Canada. Toronto, J. Ross Robertson, 1878. 128 p.

DUNFORD, JAMES ROSS Political opinion in South Waterloo, 1857-1873. Toronto, 1955. 248 leaves.

Thesis (MA) – University of Toronto.

DUNN, OSCAR Après le combat. (In *L'Opinion publique*. Montréal. v. 5, no. 7 (12 fév. 1874), p. [73]; v. 5, no. 8 (19 fév. 1874), pp. [85]-86; v. 5, no. 10 (5 mars 1874), pp. 110-111; v. 5, no. 13 (26 mars 1874), pp. [145]-147.)

Five parts in four nos.

Examines the results of the general elections held January 22, 1874.

—— La campagne electorale. (In *L'Opinion publique*. Montréal. v. 5, no. 3 (15 jan. 1874), p. 33.)

The general elections were held January 22, 1874.

—— Semaine parlementaire. Par O. D. (In *L'Opinion publique*. Montréal. v. 5, no. 16—no. 22 (16 avril—28 mai 1874.)

Summarizes proceedings during the first session of the third parliament held March 26 to May 26, 1874.

See also La fin de la session. (In *L'Opinion publique*. Montréal. v. 5, no. 23 (4 juin 1874), p. 273.)

—— Semaine parlementaire. (In *L'Opinion publique*. Montréal. v. 5, no. 21 (21 mai 1874), p. 249.)

Relates to the Canadian Pacific Railway and other matters.

—— La session fédérale. (In *L'Opinion publique*. Montréal. v. 4, no. 44 (30 oct. 1873), p. 527.)

Comments and quotes from the Speech from the Throne, delivered October 23, 1873, by Lord Dufferin.

Les Elections. (In *L'Opinion publique.* Montréal. v. 5, no. 3 (15 jan. 1874), p. 34.)

Provides a list of the candidates from Quebec for the elections held January 22, 1874.

Les Elections. (In *L'Opinion publique.* Montréal. v. 5, no. 4 (22 jan. 1874), p. 40.)

Provides a list of the candidates from Quebec.

Les Elections générales. (In *L'Opinion publique.* Montréal. v. 5, no. 5 (29 jan. 1874), p. 49.)

Discusses the general elections held January 22, 1874.

Electoral corruption. (In *The Nation.* Toronto. v. 1, no. 25 (Sept. 17, 1874), p. 297.)

Relates to practices employed by the Liberal and Conservative parties during the general elections campaign held in 1874.

FAIRHOLD, OLIVE John Robson and Confederation. (In Shelton, W. G. (ed.) *British Columbia and Confederation.* Victoria, B.C., 1967, pp. 97-123.)

FARR, DAVID MORICE LEIGH Lord Dufferin; a viceroy in Ottawa. By D. M. L. Farr. (In *Culture.* Québec. v. 19 (1958), pp. [153]-164.)

FARRELL, DAVID R. The Canada First movement and Canadian political thought. By D. R. Farrell. (In *Journal of Canadian studies.* Peterborough, Ont. v. 4, no. 4 (1969), pp. 16-26.)

FAUCHER DE SAINT-MAURICE, NARCISSE HENRY EDOUARD Lord Dufferin et le Canada-Français. Par Faucher de Saint-Maurice. (In *L'Opinion publique.* Montréal. v. 9, no. 30 (25 juil. 1878), p. 352.)

Comments arising from a speech made by Lord Dufferin in response to an address of farewell presented by the Legislature of Quebec.

La Fin de la session. (In *L'Opinion publique.* Montréal. v. 5, no. 23 (4 juin 1874), p. 273.)

Brief review at the end of the first session of the third parliament held March 26 to May 26, 1874.

The First Dominion cabinet. Some reminiscences of the men of 1867. (In *The Canadian courier.* Toronto. v. 2, no. 5 (June 29, 1907), pp. 16-17. ports.)

FORSEY, EUGENE ALFRED Government defeats in the Canadian House of Commons, 1867-73. By Eugene Forsey. (In *The Canadian journal of economics and political science.* [Toronto] v. 29 (1963), pp. 364-367.)

FOSTER, WILLIAM ALEXANDER Canada First; or, Our new nationality, an address. By W. A. Foster. Toronto, Adam, Stevenson, 1871. 36 p.

GAGAN, DAVID PAUL Canada First; a bundle of little egotisms. [London, Ont.] 1964. 144 leaves.

Thesis (MA) – University of Western Ontario.

GALBRAITH, JOHN SEMPLE A note on the Mackenzie negotiations with the Hudson's Bay Company, 1875-1878. By John S. Galbraith. (In *The Canadian historical review.* Toronto. v. 34 (1953), pp. 39-45.)

GALT, SIR ALEXANDER TILLOCH Church and State. By Sir Alex. T. Galt. Montreal, Dawson Bros., 1876. 41 p.

"The design . . . is to oppose . . . the efforts . . . made by the Roman Catholic hierarchy of Quebec, to impose upon those belonging to their communion the extreme doctrines of the Italian ecclesiastical school." – Pref.

GELINAS, AIME La Confédération dans trente ans. Par A. G. (In *L'Opinion publique.* Montréal. v. 10, no. 45 (6 nov. 1879), p. 530.)

Relates to the settlement and expansion of the North-West.

—— Echos parlementaires. Par A. G. (In *L'Opinion publique.* Montréal. v. 8, no. 7—no. 18 (14 fév.—3 mai 1877).)

Summarizes proceedings during the fourth session of the third parliament held February 8 to April 28, 1877.

—— Echos politiques. Par A. Gélinas. (In *L'Opinion publique.* Montréal. v. 8, no. 42 (18 oct. 1877), p. [493].)

Discusses the campaign held for the Drummond-Arthabaska by-election, October 27, 1877, where W. Laurier was defeated by D. O. Bourbeau.

—— Le lieutenant-gouverneur de Québec. Par A. Gélinas. (In *L'Opinion publique.* Montréal. v. 8, no. 1 (4 jan. 1877), p. [2].)

Discusses the appointment and function of the lieutenant-governor.

—— Les lieutenant-gouverneurs. Par A. Gélinas. (In *L'Opinion publique.* Montréal. v. 9, no. 51 (19 déc. 1878), p. [601].)

Government by party. (In *The Nation.* Toronto. v. 2, no. 35 (Sept. 3, 1875), pp. 414-415.)

GRAHAM, E. J. First Dominion Governor-General. (In *The Canadian courier.* Toronto. v. 2, no. 5 (June 29, 1907), p. 13.)

Concerns Sir Charles Stanley, Viscount Monck.

GRAY, JOHN HAMILTON Confederation; or, The political and parliamentary history of Canada, from the conference at Quebec, in October, 1864, to the admission of British Columbia, in July, 1871. v. 1. Toronto, Copp, Clark, printers, 1872. 432 p.

The Growth of the public debt. (In *The Nation.* Toronto. v. 3, no. 21 (May 26, 1876), pp. 243-244.)

The Guibord case. (In *The Nation.* Toronto. v. 1, no. 35 (Nov. 26, 1874), p. 416.)

With reference to the controversial issue over the burial of Joseph Guibord.

The Guibord riot. (In *The Nation.* Toronto. v. 2, no. 36 (Sept. 10, 1875), p. 427.)

Refers to the burial of Joseph Guibord.

Guibord's burial. (In *The Nation.* Toronto. v. 2, no. 46 (Nov. 19, 1875), p. 546.)

GUILLET, EDWIN CLARENCE The "Pacific scandal" seen in retrospect. By Edwin C. Guillet. (In *Saturday night.* Toronto. v. 63, no. 28 (Apr. 17, 1948), pp. [24-25].)

HAMELIN, JEAN First years of Confederation. [Translated by Joseph Levitt] Ottawa, The Centennial Commission, 1967. 25 p. (Centennial historical booklet, no. 3.)

Translation of *Les débuts de la Confédération.*

Covers the period 1867-1878.

HARDY, WILLIAM GEORGE The day Canada was born. By W. G. Hardy. (In *Maclean's.* Toronto. v. 72, no. 14 (July 4, 1959), pp. 18-19; 40.)

HARVEY, ARTHUR The Canadian census of 1871. (In *The Canadian monthly and national review.* Toronto. v. 1 (1872), pp. [97]-104.)

HARVEY, DANIEL COBB Confederation in Prince Edward Island. By D. C. Harvey. (In *The Canadian historical review.* Toronto. v. 14 (1933), pp. 143-160.)

Traces developments for Confederation from 1864 until its realization July 1, 1873.

HEICK, WELF HENRY Mackenzie and Macdonald: federal politics and politicians in Canada, 1873-1878. [Durham, N.C.] 1966. 315 leaves.

Thesis (PH D) – Duke University.

HELMCKEN, JOHN SEBASTIAN Helmcken's diary of the Confederation negotiations, 1870. (In *The British Columbia historical quarterly.* Victoria, B.C. v. 4 (1940), pp. 111-128.)

Introduction (pp. 111-115) and notes by Willard E. Ireland.

The diary was kept by the Hon. J. S. Helmcken, member of the Legislative Council for Victoria City, B.C. It illustrates certain differences between the proposals set forth by British Columbia and the final terms of union offered by the Dominion of Canada.

HILL, SIR STEPHEN Sir Stephen Hill's observations on the election of 1869 in Newfoundland. (In *The Canadian historical review.* Toronto. v. 29 (1948), pp. 278-285.)

Presented, with notes, by G. F. G. Stanley.

The correspondence deals with the subject of union between Newfoundland and the Dominion of Canada.

His Excellency the Governor-General. (In *Canadian illustrated news.* Montreal. v. 1, no. 15 (Feb. 12, 1870), pp. [225]-226.)

Concerns Sir John Young (Lord Lisgar) Governor-General of Canada, 1868-72.

History of the Guibord case. Ultra-montanism versus law and human rights. Montreal, "Witness" Print. House, 1875. vii, [3]-150 p.

Imprint on cover: Montreal, J. Dougall, 1875.

HOUGHAM, GEORGE MILLARD Canada First: a minor party in microcosm. By G. M. Hougham. (In *The Canadian journal of economics and political science.* [Toronto] v. 19 (1953), pp. 174-184.)

HOWAY, FREDERIC WILLIAM The attitude of Governor Seymour towards Confederation. By F. W. Howay. (In Royal Society of Canada. *Proceedings and transactions.* Ottawa. ser. 3, v. 14 (1920), section 2, pp. 31-49.)

"Read May meeting, 1920."

Concerns British Columbia and union with Canada.

—— Governor Musgrave and Confederation. By F. W. Howay. (In Royal Society of Canada. *Proceedings and transactions.* Ottawa. ser. 3, v. 15 (1921), section 2, pp. 15-31.)

"Read May meeting, 1921."

Concerns British Columbia and union with Canada.

HOWLAND, WILLIAM H. "Canada First". (In *The Nation*. Toronto. v. 1, no. 20 (Aug. 13, 1874), p. 234.)

Summary of an address delivered by "Mr. Howland, the President of the Dominion Board of Trade" to the Maritime National Club, August 12, 1874.

Influence or competence? (In *The Nation*. Toronto. v. 1, no. 5 (Apr. 30, 1874), pp. 56-57.)

Discusses the system of patronage.

Journalism in Canada. (In *The Nation*. Toronto. v. 3, no. 27 (July 7, 1876), p. 315.)

Comments relating to an address entitled Journalism and its duties, delivered by Goldwin Smith June 30, 1876, in Toronto, at the annual meeting of the Canadian Press Association.

The Judicial appointments. (In *The Nation*. Toronto, v. 2, no. 39 (Oct. 1, 1875), pp. 462-463.)

Concerns appointments to the Supreme Court. Considers the nominations as reflecting the standards set by Edward Blake as federal Minister of Justice.

KEENLEYSIDE, HUGH LLEWELLYN   British Columbia—annexation or confederation. (In Canadian Historical Association. *Report of the annual meeting*. Ottawa. (1928), pp. 34-40.)

LA TERREUR, MARC   Ontario et Québec depuis 1867. (In *Culture*. Québec. v. 27 (1966), pp. [151]-162.)

LAURISTON, VICTOR   Old time politics in Huron. (In *Saturday night*. Toronto. v. 44, no. 25 (May 4, 1929), p. 3.)

Concerns a contest between M. C. Cameron (Liberal) and James Colebrooke Patterson (Conservative) in 1891 in West Huron, Ont. Cameron won; Patterson won a subsequent by-election Feb. 23, 1892.

LEE, DAVID   The Dominion general election of 1878 in Ontario. (In *Ontario history*. Toronto. v. 51, no. 3 (summer 1959), pp. [172]-190.)

LEGGO, WILLIAM   The history of the administration of the Right Honourable Frederick Temple, Earl of Dufferin . . . late Governor-General of Canada. Montreal, Lovell, 1878. 901 p.

Legislation and spoliation. (In *The Nation*. Toronto. v. 3, no. 13 (Mar. 31, 1876), pp. 148-149.)

Relates to the Joint Stock Acts.

A Legislative union for the Maritime Provinces. (In *The Nation*. Toronto. v. 3, no. 16 (Apr. 21, 1876), pp. 183-184.)

LONGLEY, RONALD STEWART   The fisheries in Nova Scotia politics, 1865-71. By R. S. Longley. (In Nova Scotia Historical Society. *Collections*. Halifax. v. 25 (1942), pp. [75]-93.)

"Read before the Nova Scotia Historical Society, November 3, 1939."

Relates, as well, to the Dominion government.

LOVEKIN, L. A. M.   Letting down the pilot. Historic instances of severance between party and leader. (In *Saturday night*. Toronto. v. 42, no. 1 (Nov. 20, 1926), p. 5.)

Discusses cases involving Sir John A. Macdonald, Alexander Mackenzie, and Sir Charles Tupper.

LYALL, SIR ALFRED COMYN   The life of the Marquis of Dufferin and Ava. London, J. Murray, 1905. 2 v.

MAC BETH, RODERICK GEORGE   Schultz and Strathcona: empire builders. The parts played by two strong men in the early history of the West. By Rev. R. G. MacBeth. (In *MacLean's magazine*. Toronto. v. 27, no. 6 (Apr. 1914), pp. [24]-26.)

MC CREADY, JOHN E. BLAKENY   When the Dominion was young. The first of six historical sketches. By J. E. B. McCready. (In *The Canadian magazine of politics, science, art and literature*. Toronto. v. 27 (1906), pp. 68-70.)

Sketches the first federal parliament.

—— When the Dominion was young. The second of six historical sketches. By J. E. B. McCready. (In *The Canadian magazine of politics, science, art and literature*. Toronto. v. 27 (1906), pp. 117-119.)

Describes the opening of the first parliament.

—— When the Dominion was young. The third of six historical sketches. By J. E. B. McCready. (In *The Canadian magazine of politics, science, art and literature*. Toronto. v. 27 (1906), pp. 252-255.)

A description of Joseph Howe and Thomas D'Arcy McGee in the first session of the first parliament.

—— When the Dominion was young. The fifth of six historical sketches. By J. E. B. McCready. (In *The Canadian magazine of politics, science, art and literature*. Toronto. v. 27 (1906), pp. 453-455.)

A general description. Conjures up the tension in the House when Sir John A. Macdonald lay near death in 1870.

—— When the Dominion was young. The last of six historical sketches. By J. E. B. McCready. (In *The Canadian magazine of politics, science, art and literature*. Toronto. v. 27 (1906), pp. 556-559.)

A brief description of the election of 1872.

MAC FARLANE, RONALD OLIVER Manitoba politics and parties after Confederation. By R. O. MacFarlane. (In Canadian Historical Association. *Report of the annual meeting*. Toronto. (1940), pp. 45-55.)

Relates developments to federal politics.

MAC LEAN, JOHN Protection and free trade. Montreal, Printed by J. Lovell, 1867. 79 p.

MAC MECHAN, ARCHIBALD Confederation in Nova Scotia. (In *The University magazine*. Montreal. v. 16 (1917), pp. [573]-582.)

Discusses the attitude of Nova Scotia towards Confederation before and after 1867.

MC NAUGHT, KENNETH WILLIAM KIRKPATRICK The total environment of "Canada First". By Kenneth McNaught. (In *Saturday night*. Toronto. v. 82, no. 5 (May 1967), pp. 29-30.)

Environment 67.

Describes the Canada First movement of the 1870s.

MACSHANE, JAMES R. Census. By J. R. Macshane. (In *Stewart's quarterly*. St. John, N.B. v. 4, no. 3 (Oct. 1870), pp. 295-299.)

Comments on the first census taken by the Dominion government during 1871.

MARTIN, CHESTER BAILEY Confederation and the West. By Chester Martin. (In Canadian Historical Association. *Report of the annual meeting*. Ottawa. (1927), pp. 20-28.)

—— The first "new province" of the Dominion. By Chester Martin. (In *The Canadian historical review*. Toronto. v. 1 (1920), pp. 354-378.)

Examines the historical background leading to the creation of the province of Manitoba.

MATHEWS, JEHU The political future of Canada. (In *The Canadian monthly and national review*. Toronto. v. 8, no. 1 (July 1875), pp. 54-61; v. 8, no. 2 (Aug. 1875), pp. [89]-98.)

In two parts.

MAXWELL, JAMES ACKLEY Lord Dufferin and the difficulties with British Columbia, 1874-7. (In *The Canadian historical review*. Toronto. v. 12 (1931), pp. 364-389.)

—— Prince Edward Island and Confederation. By J. A. Maxwell. (In *The Dalhousie review*. Halifax. v. 13 (1933/34), pp. [53]-60.)

MAYO, HENRY BERTRAM How Newfoundland voted on Confederation in 1869. Will history repeat itself in 1948? By H. B. Mayo. (In *Atlantic guardian*. Montreal. v. 4, no. 4 (Jan. 1948), pp. 5-7.)

Membres élus. (In *L'Opinion publique*. Montréal. v. 5, no. 6 (fév. 1874), p. 63.)

List of members elected in the general elections of January 22, 1874.

MILLIGAN, FRANK ARCHIBALD The establishment of Manitoba's first provincial government. By F. A. Milligan. (In Historical and Scientific Society of Manitoba. *Papers*. Winnipeg. ser. 3, no. 5 (1950), pp. 5-18.)

This analysis takes into account the role of the federal government in the creation of the province of Manitoba.

Mr. Gordon Brown's defence. (In *The Nation*. Toronto. v. 2, no. 30 (July 30, 1875), p. 356.)

Concerns professional ethics in political journalism. Gordon Brown was the brother of George Brown.

MORTON, WILLIAM LEWIS The cabinet of 1867. By W. L. Morton. (In Gibson, F. W. (ed.) *Cabinet formation and bicultural relations*. [Ottawa, 1970] pp. [1]-17.)

—— The critical years; the union of British North America, 1857-1873. By W. L. Morton. [Toronto] McClelland and Stewart, 1964. xii, 322 p. (The Canadian centenary series, 12.)

"Bibliography": pp. 305-314.

MORTON, WILLIAM LEWIS (ed.) Manitoba; the birth of a province. By W. L. Morton. Altona, Man., Printed by D. W. Friesen, 1965. xxx, 265 p. (Manitoba Record Society. Publications, v. 1.)

"Seven hundred and fifty copies of this volume have been printed for the Manitoba Record Society."

An introductory essay and selection of documents relating to the entry of Manitoba into Confederation in 1870.

MORTON, WILLIAM LEWIS The West and Confederation. By W. L. Morton. Ottawa,

The Centennial Commission, 1967. 19 p. (Centennial historical booklet, no. 7.)

Covers the period 1857-1871.

—— The West and Confederation, 1857-1871. By W. L. Morton. Ottawa [Canadian Historical Association] 1962 [c1958] 19 p. (Canadian Historical Association. Historical booklets, no. 9.)

Translated into French under title: *L'Ouest et la Confédération, 1857-1871.*

MOSHER, AUSTIN   Québec in our first parliament. (In *The Canadian magazine of politics, science, art and literature.* Toronto. v. 53 (1919), pp. 312-314.)

A discussion about "the members sent from the province of Quebec to the House of Commons of Canada in the first parliament of the Confederation."

MOUSSEAU, JOSEPH ALFRED   L'affaire Guibord. Par J. A. Mousseau. (In *L'Opinion publique.* Montréal. v. 1, no. 37 (15 sept. 1870), p. 294.)

—— L'arbitrage. Par J. A. Mousseau. (In *L'Opinion publique.* Montréal. v. 1, no. 28 (14 juil. 1870), p. [217].)

Concerns "cet arbitrage prévu et ordonné par l'acte constitutionnel de 1867 et qui devait diviser et répartir entre Québec et Ontario les 'dettes, crédits, obligations, propriétés et l'actif' de la ci-devant Province unie du Haut et du Bas-Canada". Commissioners were Judge Day, chosen by Quebec, Senator McPherson, chosen by Ontario, and Colonel Gray of New Brunswick, chosen by the Privy Council.

—— L'arbitrage. Par J. A. Mousseau. (In *L'Opinion publique.* Montréal. v. 1, no. 49 (8 dec. 1870), p. [385].)

Discusses the decision handed down by the commission of arbitration concerning the division of assets and liabilities between Ontario and Quebec.

—— Le brave colonel! Par J. A. Mousseau. (In *L'Opinion publique.* Montréal. v. 1, no. 43 (27 oct. 1870), p. 338.)

Concerns Colonel J. H. Gray, member of a commission of arbitration concerning the division of assets and liabilities between Ontario and Quebec.

—— Le dernier mot de "la question épineuse". Par J. A. Mousseau. (In *L'Opinion publique.* Montréal. v. 1, no. 37 (15 sept. 1870), p. 290.)

Discusses the decision handed down by a commission of arbitration concerning the division of assets and liabilities between Ontario and Quebec (Upper and Lower Canada).

—— Guibord. Par J. A. Mousseau. (In *L'Opinion publique.* Montréal. v. 2, no. 37 (14 sept. 1871), p. 449.)

—— Le jugement dans l'affaire Guibord. Par J. A. Mousseau. (In *L'Opinion publique.* Montréal. v. 1, no. 19 (12 mai 1870), p. 150.)

—— Le procès Guibord. Par J. A. Mousseau. (In *L'Opinion publique.* Montréal. v. 1, no. 38 (22 sept. 1870), pp. [297]-298; v. 1, no. 40 (6 oct. 1870), p. 314.)

In two parts.

—— Une question de justice et une entrave constitutionnelle. Par J. A. Mousseau. (In *L'Opinion publique.* Montréal. v. 3, no. 9 (29 fév. 1872), p. [97].)

Relates to the New Brunswick schools issue.

—— Une question épineuse. Par J. A. Mousseau. (In *L'Opinion publique.* Montréal. v. 1, no. 34 (25 août 1870), pp. [265]-266; v. 1, no. 36 (8 sept. 1870), pp. [281]-282.)

In two parts.

Concerns the division of assets and liabilities between Ontario and Quebec after Confederation, by a commission of three men: Judge Day, Senator McPherson, and Colonel Gray.

—— Le recensement de 1871. Par J. A. Mousseau. (In *L'Opinion publique.* Montréal. v. 1, no. 3 (22 jan. 1870), p. 18.)

—— La semaine parlementaire. Par J. A. Mousseau. (In *L'Opinion publique.* Montréal. v. 1. no. 8—no. 19 (26 fév.—12 mai 1870.)

Summarizes proceedings during the third session of the first parliament held February 15 to May 12, 1870.

For the Speech from the Throne see Ouverture du Parlement fédéral. (In *L'Opinion publique.* Montréal. v. 1, no. 7 (19 fév. 1870), p. 50.)

—— La semaine parlementaire. Par J. A. Mousseau. (In *L'Opinion publique.* Montréal. v. 2, no. 8—no. 16 (23 fév.—20 avril 1871).)

Summarizes proceedings during the fourth session of the first parliament held February 15 to April 14, 1871.

—— Semaine parlementaire. Par J. A. Mousseau. (In *L'Opinion publique.* Montréal. v. 3, no. 17—no. 24 (25 avril—13 juin 1872).)

Summarizes proceedings during the fifth session of the first parliament held April 11 to June 14, 1872.

—— Semaine parlementaire. Les écoles catholiques du Nouveau Brunswick. Par J. A. Mousseau. (In L'Opinion publique. Montréal. v. 3, no. 22 (30 mai 1872), p. 261.)

—— Semaine parlementaire. La question des écoles. Par J. A. Mousseau. (In L'Opinion publique. Montréal. v. 3, no. 23 (6 juin 1872), pp. 273-74.)
Refers to the school question in New Brunswick.

—— Semaine parlementaire. Par J. A. Mousseau. (In L'Opinion publique. Montréal. v. 4, no. 11—no. 22 (13 mars—29 mai 1873).)
No. 22 has title: La session.
Summarizes proceedings during the first session of the second parliament held March 5 to August 13, 1873.
For comments on the prorogation of this parliament see Prorogation du parlement. (In L'Opinion publique. Montréal. v. 4, no. 34 (21 août 1873), p. 407.)

—— Ultramontains et gallicano. Par J. A. Mousseau. (In L'Opinion publique. Montréal. v. 1, no. 6 (12 fév. 1870), pp. [41]-42.)

MUISE, DELPHIN A. The federal election of 1867 in Nova Scotia: an economic interpretation. (In Nova Scotia Historical Society. Collections. [Halifax] v. 36 (1968), pp. [327]-351.)
"Read before the Nova Scotia Historical Society, April 14, 1967."

The National party. (In The Nation. Toronto. v. 2, no. 16 (Apr. 23, 1875), p. 186.)
Discusses the concepts and prospects for a nationalist party in Canada.

The New Brunswick elections. (In The Nation. Toronto. v. 1, no. 9 (May 28, 1874), pp. 105-106.)
Concerns the school question and the issue over annulling provincial legislation in the matter of separate schools.

The New Brunswick school law imbroglio. (In The Nation. Toronto. v. 2, no. 10 (Mar. 12, 1875), pp. 114-115.)

The New daily paper. (In The Nation. Toronto. v. 2, no. 5 (Feb. 5, 1875), p. 54.)
Evaluates the policy of The Liberal and discusses the general state of political journalism in Toronto.

The New province—Manitoba. (In Canadian illustrated news. Montreal. v. 1, no. 27 (May 7, 1870), p. 418.)
Editorial comment.

NEWHOOK, FRED J. Newfoundland's first rejection of Confederation. (In The Newfoundland quarterly. St. John's Nfld. v. 59, no. 3 (fall 1960), pp. [3]-6; v. 59, no. 4 (winter 1960), pp. 25-28; v. 60, no. 1 (spring 1961), pp. 32-37.)
In three parts.
Examines the Confederation issue during the years 1865-1869.

NORRIS, LEONARD Canada kept faith. By L. Norris. (In Okanagan Historical Society. Report. Vernon, B.C. 7th (1937), pp. 29-38.)
Argues that Canada honoured the agreement with British Columbia over the building of the transcontinental railway.

—— Lord Dufferin's visit to British Columbia. By L. Norris. (In Okanagan Historical Society. Report. Vernon, B.C. 11th (1945), pp. 35-48.)
The visit occurred during August and September, 1876.

—— Some aspects of the Carnarvon terms. By L. Norris. (In Okanagan Historical Society. Report. Vernon, B.C. 10th (1943), pp. 77-103.)
Refers to the dispute between the federal government and British Columbia over the building of the railway. Lord Carnarvon offered to act as an arbitrator.

—— Trutch's speech. By L. Norris. (In Okanagan Historical Society. Report. Vernon, B.C. 8th (1939), pp. 15-18.)
Discusses a speech given April 10, 1871, by J. W. Trutch, Chief Commissioner of Lands and Works in the British Columbia colonial government. The speech endorsed a resolution modifying Section 2 (the railway clause) of the Bill of Union which admitted British Columbia into the Dominion of Canada.

NORRIS, WILLIAM Canadian nationality and its opponents. (In The Canadian monthly and national review. Toronto. v. 8 (1875), pp. 237-243.)

—— The Canadian question. Montreal, Printed by the Lovell Print. and Pub. Co., 1875. 90 p.

—— The practical principles of Canadian nationalism. (In The Canadian monthly and national review. Toronto. v. 13 (1878), pp. 352-359.)

Notes on the session [of the] Dominion Parliament. (In *The Canadian monthly and national review*. Toronto. v. 3 (1873), pp. 520-536.)

Reviews and analyses the first session of the second parliament held March 5 to August 13, 1873.

Nouvelles électorales. (In *L'Opinion publique*. Montréal. v. 3, no. 33 (15 août 1872), p. 393.)

Includes tables listing electoral results from Quebec, Ontario, New Brunswick and Nova Scotia.

O'BREADY, MAURICE Le mouvement démocratique. (In Canadian Catholic Historical Association. *Rapport.* [Ottawa] (1939/40), pp. 51-66.)

Describes the principles, organization, and membership of the Institut canadien (1844-1876).

O'HANLY, JOHN LAWRENCE POWER The political standing of Irish Catholics in Canada; a critical analysis of its causes, with suggestions for its amelioration. By J. L. P. O'Hanly. Ottawa, 1872. 67 p.

O'NEILL, J. H. Canada since the union; a lecture. Quebec, 1871. 51 p.

ORMSBY, MARGARET ANCHORETTA British Columbia; a history. [Toronto] Macmillan [1958] x, 558 p.

Commissioned by the British Columbia Centennial Committee.

Chapter 10: The spoilt child of Confederation (pp. 259-292).

—— Canada and the new British Columbia. (In Canadian Historical Association. *Report of the annual meeting.* Toronto. (1948), pp. 74-85.)

—— Canadian opinion on British Columbia's entry into Confederation. By Margaret A. Ormsby. (In Okanagan Historical Society. *Report.* Vernon, B.C. 9th (1941), pp. 35-37.)

ORR, W. R. "Paddy" Loughrin looks back. Modern election campaigns pink-teas in comparison with the early battles in Ontario outposts. (In *Saturday night.* Toronto. v. 45, no. 40 (Aug. 16, 1930), p. 5.)

Reminiscences of election practices citing by-elections in Ontario during 1869 and the federal elections held in 1872 and 1874.

OSTRY, BERNARD Conservatives, Liberals and Labour in the 1870s. (In *The Canadian historical review*. Toronto. v. 41 (1960), pp. 93-127.)

Ouverture du Parlement fédéral. (In *L'Opinion publique*. Montréal. v. 1, no. 7 (19 fév. 1870), p. 50.)

Includes text of the Speech from the Throne of February 15, 1870.

P., ANNIE A chapter for the women of the Dominion. By Annie P. (In *The New Dominion monthly*. Montreal. (June 1871), pp. 328-330.)

Refers to the "women's rights" movement. Concerns, mainly, women's activities regarding the temperance movement.

PAQUET, BENJAMIN Le libéralisme; Leçons données à Université Laval. 2. éd., rév. corr. et augm. Rome, Impr. Polyglotte, 1877. 190 p.

First ed. published Quebec, 1872.

PARKER, ELIZABETH Manitoba's first Lieutenant-Governor. (In *The Dalhousie review*. Halifax. v. 10 (1930/31), pp. [519]-524.)

Concerns Adams George Archibald.

Le Parlement fédéral. (In *L'Opinion publique*. Montréal v. 7, no. 9—no. 16 (2 mars —20 avril 1876).)

Summarizes proceedings during the third session of the third parliament held February 10 to April 12, 1876.

Party politics in South Ontario. (In *The Nation*. Toronto. v. 3, no. 25 (June 23, 1876), p. 291.)

Concerns the record of George Brown and John A. Macdonald as a factor in a federal by-election held in South Ontario where the candidates were T. N. Gibbs for the Conservative Party and J. D. Edgar for the Liberal Party.

Party reconstruction. (In *Canadian illustrated news*. Montreal. v. 10, no. 15 (Oct. 10, 1874), pp. 226-227.)

An editorial comment on the state of the Liberal and Conservative parties after the fall of the Macdonald government in 1873.

PATTERSON, GEORGE GEDDIE Joseph Howe and the Anti-Confederation League. By the Hon. Judge Patterson. (In *The Dalhousie review*. Halifax. v. 10 (1930/31), pp. [397]-402.)

PEMBERTON, JOSEPH DESPARD Pemberton's letter. By J. D. Pemberton. (In Okanagan Historical Society. *Report.* Vernon, B.C. 10th (1943), pp. 114-121.]

Text of a letter which appeared in the *Victoria Colonist* of January 26, 1870, discussing whether British Columbia should unite with Canada or become annexed to the United States. Comments precede and follow the letter.

Personalities in politics. (In *The Nation*. Toronto. v. 1, no. 25 (Sept. 17, 1874), pp. 296-297.)

Discusses, briefly, the issue of personality in politics.

PETHICK, DEREK The confederation debate of 1870. (In Shelton, W. G. (ed.) *British Columbia and Confederation*. Victoria, B.C., 1967. pp. 165-194.)

The debate occurred in the British Columbia Legislature from March 9 to April 6, 1870.

PICHE, ARISTIDES Notes et commentaires. (In *Le Réveil*. Montréal. v. 1, no. 20 (7 oct. 1876), pp. 294-296.)

Discusses the contested by-election held in Charlevoix, Que., January 22, 1876, that resulted in the election of Hector Langevin to the House of Commons. The election was declared void.

—— Notes et commentaires. (In *Le Réveil*. Montréal. v. 1, no. 31 (23 déc. 1876), p. 471.)

Discusses the judgment handed down by Judge Routhier on the disputed election held at Charlevoix, Que., January 22, 1876.

Political corruption. (In *The Canadian monthly and national review*. Toronto. v. 2 (1872), pp. 366-378.)

Politics and commerce. (In *The Nation*. Toronto. v. 2, no. 11 (Mar. 19, 1875), pp. 126-127.)

Contests the contemporary assumption "that commercial development and political improvement cannot be carried on together."

Prohibition. (In *The Nation*. Toronto. v. 2, no. 13 (Apr. 2, 1875), p. 150.)

Discusses the problems of prohibition legislation.

Prorogation du Parlement. (In *L'Opinion publique*. Montréal. v. 4, no. 34 (21 août 1873), p. 407.)

PRYKE, KENNETH GEORGE Nova Scotia and Confederation, 1864-1870. [Durham, N.C., 1962] xii, 305 leaves.

Thesis (PH D) – Duke University.

Public faith. (In *The Nation*. Toronto. v. 2, no. 43 (Oct. 29, 1875), p. 510.)

Concerns political implications of the Land Act.

QUEBECENSIS Church and State in Quebec. A review of Sir Alexander Galt's pamphlet. By Quebecensis. (In *The Canadian monthly and national review*. Toronto. v. 9 (1876), pp. 418-429.)

Refers to the pamphlet: Church and State, by Sir A. T. Galt. Montreal, Dawson Bros., 1876. 41 p.

Raising the dust. (In *The Nation*. Toronto. v. 1, no. 30 (Oct. 22, 1874), pp. 356-357.)

Defends the editorial policy of *The Nation* as representing an independent journal of debate and opinion.

RATTRAY, WILLIAM JORDAN Stewart's Canada under Lord Dufferin. By William J. Rattray. (In Rose-Belford's *Canadian monthly and national review*. Toronto. v. 1 (1878), pp. 733-740.)

A review article of *Canada under the administration of the Earl of Dufferin*, by G. Stewart. Toronto, Rose-Belford, 1878.

RATZ, BETTY United Front in Toronto— 1872. (In *New frontier*. Toronto. v. 1, no. 3 (June 1936), pp. 18-20.)

Gives historical background to the passing of the Trades Union Bill in May 1872.

The Reciprocity Treaty. (In *The Nation*. Toronto. v. 1, no. 16 (July 16, 1874), p. 188.)

ROBERTSON, NANCY SUSAN (MANN) The Institut canadien; an essay in cultural history. [London, Ont., 1965] 180 leaves.

Thesis (MA) – University of Western Ontario.

ROBINS, WILLIAM Robins' political chart of Canada; a complete map of the Dominion by electoral districts. Toronto, Miles Map Publishers [c1879] 2 maps.

"A comparison of the maps exhibits . . . the changes effected by the general election of 1878."

Contents: Map 1. Political complexion of each constituency in the parliament of 1874. – Map 2. Political complexion of each constituency in the parliament of 1879.

(Located in Public Archives of Canada, Ottawa.)

RUMILLY, ROBERT Le "coup d'état". Charles de Boucherville, Luc Letellier de Saint-Just, Henry-Gustave Joly de Lotbinière. Montréal, B. Valiquette [1941] 239 p. (His *Histoire de la province de Québec*, 2.)

A political history covering the years 1875-1879.

—— Georges-Etienne Cartier. Montréal, B. Valiquette [1940] 365 p. (His *Histoire de la province de Québec*, 1.)

A political history covering the years 1867-1875.

RUSSELL, DAVID HUGH   The Ontario press and the Pacific scandal of 1873. [Kingston] 1970. xi, 185 leaves.

Thesis (MA) – Queen's University.

RYERSON, ADOLPHUS EGERTON, 1803-1882   The new Canadian dominion; dangers and duties of the people in regard to their government. By Egerton Ryerson. Toronto, Lovell & Gibson, 1867. Toronto, Canadiana House, 1968. 32 p.

Reproduction of the original edition.

Limited ed. of 100 copies.

RYERSON, STANLEY BREHAUT   Unequal union; Confederation and the roots of conflict in the Canadas, 1815-1873. [Toronto] Progress Books, 1968. 477 p.

Sequel to *The founding of Canada; beginnings to 1815*.

SAGE, WALTER NOBLE   British Columbia and Confederation. By Walter N. Sage. (In *The British Columbia historical quarterly*. Victoria, B.C. v. 15 (1951), pp. 71-84.)

Traces the historical relationship between the province of British Columbia and the federal government.

SANDS, HAROLD   Lord Dufferin in British Columbia. (In *The Canadian magazine of politics, science, art and literature*. Toronto. v. 21 (1903), pp. 461-463.)

Dufferin's visit to British Columbia occurred during August and September, 1876.

SAYWELL, JOHN TUPPER   Sir Joseph Trutch: British Columbia's first Lieutenant-Governor. (In *The British Columbia historical quarterly*. Victoria, B.C. v. 19 (1955), pp. 71-92.)

Federal-provincial relations form an integral part of this study.

SCOTT, SUSAN DICKINSON   The attitude of the colonial governors and officials towards Confederation. (In Shelton, W. G. (ed.) *British Columbia and Confederation*. Victoria, B.C., 1967. pp. 143-164.)

Considers the role of Governor Anthony Musgrave in accomplishing the union between British Columbia and Canada.

SEGUIN, NORMAND   L'opposition canadienne-française aux élections de 1867 dans la grande région de Montréal. [Ottawa, 1968] 141 leaves.

Thesis (MA) – University of Ottawa.

Semaine politique. (In *L'Opinion publique*. Montréal. v. 6, no. 16 (22 avril 1875), p. 191.)

Contains a list of "bills sanctionnés par le Gouverneur-général à la prorogation du Parlement fédéral".

The Session. (In *The Nation*. Toronto. v. 1, no. 9 (May 28, 1874), p. 104.)

Comments on the first session of the third parliament, ending May 26, 1874.

SHELTON, W. GEORGE (ed.)   British Columbia and Confederation. Edited by W. George Shelton. Victoria, B.C, Published for the University of Victoria by the Morriss Print. Co., 1967. viii, 250 p.

Contents: British Columbia and the Confederation era, by S. Higgins. – Amor de Cosmos and Confederation, by H. R. Kendrick. – John Robson and Confederation, by O. Fairholm. – "From sea to sea", by T. Trousdell. – The attitude of the colonial governors and officials towards Confederation, by S. D. Scott. – The Confederation debate of 1870, by D. Pethick. – The Confederation delegation, by B. Smith.

SIBLEY, C. LINTERN   The Inquisition in Canada. (In *The Canadian magazine of politics, science, art and literature*. Toronto. v. 33 (1909), pp. 217-223.)

Concerns the controversy over the burial of Joseph Guibord.

SISSONS, CHARLES BRUCE   Canadian political ideas in the sixties and seventies: Egerton Ryerson. (In Canadian Historical Association. *Report of the annual meeting*. Toronto. (1942), pp. 94-103.)

SMITH, BRIAN   The confederation delegation. (In Shelton, W. G. (ed.) *British Columbia and Confederation*. Victoria, B.C., 1967. pp. 195-216.)

The three official delegates from British Columbia consisted of J. W. Trutch, R. W. W. Carrall, and J. S. Helmcken. Their purpose was to negotiate British Columbia's entry into the Canadian confederation.

SMITH, GOLDWIN   Colonel Gray on Confederation. By a Bystander. (In *The Canadian monthly and national review*. Toronto. v. 2 (1872), pp. 173-183.)

A review article of *Confederation*, by J. H. Gray. Toronto, Copp Clark, 1872.

—— The Dominion Parliament. By a Bystander. (In *The Canadian monthly and national review*. Toronto. v. 2 (1872), pp. 56-67.)

Reviews the fifth session of the first parliament held April 11 to June 14, 1872.

—— The National Club. Mr. Goldwin Smith's address. (In *The Nation.* Toronto. v. 1, no. 29 (Oct. 15, 1874), pp. 346-347.)
Address delivered in the Queen's Hotel, Toronto, October 8, 1874.

—— Party politics. By a Radical. (In *The Canadian monthly and national review.* Toronto. v. 2 (1872), pp. 447-455.)

—— The political destiny of Canada. (In *The Canadian monthly and national review.* Toronto. v. 11 (1877), pp. 596-614.)
Reprinted from *The Fortnightly review.*

—— The political destiny of Canada. With a reply by Sir Francis Hincks . . . and some remarks on that reply. Toronto, Willing & Williamson, 1878. vi, 197 p.
"Reprinted from the 'Fortnightly review'." April, 1877.
"Opinion of Lord Blatchford . . . on Imperial Federation": pp. 170-182.

SMITH, R. GOLDWIN   Sir John A. Macdonald and Hon. George Brown—the bitter political enemies who joined hands to make Confederation possible. (In *Canada monthly.* London, Ont. v. 22, no. 3 (July 1917), pp. 122-123; 166-167.)

Soulless politics. (In *The Nation.* Toronto. v. 2, no. 43 (Oct. 29, 1875), pp. 510-511.)
Brief discussion on party politics.

STACEY, CHARLES PERRY   Lord Monck and the Canadian nation. By C. P. Stacey. (In *The Dalhousie review.* Halifax. v. 14 (1934/35), pp. [179]-191.)

STANLEY, GEORGE FRANCIS GILMAN   The 1870s. By George F. G. Stanley. (In Careless, J. M. S. (ed.) *The Canadians, 1867-1967.* Toronto, 1967. pp. 37-69.)

The State of the nation. (In *The Nation.* Toronto. v. 3, no. 24 (June 16, 1876), p. 279.)
Discusses critical comments made on an address by Sir A. T. Galt surveying contemporary fiscal policy.

STEWART, GEORGE   Canada under the administration of the Earl of Dufferin. Toronto, Rose-Belford, 1878. xvi, 696 p.

SULTE, BENJAMIN   Before the Militia Bill of 1868. (In *The Canadian magazine of politics, science, art and literature.* Toronto. v. 25 (1905), pp. 10-13.)
"Mr. Sulte entered the Civil Service in 1867 and retired in 1903. During that period, he was thirty-two years in the Militia Department." – p. 10.
Personal recollections.

SWAINSON, DONALD WAYNE   Ontario and Confederation. By D. Swainson. Ottawa, The Centennial Commission, 1967. 26 p. (Centennial historical booklet no. 5.)

—— The personnel of politics; a study of the Ontario members of the second federal parliament. Toronto, 1969. 585 leaves.
Thesis (PH D) – University of Toronto.

The Tariff. (In *The Nation.* Toronto. v. 3, no. 5 (Feb. 4, 1876), p. 54.)
Seen as a political issue.

TASSE, JOSEPH   Le Chemin de fer canadien du Pacifique. (In *Revue canadienne.* Montréal. t. 9 (1872), pp. [434]-471; [498]-520.)
Considers all aspects – engineering, financial, political – to the proposed venture of constructing the Canadian Pacific Railway.

The Temperance convention. (In *The Nation.* Toronto. v. 2, no. 38 (Sept. 24, 1875), p. 450.)
Discusses prohibition as a political issue.

THOMAS, GEORGINA H.   A nonagenarian remembers. (In Waterloo Historical Society. *Annual report.* Kitchener, Ont. 39th (1951), pp. 36-38.)
An anecdotal account of a meeting at Strasburg, Ont., between James Young and Samuel Merner during the campaign for the 1878 federal election.

THOMAS, WALTER KEITH   Canadian political oratory in the nineteenth century: I. By W. K. Thomas. (In *The Dalhousie review.* Halifax. v. 39 (1959/60), pp. [19]-30.)
Considers Thomas D'Arcy McGee and Edward Blake.

—— Canadian political oratory in the nineteenth century: II. By W. K. Thomas. (In *The Dalhousie review.* Halifax. v. 39 (1959/60), pp. [178]-191.)
Considers Sir John A. Macdonald and George Brown.

—— Canadian political oratory in the nineteenth century: III. By W. K. Thomas. (In *The Dalhousie review.* Halifax. v. 39 (1959/60), pp. [377]-389.)
Considers Joseph Howe. Regards Howe as the best Canadian "Victorian" political orator.

Treason in West Toronto. (In *The Nation.* Toronto. v. 2, no. 4 (Jan. 29, 1875), p. 44.)
Comments on the Reform Association whose aim is "to check the growing evil of electoral independence".

TREMBLAY, ERNEST La question du jour; le gouvernement fédéral peut-il révoquer le lieutenant-gouverneur de Québec? Montréal, 1878. 34 p.

TROUSDELL, TIM "From sea to sea"; negotiations between Ottawa and London. (In Shelton, W. G. (ed.) British Columbia and Confederation. Victoria, B.C., 1967. pp. 125-142.)

Concerns the terms of British Columbia's admission into the Canadian confederation.

TUTTLE, CHARLES RICHARD Royalty in Canada. Embracing sketches of the House of Argyll, the Right Honorable the Marquis of Lorne, Governor-General of Canada, Her Royal Highness the Princess Louise, and the members of the new government. By Charles R. Tuttle. Accompanied by a group of seventeen portrait engravings. Montreal, Tuttle & Simpson, 1878. 219 p.

"The Dominion cabinet and Administrator-general, 1878": pp. [153]-200.

"Parliamentary and legislative directory": pp. [201]-219.

The Two speeches. (In The Nation. Toronto. v. 2, no. 45 (Nov. 12, 1875), p. 534.)

Comments on speeches delivered by Edward Blake and Sir John A. Macdonald at the time of a federal by-election held in Toronto West, November 6, 1875.

Ultramontanism and civil authority. (In The Nation. Toronto. v. 3, no. 12 (Mar. 24, 1876), p. 135.)

Ultramontanism and civil duty. (In The Nation. Toronto. v. 1, no. 40 (Dec. 31, 1874), pp. 477-478.)

UNDERHILL, FRANK HAWKINS Political ideas of the Upper Canada reformers, 1867-78. (In Canadian Historical Association. Report of the annual meeting. Toronto. (1942), pp. 104-115.)

VANSTONE, JAMES P. Dufferin, Carnarvon and Canadian nationhood. (In Queen's quarterly. Kingston. v. 76 (1969), pp. [303]-311.)

WAITES, KENNETH A. Responsible government and Confederation. The popular movement for popular government. By K. A. Waites. (In The British Columbia historical quarterly. Victoria, B.C. v. 6 (1942), pp. 97-123.)

"Presidential address to the British Columbia Historical Association, January 16, 1942."

Considers the issues of responsible government and union with Canada debated in British Columbia prior to the proclamation of Confederation on July 20, 1871.

WARD, NORMAN MC QUEEN Confederation and responsible government. By Norman Ward. (In The Canadian journal of economics and political science. [Toronto] v. 24 (1958), pp. 44-56.)

A survey of parliament at the time of Confederation concentrating on its legislative aspects.

—— On the possibility that Lord Haldane was right. By Norman Ward. (In The Canadian forum. Toronto. v. 45, no. 533 (June 1965), pp. 64-66.)

Examines the historical background of the Canada Temperance Act legislated in 1878.

—— Prayers in the Commons. By Norman Ward. (In The Dalhousie review. Halifax. v. 32 (1952/53), pp. [140]-143.)

A brief discussion on the debate in 1877 concerning prayer at the opening of parliamentary sittings.

—— The Select Standing Committee on Public Accounts, 1867-78. By Norman Ward. (In The Canadian journal of economics and political science. [Toronto] v. 25 (1959), pp. 153-164.)

Who deserves the crown? (In The Nation. Toronto. v. 3, no. 12 (Mar. 24, 1876), pp. 135-136.)

Considers the ethical level of political journalism, referring to a statement citing the defunct Telegraph (Toronto) as "the most blackguard paper ever published in the Dominion".

WILLISON, SIR JOHN STEPHEN Some political leaders in the Canadian federation. (In The Federation of Canada, 1867-1917. Toronto, 1917. pp. [39]-76.)

Discusses the careers of George Brown, John A. Macdonald, Edward Blake, and others.

A Word in season. (In The Nation. Toronto. v. 3, no. 31 (Aug. 4, 1876), p. 363.)

Comments, briefly, on the political development of Canada, with an appeal to eliminate party ideology and organization.

Louis Riel and the
North-west Rebellions,
1869-70; 1885

ACHINTRE, AUGUSTE Semaine politique. Par A. Achintre. (In L'Opinion publique. Montréal. v. 6, no. 7 (18 fév. 1875), p. 83.)

Discusses the resolution to give amnesty to the rebels involved in the Red River Rebellion, 1869-70.

Affairs at Red River. (In *Canadian illustrated news*. Montreal. v. 1, no. 24 (Apr. 16, 1870), p. 371.)

An account submitted by the special correspondent of the *Toronto Leader* assigned at St. Paul, Minn.

The American view of the rebellion in the North-West. By B. (In *The Week*. Toronto. v. 2, no. 22 (Apr. 30, 1885), p. 342.)

American views of the half-breed rebellion. By B. (In *The Week*. Toronto. v. 2, no. 23 (May 7, 1885), p. 358.)

The Amnesty. (In *The Nation*. Toronto. v. 2, no. 7 (Feb. 19, 1875), p. 78.)

Refers to Louis Riel.

ANDERSON, FRANK W. 1885; the Riel Rebellion. [Calgary, Alta., Frontiers Unlimited, 1962] 80 p. [Frontier books, no. 3.]

—— Gabriel Dumont. (In *Alberta historical review*. Edmonton. v. 7, no. 3 (summer 1959), pp. 1-6.)

"This paper was given at a meeting of the Calgary branch of the [Historical Society of Alberta] on April 6, 1959."

—— Louis Riel's insanity reconsidered. (In *Saskatchewan history*. Saskatoon. v. 3, no. 3 (autumn 1950), pp. 104-110.)

Appearance of M. Riel at Ottawa. (In *The Nation*. Toronto. v. 1, no. 1 (Apr. 2, 1874), pp. 9-10.)

Comments critically on the actions of Louis Riel who paid a brief visit to Ottawa and signed the parliamentary roll on March 30, 1874, as an elected member of parliament from Provencher, Man.

BECHARD, AUGUSTE Manitoba. Par A. Béchard. (In *Revue canadienne*. Montréal. t. 13 (1876), pp. [21]-36.)

Conclusion of the Author's article on Manitoba. This article deals with the insurrection of 1869-70 led by John Bruce, Louis Riel, Ambroise D. Lépine, and William B. O'Donoghue.

BEGG, ALEXANDER The creation of Manitoba; or, A history of the Red River troubles. Toronto, A. H. Hovey, 1871. v, 408 p.

Author lived from 1839 to 1897.

—— Red River journal and other papers relative to the Red River resistance of 1869-1870. Edited with an introd. by W. L. Morton. Toronto, Champlain Society,

1956. xxiii, 636 p. (The Publications of the Champlain Society, 34.)

The Introduction provides an important background analysis of the Red River rebellion.

BENOIT, JOSEPH PAUL AUGUSTIN L'anglomanie au Canada. Observations générales. Troubles de la Rivière Rouge. Acte de Manitoba. Par Dom Benoit. (In *Le Mouvement catholique*. Trois-Rivières. v. 4 (juil.—déc. 1899), pp. 394-400.)

BLAKE, HUME "The Northwest Rebellion". Toronto, 1916. 210 leaves.

Thesis (MA) – University of Toronto.

BOISSONNAULT, CHARLES MARIE Colère en Saskatchewan. (In *La Revue de l'Université Laval*. Québec. v. 4, no. 6 (fév. 1950), pp. [489]-504.)

Concerns the second North West Rebellion, 1885.

BOULTON, CHARLES ARKOLL Reminiscences of the North-West rebellions. And a chapter on Canadian social and political life. By Charles A. Boulton. Toronto, Grip, 1886. 531 p.

BOWSFIELD, HARTWELL WALTER LEWIS (ed.) Louis Riel; rebel of the western frontier or victim of politics and prejudice? Edited by H. Bowsfield. Toronto, Copp Clark Pub. Co. [c1969] 227 p. (Issues in Canadian history.)

A selection of readings.

BRYCE, GEORGE Two provisional governments in Manitoba. Containing an interesting discussion of the Riel Rebellion, with an appendix embodying the four bills of rights verbatim. By Rev. Professor Bryce. Winnipeg, Manitoba Free Press Print, 1890. 11 p. (Historical and Scientific Society of Manitoba. Transaction 38.)

Cover title.

"Read before the Society Jan. 9th, 1890."

The captive insurgent chief. (In *The Week*. Toronto. v. 2, no. 25 (May 21, 1885), pp. 389-390.)

Concerns Louis Riel.

CHARETTE, GUILLAUME J. La rébellion de la Rivière-Rouge. (In Canadian Catholic Historical Association. *Rapport*. [Ottawa] (1948/49), pp. 81-91.)

CLARKE, CHARLES KIRK A critical study of the case of Louis Riel. By C. K. Clarke. (In *Queen's quarterly*. Kingston. v. 12 (1904/05), pp. [379]-388; v. 13 (1905/06), pp. [14]-26.)

In two parts.

[COLLINS, JOSEPH EDMUND] The story of Louis Riel; the rebel chief. Toronto, Whitby, J. S. Robertson [1885?] Toronto, Coles Pub. Co., [1970] 192 p. (Coles Canadiana collection.)

Facsim. reprint.

COOKE, BRITTON B. Famous Canadian trials: Ambroise Lepine, Riel's lieutenant. (In *The Canadian magazine of politics, science, art and literature*. Toronto. v. 45 (1915), pp. 57-60.)

Famous Canadian trials, 5.

——— Famous Canadian trials: Riel before the jury. (In *The Canadian magazine of politics, science, art and literature*. Toronto. v. 44 (1914/15), pp. 502-597.)

Famous Canadian trials, 4.

Crise de la Rivière-Rouge. (In *L'Opinion publique*. Montréal. v. 4, no. 42 (16 oct. 1873), pp. [495]-496.)

DAVID, LAURENT OLIVIER Crise à Manitoba. Par L. O. David. (In *L'Opinion publique*. Montréal. v. 4, no. 41 (9 oct. 1873), p. 491.)

Includes the text of a "protestation" signed by Louis Riel.

DAVIDSON, WILLIAM MC CARTNEY The life and times of Louis Riel. [Calgary, Albertan Printers, 1952] 114 p.

Cover title.

Text in double columns.

Published in *The Albertan* in serial form, November 1951.

——— Louis Riel, 1844-1885; a biography. Calgary, Alta., Albertan Pub. Co., 1955. 214 p.

Text in double columns.

Complete ed.

La Défense de Lépine. (In *L'Opinion publique*. Montréal. v. 5, no. 48 (26 nov. 1874), pp. [577]-578.)

An anonymous letter from Manitoba concerning the trial of Ambroise Dydime Lépine.

Edited by Oscar Dunn.

DEROUET, CAMILLE Les Métis canadiens-français. (In *La Revue canadienne*. Montréal. 32 année (1896), pp. [611]-620; [658]-675.)

Concentrates on the career of Louis Riel from 1869-70 to his execution in 1885.

DUFF, LOUIS BLAKE Amazing story of the Winghamite secretary of Louis Riel. London, Ont., Lawson Memorial Library, University of Western Ontario, 1955. 37

leaves. (Western Ontario history nuggets, no. 22.)

Cover title.

Biographical sketch of William Henry Jackson.

DUMONT, GABRIEL Gabriel Dumont's account of the North West Rebellion, 1885. (In *The Canadian historical review*. Toronto. v. 30 (1949), pp. 249-269.)

Edited, with notes, by George F. G. Stanley.

Translated text of the oral account transcribed by B. A. T. de Montigny in Montreal in December 1888: pp. 251-269.

DUNN, OSCAR L'amnistie. (In *L'Opinion publique*. Montréal. v. 4, no. 49 (4 déc. 1873), p. 587.)

Deals with Riel, Lépine, and others involved in the Red River Rebellion 1869-70.

——— L'esprit de désunion. (In *L'Opinion publique*. Montréal. v. 5, no. 47 (19 nov. 1874), p. [545].)

Deplores the lack of unity among French Canadians as reflected in the discussions on amnesty for Ambroise Lépine.

——— Le procès Lépine. (In *L'Opinion publique*. Montréal. v. 5, no. 45 (5 nov. 1874), p. 549.)

——— La question de l'amnistie. (In *L'Opinion publique*. Montréal. v. 5 no. 15 (9 avril 1874), p. [169].)

Concerns Louis Riel.

——— Riel. (In *L'Opinion publique*. Montréal. v. 5, no. 17 (23 avril 1874), p. [193].)

Relates to the amnesty question.

——— Semaine parlementaire. Par O. D. (In *L'Opinion publique*. Montréal. v. 5, no. 16 (16 avril 1874), p. [181].)

Relates to the question of amnesty and other matters.

——— Semaine parlementaire. Par O. D. (In *L'Opinion publique*. Montréal. v. 5, no. 22 (28 mai 1874), p. 261.)

Summarizes proceedings in parliament. Concerns also the question of amnesty for those involved in the Red River Insurrection, 1869-70.

——— La suite du procès Lépine. Par O. D. (In *L'Opinion publique*. Montréal. v. 5, no. 46 (12 nov. 1874), p. 561.)

FORGET, EUCHER Louis Riel et les troubles de la Rivière-Rouge. [Montréal, 1950] 1 v.

Thesis (MA) – University of Montreal.

FREGAULT, GUY Louis Riel, patriote per-
sécuté. (In L'Action nationale. Montréal.
v. 25 (jan. 1945), pp. [15]-22.)

FREMONT, DONATIEN Alfred-Norbert Provencher, 1843-1887. (In Royal Society of
Canada. Proceedings and transactions.
Ottawa. ser. 3, v. 51 (1957), section 1, pp.
29-41.)
Joseph Alfred Norbert Provencher acted
as liaison between the Métis and the Canadian government during the Riel Rebellion,
1869-70.

—— Henry Jackson et l'insurrection du
Nord-Ouest. (In Royal Society of Canada.
Proceedings and transactions. Ottawa.
ser. 3, v. 46 (1952), section 1, pp. 19-48.)

—— Les Métis de l'Ouest canadien. (In
Royal Society of Canada. Proceedings and
transactions. Ottawa. ser. 3, v. 42 (1948),
section 1, pp. 53-77.)
"A propos du livre de Marcel Giraud: Le
Métis canadien".
Includes analysis of the Red River Insur-
rection, 1869-70.

—— Les secrétaires de Riel: Louis Schmidt,
Henry Jackson, Philippe Garnot. Montréal, Editions Chantecler, 1953. 205 p.

GAGNON, FERD Louis Riel. Par Ferd. Gagnon. (In L'Opinion publique. Montréal.
v. 5, no. 32 (6 août 1874), pp. [385]-386.)

GELINAS, AIME La vérité sur l'insurrection
de Manitoba. Par A. Gélinas. (In L'Opinion publique. Montréal. v. 11, no. 23 (3
juin 1880), p. 266.)

GRAHAM, A. W. Diary of A. W. Graham
during the Red River Rebellion. (In Elgin
Historical and Scientific Institute. Reminiscences of early settlers and other records. [St. Thomas, Ont.] 1911. pp. [70]-
84.)

GROULX, LIONEL ADOLPHE Louis Riel et les
événements de la Rivière-Rouge en 1869-
1870. Par le chanoine Lionel Groulx.
Montréal, Editions de l'action nationale
[1944] 23 p.
Cover title.

HAFTER, RUTH The Riel Rebellion and
manifest destiny. (In The Dalhousie review. Halifax. v. 45, no. 4 (winter 1965/
66), pp. [447]-456.)

HOLLAND, GEORGE CLARKE When Riel
signed the roll. An historic incident in
Canadian life. (In Saturday night. Toronto. v. 37, no. 18 (Mar. 4, 1922), p. 5.)

Gives the background and events surrounding Riel's coming to Ottawa and signing the parliamentary roll of members on
March 30, 1874. Louis Riel was elected to
the House of Commons at a by-election for
Provencher, Man., on Oct. 13, 1873, and he
was re-elected in Feb. 1874. He was expelled
from the House of Commons April 16, 1874.

HOWARD, JOSEPH KINSEY Strange empire;
a narrative of the Northwest. New York,
Morrow, 1952. xii, 601 p.
An account of the rebellions in 1870 and
1885 led by Louis Riel.

—— Strange empire. [Foreword by Hartwell Bowsfield] Toronto, Swan Pub. Co.
[1965, c 1952] 480 p. (CCN 104)
On cover: Strange empire; the story of
Louis Riel.

KABIBONICA The North-West rebellion. By
Kabibonica. (In The Week. Toronto. v. 2,
no. 18 (Apr. 2, 1885), pp. 276-277.)

—— Riel's second rebellion. By Kabibonica. [In The Week. Toronto. v. 2, no. 19
(Apr. 9, 1885), pp. 292-293.]

KENNEDY, HOWARD ANGUS The North-
West Rebellion. Toronto, Ryerson Press
[1928] 32 p. (The Ryerson Canadian history readers.)
An eye-witness account.

KERR, JOHN ANDREW Gabriel Dumont: a
personal memory. (In The Dalhousie review. Halifax. v. 15 (1935/36), pp. [53]-
59.)

—— "I helped capture Ambroise Lepine".
The story of the arrest, trial of Ambroise
Lepine, chief lieutenant of Riel and his
conviction for the murder of Thomas
Scott. (In The Canadian magazine. Toronto. v. 79, no. 5 (May 1933), pp. 13;
40-41.)

KNOX, OLIVE The question of Louis Riel's
insanity. (In Historical and Scientific Society of Manitoba. Papers. Winnipeg. ser.
3, no. 6 (1951), pp. 20-34.)

KREUTZWEISER, ERWIN E. The Red River
Insurrection, its causes and events. Gar-
denvale, Que., Garden City Press [1936?]
xii, 166 p.
An interpretative study of events from
September 1869 to April 1870.

LA CHANCE, VERNON The Metis rebellions.
(In Maclean's. Toronto. v. 43, no. 20
(Oct. 15, 1930), pp. 14-15, 71-74; v. 43
no. 21 (Nov. 1, 1930), pp. 13-14, 50-54.)
In two parts.

LAMB, ROBERT EMMETT Friction between Ontario and Quebec caused by the risings of Louis Riel. [Ottawa, 1953.] xi, 492 leaves.

Thesis (PH D) – University of Ottawa.

——— Thunder in the north; conflict over the Riel risings, 1870-1885. By R. E. Lamb. New York, Pageant Press [1957] xviii, 354 p.

LAURIER, SIR WILFRID Trois discours sur Riel. Introd. par Jean Louis Gagnon. (In Ecrits du Canada français. Montréal. v. 24 (1968), pp. [163]-257.)

Contents: Laurier et la rébellion du nord-ouest. – Discours sur l'exécution de Riel.

Speeches were presented during the years 1885 and 1886.

Lepine. (In The Nation. Toronto. v. 2, no. 4 (Jan. 29, 1875), p. 42.)

Reviews the influence of party politics upon the events leading to the commutation of the sentence of Ambroise Dydime Lépine.

Lepine in the House of Lords. (In The Nation. Toronto. v. 2, no. 18 (May 7, 1875), pp. 212-213.)

Raises constitutional questions relating to Lord Dufferin's exercise of the prerogative of mercy in the case of Ambroise Dydime Lépine.

Louis Riel, martyr du Nord-Ouest; sa vie, son procès, sa mort. Publié par le journal La Presse. 6. éd. Montréal, Impr. Générale, 1885. 96 p.

MC ARTHUR, ALEX The causes of the rising in the Red River Settlement, 1896-70. [Winnipeg, 1882?] 12 p. (Manitoba Historical and Scientific Society. Publication no. 1.)

Cover title.

Dated at end: Winnipeg, Oct. 10, 1882.

"A Paper read before the Historical and Scientific Society."

MAC BETH, RODERICK GEORGE Louis Riel's stormy career. Intimate sidelights on a strange personality from an old-timer of the West. By R. G. MacBeth. (In The Canadian magazine. Toronto. [v. 67, no. 1] (Jan. 1927), pp. 15; 43.)

——— Memories of Louis Riel. The misguided but magnetic egotist who headed two risings against Canada's control of the Prairies. By R. G. MacBeth. (In Saturday night. Toronto. v. 47, no. 50 (Oct. 22, 1932), p. 3.)

——— Memories of Riel's trial. Chief Justice Lemieux one of the survivors of the legal galaxy present. By R. G. MacBeth. (In Saturday night. Toronto. v. 41, no. 38 (Aug. 7, 1926), p. 5.)

MC KENZIE, NATHANIEL MURDOCK WILLIAM JOHN Half-breed rebellion of 1885. By N. M. W. J. McKenzie. (In Thunder Bay Historical Society. Papers. [Fort William, Ont.] 11th (1920), pp. 25-30.)

MAIR, CHARLES Charles Mair: a document on the Red River rebellion. (In The Canadian historical review. Toronto. v. 40 (1959), pp. 218-226.)

Introductory remarks, by F. N. Shrive: pp. 218-220.

Text of the document: pp. 220-226.

——— Wresting the West from Riel. By Charles Mair as told to Elizabeth Bailey Price. (In Maclean's. Toronto. v. 36, no. 17 (Sept. 1, 1923), pp. 18; 44-46.)

MERCIER, HONORE La question Riel. Discours prononcé par L'Honorable M. Mercier, député de St.-Hyacinthe et chef de l'Opposition à l'Assemblée Législative de Québec le 7 mai 1886. Québec, Impr. de l'Electeur, 1886. 58 p.

MITCHELL, WILLIAM ORMOND The riddle of Louis Riel. A Maclean's flashback in two parts. (In Maclean's. Toronto. v. 65, no. 3 (Feb. 1, 1952), pp. 7-9, 43, 45; v. 65, no. 4 (Feb. 15, 1952), pp. 12-13, 41-45.)

In two parts.

M. l'abbé Ritchot. (In L'Opinion publique. Montréal. v. 1, no. 17 (28 avril 1870), p. 131.)

Reprints a report of a conversation between a correspondent and J. N. Ritchot. The source is not named.

MONTPETIT, ANDRE NAPOLEON Louis Riel à la Rivière-du-Loup. Par A. N. Montpetit. Lévis, 1885, lxii, 111 p.

MORICE, ADRIEN GABRIEL Aux sources de l'histoire manitobaine. v. – Cette infernale barrière! Par A.-G. Morice. (In La Nouvelle-France. Québec. t. 6, no. 8 (août 1907), pp. [360]-371.)

Traces the events relating to the origins of the Red River Insurrection, 1869-70.

Previous 4 parts deal with the pre-Confederation period.

——— Aux sources de l'histoire manitobaine. VI. – Métis et blanc. Par A.-G.

Morice. (In *La Nouvelle-France*. Québec. t. 6, no. 9 (sept. 1907), pp. [408]-421.)
Relates to the Red River Rebellion, 1869-70.

—— Aux sources de l'histoire manitobaine. VII. – Questions épineuses. Par A.-G. Morice. (In *La Nouvelle-France*. Québec. t. 6, no. 10 (Oct. 1907), pp. [462]-475.)
Relates to the Red River Insurrection, 1869-70.

—— Aux sources de l'histoire manitobaine. VIII. – Fidélité dans la persécution. Par A.-G. Morice. (In *La Nouvelle-France*. Québec. t. 6, no. 11 (nov. 1907), pp. [518]-530.)
Relates to the events of the Red River Insurrection, 1869-70.

—— A critical history of the Red River insurrection, after official documents and non-Catholic sources. By A. G. Morice. Winnipeg, Canadian Publishers, 1935. 375 p.

—— Louis Riel. Par A.-G. Morice. (In *Revue canadienne*. Montréal. nouv. sér., v. 1 (1908), pp. [143]-153.)
"Page inédite du Dictionnaire des Canadiens de l'Ouest."

—— La race métisse. Etude critique en marge d'un livre récent. Par Adrien-G. Morice. (In *Revue de l'Université d'Ottawa*. [Ottawa] 7. année (1937), pp. [160]-183, [364]-379, [475]-495; 8. année (1938), pp. [79]-107.)
In two parts.
A review article of *Histoire de la nation métisse dans l'Ouest canadien*, par A. H. de Trémaudan. Montréal, A. Lévesque, 1936.
Includes an extensive analysis of the Red River rebellions.

MOUSSEAU, JOSEPH ALFRED "La paix ou la guerre." Par J. A. Mousseau. (In *L'Opinion publique*. Montréal. v. 1, no. 17 (28 avril 1870), p. 130.)
Deals with the Red River Rebellion, 1869-70.

—— La Rivière Rouge. Par J. A. Mousseau. (In *L'Opinion publique*. Montréal. v. 1, no. 14 (9 avril 1870), p. [105].)

NEEDLER, GEORGE HENRY Louis Riel; the rebellion of 1885. Toronto, Burns & MacEachern, 1957. v, 81 p. plates.

The North-West question. (In *The Week*. Toronto. v. 11, no. 18 (Mar. 30, 1894), pp. 413-414.)

Nouvelles de la capitale. L'affaire Scott. (In *L'Opinion publique*. Montréal. v. 1, no. 17 (28 avril 1870), p. 131.)
Report on the parliamentary investigation of Abbé Ritchot and Alfred H. Scott, accused of complicity in the execution of Thomas Scott.

Nouvelles de la Rivière Rouge. (In *L'Opinion publique*. Montréal. v. 1, no. 9 (5 mars 1870), p. [65].)

O'DONNELL, JOHN HARRISON Manitoba as I saw it, from 1869 to date. With flashlights on the first Riel Rebellion. Toronto, Musson Book Co. [c1909] 158 p.

OSLER, EDMUND BOYD Louis Riel; un homme à pendre. Traduit de l'anglais par Rossel Vien. Montréal, Editions du Jour [1964, c1963] 295 p. (Collection: L'Histoire vivante, 2.)
Translation of *The man who had to hang: Louis Riel*.
Original English ed.: Toronto, Longmans, Green, 1961.

—— The man who had to hang: Louis Riel. [1st ed.] Toronto, Longmans, Green [1961] 320 p.

OUIMET, ADOLPHE La vérité sur la question métisse au nord-ouest. Biographie et récit de Gabriel Dumont sur les événements de 1885, par B. A. T. de Montigny. Montréal. 1899. 400 p.
Contents: Etude sur la question métisse. – Récit de Gabriel Dumont. – Procès Riel. – Accusations et refutations. – Causes véritables de son exécution. – Mémoires et documents.

PEARCE, WILLIAM Causes of the Riel Rebellion, a personal view. (In *Alberta historical review*. Calgary. v. 16, no. 4 (autumn 1968, pp. 19-26.)
"This paper is from an address 'Reminiscences concerning surveys from 1869 to 1881' given to the Alberta Land Surveyors' Association annual meeting in 1921."

POULIOT, LEON La proclamation du gouvernement provisoire de la Rivière-Rouge, 8 décembre 1869. (In *Le Bulletin des recherches historiques*. Lévis. v. 49, no. 12 (déc. 1943), pp. [353]-358.)
Considers the involvement of Rév. Georges Dugas and Mgr. J. N. Ritchot with the Proclamation.
"Texte de la Proclamation": pp. 354-357.

PRUD'HOMME, LOUIS ARTHUR Ambroise Dydime Lépine. En marge de son procès.

Par le juge L.-A. Prud'homme. (In Royal Society of Canada. *Proceedings and transactions*. Ottawa. ser. 3, v. 19 (1925), section 1, pp. 53-63.)

"Lu à la réunion de mai 1925."

Discusses the trial of Ambroise Lépine for his involvement in the execution of Thomas Scott.

—— André Nault. Par le juge L.-A. Prud'homme. (In Royal Society of Canada. *Proceedings and transactions*. Ottawa. ser. 3, v. 22 (1928), section 1, pp. 99-111.)

"Lu à la réunion de mai 1928."

Directed the firing squad at the execution of Thomas Scott.

PUCHNIAK, STANLEY A. Riel's Red River government, a legitimate government, 1869-1870. [Ottawa] 1931. 60 leaves.

Thesis (MA) – University of Ottawa.

The Red River difficulty. (In *Canadian illustrated news*. Montreal. v. 1, no. 9 (Jan. 1, 1870), pp. 130-131.)

Contains the text of the proclamation issued by W. McDougall and a counter-proclamation issued by Dr. John Shultz.

The Red River difficulty. Louis Riel. (In *Canadian illustrated news*. Montreal. v. 1, no. 11 (Jan. 15, 1870), pp. [161]-162.)

Red River Insurrection. Hon. Wm. McDougall's conduct reviewed. Montreal, Printed by J. Lovell, 1870. 69 p.

Reminiscences of the North-West rebellions. By T. M. (In *The Week*. Toronto. v. 3, no. 15 (Mar. 11, 1886), pp. 229-230.)

RICHARDSON, ROBERT LORNE Riel's second rebellion. By R. L. Richardson. (In *The Week*. Toronto. v. 2, no. 40 (Sept. 3, 1885), pp. 628-629.)

RIDD, DWIGHT NUGENT The second Riel insurrection. [Winnipeg] 1934. 123 leaves.

Thesis (MA) – University of Manitoba.

RIDD, JOHN ELWOOD The Red River Insurrection, 1859-1870. [Winnipeg] 1934. 109 leaves.

Thesis (MA) – University of Manitoba.

RIEL, LOUIS L'amnistie. Mémoire sur les causes des troubles du Nord-Ouest et sur les négociations qui ont amené leur règlement amiable. Par. M. Louis Riel, président de l'ex-gouvernement provisoire. (In *L'Opinion publique*. Montréal. v. 5, no. 8 (19 fév. 1874), pp. 86-88.)

—— The execution of Thomas Scott. (In *The Canadian historical review*. Toronto. v. 6 (1925), pp. 222-236.)

Notes and comments by A. H. de Trémaudan.

Transcript of "Affaire Scott" in which Louis Riel discusses Thomas Scott's involvement in the Red River difficulties. An English translation of the document is provided (pp. 235-236).

—— Journal de prison. (In *Ecrits du Canada français*. Montréal. v. 13 (1962), pp. [305]-353.)

—— Letter of Louis Riel and Ambroise Lépine to Lieutenant-Governor Morris, January 3, 1873. (In *The Canadian historical review*. Toronto. v. 7 (1926), pp. 137-160.)

Notes and comments and English translation by A. H. de Trémaudan.

Text of the letter provides a summary of the Red River Rebellion from a Métis viewpoint.

—— Louis Riel and the Fenian raid of 1871. (In *The Canadian historical review*. Toronto. v. 4 (1923), pp. 132-144.)

Notes and comments by A. H. de Trémaudan.

Text of minutes kept by Louis Riel for meetings held from Sept. 28, 1871, to Oct. 8, 1871. The account reflects attitudes held by Riel and the Métis leaders, during this time, toward the Canadian government.

—— Louis Riel's letter to President Grant, 1875. (In *Saskatchewan history*. Saskatoon. v. 21, no. 2 (spring 1968), pp. [67]-75.)

Text of a draft of the letter proposing a plan to re-establish himself (Riel) as head of a Provisional Government in Manitoba and the North West Territories.

RIEL, LOUIS, defendant The Queen vs. Louis Riel, accused and convicted of the crime of high treason. Report of trial at Regina. – Appeal to the Court of Queen's Bench, Manitoba. – Appeal to the Privy Council, England. – Petition for medical examination of the convict. – List of petitions for commutation of sentence, Ottawa. Ottawa, Printed by the Queen's Printer, 1886. 207 p.

Issued also in French.

RIEL, LOUIS Riel's petition to the President of the United States, 1870. (In *The Canadian historical review*. Toronto. v. 20 (1939), pp. 421-428.)

Introductory remarks by George F. G. Stanley: pp. 421-422.

Text of the petition: The memorial & petition of the people of Rupert's Land and North-West Territories, British America, to His Excellency, U. S. Grant, President of the United States (pp. 422-428).

The Riel outbreak. By C. (In *The Week*. Toronto. v. 2, no. 19 (Apr. 9, 1885), pp. 295-296.)

The Riel outbreak. By C. (In *The Week*. Toronto. v. 2, no. 20 (Apr. 16, 1885), pp. 309-310.)

SAINT-LEANDRE, SOEUR   L'œuvre véridique de Louis Riel, 1869-70. 1885. [Par] P. de M. Montréal, A. Lévesque, 1934. 186 p. (Figures canadiennes.)

The Situation. (In *Canadian illustrated news*. Montreal. v. 1, no. 13 (Jan. 29, 1870), p. 194.)
Concerns the North-West Rebellion, 1869-70.

SMITH, CARL FRANKLIN   Louis Riel; a false prophet. [Wolfville, N.S.] 1967. 1. v.
Thesis (BA Honours) – Acadia University.

SMITH, GOLDWIN   Notes on the North-West. By a Bystander. (In *The Week*. Toronto. v. 1, no. 42 (Sept. 18, 1884), pp. 659-661.)

STANLEY, GEORGE FRANCIS GILMAN   The birth of western Canada; a history of the Riel rebellion. By George F. G. Stanley. With illustrations. Maps by C. C. J. Bond. [Toronto] University of Toronto Press [1963, c1960] xiv, 475 p.
First published London, Longmans, Green, 1936.
"Notes" (bibliographical): pp. 411-452.

—— The half-breed "rising" of 1875. (In *The Canadian historical review*. Toronto. v. 17 (1936), pp. 399-412.)

—— Louis Riel. Par George F. G. Stanley. (In *Revue d'histoire de l'Amérique française*. Montréal. v. 18, no. 1 (juin 1964), pp. 14-26.)

—— Louis Riel. By George F. G. Stanley. (In McDougall, R. L. (ed.) *Canada's past and present*. [Toronto, 1967, c1965] pp. 21-40.)
Our living tradition, ser. 5.

—— Louis Riel. By George F. G. Stanley. Toronto, Ryerson Press [1969, c1963] 433 p.
"Notes" (bibliographical): pp. 377-424.

—— Louis Riel, patriot or rebel? By George F. G. Stanley. Ottawa [Canadian Historical Association, c1954] 24 p. (Canadian Historical Association. Historical booklets, no. 2.)
Translated into French under title: *Louis Riel, patriote ou rebelle?*

—— The Riel Rebellion in Canada, 1870-86. By G. F. G. Stanley. Oxford, 1933-34. 1 v.
Thesis – Oxford University.

SULTE, BENJAMIN   L'expédition militaire de Manitoba. (In *Revue canadienne*. Montréal. t. 8 (1871), pp. [500]-522; [580]-603.)
A narrative describing the military measures adopted by the federal government to quell the Insurrection of 1869-70.

TACHE, ALEXANDER ANTONIN, Abp.   L'amnistie. Par Mgr. Taché, Archevêque de St. Boniface. Montréal, Imprimée par le journal "Le Nouveau monde" 1874. 72 p.

—— Archbishop Taché, OMI, on the amnesty question with regard to the North West difficulty; communicated to "The Times" on the 6th, 7th, and 8th April, 1874. St. Boniface, Printed by the Canadian Publishing Co., 1893. 60 p.
An English ed. of *L'Amnistie*. Montréal, 1874.

—— The North West difficulty, Bishop Taché on the amnesty question, as appeared in The Times on the 6th, 7th and 8th April, 1874. [n.p., 1874?] 36 p.
Cover title.
An English ed. of *L'Amnistie*. Montréal, 1874.
Text in double column. (Cf. Peel)

TREMBLAY, ERNEST   Riel; réponse à Monsieur J. A. Chapleau. St.-Hyacinthe, Qué., Des presses à vapeur de "Union", 1885. 80 p.

The Uprising in Manitoba. By W. F. C. (In *The Week*. Toronto. v. 1, no. 3 (Dec. 20, 1883), pp. 36-37.)

WADE, FREDERICK COATE   The Riel Rebellion. By Fred C. Wade. (In *The Week*. Toronto. v. 2, no. 17 (Mar. 26, 1885), pp. 261-263.)

WELLS, JAMES EDWARD   The North-West problem. By J. E. W. (In *The Week*. Toronto. v. 1, no. 16 (Mar. 20, 1884), pp. 246-247.)

Where is Scott buried? By J. G. (In *The Canadian courier*. Toronto. v. 5, no. 13 (Feb. 27, 1909), p. 12.)
Concerns the death and burial of Thomas Scott.

WOODCOCK, GEORGE Louis Riel, defender of the past. (In *The Beaver*. Winnipeg. outfit 290 (spring 1960), pp. 24-29.)

WOODINGTON, HENRY Diary of a prisoner in Red River Rebellion. (In Niagara Historical Society. [Publications] Niagara. no. 25 (1913), pp. [32]-55.)

YEIGH, FRANK Riel's religion of rebellion. Did the North-West agitator believe in the justice of his cause and have faith in the purpose of his mission? (In *MacLean's magazine*. Toronto. v. 24, no. 5 (Sept. 1912), pp. 124-132.)

YOUNG, GEORGE Manitoba memories, 1868-1884. By Rev. George Young. Toronto. W. Briggs, 1897. 364 p.
A personal account of the Riel Rebellion, 1869-70.

THE ERA OF THE NATIONAL POLICY
1878–1896

ABERDEEN AND TEMAIR, ISHBEL MARIA (MARJORIBANKS) GORDON, MARCHIONESS OF The Canadian journal of Lady Aberdeen, 1893-1898. Edited, with an introd. by John T. Saywell. Toronto, Champlain Society, 1960. lxxxiv, 517 p. (The Pubications of the Champlain Society, 38.)
The Introduction provides a comprehensive analysis of the political situation in general and the Conservative Party in particular during this period.

ABERDEEN AND TEMAIR, JOHN CAMPBELL GORDON, 1ST MARQUIS OF "We twa." Reminiscences of Lord and Lady Aberdeen. London, W. Collins [1926] 2 v.
Vol. 2, chapt. 1-11 (pp. 1-147), covers the period of Lord Aberdeen's stay in Canada as Governor-General, 1893-1898.

ADAM, GRAEME MERCER Party manoeuvring v. useful legislation. By G. Mercer Adam. (In *The Week*. Toronto. v. 1, no. 18 (Apr. 3, 1884), p. 280.)

L'Affaire Letellier. (In *L'Opinion publique*. Montréal. v. 10, no. 17 (24 avril 1879), p. [193].)
Relates to the controversial action taken by Luc Letellier de St. Just in dismissing the Conservative government of Boucher de Boucherville in the province of Quebec.

L'Affaire Letellier. (In *L'Opinion publique*. Montréal. v. 10, no. 26 (26 juin 1879), p. [301].)

The Anti-Jesuit crusade. (In *The Week*. Toronto. v. 6, no. 31 (July 5, 1889), p. 485; v. 6, no. 32 (July 12, 1889), pp. 501-502.)
In two parts.

Appropriations and patronage. (In *The Week*. Toronto. v. 11, no. 40 (Aug. 31, 1894), pp. 940-941.)

ARMOUR, EDWARD DOUGLAS The Jesuits' Estates Act. (In *The Week*. Toronto. v. 6, no. 14 (Mar. 8, 1889), pp. 213-214.)

—— The Jesuits' Estates Act. (In *The Week*. Toronto. v. 6, no. 16 [Mar. 22, 1889), p. 245.)

—— The liquor license question. (In *The Week*. Toronto. v. 2, no. 9 (Jan. 29, 1885), pp. 132-133.)

BATHGATE, WILLIAM The Canadian tariff. By Wm. Bathgate. (In *The Week*. Toronto. v. 10, no. 18 (Mar. 31, 1893), pp. 413-415.)

BELL, JAMES W. The future of Canada. (In *The Week*. Toronto. v. 6, no. 34 (July 26, 1889), pp. 536-539.)

BERTON, PIERRE FRANCIS DE MARIGNY The last spike; the great railway, 1881-1885. By Pierre Berton. Toronto, McClelland and Stewart [c1971] xii, 478 p.
Sequel to *The national dream*.
Bibliography: pp. 451-461.

BLAKELEY, PHYLLIS RUTH The repeal election of 1886. By Phyllis R. Blakeley. (In Nova Scotia Historical Society. *Collections*. Halifax. v. 26 (1945), pp. [131]-152.)
"Read before the Nova Scotia Historical Society, Jan. 5, 1945."
Considers the movement in Nova Scotia to repeal Confederation.

BONENFANT, JEAN CHARLES Destitution d'un premier ministre et d'un lieutenant-gouverneur. (In *Les Cahiers des dix*. Montréal. no. 28 (1963), pp. [9]-31.)
Relates to the controversial action taken by Luc Letellier de St. Just in dismissing the Conservative government of Boucher de Boucherville.

BOULTON, CHARLES ARKOLL Free trade and how to raise the revenue. By C. A. Boulton. (In *The Week*. Toronto. v. 9, no. 25 (May 20, 1892), pp. 389-390.)

—— Our national progress. By C. A. Boulton. (In *The Week*. Toronto. v. 11, no. 12 (Feb. 16, 1894), pp. 277-279.)

—— Reciprocity considered. By C. A. Boulton. (In *The Week*. Toronto. v. 8, no. 37 (Aug. 14, 1891), pp. 590-591.)

—— Tariff reform. By C. A. Boulton. (In *The Week*. Toronto. v. 10, no. 50 (Nov. 10, 1893), pp. 1184-1186.)

BOURINOT, SIR JOHN GEORGE The national development of Canada. By J. G. Bourinot. (In Rose-Belford's *Canadian monthly and national review*. Toronto. v. 4 (1880), pp. [225]-237.)

—— The national sentiment in Canada. (In *University quarterly review*. Toronto. 1st quarter (Feb. 1890), pp. 3-23.)

BROWN, ROBERT CRAIG The Commercial Unionists in Canada and the United States. By R. C. Brown. (In Canadian Historical Association. *Report of the annual meeting*. [Ottawa] (1963), pp. [116]-124.)

BROWNE, ADDISON F. The campaign in Nova Scotia. (In *The Week*. Toronto. v. 4, no. 11 (Feb. 10, 1887), p. [167].)
Relates to the federal election held February 22, 1887.

BUTTERWORTH, BENJAMIN Commercial union between Canada and the United States; an address delivered before the Canadian Club of New York. By Hon. B. Butterworth. New York, E. Wiman [1887?] 39 p.

The Bystander; a . . . review of current events, Canadian and general. v. 1-3, Jan. 1880—Oct. 1883; new ser. Oct. 1889—Sept. 1890. Toronto, Hunter, Rose. 4 v.
Written and published by Goldwin Smith.
Monthly, Jan. 1880—June 1881; quarterly, Jan.—Oct. 1883; monthly, Oct. 1889—Sept. 1890.
Publication suspended, July 1881—Dec. 1882.
At head of title: Not party, but the people.

The "Bystander" on the Scott Act. By W. F. C. (In *The Week*. Toronto. v. 2, no. 1 (Dec. 4, 1884), pp. 5-6.)
Concerns the Canada Temperance Act.

CANADA. DEPT. OF PUBLIC PRINTING AND STATIONERY Electoral atlas of the Dominion of Canada as divided for the revision of the voters' lists made in the year 1894. Ottawa, Gov. Print. Bureau, 1895. [19] p. 202 maps.

Canada First. (In *The Dominion illustrated*. Montreal. v. 5, no. 130 (Dec. 27, 1890), p. 419.)

Canada First. (In *The Week*. Toronto. v. 13, no. 18 (Mar. 27, 1896), pp. 418-419.)
Presents a six-point declaration for a new Canada First party. The original Canada First movement spanned the years 1868-1876.

The *Canada Revue* case. (In *The Week*. Toronto. v. 11, no. 50 (Nov. 9, 1894), pp. 1181-1182.)
The proprietors of the *Canada Revue* vs. Archbishop E. C. Fabre of Montreal.

Canada's future. By W. E. M. (In *The Week*. Toronto. v. 2, no. 9 (Jan. 29, 1885), pp. 133-134.)

Canada's future. By G. H. M. (In *The Week*. Toronto. v. 4, no. 49 (Nov. 3, 1887), pp. [783]-785.)

The Canadian Pacific Railway. (In *The Week*. Toronto. v. 2, no. 24 (May 14, 1885), p. 373.)

Canadian political issues. (In *The Week*. Toronto. v. 11, no. 40 (Aug. 31, 1894), pp. 941-942.)

CARLOS Disintegrating forces within Confederation. By Carlos. (In *The Week*. Toronto. v. 2, no. 28 (June 11, 1885), p. 437.)

—— Is Canada a British colony? By Carlos. (In *The Week*. Toronto. v. 2, no. 33 (July 16, 1885), pp. 517-518.)
Discusses the growing political influence of French Canadians.

CARMAN, ALBERT RICHARDSON The French-Canadian member of parliament. By A. R. Carman. (In *The Week*. Toronto. v. 7, no. 16 (Mar. 21, 1890), pp. 248-249.)

CAVEN, WILLIAM The Equal Rights movement. (In *University quarterly review*. Toronto. 2d quarter (June 1890), pp. 139-145.)

CHARLESWORTH, HECTOR WILLOUGHBY Lord Mount Stephen's great career. The story of his desperate and successful fight to build the Canadian Pacific Railroad. By Hector Charlesworth. (In *Saturday night*. Toronto. v. 37, no. 6 (Dec. 10, 1921), p. 2.)
Article occasioned by Stephen's death on November 30, 1921.

CHAUVEAU, PIERRE JOSEPH OLIVIER La nationalité franco-canadienne. Par Pierre-J.-O. Chauveau. (In *Le Canada-Français*. Québec. v. 2, (1889), pp. [129]-138.)

CHOQUETTE, PHILIPPE AUGUSTE (comp.) Discours prononcés à l'Assemblée législative de la province de Québec à l'appui des résolutions Joly par les Honbles Joly, Mercier, Ross et Irvine, et par MM. Flynn, Racicot et Chs. Langelier. Suivis de l'exposé financier de l'Hon. F. Langelier Trésorier-Provincial. Compilés par P. Aug. Choquette. Québec, Imprimé par Levy et Bouchard, 1879. 121 p.

The Joly resolution concerns the controversial issue raised over the action taken by Luc Letellier de St. Just as lieutenant-governor of Quebec in dismissing the Conservative government of Boucher de Boucherville.

CLARK, LOVELL CROSBY   Canadian federal politics in the year 1879. [Kingston, Ont., 1951] 149 leaves.

Thesis (MA) – Queen's University.

COLBY, CHARLES CARROLL   Tariff re-adjustment. Canada's National Policy. Tariff revision. By C. C. Colby. Montreal, 1878. 48 p.

COLLINS, JOSEPH EDMUND   Canada under the administration of Lord Lorne. Toronto, Rose Pub. Co., 1884. xv, 567 p. (Rose's Canadian national series, v. 3.)

——   The future of the Dominion of Canada. By Edmund Collins. (In Canadian Club of New York. Canadian leaves. New York, 1887. pp. [1]-17.)

——   Party evils and a remedy. By J. E. Collins. (In The Week. Toronto. v. 1, no. 42 (Sept. 18, 1884), p. 664.)

The Coming general election. By W. (In The Week. Toronto. v. 12, no. 10 (Feb. 1, 1895), p. 223.)

Held June 23, 1896.

The Coming session. (In The Week. Toronto. v. 10, no. 9 (Jan. 27, 1893), pp. 196-197.)

Discusses matters of importance coming before Parliament: tariff reform, trade relations with the United States, Manitoba schools question.

Commercial Union Club of Toronto. Handbook of Commercial Union; a collection of papers read before the Commercial Union Club, Toronto, with speeches, letters and other documents in favour of unrestricted reciprocity with the United States. Preceded by an introd. by Goldwin Smith. Edited by G. Mercer Adam. Toronto, Hunter, Rose, 1888. xxxvi, 294 p. map.

Completing the Confederation. (In The Week. Toronto. v. 12, no. 18 (Mar. 29, 1895), pp. 413-414.)

Discusses the admission of Newfoundland to complete the federation of the British North American colonies.

COOKE, ELLEN GILLIES   The federal election of 1896 in Manitoba. [Winnipeg] 1943. 219 leaves.

Thesis (MA) – University of Manitoba.

COOPER, JOHN IRWIN   The Canadian general elections of 1887. [London, Ont.] 1933. 177 leaves.

Thesis (MA) – University of Western Ontario.

CREIGHTON, DONALD GRANT   The cabinet of 1878. By Donald G. Creighton. (In Gibson, F. W. (ed.) Cabinet formation and bicultural relations [Ottawa, 1970] pp. [19]-36.)

CROSS, W. H.   Commercial union. (In The Week Toronto. v. 4, no. 43 (Sept. 22, 1887), pp. [687]-688.)

——   The unification of Canada. (In The Week. Toronto. v. 4, no. 41 (Sept. 8, 1887), pp. [655]-[656].)

Considers the issue of clericalism in Canada.

CYRIL   Is Confederation a success? By Cyril. (In The Week. Toronto. v. 7, no. 26 (May 30, 1890), pp. 406-407.)

——   Partyism. By Cyril. (In The Week. Toronto. v. 3, no. 3 (Dec. 17, 1885), pp. [35]-36.)

DAVID, LAURENT OLIVIER   Les deux grandes questions du jour. Par L.-O. David. (In L'Opinion publique. Montréal. v. 10, no. 5 (30 jan. 1879), p. [49].)

Concerns Canada's commercial relations with other countries and protection.

——   Le tarif. Par L.-O. David. (In L'Opinion publique. Montréal. v. 10, no. 14 (3 avril 1879), p. [157].)

DAWSON, ROBERT MAC GREGOR   The gerrymander of 1882. By R. MacGregor Dawson. (In The Canadian journal of economics and political science. [Toronto] v. 1 (1935), pp. 197-221.)

Examines this Act as an example of political manipulation, and as an illustration of contemporary political corruption, with a consideration of public reaction to this legislation.

DE CELLES, ALFRED DUCLOS   Echos de la capitale. Par A.-D. DeCelles. (In L'Opi-

nion publique. Montréal. v. 13, no. 7 (16 fév. 1882), p. [73].)

Summary of the opening of the fourth session of the fourth parliament.

—— Les élections fédérales. Par A. D. D. (In *L'Opinion publique*. Montréal. v. 13, no. 22 (1 juin 1882), p. [253].)

Held June 20, 1882.

—— L'éloquence française aux Communes. Par A.-D. DeCelles. (In *L'Opinion publique*. Montréal. v. 13, no. 9 (2 mars 1882), p. [97].)

Discusses the oratory of Laurier, Royal, Langevin, and others.

DEERING, RICHARD MAURICE FERGUSON The federal election of 1891 in Nova Scotia. [Halifax, N.S.] 1968. 1 v.

Thesis (MA) – Dalhousie University.

DELTA L'affaire Letellier. Par Delta. (In *L'Opinion publique*. Montréal. v. 10, no. 15 (10 avril 1879), p. [169].)

—— L'affaire Letellier. Par Delta. (In *L'Opinion publique*. Montréal. v. 10, no. 16 (17 avril 1879), p. [181].)

—— Echos d'Ottawa. Par Delta. (In *L'Opinion publique*. Montréal. v. 8, no. 18 (3 mai 1877), p. 215.)

Summarizes the session from a personal viewpoint.

—— Echos de la capitale. Par Delta. (In *L'Opinion publique*. Montréal. v. 8, no. 13 (29 mars 1877), p. 146.)

Comments on proceedings in Parliament.

—— Echos de la capitale. Par Delta. (In *L'Opinion publique*. Montréal. v. 9, no. 8 (21 fév. 1878), pp. [85]-86.)

Summarizes proceedings in Parliament. Dated Feb. 12, 1878.

—— Echos parlementair[es]. Par Delta. (In *L'Opinion publique*. Montréal. v. 9, no. 14 (4 avril 1878), p. [157].)

Summarizes proceedings in Parliament. Dated March 26, 1878.

—— Echos parlementaires. Par Delta. (In *L'Opinion publique*. Montréal. v. 9, no. 15 (11 avril 1878), p. [169].)

Summarizes proceedings in Parliament. Dated April 2, 1878.

—— Echos parlementaires. Par Delta. (In *L'Opinion publique*. Montréal. v. 9, no. 16 (18 avril 1878), pp. [181]-182.)

Concerns the question of the lieutenant-governor in Quebec, with reference to Luc Letellier de St. Just and his dismissal of the

Boucher de Boucherville government March 2, 1878.

Dated April 13, 1878.

—— Echos parlementaires. Par Delta. (In *L'Opinion publique*. Montréal. v. 9, no. 17 (25 avril 1878), p. [193].)

Brief remarks on the Laflamme bill, the issue over the lieutenant-governor raised by the action of M. Letellier in Quebec, etc.

Dated April 20, 1878.

Les Derniers jours de la session. (In *L'Opinion publique*. Montréal. v. 10, no. 21 (22 mai 1879), p. [241].)

Summarizes the end of the first session, fourth parliament.

Diagramme de la Chambre des Communes. Sièges occupés par les membres. (In *L'Opinion publique*. Montréal. v. 10, no. 9 (27 fév. 1879), p. 102.)

Diagram (plan) of the first session of the fourth parliament.

DRAKE, EARL GORDON Pioneer journalism in Saskatchewan 1878-1887. Part I: The founding of the Territorial press. By Earl G. Drake. (In *Saskatchewan history*. Saskatoon. v. 5, no. 1 (winter 1952), pp. 17-27.)

Includes comments on the general political attitudes held by the press. Discusses the journalistic career of Nicholas Flood Davin.

Based on the Author's MA thesis, "The Territorial press in the region of present-day Saskatchewan", University of Saskatchewan, 1951.

—— Pioneer journalism in Saskatchewan 1878-1887. Part II: Some characteristics of the Territorial press. By Earl G. Drake. (In *Saskatchewan history*. Saskatoon. v. 5, no. 2 (spring 1952), pp. 41-54.)

Includes discussion on general political attitudes.

DUNN, OSCAR La dernière crise à Québec. (In *L'Opinion publique*. Montréal. v. 5, no. 40 (1 oct. 1874), p. 489; v. 5, no. 41 (8 oct. 1874), p. 501.)

In two parts.

Examines the issue over powers exercised by the lieutenant-governor.

EAYRS, CATHERINE ELIZABETH (LOFFT) The election of 1896 in western Ontario [London, Ont.] 1951. 1 v.

Thesis (MA) – University of Western Ontario.

EDGAR, SIR JAMES DAVID Titles of honour in Canada. By J. D. Edgar. (In *University quarterly review*. Toronto. 1st quarter (Feb. 1890), pp. 98-104.)

Les Elections. (In *L'Opinion publique*. Montréal. v. 13, no. 24 (15 juin 1882), p. 287.)

List of members elected by acclamation and candidates nominated in the province of Quebec for the general elections of June 20, 1882.

Les Elections. (In *L'Opinion publique*. Montréal. v. 13, no. 25 (22 juin 1882), p. 299.)

List of members elected in Quebec during the general elections held June 20, 1882.

Elections fédérales de 1896. Quelques faits soumis aux électeurs du Canada. [n.p.] 1895. 112 p.

EVANS, WILLIAM SANFORD The Canadian Club movement. (In *The Canadian magazine of politics, science, art and literature*. Toronto, v. 2, (1893/94), pp. [22]-25.)

FORSEY, EUGENE ALFRED A note on the Dominion factory bills of the eighteen-eighties. (In *The Canadian journal of economics and political science*. Toronto. v. 13 (1947), pp. 580-583.)

FOSTER, WILLIAM ALEXANDER Canada First; a memorial of the late William A. Foster. With introd. by Goldwin Smith. Toronto, Hunter, Rose, 1890. iv, 221 p.

Partial contents: Canada First; an address. – Address of the Canadian National Association. – Address to the Canadian National Association. – Party versus principle. – The Canadian confederacy. – The Canadian confederation and the Reciprocity Treaty.

The future of Canada. (In *The Week*. Toronto, v. 10, no. 8 (Jan. 20, 1893), pp. 172-173.)

GELINAS, AIMEE Le bill de M. Girouard. Par A. Gélinas. (In *L'Opinion publique*. Montréal. v. 11, no. 15 (8 avril 1880), p. 170.)

The Girouard bill dealt with marriages between brothers- and sisters-in-law.

—— Canadiens-Français et Anglais. Par A. Gélinas. (In *L'Opinion publique*. Montréal. v. 11, no. 4 (22 jan. 1880), pp. [37]-38.)

Discusses patronage in the federal government favouring English-speaking Canadians.

—— Les conséquences. Par A. Gélinas. (In *L'Opinion publique*. Montréal. v. 10, no. 32 (7 août 1879), pp. [373]-374.)

Summarizes the constitutional consequences of the Letellier affair.

—— La crise. Par A. Gélinas. (In *L'Opinion publique*. Montréal. v. 10, no. 39 (25 sept. 1879), pp. [457]-458.)

Discusses the issue of "better terms" for the provinces, especially with reference to Quebec.

—— L'indépendance commerciale. Par A. Gélinas. (In *L'Opinion publique*. Montréal. v. 10, no. 21 (22 mai 1879), p. [241].)

—— La langue français à Ottawa. Par A. Gélinas. (In *L'Opinion publique*. Montréal. v. 11, no. 21 (20 mai 1880), pp. [241]-242.)

Advocates the use of the French language when writing to officials in the federal government.

—— Le marquis de Lorne et les Canadiens-Français. Par A. Gélinas. (In *L'Opinion publique*. Montréal. v. 10, no. 25 (19 juin 1879), p. 290.)

—— La politique en action. Par A. Gélinas. (In *L'Opinion publique*. Montréal. v. 11, no. 1 (1 jan. 1880), pp. [1]-2.)

Answers the criticisms appearing in *L'Eclaireur* of the Author's article Politique pratique (In *L'Opinion publique*. Montréal. v. 10, no. 48 (27 nov. 1879), pp. [565]-566.)

—— La politique pratique. Par A. Gélinas. (In *L'Opinion publique*. Montréal. v. 10, no. 48 (27 nov. 1879), pp. [565]-566.)

Considers the work of Leonard Tilley as Minister of Finance.

—— Pratique et théorie. Par A. Gélinas. (In *L'Opinion publique*. Montréal. v. 10, no. 50 (11 déc. 1879), p. 589].)

Comments on a critical review appearing in *La Patrie* of the Author's article Politique pratique (In *L'Opinion publique*. Montréal. v. 10, no. 48 (27 nov. 1879), pp. [565]-566.) Compares and discusses the qualities of Leonard Tilley and Richard Cartwright.

—— La royauté en Canada. Par A. Gélinas. (In *L'Opinion publique*. Montréal. v. 9, no. 50 (12 déc. 1878), p. [589].)

With reference to the Marquis of Lorne.

—— Semaine parlementaire. Par A. Gélinas. (In *L'Opinion publique*. Montréal. v. 11, no. 10 (4 mars 1880), pp. [109]-110.)

A summary of proceedings in Parliament.

Concerns the question of settling the north-west boundary of Ontario, etc.

—— La session. Par A. Gélinas. (In *L'Opinion publique*. Montréal. v. 11. no. 8—no. 19 (19 fév.—6 mai 1880).)

Nos. 9, 10, 13, and 19 have title: *Semaine parlementaire*.

Summarizes proceedings during the second session of the fourth parliament held February 12 to May 7, 1880.

—— La session. Par A. Gélinas. (In *L'Opinion publique*. Montréal. v. 11, no. 12 (18 mars 1880), p. [133].)

Summary of proceedings in Parliament.

Comments on the budget of Sir Leonard Tilley, the Girouard bill concerning marriage between brothers- and sisters-in-law, etc.

—— La session. Par A. Gélinas. (In *L'Opinion publique*. Montréal. v. 11, no. 15 (8 avril 1880), p. [169].)

A summary of proceedings in Parliament. Concerns mainly the Girouard bill on marriage between brothers- and sisters-in-law.

—— La session. Par A. Gélinas. (In *L'Opinion publique*. Montréal. v. 11, no. 17 (22 avril 1880), pp. [193]-194.)

A summary of proceedings in Parliament. Concerns the Girouard bill, etc.

—— La session. Par A. Gélinas. (In *L'Opinion publique*. Montréal. v. 11, no. 18 (29 avril 1880), p. [205].)

A summary of proceedings in Parliament. Concerns an amendment to railway legislation proposed by Edward Blake, etc.

GOSNELL, R. EDWARD British Columbia politically. By R. E. Gosnell. (In *The Lake magazine*. [Toronto] v. 1, no. 5 (De. 1892), pp. [271]-276.)

Concerns the position of British Columbia in the Canadian confederation.

Government in the Territories. By E. (In *The Week*. Toronto. v. 6, no. 9 (Feb. 1, 1889), pp. 136-137.)

The Governors general. The Marquis of Lorne (1878-1883), (In *Canada month*. Montreal. v. 6, no. 5 (May 1966), p. 18. illus.)

GRANT, GEORGE MONRO Canada and the Canadian question. By G. M. Grant. (In *The Week*. Toronto. v. 8, no. 22 (May 1, 1891), pp. 348-350; v. 8, no. 24 (May 15, 1891), pp. 380-382.)

In two parts.

A review article of *Canada and the Canadian question*, by G. Smith. Toronto, Hunter, Rose, 1891.

——Canada first. (In Canadian Club of New York. *Canadian leaves*. New York, 1887. pp. [247]-267.)

—— Canada first. By Principal George Munro [sic] Grant. (In Locke, G. H. (ed.) *Builders of the Canadian commonwealth*. Freeport, N.Y. [1967] pp. 191-195.)

Excerpt from an address to the Canadian Club of New York City, 1887.

—— Canada's present position and outlook. By Principal Geo. M. Grant. (In Rose-Belford's *Canadian monthly and national review*. Toronto. v. 5 (1880), pp. 196-210.)

—— Our national objects and aims. (In National Club of Toronto. *Maple leaves*. Toronto [1891] pp. [1]-34.)

HAM, GEORGE HENRY More political memoirs: further stories of the Solons of the eighties. By Col. George H. Ham. (In *MacLean's magazine*. Toronto. v. 34, no. 5 (Mar. 1, 1921), p. 21.)

—— Solons of the eighties. By Colonel George H. Ham. (In *MacLean's magazine*. Toronto. v. 34, no. 4 (Feb. 15, 1921), pp. 27-29; 43-44. ports.)

Reminiscences about political personalities: Sir J. A. Macdonald, E. Blake, W. Laurier, Sir G. Foster, etc.

HEATON, ERNEST Canada's problems. Toronto, The Week Pub. Co., 1895. 86 p.

HENDERSON, THOMAS CHALMERS Manitoba and the National Policy. (In *The Week*. Toronto. v. 12, no. 52 (Nov. 22, 1895), pp. 1235-1236.)

—— The new N. P. (In *The Week*. Toronto. v. 11, no. 11 (Feb. 9, 1894), p. 246-247.)

Discusses the new National Policy.

HINCKS, SIR FRANCIS The political destiny of Canada. (In *The Canadian monthly and national review*. Toronto. v. 12 (1878), pp. 56-66.)

—— The political destiny of Canada. (In Rose-Belford's *Canadian monthly and national review*. Toronto. v. 2 (1879), pp. 170-182.)

The Author discusses the differences he holds with Goldwin Smith over Canadian issues.

HOCHELAGA Are French Canadian special privileges secured under treaty? By Hochelaga. (In *The Week*. Toronto. v. 4, no. 46 (Oct. 13, 1887), p. 737.)

HODSON, IAN ALBERT   Commercial Union, unrestricted reciprocity and the background of the election of 1891. [London, Ont., 1950] 414 leaves.

Thesis (MA) – University of Western Ontario.

HOPKINS, JOHN CASTELL   Lord and Lady Aberdeen. By J. Castell Hopkins. (In *The Canadian magazine of politics, science, art and literature*. Toronto. v. 2 (1893/ 94), pp. [171]-177.)

—— The position of Canada. By J. Castell Hopkins. (In *The Week*. Toronto. v. 9, no. 17 (Mar. 25, 1892), pp. 262-264.)

Jacobinism in Canada. By M. J. F. (In *The Week*. Toronto. v. 3, no. 15 (Mar. 11, 1886), pp. 228-229.)

JEFFERSON, H. B.   The great Pooh-Bah case. (In *The Atlantic advocate*. Fredericton, N.B. v. 54, no. 1 (Sept. 1963), pp. 45-51.)

Concerns John Thomas Hawke, editor of the *Moncton Transcript* and the controversial returns from Westmorland County, N.B., in the federal election held June 20, 1882.

The Jesuit claims. (In *The Week*. Toronto. v. 4, no. 14 (Mar. 3, 1887), p. 215.)

JOLY DE LOTBINIERE, SIR HENRI GUSTAVE   Mr. Joly's mission to London in the case of Lieutenant-Governor Letellier de Saint-Just. (In *The Canadian historical review*. v. 31 (1950), pp. 401-405.)

Introductory remarks by A. Joly de Lotbinière: pp. 401-402.

Joly's interview with Sir Michael Hicks Beach, Colonial Secretary, May 6, 1879: pp. 402-404.

Interview with Mr. Gladstone: pp. 404-405.

KENNEDY, DOUGLAS ROSS   The Knights of Labor in Canada. London, University of Western Ontario, 1956. 127 leaves.

Cover title.

Thesis (MA) – University of Western Ontario, 1945.

LAMPORT, W. A.   Is the Baptist position in reference to the Manitoba school question consistent? (In *The McMaster University monthly*. Toronto. v. 5, (Apr. 1896), pp. 296-304.)

Considers the issue of the relations between Church and State.

LANDON, FRED   The Canadian scene, 1880-1890. (In Canadian Historical Associa-

tion. *Report of the annual meeting*. Toronto. (1942), pp. 5-18.)

Presidential address.

LAPATRIE, C.   Le libéralisme-catholique et les élections du 23 juin, 1896. Québec, 1896. 76 p.

LAREAU, EDMOND   Libéraux et conservateurs. Montréal, En vente chez les libraires, 1879. 44 p.

LAURENDEAU, ANDRE   Deux républicains canadiens au 19ᵉ siècle. (In *L'Action nationale*. Montréal. v. 32 (nov. 1948), pp. [188]-208.)

Discusses the ideas of Honoré Mercier and Joseph Royal.

LAURISTON, VICTOR   Hot times in Haldimand. (In *Willisons monthly*. Sarnia, Ont. v. 5, no. 3 (Sept. 1929), pp. 17-18.)

Describes a political duel, involving three contested by-elections between Charles Wesley Colter (Liberal) and Walter Humphries Montague (Conservative). First by-election held November 12, 1887; second election held January 30, 1889; third and final election held February 20, 1890.

LAWDER, ROBERT H.   Reciprocity between the United States and Canada. [Part] III. (In *The Week*. Toronto. v. 10, no. 36 (Aug. 4, 1893), pp. 846-848.)

The third article considers the political policy of the reciprocity issue.

—— The reciprocity conference. (In *The Week*. Toronto. v. 10, no. 12 (Feb. 17, 1893), pp. 169-270.)

LEMIEUX, RODOLPHE   Blake—Chapleau—Laurier. Par l'honorable Rodolphe Lemieux. (In Royal Society of Canada. *Proceedings and transactions*. Ottawa. ser. 3, v. 21 (1927), section 1, pp. 51-65.)

"Lu à la réunion de mai, 1927."

LITTLE, JOHN IRVINE   The federal election of 1896 in New Brunswick. [Fredericton, N.B.] 1970 [c1971] vi, 262 leaves.

Thesis (MA) – University of New Brunswick.

LONGLEY, JAMES WILBERFORCE   Commercial union. By J. W. Longley. (In *The Week*. Toronto. v. 4, no. 46 (Oct. 13, 1887), p. 736; v. 4, no. 48 (Oct. 27, 1887), p. [767]; v. 4, no. 50 (Nov. 10, 1887), pp. [799]-800.)

In three parts.

—— The future of Canada. By J. W. Longley. (In Rose-Belford's *Canadian monthly and national review.* Toronto. v. 8 (1882), pp. 147-154.)

A discourse taken mainly from the constitutional and political point of view. Argues against the "British connection", and Americanization and for Canada as an "independent" state.

—— The future of Canada. By Hon. J. W. Longley, Attorney-General of Nova Scotia. (In *The Lake magazine.* [Toronto] v. 1, no. 2 (Sept. 1892), pp. [65]-72.)

—— Is Confederation a success? By the Hon. J. W. Longley. (In *The Week.* Toronto. v. 2, no. 47 (Oct. 22, 1885), pp. 740-742; v. 2, no. 50 (Nov. 12, 1885), pp. 789-790.)

In two parts.

—— Party in politics. By J. W. Longley. (In *The Week.* Toronto. v. 11, no. 6 (Jan. 5, 1894), pp. 126-127.)

—— Party politics. By J. W. Longley. (In *The Week.* Toronto. v. 1, no. 37 (Aug. 14, 1884), pp. 583-584.)

—— The political situation. By J. W. Longley. (In *The Week.* Toronto. v. 9, no. 31 (July 1, 1892), p. 488; v. 9, no. 32 (July 8, 1892), p. 501; v. 9, no. 33 (July 15, 1892), pp. 519-520; v. 9, no. 39 (Aug. 26, 1892), p. 613.)

In four parts.

—— Public opinion. By J. W. Longley. (In *The Week.* Toronto. v. 8, no. 34 (July 24, 1891), p. 541.)

LORNE, JOHN GEORGE EDWARD HENRY DOUGLAS SUTHERLAND CAMPBELL, MARQUIS OF Memories of Canada and Scotland. Speeches and verses by the Right Hon. the Marquis of Lorne. Montreal, Dawson Bros., 1884 [c1883] xi, 360 p.

"Speeches and addresses" delivered in Canada: pp. [179]-360.

—— L'opinion du marquis de Lorne sur la question Letellier. (In *L'Opinion publique.* Montréal. v. 10, no. 47 (20 nov. 1879), pp. 556-557.)

Text of a letter from the Marquis of Lorne to Sir Michael Hicks-Beach dated April 9, 1879.

Translated into French.

MABLE, THORPE The budget debate. By Thorpe Mable [pseud.] (In *The Week.* Toronto. v. 2, no. 16 (Mar. 19, 1885), p. 247.)

—— The budget of 1885-6. By Thorpe Mable [pseud.] (In *The Week.* Toronto.

v. 2, no. 15 (Mar. 12, 1885), pp. 229-230.)

The budget of Sir Leonard Tilley.

MC DONNELL, WILLIAM The cost of government in Canada. By W. McDonnell, Lindsay. (In Rose-Belford's *Canadian monthly and national review.* Toronto. v. 4 (1880), pp. 173-177.)

The Author was mayor of the town of Lindsay, Ont. from 1866 to 1868.

The Machine at Ottawa. By L. N. (In *The Week.* Toronto. v. 4, no. 44 (Sept. 29, 1887), pp. [703]-704.)

MC INNES, WILLIAM WALLACE BURNS Combines. By W. W. B. McInnes. (In *The Week.* Toronto. v. 8, no. 8 (Jan. 23, 1891), pp. 121-122.)

Discusses the topic as raised by N. C. Wallace and J. D. Edgar in Parliament.

MACKENZIE, GEORGE ALLEN Nationalism and reaction. By G. A. Mackenzie. (In *The Canadian monthly and national review.* Toronto. v. 12 (1878), pp. 594-601.)

Discusses the issues of a "Canadian nationality" from the viewpoints, especially, of Sir John Macdonald and Edward Blake.

MAC KIRDY, KENNETH A. The loyalty issue in the 1891 federal election campaign, and an ironic footnote. By K. A. MacKirdy. (In *Ontario history.* [Toronto] v. 55, no. 3 (Sept. 1963), pp. [143]-154. illus.)

—— National vs. provincial loyalty: the Ontario Western boundary dispute, 1883-1884. (In *Ontario history.* Toronto. v. 51, no. 3 (summer 1959), pp. [161]-198.)

MC LAUGHLIN, KENNETH MICHAEL The Canadian general election of 1896 in Nova Scotia. [Halifax, 1967] 1 v.

Thesis (MA) – Dalhousie University.

MAC LEAN, GUY ROBERTSON The Canadian offer of troops for Hong Kong, 1894. (In *The Canadian historical review.* Toronto. v. 38 (1957), pp. 275-283.)

MACLEAN, JOHN The alliance of democracy and protection. (In Rose-Belford's *Canadian monthly and national review.* Toronto. v. 2 (1879), pp. 723-727.)

—— Two of a trade. (In *The Week.* Toronto. v. 1, no. 9 (Jan. 31, 1884), pp. 135-136.)

Concerns Canadian tariff policy.

MC NAUGHT, KENNETH WILLIAM KIRKPATRICK The *Globe* and Canadian liberalism, 1880-1890. Toronto, 1946. 311 leaves.

Thesis (MA) – University of Toronto.

MAC NUTT, WILLIAM STEWART Days of Lorne. From the private papers of the Marquis of Lorne, 1878-1883, in the possession of the Duke of Argyll at Inveraray Castle, Scotland. Fredericton, N.B., Brunswick Press [1955] x, 262 p.

At head of title: Impressions of a governor-general.

—— The 1880s. By W. S. MacNutt. (In Careless, J. M. S. (ed.) The Canadians, 1867-1967. Toronto. 1967. pp. 70-107.)

MAY, J. The opening of Parliament. (In The Week. Toronto. v. 12, no. 22 (Apr. 26, 1895), p. 514.)

The opening of the fifth session of the seventh parliament.

MERCIER, HONORE L'avenir du Canada. Discours prononcé au Parc Sohmer à Montréal le 4 avril 1893. Par L'honorable Honoré Mercier. Montréal, Cie d'impr. et de Lithographie Gebhardt-Berthiaume, 1893. 91 p.

MILWARD, HENRY Politics and society at Ottawa. (In The Week. Toronto. v. 1, no. 19 (Apr. 10, 1884), pp. 297-298.)

A Minority government. By F. T. F. W. (In The Week. Toronto. v. 7, no. 14 (Mar. 7, 1890), p. 213.)

Discusses the existing system of government in the North West Territories.

MITCHELL, HARVEY Canada's negotiations with Newfoundland, 1887-1895. (In The Canadian historical review. Toronto. v. 40 (1959), pp. 277-293.)

A discussion of the Confederation issue during the years 1887-95.

MONTGOMERY, MALCOLM The Six Nations Indians and the Macdonald franchise. (In Ontario History. Toronto. v. 57, no. 1 (Mar. 1965), pp. [13]-25.)

"This paper was read before a meeting of the Institute of Iroquoian Studies, Renison College, University of Waterloo, Nov. 1964."

Refers to the Electoral Franchise Act passed July 4, 1885 and its subsequent repeal under the provisions of the Franchise Act passed June 13, 1898.

Multi-partyism in politics. (In The Week. Toronto. v. 12, no. 14 (Mar. 1, 1895), pp. 317-318.)

MURRAY, JOHN CLARK Personal vs. local representation. By J. Clark Murray. (In The Week. Toronto. v. 9, no. 28 (June 10, 1892), p. 438.)

Concerns the Redistribution Bill, at that time, before the House of Commons.

NATIONAL CLUB OF TORONTO Maple leaves. Being the papers read before the National Club of Toronto at the "National Evenings" during the winter 1890-1891. Toronto [introd. 1891] 136 p.

Contents: Our national objects and aims, by G. Grant. – Responsible government in Canada, by J. G. Bourinot. – The commercial marine of Canada, by C. H. Tupper. – Canadian nationality, by J. Young.

National Policy. By M. (In The Week. Toronto. v. 3, no. 8 (Jan. 21, 1886), p. 116.)

National Policy. By M. (In The Week. Toronto. v. 3, no. 10 (Feb. 4, 1886), p. 148.)

NORRIS, WILLIAM A review of political parties in Canada, from a Canadian standpoint. (In Rose-Belford's Canadian monthly and national review. Toronto. v. 6 (1881), pp. 614-620.)

Nouvelles de la Chambre. (In L'Opinion publique. Montréal. v. 10, no. 17 (24 avril 1879), p. 194.)

A summary of proceedings in Parliament.

NOVA SCOTIAN Elections in Nova Scotia. By Nova Scotian. (In The Week. Toronto. v. 4, no. 15 (Mar. 10, 1887), pp. 234-235.)

Relates to the general elections held February 22, 1887.

OBSERVER Some features of Canadian journalism. By Observer. (In The Week. Toronto. v. 1, no. 46 (Oct. 16, 1884), pp. 728-729.)

Concerns Canadian political journalism.

OLIVER, EDMUND HENRY The contest between Lieutenant-Governor Royal and the Legislative Assembly of the North West Territories, 1888-1893. By Edmund H. Oliver. (In Royal Society of Canada. Proceedings and transactions. Ottawa. ser. 3, v. 17 (1923), section 2, pp. 81-118.)

"Read May meeting, 1923."

Refers to Joseph Royal.

OSTRY, BERNARD Conservatives, Liberals, and labour in the 1880's. (In The Canadian journal of economics and political science. [Toronto] v. 27 (1961), pp. 141-161.)

Examines the attitude of the two federal political parties towards the young labour movement in Canada.

Our system of government. (In The Week. Toronto. v. 12, no. 21 (Apr. 19, 1895), pp. 485-486.)

Parish politics. (In *The Week*. Toronto. v. 12, no. 50 (Nov. 8, 1895), p. 1186.)
Comments on the nature of Canadian politics.

Parlement fédéral. Ouverture de la 1ère session du 4ème parlement. (In *L'Opinion publique*. Montréal. v. 10, no. 8 (20 fév. 1879), p. [85].)

Parliament and the railways. (In *The Week*. Toronto. v. 12, no. 24 (May 10, 1895), pp. 558-559.)

PEDLEY, HUGH   The study of Canadian politics. By the Rev. Hugh Pedley. (In Rose-Belford's *Canadian monthly and national review*. Toronto. v. 8 (1882), pp. 361-369.)

The Progress of the national idea. By a Canadian nationalist. (In *The Week*. Toronto. v. 1, no. 27 (June 5, 1884), pp. 421-422.)

The Provincial premiers and the veto question. By S. (In *The Week*. Toronto. v. 4, no. 52 (Nov. 24, 1887), pp. [831]-832.)

The Purification of politics. (In *The Week*. Toronto. v. 12, no. 5 (Dec. 28, 1894), p. 101.)

The Quebec agitation. By L. (In *The Week*. Toronto. v. 3, no. 1 (Dec. 3, 1885), pp. [3]-4).

READ, DAVID BREAKENRIDGE   French domination or British liberty? By D. B. Read. (In *The Week*. Toronto. v. 1, no. 33 (July 17, 1884), p. 519.)

REGEHR, THEODORE DAVID   The National Policy and Manitoba railway legislation, 1879-1888. [Kingston, Ont.] 1963. 1 v.
Thesis (MA) – Carleton University.

The Revolt against party. (In *The Week*. Toronto. v. 4, no. 16 (Mar. 17, 1887), pp. [247]-248.)

ROSS, PHILIP DANSKEN   Fair play for French Canadians, By P. D. Ross. (In *The Week*. Toronto. v. 2, no. 30 (June 25, 1885), pp. 469-470.)

ROYAL, JOSEPH   Le socialisme aux Etats-Unis et en Canada. (In Royal Society of Canada. *Proceedings and transactions*. Ottawa. [ser. 1] v. 12 (1894), section 1, pp. 49-61.)
"Lu le 23 mai 1894."

RUMILLY, ROBERT   Les "Castors". Montréal, B. Valiquette [1941] 241 p. (His *Histoire de la province de Québec*, 4.)
A political history covering the years 1882-1885.

—— Chapleau. Montréal, B. Valiquette [1941] 211 p. (His *Histoire de la province de Québec*, 3.)
A political history covering the years 1880-1881.

—— L. O. Taillon. 2. éd., rev. et augm. Montréal, B. Valiquette. [1942] 284 p. (His *Histoire de la province de Québec*, 7.)
A political history covering the years 1892-1895.

—— Les "nationaux". 2. éd. Montréal, B. Valiquette [1942] 350 p. (His *Histoire de la province de Québec*, 6.)
A political history covering the years 1888-1891.

—— Riel. Montréal, B. Valiquette [1942] 315 p. (His *Histoire de la province de Québec*, 5.)
A political history covering the years 1885-1888.

RUTHVEN, ED   The opening of Parliament. (In *The Week*. Toronto. v. 2, no. 10 (Feb. 5, 1885), p. 152.)
Concerns the third session of the fifth parliament.

—— Ottawa notes. (In *The Week*. Toronto. v. 1, no. 11 (Feb. 14, 1884), p. 168.)
Comments on the debate on the Canadian Pacific Railway resolutions.

—— Ottawa notes. (In *The Week*. Toronto. v. 1, no. 12 (Feb. 21, 1884), p. 186.)
Discusses the lobbying involved in the Canadian Pacific Loan resolution before the House.

—— Ottawa notes. (In *The Week*. Toronto. v. 1, no. 13 (Feb. 28, 1884), p. 200.)
Concerns the issue of the government granting a loan to the Canadian Pacific Railway Company.

—— Ottawa notes. (In *The Week*. Toronto. v. 1, no. 18 (Apr. 3, 1884), p. 282.)
Discusses the debates on a motion for Committee of Supply.

—— Ottawa notes. (In *The Week*. Toronto. v. 1, no. 20 (Apr. 17, 1884), pp. 312-313.)
Discusses the revival of the North Shore railway question.

RYAN, CARROLL   Political morality. (In Rose-Belford's *Canadian monthly and national review*. Toronto. v. 3 (1879), pp. 402-410.)

SAYWELL, JOHN TUPPER   The 1890s. By John T. Saywell. (In Careless, J. M. S. (ed.) *The Canadians, 1867-1967*. Toronto, 1967 pp. 108-136.)

SHEPPARD, EDMUND ERNEST   Around town. By Don [pseud.] (In *Toronto Saturday night.* Toronto. v. 8, no. 23 (Apr. 27, 1895), pp. [1]-2.)

Discusses the opening of the 5th session, 7th parliament, Lord and Lady Aberdeen, etc.

SMITH, GOLDWIN   Canada and the Canadian question. London, Macmillan, 1891 x, 325 p.

Also published Toronto, Hunter Rose, 1891.

—— Commercial union. (In *The Week.* Toronto. v. 3, no. 9 (Jan. 28, 1886), pp. [131]-132.)

—— Current events and opinions. By a Bystander. (In *The Week.* Toronto. v. 1, no. 1—v. 2, no. 5 (Dec. 6, 1883—Jan. 1, 1885.)

Aug. 14, 1884—Jan. 1, 1885, called " 'Bystander' on current events and opinions".

—— Papers, by a Bystander. no. 1. (In Rose-Belford's *Canadian monthly and national review.* Toronto. v. 2 (1879), pp. 108-119.)

Discussion of the impact of the National Policy on the Liberal and Conservative parties: pp. 113-117.

—— Papers, by a Bystander. no. 2. (In Rose-Belford's *Canadian monthly and national review.* Toronto. v. 2 (1879), pp. 230-248.)

Discussion of Canadian affairs: pp. 242-248.

—— Papers, by a Bystander. no. 3. (In Rose-Belford's *Canadian monthly and national review.* Toronto. v. 2 (1879), pp. 359-373.)

Discussion of Canadian affairs: pp. 368-373.

—— The Scott Act in Halton. (In *The Week.* Toronto. v. 5, no. 15 (Mar. 8, 1888), p. 230.)

STANLEY, GEORGE FRANCIS GILMAN   Further documents relating to the union of Newfoundland and Canada, 1886-1895. By George F. G. Stanley. (In *The Canadian historical review.* Toronto. v. 29 (1948), pp. 370-386.)

The State of the liquor law. (In *The Week.* Toronto. v. 3, no. 10 (Feb. 14, 1886), pp. [147]-148.)

STREET, WILLIAM PURVIS ROCHFORT   The Commission of 1885 to the North-West Territories. (In *The Canadian historical review.* Toronto. v. 25 (1944), pp. 38-53.)

An account of the proceedings of the Commission by W. P. R. Street who was appointed chairman: pp. 41-53.

Edited, with an introduction, by H. H. Langton.

STUART, CHARLES ALLAN   The national state. (In *The Canadian magazine of politics, science, art and literature.* Toronto. v. 1 (1893), pp. [85]-92.)

SUTHERLAND, JOHN CAMPBELL   The free trade issue. By J. C. Sutherland. (In *The Week.* Toronto. v. 9, no. 38 (Aug. 19, 1892), pp. 597-598.)

Tangled political economy. (In *The Week.* Toronto. v. 11, no. 25 (May 18, 1894), p. 581.)

Discusses the general implications of Anti-Combines legislation.

The Tariff debate. (In *The Week.* Toronto. v. 11, no. 21 (Apr. 20, 1894), pp. 485-486.)

Tariff reform. (In *The Week.* Toronto. v. 10, no. 12 (Feb. 17, 1893), pp. 268-269.)

TENNANT, GLENN ROBERT   The policy of the *Mail*, 1882-1892. Toronto, 1946. 285 leaves.

Thesis (MA) – University of Toronto.

TESSIER, ALBERT   Correspondance Taché-Laflèche. (In *Les Cahiers des dix.* Montréal. no. 23 (1958), pp. [241]-260.)

The correspondence between A. A. Taché and L. F. R. Laflèche extends over the years, 1859-1886. Deals, primarily, with the question of ultramontanism and the Riel rebellion of 1885.

THOMPSON, JOANNE EMILY   The influence of Dr. Emily Howard Stowe on the woman suffrage movement in Canada. (In *Ontario history.* [Toronto] v. 54, no. 4 (Dec. 1962), pp. [253]-266.)

Dr. Stowe organized the Dominion Woman Suffrage Association in 1893.

THOMPSON, THOMAS PHILLIPS   The Orange revolt. By Phillips Thompson. (In *The Week.* Toronto. v. 6, no. 35 (Aug. 2, 1889), pp. 554-555.)

Too much partyism. By G. C. C. (In *The Week.* Toronto. v. 2, no. 25 (May 21, 1885), p. 390.)

The Trade relations of Canada in connection with reciprocity. By J. B. (In *The Week.* Toronto. v. 7, no. 17 (Mar. 28, 1890), pp. 261-262.)

TRANT, WILLIAM Party government. (In *The Week*. Toronto. v. 8, no. 29 (June 19, 1891), pp. 458-459.)

TREMBLAY, ERNEST L'Affaire Letellier et la Constitution. Montréal, 1879. 24 p.

TROOP, CARTER Canadian opinion. (In *The Week*. Toronto. v. 4, no. 21 (Apr. 21, 1887), pp. [331]-332.)
Discusses the desirability and growth of a national opinion.

VANASSE, FABIEN A la veillée. (In *L'Opinion publique*. Montréal. v. 10, no. 7 (13 fév. 1879), pp. [73]-74.)
Remarks made before the opening of Parliament. Concerns mainly the question of protection.

―― A la veillée. (In *L'Opinion publique*. Montréal. v. 10, no. 9 (27 fév. 1879), pp. 98; 100.)
A review of the first two weeks of the first session, fourth parliament.

―― A la veillée. (In *L'Opinion publique*. Montréal. v. 10, no. 19 (8 mai 1879), pp. [217]-218.)
Includes comments on issues discussed in Parliament: constitutional questions relating to Quebec, protection, etc.

WADE, FREDERICK COATE The C.P.R. contract and monopoly. By F. C. W. [i.e. Frederick Coate Wade?] (In *The Week*. Toronto. v. 4, no. 47 (Oct. 20, 1887), pp. 752-753.)

―― The late United States consul Taylor; a true friend of Canada. By F. C. Wade. (In *The Week*. Toronto. v. 10, no. 27 (June 2, 1893), pp. 633-635.)
Deals with James Wickes Taylor.

―― Our moral obligations to the C.P.R. By F. C. W. [i.e. Frederick Coate Wade?] (In *The Week*. Toronto. v. 5, no. 6 (Jan. 5, 1888), pp. [83]-84.)

WALLACE, WILLIAM BERNARD Our bribery laws ineffective. By Wm. B. Wallace. (In *The Week*. Toronto. v. 8, no. 17 (Mar. 27, 1891), pp. 267-268.)

WARD, NORMAN MC QUEEN The raising of pigs by lieutenant-governors. By Norman Ward. (In *The Dalhousie review*. Halifax. v. 29 (1949/50), pp. [153]-156.)
Illustrates a "not unimportant point concerning the prerogatives of the Crown in the provinces . . ." Deals, humorously, with a debate in the Commons May 16, 1883, over the building of stables for the lieutenant-governor of Manitoba.

WATT, JAMES T. Anti-Catholic nativism in Canada: the Protestant Protective Association. (In *The Canadian historical review*. Toronto. v. 48 (1967), pp. 45-58.)

WELLS, JAMES EDWARD The anti-Jesuit agitation. By J. E. Wells. (In *The Week*. Toronto. v. 6, no. 15 (Mar. 15, 1889), p. 229.)

―― The Jesuits' Estates Act. By J. E. Wells. (In *The Week*. Toronto. v. 6, no. 17 (Mar. 29, 1889), p. 261.)

WICKSTEED, RICHARD J. Voting by command. (In *The Week*. Toronto. v. 9, no. 24 (May 13, 1892), p. 374.)

WIMAN, ERASTUS The feasibility of a commercial union between the United States and Canada. Interview with Erastus Wiman in the "Chicago Tribune", October 5, 1889. New York, 1889. 32 p.

YEIGH, FRANK Twenty-nine years of Confederation. (In *The Canadian magazine of politics, science, art and literature*. Toronto. v. 7 (1896), pp. [228]-235.)

―― Young men in politics. By Frank Yeigh, President, Young Men's Liberal Club, Toronto. (In *The Lake magazine*. [Toronto] v. 1, no. 3 (Oct. 1892), pp. [149]-153.)
Comparative comments.

YOUNG, JAMES Canadian nationality. (In National Club of Toronto. *Maple leaves*. Toronto. pp. [101]-135.)

The Manitoba School Question, 1890–1896

ANGLIN, TIMOTHY WARREN The school question in Manitoba. (In *The Lake magazine*. [Toronto] v. 1, no. 2 (Sept. 1892), pp. [73]-80.)
Discusses the decision in the Barrett case delivered by the Judicial Committee of the Privy Council, July 30, 1892.

ARMOUR, EDWARD DOUGLAS The Manitoba school case. (In *The Week*. Toronto. v. 12, no. 26 (May 24, 1895), pp. 607-609; v. 12, no. 27 (May 31, 1895), pp. 630-632; v. 12, no. 28 (June 7, 1895), pp. 654-656; v. 12, no. 29 (June 14, 1895), pp. 681-683.)
In four parts.
Part 4 has title: The Manitoba School Act.
For a rejoinder see Mr. Armour's dialectics, by J. S. Ewart. (In *The Week*. Toronto. v. 12, no. 33 (July 12, 1895), pp. 777-780.)

BENOIT, JOSEPH PAUL AUGUSTIN L'anglo-manie au Canada. Les lois libérales de 1890 et la persécution de la race française au Manitoba. Par Dom Benoit. (In *Le Mouvement catholique*. Trois-Rivières. v. 4 (juil. —déc. 1899), pp. [421]-430.)

——— L'anglomanie au Canada. Résistance de l'archevêque de Saint-Boniface et de la minorité catholique. Par Dom Benoit. (In *Le Mouvement catholique*. Trois-Rivières. v. 4 (juil.—déc. 1899), pp. [454]-461; pp. [478]-484; pp. [533]-536; pp. [561]-563.)
In four parts.
Concerns Mgr. A. A. Taché and the Manitoba school question.

——— Importance de la question scolaire du Manitoba. Par Dom Benoit. (In *Le Mouvement catholique*. Trois-Rivières. v. 4 (juil. —(déc. 1899), pp. 547-550.)

BRYCE, GEORGE The Manitoba school question. (In *The Canadian magazine of politics, science, art and literature*. Toronto. v. 1, (1893), pp. [511]-516.)

CHARTIER, EMILE Le Canada français; l'enseignement libre et chrétien. (In *Revue canadienne*. Montréal. nouv. sér., v. 26 (1921), pp. [7]-18.)
Includes comments on the Manitoba school question.
For a rejoinder see A propos des écoles du Manitoba, par L. O. Taillon. (In *Revue canadienne*. Montréal. nouv. sér., v. 26 (1921), pp. [286]-293.)

CLAGUE, ROBERT ERNEST The political aspects of the Manitoba school question, 1890-96. [Winnipeg] 1939. 315 leaves.
Thesis (MA) – University of Manitoba.

CLARK, LOVELL CROSBY Dialogue. David Mills and the Remedial Bill of 1896. (1) Some comments on Dr. Morton's recent article. (2) And a reply [by] W. L. Morton. By Lovell C. Clark. (In *Journal of Canadian studies*. Peterborough, Ont. v. 1, no. 3 (1966), pp. 50-53.)
The article referred to is Confederation, 1870-1896; The end of the Macdonaldian constitution and the return to duality, by W. L. Morton. (In *Journal of Canadian studies*. Peterborough, Ont. v. 1, no. 1 (1966), pp. 11-24.)

CLARK, LOVELL CROSBY (ed.) The Manitoba school question; majority rule or minority rights? Edited by Lovell Clark. Toronto, Copp Clark [1968] 230 p. (Issues in Canadian history.)
A selection of documents.

CLARKE, FRANCIS IGNATINO A new phase of the school question. By Frank I. Clarke. (In *The Week*. Toronto. v. 13, no. 6 (Jan. 3, 1896), pp. 133-134.)

CRUNICAN, PAUL EUGENE Bishop Laflèche and the mandement of 1896. By P. E. Crunican. (In Canadian Historical Association. *Historical papers*. [Ottawa] (1969), pp. [52]-61.)

——— Father Lacombe's strange mission: the Lacombe—Langevin correspondence on the Manitoba School Question 1895-96. By Rev. Paul E. Crunican. (In Canadian Catholic Historical Association. *Report*. [Ottawa] (1959), pp. 57-71.)
Refers to Albert Lacombe and Archbishop L. P. A. Langevin of St. Boniface.

——— The Manitoba school question and Canadian federal politics, 1890-1896; a study in Church-State relations. Toronto, 1968. 673 leaves.
Thesis (PH D) – University of Toronto.

DAFOE, JOHN WESLEY The Manitoba school case; a suggestion. By John W. Dafoe. (In *The Week*. Toronto. v. 12, no. 18 (Mar. 29, 1895), pp. 419-420.)

——— The school question in Manitoba. By John W. Dafoe. (In *The Week*. Toronto. v. 6, no. 51 (Nov. 22, 1889), p. 808.)

The Debate on the Remedial Bill. (In *The Week*. Toronto. v. 13, no. 15 (Mar. 6, 1896), p. 346.)

DUPONT, FLAVIEN La question scolaire manitobaine. (In *L'Action française*. Montréal. v. 8, no. 6 (déc. 1922), pp. [368]-379; v. 9, no. 1 (jan. 1923), pp. [33]-41; v. 10 (sept. 1923), pp. [168]-177.)
In three parts.
Letters of Flavien Dupont concerning the Manitoba schools issue, with introductions and conclusions by Pierre Dupont.

EWART, JOHN SKIRVING The Manitoba school question. By John S. Ewart. (In *The Canadian magazine of politics, science, art and literature*. Toronto. v. 2 (1893/94), pp. [107]-116.)

——— The Manitoba school question. Being a compilation of the legislation, the legal proceedings, the proceedings before the Governor-General-in-council. An historical account of the Red River outbreak in 1869 and 1870; its causes and its success as shewn in the treaty—the Manitoba Act and a short summary of Protestant prom-

ises. By John S. Ewart. Toronto, Copp Clark, 1894. vii, 401 p.
A pro-Catholic presentation.

—— Mr. Armour's dialectics. By John S. Ewart. (In *The Week.* Toronto. v. 12, no. 33 (July 12, 1895), pp. 777-780.)
A reply to the series of four articles The Manitoba school case, by E. D. Armour. (In *The Week.* Toronto. v. 12 (1895), pp. 607-609; 630-632; 654-656; 681-683.)

FISHER, JAMES The school question in Manitoba. A letter from James Fisher to the electors of Russell. [n.p., 1890?] 45 p.

GONTHIER, PIERRE THEOPHILE Un manifeste libéral; M. L.-O. David et le clergé canadien. [Par P. Bernard, pseud.] Québec, L. Brousseau, 1896. 2 v.
Vol. 2 has subtitle: La question des écoles du Manitoba.

GRANT, GEORGE MONRO Would federal interference with the Manitoba school system be in the general interest? By G. M. Grant. (In *The Week.* Toronto. v. 12, no. 17 (Mar. 22, 1895), pp. 392-393.)

HEATON, ERNEST The Manitoba school question and the Orange Order. (In *The Week.* Toronto. v. 13, no. 10 (Jan. 31, 1896), pp. 226-227.)

An Inconsequential debate. (In *The Week.* Toronto. v. 10, no. 16 (Mar. 17, 1893), p. 365.)
A discussion of "those clauses of Sec. 93 of the B.N.A. Act which have risen to such importance in connection with the Manitoba School question."

KRIBS, LOUIS P. The Manitoba school question considered historically, legally and controversially. Toronto, Murray Print. Co., 1895. 71 p.

"The Law allows it and the court awards it." (In *The Week.* Toronto. v. 13, no. 12 (Feb. 14, 1896), pp. 273-274.)
Concerns the Manitoba school question.

MC CARTHY, D'ALTON The Manitoba Public School Law. (In *The Canadian magazine of politics, science, art and literature.* Toronto. v. 1 (1893), pp. [3]-8.)
Examines the proceedings followed by the Privy Council of Canada with regard to its efforts to redress the decision handed down by the Judicial Committee of the Privy Council declaring the constitutionality of the School Law of Manitoba. Argues against the case presented by Sir John Thompson, Minister of Justice.

MAC GREGOR, MARGARET SCOTT Some letters from Archbishop Taché on the Manitoba school question. [Toronto] Ryerson Press [c1967] viii, 136 p.

The Manitoba question. (In *The Week.* Toronto. v. 12, no. 11 (Feb. 8, 1895), p. 245.)

The Manitoba school case. (In *The Week.* Toronto. v. 10, no. 14 (Mar. 3, 1893), pp. 317-318.)

MEEK, EDWARD The Manitoba school question and the remedial order. (In *The Canadian magazine of politics, science, art and literature.* Toronto. v. 5 (1895), pp. [90]-98.)

Mr. Ewart's dialectics. By A. B. (In *The Week.* Toronto. v. 12, no. 36 (Aug. 2, 1895), pp. 848-849.)
A response to the article Mr. Armour's dialectics, by J. S. Ewart. (In *The Week.* Toronto. v. 12, no. 33 (July 12, 1895), pp. 777-780.)

Principal Grant on the Manitoba school question. By C. (In *The Week.* Toronto. v. 12, no. 46 (Oct. 11, 1895), pp. 1086-1087.)

PRINGLE, ALLEN Sir William Dawson and separate schools. (In *The Dominion review.* Toronto. v. 1 (1896), pp. [81]-85.)

SALTER, ERNEST J. B. The Manitoba school question. Being a controversy between the Rev. E. J. B. Salter and the Rev. A. G. Morice, as published in letters to the Winnipeg Free Press. Winnipeg, West Canada Pub. Co., 1913. 86 p.

TACHE, ALEXANDRE ANTONIN, Abp. Mémoire adressé par Monseigneur Taché au gouvernement d'Ottawa au sujet des écoles du Nord-Ouest et de Manitoba. Mars 1894. Saint-Boniface, Imprimé par 'Le Manitoba', 1894. 74 p.

—— Mémoire de Monseigneur Taché sur la question des écoles en réponse au rapport du Comité de l'Honorable Conseil Privé du Canada. Montréal, C. O. Beauchemin, 1894. 64 p.
Published also in English.

—— Memorial of Archbishop Taché on the school question. In answer to a report of the Committee of the Honorable the Privy Council of Canada. Montreal, C. O. Beauchemin, 1894. 67 p.
Published also in French.

—— Une page de l'histoire des écoles de Manitoba; étude des cinq phases d'une période de 75 années. Par Mgr. Taché. Saint-Boniface, Imprimé par 'Le Manitoba', 1893. 126 p.

Issued also in English in 1893. 52 p.

TAILLON, SIR LOUIS OLIVIER A propos des écoles du Manitoba. Par. L.-O. Taillon. (In *Revue canadienne*. Montréal. nouv. sér., v. 26 (1921), pp. [286]-293.)

Comments on statements, relating to the Manitoba school question, made in the article Le Canada français; l'enseignement libre et chrétien, par E. Chartier. (In *Revue canadienne*. Montréal. nouv. sér., v. 26 (1921), pp. [7]-18.)

TARDIF, J. A. Les écoles du Manitoba. (In *La Revue franco-américaine*. Québec. t. 3, no. 6 (oct. 1909), pp. [415]-430.)

"Conférence par J. A. Tardif, président du Cercle Morin, de l'Association catholique de la jeunesse canadienne française, à Sainte-Marie, Beauce, faite devant les membres de ce cercle, le 14 février 1909."

WADE, FREDERICK COATE The Manitoba school question. By F. C. Wade. Winnipeg, Printed at the Manitoba Institution for the Deaf and Dumb, 1895. 122 p.

A popular tract supporting the position of the Manitoba government.

WILLISON, SIR JOHN STEPHEN Reminiscences, political and personal. [Pt. 11] Race and religion in Canada. By Sir John Willison. (In *The Canadian magazine of politics, science, art and literature*. Toronto. v. 52 1918/19), pp. 895-908.)

An analysis centering mainly on the Manitoba school question and briefly, the educational clauses of the Western Autonomy bills, 1905.

POLITICAL HISTORY
1896–1921

GENERAL WORKS

BROWN, ROBERT CRAIG Canada, 1896-1921; a nation transformed. By Robert Craig Brown and Ramsay Cook. [Toronto] McClelland and Stewart [c1974] xiv, 412 p. (The Canadian centenary series, 14.)

"Select bibliography of unpublished source material": pp. 339-344.

"Notes" (bibliographical): pp. 347-397.

WATT, FRANK WILLIAM The theme of "Canada's century", 1896-1920. By F. W. Watt. (In *The Dalhousie review*. Halifax. v. 38 (1958/59), p. [154]-166.)

Includes discussion of the social philosophy presented in *Industry and humanity*, by W. L. Mackenzie King.

NATIONAL DEVELOPMENT AND PRE-WAR PERIOD
1896–1914

Addresses to His Excellency Earl Grey . . . Governor General of Canada, and his speeches in reply, having relation to the resources and progress of the Dominion. Ottawa, Dawson, 1908. iv, 184 p.

AIKINS, SIR JAMES ALBERT MANNING Manitoba and its relation to Confederation. By J. A. M. Aikins, MP. (In Canadian Club of Toronto. *Addresses*. Toronto. (1911/12), pp. 127-137).

Address delivered on February 19, 1912.

ALLAN, JOHN Reciprocity and the Canadian general election of 1911. A re-examination of economic self-interest in voting. [Kingston, n.d.] v, 93 leaves.

Thesis (MA) – Queen's University.

Alphonse Verville, MP. Sketches from the House of Commons and the corridor. By H. W. A. (In *The Canadian courier*. Toronto. v. 13, no. 22 (May 3, 1913), pp. 9; 19.)

An independent Liberal representing the interests of labour groups in Canada. Classified as a Labour MP. Cf. *The Canadian directory of parliament, 1867-1967*, edited by J. K. Johnson, Ottawa, 1968 (p. 585)

AMES, HERBERT BROWN Electoral management. By H. B. Ames, MP. (In *The Canadian magazine of politics, science, art and literature*. Toronto. v. 25 (1905), pp. 26-31.)

ANDERSON, C. W. The making of titled Canadians. (In *MacLean's magazine*. Toronto. v. 22, no. 4 (Aug. 1911), pp. [65]-70.)

ANDERSON, HARRY W. From plumber to parliamentarian. (In *MacLean's magazine*. Toronto. v. 28, no. 3 (Jan. 1915), pp. [12]-13.)

Concerns Alphonse Verville, a Labour representative who "has generally given an independent support to Liberalism".

ASSELIN, OLIVAR La défense navale. (In *La Revue franco-américaine*. Québec. t. 3, no. 1 (mai 1909), pp. [27]-50.)

BARBER, MARILYN JEAN The Ontario bilingual schools issue, 1910-1916. [Kingston, Ont., 1965] iii, 177 leaves.

Thesis (MA) – Queen's University.

BELCOURT, GUILLAUME Les luttes scolaires de l'Ontario-Nord (In *Relations*. Montréal. 19. année, no 223 (juil. 1959), pp. 175-177.)

Examines briefly the issue raised between 1910 and 1927.

BENGOUGH, JOHN WILSON Cartoons of the campaign. Dominion of Canada general election, 1900. By J. W. Bengough. Reprinted from the Toronto "Daily Globe". Toronto, Poole Pub. Co. [1900] [3] p., 22 plates.

Descriptive text precedes each plate.

A Bi-lingual controversy. Summary of a great discussion which is proceeding in Ontario and Quebec. (In *The Canadian courier*. Toronto. v. 8, no. 21 (Oct. 22, 1910), pp. 5-6.)

BLACKSTOCK, GEORGE TATE Some tendencies. (In Canadian Club of Toronto. *Addresses*. Toronto. (1906/07), pp. 133-138.)

Address delivered on April 22, 1907.

General comments on parliamentary democracy in Canada.

BOCKING, DOUGLAS HENRY Political ambitions and Territorial affairs, 1900-04. By D. H. Bocking. (In *Saskatchewan history*. Saskatoon. v. 18, no. 2 (spring 1965), pp. [63]-75.)

—— Premier Walter Scott: his early career. By D. H. Bocking. (In *Saskatchewan history*. Saskatoon. v. 13, no. 3 (autumn 1960), pp. 81-99.)

Based in part on the Author's MA thesis "Premier Walter Scott: a study of his rise to political power".

Details the feud between W. Scott and Nicholas Flood Davin resulting in the election of Scott as member of parliament for West Assiniboia after the general elections held November 7, 1900.

BOGGS, THEODORE HARDING Canada and the French-Canadian. By Theodore H. Boggs. (In *The University magazine*. Montreal. v. 10 (1911), pp. [47]-67.)

BOND, F. FRASER The Confederation scheme that failed. (In *The Atlantic advocate*. Fredericton, N.B. v. 54, no. 10 (June 1964). pp. 59-64.)

Concerns the abortive attempt made in 1909 to bring Newfoundland into the Canadian federation.

BORNE, JOHN V. The power behind a vast enterprise. (In *The Busy man's magazine*. Toronto. v. 16, no. 2 (June 1908), pp. 127-131.)

Reprinted from *System magazine*.

Concerns the railway building of William Mackenzie and Donald Mann.

BOUCHETTE, ERROL French Canada and Canada. (In *The Canadian magazine of politics, science, art and literature*. Toronto. v. 14 (1899/1900), pp. 313-320.)

"This article was written and sent to the Canadian magazine before the recent discussion concerning the loyalty of the French Canadians." – Editor.

BOULTON, CHARLES ARKOLL A new National Policy. Being a plea for free trade with Great Britain in order to preserve our taxable power. By Senator Boulton. (In *The Canadian magazine of politics, science, art and literature*. Toronto. v. 13 (1899), pp. 107-111.)

—— The parting of the ways. By Senator Charles A. Boulton. (In *The Dominion review*. Toronto. v. 3, no. 5 (May 1898), pp. 168-176.)

Appeals for a policy of free trade with Great Britain.

BOURASSA, HENRI The Nationalist movement in Quebec. (In Canadian Club of Toronto. *Addresses*. Toronto. (1906/07), pp. 56-64.)

Address delivered on January 22, 1907.

Relates the implications of the Quebec movement to the rest of Canada.

—— The official languages of Canada. (In Canadian Club of Montreal. *Addresses*. [Montreal] (1913/14), pp. 257-263.)

Address delivered at the Club's annual banquet, April 27, 1914.

—— Why the Navy Act should be repealed; imperial problems. Montreal, Le Devoir [1912] 62 p.

BOYD, JOHN The Nationalist movement. (In *The Canadian magazine of politics, science, art and literature*. Toronto. v. 36 (1910/11), pp. 260-268.)

Examines the general political implications of the movement led by Henri Bourassa.

BRIDLE, AUGUSTUS The Battle of Chateauguay. Liberal seat of fifty years, won by James Morris, Conservative, with a turnover nearly 200 votes, and the heaviest polling on record. The battle of the ballots in Chateauguay is being made a national issue. (In *The Canadian courier*. Toronto v. 14, no. 20 (Oct. 18, 1913), p. 9.)

The by-election was held October 11, 1913.

—— Capturing the West. (In *The Canadian courier*. Toronto. v. 10, no. 8 (July 22, 1911), p. 9.)

A brief comment on the Western tours of Robert Borden and Wilfrid Laurier.

—— The contrasts of Parliament Hill. A moving picture of national life in three phases: scenery, statesmen and "scoundrels". (In *The Canadian courier*. Toronto. v. 7, no. 16 (Mar. 19, 1910), pp. 13-14.)

—— A day in Parliament. How members at the capital spend their time in the interests of Canada and Hansard. (In *The Canadian courier*. Toronto. v. 7, no. 18 (Apr. 2, 1910), pp. 12-13.)

—— The newspaper masquerade in Montreal. (In *The Canadian courier*. Toronto. v. 14, no. 11 (Aug. 16, 1913), pp. 10-11; 18.)

Discusses the business interests and political associations involved in the leading newspapers published in Montreal.

—— Our parliamentary masters. Not the Premier and the Leader of the Opposition but "the man from Manitoba" and the Member for St. John. (In *The Canadian courier*. Toronto. v. 13, no. 17 (Mar. 29, 1913), pp. 11-13.)

Concerns Hon. Robert Rogers, William Pugsley and others.

—— Parliamentary personalities. Casual glimpses of a few characters in Ottawa. (In *The Canadian Courier*. Toronto. v. 7, no. 23 (May 7, 1910), pp. 14-15. ports.)

Brief comments.

—— Personalities and problems. No. 19 — Henri Bourassa. Who between intellectualism and splendid delirium is always more or less misunderstood. (In *The Canadian courier*. Toronto. v. 13, no. 3 (Dec. 21, 1912), pp. 6-7; 20-21.)

BRYANT, GEORGE What Canada's public men read. (In *The Busy man's magazine*. Toronto. v. 18, no. 4 (Aug. 1909), pp. 43-46.)

Reprinted from *The Canadian bookman*.

BUCHAN, JOHN Lord Minto; a memoir. London, T. Nelson, 1924. xviii, 352 p.

The Earl of Minto (Governor-General of Canada, 1898-1904).

Canada and the Navy question. (In *The Busy man's Canada*. Toronto. v. 3, no. 1 (Aug. 1912), pp. 44-50.)

A synopsis of current opinions and comments.

CAPPON, JAMES The discussion on the naval question. (In *Queen's quarterly*. Kingston. v. 21 (1913/14), pp. [241]-250.)

Discusses the views taken by Sir Wilfrid Laurier and Robert Borden.

—— The growth of the separate school system in Canada. (In *Queen's quarterly*. Kingston. v. 19 (1911/12), pp. [429]-435.)

Traces the constitutional developments relating to the separate schools issue in Canada.

—— The principle of sectarianism in the Canadian constitution. (In *Queen's quarterly*. Kingston. v. 12 (1904/05), pp. [425]-442.)

Traces the historical development as background to argue the unconstitutionality of the Autonomy Bills under consideration by Parliament during 1905.

CARMAN, FRANCIS ASBURY Pro-Confederation sentiment in Newfoundland. (In *The Canadian magazine of politics, science, art and literature*. Toronto. v. 33 (1909), pp. 205-207.)

CHARLESON, GEORGE The historical aspect of the naval contribution. (In *The Canadian courier*. Toronto. v. 13, no. 15 (Mar. 15, 1913), pp. 11; 33-34.)

Draws upon Canadian historical background material during the 1846-1850 period as an argument against the naval policy of Premier Robert Borden.

Further discussion and clarification of views are given in a subsequent article. Is it permanent contribution? (In *The Canadian courier*. Toronto. v. 13, no. 22 (May 3, 1913), p. 10.)

—— Is it permanent contribution? (In *The Canadian courier*. Toronto. v. 13, no. 22 (May 3, 1913), p. 10.)

Answers criticisms directed at his article, The historical aspect of the naval contribution. (In *The Canadian courier*. Toronto. v. 13, no. 15 (Mar. 15, 1913), pp. 11; 33-34.)

CHARLESWORTH, HECTOR WILLOUGHBY Laurier and Tupper. By Hector Charlesworth. (In his *Candid chronicles*. Toronto, 1925. pp. 194-211.)

Personal recollections.

—— Reflections. By Hector Charlesworth. (In *Saturday night*. Toronto. [v. 40, no. 4] (Dec. 13, 1924), p. 2.)

Comments on "Lord Minto", by John Buchan. Toronto, T. Nelson, 1924.

CHARLTON, JOHN Speeches and addresses; political, literary and religious. Toronto, Morang, 1905. xi, 499 p.

CHIPMAN, GEORGE FISHER The MP factory. Recollections of the general elections. (In *The Canadian courier*. Toronto. v. 5, no. 17 (Mar 27, 1909), p. 10.)

A generalized interpretation of the political and electoral process.

CHIPMAN, GEORGE FISHER (ed.) The siege of Ottawa; being the story of the 800 farmers from Ontario, Quebec, New Brunswick, Nova Scotia, Manitoba, Saskatchewan, and Alberta, who met the government and members of Parliament in the House of Commons chamber on December 16, 1910, and demanded more equitable legislation. Edited by G. F. Chipman. Winnipeg, Grain Growers' Guide [1910?] 68 p.

Includes the Farmers' platform.

CHIPMAN, WARWICK FIELDING A word to Parliament. (In *The University magazine*. Montreal. v. 8 (1909), pp. [36]-51.)

General remarks directed to the first session of the eleventh parliament which opened January 20, 1909.

CHURCH, GORDON CAMERON Dominion government aid to the dairy industry in Western Canada, 1890-1906. By G. C. Church. (In *Saskatchewan history*. Saskatoon. v. 16, no. 2 (spring 1963), pp. [41]-58.)

Based in part on the Author's MA thesis "The origins, nature and development of the Saskatchewan Co-operative Creameries Association Limited", University of Saskatchewan, 1960.

COLQUHOUN, ARTHUR HUGH URQUHART Politics and universities. By A. H. U. Colquhoun. (In *The McGill University magazine*. Montreal. v. 5 (1905), pp. 94-96.)

—— Reciprocity trips to Washington; a page from political history. By A. H. U. Colquhoun. (In *The Canadian magazine of politics, science, art and literature*. Toronto. v. 8 (1896/97). pp. 423-429.)

Committees of the House of Commons. (In *The Canadian courier*. Toronto. v. 3, no. 7 (Jan. 18, 1908), p. 11.)

Comments briefly on the Railway Committee, the Public Accounts Committee, etc.

CONACHER, JAMES B. Reciprocity and public opinion in Canada, 1911. [Kingston, Ont.] 1939. 255 leaves.

Thesis (MA) – Queen's University.

CONRAD, ARTHUR The line-up of the financiers; a three-fold grouping of important Canadian interests. (In *MacLean's magazine*. Toronto. v. 22, no. 4 (Aug. 1911), pp. [41]-47.)

Relates to political considerations.

COOK, GEORGE RAMSAY Church, schools and politics in Manitoba, 1903-12. By G. R. Cook. (In *The Canadian historical review*. Toronto. v. 39 (1958), pp. 1-23.)

—— Church, schools and politics in Manitoba, 1903-1912. By Ramsay Cook. (In *Minorities, schools and politics*. [Toronto, c1969] pp. [19]-41.)

"Reprinted from Canadian historical review, XXXIX (1), March, 1958."

COOKE, BRITTON B. The man who wouldn't stay "dead"—Earl Grey. Some facts and inferences about the Governor-General who was supposed to be a figure-head ... (In *MacLean's magazine*. Toronto. v. 21, no. 7 (May 1911), pp. [58]-62.)

Earl Grey was Governor-General of Canada, Sept. 26, 1904–March 21, 1911.

COOPER, JOHN ALEXANDER Canada and the navy. By John A. Cooper. (In Canadian Club of Hamilton. *Addresses*. Hamilton. (1912/13), pp. 92-103.)

Address delivered February 27, 1913.

—— Churchill and the Canadian navy. By the Editor. (In *The Canadian courier*. Toronto. v. 11, no. 26 (May 25, 1912), pp. 10-11.)

Discusses Canadian naval policy.

—— The Militia Conference. By John A. Cooper. (In *The Canadian courier*. Toronto. v. 11, no. 1 (Dec. 2, 1911), pp. 6-7; 21.)

The conference convened in Ottawa, November 16-18, 1911.

—— The Militia Council. By the Editor. (In *The Canadian magazine of politics, science, art and literature.* Toronto. v. 25 (1905), pp. [3]-10.)

—— Some autonomy documents. By The Editor. (In *The Canadian magazine of politics, science, art and literature.* Toronto. v. 25 (1905), pp. 214-222.)

Concerns the subject of autonomy in the North-West. Traces the history and the changes occurring from the Haultain bill to the Ottawa bill through an examination of the texts.

—— Wanted—a new National Policy. By the Editor. (In *The Canadian courier.* Toronto. v. 9 [i.e. 8] no. 23 [i.e. 24] (Nov. 12, 1910), p. 8; v. 10 [i.e. 8] no. 24 [i.e. 25] (Nov. 19, 1910), p. 6.)

In two parts.

—— Will Canada be lopsided? A contribution to the discussion of "Wanted—a new National Policy". By the Editor. (In *The Canadian courier.* Toronto. v. 9, no. 3 (Dec. 17, 1910), p. 6.)

COPP, JOHN TERRY   The Canadian general election of 1908. [Montreal] 1962. 1 v.

Thesis (MA) – McGill University.

CORCORAN, JAMES I. W.   Henri Bourassa et la guerre sud-africaine. Traduction de Marc La Terreur. (In *Revue d'histoire de l'amérique française.* Montréal. v. 18, no. 3 (déc. 1964), pp. 343-356; v. 19 no. 1 (juin 1965), pp. 84-105; v. 19, no. 2 (sept. 1965), pp. 229-237; v. 19, no. 3 (déc. 1965), pp. 414-442.)

In four parts.

CORNISH, DESDA   Earl Carrington; prospective Governor-General of Canada. (In *The Busy man's magazine.* Toronto. v. 20, no. 1 (May 1910), pp. 21-23.)

CRANSTON, JAMES HERBERT   In the House of Commons Press Gallery. By J. H. Cranston. (In *The McMaster University monthly.* Toronto. v. 17 (Apr. 1908), pp.305-312.)

Presents impressions of contemporary political personalities: Sir Wilfrid Laurier, G. E. Foster, W. S. Fielding, etc.

CROCKET, OSWALD SMITH   New Brunswick and its relation to federation. By O. S. Crocket. (In Canadian Club of Toronto.

Addresses. Toronto. (1911/12), pp. 202-215.)

Address delivered on April 15, 1912.

"Mr. Oswald Smith Crocket . . . represents the County of York, N.S., in the House of Commons."

DONLEY, HAL B.   Canada's changed postal policy. The situation as it was. The reasons for a change as they appear to the publisher of a provincial weekly. (In *Toronto Saturday night.* Toronto. v. 20, no. 31 (May 18, 1907), p. 5.)

DONOVAN, PETER   The French Canadian Moses. By P. O. D. (In *Toronto Saturday night.* Toronto. v. 24, no. 5 (Nov. 12, 1910), p. 2.)

Concerns Henri Bourassa.

—— Opening Parliament with the Duke. By P. O. D. (In *Saturday night.* Toronto. v. 25, no. 7 (Nov. 25, 1911), pp. 4; 10.)

Describes the opening of the twelfth parliament by the Duke of Connaught.

The Driving power of conservation. A sketch of the work performed by the Commission of Conservation of Canada. (In *Saturday night.* Toronto. v. 36, no. 10 (Jan. 1, 1921), pp. [9]; 14.)

Considers the work of Clifford Sifton, chairman, 1909-1918.

DRURY, ERNEST CHARLES   The farmers and the tariff. By E. C. Drury. (In *The Canadian magazine of politics, science, art and literature.* Toronto. v. 26 (1906), pp. 556-560.)

Discusses the views presented by representatives of the farming community to the Canadian Tariff Commission.

DYDE, SAMUEL WALTERS   The Canadian constitution and the school question. By S. W. Dyde. (In *Queen's quarterly.* [Kingston] v. 13 (1905/06), pp. [59]-67.)

Presents an historical argument for the constitutionality of the Autonomy Bills considered by Parliament during 1905.

EAGER, EVELYN   The constitution of Saskatchewan. (In *Saskatchewan history.* Saskatoon. v. 15, no. 2 (spring 1962), pp. [41]-57.)

Traces the historical development and political background of the Saskatchewan Act.

An Election and a navy. (In *The Canadian courier.* Toronto. v. 9 [i.e. 8] no. 23 [i.e. 24] (Nov. 12, 1910), pp. 8; 10.)

Les Elections fédérales. Campagne de 1900. Québec, 1900. 240 p.

Electoral management: a reply to Mr. Ames. By a candidate in the late elections. (In *The Canadian magazine of politics, science, art and literature.* Toronto. v. 25 (1905), pp. 316-319.)

Refers to Ames, H. B. Electoral management. (In *The Canadian magazine of politics, science, art and literature.* Toronto. v. 25 (1905), pp. 26-31.)

ELLIS, LEWIS ETHAN   Canada's rejection of reciprocity in 1911. (In Canadian Historical Association. *Report of the annual meeting.* Toronto (1939), pp. 99-111.)

—— Reciprocity, 1911; a study in Canadian-American relations. By L. Ethan Ellis. New Haven, Yale University Press; Toronto, Ryerson Press for the Carnegie Endowment for International Peace, Division of Economics and History, 1939. x, 207 p. [The relations of Canada and the United States: a series of studies prepared under the direction of the Carnegie Endowment for International Peace, Division of Economics and History.]

EVANS, WILLIAM SANFORD   The future of the Territories: Manitoba and Territorial autonomy. By W. Sanford Evans. (In *The Canadian magazine of politics, science, art and literature.* Toronto. v. 18 (1901/02), pp. 459-461.)

EWART, JOHN SKIRVING   The Canadian flag. A suggestion for Canadian clubs. (In *The Canadian magazine of politics, science, art and literature.* Toronto. v. 30 (1907/08), pp. 332-335.)

—— Canadian sovereignty. By J. S. Ewart. (In Canadian Club of Winnipeg. *Report.* [Winnipeg] 10th (1913/14), pp. 25-28.)

Summary and excerpts of the address delivered December 4, 1913.

—— The future of Canada. By J. S. Ewart. (In Canadian Club of Ottawa. *Addresses.* Ottawa. (1910), pp. 122-127.)

—— The kingdom of Canada. By John S. Ewart. (In Canadian Club of Toronto. *Addresses.* Toronto. (1903/04), pp. 115-132.)

Address delivered March 31, 1904.

FALCONER, SIR ROBERT ALEXANDER   The necessity for breadth in the national outlook. By R. A. Falconer. (In Canadian Club of Toronto. *Addresses.* Toronto. 1907/08), pp. 17-21.)

Address delivered on November 4, 1907.

FERNOW, BERNHARD EDUARD   The forest policy in Canada. By B. E. Fernow, Dean of the School of Forestry, University of Toronto. (In Canadian Club of Toronto. *Addresses.* Toronto. (1907/08), pp. 121-128.)

Address delivered on February 24, 1908.

FLETCHER, CLYDE SHELDON   Nova Scotia and the reciprocity agreement of 1911. [Wolfville, N.S.] 1941. 1 v.

Thesis (MA) – Acadia University.

FLETCHER, JAMES HAYDEN   Newspaper life and newspaper men. By J. H. Fletcher. (In *The Prince Edward Island magazine.* Charlottetown. v. 2, no. 3 (May 1900), pp. [69]-75; v. 2, no. 4 (June 1900), pp. 107-113; v. 2, no. 5 (July 1900), pp. 149-152; v. 2, no. 6 (Aug. 1900), pp. 186-188.)

In four parts.

Includes observations on contemporary politics.

FORD, ARTHUR L.   Grain-growers at Ottawa. Western farmers invade the capital. (In *The Canadian courier.* Toronto. v. 9, no. 3 (Dec. 17, 1910), p. 10.)

Concerns the farmers' "siege of Ottawa" in December 1910.

FORD, ARTHUR RUTHERFORD   Western political dominance. (In *The Canadian magazine of politics, science, art and literature.* Toronto. v. 34 (1909/10), pp. 230-232.)

Considers the growing influence of political power in Western Canada on national politics.

FORD, FRANK   Titles of honour in Canada. (In *Queen's quarterly.* Kingston. v. 10 1902/03), pp. [155]-175.)

Presents an "account of the manner in which the prerogative of honour has been exercised" in Canada.

FOSTER, JOAN MARY VASSIE   Reciprocity and the Joint High Commission of 1898-9. (In Canadian Historical Association. *Report of the annual meeting.* Toronto. (1939), pp. 87-98.)

Contends that in 1898-99, Canadian public opinion showed signs that anticipated the rejection of reciprocity in 1911.

GADSBY, HENRY FRANKLIN   A retrospect of the session. (In *The University magazine.* Montreal. v. 11 (1912), pp. [183]-196.)

Reviews the first session of the twelfth parliament which ended April 1, 1912.

The Game of oratory. (In *The Canadian courier.* Toronto. v. 10, no. 18 (Sept. 30, 1911), p. [5].)

Comments on G. E. Foster, W. M. German, W. F. Maclean, R. Lemieux, Sir Wilfrid Laurier, etc.

GIBSON, FREDERICK W. The Alaska boundary dispute. [Kingston, Ont.] 1944. 467 leaves.

Thesis (MA) – Queen's University.

GOGGIN, DAVID JAMES North-West autonomy. By D. J. Goggin. (In Empire Club of Canada. *Addresses.* Toronto. (1904/05), pp. 196-213.)

At head of title: Empire Club speeches.
Address delivered on February 23, 1905.

GOOD, WILLIAM CHARLES A Canadian navy. By W. C. Good. (In *The University monthly.* Toronto. v. 10, no. 4 (Feb. 1910), pp. 203-211.)

—— Tariffs, bounties and the farmer. By W. C. Good. (In *The University magazine.* Montreal. v. 7 (1908), pp. [415]-436.)

GORDON, CHARLES WILLIAM The future of Canada. By Ralph Connor. (In Canadian Club of Toronto. *Addresses.* Toronto. (1904/05), pp. 146-151.)

Address delivered on April 10, 1905.

GORDON, DANIEL MINER Political purity. By Principal Gordon. (In Canadian Club of Toronto. *Addresses.* Toronto. (1904/05), pp. 67-72.)

Address delivered on January 13, 1905.

GRAHAM, WILLIAM ROGER The cabinet of 1911. By Roger Graham. (In Gibson, F. W. (ed.) *Cabinet formation and bicultural relations.* [Ottawa, 1970] pp. [47]-62.)

GRANT, WILLIAM LAWSON The Canadian elections. By W. L. Grant. (In *Queen's quarterly.* Kingston. v. 19 (1911/12), pp. [170]-180.)

Discusses the results of the general elections held September 21, 1911.

—— A note on the closure. By W. L. Grant. (In *Queen's quarterly.* Kingston. v. 20 (1912/13), pp. [467]-469.)

The Borden administration introduced a motion for closure April 9, 1912.

GREENWOOD, WILLIAM HAMAR Canada as an imperial factor. London, Collins [1913] 264 p. (The Nation's library).

GREYSON, FREDERICK The new host at Rideau Hall. (In *MacLean's magazine.* Toronto. v. 22, no. 5 (Sept. 1911), pp. [125]-130.)

Concerns Field Marshal H. R. H. The Duke of Connaught and of Strathearn (Governor-General of Canada, 1911-1916).

—— Public opinion. What are the strongest factors in molding its expression and sentiment? (In *MacLean's magazine.* Toronto. v. 23, no. 3 (Jan. 1912), pp. 290-294.)

HALL, DOUGLAS Canada's excuse for existence. (In *The Busy man's magazine.* Toronto. v. 14, no. 4 (Aug. 1907), pp. [114]-118.)

Reprinted from *The World to-day.*

HALLETT, MARY E. The fourth Earl of Grey as Governor-General of Canada. [London, Eng., 1969] 1 v.

Thesis (PH D) – University of London.

HAMILTON, CHARLES FREDERICK Canadian cost defence. By C. Frederick Hamilton. (In *The University magazine.* Montreal. v. 8 (1909), pp. [587]-602.)

—— The Canadian navy. By C. Frederick Hamilton. (In *The University magazine.* Montreal. v. 8 (1909), pp. [175]-187.)

—— Shall Canada have a navy? By C. Frederick Hamilton. (In *The University magazine.* Montreal. v. 8 (1909), pp. [375]-397.)

HAMMOND, MELVIN ORMOND The tragedy of reciprocity. By M. O. Hammond. (In *The Canadian magazine of politics, science, art and literature.* Toronto. v. 38 (1911/12), pp. 84-91.)

HARRIS, EDWARD WILLIAM Canada, the making of a nation. Toronto, 1907. 64 p.

HARRIS, JAMES G. The *News* and Canadian politics, 1903-1914; a study of the policies of the *News* under the editorship of Sir John Willison. Toronto, 1952. 288 leaves.

Thesis (MA) – University of Toronto.

HARVY, MAHLON Tariff revision called for. (In *The National monthly of Canada.* Toronto. v. 4, no. 3 (Mar. 1904), pp. [167]-169.)

Examines the attitude of the Canadian government toward tariff revision.

HAWKES, ARTHUR Why I am a suffragette. (In *The Canadian magazine of politics, science, art and literature.* Toronto. v. 33 (1909), pp. 17-21.)

HAYDON, ANDREW For the general advantage of Canada. (In *Queen's quarterly.* Kingston. v. 17 (1909/10), pp. [9]-16.)

Discusses the development of the "provincial rights" issue, citing, in particular, events which occurred during the 1906-09 parliamentary sessions.

HEROUX, MAURICE Le Canada et la défense de l'Empire, 1867-1914. (In L'Action universitaire. Montréal. no. 4 (juil. 1953), pp. [18]-31.)

—— L'opinion canadienne devant la guerre de 1914. [Montréal, 1952] 93 leaves.
Thesis (MA) – University of Montreal.

HIGHAM, WILLIAM NORWOOD The Laurier-Borden naval controversy, 1909-1913. Toronto, 1951. 115 leaves.
Thesis (MA) – University of Toronto.

HITSMAN, JOHN MAC KAY Canadian naval policy. [Kingston, Ont., 1940] ix, 208 leaves.
Thesis (MA) – Queen's University.

HOBSON, JOHN ATKINSON Canada to-day. By J. A. Hobson. London, T. F. Unwin, 1906. xiii, 143 p.

—— Canada's trade policy. A free trader's view. By John A. Hobson. (In The Canadian magazine of politics, science, art and literature. Toronto. v. 26 (1905/06), pp. 423-425.)
Reprinted from the London Daily chronicle.
The discussion is taken from the political point of view.

HOPKINS, JOHN CASTELL Historical sketch of the Canadian Club movement. By J. Castell Hopkins. With appointments and elections to the presidency of Canadian public bodies in 1907. An appendix to the Canadian annual review, 1907. [Toronto, 1907] 23 p.
Cover title.

HUNTINGFORD, E. W. Bribery and corruption; from its own point of view. By Rev. Professor E. W. Huntingford, Trinity College. (In The Canadian magazine of politics, science, art and literature. Toronto. v. 15 (1900), pp. 244-246.)

Imperialism, nationalism, or a third alternative. By a Westerner. (In The University magazine. Montreal. v. 9 (1910), pp. [339]-358.)
Includes discussion of Canadian political institutions.

The Issues of the general election. By a political onlooker. (In The Canadian magazine. Toronto. v. 14 (1899/1900), pp. 566-568.)

Concerns the federal election held Nov. 7, 1900.

JAQUES The Dominion House and the Autonomy Bill. By Jaques. (In Toronto Saturday night. Toronto. v. 18, no. 21 (Apr. 1, 1905), p. 2.)

JESOLEY, MAX The advantages of Newfoundland to the Dominion. (In The National monthly of Canada. Toronto. v. 5, no. [6] (Dec. 1904), pp. [292]-295.)
Advocates the union of Newfoundland and Canada.

JOHNSTON, HUBERT MC BEAN Canada and the census. (In Canada monthly. London, Ont. v. 11, no. 3 (Jan. 1912), pp. 197-202.)

The Judging of greatness. Sidelights on the "Courier's" voting competition. (In The Canadian courier. Toronto. v. 5, no. 3 (Dec. 19, 1908), p. 7.)
Results of a public opinion poll citing ten leading Canadian national figures: political personalities are represented.

KING, T. W. Farmers at the capital. (In The Canadian courier. Toronto. v. 9, no. 4 (Dec. 24, 1910), pp. 8-9.)
Describes the scene of the farmers' delegation in the Parliament Buildings at Ottawa, December 17, 1910.

—— The session of Parliament. (In The Canadian courier. Toronto. v. 9, no. 7 (Jan. 14, 1911), p. 12.)
Summarizes the proceedings during the third session of the eleventh parliament, held November 17, 1910, to July 29, 1911.

KINGSMILL, RODEN Back to the parliamentary grind. A forecast of the work of the session. (In The Canadian courier. Toronto. v. 1, no. 7 (Jan. 12, 1907), pp. 11-12.)
Relates to the fourth session of the tenth parliament held November 28, 1907, to July 20, 1908. Discusses reciprocity, the Keewatin partition and R. L. Borden's support for compulsory voting.

KIPLING, RUDYARD Canada's path to nationhood. (In Canadian Club of Ottawa. Addresses. Ottawa. (1903/09), pp. 118-121.)

KNOTT, H. W. H. The future of the Territories; the movement for autonomy. (In The Canadian magazine of politics, science, art and literature. Toronto. v. 18 (1901/02), pp. 453-456.)

LANHAM, PERCY ALBERT STANLEY An attempt at reciprocity; a study of the tariff issue in the election of 1911. [Winnipeg] 1935. 135 leaves.

Thesis (MA) – University of Manitoba.

LARKIN, JAMES J. Peat—a problem solved. How the government has brought fuel at $3.50 a ton to the housewife of eastern Canada. (In *Canada monthly*. London, Ont. v. 13, no. 2 (Dec. 1912), pp. 123-128.)

LASH, ZEBULON AITON The navy question. By Z. A. Lash. (In Canadian Club of Toronto. *Addresses*. Toronto. (1913/14), pp. 135-150.)

Address delivered January 5, 1914.

LAVERGNE, ARMAND RENAUD Les écoles du Nord-Ouest; discours prononcé à Montmagny. Par M. Armand Lavergne, député, le dimanche 17 septembre 1905. Suivi des différents textes et amendements de la loi, de documents et pièces justificatives. Montréal, Impr. du 'Nationaliste', 1907. 63 p.

—— The position of the French language in Canada. By Armand Lavergne. (In Canadian Club of Montreal. *Addresses*. [Montreal] (1911/12), pp. 65-73.)

Address delivered December 18, 1911.

LEACOCK, STEPHEN BUTLER The case against reciprocity. By Stephen Leacock. (In *Toronto Saturday night*. Toronto. v. 24, no. 21 (Mar. 4, 1911), p. 2; v. 24, no. 22 (Mar. 11, 1911), p. 15.)

In two parts.

—— Greater Canada: an appeal. By Stephen Leacock. (In *The University magazine*. Montreal. v. 6 (1907), pp. [132]-141.)

—— What shall we do about the navy? The policy of a united fleet. By Stephen Leacock. (In *The University magazine*. Montreal. v. 10 (1911), pp. [535]-553.)

A legal aspect of reciprocity. (In *Toronto Saturday night*. Toronto. v. 24, no. 33 (May 27, 1911), p. 4.)

"The negotiators encountered an obstacle in the existence in some of the provinces, of laws standing in the way of the freedom of the trade sought to be established."

LE ROSSIGNOL, JAMES EDWARD Railway subsidies in Canada and the United States. (In *The Canadian magazine of politics, science, art and literature*. Toronto. v. 20 (1902/03), pp. 419-424.)

A comparison of government policy.

LEX Canadian citizenship. By "Lex". (In *The National monthly of Canada*. Toronto. v. 5, no. 4 (Oct. 1904), pp. [208]-210.)

—— Les écoles dans les Territoires. Par Lex. (In *La Nouvelle-France*. Québec. t. 4, no. 5 (mai 1905), pp. [195]-207.)

—— Les écoles du Nord-Ouest. Par Lex. (In *La Nouvelle-France*. Québec. t. 9, no. 1 (jan. 1910), pp. [22]-37.)

Considers the historical background to the Autonomy Bills passed in 1905 establishing the provinces of Alberta and Saskatchewan. Argues that the government legislation is unconstitutional.

—— Les écoles du Nord-Ouest. Par Lex. (In *La Nouvelle-France*. Québec. t. 9, no. 3 (mars 1910), pp. 107-126.)

Traces pre-Confederation historical legislation: imperial acts, treaties, clauses in the British North America Act, etc.

—— Les écoles du Nord-Ouest. Par Lex. (In *La Nouvelle-France*. Québec. t. 9, no. 4 (avril 1910), pp. 159-174.)

Provides historical background in order to explain and consider the Autonomy Bills passed in 1905.

—— The right of Canada to make treaties. By Lex. (In *The National monthly of Canada*. Toronto. v. 4, no. 5 (May 1904), pp. [283]-285.)

LONGLEY, JAMES WILBERFORCE Nova Scotia at Confederation and now. By J. W. Longley. (In *The University magazine*. Montreal. v. 8 (1909), pp. [422]-435.)

—— What shall the tariff be? By the Hon. J. W. Longley, Attorney-General of Nova Scotia. (In *The Canadian magazine of politics, science, art and literature*. Toronto. v. 8. (1896/97), pp. [379]-381.)

LUPUL, MANOLY ROBERT The campaign for a French Catholic school inspector in the North West Territories, 1898-1903. By Manoly R. Lupul. (In *The Canadian historical review*. Toronto. v. 48 (1967), pp. 332-352.)

—— The campaign for a French Catholic school inspector in the North West Territories, 1898-1903. By Manoly R. Lupul. (In *Minorities, schools and politics*. [Toronto, c1969] pp. [42]-62.)

"Reprinted from Canadian historical review, XLVIII (4), December, 1967."

MC BRIDE, W. D. The faith of our fathers. (In *The University magazine*. Montreal. v. 9 (1910), pp. [239]-254.)

Comments on the historical development of the Canadian nation.

—— What of the West? (In *The University magazine*. Montreal. v. 8 (1909), pp. [274]-290.)
Considers the development of the West and its impact on the Canadian nation.

MC CONNELL, J. MILLER Canadians and imperial titles. (In *The Busy man's magazine*. Toronto. v. 17, no. 6 (Apr. 1909), pp. 23-31.)

MACDONALD, JAMES ALEXANDER Canadian democracy: its problems. By J. A. Macdonald. (In *The Canadian courier*. Toronto. v. 9, no. 23 (May 6, 1911), pp. 14; 25.)

—— Public opinion, the Canadian Club and democracy. By J. A. Macdonald. (In Canadian Club of Fort William. *Annual*. [Fort William] (1908), pp. 39-43.)
Address delivered August 31, 1908.
"J. A. Macdonald [was] editor-in-chief of the Globe, Toronto, Ont." (1902-1916).

THE MACE Told in the lobby. By the Mace. (In *Saturday night*. Toronto. v. 24, no. 7 —v. 25, no. 10 (Nov. 26, 1910—Dec. 16, 1911).)
Column dealing with national politics.

MC GRATH, SIR PATRICK THOMAS Why Newfoundland has not entered Confederation. By Hon. P. T. McGrath. (In Canadian Club of Toronto. *Addresses*. Toronto. (1913/14), pp. 123-134.)
Address delivered December 8, 1913.

MAC LEAN, ALEXANDER K. Nova Scotia and its relation to Confederation. By Hon. A. K. MacLean. (In Canadian Club of Toronto. *Addresses*. Toronto. (1911/12), pp. 173-181.)
Address delivered March 25, 1912.
"Hon. Alexander K. MacLean is the Liberal member of Parliament for the city of Halifax."

MACLEAN, JOHN BAYNE In regard to modern knights. By the Editor, [i.e. John Bayne Maclean?] (In *The Busy man's magazine*. Toronto. v. 21, no. 4 (Feb. 1911), pp. 33-39.)
Concerns Sir William Mackenzie, Sir Donald Mann, etc.

—— A Reciprocity prophecy of 1875. By the Editor [i.e. John Bayne Maclean?] (In *MacLean's magazine*. Toronto. v. 25, no. 2 (Dec. 1912), pp. 119-122.)
A discussion and excerpts from an article

by W. Dewart in the *Canadian illustrated news*, March 6, 1875.

MC LEAN, SIMON JAMES The reorganisation of the Canadian Railway Commission. By S. J. McLean. (In *The University monthly*. Toronto. v. 8, no. 7 (May 1908), pp. [237]-240.)

—— Some considerations of railway regulation. By S. J. McLean. (In Empire Club of Canada. *Addresses*. Toronto. (1908/09), pp. 220-230.)
At head of title: Empire Club speeches.
Address delivered April 29, 1909.

MACPHAIL, SIR ANDREW The appeasement of the farmer. (In *Saturday night*. Toronto. v. 25, no. 20 (Feb. 24, 1912), p. 3.)
Concerns the protective tariff.

—— Confiscatory legislation. (In *The University magazine*. Montreal. v. 10 (1911), pp. [192]-206.)

—— The interlude in politics. (In *Saturday night*. Toronto. v. 25, no. 19 (Feb. 17, 1912), p. 3.)

—— Loyalty—to what? (In *The University magazine*. Montreal. v. 6 (1907), pp. [142]-151.)
A comparative and historical discussion of the principle of loyalty as it applies to the Canadian people.

—— The navy and politics. (In *The University magazine*. Montreal. v. 12 (1913), pp. [1]-22.)

—— Protection and politics. (In *The University magazine*. Montreal. v. 7 (1908), pp. [238]-255.)

—— Reciprocity. (In *Toronto Saturday night*. Toronto. v. 23, no. 37 (June 25, 1910), p. 4.)

—— The Tariff Commission. [In *Saturday night*. Toronto. v. 25, no. 18 (Feb. 10, 1912), p. 4.)

—— The Tariff Commission. (In *The University magazine*. Montreal. v. 11 (1912), pp. [27]-40.)

—— What can Canada do? (In *The University magazine*. Montreal. v. 6 (1907), pp. 397-411.)
General reflective comments.

MAGURN, ARNOTT JAMES The Ottawa correspondent. By A. J. Magurn. (In *Massey's magazine*. Toronto. v. 3, no. 5 (May 1897), pp. [322]-327. ports.)
Describes the function and life of the political journalist.

The Marriage Law decision. That Parliament has no authority to enact the Lancaster Marriage Bill, and if it had the authority it would have no need to use it, is the Court's answer to the Government's questions. (In *The Busy man's Canada*. Toronto. v. 2, no. 6 (July 1912), pp. 39-41.)

Refers to a bill introduced by A. E. Lancaster.

MARTINEAU, PAUL   The case for separate schools. (In Canadian Club of Toronto. *Addresses*. Toronto. (1904/05), pp. 116-117.)

Address delivered on March 13, 1905.

Relates to the school issue raised during the creation of the provinces of Saskatchewan and Alberta in 1905.

MATHIESON, JOHN ALEXANDER   Celebrating Confederation. By Hon. J. A. Mathieson, Premier, Prince Edward Island. (In *The Canadian courier*. Toronto. v. 15, no. 25 (May 23, 1914), pp. 8-9; 16.)

Discusses the Charlottetown Conference, 1864, and the contemporary relationship between Prince Edward Island and the federal government in Ottawa.

MAXWELL, WILLIAM   Canada of to-day. London, Jarrold [1912] 123 p.

"These chapters have been added to, and, in some cases, modified since they appeared in the Daily Mail."

MELVILLE, JOHN   The fiasco of Isaac Ibbotson, MP. (In *The Canadian courier*. Toronto. v. 15, no. 13 (Feb. 28, 1914), pp. 10-11; 21-22.)

A fictitious character.

——— Isaac Ibbotson, MP, interviewed. The member for Moptown, Ont., clears up some misconceptions and does a little talking out in meeting about public service in the House of Commons. (In *The Canadian courier*. Toronto. v. 15, no. 20 (Apr. 18, 1914), pp. 6-7.)

Discusses party politics, parliamentary reform, etc.

This member of Parliament is a fictitious character.

MELVIN, GEORGE GIVAN   Maritime union. (In *The University magazine*. Montreal. v. 8 (1909), pp. [436]-422.)

Considers, in part, the relationship between a united Maritime region and Ottawa.

MIDDLETON, JESSE EDGAR   Bilingual schools. By J. E. Middleton. (In *The University*

monthly. Toronto. v. 13, no. 3 (Jan. 1913), pp. 120-126.)

Considers the constitutional and political aspects of the issue.

MILLS, GEORGE H.   Canada's future. A prophecy fulfilled. By G. H. Mills. (In Wentworth Historical Society. *Transactions*. Hamilton. v. 2 (1899), pp. 10-18.)

MILNER, ALFRED MILNER, 1ST VISCOUNT   Speeches delivered in Canada in the autumn of 1908. By Viscount Milner. Toronto, W. Tyrrell, 1909. 93 p.

Concentrates, mainly, upon the subject of imperial relations.

MONK, FREDERICK DEBARTZCH   Castes in Canada. By F. D. Monk, MP. (In *The Canadian courier*. Toronto. v. 1, no. 1 (Dec. 1, 1906), pp. 9-10; 17.)

Text of an address delivered before the Canadian Club of Montreal.

MONROE, NEVA MARGUERITE   Henri Bourassa and the Nationalist movement in Canada. [Madison, Wis., 1939] 112 leaves.

Thesis (MA) – University of Wisconsin.

MONTPETIT, EDOUARD   Les survivances françaises au Canada. Conférences faites à l'Ecole libre des sciences politiques les 13 et 20 juin 1913. Précédées des discours prononcés par Etienne Lamy et Louis Madelin. Paris, Typ. Plon-Nourrit, 1914. 91 p.

MORRISON, DAVID ROBERT   The politics of the Yukon Territory, 1898-1909. By David R. Morrison. [Toronto] University of Toronto Press [c1968] vi, 136 p. (Canadian studies in history and government, 12.)

This study attempts to consider "Canada's experience as an imperial power" and seeks to contribute "to the continuing debate over what form Canadian territorial government should take in the future". – Pref.

MUNRO, JOHN A. (ed.)   The Alaska boundary dispute. Edited by John A. Munro. Toronto, Copp Clark [c1970] 169 p. (Issues in Canadian history.)

A selection of readings.

MURPHY, CHARLES   Development of the Canadian national spirit. By Hon. Chas. Murphy; Secretary of State for Canada. (In Canadian Club of Fort William. *Annual*. [Fort William] (1910), pp. 31-35.)

Address delivered June 17, 1909.

NEATBY, HERBERT BLAIR   The new century. By H. Blair Neatby. (In Careless, J. M. S.

(ed.) *The Canadians, 1867-1967.* Toronto, 1967. pp. 137-171.)

An essay covering the years 1900 to 1910.

NESBITT, WALLACE   Reciprocity with the United States. (In Canadian Club of Toronto. *Addresses.* Toronto. (1910/11), pp. 51-62.)

Address delivered November 8, 1910.

NICHOLS, MARK EDGAR   A forecast of the general elections. By M. E. Nichols. (In *The Canadian magazine of politics, science, art and literature.* Toronto. v. 15 (1900), pp. 547-551.)

The general elections were held November 7, 1900.

NORTHCLIFFE, ALFRED CHARLES WILLIAM HARMSWORTH, 1ST VISCOUNT   Canada to-day and to-morrow. By Rt. Hon. Lord Northcliffe. (In Canadian Club of Ottawa. *Addresses.* Ottawa. (1910), pp. 200-206.)

Our debatable navy. By H. W. A. (In *The Canadian courier.* Toronto. v. 13, no. 5 (Jan. 4, 1913), pp. 7; 27.)

Surveys reactions in the House of Commons to the respective naval policies presented by Robert Borden and Sir Wilfrid Laurier.

OXLEY, JAMES MACDONALD   Ottawa—the political capital. By J. Macdonald Oxley. (In *The National monthly of Canada.* Toronto. v. 3, no. 6 (Dec. 1903), pp. [311]-314. illus.)

PAGE, ROBERT J. D.   The impact of the Boer War on the Canadian general election of 1900 in Ontario. [Kingston, Ont., 1965] iv, 201 leaves.

Thesis (MA) – Queen's University.

PARKER, A. S.   Military service in Canada. (In *The Busy man's magazine.* Toronto. v. 18, no. 3 (July 1909), pp. 51-56.)

PATTERSON, NORMAN   Getting close to the people. (In *The Canadian courier.* Toronto. v. 13, no. 26 (May 31, 1913), p. [7].)

Illustrates the difference in the methods used by the Conservative and Liberal parties by describing the visits made to Toronto by Robert Borden and Wilfrid Laurier.

—— New National Policy wanted. (In *The Canadian courier.* Toronto. v. 8, no. 23 (Nov. 5, 1910), pp. 17; 25.)

—— The political problem. (In *The Canadian courier.* Toronto. v. 4, no. 17 (Sept. 26, 1908), pp. 9; 17.)

Brief comparative comments on Sir Wilfrid Laurier and Robert Borden with a view to the general elections held October 26, 1908.

—— Thirty-six years of Dominion. (In *The Canadian magazine of politics, science, art and literature.* Toronto. v. 21 (1903), pp. 195-200.)

PELLETIER, JEAN GUY   La presse canadienne-française et la guerre des Boers. (In *Recherches sociographiques.* Québec. v. 4, no. 3 (sept. – déc. 1963), pp. [337]-349.)

PENLINGTON, NORMAN   Canada's entry into the Boer War. Toronto, 1937. 191 leaves.

Thesis (MA) – University of Toronto.

PETERSEN, T. A.   Grabbing legislation at Ottawa. Being a few facts and observations concerning the "gentle art of lobbying and the art of "influencing" our Parliament. (In *MacLean's magazine.* Toronto. v. 21, no. 5 (Mar. 1911), pp. [19]-22.)

PETERSON, SIR WILLIAM   Canada and the navy. (In His *Canadian essays and addresses.* London, 1915. pp. 87-107.)

An address delivered before the Empire Club, Toronto, 3 February, 1910.

—— Canadian essays and addresses. By W. Peterson. London, Longmans, Green, 1915. xi, 373 p.

Partial contents: Canada and the navy. – Mr. Borden's naval policy.

—— The navy and politics; a supplement. By W. Peterson. (In *The University magazine.* Montreal. v. 12 (1913), pp. 22-29.)

PETTYPIECE, HENRY JOHN   Do the railways own Canada? By H. J. Pettypiece, late Member, Ontario Legislative Assembly. (In *The Busy man's magazine.* Toronto. v. 21, no. 1 (Nov. 1910), pp. 125-129.)

Concerns the question of "railway taxation".

—— Railway taxation. By H. J. Pettypiece. (In *The Canadian magazine of politics, science, art and literature.* Toronto. v. 20 (1902–03), pp. 353-361.)

A comparative analysis of Canadian and American government taxation policies.

PHILLIPPS-WOLLEY, SIR CLIVE OLDNALL LONG   The Canadian naval question. Addresses delivered by Clive Phillips-Wolley. Toronto, W. Briggs, 1911. 70 p.

The Author was Vice-President of the Navy League. Cf. Introd.

PLANTE, ALBERT   Les écoles bilingues d'Ontario. (In Société historique du Nouvel-

Ontario. *Documents historiques.* Sudbury, Ont. no. 28 (1954), pp. 4-20.)

Political meetings in Canada. (In *The Canadian courier.* Toronto. v. 4, no. 18 (Oct. 3, 1908), pp. 12; 17.)
Comments on the relationship between politicians and the people.

PORRITT, EDWARD The revolt of Canada against the new feudalism; tariff history from the revision of 1907 to the uprising of the West in 1911. London, Published for the Cobden Club by Cassell and Company, 1911. x, 235 p.

—— Sixty years of protection in Canada, 1846-1907; where industry leans on the politician. London, Macmillan, 1908. xii, 478 p.
An attack on the National Policy.

—— Sixty years of protection in Canada, 1846-1907, where industry leans on the politician. 2d ed., rev. and brought up to date, by Annie G. Porritt. [Winnipeg] Winnipeg Grain Growers' Guide, 1913. xv, 476 p.

PRANG, MARGARET EVELYN Clerics, politicians and the bilingual schools issue in Ontario, 1910-1917. By Margaret Prang. (In *The Canadian historical review.* Toronto. v. 41 (1960), pp. 281-307.)

—— Clerics, politicians and the bilingual schools issue in Ontario, 1910-1917. By Margaret Prang. (In *Minorities, schools and politics.* [Toronto, c1969] pp. [85]-111.)
"Reprinted from Canadian historical review, XLI (4), December, 1960."

Quebec's demand for separate schools. Mr. Bourassa declares war. (In *The Busy man's Canada.* Toronto. v. 2, no. 3 (Apr. 1912), pp. 50-53.)
Describes the petition and circulars presented by the Constitutional Defence Association of Canada.

Quebec's loyalty to the Motherland. (In *The Busy man's Canada.* Toronto. v. 3, no. 1 (Aug. 1912), pp. 39-43.)
Presents the opposing views of Senator Rufus H. Pope and Henri Bourassa.

REGEHR, THEODORE DAVID The Canadian Northern Railway; agent of national growth, 1896-1911. [Edmonton, Alta.] 1967. 1 v.
Thesis (PH D) – University of Alberta.

The Result of the election. (In *The Week.* Toronto. v. 13, no. 31 (June 26, 1896), p. [727].)
Comments on the general elections held June 23, 1896.

RICHARDSON, ROBERT LORNE Government ownership of railways. By R. L. Richardson, MP. (In *The Canadian magazine of politics, science, art and literature.* Toronto. v. 15 (1900), pp. 404-409; v. 15 (1900), pp. 531-536; v. 16 (1900), pp. 60-66; v. 16 (1900), pp. 164-171.)
In four parts.
The Author represented Lisgar, Man., as a Liberal, in the House of Commons from 1896 to 1900.

ROBIN, MARTIN The Trades and Labor Congress of Canada and political action: 1898-1908. (In *Relations industrielles.* Québec. v. 22 (1967), pp. 187-215.)
Summary in French: Le Congrès des métiers et du travail du Canada et l'action politique (1898-1908).

ROE, J. SYDNEY The Commons of twenty years ago. By Sydney Roe. (In *Saturday night.* Toronto. v. 44, no. 14 (Feb. 16, 1929), p. 2.)
Recollects the opening of the first session of the eleventh parliament, on January 20, 1909.

ROSS, SIR GEORGE WILLIAM The evolution of Canadian sentiment. By the Hon. G. W. Ross. (In Empire Club of Canada. *Addresses.* Toronto. (1904/05), pp. 252-267.)
At head of title: Empire Club speeches.
Address delivered May 12, 1905.

—— The evolution of Canadian sentiment. By Hon. George W. Ross. (In Locke, G. H. (ed.) *Builders of the Canadian commonwealth.* Freeport, N.Y. [1967] pp. 213-218.)
Excerpt from a speech at the Empire Club, 1905.

—— Preferential trade in its relation to Canada and the Empire. By Hon. George W. Ross, Premier of Ontario. (In *The Canadian magazine of politics, science, art and literature.* Toronto. v. 21 (1903), pp. 411-416.)

RUMILLY, ROBERT Défaite de Laurier. Montréal, B. Valiquette [1945] 221 p. (His *Histoire de la province de Québec,* 16.)
A political history covering the years 1911-1912.

—— Les écoles du Keewatin. Montréal.

Montréal-Editions [1946] 244 p. (His *Histoire de la province de Québec*, 17.)

A political history covering the year 1912.

—— Les écoles du Nord-Ouest. Montréal, B. Valiquette [1944] 232 p. (His *Histoire de la province de Québec*, 12.)

A political history covering the years 1905-1907.

—— F. G. Marchand. 2. éd., rev. et augm. Montréal, B. Valiquette [1942] 317 p. (His *Histoire de la province de Québec*, 9.)

A political history covering the years 1897-1901.

—— Henri Bourassa. Montréal, B. Valiquette [1944] 213 p. (His *Histoire de la province de Québec*, 13.)

A political history covering the years 1907-1908.

—— Israël Tarte. Montréal, B. Valiquette [1943] 269 p. (His *Histoire de la province de Québec*, 10.)

A political history covering the years 1901-1903.

—— Laurier. Montréal, B. Valiquette [1942] 230 p. (His *Histoire de la province de Québec*, 8.)

A political history covering the years 1896-1897.

—— Mgr Bruchési. Montréal, B. Valiquette [1945] 211 p. (His *Histoire de la province de Québec*, 15.)

A political history covering the year 1910.

—— Le règlement 17. Montréal, Montréal-Editions [1946] 282 p. (His *Histoire de la province de Québec*, 18.)

A political history covering the years from late 1912-1914.

—— S. N. Parent. Montréal, B. Valiquette [1943] 244 p. (His *Histoire de la province de Québec*, 11.)

A political history covering the years 1903-1905.

—— Sir Lomer Gouin. Montréal, B. Valiquette [1945] 176 p. (His *Histoire de la province de Québec*, 14.)

A political history covering the years 1909-1910.

RYAN, ALONZO Caricature politique au Canada. Free lance political caricature in Canada. Drawings by Alonzo Ryan. Introductions by Lucien Lasalle and H. M. Williams. Dominion Publishing Co. Mont-real, A. T. Chapman, 1904. 112 p. (chiefly illus.)

"Limited edition, French and English."

SANDWELL, BERNARD KEBLE Political developments around the turn of the century. (In Canadian Historical Association. *Report of the annual meeting*. Toronto. (1945), pp. 49-57.)

SAVAETE, ARTHUR Voix canadiennes: vers l'abîme. Paris [1905?-22?] 14 v. (Collection Arthur Savaète.)

Vols. 13-18 (out of 20) never published? Cf. Beaulieu, A. *Guide d'histoire du Canada*. Québec, 1969 (p. 413).

Partial contents: v. 7. Les écoles du Nord-Ouest canadien. – v. 8. Ecoles du Nord-Ouest canadien.

SAYWELL, JOHN TUPPER The cabinet of 1896. By John T. Saywell. (In Gibson, F. W. (ed.) *Cabinet formation and bicultural relations*. [Ottawa, 1970] pp. [37]-45.)

—— The McInnes incident in British Columbia. (In *The British Columbia historical quarterly*. Victoria, B.C. v. 14 (1950), pp. 141-166.)

Thomas Robert McInnes held the office of Lieutenant-Governor from 1897 to 1900. He was involved in a constitutional issue over the right of a lieutenant-governor to dismiss his responsible ministers.

SELLAR, ROBERT The tragedy of Quebec; the expulsion of its Protestant farmers. 3d ed. Toronto, Ontario Press, 1910. 282, x, xxvii p.

"In this third edition . . . the book now consists of two parts, that which concerns the Protestant farmers of Quebec and that which concerns the people of the other provinces. . . . a voluminous appendix is included, giving quotations from the documents cited . . . useful for reference to those who desire to make a study of the workings of the Papacy in Canada." – Pref. 1910.

SHAW, CHARLES LEWIS The people of Parliament Hill. (In *The Canadian magazine of politics, science, art and literature*. Toronto. v. 13 (1899), pp. 304-309; pp. 438-442; pp. 557-561.)

In three parts.

General observations on the political scene in Ottawa.

SHEPPARD, EDMUND ERNEST Around town. By Don. (In *Toronto Saturday night*. Toronto. v. 1, no.1—v. 11, no. 18 (Dec. 3, 1887—Mar. 19, 1898).)

A column which includes outspoken comments on federal politics.

Written mainly by Don (Edmund E. Sheppard), with occasional articles by Mack (Joseph T. Clark).

SIEGFRIED, ANDRE   La politique canadienne, jugée à l'étranger. (In *La Revue canadienne*. Montréal. t. 40 (1901), pp. [214]-219.)

"De la Revue des questions politiques et coloniales, de Paris."

Part one. Describes politics in Canada with a view to the existence of a French-speaking and English-speaking population living under a federal political system.

SIFTON, SIR CLIFFORD   The work of the Conservation Commission of Canada. By Hon. Clifford Sifton, MP, chairman of the Commission. (In Canadian Club of Ottawa. *Addresses*. Ottawa. (1910), pp. 135-142.)

SLOAN, ROBERT W.   The Canadian West, Americanization or Canadianization? (In *Alberta historical review*. Calgary. v. 16, no. 1 (winter 1968), pp. 1-7.)

Relates, in part, to the immigration policy of the federal government.

SMITH, GOLDWIN   Canada, England and the States. (In *The Busy man's magazine*. v. 14, no. 1 (May 1907), pp. [26]-33.)

Reprinted from *The Contemporary review*.

"Dr. Goldwin Smith gives a history of Canada showing what it is receiving from England and United States. He also gives a forecast of Canadian destiny."

——   Devant le tribunal de l'histoire. Un plaidoyer en faveur des Canadiens qui ont condamné la guerre sud-africaine. Traduit de l'anglais par Henri Bourassa. Montréal, Librairie Beauchemin, 1903. 61 p.

Originally published in English under title: *In the court of history*. Toronto, 1902.

——   In the court of history; an apology for Canadians who were opposed to the South African war. Toronto, Tyrrell, 1902. 71 p.

Translated into French by Henri Bourassa under title: *Devant le tribunal de l'histoire*.

STANLEY, GEORGE FRANCIS GILMAN   A "constitutional crisis" in British Columbia. By George F. G. Stanley. (In *The Canadian journal of economics and political science*. [Toronto] v. 21 (1955), pp. 281-292.)

Discusses the case of Lieutenant-Governor Thomas R. McInnes in British Columbia in

1898 and 1900 regarding his actions of grant and refusal of dissolution.

STEVENS, HENRY HERBERT   Canada, east and west. By H. H. Stevens, MP. (In Canadian Club of Vancouver. *Addresses and proceedings*. [Vancouver] (1912/13), pp. [53]-59.)

Address delivered July 10, 1913.

STEVENS, PAUL DOUGLAS (ed.)   The 1911 general election; a study in Canadian politics. Edited by Paul Stevens. Toronto, Copp Clark [c1970] 220 p. (Issues in Canadian history.)

A selection of readings.

SWANSON, WILLIAM WALKER   Curbing the combines by boards of investigation. By W. W. Swanson. (In *Queen's quarterly*. Kingston. v. 17 (1909/10), pp. 351-356.)

Discusses the historical attempts on the part of Canadian governments to deal with the trust problem and reviews the proposed legislation of the contemporary Minister of Labor, W. L. Mackenzie King.

——   Independence in Canadian politics. By W. W. Swanson. (In *Queen's quarterly*. Kingston. v. 19 (1911/12), pp. [56]-60.)

Considers the question "To what extent should a citizen subordinate himself in order to co-operate with a political party?" relating the problem to Canadian political life.

The Ten biggest men of the Dominion. The result of the voting competition. (In *The Canadian courier*. Toronto. v. 5, no. 7 (Jan. 16, 1909), pp. [12]-[13] ports.)

The poll conducted by the *Canadian courier* resulted in the choosing of five political personalities.

THOMSON, EDWARD WILLIAM   Canadian political affairs. The navy problem in its broadest aspect. . . . (In *MacLean's magazine*. Toronto. v. 25, no. 5 (Mar. 1913), pp. 23-28.)

——   Canadian public affairs. . . . Redistribution of Representation Act . . . [and] the Premier's "Naval Aid" bill [etc.] By E. W. Thomson. (In *MacLean's magazine*. Toronto. v. 25, no. 6 (Apr. 1913), pp. 103-108.)

——   The national political situation. A review of the dominant issues of the day in Canada and the manner in which they are being met by the federal government. By E. W. Thomson. (In *MacLean's magazine*. Toronto. v. 24, no. 1 (May 1912), pp. 3-8.)

—— The national political situation. Canada and the problem of naval defence. The German peril. Armaments and taxes. Defence of British Columbia. Canadian elections probable next year. (In MacLean's magazine. Toronto. v. 24, no. 5 (Sept. 1912), pp. 31-37.)

Article no. 1.

—— The national political situation. The voluntary empire. Unity of our forefather pioneers. Under the voluntary principle all went well. Why not recast our political status? (In MacLean's magazine. Toronto. v. 24, no. 6 (Oct. 1912), pp. 25-31.)

Article no. 2.

—— The national political situation. [A discussion of the outstanding problems with which the Canadian government will deal at this session of Parliament] (In MacLean's magazine. Toronto. v. 25, no. 2 (Dec. 1912), pp. 33-38.)

Article no. 4.

—— The national political situation. . . . the tariff, civil service reform, railway matters, the navy. (In MacLean's magazine. Toronto. v. 25, no. 4 (Feb. 1913), pp. 135-141.)

Article no. 6.

—— What will the West do with Canada? By E. W. Thomson. (In The University magazine. Montreal. v. 6 (1907), pp. [3]-14.)

Discusses the impact of the development of Western Canada on the Canadian nation.

To the members of the House of Commons at Ottawa. (In The Week. Toronto. v. 13, no. 16 (Mar. 13, 1896), pp. 370-371.)

Poses five questions of national policy.

TOKER, EDWARD JOHN How a census is taken. By E. J. Toker, of the Census staff of 1891. (In The Canadian magazine of politics, science, art and literature. Toronto. v. 16 (1900/01), pp. 429-433.)

TOURANGEAU, ANDRE L'opinion du Devoir sur les événements importants de l'actualité, 1912 à 1914. [Montréal] 1964. 1 v.

Thesis (MA) – University of Montreal.

TRANT, WILLIAM "Independence" and party government. (In The Canadian magazine of politics, science, art and literature. Toronto. v. 8 (1896/97), pp. 439-442.)

TRUEMAN, WALTER H. Party government in Canada. (In The University magazine. Montreal. v. 7 (1908), pp. [37]-45.)

UNDERHILL, FRANK HAWKINS Lord Minto on his governor generalship. By Frank H. Underhill. (In Canadian historical review. Toronto. v. 40 (1959), pp. 121-131.)

Letter from Lord Minto to George R. Parkin written Sept. 26, 1904: pp. 124-131.

VAN BLARICOM, GEORGE B. How the Governor-General earns [his] salary. By G. B. Van Blaricom. (In The Busy man's magazine. Toronto. v. 18, no. 5 (Sept. 1909), pp. 19-29.)

—— What flag should Canadians fly? (In The Busy man's magazine. Toronto. v. 18, no. 3 (July 1909), pp. 87-92.)

WIGHTMAN, FREDERICK ARNOLD Our Canadian heritage; its resources and possibilities. Toronto, Briggs, 1905. 287 p.

Will there be a general election? By a politician. (In The Canadian courier. Toronto. v. 12, no. 22 (Oct. 26, 1912), p. 13.)

WILLISON, SIR JOHN STEPHEN The East and Confederation. By J. S. Willison. (In The Canadian courier. Toronto. v. 1, no. 17 (Mar. 23, 1907), p. 10.)

Extracts from a speech delivered at the opening meeting of the Halifax Canadian Club.

—— The genius of the Canadian Club. By J. S. Willison. (In The Canadian magazine of politics, science, art and literature. Toronto. v. 29 (1907), pp. 395-397.)

—— A national policy. By J. S. Willison. (In The Canadian magazine of politics, science, art and literature. Toronto. v. 20 (1902/03), pp. 515-517.)

—— The new Canada; a survey of the conditions and problems of the Dominion. By the Canadian Correspondent of "The Times". London, The Times, 1912. 118 p.

—— Northwest autonomy and the school question. By J. S. Willison. (In Canadian Club of Toronto. Addresses. Toronto. (1904/05), pp. 97-107.)

Address delivered February 27, 1905.

—— The political patronage evil. By J. S. Willison. (In The Canadian courier. Toronto. v. 1, no. 9 (Jan. 26, 1907), pp. 14-15.)

A comparative examination.

WURTELE, DOUGLAS J. The Drummond-Arthabaska by-election of 1910. (In The Dalhousie review. Halifax. v. 40, no. 1 (spring 1960), pp. [14]-33.)

CANADA DURING WORLD WAR I
AND POST-WAR YEARS
1914–1921

ALLEN, ALEXANDER RICHARD The crest and crisis of the social gospel in Canada, 1916-1927. [Durham, N.C., 1966] 1 v.
Thesis (PH D) – Duke University.

ALLEN, RALPH Conscription: the bone in Canada's throat. (In Maclean's. Toronto. v. 74, no. 19 (Sept. 23, 1961), pp. 26; 48-59.)
Excerpt from Ordeal by fire, by R. Allen. Toronto, 1961.

—— La conscription! Ce mot maléfique a ébranlé l'unité du pays deux fois; mais, le sait-on bien, les Québécois n'étaient pas les seuls à s'y opposer en 1918. (In Le Magazine Maclean. Montréal. v. 1, no. 8 (oct. 1961), pp. [30]-31; 48-51; 54.)
Adapted from Maclean's.

ALLYN, NATHANIEL CONSTANTINE The Canadian general election of 1917. [Stanford, Calif.] 1949. 185 leaves.
Thesis (MA) – Stanford University.

ALPHA A brief review of the political situation. By Alpha. (In The Onlooker. Toronto. v. 1, no. 12 (Apr. 1921), pp. 9-13.)
Concentrates on Union Government and Liberal Party opposition.

ANDERSON, HARRY W. If Canada were invaded. (In MacLean's magazine. Toronto. v. 17 [i.e. 27] no. 12 (Oct. 1914), pp. [5]-7; 142-144.)

Are the old line parties dying? (In Maclean's. Toronto. v. 34, no. 18 (Oct. 15, 1921), p. 20.)

ARMITAGE, MAY L. Major B. J. Saunders. Who foresaw the German peril and urged compulsory military training. (In Canada monthly. London, Ont. v. 18, no. 4 (Aug. 1915), p. 225; 240.)
Concerns Major Bryce Johnston Saunders of Edmonton, Alberta.

ARMSTRONG, ELIZABETH HOWARD The crisis of Quebec, 1914-18. New York, Columbia University Press, 1937. xii, 270 p.
An analysis of the conscription crisis.

ATHERTON, WILLIAM HENRY Canadian unity to win the war. A report of the first National Unity and Win the War Convention, held in Montreal, May 21-25, 1917. By W. H. Atherton. Montreal, Canadian Unity and Win the War League, 1917. 50 p.
Text in English and French.

BALAWYDER, A. The Winnipeg General Strike. Vancouver, Copp Clark [c1967] 49 p. (Problems in Canadian history.)
A selection of readings.

BASTEDO, S. T. The poor man's penny bank and the rich man's safety vault. Canadian government annuities system. (In Saturday night. Toronto. v. 30, no. 44 (Aug. 18, 1917), p. [13].)

BEATTIE, EARLE The strike that terrified all Canada. (In Maclean's. Toronto. v. 65, no. 11 (June 1, 1952), pp. 16-17; 39-40; 42; 44-45.)
A Maclean's flashback. Concerns the Winnipeg General Strike, 1919.

BEAUCHESNE, ARTHUR Dissensions et rapprochement. (In La Revue moderne. Montréal. 1 année, no. 2 (15 déc. 1919), pp. 17-18.)
Concerns relations between English- and French-speaking Canadians.

—— Pourquoi l'indépendance? (In Le Revue moderne. Montréal. 1. année, no. 8 (15 juin 1920), pp. 15-16.)
Discusses the separation of Quebec from the Canadian confederation.

Behind the Speaker's chair. (In The Statesman. Toronto. v. 1, no. 33 —no. 50 (Mar. 8, 1919—July 5, 1919).)
A weekly series of comments on proceedings in Parliament.

BERCUSON, DAVID J. The Winnipeg General Strike, collective bargaining and the One Big Union issue. (In The Canadian historical review. Toronto. v. 51 (1970), pp. [164]-176.)

BLUE BOOKE Parliamentary snap-shots. By Blue booke. (In Saturday night. Toronto. v. 32, no. 25 — [v. 34, no. 39] (Apr. 5, 1919—July 10, 1920).)
Comments on personalities in Parliament.

BOIVIN, GEORGES HENRI Canada at peace and at war. By Geo. H. Boivin, MP. (In Canadian Club of Montreal. Addresses. [Montreal] (1914/15), pp. 203-212.)
Address delivered February 22, 1915.

BORDEN, SIR ROBERT LAIRD Addresses delivered at the citizens' patriotic meeting, under the auspices of the Montreal Canadian Club, on McGill campus, Friday evening, August 4th, 1917 [i.e. 1916] by I. the Right Hon. Sir Robert L. Borden, II. the Hon. Rodolphe Lemieux. (In Canadian Club of Montreal. Addresses. [Montreal] (1916/17), pp. [19]-34.)

BOUDREAU, JOSEPH AMEDEE The enemy alien problem in Canada, 1914-1921. [Los Angeles] 1965. 203 leaves.
Thesis (PH D) – University of California, Los Angeles.

—— Western Canada's "enemy aliens" in World War One. By Joseph A. Boudreau. (In *Alberta historical review*. Edmonton. v. 12, no. 1 (winter 1964), pp. 1-9.)
"This paper was given to Calgary Branch of the Historical Society of Alberta in April, 1963."

BOURASSA, HENRI Canadian nationalism and the war. Montreal, 1916. 31 p.

—— La conscription. Montréal, Editions du Devoir, 1917. 46 p.

—— Hier, aujourd'hui, demain, problèmes nationaux. Montréal, Le Devoir, 1916. 178 p.

—— Que devons-nous à Angleterre? La défense nationale, la révolution impérialiste, Le tribut à l'empire. Montréal, 1915. x, 420 p.

BOYD, JOHN Democracy and reaction in Canada. (In *The Statesman*. Toronto. v. 1, no. 50 (July 5, 1919), pp. 7-8.)

—— The Prince on unity. (In *The Canadian nation*. Ottawa. v. 1, no. 13 (Nov. 15, 1919), pp. 10-11.)
Refers to a speech on Canadian national unity made by Edward, Prince of Wales, in Montreal during the autumn of 1919.

—— The secret of national unity. (In *La Revue moderne*. Montréal. 1. année, no. 2 (15 déc. 1919), pp. 15-16.)
Comments on public remarks made in Montreal by Edward, Prince of Wales, while visiting Canada in 1919.

—— Sir Lomer Gouin; a national figure. An appreciation of the career and character of the Prime Minister of Quebec. (In *The Canadian magazine of politics, science, art and literature*. Toronto. v. 50 (1917/18), pp. 466-471.)
The central theme of the essay revolves around the speech on the Francoeur motion delivered by Sir Lomer Gouin in the Legislative Assembly of Quebec, January 23rd, 1918. Cf. *Quebec and Confederation*, by Sir Lomer Gouin. Montreal, Beauchemin, 1918 (34 p.)

BRIDLE, AUGUSTUS The United Farmers of Canada. (In *The Canadian courier*. Toronto. v. 25, no. 4 (Nov. 22, 1919), pp. 12-13.)

—— Will Col. Lavergne enlist? By so doing he will prove himself a real nationalist. (In *The [Canadian] courier*. Toronto. v. 20, no. 21 (Oct. 21, 1916), pp. [5]-6; 22.)
Discusses French-English relations with Armand Lavergne.

BRUCE, HERBERT ALEXANDER Politics and the Canadian Army Medical Corps; a history of intrigue, containing many facts omitted from the official records, showing how efforts at rehabilitation were baulked. With introd. by Hector Charlesworth. Toronto, Briggs, 1919. 321 p.
Presents background information to the controversial Report submitted in September, 1916, to the Canadian government dealing with the administration of the Canadian Medical Service Overseas, commonly referred to as the "Bruce report".

BRUCHESI, JEAN Service national et conscription, 1914-1917. (In Royal Society of Canada. *Proceedings and transactions*. Ottawa. ser. 3, v. 44 (1950), section 1, pp. 1-18.)

BRUCHESI, LOUIS JOSEPH PAUL NAPOLEON, Abp. Le problème des races au Canada. Par S. G. Monseigneur Paul. (In Royal Society of Canada. *Proceedings and transactions*. Ottawa. ser. 3, v. 9 (1915), section 1, pp. 5-11.)
"Lu à la réunion de mai, 1915".

—— Le problème des races au Canada. Par Mgr. Bruchési. (In *Revue canadienne*. Montréal. nouv. sér., v. 16 (1915), pp. [5]-16.)
"Etude présentée à la 'Société royale' du Canada . . . le mardi 25 mai, 1915."
Touches on the political aspects of the subject.

BURY, SIR GEORGE Wanted—a national policy. (In *MacLean's magazine*. Toronto. v. 32, no. 2 (Feb. 1919), pp. [9]; 70-72.)

CAHAN, CHARLES HAZLITT Nuorteva's insidious propaganda. By C. H. Cahan. (In *MacLean's magazine*. Toronto. v. 32, no. 9 (Sept. 1919), pp. 38-39.)
Discusses Soviet propaganda and radical unrest in Canada and relates it to the strike in Winnipeg during May-June, 1919.

CAHILL, FRANK S. Can we salvage our railways. By Frank S. Cahill, MP. (In *MacLean's*. Toronto. v. 34, no. 8 (Apr. 15, 1921), pp. 20-21.)
Canada's future—colonialism or national-

ism? (In *The Canadian nation*. Calgary. v. 1, no. 1 (Mar. 15, 1919), pp. 7-10.)
Discusses the concept of Canada as a "kingdom".

Canadian nationalism and the war. Montreal, 1916. 31 p.
Contents: 1. Mr. Bourassa's views on the participation of Canada in the war – the past and the future – imperialism and nationalism. – 2. An open letter from Capt. Talbot Papineau to Mr. Henri Bourassa. – 3. Mr. Bourassa's reply to Capt. Talbot Papineau's letter. – Mr. McMaster's reply.

The Canadian revolution. (In *The Canadian nation*. Calgary. v. 1, no. 2 (1919), pp. 15-18.)
Comments on a speech Industrial problems and the condition of labor, delivered to the Canadian Club of Toronto on March 17, 1919, by Tom Moore, President of the Dominion Trades and Labour Congress.

Canadian women in the public eye. Mrs. Charles Robson. (In *Saturday night*. Toronto. v. 33, no. 16 (Jan. 31, 1920), p. 22.)
An active political party worker; Union Government supporter, etc.

CASCADEN, GORDON The Winnipeg Strike trials. (In *The Canadian nation*. Ottawa. v 1, no. 21 (Mar. 6, 1920), pp. 11-13; v. 1, no. 22 (Mar. 20, 1920), pp. 12-13.)
In two parts.
The Author conducted publicity work for the Strikers' Defence Committee. Cf. Editor's note.

The Causes of unrest in Canada. (In *The Statesman*. Toronto. v. 1, no. 45 — no. 48 (May 31 — June 21, 1919).)
In four parts.
Published during the period of the Winnipeg General Strike, May 15-June 26, 1919.

CHANTELOIS, RENE La conscription de 1917 d'après les journaux français de Montréal. [Montréal] 1967. 1 v.
Thesis (MA) – University of Montreal.

CHISHOLM, ARTHUR MURRAY Let's go after bear! By A. M. Chisholm. (In *Canadian courier*. Toronto. v. 22, no. 12 (Aug. 18, 1917), pp. [3]-4; 25-26.)
Presents, from the West, a general war policy statement for Canada.

CLARK, WILLIAM CLIFFORD Dominion by-elections. By W. C. Clark. (In *Queen's quarterly*. Kingston. v. 28 (1920/21), pp. 296-297.)
Discusses the significance of the results of federal by-elections held during 1920,

concentrating on the East Elgin by-election held November 22, 1920.

—— Political currents. By W. C. Clark. (In *Queen's quarterly*. Kingston. v. 28 (1920/21), pp. 297-301.)

COMMISSAIRES D'ECOLES CATHOLIQUES D'OTTAWA La requête des Commissaires d'écoles d'Ottawa. (In *L'Action française*. Montréal. 1. année (juin 1917), pp. [183]-189.)
"La requête . . . a été adressée au gouvernement fédéral. . . ."

Commission inquiry shows William Davies Company made large profits out of war contracts. (In *Saturday night*. Toronto. [v. 30, no. 49] (Sept. 22, 1917), pp. 3; 7; 14.)
Chairman of the Commission: G. H. Henderson.

Conscription 1917. Essays by A. H. Willms, Ramsay Cook, J. M. Bliss, Martin Robin. Introd. by Carl Berger. [Toronto] University of Toronto Press [c1969] x, 77 p. (Canadian historical readings, 8.)

Conscription, why, what, how. A clear presentation of the problem about which so many people are talking. By a military man. (In *The [Canadian] courier*. Toronto. v. 21, no. 6 (Jan. 6, 1917), pp. 5; 28.)

COOKE, BRITTON B. The breakdown of democracy—and the come-back that is already on its way. (In *Canada monthly*. London, Ont. v. 22, no. 4 (Aug. 1917), pp. 173-175.)
This article is an analysis of the conscription issue in Canada.

—— The new politics at Ottawa. (In *The [Canadian] courier*. Toronto. v. 20, no. 20 (Oct. 14, 1916), pp. [5]-6.)
Discusses changes in political party mentality, organization and personnel.

COOPER, JOHN ALEXANDER Are you government-owned? A political impertinence. By the Editor. (In *Canadian courier*. Toronto. v. 24, no. 1 (Oct. 12, 1918), pp. [5]; 11.)

—— Au revoir to democracy. By the Editor. (In *Canadian courier*. Toronto. v. 23, no. 19 (June 22, 1918), p. [5].)
Comparative remarks of the modern democratic system.

—— Canadian unity depends on liberty. By the Editor. (In *Canadian courier*. Toronto. v. 22, no. 6 (July 7, 1917), p. 12.)
Concerns the division of opinion over the conscription issue.

—— Let's be sure we lick the Kaiser; editorial. (In *Canadian courier*. Toronto. v. 22, no. 13 (Aug. 25, 1917), p. 9.)

Concerns Canadian unity and the conduct of the war.

—— A new Chamber, but the same old Commons: with a difference. Short studies of two parliamentary quartettes, who more or less dominate the 235 members from all Canada. By the Editor. (In *Canadian courier*. Toronto. v. 25, no. 12 (Mar. 13, 1920), pp. [5]; 19; 25-26.)

—— Our nebulous Dominion Day. A short study in democracy, bigotry and national indifference. By the Editor. (In *Canadian courier*. Toronto. v. 23, no. 20 (July 6, 1918), p. [5].)

—— A united Canada is the greatest need of North America. With special compliments to the international wrecking syndicate, wherever its headquarters may be. By the Editor. (In *Canadian courier*. Toronto. v. 25, no. 13 (Mar. 27, 1920), pp. 10; 29.)

COSTAIN, THOMAS BERTRAM   The farmer in politics. By T. B. Costain. (In *The University magazine*. Montreal. v. 18 (1919), pp. [454]-458.)

Contends that the success of the United Farmers of Ontario is "the most important political development in Canada since Confederation".

—— The Ginger Group. A development of war times in Canadian politics. By T. B. Costain. (In *MacLean's magazine*. Toronto. v. 31, no. 8 (June 1918), pp. [47]-49; 94-96.)

CRERAR, THOMAS ALEXANDER   The Canadian farmer in business and politics. By Hon. T. A. Crerar. (In Canadian Club of Toronto. *Addresses*. Toronto. (1920/21), pp. 221-234.)

Address delivered March 21, 1921.

A Crime against civilization. (In *The Statesman*. Toronto. v. 1, no. 30 (Feb. 15, 1919), p. 3.)

Contends that the Government is not adhering to "the laws of hospitality" as part of its duty to protect travellers and aliens resident in Canada.

CRITCHLEY, A. C.   Conscription after the war. A suggestion for compulsory training of men. By Brigadier-General Critchley. (In *MacLean's magazine*. Toronto. v. 31, no. 12 (Oct. 1918), pp. [13]-14; 104; 106.)

DEACHMAN, ROBERT JOHN   The Farmers' movement. By R. J. Deachman. (In *The Canadian nation*. Ottawa. v. 1, no. 19 (Feb. 7, 1920), pp. 14-16.)

A Demand in the Commons that Sir Joseph Flavelle be requested to resign from the chairmanship of the Imperial Munitions Board. A scathing criticism from D. D. McKenzie, MP, on the floor of the House ... From Saturday night's special Ottawa representative. (In *Saturday night*. Toronto. v. 31, no. 30 (May 11, 1918), p. 3.)

Democracy must unite. (In *The Statesman*. Toronto. v. 1, no. 47 (June 14, 1919), p. 3.)

Defends parliamentary government in post-war Canada.

DESJARDINS, LOUIS GEORGES   L'Angleterre, le Canada et la Grande Guerre. Par L. G. Desjardins. Québec, 1917. xviii, 460 p.

Published in English 1918.

A defence of the Canadian war effort.

—— England, Canada and the Great War. Quebec, Chronicle Print., 1918. xvi, 422 p.

Published in French 1917.

DEUTSCH, JOHN J.   War finance and the Canadian economy, 1914-20. By J. J. Deutsch. (In *The Canadian journal of economics and political science*. [Toronto] v. 6 (1940), pp. 525-542.)

"Paper presented to a joint meeting of the Canadian Political Science Association and the Canadian Historical Association at London, Ont., on May 23, 1940."

DICKIE, ROBERT W.   Reform or revolution? (In *The Statesman*. Toronto. v. 1, no. 47 (June 14, 1919), pp. 5-6.)

"The attitude of the Churches regarding the unrest in Canada is . . . expressed in the . . . address by Rev. Robert W. Dickie, DD, of Knox Presbyterian Church, Montreal."

DINGLE, LLOYD DENHAM   The principle of consciencious objection. [Hamilton, Ont.] 1923. 61 leaves.

Thesis (MA) – McMaster University.

An account of the policy pursued during the First World War by the Canadian government.

DURHAM, J. E.   "Gentlemen, we have with us to-night." Toastmaster, J. E. Durham. (In *Saturday night*. Toronto. v. 32, no. 23 (Mar. 22, 1919), pp. 2; 11.)

Salute to the Duke of Devonshire, the eleventh Governor-General of Canada. Presented in the form of an introductory speech.

EAYRS, HUGH SMITHURST   The new Governor-General. by Hugh S. Eayrs. (In *The Canadian magazine of politics, science, art and literature.* Toronto. v. 48 (1916/17), pp. 303-312.)
Concerns the Duke of Devonshire (Governor-General of Canada, 1916-1921).

EDMONDS, WILLIAM LEWIS   Shall we adopt Newfoundland? What Canada missed for $54,000 in 1895. (In *Canadian courier.* Toronto. v. 22, no. 7 (July 14, 1917), pp. 6; 10.)
Considers Newfoundland and the Canadian confederation.

ENNS, GERHARD   Waterloo North and conscription 1917. (In Waterloo Historical Society. *Annual volume.* Kitchener, Ont. 51st (1963), pp. 60-69.)
Bibliography: p. 69.

EWART, JOHN SKIRVING   Constitutional relations. By John S. Ewart. (In *The Statesman.* Toronto. v. 1, no. 10 (Sept. 28, 1918), p. 8; v. 1, no. 11 (Oct. 5, 1918), pp. 7-8.)
In two parts.
Comments on "the political relation in which Canada stands to the United Kingdom", with reference to the Imperial War Cabinet.

——The Grand Trunk outrage. By John S. Ewart. (In *The Canadian nation.* Ottawa. v. 1, no. 12 (Nov. 1, 1919), pp. 8-9.)

——   Responsible government—an Alberta mistake. By John S. Ewart. (In *The Canadian nation.* Ottawa. v. 1, no. 22 (Mar. 20, 1920), pp. 8-9.)
Concerns a resolution presented in the Alberta Legislature, which raised as an issue the power of dismissal by the Lieutenant-Governor.

FABIUS   52 questions on the nationalization of Canadian railways. By Fabius. Toronto, J. M. Dent [c1918] 127 p.
Stipulates the principles underlying railway nationalization.

FAIRFAX, JOHN   1918—Canada's forgotten riots. (In *The Canadian forum.* Toronto. v. 15, no. 178 (Nov. 1935), pp. 358-362.)
An essay tracing the development of resistance to the enforcement by order-in-council of the Military Service Act.

The Farmers' Party. (In *The Canadian nation.* Calgary. v. 1, no. 2 (Mar. 29, 1919), pp. 13-14.)

Includes discussion of the "Farmers' Platform" which was adopted by the Canadian Council of Agriculture at a meeting held in Winnipeg on November 29, 1918.

The Farmers' platform. (In *The Statesman.* Toronto. v. 1, no. 20 (Dec. 7, 1918), pp. 3-4.)
Examines the program issued by the Canadian Council of Agriculture.

Food profiteering on a huge scale is charge against Canadian corporations. Grave accusations made in report to the Minister of Labor. . . . (In *Saturday night.* Toronto. v. 30, no. 40 (July 21, 1917), p. [1].)
A summary of the report of the Cost of Living Commission, prepared by W. F. O'Connor.

Fooling the farmers. (In *The Statesman.* Toronto. v. 1, no. 24 (Jan 4, 1919), pp. 7-8.)
Concerns the tariff issue.

FOWKE, VERNON CLIFFORD   Allied wheat buying in relationship to Canadian marketing policy, 1914-18. By V. C. Fowke and Mitchell W. Sharp. (In *The Canadian journal of economics and political science.* Toronto. v. 6 (1940), pp. 372-389.)

FRASER, THOMAS M.   Is bolshevism brewing in Canada? (In *MacLean's magazine.* Toronto. v. 32, no. 1 (Jan. 1919), pp. 34-35; 53.)

Free trade or annexation? (In *The Canadian nation.* Calgary. v. 1, no. 1 (Mar. 15, 1919), pp. 10-13.)
Discussed as a national political issue.

The Future of Canada. (In *The Statesman.* Toronto. v. 1, no. 32 (Mar. 1, 1919), pp. 4-5.)
Discusses the question: Is Canada a nation?

GADSBY, HENRY FRANKLIN   [Commentary on national affairs] Human nature and the Kyte inquiry. By H. F. Gadsby. (In *Saturday night.* Toronto. v. 29, no. 33 (May 27, 1916), p. 4.)
Concerns the Duff-Meredith Commission and the Kyte charges against the old Shell Committee.

——   [Commentary on national affairs] Our orphan railways. By H. F. Gadsby. (In *Saturday night.* Toronto. v. 29, no. 34 (June 3, 1916), p. 4.)
Concerns the possible nationalization of the bankrupt transcontinental railways.

——   [Commentary on national affairs] Parliament regained. By H. F. Gadsby. (In

Saturday night. Toronto. v. 29, no. 38 (July 1, 1916), p. 4.)

Discusses changes that have occurred within the two major parties.

—— [Commentary on national affairs] The leaven of unrest. By H. F. Gadsby. (In *Saturday night.* Toronto. v. 30, no. 11 (Dec. 23, 1916), p. 4.)

Examines the idea of a third party in Canadian politics.

—— [Commentary on national affairs] Out of the frying-pan? By H. F. Gadsby. (In *Saturday night.* Toronto. v. 30, no. 12 (Dec. 30, 1916), pp. 4; 11.)

Discusses the proposal for a National government.

—— [Commentary on national affairs] Locating the Llama. By H. F. Gadsby. (In *Saturday night.* Toronto. v. 30, no. 13 (Jan. 6, 1917), p. 4.)

Concerns the choosing of a party leader to lead a coalition government.

—— [Commentary on national affairs] Openings I have seen. By H. F. Gadsby. (In *Saturday night.* Toronto. v. 30, no. 16 (Jan. 27, 1917), p. 4.)

Personal recollections of parliamentary openings.

—— [Commentary on national affairs] Fixing the War Horse. By H. F. Gadsby. (In *Saturday night.* Toronto. v. 30, no. 33 (June 2, 1917), p. 4.)

Concerns selective conscription.

—— [Commentary on national affairs] Coalishing. By H. F. Gadsby. (In *Saturday night.* Toronto. v. 30, no. 36 (June 23, 1917), p. 2.)

Concerns coalition government.

—— [Commentary on national affairs] Kissing him good-by. By H. F. Gadsby. (In *Saturday night.* Toronto. v. 30, no. 39 (July 14, 1917), p. 4.)

Concerns the conscription debate.

—— [Commentary on national affairs] Joseph discovered by his brethren. By H. F. Gadsby. (In *Saturday night.* Toronto. v. 30, no. 44 (Aug. 18, 1917), pp. 4-5.)

Concerns Sir Joseph Flavelle.

—— [Commentary on national affairs] Win the war with whom? By H. F. Gadsby. (In *Saturday night.* Toronto. v. 30, no. 45 (Aug. 25, 1917), p. 4.)

Comments on the position taken by political leaders within the "win-the-war" movement.

—— [Commentary on national affairs] The nigger in the CNR fence. By H. F. Gadsby. (In *Saturday night.* Toronto. v. 30, no. 48 (Sept. 15, 1917), pp. 4; 11.)

Concerns the nationalization of the Canadian Northern Railway.

—— [Commentary on national affairs] Smoke of battle. By H. F. Gadsby. (In *Saturday night.* Toronto. v. 31, no. 7 (Dec. 1, 1917), p. 4.)

Discusses the candidates for the general elections held December 17, 1917.

—— [Commentary on national affairs] The new picture. By H. F. Gadsby. (In *Saturday night.* Toronto. v. 31, no. 24 (Mar. 30, 1918), p. 4.)

Comments on the thirteenth parliament.

—— [Commentary on national affairs] Down to brass tacks. By H. F. Gadsby. (In *Saturday night.* Toronto. v. 31, no. 30 (May 11, 1918), p. 4.)

Discusses the performance of the thirteenth parliament.

—— [Commentary on national affairs] New lamps for old. By H. F. Gadsby. (In *Saturday night.* Toronto. v. 31, no. 36 (June 22, 1918), p. 4.)

Discusses the existing political party system and the possibility for political realignment in the post-World War I period.

—— [Commentary on national affairs] Open doors. By H. F. Gadsby. (In *Saturday night.* Toronto. v. 32, no. 9 (Dec. 14, 1918), pp. 4; 7.)

Comments on post-war political parties in Canada.

—— [Commentary on national affairs] Making Bolshevists. By H. F. Gadsby. (In *Saturday night.* Toronto. v. 32, no. 14 (Jan. 18, 1919), p. 4.)

Suggests a program to halt radical activities.

—— [Commentary on national affairs] Thorns in the flesh. By H. F. Gadsby. (In *Saturday night.* Toronto. v. 32, no. 15 (Jan. 25, 1919), pp. 4-5.)

Outlines problems in Canada which could fester bolshevism.

—— [Commentary on national affairs] Looking down. By H. F. Gadsby. (In *Saturday night.* Toronto. v. 32, no. 16 (Feb. 1, 1919), p. 4.)

Reflects on the Conservative and Liberal parties through the eyes of the late Sir John A. Macdonald and George Brown.

—— [Commentary on national affairs] What way the wind blows. By H. F. Gadsby. (In *Saturday night*. Toronto. v. 32, no. 27 (Apr. 19, 1919), p. 4.)

Discusses tentative election issues.

—— [Commentary on national affairs] What do I believe? By H. F. Gadsby. (In *Saturday night*. Toronto. v. 32, no. 33 (May 31, 1919), p. 4.)

Surveys the current political situation.

—— [Commentary on national affairs] Bleaching the Reds. By H. F. Gadsby. (In *Saturday night*. Toronto. v. 32, no. 34 (June 7, 1919), p. 4.)

Concerns parliamentary attitudes towards bolshevism.

—— [Commentary on national affairs] The break in the clouds. By H. F. Gadsby. (In *Saturday night*. Toronto. v. 32, no. 38 (July 5, 1919), p. 4.)

Discusses post-Union government. Considers the situation of the Liberal and Conservative parties.

—— [Commentary on national affairs] Chasing the curse. By H. F. Gadsby. (In *Saturday night*. Toronto. v. 33, no. 2 (Oct. 25, 1919), p. 4.)

Concerns prohibition and the opposition to it advanced by N. W. Rowell and George E. Foster.

—— [Commentary on national affairs] Figuring it out. By H. F. Gadsby. (In *Saturday night*. Toronto. v. 33, no. 18 (Feb. 14, 1920), pp. 4; 11.)

Part one.

Comments on Union Government, the Farmers' Party and the Labor Party.

—— [Commentary on national affairs] Freedom fighting again. By H. F. Gadsby. (In *Saturday night*. Toronto. v. 34, no. 24 (Mar. 27, 1920), p. 4.)

Concerns the liberties and privileges of the Parliamentary Press Gallery at Ottawa.

—— [Commentary on national affairs] Their swords into plowshares. By H. F. Gadsby. (In *Saturday night*. Toronto. v. 34, no. 29 (May 1, 1920), pp. 4-5.)

Discusses the Soldiers Settlement Board.

—— [Commentary on national affairs] The old familiar face. By H. F. Gadsby. (In *Saturday night*. Toronto. [v. 34, no. 37] (June 26, 1920), p. 3.)

A humorous commentary on the National Policy.

—— [Commentary on national affairs] Licking the platter. By H. F. Gadsby. (In *Saturday night*. Toronto. v. 34, no. 39 (July 10, 1920), p. 3.)

Concerns a raise in salaries for the members of the thirteenth parliament.

—— [Commentary on national affairs] There is hope. By H. F. Gadsby. (In *Saturday night*. Toronto. v. 34, no. 43 (Aug. 14, 1920), p. 4.)

Discusses the national Liberal Party and the national Conservative Party.

—— Conscription—behind the curtain. By H. F. Gadsby. (In *MacLean's magazine*. Toronto. v. 30, no. 10 (Aug. 1917), pp. 37-40.)

—— Over the Speaker's chair. [Series I] By H. F. Gadsby. (In *Saturday night*. Toronto. v. 28, no. 18—no. 28 (Feb. 13—Apr. 24, 1915).)

Weekly comments on events in Parliament.

—— Over ye Speaker's chair [Series II] By H. F. Gadsby. (In *Saturday night*. Toronto. v. 29, no. 15—no. 32 (Jan. 22—May 20, 1916).)

Weekly comments on events in Parliament.

Continued by a series without a general title.

—— Over ye Speaker's chair. By H. F. Gadsby. (In *Saturday night*. Toronto. v. 29, no. 26 (Apr. 8, 1916), pp. 4; 11.)

Comments on the Shell Committee.

—— Over ye Speaker's chair. By H. F. Gadsby. (In *Saturday night*. Toronto. v. 29, no. 32 (May 20, 1916), pp. 4; 11.)

Concerns the bilingual question.

The General election of 1921. (In *The Canadian forum*. Toronto. v. 2, no. 15 (Dec. 1921), pp. 453-454.)

The election held December 6, 1921.

GOOD, WILLIAM CHARLES The democratization of industry. (In *The Statesman*. Toronto. v. 1, no. 48 (June 21, 1919), pp. 6-7.)

Excerpts of an address delivered by W. C. Good to the Canadian Manufacturers' Association in June 1919.

—— Production and taxation in Canada; from the farmers' standpoint. Toronto, Dent, 1919. xviii, 133 p.

GOUGE, JERSE Should farmers form separate party? (In *The Statesman*. Toronto. v. 1. no. 39 [i.e. 40] (Apr. 26, 1919), pp. 5-6.)

Text of an interview reported in the *Edmonton Bulletin*.

GOUIN, SIR LOMER Quebec and Confederation. Speech of Sir Lomer Gouin, Prime Minister of the Province of Quebec on the Francoeur motion. Delivered in the Legislative Assembly of Quebec. January 23rd, 1918. [Foreword by John Boyd] Montreal, Beauchemin, 1918. 34 p.

—— Quebec and Confederation. (In Locke, G. H. (ed.) *Builders of the Canadian commonwealth.* Freeport, N.Y. [1967] pp. 277-281.)
An excerpt from a speech delivered in the Legislative Assembly of Quebec, January 23, 1918.

Government by mandate. (In *The Onlooker.* Toronto. v. 1, no. 10 (Feb. 1921), pp. 23-28.)
Contests the views held by Mackenzie King and the Liberal Party. Considers the position of both the Conservative and Liberal parties.

GRAHAM, WILLIAM ROGER Through the first World War. By Roger Graham. (In Careless, J. M. S. (ed.) *The Canadians, 1867-1967.* Toronto, 1967. pp. 172-204.)

The Grand Trunk deal. (In *The Canadian nation.* Ottawa. v. 1, no. 11 (Oct. 18, 1919), pp. 7-9.)
Comments on the proposal that the Dominion government acquire the capital stock of the Grand Trunk railway.

GREENING, E. W. The Winnipeg Strike trials. (In *Relations industrielles.* Québec. v. 20 (1965), pp. 77-85.)
Summary in French: *Le procès de la grève de Winnipeg* (pp. 84-85).

GREY, GORDON The One Big Union in Canada. (In *The Statesman.* Toronto. v. 1, no. 44 (May 24, 1919), pp. 6-8.)
Reprinted from the *New York Nation* of May 10, 1919.

GROULX, LIONEL ADOLPHE Ce cinquantenaire. Par Lionel Groulx. (In *L'Action française.* Montréal. 1. année. (juil. 1917), pp. [193]-203.)
The fiftieth anniversary of Confederation.

HALL, A. RIVES The "slacker" argument. (In *The Statesman.* Toronto. v. 1, no. 21 (Dec. 14, 1918), p. 12.)
Discusses the effectiveness of the Military Service Act.

—— The tariff question. (In *The Statesman.* Toronto. v. 1, no. 50—51 (July 5— July 12, 1919).)
In two parts.

HAMILTON, CHARLES FREDERICK A military policy. By C. F. Hamilton. (In *The University magazine.* Montreal. v. 19 (1920), pp. [96]-118.)
Advocates the adoption of a clear and permanent policy.

HAMMOND, MELVIN ORMOND Ashes of history. Events recalled by the Parliament Buildings fire at Ottawa. By M. O. Hammond. (In *The Canadian magazine of politics, science, art and literature.* Toronto. v. 46 (1915/16), pp. 473-483.)
A reflective article describing the Parliament Buildings and its historical associations and as a social institution.

Have we freedom of the press? (In *The Statesman.* Toronto. v. 1, no. 6 (Aug. 31, 1918), p. 7.)

HAWKES, ARTHUR The birthright; a search for the Canadian Canadian and the larger loyalty. With introductions by J. Z. Fraser and Mrs. G. A. Brodie. Toronto, Dent [1919] xix, 380 p.

—— Mr. Bourassa's views on the participation of Canada in the war—the past and the future—imperialism and nationalism. (In *Canadian nationalism and the war.* Montreal, 1916. pp. [5]-14.)
"This interview was written by Mr. Arthur Hawkes for the Toronto Star, and appeared in that paper, in two parts, on July 14 and 15, 1916. . . . [The interview] gives out the impressions derived by Mr. Hawkes from his conversation with Mr. Bourassa."

HAWKINS, HENRY They are all Progressives in the West. On the eve of an election. (In *Canadian courier.* Toronto. v. 22, no. 4 (June 23, 1917), pp. [3]; 18.)
Considers the provincial politics of the western Progressive movement in a federal context.

HEROUX, OMER Sur le front ontarien. (In *L'Action française.* Montréal. v. 2 (jan. 1918), pp. [14]-16.)
"Résumons, en traits rapides, les derniers faits publics."
Concerns the Ontario schools issue.

HOCKEN, HORATIO CLARENCE The inevitable Quebec. By H. C. Hocken and Hugh A. Ryan. (In *The Canadian magazine of politics, science, art and literature.* Toronto. v. 50 (1917/18), pp. 3-15.)
Contents: Striking in the national extremity; a criticism, by H. C. Hocken. –

Fair play for Quebec; a defence, by H. A. Ryan.

The article presents two differing views as to how "Quebec stands at the present time in relation to the rest of Canada". Racial animosities have been sharpened due to wartime tensions.

For a rejoinder to the article written by H. C. Hocken see Why do they defame us? by Hon. Charles Langelier. (In *The Canadian magazine of politics, science, art and literature*. Toronto. v. 50 (1917/18), pp. 208-214.)

HODGINS, JAMES COBOURG Come into my parlour. By James C. Hodgins. (In *Saturday night*. Toronto. v. 33, no. 13 (Jan. 10, 1920), p. 5.)

Concerns E. C. Drury and proportional representation.

HUGHES, SIR SAMUEL Some observations on the war. An address by Lieut.-General Sir Sam Hughes. (In Empire Club of Canada. *Addresses*. Toronto. (1916/17), pp. 265-274.)

Address delivered November 9, 1916.

HUNT, JOHN D. Democracy in Canada. Toronto, Macmillan, 1918. iv, 56 p.

A brief summary of historical events from 1763 to 1905.

HYATT, ALBERT MARK JOHN Sir Arthur Currie and conscription; a soldier's view. By A. M. J. Hyatt. (In *The Canadian historical review*. Toronto. v. 50 (1969), pp. 285-296.)

IRVINE, WILLIAM The farmers in politics. [Foreword by Rev. Salem G. Bland] Toronto, McClelland and Stewart [c1920] 253 p.

Is there a Canadian nationality? By R. (In *The Statesman*. Toronto. v. 1, no. 10 (Sept. 28, 1918), p. 7.)

JARVIS, WILLIAM HENRY POPE Democracy and returned soldiers. By W. H. P. Jarvis. (In *Canadian courier*. Toronto. v. 23, no. 24 (Aug. 31, 1918), pp. 11-12; 23.)

Concerns veterans entering politics.

KING, TOM The bilingual issue in Canada. (In *Canada monthly*. London, Ont. v. 20, no. 2 (June 1916), pp. 73-75; 113.)

—— Politics and politicians. Some of the happenings of the month on Parliament Hill. (In *Canada monthly*. London, Ont. v. 22, no. 2 (June 1917), pp. 64-65; 86.)

Reviews the seventh session of the twelfth parliament. Highlights the Royal Commis-

sion report on Canadian railway problems, the question of votes for women, etc.

—— Politics and politicians. Some of the happenings of the month on Parliament Hill. (In *Canada monthly*. London, Ont. v. 22, no. 3 (July 1917), pp. 124-125.)

Reviews the seventh session of the twelfth parliament. Cites conscription as the main issue.

—— Politics and politicians. Some of the happenings of the month on Parliament Hill. (In *Canada monthly*. London, Ont. v. 22, no. 4 (Aug. 1917), pp. 191-192; 216.)

Reviews the seventh session of the twelfth parliament. Considers the issue of conscription.

—— Politics and politicians. Some of the happenings of the month on Parliament Hill and some side lights on the coming election. (In *Canada monthly*. London, Ont. v. 22, no. 6 (Oct. 1917), pp. 316-317; 336.)

Comments on the campaign for the general elections held December 17, 1917, the Military Voters' Act, etc.

KNOX, FRANK ALBERT Canadian war finance and the balance of payments, 1914-18. By F. A. Knox. (In *The Canadian journal of economics and political science*. [Toronto] v. 6 (1940), pp. 226-257.)

Contains information on the war finance policy of the Canadian government.

Labor unrest in Canada. (In *The Statesman*. Toronto. v. 1, no. 30 (Feb. 15, 1919), p. 4.)

LAMBERT, NORMAN PLATT Western Canada and national unity. By Norman Lambert. (In *The University monthly*. Toronto. v. 18, no. 6 (Mar. 1918), pp. 212-214.)

LANCE, HENRY Railway nationalization. Can it be successful in a country beset with politics and politicians? (In *Saturday night*. Toronto. v. 30, no. 11 (Dec. 23, 1916), pp. [17]; 22.)

LANGE, FRED Bloody Saturday. (In *Canadian dimension*. Winnipeg. v. 6, no. 2 (July 1969), p. 13.)

"This interview is an eye-witness account of some of the events of June 21st, 1919." Concerns the Winnipeg General Strike.

LANGELIER, CHARLES Why do they defame us? By the Honourable Charles Langelier. (In *The Canadian magazine of politics, science, art and literature*. Toronto. v. 50 (1917/18), pp. 208-214.)

An answer to the article The inevitable Quebec, by H. C. Hocken. (In *The Canadian magazine of politics, science, art and literature*. Toronto. v. 50 (1917/18), pp. 3-15.)

The Latest "Shell" game. (In *The Statesman*. Toronto. v. 1, no. 23 (Dec. 28, 1918), pp. 6-7.)

Comments on the involvement of Sir Clifford Sifton in a financial arrangement between the Shell Transport and Trading Company and the Dominion Government.

LAUT, AGNES CHRISTINA   His feet are on the ground. By Agnes C. Laut. (In *Maclean's*. Toronto. v. 34, no. 19 (Nov. 1, 1921), pp. 13; 32.)

Concerns Herbert Greenfield and the United Farmers of Alberta. Discussion is national in scope.

——   Our election enigma—woman! By Agnes C. Laut. (In *Maclean's*. Toronto. v. 34, no. 20 (Nov. 15, 1921), pp. 20-21.)

A generalized discussion using as examples the careers of M. E. Smith, I. Parlby, and N. McClung.

LEACOCK, STEPHEN BUTLER   Politics from within. By Stephen Leacock. (In *Mac-Lean's magazine*. Toronto. v. 31, no. 2 (Dec. 1917), pp. [23]-25.)

Illustrated by C. W. Jefferys.

——   The unsolved riddle of social justice. By Stephen Leacock. Toronto, Gundy, 1920. 152 p.

LEAU, LEOPOLD   Le Canada et la guerre. Par L. Leau. (In *La Vie canadienne*. Québec. t. 1, no. 19 (nov. 14, 1918), pp. 15-18.)

The first of a two-part article.

Emphasis is placed on the position taken by Henri Bourassa.

——   Le Canada et la guerre. Par L. Leau. (In *La Vie canadienne*. Québec. t. 1, no. 20 (nov. 21, 1918), pp. 6-8.)

The second and final installment of a two-part article.

Considers, in the main, the position taken by Sir Wilfrid Laurier and the results of the general elections held December 17, 1917.

LUCIAN   The farmers on the trail. By Lucian. (In *The Statesman*. Toronto. v. 1, no. 22 (Dec. 21, 1918), p. 6.)

Comments on the farmers' movement.

LUMSDEN, E. P.   The West remembers 1919. (In *New frontier*. Toronto. v. 2, no. 3 (July/Aug. 1937), pp. 13-15.)

Concerns the Winnipeg General Strike.

MC ARTHUR, PETER   Public opinion and po-

litical life. (In Miller, J. O. (ed.) *The new era in Canada*. London, 1917. pp. 333-345.)

MC CLUNG, NELLIE LETITIA MOONEY   In times like these; addresses. By Nellie L. McClung. Toronto, McLeod and Allen [1915] 217 p.

THE MACE   [Commentary on national affairs] The worst is yet to come. By the Mace. (In *Saturday night*. Toronto. v. 36, no. 5 (Nov. 27, 1920), p. 4.)

Concerns Arthur Meighen, Mackenzie King, T. A. Crerar, and others, and their political campaigning in Western Canada.

——   [Commentary on national affairs] By the Mace. (In *Saturday night*. Toronto. v. 36, no. 6 (Dec. 4, 1920), p. 4.)

Concerns the East Elgin federal by-elections held November 22, 1920.

——   [Commentary on national affairs] The Mill begins to grind. By the Mace. (In *Saturday night*. Toronto. v. 36, no. 17 (Feb. 19, 1921), p. 4.)

Comments, generally, on the fifth session of the thirteenth parliament commencing February 14, 1921.

——   [Commentary on national affairs] The three cornered ring. By the Mace. (In *Saturday night*. Toronto. v. 36, no. 18 (Feb. 26, 1921), p. 4.)

Concerns the three-cornered political battle between Arthur Meighen, William Lyon Mackenzie King, and T. A. Crerar.

——   [Commentary on national affairs] The cross benches. By the Mace. (In *Saturday night*. Toronto. v. 36, no. 20 (Mar. 12, 1921), p. 4.)

Considers the "cross-bench" ideas.

——   [Commentary on national affairs] The real business of Parliament. By the Mace. (In *Saturday night*. Toronto. v. 36, no. 21 (Mar. 19, 1921), p. 4.)

Considers discussion and debate to be the essence of Parliament.

MC GOUN, ARCHIBALD   Finance in Canada after the war. (In *The University magazine*. Montreal v. 16 (1917), pp. [247]-262.)

MC GRATH, SIR PATRICK THOMAS   Vue de Terreneuve. (In *La Vie canadienne*. Québec. t. 1, no. 3 (25 juil. 1918), pp. 20-23.)

The Author was President of the Legislative Council of Terreneuve.

"Cet article qui a pour titre 'Quebec's disaffection' est pris de la 'Review of Reviews' américaine."

Considers the problems confronting Quebec in relation to the other Canadian provinces and to the federal government.

MACKINTOSH, WILLIAM ARCHIBALD The general election of 1921. By W. A. Mackintosh. (In *Queen's quarterly*. Kingston. v. 29 (1921/22), pp. 309-316.)

Analyses the results of the federal election held December 6, 1921.

MACLEAN, JOHN BAYNE A brighter outlook —and why. By Lieut.-Col. J. B. Maclean. (In *MacLean's magazine*. Toronto. v. 31, no. 8 (June 1918), pp. [52]; 54-56.)

—— Conscription in Quebec. (In *MacLean's magazine*. Toronto. v. 30, no. 12 (Oct. 1917), pp. [37]-38.)

—— Keep the wolf from Canada's door. Only a new government system can solve our financial problems. (In *MacLean's magazine*. Toronto. v. 31, no. 1 (Nov. 1917), pp. [17]-18; 74.)

—— Less petty politics, more common sense. By Lieut.-Col. J. B. Maclean. (In *MacLean's magazine*. Toronto. v. 31, no. 11 (Sept. 1918), pp. [49]-50.)

—— Now that the war is won. A discussion of some of the problems of reconstruction. By Lieut.-Col. J. B. Maclean. (In *MacLean's magazine*. Toronto. v. 31, no. 14 (Dec. 1918), pp. [15]; 124-125.)

—— Planning Soviet rule in Canada; tracing to the centre of the web. By Lieut.-Col. J. B. Maclean. (In *MacLean's magazine*. Toronto. v. 32, no. 8 (Aug. 1919), pp. [33]-34; 48-50.)

Concerns alien radical activities in Canada and relates them to the Winnipeg General Strike in 1919.

—— Suppressing the truth. The blind attitude of some Canadian newspapers on war problems. (In *MacLean's magazine*. Toronto. v. 31, no. 6 (Apr. 1918), pp. [45]-46; 72-74.)

—— They're all good men. By Lieut.-Col. John Bayne Maclean. (In *Maclean's*. Toronto. v. 34, no. 20 (Nov. 15, 1921), pp. 22; 33-34; 36.)

Anlyses the political situation of the national parties at the approach of the general elections held December 6, 1921.

—— Why did we let Trotzky go? Canada lost an opportunity to shorten the war. By Lieut.-Col. J. B. Maclean. (In *MacLean's magazine*. Toronto. v. 32, no. 6 (June 1919), pp. [34a]; 66a-66b.)

Leon Trotsky was arrested at Halifax, N.S., April 3, 1917.

MC LEAN, SIMON JAMES The function of railway regulation. By S. J. McLean. (In Canadian Club of Toronto. *Addresses*. Toronto. (1918/19), pp. 212-220.)

Address delivered February 10, 1919.

MC MILLAN, KENNETH The lesson of the Winnipeg Strike. (In *Canadian courier*. Toronto. v. 24, no. 23 (Aug. 16, 1919), pp. 17-19.)

MC NAUGHT, KENNETH WILLIAM KIRKPATRICK The future of the Winnipeg General Strike. By Kenneth McNaught. (In Clarkson, Stephen (ed.) *Visions 2020*. Edmonton, 1970. pp. [253]-256.)

MC NEILL, NEIL, Abp. Canadian national unity. (In Miller, J. O. (ed.) *The new era in Canada*. London, 1917. pp. 193-207.)

Discusses religion and politics, parties and races, present state of representative government.

—— "The language question." Par Mgr. McNeill. (In *L'Action française*. Montréal. v. 4 (fév. 1920), pp. 92-96.)

Text in English.

Reprint of the article which appeared in *Canadian courier* February 14, 1920.

MACPHAIL, SIR ANDREW In this our necessity. (In *The University magazine*. Montreal. v. 16 (1917), pp. [476]-483.)

General comments on wartime Canada.

MAC TAVISH, NEWTON MC FAUL The jubilee of Confederation. By the Editor. (In *The Canadian magazine of politics, science, art and literature*. Toronto. v. 49 (1917), pp. 181-201.)

Includes "statements of the present nine provincial Prime Ministers and of the Minister of Trade and Commerce". (p. 182)

—— Our national crisis. By Newton MacTavish. (In *The Canadian magazine of politics, science, art and literature*. Toronto. v. 49 (1917), pp. 351-358.)

Discusses the conscription crisis, 1917.

—— War time in Canada. By Newton MacTavish. (In *The Canadian magazine of politics, science, art and literature*. Toronto. v. 43 (1914), pp. 545-550.)

A description of the Government's steps and actions as Canada entered World War I.

MAGRATH, CHARLES ALEXANDER Some features of national service. By C. A. Magrath. (In Canadian Club of Montreal. *Addres-*

ses. [Montreal] (1916/17), pp. [157]-170.)

Address delivered January 8, 1917.

MAITLAND, FRANK   The Grain-Grower is decidedly militant. (In *Canadian courier.* Toronto. v. 24, no. 17 (May 24, 1919), pp. 14-15.)

THE MAN FROM WINDERMERE   Parliament, platforms and political leaders. By the Man from Windermere. (In *Canadian courier.* Toronto. v. 24, no. 26 (Sept. 27, 1919), pp. 12; 23-24.)

"Impartial flashlights on the Peace Parliament at Ottawa. . . ."

MASTERS, DONALD CAMPBELL CHARLES   The Winnipeg General Strike. By D. C. Masters. Toronto, University of Toronto Press, 1950. XV,159 p. (Social Credit in Alberta; its background and development, 2.)

MATTHEWMAN, OSBORNE E.   Secret party funds. (In *MacLean's magazine.* Toronto. v. 29, no. 2 (Dec. 1915), pp. [31]-33.)

THE MEMBER FOR CANADA   The Old Adam of partisanship. Party politics flourish while the Empire struggles. By the Member for Canada. (In *The Canadian courier* Toronto. v. 19, no. 13 (Feb. 26, 1916), p. 10.)

—— Ottawa's internment camp. An impartial and somewhat picturesque analysis of Parliament. By the Member for Canada. (In *The Canadian courier.* Toronto. v. 19, no. 9 (Jan. 29, 1916), p. 8.)

—— Our war Parliament. A strange mixture of mediaeval pomp and democratic business. By the Member for Canada. (In *The Canadian courier.* Toronto. v. 19, no. 8 (Jan. 22, 1916), p. 9.)

MERRITT, WILLIAM HAMILTON   Canada and national service. Toronto, Macmillan, 1917. xvi, 247 p.

MILLER, JOHN ORMSBY (ed.)   The new era in Canada; essays dealing with the upbuilding of the Canadian commonwealth. Edited by J. O. Miller. Toronto, Dent, 1917. 421 p.

Partial contents: The foundations of the new era, by C. Sifton. – Canadian national unity, by N. McNeil. – The bi-lingual question, by G. M. Wrong. – Some thoughts on the suffrage in Canada, by A. M. Plumptre. – Public opinion and political life, by P. McArthur.

MILLER, JOHN ORMSBY   The testing of our democracy. By J. O. Miller. (In *The University magazine.* Montreal. v. 15 (1916), pp. [208]-217.)

MOORE, TOM   Industrial problems and the condition of labor. (In The Canadian Club of Toronto. *Addresses.* Toronto. (1918/19), pp. 263-274.)

Delivered March 17, 1919.

MOORE, WILLIAM HENRY   The clash! A study in nationalities. London, Toronto, J. M. Dent, 1918. xxiii, 333 p.

Published in French under title: *Le Choc, étude de nationalités.* Trad. de l'anglais par Ernest Bilodeau. Montréal, Beauchemin, 1920.

—— The irresponsible Five; a new family compact. By William H. Moore. Toronto, McClelland, Goodchild & Stewart [c1917] ix, 67 p.

Discusses the Drayton-Acworth report, i.e. *Report of the Royal Commission to Inquire into Railways and Transportation in Canada.* Ottawa, Printer to the King, 1917. (cv, 86 p.)

Concerns government ownership of railways.

—— Railway nationalisation and the average citizen. By William H. Moore. Toronto, McClelland, Goodchild & Stewart [1917] x, 181 p.

—— Richardson quits no-man's land. The vigorous publisher of the Winnipeg Tribune has fought under fire from both parties. By William H. Moore. (In *The Canadian courier.* Toronto. v. 20, no. 11 (Aug. 12, 1916), pp. 5-6.)

Concerns R. L. Richardson.

MOORHOUSE, HOPKINS   Those pesky farmers out West. (In *Maclean's magazine.* Toronto. v. 32, no. 10 (Oct. 1919), pp. [41]-42.)

Concerns the Farmers' Party movement and its political implications on a national scale.

MORLEY, PERCIVAL FELLMAN   Bridging the chasm. A study of the Ontario-Quebec question. Toronto, J. M. Dent, 1919. 182 p.

Deals with the problem of national unity.

MULLOY, LORNE   National service. By Colonel Mulloy. (In Canadian Club of Montreal. *Addresses.* [Montreal] (1916/17), pp. [7]-17.)

Address delivered June 28, 1916.

Attacks the idea of a voluntary system of military service.

MUNRO, J. K. The calm at Ottawa. (In Mac-Lean's magazine. Toronto. v. 33, no. 8 (May 1, 1920), pp. [16]-17; 64.)

—— An election before fall? It is among the probable developments. (In MacLean's magazine. Toronto. v. 33, no. 2 (Feb. 1, 1920), pp. [12]-13; 75.)

—— The farmer in politics. (In MacLean's magazine. Toronto. v 32, no. 2 (Feb. 1919), pp. [20]-21; 56.)

—— The four factions at Ottawa. A review of the political possibilities. (In Mac-Lean's magazine. Toronto. v. 31, no. 12 (Oct. 1918), pp. [33]-35; 81-82.)

—— Is the group system coming? How things are shaping up in the federal arena. (In MacLean's magazine. Toronto. v. 33, no. 6 (Apr. 1, 1920), pp. [18]-19; 78-79.)

—— Opening the new book. A review of developments at Ottawa. (In MacLean's magazine. Toronto. v. 32, no. 4 (Apr. 1919), pp. [25]-26; 86-87.)

—— Ottawa is ready for the worst. Will next premier be a farmer? The rise of Lapointe. (In MacLean's magazine. Toronto. v. 32, no. 12 (Dec. 1919), pp. [24]-25; 108-109.)

—— A party in the making. Some things about the farmers' faction—and other political points. (In MacLean's magazine. Toronto. v. 32, no. 8 (Aug. 1919), pp. [29]-30; 50.)

—— Politics under the shadow. (In Mac-Lean's magazine. Toronto. v. 33, no. 1 (Jan. 1920), pp. [15]-16; 88-89.)
Concerns the farmers' movement, Grand Trunk legislation, etc.

—— The power of the West. Will the Prairies hold balance of power? (In Mac-Lean's magazine. Toronto. v. 31, no. 13 (Nov. 1918), pp. [31]-33.)

—— The rank and file. Just members— and their new way of thinking. (In MacLean's magazine. Toronto. v. 31, no. 14 (Dec. 1918), pp. [30]-32; 101.)

—— Safe in the saddle? (In MacLean's magazine. Toronto. v. 32, no. 5 (May 1919), pp. [22]-23; 88-89.)
A general review of Parliament in session.

—— Santa's political stocking. (In Mac-Lean's magazine. Toronto. v. 33, no. 23 (Dec. 15, 1920), pp. [24]-25.)
General remarks.

—— The turmoil at Ottawa; new parties, new factions, but old faces. (In Mac-Lean's magazine. Toronto. v. 32, no. 10 (Oct. 1919), pp. [15]-17.)

—— The undercurrents. (In MacLean's magazine. Toronto. v. 32, no. 6 (June 1919), pp. [29]-30; 69.)
A general review of the Canadian political situation.

—— What will Calder do? Our political pundit discusses the Conservatives' "Acrobatic turn"; "Willie King's talented entertainers"; and Crerar, the "Hired man's hero". (In MacLean's magazine. Toronto. v. 33, no. 20 (Nov. 1, 1920), pp. [16]-17; 54.)

—— Will the old parties unite? How federal politics are shaping out. (In Mac-Lean's magazine. Toronto. v. 33, no. 17 (Sept. 15, 1920), pp. [9]-10.)

Newfoundland and Canada. (In The Busy East of Canada. Sackville, N.B. v. 6, no. 2 (Sept. 1915), p. 13.)
Brief remarks on union between Newfoundland and the Dominion.

Le Nouveau règlement ontarien. (In L'Action française. Montréal. v. 2 (jan. 1918), pp. [43]-44.)
Text in English.
Reprint of a résumé of the new settlement regulations which appeared in the Globe, Toronto, January 18, 1918.

OCCIDENTALIS The Western sphinx. By "Occidentalis". (In The Onlooker. Toronto. v. 1, no. 11 (Mar. 1921), pp. 18-25.)
An analysis of politics in Western Canada.

ONLOOKER The Party spirit prevails, yet Parliament has ennui. By Onlooker. (In Canadian courier. Toronto. v. 25, no. 1 (Oct. 11, 1919), p. 11.)

The Opening of Parliament. (In The Canadian nation. Ottawa. v. 1, no. 21 (Mar. 6, 1920), pp. 19-22.)
Concerns the fourth session of the thirteenth parliament, which opened February 26, 1920.

Our new royal commissioners. The two judges who will investigate the Kyte charges in the Yoakum-Allison fuse contracts. (In The Canadian courier. Toronto. v. 19, no. 19 (Apr. 8, 1916), p. 9.)
Concerns Sir William Meredith and Sir Lyman Poore Duff.

Our next Parliament. (In The Canadian

forum. Toronto. v. 2, no. 14 (Nov. 1921), pp. 426-428.)

The federal election was held December 6, 1921.

PAPINEAU, TALBOT MERCER An open letter from Capt. Talbot Papineau to Mr. Henri Bourassa. (In *Canadian nationalism and the war*. Montreal, 1916. pp. [15]-23.)

"A copy of this letter was sent to Mr. Bourassa by Mr. Andrew R. McMaster, KC on the 18th of July, 1916. It was published on the 28th of July, in most of Montreal, Quebec, Ottawa and Toronto papers, English and French."

A Parliamentary review. (In *The Canadian nation*. Ottawa. v. 1, no. 22 (Mar. 20, 1920), pp. 18-22.)

Refers to the fourth session of the thirteenth parliament.

PAUL, CHARLES FREDERICK The new feudalism. By F. P. (In *Saturday night*. Toronto. v. 29, no. 48 (Sept. 9, 1916), p. 4.)

Discusses the new feudalism as advocated by the "Uplift" group.

—— Uplift. By F. P. (In *Saturday night*. Toronto. v. 29, no. 45 (Aug. 19, 1916), pp. 4-5.)

Discusses the "Uplifters" who are the people who would vote for the "Pink'uns".

PENTLAND, H. C. Fifty years after. (In *Canadian dimension*. Winnipeg. v. 6, no. 2 (July 1969), pp. 14-17.)

Provides an analytical account of the Winnipeg General Strike, 1919.

PETERSEN, T. A. The campaign fund in Canada. (In *The Busy man's magazine*. Toronto. v. 21, no. 4 (Feb. 1911), pp. [19]-23.)

PETERSON, CHARLES WALTER CHRISTIAN Wake up, Canada! Reflections on vital national issues. By C. W. Peterson. Toronto, Macmillan, 1919. xiv, 365 p.

Considers political and social questions raised during the post-World War I period in Canada.

PLUMPTRE, ADELAIDE MARY WYNNE (Willson) Some thoughts on the suffrage in Canada. By Adelaide M. Plumptre. (In Miller, J. O. (ed.) *The new era in Canada*. London, 1917. pp. 303-330.)

Discusses war and citizenship, war and the enfranchisement of women . . . woman suffrage from the historical standpoint, woman a non-party voter, etc.

Political probe? Pah! (In *Maclean's*. Toron-

to. v. 34, no. 8 (Apr. 15, 1921), pp. 22; 41-42.)

A nationally known businessman, interested in the railway problems of the Dominion, expresses his views on the deficit of the Canadian Government railways and makes suggestions for a solution. He remains anonymous.

PRENTICE, JAMES STUART Wartime public finance in Canada. [Kingston, Ont.] 1927. 99 leaves.

Thesis (MA) – Queen's University.

Covers federal finance from 1913 to 1925, [and] a year-by-year review of the budgets and accounts. Cf. Canadian graduate theses in the humanities and social sciences, 1921-1964. Ottawa, 1951 (p. 25)

PRITCHARD, WILLIAM A. W. A. Pritchard's address to the jury, in the Crown vs. Armstrong, Heaps, Bray, Ivens, Johns, Pritchard, and Queen . . . indicted for seditious conspiracy and common nuisance, fall assizes. Winnipeg, Manitoba, Canada, 1919-1920. Prepared by the Defense Committee . . . composed of delegates from the various labor organizations in Winnipeg, Manitoba. [Winnipeg, Printed by Wallingford Press, 1920] 219 p.

Running title: Winnipeg strike trials.

Problems of reconstruction. (In *The Statesman*. Toronto. v. 1, no. 10—no. 14 (Sept. 28—Oct. 26, 1918.)

In five parts.

QUEBEC (PROVINCE) LEGISLATURE. LEGISLATIVE ASSEMBLY Quebec and Confederation. A record of the debate of the Legislative Assembly of Quebec on the motion proposed by J.-N. Francoeur, Member for Lotbinière. Translated from the French by A. Savard and W. E. Playfair of the Quebec and Ottawa press galleries. [Quebec] 1918. 136 p.

The motion: "That this House is of the opinion that the province of Quebec would be disposed to accept the breaking of the Confederation pact of 1867 if, in the other provinces, it is believed that she is an obstacle to the union, progress and development of Canada."

A summary of "the so-called Francoeur debate. . . . The editors of this report believe that, by collecting and translating the various speeches made during that discussion, they are preserving a valuable political document." – Foreword.

The Railway question. (In *The Canadian forum*. Toronto. v. 2, no. 14 (Nov. 1921), pp. 424-426.)

READ, JOSEPH   The question of Maritime Union. By Capt. Joseph Read, MP. (In *The Busy East of Canada*. Sackville, N.B. v. 9, no. 1 (Aug. 1918), pp. 5-8; 18.)

RHODES, DAVID BERKELEY   The *Star* and the new radicalism, 1917-1926. Toronto, 1955. 199 leaves.
   Thesis (MA) – University of Toronto.

ROBIN, MARTIN   Registration, conscription and Independent Labour politics, 1916-1917. (In *The Canadian historical review*. Toronto. v. 47 (1966), pp. 101-118.)

——   Registration, conscription and Independent Labour politics, 1916-1917. (In *Conscription 1917*. [Toronto, 1969] pp. [60]-77.)
   "Reprinted from Canadian historical review, XLVII (2), June, 1966."

ROBSON, FREDERIC   Public speaking in Canada. Illustrated by photographs of prominent political speakers. (In *MacLean's magazine*. Toronto. v. 29, no. 7 (May 1916), pp. [14]-16; 118.)

ROWELL, VERNE DE WITT   Quebec the pacifist. An interview with Tancrede Marsil. (In *Canadian courier*. Toronto. v. 22, no. 10 (Aug. 4, 1917), p. 10.)
   Presents the views of Tancrède Marsil, leader and organizer of the League of Sons of Liberty. Considered within a national context.

ROY, FERDINAND   L'appel aux armes et la réponse canadienne-française; étude sur le conflit des races. 3. éd., augm. d'une réponse aux critiques et de lettres adressées à l'auteur par MM. Chapais, Garneau, Lane, LaVergne, Stuart, Wrong, etc. Québec, Garneau, 1917. 85 p.

RUMILLY, ROBERT   Alexandre Taschereau. Montréal, Chantecler [1952] 255 p. (His *Histoire de la province de Québec*, 25.)
   A political history covering the years 1920-1921.

——   L'armistice. [Montréal] Montréal-Editions [1948?] 207 p. (His *Histoire de la province de Québec*, 23.)
   A political history covering the year 1918.

——   La conscription. [Montréal] Montréal-Editions [1948?] 256 p. (His *Histoire de la province de Québec*, 22.)
   Covers the conscription crisis of 1917.

——   Courcelette. Montréal, Montréal-Editions [1947] 269 p. (His *Histoire de la province de Québec*, 21.)
   A political history covering the year 1916.

——   "1914". Montréal, Montréal-Editions [1947] 192 p. (His *Histoire de la province de Québec*, 19.)

——   Philippe Landry. Montréal, Montréal-Editions [1947] 211 p. (His *Histoire de la province de Québec*, 20.)
   A political history covering the year 1915.

——   Succession de Laurier. Montréal, Chantecler [1952] 246 p. (His *Histoire de la province de Québec*, 24.)
   A political history covering the years 1919-1920.

RUTLEDGE, J. L.   The birth of a Labor Party. (In *MacLean's magazine*. Toronto. v. 33, no. 1 (Jan. 1920), pp. [22]-23; 81; 84.)

RYDER, W. S.   Canada's industrial crisis of 1919. [Vancouver, 1920] 1 v.
   Thesis (MA) – University of British Columbia.
   Concerns the Winnipeg General Strike, 1919.

SANDWELL, BERNARD KEBLE   Railway and government. By B. K. Sandwell. (In *The University magazine*. Montreal. v. 18 (1919), pp. [459]-469.)

SCRUTATOR   Canada's next premier? By "Scrutator". (In *MacLean's*. Toronto. v. 34, no. 20 (Nov. 15, 1921), pp. 26; 41; 43-45.)
   Concerns Arthur Meighen, W. L. Mackenzie King, and T. A. Crerar. Relates to the general elections held December 6, 1921.

The Session. (In *The Canadian nation*. Ottawa. v. 1, no. 12 (Nov. 1, 1919), pp. 15-18.)
   Focuses on the debate proposing government control of the Grand Trunk railway.

The Session. (In *The Canadian nation*. Ottawa. v. 1, no. 13 (Nov. 15, 1919), pp. 15-18.)
   Reviews the third session of the thirteenth parliament Sept. 1 – Nov. 10, 1919.

Shall Quebec dominate Canada? (In *The Onlooker*. Toronto. v. 2, no. 1 (May 1921), pp. 22-27.)
   Contests the position of the Lapointe Liberals. Defends the position of Arthur Meighen and the Conservative Party.

SIBLEY, C. LINTERN   The personality of our newspapers . . . Number one: The Montreal Star. (In *The Canadian courier*. Toronto. v. 20, no. 1 (June 3, 1916), pp. 8-9.)

Concerns Sir Hugh Graham and discusses the policy of the newspaper toward politics.

Sidelights on the ending profiteering inquiry. (In *Saturday night*. Toronto. v. 30, no. 42 (Aug. 4, 1917), p. [1].)

Concerns the commission to probe the profiteering charges made in the O'Connor report. Chairman of the Commission: G. H. Henderson.

SIFTON, SIR CLIFFORD   Canada's place in the war and afterwards. (In Canadian Club of Montreal. *Addresses*. [Montreal] (1914/15), pp. 145-158.)

Address delivered January 25, 1915.

—— Conscription. (In Canadian Club of Winnipeg. *Annual report*. [Winnipeg] (1916/17), pp. 108-113.)

Address delivered July 30, 1917.

—— The foundations of the new era. (In Miller, J. O. (ed.) *The new era in Canada*. London, 1917. pp. 37-57.)

Discusses the franchise and naturalization, parliamentary representation, the patronage evil, purity of elections, reform of the Senate, the right to amend the constitution, limitations to legislative powers of Parliament.

SKELTON, OSCAR DOUGLAS   Canadian federal finance. [Part] II. By O. D. Skelton. (In *Queen's quarterly*. Kingston. v. 26 (1918/19), pp. 195-228.)

Reprinted in Bulletin no. 29 of the Departments of History and of Political and Economic Science, Queen's University.

Reviews war financial policy down to 1918 and considers some implications for post-war finance.

—— Canadian federal finance—II. By O. D. Skelton. Kingston [Ont.] Jackson Press, 1918. 34 p. (Bulletin of the Departments of History and Political and Economic Science in Queen's University, no. 29.)

Cover title.

A review of Canadian war finance.

—— The Canadian Northern. By O. D. Skelton. (In *Queen's quarterly*. Kingston. v. 22 (1914/15), pp. 102-111.)

Discusses the circumstances attending "the financial embarrassment of the Canadian Northern, and its appeal to the Dominion Government for further and possibly final aid".

—— Conscription. By O. D. Skelton. (In *Queen's quarterly*. Kingston. v. 25 (1917/18), pp. 222-230.)

Discusses the conscription issue raised during 1917.

—— The Farmers' movement. By O. D. Skelton. (In *Queen's quarterly*. Kingston. v. 27 (1919/20), pp. 326-329.)

Comments on the development of organized farmers' political movements.

—— Federal finance. By O. D. Skelton. (In *Queen's quarterly*. [Kingston] v. 23 (1915/16), pp. [60]-93.)

Reprinted in Bulletin no. 16 of the Departments of History and of Political and Economic Science, Queen's University.

Reviews the fiscal policy of the Canadian government during the early years of World War I.

—— Federal finance. By O. D. Skelton. Kingston [Ont.] Jackson Press, 1915. 34 p. (Bulletin of the Departments of History and Political and Economic Science in Queen's University, no. 16.)

Cover title.

A review of Canadian war finance.

—— The language issue in Canada. By O. D. Skelton. (In *Queen's quarterly*. Kingston. v. 24 (1916/17), pp. [438]-468.)

Reprinted in Bulletin no. 23 of the Departments of History and of Political and Economic Science, Queen's University.

Presents a brief summary of the language question in Canada as a "problem" related to Canadian politics.

—— The language issue in Canada. By O. D. Skelton. Kingston [Ont.] Jackson Press, 1917. 40 p. (Bulletin of the Departments of History and Political and Economic Science in Queen's University, no. 23.)

Cover title.

—— The political situation in Canada. By O. D. Skelton. (In *Queen's quarterly*. Kingston. v. 29 (1921/22), pp. 199-205.)

Presents the issues confronting voters before the federal election held December 6, 1921.

—— The War Franchise Act. By O. D. Skelton. (In *Queen's quarterly*. Kingston. v. 25 (1917/18), pp. 230-232.)

—— The Western strikes. By O. D. Skelton. (In *Queen's quarterly*. Kingston. v. 27 (1919/20), pp. 121-128.)

Discusses, in particular, the Winnipeg General Strike of 1919.

SMITH, DAVID EDWARD Emergency government in Canada. (In *The Canadian historical review*. Toronto. v. 50 (1969), pp. 429-448.)

Deals with the use of emergency powers during World War I.

—— Emergency government in Canada and Australia 1914-1919; a comparison. [Durham, N.C.] 1964. xi, 314 leaves.

Thesis (PH D) – Duke University.

Some speakers—. (In *The Canadian nation*. Ottawa. v. 1, no. 14 (Nov. 29, 1919), pp. 14-18.)

Evaluates speech-making in the House of Commons during 1919.

STEVENSON, JOHN A. The Winnipeg strike. By J. A. Stevenson. (In *The Statesman*. Toronto. v. 1, no. 48 (June 21, 1919), pp. 8-9.)

A brief summary citing causes of the strike.

SWANSON, WILLIAM WALKER Saskatchewan and St. Lawrence. A brief study in a peculiar kind of political unity. By W. W. Swanson. (In *Canadian courier*. Toronto. v. 22, no. 13 (Aug. 25, 1917), pp. 6-7.)

Presents a Western opinion on the national political crisis over the conscription issue.

THOMSON, EDWARD WILLIAM Concerning general elections. (In *The University magazine*. Montreal. v. 14 (1915), pp. [395]-399.)

TIPPING, FRED The Winnipeg General Strike: looking back. (In *Canadian dimension*. Winnipeg. v. 6, no. 2 (July 1969), pp. 10-12; 42.)

An interview with a member of the Strike Committee.

UNDERHILL, FRANK HAWKINS Canada and the last war. (In Martin, C. B. (ed.) *Canada in peace and war*. London, 1941. pp. 120-149.)

Unionism begets unrest. (In *The Statesman*. Toronto. v. 1, no. 25 (Jan. 11, 1919), p. 3.)

Comments on the spread of "bolshevism" in Canada.

Unrest and discontent in rural Canada. The farmers' point of view. Censored! (In *The Statesman*. Toronto. v. 1, no. 1 (July 27, 1918), pp. 9-10.)

Consists of a statement by Alex. D. Bruce, commenting on the inability of the *Statesman* to print his article "Farmers and the new draft regulations", because of censorship regulations; and, an editorial from "The Grain growers' guide" on the military situation as it affects the farmers.

Uplifting the news. By one of the Uplifted. (In *MacLean's magazine*. Toronto. v. 31, no. 10 (Aug. 1918), pp. [33]-35; 78; 80.)

Concerns the press and political reporting.

VICTOR, E. A. (ed.) Canada's future. What she offers after the war. A symposium of official opinion. Edited by E. A. Victor. Toronto, Macmillan Co. of Canada [c1916] xv, 320 p.

VINCENT, JOSEPH ULRIC La question scolaire. Par J.-U. Vincent. Ottawa, Ottawa Print. Co., [1915] 123 p.

The Week. (In *The Statesman*. Toronto. v. 1–4, no. 3 (July 27, 1918–Jan. 15, 1921).)

A weekly column which includes comments on federal political events.

What Bourassa tells Quebec. (In *Canadian courier*. Toronto. v. 22, no. 4 (June 23, 1917), pp. 4; 18.)

Presents a summary of the views expressed through articles in *Le Devoir* by Henri Bourassa.

WHITE, M. P. The eight-hour day a national matter, not a labour question alone. An address by Mr. M. P. White, of Toronto, before the National Industrial Conference. (In *Saturday night*. Toronto. v. 32, no. 51 (Oct. 4, 1919), pp. [13]; 15.)

WILLISON, SIR JOHN STEPHEN From month to month. By Sir John Willison. (In *The Canadian magazine of politics, science, art and literature*. Toronto. v. 53 (1919), pp. 326-332.)

General comments on various current topics, salaries of members of Parliament, the forthcoming national Liberal Party convention, etc.

—— From month to month. By Sir John Willison. (In *The Canadian magazine of politics, science, art and literature*. Toronto. v. 53 (1919), pp. 389-396.)

General comments on various current topics, especially the amended Civil Service Act (pp. 394-396).

—— From month to month. By Sir John

Willison. (In *The Canadian magazine of politics, science, art and literature.* Toronto. v. 54 (1919/20), pp. 343-348.)

A discussion on proportional representation (pp. 347-348).

—— From month to month. By Sir John Willison. (In *The Canadian magazine of politics, science, art and literature.* Toronto. v. 57 (1921), pp. 161-167.)

Discusses the historical background of the concept and method of "coalition" in the politics of Canada (pp. 165-166)

—— From month to month. By Sir John Willison. (In *The Canadian magazine of politics, science, art and literature.* Toronto. v. 58 (1921/22), pp. 172-178.)

Discusses the general election campaign, 1921 (pp. 174-176)

—— From month to month. By Sir John Willison. (In *The Canadian magazine of politics, science, art and literature.* Toronto. v. 58 (1921/22), pp. 262-268.)

Discusses the results of the general election, 1921 (pp. 262-266)

WILLISON, MARJORY (MAC MURCHY), LADY The woman—bless her; not as amiable a book as it sounds. By Marjory Mac-Murchy. Toronto, Gundy [1916] 155 p.

WILLMS, ABRAHAM MARTIN Conscription, 1917: a brief for the defence. By A. M. Willms. (In *The Canadian historical review.* Toronto. v. 37 (1956), pp. 338-351.)

—— Conscription 1917; a brief for the de-fence. By A. M. Willms. (In *Conscription 1917.* [Toronto, c 1969] pp. [1]-14.)

"Reprinted from Canadian historical review, XXXVII (4), December, 1956."

WINNIPEG. DEFENSE COMMITTEE "Saving the world from democracy." The Winnipeg general sympathetic strike, May—June, 1919. Trial by jury destroyed by stampede forty-five minute legislation – workers arrested and rushed to penitentiary to smash strike – leading lawyers' members of Employers' Committee of 1000 – engaged by federal government to prosecute workers. Prepared by the Defense Committee . . . composed of delegates from the various labor organizations in Winnipeg. Manitoba. [Winnipeg, 1920?] 276 p.

Running title: History of Winnipeg strike, 1919.

WOODSWORTH, JAMES SHAVER The immigrant invasion after the war—are we ready for it? By J. S. Woodsworth, Secretary Canadian Welfare League. (In Canadian Club of Winnipeg. *Annual report.* [Winnipeg] (1914/15), pp. 28-33.)

Address delivered December 15, 1914.

—— Nation building. By J. S. Woodsworth. (In *The University magazine.* Montreal. v. 16 (1917), pp. [85]-99.)

—— Some aspects of immigration. By J. S. Woodsworth. (In *The University magazine.* Montreal. v. 13 (1914), pp. [186]-193.)

POLITICAL HISTORY
1921–1948

THE TWENTIES

L'ACTION FRANCAISE Les modes d'action nationale. (In *L'Action française.* Montréal. v. 18 (déc. 1927), pp. [320]-353.)

At head of title: La doctrine l'Action française.

Places French-Canadian problems within a national context.

—— Le problème national. (In *L'Action française.* Montréal. v. 17 (fév. 1927), pp. [66]-81.)

At head of title: La doctrine de l'Action française.

Places French-Canadian problems within the context of Confederation.

Apropos of the elections. (In *The Canadian magazine.* Toronto. v. 64 (Sept. 1925), p. [227].)

Sketches a brief historical background of previous federal elections in anticipation of the general elections of 1925.

BEATTY, SIR EDWARD WENTWORTH Confederation. By E. W. Beatty, president, Canadian Pacific Railway Co. (In Canadian Club of Toronto. *Addresses.* Toronto. (1926/27), pp. 338-348.)

Address delivered on March 28, 1927.

BELCOURT, NAPOLEON ANTOINE La part réservée au bilinguisme dans l'Ontario. Par N. A. Belcourt, sénateur. (In *L'Action française*. Montréal. v. 13 (avril 1925), pp. [204]-221.)

BERGER, CARL CLINTON A Canadian Utopia: the Cooperative Commonwealth of Edward Partridge. By Carl Berger. (In Clarkson, Stephen (ed.) *Vision 2020*. Edmonton [c1970] pp. [257]-262.)
An analysis of *A War on poverty*, by E. A. Partridge. Winnipeg, Wallingford Press [1925]

BLADEN, VINCENT WHEELER The Lemieux Act. By V. W. Bladen. (In *The Canadian forum*. Toronto. v. 5, no. 54 (Mar. 1925), pp. 168-170.)
"The Industrial Disputes Investigation Act of 1907 commonly known as the Lemieux Act was drafted in accordance with the report of the then Deputy Minister of Labour, Mr. W. L. Mackenzie King after his intervention in the Lethbridge Coal Strike."

BRADY, ALEXANDER The new Dominion. (In *The Canadian historical review*. Toronto. v. 4 (1923), pp. 204-216.)

BRISCOE, R. LAIRD What are we voting for? (In *Maclean's*. Toronto. v. 38, no. 18 (Sept. 15, 1925), pp. 27; 44; 46.)
Relates to the general elections held October 29, 1925.

BRUCHESI, JEAN La jeunesse étudiante et l'avenir politique. (In *L'Action française*. Montréal. v. 9 (jan. 1923), pp. [51]-59.)

BUCHANAN, E. C. [Commentary on national affairs] Consulting the country. By E. C. B. (In *Saturday night*. Toronto. v. 40, no. 44 (Sept. 19, 1925), p. 4.)
". . . Mr. Mackenzie King announced the reorganization of his cabinet, the dissolution of the fourteenth parliament and the issue of writs for a general election on October 29. . . ." Concerns the activities of Mackenzie King and Arthur Meighen.

—— [Commentary on national affairs] The price of votes is up. By E. C. B. (In *Saturday night*. Toronto. v. 40, no. 48 (Oct. 17, 1925), p. 4.)
Concerns the political campaign for the general elections held October 29, 1925.

—— [Commentary on national affairs] The downtrodden majorities. By E. C. B. (In *Saturday night*. Toronto. v. 40, no. 49 (Oct. 24, 1025), p. 4.)

"The abiding concern of politicians everywhere and always appears to be for minorities and seldom is a voice raised in defence of majorities."

—— [Commentary on national affairs] Guiding us on. By E. C. B. (In *Saturday night*. Toronto. v. 40, no. 50 (Oct. 31, 1925), p. 4.)
Speculates on changes to be made by either King or Meighen after the general elections held October 29, 1925.

—— [Commentary on national affairs] After the battle. By E. C. B. (In *Saturday night*. Toronto. v. 40, no. 51 (Nov. 7, 1925), p. 4.)
Discusses the results of the general elections held October 29, 1925.

—— [Commentary on national affairs] All dressed up and — . By E. C. B. (In *Saturday night*. Toronto. v. 41, no. 1 (Nov. 21, 1925), p. 4.)
Concerns the results of the general elections held October 29, 1925, which gave no clear mandate to any political party to govern the country.

—— [Commentary on national affairs] Between two evils. By E. C. B. (In *Saturday night*. Toronto. v. 41, no. 3 (Dec. 5, 1925), p. 4.)
"Superficially political Ottawa continues to devote itself to speculation and rumor the while party strategists engage in all manner of subterranean negotiations looking to advantage when the issue is joined between the Government and the Conservatives in the House of Commons."

—— [Commentary on national affairs] Pay or go hungry. By E. C. B. (In *Saturday night*. Toronto. v. 41, no. 8 (Jan. 9, 1926), p. 4.)
Concerns the opening of the fifteenth parliament January 7, 1926. The Liberal government held a minority position in the House of Commons.

—— [Commentary on national affairs] The trusty triumvirate. By E. C. B. (In *Saturday night*. Toronto. v. 41, no. 13 (Feb. 13, 1926), p. 4.)
Refers to H. Bourassa, R. Forke, and J. S. Woodsworth. Discusses the political situation in Parliament.

—— [Commentary on national affairs] Drawing back the curtain. By E. C. B. (In *Saturday night*. Toronto. v. 41, no. 14 (Feb. 20, 1926), p. 4.)

Concerns the "debate on the Address in reply to the Speech from the Throne" opening the first session of the fifteenth parliament January 7, 1926.

——— [Commentary on national affairs] As bad as it seemed. By E. C. B. (In *Saturday night*. Toronto. [v. 41, no. 15] (Feb. 27, 1926), p. 4.)
Concerns the Customs Inquiry Committee investigation of scandals in the Department of Customs and Excise.

——— [Commentary on national affairs] Too much red tape. By E. C. B. (In *Saturday night*. Toronto. v. 41, no. 20 (Apr. 3, 1926), p. 4.)
Deals with the customs investigation; the diversion of waters of the Great Lakes.

——— [Commentary on national affairs] Discouraging smuggling. By E. C. B. (In *Saturday night*. Toronto. v. 41, no. 24 (May 1, 1926), p. 4.)
Concerns the customs investigation.

——— [Commentary on national affairs] Hides on the fence. By E. C. B. (In *Saturday night*. Toronto. v. 41, no. 25 (May 8, 1926), p. 4.)
Concerns the investigation of the Customs Inquiry Committee, chaired by H. H. Stevens, citing its first two witnesses: Clarence Jameson and M. J. Larochelle.

——— [Commentary on national affairs] The new co-operation. By E. C. B. (In *Saturday night*. Toronto. v. 41, no. 26 (May 15, 1926), p. 4.)
Concerns the budget debate and other matters.

——— [Commentary on national affairs] Clearing off the slate. By E. C. B. (In *Saturday night*. Toronto. v. 41, no. 29 (June 5, 1926), p. 4.)
Considers results of the Customs Inquiry Committee, chaired by H. H. Stevens.

——— [Commentary on national affairs] Stevens puts it over. By E. C. B. (In *Saturday night*. Toronto. v. 41, no. 31 (June 19, 1926), p. 4.)
Discusses the final report submitted to the House of Commons by the Customs Inquiry Committee, chaired by H. H. Stevens, investigating scandals in the Department of Customs and Excise.

——— [Commentary on national affairs] Off to the country. By E. C. B. (In *Saturday night*. Toronto. v. 41, no. 35 (July 17, 1926), p. 4.)

Comments on the dissolution of Parliament July 2, 1926.

——— [Commentary on national affairs] Midsummer chances. By E. C. B. (In *Saturday night*. Toronto. v. 41, no. 37 (July 31, 1926), p. 4.)
Discusses the campaign for the general elections of September 14, 1926.

——— [Commentary on national affairs] Where danger lies. By E. C. B. (In *Saturday night*. Toronto. v. 41, no. 38 (Aug. 7, 1926), p. 4.)
Discusses the position of the Liberal and Conservative parties, with reference to the general elections held September 14, 1926.

——— [Commentary on national affairs] Fakes and facts of the campaign. By E. C. B. (In *Saturday night*. Toronto. v. 41, no. 39 (Aug. 14, 1926), p. 4.)
Concerns the campaign for the federal election held September 14, 1926.

——— [Commentary on national affairs] Getting down to issues! By E. C. B. (In *Saturday night*. Toronto. v. 41, no. 40 (Aug. 21, 1926), p. 4.)
Discusses the campaign for the general elections held September 14, 1926.

——— [Commentary on national affairs] So's your old man. By E. C. B. (In *Saturday night*. Toronto. v. 41, no. 41 (Aug. 28, 1926), p. 4.)
Discusses the campaign for the general elections September 14, 1926.

——— [Commentary on national affairs] Nearing the finish. By E. C. B. (In *Saturday night*. Toronto. v. 41, no. 42 (Sept. 4, 1926), p. 2.)
Speculates on the results of the forthcoming general elections held September 14, 1926.

——— [Commentary on national affairs] Seeing the salvation. By E. C. B. (In *Saturday night*. Toronto. v. 41, no. 43 (Sept. 11, 1926), p. 4.)
Comments on the campaign for the general elections of September 14, 1926.

——— [Commentary on national affairs] Now for fall plowing. By E. C. B. (In *Saturday night*. Toronto. v. 41, no. 44 (Sept. 18, 1926), p. 4.)
Comments on the revenues of the Customs and Excise Department, the Civil Service, etc.

——— [Commentary on national affairs] The people prevail. By E. C. B. (In *Satur-*

day night. Toronto. v. 41, no. 45 (Sept. 25, 1926), p. 4.)

Concerns the results of the federal election of September 14, 1926.

—— [Commentary on national affairs] 'Tis but a tent. By E. C. B. (In *Saturday night.* Toronto. v. 41, no. 46 (Oct. 2, 1926), p. 20.)

Concerns Arthur Meighen and the current cabinet of Mackenzie King.

—— [Commentary on national affairs] Not a Mussolini but . . . . By E. C. B. (In *Saturday night.* Toronto. v. 41, no. 47 (Oct. 9, 1926), p. 4.)

Comments on W. L. M. King and the Conservative Party, in view of A. Meighen's decision to resign.

—— Lobby and gallery. (In *Saturday night.* Toronto. v. 41, no. 48—v. 45, no. 40, Oct. 16, 1926—Aug. 16, 1930).)

Column dealing with federal politics.

October 16, 1926—June 29, 1929 signed: E. C. B.

Title varies slightly.

—— Lobby and gallery. By E. C. B. (In *Saturday night.* Toronto. v. 41, no. 48 (Oct. 16, 1926), p. 4.)

Comments on the results of the general elections held September 14, 1926.

—— Lobby and gallery. By E. C. B. (In *Saturday night.* Toronto. [v. 42, no. 33] (July 2, 1927), p. 4.)

Concerns the Diamond Jubilee of Confederation.

—— Lobby and gallery. By E. C. B. (In *Saturday night.* Toronto. v. 43, no. 9 (Jan. 14, 1928), p. 4.)

Concerns the committee appointed to advise the government on matters relating to the St. Lawrence deep waterway and power development.

—— Lobby and gallery. By E. C. B. (In *Saturday night.* Toronto. v. 43, no. 10 (Jan. 21, 1928), p. 4.)

Concerns Sir Clifford Sifton and the St. Lawrence deep waterway and power development.

—— Lobby and gallery. The opening of Parliament. Reduction of taxation, immigration reform and the St. Lawrence canal and power project are outstanding questions for discussion. By E. C. B. (In *Saturday night.* Toronto. v. 43, no. 11 (Jan. 28, 1928), p. 4.)

—— Lobby and gallery. Analyzing the new nationhood. Have we equality of status? Pomp and circumstance at Ottawa. Mr. Meighen's comment on the new era in Parliament. By E. C. B. (In *Saturday night.* Toronto. v. 43, no. 13 (Feb. 11, 1928), p. 4.)

—— Lobby and gallery. Rules for limiting speeches work well. Government prompt with legislation. Alberta coal question. Divorce court measure's fate uncertain. By E. C. B. (In *Saturday night.* Toronto. v. 43, no. 14 (Feb. 18, 1928), p. 4.)

—— Lobby and gallery. Deadly dullness of present session. Hoary plaint about national railways, finance. Col. Hunter's partizan report on partizanship. By E. C. B. (In *Saturday night.* Toronto. v. 43, no. 16 (Mar. 3, 1928), p. 4.)

—— Lobby and gallery. Progressive drift to Conservatives. "Co-operation" in a new form. Miss MacPhail's radical suggestion. Status of St. Lawrence canal question. By E. C. B. (In *Saturday night.* Toronto. v. 43, no. 17 (Mar. 10, 1928), p. 4.)

—— Lobby and gallery. Prospects of prorogation by twenty-fourth. Estimates the biggest task of the Commons. Immigration and banking committees busy. By E. C. B. (In *Saturday night.* Toronto. v. 43, no. 22 (Apr. 14, 1928), p. 4.)

—— Lobby and gallery. Government's satisfactory stand on St. Lawrence canal proposals. Advisory committee's suggestions. Futile blockades by private members. By E. C. B. (In *Saturday night.* Toronto. v. 43, no. 24 (Apr. 28, 1928), p. 4.)

—— Lobby and gallery. By E. C. B. (In *Saturday night.* Toronto. v. 43, no. 31 (June 16, 1928), p. 4.)

Presents a general survey of the second session of the sixteenth parliament.

—— Lobby and gallery. By E. C. B. (In *Saturday night.* Toronto. v. 44, no. 4 (Dec. 8, 1928), p. 4.)

Concerns "The (Advisory) Tariff Board in connection with the tariffs on steel and steel products".

The Budget of 1928 analysed. Special correspondence of Willisons monthly. (In *Willisons monthly.* Toronto. v. 3, no. 11 (Apr. 1928), pp. 414-415.)

CANADA. PARLIAMENT. HOUSE OF COMMONS. SPECIAL COMMITTEE ON THE DOMINION ELECTIONS ACT Election Act amendments suggested by organized Labor. (In *Cana-*

dian Congress journal. Montreal. v. 8, no. 4 (Apr. 1929), pp. 11-16.)

Proceedings of the Special Committee appointed to consider the Dominion Elections Act, March 20, 1929. Convened under the chairmanship of C. G. Power.

Canadian immigration and the man who is working out the problems. By an Ottawa correspondent. (In *Saturday night.* Toronto. v. 37, no. 25 (Apr. 22, 1922), p. 3.)

Concerns W. J. Black, deputy minister of the Department of Immigration.

Canadian women in the public eye. Genevieve Lipsett-Skinner. (In *Saturday night.* Toronto. v. 40, no. 36 (July 25, 1925), p. 23.)

The first woman member of the Press Gallery.

Canadian women in the public eye. Miss Marjory Mae MacMurchy. (In *Saturday night.* Toronto. v. 38, no. 47 (Oct. 6, 1923), p. 35.)

Concerns Lady Willison.

Les Canadiens français et la Confédération canadienne. [Soixante ans de confédération] Enquête de "L'Action française". Montréal, Bibliothèque de l'Action française, 1927. 144 p.

A selection of articles covering various topics relating to the Canadian Confederation.

CARMAN, ALBERT RICHARDSON Customs jury packed by politics. By Albert R. Carman. (In *Maclean's.* Toronto. v. 39, no. 8 (Apr. 15, 1926), pp. 7-8.)

Discusses the testimonies of scandals in the Department of Customs and Excise presented to the House of Commons Customs Inquiry Committee.

CARMAN, FRANCIS ASBURY The Labour Party in Parliament. By Francis A. Carman. (In *The Dalhousie review.* Halifax. v. 2 (1922/23), pp. [444]-456.)

The Changing character of the West. Special correspondence of Willisons monthly. (In *Willisons monthly.* Toronto. v. 3, no. 2 (July 1927), pp. 61; 63.)

Considers the West within the Canadian Confederation.

CHARLESWORTH, HECTOR WILLOUGHBY The Canadian scene; sketches: political and historical. Toronto, Macmillan, 1927. 235 p.

"In the main the . . . sketches are reprinted from articles . . . a majority of them first appeared in Toronto Saturday night under the title Reflections." – Foreword.

CLARK, HUGH The day of tadpole and taper. Both the war and extension of the franchise have changed political conditions. (In *Saturday night.* Toronto. v. 41, no. 48 (Oct. 16, 1926), p. 2.)

Comments on the political situation in Canada.

—— Why I was defeated. (In *Willisons monthly.* Toronto. v. 2, no. 5 (Oct. 1926), pp. 194-196.)

Analyses the results of the federal election held September 14, 1926.

The Coming census of the Dominion. Why and how it is taken—prepared by the Dominion Statistician, Ottawa. (In *Saturday night.* Toronto. v. 36, no. 31 (May 28, 1921), p. [13].)

Concerning the election. (In *The Canadian forum.* Toronto. v. 6, no. 62 (Nov. 1925), pp. 38-40.)

Comments on the anticipated federal election held Oct. 29, 1925.

The Confessions of a she-politician. (In *Maclean's.* Toronto. v. 35, no. 11 (June 1, 1922), p. 25-26; 63.)

Contends that "experience and observation have led me to the conclusion that it is a grave mistake for women to rush into political life".

Co-operative government. (In *The Canadian forum.* Toronto. v. 7, no. 75 (Dec. 1926), pp. 70-71.)

CRERAR, THOMAS ALEXANDER Crerar backs up *MacLean's* charges. By Hon. T. A. Crerar, MP. (In *Maclean's.* Toronto. v. 37, no. 7 (Apr. 1, 1924), pp. 19; 50; 52.)

Refers to charges advanced in the series of articles, "Ottawa's orgy of extravagance", by Grattan O'Leary. (In *Maclean's.* Toronto. v. 37, no. 2-5 (1924).)

The Customs debate. (In *The Canadian forum.* Toronto. v. 6, no. 70 (July 1926), pp. 297-298.)

DAFOE, JOHN WESLEY The Dafoe-Sifton correspondence, 1919-1927. Edited by Ramsay Cook. Altona, Man., Printed by D. W. Friesen [for Manitoba Record Society] 1966. xxiii, 310 p. (Manitoba Record Society. Publications, v. 2.)

DAWSON, ROBERT MAC GREGOR The constitutional question. By R. MacG. Dawson. (In *The Dalhousie review.* Halifax. v. 6 (1926/27), pp. [332]-337.)

Concerns the constitutional issue raised between Lord Byng and W. L. Mackenzie King in 1926.

DEACHMAN, ROBERT JOHN Party vs. co-operative government. By R. J. Deachman. (In *Maclean's*. Toronto. v. 39, no. 8 (Apr. 15, 1926), pp. 17; 65.)

DEXTER, GRANT Immigrants' progress. Twenty-four members of the present House of Commons have achieved the journey from obscurity in lands across the sea to Canada's Parliament Hill. (In *Maclean's*. Toronto. v. 41, no. 14 (July 15, 1928), pp. 7; 45-47.)

—— A professor in politics. By A. G. Dexter. (In *Maclean's*. Toronto. v. 41, no. 17 (Sept. 1, 1928), pp. 16; 58; 61-62.)

Concerns John Bracken. Designated as a Liberal-Progressive; became leader of the Progressive Conservative Party in December 1942.

—— What became of our politicians? By A. G. Dexter. (In *Maclean's*. Toronto. v. 42, no. 23 (Dec. 1, 1929), pp. 19; 64-65.)

Diseases of democracy. (In *Willisons monthly*. Toronto. v. 1, no. 11 (Apr. 1926), pp. 428-429.)

Considers the problems of indolence and indifference.

Dominion Day. A plea for unity and co-operation. (In *Willisons monthly*. Toronto. v. 1, no. 2 (July 1925), pp. 45-46.)

DRURY, ERNEST CHARLES The Canadian farmer: what he is. By Hon. E. C. Drury. (In *Maclean's*. Toronto. v. 41, no. 9 (May 1, 1928), pp. 3-4; 50.)

First in a series of three articles.

—— The Canadian farmer: what he has. By Hon. E. C. Drury. (In *Maclean's*. Toronto. v. 41, no. 10 (May 15, 1928), pp. 14; 48-50.)

Second in a series of three articles.

—— The Canadian farmer: what he wants. "What is needed is a new National Policy —a policy not dominated by urban thought". By Hon. E. C. Drury. (In *Maclean's*. Toronto. v. 41, no. 12 (June 15, 1928), pp. 17; 46; 48.)

Third and concluding article.

The East and Confederation. Special correspondence of Willisons monthly. (In *Willisons monthly*. Toronto. v. 3, no. 2 (July 1927), pp. 70-73.)

The Election. (In *The Canadian forum*. Toronto. v. 6, no. 61 (Oct. 1925), pp. 3-4.)

Comments on the anticipated federal election held October 29, 1925.

Election chances. By a political correspondent. (In *The Canadian forum*. Toronto. v. 6, no. 71 (Aug. 1926), pp. 329-330.)

Considers the constitutional issue over the refusal of Lord Byng to grant Mackenzie King's request for dissolution in 1926.

EWART, JOHN SKIRVING The constitutional debate. By John E. Ewart. (In *The Dalhousie review*. Halifax. v. 6 (1926/27), pp. [1]-8.)

Discusses the parliamentary debate over the Lord Byng–Mackenzie King constitutional issue of 1926.

—— The constitutional question, 1926. By John S. Ewart. (In His *The independence papers*. Ottawa. v. 2, no. 6 (1930), pp. [176]-239.)

FOSTER, SIR GEORGE EULAS Citizenship. Sackville, Mount Allison University, 1926. 85 p.

GARDINER, JAMES GARFIELD The West and Canada's problem. By the Honourable J. G. Gardiner. (In Empire Club of Canada. *Addresses*. Toronto. (1928), pp. 161-177.)

Address delivered October 27, 1927.

GARLAND, EDWARD JOSEPH The farmers' group in politics. By J. E. [i.e. Edward Joseph] Garland, MP. (In *The Canadian forum*. Toronto. v. 6, no. 29 (June 1926), pp. 270-272.)

"Mr. Garland is member for Bow River, Alberta." – Ed.

The General election. An examination of issues and prospects. (In *Willisons monthly*. Toronto. v. 1, no. 4 (Sept. 1925), pp. 127-129.)

Concerns the federal election held October 29, 1925.

The General election and the East. Special correspondence of Willisons monthly. (In *Willisons monthly*. Toronto. v. 2, no. 5 (Oct. 1926), pp. 186-188.)

Concerns the election held September 14, 1926.

GIBSON, FREDERICK W. The cabinet of 1921. (In Gibson, F.W. (ed.) *Cabinet formation and bicultural relations*. [Ottawa, 1970] pp. [63]-104.)

GOOD, WILLIAM CHARLES The farmers' movement in Canada. By W. C. Good. (In *The Dalhousie review*. Halifax. v. 2 (1922/23), pp. [476]-484.)

GRAHAM, WILLIAM ROGER (ed.) The King-Byng affair, 1926; a question of responsible government. Edited by Roger Graham.

Toronto, Copp Clark [c1967] 140 p. (Issues in Canadian history.)

Selected readings.

HAWKES, ARTHUR Shall titles be restored? An answer to John Nelson . . . (In Maclean's. Toronto. v. 40, no. 8 (Apr. 15, 1927), pp. 7-8; 52-55.)

Rejoinder to Shall titles be restored? By J. Nelson. (In Maclean's. Toronto. v. 40, no. 6 (Mar. 15, 1927), pp. 17-18; 65).

HAYDON, J. A. P. The labor movement in Canada, 1867-1927. (In Canadian Congress journal. Montreal. v. 6, no. 6 (June 1927), pp. 15-16.)

HEATON, HUGH Three Dominion elections —some contrasts. By H. Heaton. (In The Dalhousie review. Halifax. v. 5 (1925/26), pp. [470]-480.)

Examines the three general elections of 1925 held in New Zealand, Australia, and Canada.

HEDLIN, RALPH Edmund A. Partridge. (In Historical and Scientific Society of Manitoba. Papers. Winnipeg. ser. 3, no. 15 (1960), pp. 59-68.)

Advocated ideas and practices which were expressed, after his time, through the National Progressive Party and the CCF Party.

How the West voted. Special correspondence of Willisons monthly. (In Willisons monthly. Toronto. v. 1, no. 7 (Dec. 1925), pp. 259-260.)

Relates to the results of the federal election held October 29, 1925.

How to get a stable government. (In The Canadian forum. Toronto. v. 6, no. 72 (Sept. 1926), pp. 362-363.)

Discusses the anticipated federal election held September 14, 1926.

HUDSON, ALBERT BLELLOCK Western problems. By Hon. A. B. Hudson. (In The Canadian Club of Toronto. Addresses. Toronto. (1921/22), pp. 192-200.)

Address delivered April 10, 1922.

HYATT, ALBERT MARK JOHN The King-Byng episode: a footnote to history. By A. M. J. Hyatt. (In The Dalhousie review. Halifax. v. 43, no. 4 (winter 1963/64), pp. [469]-473.)

IMRIE, JOHN A Canada forward policy. An address by Mr. John Imrie, before a joint meeting of the Empire Club of Canada and the Board of Trade of the City of Toronto. April 30, 1925. (In Empire Club of Canada. Addresses. Toronto. (1925), pp. 234-250.)

IRVINE, WILLIAM Canadian labor and the future. By Wm. Irvine. (In Canadian Congress journal. Montreal. v. 3, no. 3 (Mar. 1924), pp. 9-11.)

Outlines a policy for labour presented by the Canadian Labor Party.

—— The economics of hope. By Wm. Irvine. (In Canadian Congress journal. Montreal. v. 7, no. 6 (June 1928), pp. 9-15.)

Explains that "my purpose in writing this pamphlet is to present to Labor and Farmers . . . the financial problem in as simple a manner as possible".

Is Canada a nation? (In The Canadian forum. Toronto. v. 4, no. 43 (Apr. 1924), pp. 199-201.)

Discusses a resolution presented by J. S. Woodsworth proposing that Canada complete constitutional control over her affairs.

JACKSON, GILBERT E. An economist looks at Ottawa. (In Maclean's. Toronto. v. 39, no. 9 (May 1, 1926), pp. 18; 86.)

An article condemning "cock-fight politics".

JEFFERS, WELLINGTON Drastic re-organization of Customs Department is absolutely necessary. (In Saturday night. Toronto. v. 41, no. 13 (Feb. 13, 1926), pp. [13]-15.)

Discusses recommendations submitted by a Special Committee of the House of Commons investigating scandals in the Department of Customs and Excise.

KEMP, HUBERT RICHMOND Dominion taxation. I. The sales tax. By H. R. Kemp. (In The Canadian forum. Toronto. v. 3, no. 34 (July 1923), pp. 297-299.)

—— Dominion taxation. II. The income tax. By H. R. Kemp. (In The Canadian forum. Toronto. v. 3, no. 35 (Aug. 1923), pp. 329-330.)

LEVESQUE, ALBERT La confédération et la jeunesse canadienne-française. (In L'Action française. Montréal. v. 17 (mai/juin 1927), pp. [403]-422.)

Analyses the attitude of French Canadian youth towards the Diamond Jubilee celebrating Confederation.

LEVY, GORDON WESTRICH The Lemieux Act and Privy Council decisions of 1925. [Montreal] 1926, 1 v.

Thesis (MA) – McGill University

LOVEKIN, L. A. M. The birth of Confederation. Sixtieth anniversary of the occasion when it was first officially broached at Charlottetown, P.E.I., falls on September 1st. (In *Saturday night*. Toronto. v. 39, no. 41 (Aug. 30, 1924), pp. 4-5.)

LUCHKOVICH, MICHAEL A Ukrainian Canadian in Paliament; memoirs of Michael Luchkovich. Foreword by Alexander Gregorovich. Toronto, Ukrainian Canadian Research Foundation, 1965. xv, 128 p. (Ukrainian Canadian Research Foundation. The Canadian centennial series, 2.)

Appendix F: Ukrainian members of the House of Commons, 1926-1964 (p. 118).

The Author represented Vegreville, Alta., in the federal Parliament for the United Farmers of Alberta from 1926 to his defeat in the 1935 general elections.

MACBETH, MADGE HAMILTON (LYONS) Women who keep political secrets. Describes the work of secretaries to political figures. By Madge Macbeth. (In *Maclean's*. Toronto. v. 38, no. 18 (Sept. 15, 1925), pp. 14-15; 59-61.)

THE MACE [Commentary on national affairs] The guillotine again. By the Mace. (In *Saturday night*. Toronto. v. 36, no. 26 (April 23, 1921), p. 4.)

Discusses "closure" and the reasons behind it in the fifth session of the thirteenth parliament.

—— [Commentary on national affairs] Sandbagging a great public servant. By the Mace. (In *Saturday night*. Toronto. v. 36, no. 27 (Apr. 30, 1921), p. 4.)

Concerns a proposal to abolish the Commission of Conservation.

—— [Commentary on national affairs] Nailing it down. By the Mace. (In *Saturday night*. Toronto. v. 36, no. 33 (June 18, 1921), p. 5.)

Concerns the Yamaska by-elections held May 28, 1921.

—— [Commentary on national affairs] Ready for the fray. By the Mace. (In *Saturday night*. Toronto. v. 36, no. 46 (Sept. 17, 1921), p. 4.)

Discusses Arthur Meighen, W. L. M. King, and T. A. Crerar in view of the forthcoming election campaign.

—— [Commentary on national affairs] Beginning to boil. By the Mace. (In *Saturday night*. Toronto. v. 36, no. 47 (Sept. 24, 1921), p. 4.)

Discusses the political situation prior to the calling of the federal election held December 6, 1921.

—— [Commentary on national affairs] The riddle of Quebec. By the Mace. (In *Saturday night*. Toronto. v. 36, no. 49 (Oct. 8, 1921), p. 4.)

Sketches "the political conditions existing in Quebec at this stage in the campaign". Relates to the general elections held December 6, 1921.

—— [Commentary on national affairs] What will the harvest be? By the Mace. (In *Saturday night*. Toronto. v. 36, no. 50 (Oct. 15, 1921), pp. 5; 7.)

Concerns the general elections held December 6, 1921.

—— [Commentary on national affairs] Lo the poor tariff. By the Mace. (In *Saturday night*. Toronto. v. 36, no. 51 (Oct. 22, 1921), p. 4.)

Concerns the tariff as an issue in the general elections held December 6, 1921.

—— [Commentary on national affairs] The long, long trail. By the Mace. (In *Saturday night*. Toronto. v. 36, no. 52 (Oct. 29, 1921), p. 4.)

Concerns the long "campaign trail" relating to the general elections held December 6, 1921.

—— [Commentary on national affairs] The ready letter writers. By the Mace. (In *Saturday night*. Toronto. v. 36, no. 53 (Nov. 5, 1921), p. 4.)

Humorous commentary on Arthur Meighen and William Lyon Mackenzie King.

—— [Commentary on national affairs] To be or not to be. By the Mace. (In *Saturday night*. Toronto. v. 36, no. 54 (Nov. 12, 1921), p. 4.)

Concerns the campaign for the general elections held December 6, 1921.

—— [Commentary on national affairs] Nearing the winning post. By the Mace. (In *Saturday night*. Toronto. v. 37, no. 3 (Nov. 19, 1921), pp. 4; 10.)

Concerns the general elections held December 6, 1921.

—— [Commentary on national affairs] Looking them over. By the Mace. (In *Saturday night*. Toronto. v. 37, no. 4 (Nov. 26, 1921), p. 4.)

Discusses the election campaign and some of the candidates for the general elections held December 6, 1921.

—— [Commentary on national affairs] Elections past and present. By the Mace. (In *Saturday night*. Toronto. v. 37, no. 5 (Dec. 3, 1921), p. 4.)

With reference to the federal election held Dec. 6, 1921.

—— [Commentary on national affairs] Baron Roorbach and his doings. By the Mace. (In *Saturday night*. Toronto. v. 37, no. 9 (Dec. 31, 1921), p. 4.)

Concerns the Grand Trunk railway issue.

—— [Commentary on national affairs] New whips for old. By the Mace. (In *Saturday night*. Toronto. v. 37, no. 13 (Jan. 28, 1922), p. 4.)

Comments on the necessity for the "leaders of the three groups in the House of Commons to select new Chief Whips at the beginning of the session".

—— [Commentary on national affairs] Victors and vanquished. By the Mace. (In *Saturday night*. Toronto. v. 37, no. 14 (Feb. 4, 1922), p. 4.)

Mace looks at "some of more or less prominent members in the last parliament who have foundered".

—— [Commentary on national affairs] Danger ahead. By the Mace. (In *Saturday night*. Toronto. v. 37, no. 15 (Feb. 11, 1922), p. 4.)

Concerns the problem of a Conservative majority in the Senate during the existence of a Liberal government.

—— [Commentary on national affairs] Up goes the curtain. By the Mace. (In *Saturday night*. Toronto. v. 37, no. 19 (Mar. 11, 1922), p. 4.)

Concerns the opening of the fourteenth parliament.

—— [Commentary on national affairs] Under full sail. By the Mace. (In *Saturday night*. Toronto. v. 37, no. 21 (Mar. 25, 1922), p. 4.)

Concerns the debate on the Speech from the Throne.

—— [Commentary on national affairs] Watching the barometer. By the Mace. (In *Saturday night*. Toronto. v. 37, no. 29 (May 20, 1922), p. 4.)

Concerns the "unsettled" political conditions.

—— [Commentary on national affairs] Jogging along. By the Mace. (In *Saturday night*. Toronto. v. 37, no. 30 (May 27, 1922), p. 5.)

Discusses the "jogging along" pace of the first session of the fourteenth parliament.

—— [Commentary on national affairs] Boiling over. By the Mace. (In *Saturday night*. Toronto. v. 37, no. 32 (June 10, 1922), p. 4.)

Comments that the "political pot" is boiling over. Discusses, in part, the budget debate, the speculated departure of H. H. Stevens, etc.

—— [Commentary on national affairs] The end of the trail. By the Mace. *Saturday night*. Toronto. v. 37, no. 35 (July 1, 1922), p. 4.]

Concerns the closing of the first session, fourteenth parliament.

—— [Commentary on national affairs] The Commons, the Commission, and the railways. By the Mace. (In *Saturday night*. Toronto. v. 37, no. 37 (July 15, 1922), p. 4; v. 37, no. 38 (July 22, 1922), p. 4.)

In two parts.

—— [Commentary on national affairs] Here, there and everywhere. By the Mace. (In *Saturday night*. Toronto. v. 37, no. 39 (July 29, 1922), p. 4.)

Concerns the recall of Parliament during the summer recess. Refers to the first session of the fourteenth parliament.

—— [Commentary on national affairs] What they had they hold. By the Mace. (In *Saturday night*. Toronto. v. 38, no. 7 (Dec. 16, 1922), p. 4.)

Concerns the results of the by-elections in Halifax, Gloucester, Megantic, Lanark, and Jacques Cartier.

—— [Commentary on national affairs] New Year's resolutions. By the Mace. (In *Saturday night*. Toronto. v. 38, no. 9 [i.e. 10] (Jan. 6, 1923), p. 4.)

Prime Minister King and Arthur Meighen and their New Year's resolutions. A hypothetical setting.

—— [Commentary on national affairs] Up goes the curtain. By the Mace. (In *Saturday night*. Toronto. v. 38, no. 20 [i.e. 12] (Jan. 27, 1923), p. 4.)

The curtain goes up on the second session, fourteenth parliament.

—— [Commentary on national affairs] Putting out to sea. By the Mace. (In *Saturday night*. Toronto. v. 38, no. 15 (Feb. 17, 1923), p. 4.)

Comments on Robert Forke of the Progressive Party, Arthur Meighen, etc.

—— [Commentary on national affairs] Reds and rads in the Commons. By the Mace. (In *Saturday night*. Toronto. v. 38, no. 17 (Mar. 3, 1923), p. 4.)

Concerns Rev. James S. Woodsworth and the Rev. William Irvine, who comprise the Labour group in the House of Commons.

—— [Commentary on national affairs] Commons fads and fancies. By the Mace. (In *Saturday night*. Toronto. v. 38, no. 19 (Mar. 17, 1923), p. 4.)

Comments on the "wave of so-called moral reform . . . sweeping the House of Commons".

—— [Commentary on national affairs] Handling a burning question. By the Mace. (In *Saturday night*. Toronto. v. 38, no. 20 (Mar. 24, 1923), p. 4.)

Concerns the Dominion Fuel Board and the problem of fuel supply in Canada.

—— [Commentary on national affairs] Keeping his balance. By the Mace. (In *Saturday night*. Toronto. v. 38, no. 23 (Apr. 14, 1923), p. 4.)

Refers to Mackenzie King and the second session of the fourteenth parliament.

—— [Commentary on national affairs] On the second lap. By the Mace. (In *Saturday night*. Toronto. v. 38, no. 24 (Apr. 21, 1923), p. 5.)

Comments on the beginning of the second half of the second session, fourteenth parliament.

—— [Commentary on national affairs] Operating on the Bank Act. By the Mace. (In *Saturday night*. Toronto. v. 38, no. 27 (May 12, 1923), p. 4.)

Concerns the Banking and Commerce Committee appointed to probe into the Bank Act.

—— [Commentary on national affairs] Under observation. By the Mace. (In *Saturday night*. Toronto. v. 38, no. 33 (June 23, 1923), p. 4.)

Concerns the special House of Commons Committee's probe into the operation of the Civil Service Act.

—— [Commentary on national affairs] The curtain falls. By the Mace. (In *Saturday night*. Toronto. v. 38, no. 35 (July 7, 1923), p. 4.)

Comments on the second session, fourteenth parliament.

—— [Commentary on national affairs] Some sessional snapshots. By the Mace. (In *Saturday night*. Toronto. v. 38, no. 36 (July 14, 1923), p. 4.)

Comments on the second session, fourteenth parliament.

—— [Commentary on national affairs] Guarded from public view. By the Mace. (In *Saturday night*. Toronto. v. 38, no. 37 (July 21, 1923), p. 4.)

Comments on the activities of the Department of Justice.

—— [Commentary on national affairs] Plums on the tree. By the Mace. (In *Saturday night*. Toronto. v. 38, no. 39 (Aug. 11, 1923), p. 4.)

Concerns job vacancies in the government.

—— [Commentary on national affairs] Solving a knotty problem. By the Mace. (In *Saturday night*. Toronto. v. 38, no. 50 (Nov. 3, 1923), p. 4.)

Concerns the Mines and Minerals Committee, "what the committee had to do and what it did" with regard to the fuel supply question.

—— [Commentary on national affairs] Courting by the sea. By the Mace. (In *Saturday night*. Toronto. v. 39, no. 2 (Dec. 1, 1923), p. 4.)

Comments on party politics in Halifax past and present. Refers to Tupper, Borden, etc.

—— [Commentary on national affairs] Just around the corner. By the Mace. (In *Saturday night*. Toronto. v. 39, no. 12 (Feb. 9, 1924), p. 4.)

"There are unmistakable signs and portents that a session of parliament is just around the corner."

—— [Commentary on national affairs] Ready for the fray. By the Mace. (In *Saturday night*. Toronto. v. 39, no. 14 (Feb. 23, 1924), p. 4.)

"As the curtain rings up on the third session of the fourteenth parliament few changes in the line-up of the respective parties will be noticed."

—— [Commentary on national affairs] Up goes the curtain. By the Mace. (In *Saturday night*. Toronto. v. 39, no. 15 (Mar. 1, 1924), p. 4.)

Concerns the opening of the third session, fourteenth parliament.

—— [Commentary on national affairs]

Church union in the Commons. By the Mace. (In *Saturday night*. Toronto. v. 39, no. 16 (Mar. 8, 1924), p. 4.)

Concerns Church union proposals.

—— [Commentary on national affairs] Whips of Parliament. By the Mace. (In *Saturday night*. Toronto. v. 39, no. 25 (May 10, 1924), p. 4.)

Concerns George William Kyte, William Alves Boys, and John Frederick Johnston, chief party whips.

—— [Commentary on national affairs] The rival anglers. By the Mace. (In *Saturday night*. Toronto. v. 39, no. 27 (May 24, 1924), p. 4.)

Concerns Arthur Meighen and Prime Minister King, and budget proposals.

—— [Commentary on national affairs] An unwelcome visitor. By the Mace. (In *Saturday night*. Toronto. v. 39, no. 33 (July 5, 1924), p. 4.)

Concerns the strike of postal employees.

—— [Commentary on national affairs] On to Ottawa. By the Mace. (In *Saturday night*. Toronto. v. 40, no. 2 (Nov. 29, 1924), p. 4.)

Concerns the prohibition issue. "Indications are abroad that the next session of Parliament . . . will see a determined effort made by those who are in control of the prohibition movement to persuade the government to enact a federal law which will prohibit the importation and manufacture of intoxicating liquor."

—— [Commentary on national affairs] Watching the weather. By the Mace. (In *Saturday night*. Toronto. v. 40, no. 30 (June 13, 1925), p. 4.)

Concerns federal election prospects in Nova Scotia and New Brunswick.

—— [Commentary on national affairs] Ringing down the curtain. By the Mace. (In *Saturday night*. Toronto. v. 40, no. 32 (June 27, 1925), p. 4.)

Brief comments on the closing of the fourth session of the fourteenth parliament.

MC GRATH, SIR PATRICK THOMAS Newfoundland stands aloof. An authoritative explanation of the senior colony's disinclination to enter Confederation. By Sir Patrick McGrath. (In *Maclean's*. Toronto. v. 42, no. 21 (Nov. 1, 1929), pp. 5; 53-54.)

Lists ten reasons.

For a rejoinder see Newfoundland and Confederation, by F. A. Wightman. (In

The Busy East of Canada. Sackville, N.B. v. 23, no. 10 (May 1933), pp. 5-7; 19.)

—— Will Newfoundland join Canada? By Hon. Sir P. T. McGrath, KB. (In *Queen's quarterly*. Kingston. v. 36 (1929), pp. [253]-266.)

Argues against the union of Newfoundland with Canada.

The Author was President of the Legislative Council of Newfoundland.

MC KAY, C. Some reflections on labor policy. (In *Canadian Congress journal*. Montreal. v. 4, no. 9 (Sept. 1925), pp. 19-21.)

Argues for the development of a Labor Party in Canada.

MAC KAY, DOUGLAS The session in review. (In *Maclean's*. Toronto. v. 41, no. 13 (July 1, 1928), pp. 17; 45-56.)

Concerns the second session of the sixteenth parliament.

MC KENZIE, VERNON Customs' house-cleaning imperative—no matter whose head comes off! (In *Maclean's*. Toronto. v. 39, no. 5 (Mar. 1, 1926), pp. 24-26; 42-45.)

An analysis of the evidence collected by the Customs Investigation Committee presented to Parliament in June 1926.

MAC RAE, ARCHIBALD OSWALD What is the matter with Canada? Addresses, by "Politicus". London, Stockwell, 1928. 96 p.

MAGRATH, CHARLES ALEXANDER Organization for immigration. By C. A. Magrath. (In *Willisons monthly*. Toronto. v. 1, no. 2 (July 1925), pp. 52-55.)

Discusses Canadian immigration policy.

MARQUIS, GEORGE EMILE Le prochain recensement. Par G.-E. Marquis. (In *Le Terroir*. Québec. v. 2, no. 6 (fév. 1920), pp. 297-305.)

MASSEY, VINCENT Some Canadian problems. (In Canadian Club of Ottawa. *The Canadian Club year book*. [Ottawa] (1922/23 — 1923/24), pp. [237]-245.)

MEARS, F. C. Seven years on Parliament Hill. (In *Maclean's*. Toronto. v. 42, no. 2 (Jan. 15, 1929), pp. 13; 38-40.)

The Author was a member of the Press Gallery.

Millions lost through organized smuggling. Special correspondence of Willisons monthly. (In *Willisons monthly*. Toronto. v. 1, no. 2 (July 1925), pp. 72-75.)

Includes discussion of the application of the Customs Act and the work of the Customs Department.

Mr. Graham's ersatz navy. (In *The Canadian forum*. Toronto. v. 2, no. 21 (June 1922), pp. 646-647.)

Considers the debates on the Naval Estimates and the fulfilment of a naval policy through the provisions of the Naval Service Act of 1910.

MITCHELL, WALTER GEORGE Canadian national unity and how to attain it. By the Hon. Walter G. Mitchell. (In The Canadian Club of Toronto. *Addresses.* Toronto. (1921/22), pp. 173-181.)

Address delivered March 27, 1922.

M. Henri Bourassa. (In *L'Action française*. Montréal. v. 14 (nov. 1925), pp. [286]-293.)

MOORE, HENRY NAPIER Wanted: clean government. By H. Napier Moore. (In *Maclean's*. Toronto. v. 39, no. 14 (July 15, 1926), pp. 16; 32.)

A brief résumé of the report presented to Parliament June 18, 1926, confirming scandals in the Department of Customs and Excise.

MOORE, MARY MAC LEOD The Lady Byng of Vimy. An hour with the First Lady of the Dominion. (In *Saturday night*. Toronto. v. 36, no. 38 (July 23, 1921), p. 21.)

MORRISON, JAMES J. The political future of the UFO! By J. J. Morrison. (In *The Canadian forum*. Toronto. v. 7, no. 77 (Feb. 1927), pp. 138-140.)

Discussion is federal in scope.

MORTON, WILLIAM LEWIS The 1920s. By W. L. Morton. (In Careless, J. M. S. (ed.) *The Canadians, 1867-1967*. Toronto, 1967. pp. 205-235.)

Motors, manufacturers and taxes. (In *The Canadian forum*. Toronto. v. 6, no. 70 (July 1926), pp. 298-300.)

A general discussion of Canadian fiscal policy.

MUNRO, J. K. [Commentary on national affairs] Girding for the federal fray. (In *MacLean's magazine*. Toronto. v. 34, no. 3 (Feb. 1, 1921), pp. 17-18; 36.)

Concerns the fifth session of the thirteenth parliament opened Feb. 24, 1921.

—— [Commentary on national affairs] Funny as the owl is funny. (In *MacLean's magazine*. Toronto. v. 34, no. 5 (Mar. 1, 1921), pp. 16-17.)

Comments on the Meighen government and the Liberal Opposition under the leadership of Mackenzie King.

—— [Commentary on national affairs]

Carrying on by marking time. (In *Maclean's*. Toronto. v. 34, no. 7 (Apr. 1, 1921), pp. 18-19; 35.)

Comments on the Meighen government and the activities of the Liberal Opposition under the leadership of Mackenzie King.

—— [Commentary on national affairs] Drifting on the rocks. (In *Maclean's*. Toronto. v. 34, no. 14 (Aug. 1921), pp. 22-23; 38.)

Analyses the state of the Conservative and Liberal parties under Arthur Meighen and W. L. Mackenzie King in view of an anticipated general election.

—— [Commentary on national affairs] Plunged into the political maelstrom. (In *Maclean's*. Toronto. v. 34, no. 18 (Oct. 15, 1921), pp. 18-19; 38-39.)

Concerns the calling of the federal election held December 6, 1921.

—— [Commentary on national affairs] Funny thing, that tariff. (In *Maclean's*. Toronto. v. 34, no. 20 (Nov. 15, 1921), pp. 18-19.)

Comments on the tariff issue in the 1921 federal election campaign; sketches of Arthur Meighen, W. L. M. King, and T. A. Crerar.

—— [Commentary on national affairs] O, Demos, where is thy sting? (In *Maclean's*. Toronto. v. 35, no. 1 (Jan. 1, 1922), pp. 14-15; 44.)

A discussion of the composition of the parliament elected December 6, 1921.

—— [Commentary on national affairs] "How they love those Farmers!" (In *Maclean's*. Toronto. v. 35, no. 7 (Apr. 1, 1922), pp. 20-21.)

Concerns the Farmers' movement.

—— [Commentary on national affairs] Dog days and politicians. (In *Maclean's*. Toronto. v. 35, no. 17 (Sept. 1, 1922), pp. 18-19.)

Discusses political developments within the Liberal, Conservative, and Progressive parties.

—— [Commentary on national affairs] Precept and minor prophecy. (In *Maclean's*. Toronto. v. 35, no. 18 (Sept. 15, 1922), pp. 20-21; 41.)

A general review of the summer activities of Canadian members of Parliament, 1922.

—— [Commentary on national affairs] Politics makes strange bedfellows. (In *Maclean's*. Toronto. v. 35, no. 21 (Nov. 1, 1922), pp. 28-29.)

Traces post-war developments in Canadian political parties from the realignments which occurred at the formation of Union Government in 1917.

—— [Commentary on national affairs] Drifting back to party lines. (In Maclean's. Toronto. v. 35, no. 23 (Dec. 1, 1922), pp. 22-23; 39.)

—— [Commentary on national affairs] Girding for the fray. (In Maclean's. Toronto. v. 36, no. 1 (Jan. 1, 1923), pp. 20-21; 34.)
Discussion of the forthcoming session of Parliament, which opened January 31, 1923.

—— [Commentary on national affairs] Shaking hands before the fight. (In Maclean's. Toronto. v. 36, no. 3 (Feb. 1, 1923), pp. 22-23; 40.)
General remarks on the current session of Parliament opened January 31, 1923.

—— [Commentary on national affairs] Mediocrity can't work miracles. (In Maclean's. Toronto. v. 36, no. 9 (May 1, 1923), pp. 28-29; 44; 46.)
General comments; changes in the King cabinet, etc.

—— [Commentary on national affairs] Ottawa awakes from summer's slumbers. (In Maclean's. Toronto. v. 36, no. 20 (Oct. 15, 1923), pp. 22-23; 39-40.)
General remarks on the current political scene.

—— [Commentary on national affairs] All quiet along the Ottawa front. (In Maclean's. Toronto. v. 36, no. 22 (Nov. 15, 1923), pp. 22-23; 42.)
General remarks on the current political scene.

—— [Commentary on national affairs] All is not serene at Ottawa. (In Maclean's. Toronto. v. 37, no. 3 (Feb. 1, 1924), pp. 18-19; 42.)
General remarks on the current political scene.

—— [Commentary on national affairs] Let economy be unconfined! In Maclean's. Toronto. v. 37, no. 5 (Mar. 1, 1924), pp. 22-23; 45.)
Discussion of the general political situation.

—— [Commentary on national affairs] Varying winds blow at Ottawa. (In Maclean's. Toronto. v. 37, no. 8 (April 15, 1924), pp. 16-17; 78.)
General remarks on the current political scene.

—— [Commentary on national affairs] Commons faces vexing problems. (In Maclean's. Toronto. v. 37, no. 10 (May 15, 1924), pp. 22-23.)

—— [Commentary on national affairs] Session meanders toward its close. (In Maclean's. Toronto. v. 37, no. 12 (June 15, 1924), pp. 26-27; 58-59.)
General remarks on the third session of the fourteenth parliament.

MURRAY, W. W. The session in review. (In Maclean's. Toronto. v. 42, no. 13 (July 1, 1929), pp. 16; 54; 57.)
Concerns the third session of the sixteenth parliament.

A National appeal. (In Willisons monthly. Toronto. v. 1, no. 1 (June 1925), pp. 34-35.)
Comments on speeches made by John Imrie of Edmonton.

A National budget for the Dominion. Special correspondence of Willisons monthly. (In Willisons monthly. Toronto. v. 1, no. 4 (Sept. 1925), pp. 143-144.)

NELSON, JOHN Fifty-nine years of nation building. (In Maclean's. Toronto. v. 39, no. 13 (July 1, 1926), pp. 3-4; 37-38.)

—— Shall titles be restored? (In Maclean's. Toronto. v. 40, no. 6 (Mar. 15, 1927), pp. 17-18; 65.)
For a rejoinder see Shall titles be restored? By A. Hawkes. (In Maclean's. Toronto. v. 40, no. 8 (Apr. 15, 1927), pp. 7-8; 52-55.)

—— Wanted—a Canadian Coolidge! (In Maclean's. Toronto. v. 38, no. 19 (Oct. 1, 1925), pp. 27; 49.)
An examination of Canadian political leadership on the eve of the general election held October 29, 1925.

NORTH, NICHOLAS That man from Carstairs. (In Maclean's. Toronto. v. 35, no. 3 (Feb. 1, 1922), pp. 27; 42-43.)
Discusses Henry Wise Wood in a national perspective.

Notre avenir politique: enquête de l'Action française, 1922. Montréal, Bibliothèque de l'Action française, 1923. 269 p.

O'LEARY, MICHAEL GRATTAN Anything may happen at Ottawa. By M. Grattan O'Leary. (In Maclean's. Toronto. v. 39, no. 3 (Feb. 1, 1926), pp. 27; 37.)

—— Away with our hypocrisies! By Grattan O'Leary. (In Maclean's. Toronto. v. 36, no. 2 (Jan. 15, 1923), pp. 14-15; 29; 31.)

"Banish the shame of Canadian politics and let parties realign on a sound and honest basis."

—— The cruise of the barge Tremblay. By Grattan O'Leary. (In *Maclean's*. Toronto. v. 39, no. 11 (June 1, 1926), pp. 8; 46.)

The "Tremblay mystery" suggests a "plot around which the Parliamentary Customs Inquiry Committee has fashioned a hair-raising tale".

—— Customs disclosures rock capital. By Grattan O'Leary. (In *Maclean's*. Toronto. v. 39, no. 10 (May 15, 1926), pp. 25; 36; 38.)

Concerns a report presented to Parliament in June 1926, citing scandals in the Department of Customs and Excise.

—— Don't curse our politicians—help them! By M. Grattan O'Leary. (In *Maclean's*. Toronto. v. 37, no. 24 (Dec. 15, 1924), pp. 14; 75.)

"A biting indictment of shiftless citizenship. . . ."

—— An election: to be or not to be. By M. Grattan O'Leary. (In *Maclean's*. Toronto. v. 38, no. 9 (May 1, 1925), pp. 32; 56; 58.)

—— More revelations at Ottawa. By Grattan O'Leary. (In *Maclean's*. Toronto. v. 39, no. 12 (June 15, 1926), pp. 5; 46; 48.)

Sequel to the exploits of the barge Tremblay as revealed to the Special Customs Inquiry Committee of the House of Commons.

—— Ottawa rushes toward an election. By M. Grattan O'Leary. (In *Maclean's*. Toronto. v. 38, no. 7 (Apr. 1, 1925), pp. 31; 40.)

—— Parliament still floundering on. By M. Grattan O'Leary. (In *Maclean's*. Toronto. v. 38, no. 11 (June 1, 1925), pp. 27; 50.)

—— Party gunners seeking range. By M. Grattan O'Leary. (In *Maclean's*. Toronto. v. 38, no. 5 (Mar. 1, 1925), pp. 29; 52-53.)

—— Pussyfooting at Ottawa. By Grattan O'Leary. (In *Maclean's*. Toronto. v. 36, no. 10 (May 15, 1923), pp. 20-21.)

Concerns relations between the press and Canadian prime ministers, especially Arthur Meighen and Mackenzie King. References, also, are made to Laurier and Borden.

—— Ready for the federal fray. By M. Grattan O'Leary. (In *Maclean's*. Toronto. v. 38, no. 3 (Feb. 1, 1925), pp. 19; 35.)

Comments on the fourth session of the fourteenth parliament opened February 5, 1925.

—— When can we escape this deadlock. By M. Grattan O'Leary. (In *Maclean's*. Toronto. v. 39, no. 4 (Feb. 15, 1926), pp. 21; 44-46.)

Refers to the situation created by the results of the federal election held Oct. 29, 1925, which left Mackenzie King governing with the support of the Progressive members of Parliament.

—— Why a minister at Washington? By M. Gratton [!] O'Leary. (In *Saturday night*. Toronto. v. 41, no. 49 (Oct. 23, 1926), p. 4.)

Concerns the appointment of Vincent Massey to Washington.

—— Will 1925 be election year? By M. Grattan O'Leary. (In *Maclean's*. Toronto. v. 38, no. 1 (Jan. 1, 1925), pp. 13; 41.)

—— Zero hours before the budget. By Grattan O'Leary. (In *Maclean's*. Toronto. v. 39, no. 9 (May 1, 1926), pp. 14; 90.)

Discusses the manoeuvres of the Conservative board of strategy, the Peace River election scandal, the formation and reformation of the new Advisory Tariff Board.

OSBORNE, GLADYS Lady Byng—an intimate sketch of her character and personality. (In *Saturday night*. Toronto. v. 36, no. 36 (July 9, 1921), pp. 22; 26.)

PARLIAMENTARIAN Political sketches and anecdotes. By Parliamentarian. (In *Saturday night*. Toronto. v. 36, no. 23—no. 38 (Apr. 2—July 23, 1921).)

Parliamentary proposals to prevent smuggling. (In *Saturday night*. Toronto. v. 41, no. 32 (June 26, 1926), p. [13].)

Summary and excerpts from the report of the Customs Inquiry Committee.

PARTRIDGE, EDWARD ALEXANDER A war on poverty; the one war that can end war. Winnipeg, Wallingford Press [1925] iv, xii, 225 p.

An interpretation of the Western agrarian movement. Advances a utopian scheme for a co-operative commonwealth.

The Passing of party politics. (In *The Canadian forum*. Toronto. v. 6, no. 71 (Aug. 1926), pp. 331-332.)

PATERSON, ALEXANDER PIERCE Maritime disabilities within Confederation. By A. P. Paterson. (In *The Busy East of Canada*.

Sackville, N.B. v. 19, no. 7 (Feb. 1929), pp. 5-16.)

Text of a paper delivered before the Maritime Board of Trade annual convention held in Halifax November 21, 1928.

An historical review tracing the cause of Maritime disabilities and "a few suggestions for the betterment of these provinces within Confederation".

PATTERSON, A. DICKSON Painting Sir John A. Macdonald's portrait. By A. Dickson Patterson. (In *Saturday night*. Toronto. v. 42, no. 32 (June 25, 1927), p. 2.)

PENNER, JACOB Recollections of the early socialist movement in Winnipeg. (In *The Marxist quarterly*. Toronto. no. 2 (summer 1962). pp. 23-30.)

Includes discussion of policies advocated by the Socialist Party of Canada.

PERRAULT, ANTONIO Notre représentation à Ottawa. (In *L'Action canadienne-française*. Montréal. v. 19 (avril 1928), pp. [198]-212.)

At head of title: Quelques problèmes de l'heure.

Politics and Maritime rights. Special correspondence of Willisons monthly. (In *Willisons monthly*. Toronto. v. 2, no. 4 (Sept. 1926), pp. 150-154.)

Comments on the Royal Commission on Maritime Claims, and other matters.

Politics in the West. Special correspondence of Willisons monthly. (In *Willisons monthly*. Toronto. v. 1, no. 4 (Sept. 1925), pp. 141-142.)

Politics, parties and leaders. From a political correspondent. (In *The Canadian forum*. Toronto. v. 6, no. 64 (Jan. 1926), pp. 107-108.)

PORTER, G. C. Tom Blacklock, the Sir John A. Macdonald of the Ottawa press gallery. (In *Saturday night*. Toronto. v. 38, no. 1 (Nov. 4, 1922), p. 3.)

Prairie policies and parties. Special correspondence of Willisons monthly. (In *Willisons monthly*. Toronto. v. 1, no. 2 (July 1925), pp. 65-66.)

PRENTICE, JAMES STUART Canadian federal finance. By J. S. Prentice. (In *Queen's quarterly*. Kingston. v. 35 (1927/28), pp. 297-325.)

Surveys post-war financial policy to the close of the fiscal year 1925-26.

—— Canadian federal finance. Kingston [Ont.] Jackson Press, 1928. 29 p. (Bulletin of the Departments of History and Political and Economic Science in Queen's University, no. 55.)

Cover title.

A review of Canadian post-war finance.

The Press and party. (In *Willisons monthly*. Toronto. v. 1, no. 5 (Oct. 1925), pp. 170-171.)

Problems and prospects in Canada. (In *Willisons monthly*. Toronto. v. 1, no. 1 (June 1925), pp. 5-11.)

Prohibition and politics in the Atlantic Provinces. Special correspondence of Willisons monthly. (In *Willisons monthly*. Toronto. v. 1, no. 5 (Oct. 1925), pp. 183-184.)

Relates to the federal Liberal and Conservative parties.

Prospects at Ottawa. (In *The Canadian forum*. Toronto. v. 4, no. 38 (Nov. 1923), pp. 39-41.)

General impressions of the Mackenzie King government and the opposition led by Arthur Meighen.

RAY, JOSEPH E. The new Canada. Introd. by the Rt. Hon. Sir George Eulas Foster. London, Hutchinson [1926] 158 p.

A general survey treating trade and industry, education, literature, the Canadian constitution, etc.

Reform of the services—the next step. (In *The Canadian forum*. Toronto. v. 2, no. 20 (May 1922), pp. 614-616.)

A discussion about the Government decision to unify the control of the miltiary services.

REID, J. ADDISON Secession in Canada. I. Quebec. (In *The Canadian forum*. Toronto. v. 4, no. 45 (June 1924), pp. 264-266.)

Part 2. The Prairies (pp. 266-268) is by Thompson-Hardy.

The Result of the elections. (In *The Canadian forum*. Toronto. v. 6, no. 63 (Dec. 1925), pp. 67-68.)

Refers to the federal election held October 29, 1925.

RIDDELL, WILLIAM RENWICK What is a Canadian citizen? (In Empire Club of Canada. *Addresses*. Toronto. (1929) pp 168-188.)

Address delivered 25th April, 1929.

RIDLEY, HILDA Her Excellency the Viscountess of Willingdon—a lady of long descent and much experience in government circles in the great Dominions of the

Empire . . . (In *Saturday night*. Toronto. v. 42, no. 3 (Dec. 4, 1926), p. [41].)

ROBINETTE   A birds-eye view. By Robinette. (In *Saturday night*. Toronto. v. 36, no. 41 (Aug. 13, 1921), p. 26.)

Comments on the wives of the Governors-General of Canada.

RUMILLY, ROBERT   Camillien Houde. 2. éd. Montréal, Fides [c1958] 256 p. (His *Histoire de la province de Québec*, 30.)

A political history covering the years 1928-1929.

——   Léonide Perron. Montréal, Fides [c1959] 266 p. (His *Histoire de la province de Québec*, 31.)

A political history covering the years 1929-1930.

——   Rayonnement de Québec. Montréal, Chantecler [1953] 287 p. (His *Histoire de la province de Québec*, 26.)

A political history covering the years 1921-1923.

——   Rivalité Gouin-Lapointe. Montréal, Fides [c1955] 320 p. (His *Histoire de la province de Québec*, 27.)

A political history covering the years 1923-1925.

——   La rue Saint-Jacques. Montréal, Fides [c1955] 340 p. (His *Histoire de la province de Québec*, 28.)

A political history covering the years 1924-1926.

——   Vers l'âge d'or. Montréal, Fides [c1955] 242 p. (His *Histoire de la province de Québec*, 29.)

A political history covering the year 1927.

SANDWELL, BERNARD KEBLE   From the editor's chair. Mr. Forsey and Mr. King are not so far apart. By B. K. Sandwell. (In *Saturday night*. Toronto. v. 58, no. 42 (June 26, 1943), pp. 10-11.)

Concerns the constitutional problem of dissolution, with special reference to the constitutional issue in 1926 involving Mackenzie King and Lord Byng.

——   Mr. King and Mr. Meighen. What did we vote for in 1926? By B. K. Sandwell. (In *Saturday night*. Toronto. v. 67, no. 7 (Nov. 24, 1951), pp. 4-5.)

——   The nineteen twenty-eight budget. An address by Bernard K. Sandwell. (In Empire Club of Canada. *Addresses*. Toronto. (1928), pp. 56-68.)

Address delivered February 23, 1928.

SCANLON, JAMES P.   Printers' ink and politics. A study of the constitutional crisis of 1926; and how it affected three Canadian newspapers. [Kingston, Ont.] 1954. 176 leaves.

Thesis (MA) – Queen's University.

SCRUTATOR   And they say talk is cheap! By "Scrutator". (In *Maclean's*. Toronto. v. 36, no. 6 (Mar. 15, 1923), pp. 20-21.)

Discusses oratory in Parliament.

The Senate and the railways. (In *Willisons monthly*. Toronto. v. 1, no. 3 (Aug. 1925), pp. 88-89.)

Concerns the recommendations advanced by the Special Committee of the Senate convened to examine the railway problem.

Serving two masters. (In *The Canadian forum*. Toronto. v. 2, no. 19 (Apr. 1922), pp. 582-583.)

Discusses "a bill . . . introduced by Mr. A. R. McMaster of Brome providing that members who accepted portfolios in the Cabinet should, within fifteen days, resign all directorships previously held by him".

SINCLAIR, HUNTLY M.   Whither Canada? (In *The Canadian forum*. Toronto. v. 6, no. 66 (Mar. 1926), pp. 175-177.)

Speculates on the meaning of the returns of the general elections held October 29, 1925.

SOULSBY, E. J.   Humbug vs. humdrum. (In *The Canadian forum*. Toronto. v. 7, no. 82 (July 1927), pp. 299-300.)

General comments on the party system in Canada.

——   Sectionalism and a national policy. (In *The Canadian forum*. Toronto. v. 7, no. 74 (Nov. 1926), pp. 45-46.)

STEVENS, HENRY HERBERT   The nation as a partner. A proposal to raise revenue without draining private capital. By H. H. Stevens, MP (Vancouver). (In *Saturday night*. Toronto. v. 34, no. 34 (June 5, 1920), p. 5.)

STEVENSON, JOHN A.   The federal parliamentary session. By J. A. S. (In *Queen's quarterly*. Kingston. v. 36 (1929), pp. 538-546.)

Reviews the third session of the federal parliament ending June 15, 1929.

——   The federal political situation. By J. A. S. (In *Queen's quarterly*. Kingston. v. 36 (1929), pp. [354]-361.)

Surveys the third session of the sixteenth federal parliament.

—— From immigrant to MP. (In *Maclean's*. Toronto. v. 36, no. 12 (June 15, 1923), pp. 13-14; 48-51.)
Relates the careers of several persons.

SWEATMAN, TRAVERS Is Confederation a real success? (In Canadian Club of Toronto. *Addresses*. Toronto. (1925/26), pp. 173-189.)
Address delivered January 18, 1926.

THOMAS, ERNEST Unrepresentative government. (In *The Canadian forum*. Toronto. v. 2, no. 18 (Mar. 1922), pp. 552-554.)
An assessment of the federal election held December 6, 1921.

THOMPSON-HARDY Secession in Canada. II. The Prairies. (In *The Canadian forum*. v. 4, no. 45 (June 1924), pp. 266-268.)
Part 1. Quebec (pp. 264-266), is by J. Addison Reid.

THOMSON, DONALD WALTER The fate of titles in Canada. (In *The Canadian historical review*. Toronto. v. 10 (1929), pp. 236-246.)

THORSON, JOSEPH THARARINN The building of a nation. By J. T. Thorson. (In Empire Club of Canada. *Addresses*. Toronto. (1927), pp. 18-28.)
Address delivered February 10, 1927.

The Threat of internationalism to Canada's national policy. Special correspondence of Willisons monthly. (In *Willisons monthly*. Toronto. v. 3, no. 2 [i.e. 3] (Aug. 1927), pp. 94-95.)

TODD, IRENE The arrival of our soldier-Governor. (In *Saturday night*. Toronto. v. 36, no. 42 (Aug. 20, 1921), pp. [21]; 24.)
Description of the ceremonies at the arrival of Lord Byng in Canada, with a brief biographical sketch.

The Trend of the campaign. (In *The Canadian forum*. Toronto. v. 6, no. 72 (Sept. 1926), pp. 359-360.)
An editorial on the anticipated federal election held September 14, 1926.

Unrest in the Maritimes. Special correspondence of Willisons monthly. (In *Willisons monthly*.Toronto. v. 2, no. 3 (Aug. 1926), pp. 104-106.)
Discusses the "secessionism" movement.

VANIER, ANATOLE Le bilinguisme et l'unité nationale. (In L'*Action française*. Montréal. v. 14 (Sept. 1925), pp. [130]-141.)
—— La nouvelle chambre fédérale. (In

L'*Action française*. Montréal. v. 14 (nov. 1925), pp. 316-318.)
This House of Commons was elected October 29, 1925.

WALSH, L. P. The Labrador boundary, in dispute again? Privy Council decision is binding. (In *The Newfoundland quarterly*. St. John's, Nfld. v. 62, no. 2 (summer 1963), pp. 15-17.)
Reprinted from *Evening telegram* (St. John's, Nfld.).
Traces the historical developments leading to the Privy Council decision of 1927 which settled the dispute between the Dominion of Canada and Newfoundland over the Labrador boundary.

A Warning from the Atlantic Provinces. Special correspondence of Willisons monthly. (In *Willisons monthly*. Toronto. v. 1, no. 4 (Sept. 1925), pp. 145-146.)
Relates Maritime "local issues" to national considerations.

The West and its natural resources. Special correspondence of Willisons monthly. (In *Willisons monthly*. Toronto. v. 1, no. 11 (Apr. 1926), pp. 422-423.)
Discusses federal government policy since 1905 on natural resources.

The West in the election. Special correspondence of Willisons monthly. (In *Willisons monthly*. Toronto. v. 2, no. 6 (Nov. 1926), pp. 219-220.)
Relates to the general elections held September 14, 1926.

WHITE, SIR WILLIAM THOMAS Canada's immigration problems. By the Right Hon. Sir Thomas White. (In Empire Club of Canada. *Addresses*. Toronto. (1928), pp. 213-224.)
Address delivered October 18, 1928.
—— Canadian problems. By Sir Thomas White. (In Canadian Club of Toronto. *Addresses*. Toronto. (1925/26), pp. 338-352.)
Address delivered April 19, 1926.

WIGHTMAN, FREDERICK ARNOLD Newfoundland and Confederation. By F. A. Wightman. (In *The Busy East of Canada*. Sackville, N.B. v. 23, no. 10 (May 1933), pp. 5-7; 19.)
Examines the ten reasons against Newfoundland's joining Confederation advanced in the article Newfoundland stands aloof, by Sir Patrick McGrath. (In *Maclean's*. Toronto. v. 42, no. 21 (Nov. 1, 1929), pp. 5; 53-54.)

WILLISON, SIR JOHN STEPHEN   From month to month. By Sir John Willison. (In *The Canadian magazine of politics, science, art and literature.* Toronto. v. 59 (1922), pp. 61-68.)

Comments on political patronage (pp. 63-65), prohibition (pp. 66-67), low tariffs (p. 68).

—— From month to month. By Sir John Willison. (In *The Canadian magazine of politics, science, art and literature.* Toronto. v. 59 (1922), pp. 332-339.)

General comments on the first session of the federal Parliament under the Mackenzie King administration, 1922 (pp. 336-338).

[WILLISON, SIR JOHN STEPHEN] (ed.)   From month to month. (In *Willisons monthly.* Toronto. v. 1, no. 1—v. 2, no. 12 (June 1925—May 1927.)

Consists of running comments on current political affairs in Canada and abroad.

—— From month to month. (In *Willisons monthly.* Toronto. v. 1, no. 6 (Nov. 1925), pp. [203]-208.)

A commentary on the results of the federal election held October 29, 1925 (pp. 203-204).

—— From month to month. (In *Willisons monthly.* Toronto. v. 1, no. 7 (Dec. 1925), pp. [243]-247.)

Deals with the political deadlock in Canada resulting from the returns of the federal election held October 29, 1925 (pp. 243-246).

WILLISON, SIR JOHN STEPHEN   Sir John Willison predicts great expansion for Canada within next quarter of century. (In *The Busy East of Canada.* Sackville, N.B. v. 16, no. 4—5 (Nov.—Dec. 1925), pp. 9-11.)

Text of address delivered at the nineteenth annual convention of the Association of Life Insurance Presidents in New York City December 3, 1925.

WILLISON, MARJORY (MAC MURCHY), LADY   Canadian politics from a woman's point of view. By Marjory MacMurchy. (In *Willisons monthly.* Toronto. v. 1, no. 5 (Oct. 1925), pp. 171-172.)

—— Canadian women and public affairs. By Marjory MacMurchy. (In *Willisons monthly.* Toronto. v. 1, no. 2 (July 1925), pp. 47-48.)

WOOD, HENRY WISE   In defense of group politics. By H. W. Wood. (In *The Canadian forum.* Toronto. v. 3, no. 27 (Dec. 1922), pp. 72-74.)

WOODSWORTH, JAMES SHAVER   Besco. By J. S. Woodsworth. (In *The Canadian forum.* v. 4, no. 42 (Mar. 1924), pp. 169-171.)

Comments on the Royal Commission to Inquire into Industrial Unrest among the Steel Workers of Sydney, Nova Scotia. Ottawa, 1924. (24 p.)

BESCO is the British Empire Steel Corporation.

—— Grandsons of Confederation. By J. S. Woodsworth. (In *The Canadian forum.* Toronto. v. 6, no. 67 (Apr. 1926), pp. 205-207.)

—— The labour movement in the West. By J. S. Woodsworth. (In *The Canadian forum.* Toronto. v. 2, no. 19 (Apr. 1922), pp. 585-587.)

—— Labor's case in Parliament. A summary and compilation of the speeches of J. S. Woodsworth, MP in the Canadian House of Commons, 1921-1928. Ottawa, Canadian Brotherhood of Railroad Employees, 1929. 92 p.

—— What does radical Labor want? By James S. Woodsworth. (In *Maclean's.* Toronto. v. 35, no. 7 (Apr. 1, 1922), pp. 12; 52.)

YEIGH, FRANK   Canada's sixty-year span. (In *Willisons monthly.* Toronto. v. 2, no. 2 (July 1926), pp. 58-59.)

National Progressive Party
1920–1926

Cross currents at Ottawa. From a political correspondent. (In *The Canadian forum.* Toronto. v. 6, no. 65 (Feb. 1926), pp. 139-140.)

Assesses the influence of the Progressive Party in the Canadian Parliament.

DEXTER, GRANT   Will the Prairies go solid again? (In *Maclean's.* Toronto. v. 38, no. 20 (Oct. 15, 1925), pp. 20; 74-75.)

An examination of the Progressive Party.

The First woman in the Canadian Parliament. (In *Willisons monthly.* Toronto. v. 1, no. 5 (Oct. 1925), pp. 181-182.)

Concerns Agnes Campbell Macphail.

FORKE, ROBERT   National unity. (In *Canadian Club of Toronto. Addresses.* Toronto. (1925/26), pp. 326-337.)

Address delivered April 12, 1926.

Robert Forke was Leader of the Progressive Party in the Dominion House of Commons.

LIPSETT-SKINNER, GENEVIEVE The little farmer's daughter who became world famous. . . . (In *The Canadian magazine*. Toronto. [v. 66, no. 2] (Sept. 1926), pp. 8-9.)
Concerns Agnes Campbell Macphail.

THE MACE Hanging on the line. By the Mace. (In *Saturday night*. Toronto. v. 40, no. 22 (Apr. 18, 1925), p. 4.)
Concerns the faction within the Progressive movement led by Robert Forke.

—— Leaving the prairie schooner. By the Mace. (In *Saturday night*. Toronto. v. 39, no. 34 (July 12, 1924), p. 4.)
Concerns a break within the Progressive Party, that involved Robert Gardiner, Edward J. Garland, Donald Macbeth Kennedy, Henry E. Spencer, M. N. Campbell, and Agnes Macphail.

—— Murmurs from the West. By the Mace. (In *Saturday night*. Toronto. v. 40, no. 10 (Jan. 24, 1925), p. 4.)
Concerns Robert Alexander Hoey and the United Farmers of Manitoba.

—— Out of the ring. By the Mace. (In *Saturday night*. Toronto. v. 38, no. 4 (Nov. 25, 1922), p. 4.)
Concerns the resignation of Thomas Crerar Nov. 10, 1922, and the choosing of Robert Forke as his successor to the leadership of the Progressive Party.

—— The parting of the ways. By the Mace. (In *Saturday night*. Toronto. v. 38, no. 1 (Nov. 4, 1922), p. 4.)
Concerns Thomas A. Crerar.

A Matter of definition? (In *The Canadian forum*. Toronto. v. 3, no. 27 (Dec. 1922), pp. 70-72.)
Discusses the resignation of T. A. Crerar as leader of the Progressive Party.

Mr. Crerar at the parting of the ways By a bystander. (In *Saturday night*. Toronto. v. 37, no. 51 (Oct. 21, 1922), p. 2.)
Concerns Thomas Alexander Crerar.

MORTON, WILLIAM LEWIS Direct legislation and the origins of the Progressive movement. By W. L. Morton. (In *The Canadian historical review*. Toronto. v. 25 (1944), pp. 279-288.)

—— The Progressive Party in Canada. By W. L. Morton. Toronto, University of Toronto Press, 1950. xiii, 331 p. (Social Credit in Alberta; its background and development.)
"Bibliographical essay": pp. 307-318.
Appendices: A. The Farmers' platform

(From the Siege of Ottawa, Winnipeg, 1910). Text of the resolutions presented to the Government by the Canadian Council of Agriculture on Dec. 16, 1910 (pp. 297-299) – B. The Farmers' platform. Text of the draft drawn up by the Canadian Council of Agriculture in December 1916. (pp. 300-301) – C. The Farmers' platform (As brought up-to-date, 1921). Text of the draft revised by the Canadian Council of Agriculture, Nov. 29, 1918 (pp. 302-305).

—— The Western Progressive movement and cabinet domination. By W. L. Morton. (In *The Canadian journal of economics and political science*. [Toronto] v. 12 (1946), pp. 136-147.)
Considers the issue of group government against that of the political party system.

—— The Western Progressive movement, 1919-1921. (In Canadian Historical Association. *Report of the annual meeting*. Toronto. (1946), pp. 41-55.)

MUNRO, J. K. The Ginger Group jolts Parliament. (In *Maclean's*. Toronto. v. 37, no. 15 (Aug. 1, 1924), pp. 20-21; 36.)

NORMAN, WILLIAM HOWARD HEAL The Canadian Progressives. By W. H. H. Norman. (In *The Canadian forum*. Toronto. v. 11, no. 131 (Aug. 1931), p. 411.)

One of the three. A close-up on Thomas Alexander Crerar. By N. R. P. (In *Saturday night*. Toronto. v. 36, no. 19 (Mar. 5, 1921), p. 5.)

PATERSON, WILLIAM The progressive political movement, 1919-1930. Toronto, 1940. 191 leaves.
Thesis (MA) – University of Toronto.

PICKWELL, FREDERICK C. Embattled Progressives. Revelations of Mr. Lucas of Camrose—a sensation in the West. By Saturday night's Western correspondent [i.e. Fred C. Pickwell?] (In *Saturday night*. Toronto. v. 41, no. 41 (Aug. 28, 1926), p. 2.)
Concerns William Thomas Lucas.

Pools, Progressives and politics. Special correspondence of Willisons monthly. (In *Willisons monthly*. Toronto. v. 1, no. 8 (Jan. 1926), pp. 310-312.)

The Position at Ottawa. By a political correspondent. (In *The Canadian forum*. Toronto. v. 6, no. 67 (Apr. 1926), pp. 203-204.)
Assesses the influence of the Progressive Party in the Canadian Parliament.

Progressives and the West. Special correspondence of Willisons monthly. (In *Willisons monthly*. Toronto. v. 2, no. 11 (Apr. 1927), pp. 432-434.)

WHITE, J. FRANCIS A platform for Progressives. (In *The Canadian forum*. Toronto. v. 5, no. 55 (Apr. 1925), pp. 202-204.)

DEPRESSION YEARS
1930–1939

Advice to politicians. By a voter. (In *Saturday night*. Toronto. v. 51, no. 28 (May 16, 1936), pp. [1]; 3.)
Offers "advice to politicians as to the proper method of winning [his] vote – with especial direction to the members of the present cabinet. . . ."

ANDERSON, VIOLET Youth of Canada examines its world. (In *Saturday night*. Toronto. v. 51, no. 31 (June 6, 1936), p. 2.)
Discusses the Canadian Youth Congress, held in Ottawa, May 1936.

ANGERS, FRANCOIS ALBERT Vendrons-nous notre droit d'aînesse pour un plat de lentilles? (In *L'Action nationale*. Montréal. v. 13 (fév. 1939), pp. [140]-149.)
Discusses the idea of a federal plan for unemployment insurance.

AUSTIN, DONALD C. The merry-go-round broke down. Politicians pray for rain— burned-out farmers demand action. (In *New frontier*. Toronto. v. 2, no. 4 (Sept. 1937), pp. 14-16.)
Describes the drought in the West as a national calamity.

AYEARST, MORLEY Government by judges. (In *The Canadian forum*. Toronto. v. 17, no. 202 (Nov. 1937), pp. 276-278.)

Back to big business normalcy (In *The Canadian forum*. Toronto. v. 15, no. 178 (Nov. 1935), p. 351.)
An analysis of the results of the general elections held October 14, 1935.

BAIRD, ETHEL Women in politics. (In *The Maritime advocate and busy East*. Sackville, N.B. v. 28, no. 7 (Feb. 1938), pp. 9-10)

BALDWIN, R. W. The nation. When does Canada go to War? (In *Saturday night*. Toronto. v. 54, no. 15 (Feb. 11, 1939), p. 5.)

—— The nation. Must be done, can't be done. (In *Saturday night*. Toronto. v. 54, no. 18 (Mar. 4, 1939), p. 4.)

Comments on a national scheme of unemployment insurance; wheat legislation, etc.

—— National affairs. Refugees must try elsewhere. (In *Saturday night*. Toronto. v. 54, no. 8 (Dec. 24, 1938), p. 5.)
Comments on the feud between W. L. M. King and M. Hepburn; the opposition of R. Manion to refugee immigration into Canada.

BANKS, RIDEAU Fight to be on tariff. (In *Saturday night*. Toronto. v. 53, no. 11 (Jan. 15, 1938), p. 5.)

—— National affairs. King-maker King. (In *Saturday night*. Toronto. v. 52, no. 12 (Jan. 23, 1937), p. 4.)
Concerns J. S. Woodsworth and Mackenzie King. Refers to an objection raised by Woodsworth over a resolution passed pledging loyalty to the King.

—— National affairs. Winnipeg upsets relief cart. (In *Saturday night*. Toronto. v. 52, no. 38 (July 24, 1937), p. 5.)
Discusses a request for assistance made by the Manitoba government to the federal treasury. The request was refused.

—— Ottawa letter. New tariff idea. (In *Saturday night*. Toronto. v. 53, no. 16 (Feb. 19, 1938), p. 4.)

—— Ottawa letter. The lid is nailed down. (In *Saturday night*. Toronto. v. 53, no. 17 (Feb. 26, 1938), p. 5.)
Concerns the issue of political campaign contributions.

—— Ottawa letter. Facing reality. (In *Saturday night*. Toronto. v. 53, no. 23 (Apr. 9, 1938), p. 12.)
Comments on a debate in the House of Commons over the thesis propounded by Social Credit that the Dominion government and chartered banks assume joint responsibility for dealing with problems of poverty and economic conditions.

—— Patterns in budgets. (In *Saturday night*. Toronto. v. 52, no. 18 (Mar. 6, 1937), p. 4.)
Discusses the budget brought down during the second session of the eighteenth parliament.

—— Politics have changed. (In *Saturday night*. Toronto. v. 53, no. 9 (Jan. 1, 1938), p. 10.)
Reflections on Canadian politics of the past fifty years.

—— A poor session. (In *Saturday night*.

Toronto. v. 52, no. 24 (Apr. 17, 1937), p. 28.)

Deals with the second session of the eighteenth parliament.

—— Senate wants love. (In *Saturday night*. Toronto. v. 52, no. 21 (Mar. 27, 1937), p. 20.)

Comments on the Senate veto of a transport bill.

BEAUCHESNE, ARTHUR Les Anglo-Canadiens. (In Club canadien de Québec. *Problèmes de l'heure*. Québec, 1935. pp. 25-41.)

—— The French-Canadian. (In Canadian Club of Toronto. *Addresses*. Toronto. (1930/31), pp. 98-110.)

Address delivered November 17, 1930.

BEDER, EDWARD ARTHUR Basis for a People's Party. By E. A. Beder. (In *New frontier*. Toronto. v. 1, no. 1 (Apr. 1936), pp. 6-7.)

Part of a symposium. For the other articles see Why a People's Party, by L. Morris (pp. 8-9) and A CCF approach to a People's Party, by G. Spry (pp. 10-12).

—— A socialist program. By E. A. Beder. (In *The Canadian forum*. Toronto. v. 15, no. 182 (Mar. 1936), pp. 14-16.)

BEER, G. FRANK Time for an unemployment plan. Emergency measures and local action cannot cope with huge problem. Bureau of research on social problems is badly needed. (In *Saturday night*. Toronto. v. 48, no. 6 (Dec. 17, 1932), p. 3.)

BETTON, EUGENE A. Liberalism applied to present day conditions. (In *The Maritime advocate and busy East*. Sackville, N.B. v. 24, no. 4 (Nov. 1933), pp. 5-6.)

"An address delivered in Fredericton on November 2, 1933 before the York-Sunbury Liberal Association."

BLACK, F. M. Patrick Burns as I knew him. (In *Saturday night*. Toronto. v. 52, no. 21 (Mar. 27, 1937), p. 23.)

Senator appointed by R. B. Bennett; Burns was an Independent.

BORDEN, SIR ROBERT LAIRD Letters to Limbo. Edited by Henry Borden. [Toronto] University of Toronto Press [1971] xii, 310 p.

Includes seventy-five "letters" written between March 1933 and May 1937 covering a wide variety of subjects. Cf. Introd.

BOULANGER, JOSEPH OSCAR LEFEBRE Le sentiment national et le nouveau nationalisme. Par J.-Oscar Boulanger, MP. (In *Le Terroir*. Québec, v. 13. no. 7 (déc. 1931), pp. 14-15; v. 13, no. 8 (jan. 1932), pp. 21-23.)

In two parts.

"Conférence donnée le 5 décembre devant les membres de la Société des arts, sciences et lettres."

BOYD, HUGH New breaking; an outline of co-operation among the Western farmers of Canada. [Foreword by W. R. Motherwell] Toronto, Dent [c1938] 215 p.

BRADY, ALEXANDER Constitution hampers strong government. Increased centralization of power in Dominion required to cope with modern industrial and social problems. Present legislative divisions cripple administrative action. (In *Saturday night*. Toronto. v. 48, no. 49 (Oct. 14, 1933), p. 19.)

"Excerpt from a paper read . . . at the Conservative Summer School held recently at Newmarket, Ont." The papers were published in a collection of essays under the title: *Canadian problems as seen by twenty outstanding men of Canada*. Toronto, Oxford University Press [1933].

—— How can the civil service be improved? Private enterprise takes the cream of administrative talent. Handicap of patronage. Position of the Civil Service Commission. Need for experts to study business methods in connection with the service. (In *Saturday night*. Toronto. v. 49, no. 2 (Nov. 18, 1933), p. 2.)

An extension of an article by Professor Brady . . . "Constitution hampers strong government". This paper was read at the first annual Liberal-Conservative summer school held at Newmarket, Ont.

—— The state and economic life in Canada. By A. Brady. (In *The University of Toronto quarterly*. [Toronto] v. 2 (1932/33), pp. 422-441.)

BRASSIER, JACQUES Pour qu'on vive. (In *L'Action nationale*. Montréal. v. 4 (oct. 1934), pp. [135]-142.)

A discussion of the role of French-Canadians within Confederation.

Contents: L'avenir de la Confédération. – Les méfaits de la Confédération. – La part lamentable des nôtres. – L'éducation nationale.

Bright ideas for saving the nation. (In *Saturday night*. Toronto. v. 54, no. 44 (Sept. 2, 1939), p. 3.)

Political programs submitted to the Platform Competition held by *Saturday night*.

BRITNELL, GEORGE EDWIN Dominion legislation affecting Western agriculture, 1939. By G. E. Britnell. (In *The Canadian journal of economics and political science*. [Toronto] v. 6 (1940), pp. 275-282.)

Lists and discusses many of the Acts passed by the federal government to provide controlled methods of marketing wheat.

BROSSARD, ROGER The working of Confederation. I. A French-Canadian view, by Roger Brossard. II. A Western view, by H. F. Angus. (In *The Canadian journal of economics and political science*. [Toronto] v. 3 (1937), pp. 335-354.)

BRUCHESI, JEAN Canadian unity and the French Canadians. (In *Revue trimestrielle canadienne*. Montréal. v. 24 (juin 1938), pp. [116]-123.)

—— Defense and French Canada. The defense problem: Article 3. (In *Maclean's*. Toronto. v. 50, no. 12 (June 15, 1937), pp. 17; 33.)

BUCHANAN, DONALD W. July 28 and the UFA. (In *The Canadian forum*. Toronto. v. 11, no. 121 (Oct. 1930), pp. 7-9.)

Discusses the United Farmers of Alberta in federal politics. Refers to the general elections held July 28, 1930.

—— National affairs. Probing everything! (In *Saturday night*. Toronto. v. 49, no. 15 (Feb. 17, 1934), p. 4.)

Concerns the appointment of a special committee "to investigate the causes of the large spread between producer and consumer prices. . . ."

—— National affairs. Old and new loans. (In *Saturday night*. Toronto. v. 49, no. 21 (Mar. 31, 1934), p. 4.)

Comments on the Relief Act of 1933 and the $60,000,000 loan to the CPR.

—— National affairs. Ottawa goes "planned". (In *Saturday night*. Toronto. v. 49, no. 22 (April 7, 1934), pp. 4-5.)

Comments on the conception of a national planned economy.

—— National affairs. Relief and war-making. (In *Saturday night*. Toronto. v. 49, no. 24 (Apr. 21, 1934), pp. 4-5.)

Comments on the Relief Act; marketing legislation; revision of the BNA Act, etc.

—— National affairs. Mr. Pattullo at Ottawa. (In *Saturday night*. Toronto. v. 49, no. 26 (May 5, 1934), p. 4.)

—— National affairs. Hard on laisser-faire. (In *Saturday night*. Toronto. v. 49, no. 28 (May 19, 1934), p. 4.)

Concerns the investigation of the Imperial Tobacco Company of Canada, by the Price Spreads Committee of the House of Commons.

—— National affairs. Static in the radio. (In *Saturday night*. Toronto. v. 49, no. 31 (June 9, 1934), p. 4.)

—— National affairs. What election issue? (In *Saturday night*. Toronto. v. 49, no. 34 (June 30, 1934), p. 4.)

Comments on monetary reform; public works; report of the Bank and Commerce Committee of the House of Commons, etc.

—— National affairs. Too much to probe into. (In *Saturday night*. Toronto. v. 49, no. 47 (Sept. 29, 1934), p. 4.)

Comments on the investigations by the Royal Commission on Price Spreads.

—— National affairs. And when do we vote? (In *Saturday night*. Toronto. v. 50, no. 11 (Jan. 19, 1935), pp. 4; 9.)

Concerns an anticipated federal election.

—— National affairs. Quite a lot of reform. (In *Saturday night*. Toronto. v. 50, no. 12 (Jan. 26, 1935), pp. 4; 8.)

Comments on reform programs advocated by the Conservative, Liberal and CCF parties.

BUCHANAN, E. C. Are we for conscious progress or sleep walking. (In *Saturday night*. Toronto. v. 52, no. 35 (July 3, 1937), p. 2.)

Concerns the prospect of National Government.

—— Lobby and gallery. (In *Saturday night*. Toronto. v. 45, no. 13 (Feb. 8, 1930), p. 4.)

Concerns the state of various political parties in relation to an anticipated federal election.

—— Lobby and gallery. (In *Saturday night*. Toronto. v. 45, no. 14 (Feb. 15, 1930), p. 4.)

Concerns the Wheat Pool.

—— Lobby and gallery. (In *Saturday night*. Toronto. v. 45, no. 21 (Apr. 5, 1930), p. 20.)

Concerns an anticipated federal election.

—— Lobby and gallery. (In *Saturday*

night. Toronto. v. 45, no. 22 (Apr. 12, 1930), p. 4.)
Concerns the probability of a federal election.

—— Lobby and gallery. (In *Saturday night.* Toronto. v. 45, no. 31 (June 14, 1930), p. 4.)
Concerns issues presented in the campaign for the federal election held July 28, 1930.

—— Lobby and gallery. (In *Saturday night.* Toronto. v. 45, no. 32 (June 21, 1930), p. 3.)
Concerns issues presented in the campaign for the general elections held July 28, 1930.

—— Lobby and gallery. (In *Saturday night.* Toronto. v. 45, no. 34 (July 5, 1930), p. 4.)
Concerns the campaign for the federal election held July 28, 1930.

—— Lobby and gallery. (In *Saturday night.* Toronto. v. 45, no. 35 (July 12, 1930), p. 4.)
Concerns the election campaign conducted by Mackenzie King and R. B. Bennett.

—— Lobby and gallery. (In *Saturday night.* Toronto. v. 45, no. 39 (Aug. 9, 1930), p. 4.)
Concerns results of the federal election held July 28, 1930.

—— Mentioning many men, and morever, Meighen. (In *Saturday night.* Toronto. v. 52, no. 38 (July 24, 1937), pp. 2-3.)
Concerns the question of forming a National Government and discusses candidates for the position of prime minister.

—— National affairs. (In *Saturday night.* Toronto. v. 45, no. 43 (Sept. 6, 1930), p. 4.)
Concerns the special emergency business session called to deal with "the unemployment situation, which involves industrial and business recession. . . ."

—— National affairs. (In *Saturday night.* Toronto. v. 45, no. 48 (Oct. 11, 1930), p. 24.)
Comments on unemployment, the automobile tariff, etc.

—— National affairs. (In *Saturday night.* Toronto. v. 46, no. 3 (Nov. 29, 1930), p. 4.)
Concerns "Ottawa and the wheat situation".

—— National affairs. (In *Saturday night.* Toronto. v. 46, no. 7 [i.e. 8] (Jan. 3, 1931), p. 4.)
Discusses the post of governor-general. Relates to the departure of Lord Willingdon (Governor-General of Canada, 1926-1931).

—— National affairs. (In *Saturday night.* Toronto. v. 46, no. 18 (Mar. 14, 1931), p. 4.)
Concerns the opening of the second session of the seventeenth parliament.

—— National affairs. (In *Saturday night.* Toronto. v. 46, no. 19 (Mar. 21, 1931), p. 4.)
Concerns the debate on the Throne speech opening the second session, seventeenth parliament.

—— National affairs. (In *Saturday night.* Toronto. v. 46, no. 29 (May 30, 1931), p. 4.)
Concerns the investigation into the Beauharnois Power Concession.

—— National affairs. (In *Saturday night.* Toronto. v. 46, no. 36 (July 18, 1931), p. 4.)
Concerns the disclosures of the Beauharnois Power Concession Investigation.

—— National affairs. (In *Saturday night.* Toronto. v. 46, no. 37 (July 25, 1931), p. 4.)
Concerns the disclosures of the Beauharnois Power Concession Investigation.

—— National affairs. (In *Saturday night.* Toronto. v. 46, no. 39 (Aug. 8, 1931), p. 4.)
Relates to the conclusion of the Beauharnois affair in Parliament, "As a result of the parliamentary inquiry into the operations of the Beauharnois Power Corporations, measures have been enacted to secure the public interest against harmful exploitation of our natural resources and to safeguard the rights of bona fide investors".

—— National affairs. (In *Saturday night.* Toronto. v. 47, no. 14 (Feb. 13, 1932), p. 4.)
Comments on the Throne speech and the opening of the third session, seventeenth parliament, February 4, 1932.

—— National affairs. (In *Saturday night.* Toronto. v. 47, no. 15 (Feb. 20, 1932), pp. 4-5.)
Concerns the first week of the third session, seventeenth parliament: "For legislation substitute investigation, and you have

the business of this session of parliament in a word".

—— National affairs. (In *Saturday night*. Toronto. v. 47, no. 21 (Apr. 2, 1932), p. 4.)

Concerns the Relief Bill, E. N. Rhodes' budget, and negotiations of the St. Lawrence Waterway Treaty.

—— National affairs. (In *Saturday night*. Toronto. v. 47, no. 22 (Apr. 9, 1932), p. 20.)

Concerns the approach of Parliament to the issues of unemployment and relief.

—— National affairs. (In *Saturday night*. Toronto. v. 47, no. 24 (Apr. 23, 1932), p. 4.)

Concerns "the radio situation, the Civil Service Commission situation, the National Railways situation, and the situation in respect of unemployment and agricultural relief".

—— National affairs. (In *Saturday night*. Toronto. v. 47, no. 25 (Apr. 30, 1932), p. 4.)

Concerns the report of a special committee of the Senate appointed to "inquire into the status of the three senators" involved in the Beauharnois scandal: Wilfred Laurier McDougald, Andrew Haydon, and Maxime Raymond.

—— National affairs. (In *Saturday night*. Toronto. v. 47, no. 27 (May 14, 1932), p. 4.)

Concerns the conduct and methods of investigation followed by the inquisitorial committees set up by the government.

—— National affairs. (In *Saturday night*. Toronto. v. 47, no. 46 (Sept. 24, 1932), p. 4.)

Concerns the Duff Commission report on railway transportation.

—— National affairs. (In *Saturday night*. Toronto. v. 47, no. 47 (Oct. 1, 1932), p. 4.)

Concerns the report of the Duff Commission on Canada's transportation problems.

—— National affairs. (In *Saturday night*. Toronto. v. 47, no. 52 (Nov. 5, 1932), p. 4.)

Concerns the opposition to the Railway Bill, incorporating the principal recommendations of the Duff Commission.

—— National affairs. (In *Saturday night*. Toronto. v. 48, no. 3 (Nov. 26, 1932), p. 4.)

Concerns, primarily, the debate over the recommendations of the Duff Commission.

—— National affairs. Statecraft in the dark. By E. C. Buchanan. (In *Saturday night*. Toronto. v. 48, no. 5 (Dec. 10, 1932), p. 4.)

General comments on problems of contemporary governments; the London visit of Prime Minister Bennett; and the contest for leadership between J. S. Woodsworth and Agnes Macphail.

—— National affairs. Power without office. (In *Saturday night*. Toronto. v. 48, no. 7 (Dec. 24, 1932), p. 4.)

Comments on J. S. Woodsworth and the Co-operative Commonwealth Federation; Mr. Brownlee's appointment to the tariff board, etc.

—— National affairs. Senators work and die. (In *Saturday night*. Toronto. v. 48, no. 11 (Jan. 21, 1933), p. 4.)

Relates to the fact that the Senate still has "in hand the bill providing for the implementation of the Duff Commission's report on the railway situation. . . ."

—— National affairs. Section fight coming. (In *Saturday night*. Toronto. v. 48, no. 13 (Feb. 4, 1933), p. 4.)

Comments on the likelihood of regaining political conflict in the House of Commons.

—— National affairs. Union party rumors. (In *Saturday night*. Toronto. v. 48, no. 15 (Feb. 18, 1933), p. 4.)

Comments on the possibility of a national government.

—— National affairs. Don't neglect Ottawa. (In *Saturday night*. Toronto. v. 48, no. 18 (Mar. 11, 1933), p. 4.)

Comments on J. S. Woodsworth and the CCF Party; W. L. M. King and liberalism, etc.

—— National government by changing preposition. (In *Saturday night*. Toronto. v. 52, no. 33 (June 19, 1937), pp. 32; 37.)

Discusses National Government in the event of the retirement of R. B. Bennett and W. L. Mackenzie King.

Campaign funds—the remedy. By a defunct politician. (In *Maclean's*. Toronto. v. 44, no. 22 (Nov. 15, 1931), pp. 18; 60.)

Canadian problems as seen by twenty outstanding men of Canada. Toronto, Oxford University Press [1933] 320 p.

Added title page: Canadian problems; a collection of papers read at the first annual

Liberal-Conservative summer school held at Newmarket, Ontario.

Partial contents: Democracy on trial, by R. B. Bennett. – Public service, by G. S. Henry. – Public administration and social service, by A. Brady. An unemployment policy – some proposals, by H. M. Cassidy. – Government ownership and the Canadian scene, by H. A. Innis. – Our transportation problem, by W. T. Jackman. – A view of Canada's railway problems, by R. J. Manion. – History and aims of the Conservative Party, by L. Macaulay. – The federal problem and the British North America Act, by N. A. M. Mackenzie. – The contribution of the French Canadian to federal unity, by H. Saint-Denis. – Revolution and reaction, by G. M. Wrong. – Political changes by force and violence, by W. H. Price.

Canadian railway control; political interference. (In *Canadian comment*. Toronto. v. 2, no. 5 (May 1933), p. 16.)
Concerns recommendations set forth by the Duff Commission.

CARON, MAXIMILIEN L'actualité: M. Aberhart, le gouvernement fédéral et le désaveu. (In *L'Action nationale*. Montréal. v. 10 (oct. 1937), pp. [120]-127.)

—— Les compagnies à fonds social (In *L'Action nationale*. Montréal. v. 8 (oct. 1936), pp. [91]-108.)
Examines this issue as an argument for changes in the constitution.

—— L'organisation corporative et la constitution canadienne. (In *L'Action nationale*. Montréal. v. 11 (mars 1938), pp. [229]-244.)

—— Pour une politique nationale. (In *L'Action nationale*. Montréal. v. 9 (jan. 1937), pp. [5]-17.)

The Case of the Maritimes under Confederation (In *The Maritime advocate and busy East*. Sackville, N.B. v. 24, no. 2 (Sept. 1933), pp. 11-23.)
Reprinted from the *Saint John Telegraph* dated August 23, 1933. Text of "a 32-page brief presented to Premier Tilley and his cabinet by a committee composed of representatives of eight different groups" as an appeal to the Privy Council.

CASSIDY, HARRY M. An unemployment policy; some proposals. (In *Canadian problems as seen by twenty outstanding men of Canada*. Toronto, [1933] pp. [49]-67.)

CAYGEON, ROBERT Ko-Ko at Ottawa. (In *Saturday night*. Toronto. v. 50, no. 32 (June 1935), pp. [1]-4.)
Concerns the legislation introduced to set up a Dominion Trade and Industry Commission recommended by the Price Spreads Commission.

—— National affairs. Thunder-stealing orgy. (In *Saturday night*. Toronto. v. 50, no. 38 (July 27, 1935), p. 4.)
Concerns the manifestos presented respectively by H. H. Stevens and J. S. Woodsworth.

—— National affairs. Rebirth of a policy. (In *Saturday night*. Toronto. v. 50, no. 40 (Aug. 10, 1935), p. 4.)
Examines a series of radio speeches delivered by R. B. Bennett and Mackenzie King during the federal election campaign of 1935.

—— National affairs. Dodging real issues. (In *Saturday night*. Toronto. v. 50, no. 41 (Aug. 17, 1935), pp. 4; 6.)
Concerns the federal election campaign of 1935.

—— National affairs. In the political doldrums. (In *Saturday night*. Toronto. v. 50, no. 47 (Sept. 28, 1935), p. 4.)
Comments on the campaign for the federal election held October 14, 1935; refers to J. S. Woodsworth and socialism.

—— National affairs. A showman's election. (In *Saturday night*. Toronto. v. 50, no. 49 (Oct. 12, 1935), p. 4.)
Concerns the general elections of October 14, 1935.

—— National affairs. This socialism. (In *Saturday night*. Toronto. v. 51, no. 1 (Nov. 9, 1935), p. 4.)
Comments on socialism with reference to the CCF Party.

—— National affairs. Mr. Hepburn's future. (In *Saturday night*. Toronto. v. 51, no. 2 (Nov. 16, 1935), pp. 4; 10.)
Concerns Mitchell Frederick Hepburn.

CHALMERS, FLOYD SHERMAN The next five years in Canada. By Floyd S. Chalmers. (In Empire Club of Canada. *Addresses*. Toronto. (1935/36), pp. 365-380.)
Address delivered April 16, 1936.

—— No. 1 job-maker. A quick sketch of the dynamic head of Canada's National Employment Commission. By Floyd S. Chalmers. (In *Maclean's*. Toronto. v. 50, no. 1 (Jan. 1, 1937), p. 23.)
Concerns Arthur B. Purvis.

—— Our wheat gamble. By Floyd S. Chalmers. (In *Maclean's*. Toronto. v. 48, no. 6 (Mar. 15, 1935), pp. 14-15; 55-56.)

For a rejoinder, see Our wheat position, by J. I. McFarland. (In *Maclean's*. Toronto. v. 48, no. 9 (1935), pp. 15; 57-59.)

CLUB CANADIEN DE QUEBEC Problèmes de l'heure. Conférences prononcées devant le Club canadien de Québec en 1933 et 1934. Québec, La Cie de l'Evénement, 1935. vii, 221 p.

Partial contents: Canada, by H. H. Stevens. – Parliamentary government, by H. Guthrie. – Politique et politiciens, par E. Lapointe.

COHEN, BERNARD LANDE The railways—a plea for unification. (In *The Dalhousie review*. Halifax. v. 15 (1935/36), pp. [414]-424.)

COLWELL, A. F. What is wrong with the Maritimes. (In *The Maritime advocate and busy East*. Sackville, N.B. v. 25, no. 2 (Sept. 1934), pp. 5-7; 22.)

"An address delivered in Charlottetown before the Associated Boards of Trade . . . of Cumberland Bay, N.B."

Contends that the effects of Confederation have been negative for the Maritime provinces.

COOK, WARREN K. Will anything come of it? (In *The Canadian forum*. Toronto. v. 14, no. 167 (Aug. 1934), pp. 427-430.)

Considers the work of the price spreads and mass buying investigations, more commonly known as the Stevens Investigation.

COTE, FRANCOIS Fasciste d'un autre âge: Adrien Arcand. (In *Le Magazine Maclean*. Montréal. v. 1, no. 3 (mai 1961), pp. 21; 47-48.)

COWAN, JAMES A. Does Canada want government radio? Yes, . . . : Government control of broadcasting is the only means by which we can prevent United States domination of the Canadian air. (In *Maclean's*. Toronto. v. 43, no. 9 (May 1, 1930), pp. 9; 40; 42.)

CRAWLEY, A. M. An Englishman views Canadian politics. (In Canadian Club of Toronto. *Addresses*. Toronto. (1938/39), pp. 260-267.)

Address delivered March 20, 1939.

CREIGHTON, JAMES H. Finance Act as substitute for Central Bank. Nature of the Act's administration makes it impossible for it to fulfil functions of Central Bank.

Outstanding features are divided responsibility and lack of leadership. Cannot direct monetary policy. (In *Saturday night*. Toronto. v. 48, no. 43 (Sept. 2, 1933), pp. [17]; 24.)

CRONKITE, FREDERICK CLINTON Canada and the abdication. By F. C. Cronkite. (In *The Canadian journal of economics and political science*. [Toronto] v. 4 (1938), pp. 177-191.)

Discusses the conduct of the Canadian Parliament and the Government of Canada in dealing with the abdication of King Edward VIII and the accession to the throne of King George VI in 1937. Considers the legal and constitutional principles involved.

DAFOE, JOHN WESLEY Canada; yesterday, today and tomorrow. By John W. Dafoe. (In Canadian Club of Toronto. *Addresses*. Toronto. (1933/34), pp. 315-323.)

Address delivered February 12, 1934.

DANSEREAU, DOLLARD Le peuple veut voter! (In *L'Action nationale*. Montréal. v. 6 (oct. 1935), pp. [134]-137.)

DAVIS, ROY Primers of treachery. A startling report on the pre-war fifth-columnist activities of Nazi and Fascist schools in Canada. (In *Maclean's*. Toronto. v. 53, no. 17 (Sept. 1, 1940), pp. 9; 30.)

DAVIS, THOMAS CLAYTON National problems from the viewpoint of the man in Saskatchewan. By Hon. T. R. [!] Davis, Attorney-General, province of Saskatchewan. (In Canadian Club of Toronto. *Addresses*. Toronto. (1938/39), pp. 124-140.)

Address delivered November 28, 1938.

DAWSON, ARTHUR OSBORNE Business looks at government. "The time has come to tell the people of Canada what is right with business." No. 1. By A. O. Dawson. (In *Maclean's*. Toronto. v. 48, no. 21 (Nov. 1, 1935), p. 20.)

DEACHMAN, ROBERT JOHN Some absurd political arguments are answered. By R. J. Deachman. (In *The Maritime advocate and busy East*. Sackville, N.B. v. 26, no. 8 (Mar. 1936), pp. 13-14; 22.)

Comments on the reaction to the issue of balance of trade by the Social Credit Party, Reconstruction Party and the CCF.

DEACON, WILLIAM ARTHUR Canada's national policy. (In *The Canadian magazine*. Toronto. v. 87, no. 1 (Jan. 1937), pp. 15; 40-41.)

—— Wanted—a union government. (In

The Canadian magazine. Toronto. v. 89, no. 2 (Feb. 1938), pp. [13]; 35.)

The author considers it necessary to have a united government in order to re-write the British North America Act.

DEXTER, GRANT   Do we kill our finance ministers? By A.G. Dexter. (In *Maclean's.* Toronto. v. 43, no. 2 (Jan. 15, 1930), pp. 9; 36-37.)

"An outspoken attack on the policy that is making the portfolio of finance a passport to the grave."

—— Farm debt relief. (In *Maclean's.* Toronto. v. 48, no. 8 (Apr. 15, 1935), pp. 24; 49.)

—— Rail riddle. (In *Maclean's.* Toronto. v. 46, no. 2 (Jan. 15, 1933), pp. 13; 32-33.)

—— What did Parliament do for you? A survey of the happenings of the last parliamentary session from the viewpoint of their reaction on the interests of Mr. General Public. (In *The Canadian magazine.* Toronto. v. 77 [i.e. 76] no. 3 (Sept. 1931), pp. 13; 41-42.)

A review of the parliamentary session lasting from March 12 to August 3, 1931.

DRURY, ERNEST CHARLES   The depression. [Part] I. Its extent. By E. C. Drury. (In *Maclean's.* Toronto. v. 46, no. 10 (May 15, 1933), pp. 15; 47-49.)

—— The depression. [Part] II. Causes. By E. C. Drury. (In *Maclean's.* Toronto. v. 46, no. 11 (June 1, 1933), pp. 21; 54-55.)

—— The depression. [Part] III. Remedies. By E. C. Drury. (In *Maclean's.* Toronto. v. 46, no. 12 (June 15, 1933), pp. 17; 47; 49.)

DUROCHER, RENE   L'alliance Duplessis-Hepburn, 1936-1939. 32 leaves. (In Canadian Political Science Association. *Papers presented at the annual meeting.* Kingston. 42d (1970), v. 1, pt. 9.)

Reproduced typescript.

EDMONDS, WILLIAM LEWIS   Through sixteen campaigns. See-saw between Conservatives and Liberals since 1867 with third-party interventions. Tariff the most persistent issue. (In *Saturday night.* Toronto. v. 45, no. 37 (July 26, 1930), pp. 2-3.)

EDWARDS, FREDERICK   Does Canada want government radio? No, . . . : Government control means political control and curtailed programmes for the listener-in. (In *Maclean's.* Toronto. v. 43, no. 9 (May 1, 1930), pp. 8; 36; 38.)

—— Fascism in Canada. Blue shirts, swastikas, drills, fanaticism—they're all with us. [Part one] (In *Maclean's.* Toronto. v. 51, no. 8 (Apr. 15, 1938), pp. 10; 66-68.)

—— Fascism in Canada. Signs of disintegration have appeared following Fascism's brutality in Europe. Part two. (In *Maclean's.* Toronto. v. 51, no. 9 (May 1, 1938), pp. 15; 30.)

EPSTEIN, LOUIS   Canadian youth finds its voice. (In *New frontier.* Toronto. v. 1, no. 4 (July 1936), pp. 27-29.)

Describes the meeting of the Canadian Youth Congress at Ottawa, March 23-25, 1936.

FALCONER, SIR ROBERT   The Throne and Canada. (In *Queen's quarterly.* Kingston. v. 46 (1939), pp. [137]-144.)

Comments are related to the visit made to Canada during 1939 by King George VI and Queen Elizabeth.

Fascism in Canada. By a non-fascist. (In *Saturday night.* Toronto. v. 53, no. 22 (Apr. 2, 1938), p. 2.)

The Federal election drama. As viewed by a Conservative. (In *Canadian comment.* Toronto. v. 4, no. 8 (Aug. 1935), pp. 10-11. map.)

Election held October 14, 1935.

FERGUSON, GEORGE HOWARD   Canada must arm. By Hon. G. Howard Ferguson. (In *Maclean's.* Toronto. v. 50, no. 8 (Apr. 15, 1937), pp. 11; 75.)

FISHER, RICHARD A.   "Let 'em have housing." (In *Saturday night.* Toronto. v. 53, no. 40 (Aug. 6, 1938), pp. [1]; 3.)

Comments on the Dominion Housing Act.

For peace and order. (In *Canadian comment.* Toronto. v. 3, no. 5 (May 1934), p. 10.)

Comment on the parliamentary debate over a mandatory clause in the Relief Bill, introduced by R. B. Bennett.

FRASER, A. D.   A quota system for Canada? (In *Saturday night.* Toronto. v. 45, no. 31 (June 14, 1930), pp. 31; 38-39.)

Deals with Canada's immigration policy.

GIBSON, FREDERICK W.   The cabinet of 1935. (In his Cabinet formation and bicultural relations. [Ottawa, 1970] pp. [105]-141.)

GILBERT, GEORGE   Dominion law amendments. Bill now before Parliament represents effort to place Dominion jurisdiction of insurance beyond challenge. (In *Satur-*

day night. Toronto. v. 49, no. 17 (Mar. 3, 1934), p. 20.)

The bill was introduced in the Senate on February 20, 1934.

GIVENS, W. R.   Costing Canada a million a week. So the Canadian National costs are mounting in staggering figures that demand immediate and universal attention if we are to escape disastrous consequences. (In *The Canadian magazine.* Toronto. v. 78, no. 3 (Sept. 1932), pp. [3]; 22-23.)

Considers the political implications in a discussion of the government-owned Canadian National Railways.

GLAZEBROOK, GEORGE PARKIN DE TWENE-BROKES   Canada's defence policy. By G. de T. Glazebrook and Winslow Benson. Report of the round tables of the fourth annual conference of the Canadian Institute of International Affairs, Hamilton, Ontario, May 1937. Toronto, Canadian Institute of International Affairs, 1937. 16 p.

GOOD, WILLIAM CHARLES   My political philosophy. By W. C. Good. (In *The Canadian forum.* Toronto. v. 13, no. 155 (Aug. 1933), pp. 413-416.)

A reply to the article Mr. Good's political philosophy, by F. H. Underhill. (In *The Canadian forum.* Toronto. v. 13, no. 155 (1933), pp. 411-413.)

W. C. Good was an advocate of proportional representation.

GOUIN, PAUL   L'avenir de la jeunesse, libérale ou non. (In *Revue trimestrielle canadienne.* Montréal. v. 20 (juin 1934), pp. [148]-168.)

"Causerie donnée devant l'Association de la jeunesse libérale, le 23 avril, 1934, à la salle Saint-Sulpice."

The Granting of titles, honours and awards to Canadians. How members of the House of Commons at Ottawa voted on the proposal that the Prime Minister refrain from recommending titles for Canadians. (In *The Maritime advocate and busy East.* Sackville, N.B. v. 24, no. 9 (Apr. 1934), pp. 5-19; 28.)

Consists of the debates taken from Hansard, March 14, 1934.

GRAUER, ALBERT EDWARD   Is unemployment insurance enough? By A. E. Grauer. (In *The University of Toronto quarterly.* [Toronto] v. 4 (1934/35), pp. 514-523.)

Considers the implications of the Cana-

dian Unemployment and Social Insurance Act, 1935.

GRIFFIN, HARRY LEWIS   Public policy in relation to the wheat market. By H. L. Griffin. (In *The Canadian journal of economics and political science.* Toronto. v. 1 (1935), pp. 482-498.)

GRUBE, GEORGE MAXIMILIAN ANTONY   Defence and the House of Commons. By G. M. A. Grube. (In *The Canadian forum.* Toronto. v. 18, no. 208 (May 1938), pp. 45-47.)

Discusses the debate on the defence estimates.

HALL, JOHN S.   Dictatorship by the ballot. By J. S. Hall. (In *Saturday night.* Toronto. v. 51, no. 43 (Aug. 29, 1936), p. 8.)

Discusses the fact that in almost all recent elections, federal and provincial, one political party was elected with an overwhelming majority resulting in an absence of an effective opposition.

HAMEL, GERARD   La politique commerciale du Canada depuis 1930. (In *Etudes économiques.* Montréal. v. 6 (1936), pp. [7]-66.)

At head of title: Publications de l'Ecole des Hautes Etudes Commerciales de Montréal.

HARVEY, JEAN CHARLES   Can we achieve Canadian unity? (In Empire Club of Canada. *Addresses.* Toronto. (1938/39), pp. 184-199.)

Address delivered January 19, 1939.

——— Le cas de M. Henri Bourassa. (In *Les Idées.* Montréal. 1. année, v. 2 (1935), pp. [270]-289.)

Comments following the defeat of Henri Bourassa in the federal election held October 14, 1935, in Labelle, Que.

——— How can we build a nation? (In Empire Club of Canada. *Addresses.* Toronto. (1939/40), pp. 227-239.)

Address delivered January 11, 1940.

HEIGHINGTON, WILFRID   What is a title— and how? House of Commons resolution barring such honors for Canadians has never been tested in law and may be *ultra vires.* Conferring of knighthoods not covered by Constitution. (In *Saturday night.* Toronto. v. 46, no. 7 (Dec. 27, 1930), p. 2.)

HEPBURN, MITCHELL FREDERICK   Present day problems. By the Honourable Mitchell F. Hepburn. (In Empire Club of Canada.

Addresses. Toronto. (1938/39), pp. 153-170.)

Address delivered December 15, 1938.

HOAR, VICTOR (comp.) The great depression; essays and memoirs from Canada and the United States. Compiler: Victor Hoar. Vancouver, Copp Clark Pub. Co., c1969. vi, 232 p.

Papers first presented at a meeting of the Canadian Association for American Studies at McGill University. Cf. p. VI.

Partial contents: Federalism in crisis; a comparative study of Canada and the United States in the depression of the 1930's, by J. T. Patterson. – The Liberal way, by H. B. Neatby. – The nineteen thirties in the United States and Canada, by F. R. Scott. – The CCF Party in its formative years, by G. Spry.

HOARE, JOHN Swastika over Quebec: Arcand meeting. (In *Saturday night*. Toronto. v. 54, no. 45 (Sept. 9, 1939), p. 3.)

Reports on a meeting held by Adrien Arcand, leader of the Parti national chrétien social, held in Montreal, July 31, 1939.

—— Swastika over Quebec: party record. (In *Saturday night*. Toronto. v. 54, no. 47 (Sept. 23, 1939), p. 3.)

Concerns Adrien Arcand and the Parti national chrétien social.

HOOD, M. MC INTYRE Canada has kept faith. (In *Maclean's*. Toronto. v. 50, no. 21 (Nov. 1, 1937), pp. 11; 41-42.)

Concerns federal government aid to war veterans.

HORN, MICHIEL STEVEN DANIEL The League for Social Reconstruction: socialism and nationalism in Canada, 1931-1945. Toronto, 1969. 568 leaves.

Thesis (PH D) – University of Toronto.

HORN, MICHIEL STEVEN DANIEL Visionaries of the 1930s: The League for Social Reconstruction. By Michiel Horn. (In Clarkson, Stephen (ed.) *Visions 2020*. Edmonton [c1970] pp. [263]-267.)

HUDON, THEOPHILE Est-ce la fin de la Confédération? Avec préf. par Louis Lavoie. Montréal. Impr. du Messager, 1936. 188 p.

Discusses, in brief, amending the B.N.A. Act, the secession of Quebec from Confederation, annexation with the U.S., an equal association of the French and English peoples in Canada.

HUNTER, GRACE Divorce de luxe via the Senate. (In *Saturday night*. Toronto. v. 45, no. 16 (Mar. 1, 1930), p. 2.)

Discussion occasioned by the defeat of the bill giving divorce jurisdiction to Ontario.

HUTCHISON, BRUCE Revolt beyond the Rockies. (In *Maclean's*. Toronto. v. 47, no. 14 (July 15, 1934), pp. 16; 26.)

Premier Pattullo's struggle with the federal government to secure federal dollars for the work and wages program he wishes to set up in the province of British Columbia.

IGNATIEFF, NICHOLAS Canada's minorities. (In *Saturday night*. Toronto. v. 49, no. 30 (June 2, 1934), p. 2.)

"The proposed disfranchisement of all Doukhobors . . . which is reported to be a feature of the new Election Act now being drafted by the Dominion Government, brings up an issue of vital national importance."

IRWIN, WILLIAM ARTHUR The railway problem. An answer to the question: What's the matter with our railways? By W. A. Irwin. (In *Maclean's*. Toronto. v. 44, no. 24 (Dec. 15, 1931), pp. 19; 30; 32.)

First in a series of three articles.

—— The railway problem. An explanation of the causes that have brought about our present transportation dilemma. By W. A. Irwin. (In *Maclean's*. Toronto. v. 45, no. 1 (Jan. 1, 1932), pp. 23; 32-34.)

Second in a series of three articles.

—— The railway problem. What's "the way out" of our transportation predicament?. . . By W. A. Irwin. (In *Maclean's*. Toronto. v. 45, no. 2 (Jan. 15, 1932), pp. 23; 26; 32.)

Concludes a series of three articles.

JORDAN, HELEN C. Women and the relief boards. (In *Chatelaine*. Toronto. v. 7, no. 4 (Apr. 1933), pp. 19; 74.)

Comments on the fact that few women serve in the administration of unemployment relief.

Judge for yourself. The Davis report does not end the Bren gun case—it does change a system which the commissioner says "broke down". (In *Maclean's*. Toronto. v. 52, no. 4 (Feb. 15, 1939), pp. 9; 41-47.)

KEITH, J. E. Is Quebec going Fascist? A review of the first year of nationalist rule in French Canada. (In *Maclean's*. Toronto. v. 50, no. 15 (Aug. 1, 1937), pp. 9; 27-28.)

KELLER-WOLFF, GUSTAVE Le fascisme et le Canada. (In Les Idées. Montréal. 5. année, v. 9 (1939), pp. [551]-558.)

KEMP, HUBERT RICHMOND Is a revision of taxation powers necessary? By H. R. Kemp. (In Canadian Political Science Association. Papers and proceedings of the annual meeting. [Kingston, Ont.] v. 3 (1931), pp. [185]-201.)

KERR, WILLIAM DAVITT Ottawa begins to worry about its many Germans. (In Saturday night. Toronto. v. 54, no. 28 (May 13, 1939), p. 2.)
Concerns Germans in the public services and their relationship to the Nazi Party.

KNOX, FRANK ALBERT Dominion monetary policy, 1929-1934. A study prepared for the Royal Commission on Dominion-Provincial Relations, by F. A. Knox. Ottawa, 1939. 93 leaves.
Reproduced typescript.
Issued also in French.

LAVERGNE, ARMAND Canadiens. (In L'Action nationale. Montréal. v. 5 (jan. 1935), pp. [26]-30.)

LAWRENCE, MARGARET A simple woman sees Parliament. (In Saturday night. Toronto. v. 54, no. 13 (Jan. 28, 1939), p. 3.)

LEACOCK, STEPHEN BUTLER The riddle of the depression. By Stephen Leacock. (In Empire Club of Canada. Addresses. Toronto. (1933/34), pp. 70-83.)
Address delivered February 16, 1933.

LEAGUE FOR SOCIAL RECONSTRUCTION New national purposes. L. S. R. brief. Part III. (In The Canadian forum. Toronto. v. 18, no. 208 (May 1938), pp. 50-54.)
Brief to the Rowell Commission.

—— Obstacles to national unity. L. S. R. brief. Part II. (In The Canadian forum. Toronto. v. 18, no. 207 (Apr. 1938), pp. 441-443.)
Brief to the Rowell Commission.

—— The purpose of Confederation. L. S. R. brief. Part I. (In The Canadian forum. Toronto. v. 17, no. 206 (Mar. 1938), pp. 410-412.)
Brief to the Rowell Commission.

LE BRET, JAEN Vers le socialisme. (In Les Idées. Montréal. 1. année, v. 1 (1935), pp. [138]-150.)
Comparative remarks, with reference to Canada.

LEGGE, STUART C. The course of politics moves leftward. Addresses at Canadian Institute on Economics and Politics reveal growing conviction throughout community of need for new social order. (In Saturday night. Toronto v. 49, no. 46 (Sept. 22, 1934), p. 2.)

LEGGETT, ROBERT F. The personnel of Parliament. By Robert F. Leggett. (In The Canadian forum. Toronto. v. 17, no. 202 (Nov. 1937), pp. 272-273.)
Compares the composition of the Dominion House of Commons and the Legislative Assembly of Quebec after elections held in both the Dominion and the province of Quebec during 1936.

LEMAN, BEAUDRY Business looks at government. No. 3: "Shall we make a God of the State." (In Maclean's. Toronto. v. 49, no. 1 (Jan. 1, 1936), pp. 24; 44.)

LEWIS, DAVID Revelation according to Hansard. (In The Canadian forum. Toronto. v. 16, no. 184 (May 1936), pp. 5-6.)

LIGUE D'ACTION NATIONALE Aux Canadiens français de la province de Québec. (In L'Action nationale. Montréal. v. 11 (fév. 1938), pp. [89]-94.)
Discusses the Canadian confederation.

LIPSETT, ROBERT W. National affairs. Plebiscite bombshell. By Robert Lipsett. (In Saturday night. Toronto. v. 48, no. 19 (Mar. 18, 1933), p. 4.)
Comments on the "possibility of a plebiscite as to whether or not Canadian railway systems should be amalgamated".

—— National affairs. To bar 1933 election. By R. W. Lipsett. (In Saturday night. Toronto. v. 48, no. 29 (May 27, 1933), pp. 4; 10.)
Concerns the problem of redistribution.

—— National affairs. Rabbit's foot election. By R. W. Lipsett. (In Saturday night. Toronto. v. 48, no. 30 (June 3, 1933), p. 4.)
A review of the fourth session, seventeenth parliament.

—— National affairs. Ottawa talks union. By R. W. Lipsett. (In Saturday night. Toronto. v. 48, no. 47 (Sept. 30, 1933), p. 4.)
Concerns "rumors of impending union government".

—— National affairs. Too much sound money. By R. W. Lipsett. (In Saturday night. Toronto. v. 48, no. 50 (Oct. 21, 1933), p. 4.)
Comments on R. B. Bennett's tour of the Prairie Provinces, the 225-million-dollar refund loan, etc.

—— National affairs. Pension trouble again. By R. W. Lipsett. (In *Saturday night*. Toronto. v. 48, no. 51 (Oct. 28, 1933), p. 4.)

Comments on pensions and the Board of Pensions Commissioners.

—— National affairs. The Macmillan report. By R.W. Lipsett. (In *Saturday night*. Toronto. v. 49, no. 2 (Nov. 18, 1933), p. 4.)

Comments on the report of the Macmillan Commission on Canadian banking.

—— National affairs. Money comes first. By R. W. Lipsett. (In *Saturday night*. Toronto, v. 49, no. 4 (Dec. 2, 1933), p. 20.)

Comments on the problems of a national finance policy.

—— National affairs. See the bankers smile. By R. W. Lipsett. (In *Saturday night*. Toronto. v. 49, no. 11 (Jan. 20, 1934), p. 4.)

Comments on the banking issue and forthcoming banking legislation.

LITTLE, DALTON J. Advertising law holds threat to business. Amendment to criminal code requires impracticable prior test of quality of advertised goods and threatens to penalize owners of established trade name. (In *Saturday night*. Toronto. v. 51, no. 13 (Feb. 1, 1936), pp. [17]; 24.)

Deals with the amendment to the criminal code known as Section 406, Subsection 3, which came into force January 1, 1936, and the Dominion Trade and Industry Act.

—— Consumer is loser by codes. Canada's Supreme Court reviews legislation. Does Criminal Code put stigma on trade practices? (In *Saturday night*. Toronto. v. 51, no. 11 (Jan. 18, 1936), pp. [21]; 28.)

Deals with the Supreme Court "sitting in judgement on the constitutionality of the so-called social legislation passed by the Bennett Government last year". Concerns, in particular, Section 498A of the Criminal Code.

LOWER, ARTHUR REGINALD MARSDEN External policy and internal problems. By A. R. M. Lower. (In *The University of Toronto quarterly*. [Toronto] v. 6, (1936/37), pp. 326-337.)

Discusses Canadian attitudes toward possible war.

MC ARTHUR, DUNCAN Business and government. By D. McArthur. (In *Queen's*

quarterly. Kingston. v. 41 (1934), pp. [256]-264.)

Relates the above issue to the investigations of the Royal Commission on Price Spreads, convened in 1934 under the chairmanship of H. H. Stevens, later under that of W. W. Kennedy.

—— Parliament and people in Canada. By D. McA. (In *Queen's quarterly*. Kingston. v. 38 (1931), pp. 385-388.)

Comments on the parliamentary practice of prolonging the debate on the Address in reply to the Speech from the Throne, with special reference to the debate held from March 16 to April 21, 1931.

—— Problems of federal government. By D. McA. (In *Queen's quarterly*. Kingston. v. 40 (1933), pp. 647-651.)

Comments on the form and structure of government and its capacity to meet problems brought about by social and economic changes in post-World War I Canada.

MC CULLEY, JOSEPH Youth Congress grows in scope and influence. (In *Saturday night*. Toronto. v. 53, no. 32 (June 11, 1938), p. 2.)

MC CULLOUGH, JOHN WILLIAM SCOTT National health insurance. Says this writer "Sickness insurance is bound to come . . . it must be a unified national scheme . . . and preventive medicine must be emphasized". By John W. S. McCullough. (In *Maclean's*. Toronto. v. 51, no. 5 (Mar. 1, 1938), pp. 16; 31-33.)

MACDERMOT, TERENCE WILLIAM LEIGHTON Radical thinking in Canada. By T. W. L. Macdermot. (In *The Canadian forum*. Toronto. v. 12, no. 133 (Oct. 1931), pp. 9-11.)

MACDONALD, ANGUS LEWIS Nova Scotia and Confederation. By Hon. Angus L. Macdonald. (In Canadian Club of Toronto. *Addresses*. Toronto. (1938/39), pp. 1-16.)

Address delivered May 10, 1938.

MC DONALD, GEORGE C. Debt. (In Canadian Club of Toronto. *Addresses*. Toronto. (1932/33), pp. 342-363.)

Address delivered March 20, 1933.

Discusses "the dilemma of governmental debts in Canada".

MC FARLAND, JOHN I. Our wheat position. (In *Maclean's*. Toronto. v. 48, no. 9 (May 1, 1935), pp. 15; 57-59.)

A reply to Floyd S. Chalmers "Our wheat gamble". [In *Maclean's*. Toronto. v. 48, no. 6 (1935), pp. 14-15; 55-56.]

MAC GREGOR, DONALD CHALMERS These insignificant budgets. (In *The Canadian forum*. Toronto. v. 14, no. 166 (July 1934), pp. 386-389.)

MC KAGUE, WILLIAM ALLISON Alberta affairs moving toward a climax. Blocked in attempt to control banks and press, government must now modify policy or seek to prolong its life by employing still more radical measures. By W. A. McKague. (In *Saturday night*. Toronto. v. 52, no. 50 (Oct. 16, 1937), pp [21]; 28.)

—— Alberta versus the country. Legislation is challenge to creditors, banks, courts and Dominion authority. Four possible lines of action. By W. A. McKague. (In *Saturday night*. Toronto. v. 52, no. 41 (Aug. 14, 1937), pp. [17]; 19; 21.)

—— Control of business and our constitution. Is highly centralized government possible in Canada? — Answer is no, judging by fate of New Deal measures and division of authority under B.N.A. Act. By W. A. McKague. (In *Saturday night*. Toronto. v. 51, no. 37 (July 18, 1936), pp. [17]; 21.)

—— The mystery of ever-recurring government deficits. By W. A. McKague. (In *Saturday night*. Toronto. v. 54, no. 40 (Aug. 5, 1939), pp. [11]; 13.)

—— Stevens report urges control of business. Possibility of regulatory legislation that may seriously prejudice ability of Canadian industry to recover and absorb unemployed seen in recommendations. By W. A. McKague. (In *Saturday night*. Toronto. v. 50, no. 24 (April 20, 1935), pp. [33]; 40.)
Refers to the Royal Commission on Price Spreads; H. H. Stevens, chairman.

MAC KAY, ARMOUR Canadian youth may determine the 1939 election. (In *Saturday night*. Toronto. v. 54, no. 40 (Aug. 5, 1939), p. 2.)
Discusses the Canadian Youth Congress.

MAC KAY, ROBERT ALEXANDER After Beauharnois—what? Says this writer: "The Liberal and Conservative Parties alike have become pensioners of selfish interests. If they are to become real instruments of public welfare, drastic changes must be made in our election laws." By Robert A.

MacKay. (In *Maclean's*. Toronto. v. 44, no. 20 (Oct. 15, 1931), pp. 7-8; 61-63.)
Examines the question of campaign funds and presents suggestions aimed at reforming current practices.

MACKENZIE, NORMAN ARCHIBALD MAC RAE Our problems of defence. By N. A. M. Mackenzie. (In *Canadian comment*. Toronto. v. 12 (Dec. 1936), pp. 3-5.)

MC LEAN, J. ROSS National affairs. Needs and powers. (In *Saturday night*. Toronto. v. 50, no. 16 (Feb. 23, 1935), p. 4.)
Comments on R. B. Bennett's reform program and the CCF platform.

—— National affairs. Uninsured workers. (In *Saturday night*. Toronto. v. 50, no. 17 (Mar. 2, 1935), p. 4.)
Comments on the Unemployment Insurance Bill.

—— National affairs. Campaigns take time. (In *Saturday night*. Toronto. v. 50, no. 18 (Mar. 9, 1935), p. 4.)
Concerns speculations on a federal election.

—— National affairs. Will housing save us? (In *Saturday night*. Toronto. v. 50, no. 22 (Apr. 6, 1935), p. 4.)
Comments on the budget debate and the national housing policy.

—— National affairs. A monumental report. (In *Saturday night*. Toronto. v. 50, no. 24 (Apr. 20, 1935), p. 16.)
Concerns the Report of the Royal Commission on Price Spreads.

MACLEOD, NORMAN M. In Ottawa we trust. (In *Saturday night*. Toronto. v. 52, no. 10 (Jan. 9, 1937), pp. [1]; 2.)
Looks back over Parliament's performance in view of a forthcoming session.

—— National policy—1939 version. (In Empire Club of Canada. *Addresses*. Toronto. (1938/39), pp. 361-376.)
Address delivered April 13, 1939.

MC NAUGHT, KENNETH WILLIAM KIRKPATRICK The 1930s. By Kenneth McNaught. (In Careless, J. M. S. (ed.) *The Canadians, 1867-1967*. Toronto, 1967. pp. 236-274.)

MACPHAIL, ALEXANDER Unemployment. By A. M. (In *Queen's quarterly*. Kingston. v. 42 (1935), pp. [415]-422.)
Discusses the issue of unemployment as a matter of public policy.

MC QUEEN, R. The Price Spreads report explained (In *Queen's quarterly*. Kingston. v. 42 (1935), pp. [253]-263.)

Concerns the Report of the Royal Commission on Price Spreads. Ottawa, 1935.

MANION, ROBERT JAMES General world conditions. By Hon. R. J. Manion (In Club canadien de Québec. *Problèmes de l'heure.* Québec, 1935. pp. 11-23.)

Reprinted from "Chronicle-Telegraph, Quebec, Monday, Jan. 9, 1933".

The emphasis is on Canada in relation to world conditions.

MARKS, MERWYN The Youth Congress. (In *New frontier.* Toronto. v. 2, no. 3 (July/Aug. 1937), p. 26.)

Describes the second meeting of the Canadian Youth Congress held in Montreal during the summer of 1937.

MAROIS, ANDRE Pour vivre! (In *L'Action nationale.* Montréal. v. 7 (avril 1936), pp. [222]-234.)

Describes the attitude of the current younger generation of French Canadians toward Confederation.

Contents: Le séparatisme. – Singulier phénomène. – Ce désenchantement. – Autres découvertes. – Encore d'autres découvertes. – Et le crime de l'immigration. – Plaidoyer d'indulgence. – Race de nouilles. – Méthode d'éducation.

MONTAGNES, JAMES Nothing military about Canada's work camps. Policy is to use single unemployed men to execute public works of a type which would not ordinarily be undertaken for several years, in exchange for food, lodging and allowances. (In *Saturday night.* Toronto. v. 48, no. 28 (May 20, 1933), p. 2.)

MOORE, WILLIAM HENRY The definite national purpose. Toronto, Macmillan, 1933. xv, 161 p.

Submits recommendations for reconstructing the Canadian nation and alleviating the depression.

—— New philosophy of life needed. By W. H. Moore, MP. (In Club canadien de Québec. *Problèmes de l'heure.* Québec, 1935. pp. 43-49.)

"From the Quebec Chronicle-Telegraph of February the 13th, 1933."

MORGAN, A. E. Democracy or dictatorship? "We turn from Canadian fascism in disgust when . . . it imbrues its hands in the filth of anti-semitism." (In *Maclean's.* Toronto. v. 50, no. 9 (May 1, 1937), pp. 24; 65.)

MURRAY, GEORGE M. This campaign fund racket. A campaign manager explains why there must be money in politics. (In *Maclean's.* Toronto. v. 44, no. 21 (Nov. 1, 1931), pp. 10; 45-46.)

NADEAU, JEAN MARIE Does province of Quebec want secession? By J. M. Nadeau. (In *Saturday night.* Toronto. v. 52, no. 3 (Nov. 21, 1936), p. 2.)

Considers the fascist aspect of the separatist movement.

—— Secession sentiment in province of Quebec. By J. M. Nadeau. (In *Saturday night.* Toronto. v. 52, no. 4 (Nov. 28, 1936), p. 2.)

National affairs. [Series 1] (In *Saturday night.* Toronto. v. 45, no. 41—v. 52, no. 39; v. 53, no. 51—v. 56, no. 35 (Aug. 23, 1930—July 31, 1937; Oct. 22, 1938—May 10, 1941).)

Column on federal politics, written by E. C. Buchanan (Aug. 23, 1930–Mar. 11, 1933), Robert Lipsett, Donald W. Buchanan, J. Ross McLean, Robert Caygeon, Judith Robinson, Rideau Banks (Jan. 23–July 31, 1937), R. W. Baldwin (Oct. 22, 1938–Sept. 25, 1939), Politicus (Sept. 28, 1940–May 10, 1941), and others.

Sometimes has title: The Nation.

NESBITT, EDMUND T. Vive Laurentia! (In *Saturday night.* Toronto. v. 51, no. 19 (Mar. 14, 1936), pp. [1]-2.)

Discusses the publication of two weekly newspapers in Quebec, *La Nation* and *L'Indépendence*, which advocate the formation of an independent French-Canadian state.

A New deal in the party system. (In *The Canadian forum.* Toronto. v. 15, no. 177 (Aug. 1935), pp. 329-330.)

1939 election to swing to right. By a voter. (In *Saturday night.* Toronto. v. 54, no. 32 (June 10, 1939), p. 8.)

The Northern route; political football for fifty years. (In *Canadian comment.* Toronto. v. 1, no. 11 (Nov. 1932), pp. 9-10.)

Concerns political attitudes toward the Hudson Bay Railway.

O'BRIEN, JAMES Corporative state in Canada. (In *Saturday night.* Toronto. v. 51, no. 41 (Aug. 15, 1936), p. 8.)

Discusses the overtones of fascism (Mussolini's) in the campaign of Maurice Duplessis.

O'BRIEN, JOHN EGLI A history of the Canadian Radio League, 1930-1936. [Los Angeles, Calif., 1964] 472 leaves.

Thesis (PH D) – University of Southern California.

OLD ALBERTAN Prairie revolt. By "Old Albertan". (In *Saturday night*. Toronto. v. 53, no. 30 (May 28, 1938), pp. [1]; 2.)
Concerns the debt policy of the Aberhart government and compares it to the Riel Rebellion.

O'LEARY, MICHAEL GRATTAN Ace of our judges. By M. Grattan O'Leary. (In *Maclean's* Toronto. v. 46, no. 9 (May 1, 1933), pp. 14; 57.)
Concerns Chief Justice Lyman Poore Duff of Canada's Supreme Court.

—— Backstage at Ottawa. Another pageful of the news behind the news from the nation's capital where government and opposition now wrestle on the floor of Parliament. By a Politician with a Notebook. (In *Maclean's*. Toronto. v. 44, no. 8 (Apr. 15, 1931), pp. 6; 78-79.)

—— Backstage at Ottawa. . . . strategies and the personalities of the parliamentary struggle at the capital. By a Politician with a Notebook. (In *Maclean's*. Toronto. v. 44, no. 9 (May 1, 1931), pp. 5; 42.)

—— Backstage at Ottawa. A summary of the achievements of the second sitting of the seventeenth parliament with a forecast of probable developments during the recess. By a Politician with a Notebook. (In *Maclean's*. Toronto. v. 44, no. 15 (Aug. 1, 1931), pp. 5; 44-45.)

—— Backstage at Ottawa. Chairs are being dusted for the economic conference—the nerves of the civil service are on edge —and disillusionment hangs o'er Parliament Hill. By a Politician with a Notebook. (In *Maclean's*. Toronto. v. 45, no. 7 (Apr. 1, 1932), pp. 13; 48-49.)

—— Backstage at Ottawa. ["National government cannot come without Mr. King and Mr. Bennett going"] By a Politician with a Notebook. (In *Maclean's*. Toronto. v. 46, no. 10 (May 15, 1933), pp. 8; 39-40.)

—— Backstage at Ottawa. By a Politician with a Notebook. (In *Maclean's*. Toronto. v. 48, no. 5 (Mar. 1, 1935), pp. 15; 54.)
Discusses the issues between R. B. Bennett and Mackenzie King.

—— Backstage at Ottawa. By a Politician with a Notebook. (In *Maclean's*. Toronto. v. 48, no. 13 (July 1, 1935), pp. 16; 45.)
Concerns, mainly, the breach between R. B. Bennett and H. H. Stevens.

—— Backstage at Ottawa. By a Politician with a Notebook. (In *Maclean's*. Toronto. v. 48, no. 16 (Aug. 15, 1935), pp. 11; 35.)
Discusses the "radicalism" of R. B. Bennett, W. L. Mackenzie King, J. S. Woodsworth, and H. H. Stevens.

—— Backstage at Ottawa. Defense the next big issue. By a Politician with a Notebook. (In *Maclean's*. Toronto. v. 49, no. 22 (Nov. 15, 1936), pp. 24; 60.)

—— Backstage at Ottawa. By a Politician with a Notebook. (In *Maclean's*. Toronto. v. 50, no. 3 (Feb. 1, 1937), pp. 9; 41-42.)
Concerns defense issues.

—— Backstage at Ottawa. By a Politician with a Notebook. (In *Maclean's*. Toronto. v. 50, no. 7 (Apr. 1, 1937), pp. 14; 57; 59.)
Discusses the federal budget.

—— Backstage at Ottawa. By a Politician with a Notebook. (In *Maclean's*. Toronto. v. 50, no. 9 (May 1, 1937), pp. 16; 77.)
Concerns the issue of defense.

—— Backstage at Ottawa. By a Politician with a Notebook. (In *Maclean's*. Toronto. v. 50, no. 12 (June 15, 1937), pp. 12; 51.)
Discusses the reaction in Ottawa to Mitchell Hepburn's labour policy in Ontario, and to Hepburn's proposal for union government in Ontario.

—— Backstage at Ottawa. By a Politician with a Notebook. (In *Maclean's*. Toronto. v. 50, no. 22 (Nov. 15, 1937), pp. 14; 63.)
Discusses, mainly, Mitchell Hepburn's decisive election victory in Ontario and its effects on both the national Liberal and Conservative parties.

—— Backstage at Ottawa. "Three months of futile talk in Parliament . . . democracy can be thoroughly inefficient." "In two years . . . $1,000,000 for Royal Commissions and not one useful law to show for it." By a Politician with a Notebook. (In *Maclean's*. Toronto. v. 51, no. 10 (May 15, 1938), pp. 11; 68.)

—— Backstage at Ottawa. By a Politician with a Notebook. (In *Maclean's*. Toronto. v. 51, no. 14 (July 15, 1938), pp. 8; 36.)
Relates to the current budget; the Conservative Party leadership, etc.

—— Canada's railway crisis. By M. Grattan O'Leary. (In *Queen's quarterly*. Kingston. v. 38 (1931), pp. [724]-732.)

—— Democracy limited. By Grattan O'Leary. (In Empire Club of Canada. *Addresses*. Toronto. (1936/37), pp. 308-317.)

Address delivered April 1, 1937.

Discusses ". . . the place and the limitations of public opinion in democracy; and . . . the place of freedom in democracy". – p. 309.

—— An election in July? By a Politician with a Notebook. (In *Maclean's*. Toronto. v. 43, no. 8 (Apr. 15, 1930), pp. 21; 32; 34.)

—— Forty-nine days for taxes. Mr. average Canadian has to toil forty-nine days a year to pay the cost of government. By M. Grattan O'Leary. (In *Maclean's*. Toronto. v. 43, no. 4 (Feb. 15, 1930), pp. 5; 35-36.)

—— His Excellency. A portrait sketch of Vere Brabazon Ponsonby, ninth Earl of Bessborough, who comes to Ottawa as Canada's fourteenth Governor-General. By M. Grattan O'Leary. (In *Maclean's*. Toronto. v. 44, no. 7 (Apr. 1, 1931), pp. 7; 73-74.)

—— How far have we gone socialist? By M. Grattan O'Leary. (In *Queen's quarterly*. Kingston. v. 38 (1931), pp. [140]-150.)

—— Inside stuff—Continuing the play by play report of the political struggle at the Dominion's capital. By a Politician with a Notebook. (In *Maclean's*. Toronto. v. 43, no. 9 (May 1, 1930), pp. 16; 50.)

—— Is women's suffrage a success? By Grattan O'Leary. (In *Chatelaine*. Toronto. v. 3, no. 9 (Sept. 1930), pp. 12; 52-53.)

Examines the results of the federal election held July 28, 1930.

—— Now it can be told. In which the scribe behind the scenes spills some of the "inside stuff" of the election campaign just concluding. By a Politician with a Notebook. (In *Maclean's*. Toronto. v. 43, no. 15 (Aug. 1, 1930), pp. 9; 42; 48.)

Refers to the federal election held July 28, 1930.

—— Our cabinet ministers are underpaid. By M. Grattan O'Leary. (In *Maclean's*. Toronto. v. 43, no. 6 (Mar. 15, 1930), pp. 5; 60-61.)

—— Our politicians: explained by themselves. By M. Grattan O'Leary. Lays himself open to a charge of lese majeste in dealing with the strange quirks and foibles of the great at Ottawa. (In *The Canadian magazine*. Toronto. v. 75, no. 4 (Apr. 1931), pp. 7; 39.)

An attempt to choose the ten greatest living politicians through a mathematical approach provided by the 1931 Parliamentary guide.

—— The public and the politicians. By Grattan O'Leary. (In Empire Club of Canada. *Addresses*. Toronto. (1933/34), pp. 143-155.)

Address delivered March 30, 1933.

—— Public sucker no. 1. "The relief racket is the most vicious, most brazen, most degrading racket of our time . . . It is warping the moral fibre of thousands and making suckers out of millions." By M. Grattan O'Leary. (In *Maclean's*. Toronto. v. 50, no. 7 (Apr. 1, 1937), pp. 18-19; 52-53.)

—— Reciprocity. By M. Grattan O'Leary. (In *Maclean's*. Toronto. v. 46, no. 8 (Apr. 15, 1933), pp. 19; 36.)

—— The rival chiefs of staff. By M. Grattan O'Leary. (In *Maclean's*. Toronto. v. 43, no. 13 (July 1, 1930), pp. 8-9; 46-47.)

Concerns Major-General A. D. McRae, chief federal organizer for the Conservative Party; Senator Andrew Haydon, Rt. Hon. Mackenzie King's principal political adviser.

—— Shall knighthood flower again? By M. Grattan O'Leary. (In *Maclean's*. Toronto. v. 47, no. 4 (Feb. 15, 1934), pp. 7; 44.)

Discusses government policy on granting of titles.

—— Three score years and ten. What shall make us truly a nation?—A Dominion day confession of faith. By M. Grattan O'Leary. (In *Maclean's*. Toronto. v. 50, no. 13 (July 1, 1937), pp. 5-6.)

PARKER, J. V. The case for Western secession. (In *The Canadian forum*. Toronto. v. 16, no. 191 (Dec. 1936), pp. 10-11.)

PARKINSON, JOSEPH F. Canada in the Great Depression. By J. F. Parkinson. (In *Canadian comment*. Toronto. v. 4, no. 1 (Jan. 1935), pp. 9-10.)

Discusses, in part, government policy toward the economic situation.

PATERSON, ALEXANDER PIERCE New Brunswick's place in the confederation of Canada. An address delivered in the New Brunswick Legislature at the 1937 session, by Honorable A. P. Paterson, Minister of Education, in the Dysart Government. (In *The Maritime advocate and busy East*. Sackville, N.B. v. 27, no. 10 (May 1937), pp. 5-10; 20-23.)

PATTON, HAROLD S.   Observations on Canadian wheat policy since the World War. (In *The Canadian journal of economics and political science*. Toronto. v. 3 (1937), pp. 218-233.)

PATTULLO, THOMAS DUFFERIN   British Columbia and Confederation. By Honourable T. D. Pattullo. (In Empire Club of Canada. *Addresses*. Toronto. (1937/38), pp. 337-356.)
Address delivered April 5, 1938.

PELTON, GERALD V.   Nine nations or one? (In *Saturday night*. Toronto. v. 53, no. 7 (Dec. 18, 1937), p. 5.)
"The persistent efforts by the legislature of Alberta to usurp the functions of the Dominion Parliament, constitute the most dangerous assault upon Canadian national unity since the Riel Rebellion."

PERRAULT, JOSEPH EDOUARD   La Confédération canadienne est-elle née viable? (In *Revue de l'Université d'Ottawa*. [Ottawa] 5. année (1935), pp. [8]-25.)

PERRY, ANNE ANDERSON   Echoes from Ottawa. (In *Canadian comment*. Toronto. v. 2, no. 3 (Mar. 1933), pp. 12-14.)
Describes reactions in Parliament to a resolution concerning economic conditions, introduced February 1, 1933, by J. S. Woodsworth; debate on the Woodsworth Bill for the repeal of section 98 of the Criminal Code, etc.

—— Stag politics. (In *Chatelaine*. Toronto. v. 3, no. 5 (May 1930), pp. 10-11; 61.)
"With a federal election ahead, women must consider whether their manifest weakness in politics lies in their meek acceptance of the rule of thumb of the male politician."

—— Tempest over titles. (In *Canadian comment*. Toronto. v. 3, no. 2 (Feb. 1934), p. 13.)
Comments on reactions to a Canadian Honours list submitted January 1, 1934.

PICKWELL, FREDERICK C.   Another wheat investigation. Is underlying motive improvement of marketing position or discrediting of Board's new chairman? By F. C. Pickwell. (In *Saturday night*. Toronto. v. 51, no. 22 (Apr. 4, 1936), p. 26.)
Relates to James R. Murray.

—— Ottawa wheat policy sound. In fixing minimum price at 87½ cents, government has refused to gamble again at taxpayers' expense. By F. C. Pickwell. (In *Saturday*

night. Toronto. v. 51, no. 46 (Sept. 19, 1936), p. 23.)

—— Phantasms from the Prairies. "Left wing" of Western United Farmer Organization seeks to swing the whole agrarian class to warfare against capitalism. By F. C. Pickwell. (In *Saturday night*. Toronto. v. 47, no. 6 (Dec. 19, 1931), p. 3.)
Deals with the convention of the United Farmers of Manitoba, held in Brandon, November 1931.

—— Prairie Chartists drop secession. By F. C. Pickwell. (In *Saturday night*. Toronto. v. 46, no. 20 (Mar. 28, 1931), p. 2.)
Deals with the annual meeting of the Saskatchewan United Farmers, held in Saskatoon, February 1931, where it was proposed that a new reform party should be formed and a program was drawn up for it.

—— The West in the elections. By F. C. Pickwell. (In *Saturday night*. Toronto. v. 45, no. 36 (July 19, 1930), pp. 5; 10.)
Deals with the campaign for the federal election held July 28, 1930.

—— The West in the new House. Taxation reforms and restoration and stabilization of business conditions will be pressed on Bennett administration. By F. C. Pickwell. (In *Saturday night*. Toronto. v. 45, no. 40 (Aug. 16, 1930), p. 3.)

PLUMPTRE, ARTHUR FITZWALTER WYNNE   Canada's banking problem. By A. F. W. Plumptre. (In *Canadian comment*. Toronto. v. 3, no. 5 (May 1934), pp. 11-12.)
Considers the goals and composition of the Canadian Parliamentary Committee on Banking and Commerce.

Politics of discontent. Essays by H. J. Schultz, M. A. Ormsby, J. R. H. Wilbur, B. J. Young. Introd. by Ramsay Cook. Toronto University of Toronto Press c1967. x, 102 p. (Canadian historical readings, 4.)
Articles reprinted from the *Canadian historical review*.
Partial contents: H. H. Stevens and the Reconstruction Party, by J. R. H. Wilbur. – C. George McCullagh and the Leadership League, by B. J. Young.

POLITICUS   At Queen's Park. Mitch and Maurice grease the skids. By Politicus. (In *Saturday night*. Toronto. v. 54, no. 33 (June 19, 1939), p. 7.)
Concerns a meeting between Hepburn and Duplessis. Politicus believes the meeting was held to discuss ". . . how to put

Prime Minister King on the skids of the forthcoming federal election".

—— No, you can't ask Mr. Herridge what it all means. By Politicus. (In *Saturday night*. Toronto. v. 54, no. 36 (July 8, 1939), p. 2.)

Concerns Major the Hon. William Duncan Herridge and the New Democracy movement.

PORTER, G. C. Cattle king now a Senator. Pat Burns believes that anyone who can handle cows can handle men—was a political opponent of Hon. R. B. Bennett in the old stormy days of Calgary. (In *Saturday night*. Toronto. v. 46, no. 37 (July 25, 1931), p. 3.)

Concerns Patrick Burns.

PRANG, MARGARET EVELYN The origins of public broadcasting in Canada. (In *The Canadian historical review*. Toronto, v. 46 (1965), pp. 1-31.)

For a comment on the above, see The Origins of public broadcasting in Canada, by Graham Spry. (In *The Canadian historical review*. Toronto. v. 46 (1965), pp. 134-141.)

The Press says —. A summary of opinion on the Bren gun contract. (In *Maclean's*. Toronto. v. 52, no. 5 (Mar. 1, 1939), pp. 22; 26-27.)

PRICE, VINCENT W. Federal control of Beauharnois? B.N.A. Act gives Dominion power to take complete control of great national undertakings. Important blunders in recent legislation? (In *Saturday night*. Toronto. v. 46, no. 42 (Aug. 29, 1931), pp. [21]; 25; 27-28.)

PRO AND CON Delusion of grandeur. By Pro and Con. (In *The Canadian magazine*. Toronto. v. 90, no. 3 (Sept. 1938), pp. [32]-33; 61; 66-67.)

Pro and Con are two staff members of the *Canadian magazine*.

A general discussion of the current problems confronting the Canadian conference.

—— On the fence at Ottawa. By Pro and Con. (In *The Canadian magazine*. Toronto. v. 89, no. 6 (June 1938), pp. 8-9.)

Pro and Con are two staff members of *The Canadian magazine*. Cf. Editor's note.

A general review of the current session of Parliament. Considers the need for leadership and action to cope with Canada's "vital problems".

The Progress of reform. (In *Canadian comment*. Toronto, v. 4, no. 4 (Apr. 1935), pp. 8-10.)

Reviews the reform legislation considered during the sixth session of the seventeenth parliament.

QUINN, PETER Meet Quebec's fascists! (In *New frontier*. Toronto. v. 1, no. 5 (Sept. 1936), pp. 5-8.)

First of two articles on fascism in Quebec. Draws implications for the Canadian nation in general.

—— Quebec baits the Jew! (In *New frontier*. Toronto. v. 1, no. 6 (Oct. 1936), pp. 6-10.)

Second of two articles on fascism in Quebec. Concerns the activities of Nazi agents in Canada generally and in Quebec particularly.

RAIKES, C. F. G. Is Canada's wheat policy right or wrong? (In *The Maritime advocate and busy East*. Sackville, N.B. v. 25, no. 8 (Mar. 1935), pp. 16-17.)

RANDALL-JONES, A. R. Canadian labor in politics. (In *Saturday night*. Toronto. v. 48, no. 25 (Apr. 29, 1933), p. 5.)

Deals mainly with the Labor Party in Ontario, with reference to the National Labor Party.

—— When a premier vacates his job! Recent instances in Ontario and New Brunswick illustrate a nice constitutional point—caucus, not party at large must choose new leader. (In *Saturday night*. Toronto. v. 46, no. 32 (June 20, 1931), p. 3.)

Relates to the issue revolving around J. B. M. Baxter and Howard Ferguson.

READE, JOHN COLLINGWOOD Preparing for Canadian New Deal. Canadian Macmillan Commission must lay suitable foundations for program of reconstruction. Imminent changes foreshadowed by collapse of conference. (In *Saturday night*. Toronto. v. 48, no. 41 (Aug. 9, 1933), pp. [17]; 19; 22.)

REID, ESCOTT MEREDITH Canadian political parties; a study of the economic and racial bases of Conservatism and Liberalism in 1930. By Escott M. Reid. (In *Contributions to Canadian economics*. Toronto. v. 6 (1933), pp. 7-39.)

—— Democracy and political leadership in Canada. By Escott Reid. (In *The University of Toronto quarterly*. [Toronto] v. 4 (1934/35), pp. 534-549.)

RICHER, LEOPOLD Les Canadians françaises et les élections du 14 octobre. (In *L'Action nationale*. Montréal. v. 6 (nov. 1935), pp. [177]-182.)

Concerns the general elections held October 14, 1935.

RICHTER, LOTHAR Social insurance and politics. By L. Richter. (In *The University of Toronto quarterly*. [Toronto] v. 6 (1936/37, pp. 254-266.)

A comparative analysis.

ROBERTS, LESLIE Change here for railway prosperity. "It becomes increasingly apparent that if we leave the railway problem in the hands of those at present judging and advising upon it the riddle will remain unsolved until Time and Nature provide the answer. That is probably longer than we can afford to wait." (In *The Canadian magazine*. Toronto. v. 90, no. 3 (Sept. 1938), pp. [27]-29; 69.)

The essay considers the political relevancy of the railway problem.

—— Good word for backbenchers. (In *Saturday night*. Toronto. v. 54, no. 30 (May 27, 1939), p. 6.)

ROBERTS, LLOYD Labor MP as art patron. (In *Saturday night*. Toronto. v. 49, no. 17 (Mar. 3, 1934), pp. 2-3.)

A biographical sketch of Abraham Albert Heaps, Labour member for Winnipeg North.

ROBERTS, MARGARET A married woman in politics. (In *Saturday night*. Toronto. v. 50, no. 7 (Dec. 22, 1934), p. 15.)

Author writes of personal experience and gives advice to other women who wish to enter politics.

ROBINSON, JUDITH National affairs. Boys will be boys. (In *Saturday night*. Toronto. v. 51, no. 16 (Feb. 22, 1936), p. 4.)

Comments on the opening of the first session, eighteenth parliament.

—— National affairs. There is no daylight. (In *Saturday night*. Toronto. v. 51, no. 22 (Apr. 4, 1936), p. 4.)

Concerns the Canadian Wheat Board; an order-in-council "authorizing the payment of eight million dollars to Western farmers ..."

—— National affairs. The Senate finds a job. (In *Saturday night*. Toronto. v. 51, no. 21 (Apr. 18, 1936), p. 4.)

Comments on the Senate revision of Bill 23; the election promises of Mr. King, etc.

—— National affairs. Session highlights. (In *Saturday night*. Toronto. v. 51, no. 35 (July 4, 1936), p. 4.)

Comments on the first session of the eighteenth parliament.

ROHMER, J. Grand finale, October fourteenth. (In *Canadian comment*. Toronto. v. 4, no. 11 (Nov. 1935), p. 7.)

Conveys impressionistic observations on election night, October 14, 1935.

ROSE, FRED Fascism over Canada; an exposé. Toronto, New Era Publishers, 1938. 47 p. (Timely topics, no. 1.)

RUMILLY, ROBERT L'Action liberale nationale. Montréal, Fides [c1963] 238 p. (His *Histoire de la province de Québec*, 34.)

A political history covering the years 1934-1935.

—— L'autonomie provinciale. Montréal, Fides, [c1966] 286 p. (His *Histoire de la province de Québec*, 36.)

A political history covering the years 1936-1937.

—— Chute de Taschereau. Montréal, Fides [c1966] 252 p. (His *Histoire de la province de Québec*, 35.)

A political history covering the years 1935-1936.

—— La dépression. Montréal. Fides [c1959] 262 p. (His *Histoire de la province de Québec*, 32.)

A political history covering the years 1930-1931.

—— La plaie du chômage. Montréal, Fides [c1961] 261 p. (His *Histoire de la province de Québec*, 33.)

A political history covering the years 1931/32-1934.

—— Premier gouvernement Duplessis Montréal, Fides [c1968] 282 p. (His *Histoire de la province de Québec*, 37.)

A political history covering the years 1938-1939.

SAINT-DENIS, HENRI The contribution of the French Canadian to federal unity. (In *Canadian problems as seen by twenty outstanding men of Canada*. Toronto, 1933. pp. [259]-277.)

SANDWELL, BERNARD KEBLE Being pushed into socialism. By B. K. Sandwell. (In Empire Club of Canada. *Addresses*. Toronto. (1932), pp. 286-295.)

Address delivered November 10, 1932.

—— Break-up of old party lines comes into sight. By B. K. Sandwell. (In *Saturday night*. Toronto. v. 53, no. 37 (July 16, 1938), p. 2.)
Comments on the Conservative and Liberal parties.

—— From week to week. Leadership. By B. K. Sandwell. (In *Saturday night*. Toronto. v. 54, no. 18 (Mar. 4, 1939), p. 3.)
"The trouble with Canada at the present time is not lack of leaders, it is lack of principles by which the leaders are to lead. . . ." Comments on the political parties in Canada.

—— From week to week. Senate and railways. By B. K. Sandwell. (In *Saturday night*. Toronto. v. 54, no. 31 (June 3, 1939), p. 3.)
Refers to the Canadian National Railways.

—— From week to week. Bad in policy, good in law. By B. K. Sandwell. (In *Saturday night*. Toronto. v. 54, no. 32 (June 10, 1939), p. 3.)
Concerns Chief Justice Greenshield and the Quebec Padlock Law.

—— From week to week. Why not padlock the banks? By B. K. Sandwell. (In *Saturday night*. Toronto. v. 54, no. 33 (June 17, 1939), p. 3.)
Discusses the implications of "a series of Privy Council decisions emphasizing and extending the application of property and civil rights and reducing to the minimum the federal rights in connection with the criminal law".

—— Kingdom of Canada. By B. K. Sandwell. (In *Saturday night*. Toronto. v. 53, no. 51 (Oct. 22, 1938), p. [11].)

—— Political sidelights on the tariff agreement. By B. K. Sandwell. (In *Saturday night*. Toronto. v. 51, no. 2 (Nov. 16, 1935), p. 3.)

—— Two quarter centuries and their significance. By B. K. Sandwell. (In *Saturday night*. Toronto. v. 53, no. 9 (Jan. 1, 1938), pp. 4; 7.)
Historical reflections concerning Canada, on the occasion of the fiftieth anniversay of the founding of the magazine *Saturday night*.

—— Young men and politics. By B. K. Sandwell. (In *Queen's quarterly*. Kingston. v. 41 (1934), pp. [414]-425.)
Argues that the modernization of party

doctrine can be easily adopted by the Conservative Party, while proving to be a difficult task for the Liberal Party.

SAVAGE, HUGH Wanted: a Canadian flag. (In *Maclean's*. Toronto. v. 43, no. 13 (July 1, 1930), pp. 5; 38; 40; 42.)

SCOTT, FRANCIS REGINALD Le Canada d'aujourd'hui. Par F. R. Scott. Préf. de Edouard Montpetit. [Avant-propos de E. J. Tarr] Publié sous les auspices de l'Institut canadien des affaires internationales. Traduction de la 2. éd. anglaise. Montréal, Editions du Devoir, 1939. xvi, 221 p.

—— Canada today. A study of her national interests and national policy. By F. R. Scott. With a foreword by E. J. Tarr. Prepared for the British Commonwealth Relations Conference, 1938. Issued under the auspices of the Canadian Institute of International Affairs. 2d ed., rev. London, Toronto, Oxford University Press, 1939 [c1938] xii, 184 p.
". . . purpose is to describe the principal economic, political and social factors which determine Canada's national interests and outlook . . . and particularly to show the relations between internal forces and external policy." – Pref.
Note: Chapt. 4. Political parties. – Chapt. 6. Constitutional problems.

—— Civil liberties. By F. R. Scott. (In *Saturday night*. Toronto. v. 49, no. 52 (Nov. 3, 1934), pp. [1]; 3.)
Discusses Section 98 of the Criminal Code.

—— A decade of League for Social Reconstruction. By F. R. Scott. (In *Saturday night*. Toronto. v. 57, no. 20 (Jan. 24, 1942), p. 8.)

SCOTT, RICHARD What price votes? Votes cost money! We stand in horror at the words; but the fact remains, it still costs money to get them. (In *The Canadian* [*magazine*] Toronto. v. 84, no. 4 (Oct. 1935), pp. 3; 45-46.)
An article on election expenditures.

SEDGEWICK, JOSEPH The constitution and the radio. Dominion's right to control wave-lengths and mechanics generally is unquestioned but courts have not yet passed on the control of programmes. (In *Saturday night*. Toronto. v. 48, no. 23 (Apr. 15, 1933), p. 3.)

The Senate deplores. (In *Canadian comment*. Toronto. v. 3, no. 7 (July 1934), pp. 4-5.)

Concerns a Senate debate on Canadian naval defence, with reference to the business connections of Senator Charles Colquhoun Ballantyne.

750,000 unemployed, what will the government do with them? (In *Canadian comment.* Toronto. v. 2, no. 1 (Jan. 1933), pp. 5-7.)

SHANE, H. Canadian disunion. (In *The Dalhousie review.* Halifax. v. 18 (1938/39), pp. [157]-164.)

SHAW, CHARLES LUGRIN B.C.'s secession talk. (In *Maclean's.* Toronto. v. 49, no. 22 (Nov. 15, 1936), pp. 25-26; 50-52.)

SMITH, IRVING NORMAN Tweedsmuir of Canada. By I. Norman Smith. (In *Maclean's.* Toronto. v. 52, no. 14 (July 15, 1939), pp. 6-7; 31-33.)

Concerns John Buchan, Baron Tweedsmuir, as Governor-General of Canada.

SNIDER, CHARLES HENRY JEREMIAH The Beauharnois inquiry. By Charles H. J. Snider. Toronto, The Evening Telegram, 1931. 52 p.

Reprinted from the *Evening Telegraph* (Toronto).

SOLLOWAY, ISAAC WILLIAM CANNON Canada's destiny. By I. W. C. Solloway. Toronto, Political and Economic Pub. Co., 1934. 113 p.

—— Speculators and politicians. By I. W. C. Solloway. [n.p.] Political and Economic Pub. Co. [c1933] 223 p.

Advocates the establishment of a National Economic Council, a National Stock Exchange, government control of large financial institutions, etc. – Cf. Introd.

SOUCISSE, VICTOR C. Revolt in Quebec! Is there a separatist movement in Quebec?... (In *Maclean's.* Toronto. v. 49, no. 13 (July 1, 1936), pp. 10-11; 37-38.)

First in a series of three articles.
Concerns Quebec and Confederation.

—— Revolt in Quebec! . . . a French Canadian's interpretation of Quebec's reform movement and the viewpoint of French Canada toward Confederation. (In *Maclean's.* Toronto. v. 49, no. 14 (July 15, 1936), pp. 14-15; 40-41.)

Second in a series of three articles.

—— Revolt in Quebec! . . . a French Canadian's interpretation of the reform movement in Quebec. (In *Maclean's.* Toronto. v. 49, no. 15 (Aug. 1, 1936), pp. 16; 34-35.)

Third and last in a series of articles.

SPRY, GRAHAM The origins of public broadcasting in Canada; a comment. (In *The Canadian historical review.* Toronto. v. 46 (1965), pp. 134-141.)

Refers to the Origins of public broadcasting in Canada, by M. Prang. (In *The Canadian historical review.* Toronto. v. 46 (1965), pp. 1-31.)

Graham Spry acted as chairman of the original Radio League.

—— Politics. (In *The Canadian forum.* Toronto. v. 15, no. 177 (Aug. 1935), pp. 324-325; 339.)

A thorough discussion of the responses and general policies of the major political parties contesting in the forthcoming federal election of 1935.

STACEY, CHARLES PERRY Canada's last war —and the next. By C. P. Stacey. (In *University of Toronto quarterly.* [Toronto] v. 8 (1938/39), pp. 247-254.)

A review article of *Official history of the Canadian forces in the Great War, 1914-1919.* General series, vol. 1: From the outbreak of war to the formation of the Canadian Corps, August 1914–September 1915. By A. F. Duguid. Ottawa, King's Printer, 1938.

STEVENS, HENRY HERBERT Canada. By Hon. H. H. Stevens. (In Club canadien de Québec. *Problèmes de l'heure.* Québec, 1935. pp. 73-85.)

Speech dated: Le 7 octobre 1933.

—— The issues as I see them. By Hon. H. H. Stevens. (In *Maclean's.* Toronto. v. 48, no. 18 (Sept. 15, 1935), pp. 11; 32.)

Relates to the federal election held October 14, 1935.

Stevens probe: Cattle, cartels, Church. (In *Canadian comment.* Toronto. v. 3, no. 7 (July 1934), p. 9.)

Discusses the investigation activities of the Committee on Price Spreads, under the chairmanship of H. H. Stevens.

STEVENSON, JOHN A. The Canadian election. By J. A. Stevenson. (In *Queen's quarterly.* Kingston. v. 37 (1930), pp. [575]-586.)

Analyses the results of the general elections held July 28, 1930.

—— The Canadian political scene. By J. A. Stevenson. (In *Queen's quarterly.* Kingston. v. 38 (1931), pp. [359]-370.)

General comments on the parliamentary session held during the spring of 1931.

—— First poet to serve as Governor-General. (In *Saturday night*. Toronto. v. 50, no. 46 (Sept. 21, 1935), p. 2.)

Comments on Lord Tweedsmuir (John Buchan) (Governor-General of Canada, 1935-1940).

—— John Buchan, [Governor-General]. (In *Maclean's*. Toronto. v. 48, no. 10 (May 15, 1935), pp. 11; 59-60.)

STEWART, HERBERT LESLIE   Will Canada fight? By Herbert L. Stewart. (In *The Canadian magazine*. Toronto. v. 89, no. 3 (Mar. 1938), pp. [14-15].)

Considers the necessity of securing parliamentary approval before committing the nation to a declaration of war.

Still a white elephant. (In *Canadian comment*. Toronto. v. 3, no. 7 (July 1934), p. 8.)

Concerns the Canadian National Railways.

TARR, E. J.   Defense and national unity. The defense problem: Article 4. (In *Maclean's*. Toronto. v. 50, no. 13 (July 1, 1937), pp. 19; 36-37.)

TASCHEREAU, LOUIS ALEXANDRE   Où allons-nous? (In *Revue de l'Université d'Ottawa*. [Ottawa] 4. année (1934), pp. [8]-21.)

An historical and comparative discussion of the Canadian Confederation.

TILLEY, LEONARD PERCY DE WOLFE   Country first. By Hon. L. P. D. Tilley. (In Canadian Club of Toronto. *Addresses*. Toronto. (1934/35), pp. 304-309.)

Address delivered April 15, 1935.
Author lived from 1870 to 1947.

TILLEY, S. LEONARD   Will the Maritimes secede? (In *The Maritime advocate and busy East*. Sackville, N.B. v. 27, no. 1 (Aug. 1936), pp. 19-22; 24.)

Reprinted from *Maclean's* for August 15, 1936.

—— Will the Maritimes secede? A Maritimer speaks bluntly of "a growing feeling in favor of the Maritimes walking right out of the Confederation picture". (In *Maclean's*. Toronto. v. 49, no. 16 (Aug. 15, 1936), pp. 17; 22-24.)

TURGEON, WILLIAM FERDINAND ALPHONSE   I'd unite the Prairie Provinces. A distinguished jurist urges political union as a means to more efficient and economical government of the Prairie West. By Hon. W. F. A. Turgeon. (In *Maclean's*. Toronto. v. 45, no. 3 (Feb. 1, 1932), pp. 17; 40.)

TURNBULL, DAVID ROWAN   The Maritime Freight Rates Act. By D. R. Turnbull. (In *The Maritime advocate and busy East*. Sackville, N.B. v. 27, no. 5 (Dec. 1936), pp. 18-21.)

Text of an address delivered before the Halifax Board of Trade, November 24, 1936.
Reprinted from *The Commercial news*.

UNDERHILL, FRANK HAWKINS   Democracy and leadership in Canada. By F. H. U. (In *The Canadian forum*. Toronto. v. 14, no. 163 (Apr. 1934), pp. 246-248.)

—— "Keep Canada out of war." The defense problem. By Frank H. Underhill. (In *Maclean's*. Toronto. v. 50, no. 10 (May 15, 1937), pp. 19; 58; 60.)

—— The League for Social Reconstruction. By F. H. U. (In *The Canadian forum*. Toronto. v. 12, no. 139 (Apr. 1932), pp. 249-250.)

Text of the League's manifesto: pp. 249-250.

—— Mr. Good's political philosophy. By Frank H. Underhill. (In *The Canadian forum*. Toronto. v. 13, no. 155 (Aug. 1933), pp. 411-413.)

Review article of *Is democracy doomed*, by W. C. Good. Toronto, 1933 (32 p.).

For a reply to the comments above, see My political philosophy, by W. C. Good. (In *The Canadian forum*. Toronto. v. 13, no. 155 (1933), pp. 413-416.)

W. C. Good advocated proportional representation and the abolition of the political party system.

—— Our fantastic electoral system. By Frank H. Underhill. (In *The Canadian forum*. Toronto. v. 15, no. 178 (Nov. 1935), p. 355.)

An analysis examining the significance of the results of the general elections held October 14, 1935.

—— Our fantastic electoral system. By Frank H. Underhill. (In Courtney, J. C. (ed.) *Voting in Canada* [Scarborough, Ont., c1967] pp. [32]-34.)

Reprinted from *The Canadian forum*, XV (November) 1935.

—— Spade-workers for a new social order. The League for Social Reconstruction—what it is and what it plans to do. By Frank H. Underhill. (In *Saturday night*. Toronto. v. 49, no. 18 (Mar. 10, 1934), p. 2.)

—— Spiritual enlargement. By Frank H. Underhill. (In *The Canadian forum*. Toronto. v. 15, no. 177 (Aug. 1935), pp. 321; 344.)

A review of *Lord Minto*, by J. Buchan. London, Nelson, 1924. John Buchan as Lord Tweedsmuir held office as Governor-General of Canada, Aug. 10, 1935, to June 2, 1940.

VAN GOGH, LUCY   Radio in politics. [In *Saturday night*. Toronto. v. 50, no. 50 (Oct. 1935), p. [13].)

Discusses the importance of grassroots organization in winning elections. Refers to the federal election held October 14, 1935.

VANIER, ANATOLE   Les billets bilingues. (In *L'Action nationale*. Montréal. v. 5 (fév. 1935), pp. [100]-110.)

—— Où il faut une union sacrée. (In *L'Action nationale*. Montréal. v. 12 (déc. 1938), pp. 331-339.)

Discusses Canadian internal political attitudes toward the growing crisis in Europe.

VIEN, THOMAS   Canada and its railways. (In *Revue trimestrielle canadienne*. Montréal. v. 17 (mars 1931), pp. [138]-153.)

An address delivered to the Canadian Society of Costs Accountants at the Windsor Hotel, Montreal on January 22, 1931.

VINING, CHARLES ARTHUR MC LAREN   Mr. Massey. By R. T. L. (In *Maclean's*. Toronto. v. 46, no. 16 (Aug. 15, 1933), p. 18.)

Concerns Vincent Massey.

Voters expect action from these members of Parliament. (In *The Canadian magazine*. Toronto. v. 89, no. 1 (Jan. 1938), pp. [22-23].)

Portraits of thirty-two leading members of Parliament, with a brief comment on each.

WALTON, HENRY C.   A Commission for the West? Judicial investigation of Western grievances seems to be called for. Better feeling generally should result. (In *Saturday night*. Toronto. v. 52, no. 10 (Jan. 9, 1937), p. 24.)

WARD, BURNETT A.   Where do they go from here? (In *New frontier*. Toronto. v. 1, no. 5 (Sept. 1936), pp. 12-14.)

Concerns the system of relief camps established, as a government program, for the unemployed in Canada.

WARSHAW, LEO   Social planning for Canada. (In *New frontier*. Toronto. v. 1, no. 2 (May 1936), pp. 20-23.)

A review article of *Social planning for Canada*, by the Research Committee of the League for Social Reconstruction. Toronto, Nelson, 1935.

WEIR, GEORGE MOIR   A national health program. By Hon. G. M. Weir. (In *Maclean's*. Toronto. v. 52, no. 6 (Mar. 15, 1939), pp. 12; 54-56.)

What happened in Room 368. Startling developments in Ottawa's drama. By our Ottawa correspondent. (In *Canadian comment*. Toronto. v. 3, no. 6 (June 1934), pp. 11-12.)

Discusses the hearing conducted by the Committee on Price Spreads, under the chairmanship of H. H. Stevens.

What's wrong with Parliament? A cross section of the views of Maclean's readers on one of the vital issues of the day. (In *Maclean's*. Toronto. v. 52, no. 6 (Mar. 15, 1939), pp. 16; 42; 45.)

WHITE, J. FRANCIS   Socialism without doctrine. By J. F. W. (In *The Canadian forum*. Toronto. v. 12, no. 141 (June 1932), pp. 329-330.)

WHITE, ROBERT SMEATON   Political retrospect. By R. S. White. (In Canadian Club of Toronto. *Addresses*. Toronto. (1931/32), pp. 279-288.)

Address delivered March 14, 1932. R. S. White represented St. Antoine, Que., in the House of Commons from 1925 to 1940.

Who's who and why in Reconfederation Cabinet. (In *The Canadian magazine*. Toronto. v. 89, no. 4 (Apr. 1938), pp. 22-[23]; 36. ports.)

The Canadian magazine's selection of members for a cabinet in a union government.

Why I failed to be elected. (In *Chatelaine*. Toronto. v. 3, no. 10 (Oct. 1930), pp. 17; 37-38.)

Comments by Mrs. George Hollis, Beatrice Brigden, Mildred Low, Mrs. F. S. Greenwood, Mrs. Donald Macdonald, and Iola Saint Jean. With reference to the federal election held Aug. 10, 1930.

WILBUR, JOHN RICHARD HUMPHREY   H. H. Stevens and the antecedents of the Reconstruction Party, 1930-1935. [Kingston, Ont., 1961]. 449 leaves.

Thesis (MA) – Queen's University.

—— H. H. Stevens and the Reconstruction Party. By J. R. H. Wilbur. (In *The Canadian historical review*. Toronto. v. 45 1964), pp. 1-28.)

—— H. H. Stevens and the Reconstruction Party. By J. R. H. Wilbur. (In *Politics of discontent.* [Toronto, c1967] pp. 49-76.)

WOODSWORTH, JAMES SHAVER Co-operative government in Canada. By J. S. Woodsworth. (In *Queen's quarterly.* Kingston. v. 37 (1930), pp. [648]-655.)

YOUNG, BRIAN J. C. George McCullagh and the Leadership League. [Kingston, Ont.] 1965. 1 v.
Thesis (MA) – Queen's University.

—— C. George McCullagh and the Leadership League. (In *The Canadian historical review.* Toronto. v. 47 (1966), pp. 201-226.)

—— C. George McCullagh and the Leadership League. (In *Politics of discontent.* [Toronto, c1967] pp. [77]-102.)
"Reprinted from Canadian historical review, XLVII (3), September, 1966."

WORLD WAR II AND
POST-WAR PERIOD, 1939-1948

L'Action nationale. La guerre. (In *L'Action nationale.* Montréal. v. 14 (sept. 1939), pp. [3]-10.)

ADAMSON, ANTHONY Yes, Canada is a nation. (In *Saturday night.* Toronto. v. 57, no. 51 (Aug. 29, 1942), p. 13.)

L'Amérique serait-elle "fasciste"? Par J. S. (In *L'Action nationale.* Montréal. v. 24 (août/sept. 1944). pp. [20]-28.)
Discusses the appearance of John Roy Carlson before the Canadian Club of Montreal, March 27, 1944.

ANGERS, FRANCOIS ALBERT Le bilan canadien d'un conflit. (In *L'Action nationale.* Montréal. v. 26 (déc. 1945), pp. [251]-281.)

—— L'épée de Damoclès. (In *L'Action nationale.* Montréal. v. 17 (mai 1941), pp. [406]-417.)
Discusses the national unemployment insurance system.

—— Et nos responsabilités . . . qu'en faisons-nous? (In *L'Action nationale.* Montréal. v. 27 (avril 1946), pp. [301]-312.)
Considers the issue of conscription.

—— Fixation des prix et démocratie. (In *L'Action nationale.* Montréal. v. 18 (nov. 1941), pp. [227]-229.)

—— Le pavé de l'ours. (In *L'Action nationale.* Montréal. v. 19 (jan. 1942), pp. [30]-46.)
Deals with the question of conscription.

—— Pourquoi nous n'accepterons jamais la conscription pour service outre-mer. (In *L'Action nationale.* Montréal. v. 19 (fév./mars 1942), pp. [86]-105.)

—— Réflexions sur le budget fédéral. (In *Relations.* Montréal. 7. année. no. 78 (juin 1947), pp. 169-171.)

—— Un vote de race. Analyse mathématique et statistique du vote au plébiscite dans les cinq provinces de l'Est (In *L'Action nationale.* Montréal. v. 19 (mai 1942), pp. [299]-312.)
Concerns the national plebiscite on the issue of conscription held April 27, 1942.

—— Vues canadiennes-françaises sur le problème canadien. (In *Culture.* Québec. v. 4 (1943), pp. [482]-494.)

ARES, RICHARD Notre question nationale. Le problème politique. II. Sur le plan fédéral. (In *L'Action nationale.* Montréal. v. 20 (nov. 1942) pp. [208]-230.)

ATKINSON, L. The Japanese controversy is reviving liberalism. (In *Saturday night.* Toronto. v. 59, no. 45 (July 15, 1944), pp. 6-7.)
Reviews the debate over the clause in Bill no. 135 disfranchising Japanese Canadians.

BALDWIN, JOHN R. Parliament and liberty. (In *Saturday night.* Toronto. v. 55, no. 12 (Jan. 20, 1940), p. 3.)
Advocates that the opening of Parliament on January 25, 1940, allows for "a much-needed opportunity for thorough discussion of the government's policies of wartime regulations".

BARKWAY, MICHAEL Skeletons in Combines closet? The McGregor Flour report, a study in wartime controls and postwar embarrassment. (In *Saturday night.* Toronto. v. 65, no. 8 (Nov. 29, 1949), pp. 12-13.)

The Battle of Canada. (In *New world.* Toronto. v. 5, no. 11 (Jan. 1945), p. 18.)
Refers to the crisis over conscription.

BEAUDIN, DOMINIQUE Immigration, statistiques et histoire récente. (In *L'Action nationale.* Montréal. v. 31 (mai 1948), pp. [323]-333.)

BENSON, N. A. Charles Vining has a big job, but he's big too. (In *Saturday night.* Toronto. v. 58, no. 8 (Oct. 31, 1942), pp. 24-25.)

Concerns Charles Arthur McLaren Vining, chairman of the Wartime Information Board.

BOUCHARD, TELESPHORE DAMIEN The struggle for Quebec. By Senator T. D. Bouchard. (In *Maclean's*. Toronto. v. 57, no. 19 (Oct. 1, 1944), pp. 10; 48-49.)

BOUVIER, EMILE Innovation inquiétante à l'assurance chômage. (In *Relations*. Montréal. 6. année, no. 68 (août 1946), pp. 228-229.)

BRADY, ALEXANDER (ed.) Canada after the war; studies in political, social and economic policies for post-war Canada. Edited by Alexander Brady and F. R. Scott. Issued under the auspices of the Canadian Institute of International Affairs. Toronto, Macmillan, 1943. ix, 348 p.

Partial contents: National policy, by B. S. Keirstead. – Parliamentary democracy, by A. Brady. – The constitution and the post-war world, by F. R. Scott.

BRADY, ALEXANDER Parliamentary democracy. By A. Brady. (In his *Canada after the war*. Toronto, 1943. pp. 31-59.)

Outlines the problems relating to political reconstruction in Canada during the post-war period.

――― Reconstruction in Canada; a note on policies and plans. By A. Brady. (In *The Canadian journal of economics and political science*. Toronto. v. 8 (1942), pp. 460-468.)

BRECHIN, MARY Youth conferences pay dividends for future. (In *Saturday night*. Toronto. v. 60, no. 24 (Feb. 17, 1945), pp. 16-17.)

Deals with a conference held by the Canadian Youth Commission in Montreal in January 1945.

BREWIN, FRANCIS ANDREW Conscription in Canada. By F. A. Brewin. (In *The Canadian forum*. Toronto. v. 19, no. 229 (Feb. 1940), pp. 342-343.)

――― Must revise censorship. By F. A. Brewin. (In *Saturday night*. Toronto. v. 55, no. 19 (Mar. 9, 1940), p. 7.)

Concerns ". . . revision of Defence of Canada and Censorship regulations".

BROWN, HORACE Is Canada really a nation? (In *Saturday night*. Toronto. v. 57, no. 43 (July 4, 1942), p. 5.)

BROWN-FORBES, WILLIAM How will labour vote? C.C.F. is favourite: Liberals receive strong backing. By Wm. Brown-Forbes. (In *New world*. Toronto. v. 5, no. 11 (Jan. 1945), pp. 7-9.)

BROWNE, BEVERLY WOON Canada's reserve army. By Major-General B. W. Browne. (In *Empire Club of Canada*. *Addresses*. Toronto. (1942/43), pp. 410-425.)

Address delivered March 18, 1943.

BRYCE, R. B. Financing the war. (In Lower, A. R. M. (ed.) *War and reconstruction*. Toronto [c1942] pp. 9-15.)

BURPEE, LAWRENCE JOHNSTONE Canada and the war. By Lawrence J. Burpee. (In *Queen's quarterly*. Kingston. v. 46 (1939), pp. [385]-398.)

Presents a general description of Canadian response to the outbreak of World War II in September 1939.

CAHILL, BRIAN Confederation? Sure, let Newfoundland take over Canada! (In *Atlantic guardian*. Montreal. v. 2, no. 5 (May 1946), pp. 16-17; 42.)

CAMERON, S. G. Prospects for civil aviation. (In *The Canadian forum*. Toronto. v. 24, no. 284 (Sept. 1944), pp. 129-131.)

Discusses the issue of civil aviation as it was considered during the 1944 session of Parliament.

CANADA. AGRICULTURAL SUPPLIES BOARD Canada's food policy clarified. A statement on "Controlled prices" and other matters by the Agricultural Supplies Board. (In *Saturday night*. Toronto. v. 56, no. 26 (Mar. 8, 1941), pp. 14-15.)

CANADA. DEPT. OF NATIONAL DEFENCE. GENERAL STAFF The Canadian Army, 1939-1945; an official historical summary. By C. P. Stacey, director, Historical Section, General Staff. Illus. with paintings by Canadian Army war artists. Maps drawn by C. C. J. Bond. Ottawa, E. Cloutier, King's Printer, 1948. xv, 354 p.

"Supplements three booklets already published by the Department of National Defence under the collective title: The Canadian Army at war."

"Le Canada" on Quebec veto. (In *Saturday night*. Toronto. v. 57, no. 13 (Dec. 6, 1941), pp. 16-17.)

Article published in *Le Canada* of Montreal in reply to B. K. Sandwell's column: Week to week. The veto power of Quebec. (In *Saturday night*. Toronto. v. 57, no. 12 (Nov. 29, 1941), p. 6.)

CHAPIN, MIRIAM French Canada is ready to co-operate. (In *Saturday night.* Toronto. v. 57, no. 22 (Feb. 7, 1942), p. 24.)

CHAUVIN, FRANCIS X. Are we still at war? Hansard tells us. (In *Saturday night.* Toronto. v. 61, no. 9 (Nov. 3, 1945), pp. 18-19.)

"In his article Mr. Chauvin relies exclusively on Hansard for a definite answer to the question. His purpose is also to emphasize the value of Hansard as a source of information."

—— Is national unity really attainable in Canada? (In *Saturday night.* Toronto. v. 60, no. 11 (Nov. 18, 1944), pp. 6-7.)

—— Is there a French Canadian nation? (In *Saturday night.* Toronto. v. 59, no. 6 (Oct. 16, 1943), pp. 6-7.)

—— Proposals for building a sovereign nation. (In *Saturday night.* Toronto. v. 60, no. 46 (July 21, 1945), pp. 16-17.)

—— Socialism and racism a menace to unity. (In *Saturday night.* Toronto. v. 60, no. 16 (Dec. 23, 1944), pp. 6-7.)

CHITTY, R. M. WILLES Totalitarianism growing unheeded in Canada. (In *Saturday night.* Toronto. v. 61, no. 29 (Mar. 23, 1946), pp. 6-7.)

First published as an editorial in the *Fortnightly law journal.*

Civil liberties—1942. (In *The Canadian forum.* Toronto. v. 22, no. 257 (June 1942), pp. 69-70.)

Discusses the debate in the House of Commons over the Defense of Canada Regulations.

COADY, MOSES MICHAEL Is Confederation to blame? By M. M. Coady. (In *The Maritime advocate and busy East.* Sackville, N.B. v. 37, no. 3 (Oct. 1946), pp. 24-25.)

"Radio broadcast no. 2".

Considers Maritime prosperity in relation to its position within Confederation.

COHEN, JACOB L. Is Canada setting up a Gestapo? By J. L. Cohen. (In *Saturday night.* Toronto. v. 56, no. 11 (Nov. 23, 1940), pp. 12-13.)

Discusses Defence of Canada Regulations.

COHEN, MAXWELL ABRAHAM After the war. Federal powers are essence of Canada's problem. By Maxwell Cohen. (In *Saturday night.* Toronto. v. 58, no. 15 (Dec. 19, 1942), p. [14].)

Part one.

—— After the war. The post-war and government planning—II. By Maxwell Cohen. (In *Saturday night.* Toronto. v. 58, no. 16 (Dec. 26, 1942), p. 10.)

COLDWELL, MAJOR JAMES WILLIAM What next? By M. J. Coldwell, MP. (In *The Canadian spokesman.* Ottawa. v. 1, no. 2 (Feb. 1941), pp. [44]-48.)

Criticizes the "strict adherence to the profit incentive in the Canadian war economy".

CONROY, PAT What labor wants. Should unions be regulated? Do they favor socialization? Here's labor's viewpoint, told by a CCL leader in answer to 20 questions. By Pat Conroy as quizzed by Blair Fraser. (In *Maclean's.* Toronto. v. 60, no. 15 (Aug. 1, 1947), pp. 8; 47-48; 51.)

COOK, GEORGE RAMSAY Canadian liberalism in wartime; a study of the Defence of Canada Regulations, and some Canadians attitudes to civil liberties in wartime, 1939-1945. [Kingston, Ont.] 1956. iii, 307 leaves.

Thesis (MA) – Queen's University.

COTTERILL, MURRAY Conciliation before control at Ottawa. (In *Saturday night.* Toronto. v. 61, no. 43 (June 29, 1946), p. 18.)

"Analyzing recent government actions, Toronto Labor Council Secretary Murray Cotterill states that a clear change in government wage control policy has become evident within recent weeks."

—— Is government ready to referee wages? (In *Saturday night.* Toronto. v. 61, no. 31 (Apr. 6, 1946), pp. 6-7.)

—— Politics and labor troubles. (In *The Canadian forum.* Toronto. v. 25, no. 298 (Nov. 1945), pp. 181-182.)

COULOMBE, EDOUARD Les Sociétés Saint-Jean-Baptiste en face du plébiscite. (In *L'Action nationale.* Montréal. v. 19 (avril 1942), pp. [206]-211.)

Refers to the national plebiscite on the conscription issue held April 27, 1942.

COX, COROLYN Name in the news. Master of our statistics. (In *Saturday night.* Toronto. v. 58, no. 19 (Jan. 16, 1943), p. 2.)

A biographical sketch of Sedley Anthony Cudmore, Dominion Statistician.

—— Name in the news. Another Borden at the capital. (In *Saturday night.* Toronto. v. 58, no. 22 (Feb. 6, 1943), p. 2.)

A biographical sketch of Henry Borden, co-ordinator of Control and Chairman of the Wartime Industries Control Board.

—— Name in the news. Labor man on Coal Board. (In *Saturday night*. Toronto. v. 58, no. 23 (Feb. 13, 1943), p. 2.)
A biographical sketch of Charles Ewen Payne, labor member on the Emergency Coal Production Board.

—— Name in the news. The cabinet has a secretary. (In *Saturday night*. Toronto. v. 58, no. 24 (Feb. 20, 1943), p. 2.)
A biographical sketch of Arnold Danford, Patrick Heeney, Clerk of the Privy Council, Secretary of the Cabinet and of the War Committee of the Cabinet, and Senior Deputy Head of the Civil Service list in Ottawa.

—— Name in the news. Max is not a bureaucrat. (In *Saturday night*. Toronto. v. 58, no. 25 (Feb. 27, 1943), p. 2.)
A biographical sketch of Maxwell Weir Mackenzie, assistant to Donald Gordon, Chairman of Wartime Prices and Trade Board.

—— Name in the news. "Cliff" Clark has an old carpet. (In *Saturday night*. Toronto. v. 58, no. 34 (May 1, 1943), pp. 20-21.)
A biographical sketch of William Clifford Clark, Deputy Minister of Finance.

—— Name in the news. Searchlight on labor problem. (In *Saturday night*. Toronto. v. 58, no. 37 (May 22, 1943), p. 2.)
A biographical sketch of the Honourable Mr. Justice Charles Patrick McTague, Chairman of National War Labour Board.

—— Name in the news. He was born in Mexico, but . . . (In *Saturday night*. Toronto. v. 58, no. 40 (June 26, 1943), p. 2.)
A biographical sketch of Douglas White Ambridge, Director General of Shipbuilding, Department of Munitions and Supply, Ottawa.

—— Name in the news. J. L. Cohen has a philosophy. (In *Saturday night*. Toronto. v. 58, no. 42 (June 26, 1943), p. 2.)
A biographical sketch of the "number two member of the re-constituted three-man National War Labor Board".

—— Name in the news. A mixer, a thinker, a doer. (In *Saturday night*. Toronto. v. 59, no. 3 (Sept. 25, 1943), p. 2.)
A biographical sketch of David Sim, Deputy Minister of the Customs and Excise Branch of the Department of National Revenue.

—— Name in the news. Not a gilded success boy. (In *Saturday night*. Toronto. v. 59, no. 15 (Dec. 18, 1943), p. 2.)
A biographical sketch of J. Gerald Godsoe, Co-ordinator of Controls and Chairman of the Wartime Industries Control Board.

—— Name in the news. "Sandy" Skelton faces his second Dominion-provincial conference. (In *Saturday night*. Toronto. v. 59, no. 36 (May 13, 1944), p. 2.)
A biographical sketch of Douglas Alexander Skelton.

—— Name in the news. He is the aspirin for Canadian fuel industry's headaches. (In *Saturday night*. Toronto. v. 59, no. 48 (Aug. 5, 1944), p. 2.)
A biographical sketch of Ernest John Brunning, Coal Controller and Chairman of the Emergency Coal Production Board.

—— Name in the news. Gen. Chisholm will cure psychic ills of civil life as of army. (In *Saturday night*. Toronto. v. 60, no. 17 (Dec. 30, 1944), p. 2.)
A biographical sketch of Major-General George Brock Chisholm, Deputy Minister of the National Health section of the Department of Health and National Welfare.

—— Name in the news. One of Ottawa's bright young men handles baby bonuses. (In *Saturday night*. Toronto. v. 60, no. 24 (Feb. 17, 1945), p. 2.)
A biographical sketch of George F. Davidson, Deputy Minister of the Welfare section of the Department of National Health and Welfare.

CRAGG, ROBERT CECIL   Canadian democracy and the economic settlement. By R. Cecil Cragg. Toronto, Ryerson Press [c1947] xlii, 262 p.
The tenor of the book is expressed in the Author's opinion "that the economic solution of any problem affecting us is a political issue". – Introd. (p. xlii).
Note chapter "Postscript to an election": pp. 221-257. Refers to the federal election held June 11, 1945.

CREED, GEORGE E.   Canada's great destiny. (In *The New age*. Montreal. v. 2, no. 48 (Dec. 5, 1940), pp. 7-8; 11.)
Evaluates contemporary Canadian problems and assets.

CROSS, AUSTIN FLETCHER   I miss the women. By Austin F. Cross. (In *Chatelaine*. Toronto. v. 19, no. 2 (Feb. 1946), pp. 16; 55-56; 65-66.)

Discusses the five women sent to Parliament to date: Agnes Macphail, Mrs. Martha Louise Black, Dorise Nielsen, Cora Taylor Casselman, Gladys Strum, and laments their reduced numbers in the post-war parliament.

CUMMINGS, L. Unity? What do we do about learning French? (In *Saturday night*. Toronto. v. 59, no. 7 (Oct. 23, 1943), p. 17.)
Maintains that respect for the French language will aid national unity.

DAVIES, FRED R. 1855—responsible government; 1934—government by commission; 1946—confederation with Canada. (In *Atlantic guardian*. Montreal. v. 2, no. 4 (Apr. 1946), pp. 12-15; 39-44.)
Concerns Newfoundland and Canada.

DAWSON, ROBERT MAC GREGOR The conscription crisis of 1944. By R. MacGregor Dawson. [Toronto] University of Toronto Press [c1961] 136 p.
Appendix: The Mackenzie King ministry, September 1, 1944—December 7, 1944 (pp. [131]-132).

—— The impact of the war on Canadian political institutions. By R. MacGregor Dawson. (In *The Canadian journal of economics and political science*. [Toronto] v. 7 (1941), pp. 170-188.)
"The substance of this paper was delivered as a lecture last March at Columbia University and the College of William and Mary."

DENT, JOHN C. New deal for Indians is planned by MP. (In *Saturday night*. Toronto. v. 61, no. 30 (Mar. 30, 1946), pp. 10-11.)
"The Hon. J. A. Glen, MP for Marquette, Manitoba, advocates a Royal Commission to inquire into the needs of Canada's Indians."

DEXTER, GRANT Canada's war program. (In *Maclean's*. Toronto. v. 52, no. 21 (Nov. 1, 1939), pp. 9; 45-46.)

—— Wanted: a war cabinet. Says this writer: We need a plan to win this war and to make that plan work we need an inner War Cabinet. (In *Maclean's*. Toronto. v. 53, no. 21 (Nov. 1, 1940), pp. 11; 38-41.)

—— Whose air? Where does Canada stand in the scramble for air rights? . . . Should air be free or government controlled? (In *Maclean's*. Toronto. v. 56, no. 13 (July 1, 1943), pp. 13; 51-52; 54.)

—— Why a census? Here are reasons why Canada's national stock-taking is considered a wartime essential. (In *Maclean's*. Toronto. v. 54, no. 12 (June 15, 1941), pp. 12; 40; 45-47.)

Do you want your money spent this way? These three examples of how the Defense Department did business show why patronage must be eliminated from all government departments. (In *Maclean's*. Toronto. v. 52, no. 22 (Nov. 15, 1939), pp. 9; 48-49.)

DOUGLAS, THOMAS CLEMENT Saskatchewan's post-war plans. An address by the Honourable T. C. Douglas. (In Empire Club of Canada. *Addresses*. Toronto. (1944/45), pp. 393-408).
Address delivered April 5, 1945.
Considered within a national context.

DOUSSIN, RENE Apostilles politiques. (In *L'Action nationale*. Montréal. v. 15 (avril 1940), pp. [286]-291.)

DREW, GEORGE ALEXANDER Canada at the crossroads. By Lieutenant-Colonel George A. Drew. (In Empire Club of Canada. *Addresses*. Toronto. (1940/41), pp. 385-401.)
Address delivered March 6, 1941.
Discusses the constitutional problem relating to the legislative authority of the Dominion and provincial government (p. 390).

DUHAMEL, ROGER L'avenir du Canada. (In *L'Action nationale*. Montréal. v. 24 (déc. 1944), pp. [244]-257.)
"Le texte du message aux Canadiens-français, prononcé le 2 décembre dernier, à CKAC . . ."
Discusses the conscription issue.

—— A French Canadian speaks. What's behind Quebec's attitude on the war, the Empire and Canadian unity? Herewith a frank answer by a French-Canadian nationalist. (In *Maclean's*. Toronto. v. 58, no. 1 (Jan. 1, 1945), pp. 18; 24-25.)

—— Les jeux de la politique. (In *L'Action nationale*. Montréal. v. 14 (sept. 1939), pp. [53]-57.)
Discusses the implications of Canada's decision to enter the war.

EARL, JANE ARMSTRONG Rideau Hall's new family. (In *Chatelaine*. Toronto. v. 18, no. 10 (Oct. 1945), pp. 16; 55; 79-81.)
Concerns Field Marshal Viscount Alexander of Tunis (Governor-General of Canada, 1946-1952.)

ECKLER, S. After the war. Social security in Canada. (In *Saturday night*. Toronto. v. 57, no. 51 (Aug. 29, 1942), p. 11.)

―― After the war. A program for employment security. (In *Saturday night*. Toronto. v. 58, no. 3 (Sept. 26, 1942), p. 8.)
Concerns the Committee on Reconstruction headed by F. Cyril James, known as the James Committee, and federal training programs.

―― After the war. A program for employment security ― II. (In *Saturday night*. Toronto. v. 58, no. 4 (Oct. 3, 1942), p. 8.)
Discusses the Canadian Unemployment Insurance Act.

―― Dominion drafts charter for national health. (In *Saturday night*. Toronto. v. 58, no. 34 (May 18, 1943), p. 14.)
Discusses the draft health bill presented to the Parliamentary Social Security Committee.

EGGLESTON, WILFRID Canada at the end of the war. (In *Queen's quarterly*. Kingston. v. 52 (1945), pp. [356]-362.)
Discusses the proposed Canadian demobilization program.

―― The Ottawa letter. Saskatchewan may not be so wise in duelling with the Dominion. (In *Saturday night*. Toronto. v. 60, no. 26 (Mar. 3, 1945), p. 8.)
Concerns the "row" between the Saskatchewan government and Ottawa over seed-grain debts.

―― The Ottawa letter. Parliament will be the major sufferer if session blows up. (In *Saturday night*. Toronto. v. 60, no. 29 (Mar. 24, 1945), p. 8.)
Comments on the final days of the sixth session, nineteenth parliament.

―― The Ottawa letter. Which party in Canada can hope to win a federal majority? (In *Saturday night*. Toronto. v. 60, no. 30 (Mar. 31, 1945), p. 8.)

―― The Ottawa letter. According to the signs Mr. King has best chance of winning. (In *Saturday night*. Toronto. v. 60, no. 39 (June 2, 1945), p. 8.)
Refers to the general elections held June 11, 1945.

―― The Ottawa letter. Proportional representation might have meant a patchwork House. (In *Saturday night*. Toronto. v. 60, no. 40 (June 9, 1945), p. 8.)
With reference to the federal election held June 11, 1945.

―― The Ottawa letter. Election moral: National party must look to French-Canada. (In *Saturday night*. Toronto. v. 60, no. 41 (June 16, 1945), p. 8.)
Considers results of the federal election held June 11, 1945.

―― The Ottawa letter. People have reason to be well pleased with election result. (In *Saturday night*. Toronto. v. 60, no. 42 (June 23, 1945), p. 8.)
Concerns the federal election held June 11, 1945.

―― The Ottawa letter. New faces and untested ability a feature of new parliament. (In *Saturday night*. Toronto. v. 61, no. 1 (Sept. 8, 1945), p. 8.)
Refers to the first session of the twentieth parliament.

―― The Ottawa letter. Canada's Parliament soon should clarify "state of emergency". (In *Saturday night*. Toronto. v. 61, no. 2 (Sept. 15, 1945), p. 8.)

―― The Ottawa letter. Typical postwar budget will be between $1.5 and $2 billions. (In *Saturday night*. Toronto. v. 61, no. 5 (Oct. 6, 1945), p. 8.)

―― The Ottawa letter. Canada's new Information Board will prove itself by policies. (In *Saturday night*. Toronto. v. 61, no. 6 (Oct. 13, 1945), p. 8.)
"By an order-in-council dated September 28, [1945] the Government wound up the Wartime Information Board and established in its place the Canadian Information Service. . . ."

―― The Ottawa letter. Oh, for a poet in the House to lighten the columnist's load! (In *Saturday night*. Toronto. v. 61, no. 9 (Nov. 3, 1945), p. 8.)
Comments on colourful personalities in the House of Commons during "the good old days". e.g. Sam Jacobs, Dr. Bill Motherwell, Mitchell Hepburn, etc.

―― The Ottawa letter. Cartels revealed as enemy of national and world economy. (In *Saturday night*. Toronto. v. 61, no. 11 (Nov. 17, 1945), p. 8.)

―― The Ottawa letter. CNR 1945 statement makes the 30's seem like a nightmare. (In *Saturday night*. Toronto. v. 61, no. 12 (Nov. 24, 1945), p. 8.)
Concerns the report of the Standing Committee on Railways and Shipping.

―― The Ottawa letter. Peacetime army's three branches will cost around $250 millions. (In *Saturday night*. Toronto. v. 61, no. 22 (Feb. 2, 1946), p. 8.)

—— Ottawa letter. "Full employment" program has weathered first test period. (In *Saturday night*. Toronto. v. 61, no. 34 (Apr. 27, 1946), p. 8.)

—— Ottawa letter. Four main matters before House committee examining CBC. (In *Saturday night*. Toronto. v. 61, no. 42 (June 22, 1946), p. 8.)

—— Ottawa letter. Federal fiscal news suggests a balanced budget in 1947-48. (In *Saturday night*. Toronto. v. 61, no. 44 (July 6, 1946), p. 8.)

—— Ottawa letter. Canadian espionage report will be a best seller this year. (In *Saturday night*. Toronto. v. 61, no. 47 (July 27, 1946), p. 8.)
Concerns the report of the Taschereau-Kellock Commission on Canadian Espionage.

—— Ottawa letter. Deficit of housing units may be removed by five years' plan. (In *Saturday night*. Toronto. v. 61, no. 48 (Aug. 3, 1946), p. 8.)
Concerns the housing situation in Canada.

—— Ottawa letter. Prolonged strike brings Canada nearer edge of wild inflation. (In *Saturday night*. Toronto. v. 61, no. 49 (Aug. 10, 1946), p. 8.)
Comments on United Steel Workers' strike.

—— Ottawa letter. Canada's trade policy should be trimmed now for future needs. (In *Saturday night*. Toronto. v. 62, no. 4 (Sept. 28, 1946), p. 8.)

—— Ottawa letter. A political party's philosophy is still an elastic affair. (In *Saturday night*. Toronto. v. 62, no. 12 (Nov. 23, 1946), p. 8.)
Comments on the Liberal and Conservative parties.

—— Ottawa letter. Canada's economics and politics in 1947 likely to be stable. (In *Saturday night*. Toronto. v. 62, no. 18 (Jan. 4, 1947), p. 8.)

—— Ottawa letter. Proposed legislation to apply soil control to all Canada. (In *Saturday night*. Toronto. v. 62, no. 19 (Jan. 11, 1947), p. 8.)
Concerns a bill to extend the benefits from the Prairie Farm Rehabilitation Act (1935), to the rest of the Dominion.

—— Ottawa letter. Maritime coal issue: part of the big subsidy-control question. (In *Saturday night*. Toronto. v. 62, no. 26 (Mar. 1, 1947), p. 8.)
Comments on the debate over the Maritime coal strike.

—— Ottawa letter. Freight rates issue will stir up complex economic factors. (In *Saturday night*. Toronto. v. 6, no. 27 (Mar. 8, 1947), p. 8.)

—— Ottawa letter. The wealth of Canada's northland grows as its mystery fades. (In *Saturday night*. Toronto. v. 62, no. 34 (Apr. 26, 1947), p. 8.)
Comments on official government attitude toward the Canadian North in 1947.

—— Ottawa letter. Wheat Board Bill for external trade has domestic corollary. (In *Saturday night*. Toronto. v. 62, no. 35 (May 3, 1947), p. 8.)

—— Ottawa letter. First response to new budget was feeling of relief, then queries. (In *Saturday night*. Toronto. v. 62, no. 36 (May 10, 1947), p. 8.)
Concerns the budget address delivered by Douglas Charles Abbott.

—— Ottawa letter. Pacific Great Eastern Railway may be a four-way partnership. (In *Saturday night*. Toronto. v. 62, no. 37 (May 17, 1947), p. 8.)
"A four-way partnership – composed of the national government, the provincial government and the two railway systems. ..."

—— Ottawa letter. Practicalities keep immigration largely an academic question. (In *Saturday night*. Toronto. v. 62, no. 38 (May 24, 1947), p. 8.)
Comments on immigration policy.

—— Ottawa letter. After study, Newfoundland voter should find terms attractive. (In *Saturday night*. Toronto. v. 63, no. 8 (Oct. 25, 1947), p. 8.)

—— Ottawa letter. Decline of real national income major problem for next session. (In *Saturday night*. Toronto. v. 63, no. 12 (Nov. 22, 1947), p. 8.)

—— Ottawa letter. Renewal of Emergency Powers Act necessary before year's end. (In *Saturday night*. Toronto. v. 63, no. 14 (Dec. 6, 1947), p. 8.)

—— Ottawa letter. A strongly led, united opposition might force appeal to people. (In *Saturday night*. Toronto. v. 63, no. 15 (Dec. 13, 1947), p. 8.)

Comments on Liberal domination of the House of Commons and discusses the role of the Conservative Opposition.

—— Ottawa letter. Inflation causes beyond Canada, prices inquiry idea is futile. (In *Saturday night*. Toronto. v. 63, no. 19 (Feb. 14, 1948), p. 9.)
Concerns a House of Commons debate on a proposal to set up a parliamentary committee to inquire into the rising cost of living.

—— Ottawa letter. When rail rates make sense here, they make absurdities there. (In *Saturday night*. Toronto. v. 63, no. 27 (Apr. 10, 1948), p. 8.)

—— Ottawa letter. Both sides of Commons reluctant about election on rates issue. (In *Saturday night*. Toronto. v. 63, no. 28 (Apr. 17, 1948), p. 8.)
Concerns the issue of increased freight rates for railways.

—— Ottawa letter. The sharp debate on civil liberties discloses a non-party division. (In *Saturday night*. Toronto. v. 63, no. 29 (Apr. 24, 1948), p. 7.)

—— Ottawa letter. Most promising election role for two provincial leaders? (In *Saturday night*. Toronto. v. 63, no. 30 (May 1, 1948), p. 8.)
Refers to George Drew and Maurice Duplessis.

—— Ottawa letter. More is spent on our air defence than on Canada's army or navy. (In *Saturday night*. Toronto. v. 63, no. 39 (July 3, 1948), p. 8.)

—— Ottawa letter. End of session historic for PM, another price debate for PC's. (In *Saturday night*. Toronto. v. 63, no. 40 (July 10, 1948), p. 8.)
Concerns the fourth session of the twentieth parliament.

—— Ottawa view. Union growing pains. (In *Saturday night*. Toronto. v. 64, no. 3 (Oct. 23, 1948), p. 4.)
Comments on the problems encountered in negotiations for union of Newfoundland with Canada.

—— The report of the Royal Commission on Espionage. (In *Queen's quarterly*. Kingston. v. 53 (1946), pp. [369]-378.)
Considers the political implications relating to the issuance of the Report of the Royal Commission to Investigate the Facts Relating to and the Circumstances Surrounding the Communication, by Public

Officials and Other Persons in Positions of Trust, of Secret and Confidential Information to Agents of a Foreign Power, appointed February 5, 1946, Robert Taschereau and Roy Lindsay, commissioners.

The Election and the future. (In *The Canadian forum*. Toronto. v. 19, no. 23 (Mar. 1940), pp. 373-374.)
Concerns the federal election held March 26, 1940.

The Elections. (In *The Canadian forum*. Toronto. v. 25, no. 292 (May 1945), pp. 33-34.)
Comments on the impending general election held June 11, 1945.

EWART, T. SEATON   Citizenship fixed by three earlier Acts. By T. S. Ewart. (In *Saturday night*. Toronto. v. 62, no. 6 (Oct. 12, 1946), p. 19.)
Discussion surrounds the Canadian Citizenship Act passed into effect January 1, 1947.

FERGUSON, GEORGE HOWARD   Canada's destiny. By the Honourable G. Howard Ferguson. (In Empire Club of Canada. *Addresses*. Toronto. (1940/41), pp. 97-111.)
Address delivered October 3, 1940.

FERGUSON, GEORGE VICTOR   Ater [!] the election. By G. V. Ferguson. (In *Queen's quarterly*. Kingston. v. 47 (1940), pp. [241]-249.)
Analyses the results of the general elections held March 26, 1940.

FISHER, JOHN WIGGINS   Cobwebs. By John Fisher. (In Empire Club of Canada. *Addresses*. Toronto. (1947/48), pp. 29-42.)
Address delivered October 2, 1947.
Random thoughts on Canada.

FLAHERTY, J. FRANCIS   Big implications in Canada's new wage policy. (In *Saturday night*. Toronto. v. 56, no. 45 (July 19, 1941), pp. [30]-31.)

—— Citizenship Act clears the national status. By J. F. Flaherty. (In *Saturday night*. Toronto. v. 62, no. 1 (Sept. 7, 1946), p. 9.)
Concerns the Canadian Citizenship Act effective January 1, 1947.

—— The Ottawa letter. Debate on security conference showed reassuring agreement. By Francis Flaherty. (In *Saturday night*. Toronto. v. 60, no. 31 (Apr. 7, 1945), p. 8.)

—— The Ottawa letter. On election eve it looks as if conscription is fading issue. (In *Saturday night*. Toronto. v. 60, no. 32 (Apr. 14, 1945), p. 8.)

—— The Ottawa letter. This time Ontario will be the key in the national election. By Francis Flaherty. (In *Saturday night*. Toronto. v. 60, no. 38 (May 26, 1945), p. 8.)

The federal election held June 11, 1945.

—— Ottawa letter. Old Age Pensions Bill reaction is wish for further increase. By Frank Flaherty. (In *Saturday night*. Toronto. v. 62, no. 43 (June 28, 1947), p. 8.)

—— Ottawa letter. Though session over, more will be heard of Income Tax Bill. By Frank Flaherty. (In *Saturday night*. Toronto. v. 62, no. 47 (July 26, 1947), p. 8.)

—— Ottawa letter. Newfoundland union discussions highlight problems and a hope. By Frank Flaherty. (In *Saturday night*. Toronto. v. 62, no. 48 (Aug. 2, 1947), p. 8.)

—— Ottawa letter. Federal Board must aid fisheries with a platform under prices. By Frank Flaherty. (In *Saturday night*. Toronto. v. 62, no. 51 (Aug. 23, 1947), p. 8.)

Concerns the Fisheries Price Support Board.

FLEMING, DONALD METHUEN   The challenge we face. By Donald M. Fleming, MP. (In *Empire Club of Canada. Addresses*. Toronto. (1945/46), pp. 323-339.)

Address delivered April 4, 1946.

FLINT, IRENE   The new federal Act will clarify labor and management relations. (In *Saturday night*. Toronto. v. 63, no. 38 (June 26, 1948), p. [38].)

—— One simple labor law for Canada is intention of federal bill. (In *Saturday night*. Toronto. v. 63 no. 36 (June 12, 1948), pp. [34]-35.)

With reference to the Industrial Relations and Disputes Investigation Act, 1947.

FOWKE, EDITH MARGARET (FULTON)   Justice and Japanese Canadians. By Edith Fowke. (In *The Canadian forum*. Toronto. v. 26, no. 312 (Jan. 1947), pp. 225-226.)

—— Newfoundland: tenth province? By Edith Fowke. (In *The Canadian forum*. Toronto. v. 27, no. 317 (June 1947), pp. 59-61.)

FRASER, BLAIR   Backstage at Ottawa. By the Man with a Notebook. (In *Maclean's*.

Toronto. v. 57, no. 1 (Jan. 1, 1944), pp. 12-13.)

Comments on an anticipated federal election.

—— Backstage at Ottawa. By the Man with a Notebook. (In *Maclean's*. Toronto. v. 57, no. 3 (Feb. 1, 1944), pp. 14-15; 45.)

Concerns the retirement of Gen. McNaughton, as well as other political issues.

—— Backstage at Ottawa. By the Man with a Notebook. (In *Maclean's*. Toronto. v. 57, no. 5 (Mar. 1, 1944), pp. 14-15; 46-47.)

Discusses the census and an anticipated federal election in 1945.

—— Backstage at Ottawa. By the Man with a Notebook. (In *Maclean's*. Toronto. v. 57, no. 6 (Mar. 15, 1944), pp. 14-15; 49.)

General discussion of Quebec politics in relation to the federal situation.

—— Backstage at Ottawa. By the Man with a Notebook. (In *Maclean's*. Toronto. v. 57, no. 14 (July 15, 1944), pp. 14-15; 44.)

Discusses an anticipated federal election in 1945.

—— Backstage at Ottawa. By the Man with a Notebook. (In *Maclean's*. Toronto. v. 57, no. 15 (Aug. 1, 1944), pp. 14-15; 44.)

Discusses the forthcoming Quebec provincial election as it affects federal political matters.

—— Backstage at Ottawa. By the Man with a Notebook. (In *Maclean's*. Toronto. v. 57, no. 16 (Aug. 15, 1944), pp. 14-15; 38.)

Speculates on a future federal election.

—— Backstage at Ottawa. By the Man with a Notebook. (In *Maclean's*. Toronto. v. 58, no. 3 (Feb. 1, 1945), pp. 14-15; 49-50.)

Discusses the by-election in Grey North, Ont. where Defense Minister McNaughton ran against Mayor Case of Owen Sound for the Progressive Conservatives and Air Vice-Marshal Godfrey for the CCF. The federal by-election was held February 5, 1945.

—— Backstage at Ottawa. By the Man with a Notebook. (In *Maclean's*. Toronto. v. 58, no. 5 (Mar. 1, 1945), pp. 14-15; 51.)

Discusses the Grey North by-election involving Defence Minister McNaughton, Mayor Case of Owen Sound and Vice-

Marshal Godfrey. The federal by-election was held February 5, 1945.

―――― Backstage at Ottawa. By the Man with a Notebook. (In *Maclean's*. Toronto. v. 58, no. 7 (Apr. 1, 1945), pp. 14-15; 63.)
General comments on the King government and the Conservative Opposition.

―――― Backstage at Ottawa. "Quebec party" having difficult birth. Did Cardin turn down a Duplessis-Dorion offer of leadership of an anti-King bloc? — Montreal's flamboyant Mayor Houde plays the sphinx. By the Man with a Notebook. (In *Maclean's*. Toronto. v. 58, no. 8 (Apr. 15, 1945), p. 15.)

―――― Backstage at Ottawa. That touchy meat problem. Our failure to ration causes raised eyebrows in Washington, but what shall Ottawa do, with an election and what not on the menu? By the Man with a Notebook. (In *Maclean's*. Toronto. v. 58, no. 9 (May 1, 1945), pp. 15; 57-58.)

―――― Backstage at Ottawa. The case of the colliding elections. Drew's foes talk of contestation. Russia's facilities for feeding her zone in Europe put democracies on the spot. By the Man with a Notebook. (In *Maclean's*. Toronto. v. 58, no. 10 (May 15, 1945), pp. 15; 64-65.)

―――― Backstage at Ottawa. "Why a governor general? Why not the King?" Capital buzzes over a proposal that George VI divide his time between Britain and Canada and eliminate a governor-general. By the Man with a Notebook. (In *Maclean's*. Toronto. v. 58, no. 11 (June 1, 1945), pp. 15; 54.)

―――― Backstage at Ottawa. Quebec — key to election? Baby bonus causing headaches. Meat rationing will be tough. Labor plumps for immigration. By the Man with the Notebook. (In *Maclean's*. Toronto. v. 58, no. 12 (June 15, 1945), pp. 15; 53.)

―――― Backstage at Ottawa. Election pay-off: nobody quite happy. By the Man with a Notebook. (In *Maclean's*. Toronto. v. 58, no. 14 (July 15, 1945), pp. 15; 43-44.)
Considers results of the general elections held June 11, 1945.

―――― Backstage at Ottawa. Government housing may beat private building. By the Man with a Notebook. (In *Maclean's*. Toronto. v. 58, no. 16 (Aug. 15, 1945), pp. 15; 44.)

―――― Backstage at Ottawa. By the Man with a Notebook. (In *Maclean's*. Toronto.

v. 58, no. 18 (Sept. 15, 1945), pp. 13; 57-58.)
Discusses Canada's Pacific war effort; also, the Dominion Provincial Conference held during 1945-46. The first session held Aug. 6, 1945.

―――― Backstage at Ottawa. New Commons promises surprises. By the Man with a Notebook. (In *Maclean's*. Toronto. v. 58, no. 20 (Oct. 15, 1945), pp. 15; 66.)
Refers to the first session of the twentieth parliament opened Sept. 6, 1945.

―――― Backstage at Ottawa. How did the Reds get under the bed? By the Man with a Notebook. (In *Maclean's*. Toronto. v. 59, no. 8 (Apr. 15, 1946), pp. 15; 64; 66.)

―――― Backstage at Ottawa. Nobody's ready for an election. By the Man with a Notebook. (In *Maclean's*. Toronto. v. 59, no. 12 (June 15, 1946), p. 15.)

―――― Backstage at Ottawa. Wage policy under fire. By the Man with a Notebook. (In *Maclean's*. Toronto. v. 59, no. 15 (Aug. 1, 1946), pp. 15; 45-46.)

―――― Backstage at Ottawa. By-election blues. By the Man with a Notebook. (In *Maclean's*. Toronto. v. 59, no 21 (Nov. 1, 1946), pp. 15; 74; 76.)
Concerns the federal by-election held in Portage La Prairie, Man., October 21, 1946.

―――― Backstage at Ottawa. The sharks and the sprats. By the Man with the Notebook. (In *Maclean's*. Toronto. v. 60, no. 5 (Mar. 1, 1947, pp. 15; 65; 67.)
Discusses salaries of Canadian diplomats; the CCF party, etc.

―――― Backstage at Ottawa. Your dream house is Ottawa's nightmare as housing program bogs down . . . MPs are free to swear — but not in Hansard. By the Man with a Notebook. (In *Maclean's*. Toronto. v. 60, no. 12 (June 15, 1947), pp. 15; 69-70.)

―――― Backstage at Ottawa. We play Newfoundland poker. The prize: a tenth province — civil service hatchet men send 23,000 heads a-rolling. By the Man with a Notebook. (In *Maclean's*. Toronto. v. 60, no. 13 (July 1, 1947), pp. 15; 53.)

―――― Backstage at Ottawa. Talk of a "planned depression" in the U.S., which might help prices here. And how the CCF stole the show in l'affaire Dionne. By the Man with a Notebook. (In *Maclean's*. Toronto. v. 60, no. 14 (July 15, 1947), pp. 15; 47.)

—— Backstage at Ottawa. Insiders say Bracken won't retire—just yet. Speaking of politicos, Mike Pearson's friends think he'd be a wow. By the Man with a Notebook. (In *Maclean's*. Toronto. v. 60, no. 15 (Aug. 1, 1947), pp. 15; 46.)

—— Backstage at Ottawa. The merger and margarine. By the Man with a Notebook. (In *Maclean's*. Toronto. v. 60, no. 18 (Sept. 15, 1947), pp. 15; 82; 85.)

Discusses a union of Newfoundland with Canada.

—— Backstage at Ottawa. Sold!—for $5. By the Man with a Notebook. (In *Maclean's*. Toronto. v. 60, no. 21 (Nov. 1, 1947), pp. 15; 68.)

Concerns the old age pension bill.

—— Backstage at Ottawa. By-election blues. By the Man with a Notebook. (In *Maclean's*. Toronto. v. 60, no. 23 (Dec. 1, 1947), pp. 15; 70-71.)

Discusses national voting trends as reflected in a series of by-elections held during 1947.

—— Backstage at Ottawa. Price rocket by the tail. By the Man with a Notebook. (In *Maclean's*. Toronto. v. 61, no. 4 (Feb. 15, 1948), pp. 15; 56.)

Discusses government price controls.

—— Backstage at Ottawa. The law nobody wants. By the Man with a Notebook. (In *Maclean's*. Toronto. v. 61, no. 7 (Apr. 1, 1948), pp. 15; 65.)

Comments on income tax policy.

—— Battle of the flag. Everybody wants a Canadian flag—but at the moment choice of a design is deadlocked. (In *Maclean's*. Toronto. v. 59, no. 13 (July 1, 1946), pp. 9; 52-54.)

—— Billions for millions. Are victory loan costs too high? . . . Herewith the inside story of loan campaign expenses. (In *Maclean's*. Toronto. v. 57, no. 21 (Nov 1, 1944), pp. 6; 36-38.)

—— Crisis in Quebec. Why riots in Quebec? Why the tension, bitterness? Herewith a frank report of the story behind the story of conflict in French Canada. (In *Maclean's*. Toronto. v. 57, no. 16 (Aug. 15, 1944), pp. 5-6; 43-46.)

Relates the situation to the rest of Canada.

—— Static on the CBC. What is the matter with the CBC? Here are the pros and cons of an argument that agitates politicians,

critics, John Public—and the CBC itself. (In *Maclean's*. Toronto. v. 57, no. 11 (June 1, 1944), pp. 16; 54-59.)

—— Wanted 2,000,000 jobs. Everyone agrees we must have "full employment" to win the peace . . . Here's a blunt analysis what we have to do to get it. (In *Maclean's*. Toronto. v. 57, no. 6 (Mar. 15, 1944), pp. 7; 39; 41-44.)

Concerns post-war employment policy.

—— What's next in Quebec? Duplessis rule in Quebec . . . Social Credit supreme in Alberta . . . What does this mean for the rest of Canada? (In *Maclean's*. Toronto. v. 57, no. 18 (Sept. 15, 1944), pp. 9; 64-67.)

At head of title: Election post-mortems.

—— Where's the money go? Who's cashing in on price jumps? Here are facts and figures. (In *Maclean's*. Toronto. v. 60, no. 22 (Nov. 15, 1947), pp. 7; 79-81.)

FROMER, ANNE Canada's plans for job control after the war. (In *Saturday night*. Toronto. v. 59, no. 7 (Oct. 23, 1943), pp. 14-15.)

—— Canada's plans ready for post-war. (In *Saturday night*. Toronto. v. 59, no. 10 (Nov. 13, 1943), pp. 22-23.)

—— Post-war employment field graphed by Weir report. (In *Saturday night*. Toronto. v. 59, no. 33 (Apr. 22, 1944), p. 6.)

Concerns Dr. G. M. Weir's report to the federal government on post-war employment.

—— Social security for Canada. (In *Saturday night*. Toronto. v. 58, no. 28 (Mar. 20, 1943), p. 6.)

Discusses a report on social security submitted by Dr. Leonard Marsh.

—— What Canadian health insurance will provide. (In *Saturday night*. Toronto. v. 59, no. 17 (Jan. 1, 1944), p. 6.)

Discusses the Health Insurance Bill to be considered by the federal Parliament.

—— Will controls continue in post-war Canada? (In *Saturday night*. Toronto. v. 58, no. 44 (July 10, 1943), p. 14.)

GAGNON, JEAN LOUIS A "yes" Quebecker tells why Quebec voted "no". (In *Saturday night*. Toronto. v. 57, no. 36 (May 16, 1942), p. 8.)

Concerns the plebiscite held on the issue of conscription April 27, 1942.

GLENN, FERGUS   The conscription build-up. (In *The Canadian forum*. Toronto. v. 21, no. 249 (Oct. 1941), pp. 206-208; 210-212.)

—— Conscription—for what? (In *The Canadian forum*. Toronto. v. 21, no. 252 (Jan. 1942), pp. 306-309.)

GOBEIL, SAMUEL   The plebiscite and national unity. By Hon. S. Gobeil. (In *Saturday night*. Toronto. v. 57, no. 38 (May 30, 1942), p. 6.)
Refers to the national plebiscite on conscription held April 27, 1942.

GODBOUT, JOSEPH ADELARD   Quebec and Pan-Canadian unity. (In Empire Club of Canada. *Addresses*. Toronto. (1940/41), pp. 225-242.)
Address delivered December 4, 1940.

GORDON, H. S.   Why today's students look to socialism. (In *Saturday night*. Toronto. v. 59, no. 44 (July 8, 1944), p. 6.)

GOUZENKO, IGOR   New Soviet spy rings at work in Canada! (In *New world*. Toronto. v. 8, no. 3 (May 1947), pp. 9-13.)
An interview.

GRAHAM, JOHN   Donald Gordon, price boss. (In *Saturday night*. Toronto. v. 57, no. 17 (Jan. 3, 1942), p. 7.)
Concerns Donald Gordon, Chairman of the Wartime Prices and Trade Board.

GRANATSTEIN, JACK LAWRENCE   Conscription in the Second World War, 1939-1945; a study in political management. By J. L. Granatstein. Toronto, Ryerson Press [c1969] ix, 85 p. (The Frontenac library, 1.)

—— The York South by-election of February 9, 1942: a turning point in Canadian politics. By J. L. Granatstein. (In *The Canadian historical review*. Toronto. v. 48 (1967), pp. 142-158.)

GRUBE, GEORGE MAXIMILIAN ANTONY   Milk and our governments. By G. M. A. Grube. (In *The Canadian forum*. Toronto. v. 26, no. 310 (Nov. 1946), pp. 173-174.)
Discusses the issue of governmental subsidies for milk.

—— PC 1003—just another order-in-council. By G. M. A. Grube. (In *The Canadian forum*. Toronto. v. 24, no. 279 (Apr. 1944), pp. 6-8.)
Discusses order-in-council PC 1003 (Wartime Labour Relations Regulations) issued February 17, 1944.

—— Those defence regulations. By G. M. A. Grube. (In *The Canadian forum*. Toronto. v. 20, 240 (Jan. 1941), pp. 304-306.)
Discusses the Defence of Canada Regulations.

HACKETT, W. D. B.   Newfoundland's union with Canada favored. (In *Saturday night*. Toronto. v. 61, no. 34 (Apr. 27, 1946), p. 17.)

HAMEL, PHILIPPE   Plébiscite et conscription. A propos d'un plébiscite inopportun et injuste. (In *L'Action nationale*. Montréal. v. 19 (fév./mars 1942), pp. [108]-116.)
The national plebiscite held April 27, 1942.

Have Canadian women made the most of their political equality? (In *Chatelaine*. Toronto. v. 16, no. 9 (Sept. 1943), pp. 8-9. ports.)
Comments by Grace MacInnis, Agnes Macphail, John Bracken, George Drew, Dorise Nielsen, and others.

HOOPER, B. O.   A Youth Ministry to coordinate youth training. By Col. B. O. Hooper. (In *Saturday night*. Toronto. v. 57, no. 45 (July 18, 1942), p. 17.)
Advocates the idea of a federal Ministry of Youth.

HUMPHREY, JOHN P.   Formule pour l'unité canadienne. (In *Relations*. Montréal. 2. année, no. 26 (fév. 1943), pp. 34-35.)
Translated from the English published in the March 1943 issue of *The Canadian forum*.

—— Le Québec devant l'unité canadienne. Par John Humphrey, Hugh MacLennan, Emile Vaillancourt. (In *Relations*. Montréal. 3. année, no 25 (jan. 1943), pp. 16-19.)
"Le texte inédit d'un forum transmis de Montréal sur tout le réseau anglais de Radio-Canada."
Translated from the English.

—— A recipe for Canadian unity. (In *The Canadian forum*. Toronto. v. 22, no. 266 (Mar. 1943), pp. 345-346.)

HUTCHISON, BRUCE   Milestone; Confederation's 75th anniversary, July 1, 1942. (In *Maclean's*. Toronto. v. 55, no. 13 (July 1, 1942), pp. 5-7; 36-37.)
Written on the 75th anniversary of Confederation. Considers Canada's history and prospects.

—— Out of an empty land—a nation. (In *Maclean's*. Toronto. v. 58, no. 13 (July 1, 1945), pp. 5-6; 43-44.)

Written in honour of Canada's seventy-eighth birthday.

—— Pie in the sky Canadian style. Says this writer: "Politicians promise us post-war prosperity . . . but how do we get it? Pie in the sky by-and-by is not good enough in a time like this". (In *Maclean's*. Toronto. v. 56, no. 7 (Apr. 1, 1943), pp. 5-6; 26; 28-29.)

—— Saskatchewan landslide. What's the meaning of the Saskatchewan revolt? . . . Does it point to socialism for all Canada? (In *Maclean's*. Toronto. v. 57, no. 15 (Aug. 1, 1944), pp. 7; 41-42.)

HUTTON, ERIC The day Canada went to war. September 10, 1939. (In *Maclean's*. Toronto. v. 72, no. 19 (Sept. 12, 1959), pp. 13-17; 62-68.)

The Issue as I see it. (In *Maclean's*. Toronto. v. 53, no. 6 (Mar. 15, 1940), pp. 12-13; 53-56.)

Views given on the war issue by W. L. Mackenzie King, R. C. Manion, J. S. Woodsworth, and John H. Blackmore.

Relates to the federal election held March 26, 1940.

JAMIESON, STUART Fiscal policy and full employment. (In *The Canadian forum*. Toronto. v. 24, no. 285 (Oct. 1944), pp. 151-153.)

Part I. Decline of "private enterprise".

—— Fiscal policy and full employment. (In *The Canadian forum*. Toronto. v. 24, no. 286 (Nov. 1944), pp. 182-185.)

Part II. Subsidizing private enterprise.

JOLLIFFE, EDWARD BIGELOW Labor's post-war charter. (In *The Canadian forum*. Toronto. v. 26, no. 313 (Feb. 1947), pp. 246-248.)

Discusses the labour legislation outlined in the Industrial Relations and Disputes Investigation Act, 1947.

KAUFMAN, FRED Montreal – Cartier is a political puzzle. (In *Saturday night*. Toronto. v. 62, no. 25 (Feb. 22, 1947), p. 9.)

Concerns a forthcoming by-election in Montreal—Cartier, held March 31, 1947.

KEIRSTEAD, BURTON SEELY Canada's economic war policy. By B. S. Keirstead. Toronto, T. Nelson, 1941. 31 p. (Dalhousie University. Bulletins on public affairs, 11.)

—— National policy. By B. S. Keirstead. (In Brady, Alexander (ed.) *Canada after the war*. Toronto, 1943. pp. 1-30.)

Discusses Canadian national economic interests within the federal system in post-World War II Canadian society.

KEITH, JANET R. Rehabilitation will benefit all our farming. (In *Saturday night*. Toronto. v. 59, no. 5 (Oct. 9, 1943), p. 6.)

Concerns the application of the Prairie Farm Rehabilitation Act to all of Canada.

KETCHUM, CARLETON J. A federal district capital. (In *Saturday night*. Toronto. v. 57, no. 32 (Apr. 18, 1942), p. 6.)

Concerns a government proposal to create a federal district capital at Ottawa in order to provide rehabilitation for servicemen after the war.

KIRKCONNELL, WATSON Canada and immigration. (In Empire Club of Canada. *Addresses*. Toronto. (1943/44), pp. 374-391.)

Address delivered March 23, 1944.

A close analysis of Canadian post-war immigration policy.

LACEY, ALEXANDER Canada's tenth province? By A. Lacey. (In *University of Toronto quarterly*. [Toronto] v. 12 (1942/43), pp. 435-445.)

Discusses Newfoundland and the Canadian Confederation.

—— The case for confederation. Newfoundland should seek responsible government in local affairs as a province of Canada . . . By A. Lacey. (In *Atlantic guardian*. Montreal. v. 1, no. 4 (Apr. 1945), pp. 26-27; 30.)

The second of two articles.

—— The confederation question; its historical background. Should Newfoundland join with Canada? History records a number of attempts at union, all of which ended in failure . . . By A. Lacey. (In *Atlantic guardian*. Montreal. v. 1, no. 3 (Mar. 1945), pp. 5-7.)

First of two articles.

LAING, LIONEL H. The nature of Canada's parliamentary representation. (In *The Canadian journal of economics and political science*. [Toronto] v. 12 (1946), pp. 509-516.)

Analyses the personnel of the twentieth parliament of Canada, elected June 11, 1945.

LAURENDEAU, ANDRE Alerte aux Canadiens français! (In *L'Action nationale*. Montréal. v. 16 (nov. 1940), pp. [177]-203.)

Discussion is within a national context.

—— Can Quebec veto the draft? (In *Saturday night*. Toronto. v. 57, no. 19 (Jan. 17, 1942), p. 7.)

Translation of the author's "La conscription et le prétendu 'droit de veto' du Québec" (In *L'Action nationale*. Montréal. v. 18 (déc. 1941), pp. [258]-265.)

—— La conscription et le prétendu "droit de veto" du Québec. (In *L'Action nationale*. Montéral. v. 18 (déc. 1941), pp. [258]-265.)

—— Courrier de guerre. Par André L. (In *L'Action nationale*. Montréal v. 14 (sept. 1939), pp. [80]-88.)

—— La crise de la conscription, 1942. Montréal, Editions du Jour [c1962] 157 p.

—— Mémoires d'outre-tombe. [Quelques principes de politique extérieure énoncés par nos chefs avant la guerre] Par A. L. (In *L'Action nationale*. Montréal. v. 15 (mars 1940), pp. [229]-232.)

Part 1 of Calendrier de guerre. Part 2 is Comment le Canada est entré en guerre, by F. R. Scott.

—— Nous ne raserons pas la muraille. Le plébiscite. (In *L'Action nationale*. Montréal. v. 19 (jan. 1942), pp. [4]-13.)

Considers the issue of conscription.

LAWRENCE, MARGARET Canada has a great Parliament for a great moment. (In *Saturday night*. Toronto. v. 54, no. 46 (Sept. 16, 1939), p. 2.)

Refers to the decision to enter World War II.

LAZARUS, MORDEN Canada needs federal housing authority. (In *Saturday night*. Toronto. v. 61, no. 25 (Feb. 23, 1946), pp. 18-19.)

LEACOCK, STEPHEN BUTLER A new program for Canada. By Stephen Leacock. (In *Saturday night*. Toronto. v. 58, no. 12 (Nov. 28, 1942), p. 14.)

"Development of the land, and amelioration of social conditions: these must go hand in hand in the political program of Canada after the war."

—— Our politics, from jest to earnest. By Stephen Leacock. (In *The Canadian spokesman*. Ottawa. v. 1, no. 3 (Apr. 1941), pp. [5]-9.)

"The purpose of the present article is to make a plea for sincerity in political life in the present crisis."

EL COCQ, THELMA The woman's voice in price control. (In *Chatelaine*. Toronto. v. 18, no. 11 (Nov. 1945), pp. 16; 49; 55; 57; 59.)

Concerns Byrne Hope Saunders (editor of *Chatelaine*) as a director of the consumer branch of the Wartime Prices and Trade Board.

LEGGET, ROBERT FERGUSON A conservation policy is urgently needed. By Robert F. Legget. (In *Saturday night*. Toronto. v. 61, no. 11 (Nov. 17, 1945), pp. 22-23.)

"The conservation of natural resources . . . is a subject which appears to have been neglected by the Rowell-Sirois Commission and to a large extent, by the Dominion-Provincial Conference on Reconstruction."

LEMIEUX, EDMOND La corde va-t-elle casser? (In *L'Action nationale*. Montréal. v. 19 (avril 1942), pp. [172]-180.)

Concerns the conscription issue.

—— Les droits de la critique en temps de guerre. (In *L'Action nationale*. Montréal. v. 17 (mars 1941), pp. [222]-227.)

—— Un poulet "à la King". Notes en marge du dernier débat. (In *L'Action nationale*. Montréal. v. 19 (juil. 1942), pp. [393]-413.)

At head of title: "La conscription si . . ."

LEWIS, DAVID Labour in the war and postwar. (In Lower, A. R. M. (ed.) *War and reconstruction*. Toronto [c1942] pp. 85-91.)

L'HEUREUX, CAMILLE Le mouvement de l'immigration au Canada depuis la fin de la guerre, 1946-1950. Un documentaire. (In *L'Action nationale*. Montréal. v. 37 (mai 1951), pp. [298]-307.)

Contents: 1. La politique d'immigration canadienne d'après-guerre. – 2. Résultant de la politique d'immigration canadienne d'après-guerre.

LOUGHEED, WILLIAM FOSTER Problems of Canadian war finance. By W. F. Lougheed. (In *The Dalhousie review*. Halifax. v. 20 (1940/41), pp. [154]-160.)

LOWER, ARTHUR REGINALD MARSDEN (ed.) War and reconstruction; some Canadian issues. Edited by A. R. M. Lower and J. F. Parkinson. Toronto, Ryerson [c1942] xi, 106 p.

Addresses given at the Canadian Institute on Public Affairs, August 15 to 23, 1942.

Contents: [Pt.] 1. The war and Canada in the summer of 1942. – [Pt.] 2. Foundations of the new world. – [Pt.] 3. Rebuilding Canada.

MC ALLISTER, GEORGE A. War finance in Canada, 1939-42. [Fredericton] 1942. 121 leaves.
Thesis (MA) – University of New Brunswick.

MAC DONALD, DONALD CAMERON The deepening crisis in civil liberties. By Donald C. MacDonald. (In The Canadian forum. Toronto. v. 26, no. 308 (Sept. 1946), pp. 131-133.)

—— On Parliament Hill. By Donald C. MacDonald. (In The Canadian forum. Toronto. v. 27, no. 316 (May 1947), pp. 32-33.)
The Author contends that "The first ten weeks of the 1947 federal session have emphasized significant developments in each of the major parties".

—— Price probe. By Donald C. MacDonald. (In The Canadian forum. Toronto. v. 27, no. 326 (Mar. 1948), pp. 269-270.)
Discusses the function and work of the parliamentary committee on prices.

—— The three P's and political trends. By Donald C. MacDonald. (In The Canadian forum. Toronto. v. 26, no. 311 (Dec. 1946), pp. 199-202.)
Evaluates the impact on federal politics of the results of the three by-elections in Pontiac, Parkdale, and Portage La Prairie.

MAC EWAN, C. ROSS Ottawa background of wartime labor unrest (In Saturday night. Toronto. v. 56, no. 34 (May 3, 1941), p. 7.)

—— Weaknesses of our latest labor laws are on trial. (In Saturday night. Toronto. v. 59, no. 40 (June 10, 1944), p. 6.)

MC IVOR, RUSSEL CRAIG Canadian war-time fiscal policy, 1939-45. (In The Canadian journal of economics and political science. [Toronto] v. 14 (1948), pp. 62-93.)

MC KAY, ELSIE A. Canada is ready for a flag of its own. (In Saturday night. Toronto. v. 60, no. 50 (Aug. 18, 1945), p. 10.)

MC KENZIE, DONALD GORDON The challenge of democracy. By Honourable D. G. McKenzie. (In Empire Club of Canada. Addresses. Toronto. (1939/40), pp. 320-333.)
Address delivered February 22, 1940.

MC LEAN, F. GOULD That unemployment insurance plank. (In Saturday night. Toronto. v. 55, no. 20 (Mar. 16, 1940), pp. [11]; 13; 15-16.)
Presents this as an issue in the federal election held March 26, 1940.

—— Unemployment insurance means increased taxation. (In Saturday night. Toronto. v. 55, no. 39 (July 27, 1940), pp. [7]; 11.)
Concerns the proposed Unemployment Insurance legislation.

MC LURE, GEORGE The pacifists and Canada's military policy. (In The New age. Montreal. v. 2, no. 22 (May 30, 1940), pp. 7-8.)

MC MICHAEL, ROBERT Will "Newfie" join us? Newfoundland may soon vote for government by commission, self-government, or union with us. (In New world. Toronto. v. 6, no. 9 (Nov. 1945), pp. 9-13.)

MARTIN, CHESTER BAILEY Trends in Canadian nationhood. By Chester B. Martin. (In His Canada in peace and war. London, 1941. pp. 3-28.)

MATHESON, M. W. The mechanics of national unity. An ingenious appraisal of a Canadian problem. (In The New age. Montreal. v. 2, no. 17 (April 25, 1940), pp. 9-10.)

MATHIESON, GEORGE S. The state of [i.e. and] foreign trade. (In Empire Club of Canada. Addresses. Toronto. (1946/47), pp. 70-86.)
Address delivered November 7, 1946.

MAYO, HENRY BERTRAM Newfoundland, the tenth province of Canada; the case for union examined. By H. B. Mayo. [Oxford, 1948] 1 v.
Thesis – Oxford University.

The Meaning of the elections. (In The Canadian forum. Toronto. v. 25, no. 294 (July 1945), pp. 81-82.)
Analyses the Ontario provincial election held June 4, 1945, and the federal election held June 11, 1945.

National unity. (In The Canadian forum. Toronto. v. 24, no. 288 (Jan. 1945), pp. 225-226.)
Considers, in its historical perspective, the problem of French-Canadian–English-Canadian relations.

NEWFIELD, J. G. After the war. A plea for Canadian unity. (In Saturday night. Toronto, v. 58, no. 26 (Mar. 6, 1943), p. 9.)
Discusses the effect New Canadians have on Canadian politics.

Newfoundland goes to the poll. Referendum to determine future form of government finds electorate divided and very much

confused. (In *Atlantic guardian*. Montreal. v. 5, no. 2 (May 1948), pp. 12-13.)
Concerns Newfoundland and the Canadian Confederation.

NICHOLSON, H. F. But we already have conscription! (In *Saturday night*. Toronto. v. 56, no. 44 (July 12, 1941), p. 10.)

—— Conscription is not needed. (In *Saturday night*. Toronto. v. 56, no. 37 (May 24, 1941), p. 6.)

—— Urgently needed—a national economic policy. (In *Saturday night*. Toronto. v. 56, no. 23 (Feb. 15, 1941), p. 7.)
"Mr. Nicholson asserts that without calling in a single other person, the Deputy Ministers of the major departments could lay down the general principles which are to cover wages and prices, savings and taxation, the use of materials and labor, and other vital factors."

NICOLET, JEAN Les élections du 11 juin 1945. (In *L'Action nationale*. Montréal. v. 26 (sept. 1945), pp. [41]-46.)

—— La vie politique Les dernières sessions. (In *L'Action nationale*. Montréal. v. 23 (Jan. 1944), pp. [78]-84.)

—— Le vie politique. (In *L'Action nationale*. Montréal. v. 23 (fév. 1944), pp. [144]-152.)
Contents: "Politique en ligne droite". – Les "Comédiens liberaux au micro". – Un sénateur pour les Acadiens de l'Ile.

—— La vie politique. (In *L'Action nationale*. Montréal. v. 24 (nov. 1944), pp. [203]-210.)
Contents: La veine de M. King. – Les indépendants en politique.

NIELSEN, DORISE WINNIFRED (Webber) New worlds for women. By Dorise W. Nielsen, MP. [Toronto] Progress Books [c1944] 112 p.
Considers the position of women in postwar Canada, including their rôle in politics.

NORRIS, LEONARD Our future flag. By L. Norris. (In Okanagan Historical Society. *Report*. Vernon, B.C. 11th (1945), pp. [20]-24.)

—— The wrong flag. By L. Norris. (In Okanagan Historical Society. *Report*. Vernon, B.C. 10th (1943), pp. 9-15.)
Discusses the issue of a Canadian flag.

NORWOOD, FREDERICK W. Canada in crisis, as seen by an Australian. By Reverend Frederick W. Norwood. (In Empire Club

of Canada. *Addresses*. Toronto. (1940/41), pp. 356-369.)
Address delivered February 20, 1941.

OGILVIE, HENRY The political significance of the 1946 strikes. (In *The Canadian forum*. Toronto. v. 26, no. 311 (Dec. 1946), pp. 202-204.)

O'HEARN, DON P. Canada will be watching these men at Ottawa. (In *Saturday night*. Toronto. v. 60, no. 46 (July 21, 1945), p. 5.)
Comments on the premiers who will attend the Dominion-Provincial Conference on Reconstruction Aug. 6, 1945: A. S. MacMillan, J. B. McNair, Maurice Duplessis, G. A. Drew, J. W. Jones, T. C. Douglas, S. S. Garson, E. C. Manning, John Hart.

O'LEARY, DILLON They defend your dollar. What happened [to] the sugar shortage scare? Who broke the wool price rise? To advise, rather than to order, is the policy of Canada's Wartime Prices Board. (In *Maclean's*. Toronto. v. 53, no. 4 (Feb. 15, 1940), pp. 8; 46-47.)

O'LEARY, MICHAEL GRATTAN Backstage at Ottawa. By a Politician with a Notebook. (In *Maclean's*. Toronto. v. 53, no. 5 (Mar. 1, 1940), pp. 10; 49.)
Concerns the issues of the general elections held March 26, 1940.

—— Backstage at Ottawa. [The election: its personalities, mysteries, issues; its immediate and future consequences.] By a Politician with a Notebook. (In *Maclean's*. Toronto. v. 53, no. 9 (May 1, 1940), pp. 14; 51.)
Concerns the federal election held March 26, 1940.

—— Backstage at Ottawa. By a Politician with a Notebook. (In *Maclean's*. Toronto. v. 53, no. 20 (Oct. 15, 1940), pp. 12; 76.)
Discusses the idea of National Government and the wartime policies of the Liberal government.

—— Backstage at Ottawa. By a Politician with a Notebook. (In *Maclean's*. Toronto. v. 53, no. 23 (Dec. 1, 1940), pp. 8; 45; 48.)
General discussion of the war effort.

—— Backstage at Ottawa. By a Politician with a Notebook. (In *Maclean's*. Toronto. v. 54, no. 3 (Feb. 1, 1941), pp. 14; 39-40.)
General comments on the wartime economy.

—— Canada at war. By M. Grattan O'-Leary. (In *Queen's quarterly*. Kingston. v. 48 (1941), pp. [71]-79.)

Argues for the formation of a National War Cabinet to determine war policy.

—— Canada's G.O.C. By M. Grattan O'-Leary. (In *Maclean's*. Toronto. v. 52, no. 22 (Nov. 15, 1939), p. 12.)

Concerns Major-General A. G. L. Mc-Naughton.

—— Chief of Staff. By M. Grattan O'Lea-ry. (In *Maclean's*. Toronto. v. 53, no. 18 (Sept. 15, 1940), pp. 9; 34.)

Concerns Major-General A. McNaughton.

—— Price fixer. The young banker from Aberdeen who sets the limit on what you pay. By M. Grattan O'Leary. (In *Maclean's*. Toronto. v. 55, no. 2 (Jan. 15, 1942), p. 17.)

Concerns Donald Gordon, chairman of the Wartime Prices and Trade Board.

ORPWOOD, HELEN The Saskatoon by-election. (In *The Canadian forum*. Toronto. v. 20, no. 237 (Oct. 1940), pp. 210-211.)

"The by-election for the federal seat of Saskatoon . . . was notable chiefly for two things: first the phoenix-like rising from the ashes of the Conservative Party as a political force; and, second, the two and three-way splits in all other major parties."

The Saskatoon by-election was held August 19, 1940.

Ottawa letter. [Series I] (In *Saturday night*. Toronto. v. 53, no. 8—no. 42; v. 57, no. 21—v. 63, no. 40 (Dec. 25, 1937—Aug. 20, 1938; Jan. 31, 1942—July 10, 1948.)

Weekly comments on federal politics, written by Rideau Banks (Dec. 25, 1937—Aug. 20, 1938), G. C. Whittaker (Jan. 31, 1942—Jan. 6, 1945), Wilfrid Eggleston (Feb. 10—Mar. 31, 1945; June 2, 1945—June 21, 1947; Sept. 13, 1947—July 10, 1948) and Francis Flaherty (Apr. 7—May 26, 1945; June 28—Sept. 6, 1942).

OWEN, I. M. The frame-up of labor; editorial. (In *The Canadian forum*. Toronto. v. 26, no. 308 (Sept. 1946), pp. 126-127.)

Discusses the report issued by the Industrial Relations Committee of the House of Commons after its investigation of the steel strike.

PANABAKER, JOHN HARRY A survey of Canadian post-war monetary policy, 1946-1951. [Hamilton, Ont.] 1954. 114 [i.e. 115] leaves.

Thesis (MA) – McMaster University.

PAYNTER, SIMON Parliament before Christmas. (In *The Canadian forum*. Toronto. v. 27, no. 324 (Jan. 1948), pp. 221-223.)

A substantial article reviewing the activities of the fourth session of the twentieth parliament.

PERRAULT, JACQUES Ne votons pas par peur. (In *L'Action nationale*. Montréal. v. 19 (avril 1942), pp. [181]-189.)

Refers to the national plebiscite on the conscription issue held April 27, 1942.

PETERSON, CHARLES WALTER Home front preparedness. Peace or war, a regimenting of our economic forces is essential, says this writer, who is president and publisher of Farm and Ranch review. By C. W. Peterson. (In *Maclean's*. Toronto. v. 53, no. 7 (Apr. 1, 1940), pp. 24; 37-39.)

PHILLIPS, LESTER HENRY The impact of the Defence of Canada Regulations upon civil liberties. [Ann Arbor, 1945] viii, 348 leaves.

Thesis (PH D) – University of Michigan.

—— "Preventive detention" in Canada. (In *The Canadian forum*. Toronto. v. 26, no. 305 (June 1946), pp. 56-57.)

An analysis of the Defence of Canada Regulations.

PLUMPTRE, ARTHUR FITZWALTER WYNNE Newfoundland a province; can Canada afford it? By A. F. W. Plumptre. (In *Saturday night*. Toronto. v. 62, no. 42 (June 21, 1947), pp. 6-7.)

POIRIER, JEAN MARIE Crise au Canada. (In *Amérique française*. Montréal. (avril 1945), pp. [56]-64.)

At head of title: Politique.

Concerns the issue over conscription.

POLITICUS National affairs. "Let's face all the facts right now!" By Politicus. (In *Saturday night*. Toronto. v. 56, no. 8 (Nov. 2, 1940), p. 14.)

Concerns questions on the defence policy of Canada.

—— National affairs. It's your two-and-a-half bucks. By Politicus. (In *Saturday night*. Toronto. v. 56, no. 9 (Nov. 9, 1940), p. 9.)

Discusses the need for a parliamentary investigation into the CBC.

—— National affairs. Santa Claus came to Ottawa early. By Politicus. (In *Saturday night*. Toronto. v. 56, no. 11 (Nov. 23, 1940), p. 16.)

Comments on Premier William Aberhart's visit to Ottawa to discuss the centralization of financial power.

—— National affairs. "Friend and ally of the United States." By Politicus. (In *Saturday night*. Toronto. v. 56, no. 13 (Dec. 7, 1940), p. 14.)

Concerns the Ogdensburg Agreement, a statement on American and Canadian defence, issued jointly by President Roosevelt and Prime Minister King on August 17, 1939.

—— National affairs. National Government won't do the job. By Politicus. (In *Saturday night*. Toronto. v. 56, no. 14 (Dec. 14, 1940), p. 14.)

—— National affairs. And they're just starting now. By Politicus. (In *Saturday night*. Toronto. v. 56, no. 16 (Dec. 28, 1940), pp. 9; 29.)

Concerns the Wartime Requirements Board.

—— National affairs. Conscription for national unity. By Politicus. (In *Saturday night*. Toronto. v. 56, no. 23 (Feb. 15, 1941), p. 8.)

—— National affairs. That General McNaughton memorandum. By Politicus. (In *Saturday night*. Toronto. v. 56, no. 39 (Apr. 5, 1941), pp. 10-11.)

Concerns a memorandum arguing that "Canada should adopt a system of selectivity in dealing with its manpower in industry". It was submitted to the government on September 11, 1939.

—— National affairs. Who did support national government? By Politicus. (In *Saturday night*. Toronto. v. 56, no. 31 (Apr. 12, 1941), p. 8.)

Press election. (In *New world*. Toronto. v. 6, no. 12 (Feb. 1946), pp. 9-11.)

New world illustrated polls correspondents in the House of Commons Press Gallery to select the MP's of their choice from best speaker to best-dressed member. Presents the results of the poll.

Promoting patriotism. (In *The Canadian forum*. Toronto. v. 21, no. 252 (Jan. 1942), pp. 326-327.)

Comments on the conscription issue as presented by a small Toronto group voicing conservative opinion through a press campaign centred around the Toronto *Globe and Mail*.

PURCELL, GILLIS PHILIP Wartime press censorship in Canada. [Toronto, 1946] 156 leaves.

Thesis (MA) – University of Toronto.

Concerns World War II, 1939-45.

RAYMOND, MAXIME What does the Bloc Populaire stand for? How would Quebec's Bloc Populaire use power? Would it nationalize industry? Does it want to make Quebec a separate state; to take Canada out of the British Empire?... By Maxime Raymond, MP as quizzed by Blair Frazer. (In *Maclean's*. Toronto. v. 57, no. 1 (Jan. 1, 1944), pp. 8-10; 35-36.)

Responsible government—or union with Canada? These are the central figures in plebiscite showdown: P. J. Cashin, for responsible government; J. R. Smallwood, for Confederation; Crosbie, economic union with the U.S.; Bradley, big gun of "Confederate" party. (In *Atlantic guardian*. Montreal. v. 5, no. 2 (May 1948), pp. 14-19.)

Concerns Newfoundland and confederation with Canada.

RICHARDS, P. M. The business angle. Mr. Gordon and price control. (In *Saturday night*. Toronto. v. 57, no. 12 (Nov. 29, 1941), p. [36].)

RITCHIE, DAVID LAKIE Call Parliament. By D. L. Ritchie. (In *The New age*. Montreal. v. 1, no. 11 (Nov. 30, 1939), p. 6.)

Advocates that Parliament be convened in order to deal with wartime circumstances.

—— Divisive nationalism. By D. L. Ritchie. (In *The New age*. Montreal. v. 1, no. 8 (Nov. 9, 1939), p. 6.)

Concerns federal-provincial relations citing political relations between Quebec and the federal government.

—— Equality before the law. By D. L. Ritchie. (In *The New age*. Montreal. v. 1, no. 5 (Oct. 19, 1939), p. 6.)

Considers the national implications of actions taken by Premier Duplessis in Quebec.

—— A farmer's strike. By D. L. Ritchie. (In *The New age*. Montreal. v. 3, no. 5 (Feb. 6, 1941), pp. 6; 10.)

Considers the implications of a threatened strike by Western farmers.

—— Looking around. By D. L. Ritchie. (In *The New age*. Montreal. v. 2, no. 2 (Jan. 11, 1940), p. 6.)

Comments on the forthcoming session of Parliament, January 25, 1940.

—— National unity. By D. L. Ritchie. (In *The New age*. Montreal. v. 1, no. 13 (Dec. 14, 1939), p. 6.)

Comments on Canada during wartime.

—— Parliament assembles. By D. L. Ritchie. (In *The New age*. Montreal. v. 2, no. 44 (Nov. 7, 1940), pp. 6; 11.)

Comments on the second session of the nineteenth parliament.

—— Prospect point. By D. L. Ritchie. (In *The New age*. Montreal. v. 2, no. 14 (Apr. 4, 1940), p. 4.)

Comments, briefly, on the results of the federal election held March 26, 1940.

—— Social security. By D. L. Ritchie. (In *The New age*. Montreal. v. 2, no. 48 (Dec. 5, 1940), pp. 6; 11.)

—— A window on Ottawa. By D. L. Ritchie. (In *The New age*. Montreal. v. 3, no. 10 (June 1941), pp. 4; 7.)

Reviews the second session of the nineteenth parliament.

ROBERTS, LESLIE   Quebec and the war. Despite difficulties Jean Baptiste is doing well as a volunteer. Convince him that the Hun is at our gate, not at somebody else's gate; and he would accept conscription. (In *Maclean's*. Toronto. v. 54, no. 15 (Aug. 1, 1941), pp. 5-7; 30-31.)

—— What happened in Quebec. "The greatest single blow struck for Canadian unity in the past quarter century . . . at what seemed to be the darkest hour." (In *Maclean's*. Toronto. v. 52, no. 23 (Dec. 1, 1939), pp. 11-12.)

Concerns the defeat of the Maurice Duplessis government in the Quebec provincial election and the general implications.

—— Why Quebec feels that way. (In *Saturday night*. Toronto. v. 57, no. 19 (Jan. 17, 1942, p. 6.)

Analyses French-Canadian opposition to conscription.

ROBINSON, CHRISTOPHER C.   Income tax and increased population. (In *Saturday night*. Toronto. v. 56, no. 33 (Apr. 26, 1941), p. 13.)

Refers to the Income War Tax Act.

ROTHNEY, GORDON OLIVER   Leave Quebec alone. (In *The Canadian forum*. Toronto. v. 22, no. 260 (Sept. 1942), pp. 178-180.)

Discusses Anglo-French relations during the conscription crisis.

—— Parties and profits. (In *The Canadian forum*. Toronto. v. 20, no. 237 (Oct. 1940), pp. 204-206.)

Discusses the question of profiteering in war-time.

—— Quebec: watchful waiting. (In *The Canadian forum*. Toronto. v. 24, no. 289 (Feb. 1945), pp. 254-257.)

Analyses the political position taken toward the federal government by Quebec over the order-in-council passed on November 23, 1944, implementing conscription.

RUMILLY, ROBERT   La guerre de 1939-1945. Ernest Lapointe. Montréal, Fides [c1968] 318 p. (His *Histoire de la province de Québec*, 38.)

A political history covering the years 1939-1940.

—— La guerre de 1939-1945. Le Bloc Populaire. Montréal, Fides [c1969] 301 p. (His *Histoire de la province de Québec*, 40.)

A political history covering the years 1942-1943.

—— La guerre de 1939-1945. Duplessis reprend les rênes. Montréal, Fides [c1969] 321 p. (His *Histoire de la province de Québec*, 41.)

A political history covering the years 1944-1945.

—— La plébiscite. Montréal, Fides [c1969] 295 p. (His *Histoire de la province de Québec*, 39.)

A political history covering the years 1940-1942.

SANDERS, WILFRID   How will you vote? (In *New world*. Toronto. v. 6, no. 4 (June 1945), pp. 9-11.)

With reference to the federal election held June 11, 1945.

SANDWELL, BERNARD KEBLE   Canada's emergency powers. By B. K. Sandwell. (In *Saturday night*. Toronto. v. 54, no. 44 (Sept. 2, 1939), p. 2.)

—— Conscription and Mr. Richer. By B. K. Sandwell. (In *Saturday night*. Toronto. v. 56, no. 36 (May 17, 1941), p. 8.)

"A reply to Mr. Leopold Richer, Ottawa correspondent of 'Le Devoir', who has commented upon a proposal advanced in this paper that conscription be enforced in Canada, with the exception, if need be, of the Province of Quebec."

—— Creating a "council of perfection". By B. K. Sandwell. (In *Saturday night*.

Toronto. v. 55, no. 37 (July 13, 1940), p. 11.)

Discusses unemployment insurance and the Bennett Act of 1935.

—— The editor's chair. Conscription by back door? By B. K. Sandwell. (In *Saturday night*. Toronto. v. 57, no. 48 (Aug. 8, 1942), p. 12.)

—— The editor's chair. By McTague and Cohen. By B. K. Sandwell. (In *Saturday night*. Toronto. v. 59, no. 4 (Oct. 2, 1943), pp. 10-11.)

Concerns Justice C. P. McTague, Mr. Cohen and the McTague report on labour problems.

—— The federal election. By B. K. Sandwell. (In *Queen's quarterly*. Kingston. v. 47 (1940), pp. [89]-93.)

Comments on the war-time general elections held March 26, 1940.

—— From the editor's chair. Canada needs an economic grand strategy. By B. K. Sandwell. (In *Saturday night*. Toronto. v. 57, no. 46 (July 25, 1942), p. 8.)

—— From the editor's chair. Property has rights, even for Ukrainians. By B.K. Sandwell. (In *Saturday night*. Toronto. v. 58, no. 35 (May 8, 1943), pp. 22-23.)

Discusses the case where "the Government of Canada, acting under wartime powers conferred upon it by the War Measures Act, declared the Ukrainian Labor Farmer Temple Association an unlawful organization".

—— From the editor's chair. The campaign of the USWA. By B. K. Sandwell. (In *Saturday night*. Toronto. v. 58, no.39 (June 5, 1943), pp. 14-15.)

Concerns the "campaign of the United Steelworkers of America, Canadian national office, against the steel settlement as interpreted and administered by the National War Labor Board".

—— From the editor's chair. Are you voting for going on just as we have been? By B. K. Sandwell. (In *Saturday night*. Toronto. v. 59, no. 21 (Jan. 29, 1944), p. 10.)

Discusses *Canada after the War*, edited by A. Brady and F. R. Scott. Toronto, Macmillan, 1943.

—— From the editor's chair. Will the baby bonus provide the rallying cry against Quebec? By B. K. Sandwell. (In *Saturday night*. Toronto. v. 59, no. 50 (Aug. 19, 1944), p. 10.)

—— From the editor's chair. Problems of Canadian unity as seen by the Abbé Maheux. By B. K. Sandwell. (In *Saturday night*. Toronto. v. 60, no. 1 (Sept. 9, 1944), p. 9.)

—— From the editor's chair. Deportation order can involve big constitutional problems. By B. K. Sandwell. (In *Saturday night*. Toronto. v. 61, no. 28 (Mar. 16, 1946), p. 9.)

Concerns the orders-in-council for the deportation of Japanese-Canadians.

—— From the editor's chair. Canadian unity and separate school problem of Ontario. By B. K. Sandwell. (In *Saturday night*. Toronto. v. 61, no. 35 (May 4, 1946), pp. 16-17.)

—— From the editor's chair. A dubious future for Japanese children who get deported. By B. K. Sandwell. (In *Saturday night*. Toronto. v. 61, no. 42 (June 22, 1946), p. 12.)

Discusses the order-in-council PC 10773, dated November 26, 1942.

—— From the editor's chair. Dominion's emergency powers rest on slender foundation. By B. K. Sandwell. (In *Saturday night*. Toronto. v. 61, no. 44 (July 6, 1946), p. 10.)

Considers the Emergency Powers Extension Act.

—— From the editor's chair. When will Parliament say what is law about the steel strike? By B. K. Sandwell. (In *Saturday night*. Toronto. v. 61, no. 50 (Aug. 17, 1946), p. 14.)

—— From week to week. Conscription. By B. K. Sandwell. (In *Saturday night*. Toronto. v. 54, no. 46 (Sept. 16, 1939), p. 3.)

—— From week to week. How to work democracy. By B. K. Sandwell. (In *Saturday night*. Toronto. v. 55, no. 18 (Mar. 2, 1940), p. 3.)

—— From week to week. An abusive campaign. By B. K. Sandwell. (In *Saturday night*. Toronto. v. 55, no. 22 (Mar. 30, 1940), p. 3.)

Concerns the campaign conducted for the federal election held March 26, 1940.

—— From week to week. From Canadian history. By B. K. Sandwell. (In *Saturday night*. Toronto. v. 55, no. 32 (June 8, 1940), p. 3.)

Discusses, in an historical sense, Canadian defence policy.

—— From week to week. Democracy defends itself. By B. K. Sandwell. (In *Saturday night*. Toronto. v. 55, no. 37 (July 13, 1940), p. 3.)
Discusses the question of internment, with reference to Adrien Arcand and his fellow-conspirators.

—— From week to week. An appeal to the Senate. By B. K. Sandwell. (In *Saturday night*. Toronto. v. 55, no. 39 (July 27, 1940), p. 3.)
Pertains to unemployment insurance.

—— From week to week. The growing sense of insecurity. By B. K. Sandwell. (In *Saturday night*. Toronto. v. 56, no. 9 (Nov. 9, 1940), p. 6.)
Discusses the Defence of Canada Regulations.

—— [From] week to week. The veto power of Quebec. By B. K. Sandwell. (In *Saturday night*. Toronto. v. 57, no. 12 (Nov. 29, 1941), p. 6.)
Concerns compulsory service overseas.

—— [From] week to week. Nullification but not veto. By B. K. Sandwell. (In *Saturday night*. Toronto. v. 57, no. 17 (Jan. 3, 1942), p. 8.)
A criticism of André Laurendeau's views on conscription as expressed in his article "La conscription et le prétendu 'droit de veto' du Québec" (In *L'Action nationale*. Montreal. v. 18 (déc. 1941), pp. [258]-265.)

—— [From] week to week. Where is all this heading for? By B. K. Sandwell. (In *Saturday night*. Toronto. v. 57, no. 20 (Jan. 24, 1942), p. 15.)
Discusses the implications of two editorials from the Toronto *Globe and Mail* raising the issue of Quebec and conscription.

—— [From] week to week. Riots, 1918 and 1942. By B. K. Sandwell. (In *Saturday night*. Toronto. v. 57, no. 24 (Feb. 21, 1942), p. 19.)
Concerns the riots in Montreal over conscription.

—— The future of Confederation. By B. K. Sandwell. (In *Queen's quarterly*. Kingston. v. 49 (1942), pp. [166]-170.)
Comments on the tensions between French Canadians and English Canadians.

—— The theory behind the Marsh Report. By B. K. Sandwell. (In *Saturday night*. Toronto. v. 58, no. 29 (Mar. 27, 1943), pp. 6-7.)
Marsh report dealt with social security.

SAUNDERS, RICHARD M. The French-Canadians are ready to play ball. (In *Saturday night*. Toronto. v. 56, no. 47 (Aug. 2, 1941), p. 10.)
Concerns French Canadians and the war effort.

SCHULTZ, HAROLD J. A second term: 1940. (In *Alberta historical review*. Edmonton. v. 10, no. 1 (winter 1962), pp. 17-26.)
Examines the strategy of William Aberhart "to call a provincial election at the same time that the federal campaign was in process".

SCOTT, FRANCIS REGINALD Alignment of parties. By F. R. Scott. (In *The Canadian forum*. Toronto. v. 26, no. 314 (Mar. 1947), pp. 270-271.)

—— Comment le Canada est entré en guerre. Par Frank R. Scott. (In *L'Action nationale*. Montréal. v. 15 (mars 1940), pp. 232-240.)
Part 2 of Calendrier de guerre. Part 1 is Mémoires d'outre-tombe, by André Laurendeau.
A translation of the article which first appeared in *The Canadian forum*, v. 19, no. 229 (Feb. 1940), pp. 344-346.

—— Confederation; an assessment. By F. R. Scott. (In *The Canadian forum*. Toronto. v. 22, no. 258 (July 1942), pp. 104-106.)

—— The constitution and the war. By F. R. Scott. (In *The Canadian forum*. Toronto. v. 19, no. 226 (Nov. 1939), pp. 243-244.)

—— How Canada entered the war. By F. R. Scott. (In *The Canadian forum*. Toronto. v. 19, no. 229 (Feb. 1940), pp. 344-346.)
"Appended is a calendar of the principal events leading to Canada's entry into the war."
Contends that the phrase "Parliament will decide" is a mere slogan.

—— Parliament should decide. By F. R. Scott. (In *The Canadian forum*. Toronto. v. 19, no. 228 (Jan. 1940), pp. 311-313.)
Outlines the following issues: amendment to the Defence of Canada Regulations, profiteering and war finance, war contracts, war participation, war aims, internal reform.

—— The real vote in Quebec. By F. R. Scott. (In *The Canadian forum*. Toronto. v. 19, no. 227 (Dec. 1939), pp. 270-271.)

Considers the national significance of the results of the provincial election held October 25, 1939.

—— What did "no" mean? By F. R. Scott. (In *The Canadian forum*. Toronto. v. 22, no. 257 (June 1942), pp. 71-73.)
An analysis of the plebiscite held April 27, 1942, regarding conscription.

SCRUTINEER The Cartier by-election. By Scrutineer. (In *The Canadian forum*. Toronto. v. 23, no. 272 (Sept. 1943), pp. 126-127.)
The Cartier by-election held August 9, 1943.

SILCOX, CLARIS EDWIN Canada's need for conscription. (In *Saturday night*. Toronto. v. 57, no. 5 (Oct. 11, 1941), p. 6.)

—— The higher rationale of conscription. (In *Saturday night*. Toronto. v. 57, no. 3 (Sept. 27, 1941), p. 7.)

—— We must have faith in French Canada. (In *Saturday night*. Toronto. v. 57, no. 28 (Mar. 21, 1942), pp. 14-15.)

SOMERVILLE, HENRY Unsuspected quarters preach corporatism. (In *Saturday night*. Toronto. v. 60, no. 7 (Oct. 21, 1944), p. 8.)
Considers the views expressed in *Industry and humanity*, by W. L. Mackenzie King; and those advocated by Charles P. McTague.

STACEY, CHARLES PERRY Arms, men and governments; the war policies of Canada, 1939-1945. By C. P. Stacey. [Ottawa, Queen's Printer, 1970] xi, 681 p.
Issued by the Dept. of National Defence.
"References": pp. 607-642.

—— Through the Second World War. By Colonel C. P. Stacey. (In Careless, J. M. S. (ed.) *The Canadians, 1867-1967*. Toronto, 1967. pp. 275-308.)

STEWART, BRYCE M. War-time labour problems and policies in Canada. (In *The Canadian journal of economics and political science*. [Toronto] v. 7 (1941), pp. 426-446.)
Discusses Canadian war labour policy.

STEWART, JOHN BENJAMIN Parliament and executive in wartime Canada, 1939-1945. [New York, 1953?] 275 leaves.
Thesis (PH D) – Columbia University.

STEWART, WILLIAM JAMES Citizenship. By Hon. William J. Stewart. (In Empire Club of Canada. *Addresses*. Toronto. (1946/47), pp. 57-69.)
Address delivered October 31, 1946.

STRANGE, HARRY French Canadians will respond to honest plea. (In *Saturday night*. Toronto. v. 57, no. 50 (Aug. 22, 1942), p. 5.)
Concerns conscription.

SUMMERSKILL, EDITH Women's future. By Dr. Edith Summerskill, MP. (In *New world illustrated*. Montreal. v. 3, no. 6 (Aug. 1942), pp. 3; 44.)
Discusses the effect of the war on the emancipation of women.

TETREAU, JEAN Critique du gouvernement représentatif. (In *Amérique française*. Montréal. 5. année, no 9 (nov. 1946), pp. [38]-41.)
At head of title: Politique.
Comparative remarks.

That Bren gun contract. An independent view. (In *Maclean's*. Toronto. v. 54, no. 4 (Feb. 15, 1941), pp. 20; 35.)
"Editorial . . . from the January 10 issue of the [Winnipeg] Free Press."

THELLEND, M. La conscription et la solidarité, 1939-45. [Québec, 1961] 1 v.
Thesis (MA) – Laval University.

Those Pacific Coast contracts. Contractors selected without competition. Fortifications built on cost-plus basis. High rentals paid. Defense Department replies to criticism. (In *Maclean's*. Toronto. v. 52, no. 23 (Dec. 1, 1939), pp. 10; 51-53; 55.)

TOEWS, JOHN ARON Alternative service in Canada during World War II. [Winnipeg, 1957] 127 leaves.
Thesis (MA) – University of Manitoba.

La Triste histoire d'un débat historique. (In *L'Action nationale*. Montréal. v. 19 (fév/mars 1942), pp. [134]-144.)
Relates to the conscription issue.

TROTTER, REGINALD GEORGE Canada's partnership in freedom. By Professor Reginald Trotter. (In Empire Club of Canada. *Addresses*. Toronto. (1946/47), pp. 109-121.)
Address delivered November 28, 1946.

TURCOTTE, EDMOND A French Canadian's reply to the Bloc Populaire. (In *Maclean's*. Toronto. v. 57, no. 2 (Jan. 15, 1944), pp. 13; 45.)

—— What Canada's war effort might be. (In Lower, A. R. M. (ed.) *War and reconstruction*. Toronto [c1942] pp. 28-36.)
Discusses relations between French Canada and English Canada during wartime.

TWEED, JEAN Considerations in making a new immigration policy. (In *Saturday night.* Toronto. v. 63, no. 22 (Mar. 6, 1948), pp. 6-7.)

VAN GOGH, LUCY   He loved Canada and he made friends of Canadians. (In *Saturday night.* Toronto. v. 55, no. 16 (Feb. 17, 1940), p. 3.)
Concerns Governor-General of Canada John Buchan, Baron Tweedsmuir. A brief biographical sketch. written on the occasion of his death in Montreal Feb. 11, 1940.

VANIER, ANATOLE   Une claire idée de patrie. (In *L'Action nationale.* Montréal. v. 26 (oct. 1945), pp. [85]-93.)

VAUGHAN, ROBERT CHARLES   The railway at war. (In Empire Club of Canada. *Addresses.* Toronto. (1942/43), pp. 30-49.)
Address delivered October 1, 1942.
Centres discussion on the Canadian National Railways system.

VIGEANT, PIERRE   Session d'attente. (In *L'Action nationale.* Montréal. v. 31 (mai 1948), pp. [389]-395.)
Discusses the fourth session of the twentieth parliament.

WAKEMAN, ALBERT C.   When the government goes to the people. (In *Saturday night.* Toronto. v. 55, no. 14 (Feb. 3, 1940), pp. [11]; 13.)
"Economic interpretation of the sudden dissolution of Parliament and election announcement."

WALLACE, ROBERT CHARLES   Planning for Canada. By Robert C. Wallace. (In Royal Society of Canada. *Proceedings and transactions.* Ottawa. ser. 3, v. 35 (1941), Appendix A, pp. [63]-83.)
Presidential address.

WARING, GERALD H.   Are we doing all we should in pensions? (In *Saturday night.* Toronto. v. 60, no. 32 (Apr. 14, 1945), pp. 6-7.)

WATSON, JOHN L.   The week in radio. CBC's case in committee inquiry is upheld by majority opinion. (In *Saturday night.* Toronto. v. 61, no. 52 (Aug. 31, 1946), p. 19.)
Concerns the Parliamentary Committee appointed to inquire into the status of radio broadcasting in Canada.

WEATHERTON, WILLIAM   Remember the soldier vote in 1917? (In *Saturday night.* Toronto. v. 57, no. 31 (Apr. 11, 1942), p. 14.)
"The plebiscite on conscription this month will be the second time that the votes of soldiers on active service have been polled in a nationwide Canadian ballot. On the previous occasion the issue was also conscription."

WESTMAN, L. E.   The principle of National Selective Service. (In Lower, A. R. M. (ed.) *War and reconstruction.* Toronto [c1942] pp. 16-20.)

WHILLANS, RONALD   The Health Insurance Bill and its dental benefits. (In *Saturday night.* Toronto. v. 59, no. 26 (Mar. 4, 1944), p. 6.)

WHITTAKER, G. C.   Business men needed in planning. (In *Saturday night.* Toronto. v. 58, no. 41 (June 19, 1943), pp. 8-9.)
Proposes close co-operation between government and business in post-war planning.

——— Ottawa letter. Mr. Aberhart may be laughing. (In *Saturday night.* Toronto. v. 57, no. 28 (Mar. 21, 1942), p. 6.)
Comments on the price ceiling policy.

——— The Ottawa letter. Donald Gordon as a total war premier. (In *Saturday night.* Toronto. v. 57, no. 29 (Mar. 28, 1942), p. 13.)
Considers Donald Gordon for Prime Minister of Canada.

——— The Ottawa letter. Ottawa prepares for selective service. (In *Saturday night.* Toronto. v. 57, no. 32 (Apr. 18, 1942), p. 11.)

——— The Ottawa letter. Conscriptionists killing conscription? (In *Saturday night.* Toronto. v. 57, no. 41 (June 20, 1942), pp. 5; 14.)

——— The Ottawa letter. "Soft" recruitment policies. (In *Saturday night.* Toronto. v. 57, no. 42 (June 27, 1942), pp. 14-15.)

——— The Ottawa letter. Timidity holds up the manpower move. (In *Saturday night.* Toronto. v. 57, no. 50 (Aug. 22, 1942), p. 8.)
Concerns selective service measures.

——— Ottawa letter. Gordon turns to housing. (In *Saturday night.* Toronto. v. 58, no. 5 (Oct. 10, 1942), p. 11.)
Concerns Donald Gordon.

——— The Ottawa letter. The ceiling's the thing! (In *Saturday night.* Toronto. v. 58, no. 7 (Oct. 24, 1942), p. 16.)
Concerns controls on prices.

——— Ottawa letter. Selective Service rubber cheque. (In *Saturday night.* Toronto. v. 58, no. 12 (Nov. 28, 1942), pp. 10-11.)
Concerns the National Selective Service.

—— Ottawa letter. Price control boys are worried. (In *Saturday night*. Toronto. v. 58, no. 21 (Jan. 30, 1943), p. 14.)
Concerns anti-inflation measures.

—— The Ottawa letter. Controllers will "mobilize" newsprint industry. (In *Saturday night*. Toronto. v. 58, no. 23 (Feb. 13, 1943), p. 5.)
Discusses the effect of Donald Gordon's Wartime Prices and Trade Board Order 222 concerning newsprint production.

—— The Ottawa letter. Ottawa goes keen on production. (In *Saturday night*. Toronto. v. 58, no. 26 (Mar. 6, 1943), p. 16.)

—— The Ottawa letter. No security legislation. (In *Saturday night*. Toronto. v. 58, no. 29 (Mar. 27, 1943), p. 9.)

—— The Ottawa letter. u.s. gets tough with labor, but Canada—? (In *Saturday night*. Toronto. v. 58, no. 34 (May 1, 1943), p. 8.)
Discusses labour policy of the Canadian government.

—— The Ottawa letter. What labor is asking of NWLB. (In *Saturday night*. Toronto. v. 58, no. 36 (May 15, 1943), p. 8.)
Refers to the National War Labour Board.

—— The Ottawa letter. Labor dispute appellants need clean hands. (In *Saturday night*. Toronto. v. 58, no. 38 (May 29, 1943), p. 8.)
Concerns the ". . . refusal of Mr. Justice McTague's National War Labor Board to recognize Mr. Mosher's Canadian Brotherhood of Railway Employees as the bargaining agency for the employees of the Montreal Tramways. . . ."

—— The Ottawa letter. Our too clever Labor Department. (In *Saturday night*. Toronto. v. 58, no. 39 (June 5, 1943), p. 8.)
Concerns the ruling, in the Montreal Tramways case, by the National War Labour Board.

—— The Ottawa letter. Ministers might now be more explicit. (In *Saturday night*. Toronto, v. 58, no. 42 (June 26, 1943), pp. 8-9.)
Comments on the appointment of parliamentary assistants; the merchant marine, etc.

—— The Ottawa letter. Keeping down prices—and late hours. (In *Saturday night*. Toronto. v. 58, no. 44 (July 10, 1943), pp. 8-9.)
Comments on price control.

—— The Ottawa letter. It was not a memorable session. (In *Saturday night*. Toronto. v. 58, no. 47 (July 31, 1943), p. 8.)
Concerns the fourth session of the nineteenth parliament.

—— Ottawa letter. There may be a Dominion election. (In *Saturday night*. Toronto. v. 58, no. 52 (Sept. 4, 1943), p. 8.)
Comments on price ceilings and a possible federal election.

—— The Ottawa letter. Partial retreat from price ceilings indicated. (In *Saturday night*. Toronto. v. 59, no. 1 (Sept. 11, 1943), p. 8.)

—— Ottawa letter. Confusion in anti-inflation war. (In *Saturday night*. Toronto. v. 59, no. 2 (Sept. 18, 1943), pp. 8-9.)

—— The Ottawa letter. Shortening the anti-inflation line. (In *Saturday night*. Toronto. v. 59, no. 3 (Sept. 25, 1943), p. 8.)
Considers the report submitted as a result of the National War Labour Board inquiry on labour relations under the direction of Charles Patrick McTague.

—— The Ottawa letter. Ceiling crisis is over: line is held. (In *Saturday night*. Toronto. v. 59, no. 5 (Oct. 9, 1943), p. 8.)

—— The Ottawa letter. Don't bet on no election. (In *Saturday night*. Toronto. v. 59, no. 7 (Oct. 23, 1943), p. 8.)
Comments on a possible federal election.

—— The Ottawa letter. Will Quebec get wage parity? (In *Saturday night*. Toronto. v. 59, no. 8 (Oct. 30, 1943), p. 8.)
Urges the release of the McTague report in order to establish a new policy of wage and price controls.

—— The Ottawa letter. Signs of an early election? (In *Saturday night*. Toronto. v. 59, no. 10 (Nov. 13, 1943), p. 8.)

—— The Ottawa letter. Don't blame chairman McTague for the Labor Relations Plan. (In *Saturday night*. Toronto. v. 59, no. 19 (Jan. 15, 1944), p. 8.)

—— The Ottawa letter. Aids to business are the chief order of the day at Ottawa. (In *Saturday night*. Toronto. v. 59, no. 24 (Feb. 19, 1944), p. 8.)
Discusses policies initiated by J. A. MacKinnon and J. L. Ilsley.

—— The Ottawa letter. The boys in the ivory tower don't plan "a road back". (In *Saturday night*. Toronto. v. 59, no. 27 (Mar. 11, 1944), p. 8.)

Concerns a bill to incorporate the proposed Industrial Development Bank.

—— The Ottawa letter. With freedom from want goes much non-freedom from taxes. (In *Saturday night*. Toronto. v. 59, no. 32 (Apr. 15, 1944), p. 8.)
Discusses government finances in the post-war period.

—— The Ottawa letter. Can Canada avoid the prospect of government by log rolling? (In *Saturday night*. Toronto. v. 59, no. 48 (Aug. 5, 1944), p. 8.)
Concerns the prospect of a federal election and a divided vote.

—— The Ottawa letter. Canada prepares to spend herself out of debt after the war! (In *Saturday night*. Toronto. v. 59, no. 49 (Aug. 12, 1944), p. 8.)

—— The Ottawa letter. Provincial elections last week don't mean much federally. (In *Saturday night*. Toronto. v. 59, no. 50 (Aug. 19, 1944), p. 8.)
Comments on elections held in Alberta and Quebec.

—— The Ottawa letter. Pity we shan't have a conference on baby bonuses and suchlike. (In *Saturday night*. Toronto. v. 59, no. 51 (Aug. 26, 1944), p. 8.)

—— The Ottawa letter. After V-day Ottawa will drop most controls in a hurry. (In *Saturday night*. Toronto. v. 60, no. 4 (Sept. 30, 1944), p. 8.)

—— The Ottawa letter. Who will profit most next year out of the conscription issue? (In *Saturday night*. Toronto. v. 60, no. 15 (Dec. 16, 1944), pp. 8-9.)
Concerns the conscription issue and its impact on the outcome of a federal election.

—— The Ottawa letter. Ottawa would do well to tell us its plans for new war situation. (In *Saturday night*. Toronto. v. 60, no. 18 (Jan. 6, 1945), p. 8.)

WHITTON, CHARLOTTE Are family grants the answer we need? (In *Saturday night*. Toronto. v. 59, no. 50 (Aug. 19, 1944), pp. 6-7.)
"In this critical survey of the plan for cash family grants Dr. Whitton points out that administration properly belongs in the provincial sphere, that costs haven't been accurately estimated and that the benefits are to be distributed 'with no obligations of any kind'."

—— The baby bonus is a dog in the securi-

ty manger. (In *Saturday night*. Toronto. v. 60, no. 26 (Mar. 3, 1945), pp. 6-7.)
Second in a series of six articles.

—— Baby bonus plan involves waste and duplication. (In *Saturday night*. Toronto. v. 60, no. 28 (Mar. 17, 1945), pp. 6-7.)
Fourth in a series of six articles.

—— The feminine outlook. It's time for the woman voter to learn the facts of political life. (In *Saturday night*. Toronto. v. 62, no. 32 (Apr. 12, 1947), pp. [22-23].)

—— Is the Canadian woman a flop in politics? (In *Saturday night*. Toronto. v. 61, no. 21 (Jan. 26, 1946), pp. 6-7.)

—— Must review means as well as ways in welfare plans. (In *Saturday night*. Toronto. v. 60, no. 25 (Feb. 24, 1945), p. 6.)
First in a series of six articles.

—— National Housing Act must help low market class. (In *Saturday night*. Toronto. v. 61, no. 33 (Apr. 20, 1946), pp. 6-7.)

—— Other measures are more urgent than baby bonus. (In *Saturday night*. Toronto. v. 60, no. 29 (Mar. 24, 1945), p. 5.)
Fifth in a series of six articles.

—— We're off!! To social security confusion. (In *Saturday night*. Toronto. v. 60, no. 30 (Mar. 31, 1945), pp. 14-15.)
The last in a series of six articles.

—— What's the matter with us? (In *Chatelaine*. Toronto. v. 17, no. 12 (Dec. 1944), pp. 12-13; 39-40.)
Discusses the position of women in public life.

—— Will child bonus cripple provincial revenues? (In *Saturday night*. Toronto. v. 60, no. 27 (Mar. 10, 1945), p. 5.)
Third in a series of six articles.

—— Women hold the balance of power. (In *Chatelaine*. Toronto. v. 18, no. 5 (May 1945), pp. 7; 53; 55-56.)
Concerns the position of women in terms of voting power.

Will the Bloc Populaire win power in Quebec? (In *New world illustrated*. Toronto. v. 4, no. 10 (Dec. 1943), pp. 39-40.)
Gives a brief history and the platform of the party. Relates the development of the party to the question of Canadian unity.

WILLIAMSON, OWEN TEMPLETON GARRETT Our need is a "Canadians for Canada" party. By O. T. G. Williamson. (In *Saturday night*. Toronto. v. 57, no. 47 (Aug. 1, 1942), p. 6.)
Argues for a "Party of the Centre..."

—— We should have conscription now. By O. T. G. Williamson. (In *Saturday night*. Toronto. v. 56, no. 39 (June 7, 1941), pp. 14-15.)

WILSON, KENNETH R. Backstage at Ottawa. By the Man with a Notebook. (In *Maclean's*. Toronto. v. 52 [i.e. 55] no. 7 (Apr. 1, 1942), pp. 12-13; 43-44.)
Discusses the Victory Loan.

—— Backstage at Ottawa. By the Man with a Notebook. (In *Maclean's*. Toronto. v. 55, no. 9 May 1, 1942), pp. 14-15; 44-45.)
An analysis of the power of Donald Gordon who "derives his powers from an order in council".

—— Backstage at Ottawa. By the Man with a Notebook. (In *Maclean's*. Toronto. v. 55, no. 14 (July 15, 1942), pp. 15; 34.)
Discusses conscription; also, comments on price control.

—— Backstage at Ottawa. By the Man with a Notebook. (In *Maclean's*. Toronto. v. 55, no. 16 (Aug. 15, 1942), pp. 14-15; 30-31.)
Discusses the shortage of manpower.

—— Backstage at Ottawa. By the Man with a Notebook. (In *Maclean's*. Toronto. v. 55, no. 18 (Sept. 15, 1942), pp. 14-15; 45.)
Concerns the manpower crisis.

—— Backstage at Ottawa. By the Man with a Notebook. (In *Maclean's*. Toronto. v. 55, no. 20 (Oct. 15, 1942), pp. 14-15; 45-46.)
Discusses the Victory Loan, along with a discussion of Dieppe.

—— Backstage at Ottawa. By the Man with a Notebook. (In *Maclean's*. Toronto. v. 56, no. 6 (Mar. 15, 1943), pp. 14-15; 52.)
Comments on the Conservative Opposition, election possibilities, the McNaughton war strategy policy, etc.

—— Backstage at Ottawa. By the Man with a Notebook. (In *Maclean's*. Toronto. v. 56, no. 8 (Apr. 15, 1943), pp. 14-15; 49.)
Discusses the planning of Canada's social insurance program.

—— Backstage at Ottawa. By the Man with a Notebook. (In *Maclean's*. Toronto. v. 56, no. 10 (May 15, 1943), pp. 14-15; 59.)
Discusses manpower and labour problems.

—— Labor and the war. Canada's wartime labor policy—what it is, how it works—and why sometimes it doesn't. (In *Maclean's*. Toronto. v. 54, no. 19 (Oct. 1, 1941), pp. 16; 26-27; 30.)

—— Manpower boss. By K. R. W. (In *Maclean's*. Toronto. v. 55, no. 17 (Sept. 1, 1942), pp. 6; 35.)
Concerns Elliott M. Little appointed by the Government to head up its Wartime Bureau of Technical Personnel, February 1941.

Wipe out all patronage. A dollar wasted by any government department is a dollar less for our national war effort. (In *Maclean's*. Toronto. v. 52, no. 24 (Dec. 15, 1939), pp. 8; 33-34.)

You, the elections and civil liberty. (In *The New age*. Montreal. v. 2, no. 12 (Mar. 21, 1940), p. 8.)
"From the Bulletin of the Canadian Civil Liberties Union Montreal Branch."
Relates to the general elections held March 26, 1940.

YOUNG, EWART What would Confederation mean to Newfoundland? (In *Atlantic guardian*. Montreal. v. 3, no. 7 (July 1947), pp. 4-8.)

—— Will Newfoundland join Canada? (In *Maclean's*. Toronto. v. 59, no. 12 (June 15, 1946), pp. 7-8; 68-70.)

POLITICAL HISTORY
1948–1968

THE FIFTIES
1948–1957

ALLEN, RALPH For the sake of argument: Suppose Herbert Norman had been a Communist? (In *Maclean's*. Toronto. v. 70, no. 10 (May 11, 1957), pp. 8; 109-110.)

—— Will Dewline cost Canada its northland? (In *Maclean's*. Toronto. v. 69, no. 11 (May 26, 1956), pp. 16-17; 68-72.)

ANGERS, FRANCOIS ALBERT   A qui la faute? (In *L'Action nationale*. Montréal. v. 39 (mai 1952), pp. [261]-299.)
"Les solutions du Rapport Massey—III."
Concerns the report of the Royal Commission on National Development in the Arts, Letters and Sciences. Ottawa, E. Cloutier, Printer to the King, 1951. Commonly referred to as the Massey report.

—— Entre nous. (In *L'Action nationale*. Montréal. v. 49 (sept. 1959), pp. [21]-44.)
Contents: Un grave danger pour l'avenir du Canada et du Québec. – Le régime de l'impudence et de la grossièreté. – Le respect des contrats et la constitution! – La déclaration des anciens aumôniers de syndicats catholiques.

—— L'Ontario à signé! (In *L'Action nationale*. Montréal. v. 40 (nov. 1952), pp. [137]-161.)
Emphasizes the political aspects of federal-provincial relations.

—— Quant Ottawa s'en mêle; entretien avec Albert Lévesque, ancien Directeur provincial de l'aide à la jeunesse chômeuse. (In *L'Action nationale*. Montréal. v. 39 (avril 1952), pp. [214]-245.)
"Les solutions du Rapport Massey—II."
Concerns the report of the Royal Commission on National Development in the Arts, Letters and Sciences. Ottawa, E. Cloutier, Printer to the King, 1951. (The Massey report).

ARES, RICHARD   Précisions sur le patriotisme canadien-français. En marge du symposium de l'ACELF [i.e. Association des éducateurs de langue française]. (In *Relations*. Montréal. 17, année, no. 198 (juin 1957), pp. 157-160; 17. année, no 199 (juil. 1957), pp. (186-192.)
In two parts.

BARKWAY, MICHAEL   Constructive criticism called for. A reporter pleads for realism on defence to avoid confusion. Smart politicians are at a very heavy discount in 1951. (In *Saturday night*. Toronto. v. 66, no. 17 (Jan. 30, 1951), p. 7.)

—— "Crisis bachelors." The big wheels in defence machinery. (In *Saturday night*. Toronto. v. 66, no. 28 (Apr. 17, 1951), pp. [9]; 13.)
Concerns Crawford Gordon Jr., head of the Production Branch, and others.

—— Falling exports: rising MP's. (In *Sat-

urday night*. Toronto. v. 65, no. 26 (Apr. 4, 1950), p. 12.)
Concerns the second session of the twenty-first parliament.

—— The fifties; an Ottawa retrospect. (In *Waterloo review*. Waterloo, Ont. no. 5 (summer 1960), pp. 28-39.)

—— Freight rates tangle—gordian knot. Many agile brains are engrossed with a question that has been tied up with political expediency for several years. (In *Saturday night*. Toronto. v. 68, no. 9 (Dec. 6, 1952), pp. 9; 30; 32.)

—— Ottawa view. Combines: green, amber, green. (In *Saturday night*. Toronto. v. 67, no. 7 (Nov. 24, 1951), pp. 2-3.)
"The Government's plan to stop manufacturers from fixing retail prices has been a curious 'stop, caution, go' operation."

—— Ottawa view. This patronage business. (In *Saturday night*. Toronto. v. 67, no. 9 (Dec. 8, 1951), pp. 2-3.)

—— Ottawa view. Bold move on exchange control. Government's decision is trumpeted statement that it has no doubts about Canada's credit. (In *Saturday night*. Toronto. v. 67, no. 12 (Dec. 29, 1951), pp. 2; 6.)

—— Ottawa view. Some political shenanigans on resale price maintenance. (In *Saturday night*. Toronto. v. 67, no. 13 (Jan. 5, 1952), pp. 2; 6.)

—— Ottawa view. How Premier Frost claims to better Ottawa's offer. (In *Saturday night*. Toronto. v. 67, no. 26 (Apr. 5, 1952), pp. 2; 16.)
Concerns federal-provincial tax agreements.

—— Ottawa view. Parliament's waste of time is becoming scandalous. (In *Saturday night*. Toronto. v. 67, no. 27 (Apr. 12, 1952), pp. 2-3.)

—— Ottawa view. Elections coming up! (In *Saturday night*. Toronto. v. 67, no. 32 (May 17, 1952), pp. 2-3.)

—— Ottawa view. By-election echoes. (In *Saturday night*. Toronto. v. 67, no. 36 (June 14, 1952), pp. [2]-3.)

—— Ottawa view. New Act against combines. (In *Saturday night*. Toronto. v. 67, no. 40 (July 12, 1952), pp. 2; 16.)
Concerns revision of the Combines Investigation Act.

—— Parliaments gets under way. Taking the curse off conscription. (In *Saturday *night*. Toronto. v. 66, no. 19 (Feb. 13, 1951), p. [9].)

Refers to the fourth session of the twenty-first parliament opened January 30, 1951.

—— Parliament needn't make headlines. This has been one of the century's dullest sessions but it's been one in which much work was done. (In *Saturday night*. Toronto. v. 65, no. 41 (July 18, 1950), pp. 11; 15.)

Concerns the second session of the twenty-first parliament.

—— Parliament probes waste in defence. Civil servants are reminded of trust. They are responsible for public purse. (In *Saturday night*. Toronto. v. 67, no. 35 (June 7, 1952), pp. 10; 27.)

—— Parliament wakes up. Dollars, tempers and wheat. (In *Saturday night*. Toronto. v. 66, no. 25 (Mar. 27, 1951), pp. [9]; 16.)

Concerns the $65 million wheat bounty.

—— The political trend. (In *Saturday night*. Toronto. v. 68, no. 4 (Nov. 1, 1952), pp. [1]; 20.)

—— [Problems for the Royal Commission on Canada's Economic Prospects.] From the viewpoint of a political observer. (In Institute of Public Administration of Canada. *Proceedings of the annual conference*. Toronto. 7th (1955), pp. 19-31.)

—— This curious divorce business. (In *Saturday night*. Toronto. v. 66, no. 37 (June 19, 1951), pp. 9; 44.)

Concerns the divorce bills.

—— What defence for $5 billion? (In *Saturday night*. Toronto. v. 66, no. 20 (Feb. 20, 1951), p. 15.)

Comments on the national defence program.

BECK, JAMES MURRAY The election of 1957 and the Canadian electoral system. By J. M. Beck. (In *The Dalhousie review*. Halifax. v. 37 (1957/58), pp. [331]-340.)

Analyses the results of the general elections held June 10, 1957.

BERTON, PIERRE FRANCIS DE MARIGNY There'll always be a Massey. By Pierre Berton. (In *Maclean's*. Toronto. v. 64, no. 20 (Oct. 15, 1951), pp. [7]-9; 71-77.)

BIRD, JOHN Conservative gain of 20 to 30 seats. When the Liberals came to power in Ottawa in 1935 they controlled eight

out of nine provinces. Now they hold only three out of ten. (In *Canadian commentator*. Toronto. v. 1, no. 5 (May 1957), pp. 8-9.)

Estimates the 1957 federal election results.

—— Electoral jam spread thin. (In *Canadian commentator*. Toronto. v. 1, no. 4 (Apr. 1957), pp. 2-3.)

Discusses the impact on the forthcoming election of the preliminary report published by the Gordon Commission, the Coyne report on banking and the Fowler report on broadcasting.

—— Pearson may not want it. (In *Canadian commentator*. Toronto. v. 1, no. 3 (Mar. 1957), p. 9.)

Discusses the problems confronting both federal parties in their attempts to decide the question of leadership.

BODSWORTH, FREDERICK How serious is the defense scandal? By Fred Bodsworth. (In *Maclean's*. Toronto. v. 66, no. 3 (Feb. 1, 1953), pp. 7; 50-53.)

Analyses the Currie report.

—— Too much wheat. By Fred Bodsworth. (In *Maclean's*. Toronto. v. 67, no. 21 (Nov. 1, 1954), pp. [9]-11; 67-71.)

Examines the policy of the Canadian Wheat Board.

—— What the census man will find out. By Fred Bodsworth. (In *Maclean's*. Toronto. v. 64, no. 5 (Mar. 1, 1951), pp. 18-19; 49-51.)

—— What's behind the immigration wrangle? By Fred Bodsworth. (In *Maclean's*. Toronto. v. 68, no. 10 (May 14, 1955), pp. 12-13; 127-130.)

BRUNET, MICHEL Le rapport Massey; réflexions et observations. (In *L'Action universitaire*. Montréal. no. 2 (jan. 1952), pp. [39]-47.)

Concerns the report of the Royal Commission on National Development in the Arts, Letters and Sciences. Ottawa, 1951.

CAHILL, BRIAN Canadian politics and parties. (In *Atlantic guardian*. Montreal. v. 6, no. 4 (Apr. 1949), pp. 15-19.)

—— With our MP's at Ottawa. (In *Atlantic guardian*. v. 7, no. 2 (Feb. 1950), pp. 46-48.)

Comments on the performance of the MP's from Newfoundland during the first session of the twenty-first parliament.

CANADIAN TAX FOUNDATION The 1953 budget. Toronto [1951] 57 p. tables.
Cover title.

CLARK, JOHN ARTHUR Pick judges on merit, not politics. By J. A. Clark. (In *Saturday night*. Toronto. v. 67, no. 51 (Sept. 27, 1952), pp. 10; [14].)
"This article is based on Brigadier General Clark's presidential address to the Canadian Bar Association meeting in Vancouver. . . ."

CLAY, CHARLES Canada from sea to sea. (In *Atlantic guardian*. Montreal. v. 6, no. 3 (Mar. 1949), pp. 22-26; 29-33; 36; 39-40; 43-[53].)
"An introduction to the great Dominion of which Newfoundland now becomes a part, and a brief history of the stirring events leading up to the inclusion of the 'tenth province'."

COHEN, MAXWELL ABRAHAM Foreign policy and the election. (In *Saturday night*. Toronto. v. 72, no. 11 (May 25, 1957), pp. 10-11; 37-38.)
Refers to the federal election held June 10, 1957.

COHEN, NATHAN Television and the Massey Report. TV will creep in on soft-soled shoes. (In *Saturday night*. Toronto. v. 66, no. 38 (June 26, 1951), pp. 11; 36.)

CORBETT, DAVID CHARLES Canada's immigration policy; a critique. By David C. Corbett. Toronto, Published under the auspices of the Canadian Institue of International Affairs by University of Toronto Press, 1957. xii, 215 p.
This study is presented as "a description and explanation of Canadian immigration policy" and also as "a book of political criticism". – Pref. concerns the period after the Second World War.

CORRY, JAMES ALEXANDER Arms and the man. Defence powers and Parliament. By J. A. Corry. (In *Queen's quarterly*. Kingston. v. 62 (1955), pp. [315]-328.)
Discusses the parliamentary debate during June and July, 1955, on a bill to amend the Defence Production Act, 1951.

CRAIG, THELMA Where are the women in party politics? (In *Saturday night*. Toronto. v. 63, no. 48 (Sept. 4, 1948), p. 18.)

DANSEREAU, FERNAND La "gauche" au Canada. (In *L'Action nationale*. Montréal. v. 42 (Oct. 1953), pp. [92]-102.)

DENNIS, ERIC Hopes and fears in Canadian politics. (In *The Dalhousie review*. Halifax. v. 34 (1954/55), pp. [314]-324 [i.e. 10-20].)
Discusses the principles and methods adopted by Canadian political parties during the 1950s.

DEXTER, GRANT Politics, pipeline and Parliament. A salutary lesson? (In *Queen's quarterly*. Kingston. v. 63 (1956), pp. [323]-333.)

DINGMAN, HAROLD Pension poverty. Life on $30 a month is a better dose for our aged. But to raise pensions from the slum level would cost plenty. Can we afford it? (In *Maclean's*. Toronto. v. 62, no. 5 (Mar. 1, 1949), pp. 19; 35-38.)

Do women want women in public life? (In *Chatelaine*. Toronto. v. 21. no. 1 (Jan. 1948), pp. 12-13; 55.)
A survey of results gathered by *Chatelaine* Consumer Council reports.

EGGLESTON, WILFRID Capital comment. (In *Saturday night*. Toronto. v. 65, no. 1 –v. 67, no. 9 (Oct. 11, 1949 – Dec. 8, 1951.)
Column dealing with federal politics.

—— Capital comment. Aid for education –live issue. (In *Saturday night*. Toronto. v. 65, no. 5 (Nov. 8, 1949), p. 5.)

—— Capital comment. A resignation of protest. (In *Saturday night*. Toronto. v. 65, no. 6 (Nov. 15, 1949), p. 5.)
Concerns the resignation of Fred McGregor as a protest to the Combines Act.

—— Capital comment. The dilemma of defence. (In *Saturday night*. Toronto. v. 65, no. 7 (Nov. 22, 1949), p. 5.)

—— Capital comment. Millions for drought relief. (In *Saturday night*. Toronto. v. 65, no. 8 (Nov. 29, 1949), p. 5.)
Comments on the Prairie Farm Assistance Act.

—— Capital comment. National highway problems. (In *Saturday night*. Toronto. v. 65, no. 10 (Dec. 13, 1949), p. 5.)
Concerns the Trans-Canada Highway.

—— Capital comment. Donald Gordon has plan. (In *Saturday night*. Toronto. v. 65, no. 25 (Mar. 28, 1950), p. 3.)
Concerns the Canadian National Railways.

—— Capital comment. Saving taxpayer's dollar. (In *Saturday night*. Toronto. v. 65, no. 31 (May 9, 1950), p. 3.)
Comments on government expenditures.

—— Capital comment. Still awaits divorce remedy. (In *Saturday night*. Toronto. v. 65, no. 42 (July 25, 1950), p. 3.)

Comments on private divorce bills and Stanley Knowles's proposal to transfer jurisdiction to the Exchequer Court.

—— Capital comment. Why not a labor court? (In *Saturday night*. Toronto. v. 66, no. 1 (Oct. 10, 1950), p. 3.)

—— Capital comment. Second look at labor court. (In *Saturday night*. Toronto. v. 66, no. 3 (Oct. 24, 1950), p. 3.)

Comments on a proposal by Senator J. W. Farris.

—— Capital comment. Impact of defence on economy. (In *Saturday night*. Toronto. v. 66, no. 20 (Feb. 20, 1951), p. 3.)

—— Capital comment. Spotlight on divorce bills. (In *Saturday night*. Toronto. v. 66, no. 35 (June 5, 1951), p. 3.)

—— Capital comment. National irrigation policy. (In *Saturday night*. Toronto. v. 66, no. 45 (Aug. 14, 1951), p. 3.)

—— Capital comment. The case against fixed prices. (In *Saturday night*. Toronto. v. 67, no. 4 (Nov. 3, 1951), p. 40.)

Comments on the MacQuarrie interim report tabled Oct. 1, 1951.

—— Capital comment. This business of smuggling. (In *Saturday night*. Toronto. v. 67, no. 6 (Nov. 17, 1951), p. 45.)

Concerns A. W. Stuart's speech in the Commons regarding tariff policy.

—— Ottawa view. End of political doldrums. (In *Saturday night*. Toronto. v. 64, no. 5 (Nov. 6, 1948), p. 4.)

—— Ottawa view. Canada's defence strategy. (In *Saturday night*. Toronto. v. 64, no. 9 (Dec. 4, 1948), p. 4.)

—— Ottawa view. Last act of Confederation. (In *Saturday night*. Toronto. v. 64, no. 11 (Dec. 18, 1948), p. 4.)

Concerns the union of Newfoundland with Canada.

—— Ottawa view. Swift political change. (In *Saturday night*. Toronto. v. 64, no. 13 (Jan. 4, 1949), p. 4.)

—— Ottawa view. An election soon? (In *Saturday night*. Toronto. v. 64, no. 18 (Feb. 8, 1949), p. 4.)

—— Ottawa view. A new House spirit. (In *Saturday night*. Toronto. v. 64, no. 19 (Feb. 15, 1949), p. 4.)

—— Ottawa view. Stalemate in the offing.

A semi-miracle is now required for either old party to win. (In *Saturday night*. Toronto. v. 64, no. 22 (Mar. 8, 1949), p. 4.)

Brief comments.

—— Ottawa pattern. Vexing debate pattern. Debate on Throne Speech runs from cold weather to hot. (In *Saturday night*. Toronto. v. 64, no. 24 (Mar. 22, 1949), p. 4.)

—— Ottawa view. Talking in billions. Levelling-off figure of the budget may be cause for some concern. (In *Saturday night*. Toronto. v. 64, no. 25 (Mar. 29, 1949), p. 4.)

—— Ottawa view. Like a happy marriage. Plenty of give and take required for success of Confederation. (In *Saturday night*. Toronto. v. 64, no. 27 (Apr. 12, 1949), p. 4.)

—— Ottawa view. Last of the twentieth. Drama and suspense in House before undramatic finish. (In *Saturday night*. Toronto. v. 64, no. 31 (May 10, 1949), p. 4.)

Session ended April 30, 1949.

—— Ottawa view. Dullest and foggiest. Study of campaign literature inspires little enthusiasm. (In *Saturday night*. Toronto. v. 64, no. 32 (May 17, 1949), p. 4.)

Relates to federal election held June 27, 1949.

—— Ottawa view. Trend favors Liberals. Guess is Conservatives will gain seats but not enough to govern. (In *Saturday night*. Toronto. v. 64, no. 37 (June 21, 1949), p. 4.)

Brief comments relating to the federal election held June 27, 1949.

—— Ottawa view. Election was well timed. Economy strong until now, but worse weather may be ahead. (In *Saturday night*. Toronto. v. 64, no. 38 (June 28, 1949), p. 4.)

Brief comments on the federal election held June 27, 1949.

—— Ottawa view. More money for CBC. Since everything else is up, why not $4 radio licence? (In *Saturday night*. Toronto. v. 64, no. 50 (Sept. 20, 1949), p. 4.)

—— Ottawa view. New House of Commons. Relieves fears that many parties would impair democratic process. (In *Saturday night*. Toronto. v. 64, no. 51 (Sept. 27, 1949), p. 4.)

Refers to the first session of the twenty-first parliament which opened Sept. 15, 1949.

—— Our national budget. (In *Queen's quarterly*. Kingston. v. 57 (1950), pp. [211]-220.)

Discusses the national budget presented March 28, 1950. Contrasts, in order to consider implications, "the fiscal experience of 1945-'50 with that of the five years 1918-'23".

FERGUSON, GEORGE VICTOR Old, new strides in nationalism. Is the appointment of Vincent Massey as Governor General a new and startling departure? Or is it but one step in the long trend toward nationalism in Canada? A distinguished editor reviews our past and suggests a conclusive answer. By George V. Ferguson. (In *Saturday night*. Toronto. v. 67, no. 22 (Mar. 8, 1952), pp. 7; 17-18.)

FERLAND, PHILIPPE Il faut refaire la Confédération. (In *L'Action nationale*. Montréal. v. 44 (sept. 1954), pp. [15]-58.)

FILION, GERARD Pour un mouvement républicain. (In *L'Action nationale*. Montréal. v. 32 (oct. 1948), pp. [142]-148.)

FLAHERTY, J. FRANCIS Which Canadian will be the Governor-General? By Frank Flaherty. (In *Saturday night*. Toronto. v. 67, no. 6 (Nov. 17, 1951), pp. [11]; [29].)

FORSEY, EUGENE ALFRED The next Governor-General. By Eugene Forsey. (In *The Canadian forum*. Toronto. v. 37, no. 444 (Jan. 1958), pp. 225-226.)

Examines the qualifications to be considered in choosing a person for this position.

FOX, PAUL WESLEY Election myths. By P.W. F. (In *The Canadian forum*. Toronto. v. 37, no. 436 (May 1957), pp. 27-28.)

A discussion of the campaign preceding the general elections of June 10, 1957.

—— The score on June 10. By Paul W. Fox. (In *Canadian commentator*. Toronto. v. 1, no. 5 (May 1957), p. 17.)

With reference to the general elections held June 10, 1957.

—— A study of one constituency in the Canadian federal election of 1957. By Paul W. Fox. (In *The Canadian journal of economics and political science*. [Toronto] v. 24 (1958), pp. 230-240.)

"This article attempts to describe the process of election as it occurred in one Canadian constituency in the federal general election of June 10, 1957. . . . Constituency x is a large residential electoral district,

part of which lies within Metropolitan Toronto." The article is a hypothetical, illustrative study.

FRANCIS, ANNE Une Canadienne-anglaise juge notre attitude envers Ottawa. (In *L'Action nationale*. Montréal. v. 44 (mars 1955), pp. [616]-622.)

—— Women in politics. (In *Canadian commentator*. Toronto. v. 1, no. 5 (May 1957), pp. 9-10.)

FRASER, BLAIR Are we headed for an unemployment crisis? (In *Maclean's*. Toronto. v. 67, no. 10 (May 15, 1954), pp. 9-10; 95-99.)

—— Backstage at Ottawa. How (gulp) to pick a leader. By the Man with a Notebook. (In *Maclean's*. Toronto. v. 61, no. 15 (Aug. 1, 1948), pp. 15; 52.)

Comments on the leaders of the Dominion and provincial governments.

—— Backstage at Ottawa. Power politics. By the Man with a Notebook. (In *Maclean's*. Toronto. v. 61, no. 22 (Nov. 15, 1948), pp. 14; 68-69.)

Concerns the development of power on the St. Lawrence River.

—— Backstage at Ottawa. What the Truman upset meant to Canada. By the Man with a Notebook. (In *Maclean's*. Toronto. v. 61, no. 24 (Dec. 15, 1948), pp. 14; 42.)

—— Backstage at Ottawa. They dished the dirt at Nicolet. By the Man with a Notebook. (In *Maclean's*. Toronto. v. 62, no. 6 (Mar. 15, 1949), pp. 14; 68; 70.)

Concerns the by-election held at Nicolet-Yamaska, Que., February 7, 1949.

—— Backstage at Ottawa. Liberal—CCF coalition? No, but . . . By the Man with a Notebook. (In *Saturday night*. Toronto. v. 62, no. 10 (May 15, 1949), pp. 14; 82-83.)

—— Backstage at Ottawa. Is it time for a change? By the Man with a Notebook. (In *Maclean's*. Toronto. v. 62, no. 11 (June 1, 1949), pp. 14; 58.)

Discusses the need for a federal election.

—— Backstage at Ottawa. These experts picked the Liberals. By the Man with a Notebook. (In *Maclean's*. Toronto. v. 62, no. 14 (July 15, 1949), pp. 14; 52.)

Concerns the predictions of parliamentary reporters with regard to the federal election held June 27, 1949.

—— Backstage at Ottawa. Morale is low all round. By the Man with a Notebook.

(In *Maclean's*. Toronto. v. 62 no. 21 (Nov. 1, 1949), pp. 14; 55.)

—— Backstage at Ottawa. The whisper of conscription. (In *Maclean's*. Toronto. v. 65 [i.e. 63] no. 21 (Nov. 1, 1950), pp. 4; 52-54.)

Concerns the results of an anti-Korean War speech made in the House of Commons by Henri Courtemanche, and other matters.

—— Backstage at Ottawa. Aroused but not rattled. (In *Maclean's*. Toronto. v. 64, no. 7 (Apr. 1, 1951), pp. 5; 63.)

Random remarks covering a variety of subjects.

—— Backstage at Ottawa. Clearing up the recruiting mess. (In *Maclean's*. Toronto. v. 64, no. 15 (Aug. 1, 1951), pp. 5; 42.)

—— Backstage at Ottawa. Health insurance on the horizon. (In *Maclean's*. Toronto. v. 64, no. 16 (Aug. 15, 1951), pp. 5; 30.)

—— Backstage at Ottawa. More money for MP's and old folks. (In *Maclean's*. Toronto. v. 64, no. 20 (Oct. 15, 1951), pp. 5; 70-71.)

—— Backstage at Ottawa. How we check on loyalty. (In *Maclean's*. Toronto. v. 65, no. 2 (Jan. 15, 1952), pp. 5; 44.)

—— Backstage at Ottawa. The statue that came to life. (In *Maclean's*. Toronto. v. 65, no. 5 (Mar. 1, 1952), pp. 5; 46.)

Discusses the popularity of Viscount Alexander of Tunis as Governor-General of Canada (March 21, 1946—Feb. 1, 1952).

—— Backstage at Ottawa. A Dominion first and last. (In *Maclean's*. Toronto. v. 65, no. 6 (Mar. 15, 1952), pp. 5; 66-67.)

Discusses the arguments over constitutional phraseology that developed upon the accession to the throne of Queen Elizabeth II.

—— Backstage at Ottawa. Will the MPS get their pensions? (In *Maclean's*. Toronto. v. 65, no. 7 (Apr. 1, 1952), pp. 5; 45-46.)

—— Backstage at Ottawa. How wide is the split over NATO? (In *Maclean's*. Toronto. v. 65, no. 8 (Apr. 15, 1952), pp. 5; 49-59.)

—— Backstage at Ottawa. The scramble for seats. (In *Maclean's*. Toronto. v. 65, no. 10 (May 15, 1952), pp. 5; 76-77.)

—— Backstage at Ottawa. By-election blues. (In *Maclean's*. Toronto. v. 65, no. 11 (June 1, 1952), pp. 5; 50.)

Examines the implications for federal political parties of the by-election held in Gloucester, N.B., May 26, 1952.

—— Backstage at Ottawa. Do four wins make a trend? (In *Maclean's*. Toronto. v. 65, no. 13 (July 1, 1952), pp. 5; 44.)

The effect of provincial Quebec party politics on the federal Conservative and Liberal parties.

—— Backstage at Ottawa. Fewer guns, more butter. (In *Maclean's*. Toronto. v. 65, no. 20 (Oct. 15, 1952), pp. 5; 82.)

Discusses the 1953 election budget, CBC television and the National Film Board, and the redistribution of parliamentary seats.

—— Backstage at Ottawa. Outlook for winter: hot. (In *Maclean's*. Toronto. v. 65, no. 22 (Nov. 15, 1952), pp. 5; 94-95.)

Reviews the general political scene. Considers that the opening of the session is, in effect, "the opening of the 1953 election campaign".

—— Backstage at Ottawa. Will Ike's win hasten our election? (In *Maclean's*. Toronto. v. 65, no. 24 (Dec. 15, 1952), pp. 5; 57-58.)

—— Backstage at Ottawa. About ghosts and scandals. (In *Maclean's*. Toronto. v. 66, no. 2 (Jan. 15, 1953), pp. 5; 59.)

Discusses an immigration scandal and political speech-writing.

—— Backstage at Ottawa. Petawawa horses were overworked. (In *Maclean's*. Toronto. v. 66, no. 3 (Feb. 1, 1953), pp. 5; 54-55.)

Discusses the Currie report.

—— Backstage at Ottawa. Free speech and thin skins. (In *Maclean's*. Toronto. v. 66, no. 6 (Mar. 15, 1953), pp. 5; 74-75.)

Concerns free speech on the radio as a serious election campaign issue.

—— Backstage at Ottawa. The election mud starts to fly. (In *Maclean's*. Toronto. v. 66, no. 9 (May 1, 1953), pp. 5; 75.)

Refers to the campaign for the federal election held August 10, 1953.

—— Backstage in the campaign. Will the parties keep their leaders? (In *Maclean's*. Toronto. v. 66, no. 16 (Aug. 15, 1953), pp. 5; 55-56.)

Considers the results of the federal election held August 10, 1953.

—— Backstage at Ottawa. Should the

backbenchers pipe down? (In *Maclean's.* Toronto. v. 66, no. 24 (Dec. 15, 1953), pp. 6; 52-53.)

—— Backstage at Ottawa. Are we nearer our own flag? (In *Maclean's.* Toronto. v. 67, no. 3 (Feb. 1, 1954), pp. 5; 42.)

—— Backstage at Ottawa. More Canadians than jobs. (In *Maclean's.* Toronto. v. 67, no. 5 (Mar. 1, 1954), pp. 6; 49-50.)

—— Backstage at Ottawa. Dominion day 1954: Where do we stand? (In *Maclean's.* Toronto. v. 67, no. 13 (July 1, 1954), pp. 5; 50.)

—— Backstage at Ottawa. The divorce committee at bay. (In *Maclean's.* Toronto. v. 67, no. 14 (July 15, 1954), pp. 5; 61-62.)

—— Backstage at Ottawa. Was there a seaway sellout? (In *Maclean's.* Toronto. v. 67, no. 19 (Oct. 1, 1954), pp. 6; 86.)

—— Backstage at Ottawa. Who guards the freedom of worship? (In *Maclean's.* Toronto. v. 68, no. 9 (Apr. 30, 1955), pp. 8; 83.)
Discusses the issue as it came up for review before the Supreme Court of Canada, April 26, 1955.

—— Backstage at Ottawa. Should our flyers come home? (In *Maclean's.* Toronto. v. 68, no. 10 (May 14, 1955), pp. 6; 120.)
Discusses the problem: Should Canada continue to maintain an air division overseas while U.S. squadrons come in to guard the Canadian north?

—— Backstage at Ottawa. Even Ontario's Grits see a Tory win. (In *Maclean's.* Toronto. v. 68, no. 12 (June 11, 1955), pp. 7; 103.)

—— Backstage at Ottawa. A case of fisherman's luck? (In *Maclean's.* Toronto. v. 68, no. 16 (Aug. 6, 1955), pp. 5; 54-55.)
Discusses the issue as to the introduction of a guaranteed annual wage.

—— Backstage at Ottawa. The safe seat that wasn't. (In *Maclean's.* Toronto. v. 68, no. 23 (Nov. 12, 1955), pp. 5; 121.)
Discusses the by-election won by the Conservative Party at Restigouche-Madawaska, N.B., September 26, 1955.

—— Backstage at Ottawa. How near is health insurance? (In *Maclean's.* Toronto. v. 68, no. 24 (Nov. 26, 1955), p. 6.)

—— Backstage at Ottawa. What do civil rights mean in Quebec? (In *Maclean's.*

Toronto. v. 69, no. 1 (Jan. 7, 1956), pp. 3; 46.)

—— Backstage at Ottawa. A national health plan next year? (In *Maclean's.* Toronto. v. 69, no. 6 (Mar. 17, 1956), pp. 6; 81.)

—— Backstage at Ottawa. Could a CCF–Tory team take Ottawa? (In *Maclean's.* Toronto. v. 69, no. 18 (Sept. 1, 1956), pp. 8; 59-60.)

—— Backstage at Ottawa. Can politics compete with Howdy Doody? (In *Maclean's.* Toronto. v. 69, no. 25 (Dec. 8, 1956), pp. 10; 123.)
Discusses "whether television at a leadership convention will do good or harm to a Canadian political party".

—— Backstage at Ottawa. Where can Ottawa spend its hoarded half-billion? (In *Maclean's.* Toronto. v. 69, no. 26 (Dec. 22, 1956), pp. 5; 44.)
Concerns the spending of a budget surplus during an election year.

—— Backstage at Ottawa. The Norman case shows who's boss in the U.S. but should we let them say who's loyal in Canada too? (In *Maclean's.* Toronto. v. 70, no. 10 (May 11, 1957), p. 2.)
Reference is to Herbert Norman.

—— Backstage at Ottawa. Why both Liberals and Tories are ignoring Quebec. Why Lionel Chevrier's return made 68 MP's mad. (In *Maclean's.* Toronto. v. 70, no. 11 (May 25, 1957), p. 2.)

—— Backstage at Ottawa. Tories now think they'll pick up thirty seats and win. The Liberals admit it's not so preposterous. (In *Maclean's.* Toronto. v. 70, no. 12 (June 8, 1957), p. 2.)
Relates to the federal election held June 10, 1957.

—— Backstage at Ottawa. Sure, the political campaigns were important—but did they have to be the colossal bores they were? (In *Maclean's.* Toronto. v. 70, no. 12 [i.e. 13] (June 22, 1957), p. 2.)
Refers to the general elections held June 10, 1957.

—— Backstage at Ottawa. How will Supreme Court weight Duplessis' power? (In *Maclean's.* Toronto. v. 71, no. 12 (June 7, 1958), p. 2.)

—— Blair Fraser keeps a rendezvous with Igor Gouzenko. (In *Maclean's.* Toronto. v. 66, no. 17 (Sept. 1, 1953), pp. 9; 48-52.)

—— Can McCarthy happen here? (In *Maclean's*. Toronto. v. 67, no. 6 (Mar. 15, 1954), pp. 14-[15]; 74-78.)

—— Conscription! (In *Maclean's*. Toronto. v. 64, no. 6 (Mar. 15, 1951), pp. 14; 59-62.)

—— Election campaign. How (and why) do people get into politics? Here is the inside story of a hard clean battle now near its climax. (In *Maclean's*. Toronto. v. 62, no. 12 (June 15, 1949), pp. 8-9; 58-60.)

Concerns the federal election campaign conducted in the constituency of Durham, Ont., with a view to the general elections held June 27, 1949.

—— Houses, houses, where are the houses? The more homes we build, the greater the shortage. How come? Here's the answer, and a hint of better times—a year away. (In *Maclean's*. Toronto. v. 62, no. 5 (Mar. 1, 1949), pp. 7; 52-53.)

Concerns government housing policy.

—— How racketeers sold entry into Canada. (In *Maclean's*. Toronto. v. 65, no. 6 (Mar. 15, 1952), pp. 10-11; 61-62.)

—— A new blueprint for Confederation. (In *Maclean's*. Toronto. v. 68, no. 24 (Nov. 26, 1955), pp. [11]-13; 98-99.)

—— Ottawa's creaky divorce machine. (In *Maclean's*. Toronto. v. 68, no. 22 (Oct. 29, 1955), pp. 9-11; 61-65.)

—— The Prairies' political preachers. (In *Maclean's*. Toronto. v. 68, no. 13 (June 25, 1955), pp. 24-25; 68-75.)

Concerns Thomas Clement Douglas (CCF premier of Saskatchewan) and Ernest Charles Manning (Social Credit premier of Alberta), with reference to their relations with the federal government.

—— The truth about our Arctic defense. (In *Maclean's*. Toronto. v. 67, no. 22 (Nov. 15, 1954), pp. 20; 50-56.)

—— Various aspects of the Ottawa scene. (In Empire Club of Canada. *Addresses*. Toronto. (1949/50), pp. 160-169.)

Address delivered January 12, 1950.

—— Your stake in the U.S. election. (In *Maclean's*. Toronto. v. 69, no. 21 (Oct. 13, 1956), pp. 13-15; 109-112.)

FRECKER, HELENA M.   Vers la Confédération. (In *Relations*. Montréal. 9. année, no. 97 (Jan. 1949), pp. 5-9.)

Concerns Newfoundland.

GREENE, LORNE   One view: radio and Massey Report. New talent: who is fairy godmother? (In *Saturday night*. Toronto. v. 66, no. 40 (July 10, 1951), pp. 13; [28.].)

GREY, RODNEY   1949 budget marks turning-away from an enlightened policy. (In *Saturday night*. Toronto. v. 64, no. 26 (Apr. 5, 1949), p. [30].)

HODGETTS, JOHN EDWIN   The coming federal elections. By J. E. Hodgetts. (In *Queen's quarterly*. Kingston. v. 60 (1953), pp. [199]-207.)

Examines the Canadian electoral system in relation to the general elections held August 10, 1953.

How you did it—but not why: the vast machinery of an election. A Saturday night photostory. (In *Saturday night*. Toronto. v. 64, no. 38 (June 28, 1949), pp. 2-3. illus.)

Refers to the general elections held June 27, 1949.

HUTCHISON, BRUCE   Are we licking inflation? (In *Maclean's*. Toronto. v. 64, no. 14 (July 15, 1951), pp. 21; 29-31.)

—— The coming battle for the Columbia. (In *Maclean's*. Toronto. v. 69, no. 20 (Sept. 29, 1956), pp. 11-13; 28-35.)

—— They're killing our democracy. Who are? Politicians who feed the public myths, not facts; MP's who meekly take orders from the government; ministers who let civil servants decide policies; voters who accept double talk in lieu of the truth. (In *Maclean's*. Toronto. v. 63, no. 12 (June 15, 1950), pp. 10-11; 27-28.)

A general statement on the principles and practices of modern democracy, with special reference to the Canadian democratic system.

INGLIS, PETER   Inflation control: Ottawa hot potato. (In *Saturday night*. Toronto. v. 66, no. 51 (Sept. 25, 1951), pp. [10]; 33.)

IRVING, JOHN ALLAN   Television performance, unknown factor in winning elections. By John A. Irving. (In *Saturday night*. Toronto. v. 72, no. 10 (May 11, 1957), pp. 9; 43.)

Relates to the federal election campaign of 1957.

JEWETT, PAULINE MAE   The padlock case. By Pauline Jewett. (In *The Canadian forum*. Toronto. v. 37, no. 435 (Apr. 1957), pp. 7-8.)

Examines the decision handed down by the Supreme Court of Canada and the significance of that ruling towards the guaranteeing of fundamental freedoms assumed by the Canadian constitution.

KATZ, SIDNEY How Toronto's evening papers slanted the election news. (In *Maclean's*. Toronto. v. 62, no. 15 [i.e. 16] (Aug. 15, 1949), pp. 10-11; 53-54.)
Relates to the federal election held June 27, 1949.

—— What kind of man was Herbert Norman? (In *Maclean's*. Toronto. v. 70, no. 20 (Sept. 28, 1957), pp. 22-23; 83-92.)
Concerns the career and death of the Canadian Ambassador to Egypt.

KAUFMAN, FRED Knowledge will be their guide. Supreme Court of Canada to gain by appointment of two eminent jurists from Quebec and Ontario. By Fred Kaufman and Gordon McCaffrey. (In *Saturday night*. Toronto. v. 65, no. 18 (Feb. 7, 1950), p. 9.)
Concerns the appointment to the Supreme Court of Justice Gerald Fauteux and Justice John Cartwright.

KEENLEYSIDE, HUGH LLEWELLYN Canadian immigration policy. By H. L. Keenleyside. (In *International journal*. Toronto. v. 3 (summer 1948), pp. 222-238.)
Traces the historical background of Canadian immigration and discusses current policy.

KENNEDY, GILBERT D. Canadian divorce laws: changing views. (In *Saturday night*. Toronto. v. 68, no. 11 (Dec. 20, 1952), pp. 11; 22.)

KILBOURN, WILLIAM MORLEY The 1950s. By William Kilbourn. (In Careless, J. M. S. (ed.) *The Canadians, 1867-1967*. Toronto, 1967. pp. 309-343.)

—— Pipeline; Transcanada and the great debate; a history of business and politics. By William Kilbourn. Toronto, Clarke, Irwin, 1970. xiii, 222 p.

KLOK, PIERRE L'essentiel d'une politique d'immigration. (In *Relations*. Montréal. 15. année, no 180 (déc. 1955), pp. 315-316.)

KWAVNICK, DAVID The roots of French-Canadian discontent. By D. Kwavnick. (In *The Canadian journal of economics and political science*. [Toronto] v. 31 (1965), pp. [509]-523.)
Considers the stresses in Canadian federalism in the light of changes occurring in French Canada between 1945 and 1960. The Author attempts "to examine the manner

in which these changes have affected the basic assumptions upon which the co-existence of English and French in Canada has rested since 1867".

LAMBERT, NORMAN PLATT What wheat? Why Ottawa is in the grain business. By Norman P. Lambert. (In *Saturday night*. Toronto. v. 67, no. 46 (Aug. 23, 1952), pp. 15; 24-25.)

LAURENDEAU, ANDRE Henri Bourassa. (In *L'Action nationale*. Montréal. (sept./oct. 1952), pp. [7]-10.)
Written on the occasion of his death August 30, 1952.

—— Y a-t-il une crise du nationalisme? (In *L'Action nationale*. Montréal. v. 40 (déc. 1952), pp. [207]-225; v. 41 (jan. 1953), pp. [6]-28.)
In two parts.

LEMIEUX, EDMOND La pure Ottawa? (In *L'Action nationale*. Montréal. v. 41 (fév. 1953), pp. [145]-151.)
A discussion of the Currie report. The Report disclosed financial irregularities at the army base at Petawawa, Ont.

LEONARD, WILLIAM GEORGE The Currie report. By W. G. Leonard. (In *Queen's quarterly*. Kingston. v. 60 (1953), pp. [101]-107.)
Describes the reaction in the House of Commons to the Report investigating army expenditure irregularities at Petawawa.

LEVITT, MORTIMER Drew-Duplessis alliance. (In *The Canadian forum*. Toronto. v. 28, no. 337 (Feb. 1949), pp. 251-252.)
Contends that the alliance "has as its aim the elevation to federal power of George Drew and the emergence of Premier Duplessis as a force in Dominion politics".

LIGUE D'ACTION NATIONALE Conditions d'un Etat français dans la Confédération canadienne. (In *L'Action nationale*. Montréal. v. 43 (mars/avril 1954), pp. [328]-350.)
"Mémoire de la Ligue d'action nationale à la Commission royale d'enquête sur les relations fédérales-provinciales."
"Ce mémoire, préparé par Me Jean-Marc Léger, secrétaire de la ligue, fut présenté à la Commission Tremblay le 25 février 1954."

LIST, WILFRED Congress conventions. What's ahead on the labor scene? (In *Saturday night*. Toronto. v. 69 [i.e. 68] no. 3 (Oct. 25, 1952), pp. 13; 32a-32b.)
Discusses the position of the Trades and Labor Congress of Canada, the Canadian

Congress of Labour and brief comments on the CCF.

LIVESAY, DOROTHY Women in public life —do we want them? (In *Saturday night*. Toronto. v. 64, no. 41 (July 19, 1949), p. 17.)

LOFFT, JOHN My six weeks with the Comrades. (In *Maclean's*. Toronto. v. 67, no. 3 (Feb. 1, 1954), pp. 7-9; 54-58.)

The Author relates his experiences and reveals his contacts with youth in left-wing movements both in Canada and abroad in attending the World Youth Festival in Bucharest. Considers the membership and activities of the Canadian Peace Council and the Canadian Youth Friendship League, etc.

LONG, MARCUS And was Goliath surprised! (In *Canadian commentator*. Toronto. v. 1, no. 6 (June 1957), pp. [1]-2.)

Analyses the results of the general elections held June 10, 1957.

LOWER, ARTHUR REGINALD MARSDEN For the sake of argument: Is the RCMP a threat to our liberty? By Arthur Lower. (In *Maclean's*. Toronto. v. 70, no. 14 (July 6, 1957), pp. 8; 57-58.)

If we joined the U.S.A. If customs union led to annexation, Canada might gain a richer life at little cost—except her soul. By Arthur Lower. (In *Maclean's*. Toronto. v. 61, no. 12 (June 15, 1948), pp. 7-8; 71-74.)

MAC RAE, CHRISTOPHER FREDERICK (ed.) French Canada today: report of the Mount Allison Summer Institute. A. Davidson Dunton, chairman. Edited by C. F. MacRae. Sackville, N.B. [Mount Allison University, 1961?]

Partial contents: The role of Canadian dualism in the shaping of our federal structure, by N. Dorion.

MALLORY, JAMES RUSSELL The election and the constitution. By J. R. Mallory. (In *Queen's quarterly*. Kingston. v. 64 (1957), pp. [465]-483.)

Part I of Canadian election in retrospect. Part II, Analysing the vote, is by John Meisel (pp. [484]-495).

Analyses the results of the federal election held June 10, 1957.

MEISEL, JOHN After June 10. (In *The Canadian forum*. Toronto. v. 37, no. 438 (July 1957), pp. [73]; 96.)

General comments on the significance of the results of the federal election held June 10, 1957.

Analysing the vote. The "psephologists'" paradise. (In *Queen's quarterly*. Kingston. v. 64 (1957), pp. [484]-495.)

Part II of Canadian election in retrospect. Part I, The election and the constitution, is by J. R. Mallory (pp. [465]-483).

"This article will give a glimpse of how psephologists might tackle some problems presented by the 1957 Canadian general election."

The Canadian general election of 1957. [Toronto] University of Toronto Press [1962] xiv, 313 p. (Canadian government series, 13.)

Map: 1953 election; 1957 election (in pocket at end).

First issued as thesis (PH D) – London School of Economics, University of London, 1959.

The formulation of Liberal and Conservative programmes in the 1957 Canadian general election. (In *The Canadian journal of economics and political science*. [Toronto] v. 26 (1960), pp. 565-574.)

"This paper was presented at the annual meeting of the Canadian Political Science Association in Kingston, June 9, 1960."

Religious affiliation and electoral behaviour: a case study. (In *The Canadian journal of economics and political science*. [Toronto] v. 22 (1956), pp. 481-496.)

"This paper was presented at the annual meeting of the Canadian Political Science Association in Montreal, June 6, 1956."

Discusses a study that was made of the activities of political parties, the candidates, the press, and the radio during and after the campaigns of the 1953 federal and the 1955 provincial elections held in Kingston, Ont.

Religious affiliation and electoral behaviour; a case history. (In Courtney, J. C. (ed.) *Voting in Canada*. [Scarborough, Ont., c1967] pp. [144]-161.)

"Reprinted from The Canadian journal of economics and political science, XXII (November) 1956."

Relates the subject to an analysis of the 1953 federal election and the 1955 provincial election results in Kingston, Ont.

MORGAN, M. O. Newfoundland, our tenth province. (In *Queen's quarterly*. Kingston. v. 56 (1949), pp. [258]-267.)

Concerns the entry of Newfoundland into Confederation. Deals "with the historical background of the negotiations, the political alternatives, and the degree of Newfoundland's responsibility for the final choice".

NEWELL, I.   Newfoundland, Canada. (In *Queen's quarterly*. Kingston. v. 56 (1949), pp. [268]-276.)

Traces the developments leading to the entry of Newfoundland into confederation with Canada.

Ottawa letter. [Series II] (In *Saturday night*. Toronto. v. 68, no. 11 — v. 84, no. 3 (Dec. 20, 1952 — Mar. 1969).)

Column dealing with federal politics, written by John A. Stevenson (Dec. 20, 1952 — Sept. 13, 1958), Logan MacLean, Edwin Copps, Peter Stursberg (July 23 — Oct 1, 1960; Jan. 20 — July 7, 1962; Aug. 1963 — Oct. 1964), Raymond Rodgers, Laocoon, Mungo James, Christina Newman, and others.

Ottawa view. (In *Saturday night*. Toronto. v. 63, no. 41 — v. 68, no. 10 (July 17, 1948 — Dec. 13, 1952).)

Column dealing with federal politics, written by Wilfrid Eggleston (July 17, 1948 — June 28, 1949; Sept. 13 — Oct. 4, 1949), B. T. Richardson (July 5 — Sept. 6, 1949), Michael Barkway (Sept. 25, 1951 — Dec. 13, 1952), and others.

PELLETIER, CHARLES   Faut-il confier à Ottawa l'avenir de notre groupe ethnique? (In *L'Action nationale*. Montréal. v. 45 (sept. 1955), pp. [22]-35.)

At head of title: Notre enquête 1955 (4).

PETRIE, JOSEPH RICHARDS   Paying for government in Canada. By J. R. Petrie. (In *Public affairs*. Halifax. v. 14, no. 1 (autumn 1951), pp. [25]-33. tables.)

PHELPS, ARTHUR LEONARD   Why men fear women voters. By Arthur L. Phelps. (In *Chatelaine*. Toronto. v. 26, no. 8 (Aug. 1953), pp. 16-17.)

With reference to the federal election held August 10, 1953.

PHILIP, PERCY J.   Ottawa letter. Unemployment optimism and pirouettes. (In *Saturday night*. Toronto. v. 70, no. 24 (Mar. 19, 1955), pp. 16-17.)

PHILLIPS, ALAN   Who will win the great gas pipeline stakes? (In *Maclean's*. Toronto. v. 66, no. 19 (Oct. 1, 1953), pp. 18-19; 81-86.)

PLANTE, ALBERT   Prêts du gouvernement aux immigrants. (In *Relations*. Montréal. 16. année, no 182 (fév. 1956), pp. 33-35.)

PORTER, JOHN A.   Political parties and the political career. (In Thorburn, H. G. (ed.) *Party politics in Canada*. Toronto. [c1963] pp. 142-145.)

"Reprinted from The Canadian forum, xxxviii, June, 1958."

Comments on the downfall of the Liberal Party and the ascension of the Conservative Party to power in 1957 and 1958, relating this development in a brief examination of the failure of Canadian political leadership.

PORTER, MC KENZIE   The pulse of French Canada. (In *Maclean's*. Toronto. v. 67, no. 6 (Mar. 15, 1954), pp. 18-19; 63-68.)

RAYFIELD, FRED W.   Canada, born in age of Empires, has outlasted most of them. (In *Saturday night*. Toronto. v. 64, no. 38 (June 28, 1949), pp. 6-7.)

"Once again it is Dominion Day, a good occasion for thinking of where Canada came from, and where she is going."

REID, JOHN HOTCHKISS STEWART   Wanted: a political party for Canada. By J. H. Stewart Reid. (In *Saturday night*. Toronto. v. 71, no. 20 (Dec. 8, 1956), pp. 7-8.)

ROBINSON, JUDITH   This is on the House. With occasional observations by Grassick. Toronto, McClelland & Stewart [1957] 160 p.

Most of the articles first appeared in the *Toronto Telegram*.

This is a "record of four parliamentary years" from 1952 to 1956 during the Liberal administration of Louis St. Laurent.

SAGER, SAMUEL C.   Parliamentary control over expenditure in the fiscal year, 1957-58: the Governor General's warrants. (In *Canadian public administration*. Toronto. v. 4 (1961), pp. 310-315.)

SANDERS, WILFRID   How polls like that happen. (In *Canadian commentator*. Toronto. v. 1, no. 6 (June 1957), pp. 14-15.)

The Author: Co-Director of the Canadian Institute of Public Opinion.

Examines the election reports issued by the Canadian Institute of Public Opinion, preceding the general elections held June 10, 1957.

SANDWELL, BERNARD KEBLE   The Council for culture. By B. K. Sandwell. (In *Saturday night*. Toronto. v. 66, no. 36 (June 12, 1951), p. 7.)

Discusses the Report of the Royal Commission on Arts, Letters and Sciences, popularly known as the Massey report.

—— The Crown in Canada. By B. K. Sandwell. (In *Saturday night*. Toronto. v. 67, no. 17 (Feb. 2, 1952), pp. 3; 30.)
Concerns the forthcoming appointment of a Canadian to the post of Governor-General.

—— "Entrenched" clauses. Easy PC angle for Quebec. By B. K. Sandwell. (In *Saturday night*. Toronto. v. 67, no. 33 (May 24, 1952), pp. 4-5.)
Deals with the problem of amending the Canadian constitution.

—— Kingdom of Canada. Personal relationship of King and Canadians. By B. K. Sandwell. (In *Saturday night*. Toronto. v. 66, no. 52 (Oct. 6, 1951), pp. 4-5.)
Argues that the King should live in Canada for a portion of each year.

—— Mr. Massey's job. Delegate of King of Canada. By B. K. Sandwell. (In *Saturday night*. Toronto. v. 67, no. 19 (Feb. 16, 1952), pp. 5; 38.)
Concerns Vincent Massey (Governor-General of Canada, 1952-1959).

—— The 1949 elections. By B. K. Sandwell. (In *Queen's quarterly*. Kingston. v. 56 (1949), pp. [425]-431.)

—— Periodical press and Massey Report. Fourth estate: power or pressure? By B. K. Sandwell. (In *Saturday night*. Toronto. v. v. 66, no. 47 (Aug. 28, 1951), p. 12.)

SANFORD, JOHN X. Best man at labor's wedding. (In *Maclean's*. Toronto. v. 68, no. 17 (Aug. 20, 1955), pp. 18-19; 38-41.)
Concerns Claude Jodoin.

SCHMITT, GILBERT R. Canadian politicians and the Bench. It helps Canadian lawyers a great deal to be faithful party adherents when vacancies occur among our judges, and new ones are being chosen. (In *Saturday night*. Toronto. v. 67, no. 41 (July 19, 1952), p. 7.)

SIMONDS, GUY Where we've gone wrong on defense. By Lieut.-General Guy Simonds. (In *Maclean's*. Toronto. v. 69, no. 13 (June 23, 1956), pp. 22-23; 62-69.)

SINGER, PAUL DAVID The administration and scope of Canadian anti-monopoly policy since the Second World War. [Montreal] 1954. 1 v.
Thesis (MA) – McGill University.

SOCIETE SAINT-JEAN-BAPTISTE DE MONTREAL

Canada français et union canadienne. Mémoire présenté le 13 mai 1954 à la Commission royale d'enquête sur les problèmes constitutionnels. Lettre-préf. de Me F.-Eugène Therrien, président général. Montréal, Editions de l'Action nationale, 1954. 127 p.

STEVENSON, JOHN A. 1953: election year. (In *Saturday night*. Toronto. v. 68, no. 16 (Jan. 24, 1953), pp. [1]; 19-21.)

—— Ottawa letter. Senate is busy on Criminal Code. (In *Saturday night*. Toronto. v. 68, no. 12 (Dec. 27, 1952), pp. 4; 18.)

—— Ottawa letter. Defence spending under fire. (In *Saturday night*. Toronto. v. 68, no. 17 (Jan. 31, 1953), pp. 4; 8.)

—— Ottawa letter. Early election is possible. (In *Saturday night*. Toronto. v. 68, no. 18 (Feb. 7, 1953), pp. 14-15.)

—— Ottawa letter. Unity of the nation. (In *Saturday night*. Toronto. v. 68, no. 20 (Feb. 21, 1953), pp. 4; 8.)
Brief comments on the Currie report, defence, foreign policy, etc.

—— Ottawa letter. Humiliation in the Commons. (In *Saturday night*. Toronto. v. 68, no. 26 (Apr. 4, 1953), pp. 12-13.)
Concerns the Macnab report on the Department of National Defence, etc.

—— Ottawa letter. Coronation rush on Parliament Hill. (In *Saturday night*. Toronto. v. 68, no. 28 (Apr. 18, 1953), p. 16.)
Comments on defence spending; the position of Thomas Goode, Liberal MP for Burnaby, B.C., etc.

—— Ottawa letter. Competing for the farm vote. (In *Saturday night*. Toronto. v. 68, no. 29 (Apr. 25, 1953), pp. 14-15.)

—— Ottawa letter. Members look beyond prorogation. (In *Saturday night*. Toronto. v. 68, no. 30 (May 2, 1953), p. 9.)

—— Ottawa letter. The unmourned death of a session. (In *Saturday night*. Toronto. v. 68, no. 34 (May 30, 1953), p. 14.)
Concerns the seventh session of the twenty-first parliament.

—— Ottawa letter. As the election campaign starts. (In *Saturday night*. Toronto. v. 68, no. 35 (June 6, 1953), p. 16.)
Concerns the general election held August 10, 1953.

—— Ottawa letter. Pre-election policies

and portents. (In *Saturday night*. Toronto. v. 68, no. 38 (June 27, 1953), p. 11.)

Concerns the campaign for the federal election held August 10, 1953.

—— Ottawa letter. Platforms, promises and possibilities. (In *Saturday night*. Toronto. v. 68, no. 39 (July 4, 1953), p. 10.)

Refers to the campaign for the federal election held August 10, 1953.

—— Ottawa letter. They turn their faces to the east. (In *Saturday night*. Toronto. v. 68, no. 40 (July 11, 1953), p. 10.)

Concerns the campaign for the federal election held August 10, 1953. The Conservative and Liberal parties seek support from the Maritimes as they anticipate little support from the West.

—— Ottawa letter. Main contenders sharpen their weapons. (In *Saturday night*. Toronto. v. 68, no. 41 (July 18, 1953), p. 10.)

Comments on Louis St. Laurent, J. W. Pickersgill, J. Smallwood and George Drew with regard to the federal election held August 10, 1953.

—— Ottawa letter. Rough ground for the old parties. (In *Saturday night*. Toronto. v. 68, no. 44 (Aug. 18, 1953), p. 10.)

Concerns the status of the Liberal and Conservative parties in Alberta and British Columbia with reference to the federal election held August 10, 1953.

—— Ottawa letter. The conduct of the federal campaign. (In *Saturday night*. Toronto. v. 68, no. 45 (Aug. 15, 1953), p. 10.)

Comments on Prime Minister St. Laurent and George Drew, with reference to the federal election held August 10, 1953.

—— Ottawa letter. Decisive mandate for the Liberals. (In *Saturday night*. Toronto. v. 68, no. 46 (Aug. 22, 1953), p. 10.)

Discusses the results of the federal election held August 10, 1953.

—— Ottawa letter. Liberals, Socialists and big business. (In *Saturday night*. Toronto. v. 68, no. 47 (Aug. 29, 1953), p. 9.)

—— Ottawa letter. Behind the election's statistics. (In *Saturday night*. Toronto. v. 68, no. 48 (Sept. 5, 1953), p. 10.)

Concerns statistics on the general elections held August 10, 1953.

—— Ottawa letter. Stronger immigration policy needed. (In *Saturday night*. Toronto. v. 68, no. 50 (Sept. 19, 1953), pp. 16-17.)

—— Ottawa letter. Wanted: more crusaders in politics. (In *Saturday night*. Toronto. v. 69, no. 9 (Dec. 5, 1953), pp. 16-17.)

Comments on W. Harris, George Drew, M. J. Coldwell, S. Low, and C. D. Howe.

—— Ottawa letter. Windy debate delays legislation. (In *Saturday night*. Toronto. v. 69, no. 11 (Dec. 19, 1953), pp. 12-13.)

Concerns the debate on the Throne Speech delivered to the first session, twenty-second parliament.

—— Ottawa letter. Leadership in the new parliament. (In *Saturday night*. Toronto. v. 69, no. 13 (Jan. 2, 1954), p. 10.)

Comments on Louis St. Laurent, C. D. Howe, and George Drew.

—— Ottawa letter. Pay boosts, housing and unemployment. (In *Saturday night*. Toronto. v. 69, no. 19 (Feb. 13, 1954), p. 10.)

—— Ottawa letter. Parliament loses its insularity. (In *Saturday night*. Toronto. v. 69, no. 21 (Feb. 27, 1954), p. 10.)

—— Ottawa letter. Mortgages, jobs and by-elections. (In *Saturday night*. Toronto. v. 69, no. 23 (Mar. 13, 1954), p. 11.)

Includes comment on a by-election to be held March 22 in Elgin, Ont.

—— Ottawa letter. Changing Acts and clarifying policy. (In *Saturday night*. Toronto. v. 69, no. 25 (Mar. 27, 1954), pp. 11-12.)

Comments on the Bank Act, the Criminal Code, and Canada's relations with the government of China.

—— Ottawa letter. More questions about security checks. (In *Saturday night*. Toronto. v. 69, no. 26 (Apr. 3, 1954), pp. 11-12.)

—— Ottawa letter. The budget and the tax battle. (In *Saturday night*. Toronto. v. 69, no. 29 (Apr. 24, 1954), pp. 12-13.)

—— Ottawa letter. Interruptions in the budget debate. (In *Saturday night*. Toronto. v. 69, no. 32 (May 15, 1954), p. 17.)

Discussion of the Emergency Powers Act, provincial autonomy, the Dept. of Public Works, etc.

—— Ottawa letter. Party leaders define their positions. (In *Saturday night*. Toronto. v. 69, no. 33 (May 22, 1954), pp. 12-13.)

Concerns federal-provincial relations on taxation. Cites, especially, difficulties with Maurice Duplessis.

—— Ottawa letter. The by-elections in Quebec. (In *Saturday night*. Toronto. v. 69, no. 52 (Oct. 2, 1954), p. 12.)

Concerns the by-elections held November 8, 1954, in St.-Antoine Westmount and St. Lawrence–St. George, Quebec.

—— Ottawa letter. Political warfare and Mr. Drew's position. (In *Saturday night*. Toronto. v. 70, no. 1 (Oct. 9, 1954), pp. 12-13.)

Discusses the contention between Louis St. Laurent and Maurice Duplessis and the position of George Drew.

—— Ottawa letter. More to elections than ringing doorbells. (In *Saturday night*. Toronto. v. 70, no. 8 (Nov. 27, 1954), p. 9.)

Discusses the campaigning behind the by-elections held November 8, 1954, in St.-Antoine Westmount and St. Lawrence–St. George, Quebec.

—— Ottawa letter. The possibilities of agrarian revolt. (In *Saturday night*. Toronto. v. 70, no. 12 (Dec. 25, 1954), p. 9.)

—— Ottawa letter. Better handling of Parliament's business. (In *Saturday night*. Toronto. v. 70, no. 17 (Jan. 29, 1955), p. 9.)

Refers to the second session, twenty-second parliament.

—— Ottawa letter. Criticism from East and West. (In *Saturday night*. Toronto. v. 70, no. 19 (Feb. 12, 1955), pp. 12-13.)

Concerns a confrontation between Louis St. Laurent and Davie Fulton.

—— Ottawa letter. Plenty of work remains for Parliament. (In *Saturday night*. Toronto. v. 70, no. 23 (Mar. 12, 1955), pp. 12-13.)

Refers to the second session of the twenty-second parliament.

—— Ottawa letter. Political storms on the prairies. (In *Saturday night*. Toronto. v. 70, no. 30 (Apr. 30, 1955), p. 10.)

—— Ottawa letter. Questions of time and money in Parliament. (In *Saturday night*. Toronto. v. 70, no. 35 (July 9, 1955), pp. 16-17.)

Concerns the Defence Production Bill.

—— Ottawa letter. Heat and words. (In *Saturday night*. Toronto. v. 70, no. 36 (July 23, 1955), p. 11.)

Concerns debate on the Defence Production Bill.

—— Ottawa letter. Summing up the session. (In *Saturday night*. Toronto. v. 70, no. 37 (Aug. 6, 1955), pp. 16-17.)

Comments on the second session of the twenty-second parliament.

—— Ottawa letter. The by-elections. (In *Saturday night*. Toronto. v. 70, no. 42 (Oct. 15, 1955), pp. 13-14.)

Comments on federal by-elections held in Restigouche-Madawaska, N.B.; Temiscouata, Que.; Bellechasse, Que., and Quebec South

—— Ottawa letter. Chilly receptions. (In *Saturday night*. Toronto. v. 70, no. 46 (Dec. 10, 1955), pp. 23-24; 27.)

Comments on a possible agrarian revolt in response to government wheat policy.

—— Ottawa letter. Some contrasts in the 1955 picture. (In *Saturday night*. Toronto. v. 70, no. 48 (Jan. 7, 1956), p. 11.)

—— Ottawa letter. Political climate in the new year. (In *Saturday night*. Toronto. v. 70, no. 49 (Jan. 21, 1956), pp. 14-15.)

—— Ottawa letter. Strategy for the battles ahead. (In *Saturday night*. Toronto. v. 70, no. 50 (Feb. 4, 1956), p. 16.)

Concerns the third session of the twenty-second parliament.

—— Ottawa letter. Help in Quebec. (In *Saturday night*. Toronto. v. 72 [i.e. 71] no. 3 (Apr. 14, 1956), pp. 21-22.)

Analyses the effects of a forthcoming Quebec provincial election in June 1956 upon the position of the federal political parties.

—— Ottawa letter. New pipeline planning. (In *Saturday night*. Toronto. v. 72 [i.e. 71] no. 4 (Apr. 28, 1956), pp. 25-26.)

—— Ottawa letter. Revived by a whiff of gas. (In *Saturday night*. Toronto. v. 71, no. 7 (June 9, 1956), p. 18.)

Comments on parliamentary debating over the Trans-Canada Pipeline issue.

—— Ottawa letter. Debate in the shadow of election. (In *Saturday night*. Toronto. v. 72, no. 4 (Feb. 16, 1957), p. 24.)

Comments on the fifth session of the twenty-second parliament.

—— Ottawa letter. The press and the election. (In *Saturday night*. Toronto. v. 72, no. 7 (Mar. 30, 1957), pp. 21-22.)

Refers to the federal election held June 10, 1957.

—— Ottawa letter. Campaign in the heartland. (In *Saturday night*. Toronto. v. 72, no. 9 (Apr. 27, 1957), pp. 5-6.)

Discusses the 1957 federal election campaign conducted in Ontario and Quebec.

—— Ottawa letter. Political pilgrims' progress. (In *Saturday night*. Toronto. v. 72, no. 10 (May 11, 1957), pp. 6-7.)

Assesses the issues and personalities involved in the federal election held June 10, 1957.

—— Ottawa letter. A baffling year ahead. (In *Saturday night*. Toronto. v. 72, no. 13 (June 22, 1957), pp. 4-5.)

Discusses the results of the federal election held June 10, 1957.

STUCHEN, PHILIP Labour presents its case. (In *Queen's quarterly*. Kingston. v. 59 (1952), pp. [15]-23.)

Discusses the nature and procedure of the annual meeting held between organized labour and members of the federal cabinet.

STURSBERG, PETER Ottawa letter. The day of the great upset. (In *Saturday night*. Toronto. v. 77, no. 3 (Feb. 3, 1962), pp. 23-24.)

Retrospective comments on the federal election of June 10, 1957.

TEDMAN, JOYCE Woman of the week. Canada's ambassadress. (In *Saturday night*. Toronto. v. 65, no. 22 (Mar. 7, 1950), pp. [28]-30.)

Concerns Mme Pauline Vanier.

THOMAS, ALAN TV in Canadian politics. (In *Saturday night*. Toronto. v. 1, no. 8 (Aug. 1957), pp. [1]-2.)

Concentrates on the role played by television during the campaign for the general elections of June 10, 1957.

THOMSON, DALE C. The cabinet of 1948. (In Gibson, F. W. (ed.) *Cabinet formation and bicultural relations* [Ottawa, 1970] pp. [143]-154.)

THORBURN, HUGH GARNET Canadian government policy in the oil and gas industries. By H. G. Thorburn. (In *The Dalhousie review*. Halifax. v. 37 (1957/58), pp. [357]-362.)

—— Parliament and policy-making: the case of the Trans-Canada gas pipeline. By Hugh G. Thorburn. (In *The Canadian journal of economics and political science*. [Toronto] v. 23 (1957), pp. 516-531.)

"This paper was presented at the annual meeting of the Canadian Political Science Association in Ottawa, June 13, 1957."

TIMLIN, MABEL FRANCES Does Canada need more people? Toronto, Oxford University Press, 1951. xii, 143 p.

"Issued under the auspices of the Canadian Institute of International Affairs."

"Appendix B. Some notes on Canadian immigration and absorptive capacity, by H. Lukin Robinson": pp. [127]-140.

—— Recent changes in government attitudes towards immigration. By Mabel F. Timlin. (In Royal Society of Canada. *Proceedings and transactions*. Ottawa. ser. 3, v. 49 (1955), section 2, pp. 95-105.)

Considers contemporary immigration policy as it has developed from the time of Sir Clifford Sifton.

TRUDEAU, PIERRE ELLIOTT L'élection fédérale du 10 août 1953; prodromes et conjectures. (In *Cité libre*. Montréal. v. 3, no. 8 (1953), pp. [1]-10.)

UNDERHILL, FRANK HAWKINS Canada and the Canadian question 1954. By F. H. Underhill. (In *Queen's quarterly*. Kingston. v. 60 (1953), pp. [462]-475.)

An "appraisal of the Canadian present and the Canadian future with a strong emphasis on our essential North Americanism."

—— Canada and the Canadian question, 1954. (In his *In search of Canadian liberalism*. Toronto, 1961. pp. 214-226.)

This article was written for an issue of the *Queen's quarterly*, winter, 1953-54.

—— Canadian liberal democracy in 1955. (In his *In search of Canadian liberalism*. Toronto, 1961. pp. 227-242.)

This was an address delivered at Queen's University on 10 January, 1955.

—— The condition of Canadian politics. By F. Underhill, J. Marchand and R. Graham. (In Couchiching Conference, 25th, 1956. *Texts of addresses*. [Toronto, 1956] pp. 21-26.)

Address presented August 5, 1956.

—— How to vote. By Frank H. Underhill. (In *The Canadian forum*. Toronto. v. 33, no. 390 (July 1953), pp. [73]; 76-77.)

General comments on the state of Canadian political parties in relation to the forthcoming August 10, 1953, general election.

—— Notes on the August elections. By Frank H. Underhill. (In *The Canadian forum.* Toronto. v. 33, no. 392 (Sept. 1953), pp. [121]; 124-126.)

An analysis of the general elections held August 10, 1953.

—— Political stagnation in Canada, 1956. (In his *In search of Canadian liberalism.* Toronto, 1961. pp. 248-254.)

This article appeared in *Maclean's,* October 13, 1956.

VACHON, STANISLAS Notre politique militaire. (In *L'Action nationale.* Montréal. v. 40 (sept./oct. 1952), pp. [34]-46.)

VIGEANT, PIERRE Beaucoup d'activité, peu de changement. (In *L'Action nationale.* Montréal. v. 32 (sept. 1948), pp. [64]-71.)

Comments on the activities of the three major federal political parties in anticipating the federal general election held June 27, 1949.

—— L'élection générale de 1949 et l'influence française. (In *L'Action nationale.* Montréal. v. 34 (sept. 1949), pp. [68]-72.)

—— M. Drew et M. Saint-Laurent. (In *L'Action nationale.* Montréal. v. 32 (oct. 1948), pp. [149]-152.)

—— République ou annexion. Les tendances à Ottawa. (In *L'Action nationale.* Montréal. v. 32 (oct. 1948), pp. [133]-141.)

—— Le XXᵉ parlement et l'élection qui doit le remplacer. (In *L'Action nationale.* Montréal. v. 33 (juin 1949), pp. [451]-461.)

WALKER, HARRY W. Gubernatorial grief. (In *The Canadian forum.* Toronto. v. 32, no. 375 (Apr. 1952), pp. 8-10.)

An essay presenting an argument against the selection of a Canadian for the position of Governor-General of Canada.

WHITTON, CHARLOTTE Whither Canada? (In *Empire Club of Canada. Addresses.* Toronto. (1950/51), pp. 262-281.)

Address delivered March 1, 1951.

—— Will women ever run the country? (In *Maclean's.* Toronto. v. 65, no. 15 (Aug. 1, 1952), pp. 16-17; 31-32.)

Who owns Labrador? (In *The Newfoundland quarterly.* St. John's, Nfld. v. 53, no. 4 (Dec. 1954), p. 27.)

"Translation from an article appearing in the French language paper 'L'Unité nationale', an organ of the National Union Party."

"Why should we vote for you?" A young Canadian couple about to vote in a federal election for the first time asked the leaders of Canada's four major political parties. (In *Maclean's.* Toronto. v. 70, no. 12 (June 8, 1957), pp. 13-15; 67-72.)

Replies are given by Louis St. Laurent, John G. Diefenbaker, M. J. Coldwell, S. E. Low. With reference to the federal election held June 10, 1957.

WHYARD, FLORENCE The Mackenzie gets a vote but will share a member. (In *Saturday night.* Toronto. v. 64, no. 36 (June 14, 1949), pp. 10-11.)

"On June 27 the residents of the Mackenzie District and the Yukon Territory . . . will go to the polls to elect, between them, one member of Parliament. . . ."

WILLIAMS, JOHN RYAN Representation in the House of Commons of the twenty-first parliament: party and province. By John R. Williams. (In *The Canadian journal of economics and political science.* [Toronto] v. 18 (1952), pp. 77-87.)

This study "is an attempt to discover some of the measurable characteristics of members of the House of Commons elected June 27, 1949".

WILLIAMS, RONALD Are you a stooge for a Communist? (In *Chatelaine.* Toronto. v. 22, no. 4 (Apr. 1949), pp. 22; 90 [i.e. 91]-92; 94.)

Reports on Communist infiltration into women's public activities.

THE DIEFENBAKER–PEARSON YEARS
1957–1968

ALEXANDER, HUGH On turning 98. The great centennial boondoggle. (In *Saturday night.* Toronto. v. 80, no. 7 (July 1965), pp. 11-14.)

ALFORD, ROBERT R. The social bases of political cleavage in 1962. (In Meisel, John (ed.) *Papers on the 1962 election.* [Toronto, 1964] pp. [203]-234.)

Concerns the general elections held June 18, 1962.

—— The social bases of political cleavage in 1962. (In *Canadian society; sociological perspectives.* Edited by B. R. Blishen [and others] Toronto, 1968. pp. 410-438.)

"Reprinted in abridged form from John Meisel (ed.). Papers on the 1962 election (Toronto, 1965), pp.203-234."

Concerns the general elections held June 18, 1962.

ALLEN, PATRICK Our national purpose: no, le biculturalisme: oui, mais . . . (In *L'Action nationale*. Montréal. v. 52 (fév. 1963), pp. [606]-611.)

ALLEN, RALPH Let's say Quebec does secede —what then? (In *Maclean's*. Toronto. v. 77, no. 3 (Feb. 8, 1964), pp. 20-21; 28-32.)

ANDERSON, GRACE M. Voting behaviour and the ethnic-religious variable: a study of a federal election in Hamilton, Ontario. (In *The Canadian journal of economics and political science*. [Toronto] v. 32 (1966), pp. [27]-37.)
"The data used in this study were collected in the 'North End' district of the city of Hamilton, Ontario, in May and June, 1962. . . ."

—— Voting behaviour and the ethnic-religious variable; a study of a federal election in Hamilton, Ontario. (In *Canadian society; sociological perspectives*. Edited by B. R. Blishen [and others] Toronto, 1968. pp. 439-450.)
"Reprinted in abridged form from the Canadian journal of economics and political science, XXXII (February 1966), pp. 27-37."
"The data used in this study was collected in the 'North End' district of the city of Hamilton, Ontario in May and June 1962."

ANDREW, G. C. An educational policy for Canada. (In *The Journal of liberal thought*. [Ottawa. v.] 1, no. 1 (summer 1965), pp. 69-77.)
Reproduced typescript.

ANGERS, FRANCOIS ALBERT L'affaire du recensement éditorial. Par Le Directeur. (In *L'Action nationale*. Montréal. v. 50 (fév. 1961), pp. [497]-507.)

—— Où sont les vrais fascistes? (In *L'Action nationale*. Montréal. v. 52 (jan. 1963), pp. [477]-483.)

An Appeal for realism in politics. (In *The Canadian forum*. Toronto. v. 44, no. 520 (May 1964), pp. 29-33.)
Signed by The Committee for Political Realism: Albert Breton, Raymond Breton, Claude Bruneau, Yvon Gauthier, Marc Lalonde, Maurice Rinard, Pierre E. Trudeau.
Translation by P. M. Pitfield of Pour une politique fonctionnelle. The French version was published simultaneously in *Cité libre*, Montréal, no. 67 (mai 1964), pp. 11-17.
Introductory note by R. C., i.e. Ramsay Cook.

ARES, RICHARD André Laurendeau et la Commission B. B. (In *Relations*. Montréal. [28. année] no 329 (juil./août 1968), pp. 210-212.)

—— Balance sheet of a century. Quebec in the Canada of tomorrow. [Toronto, 1968] pp. [A-1]-A-13.
Summarizes developments within the Canadian confederation.

—— Le recensement de 1961. (In *L'Action nationale*. Montréal. v. 52 (nov. 1962), pp. [206]-216.)

—— Le recensement de 1961. II. Chez nos minorités: combien sont-ils? (In *L'Action nationale*. Montréal. v. 52 (déc. 1962), pp. [337]-355.)

—— Le recensement de 1961. III. Langues officielles et langues maternelles. (In *L'Action nationale*. Montréal. v. 52 (jan. 1963), pp. [432]-447.)

Atlantic development and the election. (In *The Atlantic advocate*. Fredericton, N.B. v. 52, no. 10 (June 1962), pp. 11-15.)
Presents policy statements issued by the four political parties regarding the Atlantic region. Relates to the general elections held June 18, 1962.

The Atlantic Development Board Act. A summary of the speeches in Parliament. (In *The Atlantic advocate*. Fredericton, N.B. v. 53, no. 5 (Jan. 1963), pp. 15-16; i-iv; 17-20; 77-80; v-vii.)
A full summary of the debate in Parliament, December 4-12, 1962.

BAIDEN, R. M. Borden calculates the odds. (In *Saturday night*. Toronto. v. 74, no. 20 (Sept. 26, 1959), pp. 22-23; 26.)
Concerns the five recommendations made by the Borden Commission investigating the Canadian oil industry and government policies regarding the industry.

—— Putting the record straight. What the Coyne affair is all about. (In *Saturday night*. Toronto. v. 76, no. 15 (July 22, 1961), pp. [11]-16.)
Refers to James E. Coyne, Governor of the Bank of Canada.

BEAU, JEAN CLAUDE Le magazine Maclean et le nationalisme au Canada, 1961 à 1967. [Montréal, 1969] 1 v.
Thesis (MA) – University of Montreal.

BEAUDIN, DOMINIQUE Un homme franc et courageux; éditorial. Par le secrétaire de la rédaction. (In *L'Action nationale*.

Montréal. v. 52 (oct. 1962), pp. [101]-106.)

"Il s'agit de M. F.-Eugène Therrien, C. R."

M. Therrien was a Commissioner on the Royal Commission on Government Organization appointed September 16, 1960.

—— Y aura-t-il une fête du centenaire? éditorial. Par le secrétaire de la rédaction. (In L'Action nationale. Montréal. v. 51 (nov. 1961), pp. [189]-203.)

BECK, JAMES MURRAY The election of 1963 and national unity. By J. M. Beck. (In The Dalhousie review. Halifax. v. 43, no. 2 (summer 1963), pp. [143]-154.)

Analyses the results of the general elections held April 8, 1963.

—— The electoral behaviour of Nova Scotia in 1965. By J. Murray Beck. (In Courtney, J. C. (ed.) Voting in Canada. [Scarborough, Ont., c1967] pp. [90]-98.)

"Reprinted from The Dalhousie review, XLVI (Spring) 1966."

—— The Maritimes. By J. Murray Beck. (In Commentator. Toronto. v. 9, no. 11 (Nov. 1965), pp. 6-7.)

One of five articles in a section called "The election campaign from coast to coast".

Examines the campaign for the federal election held November 8, 1965.

BERRY, MICHAEL Is Canada rhinocerosable? (In Canada month. Montreal. v. 4, no. 3 (Mar. 1964), p. 12.)

Concerns the "Rhinoceros Party", founded by Paul Ferron in Montreal in October 1963.

BETTS, DAVID Pre-election survey: 3. Atlantic provinces. Liberals gaining. (In The Canadian commentator. Toronto. v. 6, no. 6 (June 1962), pp. 3; 19.)

The Author is editor of the Halifax Chronicle Herald.

Relates to the general elections held June 18, 1962.

BIDDELL, J. L. Law reform; the businessman's responsibility. (In Empire Club of Canada. Addresses. [Don Mills, Ont.] (1965/66), pp. [169]-182.)

Address delivered February 3, 1966.

Discusses the relationship between government and business interests.

BIRD, JOHN Quebec—the key province. (In Canadian commentator. Toronto. v. 2, no. 3 (Mar. 1958), p. 2.)

Discusses the strategic importance of Quebec in the general elections of March 31, 1958.

—— A tinge of anti-Americanism. (In Canadian commentator. Toronto. v. 2, no. 4 (Apr. 1958), p. 2.)

Discusses the factor of Canadian nationalism in 1958 federal election campaign.

BLACK, ROBSON Canada's forest policies need reform. (In Saturday night. Toronto. v. 75, no. 7 (Apr. 2, 1960), pp. 13-14.

BLAIS, A. Les élections comme phénomène de décision collective. Les élections fédérales de 1957 à 1965 au Québec. Par A. Blais, H. Cantin et J. Crête. (In Canadian journal of political science. Toronto. v. 3 (1970), pp. [522]-539.)

BOISVERT, REGINALD Censure et liberté. Le meilleur contrôle est le contrôle de soi-même. (In Cité libre. Montréal. no. 23 (1959), pp. [15]-21.)

Concerns the controversy raised over the censoring by Radio-Canada of the text of a proposed speech by Michel Chartrand in November 1959.

BONHOMME, JEAN PIERRE The uproar in French Canada: a nation at the crossroads. (In Canada month. Montreal. v. 3, no. 4 (Apr. 1963), pp. 16-17.)

BOUTHILLETTE, JEAN La mesure canadienne-française. (In Cité libre. Montréal. no. 52 (déc. 1962), pp. 10-13.)

BOUVIER, EMILE La rapport Gill et l'assurance-chômage. (In Relations. Montréal. 23. année, no 266 (fév. 1963), pp. 42-43.)

BOYD, WINNETT Affluence for all Canadians. By Winnett Boyd and Jon W. Kieran. (In Canada month. Montreal. v. 7, no. 5 (May 1967), pp. 18-20.)

BRIEN, ROGER Une dernière chance pour la Confédération, d'ici 1967? (In L'Action nationale. Montréal. v. 51 (déc. 1961), pp. [311]-321.)

BROCHU, MICHEL L'impasse du bilinguisme au Canada. (In L'Action nationale. Montréal. v. 51 (mars 1962), pp. [596]-602.)

Discusses the political aspects of the issue.

—— La politique anglo-saxonne des contingentements du bilinguisme au Canada. (In L'Action nationale. Montréal. v. 51 (fév. 1962), pp. [491]-496.)

BUCK, TIMOTHY Automation and the leadership of the nation. By Tim Buck.

(In *The Marxist quarterly*. Toronto. no. 11 (autumn 1964), pp. 18-37.)

BURAK, MOSES J. Canada: two hundred years after the Treaty. (In *Canada month*. Montreal. v. 6, no. 2 (Feb. 1966), pp. 26-31.)

Reflective comments.

BURGHARDT, ANDREW F. What will happen if Quebec secedes from Canada? (In *The Canadian Saturday night*. Toronto. v. 78, no. 6 (June/July 1963), pp. 21; 24.)

BURNEY, DEREK HUDSON Canadian parties and the nuclear arms issue. [Kingston, Ont.] 1964. 1 v.

Thesis (MA) – Queen's University.

CAMP, DALTON KINGSLEY Opportunity for reform. By Dalton K. Camp. (In Empire Club of Canada. *Addresses*. Toronto. (1966/67), pp. [31]-42.)

Address delivered October 20, 1966.

—— Platform . . . It's power the parties are after. By Dalton Camp. (In *Maclean's*. Toronto. v. 82, no. 10 (Oct. 1969), p. 13.)

Canada month questions the Party leaders on the issues. (In *Canada month*. Montreal. v. 3, no. 4 (Apr. 1963), pp. 10-11.)

Leaders: T. C. Douglas, R. Thompson, L. B. Pearson, J. G. Diefenbaker. Refers to the federal election held April 8, 1963.

CANADIAN LABOUR CONGRESS–CO-OPERATIVE COMMONWEALTH FEDERATION JOINT NATIONAL COMMITTEE A new political party for Canada . . . A discussion outline and reference manual for weekend institutes, conferences, study groups, etc. Ottawa, 1958. 40 p.

Issued also in French.

CARRIER, ANDRE L'idéologie politique de la revue *Cité libre* telle qu'elle se dégage à travers la "nouvelle série". [Montréal] 1967. 1 v.

Thesis (MA) – University of Montreal.

CASEY, MARY Atlantic provinces—Liberal gains. The election campaign has been in low gear this time, but the Liberals may win five more seats, chiefly in Nova Scotia and P.E.I. (In *Commentator*. Toronto. v. 7, no. 4 (Apr. 1963), pp. 2-3.)

One of seven articles forming part of "Election survey".

General predictions on the outcome of the general election held April 8, 1963.

CHAPIN, MIRIAM Quebec politics in basic English. (In *Saturday night*. Toronto. v. 74, no. 8 (Apr. 11, 1959), pp. 12-13; 64; 67.)

Includes discussion of attitudes in Quebec toward the federal government and political parties.

CHAPUT, MARCEL L'avenir du Canada; séparation, intégration, ou . . .? (In Congress on Canadian Affairs, 1st, Quebec, 1961. *Le Canada expérience ratée . . . ou réussie?* Quebec, 1962. pp. [117]-131.)

—— The secession of Quebec from Canada. (In *Canadian commentator*. Toronto. v. 5, no. 7 (July—Aug. 1961), pp. 6-7.)

A discussion of Ottawa-Quebec relations. The Author "is vice-president of French Canada's Rally for National Independence".

CHAPUT-ROLLAND, SOLANGE Mon pays, Québec ou le Canada? Préf. de Claude Ryan. [Montréal] Cercle du livre de France [c1966] 181 p.

Reflections on French-Canadian–English-Canadian relations in a general historical setting.

—— My country, Canada or Quebec? Toronto, Macmillan, 1966. xi, 122 p.

Translation of *Mon pays, le Québec ou le Canada?*

First published Montréal, Cercle du livre de France, 1966.

CHILDS, LAURA Canadian defense policy. A review article. (In *Horizons*. Toronto. no. 25 (spring 1968), pp. 17-25.)

A review of the book *Canada's changing defense policy, 1957-1963; the problems of a middle power in alliance*, by J. B. McLin. Baltimore, Johns Hopkins Press, 1967.

CHISVIN, CYNTHIA What's really wrong at CBC is simple: – state ownership. (In *Canada month*. Montreal. v. 6, no. 6 (June 1966), pp. 16-17.)

CINQ-MARS, EDMOND Quand la Confédération eut 80 ans. Par E. C.-M. (In *L'Action nationale*. Montréal. v. 51 (jan. 1962), pp. 439-445.)

CLARKE, NELSON English Canada. (In *The Marxist quarterly*. Toronto. no. 7 (autumn 1963), pp. 27-36.)

—— June 18: the outcome. (In *The Marxist quarterly*. Toronto. no. 3 (autumn 1962), pp. [43]-55.)

Examines the results of the general elections held June 18, 1962.

CLARKSON, STEPHEN A programme for binational development. (In University

League for Social Reform. *Nationalism in Canada.* Toronto [1966] pp. 133-152.)

CLAUSEN, OLIVER   The election. A chance to capture new national purpose or an excuse to drift after more mirages. (In *Canada month.* Montreal. v. 2, no. 2 (Feb. 1962), pp. 18-21.)

Reviews current political issues and the state of federal political parties, with a view to a forthcoming election.

CLEVERLEY, J. C.   Tories strong in Manitoba, Saskatchewan. In these two prairie provinces the Conservatives are entrenched, though they may lose three seats to Liberals in Manitoba. (In *Commentator.* Toronto. v. 7, no. 4 (Apr. 1963), pp. 7-8.)

One of seven articles which form part of "Election survey".

General predictions on the outcome of the general elections held April 8, 1963.

CLICHE, PAUL   Double allégeance et unitarisme. (In *Cité libre.* Montréal. no. 63 (jan. 1964), pp. 13-15.)

A brief historical commentary on the political relationship between Ottawa and Quebec.

COHEN, MAXWELL ABRAHAM   National politics and foreign affairs. By Maxwell Cohen. (In *Saturday night.* Toronto. v. 73, no. 7 (Mar. 28, 1958), pp. 12-13; 38-39.)

Discusses the inter-relationship between domestic issues and international affairs.

——   Wanted now—a defence policy. By Maxwell Cohen. (In *Saturday night.* Toronto. v. 74, no. 1 (Jan. 3, 1959), pp. 14-15; 34-35.)

COLLINS, EUGENE L.   The case for a maple leaf flag. (In *Canadian commentator.* Toronto. v. 2, no. 6 (June 1958), pp. [1]-2.)

Confederation: one hundred years later, does it still work? A bilingual seminar for CBC radio and television. La Confédération, après cent ans, vaut-elle toujours? Un colloque bilingue présenté par Radio-Canada à la radio et à la télévision. [Montréal, Services d'information de Radio-Canada, 1963] 94 p.

Text in English and French.

Seminar organized by the Public Affairs Dept. of the CBC.

"Part of the series 'Citizens' Forum' . . . 1963."

COOK, GEORGE RAMSAY   Confederation of tomorrow: Premier Robarts' triumph. By

Ramsay Cook. (In *Commentator.* Toronto. v. 12, no. 1 (Jan. 1968), pp. 14-15; 18.)

——   An election without issues. By R. C. (In *The Canadian forum.* Toronto. v. 42, no. 496 (May 1962), p. 27.)

Brief comments on the forthcoming general elections held June 18, 1962.

——   Lewis Carroll's Canada. By Ramsay Cook. (In *The Canadian forum.* Toronto. v. 42, no. 499 (Aug. 1962), pp. 104-107.)

A probing essay on the significance of the results of the general elections held June 18, 1962.

——   "Un Québec fort dans une nouvelle Confédération." By Ramsay Cook. (In *The Canadian forum.* Toronto. v. 46, no. 544 (May 1966), pp. 26-28.)

Discusses the significance of the Quebec election to be held June 5, 1966, for the future of Canadian federalism.

——   Wanted: a phoenix. By R. C. (In *The Canadian forum.* Toronto. v. 42, no. 506 (Mar. 1963), pp. 266-268.)

Analyses the issues of the general elections held April 8, 1963.

COPPS, EDWIN   Ottawa: no one-man government. (In *Saturday night.* Toronto. v. 74, no. 4 (Feb. 14, 1959), pp. 16-17.)

Comments on the government of John Diefenbaker, and the performance of L. B. Pearson as leader of the Opposition.

——   Ottawa letter. Tory praise for Liberal errors. (In *Saturday night.* Toronto. v. 74, no. 16 (Aug. 1, 1959), p. 41.)

Concerns the reaction to the article A story of waste on the Mid-Canada line, by Arnold Edinborough. (In *Saturday night.* Toronto. v. 74, no. 6 (Mar. 14, 1959), pp. 9-[13]; 49.)

——   Ottawa letter. Full of wind and fury. (In *Saturday night.* Toronto. v. 75, no. 2 (Jan. 23, 1960), pp. 27-28.)

Comments on verbosity in the House of Commons, citing J. Diefenbaker, D. Fleming, and others.

——   Ottawa letter. The stubborn facts about unemployment. (In *Saturday night.* Toronto. v. 75, no. 7 (Apr. 2, 1960), pp. 25-26.)

Concerns the interpretation advanced by Michael Starr and Paul Martin.

CORBETT, EDWARD M.   Quebec confronts Canada. Baltimore, Johns Hopkins Press [1967] 336 p.

COTNAM, JAQUES   Faut-il inventer un nouveau Canada? Montréal, Fides [1967] 256 p. [Bibliothèque économique et sociale.)

Essays on French-English relations in Canada.

COURTNEY, JOHN CHILDS   Voting in a provincial general election and a federal by-election: a constituency study of Saskatoon City. By John C. Courtney and David E. Smith. (In The Canadian journal of economics and political science. [Toronto] v. 32 (1966), pp. [338]-353.)

Analyses two elections held in close succession in Saskatoon City: a provincial general election held on April 22, 1964, and a federal by-election on June 22, 1964.

CRANE, DAVID   Labor's powerful boss. (In Canada month. Montreal. v. 3, no. 11 (Nov. 1963), pp. 17-20.)

Concerns Claude Jodoin. Includes discussion of political support and the Canadian Labour Congress.

CREIGHTON, DONALD GRANT   The myth of biculturalism; or, The great French-Canadian sales campaign. The Fathers of Confederation reached a settlement which gave the French language the best chance it will ever have on this continent. By Donald Creighton. (In Saturday night. Toronto. v. 81, no. 9 (Sept. 1966), pp. 35-39.)

Crisis of Confederation. Toronto, Progress Books, 1963. 96 p.

A special issue of the Marxist quarterly.

CUMMING, ALISON A.   Are we legislating private enterprise out of Canadian business? By A. A. Cumming. (In Litvak, I. A. (ed.) The nation keepers. New York, Toronto [c1967] pp. 27-44.)

CURRIE, DON   The Manitoba school question. (In Horizons. Toronto. no. 19 (autumn 1966), pp. 86-94.)

Describes the historical background in presenting contemporary developments of the school issue.

DAIGNAULT, RICHARD   Political attitudes. (In Seminar on French Canada, Montreal, 1963. Seminar on French Canada. [Montreal, 1963] pp. 121-126.)

General comments on French-Canadian-English-Canadian political attitudes.

DANE, NAZLA   Who really won the election? (In Canadian commentator. Toronto. v. 2, no. 4 (Apr. 1958), p. 4.)

Discusses the function of women during the political campaign for the 1958 general elections.

DAVIS, E. N.   Pre-election survey: 4. Prairies. Conservatives fighting. (In The Canadian commentator. Toronto. v. 6, no. 6 (June 1962), pp. 4; 19.)

Comments on the political campaign in preparation for the general elections June 18, 1962.

DAVIS, MORRIS   Ballot behaviour in Halifax revisited. (In The Canadian journal of economics and political science. Toronto. v. 30 (1964), pp. 538-558.)

"This paper was presented at a meeting of the Canadian Political Science Association at Charlottetown, P.E.I., in June 1964."

"This paper has two aims, one substantive and the other methodological . . . the paper presents data from the April 1963 parliamentary election in Halifax. . . ."

——   Ballot behaviour in Halifax revisited. (In Courtney, J. C. (ed.) Voting in Canada. [Scarborough, Ont., c1967] pp. [130]-142.)

"Reprinted from The Canadian journal of economics and political science, XXX (November) 1964."

Concerns the 1963 federal election in Halifax.

——Did they vote for party or candidate in Halifax? (In Meisel, John (ed.) Papers on the 1962 election. [Toronto, 1964] pp. [19]-32.)

Concerns the general elections held June 18, 1962.

——   A last look at ballot behaviour in the dual constituency of Halifax. (In The Canadian journal of economics and political science. [Toronto] v. 32 (1966), pp. [366]-371.)

Compares and analyses the data gathered from the general elections held in 1962 and 1963 concentrating on the federal election of November 8, 1965.

DEAN, BASIL   For the sake of argument: We on the right have no vote. (In Maclean's. Toronto. v. 75, no. 13 (June 30, 1962), pp. 24; 32-34.)

DE MAROIS, WILLIAM   David Stanley and the Red Rabbi: two sides of the same coin? (In Canada month. Montreal. v. 5, no. 12 (Dec. 1965), pp. 30-37.)

Concerns the anti-Semitic pamphlet entitled "The Red rabbi", first distributed in Toronto in October 1964, with Abraham L. Feinberg as its subject.

DE POE, NORMAN Conservative landslide: Will the provinces rebel? (In *Saturday night*. Toronto. v. 73, no. 8 (Apr. 12, 1958), pp. 14-15; 55.)
Examines the results of the federal election held March 31, 1958.

DESBARATS, PETER HULLET The new Confederation. [Montreal] Montreal Star [1965] 25, 27 p.
Cover title.
Text in English and French.
"Reprinted from The Montreal Star."

Un Détective privé démasque le parti nazi canadien. (In *Le Magazine Maclean*. Montréal. v. 6, no. 10 (oct. 1966), p. 3.)
John Garrity is the private investigator; John Beattie is the leader of the Canadian Nazi Party.

DION, LEON The election in the province of Quebec. (In Meisel, John (ed.) *Papers on the 1962 election*. [Toronto, 1964] pp. [109]-128.)
Concerns the general elections held June 18, 1962.

DOBELL, WILLIAM M. Minority parties and majority governments. By W. M. Dobell. (In *The Journal of liberal thought*. [Ottawa v.] 2, no. 2 (spring 1966), pp. 65-73.)
Comparative comments on the campaign and general elections of November 8, 1965.

DODIER, BRIGITTE Les conventions dans la région de Québec à l'élection fédérale de 1968. Par Brigitte Dodier, Marc Pigeon et François Renaud. (In *Recherches sociagraphiques*. Québec. v. 10, no. 1 (jan.—avril 1969), pp. [83]-96.)
"Notes de recherche. Les partis politiques dans la région de Québec", by Vincent Lemieux: pp. [97]-101.

DORION, NOEL The role of Canadian dualism in the shaping of our federal structure. By the Honourable Noël Dorion, Secretary of State. (In MacRae, C. F. (ed.) *French Canada today*. Sackville, N.B. [1961?] pp. 15-21.)

DOUGLAS, THOMAS CLEMENT What politics needs most—more laughter. By Tommy Douglas. (In *Maclean's*. Toronto. v. 72, no. 7 (Mar. 28, 1959), pp. 24-25; 49-50.)

DOUPE, JACK How this flag became our flag. (In *Canada month*. Montreal. v. 4, no. 5 (May 1964), pp. 20-21.)
Refers to the Canadian Red Ensign.

DUBUC, ALFRED An anti-manifesto. (In *The Canadian forum*. Toronto. v. 45, no. 542 (Mar. 1966), pp. 272-274.)
"This article is an excerpt from 'Une interprétation économique de la constitution'". (In *Socialisme 66*. Montréal. no. 7 (jan. 1966), pp. 3-21.)
Constitutes a critical rejoinder to An appeal for realism in politics. (In *The Canadian forum*. Toronto. v. 44, no. 520 (1964), pp. 29-33.)

—— Une interprétation économique de la constitution. (In *Socialisme 66*. Montréal. no. 7 (jan. 1966), pp. 3-21.)
"La première partie de cet article a pour objet de présenter quelques matériaux pour servir à une interprétation économique de la constitution canadienne. Ces matériaux sont utilisés ensuite pour critiquer le Manifeste [Pour une politique fonctionnelle (*Cité libre*. v. 15, no 67, mai 1964, pp. 11-18)]; la deuxième partie de l'article constitue un Anti-Manifeste."
An English translation under the title: An anti-manifesto was published in *The Canadian forum*, Toronto, v. 45, no. 542 (1966), pp. 272-274.

EAYRS, JAMES Now that Canada's armed forces are nicely sorted out, what are we going to do with them? (In *Saturday night*. Toronto. v. 84, no. 8 (Aug. 1969), pp. 19-24.)
An historical discussion.

EDINBOROUGH, ARNOLD The administrative muddle of the Mid-Canada line. (In *Saturday night*. Toronto. v. 74, no. 7 (Mar. 28, 1959), pp. 9-[11]; 48.)

—— National affairs. The rape of Parliament. (In *Saturday night*. Toronto. v. 81, no. 7 (July 1966), p. 9.)
Concerns the conduct of the first sesssion of the twenty-seventh parliament.

—— National affairs. The restless electorate. (In *Saturday night*. Toronto. v. 81, no. 8 (Aug. 1966), p. 7.)
General comments.

—— National affairs. Canada and the Queen of England. (In *Saturday night*. Toronto. v. 82, no. 7 (July 1967), pp. 9; 11.)

—— National affairs. A reason for raising one small cheer for democracy emerged from last month's mess in Ottawa—TV's new impact on Parliament. (In *Saturday night*. Toronto. v. 83, no. 4 (Apr. 1968), pp. 9; 12.)

Estimates the impact on politics of television.

—— A story of waste on the Mid-Canada line. (In *Saturday night*. Toronto. v. 74, no. 6 (Mar. 14, 1959), pp. 9-[13]; 49.)

At head of title: SN/Special report.

Examines the building of the Mid-Canada radar line. The project was undertaken as a result of a decision made by the Liberal government in 1954.

—— The unpopular election. (In *Saturday night*. Toronto. v. 80, no. 11 (Nov. 1965), p. 11.)

Discusses the issues of the federal election held November 8, 1965.

EDMONDS, J. DUNCAN The Coyne affair: principles and implications. (In *The Canadian forum*. Toronto. v. 41, no. 487 (Sept. 1961), pp. [121]-122.)

ELLIOTT, G. R. Canada & Quebec should separate. (In *Canada month*. Montreal. v. 8, no. 2 (Feb. 1968), pp. 10-11.)

Argues for "an on-going Canada on the one hand and an independent Quebec on the other".

EMERSON, R. A. Turmoil in transportation. By R. A. Emerson, President and Chief Operating Officer, Canadian Pacific Railway Company. (In Empire Club of Canada. *Addresses*. Toronto. (1965/66), pp. [125]-138.)

Address delivered January 13, 1966.

Discusses, in the main, the implications of the MacPherson Report, i.e. the Report of the Royal Commission on Transportation. Ottawa, 1962. 3 v.

ETHIER-BLAIS, JEAN Rhinoceros. (In *Saturday night*. Toronto. v. 80, no. 11 (Nov. 1965), pp. 20-22.)

Concerns the "Rhinoceros Party" founded by Paul Ferron.

P. Ferron ran as a candidate in a federal by-election held in Saint-Denis, Que., February 10, 1964.

FALARDEAU, JEAN CHARLES Droits de l'homme et la politique canadienne. (In *Cité libre*. Montréal. no. 29 (août—sept. 1960), pp. 28-29.)

FARIBAULT, MARCEL Unfinished business; some thought on the mounting crisis in Quebec. Toronto, McClelland and Stewart [c1967] 186 p.

—— Why Confederation? A panel discussion led by Marcel Faribault and Robert M. Fowler. (In Empire Club of Canada.

Addresses. [Don Mills, Ont.] (1966/67), pp. [105]-124.)

Discussions were conducted December 1, 1966.

FARQUHARSON, DUART Springfield by-election. (In *Canadian commentator*. Toronto. v. 3, no. 1 (Jan. 1959), pp. 7-9.)

Analyses the federal by-election held at Springfield, Man., on December 15, 1958.

Faut-il refaire la Confédération? (In *Le Magazine Maclean*. Montréal. v. 2, no. 6 (juin 1962), pp. 17-19; 63-68.)

A panel discussion including the following participants: Jean-Jacques Bertrand, Frank Scott, Pierre de Bellefeuille, René Lévesque, Pierre Elliott Trudeau, and André Laurendeau.

FERGUSON, THOMAS M. Our unfair Income Tax Act. (In *Saturday night*. Toronto. v. 75, no. 8 (Apr. 16, 1960), pp. 13-14.)

FILLEY, WALTER O. Social structure and Canadian political parties; the Quebec case. (In Courtney, J. C. (ed.) *Voting in Canada*. [Scarborough, Ont., c1967] pp. [162]-166.)

"Reprinted from the Western political quarterly, IX (December) 1956."

"In the present analysis, the interstices of Quebec's social and political systems will be explored to ascertain the manner in which its political parties on the federal level have been or in the future may be influenced by French Canada's changing social structure."

FISHER, DOUGLAS MASON Commons comment. By D. M. Fisher. (In *The Canadian forum*. Toronto. v. 37, no. 443 (Dec. 1957), pp. 201-202.)

General comments on the first session of the twenty-third parliament.

—— Commons comment. By D. M. Fisher. (In *The Canadian forum*. Toronto. v. 38, no. 451 (Aug. 1958), pp. 101-102.)

A thorough discussion of the nature and personnel of the Canadian Press Gallery reporting on the activities of the House of Commons in Ottawa.

—— Commons comment. By D. M. Fisher. (In *The Canadian forum*. Toronto. v. 38, no. 457 (Feb. 1959), pp. 252-253.)

A general discussion on the state of the Conservative and Liberal parties at the opening of the second session of the twenty-fourth parliament January 15, 1959.

—— Commons comment. By D. M. Fisher.

(In *The Canadian forum*. Toronto. v. 39, no. 463 (Aug. 1959), pp. [97]-98.)

Concerns the report issued by the Parliamentary Broadcasting Committee.

—— Fisher on liberty. By Douglas Fisher. (In *Canada month*. Montreal. v. 3, no. 6 (June 1963), p. 25.)

—— The New Left in action as others see it. By Douglas Fisher. (In *Canadian dimensions*. Winnipeg. v. 3, no. 6 (Sept./Oct. 1966), p. 15.)

A brief comment.

—— On Parliament Hill: political instability and pre-election fever. By Douglas Fisher. (In *Commentator*. Toronto. v. 9, no. 1 (Jan. 1965), pp. 8-10.)

General elections held November 8, 1965.

FLEMING, DONALD METHUEN   Some thoughts on the Carter report. By the Hon. Donald M. Fleming. (In Empire Club of Canada. *Addresses*. [Don Mills, Ont.] (1966/67), pp. [277]-305.)

Address delivered March 16, 1967.

Discusses the Report of the Royal Commission on Taxation. Ottawa, 1966. (16 v. and index)

FONTAINE, MARIE BLANCHE   Une femme face à la Confédération. Montréal, Editions de l'Homme [1965] 156 p.

FORSEY, EUGENE ALFRED   A Canadian Fabian Society? By E. F. (In *The Canadian forum*. Toronto. v. 44, no. 522 (July 1964), pp. [73]-74.)

Outlines the background which led to the formation of an educational project named "Exchange for Political Ideas in Canada" consisting of interested members of the NDP and Liberal parties.

—— Our present discontents. By Eugene A. Forsey. [Wolfville, N.S.] Acadia University [c1968] 44 p. (The George C. Nowlan lectures, 1.)

Deals with relations between French and English Canada.

—— Our present discontents. By Eugene Forsey. (In Ontario Advisory Committee on Confederation. *Background papers and reports*. [Toronto, 1970] v. 2, pp. 60-84.)

—— The political crisis. By Eugene Forsey. (In *The Canadian forum*. Toronto. v. 42, no. 506 (Mar. 1963), pp. [265]-266.)

Comments on the parliamentary vote held February 5, 1963, which brought down the administration of John Diefenbaker, and on the resulting necessity for a general election which was scheduled April 8, 1963.

—— Present problems of Confederation, an English-Canadian view. (In *Journal of Canadian studies*. Peterborough, Ont. v. 1, no. 2 (1966), pp. 13-23.)

FOX, PAUL WESLEY   Canadian federal politics on a new tack. By Paul Fox. (In *Commentator*. Toronto. v. 8, no. 11 (Nov. 1964), pp. 15-17.)

—— A clinical picture of the election. By Paul Fox. (In *Commentator*. Toronto. v. 9, no. 12 (Dec. 1965), pp. 6-7.)

Concerns the results of the general elections held November 8, 1965.

—— Electoral post mortem. By P. W. F. (In *The Canadian forum*. Toronto. v. 38, no. 448 (May 1958), pp. 29-30.)

Discusses the results of the federal election held March 31, 1958.

—— Ontario. By Paul Fox. (In *Commentator*. Toronto. v. 9, no. 11 (Nov. 1965), pp. 10-[11].)

One of five articles in a series called "The election campaign from coast to coast".

Examines the campaign for the federal elections held November 8, 1965.

—— Ontario—Liberal stock rising. In this key province with a third of the seats in the House of Commons the Liberals have the greatest hope of making sizable gains. By Paul Fox. (In *Commentator*. Toronto. v. 7, no. 4 (Apr. 1963), pp. 5-6.)

One of seven articles which form part of "Election survey".

Predictions on the outcome of the general elections held April 8, 1963.

—— Pre-election survey: 1. Ontario, key to victory. By Paul Fox. (In *The Canadian commentator*. Toronto. v. 6, no. 2 (Feb. 1962), pp. 1; 20.)

Analyses the 1962 federal election campaign and its implications for the Conservative Party.

For other parts in this series see articles by Paul Fox, David Betts, E. N. Davis, and J. M. Minifie in the April and June 1962 issues of *The Canadian commentator*.

—— Pre-election survey: 2. Quebec scene. Duplessis' ghost lingers on. By Paul Fox. (In *Commentator*. Toronto. v. 6, no. 4 (Apr. 1962), pp. 3; 22.)

Considers the relationship between Quebec and the federal political parties.

—— A promising campaign. By P. W. F. (In *The Canadian forum*. Toronto. v. 38, no. 446 (Apr. 1958), pp. 2-3.)

Comments on the campaign preceding the general elections held March 31, 1958.

FRANCIS, ANNE   Do we really want that strong man? Diefenbaker was accused of weakness and indecision. Now the same is being said of Pearson with even less justification. (In *Commentator*. Toronto. v. 9, no. 9 (Sept. 1965), pp. 6-7; 23.)

—— Unfortunately, Diefenbaker and Pearson for ever. (In *Commentator*. Toronto. v. 10, no. 7-8 (July—Aug. 1966), pp. 13; 15; 17.)

Considers the general state of federal political affairs and is critical of the approach taken by the two political leaders.

FRASER, BLAIR   Backstage at Ottawa. The "hidden report" uproar: what it really means. (In *Maclean's*. Toronto. v. 71, no. 5 (Mar. 1, 1958), p. 2.)

The report was a survey prepared during 1957 forecasting a rise in unemployment: the report was not disclosed by the Liberal administration during the election year. The Conservative administration subsequently released the report.

—— Backstage at Ottawa. The election's mystery candidate—the dollar bill. (In *Maclean's*. Toronto. v. 71, no. 8 (Apr. 12, 1958), p. 2.)

Refers to the federal election held March 31, 1958.

—— Backstage at Ottawa. Will MPs use new statute to dictate to CBC? (In *Maclean's*. Toronto. v. 71, no. 21 (Oct. 11, 1958), p. 2.)

—— Backstage at Ottawa. What led Canada to junk the Arrow. (In *Maclean's*. Toronto, v. 71, no. 22 (Oct. 25, 1958), p. 2.)

—— Backstage at Ottawa. The CBC and "political pressure"—you can't see it, but it's always there. (In *Maclean's*. Toronto. v. 72, no. 16 (Aug. 1, 1959), p. 2.)

—— Backstage at Ottawa. The coming showdown at the CBC. Who'll fill the power vacuum Bushnell left? (In *Maclean's*. Toronto. v. 73, no. 1 (Jan. 2, 1960), p. 2.)

—— Backstage at Ottawa. The toughest puzzle of 1960: defense. What kind do we want? How much will we pay for it? (In *Maclean's*. Toronto. v. 73, no. 2 (Jan. 16, 1960), p. 2.)

—— Backstage at Ottawa. Canada has the world's worst parliament because we elect boors. (In *Maclean's*. Toronto. v. 76, no. 22 (Nov. 16, 1963), pp. 1-2.)

—— Backstage in Ottawa. The one painless way to redesign every Canadian constituency. (In *Maclean's*. Toronto. v. 77, no. 1 (Jan. 4, 1964), pp. 1-2.)

Concerns redistribution of parliamentary seats.

—— Backstage in Ottawa. So far, the defense committee is untroublesome. But wait a few weeks. (In *Maclean's*. Toronto. v. 77, no. 2 (Jan. 25, 1964), p. 2.)

Discusses Canadian defence policy.

—— Backstage in Ottawa. Why the Liberals cheered when the Tories stuck with Diefenbaker. (In *Maclean's*. Toronto. v. 77, no. 5 (Mar. 7, 1964), p. 2.)

—— Backstage in Ottawa. Parliament and the press: the steady deterioration of an old friendship. (In *Maclean's*. Toronto. v. 77, no. 6 (Mar. 21, 1964), pp. 1-2.)

—— Backstage in Ottawa. The phony little furor over every man's new number. (In *Maclean's*. Toronto. v. 77, no. 10 (May 16, 1964), p. 2.)

Discusses the opposition to the introduction of social security numbers.

—— Backstage in Ottawa. How military integration is catching some officers in a painful wringer. (In *Maclean's*. Toronto. v. 77, no. 16 (Aug. 22, 1964), pp. 2-3.)

—— Backstage in Ottawa. The handful of troublemakers who disgrace Canada's Parliament. (In *Maclean's*. Toronto. v. 77, no. 17 (Sept. 5, 1964), p. 3.)

—— Backstage in Ottawa. Poverty down on the farm, and what eleven governments are doing about it. (In *Maclean's*. Toronto. v. 77, no. 18 (Sept. 19, 1964), pp. 2-3.)

—— Backstage in Ottawa. What the man said isn't always what the press gallery says he said. (In *Maclean's*. Toronto. v. 77, no. 20 (Oct. 17, 1964), pp. 5-6.)

Discusses the reporting of parliamentary activities by the press.

—— Backstage in Ottawa. Blair Fraser on the last gasps of the flag debate. (In *Maclean's*. Toronto. v. 77, no. 21 (Nov. 2, 1964), pp. 1-2.)

—— Backstage in Ottawa. Who really invited the Queen? It was Dief, not Pearson. (In *Maclean's*. Toronto. v. 77, no. 22 (Nov. 16, 1964), pp. 2-3.)

—— Backstage in Ottawa. How the hotheads may force an election that nobody else really wants to fight. (In *Maclean's*. Toronto. v. 78, no. 4 (Feb. 20, 1965), pp. 3-4.)

—— Backstage at Ottawa. Who's a good bet to lead the Quebec Liberal MPs? Nobody. (In *Maclean's*. Toronto. v. 78, no. 7 (Apr. 3, 1965), pp. 3-4.)

—— Backstage at Ottawa. With federal medicare in the works, can an election be far behind? (In *Maclean's*. Toronto. v. 78, no. 16 (Aug. 21, 1965), pp. 1-2.)

—— Backstage at the polls. The tip-off seats to watch in this election. (In *Maclean's*. Toronto. v. 78, no. 22 (Nov. 15, 1965), pp. 1-2.)

Refers to the general elections held November 8, 1965.

—— Backstage at Ottawa. The big post-election issues: poverty and provincial tax shares. (In *Maclean's*. Toronto. v. 78, no. 23 (Dec. 1, 1965), p. 3.)

Refers to the general elections held November 8, 1965.

—— Backstage at Ottawa. This has been a Bye-Bye production; four years, $6 million, a cast of hundreds. (In *Maclean's*. Toronto. v. 79, no. 10 (May 14, 1966), pp. 1-2.)

Comments on the operation and aims of the Royal Commission on Bilingualism and Biculturalism.

—— Backstage at Ottawa. The naval broadside that missed the boat. (In *Maclean's*. Toronto. v. 79, no. 16 (Aug. 20, 1966), pp. 1-2.)

Discusses the attack on the unification of the armed services by a group of admirals led by Admiral William Landymore.

—— Backstage in Ottawa. Why cheer Carter and boo the bi-bi? (In *Maclean's*. Toronto. v. 80, no. 4 (Apr. 1967), p. 2.)

Comparative remarks about the Carter Commission on Taxation and the Dunton-Laurendeau Commission on Bilingualism and Biculturalism.

—— Backstage in Ottawa. Why the fair brought peace to Parliament. Anxious to be off to Expo, MPs showed a refreshing penchant for co-operation. (In *Maclean's*. Toronto. v. 80, no. 6 (June 1967), p. 2.)

Discussion is concerned with efficient parliamentary procedures.

—— Backstage in Ottawa. The 20 bland pieties of the Manning plan. The premier's merger proposals are remarkable for what they leave out. (In *Maclean's*. Toronto. v. 80, no. 9 (Sept. 1967), pp. 3-4.)

Discusses "Premier Ernest Manning's offer to merge the Alberta Social Credit party with the Conservatives in the federal field".

Examines the ideas presented in the book *Political realignment*, by E. C. Manning. Toronto [c1967] (94 p.).

—— The battle of nouveau Quebec. (In *Maclean's*. Toronto. v. 77, no. 10 (May 16, 1964), pp. 13-15; 66-71.)

Concerns Rene Lévesque and his struggle with Ottawa over the issue of control over the north.

—— Can the young Turks seize Parliament Hill? As Ottawa's frustrated young MPs see it, there's nothing wrong with Parliament that couldn't be fixed by throwing out the Old Guard. (In *Maclean's*. Toronto. v. 79, no. 9 (May 2, 1966), pp. 16; 35; 37-38; 40.)

—— Gerda—and Parliament. (In *Maclean's*. Toronto. v. 79, no. 8 (Apr. 16, 1966), pp. 1-3.)

An essay on the significance of the Gerda Munsinger case.

—— Party puzzle: follow what leader? (In *Maclean's*. Toronto. v. 80, no. 6 (June 1967), pp. 24; 81-82; 84.)

"Who will lead the Liberals and Conservatives into the next election? On the eve of their conventions, it's still a toss-up choice."

—— The pipeline uproar: how much smoke? How much fire? (In *Maclean's*. Toronto. v. 71, no. 14 (July 5, 1958), pp. 13; 53-55.)

FRASER, GRAHAM René Lévesque: The Anglais cheer as he calls for Canada's break-up. (In *Maclean's*. Toronto. v. 82, no. 5 (May 1969), pp. 46-50.)

Comprises, mainly, conversations with René Lévesque.

FRASER, JOHN National affairs. We love thee Newfoundland. (In *Saturday night*. Toronto. v. 82, no. 4 (Apr. 1967), pp. 9; 11.)

Comments on relations between Newfoundland and the rest of Canada.

—— Newfoundland letter. The view from the other Canada. (In *Saturday night*.

Toronto. v. 83, no. 1 (Jan. 1968), pp. 12; 15.)

Comments on relations between mainland Canada and Newfoundland.

FULFORD, ROBERT   Can these two men really figure out Canada? One reporter's inquiry into the Royal Commission on Bilingualism and Biculturalism. (In *Maclean's*. Toronto. v. 77, no. 10 (May 16, 1964), pp. 16-17; 57-60.)

Reference is to Davidson Dunton and André Laurendeau.

—— Television notebook. (In *The Canadian forum*. Toronto. v. 42, no. 506 (Mar. 1963), pp. 275-277.)

Relates the political crisis of February 5, 1963 (the fall of the Diefenbaker government) to television news broadcasting.

FULTON, EDMUND DAVIE   La Confédération, un succès . . . et un défi. Par E. Davie Fulton. (In Congress on Canadian Affairs, 1st, Quebec, 1961. *Le Canada, expérience ratée . . . ou réussie*. Québec, 1962. pp. [11]-23.)

The Future of the French fact. (In *Saturday night*. Toronto. v. 83, no. 4 (Apr. 1968), pp. 29-34.)

Verbatim discussion of the Laurendeau-Dunton report involving Claude Ryan, Jacques Yvan Morin, Richard Arès, and Yvon Groulx.

GAGNON, SERGE   Pour une conscience historique de la révolution québécoise. (In *Cité libre*. Montréal. no. 83 (jan. 1966), pp. 4-19.)

GARDNER, BARRY   Campus. (In *Canada month*. Montreal. v. 5, no. 1 (Jan. 1965), p. 27.)

Considers the results in "five recent student model parliament elections".

GELLNER, JOHN   Fantasy for the future: Canada finds a real defence policy. (In *Saturday night*. Toronto. v. 76, no. 12 (June 10, 1961), pp. [20]-22.)

"Special SN report."

—— Filling in Parliament on the future war. (In *Saturday night*. Toronto. v. 78, no. 7 (Aug. 1963), pp. 10-12.)

Examines Canadian defence policy.

—— Political parties and Canadian defence. (In *Saturday night*. Toronto. v. 76, no. 4 (Feb. 18, 1961), pp. 9-11.)

GLENDON COLLEGE FORUM, TORONTO, 1967   Quebec: year eight. [Toronto] Canadian Broadcasting Corp. [c1968] x, 127 p.

Proceedings of a forum held November 24-26, 1967.

Includes a discussion titled: Quebec and federalism, by J. L. Pépin and René Lévesque (pp. 39-67).

GOODMAN, MARTIN   The televised campaign. Politics in the parlor. (In *Saturday night*. Toronto. v. 73, no. 9 (Apr. 26, 1958), pp. 8-[9]; 41.)

Refers to the campaign for the general elections held March 31, 1958.

GORDON, DONALD   Realism or fatalism. (In Empire Club of Canada. *Addresses*. Toronto. (1961/62), pp. 213-225.)

Address delivered March 12, 1962.

Discusses the recommendations presented in volumes 1 and 2 of the Report of the Royal Commission on Transportation. Ottawa, 1962. (3v.) Commonly known as the MacPherson report.

—— The three Prairie Provinces. (In *Commentator*. Toronto. v. 9, no. 11 (Nov. 1965), pp. 12-13.)

One of five articles in a section called "The election campaign from coast to coast".

Examines the campaign for the federal election held November 8, 1965.

GORDON, WALTER LOCKHART   Troubled Canada; the need for new domestic policies. [Toronto] McClelland and Stewart [c1961] x, 134 p.

GRAHAM, CHARLES R.   I was raided by the government. (In *Saturday night*. Toronto. v. 75, no. 19 (Sept. 17, 1960), pp. [21]-22.)

Records a government investigation of alleged anti-trust practices.

GRAHAM, GWETHALYN   How two women feel about one Canada or two. [An exchange of opinions between] Gwethalyn Graham and Chaput Rolland. (In *Maclean's*. Toronto. v. 76, no. 21 (Nov. 2, 1963), pp. 19; 53-59.)

GRAY, STANLEY   New Left—Old Left. (In *Canadian dimension*. Winnipeg. v. 3, no. 1 (Nov./Dec. 1965), pp. 11-13.)

Considers the concept and programs of the Student Union for Peace (New Left) and the New Democratic Party (Old Left).

GUAY, JACQUES   Le 8 novembre. Une jeunesse socialiste et québécoise. (In *Le Magazine Maclean*. Montréal. v. 5, no. 11 (nov. 1965), p. 1.)

Discusses, in part, the decision of J.

Marchand, G. Pelletier, and P. E. Trudeau to join the Liberal Party.

—— William Houle, le petit homme qui a intimidé Pearson. (In *Le Magazine Maclean*. Montréal. v. 5, no. 10 (oct. 1965), p. 5.)

Refers to the leader of the Montreal postal workers and their efforts to secure the principle of negotiation with the federal government.

GWYN, RICHARD J. Ad-men and scientists run this election. (In Thorburn, H. G. (ed.) *Party politics in Canada*. Scarborough, Ont., [c1967] pp. [121]-123.)

Discusses the first Canadian federal election (1962) based on scientific method.

"Reprinted from The Financial post, LVI, no. 17, April 28, 1962."

GZOWSKI, PETER The B. and B.'s desperate catalogue of the obvious. (In *Saturday night*. Toronto. v. 80, no. 4 (Apr. 1965), pp. 17-19.)

Concerns the Royal Commission on Bilingualism and Biculturalism, popularly known as the Laurendeau-Dunton Commission.

—— Conversations with Quebec's revolutionaries (In *Maclean's*. Toronto. v. 76, no. 17 (Sept. 7, 1963), pp. 13-15.)

Concerns Quebec and Confederation.

—— This is the true strength of separatism. (In *Maclean's*. Toronto. v. 76, no. 21 (Nov. 2, 1963), pp. 13-18.)

Concerns Quebec and Confederation.

HALL, EMMETT MATTHEW Canada's health charter; its implications. By the Honourable Emmett M. Hall, Justice of the Supreme Court of Canada. (In Empire Club of Canada. *Addresses*. Toronto. (1965/66), pp. [107]-[120].)

Address delivered December 9, 1965.

Discusses the Report of the Royal Commission on Health Services. Ottawa, 1964 (2 v.).

HARRIS, GEORGE Which way ahead for Labor? (In *The Marxist quarterly*. Toronto. no. 4 (winter 1963), pp. [7]-21.)

Discusses general policy, including political, pursued by the organized labour movement in Canada.

HARTLE, DOUGLAS Those hidden reports. (In *The Canadian forum*. Toronto. v. 38, no. 452 (Sept. 1958), pp. 122-124.)

The "hidden reports" were "the series of confidential annual reports entitled 'Cana-

dian economic outlook . . . prepared for the Liberal government . . . by the economists in the Economics Branch of the Department of Trade and Commerce". Article discusses the intense political issue which developed between the Conservative government and the Liberal opposition created by these reports.

HEBERT, GERARD Pour un Conseil supérieur du travail rénové. (In *Relations*. Montréal. [28. année] no 325 (mars 1968), pp. 74-76.)

—— Les unités de négociation et le CCRO. (In *Relations*. Montréal. [28. année] no 323 (jan. 1968), pp. 7-8.)

Discusses Bill C-186 to amend the federal law on industrial relations.

Heckler's handbook. By the Editors. (In *Saturday night*. Toronto. v. 77, no. 12 (June 9, 1962), pp. 11-16.)

Presents the issues of the federal election held June 18, 1962.

HEYDENKORN, BENEDICT How the New Canadians will vote. (In *Canadian commentator*. Toronto. v. 2, no. 2 (Feb. 1958), pp. [1]-2.)

Relates to the general elections of March 31, 1958.

HOBSON, JOHN Is it something besides a parliamentary crisis? (In *The Marxist quarterly*. Toronto. no. 13 (spring 1965), pp. 36-39.)

Comments on the concerned public reaction to contemporary parliamentary behaviour.

HOROWITZ, GAD Creative politics. (In *Canadian dimension*. Winnipeg. v. 3, no. 1 (Nov./Dec. 1965), pp. 14-15; 28.)

Analyses contemporary Canadian politics. Relates to the ideas presented in *The vertical mosaic*, by John Porter. Toronto, University of Toronto Press, 1965.

For a continuation see the Author's article Mosaics & identity. (In *Canadian dimension*. Winnipeg. v. 3, no. 2 (Jan./Feb. 1966), pp. 17-19.)

—— The end of ideology or new (class) politics? A dialogue between Gad Horowitz and Charles Taylor. (In *Canadian dimension*. Winnipeg. v. 4, no. 1 (Nov./Dec. 1966), pp. 12-15.)

—— Mosaics & identity. (In *Canadian dimension*. Winnipeg. v. 3, no. 2 (Jan./Feb. 1966), pp. 17-19.)

Continuation of the Author's article Creative politics. (In *Canadian dimension.* Winnipeg. v. 3, no. 1 (Nov./Dec. 1965), pp. 14-15; 28.)

—— Tories, Socialists and the demise of Canada. (In *Canadian dimension.* Winnipeg. v. 2, no. 4 (May/June 1965), pp. 12-15.)

How to make the new Canada. [A symposium of prominent Canadians tell what they want their country to become.] (In *Maclean's.* Toronto. v. 77, no. 3 (Feb. 8, 1964), pp. 24-26; 36-43.)

Views of Laurier LaPierre, P. E. Trudeau, Pauline Jewett, A. R. M. Lower, Thérèse F. Casgrain, Bruce Hutchison, Wallace McCutcheon, M. J. Coldwell, Jack Scott, and others.

HOWARD, FRANK   Common sense laws to prevent strikes. (In *Saturday night.* Toronto. v. 75, no. 15 (July 23, 1960), p. 21.)

HUTCHISON, BRUCE   Inflation can kill more than our dollar. It can kill our nation. (In *Maclean's.* Toronto. v. 72, no. 3 (Jan. 31, 1959), pp. 11; 36-38.)

IRVINE, RUSSELL B.   Commons comment. (In *The Canadian forum.* Toronto. v. 43, no. 514 (Nov. 1963), pp. 173-174.)

Considers the growing concern that parliament is becoming a mere ritual.

—— Ottawa: the first session. (In *The Canadian forum.* Toronto. v. 43, no. 510 (July 1963), p. 75.)

General comments on the first session of the twenty-sixth parliament.

IRVINE, WILLIAM PETER   An analysis of voting shifts in Quebec. By W. P. Irvine. (In Meisel, John (ed.) *Papers on the 1962 election.* [Toronto, 1964] pp. [129]-143.)

Concerns the general elections held June 18, 1962.

The Issues before us in the election. By Ian Wahn, Erik Nielsen, Andrew Brewin, Robert Thompson. (In *Commentator.* Toronto. v. 9, no. 10 (Oct. 1965), pp. 8-11; 23.)

General elections held November 8, 1965.

JAENEN, CORNELIUS J.   Creighton, Confederation & conspiracy. By C. J. Jaenen. (In *Canadian dimension.* Winnipeg. v. 4, no. 4 (May/June 1967), pp. 22-25.)

Considers the view presented by Donald Creighton that the compact theory of Confederation is a contemporary and inaccurate interpretation developed by French-Canadian nationalists. Cf., for example,

The myth of biculturalism, by D. G. Creighton. (In *Saturday night.* Toronto. v. 81, no. 9 (Sept. 1966), pp. 35-39.)

JAMES, MUNGO   Ottawa letter. Press gallery. (In *Saturday night.* Toronto. v. 81, no. 7 (July 1966), pp. 10-11.)

A contemporary look at the function of the parliamentary press gallery.

—— Ottawa letter. Warlord on poverty. (In *Saturday night.* Toronto. v. 81, no. 11 (Nov. 1966), pp. 16-18.)

Concerns R. A. J. Phillips, Director of the Special Planning Secretariat, co-ordinator of the anti-poverty campaign.

JELEN, WALTER   Canada's cabinet needs more ministers. A plea for departments of industry, economics, youth and sports, and cultural affairs. (In *Commentator.* Toronto. v. 6, no. 5 (May 1962), pp. 11-12.)

JEWETT, PAULINE MAE   The major issues are blurred. By Pauline Jewett. (In *Canadian commentator.* Toronto. v. 2, no. 3 (Mar. 1958), p. 3.)

Discusses the political situation peculiar to the general elections of March 31, 1958.

JOHNSON, DANIEL   The years of the last chance. (In Hawkins, Gordon (ed.) *Concepts of federalism.* [Toronto] 1965. pp. 52-61.)

Discusses French-Canadian–English-Canadian relations in the light of a need for changes in the Canadian constitution.

JOHNSTON, HOWARD   CYC: a near-million tax dollars for upheaval. By Howard Johnston, MP. (In *Canada month.* Montreal. v. 8, no. 1 (Jan. 1968), pp. 34-35.)

Discusses the objectives and expense of the Company of Young Canadians, established in June 1966.

KETTLE, JOHN   "All the government wants to do is give you people a number." By J. K. (In *Canada month.* Montreal. v. 4, no. 5 (May 1964), pp. 18-19.)

Concerns the introduction of the social insurance number.

—— Quebec's Marcel Faribault: from the canyons of St. James Street, a man who knows what French Canada wants—a new constitution. (In *Canada month.* Montreal. v. 5, no. 5 (May 1965), pp. [12]-14.)

"A CM profile."

Presents (Faribault's) views on a new Canadian constitution.

—— Socialism in Canada: the beginning of the end. (In *Canada month*. Montreal. v. 4, no. 5 (May 1964), p. 33.)

Relates to the victory of the Liberal Party in Saskatchewan under Ross Thatcher. The provincial election was held April 23, 1964.

KIERANS, ERIC WILLIAM   Le Canada vu par Kierans. Montréal, Editions du Jour [1967] 158 p. (Collection Les Idées du jour.)

—— Challenge of confidence: Kierans on Canada. Toronto, McClelland and Stewart [c1967] 125 p.

Translation of *Le Canada vu par Kierans*.

—— The most anti-nationalist Quebecker. Interview: by Jack Doupe. (In *Canada month*. Montreal. v. 7, no. 11 (Nov. 1967), pp. 23-26.)

KNOX, DAVID N.   "Well, face it! If you're small-c you're unloved." (In *Canada month*. Montreal. v. 8, no. 8 (Aug. 1968), pp. 15-17.)

Comments on "conservatism".

KORNBERG, ALLAN   Canadian legislative behaviour; a study of the 25th parliament. New York, Holt, Rinehart and Winston [1967] x, 166 p.

The twenty-fifth parliament extended from September 27, 1962, until February 6, 1963.

KWAVNICK, DAVID   Canadians and Quebecois. Part 1. Problems & fallacies. (In *Canada month*. Montreal. v. 6, no. 9 (Sept. 1966), pp. 10-15.)

—— "Equality or independence." (In *Canada month*. Montreal. v. 6, no. 10 (Oct. 1966), pp. 12-16.)

Continuation of the author's article "Canadians and Quebecois".

—— Organized labour and government: The Canadian Labour Congress as a political interest group during the Diefenbaker and Pearson administrations. [Ottawa, 1969] 545 leaves.

Thesis (PH D) – Carleton University.

LAMARCHE, GUY   Sauf vot' respect. Si l'habit ne fait pas le moine, le drapeau ne fait pas le pays. (In *Le Magazine Maclean*. Montréal. v. 4, no. 9 (sept. 1964), pp. 28; 34; 36.)

LAMONTAGNE, MAURICE   Quebec and national unity. (In Hawkins, Gordon (ed.) *Order and good government*. Toronto, 1965. pp. 148-151.)

LAND, REGINALD BRIAN   Eglinton; The election study of a federal constituency. By Brian Land. Toronto, P. Martin Associates, 1965. vi, 160 p.

Concerns the federal election held June 18, 1962.

—— A study of Eglinton constituency in the federal election of 1962. [Toronto, 1963] 1 v.

Thesis (MA) – University of Toronto.

LANGDON, STEVEN   Canada's student movement. (In *Canada month*. Montreal. v. 8, no. 9 (Sept. 1968), pp. 12-13.)

LANGEVIN, ANDRE   Le prix: 50 millions et 3 héros. (In *Le Magazine Maclean*. Montréal. v. 5, no 11 (nov. 1965), pp. 1-2.)

Refers to the campaign for the federal election held November 8, 1965. The three "héros" are Jean Marchand, Gérard Pelletier, and Pierre Elliott Trudeau.

LAOCOON   Ottawa letter. By Laocoön. (In *Saturday night*. Toronto. v. 80, no. 9 (Sept. 1965), pp. 12-13.)

Discusses the implications drawn from the Dorion report investigating bail for Lucien Rivard.

LA PIERRE, LAURIER JOSEPH LUCIEN   Caouette and all that: an election report from Quebec. By Laurier LaPierre. (In *The Canadian forum*. Toronto. v. 43, no. 507 (Apr. 1963), pp. [1]-3.)

A discussion of the issues presented during the campaign for the general elections of April 8, 1963.

—— The Gordon affair: dialogue des sourds. By Laurier L. LaPierre. (In *The Canadian forum*. Toronto. v. 42, no. 505 (Feb. 1963), pp. 246-249.)

Analyses the reaction to remarks made by Donald Gordon concerning the promoting and appointing of French Canadians to positions in the Canadian National Railways.

—— The 1960s. By Laurier L. LaPierre. (In Careless, J. M. S. (ed.) *The Canadians*, 1867-1967. Toronto, 1967. pp. 344-382.)

—— Platform. Nationalism? Forget it! Our future is in the cities—and they need help now. By Laurier LaPierre. (In *Maclean's*. Toronto. v. 82, no. 9 (Sept. 1969), p. 13.)

LAPONCE, JEAN ANTOINE   Non-voting and non-voters: a typology. By J. A. Laponce. (In *The Canadian journal of economics and political science.* [Toronto] v. 33 (1967), pp. [75]-87.)

The data used for this study were gathered from a sample survey taken in a Vancouver federal riding at the time of the federal election held April 8, 1963.

—— People vs politics: a study of opinions, attitudes, and perceptions in Vancouver-Burrard, 1963-1965. By J. A. Laponce. [Toronto] University of Toronto Press [c1969] xii, 219 p.

The aim of this work "is simply to obtain a more precise picture of Canadian electors . . .". – Introd.

LAURENDEAU, ANDRE   For the sake of argument: The astonishing attitude of the English in Quebec. (In *Maclean's*. Toronto. v. 72, no. 10 (May 9, 1959), pp. 8; 97-98.)

—— Nos hommes politiques: Québec 1963. (In Institut canadien des affaires publiques, Montréal. *Nos hommes politiques.* Montréal [c1964]. pp. [83]-92.)

—— Y a-t-il un cas Cité Libre? (In *L'Action nationale*. Montréal. v. 37 (mars/avril 1951), pp. [222]-234.)

LAUZON, ADELE   Le Canada pris au piège de sa prospérité. (In *Le Magazine Maclean*. Montréal. v. 2, no. 9 (sept. 1962), pp. 17; 52-55.)

Examines the Canadian economy in the wake of the federal election held in June 1962.

LAXER, JAMES   The New Left as it sees itself. By James Laxer and Arthur Pape. (In *Canadian dimension*. Winnipeg. v. 3, no. 6 (Sept./Oct. 1966), pp. 14-15.)

A brief discussion.

—— Youth and Canadian politics. By James Laxer and Arthur Pape. (In *Our generation*. Montreal. v. 4, no. 3 (1966), pp. 15-21.)

LEBEL, MAURICE   The centenary of Confederation. (In *Culture*. Québec. v. 28 (1967), pp. [229]-235.)

LEFEBVRE, JEAN PAUL   Au carrefour, encore une fois? (In *Cité libre*. Montréal. no. 54 (fév. 1963), pp. 21-25.)

A conjectural answer to a question posed by Gérard Pelletier: Est-il impensable que le vieux parti libéral s'engage dans une alliance avec le nouveau parti libéral, mieux connu sous le sigle NDP?

LEMIEUX, VINCENT   Election in the constituency of Lévis. (In Meisel, John (ed.)

Papers on the 1962 election. [Toronto, 1964]. pp. [33]-52.)

Concerns general elections held June 18, 1962.

—— Quebec, la belle province. (In *Commentator*. Toronto. v. 9, no. 11 (Nov. 1965), pp. 8-[9].)

One of five articles in a section called "The election campaign from coast to coast".

Examines the campaign for the federal election held November 8, 1965.

Let's call Roly Michener home! (In *Canada month*. Montreal. v. 4 [i.e. 5] no. 4 (Apr. 1965), p. 9.)

Advances the idea of making Roland Michener leader of either the Liberal or Progressive Conservative Party.

LLOYD, TREVOR OWEN   Government as dialogue; conclusion. By Trevor Lloyd. (In University League for Social Reform. *Agenda 1970*. [Toronto, c1968]. pp. [281]-202.)

Discusses communication between government and the Canadian public.

—— The psephology of discontent. By Trevor Lloyd. (In *The Canadian forum*. Toronto. v. 43, no. 508 (May 1963), pp. 26-27.)

Discusses the general elections' results of April 8, 1963.

LONG, MARCUS   Domestic politics: the need for unity. (In *Saturday night*. Toronto. v. 74, no. 18 (Aug. 29, 1959), pp. 14-15.)

Comments on Mackenzie King, C. D. Howe, and John Diefenbaker.

—— Election outlook—the long view. (In *Canadian commentator*. Toronto. v. 2, no. 3 (Mar. 1958), pp. [1]-2.)

Comments on the political campaign for the general elections of March 31, 1958.

—— The Governor-Generalship. By M. L. (In *Canadian commentator*. Toronto. v. 1, no. 7 (July 1957), p. 5.)

Critical comments on the rumour that Louis St. Laurent was to be appointed as Governor-General of Canada.

LOUGHEED, WILLIAM FOSTER   Return to Ottawa. A review of the problems, economic and political, facing the new session of Parliament. By W. F. Lougheed. (In *Canadian commentator*. Toronto. v. 3, no. 1 (Jan. 1959), pp. 9-10.)

The second session of the twenty-fourth parliament opened January 15, 1959.

—— Spending the deficit. By W. F. Lougheed. (In *Canadian commentator*. Toronto. v. 5, no. 9 (Oct. 1961), pp. 15; 17-18.)
Discussion concerns government finance.

LOWER, ARTHUR REGINALD MARSDEN Lower on liberty. (In *Canada month*. Montreal. v. 3, no. 6 (June 1963), p. 26.)

—— Would Canada be better off without Quebec? By A. R. M. Lower. (In *Maclean's*. Toronto. v. 77, no. 24 (Dec. 14, 1964), pp. 27; 51-52.)

LYNCH, MATTHEW J. Canada's century? A centenial-plus-one appreciation. (In *Canada month*. Montreal. v. 8, no. 6 (June 1968), pp. 17-19.)

LYON, PEYTON VAUGHN The election and foreign policy discussion in Canada. "It would be naive to expect an electoral campaign to elevate foreign policy discussion . . . " By Peyton V. Lyon. (In *Commentator*. Toronto. v. 6, no. 5 (May 1962), pp. 8-[9].)
Relates foreign policy discussion to the campaign for the federal election held June 18, 1962.

—— Foreign policy is crucial. In this election, contrary to most, our parties do disagree on foreign policy, and though all have weaknesses, Pearson's is preferable. By Peyton V. Lyon. (In *Commentator*. Toronto. v. 7, no. 4 (Apr. 1963), pp. 16-17.)
Relates to the general elections held April 8, 1963.

MC CONNELL, R. K. The Carter Royal Commission report on taxation. In principle: socialistic spoliation. (In *Canada month*. Montreal. v. 7, no. 4 (Apr. 1967), pp. 20-21.)

MAC DADE, JOHN Point of view. Facing the election rhetoric. (In *Saturday night*. Toronto. v. 77, no. 3 (Feb. 3, 1962), p. 40.)
Relates to the campaign for the federal election held June 18, 1962.

MACDONALD, BRUCE JOHN STEWART Point of view. Some proper teeth for a Bill of Rights. By Bruce J. S. Macdonald. (In *Saturday night*. Toronto. v. 75, no. 22 (Oct. 29, 1960), p. 52.)

MAC DONALD, DAVID The most powerful woman's lobby in Canada. (In *Chatelaine*. Toronto. v. 29, no. 6 (June 1957), pp. 14-15; 58-61.)
Concerns the National Council of Women.

MAC KENZIE, NORMAN ARCHIBALD MAC RAE A view on education. With reference to the Atlantic Region. By Senator Norman A. MacKenzie. (In *The Atlantic advocate*. Fredericton, N.B. v. 56, no. 9 (May 1966), pp. 13-16.)

MACKINNON, FRANK Confederation after a century. [Charlottetown, P.E.I.] Prince Edward Island Centennial Committee [1964] 19 p.
Cover title.
Address delivered during Confederation Conference Centennial in P.E.I. and in cities across Canada during a Canadian Club tour. Cf. p. [1.]

MACKLIN, WILFRID HAROLD STEPHENSON Here is a defence policy for Canada. (In *The Canadian Saturday night*. Toronto. v. 78, no. 4 (Apr. 1963), pp. 25-27.)

MC LAUGHLIN, WILLIAM EARLE The coming showdown on economic policy: will the government planners take over? By W. Earle McLaughlin. (In *Canada month*. Montreal. v. 3, no. 7 [i.e. 8] (Aug. 1963), pp. 13-14.)

MAC LELLAN, JAMES W. Protest, sit-in, demonstrate! (In *Canada month*. Montreal. v. 9, no. 2 (Feb. 1969), p. 14.)
Argues "that the discrepancies between public will and parliamentary decision are too great".

MAC LENNAN, HUGH Is Quebec still the key to Canadian politics? (In *Saturday night*. Toronto. v. 72, no. 15 (July 20, 1957), pp. 10-11; 38.)

MC LEOD, JOHN TENNYSON Living in a house of minorities. By John T. McLeod. (In *The Canadian forum*. Toronto. v. 43, no. 509 (June 1963), pp. [49]-51.)
An analysis of the problems connected with minority government.

MC MENEMY, JOHN MURRAY The Columbia River Treaty, 1961-1964; a study of opposition and representation in the Canadian political system. Toronto, 1969. 2 v.
Thesis (PH D) – University of Toronto.

MC NAUGHT, KENNETH WILLIAM KIRKPATRICK Bedtime Tories. By Kenneth McNaught. (In *Saturday night*. Toronto. v. 80 [i.e. 81] no. 5 (May 1966), pp. 12; 14.)
Considers the "disintegration" of the Liberal Party and the rise of the NDP.

—— Crisis report. By Kenneth McNaught. (In *Saturday night*. Toronto. v. 83, no. 4 (Apr. 1968), pp. 35-36.)

Examines volume one of the Report of the Royal Commission on Bilingualism and Biculturalism, popularly known as the Laurendeau-Dunton report.

—— Don't disturb the floaters. Lose the issues—win the election? By Kenneth McNaught. (In *Saturday night*. Toronto. v. 77, no. 13 (June 23, 1962), p. 13.)
Refers to the federal election held June 18, 1962.

—— The failure of television in politics. By Kenneth McNaught. (In *The Canadian forum*. Toronto. v. 38, no. 451 (Aug. 1958), pp. 104-105.)

—— The majority fetish. By Kenneth McNaught. (In *Saturday night*. Toronto. v. 80, no. 11 (Nov. 1965), pp. 12-14; 16.)
Discusses the issues raised during the campaign for the general elections held November 8, 1965.

—— National affairs. By Kenneth McNaught. (In *Saturday night*. Toronto. v. 80, no. 3 (Mar. 1965), pp. 14-16.)
Discusses Canadian defence policy, with special reference to the command centre established at North Bay, Ont.

—— National affairs. By Kenneth McNaught. (In *Saturday night*. Toronto. v. 80, no. 9 (Sept. 1965), pp. 9-12.)
General comments.

—— National affairs. By Kenneth McNaught. (In *Saturday night*. Toronto. v. 80, no. 12 (Dec. 1965), pp. 13; 15-16.)
Examines the issues of the federal election held November 8, 1965.

—— National affairs. By Kenneth McNaught. (In *Saturday night*. Toronto. v. 81, no. 1 (Jan. 1966), pp. 7-8.)
Considers that Canada has developed a multi-party system.

—— Nationalism and the left. By Kenneth McNaught. (In *Saturday night*. Toronto. v. 82, no. 4 (Apr. 1967), pp. 11-12; 15.)
A comparative analysis relating to the United States, Great Britain and Canada.

—— On turning 98. It's time to talk divorce with Quebec. By Kenneth McNaught. (In *Saturday night*. Toronto. v. 80, no. 7 (July 1965), pp. 16-18.)

MACPHERSON, DUNCAN IAN Cartoons, by Macpherson. Toronto, Toronto Star [1959] v.
Cover title.
Selection of cartoons previously published in the *Toronto Star*.

Title varies.
First two volumes published 1959 and 1962, unnumbered.

MC RAE, KENNETH DOUGLAS The entrenchment of the Bill of Rights. By K. D. McRae. (In *The Canadian forum*. Toronto. v. 40, no. 476 (Sept. 1960), pp. 124-125.)

MAHAFFY, R. U. Public works: a cautious program. (In *Saturday night*. Toronto. v. 75, no. 1 (Jan. 9, 1960), pp. 25-26.)

MALONE, RICHARD S. Canada's defence; how and who? Will unification make sense in defence? By Richard S. Malone, Publisher, Winnipeg Free Press. (In Empire Club of Canada. *Addresses*. [Don Mills, Ont.] (1966/67), pp. [1]-14.)
Address delivered October 6, 1966.

Manifeste politique. Propositions programmatiques de La Revue socialiste. (In *La Revue socialiste*. Montréal. [no] 1 (printemps 1959), pp. 13-33.)

MANNING, ERNEST CHARLES Liberty, unity and prosperity. An address by the Hon. E. C. Manning. (In Empire Club of Canada. *Addresses*. Toronto. (1966/67), pp. [54]-64.)
Address delivered November 3, 1966.

—— Political realignment; a challenge to thoughtful Canadians. By the Hon. E. C. Manning. Toronto, McClelland and Stewart [c1967] 94 p.

MARCOTTE, MARCEL Vers une nouvelle loi du divorce. (In *Relations*. Montréal. [28. année] no 323 (jan. 1968), pp. 2-3.)

MARTIN, LOUIS L'existence du Canada est menacée, mais... cette constatation de la commission Laurendeau-Dunton est minimisée par les journaux anglophones. (In *Le Magazine Maclean*. Montréal. v. 5, no 7 (juil. 1965), pp. 11-13; 41.)

—— Notes de rédaction. Le 8 novembre. (In *Le Magazine Maclean*. Montréal. v. 5, no 11 (nov. 1965), p. 2.)
Refers to the federal election of November 8, 1965, and the election to the federal Parliament of J. Marchand, G. Pelletier, and P. E. Trudeau.

MATHEWS, ROBIN *Time*, Timestyle, and Canadian electioneering. (In *The Canadian forum*. Toronto. v. 42, no. 499 (Aug. 1962), pp. 101-102.)
Comments on the *Time* magazine coverage of the Canadian general elections held June 18, 1962.

MEISEL, JOHN   After the deluge—what? (In *The Canadian forum*. Toronto. v. 38, no. 448 (May 1958), pp. [25]; 48.)

Analyses the significance of the results of the 1958 general elections.

—— Conclusion; an analysis of the national (?) results [of the 1962 election] By J. Meisel. (In his *Papers on the 1962 election*. [Toronto, 1964.] pp. [272]-288.)

—— Election outcome: a breather (In *The Canadian forum*. Toronto. v. 43, no. 508 (May 1963), pp. 31-32.)

Discusses the results of the federal elections held April 8, 1963, and the significance of the election returns on the political party system.

—— The June 1962 election: break-up of our party system? (In *Queen's quarterly*. Kingston. v. 69 (1962), pp. [329]-346.)

MEISEL, JOHN (ed.)   Papers on the 1962 election. Fifteen papers on the Canadian general election of 1962. [Toronto] University of Toronto Press [1964] xii, 288 p.

Contents: St. John's West, by G. Perlin. – Did they vote for party or candidate in Halifax, by M. Davis. – The election in the constituency of Lévis, by V. Lemieux. – Three dimensions of a local political party, by H. A. Scarrow. – The campaign in Eglinton, by D. Smith. – A return to the status quo; the election in Winnipeg North Centre, by T. Peterson and I. Avakumovic. – The election in the province of Quebec, by L. Dion. – An analysis of voting shifts in Quebec, by W. P. Irvine. – The press of Ontario and the election, by T. H. Qualtar and K. A. MacKirdy. – The counter-revolution in Saskatchewan, by N. Ward. – The NDP; British Columbia's labour party, by W. D. Young. – The social bases of political cleavage in 1962, by R. L. Alford. – Group perceptions and the vote, by S. P. Regenstreif. – Political behaviour and ethnic origin, by M. A. Schwartz. – Conclusion: An analysis of the national (?) results, by J. Meisel.

—— Party images in Canada. A report on work in progress; chart and tables. [Kingston, Ont.] Queen's University [1969?] 21 leaves.

Cover title.

Statistical survey of public opinion on Canadian political parties, 1965-1968.

Reproduced typescript.

—— Some quantitative analyses of Canadian election results; an exercise in the testing of hypotheses. By John Meisel and Gilles Paquet. (In Conference on Statistics. 3d, McMaster University, 1962. *Papers*. [Toronto, 1964] pp. 1-31. 16 tables.)

This paper examines the results of the 1957 and 1958 Canadian general elections.

MELTZ, NOAH M.   Manpower policy; nature, objectives, perspectives. (In *Relations industrielles*. Québec. v. 24 (1969), pp. 33-56.)

Summary in French: De la politique de main-d'oeuvre (pp. 55-56).

An essay tracing the development of manpower policy.

"This paper was originally presented to a meeting of the University League for Social Reform at the University of Toronto on February 3, 1966."

MERCER, G.   The political party organization in a federal riding; a case-study of Burnaby/Coquitlam. [Vancouver, 1966] 144 leaves.

Thesis (MA) – Simon Fraser University.

—— For the sake of argument; We're going haywire in our security plans. (In *Maclean's*. Toronto. v. 70, no. 15 (July 20, 1957), pp. 10; 58-60.)

MINIFIE, JAMES MAC DONALD   The Canadian election in the American view. By J. M. Minifie. (In *Commentator*. Toronto. v. 9, no. 11 (Nov. 1965), pp. 22-23.)

Concerns the general elections held November 8, 1965.

—— Pre-election survey: 5. British Columbia. Anybody's guess. By J. M. Minifie. (In *The Canadian commentator*. Toronto. v. 6, no. 6 (June 1962), pp. 5; 20.)

Discusses the issues in the campaign for the general elections held June 18, 1962.

—— Quebec's in turmoil. Quebec's attitude today is reminiscent of English-Canada's revolt against Britain 40 years ago, and makes predictions difficult. By J. M. Minifie. (In *Commentator*. Toronto. v. 7, no. 4 (Apr. 1963), pp. 3-4.)

One of seven articles which form part of "Election survey".

Predictions on the outcome of the general elections held April 8, 1963.

—— What happened on June 18th? PCs' loss of 87 seats was a personal defeat for Mr. Diefenbaker . . . By James M. Minifie. (In *Commentator*. Toronto. v. 6, no. 7-8 (July—Aug. 1962), pp. 5; 22.)

Discusses the results of the general elections held June 18, 1962.

MOON, BARBARA The back-room conspiracy. (In *Maclean's*. Toronto. v. 75, no. 15 (July 28, 1962), pp. 15; 41-44.)

An essay on the strategists who plan and direct election campaigns. With special reference to the campaign for the federal election held June 18, 1962.

MOORE, HELEN G. Against socialism and fascism. The Combines Act is necessary law. (In *Saturday night*. Toronto. v. 77, no. 7 (Mar. 31, 1962), pp. [29]-30.)

MORIN, JACQUES YVAN What is equality of the two nations? (In *The Marxist quarterly*. Toronto. n. 15 (autumn 1965), pp. 9-16.)

Translation of a "paper presented to the Association des éducateurs de langue française (ACELF), and first published in Le Devoir, March 23, 1965".

MORRIS, LESLIE The April general election. (In *The Marixst quarterly*. Toronto. no. 6 (summer 1963), pp. 1-11.)

Examines the results of the general elections held April 8, 1963.

—— Mr. Pearson's "biculturalism" and the reactionary device of "cultural autonomy". (In *The Marixst quarterly*. Toronto. no. 7 (autumn 1963), pp. 6-11.)

MORTON, JOHN DESMOND Point of view. Let's put teeth in the Bill of Rights. By J. D. Morton. (In *Saturday night*. Toronto. v. 75, no. 19 (Sept. 17, 1960), p. 52.)

MOWBRAY, GEORGE Pandora's filing cabinet. (In *Canadian commentator*. Toronto. v. 2, no. 8/9 (Aug./Sept. 1958), pp. 8; 13.)

Discusses the nature and function of the Civil Service prompted by the disclosure of the "hidden reports", i.e. the report entitled "Canada's economic outlook for 1958", prepared by the Department of Trade and Commerce.

MYERS, LEONARD W. What about Western separatism? (In *Commentator*. Toronto. v. 9, no. 9 (Sept. 1965), pp. 10-11; 21.)

Discusses remarks about the secession of British Columbia from Confederation made by the Minister of Industrial Development, Trade and Commerce for British Columbia, the Hon. Ralph R. Loffmark.

NASH, C. KNOWLTON Canada needs a lobby in Washington. (In *Maclean's*. Toronto. v. 72, no. 9 (Apr. 25, 1959), pp. 24-25; 58; 60.)

National affairs. [Series II] (In *Saturday night*. Toronto. v. 80, no. 2—v. 83, no. 10 (Feb. 1965—Oct. 1968).)

Column dealing with federal politics, written by Kenneth McNaught, Arnold Edinborough, Kildare Dobbs, Christina Newman, and others.

NEATBY, HERBERT BLAIR The present discontents: a proposal. By H. Blair Neatby. (In *The Canadian forum*. Toronto. v. 43, no. 513 (Oct. 1963), pp. [145]-147.)

Considers the nature of the federal union which should involve discussion between French and English speaking Canadians.

The New Bank Act, a half-measure at best. By *** (In *Commentator*. Toronto. v. 11, no. 6 (June 1967), pp. 18-19.)

"The writer of this . . . must, because of his business affiliation, remain anonymous."

The New Confederation and its critics. A suggestion: [by] Michel Chartrand, Jacques-Yvan Morin, André L'Heureux. A critique: by E. A. Tollefson. (In *Canadian dimension*. Winnipeg. v. 1, no. 4/5 (Feb./Mar. 1964), pp. 4-6.)

NEWMAN, CHRISTINA (MC CALL) Are women 2nd-class voters? (In *Chatelaine*. Toronto. v. 35, no. 6 (June 1962), pp. [27]-44; 46; 48; 50.)

Examines the position of women in Canadian politics.

—— Canada's First Lady at home. (In *Chatelaine*. Toronto. v. 33, no. 3 (Mar. 1960), pp. 30; 83-87.)

Concerns Mme Pauline Vanier, first native-born First Lady of Canada.

—— The longest-established permanent floating chaos. By Christina Newman. (In *Saturday night*. Toronto. v. 84, no. 12 (Dec. 1969), pp. 21-22; 27.)

Reviews the scandals and the problems that confronted the Conservative and Liberal parties during the 1960s.

—— The new women in Ottawa. (In *Chatelaine*. Toronto. v. 36, no. 10 (Oct. 1963), pp. 30-31; 102; 104-108.)

Concerns Judy LaMarsh, Pauline Jewett, Jean Casselman, and Margaret Konantz.

—— Ottawa letter. Our capital? Not for Quebeckers. By Christina Newman. (In *Saturday night*. Toronto. v. 82, no. 12 (Dec. 1967), pp. 17-18.)

Discusses conditions in Ottawa for

French Canadians and some implications of the Royal Commission on Bilingualism and Biculturalism.

—— Ottawa letter. Who's up? Who's down? By Christina Newman. (In *Saturday night.* Toronto. v. 83, no. 1 (Jan. 1968), pp. 8-10.)

Comments on the reaction in the press to some political personalities: L. B. Pearson, R. Stanfield, J. Diefenbaker, T. C. Douglas, etc.

—— What's so funny about the Royal Commission on the Status of Women? By Christina Newman. (In *Saturday night.* Toronto. v. 84, no. 1 (Jan. 1969), pp. 21-24.)

NEWMAN, PETER CHARLES Backstage at Ottawa. Can we get along without U.S. dollars? By Peter C. Newman. (In *Maclean's.* Toronto. v. 73, no. 9 (Apr. 23, 1960), p. 2.)

—— Backstage at Ottawa. Inside the Defense Department: why the U.S. protects us—temporarily. By Peter C. Newman. (In *Maclean's.* Toronto. v. 73, no. 10 (May 7, 1960), p. 2.)

—— Backstage at Ottawa. The 20 men who really run Canada. By Peter C. Newman. (In *Maclean's.* Toronto. v. 73, no. 12 (June 4, 1960), p. 2.)

—— Backstage at Ottawa. The Immigration Act: St. Ellen's anachronistic dragon. By Peter C. Newman. (In *Maclean's.* Toronto. v. 73, no. 14 (July 2, 1960), p. 2.)

—— Backstage at Ottawa. How much do the provincial upsets mean nationally? By Peter C. Newman. (In *Maclean's.* Toronto. v. 73, no. 11 [i.e. 16] (July 30, 1960), p. 2.)

—— Backstage at Ottawa. Is Jack Kennedy our best hedge against depression? By Peter C. Newman. (In *Maclean's.* Toronto. v. 73, no. 18 Aug. 27, 1960), p. 2.)

—— Backstage in Newfoundland. A visit with captain Joey on his private island. By Peter C. Newman. (In *Maclean's.* Toronto. v. 73, no. 20 (Sept. 24, 1960), p. 2.)
Interviews Premier Joseph Smallwood.

—— Backstage at Ottawa. A year-end salute to Parliament's lighter moments. By Peter C. Newman. (In *Maclean's.* Toronto. v. 74, no. 1 (Jan. 7, 1961), p. 86.)

—— Backstage at Ottawa. Will a drastic new National Policy help the jobless? By Peter C. Newman. (In *Maclean's.* Toronto. v. 74, no. 3 (Feb. 11, 1961), p. 46.)

—— Backstage at Ottawa. On TV, it's John the actor versus just plain Mike. By Peter C. Newman. (In *Maclean's.* Toronto. v. 74, no. 4 (Feb. 25, 1961), p. 54.)
Concerns John Diefenbaker and Lester B. Pearson.

—— Backstage at Ottawa. Atoms, NATO and NORAD—the coming election issue. By Peter C. Newman. (In *Maclean's.* Toronto. v. 74, no. 6 (Mar. 25, 1961), p. 68.)

—— Backstage at Ottawa. Who'll pay the record shot for our next election? By Peter C. Newman. (In *Maclean's.* Toronto. v. 74, no. 9 (May 6, 1961), p. 62.)

—— Backstage at Ottawa. The election game opens. Both big parties think they have the winning move. By Peter C. Newman. (In *Maclean's.* Toronto. v. 74, no. 12 (June 17, 1961), p. 62.)

—— Backstage at Ottawa. First signs of a merger: now some planners say one way to beat the Americans is to join them. By Peter C. Newman. (In *Maclean's.* Toronto. v. 74, no. 18 (Sept. 9, 1961), p. 80.)
Discusses the argument for economic union with the United States.

—— Backstage at Ottawa. A new kind of boom—with still more unemployed. By Peter C. Newman. (In *Maclean's.* Toronto. v. 74, no. 21 (Oct. 21, 1961), p. 86.)

—— Backstage in Ottawa. The 1962 election: why both the major parties really think they'll win. By Peter C. Newman. (In *Maclean's.* Toronto. v. 75, no. 1 (Jan. 6, 1962), p. 62.)

—— Backstage in Ottawa. How to win the '62 election: catch the floating vote. By Peter C. Newman. (In *Maclean's.* Toronto. v. 75, no. 8 (Apr. 21, 1962), p. 80.)

—— Backstage in Ottawa. Coming: a night filled with surprises on June 18. By Peter C. Newman. (In *Maclean's.* Toronto. v. 75, no. 11 (June 2, 1962), p. 64.)
Concerns the 1962 general elections.

—— Backstage in Ottawa. Canada's rolling dollar: first crisis after the election. By Peter C. Newman. (In *Maclean's.* Toronto. v. 75, no. 13 (June 30, 1962), p. 50.)
Discusses the devaluation of the Canadian dollar effected May 2, 1962. Reference is to the general elections held June 18, 1962.

—— Backstage in Ottawa. The 1962 election may bring Left and Right back to Canadian politics. By Peter C. Newman. (In *Maclean's*. Toronto. v. 75, no. 15 (July 28, 1962), pp. 1-2.)

—— Backstage in Ottawa. Virgins no more: now Canada must face up to nuclear weapons. By Peter C. Newman. (In *Maclean's*. Toronto. v. 75, no. 21 (Oct. 20, 1962), pp. 1-2.)

—— Backstage in Ottawa. Who's where and why in the great Columbia Treaty debate. By Peter C. Newman. In *Maclean's*. Toronto. v. 75, no. 23 (Nov. 17, 1962), pp. 2-3.)

—— Backstage in Ottawa. Forget the "gut" issues. Nuclear arms will decide the next election. By Peter C. Newman. (In *Maclean's*. Toronto. v. 76, no. 4 (Feb. 23, 1963), p. 2.)

—— Backstage with Peter C. Newman; a special page on the campaign. The outlook: a two-party deal to run the country. A reporter's election diary: whistle-stop magic at work on the Prairies. (In *Maclean's*. Toronto. v. 76, no. 7 (Apr. 6, 1963), p. 1.)
Discusses the possibility of a formal coalition government. Relates to the elections held April 8, 1963.

—— Backstage in Ottawa. Our allies want to know where we stand; now we may even have to tell them. By Peter C. Newman. (In *Maclean's*. Toronto. v. 76, no. 8 Apr. 20, 1963), pp. 1-2.)
A discussion of Canada's future trade and defense policies.

—— Backstage in Ottawa. Diefenbaker won the campaign, but Pearson won the election. By Peter C. Newman. (In *Maclean's*. Toronto. v. 76, no. 9 (May 4, 1963), pp. 1-2.)
Concerns the results of the federal election held April 8, 1963.

—— The Canadian Bill of Rights. How we've used it, misused it, and found it unusable in the year since it became doctrine but not quite law. By Peter C. Newman. (In *Maclean's*. Toronto. v. 74, no. 16 (Aug. 12, 1961), pp. 20; 49-50.)

—— The distemper of our times; Canadian politics in transition, 1963-1968. By Peter C. Newman. Toronto, McClelland and Stewart [c1968] xiii, 558 p.

—— The French revolution, Quebec 1961. By Peter C. Newman (In *Maclean's*. To-

ronto. v. 74, no. 8 (Apr. 22, 1961), pp. [21]; 83-89.)
Considers its national impact.

—— How to tell the Grits from the Tories. By Peter C. Newman. (In *Maclean's*. Toronto. v. 75, no. 9 (May 5, 1962), pp. 14-15; 56-59.)

—— James Coyne and the great debate: Is Canada possible? By Peter C. Newman. (In *Maclean's*. Toronto. v. 74, no. 13 (July 1, 1961), pp. 14; 41-44.)

—— A nation divided; Canada and the coming of Pierre Trudeau. By Peter C. Newman. New York, Knopf, 1969 [c1968] xv, 469, xix p. (A Borzoi book)
First published Toronto, McClelland and Stewart, 1968 under title: *The distemper of our times; Canadian politics in transition, 1963-1968.*

—— National affairs. Threat of new violence in Quebec: why we should take the "Army of Liberation" seriously. By Peter C. Newman. (In *Maclean's*. Toronto. v. 77, no. 7 (Apr. 4, 1964), pp. 1-2.)

—— The Ottawa establishment [A portrait of the 37 men who execute—and sometimes make—our national policy.] By Peter C. Newman. (In *Maclean's*. Toronto. v. 77, no. 16 (Aug. 22, 1964), pp. 7; 30-38.)

—— Portrait of a nation at the bargaining table. Will we ever be "maîtres chez nous"? By Peter C. Newman. (In *Maclean's*. Toronto. v. 77, no. 3 (Feb. 8, 1964), p. 14.)
Concerns the British North America Act.

—— The sweaty fight for a single seat. By Peter C. Newman. (In *Maclean's*. Toronto. v. 75, no. 12 (June 16, 1962), pp. [13-15]; 53-60.)
A case study using the constituency of Kingston, Ont., in the general elections held June 18, 1962.

—— What are we really doing in the north? By Peter C. Newman. (In *Maclean's*. Toronto. v. 72, no. 23 (Nov. 7, 1959), pp. 17-18; 106-108; 111.)

—— What was behind the James Coyne fiasco? By Peter C. Newman. (In *Maclean's*. Toronto. v. 76, no. 20 (Oct, 19, 1963), pp. 24; 40-41; 44-47; 50-53.)

—— Who really owns Canada? By Peter C. Newman. (In *Maclean's*. Toronto. v. 69, no. 12 (June 9, 1956), pp. 11-13; 92-96.)

The Author offers "the facts in what may become a red-hot election issue".

—— Who's who in the power elite. [A form chart of the Establishment, with some notes on their similar characteristics.] (In *Maclean's*. Toronto. v. 77, no. 16 (Aug. 22, 1964), pp. 8-9.)

—— Why Diefenbaker lost Canada. By Peter C. Newman. (In *Maclean's*. Toronto. v. 75, no. 15 (July 28, 1962), pp. 10; 45-48.)

An analysis of the results of the federal election held June 18, 1962.

NICHOLSON, PATRICK   Vision and indecision. [Don Mills, Ont.] Longmans [c1968] xiv, 387 p.

Concerns "the Diefenbaker decade, from December 1956 through August 1967". - Introd.

O'DONNELL, J. R.   The twenty-sixth Canadian House of Commons; a roll call study. [Ottawa] 1966. [223] leaves.

Thesis (MA) – Carleton University.

The twenty-sixth parliament lasted from May 16, 1963, until its dissolution on September 8, 1965.

O'HEARN, PETER JOSEPH THOMAS   Articles of Confederation. While politicians and cocktail-party philosophers argued about a new constitution for Canada, Peter J. T. O'Hearn wrote one. (In *Canada month*. Montreal. v. 4, no. 12 (Dec. 1964), pp. 9-13.)

OLIVER, MICHAEL KELWAY   Confederation and Quebec. By Michael Oliver. (In *The Canadian forum*. Toronto. v. 43, no. 514 (Nov. 1963), pp. 179-183.)

"This article is reprinted from the United Steel Workers' Canadian journal 'Information' (August 1963)."

—— The future of Canada; separation, integration or . . . ? By Michael Oliver. (In *Congress on Canadian Affairs, 1st Quebec, 1961. Le Canada, expérience ratée . . . ou réussie?* Québec, 1962. pp. [133]-141.)

OLIVER, MICHAEL KELWAY (ed.)   Social purpose for Canada. Edited by Michael Oliver. [Toronto] University of Toronto Press [c1961] xii, 472 p.

Essays of social criticism assessing the principles and functions underlying Canadian social and political institutions in an attempt to define the changes occurring in Canadian society during the post-1950 era.

Partial contents: Power and freedom in Canadian democracy, by J. Porter. - The practice and theory of federalism, by P. E. Trudeau. - Social planning and Canadian federalism, by F. R. Scott. - Democratic socialist politics, by M. Oliver.

One man against the Pension Plan. (In *Canada month*. Montreal. v. 4 [i.e. 5] no. 4 (Apr. 1965), p. 10.)

Concerns John Krocker, senior administrator in the Department of Insurance.

ORMEAUX, JACQUES DES   Pour une constitution du Québec. (In *L'Action nationale*. Montréal. v. 49 (déc. 1959), pp. [279]-284.)

Ottawa letter. [Serie II] (In *Saturday night*. Toronto. v. 68, no. 11 – v. 84, no. 3 (Dec. 20, 1952 – Mar. 1969).)

Column dealing with federal politics, written by John A. Stevenson (Dec. 20, 1952 – Sept. 13, 1958), Logan MacLean, Edwin Copps, Peter Stursberg (July 23 – Oct. 1, 1960; Jan. 20 – July 7, 1962; Aug. 1963 – Oct. 1964), Raymond Rodgers, Laocoon, Mungo James, Christina Newman, and others.

PARENTEAU, ROLAND   L'Etat et la mise en valeur des ressources naturelles. (In *Cité libre*. Montréal. no. 42 (déc. 1961), pp. 20-23.)

Party organizers chase 8,000,000 votes. (In *Canada month*. Montreal. v. 3, no. 4 (Apr. 1963), p. 8.)

Refers to the federal election held April 8, 1963.

PEACOCK, DONALD   Journey to power; The story of a Canadian election. Toronto, Ryerson Press [c1968] 387 p.

Concerns the general elections held June 25, 1968. A background study.

PELLERIN, JEAN   Eric Kierans: zéro de conduite. (In *Cité libre*. Montréal. no. 84 (fév. 1966), pp. 7-11.)

—— L'Etat, c'est nous. (In *Cité libre*. Montréal. no. 81 (nov. 1965), pp. 7-12.)

—— Lettre aux nationalistes québecois. Montréal, Editions du Jour [1969] 142 p. (Cahiers de Cité libre, CL-5.)

Partial contents: 4. Les deux nations; un débat stérile. - 8. La Confédération; échec ou succès.

—— Nous n'avions rien à perdre et nous n'avions rien perdu. (In *Cité libre* Montréal. no. 57 (mai 1963), pp. 1-3.)

A commentary on the results of the general elections held April 8, 1963.

PELLETIER, GERARD   Confederation at the crossroads. [Saskatoon] University of Saskatchewan [c1965] 12 p. (University of Saskatchean, University lectures, no. 4.)

Cover title.

Public lecture delivered at the University of Saskatchewan in 1964.

Concerns English-French relations in Canada.

PENTLAND, H. C.   Labour in politics. (In The Canadian forum. Toronto. v. 48, no. 571 (Aug. 1968), pp. 100-102.)

A critical review article of Canadian labour in politics, by G. Horowitz. Toronto, University of Toronto Press, 1968.

PERLIN, GEORGE   St. John's West. (In Meisel, John (ed.) Papers on the 1962 election. [Toronto, 1964] pp. [3]-18.)

Concerns the general elections held June 18, 1962.

PETERSON, T.   A return to the status quo: the election in Winnipeg North Centre. By T. Peterson and I. Avakumovic. (In Meisel, John (ed.) Papers on the 1962 election. [Toronto, 1964.] pp. [91]-106.)

Concerns the general elections held June 18, 1962.

PHILLIPS, ALAN   What the pipeline will do for Canada. (In Maclean's. Toronto. v. 70, no. 19 (Sept. 14, 1957), pp. 26; 66-69.)

Politics; left or right, they like the middle of the road. (In Maclean's. Toronto. v. 74, no. 6 (Mar. 25, 1961), pp. 20-21; 64-65.)

Peter C. Newman and Peter Gzwoski interview six persons under thirty years old representing contemporary political viewpoints. They include Brian Mulroney, David Greenspan, John Brewin, Ted Rogers, Jean David, and Jean-Pierre Fournier.

La Politique vue par nos politiciens de demain. Qu'ils soient membres de la gauche ou de la droite nos jeunes se complaisent dans les positions du centre. (In Le Magazine Maclean. Montréal. v. 1, no. 2 (avril 1961), pp. 24-25.)

Adapted from Maclean's magazine.

Peter Gzowski and Peter C. Newman interview six persons under thirty years old representing contemporary political viewpoints.

Pour une politique fonctionnelle. Manifeste signé conjointement par Albert Breton, Raymond Breton, Claude Bruneau, Yvon Gauthier, Marc Lalonde, Maurice Pinard,

Pierre E. Trudeau (In Cité libre. Montréal. no. 67 (mai 1964), pp. 11-17.)

The English translation, entitled An appeal for realism in politics, was published simultaneously in The Canadian forum, Toronto, v. 44, no. 529 (May 1964), pp. 29-33.

For a rejoinder, see Une interprétation économique de la constitution, par A. Dubuc. [In Socialisme 66. Montréal. no. 7 (jan. 1966), pp. 3-21.]

Pour une politique fonctionnelle. Manifeste signé conjointement par Albert Breton, Raymond Breton, Claude Bruneau, Yvon Gauthier, Marc Lalonde, Maurice Pinard et Pierre E. Trudeau. (In The Journal of liberal thought. [Ottawa.] [v.] 2, no. 2 (spring 1966), pp. 23-34.)

First published in Cité libre, Montreal, no. 67 (mai 1964), pp. 11-17, and in English translation, under the title An appeal for realism in politics, in The Canadian forum, Toronto, v. 44, no. 520 (May 1964), pp. 29-33.

POZNANSKA, ALICE   Ce fut un "vote blanc"; à propos des élections du 18 juin, 1962. (In Cité libre. Montréal. no. 49 (août-sept. 1962), pp. 5-7.)

PROULX, PIERRE PAUL   A manpower policy. (In Quebec, in the Canada of tomorrow. [Toronto, 1968] pp. [DD-1]-DD-11.)

QUALTAR, TERENCE H.   The press of Ontario and the election. By T. H. Qualtar and K. A. MacKirdy. (In Meisel, John (ed.) Papers on the 1962 election. [Toronto, 1964] pp. [145]-168.)

Concerns the general elections held June 18, 1962.

QUIRIN, G. DAVID   On whom does the burden fall? An economist examines government spending. By G. D. Quirin. (In Canada month. Montreal. v. 8, no. 1 (Jan. 1968), pp. 28-29.)

RANCOURT, GERARD   Le Canada, un ou dix . . . que se passe-t-il au Québec? (In Relations industrielles. Québec. v. 23 (1968), pp. 445-465.)

Summary in English: Canada, one nation or ten . . . Quebec, what's happening? (pp. 456-465).

REFORD, ROBERT W.   How the Governor-General fills his day. (In Saturday night. Toronto. v. 75, no. 14 (July 9, 1960), pp. 12-14.)

Relates to the particular routine of Georges Vanier as Governor-General.

REGENSTREIF, SAMUEL PETER General survey: the electorate is apathetic. By Peter Regenstreif. (In *The Canadian commentator.* Toronto. v. 6, no. 6 (1962), pp. 6; 20.)

Compares the campaign for the general elections in 1958 to the one conducted in 1962.

—— Group perceptions and the vote; some avenues of opinion formation in the 1962 campaign. By S. Peter Regenstreif. (In Meisel, John (ed.) *Papers on the 1962 election.* [Toronto, 1964] pp. [235]-252.)

Concerns the general elections held June 18, 1962.

—— How Canada may vote. [Montreal] Montreal Star [1962?] 42 p.

Cover title.

Article reprinted from the *Montreal Star,* May—June 1962.

With reference to the June 18, 1962, general elections.

—— Some aspects of national party support in Canada. By S. Peter Regenstreif. (In *The Canadian journal of economics and political science.* [Toronto] v. 29 (1963), pp. 59-74.)

"This is a slightly revised version of a paper presented at the annual meeting of the Canadian Political Science Association in Hamilton, June 8, 1962."

This analysis is "based on the results of a four-page printed questionnaire mailed in one wave to a national sample of 3000 party supporters . . . in November, 1960".

ROBARTS, JOHN PARMENTER [Views on Confederation.] Document. By John Robarts. (In *Journal of Canadian studies.* Peterborough, Ont. v. 2, no. 3 (1967), pp. 52-58.)

Title from the table of contents.

". . . address by the Honourable John Robarts, Prime Minister of Ontario, . . . made to the Montmorency Conference, August 9th, 1967."

ROBERTS, LESLIE Wanted: a new approach to the Atlantic problem. (In *The Atlantic advocate.* Fredericton, N.B. v. 50, no. 5 (Jan. 1960), pp. 14-23.)

Argument is presented within a national context.

RODGERS, RAYMOND Ottawa letter. Press and Parliament: Questions. (In *Saturday night.* Toronto. v. 76, no. 1 (Jan. 7, 1961), pp. 15-16.)

—— Ottawa letter. Health plans and parties. (In *Saturday night.* Toronto. v. 76, no. 4 (Feb. 18, 1961), pp. 31-32.)

—— Ottawa letter. "Socialism" vs. "Private enterprise". (In *Saturday night.* Toronto. v. 76, no. 8 (Apr. 15, 1961), pp. 24-25.)

Discusses the position taken by the three major parties – Liberal, Conservative, and New Party (CCF).

—— Ottawa letter. Three million words for what? (In *Saturday night.* Toronto. v. 76, no. 9 (Apr. 29, 1961), pp. 19-20.)

Comments on the fourth session of the twenty-fourth parliament.

—— Ottawa letter. French Canada and education for employment. (In *Saturday night.* Toronto. v. 76, no. 11 (May 27, 1961), pp. 41-42.)

Refers to the Technical and Vocational Training Assistance Act.

—— Ottawa letter. Wanted: intelligence in the RCMP. (In *Saturday night.* Toronto. v. 76, no. 13 (June 24, 1961), pp. 25-26.)

Discusses RCMP estimates before the House of Commons.

—— Ottawa letter. Royal Commissions and Coyne. (In *Saturday night.* Toronto. v. 76, no. 15 (July 22, 1961), pp. 25-26.)

Discusses the appointment of the Royal Commission on Canada's Financial Structure and Institutions, announced by Donald Fleming on June 20, 1961.

—— Ottawa letter. Nationalism and Canadian parties. (In *Saturday night.* Toronto. v. 76, no. 17 (Aug. 19, 1961), pp. 25-26.)

—— Ottawa letter. Rural voters rule the nation. (In *Saturday night.* Toronto. v. 76, no. 18 (Sept. 2, 1961), pp. 23-24.)

—— Point of view: Canada still needs a new party. (In *Saturday night.* Toronto. v. 76, no. 19 (Sept. 16, 1961), p. 56.)

Concludes there is little or no difference between the Liberal Party and the NDP, and that there is still need for a "new" party.

—— Strange silence at Ottawa. Wanted: a debate on transport policy. (In *Saturday night.* Toronto. v. 76, no. 21 (Oct. 14, 1961), pp. 16; 19.)

ROSSINGER, ANDRE L'avenir du Canada: ou grandir ou mourir. [Traduit de l'anglais par J. P.] (In *Cité libre.* Montréal. no. 77 (mai—juin 1965), pp. 9-18.)

ROY, RAOUL Québec et la démocratie. Par R. R. (In *La Revue socialiste.* Montréal. [no] 1 (Printemps 1959), pp. 3-11.)

Discusses Un manifeste démocratique, by P. E. Trudeau. [In Cité libre. Montréal. no. 22 (oct. 1958), pp. [1]-31.]

—— Québec, une sous-colonie? (In Le Revue socialiste. Montréal. [no] 3 (hiver 1959/60), pp. 17-61.)

An historical discussion of Quebec within the Canadian confederation.

RUMILLY, ROBERT Il faut reviser le procès du Labrador. (In Nouvelle-France. Montréal. no. 20 (mars/juin 1962), pp. 224-238.)

RYAN, CLAUDE The Canadian solution. (In Kilbourn, W. M. (ed.) Canada: a guide to the peaceable kingdom. Toronto, 1970. pp. 238-241.)

Discusses "the two ways of approaching the Canadian problem" for French Canadians.

—— L'égalité, est-elle possible? (In Journal of Canadian studies. Peterborough, Ont. v. 1, no. 2 (1966), pp. 3-13.)

SAGI, DOUG In Alberta Social Credit is gaining. It's a hard province to predict, but Social Credit may win four more seats and the Liberals one or two. (In Commentator. Toronto. v. 7, no. 4 (Apr. 1963), pp. 8-9.)

One of seven articles which form part of "Election survey".

Predictions on the outcome of the general elections held April 8, 1963.

SAUVE, MAURICE Canada's need; a new consensus. (In Hawkins, Gordon (ed.) Concepts of federalism. [Toronto] 1965. pp. 17-21.)

Considers three questions in relation to effecting changes to the Canadian constitution: problem of the relationship between English-speaking Canadians and French-speaking Canadians, the cultural nature of the country, regional differences in the economy of the country.

SAYWELL, JOHN TUPPER Return to reality. By John Saywell. (In The Canadian forum. Toronto. v. 42, no. 498 (July 1962), pp. [73]-74.)

Part 1 of Two views of the election, part 2 being That uncertain feeling, by Denis Smith (pp. 74; 76-77).

Analyses the results of the general elections held June 18, 1962.

SCARROW, HOWARD A. Three dimensions of a local political party. (In Meisel, John (ed.) Papers on the 1962 election. [Toronto, 1964.] pp. [53]-67.)

Analyses the role of local provincial parties in an unnamed political constituency in Ontario with regard to the general elections held June 18, 1962.

SCHMEISER, DOUGLAS A. A strong "no" to rights entrenchment. (In Canada month. Montreal. v. 9, no. 2 (Feb. 1969), p. 17.)

Concerns the Canadian Bill of Rights.

SCHWARTZ, MILDRED ANNE Political behaviour and ethnic origin. By Mildred A. Schwartz. (In Meisel, John (ed.) Papers on the 1962 election. [Toronto, 1964.] pp. [253]-271.)

Concerns the general elections held June 18, 1962.

SEMINAR ON FRENCH CANADA, MONTREAL, 1963 Seminar on French Canada. [Montreal] The Montreal Star [1963] 140 p.

Transcript of papers presented at the seminar held in May, 1963, in the Queen Elizabeth Hotel, Montreal.

Partial contents: Quebec and the Canadian constitution, by M. Faribault. – Political attitudes, by R. Daignault.

Should this man be charged with sedition? Quebec's René Lévesque has come dangerously close to backing armed revolt. (In Canada month. Montreal. v. 4, no. 6 (June 1964), p. 9.)

Refers to an address delivered by M. Lévesque to a gathering of 400 students at Collège Sainte-Marie in Montreal on May 9, 1964.

SIMMONS, JAMES W. Voting behaviour and socio-economic characteristics: the Middlesex East federal election, 1965. (In The Canadian journal of economics and political science [Toronto] v. 33 (1967), pp. [389]-400.)

This study uses "multiple regression techniques to combine census small-area information with voting results at the poll level".

SMALLWOOD, JOSEPH ROBERTS Newfoundland. By the Honourable Joseph R. Smallwood, Premier of Newfoundland. (In Empire Club of Canada. Addresses. Toronto. (1959/60), pp. 102-113.)

Address delivered November 19, 1959.

Federal-provincial relations are discussed in the address.

—— Peril and glory. [Hull, Que., High Hill Pub. House c1966] 52 p.

Interviewed by Robert Moon.

General reflective comments on the nature and development of the Canadian nation.

SMILEY, DONALD VICTOR   The Canadian federation after the unwanted election. By Donald V. Smiley. (In *The Canadian forum*. Toronto. v. 45, no. 539 (Dec. 1965), pp. [193]-195.)

Analyses the results of the general elections held November 8, 1965.

—— Ies deux voies possible de l'égalité pour le Canada français. Par Donald Smiley. (In *Le Québec dans le Canada de demain*. Montréal. [c1967] t. 1 (pp. 76-87).)

—— Political images. By Donald Smiley. (In *The Canadian forum*. Toronto. v. 48, no. 570 (July 1968), pp. 75-76.)

"Presented on CBC—TV's 'Viewpoint'."

—— Two possible paths to equality for French Canada. (In *Quebec, in the Canada of tomorrow*. Toronto, 1968 pp. [F-1]-F-12.)

SMITH, DENIS   The campaign in Eglinton. (In Meisel, John (ed.) *Papers on the 1962 election*. [Toronto, 1964] pp. [68]-90.)

Concerns the general elections held June 18, 1962.

—— That uncertain feeling. (In *The Canadian forum*. Toronto. v. 42, no. 498 (July 1962), pp. 74; 76-77.)

Part 2 of Two views of the elections, part 1 being Return to reality, by John Saywell (pp. [73]-74).

Analyses the results of the general elections held June 18, 1962.

SMITH, F. E. W.   Competition vs. public interest. Canada needs a new airline policy. (In *Saturday night*. Toronto. v. 77, no. 8 (Apr. 14, 1962), pp. 18-19.)

SPEAIGHT, ROBERT WILLIAM   Vanier, soldier, diplomat and Governor General; a biography. By Robert Speaight. Toronto, Collins, 1970. 488 p.

STAFFORD, HAROLD   The "7 Days" crowd fooled the CBC, the people, and Parliament. By Harold Stafford, MP for Elgin County. (In *Canada month*. Montreal. v. 6, no. 8 (Aug. 1966), pp. 8-13.)

Mr. Stafford acted as a member of the Parliamentary Standing Committee on Broadcasting. Refers to the CBC television program "This hour has seven days".

STANFIELD, ROBERT LORNE   A Nova Scotian view of Confederation. By the Hon. Robert L. Stanfield. (In Empire Club of Canada.

Addresses. [Don Mills, Ont.] (1966/67), pp. [95]-104.)

Address delivered November 24, 1966.

STEVENSON, JOHN A.   J. E. Coyne: Bank Governor stirs a tempest. (In *Saturday night*. Toronto. v. 73, no. 7 (Mar. 29, 1958), pp. 14-[15]; 39.)

Examines the controversial issue over "tight money" policy.

—— Ottawa letter. The flavor of electioneering. (In *Saturday night*. Toronto. v. 72, no. 25 (Dec. 7, 1957), pp. 4-5.)

—— Ottawa letter. Election by auction. (In *Saturday night*. Toronto. v. 73, no. 5 (Mar. 1, 1958), pp. 4-5.)

Remarks on the campaign platforms presented by the Liberal and Conservative parties for the general election held March 31, 1958.

—— Ottawa letter. Electronic electioneering. (In *Saturday night*. Toronto. v. 73, no. 6 (Mar. 15, 1958), pp. 6-7.)

Considers how television has changed electioneering practices, with reference to the campaign for the federal election held March 31, 1958.

—— Ottawa letter. Votes vs. principles. (In *Saturday night*. Toronto. v. 73, no. 7 (Mar. 29, 1958), pp. 4-5.)

A critical summary of the position taken by J. Diefenbaker and L. B. Pearson during the campaign for the federal election held March 31, 1958.

—— Ottawa letter. All parties buckle down. (In *Saturday night*. Toronto. v. 73, no. 16 (Aug. 2, 1958), pp. 4-5.)

—— Ottawa letter. Good work by committees. (In *Saturday night*. Toronto. v. 73, no. 18 (Aug. 30, 1958), pp. 4-5.)

Discusses the work done by House of Commons committees, and leadership of the Conservative, Liberal, and CCF parties in the House.

—— Ottawa letter. "All Canadian parties in grave dilemma about trade policy." By J. A. Stevenson. (In *Canadian commentator*. Toronto. v. 5, no. 2 (Feb. 1961), pp. 10-13.)

—— Ottawa letter. The Gallup Poll and the Common Market are giving the government trouble. By J. A. Stevenson. (In *Canadian commentator*. Toronto. v. 5, no. 11 (Nov. 1961), pp. 23-24.)

Discusses the political implications of the Gallup Poll tabulations to the end of September 1961.

—— Ottawa letter. (In *The Canadian forum*. Toronto. v. 42, no. 496 (May 1962), pp. 38-39.)

General comments on the proceedings of the twenty-fourth federal parliament upon the occasion of its dissolution.

—— Political personalities. (In *Canadian commentator*. Toronto. v. 3, no. 12 (Dec. 1959), pp. 15-16.)

Comments on the political activities of Howard Green, Lester Pearson and Douglas Fisher.

—— Report on Ottawa. Revival of liberalism in Quebec and refusal of British Columbia to co-operate in harnessing the Columbia River challenge the government—struggle for markets abroad. By J. A. Stevenson. (In *Canadian commentator*. Toronto. v. 5, no. 5 (May 1961), pp. 15-18.)

—— Words without power. Loss of parliamentary oratory noted and regretted. By J. A. Stevenson. (In *Canadian commentator*. Toronto. v. 4, no. 3 (Mar. 1960), pp. 14-17.)

STOKES, LAWRENCE D.   The Canadian election in West Germany. (In *The Canadian forum*. Toronto. v. 42, no. 499 (Aug. 1962), pp. 100-101.)

Discusses the reaction to the Canadian general elections held June 18, 1962.

STURSBERG, PETER   Boy, this Parliament is not with it. (In *Commentator*. Toronto. v. 11, no. 1 (Jan. 1967), pp. 18-19.)

Concerns the attitude of parliamentarians to the younger generation of voters under thirty-five years of age.

—— Fortunately, Diefenbaker and Pearson for ever. (In *Commentator*. Toronto. v. 10, no. 7-8 (July—Aug. 1966), pp. 12; 14; 16.)

Considers the general state of federal political affairs and supports the actions of the two political leaders. (J. Diefenbaker and L. B. Pearson).

—— The grey morning after. (In *Commentator*. Toronto. v. 9, no. 12 (Dec. 1965), pp. 4-5.)

Brief comments on the results of the general elections held November 8, 1965.

—— Ottawa letter. The session of the "little man". (In *Saturday night*. Toronto. v. 75, no. 18 (Sept. 3, 1960), pp. 29-30.)

Summarizes the significant events of the third session, twenty-fourth parliament.

—— Ottawa letter. Election ammunition.

(In *Saturday night*. Toronto. v. 77, no. 5 (Mar. 3, 1962), pp. 25-26.)

Comments on the fifth session of the twenty-fourth parliament.

—— Ottawa letter. Murky policy on nuclear weapons. (In *Saturday night*. Toronto. v. 77, no. 7 (Mar. 31, 1962), pp. 11-12.)

—— Ottawa letter. The election personality cult. (In *Saturday night*. Toronto. v. 77, no. 11 (May 26, 1962), pp. 9-10.)

Refers to the general elections held June 18, 1962.

—— Ottawa letter. After the hoopla, a time for problems. (In *Saturday night*. Toronto. v. 77, no. 14 (July 7, 1962), pp. 8-9.)

Refers to the general elections held June 18, 1962.

—— Party splits cause Ottawa crisis. (In *Commentator*. Toronto. v. 10, no. 11 (Nov. 1966), pp. 10-12.)

The Author considers that "the crisis and revolts go much deeper than personalities; they are due to divisions within the parties and fundamental differences over policies".

—— Postmark Ottawa. (In *The Canadian Saturday night*. Toronto. v. 77, no. 15— v. 78, no. 6 (Aug. 1962—June/July 1963).)

Column dealing with federal politics.

—— Postmark Ottawa. (In *The Canadian Saturday night*. Toronto. v. 78, no. 2 (Feb. 1963), pp. 7-8.)

Discusses a proposed Royal Commission on bilingual or bicultural relations in Canada.

—— Postmark Ottawa. (In *The Canadian Saturday night*. Toronto. v. 78, no. 4 (Apr. 1963), pp. 4; 6.)

Discusses the policies and position of the four national political parties, with reference to the general elections held April 8, 1963.

—— Postmark Ottawa. (In *The Canadian Saturday night*. Toronto. v. 78, no. 5 (May 1963), pp. 7-8.)

Discusses the results of the general elections held April 8, 1963.

SULLIVAN, MARTIN   Mandate '68. Toronto, New York, Doubleday, 1968. viii, 439 p.

Describes the political developments resulting in Robert Stanfield as leader of the Progressive Conservative Party and Pierre

Elliott Trudeau as leader of the Liberal Party.

TAUBE, STANLEY We could be talking ourselves into fascism. (In *Commentator*. Toronto. v. 11, no. 4 (Apr. 1967), pp. 22-23.)
Constructs a hypothetical situation in order to explore a latent possibility.

TAYLOR, CHARLES Bâtir un nouveau Canada. (In *Cité libre*. Montréal. no. 79 (août—sept. 1965), pp. 10-14.)

—— The pattern of politics. Toronto. McClelland and Stewart [c1970] 160 p.
Concerns politics in Canada after 1963.

—— La planification fédérale-provinciale. (In *Cité libre*. Montréal. no. 76 (avril (1965), pp. 9-16.)

—— What's wrong with Canadian politics? (In *Canadian dimension*. Winnipeg. v. 2, no. 4 (May/June 1965), pp. 10-11; 20.)
Defines and explains the problems related to "dilettante politics".

THATCHER, W. ROSS A new voice in Confederation. (In Empire Club of Canada. *Addresses*. [Don Mills, Ont.] (1966/67), pp. [65]-79.)
Address delivered November 10, 1966.

This *is* Canada's flag. Keep it flying! (In *The Newfoundland quarterly*. St. John's, Nfld. v. 62, no. 1 (spring 1963), pp. [3]-4.)
Reprinted from the *Legionary*.
Argues for the adoption of the Red Ensign as the national flag of Canada.

THORBURN, HUGH GARNET Pressure groups in Canadian politics: recent revisions of the anti-combines legislation. By H. G. Thorburn. (In *The Canadian journal of economics and political science*. [Toronto] v. 30 (1964), pp. 157-174.)
Examines the general pattern of lobbying and its influence on policy decisions, citing, as an example, the pressures brought upon the 1960 amendments to the Canadian anti-combines legislation.

Top men of the four parties reveal their ideas, backgrounds, hopes, taboos. (In *Canada month*. Montreal. v. 3, no. 4 (Apr. 1963), pp. 14-15.)
Includes Alvin Hamilton, Mitchell Sharp, David Lewis, Guy Marcoux, Leslie Morris. Refers to the federal election held April 8, 1963.

TREMBLAY, JEAN NOEL La Confédération! Combien de temps encore faudra-t-il la subir? [Saint-Hyacinthe, Qué., Editions Alerte, 1961?] 16 p.
Address delivered at the closing banquet of the general congress of the Saint-Jean-Baptiste Society of Quebec, October 15, 1961.

TRUDEAU, PIERRE ELLIOTT De la notion d'opposition politique. (In *Cité libre*. Montréal. no. 27 (mai 1960), pp. 13-14.)

—— De libro, tributo . . . et quibusdam aliis. (In *Cité libre*. Montréal. no. 10 (oct. 1954), pp. [1]-16.)

—— Un manifeste démocratique. (In *Cité libre* Montréal. no.22 (oct. 1958), pp. [1]-31.)

—— The multi-national state in Canada. (In *The Canadian forum*. Toronto. v. 42, no. 497 (June 1962), pp. 52-54.)
"This article is part of a longer study entitled 'La nouvelle trahison des clercs' published in Cité libre for April, 1962. It is translated by Ramsay Cook . . . Essentially the argument is directed at the separatist movements in Quebec, but the sections printed here obviously have a wider, national interest". – Introd.

—— Note sur la conjoncture politique; à propos des élections du 18 juin, 1962. (In *Cité libre*. Montréal. no. 49 (août—sept. 1962), pp. [1]-4.)

—— La nouvelle trahison des clercs. (In *Cité libre*. Montréal. no. 46 (avril 1962), pp. 3-16.)
A shorter version of this article has been translated into English by Ramsay Cook under title: The multi-national state in Canada. (In *The Canadian forum*. Toronto. v. 42, no. 497 (1962), pp. 52-54.)

—— Le Québec est-il assiégé? (In *Cité libre*. Montréal. no. 86 (avril—mai 1966), pp. 7-10.)
Examines the political relationship of Quebec within the framework of a Canadian federation.

—— Réponses de Pierre Elliott Trudeau. Introd. de Gérard Pelletier. Montréal, Editions du Jour [c1968] 126 p.

—— Réponses de Pierre Elliott Trudeau. Introd. de Gérard Pelletier. 2. éd., augm. et mise à jour. Montréal, Editions du Jour [1968] 143 p.

—— Toward a constitutional Bill of Rights. (In *The Canadian forum*. Toronto. v. 47, no. 561 (Oct. 1967), pp. 158-159.)

"An excerpt from a speech given on September 4", 1967.

TURNER, JOHN NAPIER Politics of purpose. Politique d'objectifs. Toronto, McClelland and Stewart [c1968] xix, 216 p.

On cover: An original publication.

"Most of the essays in this book are based on speeches delivered in English". – p. xiii. Includes some text in French.

Two views of the election. (In *The Canadian forum*. Toronto. v. 42, no. 498 (July 1962), pp. [73]-74; 76-77.)

Contents: [pt.] 1. Return to reality, by J. Saywell. – [pt.] 2. That uncertain feeling, by D. Smith.

Two articles analysing the results of the general elections held June 18, 1962.

TYRWHITT, JANICE How Eric Kierans took on Réal Caouette—and won. (In *Maclean's*. Toronto. v. 76, no. 10 (May 18, 1963), pp. 22-23.)

UNDERHILL, FRANK HAWKINS The university and politics. By Frank H. Underhill. (In *Queen's quarterly*. Kingston. v. 66 (1959), pp. [217]-225.)

"Address at the Convocation for Arts and Science, Queen's University, Kingston, Ontario, May 16, 1959."

The "remarks are prompted by the last two federal general elections of 1957 and 1958". General remarks on the political function of Canadian universities.

—— The university and politics. (In his *In search of Canadian liberalism*. Toronto, 1961. pp. 263-270.)

The Convocation address delivered at Queen's University, May 16, 1959.

VALLIERES, PIERRE Les "plorines" au pouvoir. (In *Cité libre*. Montréal. no. 65 (mars 1964), pp. [1]-4.)

Questions the reason and function of Quebec within Confederation.

VAN LOON, RICHARD JEROME Canadian electoral participation; the Canadian public in the 1965 federal election. [Kingston, 1969] 1 v.

Thesis (PH D) – Queen's University.

—— Political participation in Canada; the 1965 election. By Rick Van Loon. (In *Canadian journal of political science*. Toronto. v. 3 (1970), pp. [376]-399.)

Verdict on 1962: the negative election. (In *Canada month*. Montreal. v. 2, no. 7 (July 1962), p. 10.)

Concerns the general elections held June 18, 1962.

VILLEROY, JACQUES L'élection fédérale de 1963 dans le "Grand Montréal"; analyse de sociologie électorale. [Montréal] 1968. 1 v.

Thesis (MA) – University of Montreal.

WADDINGTON, PATRICK Storm warnings from Quebec. Is Confederation in real danger? (In *Saturday night*. Toronto. v. 77, no. 3 (Feb. 3, 1962), pp. 13-[15].)

Presents the "facts" on the Quebec separatist movement.

WAITE, PETER BUSBY Confederation, then and now. By P. B. Waite. (In Royal Society of Canada. *Proceedings and transactions*. Ottawa. ser. 4, v. 2 (1964), pp. 27-33.)

At head of title: Symposium on "Confederation, then and now". – Colloque sur "La Confédération, hier et aujourd'hui."

WALKER, ROBERT The election. Pollsters say they'll call this one right on the nose. (In *Saturday night*. Toronto. v. 73, no. 6 (Mar. 15, 1958), pp. 10-11; 55.)

Examines the polling techniques of the Canadian Institute of Public Opinion, with reference to predicting the outcome of the federal election held March 31, 1958.

WALSH, SAM Some aspects of the national question in Canada. (In *Horizons*. Toronto. no. 22 (summer 1967), pp. 31-46.)

WARD, NORMAN MC QUEEN The counter-revolution in Saskatchewan. By Norman Ward. (In Meisel, John (ed.) *Papers on the 1962 election*. [Toronto, 1964] pp. [169]-180.)

Considers the reasons for the strong victory of the Conservative Party in "the only area in North America governed by a socialist party". Relates to the general elections held June 18, 1962.

WARING, GERALD How CPA escaped a takeover by Ottawa. (In *Maclean's*. Toronto. v. 78, no. 13 (July 3, 1965), p. 1.)

WATKINS, ERNEST A call for principle. (In *Canada month*. Montreal. v. 3, no. 3 (Mar. 1963), pp. 17-19.)

Discusses the current "image" of Canadian political parties.

WATKINS, ERNEST Political Canada. What will April 8 bring? (In *Canada month*. Montreal. v. 3, no. 4 (Apr. 1963), p. 13.)

Refers to the federal election held April 8, 1963.

—— Political Canada. "We" and "they". (In *Canada month*. Montreal. v. 3, no. 5 (May 1963), p. 30.)

Comments on the results of the federal election held April 8, 1963.

—— Political Canada. Misplaced effort. (In *Canada month*. Montreal. v. 3, no. 10 (Oct. 1963), pp. 40-41.)
Concerns government spending.

—— Political Canada. Happy new century! (In *Canada month*. Montreal. v. 4, no. 1 (Jan. 1964), p. 35.)
Cites three major problems: Confederation, unemployment, the decline of parliamentary democracy.

—— Political Canada. Queen & monarch. (In *Canada month*. Montreal. v. 4, no. 7 (July 1964), p. 24.)

—— Political Canada. No time for flags. (In *Canada month*. Montreal. v. 4, no. 9 (Sept. 1964), p. 33.)
Comments on the flag issue before Parliament during 1964.

—— Political Canada. Pension sickness. (In *Canada month*. Montreal. v. 4, no. 10 (Oct. 1964), pp. 35-37.)
Comments on the Canada Pension Plan.

—— Watkins on liberty. (In *Canada month*. Montreal. v. 3, no. 6 (June 1963), p. 24.)

WATKINS, MELVILLE HENRY   A new National Policy. By Mel Watkins. (In University League for Social Reform. *Agenda* 1970. [Toronto, c1968] pp. [159]-176.)
Discusses the Canadian tariff structure concentrating on "the political dimension of policies toward foreign ownership".

—— A new National Policy for Canada. (In Empire Club of Canada. *Addresses*. Toronto. (1968/69), pp. [15]-23.)
Address delivered October 17, 1968.

WEARING, JOSEPH   How to predict Canadian elections. A Canadian political scientist applies the British technique of measuring "swings" to our elections—and believes it can forecast a lot. (In *Commentator*. Toronto. v. 7, no. 2 (Feb. 1963), pp. 2-4.)

—— Party leadership and the 1966 conventions; commentary. (In *Journal of Canadian studies*. Peterborough, Ont. v. 2, no. 1 (1967), pp. 23-27.)
Remarks on the Liberal Party policy convention held in Ottawa October 12 and the Progressive Conservative national convention held in Ottawa November 13-16, 1966.

—— A prediction based on "swings". The Liberals stand to gain most by Gallup

Poll predictions of shifts in voting strength across the country—here are the key constituencies to watch. (In *Commentator*. Toronto. v. 7, no. 4 (Apr. 1963), pp. 11-12.)
One of seven articles which form part of "Election survey".
Predictions on the outcome of the general elections held April 8, 1963.

WHITTON, CHARLOTTE   Canadian women belong in politics. (In *Chatelaine*. Toronto. v. 34, no. 10 (Oct. 1961), p. 44; 150; 152; 154.)

WILSON, J. M.   Why not join the Liberals? (In *The Canadian forum*. Toronto. v. 44, no. 525 (Oct. 1964), pp. [145]-148.)
Examines the idea of an NDP—Liberal Party merger.

—— The will to win. (In *The Canadian forum*. Toronto. v. 45, no. 537 (Oct. 1965), pp. [145]-146.)
Considers the implications related to calling a federal election before the proposed redistribution of electoral seats has been put into effect.

WILSON, JOHN   The myth of candidate partisanship; the case of Waterloo South. (In *Journal of Canadian studies*. Peterborough. v. 3, no. 4 (1968), pp. 21-31.)
The federal by-election held November 9, 1964.

—— Politics and social class in Canada; the case of Waterloo South. (In *Canadian journal of political science*. Toronto. v. 1 (1968), pp. [288]-309.)
". . . a revised and shortened version of a paper read at the thirty-ninth annual meeting of the Canadian Political Science Association, Ottawa, 1967."
Analyses the federal by-election held November 9, 1964.

—— Politics and social class in Canada; the case of Waterloo South. (In Kruhlak, O. M. (comp.) *The Canadian political process*. Toronto. [c1970] pp. 245-266.)
Reprinted from *Canadian journal of political science*, v. 1 (1968), pp. 288-309.
Analyses the federal by-election held November 9, 1964.

WINKLER, ERIC   Two parties make Good Parliament. By Eric Winkler, MP (Grey-Bruce). (In *Canada month*. Montreal. v. 7, no. 6 (June 1967), pp. 19-21.)

WINTERS, ROBERT HENRY   Government and private enterprise. By the Honourable

Robert H. Winters. (In Empire Club of Canada. *Addresses*. Toronto. (1958/59), pp. 224-234.)

Address delivered February 19, 1959.

WOODS, HARRY DOUGLAS Federal government task force on labour relations. By H. D. Woods. (In *Relations industrielles*. Québec. v. 22 (1967), pp. 130-136.)

WOODSIDE, WILLSON Canada's curious new labor party. (In *Canadian commentator*. Toronto. v. 2, no. 5 (May 1958), pp. [1]-2.)

Comments on the proceedings at the Canadian Labour Congress Convention in Winnipeg April 21-25, 1958.

YOUNG, WALTER DOUGLAS BC—Liberals and NDP up. West coast Conservatives are more interested now in building a provincial party than in supporting the federal cause. By Walter Young. (In *Commentator*. Toronto. v. 7, no. 4 (Apr. 1963), pp. 10-11.)

One of seven articles which form part of "Election survey".

Predictions on the outcome of the general elections held April 8, 1963.

—— British Columbia. By Walter Young. (In *Commentator*. Toronto. v. 9, no. 11 (Nov. 1965), pp. 14-15.)

One of five articles which form part of "The election campaign from coast to coast".

Examines the campaign for the federal elections held November 8, 1965.

—— The Peterborough election: the success of a party image. By W. D. Young. (In *The Dalhousie review*. Halifax. v. 40, no. 4 (winter 1960/61), pp. [505]-519.)

Examines the campaign and results of the by-election held October 31, 1960.

YUZYK, PAUL The "third" nation—and tomorrow's Canada. By Senator Paul Yuzyk. (In *Canada month*. Montreal. v. 7, no. 1 (Jan. 1967), pp. 10-13.)

Refers to the non-English and non-French elements in the Canadian population and their impact upon Canadian society.

POLITICAL PARTIES
(INDIVIDUAL)

CONSERVATIVE PARTY

General Works

BELL, RUTH MARION Conservative Party national conventions, 1927-1956; organization and procedure. [Ottawa] 1965, c1966. iv, 215, [16] leaves.

Thesis (MA) – Carleton University.

CREIGHTON, DONALD GRANT Conservatism and national unity. By D. G. Creighton. (In Flenley, Ralph (ed.) *Essays in Canadian history*. Toronto, 1939. pp. 154-177.)

HOGAN, GEORGE W. Canadian conservatism. By George Hogan. (In *Commentator*. Toronto. v. 7, no. 3 (Mar. 1963), pp. 2-4.)

An excerpt from *The Conservative in Canada*, by G. Hogan. Toronto, McClelland and Stewart [c1963].

—— The Conservative in Canada. By George Hogan. Foreword by Leslie M. Frost. [Toronto] McClelland and Stewart [c1963] xiv, 130 p. (Canada today)

A study of the Progressive Conservative Party.

—— How conservative is the Conservative Party? By George W. Hogan, Jr. (In *Canada month*. Montreal. v. 4, no. 1 (Jan. 1964), pp. 21-23.)

MACQUARRIE, HEATH NELSON The Conservative Party. By Heath Macquarrie. Foreword by the Honourable J. M. Macdonnell. [Toronto] McClelland and Stewart [c1965] 166 p.

A survey history of the Conservative Party.

MORRISON, GREGORY JOHN Political party structure; a qualitative study of the Progressive Conservative Party of Canada. [Kingston, 1969] 1 v.

Thesis (MA) – Queen's University.

WILLIAMS, JOHN RYAN The Conservative Party of Canada, 1920-1949. Durham, NC, Duke University Press, 1956. x, 242 p. illus., diagrs., tables.

First issued as thesis (PH D), Duke University, 1951.

1867–1896

AITCHISON, JAMES HERMISTON Sir John A. Macdonald: nation-builder. By J. H. Aitchison. (In *The Canadian journal of economics and political science.* [Toronto] v. 22 (1956), pp. 549-553.)

A review article of *John A. Macdonald*, by D. Creighton. Toronto, Macmillan, 1952-55. 2 v.

AMICUS The late D'Alton McCarthy; an appreciation. By Amicus. (In *The Canadian magazine of politics, science, art and literature.* Toronto. v. 21 (1903), pp. 31-32.)

ARBOIS Profils et portraits. Sir John. Par Arbois. (In *L'Opinion publique.* Montréal. v. 9, no. 52 (26 déc. 1878), p. [613].)

A sketch of Sir John A. Macdonald.

ARCHIBALD, EDITH J. The Hon. Thomas Dickson Archibald of the Court of Queen's Bench, England, 1817-1875. By Mrs. Charles (Edith J.) Archibald. (In Nova Scotia Historical Society. *Collections.* Halifax. v. 21 (1927), pp. 45-71.)

"Read 3rd February, 1922."

ARDAGH, HENRY HATTON Life of Hon. Sir James Robert Gowan. Toronto, 1911. 328 p.

For private circulation.

ARMSTRONG, TERESA (COSTIGAN) Some Confederation reminiscences of the Hon. Senator Costigan by his daughter. (In Women's Canadian Historical Society of Ottawa. *Transactions.* [Ottawa] v. 6 (1915), pp. [113]-125.)

Concerns, primarily, the first Dominion parliament.

AUCLAIR, ELIE JOSEPH ARTHUR Le discours d'un Cartier, aux fêtes de Cartier. Par Elie J. Auclair. (In *Revue canadienne.* Montréal. nouv. sér., v. 26 (1921), pp. [51]-59.)

An account of the speech given by Louis-Joseph Cartier at the celebration held in memory of Sir George Etienne Cartier on September 28, 1919, at Saint-Antoine, Que.

—— Les fêtes du monument Cartier à Montréal. Par Elie-J. Auclair. (In *Revue canadienne.* Montréal. nouv. sér., v. 24 (1919), pp. [241]-263.)

Tribute to Sir George Etienne Cartier.

—— Sir Georges-Etienne Cartier. Par Elie-J. Auclair. (In *Revue canadienne.* Montréal. nouv. sér., v. 9 (1912), pp. [486]-503.)

—— Sir Georges-Etienne Cartier à Saint-Antoine-sur-Richelieu. Par Elie-J. Auclair. (In *Revue canadienne.* Montréal. nouv. sér., v. 14 (1914), pp. [195]-211.)

BABION, ROSS GRANT Alexander Morris, his place in Canadian history. [Kingston, Ont., 1945] 197 leaves.

Thesis (MA) – Queen's University.

BANKS, WILLIAM Reminiscences of Sir Charles Tupper. By William Banks, Jr. (In *The Canadian courier.* Toronto. v. 11, no. 5 (Dec. 30, 1911), p. 13.)

Reflects on a meeting held in Massey Hall, Toronto, June 19, 1896.

BAPTIE, SUE Edgar Dewdney. (In *Alberta historical review.* Calgary. v. 16, no. 4 (autumn 1968), pp. 1-10.)

BEAUCHESNE, ARTHUR Adolphe Chapleau. (In *La Revue moderne.* Montréal. 2. année, no 5 (15 mars 1921), pp. 17-20.)

—— Pierre Chauveau. (In *La Revue moderne.* Montréal. 3. année, no 3 (15 jan. 1922), pp. 24-26.)

BEAULIEU, J. A. Courage politique de Cartier. (In *Revue canadienne.* Montréal. nouv. sér., v. 1 (1908), pp. [303]-313.)

Concerns Sir George Etienne Cartier.

BECHARD, AUGUSTE L'honourable Joseph-G. Blanchet. Par A. Béchard. Québec, L. Brousseau, 1884. 42 p. (Galérie nationale, 2.)

BECK, JAMES MURRAY Joseph Howe. By J. M. Beck. (In McDougall, R. L. (ed.) *Our living tradition.* Fourth series. [Toronto, c1962] pp. 3-30.)

BENOIST, MARIUS Le sénateur Girard. (In Canadian Catholic Historical Association. *Rapport.* [Ottawa] (1948/49), pp. 47-54.)

Concerns Marc Amable Girard.

BERTON, PIERRE FRANCIS DE MARIGNY The improbable dream that made Sir John A. Captain Canada of 1871. By Pierre Berton. (In *Maclean's.* Toronto. v. 83, no. 11 (Nov. 1970), pp. 34-35.)

Describes the idea for a national railway.

BIGGAR, EMERSON BRISTOL Anecdotal life of Sir John Macdonald. Montreal, J. Lovell, 1891. 332 p.

BISSETT, F. W. Rt. Hon. Sir John Thompson. (In *The Dalhousie review.* Halifax. v. 25 (1945/46), pp. [323]-330.)

BLAKELEY, PHYLLIS RUTH The early career of Sir Charles Tupper. By Phyllis R. Blakeley. (In *The Atlantic advocate.* Fredericton, NB. v. 54, no. 12 (Aug. 1964), pp. 35-42.)

BLUE, CHARLES S. Famous Canadian trials: The case of Patrick James Whelan, who was hanged for the murder of Thomas D'Arcy McGee. (In *The Canadian magazine of politics, science, art and literature.* Toronto. v. 44 (1914/15), pp. 385-392.)
Famous Canadian trials, 3.

BONENFANT, JEAN CHARLES Les idées politiques de George-Etienne Cartier. (In *The Political ideas of the Prime Ministers of Canada.* Ottawa, 1969. pp. [31]-50.)

—— Sir George-Etienne Cartier. (In La-Pierre, L. J. L. (ed.) *French Canadian thinkers of the nineteenth and twentieth centuries.* Montreal, 1966. pp. 41-57.)

BOULTON, CHARLES ARKOLL Mr. Davin reviewed. By C. A. Boulton. (In *The Week.* Toronto. v. 8, no. 52 (Nov. 27, 1891), p. 829.)
For a rejoinder see Reorganization of the cabinet (sixth article), by N. F. Davin. (In *The Week.* Toronto. v. 9 (Dec. 18, 1891), p. 38.)

BOYD, JOHN The birth of the Dominion. With some personal reminiscences of Sir Charles Tupper, bart., the sole surviving Father of Confederation. (In *The Canadian magazine of politics, science, art and literature.* Toronto. v. 41 (1913), pp. 219-228.)

—— Sir George-Etienne Cartier, bart., his life and times; a political history of Canada from 1814 until 1873. Bonne entente ed. Toronto, Macmillan, 1917 [c1914] xxi, 439 p.

—— Sir George Etienne Cartier, bart.; sa vie et son temps. Histoire politique du Canada de 1814 à 1873. Ouvrage traduit de l'anglais par Sylvia Clapin. Montréal, Beauchemin [1918] xxviii, 485 p.
"En commémoration du centième anniversaire de naissance de Sir George Etienne Cartier."

—— Sir George Etienne Cartier—his work for Canada. (In Canadian Club of Hamilton. *Addresses.* Hamilton. (1912/13), pp. 125-147.)
Address delivered April 25, 1913.

—— Sir George Etienne Cartier, his work for Canada and his services to Montreal. (In Canadian Club of Montreal. *Addresses.* [Montreal] (1912/13), pp. 225-254.)
Address delivered April 7, 1913.

BRADY, ALEXANDER Thomas D'Arcy McGee. Toronto, Macmillan, 1925. 182 p. (Canadian statesmen, no. 2.)

BRIDLE, AUGUSTUS The genius of Strathcona. Who lived two complete lives before and after the age of fifty. (In *The Canadian courier.* Toronto. v. 15, no. 9 (Jan. 31, 1914), pp. 10-11.)
Written on the occasion of his death January 21, 1914.

BRYCE, GEORGE The real Strathcona. (In *The Canadian magazine of politics, science, art and literature.* Toronto. v. 45 (1915), pp. 183-189.)
Part I. A peacemaker at Fort Garry.

—— The real Strathcona. (In *The Canadian magazine of politics, science, art and literature.* Toronto. v. 45 (1915), pp. 282-287.)
Part II. The nights of Silver Heights.
Reminiscences and anecdotes covering the Author's acquaintance with Donald A. Smith.

—— The real Strathcona. (In *The Canadian magazine of politics, science, art and literature.* Toronto. v. 45 (1915), pp. 402-408.)
Part III. The glamour of the fur trade.
Donald A. Smith in his rôle of Land Commissioner and General Superintendent of Hudson's Bay Company affairs.

—— The real Strathcona. (In *The Canadian magazine of politics, science, art and literature.* Toronto. v. 45 (1915), pp. 492-496.)
Part IV. The first railway to Winnipeg.

—— The real Strathcona. (In *The Canadian magazine of politics, science, art and literature.* Toronto. v. 46 (1915/16), pp. 62-66.)
Part V. A notable legislator.

—— The real Strathcona. (In *The Canadian magazine of politics, science, art and literature.* Toronto. v. 46 (1915/16), pp. 156-162.)
Part VI. The golden spike of the Canadian Pacific Railway.

—— The real Strathcona. (In *The Canadian magazine of politics, science, art and literature.* Toronto. v. 46 (1915/16), pp. 269-272.)
Part VIII [i.e. VII]. A parthian corps from Western Canada.

—— The real Strathcona. (In *The Canadian magazine of politics, science, art and literature.* Toronto. v. 46 (1915/16), pp. 346-349.)

Part VIII. A prince of benefactors.

The Budget debate. (In *The Week.* Toronto. v. 10, no. 13 (Feb. 24, 1893), pp. 292-293.)

Concentrates on the budget speech of George Foster.

The Budget speech. (In *Canadian illustrated news.* Montreal. v. 5, no. 19 (May 11, 1872), p. 290.)

Concerns the budget of Sir Francis Hincks delivered April 30, 1872, in the House of Commons.

BUELL, JOHN PETER HAMBROOK   The political career of N. Clarke Wallace, 1872-1896. Toronto, 1961. 282 leaves.

Thesis (MA) – University of Toronto. Appendices: Election of 1896.

BURPEE, LAWRENCE JOHNSTONE   A family of nation builders; the story of the Galts. II. Sir Alexander Galt, financier and Father of Confederation. By Lawrence J. Burpee. (In *Saturday night.* Toronto. v. 42, no. 36 (July 23, 1927), pp. 4-5.)

CANADA   Royal Commission to inquire into a certain resolution moved by the Honourable Mr. Huntington in Parliament on April 2nd, 1873 relating to the Canadian Pacific Railway. Report of the Royal Commission appointed by Commission addressed to them under the Great Seal of Canada. Bearing date of the fourteenth day of August, A.D. 1873. Ottawa, 1873. 227 p.

Text printed in the Journals of the House of Commons. Appendix 1. v. 7 (1873).

Hearings held at Ottawa, September 1–October 1, 1873. Thirty-six witnesses, including Sir John A. Macdonald, appeared before the Commission. Cf. Henderson, G. F. *Federal royal commissions in Canada, 1867-1966.* Toronto, 1967. (no. 6, p. 5.)

Commissioners: Charles Dewey Day, chairman, Antoine Polette and James Robert Gowan.

——   Royal Commission to Investigate Charges Against Sir A. P. Caron. Report of the Royal Commission in reference to certain charges made against Hon. Sir A. P. Caron . . . Session, 1893. Printed by order of Parliament. Ottawa. Printed by S. E. Dawson, Printer, 1893. iv, 602 p.

Commissioners: A. B. Routhier and M. M. Tait.

CARTIER, SIR GEORGE ETIENNE, bart.   Discours de Sir Georges Cartier, baronnet. Accompagnés de notices par Joseph Tassé. Montréal, E. Senecal, 1893. viii, 817 p.

CHAMBERS, EDWARD THOMAS DAVIES   Hon. Auguste Réal Angers, Lieutenant Governor of Quebec. By E. T. D. Chambers. (In *The Week.* Toronto. v. 5, no. 42 (Sept. 13, 1888), pp. 669-670.)

Prominent Canadians: XXIV.

CHAPLEAU, SIR JOSEPH ADOLPHE   Constitution du Canada en 1867. Explication par Hubert Létourneau. (In *Le Bulletin des recherches historiques.* Lévis. v. 69, no 1 (jan. 1967), pp. 25-35; v. 69, no. 3 (juil. 1967), pp. 121-128.)

In two parts.

A report to the Colonial Secretary by the Canadian Secretary of State, J. A. Chapleau. The original text of the report was first published, in French, in the Sessional papers for 1891, no. 14, appendix E, pp. 41-52. Cf. Explication.

——   L'honorable J. A. Chapleau: sa biographie; suivie de ses principaux discours, manifestes, etc., publiés depuis son entrée au Parlement en 1867. Montréal, E. Senécal, 1887. xxx, 537 p.

——   Lettres de Joseph-Adolphe Chapleau (1870-1896). (In Quebec (Province) Archives. *Rapport.* (1959/60), pp. [23]-118.)

Edited with an introduction by Fernand Ouellet.

——   L'opinion de M. Chapleau. (In *L'Opinion publique.* Montréal. v. 5, no. 48 (26 nov. 1874), pp. 579-580.)

Quotes Chapleau's speech delivered concerning receipt of gifts for his defense of Ambroise Lépine.

CHARLESWORTH, HECTOR WILLOUGHBY   On D'Arcy McGee. By Hector Charlesworth. (In *Saturday night.* Toronto. v. 52, no. 34 (June 26, 1937), p. 12.)

——   Recollections of sixty years in Canada, by Sir Charles Tupper, bart. A review of Canadian political life by Canada's oldest statesman. By Hector Charlesworth. (In *Saturday night.* Toronto. v. 27, no. 24 (Mar. 28, 1914), pp. 3-4.)

Discusses "Recollections of sixty years", by Sir Charles Tupper. London, Cassell, 1914.

——   Reflections. By Hector Charlesworth. (In *Saturday night.* Toronto. v. 37, no. 4 (Nov. 26, 1921), p. 2.)

Comments on "Correspondence of Sir John A. Macdonald; 1840-1891", edited by Sir Joseph Pope. Garden City, N.Y., Doubleday, 1921.

CHARTIER, EMILE   Les Discours de Cartier. (In *Revue canadienne*. Montréal. nouv. sér., v. 14 (1914), pp. [280]-288.)
A study of *Discours de Sir Georges Cartier, baronnet, accompagnés de notices par Joseph Tassé*. Montréal, E. Sénécal, 1893.

CHRISTIE, MARY KATHERINE   Sir Alexander Campbell. Toronto, 1950. 199 leaves.
Thesis (MA) – University of Toronto.

CLARK, LOVELL CROSBY   The Conservative Party in the 1890's. By Lovell C. Clark. (In Canadian Historical Association. *Report of the annual meeting*. [Ottawa] (1961), pp. [58]-74.)

—— A history of the Conservative administrations, 1891 to 1896. Toronto, 1968. 2 v.
Thesis (PH D) – University of Toronto.

—— Macdonald's Conservative successors, 1891-1896. By Lovell C. Clark. (In Moir, J. S. (ed.) *Character and circumstance*. Toronto, 1970. pp. 143-162.)

CLARKE, HENRY J. O'C.   A short sketch of the life of the Hon. Thomas D'Arcy McGee, MP, for Montreal (West) late Minister of Agriculture and Immigration for Canada . . . Montreal, Printed by J. Lovell, 1868. 80 p.

COLLINS, JOSEPH EDMUND   Canada's patriot statesman; The life and career of the Right Honourable Sir John A. Macdonald, based on the work of Edmund Collins. Rev., with additions to date, by G. Mercer Adam. Toronto, Rose Pub. Co., 1891. xxiii, 613 p.
First published 1883, under title: Life and times of the Right Honourable Sir John A. Macdonald.

—— Life and times of the Right Honourable Sir John A. Macdonald, Premier of the Dominion of Canada. Toronto, Rose Pub. Co., 1883. 642 p.

COLQUHOUN, ARTHUR HUGH URQUHART (ed.)   The Hon. James R. Gowan, member of Canadian Senate; a memoir. Edited by A. H. U. Colquhoun. Toronto, 1894. 170 p.
From 1885 to 1907, Sir James Robert Gowan was a member of the Senate of Canada.
A personal friend of Sir John A. Mac-

donald, but not considered an active member of the Conservative Party.

COLQUHOUN, ARTHUR HUGH URQUHART   Sir John A.: After thirty years. By A. H. U. Colquhoun. (In *The Canadian magazine of politics, science, art and literature*. Toronto. v. 57 (1921), pp. 93-97.)

Conservatism and Conservatives. (In *The Nation*. Toronto. v. 3, no. 3 (Jan. 21, 1876), pp. 30-31.)
Examines the speech given by Sir John A. Macdonald at the S. [!] White banquet in Cooksville, Ont.

The Conservatives in convention. (In *The Nation*. Toronto. v. 1, no. 27 (Oct. 1, 1874), p. 320.)
Comment on the Conservative Party convention held in Toronto in the autumn of 1874.

COOPER, JOHN IRWIN   The political ideas of George Etienne Cartier. (In *The Canadian historical review*. Toronto. v. 23 (1942), pp. 286-294.)

CREIGHTON, DAVID   The Right Hon. Sir John A. Macdonald. (In Marquis, T. G. (ed.) *Builders of Canada from Cartier to Laurier*. Detroit, Mich. [c1903] pp. 368-391.)
List of Macdonald's ministry "as it existed, with occasional change, until . . . June 6, 1891": pp. 387-388.

CREIGHTON, DONALD GRANT   An episode in the history of the University of Toronto. By D. G. Creighton. (In *University of Toronto quarterly*. [Toronto] v. 17 (1947/48), pp. 245-256.)
"This paper, in a somewhat different form, was read to the Ontario Historical Society at its annual meeting in June, 1947."
Provides pre-Confederation background information upon the occasion of awarding an honorary degree to Sir John A. Macdonald on June 7, 1889.

—— John A. Macdonald. By Donald Creighton. Toronto, Macmillan, 1955-56 [v. 1, 1956] 2 v.
Content: v. 1. The young politician. – v. 2. The old chieftain.

—— John A. Macdonald, Confederation and the Canadian West. By Donald Creighton. (In Historical and Scientific Society of Manitoba. *Papers*. Winnipeg. ser. 3, no. 23 (1966/67), pp. 5-13.)

—— John A. Macdonald, Confederation

and the Canadian West. By D. G. Creighton. (In *Minorities, schools and politics.* [Toronto, c1969] pp. [1]-9.)

"Reprinted from Historical and Scientific Society of Manitoba, Transactions, Series III, no. 23, 1966-67."

—— John A. Macdonald, Confederation and the Canadian West. By Donald Creighton. (In Swainson. D. W. (ed.) *Historical essays on the prairie provinces.* Toronto. [c1970] pp. [60]-70.)

Reprinted from "Historical and Scientific Society of Manitoba Transactions, Series III, no. 23 (1966/67), pp. 5-13".

—— John Alexander Macdonald, the father of his country. By Donald G. Creighton. (In *Historic Kingston.* Kingston. no. 14 (1966), pp. [3]-11.)

—— Macdonald and Manitoba. The Prime Minister's approach to the task of taking over the huge Hudson's Bay Company territories for Canada as cautious and considerate, and the first provisional government of Red River was not Louis Riel's, but John A. Macdonald's. By Donald Creighton. (In *The Beaver.* Winnipeg. outfit 287 (spring 1957), pp. 12-17.)

—— Sir John A. Macdonald. (In Bissell, C. T. (ed.) *Seven Canadians.* [Toronto, 1962, c 1957] pp. 48-62.)

Our living tradition, ser. 1.

—— Sir John Macdonald and Canadian historians. By D. G. Creighton. (In *The Canadian historical review.* Toronto. v. 29 (1948), pp. 1-13.)

—— Sir John Macdonald and Canadian historians. By D. G. Creighton. (In *Approaches to Canadian history.* [Toronto, 1970, c1967] pp. [50]-62.)

"Reprinted from Canadian historical review, XXIX (1), March, 1948."

—— Sir John Macdonald and Kingston. By D. G. Creighton. (In Canadian Historical Association. *Report of the annual meeting.* [Toronto] (1950), pp. 72-80.)

CROWELL, OLIVE MAC KAY The political career of Samuel Leonard Tilley, 1850-73. [Fredericton, N.B.] 1955. x, 189 leaves.

Thesis (MA) – University of New Brunswick.

DAFOE, JOHN WESLEY The political career of Sir George Foster. (In *The Canadian historical review.* Toronto. v. 15 (1934), pp. 191-195.)

A review article of *The Memoirs of the*

Rt. Hon. Sir George Foster, by W. S. Wallace. Toronto, 1933.

DAVID, LAURENT OLIVIER Galerie nationale. Sir George. Par. L. O. D. (In *L'Opinion publique.* Montréal. v. 4, no. 22 (29 mai 1873), pp. [253]-255.)

Biographical sketch of Sir George Etienne Cartier.

—— Galerie parlementaire. Sir George Etienne Cartier. Par L. O. David (In *L'Opinion publique.* Montréal. v. 1, no. 14 (9 avril 1870), pp. 109-110.)

A biographical sketch.

—— Galerie parlementaire. Par L. O. David. (In *L'Opinion publique.* Montréal. v. 1, no. 18 (5 mai 1870), p. 141.)

Brief biographical sketch of Pierre Fortin and Hon. J. J. C. Abbott.

—— Une grave question. Par L.-O. David. (In *L'Opinion publique.* Montréal. v. 11, no. 35 (26 août 1880), pp. [413]-414.)

Discusses the question of whether the clergy is above the law. Includes references to H. Langevin and I. Tarte.

—— Sir George Et. Cartier. Par L. O. D. (In *L'Opinion publique.* Montréal. v. 4, no. 25 (19 juin 1873), pp. [289]-291.)

Written on the occasion of his death and return to Canada for burial.

DAVIN, NICHOLAS FLOOD The fair grit; or, The advantages of coalition, a farce. Toronto, 1876. 35 p.

—— The reorganization of the cabinet. [First]-fifth article. (In *The Week.* Toronto. v. 8, no. 46—no. 50 (Oct. 16—Nov. 13, 1891).)

Deals with the cabinet of Prime Minister J. J. Abbott.

—— Reorganization of the cabinet. Sixth article. (In *The Week.* Toronto. v. 9, no. 3 (Dec. 18, 1891), p. 38.)

A reply to the article Mr. Davin reviewed, by C. A. Boulton. (In *The Week.* Toronto. v. 8 (Nov. 27, 1891), p. 829.)

—— Reorganization of the cabinet. Seventh article. (In *The Week.* Toronto. v. 9, no. 16 (Mar. 18, 1892), pp. 245-246.)

DAVIS, A. R. Stories of a great statesman. The boyhood days of Sir John Macdonald. (In *The Canadian courier.* Toronto. v. 9, no. 10 (Feb. 4, 1911), pp. 12-13; 22.)

DAVISON, HELEN LOUISE Sir John A. Macdonald and imperial relations in the period, 1878-1891. Toronto, 1942. 203 leaves.

Thesis (MA) – University of Toronto.

DECARIE, MALCOLM GRAEME   The political career of Sir Charles Hibbert Tupper. [Wolfville, N.S.] 1965. 1 v.
Thesis (MA) – Acadia University.

DE CELLES, ALFRED DUCLOS   La carrière de Cartier. Par A.-D. Decelles. (In *Revue canadienne*. Montréal. nouv. sér., v. 14 (1914), pp. [212]-224.)

—— Cartier et son temps. Montréal, Beauchemin, 1907. vi, 194 p.
Bound with the Author's *LaFontaine et son temps*. Montréal, 1907.

—— Cartier et son temps. Montréal, Beauchemin, 1913. 236 p. (Bibliothèque canadienne. Collection Champlain.)

—— Papineau, Cartier. Ed. de luxe. Toronto, Morang, 1904. 136 p. (The Makers of Canada, v. 8.)

DENT, JOHN CHARLES   Hon. Joseph Howe, 1804-1873. Final instalment. (In *The Maritime advocate and busy East*. Sackville, N.B. v. 38, no. 12 (July 1948), pp. 27-32.)
Reprinted from *Canadian portrait gallery*. Toronto. J. B. Magurn, 1880.

—— The Hon. Sir Charles Tupper, 1821-1915. (In *The Maritime advocate and busy East*. Sackville, N.B. v. 38, no. 6 (Jan. 1948), pp. 9-12.)
Reprinted from *Canadian portrait gallery*. Toronto. J. B. Magurn, 1880.

DESILETS, ANDREE   Hector-Louis Langevin; un père de la Confédération canadienne, 1826-1906. Québec, Presses de l'Université Laval, 1969. 461 p. (Les Cahiers de l'Institut d'histoire, 14.)

—— La succession de Cartier 1873-1891. (In Canadian Historical Association. *Historical papers*. [Ottawa] (1968), pp. [49]-64.)

DEVITT, E. H.   Hon. Samuel Merner. (In Waterloo Historical Society. *Annual report*. Kitchener, Ont. 28th (1940), pp. 139-141.)
A biographical sketch.

DUGAS, GEORGES   L'Hon. M. Joseph Royal. Par l'abbé G. Dugas. (In *La Revue canadienne*. Montréal. t. 42 (1902), pp. [289]-293.)
Written on the occasion of the death of the Honourable Joseph Royal, August 23, 1902, in Montreal.

DUNN, OSCAR   Aurons-nous des élections générales? (In *L'Opinion publique*. Montréal. v. 5, no. 1 (1 jan. 1874), pp. [1]-2.)

Raises the question after the fall of the government of Sir John A. Macdonald.

—— Une opinion de Cartier. (In *L'Opinion publique*. Montréal. v. 4, no. 43 (23 oct. 1873), p. [507].)
Reflections.

—— Où allons-nous? (In *L'Opinion publique*. Montréal. v. 5, no. 6 (5 fév. 1874), p. [61].)
Discusses the political future of British Columbia as it relates to the completion of the Canadian Pacific Railway guaranteed by the government of Sir John A. Macdonald.

FAULKNER, RALPH DOUGLAS   Sir Alexander Tilloch Galt as politician and Finance Minister. [Wolfville, N.S., 1951] 125 leaves.
Thesis (MA) – Acadia University.

FAUTEUX, AEGIDIUS   Cartier et les minorités. (In *Revue canadienne*. Montréal. nouv. sér., v. 14 (1914), pp. [245]-255.)

FERGUSON, CHARLES BRUCE   Sir Adams G. Archibald. (In Nova Scotia Historical Society. *Collections*. [Halifax] v. 36 (1968), pp. [5]-58.)

FLYNN, LOUIS J.   Canada's greatest Scot; Sir John Alexander Macdonald, a centennial tribute. (In *Historic Kingston*. Kingston. no. 16 (1968), pp. [23]-40.)

FOLIO, TOM   Was Lord Strathcona an empire-builder? A review of W. T. R. Preston's sensational "Life and times of Lord Strathcona", in which he claims that the title "empire-builder" is a misnomer. (In *Saturday night*. Toronto. v. 28, no. 9 (Dec. 12, 1914), pp. 5; 8-9.)
Discusses the *Life and times of Lord Strathcona*, by W. T. R. Preston. London, E. Nash, 1914.

FORSEY, EUGENE ALFRED   Government defeats in the Canadian House of Commons, 1867-73. By Eugene Forsey. (In *The Canadian journal of economics and political science*. Toronto. v. 29 (1963), pp. 364-367.)

FOX, WILLIAM SHERWOOD   When Sir John A. put his foot down. [The fruits of inflation and injustice on southwestern Ontario's last frontier, the Bruce Peninsula.] London, Ont., Lawson Memorial Library, University of Western Ontario, 1961. 13 p. (Western Ontario history nuggets, no. 29.)
Cover title.
With reference to Sir John A. Mac-

donald's intervention in the Bruce Peninsula lumbering issue.

FRASER, BARBARA JEAN LOVAT   The political career of Sir Hector Langevin. Toronto, 1959. 241 leaves.

    Thesis (MA) – University of Toronto.

    Label on the page with copyright date 1965.

——   The political career of Sir Hector Louis Langevin. By Barbara Fraser. (In *The Canadian historical review*. Toronto. v. 42 (1961), pp. 93-132.)

FRASER, BLAIR   The great and gay John A. Wit, roisterer, genius, here's our first Prime Minister—but not the man you heard about in school. (In *Maclean's*. Toronto. v. 60, no. 13 (July 1, 1947), pp. 7-8; 42-44; 46.)

FRASER, GEORGE EARL MAX   Egerton Ryerson and his political relations with Sir John A. Macdonald, as disclosed by some of their correspondence between 1854 and 1872. Toronto, 1922. 23 leaves.

    Thesis (MA) – University of Toronto.

GADSBY, HENRY FRANKLIN   Marses I have met. By H. F. Gadsby. (In *Saturday night*. Toronto. v. 30, no. 9 (Dec. 9, 1916), pp. 4; 11.)

    Concerns Sir Adolphe Caron, Minister of Militia 1880-1892, and a short comment on Sir Frederick Borden.

GELINAS, AIME   L'avenir du Canada. Par A. Gélinas. (In *L'Opinion publique*. Montréal. v. 10, no. 5 (30 jan. 1879), p. [49].)

    Summarizes remarks made by Thomas White on the movement of nationalities, mainly French and English, in Canada.

——   La conférence de l'hon. M. Royal. Par A. Gélinas. (In *L'Opinion publique*. Montréal. v. 11, no. 22 (27 mai 1880), p. [263].)

    Concerns the future of Manitoba.

——   Un discours de Sir John. Par A. Gélinas. (In *L'Opinion publique*. Montréal. v. 8, no. 45 (8 nov. 1877), p. 533.)

    Comments on the speech made by Sir John A. Macdonald before the Caledonian Society in Montreal, October 31, 1877. Concerns the question of nationalities in Canada.

——   Echos. Par A. Gélinas. (In *L'Opinion publique*. Montréal. v. 10, no. 23 (5 juin 1879), pp. [265]-266.)

    Discusses changes of personnel within the cabinet of Sir John A. Macdonald involving H. Langevin, C. Tupper and M.

Campbell; residential expenses of leading government officials; the issue of conferring titles on political personalities and other matters.

George-Etienne Cartier; études par Arthur Dansereau, Benjamin Sulte, Elzéar Gérin, Mgr. Antoine Racine, suivies de discours de G. E. Cartier. Montréal, Beauchemin [1914?] 124 p.

    At head of title: Edition du centenaire, 1814-1914.

GIBSON, WILLIAM   Senator the Hon. Michael Sullivan, MD. (In Canadian Catholic Historical Association. *Report*. [Ottawa] (1938/39), pp. 85-93.)

GILLIS, DUNCAN HUGH   Sir John Thompson and Bishop Cameron. By D. Hugh Gillis. (In Canadian Catholic Historical Association. *Report*. [Ottawa] (1955), pp. 87-97.)

    Discusses the political implications of the close personal relationship between Sir John Thompson and Bishop John Cameron of Antigonish, N.S.

——   Sir John Thompson's elections. By D. Hugh Gillis. (In *The Canadian historical review*. Toronto. v. 37 (1956), pp. 23-45.)

GOUIN, JACQUES   Histoire d'une amitie; correspondance intime entre Chapleau et DeCelles (1876-1898). (In *Revue d'histoire de l'Amérique française*. Montréal. v. 18, no 3 (déc. 1964), pp. 363-386; v. 18, no. 4 (mars 1965), pp. 541-565.)

    In two parts.

    Examines the correspondence between Adolphe Joseph Chapleau and Alfred D. DeCelles.

The Government and the judgement. By A. B. (In *The Week*. Toronto. v. 12, no. 49 (Nov. 1, 1895), pp. 1164-1165.)

    Discusses the consequences of the decision handed down by the Imperial Privy Council in the Brophy case in February 1895. This decision had significance in the Manitoba School question, and to the position of the Mackenzie Bowell administration.

GRANT, GEORGE MONRO   Joseph Howe. By Rev. G. M. Grant. To which is added Howe's Essay on the organization of the Empire. 2d ed. Halifax, A. & W. MacKinlay, 1906. 110 p.

——   Memoirs of Sir John A. Macdonald. By G. M. Grant. (In *The Week*. Toronto. v. 12, no. 3 (Dec. 14, 1894), pp. 55-59.)

    A review article of *Memoirs of the Right*

Honourable Sir John Alexander Macdonald, by Joseph Pope. London, Arnold, 1894.

GRANT, WILLIAM LAWSON   The tribune of Nova Scotia; a chronicle of Joseph Howe. Toronto, Brook, 1915. xi, 163 p. (Chronicles of Canada series [v. 26].)

GREAVES, ESTHER HARRISON   Peter Mitchell, a Father of Confederation. [Fredericton, 1958] iii, 114, 45 leaves.
Thesis (MA) – University of New Brunswick.
Served as Minister of Marine and Fisheries in the Macdonald administration, 1867-72: Represented Northumberland, N.B., in the House of Commons as an Independent Liberal, 1872-78; 1882-91.

GROULX, LIONEL ADOLPHE   Les idées religieuses de Cartier. Par Lionel Groulx. (In *Revue canadienne.* Montréal. nouv. sér., v. 14 (1914), pp. [225]-235.)

GUILLET, EDWIN CLARENCE   "You'll never die, John A.!" By Edwin C. Guillet. Toronto, Macmillan, 1967. 148 p. illus., facsims., ports.
A collection of contemporary drawings, paintings, woodcuts, cartoons, etc., depicting the life and legend of Sir John A. Macdonald.

HABITANT   What of Sir Hector? By Habitant. (In *The Week.* Toronto. v. 8, no. 45 (Oct. 9, 1891), p. 717.)
Concerns Sir Hector Langevin.

HANNAY, JAMES   Wilmot and Tilley. Ed. de luxe. Toronto, Morang, 1907. 301 p. (The Makers of Canada, v. 11.)

HARKIN, WILLIAM A.   Political reminiscences of the Right Honourable Sir Charles Tupper, bart. Transcribed and edited by the late W. A. Harkin. With a biographical sketch and an appendix. London, Constable, 1914. xix, 302 p.
Also published: Toronto, Copp, Clark, 1915.

HARVEY, DANIEL COBB   The centenary of D'Arcy McGee. By D. C. Harvey. (In *The Dalhousie review.* Halifax. v. 5 (1925/26), pp. [1]-10.)

HASSARD, ALBERT RICHARD   Great Canadian orators. I. D'Arcy McGee. By A. R. Hassard. (In *The Canadian magazine of politics, science, art and literature.* Toronto. v. 53 (1919), pp. 263-269.)

—— Great Canadian orators. II. Joseph Howe. By Albert R. Hassard. (In *The Canadian magazine of politics, science,* *art and literature.* Toronto. v. 53 (1919), pp. 423-430.)

—— Great Canadian orators. III. Nicholas Flood Davin. By Albert R. Hassard. (In *The Canadian magazine of politics, science, art and literature.* Toronto. v. 53 (1919), pp. 455-463.)

—— Great Canadian orators. VIII. Sir Joseph Adolphe Chapleau. By Albert R. Hassard. (In *The Canadian magazine of politics, science, art and literature.* Toronto. v. 54 (1919/20), pp. 417-422.)

—— Great Canadian orators. X. Sir Charles Tupper. By Albert R. Hassard. (In *The Canadian magazine of politics, science, art and literature.* Toronto. v. 55 (1920), pp. 247-250.)

HEISLER, JOHN PHALEN   Sir John Thompson, 1844-1894. Toronto, 1955. 430 leaves.
Thesis (PH D) – University of Toronto.

HERAT   Sir Alexander Campbell, KCMG. Lieutenant-Governor of Ontario. By Herat. (In *The Week.* Toronto. v. 5, no. 3 (Dec. 15, 1887), pp. 42-43.)
Prominent Canadians – VII.
A close friend and associate of Sir John A. Macdonald.

Historic letters on Confederation. Correspondence of Sir Leonard Tilley reveals terms offered Prince Edward Island in 1869. (In *Saturday night.* Toronto. v. 40, no. 34 (July 11, 1925), p. 4.)
Presents two letters by L. S. Tilley printed in the *Charlottetown Guardian.*

HODGETTS, JOHN EDWIN   Public servant extraordinary. By J. E. Hodgetts. (In *The Canadian forum.* Toronto. v. 37, no. 435 (Apr. 1957), pp. 9-10.)
Concerns Pierre Fortin.

HOLLAND, GEORGE CLARKE   The assassination of Thomas D'Arcy McGee. How Whelan was caught and hanged—a contribution to Canadian history, by one who recollects the incidents. (In *Saturday night.* Toronto. v. 37, no. 26 (Apr. 29, 1922), p. 2.)

L'Hon. M. Louis Archambeault. (In *L'Opinion publique.* Montréal. v. 4, no. 36 (4 sept. 1873), pp. 424-425.)

HOPKINS, JOHN CASTELL   Life and work of the Rt. Hon. Sir John Thompson... Prime Minister of Canada, by J. Castell Hopkins. With a pref. by His Excellency the Earl of Aberdeen. Toronto, United Pub. Houses, 1895. xiii, 479 p.

—— Sir Charles Tupper. By J. Castell Hopkins. (In Marquis, T. G. (ed.) *Builders of Canada from Cartier to Laurier*. Detroit, Mich. [c1903] pp. 453-470.)
List of Tupper's ministry, May 1, 1896: p. 468.

HOWLAND, OLIVER AIKEN   Sir John Thompson. By O. A. Howland. (In *The Canadian magazine of politics, science, art and literature*. Toronto. v. 5 (1895), pp. [420]-424.)

HUTCHINSON, JOHN I.   Sir Alexander Tilloch Galt. Toronto, Ryerson Press, 1930. 32 p. (Ryerson Canadian history readers.)

HUTCHISON, BRUCE   How John A. conjured up Canada. (In *Maclean's*. Toronto. v. 77, no. 18 (Sept. 19, 1964), pp. 15-18; 54-66.)
Excerpt from *Mr. Prime Minister*, by Bruce Hutchison.

IRWIN, ARCHIBALD   Our prominent men— XII. Hon. A. A. Macdonald. By the Editor. (In *The Prince Edward Island magazine*. Charlottetown. v. 6, no. 1 (Mar. 1904), pp. 25-30.)
Concerns Andrew Archibald Macdonald.

The Kingston election. (In *The Nation*. Toronto. v. 2, no. 1 (Jan. 8, 1875), p. 6.)
Comments on the re-election of Sir John A. Macdonald to the Dominion Parliament December 28, 1874.

KOESTER, CHARLES BEVERLEY   "Mr. Davin's pamphlet on the North West": a bureaucratic comedy of errors. By C. B. Koester. (In *Saskatchewan history*. Saskatoon. v. 16, no. 1 (winter 1963), pp. 27-32.)
Concerns the circumstances surrounding the pamphlet "Homes for millions" edited by Nicholas Flood Davin and published November 2, 1891.

—— Nicholas Flood Davin: politician— poet of the Prairies. By C. B. Koester. (In *The Dalhousie review*. Halifax. v. 44 no. 1 (spring 1964), pp. [64]-74.)

—— The parliamentary career of Nicholas Flood Davin, 1887-1900. [Saskatoon, Sask.] 1964. 1 v.
Thesis (MA)–University of Saskatchewan.

LA FLAMME, JOSEPH LEON KEMNER   Cartier et son temps. Par J.-L. K.-Laflamme. (In *La Revue franço-américaine*. Montréal. t. 10, no. 5 (mars 1913), pp. [378]-402.)
"Conférence donnée, le 18 mai 1913, devant une réunion publique tenue à l'Université Laval, Québec, sous la présidence de Sir A. B. Routhier, et sous les auspices du Comité du centenaire Cartier."

LA FLAMME, JOSEPH LEON KEMNER (comp.) Le centenaire Cartier, 1814-1914. Compte rendu des assemblées manifestations, articles de journaux, conférences, etc., qui ont marqué la célébration du centenaire de la naissance de Sir George-Etienne Cartier et l'érection de monuments à la mémoire de ce grand homme d'Etat canadien. Avec une introd. par. J.-L. K.-LaFlamme. Montréal, 1927. 455 p.
At head of title: Livre-souvenir.

LAGASSE, FRANCOISE   Sir Hector Louis Langevin et l'influence indue dans l'élection du comté de Charlevoix de 1876. [Lennoxville, Qué.] 1964. 1 v.
Thesis (MA) – Bishop's University.

The Land office steal. Edmonton's controversy of 1892. (In *Alberta historical review*. Edmonton. v. 7, no. 4 (autumn 1959) pp. 1-6.)
"An edited version of the news stories carried in the June 20th and June 23rd issue [of the Edmonton Bulletin of that time]."
Involved the federal Minister of the Interior, Hon. Edgar Dewdney.

LANDON, FRED   D'Alton McCarthy and the politics of the later 'eighties. (In Canadian Historical Association. *Report of the annual meeting*. Ottawa. (1932), pp. 43-50.)

—— D'Alton McCarthy—crusader. (In *Willisons monthly*. Sarnia, Ont. v. 4, no. 11 (May 1929), pp. 360-361.)

LANGEVIN, HECTOR LOUIS   Un désaveu. (In *L'Opinion publique*. Montréal. v. 6, no. 33 (19 août 1875), pp. 387-388.)
Correspondence between H. L. Langevin and H. G. Joly with reference to the misuse of election contributions.

LA PIERRE, LAURIER JOSEPH LUCIEN   Joseph Israel Tarte; a dilemma in Canadian politics, 1874-1896. Toronto, 1957. 239 leaves.
Thesis (MA) – University of Toronto.

—— Joseph Israel Tarte: relations between the French Canadian episcopacy and a French Canadian politician (1874-1896). By Laurier L. LaPierre. (In Canadian Catholic Historical Association. *Report*. [Ottawa] (1958), pp. 23-38.)

—— Joseph Israel Tarte and the McGreevy-Langevin scandal. (In Canadian Historical Association. *Report of the annual meeting*. Ottawa (1961), pp. [47]-57.)

—— Politics, race and religion in French Canada; Joseph Israel Tarte. By Laurier LaPierre. [Toronto] 1962. v, 555 leaves.

Thesis (PH D) – University of Toronto. Abstracted in Dissertation abstracts, v. 24 (1964), no. 7, pp. 2879-2880.

The Late Hon. Alexander Morris; first Chief Justice of Manitoba, ex-Lt.-Governor of Manitoba, the North-West Territories, Keewatin, PC, etc. (In *The Dominion illustrated*. Montreal. v. 3, no. 73 (Nov. 23, 1889), pp. 330-331.)

LAURENDEAU, ARTHUR   Sir Joseph Dubuc. (In *L'Action française*. Montréal. v. 12 (1924), pp. [117]-124.)
A review article of *Sir Joseph Dubuc*, by E. Lecompte. Montréal, 1921.

LAURIER, SIR WILFRID   Death of Sir John A. Macdonald. By Wilfrid Laurier (In Locke, G. H. (ed.) *Builders of the Canadian commonwealth*. Freeport, N.Y. [1967] pp. 203-207.)
"From a speech in the House of Commons, June 8, 1891."

—— Les Discours de Sir George Cartier. Par Wilfrid Laurier. (In *La Revue canadienne*. Montréal. 30. année (1894), pp. [133]-136.)
A review article of *Discours de Sir Georges Cartier, baronnet, accompangnés de notices par Joseph Tassé*. Montréal, E. Sénécal, 1893.

LAVERGNE, CHARLES EDOUARD   Georges Etienne Cartier; homme d'Etat canadien, 1814-1873. Préf. de Edouard Montpetit. Montréal, Langevin et L'Archevêque, 1914. 89 p.

LAWDER, ROBERT H.   Hon. Mr. Bowell's speech at Kingston. (In *The Week*. Toronto. v. 10, no. 22 (Apr. 28, 1893), pp. 512-513.)
Discusses tariff policy.

The Leadership of the Opposition. (In *The Nation*. Toronto. v. 1, no. 1 (Apr. 2, 1874), p. 8.)
Estimates the political talent of Sir John A. Macdonald.

LEBEL, MAURICE   P.-J.-O. Chauveau, humaniste du dix-neuvième siècle. Discours du récipiendaire de la médaille Chauveau. (In *Royal Society of Canada. Proceedings and transactions*. Ottawa. ser. 3, v. 56 (1962), section 1, pp. 1-10.)

—— P.-J.-O. Chauveau, humaniste de XXᵉ [i.e. XIX] siècle. (In *La Revue de l'Université Laval*. Québec. v. 17 no 1 (sept. 1962), pp. [32]-42.)
"Allocution de M. Maurice Lebel, récipiendaire de la médaille Chauveau, pro-

noncée à l'Université McMaster (Hamilton), le 5 juin 1962, lors du congrès annuel de la Société royale du Canada.

LECOMPTE, EDOUARD   Sir Joseph Dubuc (1840-1914), un grand chrétien. Montréal, Impr. du Messager, 1923. 270 p.

LEFEBVRE, JEAN JACQUES   La famille Cartier. Les ascendants et les proches alliés de Sir Georges-Etienne Cartier (†1873). (In *Royal Society of Canada. Proceedings and transactions*. Ottawa. ser. 4, v. 3 (1965), section 1, pp. 77-97.)

LEMIEUX, RODOLOPHE   Memories of Chapleau. By the Honourable Rodolphe Lemieux. (In *Willisons monthly*. Sarnia, Ont. v. 5, no. 1 (July 1929), p. 8.)

LETOURNEAU, HUBERT   Un précurseur. (In *Le Bulletin des recherches historiques*. Lévis. v. 66, no 2 (avril/juin 1960), pp. 41-47.)
Concerns Sir Joseph Adolphe Chapleau.

LOCKHART, ANDREW DONALD   The contribution of Macdonald conservatism to national unity, 1854-78. (In *Canadian Historical Association. Report of the annual meeting*. Toronto. (1939), pp. 124-132.)

—— The early life of John A. Macdonald, 1815-1844. [Kingston, Ont.] 1931. 113 leaves.
Thesis (MA) – Queen's University.

LONG, MORDEN H.   Sir John Rose and the informal beginnings of the Canadian High Commissionership. (In *The Canadian historical review*. Toronto. v. 12 (1931), pp. 23-43.)

LONGLEY, JAMES WILBERFORCE   Joseph Howe. By Hon. J. W. Longley. Illustrated under the direction of A. G. Doughty. London and Toronto, Oxford University Press, 1926. viii, 313 p. (The Makers of Canada series. Anniversary ed. [v. 8].)
On cover: Confederation and expansion. General editor: W. L. Grant.
Bound with the author's *Sir Charles Tupper*. London, 1926.

—— Sir Charles Tupper. By Hon. J. W. Longley. Ed. de luxe. Toronto, Makers of Canada (Morang), 1916. 304 p. (The Makers of Canada. new ser., v. 1.)

—— Sir Charles Tupper. By Hon. J. W. Longley. Illustrated under the direction of A. G. Doughty. London and Toronto, Oxford University Press, 1926. 304 p. (The Makers of Canada series. Anniversary ed. [v. 8.])

Bound with the author's *Joseph Howe*. London, 1926.

On cover: Confederation and expansion. Edited by W. L. Grant.

LONGLEY, RONALD STEWART Cartier and McDougall, Canadian emissaries to London, 1868-9. By R. S. Longley. (In *The Canadian historical review*. Toronto. v. 26 (1945), pp. 25-41.)

Concerns the negotiations conducted by G. E. Cartier and William McDougall for the transfer of Rupert's Land and the North-Western Territory to the Canadian government.

——— Sir Francis Hincks, Finance Minister of Canada, 1869-73. By R. S. Longley. (In Canadian Historical Association. *Report of the annual meeting*. Toronto. (1939), pp. 112-123.)

LONGWORTH, ISRAEL The Hon. Sir Adams George Archibald. By the late Israel Longworth. (In *Acadiensis*. St. John, N.B. v. 2 (1920) pp. 210-213.)

A biographical sketch.

LOVEKIN, L. A. M. The Cartier memorial. (In *The Canadian magazine of politics, science, art and literature*. Toronto. v. 54 (1919/20), pp. 13-22.)

LOWER, ARTHUR REGINALD MARSDEN Sir John A. Macdonald. By A. R. M. Lower. (In *The Dalhousie review*. Halifax. v. 19 (1939/40), pp. [85]-90.)

——— Sir John Macdonald in caricature. (In Canadian Historical Association. *Report of the annual meeting*. Toronto. (1940), pp. 56-62.)

LYNE, DANIEL C. Sir John A. Macdonald and the appointment of Canada's first cardinal. (In *Journal of Canadian studies*. Peterborough, Ont. v. 2, no. 4 (1967), pp. 58-60.)

Elzéar Alexandre Taschereau was created a cardinal of the Roman Catholic Church in 1886.

MC ALDUFF, M. M. Joseph Dubuc; role and views of a French Canadian in Manitoba, 1870-1914. [Ottawa] 1967. 1 v.

Thesis (MA) – University of Ottawa.

Elected in 1878 to represent Provencher in the Canadian House of Commons as a Conservative. (Cf. *The Macmillan dictionary of Canadian biography*. 3d ed. London [1967] p. 200.)

The McCarthy reception. (In *The Week*. Toronto. v. 10, no. 21 (Apr. 21, 1893), pp. 485-486.)

Refers to D'Alton McCarthy.

MC CREADY, JOHN E. BLAKENY When the Dominion was young. The fourth of six historical sketches. By J. E. B. McCready. (In *The Canadian magazine of politics, science, art and literature*. Toronto v. 27 (1906), pp. 314-317.)

Concerns the assassination of Thomas D'Arcy McGee and the trial and execution of James Patrick Whalen.

MACDERMOT, TERENCE WILLIAM LEIGHTON John A. Macdonald; his biographies and biographers. (In Canadian Historical Association. *Report of the annual meeting*. Ottawa. (1931), pp. 77-84.)

——— The political ideas of John A. Macdonald. By T. W. L. Macdermot. (In *The Canadian historical review*. Toronto. v. 14 (1933), pp. 247-264.)

MAC DONALD, DAVID Nova Scotia's strangest son. (In *Maclean's*. Toronto. v. 66, no. 7 (Apr. 1, 1953), pp. 22; 30-34; 37.)

Concerns Joseph Howe.

MACDONALD, SIR JOHN ALEXANDER Affectionately yours; The letters of Sir John A. Macdonald and his family. Edited and with an introd. by J. K. Johnson. Toronto, Macmillan, 1969. 205 p.

——— Correspondence . . . Selections from the correspondence of the Right Honourable Sir John Alexander Macdonald, GCB, first Prime Minister of the Dominion of Canada, made by his literary executor, Sir Joseph Pope. Garden City, N.Y., Doubleday, 1921. xxvii, 502 p.

Also published: Toronto, Oxford University Press [1921].

——— The Dominion campaign! Sir John Macdonald on the questions at issue before the people, 1881. The Premier's great speech before the workingmen of Toronto, 1881. [n.p., n.d.] 22 p.

——— The letters of Sir John A. Macdonald. Edited by J. K. Johnson. Ottawa, Public Archives of Canada, 1968. (The Papers of the prime ministers.)

Contents: v. 1. 1836-1857. – v. 2. 1858-1861.

Further volumes are in progress.

——— Sir John A. Macdonald at Montreal. Speech delivered at the White banquet, Wednesday, November 24, 1875. (In *Lib-*

eral Conservative hand-book. [n.p.] 1876. pp. [3]-25.)

MC FEE, DOUGAL EDGAR   The Honourable William McDougall. [Kingston, Ont.] 1953. 307 leaves.

Thesis (MA) – Queen's University.

MC GEE, THOMAS D'ARCY   1825 — D'Arcy McGee — 1925. A collection of speeches and addresses, together with a complete report of the centennial celebration of the birth of the Honourable Thomas D'Arcy McGee, at Ottawa, April 13th, 1925. Selected and arranged by the Honourable Charles Murphy. Toronto, Macmillan, 1937. xv, 366 p. illus., ports.

MAC INTOSH, ALAN WALLACE   The career of Sir Charles Tupper in Canada, 1864-1900. Toronto, 1960. 2 v. (v, 598 leaves)

Thesis (PH D) – University of Toronto.

MC KAY, WILLIAM ANGUS   The political life and ideas of William McDougall, 1840-1880. Toronto, 1949. [240] leaves.

Thesis (MA) – University of Toronto.

MC KEEN, DAVID BRUCE   Peter Mitchell, patriot. (In *The Atlantic advocate*. Fredericton, N.B. v. 47, no. 4 (Dec. 1956), pp. 57-58; 61.)

MACLEAN, WILLIAM FINDLAY   The Canadian Themistocles. By W. F. Maclean. (In *The Canadian magazine of politics, science, art and literature*. Toronto. v. 4 (1894/95, pp. [253]-260.)

Concerns Sir John A. Macdonald.

MACLEOD, GEORGE P.   Sir Hugh John Macdonald. (In Historical and Scientific Society of Manitoba. *Papers*. Winnipeg. ser. 3, no. 14 (1959), pp. 33-53.)

MACNAUGHTON, JOHN   Lord Strathcona. Illustrated under the direction of A. G. Doughty. London and Toronto, Oxford University Press, 1926. xii, 391 p. (The Makers of Canada series. Anniversary ed. [v. 10].)

On cover: Era of national progress.

Edited by W. L. Grant.

Bound with Vaughan, Walter. *Sir William Van Horne*. London, 1926.

MACPHERSON, JAMES PENNINGTON   Life of the Right Hon. Sir John A. Macdonald... by his nephew, Lt. Col. J. Pennington Macpherson, St. John, N.B. Earle Pub. House, 1891. 2 v.

MALCHELOSSE, GERARD   Le pupitre et la chaise de Sir G-E. Cartier. (In *Le Terroir.*

Québec. v. 5. no 5 (sept. 1924), pp. 98- 99; 106.)

MARQUIS, THOMAS GUTHRIE   Sir Leonard Tilley. Toronto, Ryerson Press, 1930. 32 p. (Ryerson Canadian history readers.)

MASTERS, DONALD CAMPBELL CHARLES   Financing the CPR, 1880-5. By D. C. Masters. (In *The Canadian historical review*. Toronto. v. 24 (1943), pp. 350-361.)

Draws on the private papers of Sir John A. Macdonald to examine the financial difficulties that confronted George Stephen, Donald Smith and Macdonald in the completion of the Canadian Pacific Railway.

MEINIER   L'honorable Thomas D'Arcy McGee. (In *L'Opinion publique*. Montréal. v. 3, no. 37 (12 sept. 1872), pp. 434-435.)

MILNER, WILLIAM C.   Our lieutenant-governors. Term of Hon. Josiah Wood. By W. C. Milner. (In *The Busy East of Canada*. Sackville, N.B. v. 9, no. 5 (Dec. 1918), pp. 20-22.)

Represented Westmorland, N.B., in the Canadian House of Commons from 1882 to 1895. Held office of Lieutenant-Governor of New Brunswick from 1912 until retirement in 1917.

M. LANGEVIN and M. JOLY   (In *The Nation*. Toronto. v. 2, no. 33 (Aug. 20, 1875), p. 391.)

Refers to correspondence between the Hon. H. L. Langevin and H. G. Joly.

Mr. White's reply to Sir A. T. Galt. (In *The Nation*. Toronto. v. 3, no. 9 (Mar. 3, 1876), p. 99.)

Discusses the reply issued by Thomas White to the pamphlet Civil liberty in Lower Canada, by Sir A. T. Galt. Montreal, 1876. 16 p.

MITCHELL, PETER   Peter Mitchell on John A. Macdonald. (In *The Canadian historical review*. Toronto. v. 42 (1961), pp. 209-227.)

Introduction by A. L. Burt.

Text of a letter dated October 7, 1893, written by the Hon. Peter Mitchell of New Brunswick to A. F. Gault.

The Montreal manifesto. (In *The Nation*. Toronto. v. 2, no. 49 (Dec. 10, 1875), pp. 582-583.)

Analyses the principles of political Conservatism with reference to a speech delivered at the T. White banquet in Montreal by Sir John Macdonald, November 24, 1875.

For full text of the speech see Macdonald,

Sir John Alexander. Sir John A. Macdonald at Montreal. (In *Liberal Conservative hand-book*. [n.p.] 1876. pp. [3]-25.)

MORGAN, HAMILTON RICHARDS The centenary of Thomas D'Arcy McGee. By H. R. Morgan. (In *Saturday night*. Toronto. v. 40, no. 20 (Apr. 4, 1925), p. 3.)

MORISON, JOHN LYLE Correspondence of Sir John A. Macdonald. By J. L. Morison. (In *Queen's quarterly*. Kingston. v. 29 (1921/22), pp. 383-387.)

A review article of *Correspondence of Sir John Macdonald*, by J. Pope. Toronto, Oxford University Press, 1921.

MORTON, WILLIAM LEWIS The formation of the first federal cabinet. (In *The Canadian historical review*. Toronto. v. 36 (1955), pp. 113-125.)

—— Macdonald's greatness in his times. An address by Dr. William L. Morton. (In Empire Club of Canada. *Addresses*. Toronto. (1964/65), pp. [184]-195.)

Address delivered January 28, 1965.

MOUSSEAU, JOSEPH ALFRED Un discours de Sir George E. Cartier. Par J. A. Mousseau. (In *L'Opinion publique*. Montréal. v. 1, no. 2 (8 jan. 1870), pp. [9]-10.)

Comments on a speech made by Sir George Cartier December 23, 1869.

—— Un incident historique. Le nord-ouest et Sir Georges. Par J. A. Mousseau. (In *L'Opinion publique*. Montréal. v. 2, no. 10 (9 mars 1871), pp. 110-111; v. 2, no. 11 (16 mars 1871), pp. [121]-122; v. 2, no. 13 (30 mars 1871), pp. [145]-146.)

In three parts.

Refers to Sir George Etienne Cartier.

MURRAY, ROBERT The Honourable Sir Adams George Archibald . . . (In *The Week*. Toronto. v. 9, no. 18 (Apr. 1892), pp. 278-279.)

Prominent Canadians: XL.

NASON, HAROLD MERSEREAU The political career of Sir Samuel Leonard Tilley. [Wolfville, N.S.] 1938. 1 v.

Thesis (PH D) – Acadia University.

NEATBY, HERBERT BLAIR Chapleau and the Conservative Party in Quebec. By H. Blair Neatby and John T. Saywell. (In *The Canadian historical review*. Toronto. v. 37 (1956), pp. 1-22.)

NELSON, JOHN Sir Hibbert Tupper a chip off the old block. Many anecdotes which illustrate the human qualities of father and son. (In *Saturday night*. Toronto. v. 42, no. 25 (May 7, 1927), p. 2.)

The New administration and its opportunities. (In *The Week*. Toronto. v. 10, no. 2 (Dec. 9, 1892), pp. 28-29.

The administration of Sir John Thompson.

A New era in Canadian politics. (In *The Week*. Toronto. v. 10 no. 10 (Feb. 3, 1893), pp. 221-222.)

"The revolt of Mr. Dalton McCarthy, Col. O'Brien, and others of the old-time adherents of the Conservative Party marks the beginning of a new era in Canadian politics."

NEWMAN, PETER CHARLES The fur trader who grubstaked our nation. By Peter C. Newman. (In *Maclean's*. Toronto. v. 72, no. 8 (Apr. 11, 1959), pp. 27; 49-52.)

Concerns Donald A. Smith (Lord Strathcona).

—— Lord Strathcona. (In his *Flame of power*. [Toronto, c1959] pp. 47-[70].)

A popular account of the career of Donald Smith.

NOBLE, E. J. D'Alton McCarthy and the election of 1896. [Guelph, 1969] 1 v.

Thesis (MA) – University of Guelph.

O'HANLY, JOHN LAWRENCE POWER Sir John Thompson and his critics. By J. L. P. O'Hanly. (In *The Canadian magazine of politics, science, art and literature*. Toronto. v. 1 (1893), pp. [413]-418.)

O'LEARY, MICHAEL GRATTAN Observing the first centenary of D'Arcy McGee. By M. Grattan O'Leary. (In *Maclean's*. Toronto. v. 38, no. 7 (Apr. 1, 1925), pp. 21; 50; 56.)

OLIVER, EDMUND H. The contest between Lieutenant-Governor Royal and the Legislative Assembly of the North West Territories, 1888-1893. (In Royal Society of Canada. *Proceedings and transactions*. Ottawa. ser. 3, v. 17 (1923), section ii, pp. 81-118.)

Read May meeting, 1923.

An account of the struggle for responsible government in the North West Territories.

The Opening of the session. (In *The Week*. Toronto. v. 3, no. 13 (Feb. 25, 1886), pp. [195]-196.)

Discusses three "serious questions" facing the Government: the execution of Riel; the causes of the rebellion; finance.

O'SULLIVAN, JOSEPH FRANCIS   Dalton Mc-Carthy and the Conservative Party, 1876-1896. Toronto, 1949. 197 leaves.

Thesis (MA) – University of Toronto.

Our Canadian portrait gallery. No. 1—Hon. John Rose. (In *Canadian illustrated news*. Montreal. v. 1, no. 2 (Nov. 13, 1869), pp. [17]-18.)

Our Canadian portrait gallery. No. 2—Hon. William McDougall, CB. (In *Canadian illustrated news*. Montreal. v. 1, no. 4 (Nov. 27, 1869), pp. [49]-50.)

Our Canadian portrait gallery. No. 3—Sir Francis Hincks, CB, KCMG, Minister of Finance, Canada. (In *Canadian illustrated news*. Montreal. v. 1, no. 5 (Dec. 4, 1860), pp. [65]-66.)

Our Canadian portrait gallery No. 5—Hon. Christopher Dunkin, QC, DCL, Minister of Agriculture. (In *Canadian illustrated news*. Montreal. v. 1, no. 10 (Jan. 8, 1870), pp. [145]-146.)

Our Canadian portrait gallery. No. 6—Hon. Alexander Morris, DCL, Minister of Inland Revenue. (In *Canadian illustrated news*. Montreal. v. 1, no. 12 (Jan. 22, 1870), pp. [177]-178.)

[Our Canadian portrait gallery] No. 7—Sir John A. Macdonald, KCB, LL D, &c., Prime Minister of Canada. (In *Canadian illustrated news*. Montreal. v. 1, no. 16 (Feb. 19, 1870), p. 242.)

Our Canadian portrait gallery. No. 9—Hon. James C. Aikins, Senator, Secretary of State of Canada. (In *Canadian illustrated news*. Montreal. v. 1, no. 18 (Mar. 5, 1870), pp. 277-278.)

Our Canadian portrait gallery. No. 10—Hon. Peter Mitchell, Minister of Marine and Fisheries. (In *Canadian illustrated news*. Montreal. v. 1, no. 19 (Mar. 12, 1870), pp. 293-294.)

Our Canadian portrait gallery. No. 17—Sir George E. Cartier, bart. (In *Canadian illustrated news*. Montreal. v. 1, no. 22 (Apr. 2, 1870), p. 338.)

Our Canadian portrait gallery. No. 32—Hon. P. J. O. Chauveau, LL D, QC, MP, Premier of Quebec. (In *Canadian illustrated news*. Montreal. v. 1, no. 28 (May 14, 1870), p. 442.)

Our Canadian portrait gallery. No. 33—Hon. H. L. Langevin, QC, CB, Minister of Public Works. (In *Canadian illustrated news*. Montreal. v. 1, no. 29 (May 21, 1870), pp. 452-453.)

A brief biographical sketch. .

Our Canadian portrait gallery. No. 34—Hon. S. L. Tilley, CB, Minister of Customs. (In *Canadian illustrated news*. Montreal. v. 1, no. 29 (May 21, 1870), pp. 453-454.)

A brief biographical sketch.

Our Canadian portrait gallery. No. 43—McKenzie Bowell, esq., MP, Grand Master of the Orange Institution of B.N.A. (In *Canadian illustrated news*. Montreal. v. 2, no. 8 (Aug. 20, 1870), pp. 117-118.)

A brief biographical sketch.

Our Canadian portrait gallery. No. 50—Hon. W. P. Howland, CB, Lieut.-Governor of Ontario. (In *Canadian illustrated news*. Montreal. v. 2, no. 24 (Dec. 10, 1870), pp. [373]-374.)

A Liberal, Howland served as Minister of Internal Revenue in the Macdonald administration formed in 1867.

Our Canadian portrait gallery. No. 59—Hon. James Cockburn, QC, Speaker of the House of Commons. (In *Canadian illustrated news*. Montreal. v. 3, no. 9 (Mar. 4, 1871), pp. 132-133.)

A brief biographical sketch.

Our Canadian portrait gallery. No. 62—Hon. Joseph Howe, PC, MP, Secretary of State for the Provinces. (In *Canadian illustrated news*. Montreal. v. 3, no. 11 (Mar. 18, 1871), p. 162.)

A brief sketch.

Our Canadian portrait gallery. No. 63—Hon. Alex. Campbell, QC, PC, Postmaster-General of Canada. (In *Canadian illustrated news*. Montreal. v. 3, no. 11 (Mar. 18, 1871), p. 162.)

A brief sketch.

Our Canadian portrait gallery. No. 64—Hon. J. C. Chapais, PC, Receiver General. (In *Canadian illustrated news*. Montreal. v. 3, no. 12 (Mar. 25, 1871), pp. [177]-178.)

A brief biographical sketch.

Our Canadian portrait gallery. No. 66—The late Hon. T. D. McGee. (In *Canadian illustrated news*. Montreal. v. 3, no. 14 (Apr. 8, 1871), p. 210.)

A brief biographical sketch with an extract from an editorial dated Tuesday, April 7, 1868, in the *Ottawa Times*, describing the death of Thomas D'Arcy McGee.

Our Canadian portrait gallery. The mover

and seconder of the address in the House of Commons. (In *Canadian illustrated news*. Montreal. v. 5, no. 19 (May 11, 1872), pp. 290-291.)

Concerns Henry Nathan, MP for the city of Victoria, and Edward Carter, MP for Brome.

Our Canadian portrait gallery. No. 109 — The Hon. Col. John H. Gray. (In *Canadian illustrated news*. Montreal. v. 6, no. 10 (Sept. 7, 1872), p. 149.)

A brief sketch.

Our Canadian portrait gallery. No. 110 — H. B. Witton, esq., MP. (In *Canadian illustrated news*. Montreal. v. 6, no. 12 (Sept. 21, 1872), pp. 180-181.)

A brief biographical sketch of "the first bonâ fide workingman ever sent up to Parliament".

OXLEY, JAMES MACDONALD The Father of Confederation. By J. Macdonald Oxley. (In *The National monthly of Canada*. Toronto. v. 6, no. 4 (Apr. 1905), pp. [204]-210.)

Concerns Sir John A. Macdonald.

PAQUET, LOUIS ADOLPHE Le sénateur Landry. (In *Le Canada français*. Québec. v. 3 (1920), pp. [321]-324.)

Concerns Auguste Charles Philippe Robert Landry.

PARKINS, GEORGE ROBERT Sir John A. Macdonald. Ed. de luxe. Toronto, Morang, 1908. 372 p. (The Makers of Canada, v. 20.)

PATTERSON, FRANK H. Some incidents in the life of Sir Charles Hibbert Tupper. By Hon. Frank H. Patterson. (In Nova Scotia Historical Society. *Collections*. [Halifax] v. 35 (1966), pp. [127]-162.)

"Read before the Nova Scotia Historical Society, 15 April 1966."

PATTERSON, GEORGE G. Hon. Robert Barry Dickey. By Judge George G. Patterson. (In Nova Scotia Historical Society. *Collections*. [Halifax] v. 36 (1968), pp. [61]-64.)

PAYNE, J. LAMBERT Sir John Thompson. By J. L. Payne. (In *The Lake magazine*. [Toronto] v. 1, no. 3 (Oct. 1892), pp. [141]-145.)

At head of title: Two leaders of the Commons.

—— Sir Mackenzie Bowell. (In Marquis, T. G. (ed.) *Builders of Canada from Cartier to Laurier*. Detroit, Mich. [c1903] pp. 442-452.)

List of Mackenzie Bowell's ministry of January 1, 1895: pp. 449-450.

—— Sir Mackenzie Bowell, premier of Canada; a sketch. (In *The Canadian magazine of politics, science, art and literature*. Toronto. v. 6 (1895/96), pp. [230]-236.)

PEDLEY, JAMES WILLIAM Biography of Lord Strathcona and Mount Royal. With introd. by Sir John Willison. Toronto, Nichols [1915] 187 p. ports.

PERRAULT, ANTONIO Cartier et le droit civil canadien. (In *Revue canadienne*. Montréal. nouv. sér., v. 14 (1914), pp. [256]-279.)

PERRY, CHARLES EBENEZER Hon. N. Clarke Wallace; his action on the "remedial bill" and what led up to it. By Rev. C. E. Perry. With an appendix by Rev. W. W. Colpitts. [Mimico, Ont.] Author's Edition, 1897. 129 p.

PHELAN, JOSEPHINE The ardent exile; the life and times of Thos. D'Arcy McGee. Toronto, Macmillan, 1951. x, 317 p.

PICHE, ARISTIDES Notes et commentaires. (In *Le Réveil*. Montréal. v. 1, no. 21 (14 oct. 1876), pp. 310-311.)

Concerns Hector Langevin.

PIERCE, LORNE ALBERT William Kirby, the portrait of a Tory loyalist. By Lorne Pierce. Toronto, Macmillan, 1929. xiv, 477 p.

Partial contents: Chapt. 17. The Conservative regime, 1878-1881.

PIRIE, ALEXANDER FRASER Honourable William Macdougall, CB. By Alex. F. Pirie. (In *The Week*. Toronto. v. 5, no. 31 (June 28, 1888), pp. 492-493.)

Prominent Canadians: XX.

POPE, SIR JOSEPH The day of Sir John Macdonald; a chronicle of the first Prime Minister of the Dominion. Toronto, Brook, 1915. xi, 195 p. (Chronicles of Canada series. [v. 29].)

—— Memoirs of the Right Honourable Sir John Alexander Macdonald, GCB, first Prime Minister of the Dominion of Canada. London, E. Arnold, 1894. 2 v.

—— Memoirs of the Right Honourable Sir John Alexander Macdonald, GCB, first Prime Minister of the Dominion of Canada. With a pref. by A. G. Doughty. Rev. ed. Toronto, Oxford University Press, 1930. xxix, 816 p.

—— Memoirs of the Right Honourable Sir John Alexander Macdonald, GCB, first

Prime Minister of the Dominion of Canada. With a pref. by A. G. Doughty. Toronto, Musson [c1947?] xxix, 816 p.

—— Sir John A's first, and only, trip to the West. (In *Maclean's*. Toronto. v. 73, no. 1 (Jan. 2, 1960), pp. 24-25; 34; 36.)

Excerpt from *Public servant; the memoirs of Sir Joseph Pope*. Toronto, Oxford University Press, 1960.

This trip occurred during the summer of 1886.

POWER, LAWRENCE GEOFFREY Our first president, the Honourable John William Ritchie, 1808-1890. By the Hon. Lawrence G. Power. (In Nova Scotia Historical Society. *Collections*. Halifax. v. 19 (1918), pp. [1]-15.)

"Read, 3rd December, 1915."

J. R. Ritchie was called to the Senate in 1867.

PRESTON, WILLIAM THOMAS ROCHESTER The life and times of Lord Strathcona. London, E. Nash, 1914. ix, 324 p.

Also published: Toronto, McClelland, Goodchild and Stewart [1914].

PRUD'HOMME, LOUIS ARTHUR L'honorable Joseph Royal—sa vie—ses œuvres. Par L.-A. Prud'homme. (In Royal Society of Canada. *Proceedings and transactions.* Ottawa. ser. 2, v. 10 (1904), section 1, pp. 3-24.)

"Lu le 22 juin 1904:"

—— L'Honorable Joseph Royal, sa vie, ses œuvres. Par M. le juge L.-A. Prud'homme. (In *La Revue canadienne*. Montréal. t. 49 (1905), pp. [36]-66.)

—— Sir Joseph Dubuc. Par L.A. Prud'homme. (In *La Revue canadienne*. Montréal. nouv. sér., v. 13 (1914), pp. [386]-396; [500]-513; nouv. sér. v. 14 (1914), pp. [22]-30; [97]-112.)

In four parts.

Written on the occasion of Dubuc's death in Los Angeles, Calif., on January 7, 1914.

READE, JOHN Thomas D'Arcy McGee—the poet. (In *The New Dominion monthly*. Montreal. (Feb. 1870), pp. 12-21.)

The Reforming of the tariff. (In *The Week*. Toronto. v. 11, no. 19 (Apr. 6, 1894), pp. 437-438.)

Discusses the Government's proposals for the revision of the tariff.

RES PUBLICA Cabinet making. By Res Publica. (In *The Week*. Toronto. v. 8, no. 19 (Apr. 10, 1891), p. 300.)

The cabinet of Sir John A. Macdonald.

RICHMOND, W. R. The life of Lord Strathcona. London, Collins [1914?] 246 p. (Collins' wide world library.)

A popular account.

The Right Honourable Sir John Thompson. (In *The Week*. Toronto. v. 12, no. 4 (Dec. 21, 1894), pp. 78-79.)

Written on the occasion of his death at Windsor Castle, England, on December 12, 1894.

ROBSON, MARY EVANGELINE Sir John Alexander Macdonald as an early exponent of Canadian nationalism. [New York, 1929] 92 leaves.

Thesis (MA) – Columbia University.

ROUTHIER, SIR ADOLPHE BASILE L'Honorable P. J. O. Chauveau. Par A. B. Routhier. (In *Le Canada-Français*. Québec. v. 3 (1890), pp. [304]-349.)

RUSSELL, BENJAMIN The career of Sir John Thompson. By Mr. Justice Russell. (In *The Dalhousie review*. Halifax. v. 1 (1921/22), pp. [188]-201.)

Reminiscences of a personal friend.

RUTHVEN, ED. Ottawa notes. (In *The Week*. Toronto. v. 1, no. 14 (Mar. 6, 1884), p. 215.)

Discusses the budget speech of Sir Leonard Tilley.

SAUNDERS, EDWARD MANNING (ed.) The life and letters of the Rt. Hon. Sir Charles Tupper, bart. Edited by E. M. Saunders. With an introd. by the Rt. Hon. Sir R. L. Borden. London, Cassell, 1916. 2 v.

SAUNDERS, EDWARD MANNING Three premiers of Nova Scotia: the Hon. J. W. Johnstone, the Hon. Joseph Howe, the Hon. Charles Tupper. Toronto, W. Briggs, 1909. 628, p. ports.

SAVILLE Sir John A. Macdonald, KCB. By Saville. (In *The Week*. Toronto. v. 4, no. 49 (Nov. 3, 1887), pp. 790-791.)

Prominent Canadians – IV.

SAYWELL, JOHN TUPPER The Crown and the politicians: the Canadian succession question, 1891-1896. By John T. Saywell. (In *The Canadian historical review*. Toronto. v. 37 (1956), pp. 309-337.)

—— Sir John Thompson—the unknown. By John T. Saywell. (In *The Canadian forum*. Toronto. v. 37, no. 438 (July 1957), pp. 79-80.)

SCOTT, S. MORLEY Foster on the Thompson-Bowell succession. (In *The Canadian his-*

torical review. Toronto. v. 48 (1967), pp. 273-276.)

Presentation of a private letter written by George Eulas Foster, federal Minister of Finance, to S. D. Scott, editor of the Saint John Daily Sun, December 18, 1894.

The Second tariff debate. (In The Week. Toronto. v. 10, no. 17 (Mar. 24, 1893), pp. 389-390.)

Discusses the principles embodied in a motion by D'Alton McCarthy.

SHEPPARD, EDMUND ERNEST   Around Town. By Don. (In Toronto Saturday night. Toronto. v. 4, no. 28 (June 6, 1891), p. [1].)

A biographical sketch written on the occasion of the death of Sir John A. Macdonald June 6, 1891.

—— Around Town. By Don. (In Toronto Saturday night. Toronto. v. 8, no. 4 (Dec. 15, 1894), p. [1].)

Concerns the death of Sir John Thompson and its impact on the Conservative Party.

—— Around Town. By Don. (In Toronto Saturday night. Toronto. v. 8, no. 5 (Dec. 22, 1894), p. [1].)

Discusses the death of Sir John Thompson and its implications for the Conservative Party.

SIMPSON-HAYES, KATE   D'Arcy McGee as I saw him. (In Saturday night. Toronto. v. 42, no. 32 (June 25, 1927), p. 3.)

Sir A. Galt on Ultramontane aggression. (In The Nation. Toronto. v. 3, no. 8 (Feb. 25, 1876), pp. 88-89.)

Discusses the pamphlet Civil liberty in Lower Canada, by Sir A. T. Galt. Montreal, D. Bentley, 1876. 16 p.

Sir Alexander T. Galt. (In The Nation. Toronto. v. 2, no. 37 (Sept. 17, 1875), pp. 439-440.)

Presents the opinions and position of Sir A. T. Galt.

Sir Alexander Tilloch Galt. (In L'Opinion publique. Montréal. v. 11, no. 15 (8 avril 1880), p. 171.)

Sir J. Adolphe Chapleau. (In Société historique de Sainte-Thérèse-de-Blainville. Histoire de Sainte-Thérèse. [Joliette] 1940. pp. 271-277.)

Cahiers historiques.

Sir John A. Macdonald at Kingston. (In The Nation. Toronto. v. 1, no. 39 (Dec. 24, 1874), pp. 464-465.)

A critical evaluation of the public character and career of Sir John A. Macdonald.

Refers to a speech delivered in Kingston, Ontario, during a campaign for a by-election held December 28, 1874.

Sir John Macdonald. (In The Week. Toronto. v. 8, no. 28 (June 12, 1891), pp. 441-442.)

Written on the occasion of the death of Sir John A. Macdonald.

Sir John Thompson, KCMG, QC, Minister of Justice for Canada. By W. (In The Week. Toronto. v. 8, no. 11 (Feb. 13, 1891), pp. 171-172.)

Prominent Canadians: XXXIV.

Sir John Thompson's speech. (In The Week. Toronto. v. 10, no. 8 (Jan. 20, 1893), pp. 173-174.)

The first public statement made as Premier to the Young Men's Conservative Association of Toronto, Friday, January 13, 1893.

Sir William Pearce Howland, CB, KCMG. By G. S. A. (In The Week. Toronto. v. 6, no. 29 (June 21, 1889), pp. 457-458.)

Prominent Canadians: XXVI.

SKELTON, ISABEL   The life of Thomas D'Arcy McGee. Gardenvale, Garden City Press, 1925. vi, 554 p.

SKELTON, OSCAR DOUGLAS   Life and times of Sir Alexander Tilloch Galt. Toronto, Oxford University Press, 1920. 586 p.

—— Life and times of Sir Alexander Tilloch Galt. Edited and with an introd. by Guy Maclean. [Toronto, McClelland and Stewart c1966] xvii, 293 p. (The Carleton library, c26.)

First published Toronto, Oxford University Press, 1920.

SLATTERY, TIMOTHY PATRICK   The assassination of D'Arcy McGee. By T. P. Slattery. With illus. by the Author. Toronto, Doubleday Canada, 1968. xviii, 527 p.

A popular account for the general reader.

SMITH, DONALD WARREN   The maritime years of R. B. Bennett, 1870-1897. [Fredericton, N.B.] 1968 [c1969] ii, 209 leaves.

Thesis (MA) – University of New Brunswick.

SMITH, GOLDWIN   The government and the bank circulation. (In The Week. Toronto. v. 6, no. 5 (Jan. 4, 1889), p. 70.)

SNELL, CARROL HERBERT   The history of the Liberal-Conservative Party to 1900. [Wolfville, N.S., 1950] 189 leaves.

Thesis (MA) – Acadia University.

SOMERVILLE, R. S.   "Gentlemen, we have

with us to-night." Toastmaster, R. S. Somerville. (In *Saturday night*. Toronto. v. 34, no. 24 (Mar. 27, 1920), p. 2.)

Concerns Sir Charles Hibbert Tupper. Adopts the form of an introductory speech.

STACEY, CHARLES PERRY John A. Macdonald on raising troops in Canada for imperial service, 1885. By C. P. Stacey. (In *The Canadian historical review*. Toronto. v. 38 (1957), pp. 37-40.)

STANLEY, GEORGE FRANCIS GILMAN The Macpherson-Shaw-Macdonald connection in Kingston. By George F. G. Stanley. (In *Historic Kingston*. Kingston. no. 13 (1965), pp. [3]-20.)

A genealogical study relating to John A. Macdonald.

—— The man who made Canada, 1865-1867. An address before the Conference of the Public Relations Society of America [at the] Queen Elizabeth Hotel, November 9, 1964. [New York, Foundation for Public Relations Research and Education, c1965] 20 p.

Concerns Sir John A. Macdonald.

STAPLES, LILA The Honourable Alexander Morris: the man; his work. (In Canadian Historical Association. *Report of the annual meeting*. Ottawa. (1928), pp. 91-100.)

STAUFFER, BYRON H. Sir John A. Macdonald, empire builder; an address. (In Empire Club of Canada. *Addresses*. Toronto. (1914/15), pp. 66-67.)

Address delivered February 18, 1915.
A candid character sketch.

STAYNER, CHARLES ST. C. John William Ritchie, one of the Fathers of Confederation. (In Nova Scotia Historical Society. *Collections*. [Halifax] v. 36 (1968), pp. [183]-277.)

STEWART, ALICE ROSE The Imperial policy of Sir John A. Macdonald, Canada's first Prime Minister. [Cambridge, Mass., 1946] 2 v. (711 leaves)

Thesis (PH D) – Harvard University.

—— Sir John A. Macdonald and the Imperial Defence Commission of 1879. By Alice R. Stewart. (In *The Canadian historical review*. Toronto. v. 35 (1954), pp. 119-139.)

"The Right Hon. Sir John A. Macdonald, examined": pp. 122-139.

STEWART, GEORGE Sir Samuel Leonard Tilley, CB, KCMG, Lieutenant-Governor of

New Brunswick. By George Stewart, Jr. (In *The Week*. Toronto. v. 5, no. 9 (Jan. 26, 1888), pp. 136-137.)

Prominent Canadians –X.

—— Thomas D'Arcy McGee. (In *Stewart's literary quarterly magazine*. Saint John, NB. v. 2, no. 2 (July 1868), pp. 67-76.)

Strathcona and Sir John. A famous political quarrel of the seventies recalled. (In *Saturday night*. Toronto. v. 27, no. 16 (Jan. 31, 1914), p. 5.)

SULTE, BENJAMIN Sir George-Etienne Cartier. (In *Revue canadienne*. Montréal. t. 10 (1873), pp. [425]-436.)

—— Sir George-Etienne Cartier. Augmenté et publié par Gérard Malchelosse. Montréal, G. Ducharme, 1919. 103 p. (His Mélanges historiques, v. 4.)

Suppression, proscription. (In *Réveil*. Québec. v. 1, no. 8 (15 juil. 1876), pp. [113]-115.)

Refers to the disputed election of Hector Langevin in the constituency of Charlevoix, Que., January 22, 1876.

SWAINSON, DONALD WAYNE Alexander Campbell: general manager of the Conservative Party (Eastern Ontario Section). By Donald Swainson. (In *Historic Kingston*. Kingston. no. 17 (1969), pp. [78]-92.)

TAIT, D. H. Dr. Charles Tupper: a Father of Confederation. (In Nova Scotia Historical Society. *Collections*. [Halifax] v. 36 (1968), pp. [279]-300.)

TALON-LESPERANCE, JOHN Hon. J. A. Chapleau, MP, Secretary of State. By J. Talon-Lesperance. (In *The Week*, Toronto. v. 5, no. 13 (Feb. 23, 1888), pp. 201-202.)

Prominent Canadians – XII.

—— The Hon. Pierre Joseph Olivier Chauveau. (In *The Week*. Toronto. v. 5, no. 22 (Apr. 26, 1888), pp. 351-352.)

Prominent Canadians – XIV [i.e. XVI].

TASSE, JOSEPH Charles Joseph Coursol. (In his *Le 38me fauteuil*. Montréal, 1891. pp. [117]-164.)

—— Désiré Girouard. (In his *Le 38me fauteuil*. Montréal, 1891. pp. [227]-299.)

—— Joseph Alfred Mousseau. (In his *Le 38me fauteuil*. Montréal, 1891. pp. [1]-55.)

—— Joseph Royal. (In his *Le 38me fauteuil*. Montréal, 1891. pp. [165]-226.)

—— Louis François Roderick Masson. (In

his *Le 38me fauteuil.* Montréal, 1891. pp. [57]-116.)

—— Un parallèle. Lord Beaconsfield et Sir John Macdonald. Ottawa, 1880. 41 p.

—— Le 38me fauteuil; ou Souvenirs parlementaires. Montréal, E. Senécal, 1891. 299 p.
Contents: J. A. Mousseau. – L. F. R. Masson. – C. J. Coursol. – J. Royal. – D. Girouard.

TAYLOR, FENNINGS Thos. D'Arcy McGee; sketch of his life and death. With a life sized portrait by W. Notman. Montreal, Printed by J. Lovell, 1868. 40 p.

THIBAULT, CHARLES Biographie de Sir Charles Tupper; Ministre des chemins de fer et des canaux du Canada et Haut Commissaire canadien à Londres. Québec, L. Brousseau, 1883. 288 p.

—— Biography of Sir Charles Tupper, Minister of Railway . . . High Commissioner of Canada to England. Montreal, L'Etendard Print., 1883. 148 p.

THOMAS, EARLE SCHWARTZ Sir John Macdonald in opposition, 1873-1878. [Kingston, Ont. 1951.] 248 leaves.
Thesis (MA) – Queen's University.

TOWNSHEND, SIR CHARLES JAMES The Honourable James McDonald. By Sir Chas. Townshend. (In Nova Scotia Historical Society. *Collections.* Halifax. v. 20 (1921), pp. 139-153.)
"Read before the N. S. Society, April 4, 1919."

TUPPER, SIR CHARLES, bart. Dominion Day in London. (In *Massey's magazine.* Toronto. v. 2, no. 1 (July 1896), pp. 20-23.)

—— Recollections of sixty years. London, Cassell, 1914. 414 p.

TUPPER, SIR CHARLES HIBBERT The commercial marine of Canada. By Hon. C. H. Tupper. (In National Club of Toronto. *Maple leaves.* Toronto. [introd. 1891] pp. [84]-100.)
"Speech delivered by the Hon. C. H. Tupper, Minister of Marine, at the dinner to Mr. Plimsoll, given by the National Club."

—— The functions of a governor-general. (In *The National review.* London. v. 28 (1896/97), pp. 384-389.)
Concerns "the action of Lord Aberdeen upon the defeat of the Conservative ministry in Canada at the polls" in 1896.
For a reply, see The functions of a gov-

ernor-general, by W. A. Weir. (In *The Canadian magazine of politics, science, art and literature.* Toronto. v. 8 (1896/97), pp. 269-272.)

TUPPER, SIR CHARLES HIBBERT (ed.) Supplement to the life and letters of the Rt. Hon. Sir Charles Tupper, bart. Toronto, Ryerson, 1926. 199 p.

TURCOTTE, EILEEN How Sir John A. passed out patronage and built a nation all at once. (In *Maclean's.* Toronto. v. 79, no. 15 (Aug. 6, 1966), pp. 19; 29-30.)
An examination of the correspondence of Sir John A. Macdonald.

TURCOTTE, LOUIS PHILIPPE L'Honorable Sir G. E. Cartier, Ministre de la Milice. Par Louis P. Turcotte. Québec, Atelier typ. de L. Brousseau, 1873. 80 p. (Biographies politiques.)

TURTLE, A. J. In a reminiscent mood. Memories of Sir. John A. Macdonald. (In *Saturday night.* Toronto. v. 42, no. 9 (Jan. 15, 1927), p. 5.)

VAN BLARICOM, GEORGE B. The biggest news scoop in Canada. By G. B. Van Blaricom. (In *The Busy man's magazine.* Toronto. v. 16, no. 3 (July 1908), pp. 88-90.)
A recounting, forty years after the event, as to how the *Daily Leader* of Toronto was the first to announce the assassination of Thomas D'Arcy McGee.

WAITE, PETER BUSBY The political ideas of John A. Macdonald. By Peter B. Waite. (In *The Political ideas of the Prime Ministers of Canada.* Ottawa, 1969, pp. [51]-67.)

—— Sir John A. Macdonald: the man. By P. B. Waite. (In *Dalhousie review.* Halifax. v. 47, no. 2 (summer 1967), pp. [143]-158.)

WALLACE, WILLIAM STEWART The memoirs of the Rt. Hon. Sir George Foster. Toronto, Macmillan, 1933. vi, 291 p.

—— Sir John Macdonald. Toronto, Macmillan, 1924. 132 p. (Canadian statesmen, no. 1.)

WARD, NORMAN MC QUEEN Davin and the founding of the *Leader.* By Norman Ward. (In *Saskatchewan history.* Saskatoon. v. 6, no. 1 (winter 1953), pp. 13-16.)
Concerns Nicholas Flood Davin.

WEBSTER, THOMAS STEWART John A. Macdonald and Kingston. [Kingston, Ont.] 1944. 147 leaves.
Thesis (MA) – Queen's University.

WEIR, WILLIAM ALEXANDER   The functions of a governor-general. A reply to Sir Charles Hibbert Tupper. By W. Weir. (In *The Canadian magazine of politics, science, art and literature*. Toronto. v. 8 (1896/97), pp. 269-272.)

A reply to the article The functions of a governor-general by C. H. Tupper. (In *The National review*. London. v. 28 (1896/97), pp. 384-389.)

WHITE, THOMAS   The Liberal Conservative Party. A sketch of Canadian political history under responsible government in a speech delivered at L'Orignal, Ontario, March 5th, on the occasion of the formation of a Liberal Conservative Association. By Thos. White, Jr. Montreal, Dawson Bros., 1874. 32 p.

—— The National Policy. A speech delivered in London, Ontario, January 12, 1877. Kelowna, B.C., *Kelowna Courier* [n.d.] 39 p.

Cover title.

Concerns Sir John A. Macdonald's "National Policy" of tariff protection.

Thomas White was elected to the Canadian House of Commons in 1878. He became Minister of the Interior in 1885.

WILLISON, SIR JOHN STEPHEN   The correspondence of Sir John A. Macdonald. By Sir John Willison. (In *The Dalhousie review*. Halifax. v. 2 (1922/23), pp. [5]-25.)

A review article of Macdonald, Sir J. A. Correspondence . . . . Selections . . . made by Sir Joseph Pope. Toronto, Oxford University Press, 1921.

WILLSON, BECKLES   The life of Lord Strathcona and Mount Royal. Boston, Houghton Mifflin, 1915. 2 v.

—— The life of Lord Strathcona and Mount Royal, 1820-1914. London, Cassell, 1915. xv, 631 p.

—— Lord Strathcona; the story of his life. With forewords by the Duke of Argyll and the Earl of Aberdeen. London, Methuen, 1902. xii, 288 p.

Appendix A: Hon. Donald A. Smith's own narrative of events during the Red River rebellion, 1869-70 (pp. 252-279).

WILSON, ALAN   Fleming and Tupper; the fall of the Siamese twins, 1880. (In Moir, J. S. (ed.) *Character and circumstance*. Toronto, 1970. pp. 99-127.)

YEALLAND, FRED T.   The Hon. Sir John Carling. (In *The Canadian magazine of politics, science, art and literature*. Toronto. v. 26 (1905/06), pp. 224-226.)

Canadian celebrities, no. 67.

YORK   The results of the National Policy. By York. (In *The Week*. Toronto. v. 2, no. 12 (Feb. 19, 1885), p. 181.)

Comments on the financial policy of Sir Leonard Tilley.

1896–1921

1896–1917

ALLEN, RALPH   In this corner: Sir Sam Hughes. (In *Maclean's*. Toronto. v. 74, no. 10 (May 20, 1961), pp. [14]-17; 60-66.)

Excerpt from Ralph Allen's book *Ordeal by fire*. Toronto, 1961.

—— The misfortunes of war. (In *Maclean's*. Toronto. v. 74, no. 11 (June 3, 1961), pp. 18-19; 39-46.)

From Allen's *Ordeal by fire*. Toronto, 1961. Concerns Colonel Sam Hughes.

—— Sir Sam s'en va-t-en guerre. (In *Le Magazine Maclean*. Montréal. v. 1, no 4 (juin 1961), pp. 32-33; 59-61.)

Adapted from *Maclean's* magazine. Concerns Sir Sam Hughes.

ANDERSON, H. W.   Mainly because he is "Bob". Hon. Robert Rogers, Minister of Public Works, is picked as second man up to Sir Robert Borden. (In *The Canadian courier*. Toronto. v. 20, no. 4 (June 24, 1916), p. 13.)

ASSELIN, OLIVAR   Mes souvenirs de Sam Hughes. (In *La Revue moderne*. Montréal. 2. année, no 12 (15 oct. 1921), pp. 18-20.)

BANKS, RIDEAU   National affairs. Back in Borden's day. (In *Saturday night*. Toronto. v. 52, no. 33 (June 19, 1937), p. 34.)

Concerns Sir Robert Borden; written upon the occasion of his death in Ottawa June 10, 1937.

BASSETT, JOHN   Some leading Conservatives in the Ottawa House. (In *The Busy man's Canada*. Toronto. v. 3, no. 3 (Oct. 1912), pp. 38-43.)

BEAUCHESNE, ARTHUR   Le Très-Honorable M. R. L. Borden, premier-ministre du Canada. Montréal, 1912. 30 p.

BENNETT, RICHARD BEDFORD   Canada from

east to west. By R. B. Bennett, MP, Calgary. (In Canadian Club of Montreal. *Addresses*. [Montreal] (1911/12), pp. 189-203.)

Address delivered March 11, 1912.

Considers, in particular, the three main grievances of the West: transportation, markets, taxation.

—— The Northwest provinces and their relation to Confederation. By R. B. Bennett. (In Canadian Club of Toronto. *Addresses*. Toronto. (1911/12), pp. 192-201.)

Address delivered April 8, 1912.

"Mr. R. B. Bennett represents Calgary in the House of Commons."

BLACK, ROBSON   General-The-Honorable-Sam. An uncensored character-sketch of the Minister of Militia. (In *MacLean's magazine*. Toronto. v. 28, no. 3 (Jan. 1915), pp. [38]-40.)

Concerns Sam Hughes.

BORDEN, SIR ROBERT LAIRD   Canada and the Great War. An address by Rt. Hon. Sir Robert L. Borden, Prime Minister. (In Empire Club of Canada. *Addresses*. Toronto. (1914/15), pp. [1]-14.)

Address delivered December 5, 1914.

—— Canada and the war. By the Rt. Hon. Sir Robert L. Borden. (In Canadian Club of Montreal. *Addresses*. [Montreal] (1914/15), pp. 81-88.)

Address delivered December 7, 1914.

—— Canada at war. Speeches delivered by Rt. Hon. Sir Robert Laird Borden in Canada and the United Kingdom. [n.p.,n.d.] 28 p.

Speeches delivered December 1916—May 1917.

—— Canada at war. Speeches delivered by Rt. Hon. Sir Robert Laird Borden in England, Canada and the United States July—December, 1915. [n.p., n.d.] 58 p.

—— Democracies of the English speaking world. Address by the Right Honourable Robert L. Borden. (In Canadian Society of New York. *Year book*. [New York] (1912), pp. 60-68.)

Address delivered December 8, 1911.

Comparative remarks on the system of government in the United States and the British Dominions. (Printed by F. H. Hitchcock.)

—— From Confederation to the World War. By Sir Robert Borden. (In Locke, G. H. (ed.) *Builders of the Canadian com-*

monwealth. Freeport, N.Y. [1967] pp. 304-306.)

"From a speech delivered in 1921."

A general statement on constitutional development.

—— Mr. Borden on national ideals and dangers. The unequal distribution of wealth is a menace to the existence of democratic institutions. (In *The Busy man's Canada*. Toronto. v. 2, no. 4 (May 1912), pp. 70-71.)

"An address delivered by the Prime Minister to the Associated Press and the American Newspaper Publishers' Association at New York."

—— The Prime Minister on national dignity. (In *The Busy man's Canada*. Toronto. v. 2, no. 5 (June 1912), p. 63.)

"Speech by Mr. Borden to the American Society of International Law at Washington."

Comments on reciprocity and the boundary line between U.S.A. and Canada.

—— Robert Laird Borden; his memoirs. Edited and with a pref. by Henry Borden. With an introd. by Arthur Meighen. Toronto, Macmillan, 1938. 2 v. (xvii, 1061 p.)

—— Robert Laird Borden; his memoirs. Edited and with a pref. by Henry Borden. Abridged ed. Edited and with an introd. by Heath Macquarrie. Toronto, McClelland and Stewart [c1969] 2 v. (Carleton library, nos. 46-47.)

Original ed.: Toronto, Macmillan, 1938.

The Borden government. Characteristics—influences—and tendencies. (In *The Canadian liberal monthly*. Ottawa. v. 1, no. 1 (Sept. 1913), pp. 5-6.)

Borden's untheatrical message. The Premier's speech at Arena Gardens, Toronto. (In *The Canadian courier*. Toronto. v. 18, no. 19 (Oct. 9, 1915), p. 5.)

Describes the presentation of a speech given by Sir Robert Borden in early October 1915.

BOWKER, KATHLEEN K.   Sir Robert Borden at leisure. Impressions of a statesman who sidesteps an interview like a "parfit gentil knight". (In *The [Canadian] courier*. Toronto, v. 20, no. 18 (Sept. 30, 1916), pp. [5]-6.)

BRIDLE, AUGUSTUS   The perfect gentleman Premier; Rt. Hon. Sir Robert Borden. (In his *The masques of Ottawa*. Toronto, 1921. pp. 27-38.)

—— Personalities and problems. [No.] 2 —Hon. John Douglas Hazen. The man at the head of the naval service in Canada. (In *The Canadian courier*. Toronto. v. 12, no. 4 (June 22, 1912), pp. 6-7.)

—— Personalities and problems. [No.] 13 —Sir Rodolphe Forget. Brilliant in finance, a leader in politics and the maker of a comprehensive practical creed. (In *The Canadian courier*. Toronto. v. 12, no. 18 (Sept. 28, 1912), pp. 6-7.)

—— Personalities and problems. No. 22 — William Findlay Maclean. Newspaper man, farmer, politician, and in some respects the most remarkable William in Canada. (In *The Canadian courier*. Toronto. v. 13, no. 11 (Feb. 15, 1913), pp. 6-7.)

—— Personalities and problems. No. 24 — Hon. Robert Rogers. The man who has no illusions and to whom a majority is a machine to control Parliament. (In *The Canadian courier*. Toronto. v. 13, no. 18 (Apr. 5, 1913), pp. [5]-6.)

—— Plain Sam Hughes, plus KCB. A more or less random misappreciation of the Minister of Militia. (In *The Canadian courier*. Toronto. v. 18, no. 14 (Sept. 4, 1915), pp. 7; 20.)

—— A remarkable ninetieth birthday. Premier of Canada, 1895-96, at the age of 73, he saw Lord Elgin burned in effigy in Belleville streets in 1837. Sir Mackenzie Bowell, no. 33, "Personalities and problems". (In *The Canadian courier*. Toronto. v. 15, no. 4 (Dec. 27, 1913), pp. [5]-6; 21-22.)

—— Sir George Foster. (In his *Sons of Canada*. Toronto, 1916. pp. 221-227.)

—— Sir Robert Borden. (In his *Sons of Canada*. Toronto, 1916. pp. 11-19.)

—— Sir Sam Hughes. (In his *Sons of Canada*. Toronto, 1916. pp. 157-166.)

BROWN, ROBERT CRAIG The political ideas of Robert Borden. (In *The Political ideas of the Prime Ministers of Canada*. Ottawa, 1969. pp. [87]-106.)

—— Sir Robert Borden, the Great War and Anglo-Canadian relations. (In Moir, J. S. (ed.) *Character and circumstance*. Toronto, 1970. pp. 201-224.)

BURRELL, MARTIN Canada in war time. By Hon. M. Burrell, MP, Minister of Agriculture. (In Canadian Club of Hamilton. Addresses. Hamilton. (1914/15), pp. 284-297.)
Address delivered May 11, 1915.

A Business man's budget. The new Minister of Finance and his first financial statement. (In *The Busy man's Canada*. Toronto. v. 2, no. 3 (Apr. 1912), pp. 69-71.)
Concerns Hon. W. T. White.

Canadian government to assume ownership of Canadian Northern. Important enunciation of new railway policy from Sir Thomas White. (In *Saturday night*. Toronto. v. 30, no. 43 (Aug. 11, 1917), p. 18.)

CARMAN, FRANCIS ASBURY Borden's parliamentary manner. Notes on the Prime Minister's tricks of speech and tactics of debate. (In *The Canadian magazine of politics, science, art and literature*. Toronto. v. 39 (1912), pp. 199-204.)

—— The Finance Minister among the prophets. A curious explanation of our adverse balance of trade. By Francis A. Carman. (In *Saturday night*. Toronto. v. 26, no. 35 (June 7, 1913), p. 6.)
Refers to Sir Thomas White.

—— The naval policy. By Francis A. Carman. (In *The University magazine*. Montreal. v. 12 (1913), pp. [568]-577.)
The naval policy of the Conservative government.

—— The right hand of the Premier. A sketch of the Honourable George Halsey Perley, Minister without Portfolio in the Borden cabinet. (In *The Canadian magazine of politics, science, art and literature*. Toronto. v. 42 (1913/14), pp. 535-538.)

CARTER, J. SMITH The "Abe" Lincoln of Canada. Andrew Broder at home and abroad. His Quebec boyhood. Interesting career as merchant, farmer, legislator and story-teller. (In *The Canadian courier*. Toronto. v. 14, no. 1 (June 7, 1913), p. 14.)

CHARLESWORTH, HECTOR WILLOUGHBY The late Sir Charles Tupper. By H. C. (In *Saturday night*. Toronto. v. 29, no. 4 (Nov. 6, 1915), p. 3.)
Written on the occasion of his death in Bexley Heath, Kent, England, October 30, 1915.

—— Sir Robert Borden. By Hector Charlesworth. (In *Saturday night*. Toronto. v. 52, no. 33 (June 19, 1937), p. 37.)
Written on the occasion of his death June 10, 1937.

CHISHOLM, H. E. M. Old shibboleths will pass away. Therefore Sir Thomas White is picked as second man up to Sir Robert Borden. (In *The Canadian courier*. Toronto. v. 20, no. 8 (July 22, 1916), p. 5.)

CLARK, HUGH With Borden in the West. Effect that the tour may have on the coming election. By Hugh Clark, MPP. (In *The Canadian courier*. Toronto. v. 10, no. 9 (July 29, 1911), pp. 6-7.)

Col. Sam, a character sketch. By W. L. M. (In *The Busy man's Canada*. Toronto. v. 2, no. 2 (Feb. 1912), pp. 55-59.)
Concerns Hon. Sam Hughes, Minister of Militia.

COOKE, BRITTON B. Major-General Sam Hughes. An informal estimate and an appreciation of the Honourable the Minister of Militia and Defence. (In *The Canadian magazine of politics, science, art and literature*. Toronto. v. 45 (1915), pp. 388-394.)

Corridor comment. [Thomas Simpson Sproule] By H. W. A. (In *The Canadian courier*. Toronto. v. 13, no. 19 (Apr. 12, 1913), p. 12.)
Named Speaker of the House of Commons during the administration of R. L. Borden.

CRAICK, WILLIAM ARNOT The Bordens of Nova Scotia. By W. A. Craick. (In *MacLean's magazine*. Toronto. v. 27, no. 1 (Nov. 1913), pp. [7]-12.)

—— The Bordens of Nova Scotia. By W. A. Craick. (In *The Busy East of Canada*. Sackville, N.B. v. 6, no. 1 (Aug. 1915), pp. [3]-8.)
Reprinted from *MacLean's magazine*, Toronto, v. 27, no. 1 (Nov. 1913), pp. [7]-12.

CUFF, ROBERT DENIS The Conservative Party machine and the election of 1911 in Ontario. By Robert Cuff. (In *Ontario history*. Toronto. v. 57, no. 3 (Sept. 1965), pp. [149]-156.)
Refers to the organization of the federal Conservative Party.

DESGAGNE, RAYMOND Orateurs saguenéens. I—L'éloquence politique. Joseph Girard, 1853-1933. (In *Saguenayensia*. Chicoutimi. v. 3, no 5 (sept./oct. 1961), pp. 104-106.)

Did the Hon. Mr. White succeed in Wall Street? The story of the getting of forty-five million dollars from shrewd United States investors. (In *The Canadian courier*. Toronto. [v. 18, no. 9] (July 31, 1915), p. 19.)
Comments on government finance policy.

DONOVAN, PETER Working for the country. Patronage and Fripp, MP. By P. O. D. (In *Saturday night*. Toronto. v. 26, no. 19 (Feb. 15, 1913), p. 6.)
Concerns Alfred Ernest Fripp.

EDMONDS, WALTER EVERARD F. W. G. Haultain, Premier of the North-West Territories. By W. Everard Edmonds. (In *Alberta historical review*. Edmonton. v. 5, no. 4 (autumn 1957), pp. 11-16.)
Includes discussion of the events surrounding the formation of the provinces of Saskatchewan and Alberta in 1905.

EDMONDS, WILLIAM LEWIS The Minister of Finance. (In *The Canadian magazine of politics, science, art and literature*. Toronto. v. 48 (1916/17), pp. 385-390.)
Concerns Sir Thomas White, Minister of Finance in the Borden government.

The First public ownership candidate. (In *The Busy man's magazine*. Toronto. v. 16, no. 2 (June 1908), pp. 124-126.)
An unsigned article dealing with Alexander Whyte Wright.

FLEMING, JAMES GRANVILLE The rise of McCurdy, MP: The causes that poured oil on the flames of a youth's ambition. (In *MacLean's magazine*. Toronto. v. 27, no. 3 (Jan. 1914), pp. [27]-30.)
Concerns Fleming Blanchard McCurdy who defeated the Hon. W. S. Fielding in the riding of Queen's-Shelburne, N.S., on September 21, 1911.

FORD, ARTHUR RUTHERFORD Honest John, MP. By Arthur R. Ford. (In *Canada monthly*. London, Ont. v. 8, no. 2 (June 1910), pp. 142-144.)
Concerns John Herron.

FOSTER, SIR GEORGE EULAS Canadian addresses. By the Hon. George E. Foster. Edited by Arnold Winterbotham. Toronto, Bell & Cockburn, 1914. xxi, 324 p.
Partial contents: Reciprocity with the United States. – The naval policy of the Borden government.

—— The naval policy of the Borden government. (In his *Canadian addresses*. Toronto, 1914. pp. [254]-324.)
"A speech delivered in the House of Commons, Ottawa, December 18, 1912."

—— Reciprocity: why the United States

wants it. By the Right Honourable George E. Foster. (In *The Canadian magazine of politics, science, art and literature*. Toronto. v. 36 (1910/11), pp. 193-195.)

—— Reciprocity with the United States. By George E. Foster. (In *The University magazine*. Montreal. v. 9 (1910), pp. [550]-562.)

—— Reciprocity with the United States. (In his *Canadian addresses*. Toronto, 1914. pp. [198]-220.)
"Written for the North American review, December, 1910."

—— Sir George Foster's appeal to industrial Canada. (In *The Busy East of Canada*. Moncton, N.B. v. 5, no. 3 (Oct. 1914), pp. 15-16.)
Extracts from an official statement issued by the Minister of Trade and Commerce.

—— "Things Canadians should not forget." By Hon. Geo. E. Foster. (In Canadian Club of Vancouver. *Addresses and proceedings*. [Vancouver] (1912/13), pp. [13]-21.)
Address delivered February 17, 1913.

GADSBY, HENRY FRANKLIN As the twig is bent. How national policies are being shaped—recruiting, munition making, etc. By H. F. Gadsby. (In *MacLean's magazine*. Toronto. v. 30, no. 5 (Mar. 1917), pp. [23]-25; 71-75.)

—— The Borden cabinet. I. The Prime Minister. By H. F. Gadsby. (In *The Canadian liberal monthly*. Ottawa. v. 1, no. 2 (Oct. 1913), p. 3.)

—— The Borden cabinet. II. The Minister of Public Works. By H. F. Gadsby. (In *The Canadian liberal monthly*. Ottawa. v. 1, no. 3 (Nov. 1913), p. 27.)
Concerns Hon. Robert Rogers.

—— The Borden cabinet. III. The Minister of Trade and Commerce. By H. F. Gadsby. (In *The Canadian liberal monthly*. Ottawa. v. 1, no. 4 (Dec. 1913), p. 39.)
Concerns Hon. George E. Foster.

—— The Borden cabinet. IV. The Minister of Finance. By H. F. Gadsby. (In *The Canadian liberal monthly*. Ottawa. v. 1, no. 5 (Jan. 1914), p. 51.)
Concerns Hon. W. T. White.

—— The Borden cabinet. V. The Postmaster-General. By H. F. Gadsby. (In *The Canadian liberal monthly*. Ottawa. v. 1, no. 6 (Feb. 1914), p. 63.)
Concerns Hon. L. P. Pelletier.

—— The Borden cabinet. VI. The Minister of Militia and Defence. By H. F. Gadsby. (In *The Canadian liberal monthly*. Ottawa. v. 1, no. 7 (Mar. 1914), p. 75.)
Concerns Col. the Hon. Sam Hughes.

—— The Borden cabinet. VII. The Minister of Agriculture. (In *The Canadian liberal monthly*. Ottawa. v. 1, no. 8 (Apr. 1914), p. 87.)
Concerns Hon. Martin Burrell.

—— The Borden cabinet. VIII. The Minister of Customs. By H. F. Gadsby. (In *The Canadian liberal monthly*. Ottawa. v. 1, no. 9 (May 1914), p. 99.)
Concerns Hon. J. D. Reid.

—— The Borden cabinet. IX. The Minister of Marine and Fisheries. By H. F. Gadsby. (In *The Canadian liberal monthly*. Ottawa. v. 1, no. 10 (June 1914), p. 111.)
Concerns Hon. J. D. Hazen.

—— The Borden cabinet. X. The government leader in the Senate. By H. F. Gadsby. (In *The Canadian liberal monthly*. Ottawa. v. 1, no. 11 (July 1914), p. 123.)
Concerns Hon. James Lougheed.

—— Brickbatting Bob. By H. F. Gadsby. (In *Saturday night*. Toronto. v. 30, no. 38 (July 7, 1917), p. 4.)
Concerns the inquiry into the activities of Robert Rogers.

—— Ghosts. By H. F. Gadsby. (In *Saturday night*. Toronto. v. 30, no. 29 (May 5, 1917), pp. 4; 11.)
Concerns Sir Thomas White's free wheat order-in-council.

—— King Log. By H. F. Gadsby. (In *Saturday night*. Toronto. v. 30, no. 31 (May 19, 1917), p. 4.)
Concerns the government's "do-nothing" policy toward the high cost of living.

—— Making tummy behave. By H. F. Gadsby. (In *Saturday night*. Toronto. v. 30, no. 40 (July 21, 1917), p. 2.)
Comments on government food policy.

—— The man at the back. By H. F. Gadsby. (In *Saturday night*. Toronto. v. 32, no. 36 (June 21, 1919), pp. 4; 11.)
Discusses the career of Sir Sam Hughes.

—— Over the Speaker's Chair. By H. F. Gadsby. (In *Saturday night*. Toronto. v. 28, no. 19 (Feb. 20, 1915), p. 4.)
Discusses the budget speech of Thomas White, Minister of Finance.

—— Over ye Speaker's chair. By H. F. Gadsby. (In *Saturday night*. Toronto. v.

29, no. 18 (Feb. 12, 1916), p. 4.)
Concerns R. B. Bennett.

—— Over ye Speaker's chair. By H. F. Gadsby. (In *Saturday night*. Toronto. v. 29, no. 29 (Apr. 29, 1916), p. 4.)
Concerns Major-General Sam Hughes.

—— Sam in exile. By H. F. Gadsby. (In *Saturday night*. Toronto. v. 30, no. 17 (Feb. 3, 1917), p. 4.)
Concerns Sir Sam Hughes.

—— That man Sam. By H. F. Gadsby. (In *Saturday night*. Toronto. v. 30, no. 7 (Nov. 25, 1916), pp. 4; 12.)
Concerns Sam Hughes, Minister of Militia.

—— Tom the Tax talker. By H. F. Gadsby. (In *Saturday night*. Toronto. v. 30, no. 8 (Dec. 2, 1916), pp. 4; 12.)
Concerns Sir William Thomas White, Finance Minister of Canada and possible leader of the government.

—— Who, how and why: a financial experiment. By H. F. Gadsby. (In *MacLean's magazine*. Toronto. v. 29, no. 1 (Nov. 1915), pp. [29]-30.)
Concerns Hon. W. T. White, Minister of Finance.

—— Who, how and why: an orator from the West. By H. F. Gadsby. (In *MacLean's magazine*. Toronto. v. 28, no. 11 [i.e. 8] (June 1915), pp. [26]-27; 79.)
Concerns Richard Bedford Bennett.

—— Who, how and why: Premier Borden has found that the end justifies the Meighens. By H. F. Gadsby. (In *MacLean's magazine*. Toronto. v. 28, no. 11 (Sept. 1915), pp. [28]-29; 84.)
Concerns Arthur Meighen.

—— Who, how and why: the Canadian Abe Lincoln. By H. F. Gadsby. (In *MacLean's magazine*. Toronto. v. 28, no. 10 [i.e. 7] (May 1915), pp. [28]-29; 84.)
Concerns Andrew Broder, MP for Dundas, Ont., in the Canadian House of Commons.

—— Who, how and why: the Little Brother of the Mace. By H. F. Gadsby. (In *MacLean's magazine*. Toronto. v. 29, no. 5 (Mar. 1916), pp. [27]-28; 88.)
Concerns Albert Sévigny, Speaker of the House of Commons.

—— Who, how and why: [the new Deputy Speaker, Edgar N. Rhodes]. By H. F. Gadsby. (In *MacLean's magazine*. Toronto. v. 29, no. 6 (Apr. 1916), pp. [19]-20.)

—— Who, how and why: the raconteur of the Commons. By H. F. Gadsby. (In *MacLean's magazine*. Toronto. v. 29, no. 4 (Feb. 1916), pp. [37]-38; 84.)
Concerns Colonel Hugh Clarke, MP for Centre Bruce, Ont.

—— Who, how and why: the Wicked Partner. By H. F. Gadsby. (In *MacLean's magazine*. Toronto. v. 28, no. 12 (Oct. 1915), pp. [23]-24.)
Concerns Hon. Robert Rogers.

GIBSON, JAMES A. Sir Robert Borden. (In McDougall, R. L. (ed.) *Our living tradition*. Second and third series. [Toronto, c1959] pp. 95-122.)

Government to keep down food prices. Canada has ample supply of fuel and food-stuffs. Ottawa may impose war tax to meet decreased income. (In *Saturday night*. Toronto. v. 27, no. 45 (Aug. 22, 1914), p. 7.)

GRANT, JAMES The history of the Forgets. (In *MacLean's magazine*. Toronto. v. 22, no. 6 (Oct. 1911), pp. 243-248.)
Concerns Senator L. J. Forget and Lieut.-Col. the Hon. Rodolphe Forget, MP (i.e. Sir Joseph David Rodolphe Forget).

GREYSON, FREDERICK Menace of honesty at Ottawa. (In *MacLean's magazine*. Toronto. v. 23, no. 2 (Dec. 1911), pp. [109]-118.)
Discusses the personnel in the cabinet of R. L. Borden.

HAIG, KENNETHE MACMAHON Called to the capital. By Kennethe M. Haig. (In *The Canadian courier*. Toronto. v. 11, no. 8 (Jan. 20, 1912), p. 13.)
A character sketch of the wife of Robert Rogers, Minister of the Interior (née Aurelia Regina Widmeyer).

HAMILTON, WILLIAM BAILLIE Sir Robert Borden and the development of Canadian autonomy. [Wolfville, N.S., 1953] 1 v.
Thesis (MA) – Acadia University.

HAWKES, ARTHUR Immigration: an economic factor in Canadian progress. (In *The Busy man's Canada*. Toronto. v. 2, no. 5 (June 1912), pp. 37-40.)
Presents extracts from "the report on immigration by Mr. Arthur Hawkes, who was appointed a Special Commissioner by the Hon. Robt. Rogers, Minister of the Interior". The Report attempts to formulate a working immigration policy between the provinces and the Dominion.

HAZEN, SIR JOHN DOUGLAS Our Canadian fisheries. By Hon. J. D. Hazen, Minister of Marine and Fisheries. (In Canadian Club of Vancouver. *Addresses and proceedings.* [Vancouver] (1912/13), pp. [79]-88.)
Address delivered August 19, 1913.

HEBERT, CASIMIR L'Honorable P. E. Blondin; sénateur, ancien ministre et commandeur de la Légion d'Honneur. [n.p., 1943?] 35 p. (Essai biographique.)
Concerns Pierre Edouard Blondin.
Written on the occasion of his death October 29, 1943. Career extended from 1908 to 1935. Served in the administrations of R. L. Borden and A. Meighen and was Speaker of the Senate from 1930 to 1935.

HELLENCOURT, HENRI D' Le scandale Forget. Articles publiés dans "Le Soleil" depuis le 30 octobre 1912. Par H. d'Hellencourt. [Québec, Le Soleil, 1912?] 136 p.
Concerns Sir Joseph David Rodolphe Forget.

Hon. Frank Cochrane—a character sketch. (In *The Busy man's Canada.* Toronto. v. 3, no. 4 (Dec. 1912), pp. 62-63.)
Concerns the Minister of Railways in the Conservative government.

Hon. George Barnard Baker, KC, Senator. (In Missisquoi County Historical Society. *Report.* St. Johns, Que. 4th (1908/09), pp. 41-42. port.)
First elected to the House of Commons in 1870; called to the Senate in 1896.
Written on the occasion of his death February 9, 1910.

The Hon. W. T. White; a character sketch of the Canadian Minister of Finance. By an Old Associate. (In *MacLean's magazine.* Toronto. v. 23, no. 5 (Mar. 1912), pp. 522-531.)
William Thomas White, Minister of Finance in the cabinet of R. L. Borden. A Liberal who broke with his party and worked for the defeat of the Laurier government.

HUGHES, SIR SAMUEL The Canadian contingent and the War. By Major-General the Hon. Sam Hughes. (In Canadian Club of Montreal. *Addresses.* [Montreal] (1914/15), pp. 63-69.)
Address delivered November 23, 1914.

—— The Canadian contingent. By Major-General the Hon. Sir Sam Hughes, Minister of Militia. (In Canadian Club of Winnipeg. *Annual report.* [Winnipeg] (1914/15), pp. 39-42.)

Address delivered January 18, 1915.

LAMARCHE, PAUL EMILE Le canal de la Baie Georgienne. (In his *Oeuvres-hommages.* [Montréal, 1919] pp. [65]-100.)
This issue was debated in the House of Commons in February 1914.

—— Lamarche et la question bilingue. (In his *Oeuvres-hommages.* [Montréal, 1919] pp. [126]-157.)
The Ontario school question was an issue debated in the House of Commons on May 10, 1916.

—— Lamarche et les droits scolaires d'une minorité. (In his *Oeuvres-hommages.* [Montréal, 1919] pp. [50]-64.)
Concerns the issue of Keewatin in 1912.

—— Oeuvres-hommages. [Montréal] Bibliothèque de l'Action française. [1919] 300 p.
At head of title: In memoriam.
Lamarche was a *nationaliste* registered as a Conservative.
Elected to the House of Commons in 1911, resigned in 1916. Cf. *Canadian directory of parliament, 1867-1967.* Ottawa, 1968.

LAURISTON, VICTOR Kent's political epic. (In *Saturday night.* Toronto. v. 44, no. 20 (Mar. 20, 1929), p. 3.)
Concerns Herbert Sylvester Clements, MP for West Kent.

LINDSAY, ALEXANDER MOLLISON The effect of public opinion on the Borden administration during World War I, 1914-1918. [Wolfville, N.S., 1953] 256 leaves.
Thesis (MA) – Acadia University.

Lord Strathcona, a business statesman. By M. A. P. (In *The Busy man's magazine.* Toronto. v. 13, no. 2 (Dec. 1906), pp. [5]-7.)

LOWER, ARTHUR REGINALD MARSDEN Robert Laird Borden—his memoirs. By A. R. M. Lower. (In *Public affairs.* Halifax. v. 2 (1938), pp. 180-183.)
A review article of *Robert Laird Borden, his memoirs,* edited by H. Borden. Toronto, Macmillan, 1938, 2 v.

MACBETH, MADGE HAMILTON (LYONS) The Hon. Bob Rogers. Who has won a big name, a fair wife and a place in the cabinet. By Madge Macbeth. (In *Canada monthly.* London, Ont. v. 17, no. 5 (Mar. 1915), pp. 304-305; 327.)

—— The women in the case. By Madge Macbeth. (In *The Canadian courier.* Toronto. v. 11, no. 8 (Jan. 20, 1912), p. 12.)

Brief sketches of Mrs. M. Burrell, Mrs. T. W. Crothers, Mrs. G. E. Foster, and Mrs. S. Hughes.

MAC CORMAC, JOHN National affairs: three years of Conservative government. (In *Maclean's magazine*. Toronto. v. 27, no. 11 (Sept. 1914), pp. [5]-7; 137-138.)

THE MACE Nickle of Kingston. By the Mace. (In *Saturday night*. Toronto. v. 38, no. 40 (Aug. 18, 1923), p. 4.)
Concerns William Folger Nickle.

MACLEAN, JOHN BAYNE A gentleman! [By the Editor.] (In *Maclean's magazine*. Toronto. v. 21, no. 7 (May 1911), pp. [44]-46.)
Concerns R. L. Borden.

MAC MECHAM, ARCHIBALD MC KELLAR Justice to Premier Borden. By A. Mac-Mecham. (In *Canadian courier*. Toronto. v. 22, no. 17 [i.e. 18] (Sept. 29, 1917), pp. 6; 25.)

MACPHAIL, SIR ANDREW The conservative. (In *The University magazine*. Montreal. v. 18 (1919), pp. [419]-444.)
Advises a coalition between Sir Robert Borden and Sir Lomer Gouin.

—— Why the Conservatives failed. (In *The University magazine*. Montreal. v. 7 (1908), pp. [529]-545.)
Comments on the aftermath of the general elections held October 26, 1908.

MACQUARRIE, HEATH NELSON The formation of Borden's first cabinet. By Heath N. Macquarrie. (In *The Canadian journal of economics and political science*. Toronto. v. 23 (1957), pp. 90-104.)
"This paper was presented at the annual meeting of the Canadian Political Science Association in Montreal, June 7, 1956."
Discusses the personnel of the cabinet formed by R. L. Borden upon his assuming office in 1911.

—— Robert Borden and the election of 1911. By Heath Macquarrie. (In *The Canadian journal of economics and political science*. [Toronto] v. 25 (1959), pp. 271-286.)

—— Robert Borden — party leader. By Heath N. Macquarrie. (In *The Canadian forum*. Toronto. v. 37, no. 435 (Apr. 1957), pp. 14-17.)

MEIGHEN, ARTHUR The Borden naval policy. (In Canadian Club of Toronto. *Addresses*. Toronto. (1912/13), pp. 234-241.)

Address delivered March 22, 1913.
"Mr. Arthur Meighen represents Portage la Prairie in the House of Commons in the Conservative interest."

—— Canada's responsibility in the present crisis. By Hon. Arthur Meighen, Solicitor-General for Canada. (In Canadian Club of Winnipeg. *Annual report*. [Winnipeg] (1914/15), pp. 23-27.)
Address delivered December 5, 1914.
Concerns the Canadian position in World War I.

—— The war. An address by Hon. Arthur Meighen . . . Solicitor-General of Canada. (In Empire Club of Canada. *Addresses*. Toronto. (1914/15), pp. 15-25.)
Address delivered December 17, 1914.

—— Mr. Borden makes a tour in Ontario. (In *The Canadian courier*. Toronto. v. 8, no. 4 (June 25, 1910), p. 11.)

The New Minister of Finance. By D. B. S. (In *The Canadian courier*. Toronto. v. 10, no. 20 (Oct. 14, 1911), pp. 7; 22.)
Concerns William Thomas White.

NIAS, ANNE E. Interviews with politicians. (In *Saturday night*. Toronto. v. 25, no. 7 (Nov. 25, 1911), p. 9.)
Interviews Hon. W. T. White, Minister of Finance.

—— Interviews with politicians. (In *Saturday night*. Toronto. v. 25, no. 8 (Dec. 2, 1911), p. 9.)
Interviews Sir Samuel Hughes, Minister of Militia.

—— Interviews with politicians. (In *Saturday night*. Toronto. v. 25, no. 10 (Dec. 16, 1911), p. 9.)
Interviews Sir George Eulas Foster, Minister of Trade and Commerce.

—— Interviews with politicians. (In *Saturday night*. Toronto. v. 25, no. 12 (Dec. 30, 1911), p. 5.)
Interviews Robert Laird Borden.

NORTHRUP, MINNIE Borden's Western tour, a personal glimpse. (In *Alberta historical review*. Calgary. v. 14, no. 2 (spring 1966), pp. 22-26.)
Extracts from the diary of the wife of Will Northrup, MP for Belleville, Ont., who was a member of the party accompanying Robert Borden on his tour in 1902.

O'LEARY, MICHAEL GRATTAN Arthur Meighen; the new hope. By M. Grattan O'Leary. (In *The Canadian magazine of politics, science, art and literature*. Toronto. v. 42 (1913/14), pp. 408-410.)

—— Robert Borden; Canadian. By M. Grattan O'Leary. (In *Maclean's*. Toronto. v. 51, no. 24 (Dec. 15, 1938), pp. 12-13; 41-42; 47.)

Subtitle: Highlights from the "Memoirs" of the man of whom Smuts said: "You and I have transformed the structure of the British Empire".

Includes excerpts from *Robert Laird Borden; his memoirs*. Edited by H. Borden. Toronto, Macmillan, 1938. 2 v.

—— The wizard of Dominion politics. A sketch of the Honourable Robert Rogers, Minister of Public Works for Canada. By Grattan O'Leary. (In *The Canadian magazine of politics, science, art and literature*. Toronto. v. 42 (1913/14), pp. 316-318.)

OXLEY, JAMES MACDONALD   Lord Strathcona. By J. Macdonald Oxley. (In *The National monthly of Canada*. Toronto. v. 2, no. 6 (June 1903), pp. [321]-326.)

PATTERSON, NORMAN   Is the cement industry in danger? (In *The Canadian courier*. Toronto. v. 12, no. 4 (June 22, 1912), p. 14.)

Criticizes the cement duty policy announced by W. T. White.

—— The man who is in earnest. A character sketch of Robert Laird Borden. (In *The Canadian courier*. Toronto. v. 10, no. 14 (Sept. 2, 1911), p. 11.)

PETERSON, SIR WILLIAM   Mr. Borden's naval policy. (In his *Canadian essays and addresses*. London, 1915. pp. 149-154.)

Summary of an address delivered before the British Public Schools and Universities Club, New York, 24 May, 1913.

PROGRESSIVE CONSERVATIVE PARTY (CANADA)   The Liberal-Conservative handbook, 1911. A consideration of reciprocity and an exposition of the policy of the Liberal-Conservative Party . . . [n.p., 1911] 209 p.

Cover title.

The Railway question. Government ownership and operation. Mr. Borden's policy considered. [n.p., 1905?] 56 p.

Le Record du gouvernement Borden, 1911-1917. Montréal, 1917. 138 p.

Contents: La conscription. – La vie chère et les gros intérêts. – L'achat du Canadian Northern. – La nouvelle loi électorale. – Le gouvernement Borden avant la guerre. – Scandales administratifs. – Le gouvernement Borden pendant la guerre. – La correspond-ance Hughes-Borden. – Le gouvt. Borden et l'influence can.-française. – Le parti Conservateur dans les provinces. – La campagne de 1911.

ROGERS, ROBERT   Canada's problems during and after the war. By the Hon. Robert Rogers. (In *Canadian Club of Montreal. Addresses*. [Montreal] (1916/17), pp. [79]-86.)

Address delivered November 20, 1916.

SANDWELL, BERNARD KEBLE   From week to week. Man who didn't want power. By B. K. Sandwell. (In *Saturday night*. Toronto. v. 54, no. 1 (Nov. 5, 1938), p. 3.)

Concerns Robert Laird Borden.

—— From week to week. Weary political titan. By B. K. Sandwell. (In *Saturday night*. Toronto. v. 54, no. 2 (Nov. 12, 1938), p. 3.)

Concerns Robert Laird Borden.

SETTLEMIER, CHARLES REED   Dr. Alfred Thompson, MP. (In *The Canadian magazine of politics, science, art and literature*. Toronto. v. 25 (1905), pp. 328-329.)

Canadian celebrities; no. 63.

Dr. Thompson represented the Independent Yukon Party as a Conservative member of Parliament.

SMITH, R. GOLDWIN   Save for export. An interview with Food Controller Hon. W. J. Hanna. (In *Canada monthly*. London, Ont. v. 22, no. 4 (Aug. 1917), pp. 188-190.)

SWANSON, WILLIAM WALKER   The people and the Bank Act. By W. W. Swanson. (In *The Canadian courier*. Toronto. v. 13, no. 10 (Feb. 8, 1913), pp. 12-13; 24.)

Discusses the legislation to revise the Bank Act introduced by Thomas White, Minister of Finance.

THOMSON, EDWARD WILLIAM   The national political situation. [With comments on the outstanding issues which will confront the Borden government on the assembling of Parliament in November.] (In *MacLean's magazine*. Toronto. v. 25, no. 1 (Nov. 1912), pp. 27-32.)

Article no. 3 of a series entitled: The National political situation.

—— The national political situation. [A review of the naval policy of the Borden government as recently submitted to Parliament by Rt. Hon. R. L. Borden.] (In *MacLean's magazine*. Toronto. v. 25, no. 3 (Jan. 1913), pp. 27-32.)

Article no. 5 of a series entitled: The National political situation.

Toronto financial. Another newspaper man as Minister of Finance. By N. H. (In *Saturday night*. Toronto. v. 25, no. 1 (Oct. 14, 1911), p. 20.)
Biographical sketch of W. T. White.

TROTTER, REGINALD GEORGE   Sir Robert Borden. By Reginald G. Trotter. (In *Queen's quarterly*. Kingston. v. 46 (1939), pp. [334]-340.)
A review article of *Robert Laird Borden; his memoirs*, edited by H. Borden. Toronto, Macmillan, 1938. 2 v.

TUCKER, GILBERT NORMAN   The naval policy of Sir Robert Borden, 1912-14. (In *The Canadian historical review*. Toronto. v. 28 (1947), pp. 1-30.)

UNDERHAY, F. C.   Sir Robert Borden and imperial relations. (In *The Dalhousie review*. Halifax. v. 10 (1930/31), pp. [503]-517.)
Concerns the security of Dominion autonomy.

VINCE, DONALD M. A. R.   The acting overseas sub-militia council and the resignation of Sir Sam Hughes. (In *The Canadian historical review*. Toronto. v. 31 (1950), pp. 1-24.)

VINING, CHARLES ARTHUR MC LAREN   Sir Robert. By R. T. L. (In *Maclean's*. Toronto. v. 47, no. 8 (Apr. 15, 1934), p. 12.)
Concerns Sir Robert Borden.

WALSH, JOSEPH CHARLES   Mr. Borden and the navy. By J. C. Walsh. (In *The Canadian courier*. Toronto. v. 13, no. 2 (Dec. 14, 1912), p. 20.)

WARNER, CATHERINE LIDMILLA   Sir James P. Whitney and Sir Robert L. Borden: relations between a Conservative provincial premier and his federal party leader, 1905-1914. Toronto, 1967. 139 leaves.
Thesis (PHIL M) – University of Toronto.

WHITE, SIR WILLIAM THOMAS   Canada will do her share. (In *The Busy man's Canada*. Toronto. v. 2, no. 5 (June 1912), pp. 44-46.)
From an address delivered at the National Club, Toronto, May 17, 1912. Reply to a statement made on May 15, 1912, by Winston Churchill calling for naval contributions to an Imperial defence fleet.

—— Canadian citizenship. By Hon. W. T. White, Minister of Finance. (In Canadian Club of Montreal. *Addresses*. [Montreal] (1913/14), pp. 105-111.)
Address delivered December 22, 1913.

—— Canadian trade and finance during the war. By the Hon. Sir W. T. White. (In Canadian Club of Montreal. *Addresses*. [Montreal] (1915/16), pp. 11-23.)
Address delivered November 2, 1915.

—— The effect of the war upon Canadian finance and trade. By the Hon. W. T. White, Minister of Finance. (In Canadian Club of Montreal. *Addresses*. [Montreal] (1914/15), pp. 99-106.)
Address delivered December 14, 1914.

WINTER, CHARLES FRANCIS   Lieutenant-General, the Hon. Sir Sam Hughes, KCB, MP; Canada's war minister, 1911-1916. Recollections of service as Military Secretary at Headquarters, Canadian militia, prior to and during the early stages of the Great War. Toronto, Macmillan, 1931, xvii, 182 p.

The Woes of a Tory MP. By a Tory MP. (In *The Canadian courier*. Toronto. v. 11, no. 7 (Jan. 13, 1912), pp. 10-11.)
Discusses the practice of patronage.

WOODWARD, J. S.   He put the "go" in government. From cakeshop to cabinet, via the Grain Growers' Association and the Saskatchewan ballot box, George Langley, the farmers' friend, has made good. (In *Canada monthly*. London, Ont. v. 18, no. 2 (June 1915), pp. 100-101; 111.)
George Langley, a Liberal who served as Minister of Municipalities in the government of Robert Borden.

Union Government
1917–1920

The Anti-democratic way. (In *The Statesman*. Toronto. v. 1, no. 10 (Sept. 28, 1918), pp. 3-4.)
Compares the war cabinet of Lloyd George and the "coalition" cabinet of Sir Robert Borden.

BENBOW   "Gentlemen, we have with us tonight." Toastmaster, "Benbow". (In *Saturday night*. Toronto. v. 32, no. 27 (Apr. 19, 1919), p. 2.)
A short biographical sketch of Sir Robert Laird Borden. Presented in the form of an introductory speech.

BENNETT, RICHARD BEDFORD   R. B. Bennett and Sir Robert Borden. (In *The Canadian historical review*. Toronto. v. 45 (1964), pp. 116-124.)

Introduction by Wilfred I. Smith.

Presentation of ". . . a letter which Bennet wrote to Borden in 1918 in response to an offer to include him in a list of appointments to the Order of the British Empire". – p. 117.

BORDEN, SIR ROBERT LAIRD Canada at war. Speeches delivered by Rt. Hon. Sir Robert Laird Borden in Canada and the United Kingdom. With Robert Borden's compliments. [n.p., n.d.] 31 p.

Speeches delivered June-September 1918.

—— Borden, a modern Sisyphus. (In *The Canadian nation*. Ottawa. v. 1, no. 15 (Dec. 13, 1919), pp. 15-18.)

BRIDLE, AUGUSTUS The masques of Ottawa. By "Domino". Toronto, Macmillan, 1921. 283 p.

Impressions of leading figures in Ottawa during the period of Union Government.

—— Ottawa's lubricating oil-can. (In *Canadian courier*. Toronto. v. 24, no. 9 (Feb. 1, 1919), pp. 8-9.)

Concerns H. J. Daly, Director of Repatriation.

BRIERLEY, JAMES SAMUEL The Union government's opportunities. By James S. Brierley. (In *The University magazine*. Montreal. v. 17 (1918), pp. [14]-27.)

BROWNING, JOHN "Gentlemen, we have with us to-night." Toastmaster, John Browning. (In *Saturday night*. Toronto. v. 33, no. 16 (Jan. 31, 1920), p. 2.)

Concerns Rt. Hon. Arthur Meighen, Minister of the Interior. Adopts the form of an introductory speech.

—— "Gentlemen, we have with us to-night." Toastmaster, John Browning. (In *Saturday night*. Toronto. v. 34, no. 28 (Apr. 24, 1920), p. 2.)

Concerns Hon. James Alexander Colder. Adopts the form of an introductory speech.

CALCHAS The Government and the leading figures. I—Taking a look around. By C. A. (In *The Statesman*. Toronto. v. 1, no. 18 (Nov. 23, 1918), p. 5.)

Considers the implications of the possible retirement of Sir Robert Borden and the succession of Sir Thomas White to the leadership.

—— The government and its leading figures. II—The Prime Minister. By Calchas. (In *The Statesman*. Toronto. v. 1, no. 19 (Nov. 30, 1918), pp. 5-6.)

Concerns Sir Robert Borden.

—— The government and its leading figures. III—Sir Thomas White, KCMG. By Calchas. (In *The Statesman*. Toronto. v. 1, no. 20 (Dec. 7, 1918), p. 5.)

—— The government and its leading figures. IV—The President of the Council. By Calchas. (In *The Statesman*. Toronto. v. 1, no. 21 (Dec. 14, 1918), p. 5.)

Refers to N. W. Rowell.

CALDER, JAMES ALEXANDER There has been a radical change in Canadian immigration. By Hon. J. A. Calder, Minister of Immigration and Colonization. (In *Canadian courier*. Toronto. v. 25, no. 12 (Mar. 13, 1920), p. [14].)

Can Rowell come back? (In *The Statesman*. Toronto. v. 1, no. 1 (July 27, 1918), pp. [6]-7.)

Examines the reasons for the decline of public support for N. W. Rowell. Refers to charges made against Rowell by Hon. Charles Murphy in a House of Commons speech delivered March 19, 1918.

Canada adopts "Blue sky" measure. Ottawa. shuts down on new issues of bonds and debentures, to conserve public funds, Minister of Finance must issue permit for any new financing. (In *Saturday night*. Toronto. v. 31, no. 12 (Jan. 5, 1918), p. 14.)

Canada's next premier? (In *The Canadian nation*. Calgary. v. 1, no. 1 (Mar. 15, 1919), pp. 13-15.)

Considers Arthur L. Sifton as a candidate for the position of Prime Minister.

The Canadian press subsidy. (In *The Statesman*. Toronto. v. 1, no. 52 (July 19, 1919), pp. 5-6.)

Comments on the grant of $50,000 given to the Canadian Press Limited. Criticizes the creation of a Unionist Press.

Canadian women in the public eye. Mrs. Arthur Meighen. (In *Saturday night*. Toronto. v. 33, no. 20 (Feb. 28, 1920), p. 22.)

Canadians worth knowing: T. A. Crerar, MP. (In *The Canadian nation*. Ottawa. v. 1, no. 12 (Nov. 1, 1919), p. 10.)

Crerar resigned from the cabinet of the Unionist Government June 6, 1919.

CARVELL, FRANK BROADSTREET Financial problems of Canada. By the Hon. Frank B. Carvell, Minister of Public Works. (In Canadian Club of Montreal. *Addresses*. [Montreal] (1917/18), pp. [217]-225.)

Address delivered February 18, 1918.

The Case against the government press. (In *The Statesman*. Toronto. v. 1, no. 49 (June 28, 1919), pp. 8-10.)
Refers to the newspapers "subsidized" by the Union Government.

CHISHOLM, ARTHUR MURRAY What the country expects. What Canada will insist on is business—like action and teamwork rather than grand-stand play. The new government was elected for the specific purpose of handling affairs properly in war-time, and it must make good or make room. By A. M. Chisholm. (In *Canadian courier*. Toronto. v. 23, no. 9 (Feb. 2, 1918), pp. [5]-7.)
Presents a Western viewpoint.

CONNER, JAMES MC ARTHUR What is the cause of industrial unrest? (In *The Statesman*. Toronto. v. 1, no. 26 (Jan. 18, 1919), p. 11.)
Criticizes the orders-in-council, concerning censorship, sedition and criticism of the war effort, passed by the Union Government during 1918.

COOK, GEORGE RAMSAY Dafoe, Laurier and the formation of Union Government. (In *The Canadian historical review*. Toronto. v. 42 (1961), pp. 185-208.)

—— Dafoe, Laurier and the formation of Union Government. (In *Conscription 1917*. [Toronto, c1969] pp. [15]-38.)
"Reprinted from Canadian historical review, XLII (3), September, 1961."

COOPER, JOHN ALEXANDER Once a Liberal. By the Editor. (In *Canadian courier*. Toronto. v. 22, no. 21 (Oct. 20, 1917), p. [5].)
Concerns C. C. Ballantyne and Hugh Guthrie.

—— A retrospective estimate of Premier Borden. By the Editor. (In *Canadian courier*. Toronto. v. 25, no. 20 (July 1, 1920), pp. [5]-6.)

COSTAIN, THOMAS BERTRAM Using the whip-hand. By T. B. Costain. (In *MacLean's magazine*. Toronto. v. 31, no. 6 (Apr. 1918), pp. [21]-23; 104-105.)
Concerns Union Government, 1917.

CROWLEY, JAMES A. Borden, conscription and Union government. Ottawa, 1958. viii, 401 leaves.
Thesis (PH D) – University of Ottawa.

The Democratic way. (In *The Statesman*. Toronto. v. 1, no. 52 (July 19, 1919), p. 3.)
Critical remarks on Union Government.

EWART, JOHN SKIRVING Borden on Canadian nationhood. By John S. Ewart. (In *The Canadian nation*. Ottawa. v. 1, no. 11 (Oct. 18, 1919), pp. 10-11.)
Comments on the imperial policy of Sir Robert Borden.

Four-thousand-dollar-patriots. (In *The Canadian nation*. Ottawa. v. 1, no. 26 (May 15, 1920), pp. 21-23.)
Concerns the position of the Union Government.

GADSBY, HENRY FRANKLIN The bee and the ants. By H. F. Gadsby. (In *Saturday night*. Toronto. v. 34, no. 25 (Apr. 3, 1920), p. 4.)
Humorous commentary on Newton Wesley Rowell, and the various issues he has upheld.

—— Between the lines in two spasms. Spasm one—the Caucus. By H. F. Gadsby. (In *Saturday night*. Toronto. [v. 34, no. 40] (July 17, 1920), p. 3.)
Humorous commentary on the resignation of Sir Robert Borden.

—— Between the lines in two spasms. Spasm two—the choice. By H. F. Gadsby. (In *Saturday night*. Toronto. [v. 34, no. 41] (July 24, 1920), p. 3.)
A humorous commentary on Sir Robert Borden's choice for new Premier.

—— But why the disguise? By H. F. Gadsby. (In *Saturday night*. Toronto. v. 32, no. 41 (July 26, 1919), p. 4.)
A hypothetical dialogue between R. L. Borden and his conscience.

—— Coming home to roost. By H. F. Gadsby. (In *Saturday night*. Toronto. v. 32, no. 23 (Mar. 22, 1919), p. 4.)
Concerns government financing of the Grand Trunk Pacific.

—— Cross-indexing Tommy? By H. F. Gadsby. (In *Saturday night*. Toronto. [v. 32, no. 13] (Jan. 11, 1919), p. 3.)
Concerns the Repatriation and Employment Committee.

—— An essay in miracles. By H. F. Gadsby. (In *Saturday night*. Toronto. v. 31, no. 5 (Nov. 17, 1917), p. 4.)
Discusses Union Government.

—— Excursion and alarums. By H. F. Gadsby. (In *Saturday night*. Toronto. v. 32. no. 48 (Sept. 13, 1919), p. 4.)
Concerns Premier Borden and difficulties relating to Union Government.

—— Figuring it out. Part three. By H. F.

Gadsby. (In *Saturday night*. Toronto. v. 33, no. 20 (Feb. 28, 1920), pp. 4; 11.)
Concerns the Conservative Party and the tariff.

—— A hair cut for demos. By H. F. Gadsby. (In *Saturday night*. Toronto. v. 30, no. 51 (Oct. 6, 1917), p. 4.)
Concerns Robert Borden and the War Time Elections Act and Military Voters' Act.

—— The hangers on. By H. F. Gadsby. (In *Saturday night*. Toronto. v. 33, no. 17 (Feb. 7, 1920), p. 4.)
Humorous commentary on "the Union Government Cabinet . . .".

—— The home coming. By H. F. Gadsby. (In *Saturday night*. Toronto. v. 34, no. 32 (May 22, 1920), pp. 4; 11.)
A humorous commentary on Premier Robert Borden.

—— The inside story of the Union. The why and how of the new government. By H. F. Gadsby. (In *MacLean's magazine*. Toronto. v. 31, no. 2 (Dec. 1917), pp. [41]-43; 80-83.)

—— The lion and the lamb. By H. F. Gadsby. (In *Saturday night*. Toronto. v. 31, no. 3 (Nov. 3, 1917), p. 4.)
Concerns Union Government.

—— The little bird whispers. By H. F. Gadsby. (In *Saturday night*. Toronto. [v. 34, no. 38] (July 3, 1920), p. 3.)
". . . whispers that there will be Cabinet reorganization within two months and an election within eight."

—— Looking things over. By H. F. Gadsby. (In *Saturday night*. Toronto. v. 31, no. 20 (Mar. 2, 1918), p. 4.)
Comments on the war policy of the Union Government.

—— Love one another. By H. F. Gadsby. (In *Saturday night*. Toronto. v. 32, no. 19 (Feb. 22, 1919), p. 4.)
Humorous comment on Union Government and secrecy.

—— Making a good end. By H. F. Gadsby. (In *Saturday night*. Toronto. v. 34, no. 26 (Apr. 10, 1920), p. 4.)
Estimates the achievement of Union Government.

—— Making 'em be good. By H. F. Gadsby. (In *Saturday night*. Toronto. v. 31, no. 29 (May 4, 1918), p. 4.)
Concerns "the Orders-in-Council, the food regulations and the fuel restrictions".

—— The man behind. By H. F. Gadsby. (In *Saturday night*. Toronto. v. 31, no. 12 (Jan. 5, 1918), p. 4.)
Concerns Sir Clifffford Sifton and Union Government.

—— The mellowing years. By H. F. Gadsby. (In *Saturday night*. Toronto. v. 34, no. 27 (Apr. 17, 1920), p. 4.)
Concerns Sir George Eulas Foster.

—— The new deck. By H. F. Gadsby. (In *Saturday night*. Toronto. v. 31, no. 4 (Nov. 10, 1917), p. 4.)
Concerns Union Government and the cabinet formed October 12, 1917.

—— Not yet but soon. By H. F. Gadsby. (In *Saturday night*. Toronto. v. 33, no. 12 (Jan. 3, 1920), pp. 4; 8.)
Humorous commentary on the impending resignation of Robert Borden as Premier.

—— The propaganders. By H. F. Gadsby. (In *Saturday night*. Toronto. v. 32, no. 18 (Feb. 15, 1919), p. 4.)
Refers to propaganda and the Union Government.

—— Sweet dreams. By H. F. Gadsby. (In *Saturday night*. Toronto. v. 32, no. 49 (Sept. 20, 1919), p. 4.)
Concerns the fiscal policy and problems of R. L. Borden, presented in the form of conversation.

—— Summing it up. By H. F. Gadsby. (In *Saturday night*. Toronto. v. 31, no. 9 (Dec. 15, 1917), p. 4.)
Lists and discusses the reasons why voters might elect a Union Government, with reference to the federal election held December 17, 1917.

—— Tacks in the tariff. By H. F. Gadsby. (In *Saturday night*. Toronto. v. 32, no. 22 (Mar. 15, 1919), pp. 4; 7.)

—— Through the fire. By H. F. Gadsby. (In *Saturday night*. Toronto. v. 31, no. 16 (Feb. 2, 1918), p. 4.)
Concerns Union Government and party spirit.

—— Through the keyhole. By H. F. Gadsby. (In *Saturday night*. Toronto. v. 33, no. 14 (Jan. 17, 1920), p. 4; v. 33, no. 15 (Jan. 24, 1920), p. 4.)
In two parts.
The Author presents a hypothetical setting: Mr. Rowell and other cabinet ministers talking about what new positions they should assume to save themselves and Union Government.

—— United we stand. By H. F. Gadsby. (In *Saturday night*. Toronto. v. 31, no. 6 (Nov. 24, 1917), p. 4.)
Concerns Union Government.

—— What might be. By H. F. Gadsby. (In *Saturday night*. Toronto. v. 31, no. 14 (Jan. 19, 1918), p. 4.)
Concerns Union Government and its effect on the House of Commons.

—— What next? By H. F. Gadsby. (In *Saturday night*. Toronto. v. 31, no. 32 (May 25, 1918), p. 4.)
Comments on the function of Union Government.

—— When the dust settles. By H. F. Gadsby. (In *Saturday night*. Toronto. v. 31, no. 11 (Dec. 29, 1917), p. 4.)
Concerns Union Government and the overseas vote.

—— When the hen is on. By H. F. Gadsby. (In *Saturday night*. Toronto. v. 30, no. 46 (Sept. 1, 1917), p. 4.)
Concerns Union Government.

—— Whither do we wander? By H. F. Gadsby. (In *Saturday night*. Toronto. v. 31, no. 35 (June 15, 1918), p. 4.)
Considers post-Union Government.

—— Who spilt the beans? By H. F. Gadsby. (In *Saturday night*. Toronto. [v. 30, no. 50] (Sept. 29, 1917), p. 4.)
Concerns Sir Clifford Sifton's dealings with Robert Borden over the formation of a Union Government.

The Globe's attack on Union government. (In *The Onlooker*. Toronto. v. 1, no. 2 (June 1920), pp. 28-32.)

GREENWOOD, WILLIAM HAMAR Canada's Food Controller; a character sketch. (In *Saturday night*. Toronto. v. 31, no. 33 (June 1, 1918), p. 3.)
Concerns Henry Broughton Thomson.

HALL, A. RIVES M.S.A. a costly failure. (In *The Statesman*. Toronto. v. 1, no. 19 (Nov. 30, 1918), p. 12.)
Refers to the Military Service Act.

HODGINS, JAMES C. The Union government—an honorable truce. (In *Saturday night*. Toronto. v. 33, no. 17 (Feb. 7, 1920), p. 3.)
Analyses the contemporary political situation.

HOPKINS, JOHN CASTELL The book of the Union government; a record and souvenir of 1917. Toronto, Canadian Annual Review, 1918. 116 p.

HUTCHISON, BRUCE The Western farmer horns in. By W. Bruce Hutchison. (In *Canadian courier*. Toronto. v. 24, no. 26 (Sept. 27, 1919), pp. 9; 24-25.)
Concerns S. F. Tolmie, Minister of Agriculture.

JACKMAN, WILLIAM T. The government and the Canadian Northern Railway. By W.T. Jackman. (In *The University monthly*. Toronto. v. 18, no. 7 (Apr. 1918), pp. 258-266.)
Examines the process whereby the railway was transferred from private to government ownership.

LUCIAN Commercialized journalism. By Lucian. (In *The Statesman*. Toronto. v. 1, no. 13 (Oct. 19, 1918), p. 7.)
Comments on the support given the Borden government by the Toronto *Globe*, with reference to the latter's "renunciation" of Liberalism.

—— The first seats at the Liberal table. By Lucian. (In *The Statesman*. Toronto. v. 1, no. 21 (Dec. 14, 1918), p. 6.)
Discusses the principles of liberalism as applied to the Liberal Party, with reference to Union Government.

—— The hour has struck for Liberalism. By Lucian. (In *The Statesman*. Toronto. v. 1, no. 12 (Oct. 12, 1918), pp. 5-6.)
Concerns Union Government.

—— Tories entrench behind blue laws. By Lucian. (In *The Statesman*. Toronto. v. 1, no. 25 (Jan. 11, 1919), p. 10.)
Describes the function of the Wartime Elections Act, and its relation to Union Government.

THE MACE Returning to the fold. By the Mace. (In *Saturday night*. Toronto. v. 35, no. 51 (Oct. 16, 1920), p. 4.)
Concerns Hon. Robert Rogers and the Hon. Newton Wesley Rowell.

—— Stepping down but not out. By the Mace. (In *Saturday night*. Toronto. v. 36, no. 34 (June 25, 1921), p. 5.)
Concerns the Hon. Newton Wesley Rowell.

MAITLAND, FRANK Can Union government hold? (In *Canadian courier*. Toronto. v. 24, no. 8 (Jan. 18, 1919), pp. 11-12; 26.)

—— Going after the hard-shells. What some of the practical people in the West think of the Union government; and how they miss it. (In *Canadian courier*. Toronto. v. 22, no. 23 (Nov. 3, 1917), pp. 6; 17; 24-25.)

MALAPROP People who dislike the lime-light. Number two: Hon. N. W. Rowell, Minister of Information. By Mr. Mal-aprop. (In *Canadian courier*. Toronto. v. 24, no. 22 (Aug. 2, 1919), pp. 13; 21.)

MANION, ROBERT JAMES A surgeon in arms. Toronto, McClelland-Goodchild, 1918. 309 p.

Manning Doherty. (In *Saturday night*. Toronto. v. 33, no. 16 (Jan. 31, 1920), p. 3.)
A biographical sketch of the Minister of Agriculture.

MEIGHEN, ARTHUR Canada's natural re-sources. By Honourable Arthur Meighen, Minister of the Interior. (In *The Canadian magazine of politics, science, art and liter-ature*. Toronto. v. 52 (1919), pp. 819-828.)
Address delivered to the Royal Geograph-ical Society in London, Eng.

MUNN, W. CLEMENT Paying for the war. (In *The Statesman*. Toronto. v. 1, no. 26 (Jan. 18, 1919), pp. 7-8.)
Criticizes the tax policy of Union Gov-ernment.

MUNRO, J. K. A "close up" of Union gov-ernment. Our national executive as seen from the press gallery. (In *MacLean's magazine*. Toronto. v. 31, no. 11 (Sept. 1918), pp. [15]-17; 94-96.)

—— The idle hands at Ottawa. (In *Mac-Lean's magazine*. Toronto. v. 32, no. 11 (Nov. 1919), pp. [23]-24; 100-101.)
A general discussion of the Union Gov-ernment in office at Ottawa.

—— Union men at Ottawa. (In *Mac-Lean's magazine*. Toronto. v. 33, no. 12 (July 1, 1920), pp. [7]-8; 54-55.)
Discusses the budget presented by the Union Government and the debate in the House of Commons.

—— "We aim to please." Something about government plans and the next session. (In *MacLean's magazine*. Toronto. v. 32, no. 3 (Mar. 1919), pp. [9]-10; 86-87.)

—— White will be next premier; a pre-diction—and a rumor. (In *MacLean's magazine*. Toronto. v. 33, no. 4 (Mar. 1, 1920), pp. [9]-10; 68.)
Concerns Sir Thomas White.

A New fount of honor! (In *The Statesman*. Toronto. v. 1, no. 2 (Aug. 3, 1918), p. [1].)
Comments on the policy of the Borden

government concerning the issue of titles in Canada.

The New Victory loan. (In *The Statesman*. Toronto. v. 1, no. 9 (Sept. 21, 1918), p. 5.)
Presents a criticism of government fi-nance policy by I. W. Killam.

THE NOMAD Told on shipboard. By the Nomad. (In *The Statesman*. Toronto. v. 1, no. 23 (Dec. 28, 1918), p. 5.)
Cites four confidential anecdotes with reference to the Union Government.

Our British Columbia letter. (In *The States-man*. Toronto. v. 1, no. 24 (Jan. 4, 1919), p. 6.)
Comments on two circumstances prompt-ing negotiations between British Columbia and the Union Government.

Parliamentary government a farce. (In *The Statesman*. Toronto. v. 1, no. 9 (Sept. 21, 1918), pp. 3-4.)
Comments on the actions of Robert Bor-den and N. W. Rowell.

The Passing of Rowellism. (In *The States-man*. Toronto. v. 1, no. 52 (July 19, 1919), p. 4.)
Comments on Newton Wesley Rowell joining the Conservative Party.

PAUL, CHARLES FREDERICK Will we win the war this way? By C. F. P. [i.e. Charles Frederick Paul?] (In *Saturday night*. To-ronto. v. 31, no. 23 (Mar. 23, 1918), p. 4.)
Discusses the war policy of the govern-ment.

The Political outlook. (In *The Statesman*. Toronto. v. 1, no. 22 (Dec. 21, 1918), p. 3.)
Criticizes the position taken by the Lib-eral-Unionist press towards Union Govern-ment.

PRANG, MARGARET EVELYN The political career of N. W. Rowell. Toronto, 1959. 2 v. (728 leaves)
Thesis (PH D) – University of Toronto.

PREVOST, JULES EDOUARD Quebec and the Borden Government. By Jules-Edouard Prévost, député du comté de Terrebonne au Parlement fédéral. (In *The Statesman*. Toronto. v. 1, no. 6 (Aug. 31, 1918), p. 9.)

REID, J. ADDISON The sphinx from Alberta. (In *Canadian courier*. Toronto. v. 24, no. 7 (Jan. 4, 1919), p. 8.)
Concerns Arthur L. Sifton.

—— What does Hon. J. A. Calder want? (In *Canadian courier*. Toronto. v. 24, no. 6 (Dec. 21, 1918), p. 9.)

Repatriation of the soldier. (In *The Statesman*. Toronto. v. 1, no. 27 (Jan. 25, 1919), pp. 4-5.)

> Discusses the plan of Hon. James Calder.

ROWELL, NEWTON WESLEY   The watchword of Canada. By Hon. Newton Rowell. (In *MacLean's magazine*. Toronto. v. 31, no. 8 (June 1918), pp. 20; 107.)

Rowell as a Tory neophyte. (In *The Statesman*. Toronto. v. 1, no. 23 (Dec. 28, 1918), pp. 10-11.)

> Comments on the speech delivered by N. W. Rowell in Bowmanville on December 17, 1918, announcing his joining the Conservative Party.

The Scene shifter. Rowell dons mantle of Lloyd George. By the Scene shifter. (In *The Statesman*. Toronto. v. 1, no. 29 (Feb. 8, 1919), p. 7.)

Sir Robert Borden   (In *The Onlooker*. Toronto. v. 1, no. 4 (Aug. 1920), pp. [1]-6.)

SOMERVILLE, R. S.   "Gentlemen, we have with us to-night." Toastmaster, R. S. Somerville. (In *Saturday night*. Toronto. [v. 34, no. 36] (June 19, 1920), pp. 2; 12.)

> Concerns Henry Herbert Stevens. Presented in the form of an introductory speech.

The Story of Courtney Bay. (In *The Statesman*. Toronto. v. 1, no. 25 (Jan. 11, 1919), pp. 4-5; v. 1, no. 26 (Jan. 18, 1919), pp. 5-7; v. 1, no. 27 (Jan. 25, 1919), pp. 6-7; v. 1, no. 28 (Feb. 1, 1919), pp. 8-11.)

> In four parts.
> Concerns alleged secret arrangements for the awarding of a Dominion government contract for improvements at Courtney Bay, N.B.

Unionism under fire in Alberta. (In *The Statesman*. Toronto. v. 1, no. 15 (Nov. 2, 1918), p. 10.)

> Cites reactions to a pro-Union Government statement attributed to Michael Clark.

VERNER, JOHN   "Gentlemen, we have with us to-night." Toastmaster, John Verner. (In *Saturday night*. Toronto. v. 32, no. 17 (Feb. 8, 1919), pp. 2; 11.)

> Concerns Sir William Thomas White. Adopts the form of an introductory speech.

The Wartime premier retires. (In *MacLean's magazine*. Toronto. v. 33, no. 13 (July 15, 1920), pp. [25]; 40.)

> Concerns the retirement of Sir Robert Borden on July 10, 1920.

When Rowell came back. (In *The Statesman*. Toronto. v. 1, no. 5 (Aug. 24, 1918), pp. 5-6.)

> Discusses N. W. Rowell's support for Robert Borden and Union Government. Considers Mr. Rowell's interpretation of Liberalism.

When union isn't strength. (In *The Statesman*. Toronto. v. 1, no. 36 (Mar. 29, 1919), pp. 3-4.)

> Refers to the Union Government.

Who is to blame? (In *The Statesman*. Toronto. v. 1, no. 39 [i.e. 40] (Apr. 26, 1919), pp. 3-4.)

> Comments on a speech made by Michael Clark at the Open Forum, Toronto, Sunday, April 20, 1919. Concerns the return of Union Government.

WILLISON, SIR JOHN STEPHEN   From month to month. By Sir John Willison. (In *The Canadian magazine of politics, science, art and literature*. Toronto. v. 53 (1919), pp. 253-260.)

> General comments on various current topics, especially a sketch of Sir Robert Borden (pp. 256-257) and observations on the Winnipeg General Strike (pp. 257-260).

1921–1948

1921–1935

ACHESON, G. M.   Canada's youngest Commoner. Capt. Davis, MP, of Athabasca has proved a dynamo of the sub-Arctic. (In *Saturday night*. Toronto. v. 47, no. 25 (Apr. 30, 1932), p. 3.)

> Concerns Percy Griffith Davies; a brief biographical sketch.

ALLEN, RALPH   R. B. Bennett's noisy collision with the depression. (In *Maclean's*. Toronto. v. 74, no. 20 (Oct. 7, 1961), pp. 30-31; 65-67; 70-73.)

> Excerpt from *Ordeal by fire*, by R. Allen. Toronto, 1961.

Armand La Vergne; un patriote. Quelques témoignages. [Montréal, L'Action paroissiale, 1935] 16 p. (Oeuvres des tracts no. 190.)

> Represented Montmagny, Que. as a Conservative in 1930. Deputy Speaker of the House of Commons from 1930 until his death in Ottawa March 6, 1935.

BAGNELL, GUY P.   Interview with the Hon. H. H. Stevens, PC, LLD. (In Okanagan Historical Society. *Report*. [n.p.] 21st (1957), pp. 51-52.)

This is not a literal transcript of an interview. It is a brief chronological biographical description.

BEAVERBROOK, WILLIAM MAXWELL AITKEN, BARON Friends; sixty years of intimate personal relations with Richard Bedford Bennett . . ., Viscount Bennett of Mickleham, Surrey, and of Calgary and Hopewell, Canada; one-time Prime Minister of Canada. A personal memoir, with an appendix of letters. London, Toronto, Heinemann [1959] x, 137 p.

BENNETT, RICHARD BEDFORD Bennett party platform. (In *Saturday night*. Toronto. v. 50, no. 11 (Jan. 19, 1935), pp. 5; 9.)
Summary of the "text of Mr. Bennett's declaration of the policy of reform of capitalism", which was first published in five "talks" in the daily press. Cf. Introd. to the article.

—— The election issues as I see them. By Honourable R. B. Bennett. (In *Maclean's*. Toronto. v. 43, no. 14 (July 15, 1930), pp. 8; 36-37.)
Relates to the federal election held July 28, 1930.

—— The issues as I see them. By Rt. Hon. R. B. Bennett. (In *Maclean's*. Toronto. v. 48, no. 18 (Sept. 15, 1935), pp. 10; 26; 28.)
Relates to the federal election held October 14, 1935.

The Bennett proposals. I. Mr. Bennett's political seas made smoother. (In *Canadian comment*. Toronto. v. 4, no. 2 (Feb. 1935), pp. [3]-4; 30.)

BERNARD, GABRIEL L'honorable sénateur Lucien Moraud. (In *La Revue de l'Université Laval*. Québec. v. 6, no. 5 (jan. 1952), pp. [350]-351.)

BOYLEN, JOHN CHANCELLOR Weir of Carrot River. By J. C. Boylen. (In *The Canadian* [magazine]. Toronto. v. 83, no. 6 (June 1935), pp. 6; 19.)
Concerns the Hon. Robert Weir, Minister of Agriculture.

BRIDLE, AUGUSTUS Drayton, the practical. By the "Make-up" man. (In *Maclean's*. Toronto. v. 34, no. 16 (Sept. 15, 1921), pp. 13; 46.)
Concerns Sir Henry Drayton, Minister of Finance.

BRISCOE, R. LAIRD Is this our 1925 National Policy? (In *Maclean's*. Toronto. v. 38, no. 4 (Feb. 15, 1925), p. 21.)
A presentation of the "politico-economic

programme" of the Rt. Hon. Arthur Meighen, which the Author considers "a 1925 revised edition of the historic protectionist creed of 1874".

BUCHANAN, DONALD W. Bennett's conversion. (In *Saturday night*. Toronto. v. 50, no. 10 (Jan. 12, 1935), p. 4.)

—— National affairs. Eleven men sitting. (In *Saturday night*. Toronto. v. 49, no. 18 (Mar. 10, 1934), pp. 4; 10.)
Comments on the Hon. H. H. Stevens, chairman of the Commission on Price Spreads.

—— National affairs. What does West want? (In *Saturday night*. Toronto. v. 49, no. 25 (Apr. 28, 1934), p. 4.)
Comments on the budget brought down by E. N. Rhodes in 1934.

—— National affairs. The papers are missing! (In *Saturday night*. Toronto. v. 49, no. 41 (Aug. 12, 1934), p. 4.)
Concerns the memorandum written by Henry Herbert Stevens alleging domination of Canada by powerful financial groups.

—— National affairs. Ottawa smile contest (In *Saturday night*. Toronto. v. 49, no. 52 (Nov. 3, 1934), p. 4.)
Concerns the political career of Henry Herbert Stevens.

—— National affairs. Between the storms. (In *Saturday night*. Toronto. v. 50, no. 2 (Nov. 17, 1934), p. 4.)
Comments on the resignation of H. H. Stevens from the Bennett government; review of the B.N.A. Act, etc.

BUCHANAN, E. C. The Bagot petting party. By E. C. B. (In *Saturday night*. Toronto. v. 41, no. 5 (Dec. 19, 1925), p. 4.)
Concerns Arthur Meighen and his leadership of the Conservative Party. Reference is to the Bagot, Que., by-election held on December 7, 1925.

—— A cabinet at last. By E. C. B. (In *Saturday night*. Toronto. v. 41, no. 36 (July 24, 1926), p. 4.)
Concerns the cabinet of Arthur Meighen.

—— Lobby and gallery. By E. C. B. (In *Saturday night*. Toronto. v. 42, no. 18 (Mar. 19, 1927), p. 4.)
Concerns the Conservative Party and their effectiveness as an Opposition party

—— Lobby and gallery. By E. C. B. (In *Saturday night*. Toronto. v. 42, no. 45 (Sept. 24, 1927), p. 4.)
Comments on the forthcoming Conserva-

tive Party leadership convention held in Winnipeg, October 10-12, 1927.

—— Lobby and gallery. By E. C. B. (In *Saturday night*. Toronto. v. 42, no. 47 (Oct. 8, 1927), p. 4.)

Concerns the candidates in the Conservative Party leadership contest.

—— Lobby and gallery. By E. C. B. (In *Saturday night*. Toronto. v. 42, no. 49 (Oct. 22, 1927), p. 4.)

Concerns Richard Bennett and the first Conservative Party leadership convention held in Winnipeg, October 10-12, 1927.

—— Lobby and gallery. By E. C. B. (In *Saturday night*. Toronto. v. 42, no. 50 (Oct. 29, 1927), p. 4.)

Concerns the Conservative Party leadership convention and the party platform.

—— Lobby and gallery. The rehabilitated opposition. Mr. Bennett's reception as leader. Extending diplomatic relations. Encouraging sectional aspirations. By E. C. B. (In *Saturday night*. Toronto. v. 43, no. 12 (Feb. 4, 1928), p. 4.)

—— Lobby and gallery. Bennett makes impression on Parliament. His worth is acclaimed. The Tarriff [!] Board is in question. Coal from the West. By E. C. B. (In *Saturday night*. Toronto. v. 43, no. 19 (Mar. 24, 1928), p. 4.)

—— Lobby and gallery. (In *Saturday night*. Toronto. v. 45, no. 40 (Aug. 16, 1930), p. 4.)

Concerns the government of R. B. Bennett.

—— National affairs. (In *Saturday night*. Toronto. v. 45, no. 44 (Sept. 13, 1930), p. 4.)

Comments, primarily, on the cabinet formed by Prime Minister R. B. Bennett.

—— National affairs. (In *Saturday night*. Toronto. v. 45, no. 45 (Sept. 20, 1930), p. 4.)

Concerns Prime Minister R. B. Bennett and the problem of unemployment.

—— National affairs. (In *Saturday night*. Toronto. v. 46, no. 9 (Jan. 10, 1931), p. 4.)

Concerns the program of the Bennett government in its effort to combat the depression.

—— National affairs. (In *Saturday night*. Toronto. v. 46, no. 12 (Jan. 31, 1931), p. 4.)

Considers the legislation proposed by the Bennett government at the opening of the second session, seventeenth parliament.

—— National affairs. (In *Saturday night*. Toronto. v. 46, no. 16 (Feb. 28, 1931), p. 4.)

Concerns "the Prime Minister and Parliament" (i.e. R. B. Bennett).

—— National affairs. (In *Saturday night*. Toronto. v. 46, no. 17 (Mar. 7, 1931), p. 4.)

Concerns R. B. Bennett's opposition to communism, national railway finances, etc.

—— National affairs. (In *Saturday night*. Toronto. v. 46, no. 24 (Apr. 25, 1931), p. 4.)

Concerns the policy of the Bennett government towards unemployment; supply bill, etc.

—— National affairs. (In *Saturday night*. Toronto, v. 46, no. 25 (May 2, 1931), p. 4.)

Concerns the first budget prepared by the Bennett government and discusses the nature of the fiscal legislation advocated by the Bennett administration.

—— National affairs. (In *Saturday night*. Toronto. v. 46, no. 27 (May 16, 1931), p. 4.)

Discusses the activities of Robert Weir, Minister of Agriculture; the budget, etc.

—— National affairs. (In *Saturday night*. Toronto. v. 46, no. 31 (June 13, 1931), p. 4.)

Concerns R. B. Bennett's review of the financial conditions of the Canadian National Railways.

—— National affairs. (In *Saturday night*. Toronto. v. 47, no. 10 (Jan. 16, 1932), p. 4.)

Concerns "Cabinet-shuffle gossip".

—— National affairs. (In *Saturday night*. Toronto. v. 48, no. 4 (Dec. 3, 1932), p. 20.)

Discusses a trend towards the left in government policy.

—— Putting his foot in it! By E. C. B. (In *Saturday night*. Toronto. v. 41, no. 2 (Nov. 28, 1925), p. 20.)

Concerns Arthur Meighen and his speech of November 16, 1925 in Hamilton exposing and denouncing "methods employed against Mr. Meighen and his party in some parts of Quebec during the campaign" by the Liberal Party.

—— "Putting over" the Tory convention. A sketch of Major General McRae., MP, who has taken charge of organization work. (In *Saturday night*. Toronto. v. 42, no. 40 (Aug. 20, 1927), p. 2.)

Concerns Alexander Duncan McRae, MP.

BURTON, FRANKLIN Reforming capitalism. (In *Saturday night*. Toronto. v. 50, no. 12 (Jan. 26, 1935), pp. [1]-2.)

Concerns R. B. Bennett and his proposed reform programme.

Business is business—the Tories return to the right. (In *Canadian comment*. Toronto. v. 3, no. 11 (Nov. 1934), pp. [5]-6; 32.)

Concerns the conflict between Premier R. B. Bennett and H. H. Stevens.

CAHAN, CHARLES HAZLITT The depression; its monetary problems. By Hon. C. H. Cahan. (In Canadian Club of Toronto. *Addresses*. Toronto. (1933/34), pp. 188-205.)

Address delivered November 13, 1933.

CANADA ROYAL COMMISSION ON PRICE SPREADS Report of the Royal Commission on Price Spreads. Ottawa, J. O. Patenaude, Printer to the King, 1935. xiii, 506 p.

Chairman: Henry Herbert Stevens.

Secretary: Lester Bowles Pearson.

The Commission met in Ottawa from October 30, 1934 to February 1, 1935.

Canada's new Premier. By a man in the Press Gallery. (In *Maclean's*. Toronto. v. 43, no. 18 (Sept. 15, 1930), pp. 3-4; 66.)

Concerns Hon. R. B. Bennett.

The Canadian budget. (In *Canadian comment*. Toronto. v. 3, no. 5 (May 1931), pp. 8-9.)

Comment on the financial policy outlined by the Hon. E. N. Rhodes on April 18, 1934.

Canadian women in the public eye. Lady Tupper. (In *Saturday night*. Toronto. v. 33, no. 13 (Jan. 10, 1920), p. 18.)

Concerns Lady Janet Tupper, wife of Sir Charles Hibbert Tupper.

Canadian women in the public eye. Lady Foster. (In Saturday night. Toronto. v. 36, no. 18 (Feb. 26, 1921), p. 27.)

Née Jessie Allan.

Canadian women in the public eye. Mrs. H. H. Stevens. (In *Saturday night*. Toronto. v. 37, no. 18 (Mar. 4, 1922), p. 25.)

Née Gertrude M. Glover.

Canadian women in the public eye. Mrs. Robert Rogers. (In *Saturday night*. Toronto. v. 37, no. 20 (Mar. 18, 1922), pp. 24; 32.)

Née Aurelia Widmeyer.

Canadian women in the public eye. Mrs. George Black, FRGS. (In *Saturday night*. Toronto. v. 39, no. 10 (Jan. 26, 1924), p. 25.)

Née Martha Louise Munger. She was twice married: William Purdy, 1887-1898; George Black. As Martha Louise Black, she was elected to represent the Yukon in the federal parliament in 1935.

Canadian women in the public eye. Mrs. Hugh Guthrie. (In *Saturday night*. Toronto. v. 42, no. 22 (Apr. 16, 1927), p. 31.)

Née Maude Henrietta Scarff.

CAYGEON, ROBERT National affairs. A political paradox. (In *Saturday night*. Toronto. v. 50, no. 25 (Apr. 27, 1935), p. 4.)

Concerns Hon. Henry Herbert Stevens.

—— National affairs. Last minute strategy. (In *Saturday night*. Toronto. v. 50, no. 33 (June 22, 1935), p. 4.)

Comments on a move by the government to amend the Elections Act; the Grain Board bill; the report of the Stamp Commission, etc.

—— National affairs. Stevens makes a plea. (In *Saturday night*. Toronto. v. 50, no. 34 (June 29, 1935), p. 4.)

Concerns Hon. Henry Herbert Stevens and his speech to the House of Commons pleading for "common sense reform based on a real appreciation of values".

—— National affairs. Whom is he splitting? (In *Saturday night*. Toronto. v. 50, no. 36 (July 13, 1935), p. 4.)

Concerns H. H. Stevens and his break with the Conservative Party.

—— National affairs. Rounding first turn. (In *Saturday night*. Toronto. v. 50, no. 45 (Sept. 14, 1935), p. 4.)

Concerns R. B. Bennett and H. H. Stevens with reference to the 1935 federal election campaign.

—— National affairs. "Pa" Sage and Mr. Bennett. (In *Saturday night*. Toronto. v. 50, no. 46 (Sept. 21, 1935), p. 4.)

Concerns the federal election held October 14, 1935.

—— What about Major Herridge? (In *Saturday night*. Toronto. v. 50, no. 30 (June 1, 1935), p. 4.)

Comments on pre-election spending, the problem of leadership in the Conservative Party, and the possibility of R. B. Bennett recalling Major William D. Herridge into the cabinet.

CHARLESWORTH, HECTOR WILLOUGHBY The career of Hugh Guthrie. Entry into politics interrupted a promising legal career. Rice murder case recalled. By Hector Charlesworth. (In *Saturday night*. Toronto. v. 41, no. 49 (Oct. 23, 1926), p. 2.)

CHAUVIN, FRANCIS X. Personal glimpses. Hon. Raymond Morand. (In *Saturday night*. Toronto. v. 50, no. 19 (March 16, 1935), p. 5.)

CHURCHILL, RICHARD Canada's new agricultural policy. An exclusive . . . statement of the new farm policy . . . by Hon. Robert Weir, Minister of Agriculture. (In *Maclean's*. Toronto. v. 44, no. 6 (Mar. 15, 1931), pp. 12; 64-65.)

CLARK, HUGH Arthur Meighen. An intimate and impartial estimate of his services as leader. By Lt.-Col. Hugh Clark. (In *Saturday night*. Toronto. v. 41, no. 47 (Oct. 9, 1926), p. 2.)

——— The Tory prohibitionists. Political adventures of W. F. Nickle and Sir George Foster. By Lieut.-Col. Hugh Clark. (In *Saturday night*. Toronto. v. 42, no. 2, (Nov. 27, 1926), p. 2.)

The Conservative Party in the West. Special correspondence of Willisons monthly. (In *Willisons monthly*. Toronto. v. 3, no. 5 (Oct. 1927), pp. 180-181.)

COOPER, JOHN ALEXANDER And a prospective estimate of Premier Meighen. (In *Canadian courier*. Toronto. v. 25, no. 20 (July 1, 1920), pp. 6; 30.)
Brief comment on Arthur Meighen.

CORBETT, PERCY ELLWOOD The Prime Minister on capitalism. By P. E. Corbett. (In *Queen's quarterly*. Kingston. v. 42 (1935), pp. [121]-130.)
Concerns the policies of R. B. Bennett.

Creating a bogeyman to order. (In *The Onlooker*. Toronto. v. 1, no. 6 (Oct. 1920), pp. 24-29.)
Concerns the attitude taken by the Toronto Globe toward Arthur Meighen.

CURTIS, CLIFFORD AUSTIN Dominion legislation of 1935; an economist's review. By C. A. Curtis. (In *The Canadian journal of economics and political science*. [Toronto] v. 1 (1935), pp. 599-608.)
Reviews the work of the sixth session of the seventeenth Parliament, with special reference to the administration of R. B. Bennett.

DEACHMAN, JOHN ROBERT Mr. Bennett, the great apologist. By J. R. Deachman. (In *The Maritime advocate and busy East*. Sackville, N.B. v. 24, no. 4 (Nov. 1933), pp. 17-18; 20.)

DE BRISAY, RICHARD Mr. Bennett's embarrassment. (In *The Canadian forum*. Toronto. v. 8, no. 94 (July 1928), pp. 703-704.)

DEXTER, GRANT Cabinet portraits. Minister of National Revenue. (In *Maclean's*. Toronto. v. 47, no. 5 (Mar. 1, 1934), pp. 27; 43.)
Concerns the Hon. R. C. Matthews.

——— The Canadian political scene. (In *Queen's quarterly*. Kingston. v. 38 (1931), pp. [745]-751.)
Considers the problems confronting the Conservative government led by R. B. Bennett during 1931.

——— The political situation in Canada. (In *Queen's quarterly*. Kingston. v. 37 (1930), pp. [762]-770.)
Reviews the policies and the performance of the Conservative administration under R. B. Bennett.

——— Young Canada goes to Washington. A young man in his early forties, unknown to political fame, a man of quiet tastes, steps suddenly into a friendship with Canada's first minister and through that by a swift straight road to one of the highest honors in the gift of Canada. (In *The Canadian magazine*. Toronto. v. 75, no. 4 (Apr. 1931), pp. 3; 45.)
Concerns William Duncan Herridge. Canadian minister to Washington during the years 1931-1935.

DOYLE, LUCY SWANTON The Premier's sister. (In *Chatelaine*. Toronto. v. 4, no. 3 (Mar. 1931), pp. 16; 36.)
Concerns Mildred Bennett.

DUPIRE, LOUIS Armand LaVergne. (In *L'Action nationale*. Montréal. v. 1 (juin 1933), pp. [348]-357.)
Represented Montmagny, Que., as a Conservative member to Parliament in 1930 and was Deputy Speaker of the House of Commons, 1930-1935.

DYAS, A. E. At last, a Premier of Canada with a family. (In *Canadian courier*. Toronto. v. 25, no. 21 (July 15, 1920), p. [5].)
A domestic portrait of Mrs. Isabel Meighen.

EGGLESTON, WILFRID Mr. Stevens and our

economic ills. (In *Queen's quarterly.* Kingston. v. 41 (1934), pp. [531]-541.)

Evaluates the fiscal policy of H. H. Stevens.

—— Will Bennett go to the country soon? (In *The Canadian* [*magazine*] Toronto. [v. 82, no. 2] (Aug. 1934), pp. 17; 20.)

EWART, JOHN SKIRVING Mr. Meighen and the Bagot election. By John S. Ewart. (In his *The independence papers.* Ottawa. v. 1, no. 5 (1926), pp. 155-158.)

Comments on Arthur Meighen's Hamilton speech delivered November 16, 1925, and its impact on the by-election held in Bagot, Que., December 7, 1925.

FISHER, JOHN WIGGINS The lonely man. A radio address by John Fisher. (In *The Maritime advocate and busy East.* Sackville, N.B. v. 38, no. 1 (Aug. 1947), pp. 19-21.)

Concerns R. B. Bennett.

Address delivered on the occasion of his death June 27, 1947.

Five views of Mr. Bennett. (In *The Canadian forum.* Toronto. v. 15, no. 173 (Feb. 1935), pp. 167-170.)

Contents: St. James Street. – The West, by W. B. Herbert. – A socialist analysis, by F. H. Underhill. – An economist's view, by D. C. MacGregor.

FLAHERTY, J. FRANCIS Ottawa letter. Bennett saga is tale of an era that could never be repeated. By Frank Flaherty. (In *Saturday night.* Toronto. v. 62, no. 45 (July 12, 1947), p. 8.)

Written on the occasion of the death of R. B. Bennett June 27, 1947, at Dorking, England.

FORSEY, EUGENE ALFRED Arthur Meighen. By Eugene Forsey. (In *The Canadian forum.* Toronto. v. 40, no. 476 (Sept. 1960), pp. [121]-122.)

—— Arthur Meighen: the whole man. By Eugene Forsey. (In *Saturday night.* Toronto. v. 75, no. 25 (Dec. 10, 1960), pp. 53-54.)

A review article of *Arthur Meighen, a biography,* by Roger Graham. Toronto, Clarke Irwin, 1960-65. Vol. 1: The door of opportunity (1960).

FREEDMAN, MAX The Arthur Meighen nobody knows. (In *Saturday night.* Toronto. v. 68, no. 19 (Feb. 14, 1953), pp. [1]; 12-13.)

From month to month. (In *Willisons monthly.* Toronto. v. 3, no. 6 (Nov. 1927), pp. [203]-209.)

Deals with the first national convention of the Conservative Party held in Winnipeg October 10-12, 1927 (pp. 203-205). R. B. Bennett was elected to the leadership.

GADSBY, HENRY FRANKLIN Premier Meighen meets the Press. By H. F. Gadsby. (In *Saturday night.* Toronto. v. 34, no. 41 (July 31, 1920), p. 4.)

GORDON, WESLEY ASHTON Canadian immigration. By Hon. W. A. Gordon, Minister of Immigration. (In Canadian Club of Toronto. *Addresses.* Toronto. (1930/31), pp. 177-184.)

Address delivered February 16, 1931. Discusses the restricted immigration policy of the Conservative administration.

GRAHAM, JEAN Among those present. XLV —Rt. Hon. Arthur Meighen, BA, PC. (In *Saturday night.* Toronto. v. 48, no. 3 (Nov. 26, 1932), p. 11.)

GRAHAM, WILLIAM ROGER Arthur Meighen; a biography. By Roger Graham. Toronto, Clarke, Irwin, 1960-65. 3 v.

Contents: v. 1. The door of opportunity. – v. 2. And fortune fled. – v. 3. No surrender.

—— Arthur Meighen. By Roger Graham. Ottawa [Canadian Historical Association] 1965. 16 p. (Canadian Historical Association booklets, no. 16.)

—— Arthur Meighen and the Conservative Party in Quebec; the election of 1925. By W. R. Graham. (In *The Canadian historical review.* Toronto. v. 36 (1955), pp. 17-35.)

—— Meighen and the Montreal tycoons: railway policy in the election of 1921. By W. R. Graham. (In Canadian Historical Association. *Report of the annual meeting.* [Ottawa] (1957), pp. 71-85.)

—— Meighen in debate. The talent for controversy. By W. R. Graham. (In *Queen's quarterly.* Kingston. v. 62 (1955), pp. [24]-36.)

—— Some comments on a credible Canadian. By W. R. Graham. (In *The Canadian historical review.* Toronto. v. 39 (1958), pp. 296-311.)

A lecture delivered at the University of Toronto, February, 1958.

Concerns Arthur Meighen.

HALL, HELEN A Sunday morning call at the new Premier's home. (In *Saturday night.* Toronto. [v. 34, no. 40] (July 17, 1920), pp. 27; 30.)

Deals with the family of Arthur Meighen.

HERBERT, W. R. Bracken, butter and Bennett. (In *The Canadian forum*. Toronto. v. 12, no. 143 (Aug. 1932), pp. 408-409.)

L'Hon. Arthur Meighen dans le comté de Bagot. La vérité sur la loi du service militaire de 1917 par l'Hon. D. O. L'Espérance [n.p., préf. 1926] 36 p.

Contents: Préface par l'honorable André Fauteux. – Message de l'Hon. Arthur Meighen à l'électorat canadien-français de Bagot. – La loi du service militaire de 1917. Expliquée dans un discours de M. le sénateur D. O. L'Espérance. – Appréciations du chef conservateur par MM. Henri Bourassa et John S. Ewart.

KIPP, V. M. Hon. Robert Rogers. Conservative, yesterday, today and forever. (In *Saturday night*. Toronto. v. 42, no. 17 (Mar. 12, 1927), p. 19.)

KRISHTALKA, AARON The old Tories and fascism during the 1930s. [Montreal] 1969 [c1970] v, 369 leaves.

Thesis (MA) – McGill University.

LA TERREUR, MARC R. B. Bennett et le Québec: un cas d'incompréhension réciproque. (In Canadian Historical Association. *Historical papers*. [Ottawa] (1969), pp. [94]-102.)

LAURISTON, VICTOR The swing of the political pendulum. Can the Conservative Party prevent history repeating itself? It's odd, but ever since Confederation when a party has been in at Ottawa it has slipped in the provinces. (In *Maclean's*. Toronto. v. 44, no. 14 (July 15, 1931), pp. 11; 46.)

LEVINE, LEON The prime ministership of R. B. Bennett; a view of his political significance. [Windsor, 1960] 1 v.

Thesis (MA) – Assumption University.

LIBERAL-CONSERVATIVE PARTY (CANADA) National Convention, Winnipeg, 1927. National Liberal-Conservative convention held at Winnipeg, Manitoba, Oct. 10th to 12th, 1927. A review by John R. MacNicol. Toronto. Printed by Southam Press, 1930. 436 p.

LIPSETT, R. W. National affairs. Election? Not much. (In *Saturday night*. Toronto. v. 48, no. 21 (Apr. 1, 1933), p. 4.)

Discusses the 1933 budget brought down by E. N. Rhodes.

—— National affairs. Tory anti-titlers. (In *Saturday night*. Toronto. v. 49, no. 10 (Jan. 13, 1934), p. 4.)

Concerns R. B. Bennett's "restoration of titles of honor and distinction to His Majesty's Canadian subjects".

LUCE, P. W. B.C.'s new Conservative leader. An intimate sketch of Hon. S. F. Tolmie. (In *Saturday night*. Toronto. v. 42, no. 18 (Mar. 19, 1927), p. 5.)

Concerns Hon. Simon Fraser Tolmie who represented Victoria, B.C. in the House of Commons from 1917 to 1928.

—— George Black, MP. (In *Saturday night*. Toronto. v. 39, no. 26 (May 17, 1924), p. 3.)

MACAULAY, LEOPOLD History and aims of the Conservative Party. (In *Canadian problems as seen by twenty outstanding men of Canada*. Toronto, 1933. pp. [189]-200.)

MC CONNELL, WILLIAM HOWARD The genesis of the Canadian New Deal. By W. H. McConnell. (In *Journal of Canadian studies*, Peterborough, Ont. v. 4, no. 2 (1969), pp. 31-41.)

—— The judicial review of Prime Minister Bennett's "New Deal" legislative programme. Toronto, 1968. 413 leaves.

Thesis (PH D) – University of Toronto.

THE MACE [Commentary on national affairs] Putting the 'ME' in "Meighen". By the Mace. (In *Saturday night*. Toronto. v. 35, no. 49 (Oct. 2, 1920), p. 4.)

Concerns Arthur Meighen.

—— [Commentary on national affairs] Finding a job for Sir Robert. By the Mace. (In *Saturday night*. Toronto. v. 35, no. 52 (Oct. 23, 1920), p. 4.)

Concerns Sir Robert Laird Borden.

—— [Commentary on national affairs] Leaving it to George. By the Mace. (In *Saturday night*. Toronto. v. 36, no. 1 (Oct. 30, 1920), p. 4.)

Concerns Sir George Eulas Foster.

—— [Commentary on national affairs] Trying to rope him in. By the Mace. (In *Saturday night*. Toronto. v. 36, no. 4 (Nov. 20, 1920), p. 4.)

Concerns Arthur Meighen and French-Canadian representation in his cabinet.

—— [Commentary on national affairs] Will he take the plunge? By the Mace. (In *Saturday night*. Toronto. v. 36, no. 8 (Dec. 18, 1920), p. 4.)

Humorous commentary on Arthur Meighen and his prospects in a future federal election.

—— [Commentary on national affairs] Making New Year resolutions. By the Mace. (In *Saturday night*. Toronto. v. 36, no. 10 (Jan. 1, 1921), p. 4.)
Concerns the policy of the Meighen cabinet, presented in the form of a conversation.

—— [Commentary on national affairs] Troubled dreams. By the Mace. (In *Saturday night*. Toronto. v. 36, no. 11 (Jan. 8, 1921), p. 4.)
Humorous commentary on Arthur Meighen and issues such as the Quebec problem, cabinet reorganization, and the Farmers Movement.

—— [Commentary on national affairs] The rival suitors. By the Mace. (In *Saturday night*. Toronto. v. 36, no. 12 (Jan. 15, 1921), p. 4.)
Concerns Arthur Meighen and his political rivals, with reference to a by-election held in Peterborough West, February 14, 1921.

—— [Commentary on national affairs] Having their fortunes told. By the Mace. (In *Saturday night*. Toronto. v. 36, no. 13 (Jan. 22, 1921), p. 4.)
Humorous commentary on the future of the Meighen government.

—— [Commentary on national affairs] Welcome little stranger. By the Mace. (In *Saturday night*. Toronto. v. 36, no. 14 (Jan. 29, 1921), p. 4.)
General comments on Arthur Meighen and the fifth session of the thirteenth parliament which opened February 14, 1921.

—— [Commentary on national affairs] The pot begins to boil. By the Mace. (In *Saturday night*. Toronto v. 36, no. 15 (Feb. 5, 1921), p. 4.)
Concerns Arthur Meighen. A hypothetical presentation.

—— [Commentary on national affairs] The skipper and his crew. By the Mace. (In *Saturday night*. Toronto. v. 36, no. 16 (Feb. 12, 1921), p. 4.)
Concerns Arthur Meighen and his cabinet.

—— [Commentary on national affairs] Wanted—a man with a broom. By the Mace. (In *Saturday night*. Toronto. v. 36, no. 23 (Apr. 2, 1921), p. 4.)
Concerns the administration of Arthur Meighen.

—— [Commentary on national affairs] The power house. By the Mace. (In *Saturday night*. Toronto. v. 36, no. 25 (Apr. 16, 1921), p. 4.)
Concerns the management of public funds by the Meighen government.

—— [Commentary on national affairs] Waiting till the clouds roll by. By the Mace. (In *Saturday night*. Toronto. v. 36, no. 28 (May 7, 1921), p. 4.)
Concerns Arthur Meighen and the fifth session of the thirteenth parliament.

—— [Commentary on national affairs] Coming down the stretch. By the Mace. (In *Saturday night*. Toronto. v. 36, no. 29 (May 14, 1921), p. 4.)
Speculates on the dissolution of the current parliament and the political future of certain members in the federal cabinet.

—— [Commentary on national affairs] From George to Arthur. By the Mace. (In *Saturday night*. Toronto. v. 36, no. 35 (July 2, 1921), p. 4.)
Concerns "Sir George Foster, in his capacity of acting Prime Minister". A hypothetical presentation.

—— [Commentary on national affairs] From Arthur to George. By the Mace. (In *Saturday night*. Toronto. v. 36, no. 36 (July 9, 1921), p. 4.)
Concerns Sir George Foster and Arthur Meighen. A hypothetical presentation.

—— [Commentary on national affairs] In the doldrums. By the Mace. In *Saturday night*. Toronto. v. 36, no. 38 (July 23, 1921), p. 4.)
Concerns "Sir George Foster in his capacity of acting Prime Minister". A humorous commentary.

—— [Commentary on national affairs] The homecoming of Arthur. By the Mace. (In *Saturday night*. Toronto. v. 36, no. 39 (July 30, 1921), p. 4.)
Concerns Arthur Meighen and his return from the Imperial Conference in London.

—— [Commentary on national affairs] The pilot at the wheel again. By the Mace. (In *Saturday night*. Toronto. v. 36, no. 41 (Aug. 13, 1921), p. 4.)
Concerns Arthur Meighen as Prime Minister of Canada.

—— [Commentary on national affairs] Grooming him for the race. By the Mace. (In *Saturday night*. Toronto. v. 36, no. 42 (Aug. 20, 1921), p. 3.)
Concerns Arthur Meighen and the Na-

tional Liberal and Conservative Party and the possibility of a federal election.

—— [Commentary on national affairs] General Sir Sam. By the Mace. (In *Saturday night*. Toronto. v. 36, no. 44 (Sept. 3, 1921), pp. 4-5.)
Concerns General Sir Sam Hughes, written on the occasion of his death August 24, 1921.

—— [Commentary on national affairs] Neath the shade of the old plum tree. By the Mace. (In *Saturday night*. Toronto. v. 36, no. 45 (Sept. 10, 1921), pp. 4-5.)
Discusses the re-organization of the Meighen cabinet with a view to the general elections held December 6, 1921.

—— [Commentary on national affairs] Sweeping out the shop. By the Mace. (In *Saturday night*. Toronto. v. 36, no. 48 (Oct. 1, 1921), p. 4.)
Concerns Arthur Meighen and the selection of his cabinet ministers.

—— [Commentary on national affairs] Sir Robert in harness again. By the Mace. (In *Saturday night*. Toronto. v. 37, no. 6 (Dec. 10, 1921), p. 4.)
A review of the career of Sir Robert Borden, in view of his being chosen to represent Canada at the round-table conference in Washington.

—— [Commentary on national affairs] One of the Old Guard. By the Mace. (In *Saturday night*. Toronto. v. 37, no. 46 (Sept. 16, 1922), p. 4.)
Concerns Sir George Eulas Foster.

—— [Commentary on national affairs] The new groom. By the Mace. (In *Saturday night*. Toronto. v. 38, no. 42 [!] (Aug. 4, 1923), p. 4.)
Concerns Dr. Simon Fraser Tolmie and his appointment to the post of executive director of the Conservative Party.

—— [Commentary on national affairs] See him smiling. By the Mace. (In *Saturday night*. Toronto. v. 39, no. 7 (Jan. 5, 1924), p. 4.)
Concerns the by-election held in Kent, N.B., December 20, 1923, returning A. J. Doucet as an Independent. In 1925, he was returned as a Conservative MP.

—— [Commentary on national affairs] The gathering storm. By the Mace. (In *Saturday night*. Toronto. v. 39, no. 44 (Sept. 20, 1924), p. 4.)
Comments on the Conservative Party and the "rumblings of dissent and grumblings

about the kind of leadership it is receiving in quarters which are usually sedately orthodox".

—— [Commentary on national affairs] Still going strong. By the Mace. (In *Saturday night*. Toronto. v. 40, no. 8 (Jan. 10, 1925), p. 4.)
Concerns Sir George Eulas Foster.

MC GILLICUDDY, OWEN E.   The Conservative leader. From a struggling lawyer to one of Canada's wealthiest men and leader of His Majesty's loyal opposition at Ottawa. (In *The Canadian magazine*. Toronto. v. 68, no. 5 (Nov. 1927), pp. 14-15; 39; 42-43.)
Concerns Richard Bedford Bennett.

MC INNIS, EDGAR WARDELL   Off with their heads. By Edgar McInnis. (In *The Canadian forum*. Toronto. v. 10, no. 120 (Sept. 1930), p. 435.)
Discusses the emergence of the spoils system after the Conservative Party became the government under R. B. Bennett.

MAC KENZIE, NORMAN ARCHIBALD MAC RAE   Was it a Conservative collapse? An investigation of the political situation. By Norman MacKenzie. (In *Canadian comment*. Toronto. v. 3, no. 10 (Oct. 1934), pp. [3]-4; 32.)

MAC LEAN, ANDREW DYAS   R. B. Bennett, Prime Minister of Canada. By A. D. MacLean. Toronto, Excelsior Pub. Co., 1935 [c1934] 113 p.

MC LEAN, J. ROSS   Bennett of Tarsus. The month in Ottawa. By J. R. McLean. (In *The Canadian forum*. Toronto. v. 15, no. 173 (Feb. 1935), pp. 178-179.)

—— Four ring circus. The month in Ottawa. By J. R. McLean. (In *The Canadian forum*. Toronto. v. 15, no. 175 (Apr. 1935), pp. 258-259.)
A description of the political activities of H. H. Stevens. It was considered that Mr. Stevens was aiming to assume the leadership of a reconstituted Conservative Party.

—— National affairs. Saved by treaty power. (In *Saturday night*. Toronto. v. 50, no. 14 (Feb. 9, 1935), p. 4.)
Comments on the Unemployment Insurance Bill proposed by the R. B. Bennett government.

—— National affairs. Wheat piles up. (In *Saturday night*. Toronto. v. 50, no. 15 (Feb. 16, 1935), p. 4.)
Comments on government aid to Prairie farmers.

—— National affairs. Them's fighting words. (In *Saturday night*. Toronto. v. 50, no. 20 (Mar. 23, 1935), p. 4.)

Concerns H. H. Stevens' return to the House of Commons following his resignation from the Bennett cabinet and the division within the Conservative Party.

—— National affairs. Businesslike budget. (In *Saturday night*. Toronto. v. 50, no. 21 (Mar. 30, 1935), p. 4.)

Concerns the budget speech of E. N. Rhodes.

—— Rough justice. The month in Ottawa. By J. R. McLean. (In *The Canadian forum*. Toronto. v. 15, no. 174 (Mar. 1935), p. 219.)

Brief comments on R. B. Bennett's policies regarding the constitutional questions raised by his legislation, financial and social problems.

MACLEAN, WILLIAM FINDLAY   Some of Canada's near-by problems. By W. F. Maclean, MP. (In *The Canadian forum*. Toronto. v. 6, no. 66 (Mar. 1926), pp. 173-175.)

Discusses the railway problem, bank problem, the constitution of Canada and fiscal policy.

"Mr. Maclean is an independent Conservative protectionist and senior member of the Canadian House of Commons". – Ed.

MC LEOD, JOHN TENNYSON   He fled fortune. By John T. McLeod. (In *Commentator*. Toronto. v. 8, no. 1 (Jan. 1964), pp. 23-24.)

A review article of *Arthur Meighen: a biography* by R. Graham. Toronto, Clarke, Irwin, 1960-65. Vol. 2: And fortune fled (1963).

MANION, ROBERT JAMES   Canada's railways. By Hon. R. J. Manion. (In Canadian Club of Toronto. *Addresses*. Toronto. (1934/35), pp. 310-311.)

Address delivered May 1, 1935.
Discusses railways in relation to government policy.

—— Cutting our railway losses. By Hon. R. J. Manion. (In *The Canadian [magazine]*. Toronto. [v. 82, no. 3] (Sept. 1934), pp. 9; 38.)

—— The railway problem. By Hon. Dr. Robert J. Manion, Minister of Railways and Canals. (In Canadian Club of Toronto. *Addresses*. Toronto. (1932/33), pp. 180-194.)

Address delivered November 28, 1932.

MARSH, D'ARCY   Richard in wonderland. (In *The Canadian forum*. Toronto. v. 14, no. 165 (June 1934), pp. 346-348.)

Refers to Prime Minister Richard Bedford Bennett.

MATTHEWS, ELIZABETH ANN   Meighen and the West, 1921-1926; the National Policy revisited. [Ottawa] 1966. 1 v.

Thesis (MA) – Carleton University.

MEIGHEN, ARTHUR   The constitutional crisis, 1926. (In his *Unrevised and unrepented; debating speeches. . . .* Toronto, 1949. pp. 165-188.)

"From a speech delivered at Cobourg, Monday evening, September 13, 1926. . . . The General Election of that year took place the following day". – p. 165.

—— Hon. Mr. Meighen spoke on industrial evolution before jubilee meeting of firemen and enginemen. (In *Canadian Congress journal*. Ottawa. v. 2, no. 12 (Dec. 1923), pp. 64-74.)

Address delivered at the fiftieth anniversary celebration of the Brotherhood of Locomotive Firemen and Enginemen held December 2, 1923 at the Mount Royal Hotel in Montreal.

Text of address: pp. 70-72.

—— If I am elected? By Rt. Hon. Arthur Meighen. (In *Maclean's*. Toronto. v. 38, no. 19 (Oct. 1, 1925), pp. 29; 44; 48.)

Referring to the federal election held October 29, 1925.

—— The issues as I see them. By Rt. Hon. Arthur Meighen. (In *Maclean's*. Toronto. v. 39, no. 17 (Sept. 1, 1926), pp. 6; 32.)

Relates to the federal election held September 14, 1926.

—— Our plans for Canada. By the Rt. Hon. Arthur Meighen. (In *MacLean's magazine*. Toronto. v. 34, no. 1 (Jan. 1, 1921), pp. 14-15.)

—— Overseas addresses, June—July, 1921. By the Right Hon. Arthur Meighen. Toronto, Musson Book Co. [c1921] 82 p.

—— The price of silver. By Right Honorable Arthur Meighen. (In *Maclean's*. Toronto. v. 44, no. 13 (July 1, 1931), pp. 16; 36; 38.)

—— Simple truths. By Right Honourable Arthur Meighen. (In Club canadien de Québec. *Problèmes de l'heure*. Québec, 1935. pp. 51-65.)

—— Unrevised and unrepented; debating speeches and others. By the Right Honourable Arthur Meighen. With a foreword by M. Grattan O'Leary. Toronto, Clarke, Irwin, 1949. xiii, 470 p.

"Most of the contents of this book are debating speeches . . . a record of the position he (the Author) has taken on public issues during the past four decades of Canadian history." – Author's preface.

MENARD, C. Les lois sociales canadiennes de 1935 (lois de Bennett) [Québec, 1961] 1 v.

Thesis (MA) – Laval University.

Mr. Bennett in the West. Special correspondence of Willisons monthly. (In *Willisons monthly*. Toronto. v. 3, no. 7 (Dec. 1927), p. 254.)

Mr. Bennett issues a call. (In *Canadian comment*. Toronto. v. 4, no. 7 (July 1935), p. 6.)

Relates to the On-to-Ottawa march of the unemployed, which ended in the "Regina riot", July 1, 1935.

Mr. Bennett's lecture tour. (In *Canadian comment*. Toronto. v. 4, no. 1 (Jan. 1935), pp. 6-7.)

Comment on the policies presented by Premier R. B. Bennett.

Mr. Meighen's message. (In *The Canadian forum*. Toronto. v. 2, no. 14 (Nov. 1921), pp. 422-424.)

M. [i.e. Monsieur] Arthur Meighen. (In *L'Action française*. Montréal. v. 14 (août 1925), pp. [83]-87.)

MOORE, HENRY NAPIER Journalism's dean re-enters House. By Napier Moore. (In *Maclean's*. Toronto. v. 39, no. 3 (Feb. 1, 1926), pp. 15; 50-52.)

Concerns Robert Smeaton White, editor-in-chief of the Montreal *Gazette*; Conservative Party Member of Parliament representing the constituency of Mount Royal (Montreal Island).

MORGAN, HAMILTON RICHARDS Still father of House of Commons. R. S. White, MP for Mount Royal. By H. R. Morgan. (In *Saturday night*. Toronto. v. 46, no. 18 (Mar. 14, 1931), p. 5.)

Brief biographical sketch of R. S. White, editor of the *Montreal Gazette*.

MORRISON, ALFRED EUGENE R. B. Bennett and the imperial preferential trade agreement, 1932. [Fredericton, N.B. 1966. 1 v.

Thesis (MA) – University of New Brunswick.

MUIR, NORMA PHILLIPS The unknown Ben-

nett. (In *Saturday night*. Toronto. v. 50, no. 42 (Aug. 24, 1935), p. 5.)

MUNRO, J. K. The rise of Meighen. Being the tale of what happened at Ottawa. (In *MacLean's magazine*. Toronto. v. 33, no. 14 (Aug. 1, 1920), pp. [10]-11.)

NELSON, JOHN Harry Stevens never lost a fight. (In *Maclean's*. Toronto. v. 39, no. 9 (May 1, 1926), pp. 23; 71.)

Concerns Henry Herbert Stevens.

The New budget. Radical changes in taxation and tariffs. Wall substantially raised agaist US. (In *Saturday night*. Toronto. v. 46, no. 30 (June 6, 1931), p. 31.)

Concerns the budget brought down by the Bennett administration.

O'LEARY, MICHAEL GRATTAN Backstage at Ottawa. The candid observer reveals the news behind the news from the capital where the Bennett government faces a momentous parliamentary session. By a Politician with a Notebook. (In *Maclean's*. Toronto. v. 44, no. 4 (Feb. 15, 1931), pp. 5; 42; 44.)

—— Backstage at Ottawa. What with gold, railways, tariffs, unemployment, declining revenue, the waterway and drought relief, Mr. Bennett has certainly had his hands full. By a Politician with a Notebook. (In *Maclean's*. Toronto. v. 44, no. 24 (Dec. 15, 1931), pp. 23; 46-47.)

—— Backstage at Ottawa. By a Politician with a Notebook. (In *Maclean's*. Toronto. v. 45, no. 3 (Feb. 1, 1932), pp. 21; 34-36.)

Concerns, mainly, the taxation policy presented by the government of R. B. Bennett.

—— Backstage at Ottawa. By a Politician with a Notebook. (In *Maclean's*. Toronto. v. 46, no. 12 (June 15, 1933), pp. 13; 26.)

Concerns Prime Minister R. B. Bennett.

—— Backstage at Ottawa. By a Politician with a Notebook. (In *Maclean's*. Toronto. v. 47, no. 12 (June 15, 1934), pp. 12; 44.)

Discusses the opinions of Dr. Watson Sommerville and H. H. Stevens as representative of varying policies within the administration of R. B. Bennett.

—— Backstage at Ottawa. By a Politician with a Notebook. (In *Maclean's*. Toronto. v. 47, no. 18 (Sept. 15, 1934), pp. 18; 41.)

Discusses election pamphlets concerning H. H. Stevens.

—— Backstage at Ottawa. By a Politician with a Notebook. (In *Maclean's*. Toronto.

v. 48, no. 2 (Jan. 15, 1935), pp. 18; 51.)
Comments on R. B. Bennett and the prospect for a federal election.

—— Backstage at Ottawa. By a Politician with a Notebook. (In *Maclean's*. Toronto. v. 48, no. 5 (Mar. 1, 1935), pp. 15; 54.)
Comments on the administration of R. B. Bennett.

—— Backstage at Ottawa. Spotlighting the proposed Bennett-Roosevelt tariff reductions. By a Politician with a Notebook. (In *Maclean's*. Toronto. v. 48, no. 7 (Apr. 1, 1935), pp. 11; 57-58.)

—— Cabinet portrait—Hon. John A. Macdonald. (In *Maclean's*. Toronto. v. 44, no. 8 (Apr. 15, 1931), pp. 16; 93.)
Concerns John Alexander Macdonald, appointed Minister without Portfolio in the federal cabinet August 7, 1930.

—— Cabinet portraits: Hugh Guthrie, Dispenser of Justice; R. J. Manion, in charge of Railways. By M. Grattan O'Leary. (In *Maclean's*. Toronto. v. 43, no. 19 (Oct. 1, 1930), pp. 10; 48; 50.)

—— Cabinet portraits: Hon. E. B. Ryckman, Minister of National Revenue; Hon. Harry Stevens, Minister of Trade and Commerce. By M. Grattan O'Leary. (In *Maclean's*. Toronto. v. 43, no. 20 (Oct. 15, 1930), pp. 11; 85-87.)

—— Cabinet portraits: Sir George Perley, Minister without Portfolio; Hon. C. H. Cahan, Secretary of State. By M. Grattan O'Leary. (In *Maclean's*. Toronto. v. 43, no. 21 (Nov. 1, 1930), pp. 19; 35-38.)

—— Cabinet portraits: Hon. Robert Weir, Minister of Agriculture; Hon. Edgar N. Rhodes, Minister of Fisheries. By M. Grattan O'Leary. (In *Maclean's*. Toronto. v. 43, no. 22 (Nov. 15, 1930), pp. 19; 57-61.)

—— Cabinet portraits: Hon. Arthur Sauvé, Postmaster-General; Hon. H. A. Stewart, Minister of Public Works. By M. Grattan O'Leary. (In *Maclean's*. Toronto. v. 43, no. 23 (Dec. 1, 1930), pp. 15; 35-38.)

—— Cabinet portraits: Hon. Dr. Murray MacLaren, Minister of National Health and Pensions; Hon. Thomas Gerow Murphy, Minister of the Interior. By M. Grattan O'Leary. (In *Maclean's*. Toronto. v. 43, no. 24 (Dec. 15, 1930), pp. 14; 35-36; 40.)

—— Cabinet portraits: Hon. Gideon Robertson, Minister of Labor; Hon. Wesley Gordon, Minister of Immigration and Mines.

By M. Grattan O'Leary. (In *Maclean's*. Toronto. v. 44, no. 1 (Jan. 1, 1931), pp. 19; 32-33.)

—— Cabinet portraits: Hon. Alfred Duranleau, Minister of Marine; Hon. D. M. Sutherland, Minister of National Defense. By M. Grattan O'Leary. (In *Maclean's*. Toronto. v. 44, no. 2 (Jan. 15, 1931), pp. 19; 29-32.)

—— Conservatism's new prophet. What manner of man is the new leader of the Liberal-Conservative Party? By M. Grattan O'Leary. (In *Maclean's*. Toronto. v. 40, no. 22 (Nov. 15, 1927), pp. 3-4; 46.)
Concerns Richard Bedford Bennett.

—— The Foster of long ago. Famous public man began his career as New Brunswick professor. By M. Grattan O'Leary. (In *Saturday night*. Toronto. v. 43, no. 30 (June 9, 1928), p. 2.)
Concerns Sir George Eulas Foster.

—— A Glengarry Macdonell. By M. Grattan O'Leary. (In *Maclean's*. Toronto. v. 44, no. 22 (Nov. 15, 1931), pp. 23; 71-73.)
Concerns Major-General Archibald Hayes Macdonell; a member of the Senate.

—— The last of the old guard. Minister of Finance forty years ago, member of seven Dominion cabinets, Sir George Foster... is a living link with the Dominion's political past. By M. Grattan O'Leary. (In *Maclean's*. Toronto. v. 43, no. 10 (May 15, 1930), pp. 12; 54.)

—— Mr. Bennett: convert or realist? By M. Grattan O'Leary. (In *Maclean's*. Toronto. v. 48, no. 4 (Feb. 15, 1935), pp. 10; 51.)
Concerns R. B. Bennett.

—— Ottawa portraits: Hon. George Black, Speaker of the House of Commons. Hon. Maurice Dupré, Solicitor-General. By M. Grattan O'Leary. (In *Maclean's*. Toronto. v. 44, no. 3 (Feb. 1, 1931), pp. 13; 56-59; 63.)

—— Richard Bedford Bennett. New Conservative leader's salient characteristics as well known in London as in Ottawa. By M. Grattan O'Leary. (In *Saturday night*. Toronto. v. 42, no. 49 (Oct. 22, 1927), p. 5.)

—— What it means to be secretary to the Prime Minister. By M. Grattan O'Leary. (In *Maclean's*. Toronto. v. 44, no. 11 (June 1, 1931), pp. 12; 79.)
Concerns Arthur W. Merriam.

PERRY, ANNE ANDERSON Is versatility an asset? Can a man be a brilliant lawyer, a playwright and a political figure at one and the same time? (In *The Canadian magazine*. Toronto. v. 68, no. 4 (Oct. 1927), pp. 16-17; 41.)
Concerns Charles W. Bell, Conservative MP. for West Hamilton, Ont.

PICKWELL, FREDERICK C. After-thoughts on Winnipeg Convention. Western burnish on the new Liberal-Conservative platform. By F. C. Pickwell. (In *Saturday night*. Toronto. v. 42, no. 49 (Oct. 22, 1927), p. 3.)
Concerns the Conservative leadership convention held in Winnipeg, Manitoba, October 10-12, 1927.

PLUMPTRE, ARTHUR FITZWALTER WYNNE The Bennett proposals. II. Some economic shoals that lie beneath. By A. F. W. Plumptre. (In *Canadian comment*. Toronto. v. 4, no. 2 (Feb. 1935), pp. 5-6.)
Discusses the labour and social legislation presented by the government of R. B. Bennett.

PORTER, G. C. Corner in blue pencils. The most "colorful" episode in the political career of Canada's First Minister. (In *Saturday night*. Toronto. v. 47, no. 4 (Dec. 5, 1931), p. 19.)
Refers to Richard Bedford Bennett.

The Premier and the press. How the new Government leader appears to Canadian editors. (In *MacLean's magazine*. Toronto. v. 33, no. 14 (Aug. 1, 1920), pp. [24]; 40.)
Concerns Arthur Meighen.

The Prime Minister—a close-up. By one who followed him through his recent campaign of speech-making. (In *Saturday night*. Toronto. v. 36, no. 12 (Jan. 15, 1921), p. 5.)
Concerns Arthur Meighen.

RAYMOND, MAXIME The Bennett government and the Canadian Pacific Railway. (In *The Maritime advocate and busy East*. Sackville, N.B. v. 24, no 11 (June 1934), pp. 15; 22.)
Reprinted from the Canadian Liberal monthly.

READE, JOHN COLLINGWOOD A plea for action by Mr. Bennett. Canada must begin readjusting herself to circumstances which she cannot alter. Prices, debts and purchasing power must be brought into just relationship. (In *Saturday night*. Toronto. v. 48, no. 45 (Sept. 16, 1933), pp. [17]; 19; 24.)

RICHER, LEOPOLD Le ministère Bennett et les Canadiens français. (In *L'Action nationale*. Montréal. v. 6 (sept. 1935), pp. [42]-51.)

RIDDELL, NORMAN HAROLD The Bennett New Deal; an essay. [Saskatoon, Sask.] 1967. 1 v.
Thesis (MA)–University of Saskatchewan.

ROBERTSON, GIDEON DECKER Dominion unemployment relief. By Hon. G. D. Robertson, Dominion Minister of Labour. (In Empire Club of Canada. *Addresses*. Toronto. (1931), pp. 26-35.)
Address delivered January 29, 1931.

ROGERS, NORMAN MC LEOD Mr. Ferguson and the constitution. By Norman McL. Rogers. (In *The Canadian forum*. Toronto. v. 11, no. 122 (Nov. 1930), pp. 47-49.)
Discusses the contents of a memorandum by the Hon. Howard Ferguson to Prime Minister R. B. Bennett "on the subject of provincial rights in relation to the amendment of the British North America Act"

ROGERS, ROBERT Breaking into politics. By Hon. Robert Rogers. (In *Maclean's*. Toronto. v. 34, no. 17 (Oct. 1, 1921), pp. 14-15; 30.)

SANDWELL, BERNARD KEBLE Mr. Bennett and the next crisis. By B. K. Sandwell. (In *Saturday night*. Toronto. v. 50, no. 47 (Sept. 28, 1935), p. 3.)

——— Worm's eye view of R. B. By B. K. Sandwell. (In *Saturday night*. Toronto. v. 50, no. 8 (Dec. 29, 1934), p. [1].)
Reviews the book *R. B. Bennett*, by A. D. MacLean. Toronto, Excelsior Pub. Co. [c1934].

SAYWELL, JOHN TUPPER Turning new leaves. By John B. [i.e. T.] Saywell. (In *The Canadian forum*. Toronto. v. 44, no. 527 (Dec. 1964), pp. 211-212.)
A review article of *Arthur Meighen, a biography*, by R. Graham. Toronto, Clarke, Irwin, 1960-65. Vol. 2: And fortune fled (1963).

SCRATCH, JOHN RONALD The editorial reaction of the Alberta press to the Bennett government, 1930-1935. [Edmonton, Alta.] 1968. 1 v.
Thesis (MA) – University of Alberta.

SHERMAN, PATRICK Bennett. By Paddy Sherman. Toronto, McClelland and Stewart [c1966] xii, 316 p.

SKELTON, OSCAR DOUGLAS The Conservative leadership. By O. D. Skelton. (In

Queen's quarterly. Kingston. v. 28 (1920/21), pp. 89-93.)

Brief comments on the retirement of Sir Robert Borden and the assumption of leadership by Arthur Meighen.

SMITH, F. D. L.   Party organization and General McRae. (In *Saturday night*. Toronto. v. 44, no. 6 (Dec. 22, 1928), p. 3.)

Discusses the attempt on the part of General A. D. McRae to build a strong national Conservative Party.

SOMERVILLE, HENRY   Financing by the printing press. If Canadian Inflation Bill causes rise of domestic prices unaccompanied by rise of world prices, increased costs of production will penalize our export trade. (In *Saturday night*. Toronto. v. 49, no. 35 (July 7, 1934), pp. [17]; 24.)

Discusses R. B. Bennett's proposal to finance a program of public works "by means of an increase in the issue of dollar bills unbacked by gold".

SPARKE, QUEEN   Who's next. (In *Maclean's*. Toronto. v. 46, no. 13 (July 1, 1933), pp. 13; 38-39.)

Discusses the national implications of the political machine of Premier George Stewart Henry of Ontario.

Speaker Black; polisher of Parliament's manners. (In *Canadian comment*. Toronto. v. 1, no. 12 (Dec. 1932), p. 11.)

Concerns Hon. George Black, Speaker of the House of Commons.

STEVENSON, JOHN A.   The Canadian political scene. By J. A. Stevenson. (In *Queen's quarterly*. Kingston. v. 38 (1931), pp. 173-182.)

Reviews, in particular, the policies of the Conservative government led by R. B. Bennett.

—— Mr. Meighen's opportunity. By J. A. Stevenson. (In *The Canadian forum*. Toronto. v. 5, no. 51 (Dec. 1924), pp. 74-77.)

STUBBS, ROY ST. GEORGE   Lord Bennett. (In his *Prairie portraits*. Toronto. [c1954] pp. 25-58.)

Concerns Richard Bedford Bennett.

SWIFT, MICHAEL DAVID   R. B. Bennett and the depression, 1930-1935. [Fredericton] 1964. 1 v.

Thesis (MA) – University of New Brunswick.

VINING, CHARLES ARTHUR MC LAREN   Mr. Ferguson. By R. T. L. (In *Maclean's*. Toronto. v. 47, no. 6 (Mar. 15, 1934), p. 8.)

Concerns G. Howard Ferguson, Canadian High Commissioner in London.

—— Mr. Guthrie. By R. T. L. (In *Maclean's*. Toronto. v. 46, no. 22 (Nov. 15, 1933), p. 8.)

Concerns Hugh Guthrie.

—— Mr. Herridge. By R. T. L. (In *Maclean's*. Toronto. v. 46, no. 20 (Oct. 15, 1933), p. 8.)

Concerns William Duncan Herridge.

—— Mr. Rhodes. By R. T. L. (In *Maclean's*. Toronto. v. 46, no. 21 (Nov. 1, 1933), p. 8.)

Concerns Edgar Nelson Rhodes.

—— Senator Meighen. By R. T. L. (In *Maclean's*. Toronto. v. 46, no. 4 (Feb. 15, 1933), p. 8.)

Arthur Meighen was a member of the Senate from 1932 to 1941.

WATKINS, ERNEST   R. B. Bennett; four lives of a Prime Minister. (In *The Atlantic advocate*. Fredericton, N.B. v. 48, no. 12 (Aug. 1958, pp. 74-75.)

—— R. B. Bennett; a biography. London, Secker & Warburg [c1963] 271 p.

Published in Canada: Toronto, Kingswood House [c1963].

WEDDELL, E. C.   The Honourable Grote Stirling, PC. (In Okanagan Historical Society. *Report*. [n.p.] 17th (1953), pp. 9-12.)

Written on the occasion of his death, January 18, 1953.

WHITE, SIR WILLIAM THOMAS   The story of Canada's war finance. By Sir Thomas White. Montreal, Canadian Bank of Commerce [1921] 70 p.

Who's the Tory Moses? Will Guthrie, Rogers, Bennett, Stevens, Cahan or Ferguson don the mantle of Meighen? By a Political warrior retired. (In *Maclean's*. Toronto. v. 40, no. 16 (Aug. 15, 1927), pp. 3-5; 58-59.)

WILBUR, JOHN RICHARD HUMPHREY (ed.) The Bennett New Deal: fraud or portent? Edited by J. R. H. Wilbur. Toronto, Copp Clark [c1968] 250 p. (Issues in Canadian history.)

A selection of readings.

WILBUR, JOHN RICHARD HUMPHREY   H. H. Stevens and R. B. Bennett, 1930-34. By J. R. H. Wilbur. (In *The Canadian historical review*. Toronto. v. 43 (1962), pp. 1-16.)

—— R. B. Bennett as a reformer. By J. R. H. Wilbur. (In Canadian Historical Association. *Historical papers.* [Ottawa] (1969), pp. [103]-111.)

WILLISON, SIR JOHN STEPHEN From month to month. By Sir John Willison. (In *The Canadian magazine of politics, science, art and literature.* Toronto. v. 55 (1920), pp. 337-343.)

Comments on Arthur Meighen and James A. Calder. Brief remarks on the career of Sir Lomer Gouin (pp. 342-343).

WILLISON, MARJORY (MAC MURCHY) LADY Arthur Meighen, Canadian. A study in character. By Marjory MacMurchy. (In *The Canadian magazine of politics, science, art and literature.* Toronto. v. 57 (1921), pp. 108-115.)

WOOLLACOTT, ARTHUR P. "R.B.'s" little weaknesses. (In *Saturday night.* Toronto. v. 45, no. 2 (Nov. 23, 1929), p. 3.)

Anecdotes about the kindness and generosity of R. B. Bennett.

WRIGHT, C. P. Public works policy. (In *The Canadian forum.* Toronto. v. 14, no. 165 (June 1934), pp. 333-336.)

Discusses the policy of the Conservative government.

1935-1948

BALDWIN, R. W. The nation. An impending national loss. (In *Saturday night.* Toronto. v. 54, no. 5 (Dec. 3, 1938), p. 21.)

Comments on Richard Bedford Bennett and his retirement from federal politics.

—— The nation. Meighen re-wins debating title. (In *Saturday night.* Toronto. v. 54, no. 13 (Jan. 28, 1939), p. 5.)

Comments on Arthur Meighen and his attack on government defence policy.

—— The nation. The Tories are the nicest fellows. (In *Saturday night.* Toronto. v. 54, no. 27 (May 6, 1939), p. 5.)

Concerns J. Earl Lawson, H. H. Stevens, and W. A. Walsh.

—— The nation. Meighen appeals to people. By R. W. Baldwin. (In *Saturday night.* Toronto. v. 54, no. 32 (June 10, 1939), p. 5.)

Comments on the conflict between factions within the Conservative Party supporting Arthur Meighen and R. J. Manion.

BANKS, RIDEAU Mothballs for tariff. (In *Saturday night.* Toronto. v. 52, no. 29 (May 22, 1937), p. 4.)

Comments on the tariff policy of the Conservative Party.

—— National affairs. Are we mice or Canadians? (In *Saturday night.* Toronto. v. 52, no. 14 (Feb. 6, 1937), p. 4.)

Comments on R. B. Bennett and his concern for national unity and his desire for constitutional reform.

—— National affairs. Tories talking convention. (In *Saturday night.* Toronto. v. 52, no. 36 (July 10, 1937), p. 5.)

—— Need policy not leader. (In *Saturday night.* Toronto. v. 52, no. 28 (May 15, 1937), p. 4.)

Concerns the federal Conservative Party of Canada.

—— Ottawa letter. Two mystery men. (In *Saturday night.* Toronto. v. 53, no. 14 (Feb. 5, 1938), p. 5.)

Concerns the political activities of H. H. Stevens and W. D. Herridge.

—— Ottawa letter. Lid-lifting day here. (In *Saturday night.* Toronto. v. 53, no. 15 (Feb. 12, 1938), p. 3.)

R. B. Bennett charges that the national Liberal Association ". . . has been conducting a tollgate in connection with government contracts".

—— Ottawa letter. "R.B." says farewell. (In *Saturday night.* Toronto. v. 53, no. 19 (Mar. 12, 1938), p. 4.)

Concerns R. B. Bennett and his announcement to resign as leader of the Conservative Party.

—— Ottawa letter. The new leader—from Quebec? (In *Saturday night.* Toronto. v. 53, no. 20 (Mar. 19, 1938), p. 5.)

Considers candidates for the leadership of the federal Conservative Party, naming Dr. R. J. Manion, William Herridge, and Harry Stevens.

—— Ottawa letter. A light in the window. (In *Saturday night.* Toronto. v. 53, no. 24 (Apr. 16, 1938), p. 4.)

Comments on the forthcoming national leadership convention of the Conservative Party.

—— Ottawa letter. Policy comes first. (In *Saturday night.* Toronto. v. 53, no. 26 (Apr. 30, 1938), p. 4.)

Concerns the "status" of the Conservative Party as a representative of "conservative" opinion in the country.

—— Ottawa letter. Pre-convention. (In *Saturday night.* Toronto. v. 53, no. 32 (June 11, 1938), p. 4.)

Refers to the second national leadership

convention of the Conservative Party held in Ottawa July 5-7, 1938.

—— Ottawa letter. Mr. Bennett stands by. (In *Saturday night*. Toronto. v. 53, no. 35 (July 2, 1938), p. 4.)

Comments on the national leadership convention held by the Conservative Party in Ottawa, July 5-7, 1938, with predictions on the choice of leader: R. B. Bennett or J. Earl Lawson.

—— Ottawa letter. The machine goes into action. (In *Saturday night*. Toronto. v. 53, no. 39 (July 30, 1938), p. 4.)

Concerns the federal Conservative Party machine, directed by Robert Manion.

—— Ottawa sees three rival successors for R. B. (In *Saturday night*. Toronto. v. 52, no. 27 (May 8, 1937), p. 2.)

Refers to R. B. Bennett. The three rivals cited: M. A. MacPherson, Gordon S. Harrington, and W. D. Herridge.

—— Well, he got it. (In *Saturday night*. Toronto. v. 53, no. 37 (July 16, 1938), p. 4.)

Comments on R. J. Manion, elected leader of the federal Conservative Party during the national convention held at Ottawa, July 5-7, 1938.

BENNETT, RICHARD BEDFORD   Canada. An address by Rt. Hon. the Viscount Bennett of Mickleham, Surrey, and of Calgary and Hopewell, Canada. (In Empire Club of Canada. *Addresses*. Toronto. (1942/43), pp. 120-138.)

Address delivered October 13, 1942.

—— Retrospect and prophecy. By Right Honourable R. B. Bennett. (In Empire Club of Canada. *Addresses*. Toronto. (1939 /40), pp. 210-226.)

Address delivered December 21, 1939.

Bennett New Deal under review. Because Mr. King believes in carrying out election promises, the Court performs a painful duty. (In *Canadian comment*. Toronto. v. 5, no. 3 (Mar. 1936), p. [3].)

BIRD, JOHN   This is Bracken. (In *Maclean's*. Toronto. v. 56, no. 3 (Feb. 1, 1943), pp. 5-6; 22.)

Refers to John Bracken.

BLACK, MARTHA LOUISE   My seventy years. By Mrs. George Black, MP for the Yukon. As told to Elizabeth Bailey Price. (In *Chatelaine*. Toronto. v. 10, no. 3—no. 8 (Mar.—Aug. 1937).)

Issued in six instalments.

BRACKEN, JOHN   John Bracken says. Toronto, Oxford University Press, 1944. v, 134 p.

A collection of speeches delivered between December 1942 and October 1944.

—— What do the Progressive Conservatives stand for? By John Bracken as quizzed by Blair Fraser. (In *Maclean's*. Toronto. v. 57, no. 9 (May 1, 1944), pp. 10-11; 50-51; 53-56.)

BRUCE, HERBERT MAXWELL   Prize Conservative platform. (In *Saturday night*. Toronto. v. 54, no. 43 (Aug. 26, 1939), p. 2.)

Text of a program submitted to the Platform Competition held by *Saturday night*. The other winning entries are by R. J. Deachman (Liberal), J. C. Harris (CCF). (See *Saturday night*. Toronto. v. 54, no. 43, p. 3 and v. 54, no. 44, p. 3.)

BUCHANAN, E. C.   Not for the party R. B. stays. (In *Saturday night*. Toronto. v. 52, no. 42 (Aug. 21, 1937), p. 7.)

Concerns R. B. Bennett and his decision to remain as leader of the Conservative Party.

CAMP, DALTON KINGSLEY   The politics of survival. By Dalton K. Camp. (In *The Canadian forum*. Toronto. v. 48, no. 568 (May 1968), pp. 33-34.)

A review article of *The politics of survival; the Conservative Party of Canada, 1939-1945*, by J. L. Granatstein. Toronto, University of Toronto Press, 1967.

CHARLESWORTH, HECTOR WILLOUGHBY   Greatest adventure. By Hector Charlesworth. (In *Saturday night*. Toronto. v. 53, no. 37 (July 16, 1938), pp. [1]; 3.)

Concerns Robert James Manion, elected leader of the federal Conservative Party at the second national leadership convention held at Ottawa July 5-7, 1938.

—— Hon. Earl Rowe. By Hector Charlesworth. (In *Saturday night*. Toronto. v. 52, no. 45 (Sept. 11, 1937), p. 12.)

Concerns William Earl Rowe.

—— Nova Scotia candidate. By Hector Charlesworth. (In *Saturday night*. Toronto. v. 52, no. 20 (Mar. 20, 1937), p. 5.)

A biographical sketch of Gordon Sidney Harrington, considered a possible successor to R. B. Bennett as leader of the Conservative Party

CLAY, CHARLES   John Bracken—the Manitoba enigma. (In *Saturday night*. Toronto. v. 56, no. 16 (Dec. 28, 1940), p. 16.)

COX, COROLYN   Name in the news. Mr.

Bracken's greatest blessing. (In *Saturday night*. Toronto. v. 58, no. 27 (Mar. 13, 1943), p. 2.)

Concerns Gordon Graydon, temporary leader of the Opposition.

—— Name in the news. Building the Prog.-Con. Party. (In *Saturday night*. Toronto. v. 59, no. 13 (Dec. 4, 1943), p. 2.)

A biographical sketch of Richard Albert Bell, National Director of the Progressive Conservative Party.

—— Name in the news. Diefenbaker knows where he is going, and it's a long way. (In *Saturday night*. Toronto. v. 59, no. 34 (Apr. 29, 1944), p. 2.)

Concerns John George Diefenbaker.

—— Name in the news. Duplessis's strong man was a Bennett thirty-day minister. (In *Saturday night*. Toronto. v. 60, no. 10 (Nov. 11, 1944), p. 2.)

Concerns Onésime Gagnon.

CRAIG, THELMA   Ottawa view. Women at the convention. (In *Saturday night*. Toronto. v. 64, no. 1 (Oct. 9, 1948), p. 4.)

Concerns women at the Progressive Conservative leadership convention in 1948, including Hilda Hesson, Iva Campbell Fallis, etc.

DEACHMAN, ROBERT JOHN   The proper functions of government. By R. J. Deachman. (In *The Maritime advocate and busy East*. Sackville, N.B. v. 27, no. 10 (May 1937), pp. 11-12.)

Comments on views advanced by W. D. Herridge.

DEXTER, GRANT   Manitoba's Bracken. (In *Maclean's*. Toronto. v. 54, no. 11 (June 1, 1941), pp. 12; 47-48.)

Concerns John Bracken, Premier of Manitoba.

DREW, GEORGE ALEXANDER   Canada's armament mystery! "Canadians who may be called upon for sacrifice have a right to know . . ." What lies behind the Bren machine gun contract. By Lieut.-Col. George A. Drew. (In *Maclean's*. Toronto. v. 51, no. 17 (Sept. 1, 1938), pp. 8-9; 32-35.)

For a comment on the above, see The truth about the Bren gun article, by H. T. Hunter. (In *Maclean's*. Toronto. v. 52, no. 13 (July 1, 1939), pp. 8-9; 28-29.)

—— Drew stands by charges. Author of Bren gun article testifies before Public Accounts Committee. (In *Maclean's*. Toronto. v. 52, no. 14 (July 15, 1939), pp. 10; 36-37.)

Reference is to the article: Canada's armament, by G. A. Drew. (In *Maclean's*. Toronto. v. 51, no. 17 (1938), pp. 8-9; 32-35.)

The above consists of extracts from Colonel Drew's statements to the Public Accounts Committee.

—— Our bow-and-arrow army. "Canadian land forces have not a single piece of post-war fighting equipment." By Lieut.-Col. George A. Drew. (In *Maclean's*. Toronto. v. 49, no. 10 (May 15, 1936), pp. 19; 54-55; 57-58.)

Lieut.-Col. Drew discusses possible government solutions.

EGGLESTON, WILFRID   Ottawa letter. National organization shake-up if PC's lose York-Sunbury. (In *Saturday night*. Toronto. v. 63, no. 6 (Oct. 11, 1947), p. 8.)

Concerns the York-Sunbury by-election held October 21, 1947.

—— Ottawa letter. After by-elections, Ontario vote PC's study federal future. (In *Saturday night*. Toronto. v. 63, no. 36 (June 12, 1948), p. 8.)

—— Ottawa view. Mr. Bracken steps down. (In *Saturday night*. Toronto. v. 63, no. 43 (July 31, 1948), p. 4.)

Concerns John Bracken.

—— Ottawa view. Long or short PC plan? (In *Saturday night*. Toronto. v. 63, no. 51 (Sept. 25, 1948), p. 4.)

Concerns the fourth national leadership convention of the Progressive Conservative Party held at Ottawa September 30-October 2, 1948. George Drew was elected as party leader.

FLAHERTY, FRANCIS   A Conservative philosophy. By Francis Flaherty. (In *Saturday night*. Toronto. v. 58, no. 2 (Sept. 19, 1942), pp. 10-11.)

Refers to the conference held by the Conservative Party at Port Hope, Ont., September 5-7, 1942.

FRASER, BLAIR   Backstage at Ottawa. What's Drew up to? By a Man with a Notebook. (In *Maclean's*. Toronto. v. 61, no. 11 (June 1, 1948), p. 13.)

Concerns Premier George Drew.

—— Backstage at Ottawa. Exit Bracken, head high. By the Man with a Notebook. (In *Maclean's*. Toronto. v. 61, no. 17 (Sept. 1, 1948), pp. 15; 67.)

Discusses the resignation of John Bracken as leader of the Conservative Party.

—— Bracken the leader. (In *Maclean's*.

Toronto. v. 57, no. 9 (May 1, 1944), pp. 10; 42-44; 46.)

Concerns John Bracken.

—— Who's the opposition? Here's a revealing close-up of Bracken & Co. in action. On their shoulders rest Progressive Conservative hopes. (In *Maclean's*. Toronto. v. 60, no. 7 (Apr. 1, 1947), pp. 21; 52; 54-56.)

GARDINER, FREDERICK G.   Labor relations and the Conservative Party. (In *Saturday night*. Toronto. v. 58, no. 1 (Sept. 12, 1942), p. 6.)

GOBEIL, SAMUEL   The Conservatives and the province of Quebec. By the Hon. S. Gobeil. (In *Saturday night*. Toronto. v. 57, no. 18 (Jan. 10, 1942), p. 6.)

—— Wanted: a party to restore order. By the Hon. S. Gobeil. (In *Saturday night*. Toronto. v. 58, no. 12 (Nov. 28, 1942), pp. 6-7.)

Concerns the Conservative Party.

GOLDEN, LOU L. L.   Conservative Party—which way? By L. L. L. Golden. (In *Saturday night*. Toronto. v. 55, no. 25 (Apr. 20, 1940), p. 10.)

—— The return of Mr. Homuth. By L. L. L. Golden. (In *Saturday night*. Toronto. v. 54, no. 14 (Feb. 4, 1939), p. 8.)

Concerns Karl Homuth, MP for South Waterloo.

—— Stop-gap leader. By L. L. L. Golden. (In *Saturday night*. Toronto. v. 55, no. 33 (June 15, 1940), p. 9.)

Concerns Richard Burpee Hanson, House Leader of the Conservative Party.

Goodbye dominion status. (In *The Canadian forum*. Toronto. v. 16, no. 194 (Mar. 1937), pp. 6-7.)

Discusses a judgment handed down by the Privy Council on a reform measure presented by R. B. Bennett.

GRANATSTEIN, JACK LAWRENCE   The Conservative Party and conscription in the second World War. By Jack L. Granatstein. (In Canadian Historical Association. *Historical papers presented at the annual meeting* [Ottawa] (1967), pp. [130]-148.)

—— The Conservative Party of Canada, 1939-1945. [Durham, N.C.] 1966 [c1967] x, 377 leaves.

Thesis (PH D) – Duke University.

—— The politics of survival: the Conservative Party of Canada, 1939-1945. By J.

L. Granatstein. [Toronto] University of Toronto Press [c1967] ix, 231 p.

"A select bibliography": pp. [215]-222.

GREEN, HOWARD   Should we send the Japs back? Yes says Howard Green, MP. (In *Maclean's*. Toronto. v. 56, no. 23 (Dec. 1, 1943), pp. 12; 34-35.)

HALLETT, MARY ELIZABETH   W. D. Herridge and the New Democracy movement. [Kingston, Ont., 1964] vi, 182 leaves.

Thesis (MA) – Queen's University.

HEBB, ANDREW   Storms brewing. (In *The Canadian forum*. Toronto. v. 28, no. 334 (Nov. 1948), pp. [169]-170; 173-174.)

Concerns George Alexander Drew, Dominion leader of the Progressive Conservative Party.

HEIGHINGTON, WILFRID   A Conservative cook book. (In *Saturday night*. Toronto. v. 58, no. 7 (Oct. 24, 1942), p. 12.)

Argues that "what the Conservative Party needs is not so much platform planks as trustworthiness".

HERRIDGE, WILLIAM DUNCAN   Some Canadian problems. By Major the Hon. W. D. Herridge. (In Canadian Club of Toronto. *Addresses*. Toronto. (1936/37), pp. 121-139.)

Address delivered November 16, 1936.

HUNTER, HORACE T.   The truth about the Bren gun article. (In *Maclean's*. Toronto. v. 52, no. 13 (July 1, 1939), pp. 8-9; 28-29.)

Replies to the article Canada's armament mystery! By G. A. Drew. (In *Maclean's*. Toronto. v. 51, no. 17 (Sept. 1, 1938), pp. 8-9; 32-35.)

JACKMAN, HENRY RUTHERFORD   The Canadian war effort—a Conservative point of view. By H. R. Jackman, MP. (In *The Canadian spokesman*. Ottawa. v. 1, no. 1 (Jan. 1941), pp. [23]-30.)

KNOWLES, R. E.   Tory leader? By R. E. Knowles, Jr. (In *Saturday night*. Toronto. v. 51, no. 18 (Mar. 7, 1936), p. 12.)

Concerns William Earl Rowe.

KNOX, WILLIAM   Now the Progressive Conservatives choose a leader. (In *Saturday night*. Toronto. v. 63, no. 50 (Sept. 18, 1948), pp. 2-3. ports.)

Refers to the fourth national leadership convention of the Progressive Conservative Party held at Ottawa, September 30-October 2, 1948.

LUCE, P. W.   Watch Howard Green of B.C.—he's on the way up. (In *Saturday night*.

Toronto. v. 58, no. 10 (Nov. 14, 1942), p. 13.)

MC ANN, AIDA B. Two sons of New Brunswick are now lords of the realm. (In *The Maritime advocate and busy East*. Sackville, N.B. v. 32, no. 3 (Oct. 1941), pp. 5-9; 30.)

Concerns R. B. Bennett and Lord Beaverbrook.

MAC DONALD, HENRY BAYNE The Conservative revival. (In *Saturday night*. Toronto. v. 57, no. 23 (Feb. 14, 1942), p. 20.)

MACDONNELL, JAMES MC KERRAS Amateurs in politics. By J. M. Macdonnell. (In *Queen's quarterly*. Kingston. v. 49 (1942), pp. [385]-393.)

A discussion of the proceedings of the conference held by the Conservative Party at Port Hope, Ont. September 5-7, 1942.

—— Can we return to freedom? By J. M. Macdonnell. (In *Saturday night*. Toronto. v. 57, no. 44 (July 11, 1942), pp. 6-7.)

"This is the first of two articles on the party system and the relation of the Conservative Party in Canada to that system. ..."

—— A Conservative Party is essential in Canada. By J. M. Macdonnell. (In *Saturday night*. Toronto. v. 57, no. 45 (July 18, 1942), p. 6.)

The second of two articles.

—— The Conservatives and a new National Policy. By J. M. Macdonnell. (In *Saturday night*. Toronto. v. 57, no. 46 (July 25, 1942), p. 6.)

MAC KAY, ARMOUR The men of 1914-18 begin to take over. (In *Saturday night*. Toronto. v. 58, no. 17 (Jan. 2, 1943), p. 10.)

Concerns the third national leadership convention of the Progressive Conservative Party held at Winnipeg, December 9-11, 1942.

—— Progressive Conservatives on the middle road. (In *Saturday night*. Toronto. v. 58, no. 15 (Dec. 19, 1942), p. 16.)

—— The Winnipeg result gives us time to think. (In *Saturday night*. Toronto. v. 58, no. 18 (Jan. 9, 1943), p. 14.)

Concerns the Conservative Party convention held in Winnipeg, December 9-11, 1942. John Bracken was elected as leader.

MACKAY, KATE E. Why I intend to vote for the Progressive Conservatives. (In

Chatelaine. Toronto. v. 18, no. 6 (June 1945), pp. 13; 39; 79.)

Relates to the federal election held June 11, 1945.

MANION, ROBERT JAMES Life is an adventure. By the Honourable R. J. Manion. Toronto, Ryerson Press [1936] 360 p.

An autobiography.

MARSHALL, HENRY LYNN Sunshine or shadow for Conservative Party? (In *Saturday night*. Toronto. v. 58, no. 8 (Oct. 31, 1942), pp. 17a-17b.)

Meighen redivivus. (In *The Canadian forum*. Toronto. v. 21, no. 252 (Jan. 1942), pp. 293-295.)

MOWAT, ANGUS MC GILL I am a Conservative. By A. M. Mowat. (In *Saturday night*. Toronto. v. 51, no. 45 (Sept. 12, 1936), p. [1].)

Ironical in tone.

NAUGLER, HAROLD ADELBERT R. J. Manion and the Conservative Party, 1938-1940. [Kingston, Ont., 1966] iv, 354 leaves.

Thesis (MA) – Queen's University.

NICOLET, JEAN A l'assaut de la Confédération. (In *L'Action nationale*. Montréal. v. 27 (mars 1946), pp. [199]-203.)

Discusses proposals set forth by George Drew on federal-provincial relations.

O'HEARN, D. P. Has Premier Drew the capacity to lead a party nationally? (In *Saturday night*. Toronto. v. 63, no. 34 (May 29, 1948), pp. 6-7.)

—— Is Premier Drew ready to jump into John Bracken's shoes? (In *Saturday night*. Toronto. v. 63, no. 30 (May 1, 1948), pp. 6-7.)

O'LEARY, MICHAEL GRATTAN After Bennett what? "If the Conservative Party . . . can neither comprehend the present nor glimpse the future, its fate must be certain—and deserved—extinction." By M. Grattan O'Leary. (In *Maclean's*. Toronto. v. 50, no. 10 (May 15, 1937), pp. 11; 68-69.)

—— Backstage at Ottawa. By a Politician with a Notebook. (In *Maclean's*. Toronto. v. 50, no. 1 (Jan. 1, 1937), pp. 19; 32.)

Discusses, mainly, the possible retirement of R. B. Bennett from the leadership of the Conservative Party.

—— Backstage at Ottawa. By a Politician with a Notebook. (In *Maclean's*. Toronto. v. 51, no. 16 (Aug. 15, 1938), pp. 8; 35.)

Comments on the Conservative leadership convention held in Ottawa July 5-7, 1938.

—— Can the Conservatives come back? By M. Grattan O'Leary. (In *Maclean's*. Toronto. v. 55, no. 23 (Dec. 1, 1942), pp. 11; 38-40.)

—— Dr. Manion. A word portrait of the new leader of the national Conservative Party. By M. Grattan O'Leary. (In *Maclean's*. Toronto. v. 51, no. 16 (Aug. 15, 1938), pp. 9; 36.)

Concerns R. J. Manion elected as leader at the national convention held at Ottawa July 5-7, 1938.

—— Who'll succeed Bennett? By M. Grattan O'Leary. (In *Maclean's*. Toronto. v. 51, no. 9 (May 1, 1938), pp. 10; 52.)

POLITICUS   John Bracken of Manitoba is feeling his oats. By Politicus. (In *Saturday night*. Toronto. v. 56, no. 10 (Nov. 16, 1940), p. 4.)

—— National affairs. Can the Conservative Party be revived? By Politicus. (In *Saturday night*. Toronto. v. 56, no. 4 (Oct. 5, 1940), p. 8.)

—— National affairs. John Bracken gives his answer. By Politicus. (In *Saturday night*. Toronto. v. 56, no. 22 (Feb. 8, 1941), p. 8.)

Refers to John Bracken's opinion on the Report of the Royal Commission on Dominion-Provincial Relations (the Rowell-Sirois report).

—— National affairs. Free advice. Part III. By Politicus. (In *Saturday night*. Toronto. v. 56, no. 34 (May 3, 1941), pp. 10-11.)

To the Conservative Party, with reference to its function as the party in opposition.

PORTER, DANA   Conservative leadership material: Sidney Smith. (In *Saturday night*. Toronto. v. 57, no. 6 (Oct. 18, 1941), p. 16.)

Concerns Sidney Earle Smith.

—— Drew as Conservative chief. (In *Saturday night*. Toronto. v. 57, no. 5 (Oct. 11, 1941), pp. 14-15.)

Refers to George Alexander Drew.

—— The future of a Conservative Party. (In *University of Toronto quarterly*. [Toronto] v. 12 (1942/43), pp. 191-199.)

—— How to find a Tory leader. (In *Saturday night*. Toronto. v. 56, no. 48 (Aug. 9, 1941), p. 7.)

—— Macdonnell as Conservative leader.

(In *Saturday night*. Toronto. v. 57, no. 7 (Oct. 25, 1941), pp. 12-13.)

Concerns James McKerras Macdonnell.

—— Murdoch MacPherson as Conservative leader. (In *Saturday night*. Toronto. v. 57, no. 4 (Oct. 4, 1941), pp. 6-7.)

—— Reconstruction of the Conservative Party. (In *Saturday night*. Toronto. v. 56, no. 46 (July 26, 1941), p. 7; v. 56, no. 47 (Aug. 2, 1941), p. 14.)

PRO AND CON   The Tories call a doctor. By Pro and Con. (In *The Canadian magazine*. Toronto. v. 90, no. 2 (Aug. 1938), pp. 8-9; 37.)

Pro and Con are two staff members of *Canadian magazine*. Cf. Editor's note.

An analysis of the Conservative Party National Convention held at Ottawa, July 5-7, 1938 and the selection of R. J. Manion as leader of the Party.

The Pro and con leader. (In *The Canadian forum*. Toronto. v. 24, no. 281 (June 1944), pp. 53-54.)

Examines John Bracken as he is presented through *Maclean's* magazine.

The Pro and con party; an editorial. (In *The Canadian forum*. Toronto. v. 22, no. 264 (Jan. 1943), pp. 293-294.)

Analyses the general policies of the Progressive Conservative Party.

Red Herridge or red herring? (In *The Canadian forum*. Toronto. v. 19, no. 223 (Aug. 1939), pp. 139-140.)

An editorial comment on W. D. Herridge and the New Democracy movement.

RITCHIE, DAVID LAKIE   Looking backward. By D. L. Ritchie. (In *The New age*. Montreal. v. 2, no. 12 (Mar. 21, 1940), p. 6.)

Concerns Robert Manion as Opposition leader of the Conservative Party.

ROBERTS, LESLIE   Have they the answer? (In *The Canadian magazine*. Toronto. v. 89, no. 5 (May 1938), pp. 8; 18.)

An analysis of the prospective Conservative Party National Convention with an appraisal of Conservative Party policies.

SANDWELL, BERNARD KEBLE   The editor's chair. A great figure retires. By B. K. Sandwell. (In *Saturday night*. Toronto. v. 58, no. 15 (Dec. 19, 1942), p. [18].)

Concerns Arthur Meighen.

—— From the editor's chair. "Without Bracken they had nothing." By B. K. Sandwell. (In *Saturday night*. Toronto. v. 58, no. 16 (Dec. 26, 1942), p. 14.)

—— From week to week. The Conservative Party. By B. K. Sandwell. (In *Saturday night*. Toronto. v. 55, no. 23 (Apr. 6, 1940), p. 3.)

—— From week to week. The new Conservative strategy. By B. K. Sandwell. (In *Saturday night*. Toronto. v. 57, no. 11 (Nov. 22, 1941), pp. 20-21.)

SCOTT, FRANCIS REGINALD   The Privy Council and Mr. Bennett's "New Deal" legislation. By F. R. Scott. (In *The Canadian journal of economics and political science*. [Toronto] v. 3 (1937), pp. 234-241.)
Discusses the decisions made by the Judicial Committee of the Privy Council January 28, 1937, upon the constitutional validity of eight reform measures introduced by the government of R. B. Bennett.

SMITH, F. D. L.   Arthur Meighen and the party leadership. (In *Saturday night*. Toronto. v. 57, no. 11 (Nov. 22, 1941), p. 14.)

SMITH, HARRIET DUFF   Mrs. John Bracken. (In *Chatelaine*. Toronto. v. 16, no. 3 (Mar. 1943), pp. 44-45.)
Née Alice Wylie Bruce.

STRANGE, HARRY   Who is this John Bracken? (In *Saturday night*. Toronto. v. 58, no. 51 (Aug. 28, 1943), pp. 12-13.)

SWEEZEY, ROBERT OLIVER   Conservative Party must strengthen its ranks. By R. O. Sweezey. (In *Saturday night*. Toronto. v. 56, no. 28 (Mar. 22, 1941), p. 11.)

VAN GOGH, LUCY   John Bracken the lone wolf. (In *Saturday night*. Toronto. v. 58, no. 5 (Dec. 19, 1942), p. 36.)

WAYLING, THOMAS   John Bracken. (In *New world illustrated*. Montreal. v. 3, no. 12 (Jan. 15, 1943) [i.e. Feb. 1943], p. 38.)
A brief sketch of his career.

Whither the Tories? (In *Canadian comment*. Toronto. v. 6, no. 8 (Aug. 1937), pp. 5-6.)
Brief comment on a trend to the left in the federal Conservative Party.

WHITTAKER, G. C.   The Ottawa letter. Mr. Bracken is a very sensible man. (In *Saturday night*. Toronto. v. 58, no. 15 (Dec. 19, 1942), pp. 8-9.)
Refers to the Conservative Party National Convention held in Winnipeg, December 9-11, 1942; where John Bracken was chosen as leader.

—— The Ottawa letter. Ottawa already reacts to Bracken. (In *Saturday night*. Toronto. v. 58, no. 16 (Dec. 26, 1942), p. 15.)

—— The Ottawa letter. Mr. Bracken helps the war effort. (In *Saturday night*. Toronto. v. 58, no. 18 (Jan. 9, 1943), p. 7.)

—— The Ottawa letter. Mr. Bracken is mighty powerful. (In *Saturday night*. Toronto. v. 58, no. 22 (Feb. 6, 1943), p. 9.)

—— The Ottawa letter. Mr. Bracken sits in the gallery. (In *Saturday night*. Toronto. v. 58, no. 28 (Mar. 20, 1943), p. 8.)

—— The Ottawa letter. Bracken and McTague worrying Ottawa. (In *Saturday night*. Toronto. v. 58, no. 33 (Apr. 24, 1943), p. 8.)
Concerns John Bracken and Charles P. McTague, chairman of the National War Labour Board.

—— The Ottawa letter. Eruption coming in national broadcasting. (In *Saturday night*. Toronto. v. 59, no. 15 (Dec. 18, 1943), p. 8.)

—— The Ottawa letter. Budget talk shows Prog. Cons. are really just a Canadian GOP. (In *Saturday night*. Toronto. v. 59, no. 44 (July 8, 1944), p. 8.)

WILLIAMS, JOHN RYAN   The selection of Arthur Meighen as Conservative Party leader in 1941. By John R. Williams. (In *The Canadian journal of economics and political science*. [Toronto] v. 17 (1951), pp. 234-237.)

WILSON, KENNETH R.   Backstage at Ottawa. By the Man with a Notebook. (In *Maclean's*. Toronto. v. 55, no. 22 (Nov. 15, 1942), pp. 14-15; 55.)
Discusses the forthcoming national convention of the Conservative Party in Winnipeg, December 9-11, 1942.

—— Backstage at Ottawa. By the Man with a Notebook. (In *Maclean's*. Toronto. v. 56, no. 2 (Jan. 15, 1943), pp. 12-13; 36-37.)
Discusses the election of John Bracken as leader of the Progressive Conservative Party at the third national leadership convention held in Winnipeg December 9-11, 1942.

—— Man with a handshake. On one political trip, Gordon Graydon talked with more than 10,000 people in 19,000 miles. (In *Maclean's*. Toronto. v. 56, no. 7 (Apr. 1, 1943), pp. 10; 31-32.)

WOOD, R. C.   The handicaps of Canada's Conservative Party. (In *Saturday night*. Toronto. v. 56, no. 51 (Aug. 30, 1941), p. 8.)

1948-1968

AIKEN, GORDON Toward politics on principle. By Gordon Aiken, MP for Parry Sound-Muskoka. (In *Canada month*. Montreal. v. 7, no. 4 (Apr. 1967), pp. 10-11.)

AITKEN, MARGARET ANNE Fiorenza Drew—wife of the PC leader. By Margaret Aitken. (In *Saturday night*. Toronto. v. 64, no. 35 (June 7, 1949), p. 24.)

—— Hey Ma! I did it, by Margaret Aitken, with Byrne Hope Sanders. Decorations by Grassick. Toronto, Clarke, Irwin, 1953. xiv, 213 p.
An account of the election campaign in the constituency of York-Humber, Ont., for the federal election held August 10, 1953.

ANGERS, FRANCOIS ALBERT Conséquences des nouveaux arrangements fiscaux proposés par le gouvernement Diefenbaker. (In *Canadian public administration*. Toronto. v. 5 (1962), pp. 1-8.)
"Etude d'abord présentée en treizième congrès annuel de l'Institut d'Administration publique du Canada, du 6 au 9 septembre, 1961, à Ste. Foy, Québec."

ARES, RICHARD La déclaration canadienne des droits de l'homme. (In *Relations*. Montréal. 18. année, no 215 (nov. 1958), pp. 291-293.)
Examines the Canadian Bill of Rights advocated and pressed into legislation by John Diefenbaker.

Balloons and ballots. [Toronto, The Telegram, 1967.] 132 p.
On cover: The inside story of Robert Stanfield's victory.

BARKWAY, MICHAEL New Conservative solidarity. Are the PC's coming up? (In *Saturday night*. Toronto. v. 67, no. 7 (Nov. 24, 1951), pp. [11]; 21-22.)

—— Watch that Tory comeback. As PC's recover confidence the public renews its confidence in them. (In *Saturday night*. Toronto. v. 65, no. 28 (Apr. 18, 1950), p. 11.)

BERTON, PIERRE FRANCIS DE MARIGNY George Drew. By Pierre Berton. (In *Maclean's*. Toronto. v. 61, no. 19 (Oct. 1, 1948), pp. 7; 64-68.)
Elected as leader of the Progressive Conservative Party at the fourth national leadership convention held at Ottawa September 30-October 2, 1948.

BIRD, JOHN The Conservative convention.

(In *Canadian commentator*. Toronto. v. 1, no. 1 (Jan. 1957), pp. [1]-2.)
Comments on the Progressive Conservative leadership convention held at Ottawa December 10-12, 1956.

—— The Diefenbaker flair. (In *Canadian commentator*. Toronto. v. 1, no. 10 (Oct. 1957), p. 3.)
General comments on the Diefenbaker administration after four months in office.

—— New challenge for Smith. (In *Canadian commentator*. Toronto. v. 1, no. 9 (Sept. 1957), p. 4.)
Concerns Sidney Smith, Minister of External Affairs in the administration of John Diefenbaker. Traces the growing significance of the Department for External Affairs.

BLACK, EDWIN ROBERT Federal strains within a Canadian party. By Edwin R. Black. (In *Dalhousie review*. Halifax. v. 45, no. 3 (autumn 1965), pp. [307]-323.)
"A paper presented at the annual meeting of the Canadian Political Science Association, Charlottetown, June 12, 1964."
Examines the issue arising between federal Conservative Party leader George Drew and provincial (British Columbia) Conservative Party leader Deane Finlayson.

—— Federal strains within a Canadian party. (In Thorburn, H. G. (ed.) *Party politics in Canada*. Scarborough, Ont. [c1967] pp. [130]-140.)
"Reprinted from the Dalhousie review, XLV, 3, 1965."
Considers the dispute between the federal and provincial factions of the British Columbia Progressive Conservative Association involving federal leader George Drew and provincial leader Deane Finlayson.

BLACKBURN, CLYDE R. Hon. J. A. Brooks, Minister of Veterans Affairs and New Brunswick's representative in the federal cabinet. By Clyde Blackburn. (In *The Atlantic advocate*, Fredericton, N.B. v. 50, no. 9 (May 1960), pp. 57-59.)

—— Hon. George C. Nowlan. (In *The Atlantic advocate*, Fredericton, N.B. v. 50, no. 5 (Jan. 1960), pp. [35]-37.)

BRISBANE, R. M. Feeble defence policy cripples armed forces. (In *Saturday night*. Toronto. v. 73, no. 16 (Aug. 2, 1958), pp. 8-9; 31-32.)
Concerns, mainly, the defence policy of the Progressive Conservative government.

—— Sidney Smith: from college to cabinet.

(In *Saturday night*. Toronto. v. 72, no. 20 (Sept. 28, 1957), pp. 14-15; 47.)

CAMP, DALTON KINGSLEY   Does Canada need the Tories? By Dalton Camp and Blair Fraser. (In *Maclean's*. Toronto. v. 80, no. 9 (Sept. 1967), pp. 22; 79; 82; 84; 87-88.)

—— Gentlemen, players and politicians. By Dalton K. Camp. Toronto, McClelland and Stewart [c1970] 346 p.
". . . first of a two volume work". – Foreword.

—— Reflection on the Montmorency Conference. By Dalton Camp. (In *Queen's quarterly*. Kingston. v. 76 (1969), pp. [185]-199.)
The Progressive Conservative Party held a policy conference at Maison Montmorency in Courville, Que., August 7-10, 1967.

—— Robert Stanfield, the leader and the Party. By Dalton Camp. (In *The Atlantic advocate*. Fredericton, N.B. v. 58, no. 2 (Oct. 1967), pp. 12-13.)

Camp vs. Maloney: a survey of the voting. [Conducted by] Sandra Burt, John English, Peter Lishchynski, Martha Brook, Ronald Freeman, James Pearson. (In *The Canadian forum*. Toronto. v. 46, no. 551 (Dec. 1966), p. 197.)
Results of a survey, carried out by six political science students from the University of Waterloo, during the national leadership convention of the Progressive Conservative Party, held in Ottawa, November 13-16, 1966. The survey gathered information in order to examine the choice of delegates voting in the selection of a party president.

CAMPBELL, MARJORIE WILKINS   The Prime Minister's home town. (In *Maclean's*. Toronto. v. 71, no. 2 (Jan. 18, 1958), pp. 24-25; 36-38.)
Refers to John G. Diefenbaker and Prince Albert, Sask.

CHAMBRE DE COMMERCE DU DISTRICT DE MONTREAL   Mémoire au Très Honorable premier ministre du Canada, M. John George Diefenbaker. November 1957. [Montréal, 1957] 10, xiii, 92 leaves.
Mimeographed.

CHAPIN, MIRIAM   Point of view. Quebec: where are the goldarn Tories? (In *Saturday night*. Toronto. v. 76, no. 22 (Oct. 28, 1961), p. 54.)
Discusses the kind of alliance to be con-

sidered by the federal Conservative Party and Conservatives in Quebec.

CLARK, ROBERT MILLS   The responsibilities of the individual in facing political questions in our society. By Robert M. Clark. (In *Queen's quarterly*. Kingston. v. 71 (1964), pp. [547]-565.)
"A slightly abbreviated version of a speech given on September 9, 1964, in Fredericton, New Brunswick, at the National Conference on Canadian Goals, sponsored by the Progressive Conservative Party."

COATES, ROBERT CARMAN   The night of the knives. By Robert C. Coates. [Fredericton, N.B.] Brunswick Press, 1969. 210 p.
Traces "the events that transpired from 1966 forward" to the downfall of John Diefenbaker as leader of the Progressive Conservative Party and his replacement by Robert Stanfield.

COHEN, MAXWELL ABRAHAM   Howard Green and the direction of Canadian foreign policy. By Maxwell Cohen. (In *Saturday night*. Toronto. v. 74, no. 17 (Aug. 15, 1959), pp. [12]-13; 42.)

COOK, GEORGE RAMSAY   A big thought. By R. C. (In *The Canadian forum*. Toronto. v. 42, no. 506 (Mar. 1963), p. 271.)
A comment on the appointment of John Fisher as chairman of the National Centennial Administration.

—— Dief, Donald and Davie. By Ramsay Cook. (In *The Canadian forum*. Toronto. v. 41, no. 493 (Feb. 1962), p. 243.)
Comments on John Diefenbaker's "cabinet shuffle".

—— The future of Mr. Balcer and the Conservative Party. By Ramsay Cook. (In *The Canadian forum*. Toronto. v. 44, no. 529 (Feb. 1965), p. 245.)
Discusses the approach adopted by Léon Balcer towards the leadership question in the Progressive Conservative Party.

—— A note on Goldwaterism and Diefenbakerism. By Ramsay Cook. (In *The Canadian forum*. Toronto. v. 44, no. 527 (Dec. 1964), pp. 195-196.)

COPPS, EDWIN   Convention report. The Tories are in good heart. (In *Saturday night*. Toronto. v. 74, no. 26 (Dec. 19, 1959), pp. 11-15.)
Discusses a three-day convention held in early December 1959 by the Progressive Conservative Party in Ottawa.

—— Ottawa letter. Minding our own business. (In *Saturday night*. Toronto. v. 74, no. 1 (Jan. 3, 1959), pp. 4-5.)

Discusses the attitude of the Conservative Party government to foreign policy, the Bill of Rights, defence, unemployment, civil service, etc.

—— Ottawa letter. An act of statesmanship. (In *Saturday night*. Toronto. v. 74, no. 6 (Mar. 14, 1959), pp. 24; 27.)

Concerns John Diefenbaker's decision to cancel the Arrow fighter plane contract.

—— Ottawa letter. An earful for the PM. (In *Saturday night*. Toronto. v. 74, no. 8 (Apr. 11, 1959), pp. 28-29.)

Comments on some of the persons recommended to John Diefenbaker for the position of Secretary of State for External Affairs left vacant by the death of Sidney Smith.

—— Ottawa letter. Sanity replaces vanity. (In *Saturday night*. Toronto. v. 74, no. 9 (Apr. 25, 1959), pp. 23-24.)

Discusses the 1959/60 budget brought down by Donald Fleming.

—— Ottawa letter. Wanted: a businessman. (In *Saturday night*. Toronto. v. 74, no. 10 (May 9, 1959), p. 27.)

Comments on Douglas Fisher's criticism of the 1959/60 budget prepared by the Conservative government. Copp argues to include businessmen in the Diefenbaker government.

—— Ottawa letter. Field day for second guessers. (In *Saturday night*. Toronto. v. 74, no. 11 (May 23, 1959), p. 51.)

Discusses the criticism directed toward the White Paper on Defence (a 52-page booklet published by the Minister of National Defence, George Pearkes).

—— Ottawa letter. No Pearsonalities need apply. (In *Saturday night*. Toronto. v. 74, no. 13 (June 20, 1959), p. 48.)

Considers the procedures and reasons for the choice made by John Diefenbaker in appointing Howard Green as Secretary of State for External Affairs.

—— Ottawa letter. Hees—a jolly good fellow. (In *Saturday night*. Toronto. v. 74, no. 14 (July 4, 1959), pp. 25-26.)

Concerns George Hees.

—— Ottawa letter. The importance of being Ernest Bushnell. (In *Saturday night*. Toronto. v. 74, no. 15 (July 18, 1959), pp. 25-26.)

Ernest Bushnell was acting President of the CBC. Concerns repercussions over criticism of John Diefenbaker, expressed by

Tim Creery, on the Preview Commentary program.

—— Ottawa letter. Going John A. one better: old next year. (In *Saturday night*. Toronto. v. 74, no. 19 (Sept. 12, 1959), pp. 38-39.)

Concerns the appointment of David James Walker and Joseph Pierre Sévigny to the cabinet of John Diefenbaker.

—— Ottawa letter. Our peripatetic Prime Minister. (In *Saturday night*. Toronto. v. 74, no. 20 (Sept. 26, 1959), p. 27.)

Concerns John Diefenbaker.

—— Ottawa letter. The Tories test the market. (In *Saturday night*. Toronto. v. 74, no. 22 (Oct. 24, 1959), pp. 45-46.)

Discusses the by-election held Oct. 5, 1959 in the constituency of Russell, Ont., which resulted in the election of a Liberal, Paul Tardif. It had been considered a test for Conservative government policies.

—— Ottawa letter. Diefenbaker's strongest lieutenant. (In *Saturday night*. Toronto. v. 74, no. 23 (Nov. 7, 1959), pp. 37-38.)

Concerns Donald Methuen Fleming.

—— Ottawa letter. The remarkable Mr. Diefenbaker. (In *Saturday night*. Toronto. v. 74, no. 25 (Dec. 5, 1959), pp. 26-27.)

Reviews Diefenbaker's three years as a major political figure.

—— Ottawa letter. The pursuit of publicity and pulling the rug. (In *Saturday night*. Toronto. v. 75, no. 4 (Feb. 20, 1960), pp. 33-34.)

Comments, especially, on John Diefenbaker's flair for publicity.

—— Ottawa letter. Mr. Diefenbaker's unhappy holiday. (In *Saturday night*. Toronto. v. 75, no. 10 (May 14, 1960), pp. 29-30.)

—— Ottawa letter. The postman now rings twice. (In *Saturday night*. Toronto. v. 75, no. 13 (June 25, 1960), pp. [25]-26.)

Concerns William Hamilton, Postmaster General.

—— Ottawa: no one-man government. (In *Saturday night*. Toronto. v. 74, no. 4 (Feb. 14, 1959), pp. 16-17.)

Concerns J. G. Diefenbaker's administration.

—— The session. The Tories need a tonic. (In *Saturday night*. Toronto. v. 74, no. 17 (Aug. 15, 1959), pp. 16-17; 43.)

Reviews the second session of the

twenty-fourth parliament extending from January 15 to July 18, 1959.

CORBETT, EDWARD ANNAND   Sidney Earle Smith. By E. A. Corbett. Toronto, University of Toronto Press, 1961. vi, 72 p.

CROWE, HARRY SHERMAN   "What was heresy in June . . ." By H. S. Crowe and S. F. Wise. (In The Canadian forum. Toronto. v. 37, no. 445 (Mar. 1958), pp. [265]-266.)

The Authors argue that "the major characteristic of the 23rd parliament was a sustained attack by the Diefenbaker government upon the rights of parliament."

DALES, JOHN HARKNESS   Alice in moneyland. By J. H. Dales. (In The Canadian forum. Toronto. v. 39, no. 467 (Dec. 1959), pp. 195-196.)

Comments on the conflict over financial policy between the Diefenbaker administration and the Canadian banks.

DALY, JAMES WILLIAM   A Conservative looks at his party's future. By J. W. Daly. (In Journal of Canadian studies. Peterborough. v. 3, no. 4 (1968), pp. 48-61.)

DEMPSEY, LOTTA   With Mrs. Drew politics is a family affair. (In Chatelaine. Toronto. v. 22, no. 3 (Mar. 1949), pp. 32; 47.)
Refers to Fiorenza Drew.

DE WOLFE, JOHN   Making Canada a great power. (In Canada month. Montreal. v. 7, no. 10 (Oct. 1967), pp. 22-25.)

Outlines a national development policy for the Progressive Conservative Party. The "brainchild" of John de Wolfe, this policy was presented by the Economic Policy subcommittee, under the chairmanship of Russell Keays and John de Wolfe, at the national leadership convention held in Toronto, September 7-9, 1967.

DEXTER, SUSAN   How the Chief lost (and won) the election. When all the votes were in, John Diefenbaker had frustrated the Liberals' demand for a majority and confounded experts who had already counted him out . . . (In Maclean's. Toronto. v. 79, no. 1 (Jan. 1, 1966), pp. 16; 30-32.)

Relates to the results of the federal election held November 8, 1965.

DIEFENBAKER, JOHN GEORGE   Canada—whither? An address by the Rt. Hon. John G. Diefenbaker. (In Empire Club of Canada. Addresses. Toronto. (1967/68), pp. [386]-395.)
Address delivered March 28, 1968.

—— Le citoyen Diefenbaker. Une entrevue exclusive d'Alain Stanké. (In Le Magazine Maclean. Montréal. v. 7, no. 9 (sept. 1967), pp. 17; 40-44.)

—— The Progressive Conservative platform. A climate of progress and prosperity. By the Rt. Hon. John G. Diefenbaker. (In Saturday night. Toronto. v. 77, no. 11 (May 26, 1962), pp. 13-15.)

—— "What I will do when I form a government." By John G. Diefenbaker. (In The Canadian Saturday night. Toronto. v. 78, no. 4 (Apr. 1963), pp. 9; 27.)
Relates to the federal election held April 8, 1963.

DOUPE, JACK H.   The Tory Thinkers' Conference. No challenge to the big-government society. (In Canada month. Montreal. v. 7, no. 9 (Sept. 1967), pp. 12-13.)

Evaluates the conference held by the Progressive Conservative Party at Montmorency Falls, Que., August 7-10, 1967.

EDINBOROUGH, ARNOLD   Mr. Diefenbaker and his "Time-machine". (In Saturday night. Toronto. v. 75, no. 14 (July 9, 1960), pp. 9-11.)

Examines the coverage given to John Diefenbaker in the Canadian edition of Time magazine.

—— National affairs. Tips for Tories. (In Saturday night. Toronto. v. 81, no. 11 (Nov. 1966), p. 11.)

Draws up a hypothetical platform for the National Conservative Party convention, held in Ottawa, November 13-16, 1966.

EGGLESTON, WILFRID   Ottawa view. The PC's new platform. (In Saturday night. Toronto. v. 64, no. 2 (Oct. 16, 1948), p. 4.)

—— Ottawa view. Watch political ripples. Nicolet-Yamaska studies suggest PC odds on Quebec gains. (In Saturday night. Toronto. v. 64, no. 20 (Feb. 22, 1949), p. 4.)

—— Ottawa view. The strategy emerges. Drew revitalized final session but policy awaits testing. (In Saturday night. Toronto. v. 64, no. 28 (Apr. 19, 1949), p. 4.)

—— Ottawa view. CBC and Mr. Drew. Abolition of the licence fee would make CBC dependent. (In Saturday night. Toronto. v. 64, no. 34 (May 31, 1949), p. 4.)

ELLIOTT, BRIAN   Canada's dollar crisis. (In The Marxist quarterly. Toronto. no. 3 (autumn 1962), pp. [3]-25.)
Includes discussion of the finance policy

of the Conservative Party administration and the criticism of that policy by the opposition parties and others.

EMRYS, TREVOR   Ottawa report. The return of Mr. Diefenbaker. (In *Canadian dimension*. Winnipeg. v. 2, no. 2 (Jan./Feb. 1965), p. 5.)

ENGLISH, HARRY EDWARD   The economic consequences of June 10. By H. E. English. (In *The Canadian forum*. Toronto. v. 37, no. 439 (Aug. 1957), pp. 104-105.)
   The Author speculates about some of the general policies of the newly formed Conservative government during the summer of 1957.

FAIRCLOUGH, ELLEN LOUKS   Canadian women as citizens. By the Honourable Ellen L. Fairclough, Secretary of State for Canada. (In Empire Club of Canada. *Addresses*. Toronto. (1957/58), pp. 134-145.)
   Address delivered December 12, 1957.

FARQUHARSON, DUART   The Manitoba election. The optimistic liberalism of Roblin triumphs over cautious conservatism of the Liberals! (In *Canadian commentator*. Toronto. v. 3, no. 6 (June 1959), pp. 5-6.)
   Some consideration is given to the significance for federal politics of the provincial election campaign.

FILLEY, WALTER   The Conservative impasse. (In *The Canadian forum*. Toronto. v. 35, no. 411 (Apr. 1955), pp. [1]; 9-10.)
   Discusses the future of the Progressive Conservative Party in its relation to a Canadian two-party system on the federal level.

——   Elections have consequences. (In *The Canadian forum*. Toronto. v. 37, no. 439 (Aug. 1957), pp. 100-102.)
   An analysis of the strategy adopted by the Progressive Conservative Party in order to become the government.

FISHER, DOUGLAS MASON   Commons comment. By D. M. Fisher. (In *The Canadian forum*. Toronto. v. 37, no. 444 (Jan. 1958), pp. 221-222.)
   A critical presentation of Sydney E. Smith, Secretary of State for External Affairs.

——   Commons comment. By D. M. Fisher. (In *The Canadian forum*. Toronto. v. 40, no. 471 (Apr. 1960), pp. [1]-2.)
   General comments on the parliamentary session with emphasis on the Diefenbaker administration.

——   Commons comment. By D. M. Fisher.

(In *The Canadian forum*. Toronto. v. 40, no. 482 (Mar. 1961), pp. [265]-266.)
   Speculates on the identity of the next possible leader of the Progressive Conservative Party after John Diefenbaker.

FLEMING, DONALD METHUEN   "Distinctive conservatism"; an address. [Ottawa] Progressive Conservative Party of Canada [1956] 15 p. (incl. cover)
   Cover title.
   Address delivered before a meeting of the Progressive Conservative Business Men's Club, Toronto, November 1955.
   Issued also in French.

FORSTER, DONALD F.   Mr. Fleming's election nostrums. (In *The Canadian forum*. Toronto. v. 42, no. 496 (May 1962), pp. [25]-26.)
   General comments on the fiscal policies of the Conservative government as presented in the budget speech delivered by Donald Fleming.

FRANCIS, ANNE   Conservatives prove they can govern. (In *Canadian commentator*. Toronto. v. 2, no. 1 (Jan. 1958), pp. 5-6.)
   Comments on the 23rd parliament under the administration of John Diefenbaker.

——   Diefenbaker's calamitous course. (In *Commentator*. Toronto. v. 8, no. 12 (Dec. 1964), pp. 8-9.)

——   The swirl of rumours around the Conservative Party. (In *Commentator*. Toronto. v. 9, no. 3 (Mar. 1965), pp. 9-11.)

FRANCIS, R. A.   West coast warrior. Tory rebel still fights bureaucracy. (In *Saturday night*. Toronto. v. 68, no. 20 (Feb. 21, 1953), pp. 9; 18.)
   Concerns the Hon. Henry Herbert Stevens.

FRASER, BLAIR   Backstage at Ottawa. Quebec—Drew's problem. By the Man with a Notebook. (In *Maclean's*. Toronto. v. 61, no. 21 (Nov. 1, 1948), pp. 14; 69-70.)

——   Backstage at Ottawa. The needle for Drew—or a boomerang? By the Man with a Notebook. (In *Maclean's*. Toronto. v. 62, no. 3 (Feb. 1, 1949), p. 14.)

——   Backstage at Ottawa. A plug to stop spilt milk. (In *Maclean's*. Toronto. v. 64, no. 6 (Mar. 15, 1951), pp. 5; 63.)
   Discusses a split in the Progressive Conservative Party between the federal headquarters and the Quebec organization.

——   Backstage at Ottawa. The PCs get

spring fever. (In *Maclean's*. Toronto. v. 65, no. 9 (May 1, 1952), pp. 5; 50.)

—— Backstage at Ottawa. How the PCs muffed the Currie report. (In *Maclean's*. Toronto. v. 66, no. 10 (May 15, 1953), pp. 5; 95.)

—— Backstage at Ottawa. Tory luck can only get better. (In *Maclean's*. Toronto. v. 66, no. 19 (Oct. 1, 1953), pp. 6; 77-78.)

—— Backstage at Ottawa. Can Hees "revitalize" the Tories? (In *Maclean's*. Toronto. v. 67, no. 9 (May 1, 1954), pp. 6; 90.)

—— Backstage at Ottawa. Drew goes for the fall jack pot. (In *Maclean's*. Toronto. v. 67, no. 20 (Oct. 15, 1954), pp. 6; 118-119.)
Discusses the question of George Drew's leadership.

—— Backstage at Ottawa. Frost now batting behind Drew. (In *Maclean's*. Toronto. v. 69, no. 9 (Apr. 28, 1956), pp. 8; 105.)
Poses the question "Will Leslie Frost . . . throw his full strength behind George Drew and the national Conservative Party in next year's federal election campaign?"

—— Backstage at Ottawa. Tory dilemma: who can replace Drew? (In *Maclean's*. Toronto. v. 69, no. 22 (Oct. 27, 1956), pp. 8; 101-102.)

—— Backstage at Ottawa. It sounds crazy, but the Tories want a quick defeat in Commons and their opposition won't co-operate. (In *Maclean's*. Toronto. v. 70, no. 15 (July 20, 1957), p. 2.)

—— Backstage at Ottawa. Will the Tories make St. Laurent governor-general to win Quebec? Many Liberals also like the idea. (In *Maclean's*. Toronto. v. 70, no. 17 (Aug. 17, 1957), p. 2.)

—— Backstage at Ottawa. Will Tories' shouting protect our wheat from the Americans' "giveaway" program? (In *Maclean's*. Toronto. v. 70, no. 18 (Aug. 31, 1957), p. 2.)

—— Backstage at Ottawa. Did PC's blunder on immigration? (In *Maclean's*. Toronto. v. 70, no. 19 (Sept. 14, 1957), p. 2.)

—— Backstage at Ottawa. The man who came to dinner. (In *Maclean's*. Toronto. v. 70, no. 21 [i.e. 22] (Oct. 26, 1957), p. 2.)
Discusses the policy of the Diefenbaker government toward Commonwealth trade.

—— Backstage at Ottawa. Our haven from the big bad wolf. (In *Maclean's*. Toronto. v. 70, no. 22 [i.e. 23] (Nov. 9, 1957), p. 2.)
Discusses the Diefenbaker government's first encounter with the American cabinet.

—— Backstage at Ottawa. Trouble for tax men/buddies for bureaucrats. (In *Maclean's*. Toronto. v. 71, no. 2 (Jan. 18, 1958), p. 2.)
Discusses the attitude of the Conservative administration toward the functioning of the Dept. of National Revenue and other government departments.

—— Backstage at Ottawa. Can the PM find jobs for all those MPs? (In *Maclean's*. Toronto. v. 71, no. 9 (Apr. 26, 1958), p. 2.)
Refers to John G. Diefenbaker.

—— Backstage at Ottawa. Where is Quebec's reward for going Tory? (In *Maclean's*. Toronto. v. 71, no. 14 (July 5, 1958), p. 2.)

—— Backstage at Ottawa. Can the Tories play Santa Claus without spurring inflation? (In *Maclean's*. Toronto. v. 71, no. 25 (Dec. 6, 1958), p. 2.)

—— Backstage at Ottawa. Ottawa's big problem: how to solve our money troubles? (In *Maclean's*. Toronto. v. 72, no. 2 (Jan. 17, 1959), p. 2.)

—— Backstage at Ottawa. Under the big top: can cutting costs become a star turn? (In *Maclean's*. Toronto. v. 72, no. 3 (Jan. 31, 1959), p. 2.)
"This year, Finance Minister Donald Fleming has a uniquely difficult task in trying to cut expenditures."

—— Backstage at Ottawa. Throne speech promises: where's all the extra money coming from? (In *Maclean's*. Toronto. v. 72, no. 4 (Feb. 14, 1959), p. 2.)

—— Backstage at Ottawa. Our real defense policy: is it only to keep NATO happy? (In *Maclean's*. Toronto. v. 72, no. 7 (Mar. 28, 1959), p. 2.)

—— Backstage at Ottawa. Quebec's political dilemma: is Diefenbaker outdrawing Duplessis? (In *Maclean's*. Toronto. v. 72, no. 10 (May 9, 1959), p. 2.)

—— Backstage at Ottawa. "Tight money" stages a comeback. What can the Tories do about it? (In *Maclean's*. Toronto. v. 72, no. 13 (June 20, 1959), p. 2.)

—— Backstage at Ottawa. The government's second birthday. A quick inventory of the pros and cons. (In *Maclean's*. Toronto. v. 72, no. 14 (July 4, 1959), p. 2.)

Refers to the government of John G. Diefenbaker.

—— Backstage at Ottawa. Can the Tories streamline parliament? Yes—if Opposition leads. (In *Maclean's*. Toronto. v. 72, no. 19 (Sept. 12, 1959), p. 2.)

—— Backstage at Ottawa. The great tight-money mystery. What's changed since '56? (In *Maclean's*. Toronto. v. 72, no. 20 (Sept. 26, 1959), p. 2.)

—— Backstage at Ottawa. Why Fleming's so busy making enemies: generosity could spell calamity. (In *Maclean's*. Toronto. v. 72, no. 24 (Nov. 21, 1959), p. 2.)

—— Backstage at Ottawa. The reckless good sense of one dedicated backbencher. (In *Maclean's*. Toronto. v. 73, no. 6 (Mar. 12, 1960), p. 2.)

Concerns Edward Nasserden, Conservative MP from Rosthern, Sask.

—— Backstage in Ottawa. The next Tory pitch: "One Canada" and a new nation-binder named Balcer. (In *Maclean's*. Toronto. v. 77, no. 3 (Feb. 8, 1964), pp. 1-2.)

—— Backstage in Ottawa. Blair Fraser says: Now it's the Tories who fear an election. (In *Maclean's*. Toronto. v. 77, no. 24 (Dec. 14, 1964), pp. 2-3.)

—— Backstage at Ottawa. The difference between Keeler and Gerda: Dief knew and Macmillan didn't. (In *Maclean's*. Toronto. v. 79, no. 12 (June 18, 1966), pp. 3-4.)

Comparative remarks on the Gerda Munsinger case in Canada and the Christine Keeler affair in Great Britain.

—— Backstage at Ottawa. Will Fulton's letter to Spence cost him the Tory leadership? (In *Maclean's*. Toronto. v. 79, no. 14 (July 23, 1966), p. 3.)

Concerns Davie Fulton's letter to Justice Wishart Flett Spence, with respect to the inquiry into the Gerda Munsinger scandal.

—— Backstage in Alberta. Is Manning planning to corral Canada's Right? (In *Maclean's*. Toronto. v. 80, no. 5 (May 1967), p. 1.)

Considers "what would happen if Alberta's Premier Ernest Manning were to lead his Social Creditors into the Conservative Party this summer?"

—— Can Diefenbaker fulfill his election

promises? (In *Maclean's*. Toronto. v. 70, no. 18 (Aug. 31, 1957), pp. 18; 36; 38.)

—— Is Diefenbaker running a one-man government? (In *Maclean's*. Toronto. v. 72, no. 6 (Mar. 14, 1959), pp. 13-15; 64-70.)

—— The lone pine of Parliament Hill. (In *Maclean's*. Toronto. v. 72, no. 16 (Aug. 1, 1959), pp. 17; 49-51.)

Concerns Howard Charles Green.

—— The man who'll speak for Canada. (In *Maclean's*. Toronto. v. 70, no. 22 [i.e. 23] (Nov. 9, 1957), pp. 15-17; 79-82.)

Concerns Sidney Earle Smith.

—— The political outlook. Canada: will the Tories rule the decade? (In *Maclean's*. Toronto. v. 72, no. 23 (Nov. 7, 1959), p. [5].)

—— The Tories: 2. Stanfield in Ottawa: The end of obstruction. (In *Maclean's*. Toronto. v. 80, no. 11 (Nov. 1967), pp. 24; 100-101.)

—— Why the Conservatives are swinging to Diefenbaker. (In *Maclean's*. Toronto. v. 69, no. 24 (Nov. 24, 1956), pp. 30; 74-77.)

—— Will Diefenbaker lead the Tories? (In *Maclean's*. Toronto. v. 66, no. 23 (Dec. 1, 1953), pp. [11]; 95-98.)

FULTON, EDMUND DAVIE The Canadian union; future prospects. An address by the Honourable E. Davie Fulton. (In Empire Club of Canada. *Addresses*. Toronto. (1964/65), pp. [62]-73.)

Address delivered November 5, 1964.

—— Priorities for government. By Hon. E. Davie Fulton. (In *Canada month*. Montreal. v. 7, no. 3 (Mar. 1967), pp. 19-21.)

GARNER, HUGH Nova Scotia's "unshrinkable" Stanfield. Dedicated to the development of Nova Scotia, he has no desire to hold a federal cabinet minister's job. (In *Saturday night*. Toronto. v. 72, no. 16 (Aug. 3, 1957), pp. 14-15; 30.)

GELLNER, JOHN Point of view. Wanted: hard facts on national defence. (In *Saturday night*. Toronto. v. 76, no. 24 (Nov. 25, 1961), p. 44.)

Criticism of the defence policy pursued by the Conservative government.

GOLDING, JACK Nova Scotia's Stanfield. Interest mounts in the political future of a Maritime premier. (In *The Atlantic advocate*. Fredericton, N.B. v. 54, no. 1 (Sept. 1963), pp. 19-23.)

A character sketch of Robert Lorne Stanfield. Written with a view to the possibility of a federal political career.

GORDON, DONALD RAMSEY Gloom and good omens. By D. R. Gordon. (In *The Canadian forum*. Toronto. v. 46, no. 551 (Dec. 1966), pp. 194-196.)
A report on the Progressive Conservative Party's national convention held in Ottawa, November 13-16, 1966.

GRAFFTEY, HEWARD Pour une politique positive. [n.p., 1966] 38 p.
Cover title.
Promotes the idea of the Progressive Conservative Party.

GRAHAM, WILLIAM ROGER Can the Conservatives come back? Crisis in our party system. By W. R. Graham. (In *Queen's quarterly*. Kingston. v. 62 (1955), pp. [473]-486.)

GRAY, JOHN Quebec—Diefenbaker's problem. (In *Canadian commentator*. Toronto. v. 1, no. 7 (July 1957), pp. [1]-2.)
Explains the Quebec vote for the Liberal Party in the general elections held June 10, 1957 and its implications for the Conservative administration.

GRENIER, DAVID Will Tory policy cut dollar premium? (In *Saturday night*. Toronto. v. 72, no. 16 (Aug. 3, 1957), pp. 7; 39.)

GUEST, GOWAN T. A Canadian revolution. A new look at the way Canadians want to live, and how they think and feel about their governments. (In *Canada month*. Montreal. v. 4, no. 10 (Oct. 1964), pp. 21-28.)
A statement of Conservative political philosophy.

—— Perspicacity without perspective. (In *Commentator*. Toronto. v. 7, no. 12 (Dec. 1963), pp. 17-18.)
A review article of *Renegade in power; the Diefenbaker years*, by P. C. Newman. Toronto, McClelland and Stewart [c1963].

—— Wanted—new thinking on Canadian conservatism. A letter to the editor by a prominent Conservative makes a plea for fresh thinking on the party's traditional role in Canada. (In *Commentator*. Toronto. v. 7, no. 6 (June 1963), pp. 21-22.)
"The author . . . served as Executive Assistant to Prime Minister John Diefenbaker."

GZOWSKI, PETER Neither party can win

here, but the Tories can lose. (In *Maclean's*. Toronto. v. 75, no. 6 (Mar. 24, 1962), p. 66.)
"Quebec report".
Concerns the position of the federal Conservative Party in Quebec with regard to the general elections held June 18, 1962.

HAMILTON, ALVIN Remembering a good friend. By Hon. Alvin Hamilton. (In *Canada month*. Montreal. v. 9, no. 3 (Mar. 1969), p. 20.)
Written on the occasion of the death of Senator Wallace McCutcheon.

HARBRON, JOHN DAVISON The Conservative Party and national unity. By John D. Harbron. (In *Queen's quarterly*. Kingston. v. 69 (1962), pp. [347]-360.)

HARKNESS, DOUGLAS SCOTT The defence of the free world: Canada's role. By Hon. Douglas S. Harkness, MP. (In *Canada month*. Montreal. v. 6, no. 12 (Dec. 1966), pp. 10-12.)

HARTLE, DOUGLAS Pre-budget horrors. (In *The Canadian forum*. Toronto. v. 38, no. 458 (Mar. 1959), pp. 266-267.)
Discusses the fiscal policies of the Minister of Finance, Donald Fleming.

HOCKIN, THOMAS ALEXANDER The unmaking of a party leader. By Thomas Hockin. (In *Commentator*. Toronto. v. 10, no. 12 (Dec. 1966), pp. 14-16.)
Concerns John Diefenbaker.

HULL, RAYMOND Davie Fulton of Kamloops. The man who wants to be BC's Premier. (In *Canada month*. Montreal. v. 3, no. 5 (May 1963), pp. 17-18.)

—— Point of view. Let's have conservative Conservatism. (In *Saturday night*. Toronto. v. 75, no. 23 (Nov. 12, 1960), p. 60.)
Laments that "there is no effective conservative party in Canada".

HUTTON, ERIC Robert Stanfield: the Tory who wouldn't stay dead. (In *Maclean's*. Toronto. v. 70, no. 5 (Mar. 2, 1957), pp. 20; 40-43.)

IRVING, JOHN ALLAN Capitalism: a brief for Tory radicals. By John A. Irving. (In *Saturday night*. Toronto. v. 74, no. 24 (Nov. 21, 1959), pp. 22-23.)
Discusses the influence of Raymond Miller's ideas on John Diefenbaker.

JEWETT, PAULINE MAE Mr. Diefenbaker's proposed Bill of Rights. By Pauline Jewett. (In *The Canadian forum*. Toronto. v. 38, no. 455 (Dec. 1958), pp. 199-201.)

JOHNS, H. D. Why Canadians voted Conservative. (In *Saturday night*. Toronto. v. 72, no. 17 (Aug. 17, 1957), pp. 7; 38-39.)
Considers the results of the federal election held June 10, 1957.

JOHNSTONE, KEN The comedian who made the House of Commons. (In *Maclean's*. Toronto. v. 70, no. 20 (Sept. 28, 1957), pp. 34-35; 107-110.)
Concerns John Pratt.

KELLY, FRASER Labor Minister Starr—Service at the cleaner's shop. (In *Saturday night*. Toronto. v. 73, no. 13 (June 21, 1958), pp. [14-15]; 39-40.)

KETTLE, JOHN Dalton Camp. (In *Canada month*. Montreal. v. 6, no. 11 (Nov. 1966), pp. 14-19.)
A *Canada month* profile.

—— Donald Fleming. (In *Canada month*. Montreal. v. 7, no. 8 (Aug. 1967), pp. 22-26.)
A *Canada month* profile.

—— Hon. M. Wallace McCutcheon. (In *Canada month*. Montreal. v. 7, no. 6 (June 1967), pp. 14-18.)
A *Canada month* profile.

—— Hon. Robert Stanfield. (In *Canada month*. Montreal. v. 8, no. 5 (May 1968), pp. 14-19.)
A *Canada month* profile.

—— Hon. Roland Michener. (In *Canada month*. Montreal. v. 6, no. 10 (Oct. 1966), pp. 17-19.)
A *Canada month* profile.

—— Joseph Sedgwick. (In *Canada month*. Montreal. v. 6, no. 5 (May 1966), pp. 9-13.)
A *Canada month* profile.
Discusses J. Sedgwick's political activities and connections with the Conservative Party.

—— What they *should* have heard at Fredericton. By J. K. (In *Canada month*. Montreal. v. 4, no. 10 (Oct. 1964), p. 20.)
An introduction to "A Canadian revolution", by Gowan T. Guest (pp. 21-28). Refers to a Conference on Canadian Goals, organized by Dalton Camp, and held in the Chemistry Building at the University of New Brunswick in Fredericton, September 9-12, 1964.

KIERAN, JON W. Unemployment crisis: how will the Tories weather the winter? (In *Saturday night*. Toronto. v. 72, no. 25 (Dec. 7, 1957), pp. 7; 41-42.)

LAURENDEAU, ANDRE André Laurendeau commente l'actualité politique. Mal représentés, les Québécois se détournent d'Ottawa. (In *Le Magazine Maclean*. Montréal. v. 2, no. 5 (mai 1962), p. 3.)
Concerns Quebec representation in the government of John Diefenbaker.

—— Spécial élections: Laurendeau. Le Québec se paie une escapade avec Dief, puis une fugue avec Réal Caouette. Va-t-il cette fois s'installer dans l'aventure? (In *Le Magazine Maclean*. Montréal. v. 3, no 4 (avril 1963), pp. 1-2.)

LEFOLII, KEN Can these men run Canada better? (In *Maclean's*. Toronto. v. 75, no. 20 (Oct. 6, 1962), pp. 15; 75-77; 80-82.)
Concerns George Nowlan and M. W. McCutcheon.

LEVITT, MORTIMER Drew-Duplessis alliance. (In *The Canadian forum*. Toronto. v. 28, no. 337 (Feb. 1949), pp. 251-252.)

LIND, P. Davie Fulton's campaign for leadership, 1967. [Rochester, N.Y., 1968] 1 v.
Thesis (MA) – University of Rochester.

LOCKE, JEANNINE Young John Diefenbaker; from the family album. (In *Chatelaine*. Toronto. v. 31, no. 7 (July 1958), pp. 12-13; 39-42.)

LONG, MARCUS Advice to the Conservatives. (In *Canadian commentator*. Toronto. v. 1, no. 1 (Jan. 1957), p. 11.)

—— Mr. Diefenbaker's great power. (In *Canadian commentator*. Toronto. v. 2, no. 4 (Apr. 1958), pp. 3-4.)
Discusses John Diefenbaker's proposed Bill of Rights with its implications for Quebec and the development of strong nationalistic attitudes toward the United States.

—— The new minister. By M. L. (In *Canadian commentator*. Toronto. v. 1, no. 9 (Sept. 1957), p. 3.)
Concerns Sidney Smith, Minister of External Affairs.

LOUGHEED, WILLIAM FOSTER The Baby Budget. New policy reflects conservative principles. By W. F. Lougheed. (In *Canadian commentator*. Toronto. v. 5, no. 1 (Jan. 1961), pp. 18-20.)

—— No panacea for unemployment. Mr. Fleming has produced the best budget in four years—but not a major job-creator. By W. F. Lougheed. (In *Canadian commentator*. Toronto. v. 5, no. 7 (July—Aug. 1961), pp. 10-12.)

LYON, PEYTON VAUGHN Howard Green's

strength and weaknesses. His Sunday school teacher's role in external affairs is not enough . . . By Peyton V. Lyon. (In *The Canadian commentator*. Toronto. v. 6, no. 2 (Feb. 1962), pp. 6; 17.)

MC COOK, JAMES Four men and their party: Leon Balcer, John G. Diefenbaker, Donald M. Fleming, E. Davie Fulton. [Ottawa, Ottawa Journal, 1956] 15 p.
Cover title.
Reprinted from the *Ottawa Journal*, October 27; November 3, 10 and 24, 1956.

MACDONALD, HUGH IAN Challenge to Conservatives. By H. I. Macdonald. (In *Canadian commentator*. Toronto. v. 3, no. 1 (Jan. 1959), pp. 2-4.)
Part one.
The Author proposes to "look backward at the record of the past eighteen months in an attempt to diagnose policy symptoms".

—— Challenge to Conservatives. By H. I. Macdonald. (In *Canadian commentator*. Toronto. v. 3, no. 2 (Feb. 1959), pp. 8-10.)
Part two.
Anticipates certain problems, especially economic, to concern the Conservative government.

—— Churchill, Coyne and Fleming. Our "exotic economic patterns" reflected in confused controversy. By H. I. Macdonald. (In *Canadian commentator*. Toronto. v. 4, no. 6 (June 1960), pp. 10-12.)

—— First Conservative budget of Keynesian era. By H. I. Macdonald. (In *Canadian commentator*. Toronto. v. 2, no. 7 (July 1958), pp. 9-10.)
Examines the budget presented by Finance Minister Donald Fleming June 17, 1958.

MAC DONALD, RON Stanfield—the man. On tour with an unusual politician. (In *The Atlantic advocate*. Fredericton, N.B. v. 58, no. 2 (Oct. 1967), pp. 14-16.)

MACDONNELL, JAMES MC KERRAS In and out of Parliament. By J. M. Macdonnell. (In *Queen's quarterly*. Kingston. v. 70 (1963), pp. [64]-68.)

—— The Progressive Conservative Party: a stock-taking. By J. M. Macdonnell. (In *The Canadian forum*. Toronto. v. 32, no. 378 (July 1952), pp. 81-83.)
"Mr. Macdonnell, financial critic of the Progressive Conservative opposition in the federal Parliament, reviews the state of his party."

MC GRATH, PAUL Musical chairs at Ottawa? Cabinet splits and the next election. (In *Saturday night*. Toronto. v. 76, no. 24 (Nov. 25, 1961), pp. 15-16.)
Reference is to the cabinet of John Diefenbaker.

MC GREGOR, ALEX Farewell O Chief. (In *Canadian dimension*. Winnipeg. v. 5, no. 1 (Nov./Dec. 1967), pp. 8-9.)
Concerns the fall of John Diefenbaker.

MACKLIN, W. H. S. Let's get our money's worth of defence. By Major-General W. H. S. Macklin. (In *Saturday night*. Toronto. v. 72, no. 18 (Aug. 31, 1957), pp. 8; 35-36.)
Offers suggestions to the newly elected Conservative government.

MAC LEAN, LOGAN Henry Borden: probing the pipeline. (In *Saturday night*. Toronto. v. 72, no. 24 (Nov. 23, 1957), pp. 8-9; 34.)
Poses the question: "Is Mr. Diefenbaker hoping Henry Borden will take the government off the hook? Has he changed his mind on the hotly debated Trans-Canada Pipeline argument?"

—— Ottawa letter. That Bill of Rights. (In *Saturday night*. Toronto. v. 73, no. 20 (Sept. 27, 1958), pp. 6-7.)
Comments on the measure introduced to the House of Commons on September 5, 1958.

—— Ottawa letter. No help wanted. (In *Saturday night*. Toronto. v. 73, no. 22 (Oct. 25, 1958), pp. 6-7.)
Comments on John Diefenbaker's choice for Governor-General of Canada, and other matters.

MC LIN, JON B. Canada's changing defense policy; 1957-1963. The problems of a middle power in alliance. Baltimore, Johns Hopkins Press, 1967. xii, 251 p.
An interpretation of the defense policy followed by the John Diefenbaker government.

MC NAUGHT, KENNETH WILLIAM KIRKPATRICK National affairs. The Tories in search of a leader. By Kenneth McNaught. (In *Saturday night*. Toronto. v. 82, no. 9 (Sept. 1967), pp. 9; 11.)
Discusses the national convention of the Progressive Conservative Party held in Toronto September 7-9, 1967.

—— What the Tories *still* don't know

about running Canada. By Kenneth Mc-Naught. (In *Saturday night*. Toronto. v. 80, no. 4 (Apr. 1965), pp. 25-26.)

MAHAFFY, R. U. Spending your money. Behind the scenes look at the budget. (In *Saturday night*. Toronto. v. 76, no. 8 (Apr. 15, 1961), pp. [9]-11.)
Concerns the budget for the fiscal year 1961/62.

MARSHALL, DOUGLAS Robert Lorne Stanfield. Okay, so he's no swinger, but . . . (In *Maclean's*. Toronto. v. 81, no. 3 (Mar. 1968), pp. [22]-23; 46-51.)

MUNGALL, CONSTANCE Chatelaine drops in on Mrs. Robert Stanfield. (In *Chatelaine*. Toronto. v. 40, no. 12 (Dec. 1967), pp. 26-27; 82; 84-85.)

NEUFELD, EDWARD PETER Basis of the budget: free enterprise. By E. P. Neufeld. (In *Saturday night*. Toronto. v. 75, no. 9 (Apr. 30, 1960), pp. 15-16.)
Concerns the budget presented in the House of Commons by Donald M. Fleming March 31, 1960.

—— Mr. Fleming's budget. By E. P. Neufeld. (In *The Canadian forum*. Toronto. v. 38, no. 450 (July 1958), pp. [73]; 96.)
Tabled June 17, 1958.

NEWMAN, CHRISTINA (MC CALL) So Stanfield slew the Chief. Now what happens? By Christina Newman. (In *Saturday night*. Toronto. v. 82, no. 11 (Nov. 1967), pp. 37-40.)

NEWMAN, PETER CHARLES Backstage at Ottawa. Diefenbaker's non-Tory Tories. He's got socialist and big businessmen both off balance. By Peter C. Newman. (In *Maclean's*. Toronto. v. 73, no. 7 (Mar. 26, 1960), p. 2.)

—— Backstage at Ottawa. Ottawa: the Diefenbaker government will go to the country on June 5, 1961 . . . political strategists making this prediction believe... . By Peter C. Newman. (In *Maclean's*. Toronto. v. 73, no. 11 (May 21, 1960), p. 2.)

—— Backstage at Ottawa. The PM's puritan stand on MPS' pay—even his own. By Peter C. Newman. (In *Maclean's*. Toronto. v. 73, no. 10 [i.e. 15] (July 16, 1960), p. 2.)

—— Backstage at Ottawa. The PM's election role: the Paul Revere of Canada. By Peter C. Newman. (In *Maclean's*. Toronto. v. 73, no. 19 (Sept. 10, 1960), p. 2.)

—— Backstage at Ottawa. Diefenbaker's

new vision—agriculture—and his new visionary—Alvin Hamilton. By Peter C. Newman. (In *Maclean's*. Toronto. v. 73, no. 25 (Dec. 3, 1960), p. 2.)

—— Backstage at Ottawa. The PM's problem: how to keep his party moving left. By Peter C. Newman. (In *Maclean's*. Toronto. v. 73, no. 26 (Dec. 17, 1960), p. 2.)

—— Backstage at Ottawa. The 1961 budget: the tax laws will change, but there's almost no hope of tax cuts. By Peter C. Newman. (In *Maclean's*. Toronto. v. 74, no. 8 (Apr. 22, 1961), p. 92.)

—— Backstage at Ottawa. Why Kennedy will try to enlist John Diefenbaker as his next New Frontiersman. By Peter C. Newman. (In *Maclean's*. Toronto. v. 74, no. 10 (May 20, 1961), p. 70.)

—— Backstage at Ottawa. Hope comes into the prisons. Fulton's plan: improve the con's lot—and chances. By Peter C. Newman. (In *Maclean's*. Toronto. v. 74, no. 13 (July 1, 1961), p. 54.)
Reference is to Davie Fulton, Minister of Justice.

—— Backstage at Ottawa. Fleming's double game: can he get the nation and his party out of hock? By Peter C. Newman. (In *Maclean's*. Toronto. v. 74, no. 14 (July 15, 1961), p. 46.)

—— Backstage at Ottawa. The Tory future: it looks a lot better than the past. By Peter C. Newman. (In *Maclean's*. Toronto. v. 74, no. 19 (Sept. 23, 1961), p. 76.)

—— Backstage at Ottawa. Howard Green: a friendly peacemaker toughens up. By Peter C. Newman. (In *Maclean's*. Toronto. v. 74, no. 20 (Oct. 7, 1961), p. 108.)

—— Backstage at Ottawa. The PM's new vision: a national power grid. By Peter C. Newman. (In *Maclean's*. Toronto. v. 74, no. 22 (Nov. 4, 1961), p. 78.)

—— Backstage in Ottawa. How Fleming lost his battle with the heavy spenders. By Peter C. Newman. (In *Maclean's*. Toronto. v. 75, no. 2 (Jan. 27, 1962), p. 50.)
Concerns a conflict over fiscal policy between the Minister of Finance, Donald Fleming and Prime Minister John Diefenbaker.

—— Backstage in Ottawa. The Tories think the decisive votes are in suburbia. By Peter C. Newman. (In *Maclean's*. Toronto. v. 75, no. 4 (Feb. 24, 1962), p. 58.)

—— Backstage in Ottawa. New Tory election game: baiting Liberal comsymps. By Peter C. Newman. (In *Maclean's*. Toronto. v. 75, no. 9 (May 5, 1962), p. 62.)

—— Backstage in Ottawa. Why Diefenbaker thinks the press is against him. By Peter C. Newman. (In *Maclean's*. Toronto. v. 75, no. 10 (May 19, 1962), p. 78.)

—— Backstage in Ottawa. The defense plea was the same but the jury's mood changed. By Peter C. Newman. (In *Maclean's*. Toronto. v. 75, no. 14 (July 14, 1962), pp. 1-2.)

—— Backstage in Ottawa. There are still some taxes the government hasn't levied. But they'll have to come. By Peter C. Newman. (In *Maclean's*. Toronto. v. 75, no. 16 (Aug. 11, 1962), pp. 1-2.)

—— Backstage in Ottawa. The cabinet shuffle means one-man rule continues as before. By Peter C. Newman. (In *Maclean's*. Toronto. v. 75, no. 18 (Sept. 8, 1962), pp. 1-2.)
Refers to the cabinet of John Diefenbaker.

—— Backstage in Ottawa. Could the Tories win by making Pearson Prime Minister? By Peter C. Newman. (In *Maclean's*. Toronto. v. 75, no. 20 (Oct. 6, 1962), pp. 1-2.)

—— Backstage in Ottawa. The "third-force" Tories: they're aiming at '67 —without John Diefenbaker. By Peter C. Newman. (In *Maclean's*. Toronto. v. 75, no. 25 (Dec. 15, 1962), pp. 1-2.)
Considers the leadership crisis within the Conservative Party.

—— Backstage in Ottawa. Tribute: a young minister goes West. By Peter C. Newman. (In *Maclean's*. Toronto. v. 76, no. 1 (Jan. 5, 1963), pp. 1-2.)
Concerns E. Davie Fulton.

—— Backstage with Peter C. Newman; a special page on the campaign. Trouble at the top: four shaky ministers. Power at the bottom: last chance for the old-time ward bosses. (In *Maclean's*. Toronto. v. 76, no. 5 (Mar. 9, 1963), p. 1.)
The ministers: George Nowlan, Ellen Fairclough, Gordon Churchill, and Howard Green.
Relates to the general elections held April 8, 1963.

—— Backstage in Ottawa. Diefenbaker will lead the toughest, loudest Opposition in history. By Peter C. Newman. (In *Maclean's*. Toronto. v. 76, no. 10 (May 18, 1963), p. 2.)

—— The Diefenbaker legend will live on. By Peter Newman. (In Kilbourn, W. M. (ed.) *Canada; a guide to the peaceable kingdom*. Toronto, 1970. pp. 231-234.)

—— Donald Fleming: the man who spends your money. By Peter C. Newman. (In *Maclean's*. Toronto. v. 73, no. 8 (Apr. 9, 1960), pp. 17; 63-70.)

—— Douglas Harkness: the lonely ordeal of a Tory rebel. By Peter C. Newman. (In *Maclean's*. Toronto. v. 77, no. 1 (Jan. 4, 1964), p. 1.)

—— George Hees; Ottawa's biggest surprise package. By Peter C. Newman. (In *Maclean's*. Toronto. v. 72, no. 13 (June 20, 1959), pp. 18-19; 64-69.)

—— How Alvin Hamilton keeps the Prairies in his pocket. By Peter C. Newman. (In *Maclean's*. Toronto. v. 76, no. 16 (Aug. 24, 1963), pp. 16; 32-33.)

—— John Diefenbaker. By Peter C. Newman. (In *Maclean's*. Toronto. v. 76, no. 6 (Mar. 23, 1963), pp. [15-17]; 46-53.)

—— National affairs. Some federal Tories like Diefenbaker. Some don't. But they all like Roblin. By Peter C. Newman. (In *Maclean's*. Toronto. v. 77, no. 1 (Jan. 4, 1964), p. 2.)

—— Renegade in power: the Diefenbaker years. By Peter C. Newman. Toronto, McClelland and Stewart [1964, c1963] xvi, 411 p.

—— The second most powerful Tory . . . is Davie Fulton . . . By Peter C. Newman. (In *Maclean's*. Toronto. v. 71, no. 1 (Jan. 4, 1958), pp. 17; 32-34.)

—— Women are equal—especially Ellen Fairclough. By Peter C. Newman. (In *Maclean's*. Toronto. v. 71, no. 18 (Aug. 30, 1958), pp. 22-23; 27-28.)

O'HEARN, DON A new career for George Drew. (In *Saturday night*. Toronto. v. 72, no. 19 (Sept. 14, 1957), pp. 14-15; 39.)
Concerns his appointment as Canadian High Commissioner in London.

O'LEARY, DILLON Diefenbaker—overboard in February? The Tory leader may survive his party's February meeting but "he likely will be gunned down by his own followers before the end of '64". (In *Commentator*. Toronto. v. 8, no. 1 (Jan. 1964), pp. 6-7.)

—— How they tried to get rid of Diefenbaker. (In *Commentator*. Toronto. v. 7, no. 7-8 (July—Aug. 1963), pp. 2-6.)

O'NEIL, PIERRE Seul le peuple peut déloger Diefenbaker. (In *Le Magazine Maclean*. Montréal. v. 5, no 1 (jan. 1965), p. 4.)
Brief remarks.

PCs search for truth. By D. L. C. (In *Canada month*. Montreal. v. 2, no. 11 (Nov. 1962), pp. 19-20.)

PAYZANT, GEOFFREY The victory of the Philistines. (In *Canadian commentator*. Toronto. v. 2, no. 4 (Apr. 1958), pp. [1]-2.)
The editor of *The Canadian music journal* considers the policy of the Conservative administration towards the CBC, the Canada Council, the Film Board, and other Canadian cultural institutions.

PEACOCK, DON Free enterprise: a government definition. (In *Saturday night*. Toronto. v. 74, no. 24 (Nov. 21, 1959), pp. 26-29.)
Discusses the proposed revision of two sections of the Combines Investigation Act, by the Diefenbaker administration.

PELLERIN, JEAN Le roman d'une crise; celle des relations canado-américaines (In *Cité libre*. Montréal. no. 56 (avril 1963), pp. 1-7.)
A review of the policy of the Diefenbaker administration before the election of April 8, 1963.

PEPIN, JEAN LUC Diefenbaker le voyant, principal atout électoral de son parti. (In *Le Magazine Maclean*. Montréal. v. 1, no 3 (mai 1961), p. 2.)

—— Pourquoi Diefenbaker ne donne-t-il pas sa faveur à Dorion? (In *Le Magazine Maclean*. Montréal. v. 1, no 7 (sept. 1961), p. 2.)
Refers to Noël Dorion.

PHILLIPS, ALAN The last angry Tory. (In *Maclean's*. Toronto. v. 71, no. 12 (June 7, 1958), pp. 22-23; 65-71.)
Concerns Grattan O'Leary.

PORTER, JOHN A. Conserving the bureaucracy. By John Porter. (In *The Canadian forum*. Toronto. v. 38, no. 448 (May 1958), pp. 27-28.)
Discusses a prevailing assumption that there exists strained relations between the Conservative administration and senior civil servants.

PORTER, JULIAN Conservative convention, three views. 1. View from the right, by Julian Porter. 2. View from the seats, by Alastair Sweeney. 3. View from Montmorency, by J. L. Granatstein. (In *The Canadian forum*. Toronto. v. 47, no. 561 (Oct. 1967), pp. 148-151.)
The national convention of the Progressive Conservative Party held September 7-9, 1967.

The Private side of politics: John Diefenbaker. (In *Maclean's*. Toronto. v. 71, no. 7 (Mar. 29, 1958), pp. 15; 54-58.)
The private side of politics; a *Maclean's* panel talks informally with John Diefenbaker and L. B. Pearson. Panelists: Hugh MacLennan, Barbara Moon, James Bannerman.

PROGRESSIVE CONSERVATIVE PARTY (CANADA) Conservative action. An up-to-date summary of the achievements of the Progressive Conservative government of Prime Minister John Diefenbaker, June 1957 to date. [Ottawa, 1961] 43 p.

—— 1953 campaign handbook for Progressive Conservative candidates and workers in the federal election. [Ottawa, 1953] x, 136 p.
Cover title.
At head of title: Confidential.
Spiral binding.

—— The record speaks! [Ottawa, 1960] 72 p.
Compiled from official sources and written by Pat Macadam.

—— Where we stand. Statements on policy by Progressive Conservative members of Parliament. [Ottawa, 1966-67] 2 v.
Cover title.
Excerpts from Hansard compiled by Mrs. Leslie Hatheway.
Contents: [v. 1] 27th parliament, 1st session, Jan. 18—Sept. 9, 1966. – v. 2. 27th parliament, 1st session, Oct. 5, 1966—Jan. 27, 1967.

REED, LORNE H. Grass-roots non-politicking. (In *Canada month*. Montreal. v. 8, no. 7 (July 1968), pp. 24-25.)
Concerns an association called the New Tories. The group originated in Alberta and sought legal counsel on the constitutionality of federal medicare legislation.

REFORD, ROBERT W. How vulnerable is the Tory majority? By Robert W. Reford. (In *Saturday night*. Toronto. v. 75, no. 6 (Mar. 19, 1960), pp. 18-19.)

REGENSTREIF, SAMUEL PETER The Diefenbaker interlude; parties and voting in Canada, an interpretation. [Toronto] Longmans [c1965] xiv, 194 p.

'Renegade in power.' A review of Peter C. Newman's controversial book about John Diefenbaker. By J. W. B. (In *The Atlantic advocate*. Fredericton, N.B. v. 54, no. 4 (Dec. 1963), pp. 41-43.)

RICHARDSON, BURTON TAYLOR   Canada and Mr. Diefenbaker. By B. T. Richardson. [Toronto] McClelland and Stewart [c1962] 120 p.

RODGERS, RAYMOND   Ottawa letter. Does the cabinet govern Canada? (In *Saturday night*. Toronto. v. 75, no. 23 (Nov. 12, 1960), pp. 33-34.)
Relates, specifically, to the government of John Diefenbaker.

—— Ottawa letter. We need specialists in government. (In *Saturday night*. Toronto. v. 75, no. 25 (Dec. 10, 1960), pp. 28-29.)
Relates this idea to the John Diefenbaker cabinet, citing the background of its members.

—— Ottawa letter. Diefenbaker looks east —dimly. (In *Saturday night*. Toronto. v. 76, no. 2 (Jan. 21, 1961), pp. 21-22.)
Concerns the government's program for the Atlantic Provinces.

—— Ottawa letter. The Pro-Cons and pro-Canadians. (In *Saturday night*. Toronto. v. 76, no. 6 (Mar. 18, 1961), p. 33.)
Comments on the agenda for the annual general meeting of the Progressive Conservative Association held March 16-18, 1961.

—— Ottawa letter. Crossing the Tory party lines? (In *Saturday night*. Toronto. v. 76, no. 7 (Apr. 1, 1961), pp. 25-26.)
"If the real divisions in Canada are between levels of government . . . why do we have such emphasis on party discipline . . .?"

—— Ottawa letter. What O'Leary really wanted. (In *Saturday night*. Toronto. v. 76, no. 24 (Nov. 25, 1961), pp. 25-26.)
Refers to the Royal Commission on Publications under the chairmanship of Grattan O'Leary. Discusses the difference in interpretation of Conservative (Tory) principles held by Grattan O'Leary and John Diefenbaker.

ROSS, ALEXANDER   Dalton Camp; the man who finally belled the cat. (In *Maclean's*. Toronto. v. 80, no. 2 (Feb. 1967), pp. 20-21; 73-75.)

ROSS, MARY LOWREY   Ellen Fairclough: first woman in the cabinet. (In *Saturday night*. Toronto. v. 72, no. 18 (Aug. 31, 1957), pp. 14-15; 34.)

RUDDY, JON   The Tories: 1. The day the balloon went up for Wallace McCutcheon. A wistful drama in two acts. (In *Maclean's*. Toronto. v. 80, no. 11 (Nov. 1967), pp. 23; 95-98.)

SEVIGNY, JOSEPH PIERRE   Pierre Sévigny: "This is what really happened." [An] interview with Susan Dexter. (In *Maclean's*. Toronto. v. 79, no. 15 (Aug. 6, 1966), pp. 14-17; 39-41.)
With reference to the Gerda Munsinger case.

—— This game of politics. By Pierre Sévigny. Toronto, McClelland and Stewart [c1965] xi, 324 p.
Autobiographical. Deals mainly with events from 1956 to 1963.

SHAW, STUART J.   Tory prospects in the West. (In *Saturday night*. Toronto. v. 70, no. 35 (July 9, 1955), pp. 7-8.)

SHAW, W. F.   How Union Nationale tricked the Tories. (In *Canada month*. Montreal. v. 7, no. 10 (Oct. 1967), p. 26.)
Refers to the "deux nations" phrasing in a constitutional reform resolution presented at the national convention of the Progressive Conservative Party, held in Toronto, September 7-9, 1967.

SMITH, DENIS   The Conservatives are confused. (In *Canadian commentator*. Toronto. v. 1, no. 5 (May 1957), pp. 3-4.)
Analyses the politics presented by John Diefenbaker.

—— Rhetorical radical. (In *The Canadian forum*. Toronto. v. 43, no. 515 (Dec. 1963), pp. 203-205.)
A review article of *Renegade in power; the Diefenbaker years*, by P. C. Newman. Toronto, McClelland & Stewart [c1963].

STEVENS, HENRY HERBERT   Fifty years a politician. First elected an MP in 1911, B.C.'s Grand Old Man of politics is 85. [Interviewed] By Raymond Hull. (In *Canada month*. Montreal. v. 3, no. 12 (Dec. 1963), p. 9.)

STEVENSON, JOHN A.   The cautious optimist. (In *Saturday night*. Toronto. v. 73, no. 14 (July 5, 1958), pp. 14-15; 34-35.)
Concerns Donald Fleming.

—— Letter from Ottawa. Reflections on the budget and political promises. (In

Canadian commentator. Toronto. v. 3, no. 5 (May 1959), pp. 10-11.)

Comments on the policies and procedures of John Diefenbaker's administration.

—— Men and politics. A critical survey of the strength and weakness of the Diefenbaker government. (In *Canadian commentator.* Toronto. v. 3, no. 9 (Sept. 1959), pp. 7-9.)

—— Ottawa letter. Political possibilities in Quebec. (In *Saturday night.* Toronto. v. 68, no. 37 (June 20, 1953), pp. 14-15.)

Refers to the prospects of the Progressive Conservative Party in Quebec.

—— Ottawa letter. The political situation in Quebec. (In *Saturday night.* Toronto. v. 68, no. 42 (July 25, 1953), p. 10.)

Considers the position of the Conservative Party under George Drew relating to Quebec in the federal election held August 10, 1953.

—— Ottawa letter. The failure of the Opposition. (In *Saturday night.* Toronto. v. 71, no. 13 (Sept. 1, 1956), p. 13.)

—— Ottawa letter. The prospects of John Diefenbaker. (In *Saturday night.* Toronto. v. 72, no. 2 (Jan. 19, 1957), pp. 12-13.)

Diefenbaker was elected leader at the fifth national convention of the Progressive Conservative Party held at Ottawa December 10-12, 1956.

—— Ottawa letter. Wealthy Tories quitting the Party? (In *Saturday night.* Toronto. v. 72, no. 6 (Mar. 16, 1957), pp. 16-17.)

—— Ottawa letter. New cabinet problems. (In *Saturday night.* Toronto. v. 72, no. 14 (July 6, 1957), pp. 4-5.)

Discusses the cabinet formed by John Diefenbaker.

—— Ottawa letter. Tariff snags for the Tories. (In *Saturday night.* Toronto. v. 72, no. 15 (July 20, 1957), pp. 4-5.)

—— Ottawa letter. Can the PM do two jobs? (In *Saturday night.* Toronto. v. 72, no. 17 (Aug. 17, 1957), pp. 4-5.)

Discusses John Diefenbaker's responsibilities as Prime Minister and as director of the Department of External Affairs.

—— Ottawa letter. Flying Prime Minister. (In *Saturday night.* Toronto. v. 72, no. 19 (Sept. 14, 1957), pp. 4-5.)

Refers to John Diefenbaker.

—— Ottawa letter. Diefenbaker cracks down. (In *Saturday night.* Toronto. v. 72, no. 21 (Oct. 12, 1957), pp. 4-5.)

—— Ottawa letter. Tories drop "big business". (In *Saturday night.* Toronto. v. 72, no. 23 (Nov. 9, 1957), pp. 4-5.)

—— Ottawa letter. Is Diefenbaker bluffing? (In *Saturday night.* Toronto. v. 72, no. 24 (Nov. 23, 1957), pp. 4-5.)

Concerns the issue of the dissolution of Parliament.

—— Ottawa letter. Tory tempers frayed. (In *Saturday night.* Toronto. v. 73, no. 1 (Jan. 4, 1958), pp. 4-5.)

Cites conflict over the approach and attitude shown by the Conservative Party in power regarding the parliamentary process.

—— Ottawa letter. Tories seek defeat. (In *Saturday night.* Toronto. v. 73, no. 2 (Jan. 18, 1958), pp. 4-5.)

—— Ottawa letter. The PM and Parliament. (In *Saturday night.* Toronto. v. 73, no. 4 (Feb. 15, 1958), pp. 4-5.)

Concerns John Diefenbaker.

—— Ottawa letter. A political revolution. (In *Saturday night.* Toronto. v. 73, no. 8 (Apr. 12, 1958), pp. 6-7.)

Examines the results of the general elections held March 31, 1958.

—— Ottawa letter. Second thoughts about March. (In *Saturday night.* Toronto. v. 73, no. 9 (Apr. 26, 1958), pp. 4-5.)

Concerns primarily the Progressive Conservative government, with reference to the results of the general elections held March 31, 1958.

—— Ottawa letter. Tariff pleas plague PM. (In *Saturday night.* Toronto. v. 73, no. 10 (May 10, 1958), pp. 6-7.)

—— Ottawa letter. Scant comfort for PCs. (In *Saturday night.* Toronto. v. 73, no. 12 (June 7, 1958), pp. 4-5.)

Discusses debates in the House of Commons over significant issues.

—— Ottawa letter. New Tories, old principles. (In *Saturday night.* Toronto. v. 73, no. 13 (June 21, 1958), pp. 4-5.)

—— Ottawa letter. Morality in high places. (In *Saturday night.* Toronto. v. 73, no. 14 (July 5, 1958), pp. 4-5.)

Includes discussion of the federal budget for 1958/59 presented by Donald Fleming on June 18, 1958.

—— Ottawa letter. Fickle fortune's favors. (In *Saturday night.* Toronto. v. 73, no. 15 (July 19, 1958), pp. 4-5.)

Comments on the position of the Conservative Party in office.

—— Ottawa letter. A radical administration. (In *Saturday night*. Toronto. v. 73, no. 17 (Aug. 16, 1958), pp. 4-5.)

Comments on the first year of the John Diefenbaker ministry and other matters.

—— Ottawa letter. Mr. Diefenbaker and his team; their qualifications and problems. (In *Canadian commentator*. Toronto. v. 3, no. 2 (Feb. 1959), pp. 5-7.)

—— Ottawa letter. Liberal Senator urges government to be conservative in fact as well as name. (In *Canadian commentator*. Toronto. v. 3, no. 3 (Mar. 1959), pp. 7-8.)

Refers to the speech delivered in the Senate on February 3, 1959, by A. K. Hugessen.

—— Ottawa letter. The Manitoba election and the Gallup poll give contradictory estimates of Conservative popularity. (In *Canadian commentator*. Toronto. v. 3, no. 6 (June 1959), pp. 8-9.)

Analyses the nature and degree of public support remaining for the Diefenbaker administration.

—— Ottawa letter. (In *Canadian commentator*. Toronto. v. 4, no. 5 (May 1960), pp. 11-13.)

Concerns the debate on the budget presented by Donald Fleming.

—— Ottawa letter. By J. A. Stevenson. (In *Canadian commentator*. Toronto. v. 4, no. 11 (Nov. 1960), pp. 26-27.)

Brief remarks on the general condition of the federal Progressive Conservative Party.

—— Politicians and promises. (In *Canadian commentator*. Toronto. v. 3, no. 11 (Nov. 1959), pp. 11-12.)

Comments on the financial and trade policies of the Conservative government and the career of Ross Thatcher.

—— Professional optimists. A rosy view of defence and economy offered in Ottawa. By J. A. Stevenson. (In *Canadian commentator*. Toronto. v. 4, no. 4 (Apr. 1960), pp. 7-8.)

—— Program for Canada. Thin political gruel for the feeding of the nation. By J. A. Stevenson. (In *Canadian commentator*. Toronto. v. 4, no. 2 (Feb. 1960), pp. 8-11.)

General comments on the Speech from the Throne opening the third session of the twenty-fourth parliament.

—— Report on Ottawa. Despite its own deficit, the government labours mightily to revive business; and speaks with frankness about Cuba to the U.S.A. By J. A. Stevenson. (In *Canadian commentator*. Toronto. v. 5, no. 6 (June 1961), pp. 17-19.)

—— Tories in trouble. Recent provincial elections suggest growing disillusionment. By J. A. Stevenson. (In *Canadian commentator*. Toronto. v. 4, no. 10 (Oct. 1960), pp. 8-10.)

Relates provincial political developments to the federal Progressive Conservative Party.

—— The Tory convention. In which Mr. Diefenbaker sometimes flirted with the truth. By J. A. Stevenson. (In *Canadian commentator*. Toronto. v. 4, no. 1 (Jan. 1960), pp. 12-14.)

Held in Ottawa, December 1959.

STURSBERG, PETER Ottawa letter. A cabinet shuffle coming up. (In *Saturday night*. Toronto. v. 75, no. 17 (Aug. 20, 1960), pp. 22-23.)

Compares the situation which compelled a cabinet reorganization by Mackenzie King in 1940 and 1945 and John Diefenbaker in 1960.

—— Ottawa letter. The pre-election Throne Speech. (In *Saturday night*. Toronto. v. 77, no. 2 (Jan. 20, 1962), pp. 25-26.)

". . . this session's Throne Speech is fully expected to become the Conservative government's election manifesto."

—— Ottawa letter. The last Conservative. (In *Saturday night*. Toronto. v. 77, no. 4 (Feb. 17, 1962), pp. 34-35.)

Concerns Earl Rowe.

—— Ottawa letter. Wanted: a leader from Quebec. (In *Saturday night*. Toronto. v. 77, no. 9 (Apr. 28, 1962), pp. 11-12.)

Deals mainly with relations between the federal and provincial Conservative parties.

—— Ottawa letter. A look at the government record. (In *Saturday night*. Toronto. v. 77, no. 10 (May 12, 1962), pp. 11-12.)

Refers to the Conservative Party administration led by John Diefenbaker.

—— Postmark Ottawa. (In *The Canadian Saturday night*. Toronto. v. 77, no. 15 (Aug. 1962), pp. 33-34.)

Discusses policies advanced by the Conservative Party administration following the federal election held June 18, 1962.

—— Postmark Ottawa. (In *The Canadian Saturday night*. Toronto. v. 78, no. 3 (Mar. 1963), pp 7-9.)

Discusses nuclear weapons policy and the move within the Conservative Party to force the resignation of John Diefenbaker.

—— Why do the Conservatives behave like lemmings? There are historical reasons that explain the Conservatives' strange tendency to commit political hara-kiri when things go well, or could go well, for them. (In *Commentator*. Toronto. v. 9, no. 4 (Apr. 1965), pp. 21-22.)
Examines the recurrence of leadership crisis within the Conservative Party.

TREPANIER, VICTOR   L'élection du 10 août [1953]. Une question de vie ou de mort pour les droits provinciaux. Plaidoyer, autonomiste pour les nationalistes, les indépendants et les vrais libéraux. [Québec, 1953] 89 p.

TRUDEAU, PIERRE ELLIOTT   Diefenbaker monte en ballon. (In *Cité libre*. Montréal. no. 26 (avril 1960), pp. 15-16.)

VAN DUSEN, THOMAS   The Chief. New York, Toronto, McGraw-Hill [c1968] ix, 278 p.
Concerns John G. Diefenbaker.

VAN STEEN, MARCUS   The rising Tory star in Nova Scotia. (In *Saturday night*. Toronto. v. 71, no. 19 (Nov. 24, 1956), pp. 7-8.)
Concerns Robert Lorne Stanfield.

VINEBERG, MICHAEL   The Progressive Conservative leadership convention of 1967. [Montreal] 1968 [c1969] ii. [62] leaves.
Thesis (MA) – McGill University.

WALKER, DAVID JAMES   What we are doing and what you can do about employment. By the Honourable David J. Walker, Minister of Public Works. (In Empire Club of Canada. *Addresses*. Toronto. (1960/61), pp. 116-125.)
Address delivered December 1, 1960.

WALWYN, ARTHUR   Why this Conservative believes George Drew must win in 1949. (In *Saturday night*. Toronto. v. 64, no. 20 (Feb. 22, 1949), pp. 6-7.)

WARD, NORMAN MC QUEEN   Will the Tories restore Parliament's power? By Norman Ward. (In *Saturday night*. Toronto. v. 72, no. 17 (Aug. 17, 1957), pp. 8-9; 34-35.)

WARDELL, MICHAEL   Thank you, Mr. Diefenbaker! (In *The Atlantic advocate*. Fredericton, N.B. v. 58, no. 4 (Dec. 1967), pp. 14-18.)
Concerns John Diefenbaker and the

establishment of the Atlantic Development Board.

WATKINS, ERNEST   Political Canada. Leader in a void. (In *Canada month*. Montreal. v. 4, no. 2 (Feb. 1964), p. 34.)
Refers to John Diefenbaker.

—— Political Canada. Who should shake the money tree? (In *Canada month*. Montreal. v. 4, no. 11 (Nov. 1964), p. 26.)
Comments on "A Canadian revolution", by G. T. Guest. (In *Canada month*. Montreal. v. 4, no. 10 (Oct. 1964), pp. 21-28.)

—— Political Canada. Conservatives must define direction. (In *Canada month*. Montreal. v. 4, no. 12 (Dec. 1964), p. 30.)
Draws comparisons between Barry Goldwater and John Diefenbaker.

—— The Tory annual meeting. A love feast with a deeper meaning. (In *Saturday night*. Toronto. v. 76, no. 8 (Apr. 15, 1961), pp. [12]-[14].)
This particular meeting was held March 16-18, 1961.

WEARING, JOSEPH   A convention for professionals; the PCs in Toronto. (In *Journal of Canadian studies*. Peterborough, Ont. v. 2, no. 4 (1967), pp. 3-15.)
Refers to the national convention held by the Progressive Conservative Party in Toronto September 7-9, 1967.

Why Harkness resigned—and what followed. By J. H. S. D., J. K. (In *Canada month*. Montreal. v. 3, no. 3 (Mar. 1963), pp. 12-16.)

WUORIO, EVA-LIS   Ellen goes to Ottawa. (In *Maclean's*. Toronto. v. 63, no. 15 (Aug. 1, 1950), pp. 14; 36-37.)
Concerns Ellen Fairclough.

YOUNG, SCOTT   Why I'm voting Conservative. (In *Maclean's*. Toronto. v. 66, no. 15 (Aug. 1, 1953), pp. 9; 50-51.)
Refers to the federal election held August 10, 1953.

LIBERAL PARTY

General Works

HEPPE, PAUL HARRY   The Liberal Party of Canada. Ann Arbor, University Microfilms [1957] 2 v. (v, 491 leaves)
Thesis (PH D) – University of Wisconsin.

Les Origines du Parti libéral canadien. (In *La Revue moderne*. Montréal. 5 année, no 4 (fév. 1924), pp. 17-20.)

PICKERSGILL, JOHN WHITNEY The Liberal Party. Introd. by L. B. Pearson. [Toronto] McClelland and Stewart [1962] xiii, 146 p.

—— Le Parti libéral. Préf. de Lionel Chevrier. Traduit par David-Armand Gourd. Montréal, Editions du Jour [c1963] 124 p.
Translation of part of the author's The Liberal Party.
Appendix (pp. [115]-124): Associés égaux dans la Conféderation. Discours prononcé à la Chambre des Communes le 17 décembre 1962, par L. B. Pearson.

REGENSTREIF, SAMUEL PETER The Liberal Party of Canada; a political analysis. [Ithaca, N.Y., 1963] v, 555 leaves.
Thesis (PH D) – Cornell University.
Abstracted in Dissertation abstracts, v. 24 (1963), no. 2, p. 813.

1867–1896

ACHINTRE, AUGUSTE Emigration colonisation. Rapport du Ministre de l'agriculture du Canada pour l'année 1874. Par A. Achintre. (In L'Opinion publique. Montréal. v. 6, no. 42 (21 oct. 1875), p. [493]; v. 6, no. 43 (28 oct. 1875), pp. [505]-506.)
In two parts.

—— L'Hon. Hector Fabre, sénateur. Par A. Achintre. (In L'Opinion publique. Montréal. v. 6, no. 9 (4 mars 1875), pp. [97]-98.)

—— Semaine politique. Le Budget. Par A. A. (In L'Opinion publique. Montréal. v. 6, no. 8 (25 fév. 1875), p. 95.)

ARBOIS Croquis et portraits. M. Blake. Par Arbois. (In L'Opinion publique. Montréal. v. 10, no. 1 (2 jan. 1879), p. [1].)

—— Croquis et portraits. M. Holton. Par Arbois. (In L'Opinion publique. Montréal. v. 10, no. 3 (16 jan. 1879), p. [25].)
Concerns L. H. Holton.

The Aurora illumination. (In The Nation. Toronto. v. 1, no. 29 (Oct. 15, 1874), p. 344.)
Brief comment on the speech delivered by Edward Blake, at Aurora, Ont., October 3, 1874.

BANKS, MARGARET AMELIA The change in Liberal Party leadership, 1887. (In The Canadian historical review. Toronto. v. 38 (1957), pp. 109-128.)

—— Edward Blake's relations with Canada during his Irish career, 1892-1907. By Margaret A. Banks. (In The Canadian his-

torical review. Toronto. v. 35 (1954), pp. 22-42.)

BEAUCHAMP, J. CLEM The last of the Old Guard passes. Albert Hagar who died recently in his 98th year served in Canada's first parliament, was a member of the Commons from 1867 to 1878. (In Saturday night. Toronto. v. 39, no. 47 (Oct. 11, 1924), p. 3.)
Written on the occasion of his death, September 14, 1924.

BEAUCHESNE, ARTHUR Honoré Mercier. (In La Revue moderne. Montréal. 2 année, no 2 (15 déc. 1920), pp. 12-13.)
Represented Rouville, Que., in the Canadian House of Commons, 1872-1874.

BEAUGRAND, HONORE Honourable Honoré Mercier, QC, Premier of Quebec. By H. Beaugrand. (In The Week. Toronto. v. 5, no. 29 (June 14, 1888), pp. 460-461.)
Prominent Canadians: XIX.

BLAKE, EDWARD Edward Blake to the electors. He pointedly condemns unrestricted reciprocity. Would certainly lead to annexation. Unable to sanction it. He reluctantly retired from public life. Full text of his letter. Toronto, The Empire [1892] ¼ p. (newspaper size)
Reprinted in The Empire (Toronto) January 19, 1892.

—— Edward Blake's Aurora speech, 1874. (In The Canadian historical review. Toronto. v. 2, (1921), pp. 249-271.)
Reprint of complete text of the speech delivered October 3, 1874.
Introductory remarks by W. S. Wallace.

—— Edward Blake's interview with Lord Cairns on the Supreme Court Act, July 5, 1876. (In The Canadian historical review. Toronto. v. 19 (1938), pp. 292-294.)
Text of a letter dated July 5, 1876 to Alexander Mackenzie.
Introductory remarks by Frank H. Underhill.

—— An exposition of national sentiment. (In The Nation. Toronto. v. 1, no. 28 (Oct. 8, 1874), pp. 330-331.)
Extracts taken from the Toronto Globe.
Refers to Edward Blake's Aurora speech.

—— Letter of the Hon. Edward Blake to the West Durham Reform Convention. To which is appended correspondence as to the Inverary meeting. Toronto, Budget Print. and Publ. Co., 1891. 10 p.
Published March 5, 1891.

—— Mr. Blake's speech on the School Bill.

With analysis of amendments. Toronto, Globe Print. Co., 1871. 39 p.

—— "A national sentiment!" Speech of Hon. Edward Blake, MP at Aurora. With the comments of some of the Canadian press thereon. Ottawa, E. A. Perry, 1874. 107, 2p.
Reprinted from Toronto Globe, 12th October, 1874. Speech delivered at Aurora, Ont., October 3, 1874.

—— Speeches by Hon. Edward Blake on the political questions of the day, delivered in the province of Ontario. Toronto, Hunter Rose, 1887. 424 p.
(Cf. Watters, R. E. A checklist of Canadian literature. 2d ed. Toronto, 1972. p. 604.)

BLAKELEY, PHYLLIS RUTH   Jonathan McCully, Father of Confederation. By Phyllis R. Blakeley. (In Nova Scotia Historical Society. Collections. [Halifax] v. 36 (1968), pp. [143]-181.)
"Read before the Nova Scotia Historical Society, November 12, 1965."

BOGGS, BEAUMONT   What I remember of Hon. Amor DeCosmos. (In British Columbia Historical Association. Report and proceedings. [Victoria, B.C.] 4th (1925/29), pp. 54-58.)
Address delivered May 3, 1929.

BOURINOT, SIR JOHN GEORGE   Alexander Mackenzie's place in Canadian history. By J. G. Bourinot. (In The Week. Toronto. v. 9, no. 51 (Nov. 18, 1892), pp. 808-810.)

BRIGGS, GEORGE ELMER   Edward Blake-Alexander Mackenzie; rivals for power. [Hamilton] 1965. 1 v.
Thesis (MA) – McMaster University.

British Columbia. (In The Nation. Toronto. v. 1, no. 11 (June 11, 1874), p. 128.)
Concerns points of negotiation between the Liberal Government and British Columbia as revealed in correspondence involving Prime Minister Mackenzie, J. D. Edgar, and Mr. Walker, Attorney-General for British Columbia, and others.

BRUCHESI, JEAN   Eustache Letellier de Saint-Just. (In Amérique française. Montréal. v. 10, no. 5 (sept./oct. 1952), pp. 46-49.)

BUCKINGHAM, WILLIAM   The Hon. Alexander Mackenzie; his life and times. By William Buckingham and Hon. Geo. W. Ross. Toronto, Rose Pub. Co., 1892. 678 p.
Reprinted New York, Haskell House, 1969.

The Budget. (In The Nation. Toronto. v. 1, no. 4 (Apr. 23, 1874), p. 44.)
Concerns the budget for 1874-75 presented by Richard Cartwright, Minister of Finance.

The Budget. (In The nation. Toronto. v. 2, no. 7 (Feb. 19, 1875), pp. 78-79.)
Concerns the budget of Richard Cartwright.

The Budget. (In The Nation. Toronto. v. 3, no. 9 (Mar. 3, 1876), pp. 99-100.)
Concerns the financial statement presented by Richard Cartwright.

BURKE, TERESA AVILA   Mackenzie and his cabinet, 1873-1878. (In The Canadian historical review. Toronto. v. 41 (1960), pp. 128-148.)

CAMPBELL, ROBERT ELLIS   George Brown's attempted reciprocity treaty in 1874. Toronto, 1936. ii, 246 leaves.
Thesis (MA) – University of Toronto.

CAPPON, JAMES   Reciprocity and Imperial preference. (In Queen's quarterly. [Kingston] v. 11 (1903/04), pp. 332-334.)
Discusses briefly the reciprocity issue and its historical relationship to the policy of the Liberal Party and, especially, the views of Edward Blake.

CARELESS, JAMES MAURICE STOCKFORD   Brown of The Globe. Toronto, Macmillan, 1959 [i.e. 1960]-1963. 2 v.
Contents: v. 1. The voice of Upper Canada, 1818-1859. – v. 2. Statesman of Confederation, 1860-1880.

—— George Brown. By J. M. S. Careless. (In McDougall, R. L. (ed.) Our living tradition. Second and third series. [Toronto, c1959] pp. 31-54.)

—— The political ideas of George Brown. By J. M. S. Careless. (In The Canadian forum. Toronto. v. 36, no. 433 (Feb. 1957), pp. 247-250.)

—— Who was George Brown? By J. M. S. Careless. (In Ontario history. Toronto. v. 42, no. 2 (Apr. 1950), pp. [57]-66.)

CARTWRIGHT, HENRY L.   The Cartwrights of Kingston. (In Historic Kingston. no. 16 (1968), pp. [41]-47.)
Includes the career of Sir Richard Cartwright..

CASGRAIN, PHILIPPE BABY   Letellier de Saint-Just et son temps; étude historique. Par P.-B. Casgrain. Québec, C. Darveau, 1885. 470 p.

CHARLTON, JOHN   How Mackenzie failed. (In The Canadian magazine of politics, *science, art and literature.* Toronto. v. 28 (1906/07), pp. 558-559.)

"Reminiscences of the famous Dominion general elections of 1878, with a defence of Mackenzie's administration of the treasury."

—— Speech of Mr. J. Charlton, MP on Jesuits' Estates Act. Delivered in the House of Commons, Ottawa, on Thursday, March 28th, 1889. Ottawa, Printed for the Queen's Printer, by A. Sénécal, Supt. of Printing, 1889. 28 p.

Cover title.

CLARK, JOSEPH T.   Around town. By Mack. (In *Toronto Saturday night.* Toronto. v. 8, no. 41 (Aug. 31, 1895), p. 1.)

Concerns Wilfrid Laurier's position on the school question.

The Coming Liberal convention. (In *The Week.* Toronto. v. 10, no. 29 (June 16, 1893), pp. 677-678.)

The national Liberal convention held at Ottawa June 20-21, 1893.

COOKE, BRITTON B.   The rails that wrecked the government. By B. B. Cooke. (In *The Busy man's magazine.* Toronto. v. 21, no. 1 (Nov. 1910), pp. 41-42.)

Concerns Alexander Mackenzie's administration, 1873-78.

Countervailing commercial legislation. (In *The Nation.* Toronto. v. 2, no. 16 (Apr. 23, 1875), pp. 186-187.)

Considers "the whole question of the legitimacy of duties intended to countervail hostile foreign legislation", with reference to current government policy.

DAVID, LAURENT OLIVIER   L'Hon. George Brown. Par L.-O. David. (In *L'Opinion publique.* Montréal. v. 1, no. 18 (5 mai 1870), p. [137].)

A biographical sketch.

—— L'Hon. George Brown. Par L.-O. David. (In *L'Opinion publique.* Montréal. v. 11, no. 21 (20 mai 1880), p. [241].)

—— L'Hon. Louis Renaud. Par L.-O. David. (In *L'Opinion publique.* Montréal. v. 9, no. 47 (21 nov. 1878), p. 556.)

Written on the occasion of his death November 13, 1878.

—— L'Hon. Wilfrid Laurier. Par. L.-O. David. (In *L'Opinion publique.* Montréal. v. 8, no. 43 (25 oct. 1877), p. [505].)

—— M. Mercier. Par L.-O. David. (In *L'Opinion publique.* Montréal. v. 10, no. 19 (8 mai 1879), p. [217].)

—— M. Pierre-Alexis Tremblay. Par L.-O. D. (In *L'Opinion publique.* Montréal. v. 10, no. 4 (23 jan. 1879), p. 38.)

Written on the occasion of his death January 5, 1879. Quotes also the comments of Achintre and Fabre on Tremblay.

DENT, JOHN CHARLES   The Hon. Sir Albert James Smith, 1824-1883. (In *The Maritime advocate and busy East.* Sackville, N.B. v. 38, no. 5 (Dec. 1947), pp. 9-10.)

Reprinted from *Canadian portrait gallery.* Toronto, J. B. Magurn, 1880.

DESILETS, ANDREE   Une figure politique du 19ᵉ siècle, François-Xavier Lemieux. Par sœur Andrée Désilets. (In *Revue d'histoire de l'Amérique française.* Montréal. v. 20, no 4 (mars 1967), pp. 572-592; v. 21, no 2 (sept. 1967), pp. 243-267; v. 22, no. 2 (sept. 1968), pp. 223-255.)

In three parts.

Sir François Xavier Lemieux acted as counsel for Louis Riel at Regina in 1885 and defended Honoré Mercier before the Royal Commission of 1892. (Cf. W. S. Wallace. *The Macmillan dictionary of Canadian biography.* 3d ed. p. 407.)

DESJARDINS, LOUIS GEORGES   M. [i.e Monsieur] Laurier devant l'histoire; les erreurs de son discours et les véritables principes du Parti conservateur [par L. G. Desjardins] Québec, Impr. du "Canadien", 1877. 32 p.)

Includes the Author's *La marche triomphale de Sir John A. Macdonald dans les cantons de l'Est* (pp. [19]-25).

DUNN, OSCAR   Changement de ministère. (In *L'Opinion publique.* Montréal. v. 4, no. 46 (13 nov. 1873), p. 551.)

Discusses the formation of the Alexander Mackenzie cabinet.

—— L'Hon. A. A. Dorion. (In *L'Opinion publique.* Montréal. v. 5, no. 25 (18 juin 1874), pp. [289]-290.)

—— L'Hon. Alexander Mackenzie. (In *L'Opinion publique.* Montréal. v. 4, no. 47 (20 nov. 1873), p. [555].)

—— L'Hon. Edward Blake, Ministre sans portefeuille. (In *L'Opinion publique.* Montréal. v. 4, no. 48 (27 nov. 1873), pp. [567]-568.)

—— La réforme du tarif. Par O. D. (In *L'Opinion publique.* Montréal. v. 5, no. 18 (30 avril 1874), pp. [205]-206.)

Proposed by R. Cartwright.

Echos parlementaires d'Ottawa. Le budget.

(In *L'Opinion publique*. Montréal. v. 9, no. 10 (7 mars 1878), p. [109].)
Concerns the budget brought down by Richard Cartwright.

EDGAR, SIR JAMES DAVID   The Honourable Wilfrid Laurier, MP. By J. D. Edgar. (In *The Week*. Toronto. v. 5, no. 25 (May 17, 1888), p. 397.)
Prominent Canadians – XVIII.

EWAN, JOHN ALEXANDER   Edward Blake and Ireland. By John A. Ewan. (In *The Lake magazine*. [Toronto] v. 1, no. 1 (Aug. 1892), pp. [9]-15.)
Includes discussion of Blake's career in Canada.

——   Hon. Wilfrid Laurier. By John A. Ewan. (In *The Lake magazine*. [Toronto] v. 1, no. 3 (Oct. 1892), pp. 145-148. port.)
At head of title: Two leaders of the Commons.

FAUTEUX, AEGIDIUS   Antoine Aimé Dorion. (In *Les Cahiers des dix*. Montréal. no. 26 (1961), pp. [211]-217.)

FIELD, MRS. ARTHUR   Honorable Edward Blake, 1833-1912. London, Ont., Lawson Memorial Library, University of Western Ontario, 1963. 10 p. (Western Ontario historical notes, v. 19, no. 1.)
Mimeographed.

FORSEY, EUGENE ALFRED   Alexander Mackenzie's memoranda on the appointment of extra senators, 1873-4. (In *The Canadian historical review*. Toronto. v. 27 (1946), pp. 189-194.)

Free discussion. (In *The Nation*. Toronto. v. 2, no. 2 (Jan. 15, 1875), p. 16.)
Concerns controversial discussion over the issue of Canadian independence, with reference to a speech given by Edward Blake in East Toronto.

Free traders and their methods. (In *The Canadian manufacturer and industrial world*. Toronto. v. 30, no. 6 (Mar. 15, 1895), pp. 247-248.)
An editorial comment on the "free trade as they have it in Britain" policy of Wilfred Laurier and the Liberal Party.

GELINAS, AIME   A propos de politique. Par A. Gélinas. (In *L'Opinion publique*. Montréal. v. 8, no. 30 (26 juil. 1877), p.[349].)
Relates to the speech Discours sur le libéralisme politique, delivered by Wilfrid Laurier in Quebec on June 20, 1877.

——   La politique. Par A. Gélinas. (In *L'Opinion publique*. Montréal. v. 8, no. 45 (8 nov. 1877), pp. 532-533.)

Discusses the Drummond-Arthabaska by-election held October 27, 1877, and the defeat of Wilfrid Laurier by D. O. Bourbeau.

GOUIN, LEON MERCIER   L'idéal patriotique d'Honoré Mercier. (In *Revue de l'Université d'Ottawa*. [Ottawa] 11. année (1941), pp. [159]-175.)

Government management of railways. (In *The Nation*. Toronto. v. 1, no. 3 (Apr. 16, 1874), pp. 33-34.)
Concerns Liberal government policy regarding the Canadian Pacific railway.

GRAHAM, JANE ELIZABETH   The Riel amnesty and the Liberal Party in central Canada, 1869-1875. [Kingston, Ont.] 1967. 1 v.
Thesis (MA) – Queen's University.

GRAHAM, WILLIAM ROGER   The Alexander MacKenzie administration, 1873-78; a study of Liberal tenets and tactics. Toronto, 1944. 264 leaves.
Thesis (MA) – University of Toronto.
Thesis accepted 1945.

——   Liberal nationalism in the eighteen-seventies. By W. R. Graham. (In Canadian Historical Association. *Report of the annual meeting*. Toronto. (1946), pp. 101-119.)

——   Sir Richard Cartwright and the Liberal Party, 1863-1896. Toronto, 1950. 358 leaves.
Thesis (PH D) – University of Toronto.

——   Sir Richard Cartwright, Wilfrid Laurier and Liberal Party trade policy, 1887. By W. R. Graham. (In *The Canadian historical review*. Toronto. v. 33 (1952) pp. 1-18.)

GREENING, WILLIAM EDWARD   The *Globe* and Canadian politics, 1890-1902; a study of the policies of the *Globe* and their influence on Liberal policies. [Toronto] 1939. 134 leaves.
Thesis (MA) – University of Toronto.

HARRIS, EDWARD   Mr. Blake's letter, and the ethics of opposition. (In *The Week*. Toronto. v. 8, no. 19 (Apr. 10, 1891), pp. 297-298.)
Discusses Edward Blake's letter to the West Durham Reform Convention published on March 5, 1891, and Blake's retirement.

Has served under four premiers. (In *The Busy man's magazine*. Toronto. v. 16, no. 3 (July 1908), pp. 79-80.)
Concerns the Hon. Sir Richard William Scott.

"Mr. Scott was a Conservative, but joined the Liberal ranks in 1871." – p. 80.

HASSARD, ALBERT RICHARD   Great Canadian orators. VI. Edward Blake. By Albert R. Hassard. (In *The Canadian magazine of politics, science, art and literature.* Toronto. v. 54 (1919/20), pp. 240-246.)

HENDERSON, GEORGE FLETCHER   Alexander Mackenzie and the Canadian Pacific Railway, 1871-1878. [Kingston, Ont.] 1964. 1 v.
Thesis (MA) – Queen's University.

HISTORICUS   Blake, Mowat, Laurier. By "Historicus". (In *Saturday night.* Toronto. v. 37, no. 13 (Jan. 28, 1922), p. 2.)

——— Memories of Blake and other Liberals. By Historicus. (In *Saturday night.* Toronto. v. 32, no. 32 (May 24, 1919), p. 3.)

HORTON, WILLIAM, OF LONDON, CANADA   Memoir of the late Thomas Scatcherd, barrister-at-law, Queen's Counsel and Member of Parliament for the North Riding of Middlesex, Canada. A family record. London, Ontario, 1878. 212 p.

HUGHES, KATHERINE   Honourable David Laird. (In *The Canadian magazine of politics, science, art and literature.* Toronto. v. 27 (1906), pp. 400-403.)
Canadian celebrities, no. 72.

Isaac Erb Bowman. (In *Waterloo Historical Society. Annual report.* Kitchener, Ont. 20th (1932), pp. 334-335.)
A short biographical sketch.

JACKSON, ERIC VIVIAN   The organization of the Canadian Liberal Party, 1867-1896. With particular reference to Ontario. Toronto, 1962. 270 leaves.
Thesis (MA) – University of Toronto.

James Livingston. (In *Waterloo Historical Society. Annual report.* Kitchener, Ont. 9th (1921), pp. 189-191.)
A short biographical sketch.

John Macdonald, Senator. By G. S. A. (In *The Week.* Toronto. v. 6, no. 31 (July 5, 1889), pp. 488-490.)
Prominent Canadians: XXVII.

JOHNSTON, HUGH   A merchant prince; life of Hon. Senator John Macdonald. Toronto, W. Briggs, 1893. 321 p.
"In 1887 he (Hon. John Macdonald) was made a Senator of Canada, the only Liberal ever appointed to the Upper House on the nomination of Sir John Macdonald." – (W. S. Wallace. *The Macmillan Dictionary of Canadian biography.* 3d ed. p. 439.)

Judge Wilson and the "Globe". (In *The Nation.* Toronto. v. 3, no. 28 (July 14, 1876), p. 327.)
Refers to attacks by George Brown on Judge Adam Wilson over the interpretation of the "Big Push" letter, written by Brown to Senator John Simpson in 1872.

KENDRICK, H. ROBERT   Amor de Cosmos and Confederation. (In Shelton, W. G. (ed.) *British Columbia and Confederation.* Victoria, B.C., 1967. pp. 67-96.)

KNOXONIAN   Hon. Alexander Mackenzie, MP. By Knoxonian. (In *The Week.* Toronto. v. 5, no. 7 (Jan. 12, 1888), pp. 104-105.)
Prominent Canadians – IX.

LANDON, FRED   When Laurier met Ontario. (In Royal Society of Canada. *Proceedings and transactions.* Ottawa. ser. 3, v. 35 (1941), section 2, pp. [1]-14.)
Presidential address.
Concerns tours through Ontario made by Wilfrid Laurier during 1886 and 1888.

LANGELIER, CHARLES   Souvenirs politiques; récits, études et portraits. Par l'Hon. Chs. Langelier. Québec, Dussault & Proulx, 1909-12. 2 v.
Contents: [t. 1] De 1878 à 1890. – [t. 2.] 1890 à 1896. Mercier, son renvoi d'office, son procès, sa mort.
Records observations on Quebec and federal politics.

LA TERREUR, MARC   Sir Wilfrid Laurier écrit à Emilie Lavergne. (In *Le Magazine Maclean.* Montréal. v. 6, no. 1 (jan. 1966), pp. [14-15]; 36-41.)
The correspondence consisted of 41 letters written during 1891-1893.

LAURIER, SIR WILFRID   Discours sur le libéralisme politique. Prononcé par M. W. Laurier, député fédéral, le 20 juin 1877, à la Salle de musique, sous les auspices du Club canadien. Québec, Impr. de l'Evénement, 1877. 32 p.

——— Lecture on political liberalism. Delivered by Wilfrid Laurier, MP, on the 20th June, 1877, in the Music Hall, Quebec, under the auspices of Le Club canadien. Quebec, Printed at the Morning Chronicle Office, 1877. 44 p.

———Political liberalism; definition of the liberal idea. Mr. Laurier, an admirer and disciple of the English liberal school. (In his *Wilfrid Laurier on the platform.* Quebec, 1890. pp. [51]-80.)

Translation of *Discours sur le libéralisme politique.*

"Lecture delivered at the Academy of Music, Quebec, on the invitation of the Club canadien, on the 26th [sic] June, 1877."

—— Political liberalism. By Wilfrid Laurier. (In Locke, G. H. (ed.) *Builders of the Canadian commonwealth.* Freeport, NY. [1967] pp. 183-186.)

An excerpt from the speech delivered before the Club canadien in Quebec, June 20, 1877.

—— Quebec the shuttlecock of Tory Party. (In *The Statesman.* Toronto. v. 1, no. 33 (Mar. 8, 1919), p. 9.)

Extract from a speech delivered before the Young Men's Liberal Club of Toronto, December 10, 1886.

—— Sir Antoine Aimé Dorion. By Wilfrid Laurier. (In *The Week.* Toronto. v. 7, no. 43 (Sept. 26, 1890), pp. 677-679.)

Prominent Canadians: xxx.

—— Wilfrid Laurier à la tribune; recueil des principaux discours prononcés au Parlement ou devant le peuple par l'honorable W. Laurier . . . député de Québec-Est aux communes, depuis son entrée dans la politique active en 1871. Edition française. Compilée par Ulric Barthe . . . et précédé d'une étude sur sa carrière et son œuvre. Québec, Des Presses de Turcotte & Menard, 1890. xxxii, 617, x p.

At head of title: 1871-1890.

—— Wilfrid Laurier on the platform; a collection of the principal speeches made in Parliament or before the people, by the Honorable Wilfrid Laurier, member for Quebec East in the Commons since his entry into active politics in 1871. Compiled by Ulric Barthe . . . and prefaced with a sketch of his career and work. Quebec, Turcotte & Menard's Stream Print. Office, 1890. xxxii, 624 p.

At head of title: 1871-1890.

LAWDER, ROBERT H. Hon. Jas. Young's letters to the "Globe". (In *The Week.* Toronto. v. 11, no. 19 (Apr. 6, 1894), pp. 438-439.)

Mr. Young appears to have been invited to write a series of letters, addressed to the *Globe*, on the subject of Canadian national policy.

LEDERLE, JOHN W. The Liberal convention of 1893. (In *The Canadian journal of economics and political science.* [Toronto] v. 16 (1950), pp. 42-52.)

". . . the object is to investigate the patterns and precedents which the 1893 convention established for subsequent Liberal and Conservative convention."

LEMIEUX, RODOLPHE Edward Blake. By the Honourable Rodolphe Lemieux. (In *Willisons monthly.* Sarnia, Ont. v. 4, no. 12 (June 1929), pp. 392-394.)

Letellier de Saint Just. By W. (In *The Week.* Toronto. v. 3, no. 33 (July 15, 1886), pp. [523]-524.)

A review article of *Letellier de Saint Just et son temps; étude historique,* par P. B. Casgrain. Québec, 1885.

LEWIS, JOHN Famous Canadian trials: George Brown for contempt of court. (In *The Canadian magazine of politics, science, art and literature.* Toronto. v. 45 (1915), pp. 101-103.)

Famous Canadian trials, 7.

The case was heard in December 1876 and involved Senator George Brown and Judge Adam Wilson. Brown issued a critical editorial statement in the *Globe* July 8, 1876, objecting to remarks made by Judge Wilson with regard to the "big push" letter exchanged between Brown and Senator John Simpson in 1872.

—— George Brown. Ed. de luxe. Toronto, Morang, 1906. 281 p. (The Makers of Canada, v. 15.)

The Liberal opposition. (In *The Week.* Toronto. v. 4, no. 28 (June 9, 1887), p. [443].)

Comments are made on the occasion of the resignation of Edward Blake as leader of the federal Liberal Party.

LIBERAL PARTY (CANADA) Official report of the Liberal Convention held in response to the call of Hon. Wilfrid Laurier, leader of the Liberal Party of the Dominion of Canada. Ottawa, Tuesday, June 20th and Wednesday, June 21st, 1893. Toronto, Published by the Budget Print. & Pub. Co., 1893. 160 p.

The Liberal Party. By F. W. F. (In *The Week.* Toronto. v. 9, no. 22 (Apr. 29, 1892), pp. 346-347.)

The Liberal platform. (In *The Week.* Toronto. v. 10, no. 31 (June 30, 1893), pp. 725-726.)

The Liberal policy. By F. W. F. (In *The Week.* Toronto. v. 10, no. 13 (Feb. 24, 1893), pp. 299-300.)

The Liberal policy on commercial union.

The Liberals and their leaders. (In *The Nation*. Toronto. v. 3, no. 13 (Mar. 31, 1876), pp. 147-148.)

Examines the policy of the Liberal Party and the idea of coalition government.

Liberty of the Press vs. liberty of the Bench. (In *The Nation*. Toronto. v. 3, no. 29 (July 21, 1876), p. 340.)

Concerns the attack by the *Globe* on Judge Wilson over interpretation of the "Big push" letter written by George Brown to Senator John Simpson in 1872.

LOUDON, JAMES Edward Blake. By J. Loudon. (In *The University monthly*. Toronto. v. 12, no. 7 (May 1912), pp. 325-338.)

Personal recollections.

MABLE, THORPE M. Letellier de Saint-Just. By Thorpe Mable [pseud.] (In *The Week*. Toronto. v. 2, no. 22 (Apr. 30, 1885), pp. 340-341.)

A review article of *Letellier de Saint-Just et son temps; étude historique*, par P. B. Casgrain. Québec, 1885.

MC GILLICUDDY, DAN M. C. Cameron; as I knew him. A character sketch. (In *The Canadian magazine of politics, science, art and literature*. Toronto. v. 12 (1898/99), pp. 57-60.)

Concerns Malcolm Colin Cameron, Lieutenant-Governor of the North-West Territories; Member of Parliament for the Liberal Party from Huron County in the first federal parliament.

MACKENZIE, ALEXANDER The life and speeches of Hon. George Brown. By Alex. Mackenzie. Toronto, Globe Print. Co., 1882. viii, 381 p.

―――― Speeches of the Hon. Alexander Mackenzie during his recent visit to Scotland, with his principal speeches in Canada since the session of 1875. Accompanied by portrait and sketch of his life and public services. Toronto, J. Campbell, 1876. 219 p.

MAC KINNON, FRANK David Laird of Prince Edward Island. (In *The Dalhousie review*. Halifax. v. 26 (1946/47), pp. [405]-421.)

MAC LAREN, A. MARGARET Edward Blake and imperial relations. Toronto, 1935. 207 leaves.

Thesis (MA) – University of Toronto.

MC LENNAN, C. P. Hon. William Stevens Fielding, Premier of Nova Scotia. (In *The*

Week. Toronto. v. 5, no. 5 (Dec. 29, 1887), pp. 74-75.)

Prominent Canadians – VIII.

MC NAUGHT, CARLTON Hon. James Young: Canadian patriot. (In Waterloo Historical Society. *Annual report*. Kitchener, Ont. 6th (1918), pp. 37-43.)

A biographical sketch.

MARQUIS, THOMAS GUTHRIE Hon. Alexander Mackenzie. (In his *Builders of Canada from Cartier to Laurier*. Detroit, Mich. [c1903] pp. 392-418.)

List of Mackenzie's Ministry: p. 410.

MARTELL, L. H. Joe Howe's last opponent. (In *Maclean's magazine*. Toronto. v. 28, no. 6 (Apr. 1915), pp. [31]-32.)

Concerns Monson H. Goudge, Liberal Member of Parliament representing Hants County, N.S.

MEAGHER, NICHOLAS HOGAN Life of the Hon. Jonathan McCully, 1809-1877. By the Hon. Nicholas H. Meagher. (In Nova Scotia Historical Society. *Collections*. Halifax. v. 21 (1927), pp. 73-114.)

"Read 15th December, 1922."

Mr. Blake's Aurora speech. (In *The Nation*. Toronto. v. 1, no. 28 (Oct. 8, 1874), p. 332.)

A brief comment on the address delivered at Aurora, Ont., October 3, 1874.

Mr. Blake's speech. (In *The Nation*. Toronto. v. 2, no. 23 (June 11, 1875), pp. 270-271.)

A summary and comment.

Mr. Brown on his treaty. (In *The Nation*. Toronto. v. 2, no. 8 (Feb. 26, 1875), p. 90.)

Concerns George Brown and his presentation of the draft Reciprocity Treaty. Considers the nature of the political roles of Prime Minister Alexander Mackenzie and George Brown, Canadian delegate to Washington.

Mr. George Brown's letters. (In *The Nation*. Toronto. v. 2, no. 40 (Oct. 8, 1875), pp. 474-475.)

Refers to "the unearthing of his corrupt correspondence in 1872", especially a letter (the "big push" letter) dated August 15, 1872, addressed to Senator John Simpson of Bowmanville, Ont.

MOODY, BARRY MORRIS Edward Blake, Canadian nationalist. [Wolfville, NS] 1967. 1 v.

Thesis (BA Honours) – Acadia University.

MOWAT, OLIVER The Reform Party and

Canada's future. An open letter from the Hon. Oliver Mowat, Premier of Ontario, to the Hon. Alexander Mackenzie, MP for East York and formerly Prime Minister of Canada. With an appendix. Toronto, Printed by Hunter, Rose, 1891. 40 p.

MURRAY, JOHN CLARK Mr. Edward Blake. By J. Clark Murray. (In The Week. Toronto. v. 4, no. 32 (July 7, 1887), pp. [511]-512.)

A National tariff. (In The Nation. Toronto. v. 3, no. 9 (Mar. 3, 1876), p. 100.)
Considers the idea as presented in the budget statement of Finance Minister, Richard Cartwright.

A New departure. (In The Nation. Toronto. v. 3, no. 2 (Jan. 14, 1876), p. 19.)
Concerns a speech by L. S. Huntington attacking Ultramontanism.

The New tariff. (In The Nation. Toronto. v. 1, no. 4 (Apr. 23, 1874), pp. 44-45.)
Discusses the policy adopted by Richard Cartwright relating to customs and excise duties.

The New tariff renewed. (In The Nation. Toronto. v. 1, no. 6 (May 7, 1874), pp. 68-69.)
Discusses the adjustments to the tariff proposals contained in an original budget presented by Richard Cartwright, Minister of Finance.

Le Nouveau ministre. (In L'Opinion publique. Montréal. v. 8, no. 5 (1 fév. 1877), p. [49].)
Concerns Charles-Pantaléon Pelletier, Minister of Agriculture.

OBAY, L. Le Parti libéral et l'exécution du complot maçonnique. La question des écoles du Manitoba. (In Le Mouvement catholique. Trois-Rivières. v. 1 (jan.—juin 1898), pp. 321-329.)

ONTARIO Mr. Laurier's new departure. By Ontario. (In The Week. Toronto. v. 9, no. 3 (Dec. 18, 1891), pp. 37-38.)

ORMSBY, MARGARET ANCHORETTA Prime Minister Mackenzie, the Liberal Party and the bargain with British Columbia. By Margaret A. Ormsby. (In The Canadian historical review. Toronto. v. 26 (1945), pp. 148-173.)

—— The quarrel between the Governor-General and the Prime Minister, 1876. By Margaret A. Ormsby. (In Okanagan Historical Society. Report. Vernon, B.C. 11th (1945), pp. 49-55.)

Concerns Lord Dufferin and Alexander Mackenzie with reference to the dispute between the federal government and British Columbia over railway terms.

Our Canadian portrait gallery. No. 25—Hon. George Brown. (In Canadian illustrated news. Montreal. v. 1, no. 26 (Apr. 30, 1870), pp. [401]-402.)

Our Canadian portrait gallery. No. 57—Hon. Joseph E. Cauchon, Speaker of the Senate. (In Canadian illustrated news. Montreal. v. 3, no. 8 (Feb. 25, 1871), p. 114.)

Our Canadian portrait gallery. [No.] 111—L. A. Jetté, esq., MP. (In Canadian illustrated news. Montreal. v. 6, no. 12 (Sept. 21, 1872), pp. 181-182.)
A brief biographical sketch.

The Outlook at Ottawa. (In The Nation. Toronto. v. 1, no. 1 (Apr. 2, 1874), p. 11.)
Brief comments on the prospects for the government of Alexander Mackenzie.

The Pacific Railway and British Columbia. (In The Nation. Toronto. v. 1, no. 8 (May 21, 1874), p. 94.)
Concerns the proposed policy of the Liberal Government regarding the building of the railway and subsidy terms with British Columbia.

PELLAND, JOSEPH OCTAVE Biographie, discours, conférences, etc. de l'Hon. Honoré Mercier . . . premier ministre de la province de Québec. Par J. O. Pelland. Montréal, 1890. 814 p.
Mercier represented Rouville for the Parti national in the House of Commons, 1872-74 and then retired from federal politics. – Encyclopedia Canadiana. 1966 ed. v. 7, p. 29.

PHELPS, EDWARD A Liberal back-bencher in the Macdonald regime: the political career of John Henry Fairbank of Petrolia. London, Ont., Lawson Memorial Library, University of Western Ontario, 1966. 45 p. (Western Ontario historical notes, v. 22, no. 1.)
Mimeographed.

PICHE, ARISTIDES L'affaire Cotté. (In Le Réveil. Montréal. v. 1, no. 24 (4 nov. 1876), pp. 359-360.)
Discusses the pressure brought to bear on the Quebec government by Edward Blake to bring Cotté to justice.

—— Notes et commentaires. (In Le Réveil. Montréal. v. 1, no. 28 (2 déc. 1876), pp. 423-424.)
Discusses the election of T. A. R. La-

flamme in the by-election held in the constituency of Jacques-Cartier, Que., November 28, 1876.

A Policy of hush up. (In The Nation. Toronto. v. 2, no. 42 (Oct. 22, 1875), pp. 499-500.)
Further comments on the letter sent in August 1872 to Senator John Simpson by George Brown.

The Political situation. By a Canadian Liberal. (In The Week. Toronto. v. 7, no. 35 (Aug. 1, 1890), pp. 550-551.)

The Premier's speech. (In The Nation. Toronto. v. 2, no. 42 (Oct. 22, 1875), pp. 498-499.)
Examines a statement presented by Alexander Mackenzie in an address at Sarnia, Ont., October 11, 1875. Cf. Full text of speech under title: Exposition of policy at Sarnia. (In Mackenzie, Alexander. Speeches. Toronto, 1876. pp. [136]-173.)

Reform government in the Dominion. The Pic-Nic speeches delivered in the province of Ontario during the summer of 1877 by the Hon. A. Mackenzie, Premier and Minister of Public Works, Hon. E. Blake, President of the Council, Hon. R. J. Cartwright, Minister of Finance, Hon. L. S. Huntington, Postmaster-General and Hon. D. Mills, Minister of the Interior. Toronto, Printed by the Globe Print. and Pub. Co., 1878. 188 p.

RINFRET, THIBAUDEAU Le juge Télesphore Fournier. (In Revue trimestrielle canadienne. Montréal. v. 12 (1926), pp. [1]-16.)
"Cette conférence à été donné au Cercle universitaire, le 22 janvier 1926 . . . ."

RIVET, LOUIS ALFRED ADHEMAR Honoré Mercier; patriote et homme d'Etat. Conférence prononcée, le 14 décembre 1922... à Montréal, sous la présidence d'honneur de Sir Lomer Gouin, ministre de la Justice. [Préf. par L.-O. David] Montréal, Beauchemin [1924] 140 p.

ROBERTSON, BARBARA ANNE The federal Liberal Party in Canada; a study of its representatives and representation, 1878-1896. [Kingston, Ont.] 1957. 272 leaves.
Thesis (MA) – Queen's University.

ROBINSON, JOHN R. Canadian celebrities: the Hon. Joseph Martin. (In The Canadian magazine of politics, science, art and literature. Toronto. v. 13 (1899), pp. 424-428.)
Canadian celebrities: no. 7.

ROSS, MARGARET Amor de Cosmos, a British Columbia reformer. [Vancouver] 1931. 200 leaves.
Thesis (MA) – University of British Columbia.

ROWAN, CHARLES MICHAEL Timothy Warren Anglin; journalist and politician, portraying New Brunswick's reaction to Confederation during the years 1867-1872. [Fredericton, 1953] 130 leaves.
Thesis (MA) – University of New Brunswick.

ROY, PAUL EUGENE L. A. Olivier. Par P. E. Roy. Levis, Qué., 1891. 30 p.
Louis Auguste Olivier was appointed to the Senate in 1867.

Les Ruines libérales. Quelques pages de politique. Montréal, 1878. 160 p.
A presentation of the case of Luc Letellier de St. Just.

RUMILLY, ROBERT Mercier. Montréal, Editions du Zodiaque [1936] 545 p. (Collection du Zodiaque '35, no. 1865.)

RUTHVEN, ED. Ottawa notes. (In The Week. Toronto. v. 1, no. 17 (Mar. 27, 1884), pp. 266-267.)
Discusses the speech made by Edward Blake on the occasion of "the annual Orange Bill episode" and the "revival of the talk about a union of forces by him (Blake) and Sir Hector Langevin".

SAGE, WALTER NOBLE Amor de Cosmos, journalist and politician. By Walter N. Sage. (In The British Columbia historical quarterly. Victoria, B.C. v. 8 (1944), pp. 189-212.)
Amor de Cosmos was born William Alexander Smith. In 1871 he was elected to represent Victoria, B.C., in the federal Parliament and, at the same time, served as a member in the Legislative Assembly of British Columbia.

SAVILLE Hon. Henry Gustave Joly. By Saville. (In The Week. Toronto. v. 5, no. 20 (Apr. 12, 1888), p. 315.)
Prominent Canadians – xv.
Concerns Sir Henry Gustave Joly de Lotbinière.

SELLAR, ROBERT George Brown, the Globe, Confederation. Toronto, Britnell's Bookstore [1917] 32 p.

SHEPPARD, EDMUND ERNEST Around town. By Don. (In *Toronto Saturday night*. Toronto. v. 8, no. 46 (Oct. 5, 1895), p. 1.)

Discusses Wilfrid Laurier's statement "Thank God, there is not an Orangeman among the Liberals".

—— Around town. By Don. (In *Toronto Saturday night*. Toronto. v. 9, no. 19 (Mar. 28, 1896), pp. 1-2.)

Comments on Wilfrid Laurier and remedial legislation, with reference to the Manitoba Schools issue.

—— Hon. Edward Blake's letter. By Don. (In *Toronto Saturday night*. Toronto. v. 4, no. 16 (Mar. 14, 1891), pp. [1]-2.)

Discusses Blake's letter to the West Durham Reform Convention, published on March 5, 1891, dealing with unrestricted reciprocity.

SNELL, JAMES The West Toronto by-election of 1873 and Thomas Moss. (In *Ontario history*. Toronto. v. 58, no. 4 (Dec. 1966), pp. [237]-256.)

SPLANE, RICHARD BEVERLEY The Upper Canada Reform Party, 1867-1878. Toronto, 1948, 2 v.

Thesis (MA) – University of Toronto.

Contains material on Edward Blake.

STAMP, ROBERT MILES J. D. Edgar and the Liberal Party; 1867-96. By Robert M. Stamp. (In *The Canadian historical review*. Toronto. v. 45 (1964), pp. 93-115.)

—— J. D. Edgar and the Pacific Junction Railway: the problems of a nineteenth century Ontario railway promoter. By Robert M. Stamp. (In *Ontario history*. [Toronto] v. 55, no. 3 (Sept. 1963), pp. [119]-130.)

—— The public career of Sir James David Edgar. Toronto, 1962. 453 leaves.

Thesis (MA) – University of Toronto.

The Stormy petrel of Canadian politics. Hon. Joseph Martin, of Vancouver, passes away after unique career. (In *Saturday night*. Toronto. v. 38, no. 19 (Mar. 17, 1923), p. 3.)

Written on the occasion of his death March 2, 1923.

STUBBS, ROY ST. GEORGE Hon. Edmund Burke Wood. (In Historical and Scientific Society of Manitoba. *Papers*. Winnipeg. ser. 3, no. 13 (1958), pp. 27-47.)

SWAINSON, DONALD WAYNE Richard Cartwright joins the Liberal Party. By Donald Swainson. (In *Queen's quarterly*. Kingston. v. 75 (1968), pp. [124]-134.)

THOMSON, DALE C. Alexander Mackenzie; Clear Grit. Toronto, Macmillan, 1960. vii, 436 p.

TUSCARORA Sir Richard John Cartwright, KCMG, MP. By Tuscarora. (In *The Week*. Toronto. v. 5, no. 15 (Mar. 8, 1888), pp. 230-231.)

Prominent Canadians – XIII.

UNDERHILL, FRANK HAWKINS Edward Blake. By Frank H. Underhill. (In Bissell, C. T. (ed.) *Seven Canadians*. [Toronto, 1962, c1957] pp. 3-28.)

Our living tradition, ser. 1.

—— Edward Blake and Canadian Liberal nationalism. By Frank H. Underhill. (In Flenley, Ralph (ed.) *Essays in Canadian history*. Toronto, 1939. pp. 132-153.)

—— Edward Blake, the Liberal Party and unrestricted reciprocity. (In Canadian Historical Association. *Report of the annual meeting*. Toronto. (1939), pp. 133-141.)

—— Edward Blake, the Supreme Court Act and the appeal to the Privy Council, 1875-6. (In *The Canadian historical review*. Toronto. v. 19 (1938), pp. 245-263.)

"A note upon the references to the Supreme Court Act, 1875, in certain books on the Canadian constitution": pp. 262-263.

—— Laurier and Blake, 1882-1891. (In *The Canadian historical review*. Toronto. v. 20 (1939), pp. 392-408.)

—— Laurier and Blake, 1891-2. (In *The Canadian historical review*. Toronto. v. 24 (1943), pp. 135-155.)

VANASSE, FABIEN A la veillée. (In *L'Opinion publique*. Montréal. v. 9, no. 10 (7 mars 1878), pp. 110; 112.)

Comments on the details of the budget brought down by R. Cartwright.

WALLACE, CARL Albert Smith, Confederation and reaction in New Brunswick, 1852-1882. (In *The Canadian historical review*. Toronto. v. 44 (1963), pp. 285-312.)

WALLACE, WILLIAM STEWART The mystery of Edward Blake. By W. S. Wallace. (In *The Canadian magazine of politics, science, art and literature*. Toronto. v. 39 (1912), pp. 395-400.)

WELLS, JAMES EDWARD Alexander Mackenzie. By J. E. Wells. (In *The McMaster*

University monthly. Toronto. v. 2 (Nov. 1892), pp. [57]-65.)

—— Hon. Oliver Mowat, QC, LL D. By J. E. Wells. (In *The Week*. Toronto. v. 4, no. 43 (Sept. 22, 1887), pp. 694-695.)
Prominent Canadians – I.

WESTERN, MAURICE ALBAN WALTER Edward Blake as leader of the opposition, 1880-1887. Toronto, 1940. 288 leaves.
Thesis (MA) – University of Toronto.

WILD, ROLAND GIBSON Amor De Cosmos. Foreword, by W. A. C. Bennett. Toronto, Ryerson Press [1958] xi, 146 p.

WILLISON, SIR JOHN STEPHEN The premiers of Ontario since Confederation. By J. S. Willison. (In *The Canadian magazine of politics, science, art and literature*. Toronto. v. 10 (1897/98), pp. 16-31.)
Includes a section devoted to Edward Blake (pp. 22-27).

—— Reminiscences, political and personal. [Pt. 3] Mr. John Cameron and the Blake wing. (In *The Canadian magazine of politics, science, art and literature*. Toronto. v. 51 (1918), pp. 229-240.)

—— Reminiscences, political and personal. [Pt. 10] A letter and a mystery. (In *The Canadian magazine of politics, science, art and literature*. Toronto. v. 52 (1918/ 19), pp. 873-882.)
A background study on Edward Blake's West Durham letter opposing unrestricted reciprocity published March 5, 1891.

ZOLTVANY, YVES Les Libéraux du Québec, leur parti et leur pensée, 1867-1873. [Montréal, 1960] 1 v.
Thesis (MA) – University of Montreal.

1896–1921

ABERCROMBIE, CLINTON WILLIAM The part played by Sir Wilfrid Laurier in the development of Canada. Vancouver, 1929. 167 leaves.
Thesis (MA) – University of British Columbia.

ALLEN, PATRICK Bourassa et l'impérialisme anglais. (In *L'Action nationale*. Montréal. v. 43 (jan. 1954), pp. [57]-82.)

ANDERSON, HARRY W. Building up a powerful opposition at Ottawa. By Harry W. Anderson, in Toronto *Globe*. (In *The Busy man's Canada*. Toronto. v. 3, no. 3 (Oct. 1912), pp. 30-37.)
Concerns the Liberal Party in opposition.

—— National affairs: the men around the white plume. (In *MacLean's magazine*. Toronto. v. 27, no. 10 (Aug. 1914), pp. [7]-9; 137-141.)
Concerns the colleagues surrounding Sir Wilfrid Laurier.

—— The party bolter—Clifford Sifton. By H. W. Anderson. (In *MacLean's magazine*. Toronto. v. 21, no. 6 (Apr. 1911), pp. [27]-28.)

—— Red Michael. An appreciation of the character and talents of Dr. Michael Clark, Member of Parliament for Red Deer, Alberta. (In *The Canadian magazine of politics, science, art and literature*. Toronto. v. 42 (1913/14), pp. 584-589.)

ARMSTRONG, WALTER S. B. From grocer's apprentice to Senator. (In *The Busy man's magazine*. Montreal, Toronto. v. 12, no. 1 (May 1906), pp. [5]-8.)
Concerns the career of Hon. Robert Jaffray, created a Senator in March 1906.

ASSELIN, OLIVAR Sir Wilfrid Laurier. (In his *Pensée française*. Montréal [1937] pp. [101]-113.)

ATKINSON, WILLIAM DAVID Organized labour and the Laurier administration; the fortunes of a pressure group. [Ottawa, 1957] 196 leaves.
Thesis (MA) – Carleton University.

AUCLAIR, ELIE JOSEPH ARTHUR Sir Wilfrid Laurier. Par l'abbé Elie-J. Auclair. (In *Revue canadienne*. Montréal. nouv. sér., v. 23 (1919), pp. [161]-175.)
Written on the occasion of the death of Sir Wilfrid Laurier in Ottawa on February 17, 1919.

AUNT ADELAIDE Mainly about women. By Aunt Adelaide. (In *The Statesman*. Toronto. v. 1, no. 19 (Nov. 30, 1918), p. 14.)
States a position taken by women supporting the Liberal Party towards "Toryism" and the Women's Party.

BANKS, MARGARET AMELIA Toronto opinion of French Canada during the Laurier régime, 1896-1911. Toronto, 1950. 159 leaves.
Thesis (MA) – University of Toronto.

BARBEAU, ROBERT L'idée de libre-échange chez Wilfrid Laurier. (In *Economie québécoise*. [Québec] 1969. pp. [363]-369.)

BARKER, AILEEN ELIZABETH Laurier, French Canada and the Boer War. [Vancouver] 1961. 1 v.
Thesis (MA) – University of British Columbia.

BARRON, JOHN AUGUSTUS The Honorable Wilfrid Laurier. (In *The Canadian magazine of politics, science, art and literature.* Toronto. v. 6 (1895/96), pp. [237]-241.)

BEAUCHESNE, ARTHUR Les dernières sessions parlementaires de Laurier. (In *La Revue moderne.* Montréal. 1. année, no 6 (15 avril 1920), pp. 9-11.)

—— Israël Tarte. (In *La Revue moderne.* Montréal. 1. année, no 11 (15 sept. 1920), pp. 14-15.)

The Beginning of Sir Wilfrid Laurier. (In *The Canadian courier.* Toronto. v. 2, no. 5 (June 29, 1907), p. 15.)

BEIQUE, CAROLINE ANGELINAS (DESSAULLES) Quatre-vingts ans de souvenirs. Par Mme. F.L. Béique. Montréal, B. Valiquette, A[ction] c[anadienne] f[rançaise, 1939] 287 p.
Half-title: Histoire d'une famille.
Frédéric Ligori Béique was a member of the Canadian Senate from 1902 to 1933.
Partial contents: Sir Wilfrid Laurier. – Quelques hommes politiques.

BENOIT, JOSEPH PAUL AUGUSTIN Les élections de 1896. Le réglement Laurier-Greenway. Par Dom Benoît. (In *Le Mouvement catholique.* Trois-Rivières. v. 4 (juil.—déc. 1899), pp. 536-547.)

—— Le libéralisme et le Parti libéral. Par Dom Benoît. (In *Le Mouvement catholique.* Trois-Rivières. v. 5 (jan.—juin 1900), pp. [37]-45.)

BENTLEY, MARY PATRICIA The budget of 1909; a study of contemporary interpretation of Liberal financial policy. [Kingston, Ont.] 1967. 1 v.
Thesis (MA) – Queen's University.

BERGEVIN, ANDRE Henri Bourassa; biographie, index des écrits, index de la correspondance publique, 1895-1924. Par André Bergevin, Cameron Nish et Anne Bourassa. [Préf. de François-Albert Angers] [Montréal] Editions de l'Action nationale, 1966. lxii, 150 p.
Contents: Introduction: Biographie d'Henri Bourassa, par Anne Bourassa. – Index des ouvrages, des articles, des discours, des conférences d'Henri Bourassa, préparé par André Bergevin. – Index de la correspondance publique d'Henri Bourassa, 1895-1924, préparé par Cameron Nish.

—— Les œuvres de Bourassa. Index par sujet des ouvrages, articles et conférences.

(In *L'Action nationale.* Montréal. v. 43 (jan. 1954), pp. [199]-244.)
Contents: 1. Ouvrages et brochures. – 2. Articles, discours et conférences.

BIGGAR, CHARLES ROBERT WEBSTER Sir Oliver Mowat; a biographical sketch. Toronto, Warwick & Rutter, 1905. 2 v.

BILKEY, PAUL Who is second man up to Sir Wilfrid? Hazard number one, a Conservative opinion. (In *The Canadian courier.* Toronto. v. 20, no. 1 (June 3, 1916), p. [3].)
Advocates Hon. William Pugsley.

BRAY, ROBERT MATTHEW The role of Sir Clifford Sifton in the formulation of the editorial policy of the *Manitoba Free Press,* 1916 to 1921. [Winnipeg] 1968. iv, 161 leaves.
Thesis (MA) – University of Manitoba.

BRIDLE, AUGUSTUS After all, what a man he was! (In *Canadian courier.* Toronto. v. 24, no. 12 (Mar. 15, 1919), pp. 14-15; 22-23. illus.)
Concerns Sir Wilfrid Laurier.

—— The greatest spender in Canada. (In *The Canadian courier.* Toronto. v. 4, no. 19 (Oct. 10, 1908), p. 9.)
Concerns W. S. Fielding, Minister of Finance.

—— Henri Bourassa. (In his *Sons of Canada.* Toronto, 1916. pp. 95-106.)
A character sketch.

—— A political solar system; Rt. Hon. Sir Wilfrid Laurier. (In his *The masques of Ottawa.* Toronto, 1921. pp. 39-51.)

—— Sir Clifford Sifton. (In his *Sons of Canada.* Toronto, 1916. pp. 79-86.)
A character sketch.

—— Sir Wilfrid Laurier. (In his *Sons of Canada.* Toronto, 1916. pp. 29-40.)
A character sketch.

—— Sir William Mulock. (In his *Sons of Canada.* Toronto, 1916. pp. 207-214.)
A character sketch.

BROWNING, JOHN "Gentlemen, we have with us tonight." Toastmaster, John Browning. (In *Saturday night.* Toronto. v. 32, no. 43 (Aug. 9, 1919), p. 2.)
Salutes Daniel Duncan Mackenzie. Presented in the form of an introductory speech.

—— "Gentlemen, we have with us tonight." Toastmaster, John Browning. (In *Saturday night.* Toronto. v. 33, no. 6 (Nov. 22, 1919), p. 2.)

A short biographical sketch of Ernest Lapointe. Presented in the form of an introductory speech.

BRUCHESI, JEAN Sir Wilfrid Laurier et Monseigneur Bruchési. (In Royal Society of Canada. *Proceedings and transactions.* Ottawa. ser. 3, v. 40 (1946), section 1, pp. 3-22.)

BURKE, JOHN E. Eloquent tribute to Laurier's life work. (In *The Statesman.* Toronto. v. 1, no. 32 (Mar. 1, 1919), pp. 6-7.)
An eulogy.

BURRELL, MARTIN British Columbia and its relation to Confederation. By Hon. Martin Burrell. (In Canadian Club of Toronto. *Addresses.* Toronto. (1911/12), pp. 147-158.)
Address delivered March 4, 1912.
"Hon. Martin Burrell, MP, Minister of Agriculture in the Dominion government, represents in Parliament the immense constituency of Yale and Cariboo, British Columbia."

CAMERON, A. KIRK Sir Wilfrid Laurier. (In *Queen's quarterly.* Kingston. v. 26 (1918/19), pp. 420-431.)

Canadian celebrities. No. XII. Senator George A. Cox. [By J. K. M.] (In *The Canadian magazine of politics, science, art and literature.* Toronto. v. 14 (1899/1900), pp. 504-507.)

Canadians worth knowing: Ernest Lapointe, MP. (In *The Canadian nation.* Ottawa. v. 1, no. 11 (Oct. 18, 1919), p. 12.)

CAPPON, JAMES Sir Wilfrid Laurier's liberalism. (In *Queen's quarterly.* [Kingston] v. 11 (1903/04), pp. 334-340.)

CARRIER, MAURICE Laurier, citoyen d'Arthabaska. [Par Frère Antoine] Ottawa, 1961. v, 167 leaves.
Thesis (MA) – University of Ottawa.

CARROL, C. A. Reforms for the militia. (In *The National monthly of Canada.* Toronto. v. 5, no. 5 (Nov. 1904), pp. [235]-237.)
Refers to Liberal government legislation to revise the method of managing the militia.

CARTER, J. SMITH Hon. George P. Graham. Who has been in Washington at the peace-with-honour Tariff Conference. (In *The Canadian courier.* Toronto. v. 7, no. 19 (Apr. 9, 1910), pp. 12-13.)

—— A solver of labour troubles. Something of the early life and training of the

Minister of Labour. (In *The Canadian courier.* Toronto. v. 10, no. 11 (Aug. 12, 1911), pp. 6-7.)
Concerns W. L. Mackenzie King.

CARTWRIGHT, SIR RICHARD JOHN Memories of Confederation. By Sir Richard Cartwright. (In Canadian Club of Ottawa. *Addresses.* Ottawa. (1903/09), pp. 87-94.)

—— Reminiscences. By the Right Honourable Sir Richard Cartwright. [Pref. by J. M. Courtney.] Toronto, W. Briggs, 1912. xiv, 405 p.

Catherine, Forêt Acadienne, bisaïeule maternelle de Sir Wilfrid Laurier. (In *Le Pays laurentien.* Montréal. 3. année, no 2 (fév. 1918), pp. 36-39.)

CHAPLEAU, SIR JOSEPH ADOLPHE Lettre de l'hon. J. A. Chapleau à A. D. DeCelles. (In *Le Bulletin des recherches historiques.* Lévis. v. 69, no 4 (oct. 1967), pp. 157-159.)
Text of a letter dated November 3, 1897. Considers factions within the Liberal Party and states his (Chapleau) personal position at this time. Chapleau was a member of the Conservative Party.

CHARLESWORTH, HECTOR WILLOUGHBY Reflections. By Hector Charlesworth. (In *Saturday night.* Toronto. v. 32, no. 20 (Mar. 1, 1919), p. 2.)
Concerns Sir Wilfrid Laurier. Written on the occasion of his death February 17, 1919.

—— Reflections. By Hector Charlesworth. (In *Saturday night.* Toronto. v. 37, no. 11 (Jan. 14, 1922), p. 2.)
Comments on *Life and letters of Sir Wilfrid Laurier*, by O. D. Skelton. Toronto, S. B. Gundy, 1921. 2 v.

CHEVRIER, BERNARD Le ministère de Félix-Gabriel Marchand (1897). (In *Revue d'histoire de l'Amérique française.* Montréal. v. 22, no 1 (juin 1968), pp. 35-46.)
Discusses the influence of the federal Liberal government under Sir Wilfrid Laurier upon the Quebec provincial election held May 11, 1897, and the formation of the Marchand administration.

CHOQUETTE, PHILIPPE AUGUSTE Un demi-siècle de vie politique. Préf. de Robert Rumilly. [Montréal] Beauchemin, 1936. 352 p.
P. A. Choquette was called to the Senate September 30, 1904; resigned from the Senate December 29, 1919. He died in 1948.

CLARK, MICHAEL Direct vs. indirect taxation. By Dr. Michael Clark, MP. (In *The*

Canadian courier. Toronto. v. 11, no. 14 (Mar. 2, 1912), p. 7.)

CLIFFE, C. D. A leader who stands for high ideals. (In *The Busy man's magazine.* Toronto. v. 16, no. 3 (July 1908), pp. 129-132.)

The Hon. Lomer Gouin, Prime Minister of Quebec. Includes views relating to federal matters.

COLVIN, JAMES A. Sir Wilfrid Laurier and the British preferential tariff system. (In *Canadian Historical Association. Report of the annual meeting.* [Ottawa] (1955), pp.13-23.)

—— Sir Wilfrid Laurier and the imperial problem, 1896-1906. London, 1955. 1 v.
Thesis (PH D) – University of London.

COOKE, BRITTON B. Did Laurier betray us? (In *MacLean's magazine.* Toronto. v. 22, no. 4 (Aug. 1911), pp. [3]-8.)

A discussion of Laurier's representation of Canada at the Imperial Conference, 1911.

COOPER, JOHN ALEXANDER Picturesque Parliament once more. By the Editor. (In *Canadian courier.* Toronto. v. 24, no. 10 (Feb. 15, 1919), pp. 5-6.)

A commentary concentrating on the career of Sir Wilfrid Laurier.

Corridor comment. [Hon. William Pugsley] By H. W. A. (In *The Canadian courier.* Toronto. v. 13, no. 18 (Apr. 15, 1913), p. 12.)

COUTTS, ROBERT MORTIMER The railway policy of Sir Wilfrid Laurier: the Grand Trunk Pacific-National Transcontinental. Toronto, 1968. 222 leaves. maps.
Thesis (MA) – University of Toronto.

CROWLEY, TERENCE A. Mackenzie King and the 1911 election. (In *Ontario history.* Toronto. v. 61, no. 4 (Dec. 1969), pp. [181]-196.)

CUFF, ROBERT DENIS The Toronto eighteen and the election of 1911. By Robert D. Cuff. (In *Ontario history.* Toronto. v. 57, no. 4 (Dec. 1965), pp. [169]-180.)

Refers to the revolt of eighteen members of the Liberal Party.

DAFOE, JOHN WESLEY Clifford Sifton in relation to his time. Toronto, Macmillan, 1931. xxix, 547 p.

—— Laurier; a study in Canadian politics. Toronto, T. Allen [1922] 182 p.

—— Laurier; a study in Canadian politics. With an introd. by Murray S. Donnelly.

[Toronto] McClelland and Stewart [1963] 109 p. (Carleton library, no. 3.)
First published in 1922.

The Daughter of the Old Reformers. The Liberal re-union. By the Daughter of the Old Reformers. (In *The Statesman.* Toronto. v. 1, no. 52 (July 19, 1919), pp. 6-8.)

DAVID, LAURENT OLIVIER Au soir de la vie. Par L.-O. David (Sénateur) Montréal, Beauchemin [1924] 358 p.

"On y trouvera un peu de tout: des souvenirs historiques, des études religieuses, patriotiques et morales, des observations sur notre situation politique et nationale et sur nos destinées." – Avant-propos.

—— La croix et l'épée au Canada. Montréal, Beauchemin, 1926. 123 p. (Bibliothèque canadienne. Collection Montcalm, no. 433 B.)

"Ils y trouveront un aperçu de toutes les questions religieuses, politiques et nationales qui ont agité l'opinion publique pendant cette longue [de soixante ans]." – Avant-propos.

Note: Mission des gouvernements (ptie. I et ptie. II) pp. [38]-48.

—— Les gerbes canadiennes. Montréal, Beauchemin [1921] 328 p.

"Des écrits . . . un bon nombre sont inédits, d'autres ont été publiés, depuis cinquante ans, dans divers journaux". – Avant-propos.

—— Laurier; sa vie, ses œuvres. Par L. O. David. Beauceville, Qué., L'Eclaireur, 1919. 268 p.

—— Laurier et son temps. [Lettre-préface à l'honorable M. David par A. D. De Celles] Montréal, La Cie de publication de "La Patrie", 1905. 143 p.

—— Sir Wilfrid Laurier. By L. O. David. (In *The Canadian magazine of politics, science, art and literature.* Toronto. v. 19 (1902), pp. 140-147.)
Canadian celebrities, no. 35.
Translated by Capt. E. J. Chambers.

DE CELLES, ALFRED DUCLOS Laurier et son temps. Montréal, Beauchemin, 1920. 228 p.

DESGAGNE, RAYMOND Orateurs saguenéens. I—L'éloquence politique. Le docteur Edmond Savard, MP (1862-1925). (In *Saguenayensia.* Chicoutimi. v. 3, no 3/4 mai/août 1961), pp. 76-78.)

DONOVAN, PETER When Sir Wilfrid walloped the Borden Bill. By P. O. D. (In *Sat-*

urday night. Toronto. v. 26, no. 11 (Dec. 21, 1912), p. 3.)

DRURY, KEN C.   Last political pow-wows. Touring big chiefs from Ottawa return from Prince Rupert. (In *The Canadian courier.* Toronto. v. 8, no. 16 (Sept. 17, 1910), pp. 11-12.)

Refers to a three-month Western tour made by Sir Wilfrid Laurier and others starting in June 1910.

DUNSMUIR, JAMES   British Columbia's appeal to Sir Wilfrid Laurier for better terms. (In *The Canadian historical review.* Toronto. v. 17 (1936), pp. 423-430.)

Introductory note by Harold P. Johns.

"The following [is a] hitherto unpublished letter of January 7, 1902 from the 'Premier's letter books' on file in the premier's office. Victoria . . .". – (p. 425.)

Text of letter: pp. 426-403.

DUPASQUIER, MAURICE   Laurier et l'extension des relations franco-canadiennes. Ottawa, 1960. x, 137 leaves.

Thesis (MA) – University of Ottawa.

DWYER, MELVA JEAN   Laurier and the British Columbia Liberal Party, 1896-1911; a study in federal-provincial party relations. [Vancouver] 1961. 1 v.

Thesis (MA) – University of British Columbia.

EAGER, EVELYN   Separate schools and the cabinet crisis of 1905. (In *The Lakehead University review.* [Port Arthur, Ont.] v. 2 (1969), pp. [89]-115.)

ECCLES, H. LINTON   The political star of Senator Dandurand. (In *MacLean's magazine.* Toronto. v. 26, no. 4 (Aug. 1913), pp. 47-51.)

EGGLESTON, WILFRID   Ottawa letter. Record career of Mackenzie King had turning point as newsman. (In *Saturday night.* Toronto. v. 61, no. 40 (June 8, 1946), p. 8.)

Deals with Mackenzie King's early career as journalist. Comments on King's investigation of the sweating system in the garment industry in Toronto for the *Mail and Empire,* Toronto, in 1897.

ELLIS, ROBERT JOSEPH   Relationships of Mackenzie and Mann with the Laurier government. [London, Ont.] 1938. 107 leaves.

Thesis (MA) – University of Western Ontario.

EMMERSON, HENRY ROBERT   The fulfilment of a prophecy in transportation. By Hon.

H. R. Emmerson, Minister of Railways. (In Canadian Club of Toronto. *Addresses.* Toronto. (1906/07), pp. 78-86.)

Address delivered February 11, 1907.

EWART, JOHN SKIRVING   Laurier and the Kingdom of Canada. By John S. Ewart. (In *The Statesman.* Toronto. v. 1, no. 34 (Mar. 15, 1919), p. 6.)

FERGUSON, CHARLES BRUCE   Hon. W. S. Fielding. By Bruce Ferguson. Windsor, N.S., Lancelot Press [1970-71] 2 v.

Contents: v. 1. The mantle of Howe. – v. 2. Minister of Finance.

FERNS, HENRY STANLEY   Mackenzie King and the first World War. By H. S. Ferns and Bernard Ostry. (In *The Canadian historical review.* Toronto. v. 36 (1955), pp. 93-112.)

FIELDING, WILLIAM STEVENS   Bearing the burden. By Hon. W. S. Fielding. (In *MacLean's magazine.* Toronto. v. 29, no. 9 (July 1916), pp. [33]-34.)

Concerns wartime finance policy.

The Fielding banquet. An account of the dinner given by the Liberals of Nova Scotia to Hon. W. S. Fielding, Minister of Finance of Canada, Halifax, N.S., Dec. 11th, 1902. Halifax, McAlpine, 1903. 112 p.

FORD, ARTHUR   The man from Brockville. Hon. George P. Graham, ex-Minister of Railways, is the man picked for second man up to Sir Wilfrid Laurier. (In *The Canadian courier.* Toronto. v. 20, no. 6 (July 8, 1916), p. 10.)

FRECHETTE, LOUIS HONORE   The Right Hon. Sir Wilfrid Laurier. (In Marquis, T. G. (ed.) *Builders of Canada from Cartier to Laurier.* Detroit, Mich. [c1903] pp. 525-538.)

List of Laurier's Ministry, July 13, 1896: p. 532.

GADSBY, HENRY FRANKLIN   [Commentary on national affairs] The Old Man's mind. By H. F. Gadsby. (In *Saturday night.* Toronto. v. 30, no. 37 (June 30, 1917), pp. 4-5.)

Reflects on Sir Wilfrid Laurier's position on coalition government, conscription, etc.

—— [Commentary on national affairs] The cuckoos. By H. F. Gadsby. (In *Saturday night.* Toronto. [v. 30, no. 53] (Oct. 20, 1917), p. 4.)

Concerns Sir Wilfrid Laurier and those who attempted to replace him as leader.

—— [Commentary on national affairs]

Throwing the Old Man. By H. F. Gadsby. (In *Saturday night*. Toronto. v. 31, no. 10 (Dec. 22, 1917), p. 4.)
Concerns Sir Wilfrid Laurier.

—— [Commentary on national affairs] The vacant chair. By H. F. Gadsby. (In *Saturday night*. Toronto. v. 32, no. 21 (Mar. 8, 1919), p. 4.)
Concerns Sir Wilfrid Laurier. Written on the occasion of his death in Ottawa, February 17, 1919.

—— [Commentary on national affairs] On the brink. By H. F. Gadsby. (In *Saturday night*. Toronto. v. 32, no. 42 (Aug. 2, 1919), p. 4.)
Concerns the Liberal Party leadership convention held August 5-7, 1919.

—— [Commentary on national affairs] The love feast. By H. F. Gadsby. (In *Saturday night*. Toronto. [v. 32, no. 44] (Aug. 16, 1919), p. 3.)
Concerns the National Liberal Convention held August 5-7, 1919.

—— [Commentary on national affairs] A word to the wise. By H. F. Gadsby. (In *Saturday night*. Toronto. [v. 32, no. 47] (Sept, 6, 1919), p. 4.)
Concerns William Lyon Mackenzie King. A hypothetical conversation between King and Sir Wilfrid Laurier.

—— [Commentary on national affairs] Figuring it out. Part two. By H. F. Gadsby. (In *Saturday night*. Toronto. v. 33, no. 19 (Feb. 21, 1920), pp. 4; 11.)
Concerns the policy of the Liberal Party on the returned Canadian war veterans.

—— [Commentary on national affairs] The good old game. By H. F. Gadsby. (In *Saturday night*. Toronto. v. 33, no. 23 (Mar. 20, 1920), p. 4.)
Concerns Mackenzie King and his motion for an election.

—— [Commentary on national affairs] A lively horoscope. By H. F. Gadsby. (In *Saturday night*. Toronto. v. 34, no. 46 (Sept. 4, 1920), p. 4.)
Concerns the Liberal Party.

—— The four Lauriers. Being an impressionistic, but not unfriendly, view of Canada's great men. (In *MacLean's magazine*. Toronto. v. 22, no. 6 (Oct. 1911), pp. [249]-254.)

—— "Gentlemen, we have with us tonight." Toastmaster, H. F. Gadsby. (In *Saturday night*. Toronto. v. 32, no. 15 (Jan. 25, 1919), p. 2.)

Salutes Sir Wilfrid Laurier. Presented in the form of an introductory speech.

—— Has Canada a political boss? Something about Sir Clifford Sifton and his habit of swinging elections. By H. F. Gadsby. (In *MacLean's magazine*. Toronto. v. 31, no. 5 (Mar. 1918), pp. [38]-40; 75-76.)

—— He may be leader some day; being a sketch of Hon. Wm. Pugsley. By F. H. [i.e. H. F.] Gadsby. (In *MacLean's magazine*. Toronto. v. 29, no. 8 (June 1916), pp. [21]-22; 89-90.)
Concerns the Hon. William Pugsley of St. John, N.B.

—— Hon. J. I. Tarte. (In *The Canadian magazine of politics, science, art and literature*. Toronto. v. 23 (1904), pp. 32-35.)
Canadian celebrities, no. 51.

—— Red Michael, the tariff crusader. By H. F. Gadsby. (In *MacLean's magazine*. Toronto. v. 29, no. 10 (Aug. 1916), pp. [25]-26.)
Concerns Michael Clark.

—— Sir William Mulock. (In *The Canadian magazine of politics, science, art and literature*. Toronto. v. 22 (1903/04), pp. 145-146.)
Canadian celebrities, no. 49.

—— W. S. Fielding, maker of tariffs. By H. F. Gadsby. (In *The Busy man's magazine*. Montréal, Toronto. v. 11, no. 4 (Feb. 1906), pp. [7]-12.)

—— Who, how and why: a Liberal white hope. By H. F. Gadsby. (In *MacLean's magazine*. Toronto. v. 28, no. 6 (Apr. 1915), pp. [26]-27.)
Concerns Hugh Guthrie. Entered Parliament in 1900 as the Member from the constituency of South Wellington, Ont.

—— Who, how and why: an official sunshine maker. By H. F. Gadsby. (In *MacLean's magazine*. Toronto. v. 29, no. 7 (May 1916), pp. [34]-35.)
Concerns Rodolphe Lemieux.

—— Who, how and why: the Liberal stage manager. By H. F. Gadsby. (In *MacLean's magazine*. Toronto. v. 29, no. 2 (Dec. 1915), pp. [26]-27.)
Concerns Frederick Forsythe Pardee.

—— Who, how and why: the original why why of the Commons. By H. F. Gadsby. (In *MacLean's magazine*. Toronto. v. 28, no. 10 (Aug. 1915), pp. [29]-30.)
Concerns Frank Broadstreet Carvell, MP for Carleton, N.B.

—— William Stevens Fielding. (In *The Canadian magazine of politics, science, art and literature*. Toronto. v. 21 (1903), pp. 310-313.)

Canadian celebrities, no. 45.

GONTHIER, PIERRE THEOPHILE DOMINIQUE CESLAS Un manifeste libéral; M. L. O. David et le clergé canadien. Par P. Bernard [pseud.] Québec, L. Brousseau, 1896. 2 v.

Vol. 2 has subtitle: La question des écoles du Manitoba.

GRAHAM, GEORGE PERRY Transportation. By Hon. Geo. P. Graham. (In Canadian Club of Montreal. *Addresses*. [Montreal] (1911/12), pp. 231-242.)

Address delivered April 1, 1912.

GRANT, WILLIAM LAWSON Sir Richard Cartwright. By Professor W. L. Grant. (In *The Canadian magazine of politics, science, art and literature*. Toronto. v. 40 (1912/13), pp. 289-293.)

GUNDY, HENRY PEARSON Sir Wilfrid Laurier and Lord Minto. (In Canadian Historical Association. *Report of the annual meeting*. [Ottawa] (1952), pp. 28-38.)

HACKER, ALBERT E. Laurier's last message. (In *The Maritime advocate and busy East*. Sackville, N.B. v. 32, no. 8 (Mar. 1942), pp. 13-14.)

Reprinted from the *Liberal advocate*.

Discusses the address delivered before the Eastern Ontario Liberal Association on January 14, 1919.

HAL The Minister of Railways; his Toronto speech and some observations thereon. By Hal. (In *Toronto Saturday night*. Toronto. v. 20, no. 15 (Feb. 16, 1907), p. 11.)

Concerns Henry R. Emmerson's "The fulfillment of a prophecy in transportation".

HAMMOND, MELVIN ORMOND In the barefoot prints of Sir Wilfrid. Illustrated with photographs. By M. O. Hammond. (In *Canada monthly*. London, Ont. v. 8, no. 5 (Sept. 1910), pp. 361-368.)

Describes the youth of Sir Wilfrid Laurier as spent in the county of L'Assomption, Quebec.

HARVEY, DANIEL COBB Fielding's call to Ottawa. By D. C. Harvey. (In *The Dalhousie review*. Halifax. v. 28 (1948/49), pp. [369]-385.)

Concerns the entrance of W. S. Fielding into the cabinet of Wilfrid Laurier in 1896.

HASSARD, ALBERT RICHARD Great Canadian orators. XII. Sir George Ross. By Albert R. Hassard. (In *The Canadian magazine of politics, science, art and literature*. Toronto. v. 56 (1920/21), pp. 170-172.)

Represented West Middlesex, Ont. in the House of Commons, 1872-1883; served in the Senate, 1907-1914.

Hommage à Henri Bourassa. [Montréal, 1952] 216 p.

Texte in double columns.

(Reproduit du numéro souvenir paru dans *Le Devoir*, du 25 octobre 1952.

Hommage à Henri Bourassa (1868-1952). Montréal, 1952. 40 p.

Supplement to the Saturday, October 25, 1952, issue of *Le Devoir*.

The Honourable Sir Frederick Borden, KCMG. (In *The Canadian liberal monthly*. Ottawa. v. 4, no. 5 (Jan. 1917), pp. 73-74.)

Issued on the occasion of his death January 6, 1917.

HOWARD, SID H. Lacrymosa dies illa, February 22, 1919. By S. H. Howard. (In *Canadian courier*. Toronto. v. 24, no. 12 (Mar. 15, 1919), pp. 18-19.)

Observations recorded at the funeral of Sir Wilfrid Laurier.

—— Reuben Truax, saw-miller and MP-elect. By Sid H. Howard. (In *The Canadian courier*. Toronto. v. 14, no. 24 (Nov. 15, 1913), p. 7.)

HUTCHEON, ROBERT J. Sir Wilfrid Laurier. (In *Queen's quarterly*. Kingston. v. 29 (1921/22), pp. 243-255.)

A review article of *The life and letters of Sir Wilfrid Laurier*, by O. D. Skelton. Toronto, Oxford University Press, 1922.

"The Issue is reciprocity." Sir Wilfrid Laurier at Simcoe, Ont., August 15. (In *The Canadian courier*. Toronto. v. 10, no. 13 (Aug. 26, 1911), p. 9.)

Mainly illustrations.

JOHNSTON, HUBERT MC BEAN Honourable Charles S. Hyman. (In *The Canadian magazine of politics, science, art and literature*. Toronto. v. 24 (1904/05), pp. 216-218.)

Canadian celebrities, no. 58.

Judas Iscariote Tarte; sa carrière politique d'après divers auteurs. [n.p.] 1903. 318 p.

On spine: Judas Iscariote Tarte: brochures politiques.

In 1891, Joseph Israel Tarte was elected as a Conservative to represent L'Islet in the

Canadian House of Commons. But he went over to the Liberal Opposition and served as Minister of Public Works for Canada, 1896-1902. (Cf. W. S. Wallace. *The Macmillan Dictionary of Canadian biography.* 3d ed. p. 736.)

KING, TOM Politics and politicians. Some of the happenings of the month on Parliament Hill and some comments on the Winnipeg Convention. (In *Canada monthly.* London, Ont. v. 22, no. 5 (Sept. 1917), pp. 254-256.)

Reviews the seventh session of the twelfth parliament. Concerns the Liberal Party convention in Winnipeg, the conscription issue and the railway situation.

—— Sir Wilfrid at Maisonneuve. (In *The [Canadian] courier.* Toronto. v. 20, no. 19 (Oct. 7, 1916), p. [5].)

A brief comment on the meeting held at Maisonneuve, September 27, 1916.

—— Will N. W. Rowell become Premier of Canada? (In *The Canadian courier.* Toronto. v. 20, no. 14 (Sept. 2, 1916), p. 8.)

Considers the succession of Mr. Rowell to Sir Wilfrid Laurier as leader of the Liberal Party.

KING, WILLIAM LYON MACKENZIE Canada and the navy. By Hon. W. L. Mackenzie King. (In Canadian Club of Toronto. *Addresses.* Toronto. (1912/13), pp. 215-225.)

Address delivered March 10, 1913.

—— Four parties to industry. By the Hon. W. L. Mackenzie King. (In Canadian Club of Montreal. *Addresses.* [Montreal] (1918 /19), pp. [211]-221.)

Address delivered March 17, 1919.

—— Industrial peace. By Mackenzie King. (In Canadian Club of Vancouver. *Addresses.* Vancouver. (1906/08), pp. 102-106.)

Summary of address delivered November 18, 1907.

Summarizes and quotes excerpts from a speech discussing the formation of the Department of Labour in 1900 and the Industrial Disputes Conciliation Act (1907).

—— Industry and humanity; study in the principles underlying industrial reconstruction. Toronto, T. Allen [1918] xx, 567 p.

—— Industry and humanity; a study in the principles underlying industrial reconstruction. By the Right Honourable W. L. Mackenzie King, MP. New and

shorter ed. Toronto, Macmillan, 1935. xx, 269 p.

An abridgment of the original published in 1918. It is not in any other sense a revision. Cf. Publisher's note.

—— Laurier. (In his *The message of the carillon.* Toronto, 1928. pp. 46-60.)

—— Liberal solution of labor problem. (In *The Statesman.* Toronto. v. 1, no. 27 (Jan. 25, 1919), pp. 8-9.)

Text of an address delivered at Montreal on January 11, 1919.

—— Liberalism and reconstruction. By Wm. L. Mackenzie King. (In Locke, G. H. (ed.) *Builders of the Canadian commonwealth.* Freeport, N.Y. [1967] pp. 287-291.)

"Excerpts from speeches delivered to Liberal supporters, August, 1919."

—— Mackenzie King looks at two 1911 elections. Edited by Charles W. Humphries. (In *Ontario history.* Toronto. v. 56, no. 3 (Sept. 1964), pp. [203]-206.)

Cites a letter from W. L. M. King to Violet Markham concerning the Ontario provincial election held December 11, 1911, and the federal election held September 21, 1911.

—— La question sociale et le Canada, industrie et humanité. Par W.-L. Mackenzie King. Traduction de Altiar. Préf. de Gabriel Hanotaux. Paris, F. Alcan, 1925. iv, 252 p. (Bibliothèque France-Amérique.)

French translation of *Industry and humanity,* by W. L. M. King. Toronto, Allen, 1918.

—— The secret of heroism; a memoir of Henry Albert Harper. By W. L. Mackenzie King. New York, F. H. Revell Co. [c1906] 161 p.

H. A. Harper was a civil servant, an associate editor of the *Labour gazette,* in the Department of Labour during the time W. L. M. King was Deputy Minister of Labour.

L.-O. David. (In *L'Action française.* Montréal. v. 16 (sept. 1926), pp. [154]-157.)

Written on the occasion of his death August 24, 1926.

LAMBERT, NORMAN PLATT Dunning came up through. By Norman Lambert. (In *The [Canadian] courier.* Toronto. v. 21, no. 12 (Feb. 17, 1917), pp. [5]-6.)

Concerns Charles A. Dunning.

LANDER, J. A. Grave problème à résoudre. (In *La Vie canadienne.* Québec. t. 2, no. 2

(25 jan. 1919), pp. 3-5; t. 2, no. 3 (10 fév. 1919), pp. 5-8.)

In two parts.

Discusses the ideas of W. L. Mackenzie King regarding labour and industrial questions which were presented at a meeting of the Reform Club of Montreal.

LANDON, FRED   A Canadian cabinet episode of 1897. (In Royal Society of Canada. *Proceedings and transactions*. Ottawa. ser. 3, v. 32 (1938), section 2, pp. 49-56.)

Concerns the appointment of David Mills as Minister of Justice in the cabinet of Sir Wilfrid Laurier.

—— David Mills, the philosopher from Bothwell. (In *Willisons monthly*. Sarnia, Ont. v. 5, no. 3 (Sept. 1929), pp. 8-9.)

Served as Minister of the Interior in the Mackenzie government, 1876-1878; held the position of Minister of Justice in the Laurier administration, 1897-1902.

The Late Robt. Bickerdike. Career of a famous Canadian. (In *Saturday night*. Toronto. v. 44, no. 13 (Feb. 9, 1929), p. 3.)

Written on the occasion of his death December 28, 1928.

LA TERREUR, MARC   Armand Lavergne: son entrée dans la vie publique. (In *Revue d'histoire de l'Amérique française*. Montréal. v. 17, no 1 (juin 1963), pp. 39-54.)

"Travail présenté à la réunion générale de l'Institute d'histoire de l'Amerique française, le 27 avril 1963."

—— Correspondance Laurier–Mme Joseph Lavergne, 1891-1893. (In Canadian Historical Association. *Report of the annual meeting*. [Ottawa] (1964), pp. [37]-51.)

LAURENDEAU, ANDRE   Armand LaVergne; un témoignage. (In *L'Action nationale*. Montréal. v. 5 (juin 1935), pp. [335]-364.)

—— Henri Bourassa. (In McDougall, R. L. (ed.) *Our living tradition*. Fourth series. [Toronto, c1962] pp. 135-158.)

—— Le nationalisme de Bourassa. (In *L'Action nationale*. Montréal. v. 43 (jan. 1954), pp. [9]-56.)

LAURIER, SIR WILFRID   Discours à l'étranger et au Canada. Montréal, Beauchemin [1909] xcix, 472 p.

"Introduction", biographical, unsigned: p. vii-lxxv. "Souvenirs", signed, L. O. David: p. lxxvii-xcix.

—— Discours de M. Wilfrid Laurier. (In Société Saint Jean Baptiste de Québec.

Jubilé sacerdotal de S. E. le Cardinal E. A. Taschereau. Québec, 1892. pp. 165-173.)

Touches on a variety of subjects.

—— Discours de Sir Wilfrid Laurier. Edités par Alfred D. DeCelles. Montréal, Beauchemin, 1920. 2 v. in 1.

Contents: t. 1. De 1889 à 1911. – t. 2. De 1911 à 1919.

—— Le fédéralisme. (In *Revue trimestrielle canadienne*. Montréal. v. 4 (août 1918), pp. [219]-221.)

Ideas expressed in a letter dated 18 July 1918.

—— The Liberal chieftain, the Right Honourable Sir Wilfrid Laurier, KC, GCMG, MP, delivers address at his birthplace, St. Lin, Que. (In *The Canadian liberal monthly*. Ottawa. v. 2, no. 12 (Aug. 1915), pp. 141-142.)

Excerpts from the speech presented at St. Lin, Que., August 7, 1915. Concerns the issue of military recruitment.

—— Sir Wilfrid Laurier; letters to my father and mother. Selected and edited by Lucien Pacaud. Toronto, Ryerson Press [1935] viii, 148 p.

Letters to Ernest Pacaud and his wife.

—— Sir Wilfrid Laurier; lettres à mon père et à ma mère, 1867-1919. [Publiées par] Lucien Pacaud. [Arthabaska, P.Q., L'Impr. d'Arthabaska, 1935] 349 p.

Letters to Ernest Pacaud and his wife.

—— Sir Wilfrid Laurier at Montreal. Quotations from speech delivered before Montreal Reform Club, December 13, 1914. (In *The Canadian liberal monthly*. Ottawa. v. 2, no. 5 (Jan. 1915), pp. [52]-53.)

Concerns Canada and the war.

—— Sir Wilfrid Laurier at Montreal. Speech at Monument national, December 9, 1915. (In *The Canadian liberal monthly*. Ottawa. v. 3, no. 5 (Jan. 1916), pp. 51-53.)

Excerpts from the speech. Involves issues of defense, Liberal Party attitude towards participation in the war, principles of Canadian patriotism, etc.

—— Sir Wilfrid Laurier at Montreal. Speech on call for recruits for French-Canadian regiment. (In *The Canadian liberal monthly*. Ottawa. v. 2, no. 3 (Nov. 1914), pp. 27-30.)

Text of the speech delivered at Sohmer Park, Montreal, October 15, 1914.

—— Sir Wilfrid Laurier at Toronto. Quotations from speech before Liberal Club Federation of Ontario at Toronto, May 21, 1915. (In *The Canadian liberal monthly.* Ottawa. v. 2, no. 10 (June 1915), pp. 116-117.)

Touches on several issues.

—— Sir Wilfrid Laurier's speech St. Joseph Boulevard, Maisonneuve, Quebec, September 27th, 1916. (In *The Canadian liberal monthly.* Ottawa. v. 4, no. 2 (Oct. 1916), pp. 15-16.)

Extracts.

—— When Great Britain is at war we are at war. (In Locke, G. H. (ed.) *Builders of the Canadian commonwealth.* Freeport, N.Y. [c1967] pp. 245-248.)

"From an address in the House of Commons, Ottawa August 19, 1914."

Laurier and liberalism. (In *The Statesman.* Toronto. v. 1, no. 32 (Mar. 1, 1919), pp. 3-4.)

LAVERGNE, ARMAND RENAUD Armand Lavergne. Textes choisis et présentés par Marc LaTerreur. Montréal, Fides [1968] 95 p. (Collection Classiques canadiens, 31.)

—— Trente ans de vie nationale. Montréal, Editions du Zodiaque [1934] 228 p. (Collection du Zodiaque '35.)

The Author was "successively a Liberal, a Nationalist and a Conservative. . . . he was Deputy Speaker of the House from 1930 to his death . . . on March 6, 1935." (Cf. W. S. Wallace. *The Macmillan dictionary of Canadian biography.* 3d ed. p. 399.)

LEDERLE, JOHN W. The Liberal Convention of 1919 and the selection of Mackenzie King. (In *The Dalhousie review.* Halifax. v. 27 (1947/48), pp. [85]-92.)

LEFEBVRE, JEAN JACQUES Famille Laurier. Sir Wilfrid Laurier (†1919), sa famille et ses proches alliés. (In *Royal Society of Canada. Proceedings and transactions.* Ottawa. ser. 4, v. 6 (1968), section 1, pp. 143-158.)

LEMIEUX, RODOLPHE Memories of Laurier. By the Honourable Rodolphe Lemieux. (In *Willisons monthly.* Sarnia, Ont. v. 5, no. 2 (Aug. 1929), pp. 8-10.)

—— Sir Wilfrid Laurier. (In *Revue trimestrielle canadienne.* Montréal. v. 5 (mai 1919), pp. [3]-10.)

—— Wilfrid Laurier; conférence devant le Club national de Montréal. Montréal, C. Theoret, 1897. 58 p.

LEON Le libéralisme canadien. Par Léon. (In *Le Mouvement catholique.* Trois-Rivières. v. 1 (jan.—juin. 1898), pp.[314]-317.)

Discusses the liberal political policy and program of Wilfrid Laurier.

LEVITT, JOSEPH La perspective nationaliste d'Henri Bourassa 1896-1914. Richard Jones: commentaire. (In *Revue d'histoire de l'Amérique française.* Montréal. v. 22, no. 4 (mars 1969), pp. [567]-585.)

This study bears relevance to the political events occurring during the time span from the election of Sir Wilfrid Laurier as Prime Minister of Canada to the outbreak of the First World War.

Liberal elections of 1908. Liberal regime, 1897-1908. Eleven years of financial improvements and fruitful administration. Quebec, 1908. 184 p.

The Liberal leadership. (In *The Statesman.* Toronto. v. 1, no. 23 (Dec. 28, 1918), p. 3.)

Argues that Sir Wilfrid Laurier continue as leader of the Liberal Party.

LIBERAL PARTY (CANADA) National Convention, 2d, Ottawa, 1919. Historique de la convention et rapport des délibérations. [Montréal, 1919] 222 p.

Convention held August 5, 6, and 7, 1919.

—— National Convention, 2d, Ottawa, 1919. The story of the convention and the report of its proceedings. [Ottawa, 1919?] 214 p.

On cover: The National Liberal Convention. Ottawa, August 5, 6, 7 1919.

The Liberal record on tariff issue. (In *The Statesman.* Toronto. v. 1, no. 27 (Jan. 25, 1919), pp. 10-11.)

Liberalism is vindicated! (In *The Statesman.* Toronto. v. 1, no. 4 (Aug. 17, 1918), p. 5.)

Surveys, briefly, the record of Sir Wilfrid Laurier.

Liberals and the new era. (In *The Statesman.* Toronto. v. 1, no. 36 (Mar. 29, 1919), p. 3.)

LUCIAN Dissenting Liberals vindicate Laurier. By Lucian. (In *The Statesman.* Toronto. v. 1, no. 20 (Dec. 7, 1918), p. 6.)

Discusses, in particular, the position taken by W. S. Fielding.

MC ARTHUR, PETER Sir Wilfrid Laurier. London, Toronto, Dent, 1919. 183 p.

MACBETH, MADGE HAMILTON (LYONS) A

cabinet minister's canoe trip. How Honourable Frank Oliver sought to learn a little more about his constituency. By Madge Macbeth. (In *MacLean's magazine.* Toronto. v. 21, no. 6 (Apr. 1911), pp. [38]-44.)

—— The lady of the gentle heart. By Madge Macbeth. (In *Canada monthly.* Winnipeg. v. 9, no. 5 (Mar. 1911), pp. 356-361.)

A domestic sketch of Lady Laurier. (née Zoé Lafontaine)

—— The other side of government. By Madge Macbeth. (In *Canada monthly.* Winnipeg. v. 10, no. 2 (June 1911), pp. 113-119.)

Portrait sketch of Mrs. Frank Oliver (née Harriet Dunlop) and Mrs. Cecil Kerr.

MC CORMACK, A. R.   Arthur Puttee and the Liberal Party, 1899-1904. (In *The Canadian historical review.* Toronto. v. 51 (1970), pp. [141]-163.)

The first Independent Labor member elected to the federal Parliament in the general election of 1900.

MC GREGOR, FRED ALEXANDER   The fall & rise of Mackenzie King, 1911-1919. By Fred A. McGregor. Toronto, Macmillan, 1962 [i.e. 1963] 358 p.

MAC KINNON, FRANK   A statesman's centenary: Sir Louis Davies. (In *The Dalhousie review.* Halifax. v. 25 (1945/46), pp. [15]-21.)

MC LEOD, A.   Where Manitoba Liberals stand. (In *The Statesman.* Toronto. v. 1, no. 24 (Jan. 4, 1919), p. 5.)

Text of an address delivered at the Conference of Liberals, held in Winnipeg December 19-20, 1918.

MC LEOD, JOHN TENNYSON   The Laurier legend. By John T. McLeod. (In *Saturday night.* Toronto. v. 81, no. 1 (Jan. 1966), pp. 29; 31-33.)

A review article of *Laurier, the first Canadian,* by Joseph Schull. Toronto, Macmillan, 1965.

—— The political thought of Sir Wilfrid Laurier; a study in Canadian party leadership. Toronto, 1965. 337 leaves.

Thesis (PH D) – University of Toronto.

MC MASTER, ANDREW ROSS   Impressions of a new member. By Andrew R. McMaster, member for Brome. (In *The Statesman.* Toronto. v. 1, no. 2 (Aug. 3, 1918), pp. 5-6.)

MC MURCHY, DONALD JOHN ARNOLD   David Mills, nineteenth century Canadian liberal. [Rochester, N.Y.] 1968. ix, 650 leaves.

Thesis (PH D) – University of Rochester.

MACPHAIL, SIR ANDREW   Why the Liberals failed. (In *The University magazine.* Montreal. v. 10 (1911), pp. [566]-580.)

Comments on the aftermath of the general elections of 1911.

MAC TAVISH, NEWTON MC FAUL   W. L. Mackenzie King, the new leader of the Liberal Party in Canada. By Newton MacTavish. (In *The Canadian magazine of politics, science, art and literature.* Toronto. v. 54 (1919/20), pp. 71-74.)

MAGURN, ARNOTT JAMES   Hon. Clifford Sifton. By A. J. Magurn. (In *The Canadian magazine of politics, science, art and literature.* Toronto. v. 21 (1903), pp. 502-505.)

MAITLAND, FRANK   "Gentlemen, we have with us to-night." Toastmaster Frank Maitland. (In *Saturday night.* Toronto. v. 32, no. 45 (Aug. 23, 1919), pp. 2; 10.)

Concerns Hon. Charles Avery Dunning. Adopts the form of an introductory speech.

MALAPROP, MR.   People who dislike limelight. Number three: Hon. William Lyon Mackenzie King. By Mr. Malaprop. (In *Canadian courier.* Toronto. v. 24, no. 24 (Aug. 30, 1919), pp. 14; 21.)

MARQUIS, THOMAS GUTHRIE   Hon. Andrew G. Blair. By T. G. Marquis. (In *The Canadian magazine of politics, science, art and literature.* Toronto. v. 24 (1904/5), pp. 144-147.)

Canadian celebrities, no. 57.

—— Sir Wilfrid Laurier. By T. G. Marquis. Toronto, Ryerson Press, 1930. 30 p. (Ryerson Canadian history readers.)

MASSICOTTE, EDOUARD ZOTIQUE   L'ancêtre de Sir Wilfrid Laurier. Par E. Z. Massicotte. (In *Bulletin des recherches historiques.* Lévis. v. 26, no 2 (fév. 1920), pp. 53-55.)

A Master mind. (In *The Canadian courier.* Toronto. v. 8, no. 6 (July 9, 1910), p. 8.)

A brief sketch of Hon. A. B. Aylesworth.

MATTHEWS, C. A.   Canadian celebrities. No. XI. Hon. Frederick William Borden, Minister of Militia. (In *The Canadian magazine of politics, science, art and literature.* Toronto. v. 14 (1899/1900), pp. 448-452.)

THE MEMBER FOR CANADA   Press, Parliament

and piffle. Observations on the Carvell-Free Press controversy at Ottawa. By the Member for Canada. (In *The Canadian courier*. Toronto. v. 19, no. 10 (Feb. 5, 1916), p. 11.)
Refers to Frank Carvell and the *Ottawa Free Press*.

MILES, KATE HAWS Motoring with an MP. Sidelights on the member for Carleton, N.B. (In *The Canadian courier*. Toronto. v. 10, no. 11 (Aug. 12, 1911), p. 7.)
Concerns F. B. Carvell.

MILLER, CARMAN The public life of Sir Frederick Borden. [Halifax, 1964] 1 v.
Thesis (MA) – Dalhousie University.

—— Sir Frederick William Borden and military reform, 1896-1911. (In *The Canadian historical review*. Toronto. v. 50 (1969), pp. 265-284.)

Mrs. Iama Peach hears Mr. King. By J. S. K. (In *Saturday night*. Toronto. v. 36, no. 2 (Nov. 6, 1920), p. 2.)
A "letter" to the Editor conveying impressions of W. L. Mackenzie King.

MOASE, ROBERT MAJOR Sir Wilfrid Laurier; his efforts to allay religious and racial intolerance. [Sackville, N.B.] 1962. 1 v.
Thesis (MA) – Acadia University.

MOORE, WILLIAM HENRY My last interview with Sir Wilfrid. By W. H. Moore. (In *Canadian courier*. Toronto. v. 24, no. 11 (Mar. 1, 1919), p. [5].)
Written on the occasion of the death of Sir Wilfrid Laurier February 17, 1919.

MOREAU, HENRI Sir Wilfrid Laurier, premier ministre du Canada. Paris, Plon-Nourrit, 1902. 299 p. [Librairie Plon.)

MOTHERWELL, WILLIAM RICHARD The trail of Sifton and Calder. By W. L. [*sic*] Motherwell. (In *The Statesman*. Toronto. v. 1, no. 33 (Mar. 8, 1919), pp. 6-7.)
Text of a speech delivered Thursday, March 6, 1919.

MUNRO, J. K. Why King won Laurier's mantle. (In *MacLean's magazine*. Toronto. v. 32, no. 9 (Sept. 1919), pp. [35]-37; 39.)
Refers to the election of W. L. M. King as leader at the National Convention of the Liberal Party held August 5-7, 1919.

—— Why Laurier will wait. (In *MacLean's magazine*. Toronto. v. 32, no. 1 (Jan. 1919), pp. [20]-21; 59-60.)

MURROW, CASEY Henri Bourassa and French-Canadian nationalism; opposition

to Empire. Montreal, Harvest House [c1968] 143 p.

The National Liberal Advisory Committee. (In *The Canadian liberal monthly*. v. 3, no. 5 (Jan. 1916), pp. 54-56.)
Convened in Ottawa, December 20-21, 1915, under the chairmanship of Sir Wilfrid Laurier. This committee was established as a general advisory body of the Liberal Party to formulate policy and draw up procedures relevant to the changing economic and political conditions of Canadian society.

The National Liberal Advisory Committee. (In *The Canadian liberal monthly*. Ottawa. v. 3, no. 12 (Aug. 1916), pp. 147-149.)
Presents a report of the meeting held by the Committee in Ottawa during July 1916.

NEATBY, HERBERT BLAIR Laurier and a Liberal Quebec; a study in political management. Toronto, 1956. 428 leaves.
Thesis (PH D) – University of Toronto.

—— Laurier and a Liberal Quebec; a study in political management. By H. Blair Neatby. Edited with an introd. by Richard T. Clippingdale. [Toronto] McClelland and Stewart [1973] xviii, 244 p. (The Carleton library, no. 63.)
"A note on sources and suggestions for further reading": pp. [232]-237.

—— Laurier and Canadian nationhood. By H. B. Neatby. (In *The Canadian forum*. Toronto. v. 37, no. 437 (June 1957), pp. 56-57.)

—— Laurier and imperialism. (In Canadian Historical Association. *Report of the annual meeting*. [Ottawa] (1955), pp. 24-32.)

NELSON, JOHN Senator Templeman. (In *The Canadian magazine of politics, science, art and literature*. Toronto. v. 19 (1902), pp. 45-47.)
Canadian celebrities, no. 34.
Concerns the Hon. William Templeman.

OBAY, L. Le Parti libéral et l'exécution du complot maçonnique. (In *Le Mouvement catholique*. Trois-Rivières. v. 1 (jan.—juin 1898), pp. 174-178.)

—— Le Parti libéral et l'exécution du complot maçonnique. La question des réformes scolaires. (In *Le Mouvement catholique*. Trois-Rivières. v. 1 (jan.—juin 1898), pp. [340]-350; [373]-383.)
In two parts.

—— Le Parti libéral et l'exécution du complot maçonnique. Les réformes scolaires. (In *Le Mouvement catholique*. Trois-Rivières. v. 1 (jan.—juin 1898), pp. 427-430.)

Obstacles to a Liberal re-union. (In *The Statesman*. Toronto. v. 1, no. 25 (Jan. 11, 1919), pp. 5-6.)

O'CONNELL, MARTIN PATRICK Henri Bourassa and Canadian nationalism. [Toronto] 1954. 304 leaves.

Thesis (PH D) – University of Toronto.

—— The ideas of Henri Bourassa. By M. P. O'Connell. (In *The Canadian journal of economics and political science*. [Toronto] v. 19 (1953), pp. 361-376.)

"This paper was presented at the annual meeting of the Canadian Political Science Association in London, June 4, 1953."

O'CONNOR, T. P. Sir Wilfrid Laurier as seen by T. P. O'Connor. An interesting personal sketch of the Canadian Premier by the celebrated London journalist. (In *Toronto Saturday night*. Toronto. v. 20, no. 24 (Mar. 30, 1907), p. 12.)

O'HAGAN, THOMAS Sir Wilfrid Laurier. (In *The Statesman*. Toronto. v. 1, no. 34 (Mar. 15, 1919), pp. 4-5.)

OLIVER, FRANK The building of Canada. By Hon. Frank Oliver, Minister of Interior. (In Canadian Club of Vancouver. *Addresses*. Vancouver. (1906/08), pp. 65-69.)

Address delivered August 17, 1907.

Oratory in the Dominion House. (In *The Statesman*. Toronto. v. 1, no. 39 (Apr. 19, 1919), p. 7.)

Considers briefly the oratorical style of W. S. Fielding, Rodolphe Lemieux, Lucien Cannon, and Joseph Archambault.

Our prominent men—Horace Haszard, MP. (In *The Prince Edward Island magazine*. Charlottetown. v. 5, no. 12 (Feb. 1904), pp. 387-389.)

PATTERSON, NORMAN From Parliament to the public. Sir Wilfrid Laurier seeks a new jury. (In *The Canadian courier*. Toronto. v. 13, no. 24 (May 17, 1913), p. 11.)

—— Mr. Willison's "Laurier". (In *The Canadian magazine of politics, science, art and literature*. Toronto. v. 20 (1902/03), pp. 474-475.)

A review article of *Sir Wilfrid Laurier and the Liberal Party*, by J. S. Willison, Toronto, 1903. 2 v.

PEAU D'OURS Le pseudo-Jules Evrard déraisonne. Par Peau d'Ours. (In *L'Action nationale*. Montréal. v. 8 (nov. 1936), pp. [76]-180.)

A criticism of an article by Jules Evrard, entitled "Armand Lavergne fut-il le grand patriote qu'on dit?", which appeared in *Le Canada*, October 1 and 3.

La Pensée de Henri Bourassa, par Patrick Allen, F. A. Angers, J. P. Archambault, Richard Arès, André Laurendeau, Anne Bourassa, Roland Parenteau et André Bergevin. [Montréal] L'Action nationale [1954] 244 p.

Articles from *L'Action nationale*, Jan. 1954.

PERRAULT, ANTONIO Joseph-Israel Tarte. (In *Revue canadienne*. Montréal. nouv. sér. v. 1 (1908), pp. [104]-124.)

PRANG, MARGARET EVELYN Mackenzie King woos Ontario, 1919-1921. By Margaret Prang. (In *Ontario history*. Toronto. v. 58, no. 1 (Mar. 1966), pp. [1]-20.)

PUCK Behind the Speaker's chair. By Puck. (In *The Week*. Toronto. v. 13, no. 44 (Sept. 25, 1896), pp. 1043-1044.)

A sketch of the Liberal administration.

RAYMOND, MAXIME A la mémoire d'Henri Bourassa. (In *L'Action universitaire*. Montréal. no. 2 (jan. 1953), pp. [3]-23.)

Reconstruction problems. (In *The Statesman*. Toronto. v. 1, no. 21 (Dec. 14, 1918), p. 8.)

Comments on an address delivered by Sydney Fisher, Minister of Agriculture in the Laurier cabinet previous to 1911.

Reflections by a Winnipeg Conservative on the Liberal Convention. (In *Canadian courier*. Toronto. v. 22, no. 13 (Aug. 25, 1917), pp. 8; 23-25.)

Comments on the Liberal Party convention held in Winnipeg, August 7-9, 1917.

ROE, SYDNEY When Laurier reigned supreme. (In *Saturday night*. Toronto. v. 45, no. 16 (Mar. 1, 1930), p. 3.)

Reminisces about the first session of the tenth parliament which opened on January 11, 1905.

ROSICRUCIAN Party government in Canada. (In *The Statesman*. Toronto. v. 1, no. 44 (May 24, 1919), pp. 8-9.)

Discusses the place of the Liberal Party in post-war Canada.

ROSS, SIR GEORGE WILLIAM Getting into Parliament and after. Toronto, W. Briggs, 1913. viii, 343 p.

ROSS, MARGARET Sir George W. Ross; a biographical study. Toronto, Ryerson Press, 1924. 195 p.

A Rowell boom in Quebec. (In *The Statesman*. Toronto. v. 1, no. 10 (Sept. 28, 1918), pp. 4-5.)
Discusses the conflict between Liberal supporters of N. W. Rowell and Sir Wilfrid Laurier.

The Rowell phase. (In *The Statesman*. Toronto. v. 1, no. 23 (Dec. 28, 1918), pp. 3-4.)
Comments on Hon. Newton Wesley Rowell joining the Conservative Party.

ROY, JAMES ALEXANDER The Honourable Richard Cartwright. (In Canadian Historical Association. *Report of the annual meeting*. [Ottawa?] (1950), pp. 64-71.)

RUMILLY, ROBERT Henri Bourassa, la vie publique d'un grand Canadien. Montréal, Editions Chantecler [1953] 791 p.
Reprinted: Montréal, Editions de l'Homme [1969].

—— Sir Wilfrid Laurier, Canadien. Préf. de René Doumic. [Paris] E. Flammarion [c1931] 209 p. (Chefs de file.)

RUSSELL, BENJAMIN Recollections of W. S. Fielding. By the Hon. B. Russell. (In *The Dalhousie review*. Halifax. v. 9 (1929/30), pp. [326]-340.)

RUSSELL, ROBERT "The young Napoleon of the West." (In *The Busy man's magazine*. Toronto. v. 16, no. 2 (June 1908), pp. 30-32.)
Concerns Clifford Sifton.

SAINT PIERRE, HENRI CESAIRE Affaire de W. A. Grenier, propriétaire du journal *La Libre parole*, accusé de libelle par l'Honorable J. Israel Tarte, Ministre des travaux publics. Plaidoyer de Mtre H. C. St-Pierre, pour la poursuite. Suivi du résumé des débats par l'Hon. Juge Wurtele. Audience du 2 octobre 1897. [Introd. par Charles Avila Wilson] Montréal, C. Theoret [1897?] x, 145 p.
At head of title: Cour du banc de la reine. Juridiction criminelle. Présidence de l'Honorable Juge Wurtele.

SANDWELL, BERNARD KEBLE Prophetic French Canadian. Bourassa: ahead of his times. By B. K. Sandwell. (In *Saturday*

night. Toronto. v. 67, no. 50 (Sept. 20, 1952), pp. 7; 10.)
Concerns Joseph Henri Napoléon Bourassa. Written on the occasion of his death August 30, 1952.

SAYWELL, JOHN TUPPER Liberal politics, federal policies, and the Lieutenant-Governor: Saskatchewan and Alberta 1905. (In *Saskatchewan history*. Saskatoon. v. 8, no. 3 (autumn 1955), pp. 81-88.)

—— Liberal politics, federal policies, and the Lieutenant-Governor: Saskatchewan and Alberta, 1905. (In Swainson, D. W. (ed.) *Historical essays on the Prairie Provinces*. Toronto [c1970] pp. [179]-190.)
"Reprinted from Saskatchewan History, vol. VIII no. 3 (autumn 1955), pp. 81-88."

THE SCENE SHIFTER Choosing the Liberal leader. By the Scene Shifter. (In *The Statesman*. Toronto. v. 1, no. 23 (Dec. 28, 1918), p. 6.)

SCHULL, JOHN JOSEPH Laurier; the first Canadian. By Joseph Schull, Toronto, Macmillan, 1965. 658 p.

—— Laurier. Par Joseph Schull. Traduit par Hélène J. Gagnon. [Montréal] HMH [1968] 530 p.
Translation of *Laurier; the first Canadian*. Toronto, Macmillan, 1965.

Senator Robert Jaffray. (In *The Canadian liberal monthly*. Ottawa. v. 2, no. 5 (Jan. 1915), p. 53.)
A brief statement presented on the occasion of his death in Toronto, December 16, 1914.

SHEPPARD, EDMUND ERNEST An open letter to Right Hon. Sir Wilfrid Laurier, GCMG, PC, President of the King's Privy Council in Canada. By Edmund E. Sheppard. (In *Toronto Saturday night*. Toronto. v. 18, no. 28 (May 20, 1905), p. [1].)
Concerns the withdrawal of Israel Tarte from the Laurier cabinet.

—— Second open letter to Right. Hon. Sir Wilfrid Laurier, GCMG, PC, President of the King's Privy Council in Canada. By Don. (In *Toronto Saturday night*. Toronto. v. 18, no. 29 (May 27, 1905), p. 1.)
With reference to the Autonomy bills of 1905.

SIEGFRIED, ANDRE La politique canadienne, jugée à l'étranger. (In *La Revue canadienne*. Montréal. t. 40 (1901), pp. [284]-291.)
Part two. Examines the essence of the political success of Sir Wilfrid Laurier.

SIFFORD, CLIFTON   Rowell vs. Dewart. "Globe" intervening. No. I. By Clifton Sifford [pseud.] (In *Saturday night*. Toronto. v. 32, no. 43 (Aug. 9, 1919), p. 5.)
Concerns N. W. Rowell.

—— What's the matter with Rowell? No. II. By Sifford-Clifton [pseud.] (In *Saturday night*. Toronto. [v. 32, no. 44] (Aug. 16, 1919), p. 4.)
Reference is to Newton Wesley Rowell.

SIFTON, SIR CLIFFORD   Canadian immigration. By Hon. Clifford Sifton. (In Canadian Club of Toronto. *Addresses*. Toronto. (1903/04), pp. 35-38.)
Address delivered January 4, 1904.

—— The needs of the Northwest. By Hon. Clifford Sifton, Minister of the Interior. (In *The Canadian magazine of politics, science, art and literature*. Toronto. v. 20 (1902/03), pp. 425-428.)

—— Sir Clifford Sifton's strong plea for a united front against the common enemy. (In *Saturday night*. Toronto. v. 30, no. 42 (Aug. 4, 1917), p. 2.)
An open letter, dated Ottawa, July 1917, addressed to Senator Bostock.

—— What Canada should accomplish. By Clifford Sifton. (In Canadian Club of Toronto. *Addresses*. Toronto. (1904/05), pp. 139-145.)
Address delivered April 3, 1905.

Sir Wilfrid Laurier, premier ministre du Canada. (Traduction d'une étude parue dans la revue "The Messenger" de New York, publiée par les R. P. jésuites) [n.p., 19—] 30 p.
Caption title.

Sir Wilfrid Laurier, rebel and patriot. By H. (In *The Rebel*. Toronto. v. 3 (1919), pp. 215-218.)

Sir Wilfrid Laurier—the man and his work. By a Canadian. (In *The National monthly of Canada*. Toronto. v. 2, no. 4 (Apr. 1903), pp. [192]-195.)

SKELTON, OSCAR DOUGLAS   Dafoe's Sifton. By O. D. Skelton. (In *Queen's quarterly*. Kingston. v. 39 (1932), pp. [1]-11.)
A review article of *Clifford Sifton in relation to his times*, by J. W. Dafoe. Toronto, Macmillan, 1931.

—— The day of Sir Wilfrid Laurier; a chronicle of our own times. Toronto, Brook, 1916. xi, 340 p. (The Chronicles of Canada [v. 30].)

—— Life and letters of Sir Wilfrid Laurier. Illustrated with photographs. Toronto, S. B. Gundy, 1921. 2 v.

—— Life and letters of Sir Wilfrid Laurier. Illustrated with photographs. London, Oxford University Press, 1922. 2 v.

—— Life and letters of Sir Wilfrid Laurier. Edited, and with an introd. by David M. L. Farr. [Abridged ed. Toronto] McClelland and Stewart [c1965] 2 v. (The Carleton library, no. 21-22.)
First ed. Toronto. S. B. Gundy, 1921.

SMALLEY, GEORGE W.   An English impression of Laurier. (In *The Busy man's magazine*. Toronto. v. 19, no. 2 (Dec. 1909), pp. 86-87.)
Gives the text of a conversation between Smalley and Laurier over the Alaska boundary question.

SMITH, F. CLIFFORD   Mr. L. O. David. (In *The Canadian magazine of politics, science, art and literature*. Toronto. v. 17 (1901), pp. 431-433.)
Canadian celebrities, no. 27.
Laurent Olivier David was appointed to the Senate of Canada in 1903.

SMITH, GRAY   Henri Bourassa; product and champion of French Canada, 1900-1914. Kingston, Ont. 1954. 305 leaves.
Thesis (MA) – Queen's University.

SMITH, PAMELA EDEN   Henri Bourassa and Sir Wilfrid Laurier. Toronto, 1948. 245 leaves.
Thesis (MA) – University of Toronto.

SMITH, V. C.   Moral crusader: Henri Bourassa and the Empire, 1900-1916. (In *Queen's quarterly*. Kingston. v. 76 (1969), pp. [635]-647.)
Considers the nature of Bourassa's contribution to Canada and the Empire.

SOMERVILLE, JAMES NORMAN   Canada's need is Liberalism. (In *The Statesman*. Toronto. v. 1, no. 21 (Dec. 14, 1918), pp. 8-9.)
Advocates the "Laurier principle".

SPALDING, GORDON LOW   The *Toronto Daily Star* as a Liberal advocate, 1899-1911. Toronto, 1954. 365 leaves.
Thesis (MA) – University of Toronto.

STERNER, W. E.   Sir Clifford as a young campaigner. (In *Saturday night*. Toronto. v. 44, no. 24 (Apr. 27, 1929), p. 3.)
Concerns Sir Clifford Sifton.

STEVENS, PAUL DOUGLAS   Laurier and the Liberal Party in Ontario, 1887-1911. Toronto, 1966 424 leaves.
Thesis (PH D) – University of Toronto.

—— Laurier, Aylesworth and the decline of the Liberal Party in Ontario. (In Canadian Historical Association. *Historical papers.* [Ottawa] (1968), pp. [94]-113.)

—— Wilfrid Laurier: politician. (In *The Political ideas of the Prime Ministers of Canada.* Ottawa, 1969. pp. [69]-85.)

SUTHERLAND, ROBERT FRANKLIN   National topics. By Hon. R. F. Sutherland, Speaker, House of Commons. (In Canadian Club of Vancouver. *Addresses.* Vancouver. (1906/08), pp. 88-91.)
Summary of address delivered September 6, 1907.

TANGHE, RAYMOND   Laurier; architect of Canadian unity. Translated by Hugh Bingham Myers. Montreal, Harvest House [1967, c1966] xiv, 124 p.
Translation of *Laurier, artisan de l'unité canadienne, 1841-1919.*
First published: Tours, Mame, 1960.

—— Laurier; artisan de l'unité canadienne, 1841-1919. [Tours] Mame [c1960] 191 p. (Figures canadiennes, 4.)

THOMSON, D. WALTER   Frank Oliver's West. (In *Saturday night.* Toronto. v. 48, no. 27 (May 13, 1933), p. 10.)
Deals with the "founding and growth of the Edmonton Bulletin" and Frank Oliver's connection with the newspaper and the West. He died in Ottawa, March 31, 1933.

TIMLIN, MABEL FRANCES   Canada's immigration policy, 1896-1910. By Mabel F. Timlin. (In *The Canadian journal of economics and political science.* [Toronto] v. 26 (1960), pp. 517-532.)
"Presidential address delivered at Kingston, June 10, 1960, at the annual meeting of the Canadian Political Science Association."
Considers the personalities of Sir Wilfrid Laurier and Clifford Sifton as a basic element in the formulation of immigration policy.

TROY, JOSEPH   The Laurier regime. (In *The Statesman.* Toronto. v. 1, no. 36 (Mar. 29, 1919), p. 10.)

TURGEON, JEAN MARIE   Un pélerinage à la maison de Laurier à Arthabaska. Par J. M. Turgeon. (In *Le Terroir.* Québec. v. 2, no 3/4 (nov./déc. 1919), pp. 171-179.)

VAN BLARICOM, GEORGE B.   A day with Canada's Premier. By G. B. Van Blaricom. (In *The Busy man's magazine.* Toronto. v. 18, no. 2 (June 1909), pp. 19-27.)
Concerns Sir Wilfrid Laurier.

WADDELL, WILLIAM S.   Frank Oliver and the *Bulletin.* By W. S. Waddell. (In *Alberta historical review.* Edmonton. v. 5, no. 3 (summer 1957), pp. 7-12.)
Based on the author's MA thesis, University of Alberta, 1950.

—— The Honorable Frank Oliver. Edmonton, 1950 2 v. (356 leaves)
Thesis (MA) – University of Alberta.

WADE, MASON   Sir Wilfrid Laurier. (In Bissell, C. T. (ed.) *Seven Canadians.* [Toronto, 1962, c1967] pp. 89-104.)
Our living tradition, ser. 1.

WALLACE, WILLIAM STEWART   An examination of our immigration policy. By W. S. Wallace. (In *The University of Toronto monthly.* Toronto. v. 6, no. 6 (Apr. 1906), pp. 150-155.)
Discusses the policy as advocated by Clifford Sifton.

Where is the Liberal Party to be found? (In *The Statesman.* Toronto. v. 1, no. 36 (Mar. 29, 1919), p. 11.)

Where is the logic? (In *The Statesman.* Toronto. v. 1, no. 35 (Mar. 22, 1919), pp. 3-4.)
Examines points covered in a statement made by W. S. Fielding in the House of Commons, Friday, March 14, 1919.

Where Nova Scotia stands. (In *The Statesman.* Toronto. v. 1, no. 22 (Dec. 21, 1918), p. 8.)
With reference to the national Liberal Party.

Why was this suppressed? (In *The Canadian nation.* Calgary. v. 1, no. 3 (Apr. 12, 1919), p. 9.)
Prints a resolution passed at a Liberal Party convention in Ontario, which went unreported by leading newspapers.

WILLIAMS, FRED G. H.   L. P. Brodeur; the man behind the navy. (In *The Canadian magazine of politics, science, art and literature.* Toronto. v. 36 (1910/11), pp. 295-301.)
Discusses the career of the Hon. Louis Philippe Brodeur, Minister of Marine and of Naval Affairs.

WILLISON, SIR JOHN STEPHEN   Reminiscences, political and personal. [Pt. 13] Laurier and the Empire. (In *The Canadian magazine of politics, science, art and literature.* Toronto. v. 53 (1919), pp. 55-66.)

—— Sir Wilfrid Laurier. London, Oxford University Press, 1926. xii, 472, 526 p. (The Makers of Canada series. Anniversary ed. v. 11.)

On cover: Era of national progress.

"The first twenty-seven chapters of this book were . . . published in . . . 1903." – Author's note.

—— Sir Wilfrid Laurier and the Liberal Party; a political history. Toronto, G. N. Morang, 1903. 2 v.

WILLMS, ABRAHAM MARTIN Decision making: the case of the Ross rifle. By A. M. Willms. (In Canadian public administration. Toronto. v. 2 (1959), pp. 202-213.)

A case study concerning the decision of Sir Frederick Borden, Minister of Militia in the Laurier government, "to have a distinctive Canadian rifle manufactured in Canada for use by Canadian forces."

A Word to the protectionist Liberals. (In The Onlooker. Toronto. v. 1, no. 11 (Mar. 1921), pp. [1]-10.)

1921–1948

1921–1935

ALLAN, HOWARD Cabinet portraits: Hon. W. D. Euler. (In Maclean's. Toronto. v. 39, no. 22 (Nov. 15, 1926), pp. 5; 49.)

Concerns W. D. Euler, Minister of Customs.

ALPHA How the mighty have fallen. By Alpha. (In The Onlooker. Toronto. v. 1, no. 11 (Mar. 1921), pp. 15-18.)

Comments on the Liberal Party and Mackenzie King.

BISHOP, CHARLES "George P." becomes a tariff judge. (In Maclean's. Toronto. v. 39, no. 8 (Apr. 15, 1926), pp. 21; 43.)

Concerns George P. Graham.

BLUE BOOKE A maker of budgets. A sidelight or two on Hon. J. A. Robb, Minister of Finance. By Blue Booke. (In Saturday night. Toronto. v. 42, no. 16 (Mar. 5, 1927), p. 5.)

—— The new Secretary of State. An intimate glimpse of Fernand Rinfret. By Blue Booke. (In Saturday night. Toronto. v. 41, no. 48 (Oct. 16, 1926), p. 3.)

BRENNAN, J. WILLIAM C. A. Dunning and the challenge of the Progressives: 1922-1925. (In Saskatchewan history. Saskatoon. v. 22, no. 1 (winter 1969), pp. [1]-12.)

Based in part on the author's MA thesis "The public career of Charles Avery Dunning in Saskatchewan."

BRIDLE, AUGUSTUS Gouin, the sagacious. By "the Make-up man". (In Maclean's. Toronto. v. 34, no. 14 (Aug. 1921), pp. 9-10; 61-62.)

"A . . . biographical sketch from 'Ottawa in masquerade', a book to be published . . . ."

Concerns Sir Lomer Gouin.

BRODERICK, RALPH J. The young Liberal movement. (In The Maritime advocate and busy East. Sackville, N.B. v. 24, no. 11 (June 1934), pp. 16; 22.)

Traces the development of the 20th Century Liberal Association of Canada. Its inaugural meeting was held in Ottawa on March 19, 1930.

BROWN, E. W. Mackenzie King of Canada. (In The Maritime advocate and busy East. Sackville, N.B. v. 33, no. 6 (Jan. 1943), pp. 14-18; 31-32.)

Reprinted from Harper's magazine, January 1943.

BUCHANAN, E. C. [Commentary on national affairs] The deciding factor. By E. C. B. (In Saturday night. Toronto. v. 40, no. 42 (Sept. 5, 1925), p. 4.)

"The great problem of the cabinet these two months has not been tariff policy or the railways or Senate reform. The problem has been currency."

—— [Commentary on national affairs] Mr. King sees it through. By E. C. B. (In Saturday night. Toronto. [v. 40, no. 52] (Nov. 14, 1925), p. 3.)

Discusses the post-election result and the decision of Mackenzie King to withhold pronouncement.

—— [Commentary on national affairs] Swimming among the sharks. By E. C. B. (In Saturday night. Toronto. v. 41, no. 6 (Dec. 26, 1925), p. 4.)

Concerns, mainly, the invitation extended by Mackenzie King to Charles Avery Dunning to become a member of the Privy Council.

—— [Commentary on national affairs] The first fifty days. By E. C. B. (In Saturday night. Toronto. v. 41, no. 9 (Jan. 16, 1926), p. 4.)

Concerns the issue as to the right of Mr. King to return to office: . . . "Mr. Lapointe moved at once that the House approve of the course of the Government in retaining office following the elections and that it formally record its confidence in the Administration".

—— [Commentary on national affairs] Confounding the constitution. By E. C. B. (In *Saturday night*. Toronto. [v. 41, no. 10] (Jan. 23, 1926), p. 4.)
Concerns a vote of confidence given the Mackenzie King government.

—— [Commentary on national affairs] Probing the promises. By E. C. B. (In *Saturday night*. Toronto. v. 41, no. 11 (Jan. 30, 1926), p. 4.)
Concerns the Speech from the Throne, with specific reference to the issue of coal.

—— [Commentary on national affairs] Co-operation's the thing. By E. C. B. (In *Saturday night*. Toronto. v. 41, no. 12 (Feb. 6, 1926), p. 4.)
Comments on the general position of the Mackenzie King government.

—— [Commentary on national affairs] Party versus the public? By E. C. B. (In *Saturday night*. Toronto. v. 41, no. 16 (Mar. 6, 1926), p. 4.)
Concerns the political relationship of Mackenzie King to the Railway Commission.

—— [Commentary on national affairs] Coming home to roost. By E. C. B. (In *Saturday night*. Toronto. v. 41, no. 18 (Mar. 20, 1926), p. 4.)
Discusses the negotiations between W. L. M. King and Robert Forke of the Progressive Party for the latter's support of the government.

—— [Commentary on national affairs] Bounties of the budget. By E. C. B. (In *Saturday night*. Toronto. v. 41, no. 23 (Apr. 24, 1926), p. 4.)
Concerns the budget presented by James Alexander Robb.

—— [Commentary on national affairs] Quiet on the frontier. By E. C. B. (In *Saturday night*. Toronto. v. 41, no. 30 (June 12, 1926), p. 4.)
Considers the leadership qualities of Mackenzie King.

—— [Commentary on national affairs] Struggling strategists. By E. C. B. (In *Saturday night*. Toronto. v. 41, no. 32 (June 26, 1926), p. 4.)
Concerns the impact of the Customs Inquiry report on the government of Mackenzie King.

—— [Commentary on national affairs] Supporting the Premier. By E. C. B. (In *Saturday night*. Toronto. v. 41, no. 33 (July 3, 1926), p. 4.)
Concerns the defeat of the Mackenzie King government in the House of Commons.

—— [Commentary on national affairs] Now up to the country. By E. C. B. (In *Saturday night*. Toronto. v. 41, no. 34 (July 10, 1926), p. 4.)
Concerns the constitutional crisis of 1926 occurring when the Governor-General (Lord Byng) refused to grant a dissolution of Parliament to Mackenzie King.

—— Lobby and gallery. By E. C. B. (In *Saturday night*. Toronto. v. 42, no. 10 (Jan. 22, 1927), p. 4.)
Concerns the government of Mackenzie King and patronage.

—— Lobby and gallery. By E. C. B. (In *Saturday night*. Toronto. v. 42, no. 15 (Feb. 26, 1927), p. 4.)
Concerns the federal budget brought down by James Alexander Robb.

—— Lobby and gallery. By E. C. B. (In *Saturday night*. Toronto. v. 42, no. 19 (Mar. 26, 1927), p. 4.)
Concerns Mackenzie King and Maritime legislation.

—— Lobby and gallery. By E. C. B. (In *Saturday night*. Toronto. v. 42, no. 21 (Apr. 9, 1927), p. 4.)
Concerns Mackenzie King and the Georgian Bay canal water power bill.

—— Lobby and gallery. By E. C. B. (In *Saturday night*. Toronto. v. 42, no. 28 (May 28, 1927), p. 4.)
Concerns Mackenzie King and the restored independence of the Railway Commission.

—— Lobby and gallery. By E. C. B. (In *Saturday night*. Toronto. v. 43, no. 1 (Nov. 19, 1927), p. 4.)
Discusses the indecision of the Mackenzie King government; the Dominion Inter-provincial Conference.

—— Lobby and gallery. By E. C. B. (In *Saturday night*. Toronto. v. 43, no. 3 Dec. 3, 1927), p. 4.)
Concerns the political struggle between Mackenzie King and L. A. Taschereau.

—— Lobby and gallery. By E. C. B. (In *Saturday night*. Toronto. v. 43, no. 5 (Dec. 17, 1927), p. 4.)

Comments relate, mainly, to James Robb, Minister of Finance.

—— Lobby and gallery. Hon. Mr. Robb's fifth budget does not please everybody but is a sensible document. Its provisions analyzed. Important matters ignored. By E. C. B. (In *Saturday night*. Toronto. v. 43, no. 15 (Feb. 25, 1928), p. 4.)

—— Lobby and gallery. By E. C. B. (In *Saturday night*. Toronto. v. 43, no. 49 (Oct. 20, 1928), p. 4.)
Comments on Mackenzie King and his government.

—— Lobby and gallery. By E. C. B. (In *Saturday night*. Toronto. v. 44, no. 7 (Dec. 29, 1928), p. 4.)
Concerns the Beauharnois power project approved by the federal government.

—— Lobby and gallery. Giving Canada stable government. By E. C. B. (In *Saturday night*. Toronto. v. 44, no. 9 (Jan. 12, 1929), p. 4.)
Concerns the policies and leadership of Mackenzie King.

—— Lobby and gallery. By E. C. B. (In *Saturday night*. Toronto. v. 44, no. 11 (Jan. 26, 1929), p. 4.)
Concerns the approval for the Beauharnois power development concession.

—— Lobby and gallery. By E. C. B. (In *Saturday night*. Toronto. v. 44, no. 14 (Feb. 16, 1929), p. 4.)
Concerns the program of the King government for the third session, sixteenth parliament.

—— In lobby and gallery. (In *Saturday night*. Toronto. v. 44, no. 48 (Oct. 12, 1929), p. 24.)
Concerns W. D. Euler and his disagreement with the King government over the issue of liquor-running.

—— In lobby and gallery. (In *Saturday night*. Toronto. v. 44, no. 52 (Nov. 9, 1929), p. 4.)
Concerns Mackenzie King and the tariff situation, the Ottawa and Ontario election and James Robb's illness.

—— In lobby and gallery. (In *Saturday night*. Toronto. v. 45, no. 2 (Nov. 23, 1929), p. 4.)
Discusses the political implications arising from the death of James Alexander Robb November 11, 1929.

—— Lobby and gallery. (In *Saturday night*. Toronto. v. 45, no. 4 (Dec. 7, 1929), p. 4.)

Concerns the reorganization of the Mackenzie King cabinet.

—— Lobby and gallery. (In *Saturday night*. Toronto. v. 45, no. 5 (Dec. 14, 1929), p. 4.)
Concerns Mackenzie King and the "tariff question and the proposed upward revision of the United States tariff on Canadian products".

—— Lobby and gallery. (In *Saturday night*. Toronto. v. 45, no. 15 (Feb. 22, 1930), p. 4.)
Discusses the appointment of the first woman to the Senate, Mrs. Norman Wilson (née Cairine Reay Mackay). Concerns, in addition, tariff policy, civil service salaries, etc.

—— Lobby and gallery. (In *Saturday night*. Toronto. v. 45, no. 16 (Mar. 1, 1930), p. 4.)
Comments on the Speech from the Throne at the opening of the fourth session, sixteenth parliament.

—— Lobby and gallery. (In *Saturday night*. Toronto. v. 45, no. 23 (Apr. 19, 1930), p. 4.)
Concerns Mackenzie King's decision to dissolve Parliament.

—— Lobby and gallery. (In *Saturday night*. Toronto. v. 45, no. 26 (May 10, 1930), p. 4.)
Concerns the budget presented by Finance Minister C. A. Dunning.

—— Lobby and gallery. (In *Saturday night*. Toronto, v. 45, no. 29 (May 31, 1930), p. 4.)
Concerns John Campbell Elliott, Minister of Public Works, and the Beauharnois power concession.

—— National affairs. (In *Saturday night*. Toronto. v. 46, no. 20 (Mar. 28, 1931), p. 4.)
Concerns the "condition of the Senate" and Mackenzie King's "contention that the deputy speaker of the House of Commons should refrain from participation in debate", etc.

—— National affairs. (In *Saturday night*. Toronto. v. 47, no. 26 (May 7, 1932), p. 4.)
Concerns the endorsement by the Liberal minority in the Senate of Messers. McDougald and Haydon, the senators involved in the Beauharnois scandal.

—— National affairs. (In *Saturday night.* Toronto. v. 47, no. 48 (Oct. 8, 1932), p. 20.)

Relates to an address delivered by Mackenzie King to the electors of South Huron, Ont. during the campaign for the by-election held October 3, 1932.

Canada's railway policy. Hon. W. C. Kennedy, Minister of Railways, announces co-ordinated operation of Canadian National and Grand Trunk railways under one Board of Directors. (In *Saturday night.* Toronto. v. 37, no. 25 (Apr. 22, 1922), p. [13].)

Includes quotations from the speech made by W. C. Kennedy in Parliament.

Canadian women in the public eye. Mrs. Charles Stewart. (In *Saturday night.* Toronto. v. 37, no. 32 (June 10, 1922), p. 24.)

Concerns the wife of the Minister of the Interior (née Jane R. Sneath).

Canadian women in the public eye. Mrs. Copp. (In *Saturday night.* Toronto. v. 39, no. 23 (Apr. 26, 1924), pp. 35-36.)

Concerns Mrs. Arthur Copp (née Elizabeth Bell), wife of Canada's Secretary of State.

Canadian women in the public eye. Mrs. J. H. King. (In *Saturday night.* Toronto. v. 40, no. 25 (May 9, 1925), p. 35.)

Wife of J. H. King, Minister of Public Works (née Nellie Sadler).

CAYGEON, ROBERT Ernest Lapointe, a genuine Liberal. The former Minister of Justice more interested in principles than in policies. (In *Saturday night.* Toronto. v. 48, no. 49 (Oct. 14, 1933), p. 18.)

—— Hepburn, Liberal St. George. A young man with old ideas, he is out to slay the Tory dragon. (In *Saturday night.* Toronto. v. 49, no. 1 (Nov. 11, 1933), p. 3.)

Concerns Mitchell Frederick Hepburn.

—— King's mandate. (In *Saturday night.* Toronto. v. 50, no. 50 (Oct. 19, 1935), p. 16.)

Considers the results of the general elections held October 14, 1935.

—— Letter from a parliamentarian to his son. (In *Saturday night.* Toronto. v. 50, no. 23 (Apr. 13, 1935), p. 3.)

A ficticious letter from Mackenzie King to Mitchell Hepburn.

—— Mackenzie King—an old-fashioned liberal. (In *Saturday night.* Toronto. v. 48, no. 41 (Aug. 19, 1933), p. 3.)

—— National affairs. The Liberal old guard. (In *Saturday night.* Toronto. v. 50, no. 48 (Oct. 5, 1935), p. 4.)

Comments on the Liberal Party.

—— Vincent Massey and the Liberal future. (In *Saturday night.* Toronto. v. 48, no. 37 (July 22, 1933), p. 3.)

CHARLESWORTH, HECTOR WILLOUGHBY From parochialism to nationalism. Sir William Mulock, the most eminent survivor of the youths of 1867, talks of Canada's story. An interview by Hector Charlesworth. (In *Saturday night.* Toronto. [v. 42, no. 33] (July 2, 1927), p. 2.)

CLEMENT, NOEL Mister Speaker! (In *Maclean's.* Toronto. v. 40, no. 4 (Feb. 15, 1927), pp. 11; 41-42; 45.)

Concerns Rodolphe Lemieux, Speaker of the fourteenth, fifteenth, and sixteenth Canadian parliaments.

COPPS, EDWIN Ottawa letter. A distorted image of Mackenzie King. (In *Saturday night.* Toronto. v. 75, no. 8 (Apr. 16, 1960), pp. 27-28.)

Criticizes a CBC televised biography.

CROWELL, HORATIO C. Cabinet portraits: Hon. James L. Ralston. (In *Maclean's.* Toronto. v. 40, no. 2 (Jan. 15, 1927), pp. 10; 51.)

DANDURAND, RAOUL Mémoires (1861-1942) Edités par Marcel Hamelin. Québec, Presses de l'Université Laval, 1967. xiv, 374 p.

Called to the Senate in 1898. Served as representative in the Senate for the King government of 1921, 1926, and 1935. He died in Ottawa, March 18, 1942.

DAWSON, ROBERT MAC GREGOR Mackenzie King as leader. (In Thorburn, H. G. (ed.) *Party politics in Canada.* Scarborough, Ont. [c1967] pp. [124]-129.)

Reprinted from the Author's *William Lyon Mackenzie King; a political biography.* [Toronto] University of Toronto Press, 1958.

—— William Lyon Mackenzie King; a political biography, 1874-1923. By R. MacGregor Dawson. [Toronto] University of Toronto Press [1958] xiii, 521 p.

Continued by H. B. Neatby's *William Lyon Mackenzie King; 1924-1932, The lonely heights.*

—— William Lyon Mackenzie King; a political biography, 1874-1923. [Kingsmere ed. Toronto] University of Toronto Press [1958] xiii, 521 p.

Limited edition of 350 numbered copies. Continued by H. B. Neatby's *William Lyon Mackenzie King; 1924-1932, the Lonely heights.*

DEXTER, GRANT From Ox-plow to cabinet. (In *Maclean's.* Toronto. v. 43, no. 6 (Mar. 15, 1930), pp. 16; 53-54.)
Concerns W. R. Motherwell, Minister of Agriculture in the federal cabinet.

—— The new finance minister and his policy. By A. G. Dexter. (In *Maclean's.* Toronto. v. 43, no. 3 (Feb. 1, 1930), pp. 5; 43-44.)
Concerns Charles A. Dunning.

—— The rise of Raoul Dandurand. Brilliant career of Canada's representative on the Council of the League of Nations. (In *Saturday night.* Toronto. v. 43, no. 6 (Dec. 24, 1927), p. 2.)
Concerns Raoul Dandurand.

—— Stewart of Alberta. By A. G. Dexter. (In *Maclean's.* Toronto. v. 42, no. 20 (Oct. 15, 1929), pp. 11; 46.)
Concerns Charles Stewart, Minister of the Interior.

—— This man Mackenzie King. (In *Saturday night.* Toronto. v. 50, no. 46 (Sept. 21, 1935), pp. 5; 8.)

DILLON, JOHN T. A. Crerar, prodigal son. (In *Maclean's.* Toronto. v. 43, no. 4 (Feb. 15, 1930), pp. 9; 42; 45.)

DOYLE, FRANK W. Cabinet portraits: Hon. Peter J. Veniot. (In *Maclean's.* Toronto. v. 39, no. 24 (Dec. 15, 1926), pp. 6; 67.)

DUTHIE, SCOTT I. T. A. Low: business man in politics. (In *Maclean's.* Toronto. v. 37, no. 12 (June 15, 1924), pp. 19; 61-62.)
Concerns Hon. Thomas Andrew Low, Minister of Trade and Commerce.

EGGLESTON, WILFRID Capital comment. The stature of Mackenzie King. (In *Saturday night.* Toronto. v. 65, no. 44 (Aug. 8, 1950), p. 3.)
Written on the occasion of his death July 22, 1950.

—— "Ed" Young. (In *Saturday night.* Toronto. v. 52, no. 31 (June 5, 1937), p. 12.)
A biographical sketch of Edward James Young, Liberal member for Weyburn, Sask.

FERNS, HENRY STANLEY The age of Mackenzie King: the rise of the leader. By H. S. Ferns and B. Ostry. London, Heinemann [1955] xii, 356 p.

—— The ideas of Mackenzie King. By H. S. Ferns. (In *The Manitoba arts review.* Winnipeg. v. 6, no. 2/3 (winter 1948/49), pp. 4-11.)

—— Mackenzie King of Canada. By H. S. Ferns. (In *The Canadian forum.* Toronto. v. 28, no. 334 (Nov. 1948), pp. 174-177; v. 28, no. 335 (Dec. 1948), pp. 200-201; v. 28, no. 336 (Jan. 1949), pp. 226-228.)
In three parts.

FIGLER, BERNARD Sam Jacobs, Member of Parliament (Samuel William Jacobs, KC, MP) 1871-1938. Foreword by H. Carl Goldenberg. [Ottawa, Author, 1970, c1959] 282 p.
First elected to the House of Commons in 1917.

FORSEY, EUGENE ALFRED Constitutional annus mirabilis. By Eugene Forsey. (In *Public affairs.* Halifax. v. 14, no. 1 (autumn 1951), pp. [43]-45.)
Concerns a constitutional issue in 1926 over an attempt by the government of Nova Scotia to abolish the Legislative Council. Mackenzie King thwarted this attempt.

—— Mr. King and parliamentary government. By Eugene Forsey. (In *The Canadian journal of economics and political science.* [Toronto] v. 17 (1951), pp. 451-467.)
"This paper was presented at the annual meeting of the Canadian Political Science Association and the Canadian Historical Association in Montreal, June 6, 1951."

—— A new telling of the King-Byng story. A gamble and the constitution. By Eugene Forsey. (In *Saturday night.* Toronto. v. 68, no. 13 (Jan. 3, 1953), pp. 9; 19; 34.)
A criticism of Bruce Hutchison's article "How Mackenzie King won his greatest gamble". [In *Maclean's.* Toronto. v. 65, no. 21 (Nov. 1, 1952), pp. 16-17; 37-48.]

FORSTER, DONALD F. The politics of combines policy: Liberals and the Stevens Commission. (In *The Canadian journal of economics and political science.* [Toronto] v. 28 (1962), pp. 511-526.)
"A revised version of a paper read at the annual meetings [!] of the Canadian Political Science Association at the McMaster University, Hamilton, on June 8, 1962."
This paper "is an attempt to show how the opposition Liberal Party developed a strategy to deal with the important issues of economic policy raised by the investigation" undertaken by the Royal Commission

on Price Spreads and Mass Buying constituted July 7, 1934 under the chairmanship of H. H. Stevens.

FRASER, BLAIR The secret life of Mackenzie King, spiritualist. (In *Maclean's*. Toronto. v. 64, no. 24 (Dec. 15, 1951), pp. 7-9; 60-61.)

FRASER, THOMAS M. " 'The little grey man'." A personal sketch of Hon. W. S. Fielding. By T. M. Fraser. (In *Maclean's*. Toronto. v. 36, no. 10 (May 15, 1923), pp. 25; 40; 43-48.)

—— The new government in action. By T. M. Fraser. (In *The Canadian magazine of politics, science, art and literature*. Toronto. v. 59 (1922), pp. 3-13.)
The government of W. L. Mackenzie King.

FRENCH, GOLDWIN. Some comments on the "incredible Canadian". (In *Waterloo review*. Waterloo, Ont. v. 2, no. 1 (summer 1959), pp. 37-40.)
Concerns the two biographies of Mackenzie King, written by Bruce Hutchison and R. MacGregor Dawson respectively.

The Government takes the offensive. By a political correspondent. (In *The Canadian forum*. Toronto. v. 6, no. 68 (May 1926), pp. 235-236.)
Discusses the positive effect on the Liberal Party resulting from its budget statement.

GRAHAM, JEAN Among those present. XXVI —Hon. Cairine Wilson. (In *Saturday night*. Toronto. v. 47, no. 32 (June 18, 1932), pp. 5; 10.)

—— Among those present. XXXI—Mr. W. H. Moore, MP. (In *Saturday night*. Toronto. v. 47, no. 38 (July 30, 1932), p. 10.)

GRIERSON, FRANK William Lyon Mackenzie King; a memoir. Presented for the earnest consideration of all patriotic Canadians. [Ottawa, Priv. print., 1952] 110 p.
On cover: Histology and vision.
Edition limited to 1000 copies.

HARDY, HENRY REGINALD Mackenzie King of Canada; a biography. London, Oxford University Press, 1949. xii, 390 p.

Hats off to the win-the-war Liberals. (In *The Onlooker*. Toronto. v. 1, no. 11 (Mar. 1921), pp. 10-15.)

HAYDON, ANDREW Mackenzie King and the Liberal Party. Toronto, T. Allen, 1930. 54 p.

HAYDON, J. A. P. The new Canadian government. (In *Canadian Congress journal*. Montreal. v. 5, no. 10 (Oct. 1926), pp. 19-20.)
Concerns the Liberal government under the leadership of W. L. Mackenzie King.

L'Hon. Rodolphe Lemieux. (In *L'Action canadienne-française*. Montréal. v. 19 (juin 1928), pp. [353]-356.)

HUTCHISON, BRUCE How Mackenzie King won his greatest gamble. (In *Maclean's*. Toronto. v. 65, no. 21 (Nov. 1, 1952), pp. 16; 17; 37-48.)
Concerns the constitutional crisis of 1926.
For a critical commentary, see A new telling of the King-Byng story, by E. Forsey. [In *Saturday night*. Toronto. v. 68, no. 13 (Jan. 3, 1953), p. 9; 19; 34.]

—— The incredible Canadian; candid portrait of Mackenzie King, his works, his times and his nation. [1st ed.] Toronto, Longmans, Green, 1952. 454 p.

—— The incredible Canadian; a candid portrait of Mackenzie King, his works, his times, and his nation. [1st American ed.] New York, Longmans, Green, 1953. 454 p.

—— Mackenzie King; the incredible Canadian. London, Longmans, Green [1953] xi, 456 p.
"First published in Canada in 1952 under the title: The incredible Canadian."

—— Seven Mackenzie Kings Canadians never knew. (In *Maclean's*. Toronto. v. 77, no. 19 (Oct. 3, 1964), pp. 12-13; 28-35.)
Excerpts from Mr. Prime Minister, by Bruce Hutchison. [Don Mills, Ont., c1964].

—— Thoughts on Mackenzie King. (In *Maclean's*. Toronto. v. 65, no. 22 (Nov. 15, 1952), pp. 30-31; 70-73.)

Industry and humanity. Mackenzie King and a new social order. (In *The Maritime advocate and busy East*. Sackville, N.B. v. 24, no. 7 (Feb. 1934), pp. 5-8.)
"Reprinted from the Toronto Daily star, January 10 and 12, 1934."
Considers the principles advocated in *Industry and humanity*, by W. L. M. King. Toronto, Allen, 1918.

IRWIN, W. A. Cabinet portraits: Hon. J. Malcolm. (In *Maclean's*. Toronto. v. 39, no. 23 (Dec. 1, 1926), pp. 8; 34-38.)
Concerns James Malcolm, Minister of Trade and Commerce in the federal government.

KING, WILLIAM LYON MACKENZIE   The aim of the Liberal Party in Canada to-day. By the Hon. W. L. Mackenzie King. (In *Mac-Lean's magazine*. Toronto. v. 34, no. 2 (Jan. 15, 1921), pp. 20-21; 37.)

—— Canada's legations abroad. (In *The Canadian nation*. Ottawa. v. 2, no. 1 (Mar./Apr. 1929), pp. 5-7; 24-26.)

—— The election issues as I see them. By Rt. Hon. W. L. Mackenzie King. (In *Maclean's*. Toronto. v. 43, no. 14 (July 15, 1930), pp. 9; 37-39; 41.)
Relates to the federal election held July 28, 1930.

—— If I am re-elected? By Rt. Hon. W. L. Mackenzie King. (In *Maclean's*. Toronto. v. 38, no. 19 (Oct. 1, 1925), pp. 28; 44.)
Referring to the federal election held October 29, 1925.

—— The issues as I see them. By Rt. Hon. W. L. Mackenzie King. (In *Maclean's*. Toronto. v. 39, no. 17 (Sept. 1, 1926), pp. 7; 32; 36.)
Relates to the federal election held September 14, 1926.

—— The issues as I see them. By Rt. Hon. W. L. Mackenzie King. (In *Maclean's*. Toronto, v. 48, no. 18 (Sept. 15, 1935), pp. 10; 29-31.)
Relates to the federal election held October 14, 1935.

—— The Liberal Party and the tariff; a review of the 1924 budget proposals and principles underlying Liberal policy. By the Rt. Hon. W. L. Mackenzie King, MP, Prime Minister of Canada. [Ottawa? 1924?] 71 p.
A speech delivered in reply to the Leader of the Opposition in the debate on the budget, House of Commons, May 15th, 1924.

—— The message of the carillon and other addresses. By the Right Honourable W. L. Mackenzie King . . . Prime Minister of Canada. Toronto, Macmillan, 1928. x, 274 p.
A collection of addresses published for the occasion of the sixtieth anniversary of Confederation.

—— The practice of liberalism. (In *Liberal Summer Conference*, 1st, Port Hope, Ont., 1933. Toronto, 1933. pp. 269-287.)

—— Whither are we tending to-day? Dictatorship looms in Canada; a view of Rt. Hon. W. L. Mackenzie King. (In *The Maritime advocate and busy East*. Sack-ville, N.B. v. 26, no. 1 (Aug. 1935), pp. 5-14.)
Text of an address delivered "over a national hook up of the Canadian Radio Commission".

KIPP, V. M.   The dynamic Dunning. A close-up of the Saskatchewan man who's Minister of Railways. By V. M. Kepp [!] (In *Saturday night*. Toronto. v. 42, no. 8 (Jan. 8, 1927), p. 2.)
Concerns Charles Avery Dunning.

—— Mr. Forke's lucky smile. Story of one cabinet minister whose face was his fortune. By V. M. Kipp. (In *Saturday night*. Toronto. v. 42, no. 18 (Mar. 19, 1927), p. 2.
Concerns Robert Forke.

LANCTOT, GUSTAVE   Mackenzie King d'après ses mémoires. (In *La Revue de l'Université Laval*. Québec. v. 13, no. 9 (mai 1959), pp. [826]-829.)
A review article of *William Lyon Mackenzie King; a political biography, 1874-1923*, by R. M. Dawson. Toronto, University of Toronto Press [1958].

LAPOINTE, ERNEST   Politique et politiciens. Par l'Hon. Ernest Lapointe. (In *Club canadien de Québec. Problèmes de l'heure*. Québec, 1935. pp. 147-165.)
Speech dated January 10, 1934.

—— "Unity in diversity." By the Honourable Ernest Lapointe. (In *The Canadian nation*. Ottawa. v. 1, no. 1 (Feb. 1928), pp. [9-11].)
"An abridged report of an address before the annual banquet of the Association of Canadian Clubs, on Sept. 16, 1927."

LAUT, AGNES CHRISTINA   Bridging a commercial chasm. By Agnes C. Laut. (In *Maclean's* Toronto. v. 35, no. 6 (Mar. 15, 1922), pp. 17; 42; 44.)
Issues confronting the government of Mackenzie King.

—— Get behind the Premier. By Agnes C. Laut. (In *Maclean's*. Toronto. v. 35, no. 5 (Mar. 1, 1922), pp. 7-8.)
Issues confronting the government of Mackenzie King.

LE SARGE, JOHN EVERETT   The liberalism of Mackenzie King. [Toronto, 1963] 1 v.
Thesis (MA) – University of Toronto.

LEWIS, JOHN   Mackenzie King, the man: his achievement. Toronto, Morang, 1925. 136 p.

—— Parliament's new problem; a Liberal point of view. By Senator John Lewis. (In *The Canadian forum*. Toronto. v. 6, no. 68 (May 1926), pp. 243-244.)

A Liberal budget. (In *The Canadian forum*. Toronto. v. 4, no. 44 (May 1924), pp. 234-235.)

The Liberal Party's position. (In *The Maritime advocate and busy East*. Sackville, N.B. v. 24, no. 8 (Mar. 1934), pp. 5-10; 27.)
A selection of comments relating to the policies of the Liberal Party regarding contemporary problems. Reprinted from the Canadian Liberal monthly, January 1934.

LIBERAL SUMMER CONFERENCE, 1ST, PORT HOPE, ONT., 1933 The Liberal way. A record of opinion on Canadian problems as expressed and discussed at the first Liberal Summer Conference, Port Hope, September, 1933. Toronto, Dent [1933] x, 294 p.
Partial contents: The relations between government and business in Canada, by F. Hankin. – Federal provincial relations, by N. M. Rogers. – Electoral reform, by O. M. Biggar. – The practice of liberalism, by W. L. M. King.

The Liberal Summer Conference at Port Hope. (In *The Maritime advocate and busy East*. Sackville, N.B. v. 24, no. 4 (Nov. 1933), pp. 15-16.)
A factual account of the proceedings sent out from National Liberal Headquarters, Ottawa.

The Liberals go to school. By a liberal. (In *The Canadian forum*. Toronto. v. 14, no. 157 (Oct. 1933), pp. 6-8.)
A report on the Liberal Summer Conference held at Port Hope, Ont., September 4-9, 1933.

LOGAN, JOHN DANIEL The Prime Minister as a man of letters. By J. D. Logan. (In *The Canadian magazine of politics, science, art and literature*. Toronto. v. 61 (1923), pp. 211-217.)
Discusses the literary merits of W. L. Mackenzie King.

LOWER, ARTHUR REGINALD MARSDEN Monument amid the tombstones. Dawson's "Mackenzie King.". By A. R. M. Lower. (In *Queen's quarterly*. Kingston. v. 66 (1959), pp. [146]-150.)
A review article of *William Lyon Mackenzie King; a political biography, 1874-1923*. By R. M. Dawson. Toronto, University of Toronto Press, 1958.

LUDWIG, EMIL Mackenzie King; a portrait sketch. Toronto, Macmillan, 1944. 62 p.

—— Mackenzie King; esquisse d'un portrait. Traduit par André Champroux. Montréal, Editions de L'Arbre [c1944] 95 p.

THE MACE [Commentary on national affairs] Courting the farmer. By the Mace. (In *Saturday night*. Toronto. v. 35, no. 50 (Oct. 9, 1920), p. 4.)
Concerns William Lyon Mackenzie King's "courtship" of the farmers.

—— [Commentary on national affairs] The passing of Mr. Sifton. By the Mace. (In *Saturday night*. Toronto. v. 36, no. 14 (Jan. 29, 1921), p. 3.)
Concerns Arthur Lewis Sifton. Written on the occasion of his death, January 21, 1921.

—— [Commentary on national affairs] Family quarrels. By the Mace. (In *Saturday night*. Toronto. v. 36, no. 19 (Mar. 5, 1921), p. 4.)
Concerns Rodolphe Lemieux and Ernest Lapointe.

—— [Commentary on national affairs] Supply and supplies. By the Mace. (In *Saturday night*. Toronto. v. 36, no. 22 (Mar. 26, 1921), p. 4.)
Concerns the passing of a government interim supply bill.

—— [Commentary on national affairs] The new broom. By the Mace. (In *Saturday night*. Toronto. [v. 37, no. 7] (Dec. 17, 1921), p. 4.)
Comments on the election of W. L. M. King as Prime Minister of Canada.

—— [Commentary on national affairs] The little gray man. By the Mace. (In *Saturday night*. Toronto. v. 37, no. 8 (Dec. 24, 1921), p. 4.)
Concerns William Stevens Fielding and the "development of the 'bloc' habit by provinces other than Quebec".

—— [Commentary on national affairs] New Year's greetings. By the Mace. (In *Saturday night*. Toronto. v. 37, no. 10 (Jan. 7, 1922), p. 4.)
Comments, mainly, on W. L. M. King and his cabinet.

—— [Commentary on national affairs] Getting down to business. By the Mace. (In *Saturday night*. Toronto. v. 37, no. 11 (Jan. 14, 1922), p. 4.)

Concerns the fourteenth parliament and a proposal to nominate Rodolphe Lemieux as Speaker of the House.

—— [Commentary on national affairs] Three of a kind. By the Mace (In *Saturday night*. Toronto. v. 37, no. 12 (Jan. 21, 1922), p. 4.)

Comments on members of the King cabinet: George Perry Graham, Daniel Duncan McKenzie, and William Costelle Kennedy.

—— [Commentary on national affairs] Editing the estimates. By the Mace. (In *Saturday night*. Toronto. v. 37, no. 17 (Feb. 25, 1922), p. 4.)

Concerns W. S. Fielding, Minister of Finance, and editing of the "estimates for the approaching fiscal year".

—— [Commentary on national affairs] Sir Lomer lifts the veil. By the Mace. (In *Saturday night*. Toronto. v. 37, no. 22 (Apr. 1, 1922), p. 4.)

Concerns Sir Jean-Lomer Gouin and his election to the House.

—— [Commentary on national affairs] After the slums again. By the Mace. (In *Saturday night*. Toronto. v. 37, no. 23 (Apr. 8, 1922), p. 4.)

Considers that "the chief problem on the hands of Mr. King and his colleagues is the unemployment rife among those who voted them into power".

—— [Commentary on national affairs] Rounding into form. By the Mace. (In *Saturday night*. Toronto. v. 37, no. 24 (Apr. 15, 1922), p. 4.)

Considers the performance of the King administration to date.

—— [Commentary on national affairs] Tackling a big job. By the Mace. (In *Saturday night*. Toronto. v. 37, no. 26 (Apr. 29, 1922), p. 4.)

Concerns Mackenzie King and the railway problem.

—— [Commentary on national affairs] Uneasy lies the head. By the Mace. (In *Saturday night*. Toronto. v. 37, no. 27 (May 6, 1922), p. 4.)

Concerns Mackenzie King. Comments that "Mr. King is treading warily the sessional path".

—— [Commentary on national affairs] Wrestling with the budget. By the Mace. (In *Saturday night*. Toronto. v. 37, no. 28 (May 13, 1922), p. 4.)

Concerns W. S. Fielding and his budget proposals.

—— [Commentary on national affairs] The Master at the helm. By the Mace. (In *Saturday night*. Toronto. v. 37, no. 31 (June 3, 1922), p. 4.)

Concerns W. S. Fielding and his sixteenth budget.

—— [Commentary on national affairs] A feather in his cap. By the Mace. (In *Saturday night*. Toronto. v. 37, no. 33 (June 17, 1922), p. 5.)

Concerns Mackenzie King and his promotion to the rank of an Imperial Privy Councillor.

—— [Commentary on national affairs] In deep water. By the Mace. (In *Saturday night*. Toronto. v. 37, no. 34 (June 24, 1922), p. 4.)

Concerns Mackenzie King's government with a small Liberal majority.

—— [Commentary on national affairs] The curtain falls. By the Mace. (In *Saturday night*. Toronto. v. 37, no. 36 (July 8, 1922), p. 4.)

"Mr. King comes through the fiery furnace of the session with his position of leader consolidated." Refers to the first session, fourteenth parliament.

—— [Commentary on national affairs] Back to the fold. By the Mace. (In *Saturday night*. Toronto. v. 37, no. 41 (Aug. 12, 1922), p. 4.)

Concerns William Pugsley and his possible entrance into the Senate.

—— [Commentary on national affairs] Helping the returned man. By the Mace. (In *Saturday night*. Toronto. v. 37, no. 43 (Aug. 26, 1922), p. 4; v. 37, no. 44 (Sept. 2, 1922), p. 4.)

In two parts.

Concerns the programme of the government relating to war veterans.

—— [Commentary on national affairs] The new broom at work. By the Mace. (In *Saturday night*. Toronto. v. 37, no. 47 (Sept. 23, 1922), p. 4.)

Concerns Charles Murphy, Postmaster General, and changes introduced in the Public Service.

—— [Commentary on national affairs] A hard nut to crack. By the Mace. (In *Saturday night*. Toronto. v. 37, no. 52 (Oct. 28, 1922), p. 4.)

Concerns the immigration policy of Charles Stewart, Minister of the Interior and Immigration.

—— [Commentary on national affairs] A test of strength. By the Mace. (In *Saturday night*. Toronto. v. 38, no. 2 (Nov. 11, 1922), p. 4.)

Concerns Mackenzie King's considerations filling the "five vacancies in the constituencies of Gloucester, N.B., Lanark, Jacques Cartier, Megantic and Halifax".

—— [Commentary on national affairs] Starting out for himself. By the Mace. (In *Saturday night*. Toronto. v. 38, no. 3 (Nov. 18, 1922), p. 4.)

Concerns the candidates for the job of Canadian representative at Washington: W. S. Fielding, Sir Charles Fitzpatrick, and C. A. Magrath.

—— [Commentary on national affairs] Flying the flag again. By the Mace. (In *Saturday night*. Toronto. v. 38, no. 6 (Dec. 9, 1922), p. 4.)

Concerns Charles Stewart and his immigration policy.

—— [Commentary on national affairs] Turning over a new leaf. By the Mace. (In *Saturday night*. Toronto. v. 38, no. 8 [i.e. 9] (Dec. 30, 1922), p. 4.)

Reviews the first year in office of the Mackenzie King government.

—— [Commentary on national affairs] The vacant chair. By the Mace. (In *Saturday night*. Toronto. v. 38, no. 13 (Feb. 3, 1923), p. 4.)

Concerns the successor to the late William Costelle Kennedy.

—— [Commentary on national affairs] Off to a good start. By the Mace. (In *Saturday night*. Toronto. v. 38, no. 16 (Feb. 24, 1923), p. 4.)

Concerns the first divisions of the session and the fact that the "government has been sustained by large majorities".

—— [Commentary on national affairs] The Daddy of the House. By the Mace. (In *Saturday night*. Toronto. v. 38, no. 18 (Mar. 10, 1923), p. 4.)

Concerns William Stevens Fielding.

—— [Commentary on national affairs] Pulling against the stream. By the Mace. (In *Saturday night*. Toronto. v. 38, no. 21 (Mar. 31, 1923), p. 4.)

Concerns Charles Stewart and the problem of immigration.

—— [Commentary on national affairs] Letting George do it. By the Mace. (In *Saturday night*. Toronto. v. 38, no. 22 (Apr. 7, 1923), p. 4.)

Concerns George Perry Graham, Minister of Defence.

—— [Commentary on national affairs] Hail and farewell. By the Mace. (In *Saturday night*. Toronto. v. 38, no. 25 (Apr. 28, 1923), p. 4.)

Concerns Edward Mortimer Macdonald and Daniel Duncan McKenzie.

—— [Commentary on national affairs] A maker of budgets. By the Mace. (In *Saturday night*. Toronto. v. 38, no. 26 (May 5, 1923), p. 4.)

Concerns William Stevens Fielding.

—— [Commentary on national affairs] The merry-go-round. By the Mace. (In *Saturday night*. Toronto. v. 38, no. 28 (May 19, 1923), p. 4.)

Comments on the appointment of the many committees by the government of Mackenzie King.

—— [Commentary on national affairs] Cutting loose. By the Mace. (In *Saturday night*. Toronto, v. 38, no. 31 (June 9, 1923), p. 4.)

Concerns Andrew McMaster's break with the Liberal Party.

—— [Commentary on national affairs] One of the Old Guard. By the Mace. (In *Saturday night*. Toronto. v. 38, no. 41 (Aug. 25, 1923), p. 4.)

Concerns Sir Charles Fitzpatrick.

—— [Commentary on national affairs] Shuffling the pack. By the Mace. (In *Saturday night*. Toronto. v. 38, no. 42 (Sept. 1, 1923), p. 4.)

Concerns the cabinet shuffles in the King government.

—— [Commentary on national affairs] A new member of the crew. By the Mace. (In *Saturday night*. Toronto. v. 38, no. 46 (Sept. 29, 1923), p. 4.)

Concerns Edward James McMurray.

—— [Commentary on national affairs] Stepping down. By the Mace. (In *Saturday night*. Toronto. v. 38, no. 47 (Oct. 6, 1923), p. 4.)

Concerns the resignation of Louis-Philippe Brodeur.

—— [Commentary on national affairs] From Billy to Billy. By the Mace. (In *Saturday night*. Toronto. v. 38, no. 48 (Oct. 13, 1923), p. 4.)

Concerns W. S. Fielding as acting leader for the Government in the House of Commons.

—— [Commentary on national affairs] The first Commoner. By the Mace. (In *Saturday night*. Toronto. v. 38, no. 48 (Oct. 20, 1923), p. 4.)

Concerns Rodolphe Lemieux and the position of Speaker in the Commons.

—— [Commentary on national affairs] The call of the West. By the Mace. (In *Saturday night*. Toronto. v. 38, no. 49 (Oct. 27, 1923), p. 4.)

Concerns Thomas Andrew Low.

—— [Commentary on national affairs] The winning smile. By the Mace. (In *Saturday night*. Toronto. v. 38, no. 51 (Nov. 10, 1923), p. 4.)

Comments on Edward James McMurray and the by-election of Winnipeg North held October 24, 1923.

—— [Commentary on national affairs] Coming back again. By the Mace. (In *Saturday night*. Toronto. v. 38, no. 52 (Nov. 17, 1923), p. 4.)

Concerns Thomas A. Crerar and his return from retirement.

—— [Commentary on national affairs] Still going strong. By the Mace. (In *Saturday night*. Toronto. v. 39, no. 3 (Dec. 8, 1923), p. 4.)

Concerns William Stevens Fielding.

—— [Commentary on national affairs] Turning another page. By the Mace. (In *Saturday night*. Toronto. v. 39, no. 6 (Dec. 29, 1923), p. 4.)

Reviews, briefly, the performance of the King government over the period of a year.

—— [Commentary on national affairs] Coming and going. By the Mace. (In *Saturday night*. Toronto. v. 39, no. 9 (Jan. 19, 1924), p. 4.)

Concerns the departure of Sir Lomer Gouin from the King administration.

—— [Commentary on national affairs] Leaving the door ajar. By the Mace. (In *Saturday night*. Toronto. v. 39, no. 10 (Jan. 26, 1924), p. 4.)

Concerns cabinet shuffles in the King government.

—— [Commentary on national affairs] The Handy man. By the Mace. (In *Saturday night*. Toronto. v. 39, no. 11 (Feb. 2, 1924), p. 4.)

Concerns James Alexander Robb.

—— [Commentary on national affairs] Prepared for heavy weather. By the Mace. (In *Saturday night*. Toronto. v. 39, no. 13 (Feb. 16, 1924), p. 4.)

Comments on the strategy of the King government with a view to the forthcoming session of parliament opening February 28, 1924.

—— [Commentary on national affairs] On the operating table. By the Mace. (In *Saturday night*. Toronto. v. 39, no. 18 (Mar. 22, 1924), p. 4.)

Concerns proposed tariff amendments considered by the King government.

—— [Commentary on national affairs] Sitting on the lid. By the Mace. (In *Saturday night*. Toronto. v. 39, no. 20 (Apr. 5, 1924), p. 4.)

Comments on the "pruning of expenditures" by the King government.

—— [Commentary on national affairs] Budgets past & present. By the Mace. (In *Saturday night*. Toronto. v. 39, no. 22 (Apr. 19, 1924), p. 4.)

Comments on Sir Thomas White and W. S. Fielding.

—— [Commentary on national affairs] Familiar fighting ground. By the Mace. (In *Saturday night*. Toronto. v. 39, no. 23 (Apr. 26, 1924), p. 4.)

Concerns tariff proposals presented by the King government.

—— [Commentary on national affairs] Off again, on again. By the Mace. (In *Saturday night*. Toronto. v. 39, no. 28 (May 31, 1924), p. 4.)

Concerns Walter G. Mitchell and Andrew Ross McMaster and their stepping off and on the "government bandwagon".

—— [Commentary on national affairs] A pair of veterans. By the Mace. (In *Saturday night*. Toronto. v. 39, no. 30 (June 14, 1924), p. 4.)

Concerns George Perry Graham and the railway budget, etc.

—— [Commentary on national affairs] A varied menu. By the Mace. (In *Saturday night*. Toronto. v. 39, no. 31 (June 21, 1924), p. 4.)

Comments on Mackenzie King's agenda for the House, which involves "legislation arising out of the reports of the various committees . . ."; these include Banking and Commerce, Redistribution, etc.

—— [Commentary on national affairs] The cares of office. By the Mace. (In *Saturday night*. Toronto. v. 39, no. 42 (Sept. 6, 1924), p. 4.)

Refers to Mackenzie King.

—— [Commentary on national affairs] On the Western trail. By the Mace. (In *Saturday night*. Toronto. v. 39, no. 45 (Sept. 27, 1924), p. 4.)

Comments on Mackenzie King and his forthcoming Western tour.

—— [Commentary on national affairs] Under the plum tree. By the Mace. (In *Saturday night*. Toronto. v. 39, no. 46 (Oct. 4, 1924), p. 4.)

Concerns various vacant positions in the government.

—— [Commentary on national affairs] Back to his post. By the Mace. (In *Saturday night*. Toronto. v. 39, no. 48 (Oct. 18, 1924), p. 4.)

Concerns Charles Murphy, Postmaster General.

—— [Commentary on national affairs] New feathers in his cap. By the Mace. (In *Saturday night*. Toronto. v. 39, no. 49 (Oct. 25, 1924), p. 4.)

Comments on Mackenzie King and the German debts settlement, etc.

—— [Commentary on national affairs] Wearing the crown. By the Mace. (In *Saturday night*. Toronto. v. 39, no. 51 (Nov. 8, 1924), p. 4.)

Concerns George Perry Graham.

—— [Commentary on national affairs] Back into harness again. By the Mace. (In *Saturday night*. Toronto. v. 40, no. 1 (Nov. 22, 1924), p. 4.)

Comments on Mackenzie King's return from his Western tour and discusses the issues waiting his consideration.

—— [Commentary on national affairs] For old times sake. By the Mace. (In *Saturday night*. Toronto. v. 40, no. 3 (Dec. 6, 1924), p. 4.)

Concerns Rodolphe Lemieux.

—— [Commentary on national affairs] Sitting on the treasury list. By the Mace. (In *Saturday night*. Toronto. v. 40, no. 11 (Jan. 31, 1925), p. 4; v. 40, no. 12 (Feb. 7, 1925), p. 4; v. 40, no. 13 (Feb. 14, 1925), p. 4.)

In three parts.

Concerns the financial policy of the government led by Mackenzie King.

—— [Commentary on national affairs] Trimming the tree. By the Mace. (In *Saturday night*. Toronto. v. 40, no. 15 (Feb. · 28, 1925), p. 4.)

Concerns the estimates presented by the Mackenzie King government.

—— [Commentary on national affairs] Making both ends meet. By the Mace. (In *Saturday night*. Toronto. v. 40, no. 19 (Mar. 28, 1925), p. 4.)

Concerns James Alexander Robb and the 1925 budget.

—— [Commentary on national affairs] Some budget sidelights. By the Mace. (In *Saturday night*. Toronto. v. 40, no. 20 (Apr. 4, 1925), p. 4.)

Concerns the budget of 1925.

—— [Commentary on national affairs] A familiar role. By the Mace. (In *Saturday night*. Toronto. v. 40, no. 27 (May 23, 1925), p. 4.)

Concerns George Perry Graham and his annual statement on government railway policy.

MC GILLICUDDY, OWEN ERNEST   The laird of Pipestone. A personality study of Honourable Robert Forke, who emigrated from Scotland in 1882 and became Minister of Immigration for Canada in 1926. By Owen E. McGillicuddy. (In *The Canadian magazine*. Toronto. v. 69, no. 4 (Apr. 1928), pp. 13; 33; 35.)

—— The making of a premier; an outline of the life story of W. L. Mackenzie King. With a pref. by John Lewis. Toronto, Musson [1922] xiii, 91 p.

MACPHAIL, ALEXANDER   The federal election: Mr. King. By A. M. (In *Queen's quarterly*. Kingston. v. 42 (1935), pp. [523]-529.)

Analyses the results of the general elections held October 14, 1935, which returned the Liberal Party as the government.

MAC TAVISH, NEWTON MC FAUL   The King family in literature. By Newton MacTavish. (In *Maclean's*. Toronto. v. 49, no. 6 (Mar. 15, 1936), p. 22.)

Outlines the literary background and published works of W. L. Mackenzie King.

—— The vision of immortality. A reconsideration of the Rt. Hon. Mackenzie King's remarkable book "The secret of heroism". By Newton MacTavish. (In *The Canadian magazine*. Toronto. v. 64 (Apr. 1925), pp. 70-71; 85.)

Article on "The secret of heroism; a memoir of Henry Albert Harper", published Toronto, 1906, by Revell. Harper was a civil servant in Ottawa, who worked "in close association and friendship with Mr. W. L. Mackenzie King . . . at that time (1901) Deputy Minister of Labor".

MARCH, J. EDGAR   Go easy—let others spread out. (In *Maclean's*. Toronto. v. 37, no. 11 (June 1, 1924), pp. 19; 62-64.)
Concerns James A. Robb, Minister of Finance.

MARSH, D'ARCY   The appeal of reason. (In *The Canadian forum*. Toronto. v. 15, no. 174 (Mar. 1935), p. 228.)
Concerns Humphrey Mitchell who was Labour MP for East Hamilton, 1931-35. He served, later, as Minister of Labour during the years 1941-1950.

——   Liberalism on the march. (In *The Canadian forum*. Toronto. v. 14, no. 164 (May 1934), p. 298.)
Concerns Ian Mackenzie.

MELROSE, G. H.   The fine tact of Hon. C. H. Mackintosh. (In *Saturday night*. Toronto. v. 44, no. 10 (Jan. 19, 1929), p. 5.)
Concerns Charles Herbert Mackintosh; a brief biographical sketch.

Mr. King's opportunity. (In *The Canadian forum*. Toronto. v. 7, no. 73 (Oct. 1926), pp. 394-395.)
Assesses the results of the general elections held September 14, 1926.

Mr. Robb's tax reduction problem. Special correspondence of Willisons monthly. (In *Willisons monthly*. Toronto. v. 2, no. 9 (Feb. 1927), pp. 331-332.)

M. [i.e. Monsieur] Ernest Lapointe. (In *L'Action française*. Montréal. v. 12 (sept. 1924), pp. [145]-149.)

M. [i.e. Monsieur] Mackenzie King. (In *L'Action française*. Montréal. v. 13 (juin 1925), pp. [346]-349.)

MOORE, WILLIAM HENRY   Mackenzie King and the obstinate idealist. By W. H. Moore. (In *The Maritime advocate and busy East*. Sackville, N.B. v. 26, no. 2 (Sept. 1935), pp. 19-20.)
An article reprinted from *Public life*.
Concerns the personality and background of W. L. M. King.

——   Mackenzie King and the wage earner. (In *The Maritime advocate and busy East*. Sackville, N.B. v. 26, no. 2 (Sept. 1935), pp. 5; 24-25.)
An article reprinted from *Public life*.

MUNRO, J. K.   After the conference is over. (In *Maclean's*. Toronto. v. 36, no. 24 (Dec. 15, 1923), pp. 18-19.)
Comments on the current political situation; concentrates on the activities of Sir Lomer Gouin and Ernest Lapointe.

——   "Little grey man" trips in his balancing act. (In *Maclean's*. Toronto. v. 36, no. 11 (June 1, 1923), pp. 20-21; 50-51.)
"Little grey man" is W. S. Fielding.

——   Made in Montreal? (In *Maclean's*. Toronto. v. 35, no. 3 (Feb. 1, 1922), pp. 14-15; 40.)
Discusses the influence of Sir Lomer Gouin in selecting the cabinet for the Mackenzie King government.

——   Rule by oratory is ended. (In *Maclean's*. Toronto. v. 35, no. 11 (June 1, 1922), pp. 20-21; 46.)
Concerns, mainly, the composition and the performance of the King government in Parliament.

——   When Fielding came back. (In *Maclean's*. Toronto. v. 36, no. 5 (Mar. 1, 1923), pp. 18-19.)
Concerns W. S. Fielding.

NEATBY, HERBERT BLAIR   Mackenzie King and the national identity. By Blair Neatby. (In Historical and Scientific Society of Manitoba. *Papers*. Winnipeg. ser 3, no. 24 (1967/68), pp. 77-87.)

——   William Lyon Mackenzie King. By Blair Neatby. (In McDougall, R. L. (ed.) *Canada's past and present*. [Toronto, 1967, c1965] pp. 1-20.)
Our living tradition, ser. 5.

——   William Lyon Mackenzie King; 1924-1932, the lonely heights. By H. Blair Neatby. [Toronto] University of Toronto Press [c1963] xii, 452 p.
Continuation of R. M. Dawson's *William Lyon Mackenzie King; a political biography, 1874-1923*.
The complete biographical work is in progress.

——   William Lyon Mackenzie King; 1924-1932, the lonely heights. By H. Blair Neatby. [Kingsmere ed. Toronto] University of Toronto Press [c1963] xii, 452 p.
Limited edition of 350 numbered copies.
Continuation of R. M. Dawson's *William Lyon Mackenzie King; a political biography, 1874-1923*.
The work is in progress.

NELSON, JOHN Dunning dares to take a chance. (In *Maclean's*. Toronto. v. 39, no. 11 (June 1, 1926), pp. 16; 61.)

Concerns Charles Dunning, Minister of Railways and Canals in the Mackenzie King government.

O'LEARY, MICHAEL GRATTAN The "Father of the House". Mr. Speaker Lemieux's thirty years in Parliament. By M. Grattan O'Leary. (In *Saturday night*. Toronto. v. 42, no. 4 (Dec. 11, 1926), p. 5.)

Concerns Rodolphe Lemieux.

—— Fielding: link with Confederation. By M. Grattan O'Leary. (In *Saturday night*. Toronto. v. 42, no. 31 (June 18, 1927), p. 3.)

Concerns William Stevens Fielding.

—— Government by stagnation. By M. Grattan O'Leary. (In *Maclean's*. Toronto. v. 39, no. 5 (Mar. 1, 1926), pp. 23; 40-41.)

Comments on the Liberal administration.

—— Keeper of Taschereau's purse. By M. Grattan O'Leary. (In *Maclean's*. Toronto. v. 42, no. 24 (Dec. 15, 1929), pp. 9; 59.)

Concerns Andrew McMaster, Provincial Treasurer of Quebec. Represented the riding of Brome in the federal parliament of 1917.

—— Lapointe. By M. Grattan O'Leary. (In *Maclean's*. Toronto. v. 42, no. 15 (Aug. 1, 1929), pp. 7; 50; 53.)

Concerns Ernest Lapointe, Minister of Justice in the Mackenzie King government.

—— The play re-opens at Ottawa. By Grattan O'Leary. (In *Maclean's*. Toronto. v. 39, no. 7 (Apr. 1, 1926), pp. 29; 46-49.)

Concerns the reconstruction of the Mackenzie King cabinet, etc.

—— The political scene. By M. Grattan O'Leary. (In *Queen's quarterly*. Kingston. v. 37 (1930), pp. 205-213.)

Comments on the death of James Robb, Minister of Finance, and the appointment of Charles A. Dunning.

—— Prosperity's silent prophet. Quebec owes much of her new-found progress to the man who is now her Lieutenant-Governor. By M. Grattan O'Leary. (In *Maclean's*. Toronto. v. 42, no. 2 (Jan. 15, 1929), pp. 5; 55.)

Concerns Sir Lomer Gouin.

—— Senator George P. Graham. Laughing philosopher of the Commons goes to new surroundings. By M. Grattan O'Leary.

(In *Saturday night*. Toronto. v. 42, no. 8 (Jan. 8, 1927), p. 3.)

Concerns George Perry Graham, appointed to the Senate December 20, 1926.

OLIVER, FRANK A government wheat guarantee? By the Hon. Frank Oliver. (In *Saturday night*. Toronto. v. 46, no. 4 (Dec. 6, 1930), pp. [69]; 71; 73.)

The Opposition: "Outworn and moribund". (In *Canadian comment*. Toronto. v. 4, no. 1 (Jan. 1935), p. 7.)

Brief comment on the Liberal Party.

PAUL, CHARLES FREDERICK A day with the budget. By Frederick Paul. (In *Saturday night*. Toronto. v. 39, no. 22 (Apr. 19, 1924), p. 2.)

Comments on the budget brought down by Hon. James A. Robb, Acting Minister of Finance.

Pepping up the debate. (In *Canadian comment*. Toronto. v. 3, no. 7 (July 1934), p. 6.)

Refers to the Hon. W. R. Motherwell and his position on the Marketing Bill voted on June 8, 1934.

PERRY, ANNE ANDERSON Women begin to speak their minds. (In *Chatelaine*. Toronto. v. 1, no. 4 (June 1928), pp. 6; 61-62.)

Describes the national convention held by women in the Liberal Party at Ottawa, April 1928.

PICKERSGILL, JOHN WHITNEY Mackenzie King's speeches. By J. W. Pickersgill. (In *Queen's quarterly*. Kingston. v. 57 (1950), pp. [304]-311.)

PICKWELL, FREDERICK C. The new Premier of Saskatchewan. How James G. Gardiner worked his way from the bottom to the top. By F. C. Pickwell. (In *Saturday night*. Toronto. v. 41, no. 17 (Mar. 13, 1926), p. 5.)

James Garfield Gardiner was federal Minister of Agriculture, 1935-1957.

RALSTON, JAMES LAYTON Misery and suffering as a result of Tory policies. By J. L. Ralston. (In *The Maritime advocate and busy East*. Sackville, N.B. v. 25, no. 11 (May 1935), pp. 14; 28.)

Reply to the Budget speech reprinted from the Canadian Liberal monthly.

REGENSTREIF, SAMUEL PETER A threat to leadership: C. A. Dunning and Mackenzie King. By S. Peter Regenstreif. (In *The Dalhousie review*. Halifax. v. 44, no. 3 (autumn 1964), pp. [272]-289.)

ROBERTS, LESLIE   The silent senator . . . (In *The Canadian* [magazine] Toronto. v. 72, no. 6 (Dec. 1929), pp. 15; 46-47.)
Concerns Donat Raymond.

—— The wife of a politician. (In *Chatelaine*. Toronto. v. 4, no. 5 (May 1931), pp. 9; 75-76.)
Relates a conversation with the wife of Ernest Lapointe (née Emma Pratte).

ROBERTS, LLOYD   Have you met Sam Jacobs? (In *Saturday night*. Toronto. v. 49, no. 35 (July 7, 1934), p. 16.)
A character sketch of Samuel W. Jacobs, Liberal MP for Cartier, Que.

ROE, SYDNEY   The little grey man from Nova Scotia. Rt. Hon. W. S. Fielding in the twilight of his eventful life. (In *Saturday night*. Toronto. v. 43, no. 51 (Nov. 3, 1928), pp. 2; 3.)

—— "Silent Jim" Robb's debut. (In *Saturday night*. Toronto. v. 45, no. 2 (Nov. 23, 1929), p. 5.)
Concerns James Alexander Robb.

ROGERS, NORMAN MC LEOD   Mackenzie King. A revised and extended ed. of a biographical sketch by John Lewis. Toronto, Morang, 1935. xii, 212 p.

ROSKIES, ETHEL   The liberalism of William Lyon Mackenzie King. [Montreal] 1960. 518 leaves.
Thesis (MA) – McGill University.

SANDWELL, BERNARD KEBLE   Mr. King: politician vs human being. By B. K. Sandwell. (In *Saturday night*. Toronto. v. 65, no. 7 (Nov. 22, 1949), p. 13.)

SCOTT, JOHN LESLIE   Our new woman senator. (In *Maclean's*. Toronto. v. 43, no. 7 (Apr. 1, 1930), pp. 16; 97-98.)
Concerns Cairine Reay Wilson, appointed to the Senate February 15, 1930.

Le Sénateur Belcourt. (In *L'Action française*. Montréal. v. 11 (mars 1924), pp. [141]-145.)
Concerns Napoléon Antoine Belcourt.

SIFTON, SIR CLIFFORD   The immigrants Canada wants. (In *Maclean's*. Toronto. v. 35, no. 7 (Apr. 1, 1922), pp. 16; 32-34.)

Sir Lomer Gouin. (In *L'Action française*. Montréal. v. 10 (déc. 1923), pp. [330]-333.)

SLACK, JOHN BOLTON   The external policy of the Right Honourable W. L. Mackenzie King; a dissertation on the development of Canadian foreign policy, 1919-1944. [Kingston, Ont.] 1946. 317 leaves.
Thesis (MA) – Queen's University.

Some problems of tax reduction. Special correspondence of Willisons monthly. (In *Willisons monthly*. Toronto. v. 3, no. 8 (Jan. 1928), pp. 292-294.)
Discusses tax policy in consideration of a budget to be presented by the Minister of Finance, J. A. Robb.

STEELE, CHARLES FRANKLIN   Prairie editor; the life and times of Buchanan of Lethbridge. By C. Frank Steele. Foreword by Arthur R. Ford. Toronto, Ryerson Press [c1961] viii, 196 p. port.
Concerns Senator William Francis Asbury Buchanan, owner of the Lethbridge *Herald*. Appointed to the Senate, September 5, 1925.

STEVENSON, JOHN A.   The parliamentary session. By J. A. Stevenson. (In *Queen's quarterly*. Kingston. v. 38 (1931), pp. 563-571.)
Discusses, in particular, the political scandal involving the Beauharnois Corporation and the Liberal Party.

STUBBS, ROY ST. GEORGE   E. J. McMurray (In his *Prairie portraits*. Toronto. [c1954] pp. 143-176.)
Elected as a Liberal to represent North Winnipeg in the federal election of 1921.

UNDERHILL, FRANK HAWKINS   Concerning Mr. King. By Frank H. Underhill. (In *The Canadian forum*. Toronto. v. 30, no. 356 (Sept. 1950), pp. [121]-122; 125-127.)
An essay depicting the career of the late William Lyon Mackenzie King.

—— The Dawson biography of Mackenzie King. By F. H. Underhill. (In *The Canadian forum*. Toronto. v. 39, no. 463 (Aug. 1959), pp. 102-103.)
A review article of *William Lyon Mackenzie King*, by R. M. Dawson. Toronto, University of Toronto Press, 1958.

—— The Liberal programme. By F. H. U. (In *The Canadian forum*. Toronto. v. 13, no. 146 (Nov. 1932), pp. 45-46.)

—— W. L. Mackenzie King. (In his *In search of Canadian liberalism*. Toronto, 1961. pp. 114-140.)

VEZINA, FRANCOISE   L'exposé budgétaire de M. Fielding. (In *Revue trimestrielle canadienne*. Montréal. v. 9 (sept. 1923), pp. [287]-298.)
Discusses the budget for 1923/24.

VINING, CHARLES ARTHUR MC LAREN   Mr. Dunning. By R. T. L. (In *Maclean's*. Toronto. v. 46, no. 17 (Sept. 1, 1933), p. 12.)
Concerns C. A. Dunning.

—— Mr. Gardiner. By R. T. L. (In *Maclean's*. Toronto. v. 47, no. 18 (Sept. 15, 1934), p. 12.)
Concerns James Garfield Gardiner.

—— Mr. Lapointe. By R. T. L. (In *Maclean's*. Toronto. v. 46, no. 23 (Dec. 1, 1933), p. 8.)
Concerns Ernest Lapointe.

—— Sir William. By R. T. L. (In *Maclean's*. Toronto. v. 46, no. 15 (Aug. 1, 1933), p. 12.)
Concerns Sir William Mulock.

—— This man Hepburn. By Charles Vining. (In *Saturday night*. Toronto. v. 49, no. 25 (Apr. 28, 1934), pp. 5; 7.)
Concerns Mitchell Frederick Hepburn.

WARD, NORMAN MC QUEEN   Dawson on King. By Norman Ward. (In *The Canadian forum*. Toronto. v. 38, no. 457 (Feb. 1959), pp. 251-252.)
A review article of *William Lyon Mackenzie King*, by R. M. Dawson. Toronto, University of Toronto Press, 1958.

WAYLING, THOMAS   Heenan, called Peter. By Tom Wayling. (In *Maclean's*. Toronto. v. 43, no. 1 (Jan. 1, 1930), pp. 12; 44-46.)
Concerns Peter Heenan, Minister of Labour in the King government.

—— Therese Casgrain. (In *Saturday night*. Toronto. v. 48, no. 26 (May 6, 1933), p. 14.)
The wife of Pierre Casgrain, chief Liberal whip in the House of Commons.

WEILBRENNER, BERNARD   Les idées politiques de Lomer Gouin. (In Canadian Historical Association. *Report of the annual meeting*. [Ottawa] (1965), pp. 46-57.)

WEIR, WILLIAM GILBERT   Twenty-two years in Parliament. By W. "Gibb" Weir, MP. [Ottawa, 1953] 32 p.
Cover title.
First elected to the House of Commons in 1930.

What the budget means. (In *The Canadian forum*. Toronto. v. 7, no. 78 (Mar. 1927), pp. 165-166.)
The budget presented by J. A. Robb.

1935-1948

ABBOTT, DOUGLAS CHARLES   A new look at Canada. By the Hon. Charles Abbott. (In Empire Club of Canada. *Addresses*. Toronto. (1947/48), pp. 285-298.)
Address delivered March 11, 1948.

ALWAY, RICHARD MARTIN HOLDEN   Hepburn, King and the Rowell-Sirois Commission. By Richard M. H. Alway. (In *The Canadian historical review*. Toronto. v. 48 (1967), pp. 113-141.)

—— Mitchell F. Hepburn and the Liberal Party in the province of Ontario, 1937-1943. ix, 395 leaves.
Thesis (MA) – University of Toronto.
Federal-provincial relations are touched upon frequently in this analysis.

ANGERS, FRANCOIS ALBERT   Pourquoi M. King n'est pas délié. (In *L'Action nationale*. Montréal. v. 19 (mai 1942), pp. [251]-262.)
Discusses the results of the national plebiscite on the matter of conscription held April 27, 1942.

ANGUS, HENRY FORBES   Liberalism stoops to conquer. By H. F. Angus. (In *The Canadian forum*. Toronto. v. 15, no. 179 (Dec. 1935), pp. 389-390.)
Discusses the political motivation of Liberal Party candidates in British Columbia, who opposed the enfranchisement of Oriental Canadians during the federal election campaign of 1935.

BALDWIN, R. W.   The nation. Mr. King is sentimental. (In *Saturday night*. Toronto. v. 54, no. 3 (Nov. 19, 1938), p. 5.)
Comments on an Armistice Day speech made by Mackenzie King.

—— The nation. Mr. Pouliot is a Liberal. (In *Saturday night*. Toronto. v. 54, no. 20 (Mar. 18, 1939), p. 5.)
Refers to Jean François Pouliot. Comments on the Defence Purchasing Board legislation.

—— The nation. Who gets lost Liberal votes? (In *Saturday night*. Toronto. v. 54, no. 33 (June 17, 1939), p. 5.)

—— National affairs. Ottawa declares war on "Mitch". (In *Saturday night*. Toronto. v. 54, no. 7 (Dec. 17, 1938), p. 4.)
Refers to the conflict between W. L. M. King and Mitchell Hepburn.

—— National affairs. Cabinet shuffle is in the air. (In *Saturday night*. Toronto. v. 54, no. 22 (Apr. 1, 1939), p. 4.)
Refers to the cabinet of W. L. M. King.

BANKS, RIDEAU   Mitch ready to march. (In *Saturday night*. Toronto. v. 52, no. 32 (June 12, 1937), p. 5.)
Concerns Mitchell F. Hepburn and his criticism of Mackenzie King.

—— National affairs. Mr. King is ready. (In *Saturday night*. Toronto. v. 52, no. 15 (Feb. 13, 1937), p. 4.)
Comments on the "enlarged defence appropriations".

—— National affairs. Rivers in dry land. (In *Saturday night*. Toronto. v. 52, no. 16 (Feb. 20, 1937), p. 4.)
Concerns Pierre Joseph Arthur Cardin and James Garfield Gardiner.

—— The Ottawa letter. Why they fight. (In *Saturday night*. Toronto. v. 53, no. 8 (Dec. 25, 1937), p. 5.)
Concerns the feud between M. Hepburn and W. L. M. King over export of hydro electric power to us.

—— Ottawa letter. Mr. Howe's way. (In *Saturday night*. Toronto. v. 53, no. 22 (Apr. 2, 1938), p. 4.)
Comments on the activities of Clarence Decatur Howe.

—— Ottawa letter. King's new strategy. (In *Saturday night*. Toronto. v. 53, no. 30 (May 28, 1938), p. 5.)
Concerns Mackenzie King's plan to unite Great Britain, the u.s. and Canada in a three-way trade treaty.

—— Ottawa letter. An appeasing budget. (In *Saturday night*. Toronto. v. 53, no. 34 (June 25, 1938), p. 4.)
Concerns the 1938 federal budget presented by C. A. Dunning.

—— Rah for independence! (In *Saturday night*. Toronto. v. 52, no. 20 (Mar. 20, 1937), p. 4.)
Concerns William Henry Moore and his vote "against the government on the major occasion of the Conservative want-of-confidence amendment to the budget . . ."

BEDER, EDWARD ARTHUR   Tariffs are trifles. By E. A. Beder. (In *The Canadian forum*. Toronto. v. 27, no. 324 (Jan. 1948), pp. 224-225.)
Examines the political implications of the announcement on the tariff made November 17, 1947, by Prime Minister King and Finance Minister Abbott.

BENSON, NATHANIEL ANKETELL MICHAEL   None of it came easy; the story of James Garfield Gardiner. With a foreword by Burton T. Richardson. Toronto, Burns & MacEachern, 1955. 272 p.

BOUCHARD. TELESPHORE DAMIEN   Mémoires. Montréal, Editions Beauchemin, 1960. 3 v.
Contents: t. 1. Ma vie privée. Préf. de Arthur Maheux. – t. 2. Gravissant la colline. Préf. de Albert Milot. – t. 3. "Quarante ans dans la tourmente politico-religieuse". Préf. de Claude-Henri Grignon.
T. D. Bouchard was called to the Senate March 3, 1944; he died November 13, 1962.

The Case for Mr. Hepburn. By a Hepburn Liberal. (In *Saturday night*. Toronto. v. 52, no. 43 (Aug. 28, 1937), p. 5.)

CAYGEON, ROBERT   Even Libs. have worries. (In *Saturday night*. Toronto. v. 51, no. 4 (Nov. 30, 1935), p. 4.)
Comments on Mitchell Hepburn; the forthcoming Dominion-provincial Conference, etc.

—— National affairs. Pragmatic Grits. (In *Saturday night*. Toronto. v. 50, no. 51 (Oct. 26, 1935), p. 4.)
Concerns the formation of a cabinet by Mackenzie King.

CHARLESWORTH, HECTOR WILLOUGHBY   Ralston is back. By Hector Charlesworth. (In *Saturday night*. Toronto. v. 54, no. 46 (Sept. 16, 1939), p. 5.)

CHAUVIN, FRANCIS X.   The member for Essex East. (In *Saturday night*. Toronto. v. 51, no. 9 (Jan. 4, 1936), p. 8.)
A biographical sketch of Paul Martin.

CLARK, GREGORY   With the Prime Minister in Great Britain. (In Empire Club of Canada. *Addresses*. Toronto. (1941/42), pp. 39-53.)
Address delivered September 23, 1941. Refers to W. L. Mackenzie King.

CLAXTON, BROOKE   What's wrong with Parliament? By Brooke Claxton, MP. (In *Maclean's*. Toronto. v. 56, no. 5 (Mar. 1, 1943), pp. 13; 39-40.)

The Close of an era; twenty-five years of Mr. Mackenzie King. (In *The Canadian forum*. Toronto. v. 24, no. 284 (Sept. 1944), pp. 125-126.)
An editorial.

COHEN, MAXWELL ABRAHAM   The problem of manpower. By Maxwell Cohen. (In *Saturday night*. Toronto. v. 58, no. 7 (Oct. 24, 1942), pp. 6-7.)
"Not until the Government has decided on its military policy . . . can anything much be done about the allocation of the nation's manpower."

CONNICK, MARK   Futility fair. (In *Canadian magazine*. Toronto. v. 91, no. 2 (Feb. 1939), pp. 16-17; 63.)

A critical discussion of the general policies of the re-elected Liberal government as outlined in the Speech from the Throne.

CONNOLLEY, JOHN S.   An open letter to Mr. King. An editorial. (In *The Canadian spokesman*. Ottawa. v. 1, no. 3 (Apr. 1941), pp. [1]-4.)

Criticizes the war leadership of W. L. Mackenzie King.

COURTEAU, GUY   Le docteur Joseph-Raoul Hurtubise, MD, sénateur. (In *Canadian Catholic Historical Association. Rapport*. Ottawa (1960), pp. 53-70.)

First elected to the House of Commons in 1930; appointed to the Senate in 1945.

COX, COROLYN   Name in the news. First parliamentary assistant. (In *Saturday night*. Toronto. v. 58, no. 39 (June 5, 1943), p. 2.)

Concerns Brooke Claxton.

—— Name in the news. Chevrier is oh so bilingual. (In Saturday night. Toronto. v. 58, no. 44 (July 10, 1943), p. 2.)

Concerns Lionel Chevrier.

—— Name in the news. Well up the political ladder. (In *Saturday night*. Toronto. v. 58, no. 47 (July 31, 1943), p. 2.)

Concerns Paul Joseph James Martin.

—— Name in the news. Why the war costs so much. (In *Saturday night*. Toronto. v. 59, no. 4 (Oct. 2, 1943), p. 2.)

Concerns Hughes Cleaver, MP, chairman of the War Expenditures Committee of the House of Commons.

—— Name in the news. Right-hand man to Mr. Ilsley. (In *Saturday night*. Toronto. v. 59, no. 8 (Oct. 30, 1943), p. 2.)

A biographical sketch of Douglas Charles Abbott, parliamentary assistant to Hon. J. L. Ilsley, Minister of Finance.

—— Name in the news. James Sinclair, Rhodes scholar, is "one of Weir's young men". (In *Saturday night*. Toronto. v. 59, no. 28 (Mar. 18, 1944), p. 2.)

—— Name in the news. Alan Chambers was chokerman; is now soldier and reformer. (In *Saturday night*. Toronto. v. 59, no. 29 (Mar. 25, 1944), p. 2.)

Biographical sketch of Alan Chambers, MP.

—— Name in the news. Rubber-down for the Liberal Party is doing a nice job. (In *Saturday night*. Toronto. v. 59, no. 35 (May 6, 1944), p. 2.)

A biographical sketch of Andrew Wilfrid Hamilton, National Secretary of the National Liberal Federation.

—— Name in the news. "Mike" Pearson, product of the Old Manse, is big man in UNRRA. (In *Saturday night*. Toronto. v. 59, no. 37 (May 20, 1944), p. 2.)

—— Name in the news. Stuart Garson is a non-partisan premier and a Liberal leader. (In *Saturday night*. Toronto. v. 59, no. 41 (June 17, 1944), p. 2.)

Concerns Stuart Sinclair Garson, Premier of Manitoba.

—— Name in the news. Outspoken French senator takes all Canada for his homeland. (In *Saturday night*. Toronto. v. 59, no. 49 (Aug. 12, 1944), p. 2.)

A biographical sketch of Senator Télesphore Damien Bouchard.

—— What it means to be a Liberal. (In *National home monthly*. Winnipeg. v. 45, no. 10 (Oct. 1944), pp. 7; 20; 22; 24; 26.)

An article based on an interview with W. L. Mackenzie King.

CUMMING, JOHN   Dr. King's panacea. By John Cumming and Edith Fowke. (In *The Canadian forum*. Toronto. v. 28, no. 329 (June 1948), pp. 54-55.)

Discusses the national health plan of the Liberal government.

DAWSON, WALTER   Alberta's new hope at Ottawa. (In *Saturday night*. Toronto. v. 55, no. 29 (May 18, 1940), p. 8.)

Concerns James Angus MacKinnon.

—— The new lady member. (In *Saturday night*. Toronto. v. 56, no. 48 (Aug. 9, 1941), p. 13.)

A biographical sketch of Mrs. Cora Taylor (Watt) Casselman, MP for Edmonton East.

DEACHMAN, ROBERT JOHN   Prize Liberal platform. By R. J. Deachman, MP. (In *Saturday night*. Toronto. v. 54, no. 43 (Aug. 26, 1939), p. 3.)

Text of a program submitted to the Platform Competition held by *Saturday night*. The other winning entries are by H. M. Bruce (Conservative) and J. C. Harris (CCF) [see *Saturday night*. Toronto. v. 54, no. 43, p. 2 and v. 54, no. 44, p. 3.]

—— What the budget means. By R. J. Deachman. (In *Maclean's*. Toronto. v. 53, no. 16 (Aug. 15, 1940), pp. 10; 33-35.)

Discusses the financial policy of the Liberal government.

Defenseman. By K. B. (In *Maclean's*. Toronto. v. 54, no. 23 (Dec. 1, 1941), pp. 14; 76.)

Concerns J. L. Ralston, Minister of Defense.

DELL, MARTIN   A cabinet minister on postwar "reconstruction". (In *The Canadian forum*. Toronto. v. 22, no. 262 (Nov. 1942), pp. 232-235.)

Questions statements made by Ian Mackenzie, Minister of Pensions and National Health, at the opening session of the Special Committee on Reconstruction and Reëstablishment.

DEXTER, GRANT   Cabinet portraits. Thumbnail sketches of the men who will hold the reins of power at Ottawa for the next five years. Part I. By A. Grant Dexter. (In *Maclean's*. Toronto. v. 48, no. 23 (Dec. 1, 1935), pp. 14; 34.)

Concerns cabinet ministers in the Mackenzie King government.

—— Cabinet portraits. Herewith, the "new men" of the King government . . . Conclusion. By A. Grant Dexter. (In *Maclean's*. Toronto. v. 48, no. 24 (Dec. 15, 1935), pp. 14; 28; 30.)

—— "First lord." (In *Maclean's*. Toronto. v. 52 [i.e. 55] no. 6 (Mar. 15, 1942), pp. 13; 40-41.)

Concerns Angus Macdonald, Minister of Defence for Naval Services.

—— Ilsley the man. (In *Maclean's*. Toronto. v. 55, no. 20 (Oct. 15, 1942), pp. 9; 49-50.)

Concerns James L. Ilsley, Minister of Finance.

—— Joe Thorson. A quick sketch of the new Minister of National War Services, whose job—by any other name—is propaganda. (In *Maclean's*. Toronto. v. 54, no. 16 (Aug. 15, 1941), pp. 17; 27-28.)

Concerns J. T. Thorson.

—— Minister of Supply. (In *Maclean's*. Toronto. v. 55, no. 10 (May 15, 1942), pp. 9; 57-58; 60.)

Concerns C. D. Howe, Minister of Munitions and Supply.

—— Mr. King. (In *Maclean's*. Toronto. v. 48, no. 22 (Nov. 15, 1935), pp. 19; 39-40.)

Concerns William Lyon Mackenzie King.

DRENNON, HERBERT NEAL   The industrial relations policy of the Canadian Dominion Government, 1939-1948. [Durham, N.C., 1951] 298 leaves.

Thesis (PH D) – Duke University.

EDWARDS, FREDERICK   Norman McLarty. A word portrait of Canada's new Postmaster General. (In *Maclean's*. Toronto. v. 52, no. 7 (Apr. 1, 1939), pp. 8; 32; 34.)

—— Youth in training. (In *Maclean's*. Toronto. v. 51, no. 1 (Jan. 1, 1938), pp. 14-15; 31-32.)

Concerns the Dominion government youth training plan.

EGGLESTON, WILFRID   The Ottawa letter. Apparently Mr. King misjudged the resentment of the people. (In *Saturday night*. Toronto. v. 60, no. 24 (Feb. 17, 1945), p. 8.)

Discusses the by-election in Grey North, Ont., held February 5, 1945, and won by W. G. Case for the Progressive Conservative Party.

—— The Ottawa letter. In facing this postwar we have some factors to our advantage. (In *Saturday night*. Toronto. v. 60, no. 28 (Mar. 17, 1945), p. 8.)

With reference to a press conference given by C. D. Howe presenting an outline of a proposed post-war reconstruction program.

—— The Ottawa letter. Many contenders will be in field when Liberals seek new leader. (In *Saturday night*. Toronto. v. 60, no. 44 (July 7, 1945), p. 9.)

Discusses a replacement for Mackenzie King. Candidates include Robert Manion, Mitchell Hepburn, James Gardiner, and others.

—— The Ottawa letter. Mr. Howe encouraging formation labor-management committees. (In *Saturday night*. Toronto. v. 60, no. 46 (July 21, 1945), p. 8.)

Concerns Clarence D. Howe, Minister of Reconstruction.

—— The Ottawa letter. Dominion will do its postwar job with or without cooperation. (In *Saturday night*. Toronto. v. 60, no. 48 (Aug. 4, 1945), p. 8.)

Refers to a comment made by Louis St. Laurent affirming that the Dominion government would undertake a program of postwar reconstruction.

—— The Ottawa letter. The cabinet, it would seem, lags behind the "Bright young men". (In *Saturday night*. Toronto. v. 60, no. 52 (Sept. 1, 1945), p. 9.)

Concerns a program for post-war reconstruction.

—— The Ottawa letter. Hapless cabinet members have to meet much captious criticism. (In *Saturday night*. Toronto. v. 61, no. 3 (Sept. 22, 1945), p. 9.)

Comments on the difficult adjustment period as the Government undergoes changes from a war-time to a peace-time economy.

—— The Ottawa letter. Revolutionary nature of wheat policy overlooked in comment. (In *Saturday night*. Toronto. v. 61, no. 4 (Sept. 29, 1945), p. 8.)

—— The Ottawa letter. Budget aims to avoid inflation and to speed reconversion. (In *Saturday night*. Toronto. v. 61, no. 7 (Oct. 20, 1945), p. 8.)

—— The Ottawa letter. King government probably lost ground during past session. (In *Saturday night*. Toronto. v. 61, no. 17 (Dec. 29, 1945), p. 8.)

Refers to the first session of the twentieth parliament.

—— Ottawa letter. Government's program reflects uncertain state of world. (In *Saturday night*. Toronto. v. 61, no. 29 (Mar. 23, 1946), p. 8.)

Comments on the domestic program of the Liberal government.

—— Ottawa letter. King reproves labor's attitude as likely to foment strife. (In *Saturday night*. Toronto. v. 61, no. 32 (Apr. 13, 1946), p. 8.)

Concerns a rebuke administered to the Canadian Congress of Labor.

—— Ottawa letter. Question of King's successor is prompting survey of eligibles. (In *Saturday night*. Toronto. v. 61, no. 43 (June 29, 1946), p. 8.)

Contenders include James Gardiner, J. L. Ilsley and Louis St. Laurent.

—— Ottawa letter. Wide range of political tenets is a Liberal Party weakness. (In *Saturday night*. Toronto. v. 62, no. 2 (Sept. 14, 1946), p. 8.)

—— Ottawa letter. Milk price issue shows variance of opinion on state control. (In *Saturday night*. Toronto. v. 62, no. 5 (Oct. 5, 1946), p. 8.)

Concerns the Government's decision to terminate wartime subsidies.

—— Ottawa letter. Liberals still have fair margin; uncertainty in next election. (In *Saturday night*. Toronto. v. 62, no. 9 (Nov. 2, 1946), p. 8.)

—— Ottawa letter. Cabinet shuffle retains the old guard and bolsters defences. (In *Saturday night*. Toronto. v. 62, no. 16 (Dec. 21, 1946), p. 8.)

Concerns a cabinet shuffle in the Mackenzie King government.

—— Ottawa letter. Mr. Abbott's new tax formulas near Rowell-Sirois objective. (In *Saturday night*. Toronto. v. 62, no. 22 (Feb. 1, 1947), p. 8.)

—— Ottawa letter. Recent events inspire a Liberal Party reappraisal of policy. (In *Saturday night*. Toronto. v. 62, no. 24 (Feb. 15, 1947), p. 8.)

—— Ottawa letter. Will new phase of Government's emergency powers be the last? (In *Saturday night*. Toronto. v. 62, no. 30 (Mar. 29, 1947), p. 8.)

—— Ottawa letter. Old constitutional sore spot is touched by Justice Minister. (In *Saturday night*. Toronto. v. 62, no. 31 (Apr. 5, 1947), p. 8.)

Comments on a Privy Council decision dealing with the Canada Temperance Act.

—— Ottawa letter. Upset of two political traditions if Mr. St. Laurent became PM. (In *Saturday night*. Toronto. v. 63, no. 9 (Nov. 1, 1947), p. 8.)

—— Ottawa letter. Party convention should debate Liberal platform for future. (In *Saturday night*. Toronto. v. 63, no. 17 (Jan. 31, 1948), p. 8.)

—— Ottawa letter. Process of reaching conclusions about the Liberal leadership. (In *Saturday night*. Toronto. v. 63, no. 20 (Feb. 21, 1948), p. 8.)

—— Ottawa letter. Heart-searching, not smugness, should be convention keynote. (In *Saturday night*. Toronto. v. 63, no. 25 (Mar. 27, 1948), p. 9.)

Concerns the forthcoming Liberal Party convention.

—— Ottawa letter. Our best house-building year but still not good enough. (In *Saturday night*. Toronto. v. 63, no. 32 (May 15, 1948), p. 8.)

Reviews federal housing policy.

—— Ottawa letter. Reactions to health proposals reflect triumph and chagrin. (In *Saturday night*. Toronto. v. 63, no. 33 (May 22, 1948), p. 8.)

Concerns Mackenzie King's program for enlarged public health services.

—— Ottawa letter. Abbott budget seen as test case of cyclical budgeting theory. (In *Saturday night*. Toronto. v. 63, no. 34 (May 29, 1948), p. 8.)

—— Ottawa letter. Abbott budget passes judgment on some prices inquiry issues. (In *Saturday night*. Toronto. v. 63, no. 35 (June 5, 1948), p. 8.)

—— Ottawa letter. Liberal strategy deeply affected by past and imminent events. (In *Saturday night*. Toronto. v. 63, no. 37 (June 19, 1948), p. 8.)

—— Ottawa letter. Liberals probing for discontent which led to CCF victories. (In *Saturday night*. Toronto. v. 63, no. 38 (June 26, 1948), p. 8.)
Relates to by-elections held in Yale, B.C., Vancouver Centre, B.C., and in Ontario.

—— Ottawa view. Liberal leadership race. (In *Saturday night*. Toronto. v. 63, no. 41 (July 17, 1948), p. 4.)

—— Ottawa view. The Liberals' dilemma. (In *Saturday night*. Toronto. v. 63, no. 42 (July 24, 1948), p. 4.)

—— Ottawa view. Duplessis and deflation. (In *Saturday night*. Toronto. v. 63, no. 44 (Aug. 7, 1948), p. 4.)
Comments on Maurice Duplessis's election victory and its effect on future Dominion-provincial relations.

—— Ottawa view. Appointing a liquidator. (In *Saturday night*. Toronto. v. 63, no. 45 (Aug. 14, 1948), p. 4.)
Concerns the election of Louis St. Laurent as leader of the national Liberal Party.

—— Ottawa view. Mackenzie King's era. (In *Saturday night*. Toronto. v. 64, no. 7 (Nov. 20, 1948), p. 4.)

Fergusons v. Woodsworths. (In *Canadian comment*. Toronto. v. 6, no. 3 (Mar. 1937), pp. 4-5.)
Comments on the defence policy of W. L. Mackenzie King.

FLAHERTY, J. FRANCIS Canada's new Labor Minister gets things done. By Francis Flaherty. (In *Saturday night*. Toronto. v. 57, no. 16 (Dec. 27, 1941), p. 11.)
Concerns Humphrey Mitchell.

—— Federal plan may keep housing prices high. By J. F. Flaherty. (In *Saturday night*. Toronto. v. 63, no. 39 (July 3, 1948), p. 23.)
"Mr. Flaherty . . . reviews the important points of Mr. Howe's amendment to the National Housing Act . . ."

—— The Ottawa letter. Mr. King got his usual surprises and perhaps a minor setback. By Francis Flaherty. (In *Saturday night*. Toronto. v. 60, no. 33 (Apr. 21, 1945), p. 8.)
The federal election held June 11, 1945.

—— The Ottawa letter. Will King get away with reform of method of cabinet selection? By Francis Flaherty. (In *Saturday night*. Toronto. v. 60, no. 34 (Apr. 28, 1945), p. 8.)

FORSEY, EUGENE ALFRED The budget. By Eugene Forsey. (In *The Canadian forum*. Toronto. v. 19, no. 221 (June 1939), pp. 76-77.)
Discusses the budget of Charles Dunning.

—— The budget. By Eugene Forsey. (In *The Canadian forum*. Toronto. v. 20, no. 235 (Aug. 1940), pp. 136-137.)
Discusses Colonel J. L. Ralston's budget.

—— Mr. King and the Government's labor policy. By Eugene Forsey. (In *The Canadian forum*. Toronto. v. 21 no. 250 (Nov. 1941), pp. 231-232.)

—— Mr. King, Parliament, the constitution and labor policy. By Eugene Forsey. (In *The Canadian forum*. Toronto. v. 21, no. 252 (Jan. 1942), pp. 296-298.)

—— Mr. Lapointe and the Padlock. By Eugene Forsey. (In *The Canadian forum*. Toronto. v. 18, no. 211 (Aug. 1938), pp. 148-150.)
The Padlock (an Act Respecting Communist Propaganda) passed into law in 1937 giving the Attorney General of the province of Quebec power to padlock the premises of any organization considered to be subversive.

—— Parliament is endangered by Mr. King's principle. By Eugene Forsey. (In *Saturday night*. Toronto. v. 64, no. 1 (Oct. 9, 1948), pp. 10-11.)
"When Prime Minister King announced the appointment of L. B. Pearson to the cabinet, he said that the civil service should be regarded as 'the stepping-stone to the Ministry'. This would result in a major change of job for the civil servant, traditionally an impartial expert who advises his minister without political bias."

FOWKE, EDITH MARGARET (Fulton) Democracy and the Japanese Canadian. By Edith Fowke and A. G. Watson. (In *The Canadian forum*. Toronto. v. 25, no. 294 (July 1945), pp. 87-89.)

An analysis of the policy of the Liberal government towards Japanese v. Canadians during the Second World War.

—— Japanese Canadians. By Edith Fowke. (In The Canadian forum. Toronto. v. 25, no. 300 (Jan. 1946), pp. 231-232.)

An analysis of "the Government's present position on the Japanese Canadian question [as] set forth by Hon. Humphrey Mitchell, Minister of Labor, on November 21, 1945."

FRASER, BLAIR Backstage at Ottawa. By the Man with a Notebook. (In Maclean's. Toronto. v. 57, no. 23 (Dec. 1, 1944), pp. 14-15; 47.)

Discusses the reasons behind Col. J. L. Ralston's resignation from the federal cabinet.

—— Backstage at Ottawa. By the Man with a Notebook. (In Maclean's. Toronto. v. 57, no. 24 (Dec. 15, 1944), pp. 12-13; 53.)

Discusses Mackenzie King's adoption of conscription.

—— Backstage at Ottawa. By the Man with a Notebook. (In Maclean's. Toronto. v. 58, no. 1 (Jan. 1, 1945), pp. 14-15; 49.)

Concerns Mackenzie King's adoption of conscription.

—— Backstage at Ottawa. Tax relief in sight? By the Man with a Notebook. (In Maclean's. Toronto. v. 58, no. 13 (July 1, 1945), pp. 15; 47.)

Discusses the fiscal policy of the Liberal government.

—— Backstage at Ottawa. Pearkes vs. Gardiner, headline bout. By the Man with a Notebook. (In Maclean's. Toronto. v. 58, no. 17 (Sept. 1, 1945), pp. 15; 46-47.)

Concerns Major-Gen. Pearkes and James Gardiner, Minister of Agriculture.

—— Backstage at Ottawa. Mr. King rebuilding cabinet. By the Man with a Notebook. (In Maclean's. Toronto. v. 58, no. 19 (Oct. 1, 1945), pp. 15; 65.)

—— Backstage at Ottawa. Pro or anti-tariff? Cabinet put on spot? By the Man with a Notebook. (In Maclean's. Toronto. v. 58, no. 23 (Dec. 1, 1945), pp. 15; 58-59.)

—— Backstage at Ottawa. General Ilsley beats a slow retreat. (In Maclean's. Toronto. v. 59, no. 9 (May 1, 1946), pp. 15; 77-78.)

Concerns Finance Minister Ilsley's policy

of "orderly retreat" from wartime price-ceiling levels.

——Backstage at Ottawa. Mr. Howe flies the great circle. By the Man with a Notebook. (In Maclean's. Toronto. v. 59, no. 19 (Oct. 1, 1946), p. 15.)

—— Backstage at Ottawa. Handwriting on a Quebec wall. By the Man with a Notebook. (In Maclean's. Toronto. v. 60, no. 1 (Jan. 1, 1947), pp. 15; 43-44.)

Discusses implications for the Liberal government of the Richelieu-Verchères, Que., by-election held December 23, 1946.

—— Backstage at Ottawa. Chubby recovers from social leprosy. By the Man with a Notebook. (In Maclean's. Toronto. v. 60, no. 6 (Mar. 15, 1947), pp. 15; 72.)

Concerns Hon. C. G. Power.

—— Backstage at Ottawa. The government bets its shirt. By the Man with a Notebook. (In Maclean's. Toronto. v. 60, no. 7 (Apr. 1, 1947), pp. 15; 74-75.)

Discusses the government's amendments to the Wheat Board Act.

—— Backstage at Ottawa. Mr. Abbott's budget hints at a Liberal right shift . . . By the Man with a Notebook. (In Maclean's. Toronto. v. 60, no. 11 (June 1, 1947), pp. 15; 78.)

—— Backstage at Ottawa. Up, St. Laurent. By the Man with a Notebook. (In Maclean's. Toronto. v. 60, no. 20 (Oct. 15, 1947), pp. 15; 86.)

Concerns Louis St. Laurent.

—— Backstage at Ottawa. Crisis coming up. By the Man with a Notebook. (In Maclean's. Toronto. v. 60, no. 22 (Nov. 15, 1947), pp. 15; 73.)

Discusses the probability of Mackenzie King's retirement.

—— Backstage at Ottawa. Fiasco in dog sleds. By the Man with a Notebook. (In Maclean's. Toronto. v. 61, no. 2 (Jan. 15, 1948), pp. 15; 51.)

Concerns Edmond Turcotte's appointment as Consul General in Canada.

—— Backstage at Ottawa. Saved by a blunder. By the Man with a Notebook. (In Maclean's. Toronto. v. 61, no. 3 (Feb. 1, 1948), p. 15.)

Discusses Mackenzie King's "dollar-saving" program.

—— Backstage at Ottawa. By the Man with a Notebook. (In Maclean's. Toronto. v. 61, no. 5 (Mar. 1, 1948), p. 15.)

Comments on the speculated retirement of Mackenzie King.

—— Burning issue. Are Canadians going to get enough coal this winter? . . . Here's the lowdown on a crisis which affects all of us. (In *Maclean's*. Toronto. v. 56, no. 21 (Nov. 1, 1943), pp. 7; 34; 48-51.)
Concerns the fuel policy of the federal government.

—— Howe at the controls. (In *Maclean's*. Toronto. v. 61, no. 3 (Feb. 1, 1948), pp. 11; 43-44.)
Concerns Clarence Decatur Howe, Minister of Reconstruction.

—— Mackenzie King, as I knew him. (In *Maclean's*. Toronto. v. 63, no. 17 (Sept. 1, 1950), pp. 7-8; 52-54.)

—— Mr. King. (In *Maclean's*. Toronto. v. 58, no. 3 (Feb. 1, 1945), pp. 10; 45; 47-48.)
Refers to William Lyon Mackenzie King.

—— The Prime Minister. Prime Minister longer than any other Canadian—that will be Mr. King's record on June 8. Here's the story of how he handles his job. (In *Maclean's*. Toronto. v. 59, no. 11 (June 1, 1946), pp. 7-8; 79-81.)

—— This is Raymond. (In *Maclean's*. Toronto. v. 57, no. 1 (Jan. 1, 1944), pp. 9; 30-31.)
Concerns Maxime Raymond, leader of the Bloc Populaire; an MP representing Beauharnois–La Prairie, Que.

—— Where does St. Laurent stand? Here's a close-up of the next PM's views on controls, taxes, trade unions, defense, subsidies and other national issues. (In *Maclean's*. Toronto. v. 61, no. 18 (Sept. 15, 1948), pp. 7-8; 73-77.)

GARDINER, JAMES GARFIELD What will we eat this year? Says Canada's Minister of Agriculture—no Canadian consumer should be worried about having a well-supplied table in 1943. By Hon. James G. Gardiner. (In *Maclean's*. Toronto. v. 56, no. 9 (May 1, 1943), pp. 17; 42-43.)

GAUDRAULT, P. M. Ernest Lapointe. (In *La Revue dominicaine*. St. Hyacinthe, Qué. v. 48 (jan. 1942), pp. 1-9.)

GOLDEN, LOU L. L. Gardiner, Western colossus. By L. L. L. Golden. (In *Saturday night*. Toronto. v. 55, no. 42 (Aug. 17, 1940), pp. 19-20.)
A biographical sketch of James Garfield Gardiner.

—— The minister who has fun. By L. L. L. Golden. (In *Saturday night*. Toronto. v. 55, no. 30 (May 25, 1940), p. 5.)
Concerns Charles Gavan (Chubby) Power.

—— National affairs. The Naval Minister. By L. L. L. Golden. (In *Saturday night*. Toronto. v. 55, no. 40 (Aug. 3, 1940), p. 5.)
Concerns Angus Lewis Macdonald.

GRAHAM, JOHN Our national cheerleader. (In *Saturday night*. Toronto. v. 57, no. 3 (Sept. 27, 1941), p. 12.)
Concerns Joseph Thararinn Thorson, Minister of National War Services.

GRUBE, GEORGE MAXIMILIAN ANTONY The steel crisis. By G. M. A. Grube. (In *The Canadian forum*. Toronto. v. 22, no. 261 (Oct. 1942), pp. 205-207; 210.)
Analyses government policy towards labour.

—— Wanted: a minister of labor. By G. M. A. Grube. (In *The Canadian forum*. Toronto. v. 22, no. 258 (July 1942), pp. 110-113.)
Discusses relations between organized labour and the Liberal government. Critical of the actions of Humphrey Mitchell.

GULLEY, E. VINCENT It's up to Ottawa. (In *The Canadian magazine*. Toronto. v. 89, no. 1 (Jan. 1938), pp. 14-15.)
The author asserts that the Canadian public want statements of policy and action from the Mackenzie King administration.

HAWKINS, GERALD Once party outcast, is now cabinet member. (In *Saturday night*. Toronto. v. 61, no. 27 (Mar. 9, 1946), pp. [12-13].)
Concerns Hedley Francis Gregory Bridges, Minister of Fisheries.

HAWKINS, JOHN The life and times of Angus L. Windsor, N.S., Lancelot Press [1969]. 268 p.
Concerns Angus L. Macdonald, Minister of National Defence for Naval Services, 1940-45.

HEENEY, ARNOLD DANFORD PATRICK Mackenzie King and the cabinet secretariat. By A. D. P. Heeney (In *Canadian public administration*. Toronto. v. 10 (1967), pp. 366-375.)
A Secretary to the Cabinet was first appointed in March 1940.

HOWE, CLARENCE DECATUR Canada at war. By the Honourable C. D. Howe. (In Empire Club of Canada. *Addresses*. Toronto. (1940/41), pp. 50-69.)

Address delivered September 4, 1940.

—— Canada's coal problems. By Right Honourable C. D. Howe. (In Empire Club of Canada. *Addresses*. Toronto. (1946/47), pp. 200-227.)

Address delivered February 13, 1947.

Discusses, essentially, the Report of the Royal Commission on Coal. Ottawa, 1947. (1 v.)

—— Government and transport. By C. D. Howe, Minister of Transport. (In *The Maritime advocate and busy East*. Sackville, N.B. v. 27, no. 4 (Nov. 1936), pp. 25-27.)

Text of address delivered to the Canadian Club, Montreal, November 2, 1936.

—— Government and transportation. By the Hon. C. D. Howe, Minister of Transport. (In Canadian Club of Toronto. *Addresses*. Toronto. (1936/37), pp. 305-314.)

Address delivered April 19, 1937.

"I propose to discuss today the work of my own Department." – The Author.

HUTCHISON, BRUCE Crerar's career deserves understanding. (In *Canada month*. Montreal. v. 7, no. 8 (Aug. 1967), p. 18.)

Reprint of a tribute written on the occasion of T. A. Crerar's retirement from public life in 1966.

—— Mackenzie King and the "revolt" of the army. (In *Maclean's*. Toronto. v. 65, no. 20 (Oct. 15, 1952), pp. 7-9; 57-70.)

—— Mackenzie King and the "revolt" of the army. A postscript. (In *Maclean's*. Toronto. v. 66, no. 10 (May 15, 1953), pp. 20; 57-58.)

—— Words are weapons. Says this writer: "In a war of ideas that is being waged against us, to confuse and divide us, we must use ideas as weapons for our own salvation." (In *Maclean's*. Toronto. v. 55, no. 22 (Nov. 15, 1942), pp. 18; 24-25.)

Refers to Prime Minister King's appointment of Charles Vining and his assignment to create a wartime ideolgy for Canada.

ILSLEY, JAMES LORIMER War loan quiz. Honorable James L. Ilsley, Canada's Minister of Finance, answers a 21-question quiz on war finance. Why such high income taxes? Why compulsory savings? Why not borrow from the banks? Can we pay our war debt? Here are the answers from the man who has to pay the

bills. (In *Maclean's*. Toronto. v. 55, no. 20 (Oct. 15, 1942), pp. 7-9; 51-54.)

JONES, C. TREVOR King may even get an over-all majority. (In *Saturday night*. Toronto. v. 60, no. 40 (June 9, 1945), pp. 10-11.)

Refers to the general elections held June 11, 1945.

KEYES, T. E. Hero of the hustings. (In *Saturday night*. Toronto. v. 53, no. 36 (July 9, 1938), p. 6.)

Deals with the role James G. Gardiner played in the Saskatchewan provincial election.

KING, WILLIAM LYON MACKENZIE Canada and the fight for freedom. By the Right Honourable W. L. Mackenzie King. [Introd. by Eric Estorick and B. K. Sandwell] Toronto, Macmillan, 1944. xxiv, 326 p.

Consists of a selection of speeches delivered from September 1941 to June 1944.

Partial contents: National selective service. – Overseas service; historical considerations. – Overseas service in relation to a total war effort. – Politics and the war.

—— Canada in a world at war. By Right Honorable W. L. Mackenzie King. (In *The Maritime advocate and busy East*. Sackville, N.B. v. 35, no. 12/13 (July/Aug. 1944), pp. 12-15; 29-30.)

"An address delivered to the members of both Houses of Parliament, Westminster, on May 11, 1944."

—— The Mackenzie King record. Edited by J. W. Pickersgill and D. F. Forster. [Toronto] University of Toronto Press [1960-70] 4 v.

Contents: v. 1. 1939-1944. – v. 2. 1944-1945. – v. 3. 1945-1946. – v. 4. 1947-1948.

—— An outstanding radio address. By the Rt. Hon. W. L. Mackenzie King. (In *The Maritime advocate and busy East*. Sackville, N.B. v. 32, no. 3 (Oct. 1941), pp. 10-12; 30-31.)

Text of address delivered September 4, 1941, at the Mansion House, London, Eng.

—— Politics and the war. (In his *Canada and the fight for freedom*. Toronto, 1944. pp. 275-298.)

Speech delivered at the Château Laurier in Ottawa, September 27, 1943.

—— What do the Liberals stand for? By Rt. Hon. W. L. Mackenzie King as quizzed by Blair Fraser. (In *Maclean's*. Toronto. v. 58, no. 3 (Feb. 1, 1945), pp. 10-11; 38-40.)

KNOWLES, R. E. Personal glimpses. Samuel Factor, MP. By R. E. Knowles, Jr. (In *Saturday night*. Toronto. v. 51, no. 4 (Nov. 30, 1935), p. 12.)

"First Jewish MP from Ontario and the third in the Dominion." Elected in the riding of Toronto West Centre in 1930.

LAPOINTE, ERNEST League for democracy. By the Hon. Ernest Lapointe. (In *Saturday night*. Toronto. v. 52, no. 28 (May 15, 1937), p. [8].)

Portion of a speech in which E. Lapointe proposed the formation "of a League for educational work looking to the preservation of the democratic state in Canada".

Lapointe; Sir Wilfrid Laurier's great successor. (In *New world illustrated*. Montreal. v. 2, no. 7 (Sept. 1941), pp. 20-21; 56.)

Brief biographical sketch of Ernest Lapointe.

LAWRENCE, MARGARET Norman Rogers. (In *Saturday night*. Toronto. v. 55, no. 33 (June 15, 1940), p. 6.)

Written on the occasion of his death June 10, 1940.

LE COCQ, THELMA His first century. (In *Maclean's*. Toronto. v. 56, no. 5 (Mar. 1, 1943), pp. 9; 37-38.)

Concerns Sir William Mulock.

—— Mitch Hepburn. (In *Maclean's*. Toronto. v. 56, no. 6 (Mar. 15, 1943), pp. 9; 44; 46-48.)

LEMIEUX, EDMOND De M. Fournier à M. King. (In *L'Action nationale*. Montréal. v. 19 (jan. 1942), pp. [14]-29.)

Concerns the conscription issue.

LEWIS, DAVID Big business in the saddle. (In *The Canadian forum*. Toronto. v. 20, no. 235 (Aug. 1940), pp. 142-143.)

Comments on wartime policies of the Liberal government.

LIBERAL PARTY (CANADA) NATIONAL CONVENTION, 3D, OTTAWA, 1948 Report of the proceedings of the National Liberal convention. Called by the National Liberal Federation of Canada at the request of Rt. Hon. W. L. Mackenzie King. Thursday, Friday, Saturday August 5th, 6th, 7th 1948, the Coliseum, Ottawa, Canada. [Ottawa, 1948?] 259 p.

"First edition."

The Liberal Party and labor. (In *The Maritime advocate and busy East*. Sackville, N.B. v. 25, no. 11 (May 1935), p. 15.)

Itemizes the labour legislation passed by the Liberal Party under Laurier and the Conservative Party under R. B. Bennett.

Reprinted from the Canadian Liberal monthly.

LOWER, ARTHUR REGINALD MARSDEN Mackenzie King through his diaries. (In *Queen's quarterly*. Kingston. v. 68 (1961), pp. [169]-173.)

A review article of *The Mackenzie King record*, edited by J. W. Pickersgill. Toronto, University of Toronto Press, 1960-70. Vol. 1, 1939-1944 (1960).

MC COLL, DENNIS Hepburn. (In *New frontier*. Toronto. v. 2, no. 5 (Oct. 1937), pp. 6-7.)

An appraisal of Mitchell Hepburn.

MACDONALD, ANGUS LEWIS Speeches. With a biographical note by T. A. Crerar and a foreword by the Hon. J. L. Ilsley. [1st ed.] Toronto, Longmans, Green [1960] xxvii, 227 p.

MACDONALD, EDWARD MORTIMER Recollections; political and personal. By E. M. Macdonald. 3d ed. Toronto, Ryerson Press [1938] xi, 584 p.

First published in 1938.

MC DOWELL, KATHLEEN Ladies of the cabinet. (In *Saturday night*. Toronto. v. 51, no. 30 (May 30, 1936), p. 11.)

Concerns Mrs. C. G. Howe (née Alice Martha Worcester) and Mrs. J. L. Ilsley (née Evelyn Wilhelmina Smith).

—— Madame Therese Casgrain. (In *Saturday night*. Toronto. v. 51, no. 37 (July 18, 1936), p. 16.)

Née Marie Thérèse Forget.

MC KAGUE, WILLIAM ALLISON This is a budget to get at the middle classes. By W. A. McKague. (In *Saturday night*. Toronto. v. 55, no. 35 (June 29, 1940), p. 2.)

Comments on the budget brought down by Finance Minister J. L. Ralston.

MC KENTY, NEIL Mitch Hepburn. Toronto. McClelland and Stewart [c1967] 307 p.

MAC KENZIE, NORMAN ARCHIBALD MAC RAE The Liberals return! By N. A. M. MacKenzie. (In *Canadian comment*. Toronto. v. 4, no. 11 (Nov. 1935), pp. [3]-4; 19.)

Analyses the political situation as a result of the general elections held October 14, 1935.

Mackenzie King, step by step. (In *New world illustrated*. Montreal. v. 1, no. 1 (Mar. 1940), pp. 3-6; 49.)

Reviews the career of W. L. M. King.

MC LARTY, NORMAN ALEXANDER   The labour battle-front. By the Honourable Norman A. McLarty. (In *The Canadian spokesman*. Ottawa. v. 1, no. 2 (Feb. 1941), pp. [14]-18.)
Describes the war effort of the Department of Labour.

MAC LEOD, NORMAN A.   National affairs. Help for "Mitch"? (In *Saturday night*. Toronto. v. 52, no. 11 (Jan. 16, 1937), p. 4.)
Concerns Mitchell Hepburn and his dealings with Ottawa, with reference to his contention with Quebec over hydro-electric power interests.

MC NAUGHT, KENNETH WILLIAM KIRKPAT-RICK   Swan song of an old Progressive. By Kenneth McNaught. (In *Saturday night*. Toronto. v. 81, no. 8 (Aug. 1966), pp. 8-9; 11.)
Discusses the career of Thomas Alexander Crerar on the occasion of his retirement from the Senate, May 31, 1966.

MALLORY, JAMES RUSSELL   A note on the King era. By James Mallory. (In *The Canadian forum*. Toronto. v. 30, no. 357 (Oct. 1950), p. 152.)

MARTIN, PAUL JOSEPH JAMES   Canada's manpower policy. By Paul Martin, MP. (In *University of Toronto quarterly*. [Toronto] v. 13 (1943/44), pp. 196-206.)

MICHAUD, JOSEPH ENOIL   Canada at war two years. By Hon. J. E. Michaud, Minister of Fisheries. (In *The Maritime advocate and busy East*. Sackville, N.B. v. 32, no. 3 (Oct. 1941), pp. 13-14; 31-32.)
Reprinted from the *Liberal advocate*, September 1941.

Mr. King as issue. By another voter. (In *Saturday night*. Toronto. v. 54, no. 35 (July 1939), pp. 4-5.)

Mr. King is no Santa Claus. (In *Canadian comment*. Toronto. v. 5, no. 1 (Jan. 1936), pp. 5-6.)
Discusses the Dominion-provincial conference held in Ottawa December 9-13, 1935.

Mr. King picks up the gage. (In *The New age*. Montreal. v. 2, no. 5 (Feb. 1, 1940), pp. 2-3.)
Comments on issues with reference to the general elections held March 26, 1940.

MUNROE, DUFF   Labor legislation 1939. (In *The Canadian forum*. Toronto. v. 19, no. 221 (June 1939), pp. 74-75.)

Discusses the legislation in Ontario proposed by David Croll and the federal legislation introduced by Ernest Lapointe.

National Employment Commission Bill. (In *Canadian comment*. Toronto. v. 5, no. 5 (May 1936), pp. 7-8.)
Presents policy as advocated by Norman McLeod Rogers, Minister of Labour.

National unity. (In *The Canadian forum*. Toronto. v. 24, no. 288 (Jan. 1945), pp. 225-226.)
An editorial.
Compares the methods used by W. L. M. King in meeting the conscription crisis of 1944 to the policies adopted by Macdonald and Laurier in dealing with crises arising between French and English Canadians.

NEATBY, HERBERT BLAIR   The Liberal way; fiscal and monetary policy in the 1930's. By H. Blair Neatby. (In *The Great depression*. [Toronto, c1969] pp. 84-114.)
Examines the impact of William Lyon Mackenzie King as a political leader.

The New parliament and its opportunity. (In *The Maritime advocate and busy East*. Sackville, N.B. v. 26, no. 6 (Jan. 1936), pp. 12; 19.)
Reprinted from the *Montreal Daily Star*, January 8, 1936.
Relates to the Mackenzie King government.

The New Prime Minister. His policies. A return to cabinet government. "Recovery before reform." (In *The Canadian forum*. Toronto. v. 15, no. 181 (Feb. 1936), pp. 3-4.)
Editorial comments on the Liberal government under the leadership of Mackenzie King.

NICOLET, JEAN   Y a-t-il un cas Cardin? (In *L'Action nationale*. Montréal. v. 20 (oct. 1942), pp. [155]-163.)
Concerns the Hon. Pierre Cardin.

Norman McLarty. Unemployment is no longer his problem. (In *New world illustrated*. Montreal. v. 2, no. 8 (Oct. 1941), p. 25.)

O'HEARN, D. P.   In the public eye. Connolly said "no" to Mr. King; he likes to stay in Maritimes. (In *Saturday night*. Toronto. v. 62, no. 16 (Dec. 21, 1946), p. 12.)
Refers to Harold Joseph Connolly.

O'LEARY, MICHAEL GRATTAN   Backstage at Ottawa. By a Politician with a Notebook.

(In *Maclean's*. Toronto. v. 48, no. 23 (Dec. 1, 1935), pp. 19; 34.)
Concerns, primarily, the forming of the Mackenzie King cabinet.

—— Backstage at Ottawa. By a Politician with a Notebook. (In *Maclean's*. Toronto. v. 49, no. 6 (Mar. 15, 1936), pp. 14; 24; 26.)
Concerns, mainly, problems confronting the King government.

—— Backstage at Ottawa. By a Politician with a Notebook. (In *Maclean's*. Toronto. v. 50, no. 14 (July 15, 1937), pp. 9; 44.)
Concerns the strained relations between Mackenzie King and Mitchell Hepburn.

—— Backstage at Ottawa. By a Politician with a Notebook. (In *Maclean's*. Toronto. v. 50, no. 18 (Sept. 15, 1937), pp. 11; 42-43.)
Discusses, mainly, the implications of the breach between Mackenzie King and Mitchell Hepburn, involving, as well, R. B. Bennett, M. Duplessis, and others.

—— Backstage at Ottawa. By a Politician with a Notebook. (In *Maclean's*. Toronto. v. 51, no. 2 (Jan. 15, 1938), pp. 13; 34.)
Concerns the budget and the Hepburn-King feud.

—— Backstage at Ottawa. By a Politician with a Notebook. (In *Maclean's*. Toronto. v. 51, no. 21 (Nov. 1, 1938), pp. 14; 49.)
Concerns Prime Minister King's cabinet reorganization and also comments on R. J. Manion.

—— Backstage at Ottawa. The King-Hepburn clash. By a Politician with a Notebook. (In *Maclean's*. Toronto. v. 52, no. 2 (Jan. 15, 1939), pp. 7; 34.)

—— Backstage at Ottawa. By a Politician with a Notebook. (In *Maclean's*. Toronto. v. 52, no. 15 (Aug. 1, 1939), pp. 8; 36.)
Considers whether Prime Minister W. L. Mackenzie King will call a federal election and discusses the issues.

—— Backstage at Ottawa. By a Politician with a Notebook. (In *Maclean's*. Toronto. v. 52, no. 17 (Sept. 1, 1939), p. 8.)
Concerns the cabinet of Mackenzie King.

—— Backstage at Ottawa. By a Politician with a Notebook. (In *Maclean's*. Toronto. v. 52, no. 20 (Oct. 15, 1939), pp. 10; 62.)
Concerns Mackenzie King's war policy and program.

—— Backstage at Ottawa. By a Politician with a Notebook. (In *Maclean's*. Toronto.

v. 53, no. 3 (Feb. 1, 1940), pp. 12; 35-36.)
Discusses the wartime policies of the King government.

—— Backstage at Ottawa. By a Politician with a Notebook. (In *Maclean's*. Toronto. v. 53, no. 5 (Mar. 1, 1940), pp. 10; 49.)
Concerns Mackenzie King's dissolution of Parliament and the federal election held March 26, 1940.

—— Backstage at Ottawa. By a Politician with a Notebook. (In *Maclean's*. Toronto. v. 53, no. 13 (July 1, 1940), pp. 8; 29.)
Comments on Mackenzie King's government.

—— Backstage at Ottawa. By a Politician with a Notebook. (In *Maclean's*. Toronto. v. 53, no. 16 (Aug. 15, 1940), pp. 14; 43.)
Discusses the Mackenzie King government.

—— Backstage at Ottawa. By a Politician with a Notebook. (In *Maclean's*. Toronto. v. 54, no. 1 (Jan. 1, 1941), pp. 8; 33.)
Comments on Liberal government policy.

—— Backstage at Ottawa. By a Politician with a Notebook. (In *Maclean's*. Toronto. v. 54, no. 5 (Mar. 1, 1941), pp. 8; 44.)
Comments on rumours concerning National Government and discusses a currency issue raised between Mackenzie King and Mitchell Hepburn.

—— The man behind Ilsley. By M. Grattan O'Leary. (In *Maclean's*. Toronto. v. 58, no. 9 (May 1, 1945), pp. 12; 28; 30.)
Concerns William Clifford Clark, Deputy Minister of Finance.

—— Minister for Air. "Chubby" Power—the man Ottawa thought it knew and didn't. (In *Maclean's*. Toronto. v. 54, no. 18 (Sept. 15, 1941), pp. 11; 41.)
Concerns Charles Gavan Power.

—— Mr. St. Laurent. By M. Grattan O'Leary. (In *Maclean's*. Toronto. v. 60, no. 4 (Feb. 15, 1947), pp. 12; 52-54.)

Paean in praise of Mr. Pouliot. By a taxpayer. (In *Saturday night*. Toronto. v. 52, no. 24 (Apr. 17, 1937), p. [22].)
Concerns Jean-François Pouliot, member for Temiscouata, Que.

PAINE, JACK   Unselective service. (In *The Canadian forum*. Toronto. v. 22, no. 265 (Feb. 1943), pp. 319-320.)
Concerns the work and resignation of Elliott Little as Director of National Selective Service.

PER ARDUA The Information Minister is mis-informed. By Per ardua. (In *Saturday night*. Toronto. v. 56, no. 1 (Sept. 14, 1940), p. 5.)

Refers to James G. Gardiner and public information.

PERKS, A. E. Bouchard getting his heavy guns ready. (In *Saturday night*. Toronto. v. 60, no. 3 (Sept. 23, 1944), p. 16.)

Concerns Télesphore Damien Bouchard.

PICKERSGILL, JOHN WHITNEY Senator Norman Lambert—an appreciation. By The Honourable J. W. Pickersgill. (In *The Journal of liberal thought*. [Ottawa. v.] 2, no. 2 (spring 1966), pp. 140-141.)

Called to the Senate January 20, 1938. Written on the occasion of his death November 4, 1965.

PLAUNT, ALAN B. Canadian radio. (In *Saturday night*. Toronto. v. 51, no. 22 (Apr. 4, 1936), p. 11.)

Discusses "the draft act submitted by the Hon. C. D. Howe as a basis of discussion for the Parliamentary Committee on Radio. . . ."

POLITICUS At Queen's Park. The worms are turning. By Politicus. (In *Saturday night*. Toronto. v. 54, no. 38 (July 22, 1939), p. 5.)

Observes that the Ontario Liberals will support the federal Liberal Party in a general election.

—— [At Queen's Park] This coming election. Quarter mile from Queen's Park. By Politicus. (In *Saturday night*. Toronto. v. 54, no. 42 (Aug. 19, 1939), p. 5.)

Refers to the relationship between W. L. M. King and Mitchell Hepburn.

—— At Queen's Park. The for-and-against King men. By Politicus. (In *Saturday night*. Toronto. v. 55, no. 15 (Feb. 10, 1940), p. 5.)

Comments on the relationship between Ontario politicians and Prime Minister King, with reference to the federal election held March 26, 1940.

—— At Queen's Park. It's Mr. Hepburn's move. By Politicus. (In *Saturday night*. Toronto. v. 55, no. 17 (Feb. 24, 1940), p. 5.)

Concerns Mitchell Hepburn's "resolution condemning the King government for lack of drive in its war effort".

—— National affairs. Mitchell Hepburn, the new appeaser. By Politicus. (In *Satur-*

day night. Toronto. v. 56, no. 6 (Oct. 19, 1940), p. 14.)

—— National affairs. Mr. Howe: "Take off your uniform". By Politicus. (In *Saturday night*. Toronto. v. 56, no. 12 (Nov. 30, 1940), p. 12.)

Refers to a statement made by C. D. Howe, in the House of Commons, directed at Captain George White.

—— National affairs. What size shoes does Mitch wear? By Politicus. (In *Saturday night*. Toronto. v. 56, no. 17 (Jan. 4, 1941), p. 12.)

Concerns Mitchell Hepburn and Mackenzie King, with reference to a forthcoming Dominion-provincial constitutional conference.

—— National affairs. Well, little men, and what now? By Politicus. (In *Saturday night*. Toronto. v. 56, no. 20 (Jan. 25, 1941), p. 23.)

Discusses the meeting of the provincial premiers and Mackenzie King to discuss the Report of the Royal Commission on Dominion-Provincial Relations (the Rowell-Sirois report).

—— National affairs. It's your baby, Willie! By Politicus. (In *Saturday night*. Toronto. v. 56, no. 21 (Feb. 1, 1941), p. 12.)

Refers to the position of W. L. M. King with regard to a final decision on the part of the Liberal Party to force Mitchell Hepburn out of the party.

—— National affairs. The strange case of Harvey MacMillan. By Politicus. (In *Saturday night*. Toronto. v. 56, no. 24 (Feb. 22, 1941), p. 11.)

Concerns the clash between H. R. MacMillan, chairman of the Wartime Requirements Board, and Clarence D. Howe.

—— National affairs. Mr. Lapointe, what do you say? By Politicus. (In *Saturday night*. Toronto. v. 56, no. 25 (Mar. 1, 1941), pp. 8-9.)

Concerns Ernest Lapointe and civil liberties.

—— National affairs. Mr. Lapointe and those journalists. (In *Saturday night*. Toronto. v. 56, no. 27 (Mar. 15, 1941), p. 7.)

Refers to the work of the Royal Canadian Mounted Police in "investigating" journalists: Judith Robinson and Oakley Dalgleish.

—— National affairs. Mr. Lapointe and some non-journalists. By Politicus. (In *Saturday night*. Toronto. v. 56, no. 28 (Mar. 22, 1941), p. 8.)

Refers to a government investigation of Lieut.-Col. C. E. Reynolds, Lieut-Col. George Alexander Drew, and the *Globe and Mail*.

—— National affairs. "Chubby" Power brings sweetness and light. By Politicus. (In *Saturday night*. Toronto. v. 56, no. 29 (Mar. 29, 1941), p. 8.)
Concerns Charles Gavan Power.

—— National affairs. Free advice. Part I. By Politicus. (In *Saturday night*. Toronto. v. 56, no. 32 (Apr. 19, 1941), p. 8.)
To W. L. M. King, with reference to strong government.

—— National affairs. Free advice: Part II. By Politicus. (In *Saturday night*. Toronto. v. 56, no. 33 (Apr. 26, 1941), p. 16.)
To C. D. Howe, Minister of Munitions and Supply.

—— National affairs. Free advice: Part IV. By Politicus. (In *Saturday night*. Toronto. v. 56, no. 35 (May 10, 1941), p. 16.)
To W. L. M. King, with reference to efficient government.

POWER, CHARLES GAVAN A party politician; the memoirs of Chubby Power. Edited by Norman Ward. Toronto, Macmillan, 1966. 419 p.

—— What's wrong with the Liberals? "The Liberal Party is travelling in the ditches of expediency, first right, then left." By the Hon. C. G. Power. (In *Maclean's*. Toronto. v. 60, no. 3 (Feb. 1, 1947), pp. 13; 46-48.)

Premier King, cunctator. (In *Canadian comment*. Toronto. v. 6, no. 8 (Aug. 1937), p. 5.)
Comments on the tactics pursued by Mackenzie King regarding intervention by Canada in the event of an outbreak of war.

PRO AND CON Whither drifting? By Pro and Con. (In *Canadian magazine*. Toronto. v. 90, no. 4 (Oct. 1938), pp. [32]-33; 41-42.)
Pro and Con are two staff members of the *Canadian magazine*.
A discussion of the general policies of the Liberal government from 1935 to 1938.

QUINN, HERBERT FURLONG The third national convention of the Liberal Party. (In *The Canadian journal of economics and political science*. Toronto. v. 17 (1951), pp. 228-233.)
Held in Ottawa, August 5-7, 1948.

Ralston; realist in the Defence office. (In

New world illustrated. Montreal. v. 2, no. 6 (Aug. 1941), pp. 19; 56.)
Brief biographical sketch of J. L. Ralston.

REID, ESCOTT MEREDITH Canada and the threat of war. A discussion of Mr. Mackenzie King's foreign policy. By Escott Reid. (In *The University of Toronto quarterly*. [Toronto] v. 6 (1936/37), pp. 242-253.)

—— Mr. Mackenzie King's foreign policy, 1935-36. By Escott Reid. (In *Canadian journal of economics and political science*. [Toronto] v. 3 (1937), pp. 86-97.)
The Author is concerned "mostly with the attitude of [Mackenzie King's] government on the ultimate question of peace and war" and concentrates on the "political foreign policy" of the King administration.

RICHARDS, P. M. The business angle. A confidence-creating budget. (In *Saturday night*. Toronto. v. 61, no. 7 (Oct. 20, 1945), p. 42.)
Concerns the budget brought down by J. L. Ilsley in 1945.

—— The business front. The Ralston budget. (In *Saturday night*. Toronto. v. 55, no. 36 (July 6, 1940), p. [7].)

RICHER, LEOPOLD Ernest Lapointe. (In *L'Action nationale*. Montréal. v. 18 (déc. 1941), pp. [272]-277.)

RITCHIE, DAVID LAKIE The famine of ideas. By D. L. Ritchie. (In *The New age*. Montreal. v. 2, no. 15 (Apr. 11, 1940), p. 5.)
Evaluates the Liberal Party after the federal election held March 26, 1940.

ROBERTS, LLOYD Mackenzie King, the man. (In *The Maritime advocate and busy East*. Sackville, N.B. v. 26, no. 5 (Dec. 1935), pp. 11-12; 28.)
Reprinted from the *Christian Science Monitor*, Boston, Mass., December 4, 1935.

ROBINSON, JUDITH Lacroix of Beauce. (In *Saturday night*. Toronto. v. 51, no. 34 (June 27, 1936), p. 5.)
Describes Edouard Lacroix, Liberal member of parliament for Beauce, Que.

—— Objective Liberal. (In *Saturday night*. Toronto. v. 51, no. 19 (Mar. 14, 1936), pp. 5; 10.)
Concerns Jean-François Pouliot; "Objective Liberal member for Temiscouata, P.Q."

ROGERS, NORMAN MC LEOD The present challenge to Canada. By the Honourable

Norman McLeod Rogers. (In Empire Club of Canada. *Addresses*. Toronto. (1940/41), pp. 19-32.)

Delivered by Colonel James Mess due to the death of N. M. Rogers while en route from Ottawa to present the above address on June 10, 1940.

ROTHNEY, GORDON OLIVER   A Liberal decade. By Gordon O. Rothney. (In *The Canadian forum*. Toronto. v. 25, no. 299 (Dec. 1945), pp. 203-204.)

An historical commentary on the era of Mackenzie King.

—— Quebec saves our King. By Gordon O. Rothney. (In *The Canadian forum*. Toronto. v. 25, no. 294 (July 1945), pp. 83-84.)

An analysis of the Quebec electorate and its relationship to the federal Liberal Party under the leadership of Mackenzie King.

RUFUS II   The war budget. By Rufus II. (In *The Canadian forum*. Toronto. v. 19, no. 230 (Mar. 1940), pp. 376-378.)

Discusses the first war budget of the Liberal government.

RUSSENHOLT, MRS. E. S.   Why I intend to vote for the Liberals. (In *Chatelaine*. Toronto. v. 18, no. 6 (June 1945), pp. 12; 32; 39.)

Relates to the federal election held June 11, 1945.

SANDWELL, BERNARD KEBLE   From the editor's chair. Mr. St. Laurent undertakes to prove a great deal too much. By B. K. Sandwell. (In *Saturday night*. Toronto. v. 61, no. 43 (June 29, 1946), p. 17.)

Comments on Louis St. Laurent's position on amending the Canadian constitution.

—— From the editor's chair. Prime Ministership has become a vast power in Mr. King's hand. By B. K. Sandwell. (In *Saturday night*. Toronto. v. 64, no. 6 (Nov. 13, 1948), pp. 10; 48.)

—— From week to week. The King has a right to Mr. King. By B. K. Sandwell. (In *Saturday night*. Toronto. v. 54, no. 28 (May 13, 1939), p. 10.)

Argues that Mackenzie King should accompany King George VI during the latter's visit to Canada.

—— From week to week. In the path of Laurier. By B. K. Sandwell. (In *Saturday night*. Toronto. v. 55, no. 1 (Nov. 4, 1939), p. 2.)

Concerns Ernest Lapointe.

—— From week to week. Parliament's function. By B. K. Sandwell. (In *Saturday night*. Toronto. v. 55, no. 15 (Feb. 10, 1940), p. 3.)

Comments on Mackenzie King and his procedure in the dissolution of parliament.

—— From week to week. Mr. King and what to do about him. By B. K. Sandwell. (In *Saturday night*. Toronto. v. 56, no. 34 (May 3, 1941), p. 12.)

—— From week to week. Should Mr. King go to London? By B. K. Sandwell. (In *Saturday night*. Toronto. v. 56, no. 37 (May 24, 1941), p. 13.)

Considers Mackenzie King's participation in an Empire War Cabinet.

—— [From] week to week. The government's massage party. By B. K. Sandwell. (In *Saturday night*. Toronto. v. 57, no. 13 (Dec. 6, 1941), p. 11.)

Concerns the question of price control.

—— How Mr. King kept power. He had intense conviction that Canada's national destiny demanded unity. By B. K. Sandwell. (In *Saturday night*. Toronto. v. 65, no. 43 (Aug. 1, 1950), pp. 12; 34.)

SCOTT, FRANCIS REGINALD   Labor learns the truth. By F. R. Scott. (In *The Canadian forum*. Toronto. v. 26, no. 304 (May 1946), pp. 29-30.)

Discusses the Liberal government's attitude toward the demands made by the Trades and Labor Congress and the Canadian Congress of Labor.

—— Mr. King and the King makers. By F. R. Scott. (In *The Canadian forum*. Toronto. v. 30, no. 359 (Dec. 1950), pp. 197-199.)

A critical analysis of the "qualities of leadership" possessed by the late William Lyon Mackenzie King.

SHAW, CHARLES L.   Pattullo takes a poll. After a right-about-face B.C.'s Premier is ready to try his strength. (In *Maclean's*. Toronto. v. 54, no. 20 (Oct. 15, 1941), pp. 12; 53-55.)

Concerns T. D. Pattullo's relations with Ottawa.

SMALL, FRANKLIN   What manner of man is the Secretary of State? (In *Saturday night*. Toronto. v. 56, no. 4 (Oct. 5, 1940), p. 13.)

Concerns Pierre François Casgrain.

SMITH, F. D. L.   Why there's no statue of Laurier in Quebec. (In *Saturday night*. Toronto. v. 62, no. 8 (Oct. 26, 1946), p. 21.)

SMITH, HARRIET W. "His first thought was for Canada's women." (In *Saturday night.* Toronto. v. 56, no. 31 (Apr. 12, 1941), p. [25].)

Concerns Dr. John Power Howden, MP, from Norwood Grove, Manitoba.

SMITH, IRVING NORMAN How Mackenzie King fought the war. By I. Norman Smith. (In *Saturday night.* Toronto. v. 75, no. 21 (Oct. 15, 1960), pp. [25]-26.)

A review article of *The Mackenzie King record,* edited by J. W. Pickersgill. Toronto, University of Toronto Press, 1960-70. Vol. 1, 1939-1944 (1960).

—— King and the conscription crisis. By I. Norman Smith. (In *Saturday night.* Toronto. v. 75, no. 22 (Oct. 29, 1960), pp. 9-10.)

Refers to the crisis which arose in Canada during the Second World War.

STACEY, CHARLES PERRY Canadian defence policy. By C. P. Stacey. (In *The Canadian journal of economics and political science.* [Toronto] v. 4 (1938), pp. 490-504.)

"This paper is a somewhat abbreviated and considerably revised version of that entitled 'New trends in Canadian defence policy', which was . . . published in the series of Canadian supplementary papers presented to the recent British Commonwealth Relations Conference at Sydney, Australia."

Describes defence policy as administered by the Hon. Ian A. Mackenzie, Minister of National Defence.

STAEBLER, H. L. Mackenzie King. (In Waterloo Historical Society. *Annual report.* [Kitchener, Ont.] 38th (1950), pp. 10-13.)

Written on the occasion of his death July 22, 1950.

THOMAS, A. VERNON In the public eye. From switchman to statesman in Western success story. (In *Saturday night.* Toronto. v. 63, no. 46 (Aug. 21, 1948), p. [14].)

A biographical sketch of Ralph Maybank, parliamentary assistant to Hon. Paul Martin, Minister of Health and Welfare, and vice-chairman of the Prices Committee.

THOMAS, J. K. Mackenzie King at 70; the paradox of the Prime Minister. (In *New world.* Toronto. v. 5, no. 10 (Dec. 1944), pp. 9-13.)

THORSON, JOSEPH THARARINN The Canadian war effort—as a Liberal sees it. By J. T. Thorson, MP. (In *The Canadian spokesman.* Ottawa. v. 1, no. 1 (Jan. 1941), pp. [17]-22.)

TOLBRIDGE, R. B. CBC and the government. (In *The Canadian forum.* Toronto. v. 22, no. 264 (Jan. 1943), pp. 299-301.)

Tough-minded "Mike". (In *New world.* Toronto. v. 5, no. 8 (Oct. 1944), p. 16.)

Brief character sketch of Lester Bowles Pearson.

Twenty years as Prime Minister. (In *The Canadian forum.* Toronto. v. 26, no. 306 (July 1946), pp. 77-78.)

Discusses the career of William Lyon Mackenzie King.

UNDERHILL, FRANK HAWKINS The end of the King era. By Frank H. Underhill. (In *The Canadian forum.* Toronto. v. 28, no. 331 (Aug. 1948), pp. [97]-98; v. 28, no. 332 (Sept. 1948), pp. [121]-122, 126-127.)

In two parts.

VIGEANT, PIERRE L'ascension de M. Saint-Laurent. (In *L'Action nationale.* Montréal. v. 31 (fév. 1948), pp. [143]-148.)

—— La dernière session de M. King. (In *L'Action nationale.* Montréal. v. 30 (nov. 1947), pp. [232]-238.)

WAKEMAN, ALBERT C. Industry bears burden of budget changes. Increases in taxation will be passed on to consumers. Latter compensated by reductions in duties on imports. Closer competition for Canadian industry. (In *Saturday night.* Toronto. v. 51, no. 27 (May 9, 1936), pp. [21]; 25; 28.)

Discusses the budget brought down by C. A. Dunning, May 2, 1936.

WARD, WALLACE They're setting up the Liberal convention. (In *Saturday night.* Toronto. v. 63, no. 43 (July 31, 1948), pp. 2-3. ports.)

The National Liberal leadership convention held August 5-7, 1948.

WATT, C. D. The problem of co-ordination. (In *The Canadian forum.* Toronto. v. 22, no. 257 (June 1942), pp. 76-79.)

Discusses government policy with regard to Canada's war effort.

Well within ninety days. The Prime Minister promised a trade agreement with the United States within 90 days of his election, and here it is. (In *Canadian comment.* Toronto. v. 4, no. 12 (Dec. 1935), pp. [5]-6; 31.)

With reference to Mackenzie King.

WHITTAKER, G. C. Ottawa letter. Will Meighen unite Liberals? (In *Saturday night*. Toronto. v. 57, no. 22 (Feb. 7, 1942), p. 13.)

—— The Ottawa letter. Ottawa says something must happen now. (In *Saturday night*. Toronto. v. 57, no. 37 (May 23, 1942), p. 11.)
Concerns W. L. M. King and the issue of conscription.

—— Ottawa letter. Mr. King in his tightest corner. (In *Saturday night*. Toronto. v. 57, no. 39 (June 6, 1942), pp. 6-7.)
Refers to W. L. Mackenzie King and his dilemma over conscription.

—— The Ottawa letter. Taxing us into forgetting conscription. (In *Saturday night*. Toronto. v. 57, no. 43 (July 4, 1942), p. 8.)
Refers to the budget presented by J. L. Ilsley.

—— Ottawa letter. Ministerial revolt is possible. (In *Saturday night*. Toronto. v. 57, no. 45 (July 18, 1942), p. 16.)
Concerns conscription as a matter of contention within the cabinet of Mackenzie King.

—— The Ottawa letter. The budget is still being amended. (In *Saturday night*. Toronto. v. 57, no. 51 (Aug. 29, 1942), p. 7.)

—— The Ottawa letter. General LaFleche as Minister of War Services. (In *Saturday night*. Toronto. v. 58, no. 1 (Sept. 12, 1942), p. 7.)
Concerns Léo Richer Laflèche.

—— The Ottawa letter. LaFleche will be a power in the cabinet. (In *Saturday night*. Toronto. v. 58, no. 6 (Oct. 17, 1942), p. 8.)
Concerns Hon. Léo Richer Laflèche.

—— The Ottawa letter. Absenteeism and high taxes. (In *Saturday night*. Toronto. v. 58, no. 10 (Nov. 14, 1942), p. 8.)
Concerns J. L. Ilsley's taxation policy.

—— The Ottawa letter. Don't insult the Director of Selective Service. (In *Saturday night*. Toronto. v. 58, no. 13 (Dec. 5, 1942), p. 6.)
Concerns Elliott Little and his draft of the Selective Service law intended to be put through by order-in-council. Resulted in a feud between Humphrey Mitchell and Elliott Little over policy.

—— The Ottawa letter. Producer prices out of Gordon's hands. (In *Saturday night*.

Toronto. v. 58, no. 24 (Feb. 20, 1943), p. 8.)
Refers to government control over Donald Gordon with regard to fixing producer prices of primary products.

—— Ottawa letter. Parliament takes more interest. (In *Saturday night*. Toronto. v. 58, no. 30 (Apr. 3, 1943), p. 15.)
Discusses Parliament's questioning of J. L. Ilsley and actions taken by those within his jurisdiction.

—— Ottawa letter. The Labor Department's Waterloo. (In *Saturday night*. Toronto. v. 59, no. 14 (Dec. 11, 1943), pp. 8-9.)
Comments on the McTague report on labor relations and the decision of the government to adopt the major provisions of the report.

—— The Ottawa letter. The political course of 1944 up to Mr. King and the gods. (In *Saturday night*. Toronto. v. 59, no. 18 (Jan. 8, 1944), p. 8.)

—— The Ottawa letter. Canada's new deal puts all the other new deals in the shade. (In *Saturday night*. Toronto. v. 59, no. 22 (Feb. 5, 1944), p. 11.)
Refers to the policies of W. L. Mackenzie King.

—— The Ottawa letter. Labor code, while belated, is big step in right direction. (In *Saturday night*. Toronto. v. 59, no. 25 (Feb. 26, 1944), p. 11.)
Concerns the compulsory collective bargaining formula drawn up by the Department of Labor under Humphrey Mitchell.

—— The Ottawa letter. Utmost freedom of trade in all directions. is King's policy. (In *Saturday night*. Toronto. v. 59, no. 26 (Mar. 4, 1944), pp. 8-9.)
Concerns the trade policy of the Mackenzie King government.

—— The Ottawa letter. Mr. Howe doesn't want the CPR to play in his aviation yard. (In *Saturday night*. Toronto. v. 59, no. 29 (Mar. 25, 1944), p. 8.)
Concerns the air policy of C. D. Howe.

—— The Ottawa letter. Lobby raiders getting ready to blast Howe's air policy. (In *Saturday night*. Toronto. v. 59, no. 30 (Apr. 1, 1944), p. 9.)

—— The Ottawa letter. Donald Gordon is letting his horse have a free rein. (In *Saturday night*. Toronto. v. 59, no. 39 (June, 3, 1944), p. 8.)

Concerns the loosening of controls over business.

——— The Ottawa letter. What new strategy will King adopt to meet the CCF? (In *Saturday night*. Toronto. v. 59, no. 42 (June 24, 1944), p. 8.)

Relates to the significant gains made by the CCF in the 1943 Ontario election.

——— The Ottawa letter. Ottawa's pundits shaking heads over Mr. King and baby bonus. (In *Saturday night*. Toronto. v. 59, no. 43 (July 1, 1944), p. 10.)

——— The Ottawa letter. These taxation experts are a pretty tough kind of people. (In *Saturday night*. Toronto. v. 59, no. 45 (July 15, 1944), p. 8.)

Concerns James Lorimer Ilsley and his performance as Minister of Finance in wartime.

——— The Ottawa letter. Will Mr. King remain Premier by making arrangement with CCF? (In *Saturday night*. Toronto. v. 59, no. 46 (July 22, 1944), pp. 8-9.)

——— The Ottawa letter. If Mr. King wants a fall election he can easily find an excuse. (In *Saturday night*. Toronto. v. 60, no. 1 (Sept. 9, 1944), p. 8.)

——— The Ottawa letter. Gordon system of spend to make promises an excess of riches. (In *Saturday night*. Toronto. v. 60, no. 3 (Sept. 23, 1944), p. 8.)

Concerns Donald Gordon's plan to convert from a wartime to a peacetime economy.

——— The Ottawa letter. Mr. King busy tidying his house but this year not likely. (In *Saturday night*. Toronto. v. 60, no. 7 (Oct. 21, 1944), p. 10.)

——— The Ottawa letter. Does King mean to appeal from Parliament to the electors? (In *Saturday night*. Toronto. v. 60, no. 11 (Nov. 18, 1944), p. 8.)

Concerns W. L. Mackenzie King and the conscription issue.

——— The Ottawa letter. Well, the opposition has helped Mr. King out of many holes. (In *Saturday night*. Toronto. v. 60, no. 12 (Nov. 25, 1944), pp. 8-9.)

Concerns Mackenzie King's summoning of the House of Commons to discuss a voluntary system of raising reinforcements.

——— The Ottawa letter. Mr. King got in the stream and made his stand in the middle. (In *Saturday night*. Toronto. v. 60, no. 13 (Dec. 2, 1944), pp. 8-9.)

Discusses the position of Prime Minister King on conscription.

——— The Ottawa letter. Future of the Canadian nation has been in balance at Ottawa. (In *Saturday night*. Toronto. v. 60, no. 14 (Dec. 9, 1944), pp. 10-11.)

Concerns Mackenzie King and the issue over conscription.

Who will succeed King? (In *New world*. Toronto. v. 7, no. 6 (Aug. 1946), pp. 9-11.)

Will the West's Jimmy Gardiner become Prime Minister of Canada? (In *New world*. Toronto. v. 8, no. 5 (July 1947), pp. 10-11; 43.)

WILSON, KENNETH R. Backstage at Ottawa. By the Man with a Notebook. (In *Maclean's*. Toronto. v. 54, no. 8 (Apr. 15, 1941), pp. 12; 60; 62.)

Comments, mainly, on the personality of Mackenzie King and Liberal government activities.

——— Backstage at Ottawa. By the Man with a Notebook. (In *Maclean's*. Toronto. v. 54, no. 14 (July 15, 1941), pp. 10; 41; 43.)

Considers the wartime policies, including conscription, of Mackenzie King, etc.

——— Backstage at Ottawa. By the Man with a Notebook. (In *Maclean's*. Toronto. v. 55, no. 1 (Jan. 1, 1942), pp. 11; 34-35.)

Considers the choosing of a replacement for Ernest Lapointe following his death November 26, 1941.

——— Backstage at Ottawa. By the Man with a Notebook. (In *Maclean's*. Toronto. v. 55, no. 2 (Jan. 15, 1942), pp. 11; 37.)

Discusses the issue of conscription, etc.

——— Backstage at Ottawa. By the Man with a Notebook. (In *Maclean's*. Toronto. v. 55, no. 4 (Feb. 15, 1942), pp. 14-15; 47-49.)

Discusses a proposed national plebiscite to release Mackenzie King from his pledge not to invoke conscription.

——— Backstage at Ottawa. By the Man with a Notebook. (In *Maclean's*. Toronto. v. 52 [i.e. 55] no. 5 (Mar. 1, 1942), pp. 10-11; 38-39.)

Discusses a proposed national plebiscite to release Mackenzie King from his pledge that there would be no use made of conscription.

—— Backstage at Ottawa. By the Man with a Notebook. (In *Maclean's*. Toronto. v. 55, no. 7 (Apr. 1, 1942), pp. 12-13; 43-44.)

Discusses the wartime policies and activities of the Liberal government.

—— Backstage at Ottawa. By the Man with a Notebook. (In *Maclean's*. Toronto. v. 55, no. 8 (Apr. 15, 1942), pp. 14-15; 52-53.)

Discusses government policy for wartime industrial production.

—— Backstage at Ottawa. By the Man with a Notebook. (In *Maclean's*. Toronto. v. 55, no. 11 (June 1, 1942), pp. 14; 39-40.)

Considers, mainly, the results of the national plebiscite to release Mackenzie King from his "no conscription" commitment. The plebiscite was held April 27, 1942.

—— Backstage at Ottawa. By the Man with a Notebook. (In *Maclean's*. Toronto. v. 55, no. 12 (June 15, 1942), pp. 14-15; 49.)

Discusses Mackenzie King's removal of clause 3 from the National Resources Mobilization Act (the clause in this act prevents the conscription of men for overseas service).

—— Backstage at Ottawa. By the Man with a Notebook. (In *Maclean's*. Toronto. v. 55, no. 15 (Aug. 1, 1942), p. 14.)

Dicusses J. L. Ilsley's budget and other issues.

—— Backstage at Ottawa. By the Man with a Notebook. (In *Maclean's*. Toronto. v. 55, no. 19 (Oct. 1, 1942), pp. 14-15; 44-45.)

Discusses the wartime policy of the federal government.

—— Backstage at Ottawa. By the Man with a Notebook. (In *Maclean's*. Toronto. v. 55, no. 21 (Nov. 1, 1942), pp. 14-15; 47; 49.)

Discusses the program of the federal government to curtail non-essential civilian industries.

—— Backstage at Ottawa. By the Man with a Notebook. (In *Maclean's*. Toronto. v. 55, no. 24 (Dec. 15, 1942), pp. 14-15; 45; 49.)

Discusses the "Little-Mitchell" (Elliott Little and Hon. Humphrey Mitchell) feud over policy concerning manpower and its use during the war.

—— Backstage at Ottawa. By the Man with a Notebook. (In *Maclean's*. Toronto. v. 56, no. 13 (July 1, 1943), pp. 14-15; 58-59.)

Concerns C. G. Power's annual report to the House of Commons on the Royal Canadian Air Force.

—— Backstage at Ottawa. By the Man with a Notebook. (In *Maclean's*. Toronto. v. 56, no. 19 (Oct. 1, 1943), pp. 14-15; 61.)

Discusses the administration of Mackenzie King.

—— Backstage at Ottawa. By the Man with a Notebook. (In *Maclean's*. Toronto. v. 56, no. 20 (Oct. 15, 1943), pp. 14-15; 65.)

Concerns the McTague report on inflation and Finance Minister Ilsley's argument to implement wage and price controls.

—— Manpower. (In *Maclean's*. Toronto. v. 55, no. 17 (Sept. 1, 1942), pp. 5-7; 32-34.)

Analyses Government policy and the role of Elliott M. Little, appointed Director of National Selective Service in March, 1942.

—— Why Canadianize the air force? The Minister of National Defence for Air explains why he believes Canada should control her own airmen overseas. (In *Maclean's*. Toronto. v. 55, no. 22 (Nov. 15, 1942), pp. 11; 28-30.)

An interview with C. G. Power.

WISMER, L. E. Interim budget. (In *The Canadian forum*. Toronto. v. 27, no. 317 (June 1947), p. 54.)

Discusses the budget statement delivered in the House of Commons on Tuesday, April 29, 1947.

WOOD, R. C. Should Mr. King lead anti-CCF front? (In *Saturday night*. Toronto. v. 60, no. 33 (Apr. 21, 1945), pp. 6-7.)

WRIGHT, C. P. A platform of boards. (In *The Canadian forum*. Toronto. v. 16, no. 186 (July 1936), pp. 8-10.)

A full discussion of Liberal government policy on the National Employment Commission Act, the Canadian National Railways and the change in directorate of the Bank of Canada.

1948–1968

1948–1957

ABBOTT, DOUGLAS CHARLES   Some economic and financial consequences of defence. An address by the Hon. Douglas Charles Abbott, Minister of Finance. (In Empire Club of Canada. *Addresses.* Toronto. (1950/51), pp. 133-143.)
Address delivered December 14, 1950.

ANGERS, FRANCOIS ALBERT   Deux modèles d'inconscience: le premier Saint-Laurent et le Commissaire Lévesque. (In *L'Action nationale.* Montréal. v. 38 (nov. 1951), pp. [180]-210.)
"Les antécédents du Rapport Massey-Lévesque."
Concerns the report of the Royal Commission on National Development in the Arts, Letters and Sciences. Ottawa, 1951.

——— Idées croches et petite politique. (In *L'Action nationale.* Montréal. v. 39 (juin/juil. 1952), pp. 409-417.)
Discusses the ideas of Stuart Garson, Minister of Justice, regarding federal aid to education.

——— Mais où sont les convictions d'antan? (In *L'Action nationale.* Montréal. v. 35 (juin 1950), pp. [460]-475.)
Discusses the military budget.

APOLLONIA, LUIGI D'   L'explication insuffisante de M. Pearson. (In *Relations.* Montréal. 17. année, no 198 (juin 1957), pp. 145-147.)
Concerns the career of Ambassador E. Herbert Norman.

ARMSTRONG, P. C.   The inflationary prospect. (In *Public affairs.* Halifax. v. 14, no. 2 (winter 1952), pp. [41]-46.)
Discusses government policy.

BAIN, GEORGE   The forgotten man of Parliament Hill. (In *Maclean's.* Toronto. v. 67, no. 21 (Nov. 1, 1954), pp. 20-21; 51-54.)
Concerns David Arnold Croll.

——— The wordiest MP in Ottawa. (In *Maclean's.* Toronto. v. 67, no. 18 (Sept. 15, 1954), pp. 17; 94-98.)
Concerns Jean François Pouliot, Liberal Member of Parliament for Temiscouata, Quebec.

BARKWAY, MICHAEL   Back-room minister. (In *Saturday night.* Toronto. v. 67, no. 39 (July 5, 1952), cover; p. 19.)
Concerns Walter Edward Harris.

——— The happy Finance Minister. (In *Saturday night.* Toronto. v. 68, no. 6 (Nov. 15, 1952), pp 1; 20-22.)
Concerns Douglas Charles Abbott.

——— Lester Pearson: reluctant politician. (In *Saturday night.* Toronto. v. 67, no. 29 (Apr. 26, 1952), pp. 13; [37].)

——— Ottawa view. Defence budget near decision. Total higher but NATO aid still uncertain. (In *Saturday night.* Toronto. v. 67, no. 15 (Jan. 19, 1952), pp. 2-3.)

——— Ottawa view. King, Governor General, PM. (In *Saturday night.* Toronto. v. 67, no. 19 (Feb. 16, 1952), pp. 4; 18.)
Concerns the appointment of Vincent Massey as Governor-General of Canada.

——— Ottawa view. Budget had some puzzles. (In *Saturday night.* Toronto. v. 67, no. 28 (Apr. 19, 1952), pp. 2-3.)
Comments on Douglas Abbott's budget.

——— Ottawa view. St. Laurent opens campaign. (In *Saturday night.* Toronto. v. 67, no. 51 (Sept. 27, 1952), pp. 4; 36.)

——— Ottawa view. Contradictions on immigration. (In *Saturday night.* Toronto. v. 67, no. 52 (Oct. 4, 1952), pp 4; 8.)
Comments on immigration policy.

——— Ottawa view. Up or down, prices get blamed. (In *Saturday night.* Toronto. v. 68, no. 4 (Nov. 1, 1952), pp. 4; 8.)
Refers to the budget presented by D. C. Abbott.

——— Parliament's not dull. Even a powerful government blushes and shudders when cats escape the bag. (In *Saturday night.* Toronto. v. 65, no. 10 (Dec. 13, 1949), pp. 14; 46.)
Comments on the Liberal government and its ten-month suppression of the McGregor report on the flour-milling combine.

——— Wheat bounty: fact and fiction. (In *Saturday night.* Toronto. v. 66, no. 24 (Mar. 20, 1951), p. 7.)
Concerns J. G. Gardiner's defence in the House of Commons of the $65 million wheat bounty.

BIRD, JOHN   A prophet in Ottawa. (In *Canadian commentator.* Toronto. v. 1, no. 2) (Feb. 1957), pp. [1]-2.)
Concerns Walter Gordon and the reaction to the publication of the preliminary report of the Royal Commission on Canada's Economic Prospects. Ottawa, 1956.

—— When the Liberals lost the press. (In *Canadian commentator*. Toronto. v. 1, no. 6 (June 1957), p. 3.)

Considers the Trans-Canada Pipeline debate and the criticism launched against the Government by the press, which contributed, in the main, to the defeat of the Liberals in the federal election of June 10, 1957.

CHEVRIER, LIONEL   The St. Lawrence Seaway. By the Hon. Lionel Chevrier, MP. Toronto, Macmillan, 1959. x, 174 p. illus., maps, plates.

—— La voie maritime du Saint-Laurent. Par l'Hon. Lionel Chevrier. [Montréal] Cercle de Livre de France [c1959] 184 p. illus., maps, plates.

CLAXTON, BROOKE   Men, materials, money for Canada's defence. By Hon. Brooke Claxton, Minister of National Defence. (In Empire Club of Canada. *Addresses*. Toronto. (1950/51), pp. 192-205.)

Address delivered January 25, 1951.

—— Military preparedness policy. By the Honourable Brooke Claxton. (In *Public affairs*. Halifax. v. 13, no. 3 (spring 1951), pp. [4]-6.)

DESCHAMPS, JEAN   Commentaire sur le discours Winters. (In *L'Action nationale*. Montréal. v. 34 (déc. 1949), pp. [300]-307.)

Speech delivered by the Hon. Robert G. Winters in the House of Commons, September 21, 1949.

EGGLESTON, WILFRID   Canadian politics: the old era and the new. (In *Queen's quarterly*. Kingston. v. 55 (1948), pp. [476]-488.)

Reviews the era of Mackenzie King and comments on the new administration led by Louis St. Laurent at the time of the transfer of power (from Mr. King to Mr. St. Laurent) on November 15, 1948.

—— Capital comment. St. Laurent versus Duplessis. (In *Saturday night*. Toronto. v. 65, no. 4 (Nov. 1, 1949), p. 5.)

Dispute over constitutional reform.

—— Capital comment. Opposition has a big job. (In *Saturday night*. Toronto. v. 65, no. 9 (Dec. 6, 1949), p. 5.)

Refers to the large majority held by the Liberal government in Parliament.

—— Capital comment. What price adequate defence? (In *Saturday night*. Toronto. v. 65, no. 49 (Sept. 19, 1950), p. 3.)

Comments on the "Korean war budget" presented by Douglas Abbott.

—— Capital comment. Budget honeymoon is over. (In *Saturday night*. Toronto. v. 65, no. 28 (Apr. 18, 1950), p. 3.)

Comment on the budget speech by D. C. Abbott.

—— Capital comment. Analyzing the surplus. (In *Saturday night*. Toronto. v. 67, no. 1 (Oct. 13, 1951), p. [35].)

Refers to the budget presented by D. C. Abbott.

—— Ottawa view. Concentration of power. (In *Saturday night*. Toronto. v. 63, no. 46 (Aug. 21, 1948), p. 4.)

Comments on the charge made by C. G. Power that the Government is "abandoning responsible government by allowing the Executive and the Bureaucracy to usurp the rightful powers of Parliament."

—— Ottawa view. A job for Mr. St. Laurent. (In *Saturday night*. Toronto. v. 63, no. 49 (Sept. 11, 1948), p. 4.)

—— Ottawa view. Mr. Pearson's new job. (In *Saturday night*. Toronto. v. 63, no. 50 (Sept. 18, 1948), p. 4.)

Concerns Lester Pearson's appointment to the position of Minister of External Affairs.

—— Ottawa view. Seven Liberal problems. (In *Saturday night*. Toronto. v. 64, no. 8 (Nov. 27, 1948), p. 4.)

The problems are: national defence and the North Atlantic Treaty, export trade and the dollar problem, need for a ten-province dominion-provincial pact, housing, freight rates, revision and reduction of taxes, and the imminence of a general election.

—— Ottawa view. Liberal hopes rising. Survey of Quebec and the West reason for new confidence. (In *Saturday night*. Toronto. v. 64, no. 33 (May 24, 1949), p. 4.)

FORSEY, EUGENE ALFRED   Mr. McGregor's garden—keep out! By Eugene Forsey. (In *Public affairs*. Halifax. v. 15, no. 2 (winter 1953), pp. [20]-29.)

Discusses events leading to the resignation of F. A. McGregor as Commissioner of the Combines Investigation Act on October 29, 1949.

—— Never have so many been in so long. By Eugene Forsey. (In *Canadian commentator*. Toronto. v. 1, no. 5 (May 1957), pp. [1]-2.)

A critical analysis of the contemporary Liberal Party.

FOX, PAUL WESLEY The Liberal Party. By Paul Fox. (In *The Canadian forum*. Toronto. v. 35, no. 418 (Nov. 1955), pp. 172-174.)

—— Why the Liberal debacle? By P. W. F. (In *The Canadian forum*. Toronto. v. 37, no. 438 (July 1957), p. 75.)
Discusses the causes for the defeat of the Liberal Party in the general elections held June 10, 1957.

FRASER, BLAIR Backstage at Ottawa. Mike for PM? By the Man with a Notebook. (In *Maclean's*. Toronto. v. 61, no. 19 [i.e. 20] (Oct. 15, 1948), pp. 14; 66.)
Concerns Lester Pearson.

—— Backstage at Ottawa. A win for Louis —and Limbo? By the Man with a Notebook. (In *Maclean's*. Toronto. v. 62, no. 9 (May 1, 1949), pp. 14; 83.)
Concerns Louis St. Laurent and the Liberal Party.

—— Backstage at Ottawa. Only Liberals need apply. By the Man with a Notebook. (In *Maclean's*. Toronto. v. 62, no. 15 [i.e. 16] (Aug. 15, 1949), pp. 14; 58.)
Concerns the 14 Senate vacancies held unfilled by Louis St. Laurent until the election.

—— Backstage at Ottawa. No more vinegar budgets. (In *Maclean's*. Toronto. v. 64, no. 3 (Feb. 1, 1951), pp. 5; 46.)
Concerns fiscal policy of the Liberal government.

—— Backstage at Ottawa. Has Jimmy Gardiner won his last fight? (In *Maclean's*. Toronto. v. 64, no. 8 (Apr. 15, 1951), pp. 5; 68.)

—— Backstage at Ottawa. The Liberals have Quebec trouble too. (In *Maclean's*. Toronto. v. 64, no. 9 (May 1, 1951), pp. 5; 70.)

—— Backstage at Ottawa. Warm for October on Liberal benches. (In *Maclean's*. Toronto. v. 64, no. 18 (Sept. 15, 1951), pp. [65]-66.)

—— Backstage at Ottawa. The Grits write off Ontario. (In *Maclean's*. Toronto. v. 64, no. 22 (Nov. 15, 1951), pp. 5; 81-82.)

—— Backstage at Ottawa. Cigarette smugglers beware. (In *Maclean's*. Toronto. v. 65, no. 3 (Feb. 1, 1952), pp. 5; 50.)
Discusses the Government's determination to enforce an extra tax on cigarettes.

—— Backstage at Ottawa. "Save" is a four-letter word. (In *Maclean's*. Toronto.

v. 65, no. 12 (June 15, 1952), pp. 5; 68-69.)
Discusses W. Ross Thatcher's criticism of Government expenditure.

—— Backstage at Ottawa. Quebec Grits learn to like it. (In *Maclean's*. Toronto. v. 65, no. 14 (July 15, 1952), pp. 5; 52.)
Examines the relations of the federal Liberal Party to the provincial Liberal Party of Quebec.

—— Backstage at Ottawa. The Grits get stuck with a fork. (In *Maclean's*. Toronto. v. 65, no. 15 (Aug. 1, 1952), pp. 3; 38.)
Discusses the relationship between the 1952 budget speech and the decline of Liberal Party morale.

—— Backstage at Ottawa. The false bottom in Abbott's hat. (In *Maclean's*. Toronto. v. 66, no. 7 (Apr. 1, 1953), pp. 5; 80-81.)
An analysis of the tax cuts presented in Douglas Abbott's 1953 budget.

—— Backstage at Ottawa. The coach gets a chance to score. (In *Maclean's*. Toronto. v. 66, no. 13 (July 1, 1953), pp. 5; 54-55.)
Concerns J. W. Pickersgill.

—— Backstage at Ottawa. Last round coming up for the Liberals? (In *Maclean's*. Toronto. v. 66, no. 15 (Aug. 1, 1953), pp. 5; [43]-44.)

—— Backstage at Ottawa. Is Duplessis challenging St. Laurent? (In *Maclean's*. Toronto. v. 67, no. 11 (June 1, 1954), pp. 6; 85.)

—— Backstage at Ottawa. Why Abbott and Claxton said good-by. (In *Maclean's*. Toronto. v. 67, no. 17 (Sept. 1, 1954), pp. 5; 35-36.)

—— Backstage at Ottawa. Has Louis lost Liberal Quebec? (In *Maclean's*. Toronto. v. 68, no. 5 (Mar. 5, 1955), pp. 6; 52-53.)
Refers to Louis St. Laurent.

—— Backstage at Ottawa. They're paring down the estimates. (In *Maclean's*. Toronto. v. 68, no. 6 (Mar. 19, 1955), pp. 6; 75-76.)

—— Backstage at Ottawa. Back to old-fashioned budgets. (In *Maclean's*. Toronto. v. 68, no. 7 (Apr. 2, 1955), pp. 6; 84; 86.)
Comments on the first budget presented by Walter Harris.

—— Backstage at Ottawa. Should they censor the King papers? (In *Maclean's*.

Toronto. v. 68, no. 11 (May 28, 1955), pp. 6; 61-62.)
The papers of W. L. Mackenzie King.

—— Backstage at Ottawa. Was Guy Simonds really sacked? (In *Maclean's*. Toronto. v. 68, no. 15 (July 23, 1955), pp. 5; 41-42.)
General Guy Simonds was Chief of the General Staff.

—— Backstage at Ottawa. How C. D. Howe was humbled. (In *Maclean's*. Toronto. v. 68, no. 17 (Aug. 20, 1955), pp. 6; 65-66.)

—— Backstage at Ottawa. The wreckers eye the West Block. (In *Maclean's*. Toronto. v. 68, no. 19 (Sept. 17, 1955), pp. 6; 111.)
Discusses the decision to be made by Robert Winters, Minister of Public Works, concerning the retention or destruction of the West Block of the original Parliament Buildings.

—— Backstage at Ottawa. Can the immigration issue lick the Liberals? (In *Maclean's*. Toronto. v. 68, no. 25 (Dec. 10, 1955), pp. 8; 121-122.)

—— Backstage at Ottawa. Why the CBC shunned the King story. (In *Maclean's*. Toronto. v. 69, no. 7 (Mar. 31, 1956), pp. 5; 58-59.)
Concerns the cancellation of a televised review of the biography: *The age of Mackenzie King*, by H. S. Ferns and B. Ostry. London, Heinemann [1955].

—— Backstage at Ottawa. How much will Ottawa help the arts? (In *Maclean's*. Toronto. v. 69, no. 8 (Apr. 14, 1956), pp. 6; 106-107.)
Discusses Liberal government policy toward the Canada Council.

—— Backstage at Ottawa. Will the Liberals take over the pipeline? (In *Maclean's*. Toronto. v. 69, no. 10 (May 12, 1956), pp. 10; 113.)

—— Backstage at Ottawa. How the Grits' power play backfired. (In *Maclean's*. Toronto. v. 69, no. 14 (July 7, 1956), pp. 8; 56.)

—— Backstage at Ottawa. Why the steel strike gives the Liberals nightmares. (In *Maclean's*. Toronto. v. 69, no. 17 (Aug. 18, 1956), pp. 8; 66.)

—— Backstage at Ottawa. Ross Thatcher's glum conversion. (In *Maclean's*. Toronto. v. 69, no. 19 (Sept. 15, 1956), pp. 8; 93-94.)

Converted from the CCF to the Liberal Party.

—— Backstage at Ottawa. Has Ottawa broken Duplessis' grip on Quebec's universities? (In *Maclean's*. Toronto. v. 69, no. 24 (Nov. 24, 1956), pp. 8; 85-86.)

—— The cabinet minister who never sleeps. (In *Maclean's*. Toronto. v. 65, no. 11 (June 1, 1952), pp. 7-9; 31-32; 35-36.)
Concerns Brooke Claxton, Minister of National Defence.

—— Is the Liberal Party on the ropes? (In *Maclean's*. Toronto. v. 65, no. 22 (Nov. 15, 1952), pp. 20-21; 88-90.)

—— Meet Mike Pearson. (In *Maclean's*. Toronto. v. 64, no. 8 (Apr. 15, 1951), pp. 7; 57-60.)
Concerns Lester Bowles Pearson.

—— Who will the Liberals choose after Louis? (In *Maclean's*. Toronto. v. 69, no. 17 (Aug. 18, 1956), pp. 16-17; 60-65.)
Refers to Louis St. Laurent.

—— Will Walter Harris be our next Prime Minister? (In *Maclean's*. Toronto. v. 67, no. 16 (Aug. 15, 1954), pp. 7-9; 55-58.)

GARNER, HUGH Martin's millions and Mrs. Finch. (In *Saturday night*. Toronto. v. 68, no. 33 (May 23, 1953), pp. 7-8.)
Concerns the Hon. Paul Martin and the National Health program.

GARSON, STUART SINCLAIR The Empire, Canada and the provinces, 1949. An address by Honourable Stuart S. Garson, Minister of Justice and Attorney General of Canada. (In Empire Club of Canada. *Addresses*. Toronto. (1949/50), pp. 170-182.)
Address delivered January 19, 1950.

HARDY, REGINALD Our fantastic legacy from Mackenzie King. (In *Maclean's*. Toronto. v. 64, no. 14 (July 15, 1951), pp. 7-9; 38-39.)

HODGETTS, JOHN EDWIN The Liberal and the bureaucrat. A rose by any other name. By J. E. Hodgetts. (In *Queen's quarterly*. Kingston. v. 62 (1955), pp. [176]-183.)
Queries the possible connection between the long tenure in office of the Liberal Party and a growing Canadian bureaucracy.

HOWE, CLARENCE DECATUR Canada's trade policy. By Rt. Hon. C. D. Howe. (In *Public affairs*. Halifax. v. 12, no. 3 (spring 1950), pp. [9]-12.)

—— Preparedness and the Canadian economy. An address by Rt. Hon. C. D. Howe, Minister of Trade and Commerce. (In Empire Club of Canada. *Addresses.* Toronto. (1950/51), pp. 252-261.)

Address delivered February 26, 1951.

KNOTT, LEONARD Canada salesman. Romuald Bourque: Ottawa crusader. (In *Saturday night.* Toronto. v. 68, no. 4 (Nov. 1, 1952), p. 17.)

A biographical sketch.

LAPORTE, PIERRE Exposé du problème. (In *L'Action nationale.* Montréal. v. 44 déc. 1954 [i.e. jan. 1955]), pp. [426]-430.)

At head of title: Notre enquête 1955 [no] 1.

Comments on the attitude of Prime Minister Louis Saint-Laurent towards the province of Quebec.

LEMIEUX, EDMOND M. Abbott se confesse. (In *L'Action nationale.* Montréal. v. 41 (mai 1953), pp. [368]-379.)

LESAGE, JEAN Canadian resource policy. By the Hon. Jean Lesage, MP, Minister of Northern Affairs and National Resources, Ottawa. (In Empire Club of Canada. *Addresses.* Toronto. (1956/57), pp. 137-151.)

Address delivered December 13, 1956

LIGUE D'ACTION NATIONALE Les sophismes de Monsieur Saint-Laurent. (In *L'Action nationale.* Montréal. v. 44 (oct. [i.e. nov.] 1954), pp. [181]-187.)

—— Unissons-nous contre l'envahisseur! (In *L'Action nationale.* Montréal. v. 43 (mars/avril 1954), pp. [304]-313.)

MACKLIN, WILFRID HAROLD STEPHENSON The costly folly of our defence policy. By Major-Gen. W. H. S. Macklin. (In *Maclean's.* Toronto. v. 69, no. 4 (Feb. 18, 1956), pp. 20-[21]; 50-56.)

MAC LENNAN, HUGH Why I'm voting Liberal. (In *Maclean's.* Toronto. v. 66, no. 15 (Aug. 1, 1953), pp. 8; 50.)

Refers to the federal election held August 10, 1953.

MARTIN, PAUL JOSEPH JAMES A health programme for the Atlantic Provinces. By Hon. Paul Martin, Minister of National Health and Welfare. (In *The Atlantic advocate.* Fredericton, N.B. v. 47, no. 3 (Nov. 1956), pp 13-15.)

MICHENER, DANIEL ROLAND Parliament and centralization. The impact of Liberal longevity. By D. R. Michener. (In *Queen's*

quarterly. Kingston. v. 63 (1956), pp. [491]-502.)

MOORE, A. M. Budget decisions geared to employment level. (In *Saturday night.* Toronto. v. 70, no. 31 (May 14, 1955), pp. 55; 57.)

NATIONAL LIBERAL FEDERATION OF CANADA Liberal action for a greater Canada; speaker's handbook. Federal general election, 1957. [Ottawa, 1957] 384 p.

Issued also in French.

—— Le Parti libéral au pouvoir pour le plus grand bien du Canada. Guide de l'orateur, élection fédérale générale 1957. [Ottawa, 1957] 264 p.

Issued also in English.

The New Minister. (In *The Canadian forum.* Toronto. v. 28, no. 333 (Oct. 1948), p. [145].)

Concerns Lester B. Pearson, Minister of External Affairs.

O'HAGAN, RICHARD The N.B. Senator who doubles in spuds. Frederick William Pirie grows more potatoes than anyone in Canada, and is the biggest producer in his province's flourishing industry. (In *Saturday night.* Toronto. v. 68, no. 9 (Dec. 6, 1952), pp. 12; 37; 39.)

PERRY, J. HARVEY Defence is here to stay. The philosophy behind the budget. (In *Saturday night.* Toronto. v. 68, no. 17 (Jan. 31, 1953), pp. 12; 20.)

Persona grata. Blessed is the peacemaker. (In *Saturday night.* Toronto. v. 70, no. 48 (Jan. 7, 1956), pp. 9-10.)

A biographical sketch of Lester Bowles Pearson.

Persona grata. With halo or horns? (In *Saturday night.* Toronto. v. 70, no. 52 (Mar. 3, 1956), pp. 9-10.)

Concerns John Whitney Pickersgill.

RAHMEL, FERN Senator from the Island. (In *Saturday night.* Toronto. v. 70, no. 45 (Nov. 26, 1955), pp. 51-52.)

Concerns Florence Elsie Inman.

RICHARDSON, BURTON TAYLOR Ottawa view. The Pearson doctrine. Couchiching speech on control adds to Minister's stature. By B. T. Richardson. (In *Saturday night.* Toronto. v. 64, no. 47 (Aug. 30, 1949), p. 4.)

Brief comments on L. B. Pearson and other topics.

ROBERTS, LESLIE C. D.; The life and times of Clarence Decatur Howe. Toronto, Clarke, Irwin, 1957. 246 p.

—— Persona grata. Mr. Howe and Parliament. (In *Saturday night*. Toronto. v. 71, no. 10 (July 21, 1956), pp. 17-18.)
Concerns Clarence Decatur Howe.

—— The troubled Liberals. (In *Saturday night*. Toronto. v. 72, no. 3 (Feb. 2, 1957), pp. 5-6.)

ROSS, MARTIN Through troubled waters. Macdonald, Commons skipper. (In *Saturday night*. Toronto. v. 66, no. 45 (Aug. 14, 1951), pp. 8; 33.)
Concerns Hon. William Ross Macdonald.

ROSS, MARY LOWREY First Lady of the Senate. (In *Saturday night*. Toronto. v. 70, no. 33 (June 11, 1955), pp. 51-53.)
Concerns Cairine Reay Wilson. Called to the Senate, February 15, 1930.

SCLANDERS, IAN How the Prime Minister became Uncle Louis. (In *Maclean's*. Toronto. v. 68, no. 1 (Jan. 1, 1955), pp. 5-7; 41-43.)
Refers to Louis St. Laurent.

SHAW, STUART West holds balance of power. The Liberals are the only national party operating in the West. Their defeat might bring bloc government. (In *Saturday night*. Toronto. v. 71, no. 17 (Oct. 27, 1956), pp. 7-8.)

SMITH, HARRIET DUFF Mrs. Garson goes to Ottawa. (In *Saturday night*. Toronto. v. 64, no. 48 (Sept. 6, 1949), p. 17.)
Concerns Mrs. Stuart S. Garson (née Emily Topper).

STEVENSON, JOHN A. Ottawa letter. Civil service neutrality. (In *Saturday night*. Toronto. v. 68, no. 11 (Dec. 20, 1952), pp. 4-8.)
Concerns the presence of J. W. Pickersgill on a tour of the West made by Louis St. Laurent.

—— Ottawa letter. Wheat price and the cabinet. (In *Saturday night*. Toronto. v. 68, no. 16 (Jan. 24, 1953), pp. 4; 32.)

—— Ottawa letter. Policies and tactics. (In *Saturday night*. Toronto. v. 68, no. 19 (Feb. 14, 1953), pp. 4; 8.)
Discusses discontent within the Liberal Party.

—— Ottawa letter. Defensive battle for the Liberals. (In *Saturday night*. Toronto. v. 68, no. 24 (Mar. 21, 1953), pp. 16-17.)

—— Ottawa letter. Danger depends on the viewpoint. (In *Saturday night*. Toronto. v. 68, no. 27 (Apr. 11, 1953), pp. 14-15.)
Comments on Brooke Claxton and Canada's aerial defence program, etc.

—— Ottawa letter. Destruction of moral authority. (In *Saturday night*. Toronto. v. 68, no. 31 (May 9, 1953), pp. 14-15.)
Refers to the Liberal government.

—— Ottawa letter. Bitter dose of political medicine. (In *Saturday night*. Toronto. v. 68, no. 32 (May 16, 1953), p. 16.)
Comments on the resignation from the House of Commons of A. E. Dewar, etc.

—— Ottawa letter. Liberalism, agriculture and Mr. Gardiner. (In *Saturday night*. Toronto. v. 68, no. 36 (June 13, 1953), p. 16.)
Concerns a speech made by Hon. J. G. Gardiner on the CBC, May 26, 1953.

—— Ottawa letter. Prospects in Manitoba and Saskatchewan. (In *Saturday night*. Toronto. v. 68, no. 43 (Aug. 1, 1953), p. 10.)
Examines the status of the Liberal Party relating to the federal election held August 10, 1953.

—— Ottawa letter. The duties of ministers and generals. (In *Saturday night*. Toronto. v. 68, no. 51 (Sept. 26, 1953), pp. 10-11.)
Refers to Louis St. Laurent, Gen. Guy Simonds, and C. D. Howe.

—— Ottawa letter. Problems for the federal cabinet. (In *Saturday night*. Toronto. v. 69, no. 3 (Oct. 24, 1953), p. 16.)

—— Ottawa letter. Speakers, speeches and surpluses. (In *Saturday night*. Toronto. v. 69, no. 4 (Oct. 31, 1953), p. 9.)
Concerns the appointment of Wishart Robertson to the Speakership of the Senate and René Beaudoin to the Speakership of the House of Commons.

—— Ottawa letter. The varying moods of ministers. (In *Saturday night*. Toronto. v. 69, no. 6 (Nov. 14, 1953), pp. 16-17.)
Comments on the issue raised over the appointment of René Beaudoin to Speakership of the House of Commons.

—— Ottawa letter. Appointment displeases many Liberals. (In *Saturday night*. Toronto. v. 69, no. 17 (Jan. 30, 1954), p. 11.)
Comments on the appointment of Senator Ross Macdonald to the office of Solicitor-General.

—— Ottawa letter. The purpose of the Prime Minister's tour. (In *Saturday night*. Toronto. v. 69, no. 20 (Feb. 20, 1954), pp. 13-14.)

Comments on Louis St. Laurent's tour to foreign capitals. Also comments on federal expenditure estimates for fiscal year 1954/55.

—— Ottawa letter. Discontent among the Liberal members. (In *Saturday night*. Toronto. v. 69, no. 22 (Mar. 6, 1954), pp. 11-12.)

—— Ottawa letter. Budget inspires more sorrow than savagery. (In *Saturday night*. Toronto. v. 69, no. 30 (May 1, 1954), pp. 21-22.)

—— Ottawa letter. The troubles of party leaders. (In *Saturday night*. Toronto. v. 69, no. 35 (June 5, 1954), pp. 12-13.)

Comments on difficulties with Maurice Duplessis over taxation; cabinet re-organization, etc.

—— Ottawa letter. The chances in the cabinet. (In *Saturday night*. Toronto. v. 69, no. 41 (July 17, 1954), p. 12.)

Refers to the cabinet of Louis St. Laurent.

—— Ottawa letter. Sudden sweetness and light. (In *Saturday night*. Toronto. v. 70, no. 3 (Oct. 23, 1954), pp. 12-13.)

Discusses a meeting held between Louis St. Laurent and Maurice Duplessis in an attempt to settle differences.

—— Ottawa letter. A change of heart by the Prime Minister? (In *Saturday night*. Toronto. v. 70, no. 4 (Oct. 30, 1954), pp. 12-13.)

Refers to Louis St. Laurent.

—— Ottawa letter. The strategy of Mr. St. Laurent. (In *Saturday night*. Toronto. v. 70, no. 6 (Nov. 13, 1954), pp. 13-14.)

—— Ottawa letter. A new target for the opposition. (In *Saturday night*. Toronto. v. 70, no. 22 (Mar. 5, 1955), p. 12.)

Comments on Opposition attacks on J. W. Pickersgill.

—— Ottawa letter. Cabinet revolt on the pipeline. (In *Saturday night*. Toronto. v. 70, no. 26 (Apr. 2, 1955), pp. 11-12.)

Concerns the Trans-Canada Pipeline.

—— Ottawa letter. Thankfulness for small blessings. (In *Saturday night*. Toronto. v. 70, no. 29 (Apr. 23, 1955), pp. 16-17.)

Comments on the budget introduced by W. E. Harris.

—— Ottawa letter. Avoiding the big issue in the West. (In *Saturday night*. Toronto. v. 70, no. 41 (Oct. 1, 1955), pp. 13-14.)

Comments on a Western tour undertaken by Premier Louis St. Laurent.

—— Ottawa letter. The PM's troubles. (In *Saturday night*. Toronto. v. 70, no. 45 (Nov. 26, 1955), pp. 39-40.)

Refers to Louis St. Laurent.

—— Ottawa letter. Senile decay in the cabinet. (In *Saturday night*. Toronto. v. 70, no. 52 (Mar. 3, 1956), p. 13.)

Comments on the cabinet of Louis St. Laurent.

—— Ottawa letter. Howe as leader? (In *Saturday night*. Toronto. v. 72 [i.e. 71] no. 5 (May 12, 1956), pp. 31-32.)

—— Ottawa letter. Howe shows who's the boss. (In *Saturday night*. Toronto. v. 71, no. 6 (May 26, 1956), p. 18.)

Refers to C. D. Howe and the Trans-Canada Pipeline.

—— Ottawa letter. Murder of the 22nd parliament. (In *Saturday night*. Toronto. v. 71, no. 8 (June 23, 1956), p. 12.)

Cites, especially, the behaviour of Louis St. Laurent, C. D. Howe, and René Beaudoin.

—— Ottawa letter. Liberals' election problems. (In *Saturday night*. Toronto. v. 71, no. 10 (July 21, 1956), p. 12.)

—— Ottawa letter. More important than Parliament. (In *Saturday night*. Toronto. v. 71, no. 11 (Aug. 4, 1956), p. 12.)

Comments on the behaviour and resignation of René Beaudoin.

—— Ottawa letter. Liberals think of earlier election. (In *Saturday night*. Toronto. v. 72, no. 5 (Mar. 1957), p. 14.)

—— Ottawa letter. Liberal GOM and after. (In *Saturday night*. Toronto. v. 72, no. 8 (Apr. 13, 1957), pp. 8-10.)

Concerns the "Grand Old Man" of Liberalism: Louis St. Laurent. Relates to the federal election campaign of 1957.

—— Ottawa letter. PM's decline in the West. (In *Saturday night*. Toronto. v. 72, no. 11 (May 25, 1957), pp. 4-5.)

Refers to Louis St. Laurent and his tour of the West during the campaign for the federal election held June 10, 1957.

—— Ottawa letter. More modest Liberal victory? (In *Saturday night*. Toronto. v. 72, no. 12 (June 8, 1957), pp. 4-5.)

Assesses prospects for the Liberal Party in the general elections held June 10, 1957.

—— Ottawa letter. The St. Laurent record. (In *Saturday night*. Toronto. v. 72, no. 20 (Sept. 28, 1957), p. 6.)

Written on the occasion of the retirement from public life of Louis St. Laurent.

STEWART, WILLIAM The wife of Canada's Prime Minister. (In *Saturday night*. Toronto. v. 64, no. 34 (May 31, 1949), p. 23.)

Concerns Mme Jeanne St. Laurent (née Renault).

THOMSON, DALE C. Louis St. Laurent, Canadian. Toronto, Macmillan, 1967. x, 564 p.

"Published on the occasion of the Centennial of Canadian Confederation." – p. [1].

—— Louis St.-Laurent, Canadien. Traduction de F. Dufau-Labeyrie. Montréal. Cercle du Livre de France, 1968. 570 p.

Translation of *Louis St. Laurent; Canadian*. Toronto, Macmillan, 1967.

—— Louis Stephen St. Laurent; Eastern Township boy. (In *Journal of Canadian studies*. Peterborough, Ont. v. 1, no. 3 (1966), pp. 31-39.)

VIGEANT, PIERRE Les débuts de M. Saint-Laurent. (In *L'Action nationale*. Montréal. v. 33 (fév. 1949), pp. [106]-114.)

—— La prochaine convention libérale. (In *L'Action nationale*. Montréal. v. 31 (juin 1948), pp. [458]-465.)

WARD, NORMAN MC QUEEN The departure of C. D. Howe. By Norman Ward. (In *The Canadian forum*. Toronto. v. 37, no. 439 (Aug. 1957), pp. 105-106.)

1957–1968

ANDERSON, WILLIAM M. A business reaction to leaping government costs. (In *Canada month*. Montreal. v. 8, no. 1 (Jan. 1968), pp. 22-23.)

Criticizes the expenditures of the Liberal government.

ANGERS, FRANCOIS ALBERT Le nouveau programme du Parti libéral fédéral. Par F.-A. A. (In *L'Action nationale*. Montréal. v. 51, mars 1962), pp. [629]-633.)

The Atlantic Development Board and the Pearson government; editorial. (In *The Atlantic advocate*. Fredericton, N.B. v. 53, no. 9 (May 1963), pp. 14-15.)

AXWORTHY, TOM Innovation and the party system; an examination of the career of Walter L. Gordon and the Liberal Party. [Kingston, Ont.] 1970 [c1971] viii, 268 leaves.

Thesis (MA) – Queen's University.

BEAL, JOHN ROBINSON Pearson of Canada. New York, Duell, Sloan and Pearce [c1964] xi, 210 p.

"First edition."

Published in Canada under title: *The Pearson phenomenon*.

—— The Pearson phenomenon. Toronto, Longmans [c1964] xi, 210 p.

Published in the United States under title: *Pearson of Canada*.

—— Les trois vies de Pearson. Par John R. Beal. Traduit par Jean Marc Poliquin. Montréal, Editions de l'Homme [c1968] 269 p.

Translation of *The Pearson phenomenon*. Toronto, Longmans [c1964].

BECK, JAMES MURRAY The Pearson government after six months. By J. M. Beck. (In *Queen's quarterly*. Kingston. v. 70 (1963), pp. [465]-474.)

BLAIN, MAURICE Les colombes et le pouvoir politique; observations sur une hypothèse. (In *Cité libre*. Montréal. no. 28 (déc. 1965), pp. 7-12.)

"Les trois colombes": Jean Marchand, Gérard Pelletier et Pierre Elliott Trudeau.

BROADBENT, EDWARD JOHN The Liberal rip-off; Trudeauism vs. the politics of equality. By Ed. Broadbent. [Toronto] New Press, 1970. xi, 84 p.

CAMP, DALTON KINGSLEY A Tory looks at the Liberal convention. By Dalton K. Camp. (In *The Atlantic advocate*. Fredericton, N.B. v. 48, no. 6 (Feb. 1958), pp. 11-15.)

The Liberal Party leadership convention held in Ottawa January, 14-16, 1958.

CASSIDY, MICHAEL New deal for Canadian public transportation. (In *Commentator*. Toronto. v. 10, no. 10 (Oct. 1966), pp. 18-19.)

Comments on the transportation policy introduced for legislation by John W. Pickersgill.

CHAPIN, MIRIAM Quebec or French-Canada? (In *Saturday night*. Toronto. v. 75, no. 25 (Dec. 10, 1960), pp. 11-12.)

Suggests future implications may include Jean Lesage's bid to become leader of the federal Liberal Party.

CLARKE, PHYLLIS The Trudeau phenomenon. (In *Horizons*. Toronto. no. 27 (autumn 1968), pp. 7-10.)

COOK, GEORGE RAMSAY A new Liberal government? By R. C. (In *The Canadian forum*. Toronto. v. 43, no. 508 (May 1963), pp. [25]-26.)

Comments on the results, as they affected the Liberal Party, of the general elections held April 8, 1963.

—— Not right, not left, but forward. By Ramsay Cook. (In *The Canadian forum*. Toronto. v. 40, no. 481 (Feb. 1961), pp. [241]-242.)

Discusses the general policy and platform of the Liberal Party, as drawn up and presented at the Liberal rally held at Ottawa January 9-11, 1961.

COPPS, EDWIN The Liberal line in the new session. (In *Saturday night*. Toronto. v. 74, no. 2 (Jan. 17, 1959), pp. 10-11; 38.)

COURTNEY, JOHN CHILDS What do the Western Liberals want? (In *The Canadian forum*. Toronto. v. 46, no. 548 (Sept. 1966), pp. [121]-122.)

A report on the Saskatoon Conference held August 12-13, 1966, where delegates and observers from the four Western provinces met in an "attempt to examine the organization and policies of the federal Liberal Party".

COWAN, JOHN SCOTT The White Paper façade. (In *Commentator*. Toronto. v. 8, no. 10 (Oct. 1964), pp. 16-18.)

Comments on the White Paper on Defence, March 1964, issued by the Department of National Defence. Ottawa, Queen's Printer, 1964 (30 p.).

CRANE, DAVID Crime and politics. (In *Saturday night*. Toronto. v. 80, no. 11 (Nov. 1965), pp. 16-18; 20.)

Discusses corruption in political life with special reference to the Dorion report investigating the raising of bail for Lucien Rivard, which implicated members of the Liberal Party.

—— Will Liberals make free enterprise vs. socialism THE election issue? Where *is* the Liberal Party really headed? (In *Canada month*. Montreal. v.2, no. 6 (June 1962), pp. 15; 17.)

The general elections held June 18, 1962.

DAHRIN, RICHARD The media and the rise of P. E. Trudeau. (In *Canadian dimen-*

sion. Winnipeg. v. 5, no. 5 (June/July 1968), pp. 5-6.)

Editorial.

Defense—Hellyer. By D. L. C. (In *Canada month*. Montreal. v. 3, no. 7 (July 1963), pp. 12-13.)

DESBARATS, PETER Jean Lesage of Quebec. (In *The Canadian forum*. Toronto. v. 42, no. 501 (Oct. 1962), pp. 150-152.)

DEUTSCH, ANTAL Mr. Gordon's budget: an arm-chair view. (In *The Canadian forum*. Toronto. v. 45, no. 533 (June 1965), pp. 53-54.)

DEWAR, KEN Pierre Elliott Trudeau and the Liberal Party: continuity & change. (In *Canadian dimension*. Winnipeg. v. 5, no. 5 (June/July 1968), pp. 7-9.)

An historical and comparative analysis of the leadership of the Liberal Party.

DEXTER, SUSAN How Joe Greene figgers to keep 'em happy down on the farm. (In *Maclean's*. Toronto. v. 79, no. 8 (Apr. 16, 1966), pp. 22; 34-35.)

DIXON, BRIAN Sharp goes for freer trade. What the Trade Minister's bargaining at GATT will mean to business. (In *Canada month*. Montreal. v. 3, no. 12 (Dec. 1963), pp. 7-8.)

An interview with Mitchell Sharp, Minister of Trade and Commerce.

DOBBS, KILDARE National affairs. Hellyer and the admirals. (In *Saturday night*. Toronto. v. 81, no. 9 (Sept. 1966), p. 21.)

DORVAL, S. Attitude du gouvernement du Canada concernant l'immigration dans les années qui suivirent la guerre 1939-1945. [Québec, 1960] 1 v.

Thesis (MA) – Laval University.

Doug Connor's five-year fight against "pernicious political interference" in his business. (In *Canada month*. Montreal. v. 5, no. 6 (June 1965), pp. 9-10.)

Concerns an issue over a contract for government work. Involves C. M. Drury, J. W. Pickersgill, and G. J. McIlraith.

DOUPE, JACK H. The new Cabinet's plans and principles: industry—Bud Drury. By J. H. D. [i.e. Jack H. Doupe?] (In *Canada month*. Montreal. v. 3, no. 6 (June 1963), pp. 27-28.)

Charles M. Drury.

—— The new Cabinet's plans and principles: trade—Mitchell Sharp. By J. H. D. [i.e. Jack H. Doupe?] (In *Canada month*.

Montreal. v. 3, no. 7 (July 1963), pp. 11-12.)

—— The temptation toward Hon. Pierre Trudeau. (In *Canada month*. Montreal. v. 8, no. 4 (Apr. 1968), pp. 15-16.)

—— When separatism became respectable. (In *Canada month*. Montreal. v. 7, no. 10 (Oct. 1967), p. 27.)
Concerns the conflict in the Liberal Party over the "deux nations" concept. Cites the differences between federal Liberal Pierre Trudeau and Quebec Liberals.

EAYRS, JAMES The scrutable Canadian: Lester Pearson. (In Kilbourn, W. M. (ed.) *Canada; a guide to the peaceable kingdom*. Toronto, 1970. pp. 228-230.)

EDINBOROUGH, ARNOLD Pierre Elliott Trudeau. The leader tomorrow, by Arnold Edinborough. The man today, by Peter Desbarats. (In *Saturday night*. Toronto. v. 83, no. 3 (Mar. 1968), pp. [28-30].)

—— This month. The left wing must be clipped. (In *Saturday night*. Toronto. v. 78, no. 10 (Nov. 1963), p. 9.)
Refers to the "left wing" of the Liberal Party.

EDMONDS, ALAN Can Ralph Cowan defeat the French single-handed? A report on the Toronto MP who's become a one-man WASP backlash, and Ottawa's angriest man. (In *Maclean's*. Toronto. v. 80, no. 8 (Aug. 1967), pp. 30; 41-45.)

EMRYS, TREVOR Ottawa report. Liberal government studies the Hall Commission report on medicare. (In *Canadian dimension*. Winnipeg. v. 1, no. 8 (Sept./Oct. 1964), p. 4.)

FISHER, DOUGLAS MASON Trudeauism. By Douglas Fisher and Harry Crowe. (In *Canadian dimension*. Winnipeg. v. 5, no. 2-3 (Jan./Mar. 1968), pp. 18-19.)
Part 2 of The Constitutional crisis.
Describes the philosophy of federalism advocated by Pierre Elliott Trudeau.

—— Who is Jean Marchand? By Douglas Fisher. (In *Canadian dimension*. Winnipeg. v. 2, no. 6 (Sept./Oct. 1965), pp. 5; 9.)

FORSEY, EUGENE ALFRED The November election and redistribution. To call an election at this time, just before redistribution takes effect, was cheap politicking unworthy of a man of Prime Minister's stature. By Eugene Forsey. (In *Commen-*

tator. Toronto. v. 9, no. 10 (Oct. 1965), pp. 12-13.)
Criticizes the action of the Liberal Party.

FOURNIER, JEAN PIERRE Guy Favreau, Rouge à Ottawa. (In *Le Magazine Maclean*. Montréal. v. 4, no 9 (sept. 1964), pp. 17-19; 52-58.)

—— La vieille garde libérale croule. L'âge, les scandales et des réformes-clés en ont eu raison. Des hommes neufs s'apprêtent à prendre la relève. (In *Le Magazine Maclean*. Montréal. v. 5, no 10 (oct. 1965), pp. 15; 54-57.)

FOX, PAUL WESLEY The Liberals choose Trudeau—pragmatism at work. By Paul Fox. (In *The Canadian forum*. Toronto. v. 48, no. 568 (May 1968), pp. 27-28.)
Refers to the national Liberal leadership convention held at Ottawa April 4-6, 1968.

—— Liberals convene but can they convince? By P. W. F. (In *The Canadian forum*. Toronto. v. 37, no. 445 (Feb. 1958), pp. 241; 264.)
Comments on the fourth national convention of the Liberal Party held at Ottawa January 14-16, 1958.

FRASER, BLAIR Backstage at Ottawa. "Just wait until we're in opposition!" the Liberals always boasted. Well, let's see what they can do! (In *Maclean's*. Toronto. v. 70, no. 14 (July 6, 1957), p. 2.)

—— Backstage at Ottawa. The Liberals after St. Laurent. (In *Maclean's*. Toronto. v. 70, no. 20 (Sept. 28, 1957), p. 2.)

—— Backstage at Ottawa. Questions the Liberals wish they'd never asked. (In *Maclean's*. Toronto. v. 70, no. 25 (Dec. 7, 1957), p. 2.)

—— Backstage at Ottawa. Why there's new zest on the Opposition benches. (In *Maclean's*. Toronto. v. 71, no. 1 (Jan. 4, 1958), p. 2.)

—— Backstage at Ottawa. Liberal dilemma: hang on or topple the Tories? (In *Maclean's*. Toronto. v. 71, no. 3 (Feb. 1, 1958), p. 2.)

—— Backstage in the campaign. Pearson likes tough questions—and has them. (In *Maclean's*. Toronto. v. 71, no. 7 (Mar. 29, 1958), p. 2.)
Relates to the federal election held March 31, 1958.

—— Backstage at Ottawa. Can the Liberals muster enough snipers? (In *Maclean's*. Toronto. v. 71, no. 11 (May 24, 1958), p. 2.)

—— Backstage at Ottawa. What chances for a Liberal comeback? (In *Maclean's*. Toronto. v. 71, no. 26 (Dec. 20, 1958), p. 2.)

—— Backstage at Ottawa. Can the Liberal Gulliver get back on his feet? Leaders are lacking but funds are swelling. (In *Maclean's*. Toronto. v. 72, no. 25 (Dec. 5, 1959), p. 2.)

—— Backstage in Ottawa. Why the CBC won't let you see the film about Mike Pearson, human being. (In *Maclean's*. Toronto. v. 77, no. 13 (July 4, 1964), p. 2.)
Concerns the film "Mr. Pearson" directed by Richard Ballentine.

—— Backstage in Ottawa. How Walter Gordon has recovered from Parliament's biggest pratfall. (In *Maclean's*. Toronto. v. 77, no. 14 (July 25, 1964), pp. 2-3.)

—— Backstage in Ottawa. Why the Liberals fear a fall election—even though they'd gain seats. (In *Maclean's*. Toronto. v. 77, no. 15 (Aug. 8, 1964), pp. 1-3.)

—— Backstage at Ottawa. Now who's keeping Lester B. Pearson in power? Why, John G. Diefenbaker—almost single-handed. (In *Maclean's*. Toronto. v. 78, no. 2 (Jan. 23, 1965), p. 1.)

—— Backstage at Ottawa. How the scandals could tie Pearson's hands as he tries to shuffle his cabinet. (In *Maclean's*. Toronto. v. 78, no. 3 (Feb. 6, 1965), pp. 1-2.)

—— Backstage at Ottawa. An election soon? Yes—if Mike gets a push. (In *Maclean's*. Toronto. v. 78, no. 10 (May 15, 1965), p. 1.)

—— Backstage in Ottawa. The Liberal "cleanup" in Quebec: how the Old Guard still hang on. (In *Maclean's*. Toronto. v. 78, no. 12 (June 19, 1965), pp. 3-4.)

—— Backstage at Ottawa. How to make speeches and alienate farmers. (In *Maclean's*. Toronto. v. 78, no. 14 (July 24, 1965), p. 1.)
Concerns Maurice Sauvé while Minister of Forestry.

—— Backstage at Ottawa. If Lesage wins friends out West, will he wind up in federal politics? (In *Maclean's*. Toronto. v. 78, no. 19 (Oct. 2, 1965), pp. 1-2.)

—— Backstage at Ottawa. Exit Gordon, nobly: a hard act to follow. (In *Maclean's*. Toronto, v. 78, no. 24 (Dec. 15, 1965), pp. 1-2.)
Concerns Walter Gordon.

—— Backstage at Ottawa. John Turner's a minister without a portfolio but with a bright future. (In *Maclean's*. Toronto. v. 79, no. 2 (Jan. 22, 1966), pp. 3-4.)

—— Backstage at Ottawa. How Quebec's three wise men have laid their careers on the line. (In *Maclean's*. Toronto. v. 79, no. 9 (May 2, 1966), pp. 1-2.)
Concerns Pierre Elliott Trudeau, Jean Marchand and Gérard Pelletier.

—— Backstage at Ottawa. The Liberals have a Cowan quandary. He's a nuisance but he's Grit to the core. (In *Maclean's*. Toronto. v. 79, no. 11 (June 4, 1966), pp. 2-3.)
Concerns Ralph Cowan.

—— Backstage at Ottawa. With Lesage gone, it's easier for Ottawa to say no to Quebec's demands. (In *Maclean's*. Toronto. v. 79, no. 13 (July 2, 1966), pp. 1-2.)

—— Backstage at Ottawa. Defense assistant Bill Lee may talk out of turn—but at least he talks. (In *Maclean's*. Toronto. v. 79, no. 18 (Sept. 17, 1966), pp. 2-3.)
Concerns Defense Minister Paul Hellyer's executive assistant, Group Captain William Maurice Lee.

—— Backstage at Ottawa. Why Sudbury really shook the Liberals. The NDP's by-election gain could mean another general election early next year. (In *Maclean's*. Toronto. v. 80, no. 7 (July 1967), pp. 2-3.)
Concerns the federal by-election won by M. B. Germa in Sudbury, Ont., May 29, 1967.

—— Backstage in Ottawa. Why Liberals almost wish Dief was back. (In *Maclean's*. Toronto. v. 80, no. 12 (Dec. 1967), pp. 6-7.)

—— Backstage in Ottawa. How some Grits managed to keep their cool. (In *Maclean's*. Toronto. v. 81, no. 4 (Apr. 1968), p. 2.)
Comments on the Liberal leadership campaign.

—— Can an ex-private bring common sense to our defense policy? (In *Maclean's*. Toronto. v. 77, no. 2 (Jan. 25, 1964), pp. 12-13; 35-37.)
Concerns Paul Hellyer.

—— Favreau, Pearson and a sick feeling inside. (In *Maclean's*. Toronto. v. 78, no. 1 (Jan. 2, 1965), p. 2.)

—— How Lesage unsettled the West. (In *Maclean's*. Toronto. v. 78, no. 22 (Nov. 15, 1965), pp. [16-17]; 56-58.)

—— Rise of a soft-spoken strong man. (In *Maclean's.* Toronto. v. 76, no. 23 (Dec. 2, 1963), pp. 11; 66-72.)
Concerns Mitchell W. Sharp.

—— The Sharp/Gordon debate. (In *Maclean's.* Toronto. v. 79, no. 14 (July 23, 1966), pp. 8-9; 36-38.)
An analysis of the positions taken within the Liberal Party by Mitchell Sharp and Walter Gordon.

—— The sudden rise of Pierre Elliott Trudeau. (In *Maclean's.* Toronto. v. 81, no. 4 (Apr. 1968), pp. [24]; 62; 65-68.)

—— The Three: Quebec's new face in Ottawa. (In *Maclean's.* Toronto. v. 79, no. 2 (Jan. 22, 1966), pp. 16-17; 37-38.)
Concerns Pierre Elliott Trudeau, Jean Marchand, and Gérard Pelletier.

—— What Pearson won by losing. (In *Maclean's.* Toronto. v. 75, no. 15 (July 28, 1962), pp. 9; 39-40.)
An analysis of the results of the general elections held June 18, 1962.

—— Your guide to the new split-level cabinet. (In *Maclean's.* Toronto. v. 77, no. 7 (Apr. 4, 1964), pp. 18-19; 30-34.)
The cabinet of Lester B. Pearson.

FULFORD, ROBERT Lester B. Pearson. (In *Maclean's.* Toronto. v. 76, no. 7 (Apr. 6, 1963), pp. 13-15; 50-56.)

GELLNER, JOHN A short guide through the White Paper. (In *Commentator.* Toronto. v. 8, no. 5 (May 1964), pp. 5-8.)
Examines the "White Paper on Defence which Hon. Paul Hellyer tabled in the Commons on March 26" 1964.

GONICK, C. W. Pierre Elliott Trudeau and "the new politics". By C. W. G. (In *Canadian dimension.* Winnipeg. v. 5, no. 4 (Apr./May 1968), pp. 3-4.)
Editorial.

GREENE, JOHN JAMES The Liberal tomorrow. By J. J. Greene [Ottawa, Accurate Print. Service, 1968] 86 p.
Cover title.
With an introduction by Emmett O'Grady.

GWYN, RICHARD J. The new Pearson and his brains trust. (In *Saturday night.* Toronto. v. 75, no. 19 (Sept. 17, 1960), pp. 12-14.)
"Political fall fair."

—— The shape of scandal; a study of a government in crisis. Toronto, Clarke, Irwin, 1965. 248 p.

An analysis concerning the "scandals which plagued the government of Lester Pearson from November 1964 until July 1965 . . . ." – Author's note.

GZOWSKI, PETER Un capitaliste socialisant: Pierre-Elliott Trudeau. (In *Le Magazine Maclean.* Montréal. v. 2, no 3 (mars 1962), pp. 25; 52-55.)

—— The new women in politics. (In *Maclean's.* Toronto. v. 75, no. 8 (Apr. 21, 1962), pp. 30-31; 52-54.)
Concerns July LaMarsh and Pauline Jewett.

—— Portrait of an intellectual in action. (In *Maclean's.* Toronto. v. 75, no. 4 (Feb. 24, 1962), pp. 23; 29-30.)
Concerns Pierre Elliott Trudeau.

HAGGART, RON The virtues of minority government. (In *Canadian dimension.* Winnipeg. v. 2, no. 2 (Jan./Feb. 1965), pp. 5; 22.)
Concerns the Liberal government under Lester Pearson.

HARBRON, JOHN DAVISON This is Trudeau. By John D. Harbron. [Don Mills, Ont., Longmans Canada, c1968] 119 p.
Concerns Pierre Elliott Trudeau.

HELLYER, PAUL THEODORE The Liberal Party and national defence. NATO, yes; NORAD, perhaps. By Paul T. Hellyer. (In *Canadian commentator.* Toronto. v. 5, no. 4 (Apr. 1961), pp. 5-6; 9.)

—— Unification: the Defence Minister reports. By Hon. Paul Hellyer. (In *Canada month.* Montreal. v. 6, no. 11 (Nov. 1966), pp. 10-13.)

Hellyer's defense plans are good business, too. Cutting defense costs means Canada will have more money for new equipment. (In *Canada month.* Montreal. v. 4, no. 9 (Sept. 1964), p. 16.)

HOCKIN, THOMAS ALEXANDER In the federal cabinet: French Canada on the up and up. By Thomas Hockin. (In *Commentator.* Toronto. v. 11, no. 5 (May 1967), pp. 22-24.)
Examines the significance of the federal cabinet formed April 4, 1967, by Lester Pearson in which French Canadians from Quebec held 10 out of 27 posts.

—— Mr. Hellyer and his critics. By Thomas Hockin. (In *Commentator.* Toronto. v. 11, no. 3 (Mar. 1967), pp. 22-25.)
Discusses the policy for the unification of the armed forces.

—— Off and running. By Thomas A. Hockin. (In *The Canadian forum*. Toronto. v. 47, no. 565 (Feb. 1968), pp. [241]-243.)

Examines the implications of the national Liberal leadership convention held April 4-6, 1968.

—— Retrograde in power. By Thomas Hockin. (In *The Canadian forum*. Toronto. v. 48, no. 575 (Dec. 1968), pp. 194-195.)

Discusses the significance of the Pearson years in a review article of *The distemper of our times; Canadian politics in transition, 1963-1968*, by P. C. Newman. Toronto, McClelland and Stewart, c1968.

HOOD, WILLIAM C.   Recent federal economic policy in Canada. By Wm. C. Hood. (In *Queen's quarterly*. Kingston. v. 71 (1964), pp. [16]-30.)

Concerns the policy of the Liberal Party government.

HOROWITZ, GAD   The Trudeau doctrine. (In *Canadian dimension*. Winnipeg. v. 5, no. 5 (June/July 1968), pp. 9-11.)

A critical presentation of the political thought of P. E. Trudeau.

—— Trudeau vs. Trudeauism. (In *The Canadian forum*. Toronto. v. 48, no. 568 (May 1968), pp. 29-30.)

HUNTER, G. D.   What price interregnum? The Liberal performance. (In *Canadian dimension*. Winnipeg. [v. 1, no. 3] (Dec./Jan. 1963/64), pp. 18-20.)

Assesses the achievement of the Liberal government under Lester Pearson.

HUTCHISON, BRUCE   A day with Brock Chisholm: another incredible Canadian. (In *Maclean's*. Toronto. v. 74, no. 18 (Sept. 9, 1961), pp. 20; 45-50.)

"INSIDE OTTAWA"   Pearson's desperate gamble for Quebec. Trying to satisfy Quebec's demands endangers the Prime Minister's English-Canadian support—but he's playing for the highest stakes. By "Inside Ottawa". (In *Commentator*. Toronto. v. 7, no. 6 (June 1963), pp. 2-3.)

IRVINE, RUSSELL B.   Commons comment. (In *The Canadian forum*. Toronto. v. 43, no. 511 (Aug. 1963), pp. 102-103.)

A critical discussion of the budgetary decisions of Walter Gordon, Minister of Finance.

—— Commons comment. (In *The Canadian forum*. Toronto. v. 43, no. 515 (Dec. 1963), pp. 198-199.)

Comments on the behaviour of the Liberal government when legislating the Canada Pension Plan and the Canada Development Corporation.

IRVINE, WILLIAM PETER   The federal Liberal Party and the new Quebec; a study in national unity. [Kingston, 1964] iv, 136 leaves.

Thesis (MA) – Queen's University.

—— The federal Liberal Party and the new Quebec; a study in national unity. By W. P. Irvine. [Kingston, Ont.] Queen's University [n.d.] 136 p. (Queen's political studies, 1.)

Cover title.

Reprint of the Author's thesis (MA) – Queen's University, 1964.

"This study traces the degree of success with which the Liberal Party has appealed to certain groups in Quebec society" through the federal elections of 1957, 1958 and 1962.

JACKSON, JAMES   Mr. Hellyer and the officers. Why unification is not the issue. (In *Saturday night*. Toronto. v. 82, no. 4 (Apr. 1967), pp. 23-25.)

JAMES, MUNGO   Shake the hand that ends the arm that once held Princess Margaret. John Turner: the dreamboat politician. (In *Saturday night*. Toronto. v. 80 [i.e. 81] no. 5 (May 1966), pp. 33-35.)

JEWETT, PAULINE MAE   Clarence Decatur Howe By Pauline Jewett. (In *The Canadian forum*. Toronto. v. 37, no. 440 (Sept. 1957), pp. 126-127.)

KETTLE, JOHN   Defence Minister Hellyer: clear-sighted businessman and parliamentary prodigy who's unifying the Army, Navy, and Air Force. (In *Canada month*. Montreal. v. 5, no. 6 (June 1965), pp. [12]-14.)

"A CM profile."

—— Hon. Jean Marchand, the Minister of Manpower and Immigration (In *Canada month*. Montreal. v. 7, no. 1 (Jan. 1967), pp. 14-18.)

A *Canada month* profile.

—— Hon. Mitchell Sharp, the Minister of Finance. (In *Canada month*. Montreal. v. 7, no. 2 (Feb. 1967), pp. 12-17.)

A *Canada month* profile.

—— John R. Nicholson of Labour. (In *Canada month*. Montreal. v. 6, no. 8 (Aug. 1966), pp. 18-23.)

A *Canada month* profile.

—— Liberal—NDP merger: the facts. (In *Canada month*. Montreal. v. 4, no. 2 (Feb. 1964), pp. 10-11.)

A telephone interview with Keith Davey, national organizer of the Liberal Party.

—— Manpower's Deputy Minister Tom Kent: the philosopher of welfarism who helped mould today's Liberal Party. (In *Canada month*. Montreal. v. 6, no. 2 (Feb. 1966), pp. 14-20.)

—— Minister of a workless future. Hon. Allan J. MacEachen, National Health & Welfare. (In *Canada month*. Montreal. v. 7, no. 5 (May 1967), pp. 12-15.)

A *Canada month* profile.

—— The new Liberal idea—is it collectivism? (In *Canada month*. Montreal. v. 3, no. 8 [i.e. 9] (Sept. 1963), pp. 22-27.)

Discusses the ideology and program of the Liberal Party with Pauline Jewett and Jack Davis.

—— Paul Hellyer. (In *Canada month*. Montreal. v. 8, no. 4 (Apr. 1968), pp. 11-14.)

A *Canada month* profile.

—— Registrar General, Hon. John Turner. (In *Canada month*. Montreal. v. 7, no. 10 (Oct. 1967), pp. 14-19.)

A *Canada month* profile.

LA MARSH, JULIA VERLYN   Memoirs of a bird in a gilded cage. By Judy LaMarsh. Toronto, McClelland and Stewart [c1969] 367 p.

LA PIERRE, LAURIER JOSEPH LUCIEN   Quebec Liberals: changing of the guard? (In *Canadian forum*. Toronto. v. 45, no. 535 (Aug. 1965), pp. [97]-100.)

Analyses the changing developments within the Quebec wing of the federal Liberal Party.

LAUZON, ADELE   Gérard Pelletier: des ennemis à la douzaine. (In *Le Magazine Maclean*. Montréal. v. 4, no 11 (nov. 1964), pp. 24; 60-66.)

—— Jean Marchand est-il perdue pour les ouvriers? Après 23 ans de luttes syndicales, le président de la C. S. N. démissionne. Pourquoi? (In *Le Magazine Maclean*. Montréal. v. 5, no 9 (sept. 1965), pp. 18; 32-38.)

LE DUC, LAWRENCE   Ballot behaviour in a national convention. A research report on the leadership selection process in Canada based on a study of the 1968 Liberal convention. [n.p. 1970?] 36, [3], 16 leaves.

(In *Canadian Political Science Association. Papers presented at the annual meeting*. Kingston. 42d (1970), v. 2, pt. 20.)

Reproduced typescript.

LIBERAL PARTY (CANADA) NATIONAL CONVENTION, 4TH, OTTAWA, 1958   Liberal Convention resolutions affecting the Atlantic Provinces. (In *The Atlantic advocate*. Fredericton, N.B. v. 48, no. 6 (Feb. 1958), p. 18.)

Text of the Atlantic Provinces and Fisheries Resolutions accepted at the Liberal Party convention held in Ottawa, January 14-16, 1958.

—— New statements of Liberal policy, 1958, for a greater Canada; resolutions adopted. [Ottawa, 1958] 48 p.

Convention held in Ottawa, January 14-16, 1958.

Issued also in French.

—— Nouvel exposé de la politique libérale, 1958, pour le plus grand bien du Canada; texte des résolutions adoptées. [Ottawa, 1958] 48 p.

Convention held in Ottawa, January 14-16, 1958.

Issued also in English.

—— Report of the proceedings of the National Liberal Convention. Called by the National Liberal Federation of Canada, at the request of Rt. Hon. Louis St. Laurent... [Ottawa, National Liberal Federation of Canada, 1966?] 25, xvi, 268 p.

A "verabatim transcript of the 4th National Liberal Convention" held Tuesday, Wednesday, Thursday, January 14th, 15th, 16th, 1958, at the Coliseum, Ottawa, Canada.

"First edition."

Editors' note dated Sept. 1961.

LONG, MARCUS   The Liberal crisis. (In *Canadian commentator*. Toronto. v. 1, no. 9 (Sept. 1957), pp. [1]-2.)

Considers Lester B. Pearson as the candidate most suitable for leadership of the Liberal Party.

LOWER, ARTHUR REGINALD MARSDEN   Beginning of a new political era. By Arthur Lower. (In *Canadian commentator*. Toronto. v. 2, no. 5 (May 1958), pp. 3-4.)

Examines the state of the Liberal Party after the general elections held in June 1957 and March 1958.

—— Pearson and the mantle of Laurier. By Arthur Lower. (In *Canadian commentator*. Toronto. v. 2, no. 2 (Feb. 1958), p. 3.)

MAC EACHEN, ALLAN JOSEPH "The Freed-man report on railway run-throughs." By the Honourable Allan J. MacEachen. (In *The Journal of liberal thought.* [Ottawa. v.] 2, no. 2 (spring 1966), pp. 97-102.)

Comments on the Report of the Industrial Inquiry Commission on Canadian National Railway "Run-throughs". Ottawa, 1965. The Honourable Mr. Justice Samuel Freedman, commissioner.

—— The future of redistribution of income by governments. By Hon. Allan J. MacEachen. (In *Canada month.* Montreal. v. 8, no. 3 (Mar. 1968), pp. 21-23.)

MC LEOD, JOHN TENNYSON Moses with a maple-leaf. One man's view of Walter Gordon. By John T. McLeod. (In *Saturday night.* Toronto. v. 81, no. 7 (July 1966), pp. 21-24.)

MC LUHAN, MARSHALL The man in the mask: Pierre Trudeau. (In Kilbourn, W. M. (ed.) *Canada; a guide to the peaceable kingdom.* Toronto, 1970. pp. 225-227.)

MC NAUGHT, KENNETH WILLIAM KIRKPAT-RICK National affairs. By Kenneth Mc-Naught. (In *Saturday night.* Toronto. v. 80, no. 10 (Oct. 1965), pp. 11-16.)

Discusses differences between the political approach of Mackenzie King and Lester Pearson.

—— National affairs. No millionaires on the left. By Kenneth McNaught. (In *Saturday night.* Toronto. v. 83, no. 1 (Jan. 1968), pp. 7-8.)

Discusses the ideas and political activities of Eric Kierans.

—— Pearson: caution and compromise everywhere. By Kenneth McNaught. (In *Saturday night.* Toronto. v. 80, no. 6 (June 1965), pp. 21-[23].)

The pattern of North American leadership, II.

Marchand, Pelletier, Trudeau et le 8 novembre. [L'équipe de rédaction de Cité libre. Jean Pellerin, Maurice Blain, Jacques Tremblay, Charles Taylor.] (In *Cité libre.* Montréal. no. 80 (oct. 1965), pp. [1]-3.)

Relates to the general elections held November 8, 1965.

A Matter of image. (In *Maclean's.* Toronto. v. 81, no. 3 (Mar. 1968), pp. 34-35.)

Maclean's magazine chose four leading Liberals and asked five image makers and marketing experts to comment and advise on the public appeal of these politicians:

Paul Hellyer, Eric Kierans, Paul Martin, Mitchell Sharp.

MOON, ROBERT JAMES Pearson. [Hull, Que., High Hill Pub. House, c1963] 60 p.

Cover title: Pearson: confrontation years against Diefenbaker.

Series of articles, first published in the *Regina Leader-post* and the *Saskatoon Star-phoenix*, on the political career of Lester Bowles Pearson.

MOORE, ELLEN Man's right to life and freedom. (In *Canada month.* Montreal. v. 9, no. 3 (Mar. 1969), pp. 23-24.)

Discusses the concept of a "just society" as advocated by Pierre Elliott Trudeau.

—— The morality of dictatorship. (In *Canada month.* Montreal. v. 7, no. 11 (Nov. 1967), pp. 20-22.)

Responds to views expressed by Hon. Allan MacEachen in the article, Minister of a workless future, by J. Kettle [In *Canada month.* Montreal. v. 7, no. 5 (May 1967), pp. 12-15.]

MORRIS, LESLIE TOM Liberal plans and you. [Toronto, Published by Progress Books for the Communist Party of Canada, 1963] 23 p.

Cover title.

The New Cabinet's plans and principles. Paul Martin. By D. L. C. (In *Canada month.* Montreal. v. 3, no. 7 [i.e. 8] (Aug. 1963), pp. 11-12.)

NEWMAN, CHRISTINA (MC CALL) Ottawa letter. The inglorious end of an era. By Christina Newman. (In *Saturday night.* Toronto. v. 83, no. 2 (Feb. 1968), pp. 9-10.)

An evaluation of the era of Lester B. Pearson.

—— Ottawa letter. "This was a very clever plan focussed on making one feel that an anti-Trudeau vote was a vote against the future of Canada." By Christina Newman. (In *Saturday night.* Toronto. v. 83, no. 5 (May 1968), pp. 7; 9; 12.)

Analyses the selection of Pierre Elliott Trudeau as leader of the Liberal Party at the National Liberal Convention held at Ottawa April 4-6, 1968.

NEWMAN, PETER CHARLES Backstage at Ottawa. The man behind the party's new Mike Pearson—he's still a diplomat in politics. By Peter C. Newman. (In *Maclean's.* Toronto. v. 73, no. 22 (Oct. 22, 1960), p. 2.)

—— Backstage at Ottawa. How the Tories trust a Liberal braintruster's brains. By Peter C. Newman. (In *Maclean's*. Toronto. v. 74, no. 2 (Jan. 28, 1961), p. 52.)
Concerns Walter Gordon.

—— Backstage at Ottawa. Louis St. Laurent today: the Liberals' patron saint. By Peter C. Newman. (In *Maclean's*. Toronto. v. 74, no. 7 (Apr. 8, 1961), p. 70.)

—— Backstage at Ottawa. Yes, there is a new Mike Pearson; now he wants to be Prime Minister. By Peter C. Newman. (In *Maclean's*. Toronto. v. 74, no. 17 (Aug. 26, 1961), p. 50.)

—— Backstage in Ottawa. The winter book on prospects for a Liberal cabinet. By Peter C. Newman. (In *Maclean's*. Toronto. v. 75, no. 5 (Mar. 10, 1962), p. 52.)
Considers personnel for a cabinet under a Liberal Party administration.

—— Backstage in Ottawa. The stakes in Quebec: if Lesage loses, so does Pearson. By Peter C. Newman. (In *Maclean's*. Toronto. v. 75, no. 22 (Nov. 3, 1962), pp. 1-2.)

—— Backstage in Ottawa. The Drury approach to defense: stop fighting World War II. By Peter C. Newman. (In *Maclean's*. Toronto. v. 75, no. 24 (Dec. 1, 1962), pp 1-2.)
Concerns the views on defense policy advocated by C. M. Drury, Liberal MP for St. Antoine–Westmount, Que.

—— Backstage in Ottawa. Pearson can stop Caouette—but only if he finds a fighting Quebecker. By Peter C. Newman. (In *Maclean's*. Toronto. v. 76, no. 3 (Feb. 9, 1963), p. 2.)
Refers to Réal Caouette, leader of the Social Credit Party in Quebec.

—— Backstage with Peter C. Newman; a special page on the campaign. The Liberal plan: 100 days to get the country rolling. A reporter's election diary: two tough fights and a few wild promises. (In *Maclean's*. Toronto. v. 76, no. 6 (Mar. 23, 1963), p. [1].)
Relates to the general elections held April 8, 1963.

—— Backstage in Ottawa. The cabinet's problem: keep civil servants in their place. By Peter C. Newman. (In *Maclean's*. Toronto. v. 76, no. 11 (June 1, 1963), pp. 2-3.)
The cabinet of Lester Pearson.

—— Backstage in Ottawa. The Liberal program runs right down the middle of C. D. Howe's road. By Peter C. Newman. (In *Maclean's*. Toronto. v. 76, no. 12 (June 15, 1963), pp. 1-2.)

—— Backstage in Ottawa. The centre of power in the cabinet is now shifting toward the right. By Peter C. Newman. (In *Maclean's*. Toronto. v. 76, no. 14 (July 27, 1963), pp. 1-2.)
The cabinet of Lester Pearson.

—— Backstage in Ottawa. If there's a statesman who can save Confederation, Pearson can't find him. By Peter C. Newman. (In *Maclean's*. Toronto. v. 76, no. 15 (Aug. 10, 1963), p. 2.)

—— Backstage in Ottawa. Guy Favreau: a new Liberal heavyweight and a new kind of Immigration Minister. By Peter C. Newman. (In *Maclean's*. Toronto. v. 76, no. 16 (Aug. 24, 1963), pp. 1-2.)

—— Backstage in Ottawa. Bud Drury's new orders: back industry, beat unemployment, save the nation. By Peter C. Newman. (In *Maclean's*. Toronto. v. 76, no. 17 (Sept. 7, 1963), p. 2.)

—— Backstage in Ottawa. Paul Hellyer proves he's no patsy for the armed forces. By Peter C. Newman. (In *Maclean's*. Toronto. v. 76, no. 19 (Oct. 5, 1963), pp. 5-6.)

—— Backstage in Ottawa. The Liberals are courteous, chummy and—already—very, very cocky. (In *Maclean's*. Toronto. v. 76, no. 20 (Oct. 19, 1963), pp. 1-2.)

—— Backstage in Ottawa. The most dangerous caucus in Liberal history may still save the Liberals. By Peter C. Newman. (In *Maclean's*. Toronto. v. 76, no. 21 (Nov. 2, 1963), pp. 1-2.)

—— Jack Pickersgill's third contentious life on Parliament Hill. By Peter C. Newman. (In *Maclean's*. Toronto. v. 73, no. 22 (Oct. 22, 1960), pp. 20-21; 59; 62-63.)

—— Lesage: Why Quebec's Premier holds the key to Canada's future. By Peter C. Newman. (In *Maclean's*. Toronto. v. 76, no. 11 (June 1, 1963), pp. 13-15; 54-59.)

—— National affairs. Pearson's—and Canada's—one chance: a kind of federalism we've never known. By Peter C. Newman. (In *Maclean's*. Toronto. v. 76, no. 24 (Dec. 14, 1963), p. 2.)
Concerns federal-provincial relations.

—— National affairs. Despite the budget, Gordon is still an economic nationalist—and the cabinet is still with him. (In *Maclean's*. Toronto. v. 77, no. 8 (Apr. 18, 1964), pp. 4-5.)

Refers to Walter Gordon.

—— National affairs. The grey, quiet failure of the Liberal administration. By Peter C. Newman. (In *Maclean's*. Toronto. v. 77, no. 13 (July 4, 1964), pp. 3-4.)

—— National affairs. Maurice Sauvé; the Liberals' leading Liberal-fighter. (In *Maclean's*. Toronto. v. 77, no. 15 (Aug. 8, 1964), pp. 3-4.)

—— What really happened to Walter Gordon. By Peter C. Newman. (In *Maclean's*. Toronto. v. 76, no. 20 (Oct. 19, 1963), pp. 22; 76-79.)

O'NEIL, PIERRE C. Why Trudeau won. (In *Commentator*. Toronto. v. 12, no. 5 (May 1968), pp. 9-12.)

Analyses the outcome of the National Liberal Convention which chose Pierre Elliott Trudeau as leader on April 6, 1968.

PATRICK, STEPHEN Ralph Cowan, MP: individualist and welfarist all in one fiery package. (In *Canada month*. Montreal. v. 5, no. 12 (Dec. 1965), pp. 22-23.)

PEARSON, LESTER BOWLES Canadian unity. An address by the Right Honourable Lester B. Pearson. (In Empire Club of Canada. *Addresses*. Toronto. (1964/65), pp. [35]-46.)

Address delivered October 15, 1964.

—— Le citoyen Pearson. (In *Le Magazine Maclean*. Montréal. v. 7, no 7 (juil. 1967), pp. 28; 45-51.)

Interview conducted by Alexander Ross for *Maclean's* magazine. Adapted for *Le Magazine Maclean* by Massue Belleau.

—— The Liberal platform. Tested principles and policies. By the Hon. Lester B. Pearson. (In *Saturday night*. Toronto. v. 77, no. 11 (May 26, 1962), pp. 16-17.)

—— The long, happy life of Lester Pearson. An intimate interview with Alexander Ross. (In *Maclean's*. Toronto. v. 80, no. 7 (July 1967), pp. 11; 48; 50-55.)

—— A national purpose. An address by the Right Honourable Lester B. Pearson. (In Empire Club of Canada. *Addresses*. [Don Mills, Ont.] (1963/64), pp. [17]-27.)

Address delivered October 10, 1963.

—— A new kind of peace force. A proposal by Lester B. Pearson. (In *Maclean's*. Toronto. v. 77, no. 9 (May 2, 1964), pp. 9-11.)

—— Straight talk from Mike Pearson. The man who speaks for Canada abroad says bluntly in this exclusive tape-recorded interview for Maclean's that we won't be anybody's satellite. Here's our foreign policy, nailed down plank by plank. (In *Maclean's*. Toronto. v. 62, no. 20 (Oct. 15, 1949), pp. 8-9; 62-67.)

"Interview . . . between the Minister of External Affairs, Hon. Lester Bowles Pearson, OBE, and Arthur Irwin . . . and Blair Fraser . . . ."

—— "What I will do when I form a government." By Lester B. Pearson. (In *The Canadian Saturday night*. Toronto. v. 78, no. 4 (Apr. 1963), pp. 10; 36.)

Relates to the federal election held April 8, 1963.

PELLERIN, JEAN Pearson; prisonnier de la droite. Par. J. P. (In *Cité libre*. Montréal. no. 82 (déc. 1965), pp. 1-4.)

PICKERSGILL, JOHN WHITNEY The future of Liberalism in Canada. By Jack Pickersgill, D. M. Fisher and Ernest Watkins. (In *Waterloo review*. Waterloo, Ont. no. 5 (summer 1960), pp. 51-67.)

Contents: The future of Liberalism in Canada, by J. Pickersgill. – My liberalism, by D. M. Fisher. – Liberalism from a Conservative viewpoint, by E. Watkins.

Comments are directed, primarily, toward the status of the Liberal Party in Canada.

The Private side of politics: Mike Pearson. (In *Maclean's*. Toronto. v. 71, no. 7 (Mar. 29, 1958), pp. 17; 58-63.)

The private side of politics; a *Maclean's* panel talks informally with John Diefenbaker and L. B. Pearson, Panelists: Hugh MacLennan, Barbara Moon, James Bannerman.

REGENSTREIF, SAMUEL PETER Note on the "alternation" of French and English leaders in the Liberal Party of Canada. By Peter Regenstreif. (In *The Canadian journal of political science*. Toronto. v. 2 (1969), pp. [118]-122.)

ROBICHAUD, HEDARD J. Atlantic fisheries. Blueprint for an orderly revolution. By Hon. H. J. Robichaud. (In *The Atlantic advocate*. Fredericton, N.B. v. 57, no. 2 (Oct. 1966), pp. [13]; 15-16.)

—— Atlantic fisheries in review. By the Hon. H. J. Robichaud, federal Minister of Fisheries. (In *The Atlantic advocate*. Fredericton, N.B. v. 55, no. 2 (Oct. 1964), pp. 19-23.)

RODGERS, RAYMOND Ottawa letter. Three premiers and the Liberal left. (In *Saturday night*. Toronto. v. 76, no. 3 (Feb. 4, 1961), pp. 22-23.)

Considers the influence of J. Smallwood, H. Robichaud, and T. C. Douglas on the national Liberal rally held in January 1961.

ROGERS, GEORGE J. "Lower our taxes!" (In *Canada month*. Montreal. v. 7, no. 5 (May 1967), pp. 24-25.)

Discusses government finance policy.

RYAN, CLAUDE On Canada: Canada and the tasks that lie ahead. (In *The Journal of liberal thought*. Ottawa. [v.] 3, no. 1 (winter 1966/67), pp. 51-62.)

"The Liberals' responsibility with regard to the future tasks confronting Canada."

Preceded by the French version, pp. 38-50.

—— Sur le Canada: les tâches de l'avenir au Canada. (In *The Journal of liberal thought*. Ottawa. [v.] 3, no. 1 (winter 1966/67), pp. 38-50.)

"La responsabilité des libéraux devant les tâches de l'avenir au Canada."

Article is followed by the English version, pp. 51-62.

SAUVE, MAURICE Document. Statement by the Hon. Maurice Sauvé concerning alleged irregularities during the elections held on November 8, 1965 in the federal county of the Magdalen Islands. (In *Journal of Canadian studies*. Peterborough, Ont. v. 1, no. 1 (1966), pp. 35-49.)

—— Economic nationalism or economic planning: the way ahead for the Canadian economy. (In *The Journal of liberal thought*. Ottawa. [v.] 3, no. 1 (winter 1966/67), pp. 166-174.)

"Notes of a speech delivered by the Honourable Maurice Sauvé, Minister of Forestry and Rural Development, to the Club St-Laurent Kiwanis de Montréal Inc., Wednesday, March 1st, 1967."

—— The need for unity in Canada. (In Empire Club of Canada. *Addresses*. [Don Mills, Ont.] (1965/66), pp. [139]-154.)

Address delivered January 20, 1966.

Discusses the problem of rural poverty in Canada.

SHARP, MITCHELL WILLIAM Learning to be a Canadian. By Mitchell Sharp. (In *Queen's quarterly*. Kingston. v. 72 (1965), pp. [304]-312.)

"This paper is the text of an address to the Canadian Club of Montreal delivered on November 23, 1964."

A personal statement.

SLATER, DAVID WALTER Gordon's new book. By David W. Slater. (In *The Canadian forum*. Toronto. v. 46, no. 545 (June 1966), pp. [49]-51.)

A review article of *A choice for Canada*, by W. L. Gordon. Toronto, McClelland and Stewart, 1966.

Incorporates a discussion of general policies for Canada.

SMITH, LAWRENCE B. Housing and inflation: the government's dilemma. (In *The Canadian forum*. Toronto. v. 46, no. 552 (Jan. 1967), pp. [217]-218.)

STEVENSON, JOHN A. Ottawa letter. Liberals lean leftwards. (In *Saturday night*. Toronto. v. 72, no. 18 (Aug. 31, 1957), pp. 4-5.)

—— Ottawa letter. Middle-of-the-road policies. (In *Saturday night*. Toronto. v. 73, no. 3 (Feb. 1, 1958), pp. 4-5.)

Concerns the fourth National Convention of the Liberal Party held January 14-16, 1958, which elected Lester B. Pearson as leader.

—— The Ottawa story. Growing weariness at Ottawa: new life for Liberals. By J. S. Stevenson. (In *Canadian commentator*. Toronto. v. 4, no. 7-8 (July–Aug. 1960), pp. 13-15; 23-24.)

General remarks on the Canadian political situation.

—— Peacemaking to politicking. (In *Saturday night*. Toronto. v. 73, no. 1 (Jan. 4, 1958), pp. [14]; 38.)

Concerns Lester B. Pearson.

STUEBING, DOUGLAS Trudeau; a man for tomorrow. By Douglas Stuebing, with John Marshall and Gary Oakes. Toronto, Clarke, Irwin [c1968] 187 p.

—— Trudeau: l'homme de demain. Par Douglas Stuebing, John Marshall et Gary Oakes. [Montréal] HMH [c1969] 238 p.

Translation of *Trudeau; a man for tomorrow*. Toronto, Clarke, Irwin, 1968.

STURSBERG, PETER How they twisted Pearson's arm. (In *Commentator*. Toronto. v. 9, no. 10 (Oct. 1965), pp. 6-7.)

Concerns the decision to call a federal election for November 8, 1965.

—— Musings on the Liberal hopefuls. (In *Commentator*. Toronto. v. 12, no. 3 (Mar. 1968), pp. 7-8.)

Considers the candidates for the leadership of the Liberal Party at the national convention held in Ottawa April 4-6, 1968.

—— Ottawa letter. Judy's punch with the pensions. (In *Saturday night*. Toronto. v. 78, no. 8 (Sept. 1963), pp. 9-10.)

Concerns Judy LaMarsh.

—— Ottawa letter. (In *Saturday night*. Toronto. v. 79, no. 9 (Sept. 1964), pp. 9-10.)

Discusses the nationalist policy and the attempt to implement that policy by Walter Gordon.

—— Our foreign policy and the man who makes it. A special interview with Paul Martin. (In *Saturday night*. Toronto. v. 78, no. 10 (Nov. 1963), pp. 15-20.)

—— Pépin and Lévesque, two Quebec leaders to reckon with. (In *Commentator*. Toronto. v. 10, no. 2 (Feb. 1966), pp. 20-21.)

Discusses the significance of René Lévesque and Jean Luc Pépin in a federal context.

—— Politics is not for amateurs. (In *Commentator*. Toronto. v. 9, no. 1 (Jan. 1965), pp. 5-7.)

Comments on the political performance of three members of the Liberal cabinet: Guy Favreau, Walter Gordon, and Maurice Lamontagne.

—— Postmark Ottawa. (In *The Canadian Saturday night*. Toronto. v. 78, no. 6 (June/July 1963), pp. 7-8.)

Concerns the cabinet of Lester B. Pearson.

SWAINSON, DONALD WAYNE   The Liberal Party: a party of national unity? By Donald Swainson. (In *Canadian dimension*. Winnipeg. v. 2, no. 3 (Mar./Apr. 1965), pp. 14-15.)

THOMSON, DALE C.   Liberals settle for the middle road. (In *Saturday night*. Toronto. v. 76, no. 3 (Feb. 4, 1961), pp. 7-11.)

Discusses the program of the national Liberal Party rally held at Ottawa January 9-11, 1961.

TROTTER, BERNARD   Canadian Broadcasting Act IV: Scene '67; or, Double talk and the single system. (In *Queen's quarterly*. Kingston. v. 73 (1966), pp. [461]-482.)

Concerns the policy of the Liberal Party on the structure and management of the Canadian broadcasting system.

TRUDEAU, PIERRE ELLIOTT   A l'Ouest rien de nouveau. (In *Cité libre*. Montréal. no. 34 (fév. 1961), pp. 8-9.)

Discusses the "Rassemblement libéral national" held in Ottawa January 9-11, 1961.

—— Pearson ou l'abdication de l'esprit. (In *Cité libre*. Montréal. no. 56 (avril 1963), pp. 7-12.)

A strong statement opposing Lester Pearson's public position on nuclear weapons.

—— Pelletier et Trudeau s'expliquent. Par Pierre Trudeau et Gérard Pelletier. (In *Cité libre*. Montréal. no 80 (Oct. 1965), pp. 3-5.)

WARD, NORMAN MC QUEEN   The Liberals in convention. Revised and unrepentant. By Norman Ward. (In *Queen's quarterly*. Kingston. v. 65 (1958), pp. [1]-11.)

Discusses the Liberal Party leadership convention held January 14-16, 1958.

—— The Liberals in convention. By Norman Ward. (In Thorburn, H. G. *Party politics in Canada*. Scarborough, Ont. [c1967] pp. [96]-103.)

"Reprinted from Queen's quarterly, LXV, no. 1, 1958."

Discusses the Liberal Party leadership convention held January 14-16, 1958.

WATKINS, ERNEST   Political Canada. The budget's lessons. (In *Canada month*. Montreal. v. 3, no. 7 [i.e. 8] (Aug. 1963), p. 30.)

Refers to the budget presented by Walter Gordon.

WEARING, JOSEPH   The Liberal choice. (In *Journal of Canadian studies*. Peterborough. v. 3, no. 2 (1968), pp. 3-20.)

Concerns the national leadership convention of the Liberal Party held at Ottawa April 4-6, 1968. The "choice" was Pierre Elliott Trudeau.

WHALEN, HUGH   Speech from the Throne: trends and portents. (In *The Canadian forum*. Toronto. v. 45, no. 532 (May 1965), pp. 27-29.)

An extensive discussion of the proposed program of the Liberal government.

What's behind Ottawa's bid for wildlife control. (In *Canada month*. Montreal. v. 5, no. 8 (Aug. 1965), p. 14.)

Refers to Arthur Laing, Minister of National Resources.

WHEALEN, J. P. Meet Paul Martin; a personal sketch. Winnipeg, Greywood Pub. [1968] 111 p. (Greywood paperback original, 108.)

WILSON, J. M. Why Mr. Pearson did not wait for redistribution. (In *Canadian dimension*. Winnipeg. v. 2, no. 6 (Sept./Oct. 1965), pp. 6; 27.)

WINTERS, ROBERT HENRY Business and government in relation to our economy. By Hon. R. H. Winters, Minister of Trade and Commerce. (In Empire Club of Canada. *Addresses*. [Don Mills, Ont.] (1965/66), pp. 276-288.)
Address delivered March 21, 1966.

YOUNG, WALTER DOUGLAS Pierre Elliott Trudeau and the intellectuals. By Walter Young. (In *Canadian dimension*. Winnipeg. v. 5, no. 5 (June/July 1968), pp. 11-12.)

ZIEGEL, JACOB S. Towards a policy for consumer protection. By Jacob S. Ziegel and Mrs. A. F. W. Plumptre. (In *The Journal of liberal thought*. Ottawa. [v.] 3, no. 1 (winter 1966/67), pp. 146-160.)
"This working paper was presented in the section on Consumer Problems at the Liberal Party Policy Conference held in Ottawa in October, 1966 . . . This paper has been slightly modified for the purposes of publication."

CO-OPERATIVE COMMONWEALTH FEDERATION (CCF)

1932–1961

ANDERSON, LINDA LOUISE Focus of appeal in the analysis of parties, CCF–NDP. [Edmonton, 1969] 1 v.
Thesis (MA) – University of Alberta.

ANGERS, FRANCOIS ALBERT La nouvelle CCF est-elle socialiste? Par Albert Angers. (In *L'Action nationale*. Montréal. v. 46 (oct. 1956), pp. [105]-115.)

—— La nouvelle déclaration du parti CCF. (In *L'Action nationale*. Montréal. v. 46 (sept. 1956), pp. [11]-26.)
"La déclaration de Winnipeg": pp. 21-26. Concerns the 1956 Winnipeg Declaration of Principles of the Co-operative Commonwealth Federation presented at the annual national convention of the CCF held at Winnipeg, August 1-3, 1956.

—— Le parti CCF et la centralisation. (In *L'Action nationale*. Montréal. v. 46 (nov. 1956), pp. [222]-231.)

ARMSTRONG, MYRTLE MAY The development of trade union political activity in the CCF [Toronto, 1959] 136 leaves.
Thesis (MA) – University of Toronto.

BALLANTYNE, MURRAY G. The Catholic Church and the CCF. (In Canadian Catholic Historical Association. *Report*. [Ottawa] (1963), pp. 33-45.)

Balloting for a better world; editorial. (In *The Canadian forum*. Toronto. v. 23, no. 271 (Aug. 1943), pp. 101-102.)
Argues for the adoption of CCF policy to cope with the problem of "the ordering of our national economy so that full use shall be made of our resources for the common benefit".

BECK, JAMES MURRAY Labour parties, new and old. By J. M. Beck and D. J. Dooley. (In *The Dalhousie review*. Halifax. v. 40, no. 3 (fall 1960), pp. [323]-328.)
Discusses the CCF and the New Party.

BEDER, EDWARD ARTHUR Changes in socialist thinking. By E. A. Beder. (In *The Canadian forum*. Toronto. v. 30, no. 358 (Nov. 1950), pp. 173-175.)
Considers a revised Regina Manifesto to be submitted by the National Council of the CCF Party to the 1952 national convention.

—— First term program. By E. A. Beder. (In *The Canadian forum*. Toronto. v. 28, no. 336 (Jan. 1949), pp. 221-222.)
An examination of the CCF first-term program.
For a rejoinder to the above, see Mr. Beder's first-term program, by G. M. A. Grube. (In *The Canadian forum*. Toronto. v. 28, no. 337 (1939), pp. 249-250.)

BELL, CHARLES E. Labor pains in Canada's newest Party. (In *Saturday night*. Toronto. v. 75, no. 19 (Sept. 17, 1960), pp. 9-11.)
"Political fall fair."
Examines the political alignment between the CCF Party and the Canadian Labour Congress to form a new national party.

BLOOM, LLOYD H. A CCF crusader. (In *Saturday night*. Toronto. v. 48, no. 42 (Aug. 26, 1933), p. 3.)
A brief biographical sketch of Elmore Philpott, a Liberal candidate in the 1931 by-election in West Hamilton, who later joined the CCF Party.

BREWIN, FRANCIS ANDREW   CCF enters new phase. By Andrew Brewin. (In *The Canadian forum*. Toronto. v. 26, no. 308 (Sept. 1946), pp. 129-130.)

—— The future of the CCF. By A. F. Brewin. (In *Saturday night*. Toronto. v. 56, no. 52 (Sept. 6, 1941), p. 8.)

—— Labour legislation. By F. Andrew Brewin. (In Co-operative Commonwealth Federation (Ontario). *Planning for freedom*. 2d ed. [Toronto] 1944. pp. 114-124.)
Lecture delivered March 6, 1944.

—— Next step for the CCF—government or opposition? By Andrew Brewin. (In *The Canadian forum*. Toronto. v. 23, no. 273 (Oct. 1943), pp. 150-152.)

—— What the CCF needs. By Andrew Brewin. (In *The Canadian forum*. Toronto. v. 25, no. 301 (Feb. 1946), pp. 254-256.)

BUCHANAN, DONALD W.   The CCF's young man. (In *Saturday night*. Toronto. v. 49, no. 42 (Aug. 25, 1934), p. 8.)
Biographical sketch of Graham Spry, CCF candidate in a federal by-election held in Toronto East, Sept. 24, 1934 (i.e., Toronto-Broadview).

The CCF charts the future. (In *The Canadian forum*. Toronto. v. 22, no. 260 (Sept. 1942), pp. 166-168.)
Discusses the CCF seventh national convention held in Toronto July 1942.

The CCF's opportunity. (In *The Canadian forum*. Toronto. v. 17, no. 199 (Aug. 1937), pp. 154-155.)

Canadian third party. (In *Canadian comment*. Toronto. v. 2, no. 1 (Jan. 1933), pp. 13-14.)
Concerns the CCF Party.

CAYGEON, ROBERT   Agnes Macphail—a romantic evangelist. (In *Saturday night*. Toronto. v. 48, no. 38 (July 29, 1933), p. 3.)
Concerns Agnes Campbell Macphail.

—— A voice in the Canadian wilderness. Mr. J. S. Woodsworth, who comes to prepare the way. His doctrine of the state as the custodian of the common interests. Economic parasitism and the planned economy. Not a strong leader but an effective missionary. (In *Saturday night*. Toronto. v. 48, no. 44 (Sept. 9, 1933), pp. 2; 6.)

CLARK, SAMUEL DELBERT   The CCF and Alberta politics. By S. Delbert Clark. (In *The Canadian forum*. Toronto. v. 14, no. 159 (Dec. 1933), pp. 90-91.)
For a rejoinder, see *The CCF in Alberta*, by E. E. Roper. (In *The Canadian forum*. Toronto. v. 14, no. 161 (1934), pp. 173-175.)

COLDWELL, MAJOR JAMES WILLIAM   Canadian progressives on the march; The story of the rise of the CCF. By M. J. Coldwell . . . Regina manifesto. Postwar program, CCF. New York, League for Industrial Democracy [1944] 32 p. (L.I.D. pamphlet series.)
Address delivered in New York, January 15, 1944. Cf. Foreword.

—— The case for price controls. By M. J. Coldwell. (In *Public affairs*. Halifax. v. 14, no. 2 (winter 1952), pp. [18]-20.)

—— Left turn, Canada. By M. J. Coldwell. London, V. Gollancz, 1945. 192 p. (Left book club edition.)

—— Left turn, Canada. By M. J. Coldwell. With an introd. by Eric Estorick. New York, Duell, Sloan and Pearce [1945] xv, 247 p. (British Commonwealth series.)

—— Some regional problems of Canada. By M. J. Coldwell, parliamentary leader of the Co-operative Commonwealth Federation. (In Empire Club of Canada. *Addresses*. (1955/56), pp. 111-125.)
Address delivered November 24, 1955.

—— What does the CCF stand for? By M. J. Coldwell, MP as quizzed by Bruce Hutchison. (In *Maclean's*. Toronto. v. 56, no. 17 (Sept. 1, 1943), pp. 12-13; 38; 40-42.)

—— What's Left. By M. J. Coldwell. (In *The Canadian forum*. Toronto. v. 32, no. 376 (May 1952), pp. 28-29.)
A brief statement outlining the principal aims of the CCF Party.

Co-operative Commonwealth Federation. CCF Cooperative Commonwealth Federation 25th anniversary souvenir. [Ottawa, 1957] 126 p.
Cover title.
Title page and text partly in French
Editors: G. MacInnis, M. Lazarus.

—— Let's go forward; the national CCF program. [Ottawa, 1958] 8 p.
Caption title.
Official national program, drawn up by the National Council, January 1958, on the basis of resolutions approved at CCF national conventions. Cf. p. 1.

CO-OPERATIVE COMMONWEALTH FEDERATION (ONTARIO) Planning for freedom; 16 lectures on the CCF, its policies and program. 2d ed. [Toronto. Printed for the Ontario CCF by Thistle Print. Co.] 1944. 180 p.

Partial contents: The nature of economic planning, by F. R. Scott. – Freedom and the CCF, by G. M. A. Grube. – Socialized health services, by T. F. Nicholson. – Marching home to what? by C. Gillis. – Social ownership; dominion and provincial, by E. B. Jolliffe. – The CCF policy on money, by E. Forsey. – The farmer and the world of tomorrow, by T. C. Douglas. – Labour legislation, by F. A. Brewin. – A program for education, by J. W. Noseworthy. –Dominion-provincial relations, by F. H. Underhill. – The structure of the CCF, by D. Lewis.

COPPS, EDWIN Ottawa letter. Disenchantment of an idealist. (In Saturday night. Toronto. v. 74, no. 21 (Oct. 10, 1959), pp. 41-43.)

Presents the reasons given by Douglas Mason Fisher for his retirement from Canadian politics.

CORBETT, PERCY ELLWOOD Canadian and European socialism differ. Organization here is only now becoming nation-wide and has still no particular international outlook. Is the small farmer-owner lost to capitalism? By P. E. Corbett. (In Saturday night. Toronto. v. 48, no. 17 (Mar. 4, 1933), p. 2.)

Concerns the CCF Party.

COUTURE, LUC CCF, une étude canadienne. [Ottawa] 1943. 67 leaves.

Thesis (L SC POL: MA) – University of Ottawa.

COX, COROLYN Name in the news. National leader of the CCF. (In Saturday night. Toronto. v. 58, no. 14 (Dec. 12, 1942), p. 2.)

Concerns Hon. Major James William Coldwell.

—— Name in the news. Bialystok, McGill-Oxford-Ottawa. (In Saturday night. Toronto. v. 58, no. 30 (Apr. 3, 1943), p. 2.)

A biographical sketch of David Lewis.

CRAIK, GALEN The CCF at Calgary was chafing at the bit. (In Saturday night. Toronto. v. 59, no. 4 (Oct. 2, 1943), p. 14.)

CROSS, AUSTIN FLETCHER Coldwell . . . the man. By Austin Cross. (In National home

monthly. Winnipeg. v. 49, no. 10 (Oct. 1948), pp. 14-15; 30-31.)

DEACHMAN, ROBERT JOHN Labour rushes to the rescue. By R. J. Deachman. (In The Maritime advocate and busy East. Sackville, N.B. v. 26, no. 9 (Apr. 1936), pp. 14; 24.)

Examines a resolution on retirement allowances proposed by A. A. Heaps and A. MacInnis.

DEMPSON, PETER W. Canada's first CCF Premier a fighter. By P. W. Dempson. (In Saturday night. Toronto. v. 59, no. 43 (July 1, 1944), p. 6.)

Concerns Thomas Clement Douglas.

—— Will Coldwell call it a day? (In Saturday night. Toronto. v. 73, no. 10 (May 10, 1958), pp. 16-[17]; 46; 48-49.)

DEXTER, GRANT Coldwell the man. (In Maclean's. Toronto. v. 56, no. 17 (Sept. 1, 1943), pp. 13; 50-52.)

DIBNEY, DORA Parliament's lone lady. (In Chatelaine. Toronto. v. 18, no. 8 (Aug. 1945), pp. 54; 60; 64.)

Concerns Gladys Strum, MP for Qu'Appelle, who defeated former member E. E. Perley and Gen. A. G. L. McNaughton.

DOUGLAS, THOMAS CLEMENT The farmer and the world of tomorrow. By Hon. T. C. Douglas. (In Co-operative Commonwealth Federation (Ontario). Planning for freedom. 2d ed. [Toronto] 1944. pp. 103-113.)

Lecture delivered Feb. 28, 1944.

EGGLESTON, WILFRID Behind the scenes with the CCF. Informal notes on members of the Ottawa group of the new party— they're really human! (In Saturday night. Toronto. v. 48, no. 45 (Sept. 16, 1933), p. 3.)

—— Ottawa view. The future of the CCF. (In Saturday night. Toronto. v. 63, no. 47 (Aug. 28, 1948), p. 4.)

—— Ottawa view, CCF and the Liberals. Third party probably permanent but founder's dream is mirage. (In Saturday night. Toronto. v. 64, no. 30 (May 3, 1949), p. 4.)

ELYOT, STEPHEN The new Commonwealth. A critical study of the Cooperative Commonwealth Federation. (In The Canadian forum. Toronto. v. 13, no. 146 (Nov. 1932), pp. 51-52.)

ENGELMANN, FREDERICK CHARLES The Co-operative Commonwealth Federation of Canada; a study of membership participation in party policy-making. By Frederick C. Engelmann. [New Haven, Conn.] 1954. vi, 262 leaves.

Thesis (PH D) – Yale University.

—— Membership participation in policy-making in the CCF. By Frederick C. Engelmann. (In The Canadian journal of economics and political science. [Toronto] v. 22 (1956), pp. 161-173.)

Discusses the practice of a political party which allows its membership to determine policy by means of an active participation in all its policy-making agencies and channels.

FISHER, DOUGLAS MASON An interesting campaign. (In The Canadian forum. Toronto. v. 37, no. 440 (Sept. 1957), pp. [121]; 143-144.)

The Author discusses the campaign conducted in Port Arthur, Ont., in which he defeated C. D. Howe in the federal election held June 10, 1957.

—— The last CCF roundup. By D. M. Fisher. (In The Canadian forum. Toronto. v. 40, no. 476 (Sept. 1960), pp. 122-123.)

Describes the CCF national convention in Regina August 9-11, 1960, which approved the founding of the New Party. Comments on speculations as to whom will be selected leader of the Party in mid-1961.

For a rejoinder, see A reply to Mr. Fisher, by L. Ingle. [In The Canadian forum. Toronto. v. 40, no. 478 (1960), pp. 183-184.]

FORREST, A. C. Political agnosticism big factor in CCF rise. (In Saturday night. Toronto. v. 59, no. 4 (Oct. 2, 1943), p. 8.)

FORSEY, EUGENE ALFRED The CCF policy on money. By Dr. Eugene Forsey. (In Co-operative Commonwealth Federation (Ontario). Planning for freedom. 2d ed. [Toronto] 1944. pp. 85-91.)

Lecture delivered Jan. 31, 1944.

—— The Crown, the constitution and the CCF. By Eugene Forsey. (In The Canadian forum. Toronto. v. 23, no. 269 (June 1943), pp. 54-56.)

—— Planning from the bottom—can it be done? By Eugene Forsey. (In The Canadian forum. Toronto. v. 24, no. 290 (Mar. 1945), pp. 277-279; v. 25, no. 291 (Apr. 1945), pp. 20-23.)

In two parts.

"An address delivered . . . to the CCF Leadership School."

—— The question of a provincial bank. By Eugene Forsey. (In The Canadian forum. Toronto. v. 16, no. 188 (Sept. 1936), pp. 12-13.)

Discusses CCF policy on chartering banks.

FORSEY, HARRIET ROBERTS Will women win the peace? (In The Canadian forum. Toronto. v. 24, no. 283 (Aug. 1944), pp. 106-108.)

Advocates that the CCF Party define and present its policy on the position of women.

FRASER BLAIR Backstage at Ottawa. Crowding on the left. By the Man with a Notebook. (In Maclean's. Toronto. v. 59, no. 24 (Dec. 15, 1946), pp. 15; 71.)

Concerns the CCF Party.

—— Backstage at Ottawa. Flag-waving on the left. By the Man with a Notebook. (In Maclean's. Toronto. v. 60, no. 19 (Oct. 1, 1947), p. 15.)

Concerns the CCF Party.

—— Backstage at Ottawa. The new third party. Can farmers and labor get together? (In Maclean's. Toronto. v. 72, no. 18 (Aug. 29, 1959), p. 2.)

Discusses the Joint National Committee of the CCF and the Canadian Labour Congress.

—— The saintly failure who changed Canada. (In Maclean's. Toronto. v. 64, no. 21 (Nov. 1, 1951), pp. 16; 52-55.)

Concerns J. S. Woodsworth.

FRENCH, DORIS Agnes Macphail, 1890-1954. (In Innis, M. Q. (ed.) The clear spirit. [Toronto] University of Toronto Press [c1966] pp. [179]-197.)

GALLOWAY, JEAN LOVE Nora Coldwell: gallant lady of the CCF. (In Saturday night. Toronto. v. 64, no. 36 (June 14, 1949), p. 29.)

GILBERT, GEORGE CCF attacks life insurance. (In Saturday night. Toronto. v. 59, no. 18 (Jan. 8, 1944), p. 26.)

GILLIS, CLARENCE Marching home to what? Plans for the rehabilitation of the personnel of the Canadian armed forces. (In Co-operative Commonwealth Federation (Ontario). Planning for freedom. 2d ed. [Toronto] 1944. pp. 49-62.)

Lecture delivered April 17, 1944.

Gillis was elected from Cape Breton South to the House of Commons from 1940 to 1953.

GODFREY, WILLIAM GERALD The 1933 Regina convention of the Co-operative Commonwealth Federation. [Waterloo, Ont.] 1965. iv, 151 leaves.

Thesis (MA) – University of Waterloo.

GOLDEN, LOU L. L. A CCF maritimer! By L. L. L. Golden. (In *Saturday night*. Toronto. v. 55, no. 39 (July 27, 1940), p. 19.)

Concerns Clarence Gillis.

—— Out of the needs of the people. By L. L. L. Golden. (In *Saturday night*. Toronto. v. 55, no. 34 (June 22, 1940), p. 4.)

A biographical sketch of Dorise Winnifred Nielsen, MP (née Webber).

GORDON, J. KING The CCF convention. By King Gordon. (In *The Canadian forum*. Toronto. v. 17, no. 200 (Sept. 1937), pp. 189-191.)

Refers to the fourth national convention held in Winnipeg July 27-28, 1937

GOULD, EMILY Dorise Nielsen, MP. (In *Chatelaine*. Toronto. v. 13, no. 6 (June 1940), pp. 16; [69].)

GRUBE, GEORGE MAXIMILIAN ANTONY Freedom and the CCF. By G. M. A. Grube. (In Co-operative Commonwealth Federation (Ontario). *Planning for freedom*. 2d ed. [Toronto] 1944. pp. 12-24.)

Lecture delivered January 17, 1944.
Concerns political and civil liberties.

—— Mr. Beder's first term program. By G. M. A. Grube. (In *The Canadian forum*. Toronto. v. 28, no. 337 (Feb. 1949), pp. 249-250.)

The above is a reply to the article *First term program*, by E. A. Beder. (In *The Canadian forum*. Toronto. v. 28, no. 336 (1949), pp. 221-222.)

HARRIS, J. C. Prize CCF platform. (In *Saturday night*. Toronto. v. 54, no. 44 (Sept. 2, 1939), p. 3.)

Text of a program submitted to the Platform Competition held by *Saturday night*. The other winning entries are by H. M. Bruce (Conservative) and R. J. Deachman (Liberal). (See *Saturday night*. Toronto. v. 54, no. 43, p. 2 and p. 3.)

HARWOOD, WALTER An embarrassed editor. (In *The Canadian forum*. Toronto. v. 18, no. 214 (Nov. 1938), pp. 232-233.)

Discusses the attitude of J. W. Dafoe toward the CCF Party and its policies.

HEAPS, LEO The rebel in the House; the life and times of A. A. Heaps, MP. London [Ont.] Niccolo Pub. Co., 1970. 168 p.

Concerns Abraham Albert Heaps, 1889-1954.

HODGSON, FRED Leftward ho! (In *New frontier*. Toronto. v. 1, no. 5 (Sept. 1936), pp. 9-10.)

Discusses the CCF national convention held in Toronto August 3-5, 1936.

HOROWITZ, GAD Canadian labor in politics; the trade unions and the CCF–NDP, 1937-62. [Cambridge, Mass.] 1965. 1 v.

Thesis (PH D) – Harvard University.

—— Canadian labour in politics. [Toronto] University of Toronto Press [c1968] 273 p. (Studies in the structure of power: decision-making in Canada, 4.)

—— The rise & fall of the CCF. (In *Canadian dimension*. Winnipeg. v. 1, no. 8 (Sept./Oct. 1964), pp. 20-22.)

A review article of *A protest movement becalmed*, by L. Zakuta. Toronto, University of Toronto Press, 1964.

HOWARD, H. C. The CCF as a working political force. Present weaknesses of leadership and organization make its future effectiveness a debatable question. (In *Saturday night*. Toronto. v. 49, no. 41 (Aug. 18, 1934), p. 2.)

HUESTIS, CHARLES HERBERT A United Front in Canada? (In *New frontier*. Toronto. v. 1, no. 9 (Jan. 1937), pp. 20-21.)

Concentrates on the position of the CCF Party.

HUTCHISON, BRUCE Freedom in the balance. "The central issue of our time is . . . whether we shall give up liberty of thought . . . for a promise of security." (In *Maclean's*. Toronto. v. 56, no. 22 (Nov. 15, 1943), pp. 13; 45-48.)

Concerns M. J. Coldwell and the CCF Party.

IGNATIEFF, NICHOLAS Is the CCF a national movement? (In *Canadian comment*. Toronto. v. 2, no. 11 (Nov. 1933), pp. [5]-6; 32.)

IRVING, JOHN ALLAN The CCF: a record of failure. By John A. Irving. (In *Saturday night*. Toronto. v. 70, no. 46 (Dec. 10, 1955), pp. 7-8.)

JAMES, HESTER I canvassed for Noseworthy. (In *The Canadian forum*. Toronto. v. 22, no. 255 (Apr. 1942), pp. 16; 18.)

Records experience in the York South, Ont., by-election held February 9, 1942.

JAMIESON, STUART Growing support for CCF expected from workers. (In *Saturday night*. Toronto. v. 64, no. 4 (Oct. 30, 1948), p. 34.)

JOLLIFFE, EDWARD BIGELOW Social ownership—dominion and provincial. By E. B. Jolliffe. (In Co-operative Commonwealth Federation (Ontario). *Planning for freedom*. 2d ed. [Toronto] 1944. pp. 63-76.)

Lecture delivered Feb. 7, 1944.

KENNY, MARTIN J. CCF shows its hand. Pickering, Ont., Printers' Guild, 1944. 64 p.

Argues the case against socialism.

KEY, ARCHIBALD Creating a national Federation. (In *The Canadian forum*. Toronto. v. 12, no. 144 (Sept. 1932), pp. 451-453.)

A report on the convention at Calgary August 1, 1932, which founded the Co-operative Commonwealth Federation.

KING, CARLYLE The CCF sweeps Saskatchewan. (In *The Canadian forum*. Toronto. v. 24, no. 282 (July 1944), p. 79.)

Suggests that the CCF victory in the June 15 election represents, in part, a protest vote against the Liberal and Conservative federal parties.

KNIGHT, ROY R. Great progress by CCF in 17 years of life. (In *Saturday night*. Toronto. v. 64, no. 33 (May 24, 1949), pp. 18-19.)

KNOWLES, STANLEY HOWARD Business, labour and politics. By Stanley Knowles. (In Greenslade, J. G. (ed.) *Canadian politics*. Sackville, N.B. [1959?] pp. 33-46.)

—— The new political party. By Stanley Knowles. (In *Canadian commentator*. Toronto. v. 3, no. 3 (Mar. 1959), pp. 4-5.)

—— The new political party. By Stanley Knowles. Part two. (In *Canadian commentator*. Toronto. v. 3, no. 12 (Dec. 1959), pp. 3-4; 10-12.)

Discusses the reasons for a third political party and the possibilities for its exercising effective action.

Part one entitled "Labour and society" appeared in the November 1959 issue of the *Canadian commentator*. The article dealt with the aims and organization of the Canadian Labour Congress.

Parts one and two are excerpts from an address delivered by Mr. Knowles in August 1959 to the Summer Institute of Mount Allison University and published in J. G. Greenslade's *Canadian politics*. Sackville, N.B. [1959?].

Labor takes political action. (In *The Canadian forum*. Toronto. v. 27, no. 322 (Nov. 1947), pp. 174-175.)

Discusses the political support given by the Canadian Congress of Labour to the CCF Party and the political direction of the Trades and Labor Congress of Canada.

LAWRENCE, SIDNEY Whence does the CCF draw its recruits? A shrewd and impartial estimate of the sources of the new party's membership—ten widely differing types sketched by one who says CCF-ers are "easy to spot". (In *Saturday night*. Toronto. v. 48, no. 22 (Apr. 8, 1933), p. 14.)

LE COCQ, THELMA Fighting lady. (In *Chatelaine*. Toronto. v. 21, no. 5 (May 1948), pp. 36; 42-46.)

Concerns Thérèse Casgrain. Mme Casgrain left the Liberal Party in 1946 to join the CCF.

LEFOLII, KEN The poet who outfought Duplessis. (In *Maclean's*. Toronto. v. 72, no. 8 (Apr. 11, 1959), pp. 16-17; 70; 72; 74-76.)

Concerns Frank Scott. Includes discussion of his involvement with the Canadian socialist movement and the CCF Party.

LEVESQUE, GEORGES HENRI Socialisme canadien. La CCF. (In *L'Action nationale*. Montréal. v. 2 (oct. 1933), pp. [91]-116.)

LEVITT, JOSEPH The CCF and French Canadian "radical" nationalism; a comparison in policy, 1933-1942. Toronto, 1964. 213 leaves.

Thesis (MA) – University of Toronto.

LEWIS, DAVID The CCF convention. (In *The Canadian forum*. Toronto. v. 16, no. 188 (Sept. 1936), pp. 6-8.)

Discusses the third national convention held in Toronto August 3-5, 1936.

—— Make this your Canada; a review of CCF history and policy. By David Lewis and Frank Scott. With a foreword by M. J. Coldwell. Toronto [Central Canada Pub. Co.] 1943. xii, 223 p.

Statement prepared by the National Secretary and the National Chairman of the CCF Party.

Appendix A: Regina Manifesto. Adopted at first national convention held at Regina, Sask., July 19-21, 1933 (pp. 199-207).

Appendix B: For victory and reconstruction. Adopted at seventh national convention held at Toronto, Ont., July 1942 (pp. 208-213).

—— The structure of the CCF. (In Co-operative Commonwealth Federation (Ontario). *Planning for freedom.* 2d ed. [Toronto] 1944. pp. 173-180.)
Lecture delivered January 24, 1944.

—— Wanted: brawn as well as brains. (In *The Canadian forum.* Toronto. v. 20, no. 233 (June 1940), pp. 76-78.)
Discusses "the results of the federal election, particularly as they affect the CCF."
Refers to the federal election held March 26, 1940.

MAC EWAN, C. ROSS Saskatchewan secures CCF labor beachhead. (In *Saturday night.* Toronto. v. 60, no. 2 (Sept. 16, 1944), p. 20.)
Comments on "Tommy" Douglas and the CCF Party in Saskatchewan and the significance of the national CCF Party.

MC HENRY, DEAN EUGENE The third force in Canada; the Cooperative Commonwealth Federation, 1932-1948. Berkeley, University of California Press; Toronto, Oxford University Press, 1950. viii, 351 p.

MAC INNIS, ANGUS Should we send the Japs back? No says Angus MacInnis, MP. (In *Maclean's.* Toronto. v. 56, no. 23 (Dec. 1, 1943), pp. 12; 37-38.)

MAC INNIS, GRACE (WOODSWORTH) J. S. Woodsworth; a man to remember. Toronto, Macmillan, 1953. 336 p.

—— J. S. Woodsworth; personal recollections. (In Historical and Scientific Society of Manitoba. *Papers.* Winnipeg. ser. 3, no. 24 (1967/68), pp. 17-26.)

MC NAUGHT, KENNETH WILLIAM KIRKPATRICK CCF: town and country. By K. W. McNaught. (In *Queen's quarterly.* Kingston. v. 61 (1954), pp. [213]-219.)
Questions the thesis that the CCF Party represents, primarily, prairie farm interests. Concentrates on the urban and intellectual basis of the Party.

—— J. S. Woodsworth and a political party for Labour, 1896-1921. By Kenneth McNaught. (In *The Canadian historical review.* Toronto. v. 30 (1949), pp. 123-143.)
". . . an attempt to analyse J. S. Woodsworth's philosophy against the background of the major influences in his life between 1896 and 1921."

—— J. S. Woodsworth and a political party for Labour, 1896 to 1921. By Kenneth McNaught. (In Swainson, D. W. (ed.) *Historical essays on the Prairie Provinces.* Toronto. [c1970] pp. [230]-253.)
Reprinted from "Canadian Historical Review, vol. XXX (1949), pp. 123-43".

—— James Shaver Woodsworth; from social gospel to social democracy, 1874-1921. Toronto, 1950. 274 leaves.
Thesis (PH D) – University of Toronto.

—— A prophet in politics; a biography of J. S. Woodsworth. By Kenneth McNaught. [Toronto] University of Toronto Press [1960] 339 p.
Appendix: Co-operative Commonwealth Federation programme. Adopted at first national convention held at Regina, Sask., July 19-21, 1933 (pp. [321]-330).

MACPHAIL, AGNES CAMPBELL If I were Prime Minister. By Agnes Macphail. (In *Chatelaine.* Toronto. v. 7, no. 1 (Jan. 1933), pp. 13; 46.)

—— Out of my experiences. By Agnes G. [sic] Macphail. (In Canadian Club of Toronto. *Addresses.* Toronto. 1934/35), pp. 242-253.)
Address delivered March 4, 1935.

MAC PHERSON, IAN The 1945 collapse of the CCF in Windsor. (In *Ontario history.* Toronto. v. 61, no. 4 (Dec. 1969), pp. [197]-212.)
Refers to the Ontario provincial and federal elections held June 4 and June 11, 1945, respectively.

Maligning the CCF. (In *The Canadian forum.* Toronto. v. 22, no. 261 (Oct. 1942), pp. 198-199.)
Discusses the war policy of the CCF.

MARSH, D'ARCY Demagogues beware. (In *The Canadian forum.* Toronto. v. 15, no. 171 (Dec. 1934), p. 102.)
Concerns J. S. Woodsworth.

MARSHALL, JOHN On to Ottawa—or back to the people. (In *The Canadian forum.* Toronto. v. 24, no. 287 (Dec. 1944), pp. 198-199.)
Discusses the prospects of the CCF Party taking on the responsibilities of power in federal politics.

METCALF, JOHN FRANKLIN Intraparty democracy in the Co-operative Commonwealth Federation. [Montreal, 1949] 1 v.
Thesis (MA) – McGill University.

MOWBRAY, GEORGE   Cyprus settlement. (In *Canadian commentator*. Toronto. v. 3, no. 5 (May 1959), pp. 7-8.)
Discusses the formation of a new socialist third political party with the support of the Canadian Labour Congress.

MULROONEY, P. J.   The Catholic hierarchy and the CCF. (In *Saturday night*. Toronto. v. 59, no. 14 (Dec. 11, 1943), pp. 14-15.)

NESTER, M. S.   "Make it your Canada" and you'll regret it. (In *Saturday night*. Toronto. v. 60, no. 8 (Oct. 28, 1944), p. [18].)
A critical review of *Make this your Canada*, by D. Lewis and F. R. Scott. Toronto, 1943.

NICHOLSON, T. F.   Socialized health services. By Dr. T. F. Nicholson. (In Co-operative Commonwealth Federation (Ontario). *Planning for freedom*. 2d ed. [Toronto] 1944. pp. 25-36.)
Lecture delivered March 20, 1944.

NOSEWORTHY, JOSEPH WILLIAM   A program for education. By J. W. Noseworthy. (In Co-operative Commonwealth Federation (Ontario). *Planning for freedom*. 2d ed. [Toronto] 1944. pp. 125-136.)
Lecture delivered March 13, 1944.

O'LEARY, MICHAEL GRATTAN   Backstage at Ottawa. By a Politician with a Notebook. (In *Maclean's*. Toronto. v. 47, no. 15 (Aug. 1, 1934), pp. 16; 32-33.)
Discusses the third-party influence – CCF.

ORLIFFE, HERBERT   Proportional representation? (In *The Canadian forum*. Toronto. v. 17, no. 205 (Feb. 1938), pp. 388-390.)
Analyses the relevancy of proportional representation to the CCF Party.

PALMER, JAMES B.   Agnes Macphail—a biographical sketch. (In *The Quarterly*, McMaster University. Hamilton. v. 45, no. 2 (Jan. 1936), pp. [29]-35.)

PARKINSON, JOSEPH F.   The new Party writes a platform. By J. F. Parkinson. (In *Canadian comment*. Toronto. v. 2, no. 8 (Aug. 1933), pp. 13-14.)
Concerns the CCF Party.

PARR, JACK   Liberals, liars and the United Front. (In *New frontier*. Toronto. v. 1, no. 6 (Oct. 1936), pp. 11-13.)
Concentrates on CCF attitudes toward a national Popular Front.

PECHEY, DOROTHY   The feminine outlook. Mrs. Gladys Strum: lone woman MP in Dominion Parliament. (In *Saturday night*.

Toronto. v. 60, no. 44 (July 7, 1945), pp. 22-23.)

PEMBERTON, R. E. K.   The CCF and the Communists. (In *The New age*. Montreal. v. 2, no. 32 (Aug. 15, 1940), pp. 7-8; 12.)

—— The CCF should get wise to itself. (In *The Canadian forum*. Toronto. v. 25, no. 297 (Oct. 1945), pp. 154-156.)

—— The CCF, the election and the future. (In *The Canadian forum*. Toronto. v. 20, no. 232 (May 1940), pp. 38-40.)
Refers to the federal election held March 26, 1940.

PETERSON, CHARLES W.   Answer to the CCF. Under the policy outlined by M. J. Coldwell Canadians would be "conscripts working for our board and lodging". (In *Maclean's*. Toronto. v. 56, no. 20 (Oct. 15, 1943), pp. 10; 53-56.)

PICKWELL, FREDERICK   Asking farmers to abandon profits. Western wiseacres launch "The Canadian Co-operative Commonwealth". By F. C. Pickwell. (In *Saturday night*. Toronto. v. 47, no. 46 (Sept. 24, 1932), p. 2.)

Politics is not enough; editorial. (In *The Canadian forum*. Toronto. v. 23, no. 274 (Nov. 1943), pp. 173-174.)
An analysis of the CCF Party.

The Real meaning of the Ontario elections; editorial. (In *The Canadian forum*. Toronto. v. 23, no. 272 (Sept. 1943), pp. 125-126.)
"The real significance of the Ontario elections lies . . . in the clear indication given of growing popular support for the CCF." The implications are considered in general terms.

The Record of the CCF. How wrong can a political party be? Winnipeg, 1953. 22 p.
"Reprinted from the files of the Winnipeg Free Press." Excerpts from speeches of M. J. Coldwell and other CCF members, with comments.

RODGERS, RAYMOND   Hazen Argue of the CCF—Profile of a hopeful party leader. (In *Saturday night*. Toronto. v. 76, no. 13 (June 24, 1961), pp. 13-14.)

ROGERS, D. B.   CCF show window. After 18 months of socialist government, Saskatchewan is a small-scale display of what the party would like to do with the rest of Canada. By D. B. Rogers and Victor J. Mackie. (In *Maclean's*. Toronto. v. 59, no. 2 (Jan. 15, 1946), pp. 13; 39; 42.)

ROPER, ELMER E. The CCF in Alberta. (In *The Canadian forum*. Toronto. v. 14, no. 161 (Feb. 1934), pp. 173-175.)

A rejoinder to *The CCF and Alberta politics*, by S. D. Clark. [In *The Canadian forum*. Toronto. v. 14, no. 159 (1933), pp. 90-91.]

ROSS, MARY LOWREY Joe Noseworthy. A quick sketch of the man who beat Meighen. (In *Maclean's*. Toronto. v. 52 [i.e. 55] no. 7 (Apr. 1, 1942), pp. 20; 49.)

Concerns Joseph William Noseworthy.

ROY, RAOUL Le PSD, Parti social despotique. (In *La Revue socialiste*. Montréal. [no] 4 (été 1960), pp. 15-27.)

Comments on the attitude taken by the federal CCF/NDP in Quebec.

SANDWELL, BERNARD KEBLE The editor's chair. CCF and Senate. By B. K. Sandwell. (In *Saturday night*. Toronto. v. 59, no. 14 (Dec. 11, 1943), p. 18.)

—— The sisters pacifism and communism. By B. K. Sandwell. (In *Saturday night*. Toronto. v. 47, no. 47 (Oct. 1, 1932), p. 3.)

Concerns J. S. Woodsworth.

SCOTT, FRANCIS REGINALD The CCF convention. By F. R. Scott. (In *The Canadian forum*. Toronto. v. 18, no. 156 (Sept. 1933), pp. 447-449.)

The first national convention held at Regina, Sask., July 19-21, 1933.

—— The CCF in convention. By F. R. Scott. (In *The Canadian forum*. Toronto. v. 18, no. 212 (Sept. 1938), pp. 166-167.)

The fifth national convention held in 1938.

—— The nature of economic planning. By F. R. Scott. (In Co-operative Commonwealth Federation (Ontario). *Planning for freedom*. 2d ed. [Toronto] 1944. pp. 5-11.)

Lecture delivered April 24, 1944.

—— The nineteen thirties in the United States and Canada. By F. R. Scott. (In Hoar, Victor (comp.) *The Great depression*. [Toronto, c1969] pp. 169-185.)

Discusses the League for Social Reconstruction and the CCF Party.

—— Social reconstruction and the BNA Act. By F. R. Scott. Toronto, T. Nelson, 1934. 38 p. (LSR pamphlet, no. 4.)

Discusses the question "Is the CCF programme possible under the British North America Act?"

SHACKLETON, PHIL A CCFer looks at the CCF. (In *Saturday night*. Toronto. v. 67, no. 43 (Aug. 2, 1952), p. 9.)

—— The Island's "extra" MP. (In *Atlantic guardian*. Montreal. v. 8, no. 6 (June 1951), pp. 29-32.)

Newfoundlander's [!] abroad, no. 24.
Concerns Joseph William Noseworthy, born in Lewisporte, Newfoundland.

SILCOX, CLARIS EDWIN Why I shall not vote for the CCF. (In *Canadian Commentator*. Toronto. v. 1, no. 5 (May 1957), p. 7.)

With reference to the general elections held June 10, 1957.

SINCLAIR, LISTER Why I'm voting CCF. (In *Maclean's*. Toronto. v. 66, no. 15 (Aug. 1, 1953), pp. 10; 52-53.)

Refers to the federal election held August 10, 1953.

SISSONS, CHARLES BRUCE The life story of James Shaver Woodsworth. By C. B. Sissons. (In *Saturday night*. Toronto. v. 57, no. 29 (Mar. 28, 1942), p. 14.)

Written on the occasion of his death March 21, 1942.

SMITH, JOHN The CCF Press. (In *The Canadian forum*. Toronto. v. 29, no. 350 (Mar. 1950), pp. 271-273.)

A discussion of the aims and content of some newspapers founded and supported by the CCF Party.

SMITH, MARY MARCIA The ideological relationship between the United Farmers of Alberta and the Co-operative Commonwealth Federation. [Montreal, 1967] 1 v.

Thesis (MA) – McGill University.

Socialist leader. (In *New world illustrated*. Montreal. v. 3, no. 5 (July 1942), pp. 32-33; 48.)

Concerns Major James Coldwell. A popular account of his career and objectives.

Socialists meet. (In *Saturday night*. Toronto. v. 52, no. 40 (Aug. 7, 1937), p. 5.)

Discusses the CCF Convention held in Winnipeg, July 27 and 28, 1937.

SPRY, GRAHAM A CCF approach to a People's Party. (In *New frontier*. Toronto. v. 1, no. 1 (Apr. 1936), pp. 10-12.)

Part of a symposium. For other articles see Basis for a People's Party, by E. A. Beder (pp. 6-7) and Why a People's Party, by L. Morris (pp. 8-9).

—— CCF Party in its formative years. (In Hoar, Victor (comp.) *The Great depression*. [Toronto, c1969] pp. 212-232.)
Consists of "an undocumented recollection" of the Author's political career as a member of the CCF party from 1932 to 1937.

STEVENSON, JOHN A. Canada under CCF socialism. By J. A. Stevenson. (In *National home monthly*. Winnipeg. v. 49, no. 10 (Oct. 1948), pp. 9-11; 46.)

—— Ottawa letter. New Russian trade menace. (In *Saturday night*. Toronto. v. 73, no. 11 (May 24, 1958), pp. 4-5.)
Includes a section dealing with the movement to form an alliance between the Canadian Labour Congress and the CCF Party.

STEWART, MARGARET DOROTHY (MC CALL) Ask no quarter; a biography of Agnes Macphail. By Margaret Stewart and Doris French. Toronto, Longmans, Green, 1959. 311 p.

STEWART, MILLER A CCF leader analyses election, seeks reasons for set-back. (In *Saturday night*. Toronto. v. 64, no. 42 (July 26, 1949), pp. 6-7.)
Analyses the results of the federal election held June 27, 1949.

SWAN, JAMES BANYMAN The Co-operative Commonwealth Federation. [Wolfville, N.S., 1950] 56 leaves.
Thesis (MA) – Acadia University.

THOMAS, C. P. The popes and socialism. (In *The Canadian forum*. Toronto. v. 23, no. 267 (Apr. 1943), pp. 20-21.)
Discusses Roman Catholic political support and the CCF Party.

THOMAS, ISABEL Why I intend to vote for the CCF. (In *Chatelaine*. Toronto. v. 18, no. 6 (June 1945), pp. 12-13; 64; 78-79.)
Relates to the federal election held June 11, 1945.

THOMPSON, LESLIE The CCF and communism. (In *The Canadian forum*. Toronto. v. 28, no. 332 (Sept. 1948), pp. 128-129.)

UNDERHILL, FRANK HAWKINS The CCF convention and after. By Frank H. Underhill. (In *The Canadian forum*. Toronto. v. 14, no. 168 (Sept. 1934), pp. 463-465.)
The second national convention.

—— The CCF takes stock. By Frank H. Underhill. (In *The Canadian forum*. Toronto. v. 16, no. 187 (Aug. 1936), pp. 9-10.)

—— The Cooperative Commonwealth Federation. By F. H. U. (In *The Canadian forum*. Toronto. v. 12, no. 144 (Sept. 1932), pp. 445-446.)

—— English labour and the CCF. By F. H. U. (In *The Canadian forum*. Toronto. v. 13, no. 151 (Apr. 1933), pp. 246-247.)

—— J. S. Woodsworth. (In his *In search of Canadian liberalism*. Toronto, 1961. pp. 148-163.)
"This was an address given . . . to inaugurate the Ontario Woodsworth Memorial Foundation in Toronto on October 7, 1944."

—— James Shaver Woodsworth; untypical Canadian; an estimate of his life and ideas. By Frank H. Underhill. Toronto, Ontario Woodsworth Memorial Foundation, 1944. 36 p.
An address delivered at the dinner to inaugurate the Ontario Woodsworth Memorial Foundation, Toronto, Saturday, October 7th, 1944.

—— The Winnipeg Declaration of the CCF. (In his *In search of Canadian liberalism*. Toronto, 1961. pp. 243-247.)
"This appeared in the Toronto *Globe and Mail*, 21 August, 1956, on the occasion of the new declaration of policy made by the CCF at its Winnipeg convention in the summer of 1956."

—— Without trumpets. By Frank Underhill. (In *Saturday night*. Toronto. v. 49, no. 38 (July 28, 1934), pp. [1]; 3.)
Traces the historical origins of the CCF Party.

VINING, CHARLES ARTHUR MC LAREN Miss Macphail. By R. T. L. (In *Maclean's*. Toronto. v. 46, no. 12 (June 15, 1933), p. 12.)
Concerns Agnes Macphail.

—— Mr. Woodsworth. By R. T. L. (In *Maclean's*. Toronto. v. 46, no. 3 (Feb. 1, 1933), p. 8.)
Concerns J. S. Woodsworth.

WILLS, HAROLD A. The constitution and the CCF. The constitution enters politics. What Canada's new political party could do—and how. (In *Saturday night*. Toronto. v. 48, no. 38 [i.e. 39] (Aug. 5, 1933), pp. 2; 7.)

WOODSWORTH, JAMES SHAVER The issues as I see them. By J. S. Woodsworth. (In *Maclean's*. Toronto. v. 48, no. 18 (Sept. 15, 1935), pp. 31-32.)
Relates to the federal election held October 14, 1935.

—— My neighbor; a study of city conditions, a plea for social service. B. J. S. Woodsworth. 2d ed. Toronto, Missionary Society of the Methodist Church, Forward movement [1913, c1911] 341 p. ([Methodist Church (Canada)] Missionary Society. The Young People's Forward Movement Dept. Text-book, no. 7.)

—— Strangers within our gates; or, Coming Canadians. By James S. Woodsworth. Toronto, F. C. Stephenson [c1909] 356 p. (Missionary Society of the Methodist Church, Canada. Young People's Forward Movement Dept. Text-book, no. 5.)

—— Toward socialism. Selections from the writings of J. S. Woodsworth. Edited by Edith Fowke. [Toronto] Ontario Woodsworth Memorial Foundation [c1948] 48 p.

YOUNG, WALTER DOUGLAS The anatomy of a party: the national CCF, 1932-61. [Toronto] University of Toronto Press [c1969] 328 p.

Appendix A: Calgary programme (pp. 303-304); Regina manifesto (pp. 304-313); 1956 Winnipeg Declaration of Principles of the Co-operative Commonwealth Federation (pp. 313-317).

Appendix B: Table 1. Election results 1935-62. – Table 2. Gallup poll results, 1942-61. – Table 3. CCF membership, 1947-60.

—— The national CCF; political party and political movement. Toronto, 1965. 2 v.
Thesis (PH D) – University of Toronto.

ZAKUTA, LEO The CCF-NDP; membership in a becalmed protest movement. (In Thorburn, H. G. (ed.) Party politics in Canada. Toronto [c1963] pp. 96-108.)
Reprinted from The Canadian journal of economics and political science, Toronto, v. 24, (1958), pp. 190-202.
First published under title: Membership in a becalmed protest movement.
Traces the historical development and organization of the CCF Party.

—— The CCF: the road back? (In The Canadian forum. Toronto. v. 38, no. 448 (May 1958), pp. 28-29.)
An analysis of the results of the 1958 general elections as they affected the general state of the CCF Party.

—— Membership in a becalmed protest movement. (In The Canadian journal of economics and political science. [Toronto] v. 24 (1958), pp. 190-202.)

"This paper was presented at the annual meeting of the Canadian Political Science Association in Ottawa, June 14, 1957."
Traces, historically, the ideology, organization and morale of the CCF Party.

—— A protest movement becalmed; a study of change in the CCF. [Toronto] University of Toronto Press [c1964] viii, 204 p. (Canadian studies in sociology, 1.)

ZIEGLER, OLIVE Woodsworth; social pioneer. Authorized sketch. Foreword by Dr. Salem Bland. Toronto, Ontario Pub. Co., 1934. xii, 202 p.

NEW DEMOCRATIC PARTY
(NDP)

ALLEN, RALPH What the New Party wants that Tommy Douglas has. (In Maclean's. Toronto. v. 74, no. 7 (Apr. 8, 1961), pp. 16-17; 55; 58-62.)

ANGERS, FRANCOIS ALBERT Le congrès du Nouveau Parti. Par F.-A. A. (In L'Action nationale. Montréal. v. 51 (sept. 1961), pp. [72]-75.)
The convention founding the NDP was held at Ottawa July 31-August 4, 1961.

BAKER, WALTER The New Democratic Party and Canadian politics. By W. Baker and T. Price. (In Thorburn, H. G. (ed.) Party politics in Canada. Scarborough, Ont. [c1967] pp. [168]-179.)

BELL, CHARLES E. Tommy Douglas has a plan. Saskatchewan sets pattern for the NDP. (In Saturday night. Toronto. v. 76, no. 21 (Oct. 14, 1961), pp. 21-33.)
Analyses the CCF program carried out in Saskatchewan during the premiership of T. C. Douglas, relating it to the policies proposed by the New Democratic Party under the leadership of T. C. Douglas.

BROADBENT, JOHN EDWARD Industrial democracy: a proposal. By Edward Broadbent. (In The Canadian forum. Toronto. v. 49, no. 583 (Aug. 1969), pp. 106-109.)
"Presented to the Federal Council of the New Democratic Party, Montreal, June 1969."

BRYDEN, KEN Planning is more than talking about it. (In Commentator. Toronto. v. 6, no. 10 (Oct. 1962), pp. 10-11.)
The Author argues that, unlike the Conservative and the Liberal parties, the New Democratic Party possesses a distinct policy on planning.

CAMERON, COLIN For the sake of argument. The New Party will die if it's a mere Liberal splinter. (In *Maclean's*. Toronto. v. 74, no. 15 (July 29, 1961), pp. 5; 46.)

—— A new program for the NDP. (In *Canadian dimension*. Winnipeg. v. 4, no. 6 (Sept./Oct. 1967), pp. 28-29.)
Outlines an economic policy.

COOK, GEORGE RAMSAY Crisis in the NDP. By Ramsay Cook. (In *The Canadian forum*. Toronto. v. 43, no. 511 (Aug. 1963), pp. 111-113.)
Examines the relationship of the Quebec NDP to the federal NDP. Considers the concept of two nations in Canada and the problems involved in an attempt to realize this idea.

—— Deserting a sinking ship. By Ramsay Cook. (In *The Canadian forum*. Toronto. v. 41, no. 494 (Mar. 1962), p. 267.)
Discusses the resignation of Hazen Argue from the New Democratic Party.

—— The labor-socialist wedding. Moderation wins down the line in NDP. By Ramsay Cook. (In *Saturday night*. Toronto. v. 76, no. 18 (Sept. 2, 1961), pp. 9-12.)

—— The old man, the old manifesto, the old party. By Ramsay Cook. (In *The Canadian forum*. Toronto. v. 41, no. 484 (May 1961), pp. [25]-27.)
A reply to J. S. Woodsworth and the New Party, by Kenneth McNaught. [In *The Canadian forum*. Toronto. v. 40, no. 482 (1961), pp. 280-281.]

—— Prosperity in the midst of affluence. By Ramsay Cook. (In *The Canadian forum*. Toronto. v. 41, no. 486 (July 1961), pp. 77-78.)
A comparison of "The New Party draft program" issued in 1961 with the Regina Manifesto issued by the CCF Party in 1933.

—— Three issues of the New Party convention. (In *The Canadian forum*. Toronto. v. 41, no. 487 (Sept. 1961), pp. 123-126.)
Contents: A calculated risk, by R. Cook. - Le Nouveau Parti fédéral, by H. B. Neatby. - Democracy at the convention, by P. Fox.

DOUGLAS, THOMAS CLEMENT Canada; a nation or a satellite. By the Honourable Thomas C. Douglas. (In Empire Club of Canada. *Addresses*. [Don Mills, Ont.] (1963/64), pp. [339]-350.)
Address delivered April 16, 1964.

—— The case for the New Democratic Party. Peace, prosperity and human dignity. By T. C. Douglas. (In *Saturday night*. Toronto. v. 77, no. 10 (May 12, 1962), pp. 15-17.)

—— A socialist looks at business By T. C. Douglas. (In *Canada month*. Montreal. v. 3, no. 12 (Dec. 1963), pp. 17-19.)

—— "What I will do when I form a government." By T. C. Douglas. (In *The Canadian Saturday night*. Toronto. v. 78, no. 4 (Apr. 1963), pp. 12; 36.)
Relates to the federal election held April 8, 1963.

Drawing battle lines for the next election. By S. J. B. S. (In *Canada month*. Montreal. v. 1, no. 1 (Oct. 6, 1961), pp. 33-35.)
Discusses the policies and platform of the New Democratic Party.

DREA, FRANK The New Party faces the checkoff issue. (In *Saturday night*. Toronto. v. 76, no. 3 (Feb. 4, 1961), pp. 17-19.)
Discusses "The basic proposition that unions affiliate in blocks with the New Party and arrange for an automatic deduction of five cents a member per month".

—— Trouble for the New Party? Newfoundland fight splits labor ranks. (In *Saturday night*. Toronto. v. 76, no. 16 (Aug. 5, 1961), pp. [29]-31.)

DUMAS, EVELYN The NDP since its founding. By Evelyn Dumas and Edward Smith. (In *Our generation*. Montreal. v. 6, no. 4 (1969), pp. 74-80.)

FRASER, BLAIR The LaPierre generation: can it make the NDP win? (In *Maclean's*. Toronto. v. 80, no. 10 (Oct. 1967), pp. 19; 92-96.)
Reference is to Laurier LaPierre.

—— Will the NDP turn Parliament upside down? (In *Maclean's*. Toronto. v. 78, no. 14 (July 24, 1965), pp. 13; 38-42.)

GAGNE, WALLACE Some aspects of New Democratic Party urban support in 1965. By Wallace Gagne and Peter Regenstreif. (In *The Canadian journal of economics and political science*. [Toronto] v. 33 (1967), pp. [529]-550.)
"This article analyses survey findings that shed some light on the NDP phenomenon in the 1960s in four cities in English Canada."

GAUTHIER, DAVID P. A candidate looks at his party. (In *The Canadian commentator*. Toronto. v. 6, no. 9 (Sept. 1962), pp. 9-10.)

"The first of a two part examination of the New Democratic Party by its recent candidate in Eglinton, Toronto."

For Part 2 see the author's What went wrong with the NDP?

—— An NDP-Liberal marriage is impossible. (In *Commentator*. Toronto. v. 8, no. 4 (Apr. 1964), pp 8-9.)

—— What went wrong with the NDP? Part II. By David Gauthier. (In *Commentator*. Toronto. v. 6, no. 10 (Oct. 1962), pp. 2-4.)

For Part I see the Author's A candidate looks at his Party.

GONICK, CYRIL WOLFE   The NDP federal convention—1967. By C. W. G. (In *Canadian dimension*. Winnipeg. v. 4, no. 6 (Sept./Oct. 1967), pp. 4; 37.)

—— The New Democratic Party convention. By C. W. Gonick. (In *Canadian dimension*. Winnipeg. v. 2, no. 6 (Sept./Oct. 1965), pp. 22-23.)

Concerns the third national convention of the NDP held in Toronto, July 12-15, 1965.

GRAY, STANLEY   The New Democratic Youth convention. (In *Canadian dimension*. Winnipeg. v. 2, no. 6 (Sept./Oct. 1965), p. 23.)

A brief comment on the convention held in Toronto, July 12-15, 1965.

GZOWSKI, PETER   A report from the changing heartland of Canada. (In *Maclean's*. Toronto. v. 77, no. 14 (July 25, 1964), pp. [10-11]; 28-31.)

Discusses the CCF Party in Saskatchewan, with a view to its national influence.

HARDING, JAMES   The NDP, the Regina Manifesto, and the New Left. (In *Canadian dimension*. Winnipeg. v. 4, no. 1 (Nov./Dec. 1966), pp. 18-19.)

HOROWITZ, GAD   The future of the NDP. (In *Canadian dimension*. Winnipeg. v. 3, no. 5 (July/Aug. 1966), pp. 23-24.)

Discusses the results of a survey conducted by *Canadian dimension* in 1965.

—— Quebec collectivism—socialism—NDP? (In *Canadian dimension*. Winnipeg. v. 2, no. 5 (July/Aug. 1965), pp. 16-17.)

At head of title: Nouveau parti démocratique. The New Democratic Party in Quebec.

"This article was presented originally as a Viewpoint talk over CBC-TV."

HUNTER, W. D. G.   The New Democratic Party: antecedents, policies, prospects. (In

Queen's quarterly. Kingston. v. 69 (1962), pp. [361]-376.)

—— Paralytic New Democracy. (In *Canadian dimension*. Winnipeg. v. 4, no. 5 (July/Aug. 1967), pp. 8-10.)

Concerns the federal New Democratic Party.

INGLE, LORNE   A reply to Mr. Fisher. (In *The Canadian forum*. Toronto. v. 40, no. 478 (Nov. 1960), pp. 183-184.)

A reply to The last CCF roundup, by D. M. Fisher. (In *The Canadian forum*. Toronto. v. 40, no. 476 (1960), pp. 122-123.)

JEWETT, PAULINE MAE   Voting in the 1960 federal by-elections at Peterborough and Niagara Falls: who voted New Party and why? By Pauline Jewett. (In *The Canadian journal of economics and political science*. [Toronto] v. 28 (1962), pp. 35-53.)

"This paper was presented at the annual meeting of the Canadian Political Science Association in Montreal, June 9, 1961."

—— Voting in the 1960 federal by-elections at Peterborough and Niagara Falls. Who voted New Party and why? By Pauline Jewett. (In Courtney, J. C. (ed.) *Voting in Canada*. [Scarborough, Ont., c1967] pp. [50]-70.)

"Reprinted from The Canadian journal of economics and political science, XXVIII (February) 1962."

KETTLE, JOHN   Parliament— discussed and defended. (In *Canada month*. Montreal. v. 9, no. 2 (Feb. 1969), pp. 11-13.)

A *Canada month* profile.

Interviews Stanley Knowles.

KNOWLES, STANLEY HOWARD   The New Party. By Stanley Knowles. [Toronto] McClelland and Stewart [1961] vi, 136 p.

—— The New Party. By Stanley Knowles. [2d print. Toronto] McClelland and Stewart [1961] vi, 136 [46] p.

First published in 1961, without the appendices.

Appendices (46 p. at end): [1] Draft constitution . . . – [2] Draft program . . .

—— Le Nouveau Parti. Traduit de l'anglais par Michel van Schendel. Préf. de Gérard Filion. Montréal, Editions du Jour [1961] 158 p.

LAURENDEAU, ANDRE   Le Nouveau Parti gagnera-t-il les Québécois au socialisme? (In *Le Magazine Maclean*. Montréal. v. 1, no 5 (juil. 1961), p. 3.)

LAUZON, ADELE Le Nouveau Parti Démocratique est-il viable dans le Québec? (In *Le Magazine Maclean*. Montréal. v. 2, no 3 (mars 1962), pp. 26-27; 49-51.)

LEGER, JEAN MARC Has French Canadian socialism been born? (In *The Canadian forum*. Toronto. v. 43, no. 511 (Aug. 1963), pp. 100-101.)

> From *Le Devoir*, 3 July 1963.
> Discusses the relationship between the federal and Quebec NDP.

LYONS, WILLIAM ELMER The New Democratic Party in the Canadian political system. [University Park, 1965] vi, 458 leaves.

> Thesis (PH D) – Pennsylvania State University.

MC LEOD, JOHN TENNYSON Taylor vs. Young: amateurs vs. pros. By John T. McLeod. (In *The Canadian forum*. Toronto. v. 43, no. 514 (Nov. 1963), p. 175.)

> A discussion of two articles: Regina, thirty years later, by Walter Young. (In *The Canadian forum*. Toronto. v. 43, no. 512 (1963), pp. 124-126) and Regina revisited, by Charles Taylor (In *The Canadian forum*. Toronto. v. 43, no. 513 (1963), pp. 150-151).

MC NAUGHT KENNETH WILLIAM KIRKPATRICK J. S. Woodsworth and the New Party. By Kenneth McNaught. (In *The Canadian forum*. Toronto. v. 40, no. 482 (Mar. 1961), pp. 280-281.)

> For a rejoinder, see The old man, the old manifesto, the old party, by Ramsay Cook. (In *The Canadian forum*. Toronto. v. 41, no. 484 (1961), pp. [25]-27.)

—— National affairs. The NDP'S special status kick. By Kenneth McNaught. (In *Saturday night*. Toronto. v. 82, no. 10 (Oct. 1967), pp. 12; 15.)

> Discusses NDP attempts to define the position of Quebec within Confederation.

MALLORY, JAMES RUSSELL Vacation of seats in the House of Commons: the problem of Burnaby-Coquitlam. By. J. R. Mallory. (In *The Canadian journal of economics and political science*. [Toronto] v. 30 (1964), pp. 125-130.)

> Examines the case in Burnaby-Coquitlam, British Columbia, where Erhart Regier, who had been re-elected to the House of Commons in the general elections of June 18, 1962, resigned his seat to T. C. Douglas,

leader of the New Democratic Party, who had been defeated by his Regina City constituency in the federal election.

MARTIN, LOUIS Le NDP: une image rassurante. (In *Le Magazine Maclean*. Montréal. v. 7, no 5 (mai 1967), p. 1.)

> Concerns Robert Cliche.

MORTON, DESMOND PAUL With your help; an election manual. [Ottawa] New Democratic Party [n.d.] 49 p.

> Cover title.

The NDP: after two years, a new look? (In *Canada month*. Montreal. v. 3, no. 7 (July 1963), p. 14.)

NATIONAL COMMITTEE FOR THE NEW PARTY Convention call for the first constitutional convention; a new political party for Canada. [Ottawa, 1961] [4, 4] p.

> Caption title.
> Text bilingual, English and French.
> Convention held in Ottawa, July 31 – August 4, 1961.

—— Delegates to the New Party Founding Convention, Ottawa, Ontario, July 31 – August 4, 1961. Délégués à la [sic] Congrès de fondation du Nouveau Parti, Ottawa, Ontario, juillet 31 – août 4, 1961. [Ottawa, 1961] 48 p.

> Cover title.
> Title and headings in English and French.

—— Draft constitution. Ottawa, 1961. 15 p.

> At head of title: The New Party.
> On cover: Founding Convention. Ottawa, July 31 – Aug. 4, 1961.

—— Draft program. Ottawa, 1961. 30 p.

> At head of title: The New Party.
> On cover: Founding Convention. Ottawa, July 31 – Aug. 4, 1961.

—— New Party Founding Convention program, agenda, convention committees and rules of order. [Ottawa, 1961] 11, 11 p.

> Cover title.
> Text bilingual, English and French.
> Convention held in Ottawa July 31 – Aug. 4, 1961.

—— Report to the Founding Convention of the National Committee for the New Party, Ottawa, July 31, 1961. [Ottawa, 1961] [4, 4] p.

> Cover title.
> Text bilingual, English and French.

—— Resolutions submitted to the New Party Founding Convention, Ottawa, Ontario, July 31—August 4, 1961. [Ottawa, 1961] 131 p.
Cover title.

—— Study paper on programme of the proposed new political party for Canada. Ottawa, 1960. 19 p.
Cover title: A new party for Canada; study paper on programme.
Issued also in French.

NEW DEMOCRATIC PARTY (CANADA) The federal constitution of the New Democratic Party, adopted by its Founding Convention, Ottawa, July 31—August 4, 1961. [Ottawa, 1961] 17 p.

—— The federal program of the New Democratic Party, adopted by its Founding Convention, Ottawa, July 31—August 4, 1961. [Ottawa, 1961] 29 p.

NEWMAN, PETER CHARLES Backstage at Ottawa. Choosing a leader isn't the New Party's only problem. By Peter C. Newman. (In Maclean's. Toronto. v. 73, no. 17 (Aug. 13, 1960), p. 4.)

—— Backstage at Ottawa. The fight to lead the New Party is lopsided but real. By Peter C. Newman. (In Maclean's. Toronto. v. 74, no. 5 (Mar. 11, 1961), p. 64.)

—— Backstage at Ottawa. Tommy Douglas' vision of the carefully-planned, fully-insured promised land. By Peter C. Newman. (In Maclean's. Toronto. v. 74, no. 16 (Aug. 12, 1961), p. 54.)

—— Backstage in Ottawa. Tommy Douglas' first six months. Where the NDP will seek votes: among the Tories. By Peter C. Newman. (In Maclean's. Toronto. v. 75, no. 3 (Feb. 10, 1962), p. 50.)

—— Backstage in Ottawa. The last angry idealist becomes a political power. By Peter C. Newman. (In Maclean's. Toronto. v. 76, no. 2 (Jan. 26, 1963), p. 1.)
Concerns David Lewis.

—— Dilemma of a maverick politician: too many ideas to be a success. By Peter C. Newman. (In Maclean's. Toronto. v. 74, no. 9 (May 6, 1961), pp. 26; 30; 34.)
Concerns Douglas Fisher.

NOBLE, HOWAT PEARSON Membership participation and political organization; a study of the New Democratic Party in five provincial ridings in the inter-election period, 1963-65. [Ottawa] 1966. 1 v.
Thesis (MA) – Carleton University.

PENTLAND, HARRY CLARE Guaranteed full employment: a critique of the New Democratic Party program. (In Canadian dimension. Winnipeg. v. 2, no. 1 (Nov./Dec. 1964), pp. 11-14.)
Article no. 2 of Three approaches to unemployment.

ROBIN, MARTIN The New Democratic Party after Sask. (In Canadian dimension. Winnipeg. v. 1, no. 7 (July/Aug. 1964), pp. 5-7.)
Considers the prospects for a third party in Canadian politics.

RODGERS, RAYMOND Point of view. Canada still needs a new Party. (In Saturday night. Toronto. v. 76, no. 19 (Sept. 16, 1961), p. 56.)
A criticism of the New Democratic Party.

ROHMER, RICHARD Government by caucus. (In Canada month. Montreal. (July 1, 1961), pp. 17-18.)
Considers the principles and organization of the New Party. The founding convention of the New Democratic Party was held in Ottawa July 31—August 4, 1961.

SAYWELL, JOHN TUPPER How new will the New Party be? By John Saywell. (In Saturday night. Toronto. v. 76, no. 9 (Apr. 29, 1961), pp. 27-28.)
A review article of The New Party, by Stanley Knowles. Toronto, McClelland & Stewart [1961].

SCHLESINGER, RUDOLPH Socialism and the New Democratic Party. A view from Europe. (In Canadian dimension. Winnipeg. v. 4, no. 1 (Nov./Dec. 1966), pp. 16-17.)

SCOTT, VAL The Scott letter: The future of the NDP. "Where do we go from here?" was the question. Val Scott asked his leader, Tommy Douglas, in a letter partially reproduced here. (In Commentator. Toronto. v. 7, no. 12 (Dec. 1963), pp. 15-16.)

SHERWOOD, DAVID HENRY The NDP and French Canada, 1961-1965. [Montreal] 1966. 1 v.
Thesis (MA) – McGill University.

SPARHAM, DESMOND "Who is Right and what is Left." (In Canadian dimension. Winnipeg. v. 1, no. 8 (Sept./Oct. 1964), pp. 17-18.)
Considers differences of emphasis within the New Democratic Party.

STEIN, DAVID LEWIS   The birth of a labor party? (In *Maclean's*. Toronto. v. 75, no. 15 (July 28, 1962), p. 14.)

Concerns the New Democratic Party and the results of the federal election held June 18, 1962.

STEVENSON, JOHN A.   The New Party. Success in by-elections of concern to old-party leaders. By J. A. Stevenson. (In *Canadian commentator*. Toronto. v. 4, no. 12 (Dec. 1960), pp. 10-12.)

STINSON, LLOYD   Exchange. Reply to the New Left. (In *Canadian dimension*. Winnipeg. v. 3, no. 3-4 (Mar.—Apr., 1966), pp. 56-57.)

A reply to the article New Left, old Left, by S. Gray. (In *Canadian dimension*. Winnipeg. v. 3, no. 1 (Nov. 1965), pp. 11-13).

Concentrates on the objectives and approach of the New Democratic Party.

STURSBERG, PETER   Ottawa letter. (In *Saturday night*. Toronto. v. 79, no. 8 (Aug. 1964), pp. 7-8.)

Concerns Douglas Fisher and rumours of his involvement in promoting an NDP–Liberal Party merger.

TAYLOR, CHARLES   Regina revisited: reply to Walter Young. (In *The Canadian forum*. Toronto. v. 43, no. 513 (Oct. 1963), pp. 150-151.)

A reply to Regina, thirty years later, by Walter Young (In *The Canadian forum*. Toronto. v. 43, no. 512 (1963), pp. 124-126.) For a rejoinder see Taylor vs. Young, by John T. McLeod (In *The Canadian forum*. Toronto. v. 43, no. 514 (1963), p. 175.)

TOWER, COURTNEY   A new direction for the New Democrats: Left! (In *Maclean's*. Toronto. v. 82, no. 10 (Oct. 1969), pp. 1-6.)

UNDERHILL, FRANK HAWKINS   New Canadian frontier? By Frank H. Underhill. (In *Queen's quarterly*. Kingston. v. 69 (1962), pp. [294]-301.)

A review article of *Social purpose for Canada*, edited by M. Oliver. Toronto, University of Toronto Press, 1961.

Comments on the goals of the New Democratic Party.

——— Old wine in new bottles. By Frank H. Underhill. (In *The Canadian forum*. Toronto. v. 41, no. 484 (May 1961), pp. 35-36.)

A review article of *The New Party*, by S. Knowles. Toronto, McClelland & Stewart, 1961.

WALKER, A.   Social purpose for Canada: a review. (In *The Marxist quarterly*. Toronto. no. 2 (summer 1962), pp. 77-83.)

A review article of *Social purpose for Canada*, edited by M. Oliver. Toronto, University of Toronto Press [c1961]

Discusses the book in terms of its "projecting an ideological basis for the NDP".

WILBUR, RICHARD   The Maritimes; continuous failure. (In *Canadian dimension*. Winnipeg. v. 4, no. 5 (July/Aug. 1967), pp. 18-19.)

Considers the position of the New Democratic Party in the Maritimes.

WILSON, J. M.   Waterloo South breakthrough for the NDP? (In *The Canadian forum*. Toronto. v. 44, no. 527 (Dec. 1964), pp. 196-198.)

The by-election was held November 9, 1964.

YOUNG, WALTER DOUGLAS   The NDP: British Columbia's labour party. By Walter D. Young. (In Meisel, John (ed.) *Papers on the 1962 election*. [Toronto, 1964] pp. [181]-200.)

——— Regina, thirty years later. By Walter Young. (In *The Canadian forum*. Toronto. v. 43, no. 512 (Sept. 1963), pp. 124-126.)

A report on the second convention held by the New Democratic Party in Regina, August 6-9, 1963. Compares the policies and the problems of the NDP to those of its predecessor, the CCF Party.

For a rejoinder see Regina revisited, by Charles Taylor. (In *The Canadian forum*. Toronto. v. 43, no. 513 (1963), pp. 150-151) and also Taylor vs. Young, by John T. McLeod (In *The Canadian forum*. Toronto. v. 43, no. 514 (1963), p. 175.)

ZAKUTA, LEO   The New Party. (In *The Canadian forum*. Toronto. v. 39, no. 469 (Feb. 1960), pp. 251-252.)

SOCIAL CREDIT PARTY OF CANADA

Anthony Hlynka. (In *New world illustrated*. Montreal. v. 2, no. 9 (Nov. 1941), pp. 19; 64.)

Brief sketch.

BARTHA, PETER   Social Credit has a field day with the Bank Act. The decennial revision of the Bank Act gives Socreds and Créditistes an opportunity to play again their quaint familiar tunes. (In *Commentator*. Toronto. v. 9, no. 6 (June 1965), pp. 18-20.)

BOWMAN, ROBERT Why I'm voting Social Credit. By Bob Bowman. (In *Maclean's*. Toronto. v. 66, no. 15 (Aug. 1, 1953), pp. 11; 52.)
Refers to the federal election held August 10, 1953.

BRYCE, ROBERT B. What is wrong with Social Credit? (In *Public affairs*. Halifax. v. 1, no. 2 (Dec. 1937), pp. [47]-49.)

CAOUETTE, REAL Réal Caouette vous parle. [Montréal] Editions du Caroussel [sic] [1962] 96 p.
Contents: Réal Caouette vous parle. – Conférence de presse. – Les chefs du Crédit social s'expliquent, par R. Caouette et G. Grégoire.

COX, COROLYN Name in the news. Canada needs no more imported capital says S. C. Treasurer. (In *Saturday night*. Toronto. v. 59, no. 47 (July 29, 1944), p. 2.)
A biographical sketch of Solon Low.

DEACHMAN, ROBERT JOHN The myths of Social Credit. By R. J. Deachman. (In *The Maritime advocate and busy East*. Sackville, N.B. v. 26, no. 12 (July 1936), pp. 11-12.)

EDINBOROUGH, ARNOLD The shade of "Bible Bill"? Social Credit: a party "on the move". (In *Saturday night*. Toronto. v. 76, no. 16 (Aug. 5, 1961), pp. 12-14.)
Concerns the first national convention of the Social Credit Party held at Ottawa July 4-6, 1961.

EGGLESTON, WILFRID Capital comment. SC still harps on one string. (In *Saturday night*. Toronto. v. 66, no. 4 (Oct. 31, 1950), p. 3.)
Comments on a national convention held by the Social Credit Party in Regina.

—— The Ottawa letter. Social Creditors claim to be Bretton Woods specialists. (In *Saturday night*. Toronto. v. 61, no. 16 (Dec. 22, 1945), p. 8.)
Refers to the United Nations Monetary and Financial Conference held at Bretton Woods, New Hampshire, during 1944.

FRASER, BLAIR Backstage at Ottawa. Social Credit feels its oats. (In *Maclean's*. Toronto. v. 66, no. 8 (Apr. 15, 1953), pp. 5; 95.)

—— Backstage at Ottawa. How the Socred blitzkrieg failed. (In *Maclean's*. Toronto. v. 69, no. 16 (Aug. 4, 1956), pp. 7; 51.)

—— The rise and fall of Social Credit. (In *Maclean's*. Toronto. v. 71, no. 10 (May 10, 1958), pp. 26; 96-100.)

GALLOWAY, JEAN LOVE Alice Low: she married the teacher. (In *Saturday night*. Toronto. v. 64, no. 37 (June 21, 1949), p. 27.)

GRENIER, JEAN Le Crédit social au lieu du socialisme. (In *L'Action nationale*. Montréal. v. 43 (juil./août 1954), pp. [566]-582.)

GZOWSKI, PETER A strongman's road to power. (In *Maclean's*. Toronto. v. 75, no. 15 (July 28, 1962), pp. 11; 33-35.)
Concerns Réal Caouette and the results of the federal election held June 18, 1962.

HALLETT, MARY ELIZABETH The Social Credit Party and the New Democratic movement, 1939-1940. (In *The Canadian historical review*. Toronto. v. 4 (1966), pp. 301-325.)

HALLIDAY, HUGH ALAN Social Credit as a national party in Canada. [Ottawa, 1966] 197 leaves.
Thesis (MA) – Carleton University.

IRVING, JOHN ALLAN The conscience of conservatism: Social Credit's new man of destiny. By John A. Irving. (In *Saturday night*. Toronto. v. 76, no. 12 (June 10, 1961), pp. 9-11.)
Concerns Robert N. Thompson.

—— The evolution of the Social Credit movement. By John A. Irving. (In *The Canadian journal of economics and political science*. Toronto. v. 14 (1948), pp. 321-341.)

—— Social Credit: prophet and the doctrine. By John A. Irving. (In *Saturday night*. Toronto. v. 68, no. 23 (Mar. 14, 1953), pp. 7-8.)

—— Social Credit's future as a federal force. By John A. Irving. (In *Saturday night*. Toronto. v. 68, no. 28 (Apr. 18, 1953), pp. 7-8.)

KETTLE, JOHN They have nothing to lose. By J. K. (In *Canada month*. Montreal. v. 3, no. 4 (Apr. 1963), pp. 19-21.)
Discusses the Social Credit Party.

KOSTAKEFF, JORDAN Qu'est-ce que le Crédit social? Montréal, Editions du Jour [c1962] 128 p.
On cover: Yordan Kostakeff.

LEMIEUX, VINCENT Les dimensions sociologiques du vote Créditiste au Québec. (In *Recherches sociographiques*. Québec. v. 6, no 2 (mai—août 1965), pp. [181]-195.)
Examines the federal elections held in 1962 and 1963.

LOW, SOLON   What does Social Credit stand for? By Solon Low as quizzed by Blair Fraser. (In *Maclean's*. Toronto. v. 58, no. 8 (Apr. 15, 1945), pp. 10-11; 31-34.)

MAHEU, PIERRE   L'ambiguité du peuple. (In *Parti pris*. Montréal. v. 3, no. 8 (mars 1966), pp. 6-14.)

Examines the theory and political party of Social Credit.

MALLORY, JAMES RUSSELL   Inquest on Social Credit. By J. R. Mallory. (In *The Canadian forum*. Toronto. v. 38, no. 449 (June 1958), pp. [49]; 72.)

Analyses the impact on the Social Credit Party of the federal election results of March 31, 1958.

—— Social Credit and the federal power in Canada. Toronto, University of Toronto Press, 1954. xii, 204 p. (Social Credit in Alberta; its background and development, 5.)

—— Social Credit: party or movement? By J. R. Mallory. (In *The Canadian forum*. Toronto. v. 35, no. 413 (June 1955), pp. 52-55.)

MARCHAND, JEAN   "Les Béréts blancs" sont les seuls vrais créditistes. (In *Cité libre*. Montréal. v. 53 (jan. 1963), pp. 15-17.)

MAYO, HENRY BERTRAM   What has Social Credit to offer? By H. B. Mayo. (In *Canadian commentator*. Toronto. v. 1, no. 5 (May 1957), pp. 5-6.)

MORIN, ROLAND   Crédit social. [Québec, 1947] 1 v.

Thesis (M SC SOC) – Laval University.

NEILL, ROBERT FOLIET   Social Credit and national policy in Canada. By R. F. Neill. (In *Journal of Canadian studies*. Peterborough. v. 3, no. 1 (1968), pp. 3-13.)

NEWMAN, PETER CHARLES   Backstage in Ottawa. Flash: the Socreds are . . . well, antisemantic. By Peter C. Newman. (In *Maclean's*. Toronto. v. 75, no. 19 (Sept. 22, 1962), pp. 1-2.)

PARKINSON, JOSEPH F.   Social Credit—a monetary anaesthetic for a diseased economic order. By J. F. Parkinson. (In *Canadian comment*. Toronto. v. 4, no. 7 (July 1935), pp. [3]-5.)

PELLERIN, JEAN   Le messianisme créditiste, ou le néo-charlatanisme. (In *Cité libre*. Montréal. no. 53 (jan. 1963), pp. 10-14.)

PELLETIER, GERARD   Profil d'un démagogue: M. Réal Caouette. (In *Cité libre*. Montréal. no. 53 (jan. 1963), pp. [1]-9.)

English translation published under title: Réal Caouette: portrait of a demagogue. (In *The Canadian forum*. Toronto. v. 43, no. 507 (1963), pp. 6-9.)

—— Réal Caouette: portrait of a demagogue. (In *The Canadian forum*. Toronto. v. 43, no. 507 (Apr. 1963), pp. 6-9.)

"Translation by Dawn Smith."

First published under title: Profil d'un démagogue: M. Réal Caouette. (In *Cité libre*. Montréal. no. 53 (jan. 1963), pp. [1]-9.)

PEPIN, JEAN LUC   Un slogan pour le moins douteux: le Crédit social s'en vient. (In *Le Magazine Maclean*. Montréal. v. 1, no. 5 (juil. 1961), p. 2.)

PILOTTE, HELENE   Réal Caouette, führer ou Don Quichotte? (In *Le Magazine Maclean*. Montréal. v. 2, no 9 (sept. 1962), pp. 18-20; 34-35; 38.)

PINARD, MAURICE   One-party dominance and third parties. (In *The Canadian journal of economics and political science*. [Toronto] v. 33 (1967), pp. [358]-373.)

"This is a revised and shortened version of a paper read at the thirty-sixth annual meeting of the Canadian Political Science Association, Charlottetown, 1964, under the title of 'Political factors in the rise of Social Credit in Quebec'."

"The purpose of this paper is, first, to show in what ways the political situation at the federal level in Quebec was particularly conducive to the rise of the Social Credit party and, second, to present a general hypothesis concerning the political factors which account for the rise of third parties during other periods, and elsewhere in Canada."

RICHARDSON, BURTON TAYLOR   Solon Low. By B. T. Richardson. (In *Maclean's*. Toronto. v. 58, no. 8 (Apr. 15, 1945), pp. 10; 24.)

Concerns Solon Low leader of the Social Credit Party.

SANDWELL, BERNARD KEBLE   From the editor's chair. Social Credit has a gospel, a creed and a very satisfactory devil. By B. K. Sandwell. (In *Saturday night*. Toronto. v. 59, no. 32 (Apr. 15, 1944), p. 10.)

SMILEY, DONALD VICTOR   Canada's Poujadists: a new look at Social Credit. By Donald V. Smiley. (In *The Canadian forum*. Toronto. v. 42, no. 500 (Sept. 1962), pp. [121]-123.)

Social Credit Association of Canada. Manuel du Crédit social. Ottawa, 1958. 64 (i.e. 65) leaves.

—— Social Credit explained. [Ottawa, 1958?] 48 leaves. diagrs., tables.

Cover title.
Mimeographed.

Socialist Credit. By a pessimist. (In Saturday night. Toronto. v.53, no. 20 (Mar. 19, 1938), pp. [1]; 3.)

Critical comments on Social Credit and the socialist policy of unemployment relief.

STURSBERG, PETER   Postmark Ottawa. (In The Canadian Saturday night. Toronto. v. 77, no. 18 (Nov. 1962), pp. 38-40.)

Concerns the Social Credit Party.

THOMPSON, ROBERT NORMAN   The case for Social Credit. Canada's gateway to greatness. By Robert N. Thompson. (In Saturday night. Toronto. v. 77, no. 10 (May 12, 1962), pp. 17-19.)

—— Commonsense for Canadians; a selection of speeches analysing today's opportunities and problems. Edited by Patrick Nicholson. Toronto, McClelland and Stewart [c1965] 162 p.

On Social Credit policies for Canada.

—— "What I will do when I form a government." By Robert N. Thompson. (In The Canadian Saturday night. Toronto. v. 78, no. 4 (Apr. 1963), pp. 11; 36.)

Relates to the federal election held April 8, 1963.

TROYER, WARNER   The real Caouette, new political missile? A personal assessment of Quebec's Social Credit leader by a reporter who has dealt with him close-up. (In The Canadian commentator. Toronto. v. 6, no. 9 (Sept. 1962), pp. 4-5.)

WATKINS, ERNEST   Point of view. Social Credit has no social conscience. (In Saturday night. Toronto. v. 76, no. 15 (July 22, 1961), pp. 36-[37].)

WILLIAMSON, COLWYN   Anti-semitism & Social Credit. (In Canadian dimension. Winnipeg. v. 2, no. 6 (Sept./Oct. 1965), pp. 13-16.)

WILSON, CHARLES F.   Social Credit: our next panacea. Alluring picture painted by Social Credit-ers. State dividends to replace taxes; unemployment and national debt to vanish. Are premises of doctrine sound? (In Saturday night. Toronto. v. 49, no. 51 (Oct. 27, 1934), pp. [17]; 24.)

COMMUNIST PARTY OF CANADA

ABELLA, IRVING MARTIN   The CIO, the Communist Party and the formation of the Canadian Congress of Labour, 1936-1941. By I. M. Abella. (In Canadian Historical Association. Historical papers. [Ottawa] (1960), pp. [112]-128.)

ALLEN, RALPH   The case history of Comrade Buck. (In Maclean's. Toronto. v. 64, no. 6 (Mar. 15, 1951), pp. 7-9; 54-58.)

Concerns Tim Buck.

BELOFF, MAX   Canada and Communism. (In Canadian life. Toronto. v. 1, no. 1 (Mar./Apr. 1949), pp. 6; 34.)

Part 1.

—— Canada and Communism. The Communist as such has only a single allegiance—to the Revolution, and through it, to the Soviet Union. (In Canadian life. Toronto. v. 1, no. 2 (July 1949), pp. 4; 35.)

Part 2.

BUCK, TIMOTHY   Canada; the communist viewpoint. By Tim Buck. [Foreword by Stanley B. Ryerson] Toronto, Progress Books [c1948] 288 p.

—— An indictment of capitalism; the speech of Tim Buck. Address to the jury on November 12th, 1931 at the trial of the eight leaders of the Communist Party of Canada during November 2nd to November 13th, 1931. With an explanatory introd. by A. E. Smith. Toronto, Canadian Labor Defense League, National Executive Committee [pref. 1932] 86 p.

—— A labor policy for victory. Submission presented by Tim Buck on behalf of the Dominion Communist-Labor Total War Committee to the National War Labor Board Inquiry into Labor Relations. May 28th, 1943. [Toronto, Printed by Eveready Printers, 1943?] 90 p.

—— Our fight for Canada; selected writings, 1923-1959. Introd. by Leslie Morris. [Toronto, Progress Books, 1959] 407 p.

Issued by the National Executive Committee of the Communist Party of Canada.

—— Put Canada first. [Report to the 5th National Convention Labor-Progressive Party, March 25th, 1954. By Tim Buck. Toronto, National Committee, Labor-Progressive Party, 1954] 46 p.

—— Thirty years, 1922-1952; the story of the Communist movement in Canada. By

Tim Buck. [Foreword by Leslie Morris] Toronto, Progress Books [c1952], 224 p.

—— What we propose. By Tim Buck. [Toronto, Communist Party of Canada, 1936] 79 p.
Cover title.

—— Why I support Mackenzie King. By Tim Buck. (In New world. Toronto. v. 5, no. 6 (Aug. 1944), pp. [28]-31.)

Canada's Communist network. (In New world. Toronto. v. 7, no. 12 (Feb. 1947), pp. 9-11; 35.)

Canadian Communist and the French-Canadian nation (In The Marxist quarterly. Toronto. no. 15 (autumn 1965), pp. 27-35.)
A compilation of brief excerpts spanning the years 1929-1964.

CLARKE, FREDERICK NELSON Two nations, one country; the Communist proposals for a democratic solution of the crisis of Confederation. Toronto, Published for the Communist Party by Progress Books, 1965. 29 p.
Cover title.

COMMUNIST PARTY OF CANADA Constitution of the Labor-Progressive Party, as amended at Fourth National Convention, January 25-28, 1951. [Toronto, 1951?] 31 p.
Cover title.

—— A new constitution for Canada. (In The Marxist quarterly. Toronto. no. 15 (autumn 1965), pp. 78-85.)
"Excerpt from the brief submitted by the Communist Party of Canada to the Laurendeau-Dunton Royal Commission."

—— Toward democratic unity for Canada. Submission of the Dominion Committee, Communist Party of Canada to the Royal Commission on Dominion-Provincial Relations. Rev. ed. [Toronto, New Era Publishers, 1939] 123 p.
"Prepared under the editorship of Alderman Stewart Smith of Toronto."

—— National Convention, 2d, Toronto, 1946. For peace, progress, socialism. [Foreword by William Kashtan. Toronto, Printed by Eveready Printers [n.d.] 104 p.
Cover title.
"This booklet contains the main report and summary delivered by Tim Buck, National Leader of the Labor-Progressive Party to the second national convention, which met in Toronto, June 1-5, 1946." - Foreword.

—— NATIONAL EXECUTIVE COMMITTEE Canadian Independence and a people's parliament: Canada's path to socialism. [Toronto, 1954] 32 p.
On cover: Program of the Labor-Progressive Party.

—— QUEBEC PROVINCIAL COMMITTEE Une politique sociale au lieu d'une politique bourgeoise. [Toronto, Progress Books, 1964] 31 p.
Text signed: Samuel Walsh, président du Comité.

COX, COROLYN Name in the news. How Tim Buck got that way. (In Saturday night. Toronto. v. 58, no. 41 (June 19, 1943), p. 2.)
A biographical sketch.

—— Name in the news. Dutch and French strains blend in this Lab.-Prog. leader. (In Saturday night. Toronto. v. 59, no. 26 (Mar. 4, 1944), p. 2.)
A biographical sketch of Stanley B. Ryerson, Education Director for the Labor-Progressive Party.

—— Name in the news. First Communist in Commons was in the "Battle of Queen's Park". (In Saturday night. Toronto. v. 59, no. 33 (Apr. 22, 1944), p. 2.)
Concerns Fred Rose. MP.

DREA, FRANK Red infiltration fails. Canadian labor ousts Communism. (In Saturday night. Toronto. v. 77, no. 4 (Feb. 17, 1962), pp. 20; 22-34.)

DREW, GEORGE ALEXANDER Dr. Drew on the menace of Communism. By George A. Drew. (In Revue de l'Université d'Ottawa. 18. année (1948), pp. [9]-13.)
"A speech by the Honourable George Drew at the Convocation of the University of Ottawa, Wednesday, December 3rd, 1947."

EGGLESTON, WILFRID Capital comment. How to deal with Communists. (In Saturday night. Toronto. v. 65, no. 32 (May 16, 1950), p. 3.)
Concerns a debate initiated by a motion introduced by George Drew on May 2, 1950.

FRASER, BLAIR Backstage at Ottawa. Door-to-door spy hunt in Ottawa. By the Man with a Notebook. (In Maclean's. Toronto. v. 62, no. 17 (Sept. 1, 1949), pp. 16; 67-68.)
Concerns RCMP officers searching for those who may be members of the Canadian Communist Party.

—— The Commies aren't so hot, at that. (In *Maclean's*. Toronto. v. 64, no. 14 (July 15, 1951), pp. 10-11; 50-52.)

—— The Commies muscle in. "Control or destroy"—that's the Communist labor line. Reds control nine unions, but foment trouble everywhere. (In *Maclean's*. Toronto. v. 60, no. 2 (Jan. 15, 1947), pp. 13; 40-42.)

How Dr. Endicott fronts for the Reds. (In *Maclean's*. Toronto. v. 65, no. 14 (July 15, 1952), pp. 7; 9; 49-51.)
Concerns James Gareth Endicott.

The Future of the Communist Party; editorial. (In *The Canadian forum*. Toronto. v. 23, no. 270 (July 1943), pp. 77-78.)

GELBER, MARVIN B.   Clench the fist and smash the party. (In *The Canadian forum*. Toronto. v. 17, no. 195 (Apr. 1937), pp. 14-16.)
References are made to Communism in Canada.

GRIMSON, COLIN DONALD   The Communist Party of Canada, 1922-1946. [Montreal, 1966] iv, 221 leaves.
Thesis (MA) – McGill University.

HART, JOSEPH TATE   The Communist Party of Canada. [Durham, N.C., 1953] 183 leaves.
Thesis (MA) – Duke University.

Here we go gathering nuts in May. (In *The Canadian forum*. Toronto. v. 37, no. 437 (June 1957), pp. 50-51.)
Discusses the resignation of J. B. Salsberg from the Labor-Progressive Party.

HICHIN, CARL   Communism's false front. An insider's revelation of the strategy behind the "campaign for democracy". (In *Maclean's*. Toronto. v. 52, no. 3 (Feb. 1, 1939), pp. 7; 34; 36-39.)
Reveals the strategy behind the "campaign for democracy" advocated by the Communist Party of Canada.

KASHTAN, WILLIAM   Diagnosing anti-communism. By W. Kashtan. (In *The Marxist quarterly*. Toronto. no. 3 (autumn 1962), pp. [74]-89.)
A comparative analysis.

KETTLE, JOHN   The plans and methods of the Communists' new leader. (In *Canada month*. Montreal. v. 4 [i.e. 5] no. 3 (Mar. 1965), p. 9.)
Concerns William Kashtan.

KIRKCONNELL, WATSON   Canadian Communists and the Comintern. (In Royal

Society of Canada. *Proceedings and transactions*. Ottawa. ser. 3, v. 42 (1948), section 2, pp. 91-105.)

—— Communism in Canada and the U.S.A. (In Canadian Catholic Historical Association. *Report*. [Ottawa] (1947/48), pp. 41-51.)

—— Les communistes canadiens. (In *Relations*. Montréal. 3. année, no 33 (sept. 1943), pp. 243-245.)

MACDONALD, JACK   The Communist platform. (In *The Canadian forum*. Toronto. v. 6, no. 70 (July 1926), pp. 302-304.)
"Mr. Macdonald is president of the Canadian Labour Party and secretary of the Communist Party in Canada." – Ed.

MAC EWAN, ROSS   The boys are at it again. (In *The Canadian forum*. Toronto. v. 22, no. 266 (Mar. 1943), pp. 342-343.)
Comments on the "infiltration" of the Communist Party of Canada into the ranks of the Boilermakers and Iron Shipbuilders Union.

MC EWEN, TOM   He wrote for us; the story of Bill Bennett, pioneer socialist journalist. Vancouver, Tribune Pub. Co., 1951. 159 p.
"William (Ol' Bill) Bennett was a Communist, a founder and life-long member of the Communist movement in Canada." – Introd.

MC MANUS, T. G.   Death of a union. By T. G. McManus. (In *Maclean's*. Toronto. v. 63, no. 23 (Dec. 1, 1950), pp. 18-19; 58-59.)
The Author writes as a former member of the Communist Party of Canada who served as Secretary-Treasurer of the Canadian Seamen's Union.

—— The Reds are ready to wage war inside Canada. (In *Maclean's*. Toronto. v. 63, no. 22 (Nov. 15, 1950), pp. 7; 61-63; 65-67.)
The Author writes as a former member of the Communist Central Committee for Canada.

MORRIS, LESLIE TOM   Labor-farmer political action. [Toronto, Published by Progress Books for the Labor-Progressive Party, 1959] 23 p.
Cover title.

—— Look on Canada, now. Selected writings of Leslie Morris, 1923/1964. Toronto, Progress Books, 1970. xxiv, 213 p.

—— Why a People's Party. By Leslie Morris. (In *New frontier*. Toronto. v. 1, no. 1 (Apr. 1936), pp. 8-9.)

Part of a symposium. For the other articles see Basis for a People's Party, by E. A. Beder (pp. 6-7) and A CCF approach to a People's Party, by G. Spry (pp. 10-12).

The author is a member of the Canadian Communist Party and presents the position of the Party.

O'HEARN, D. P. Communist convention will decide "line". (In *Saturday night*. Toronto. v. 61, no. 39 (June 1, 1946), p. 9.)

Concerns the national convention of the Labor-Progressive Party held at Toronto in June 1946.

PELT, MELVYN LEONARD The Communist Party of Canada, 1929-1942. Toronto, 1964. 192 leaves.

Thesis (MA) – University of Toronto.

PHILLIPS, ALAN The thirty years' war with the Commies. (In *Maclean's*. Toronto. v. 67, no. 17 (Sept. 1, 1954), pp. 18-19; 56-62.)

A report on the Royal Canadian Mounted Police and the Canadian Communist Party.

RASKY, FRANK Canada's Communists wither away. (In *Saturday night*. Toronto. v. 72, no. 21 (Oct. 12, 1957), pp. 10-11; 29.)

Reviews the career of Joseph Salsberg.

RODNEY, WILLIAM A history of the Communist Party of Canada, 1919-1929. London, 1961. 412 leaves.

Thesis (PH D) – London School of Economics, University of London.

—— Soldiers of the International; a history of the Communist Party of Canada, 1919-1929. [Toronto] University of Toronto Press [c1968] xii, 204 p. (Canadian studies in history and government, 10.)

ROSS, MARTIN The enemy within. Domestic Communists require very careful watching. Foreign language groups are red hot-beds. (In *Saturday night*. Toronto. v. 65, no. 48 (Sept. 12, 1950), pp. 9; 38.)

ROWLAND, D. Canadian communism, the post-Stalinist phase. Winnipeg, 1964. 1 v.

Thesis (MA) – University of Manitoba.

ST. PIERRE, FREDERIC Le communisme au Canada. (In *Le Terroir*. Québec. v. 12, no. 9 (fév. 1931), pp. 18-22; v. 12, no. 10 (mars. 1931), pp. 15-18; v. 12, no. 11 (avril 1931), pp. 21-22.)

In three parts.

SANDWELL, BERNARD KEBLE From the editor's chair. Saints and heroes of the new party. By B. K. Sandwell. (In *Saturday night*. Toronto. v. 59, no. 2 (Sept. 18, 1943), pp. 14-15.)

Concerns Tim Buck and the Labor-Progressive Party.

—— From the editor's chair. Capitalism is now OK, but where does Mr. Tim Buck go to next? By B. K. Sandwell. (In *Saturday night*. Toronto. v. 59, no. 20 (Jan. 22, 1944), p. 11.)

—— New Communist strategy. Canadian comrades have received their orders from Salsberg; give up top-level unionists, go for rank and file. By B. K. Sandwell. (In *Saturday night*. Toronto. v. 66, no. 1 (Oct. 10, 1950), p. 7.)

SCOTT, FRANCIS REGINALD Communists, senators and all that. By F. R. Scott. (In *The Canadian forum*. Toronto. v. 12, no. 136 (Jan. 1932), pp. 127-129.)

Discusses the outlawing of the Communist Party of Canada. Comments are centred around "a bill to amend the Criminal Code by repealing section 98".

—— The trial of the Toronto Communists. By F. R. Scott. (In *Queen's quarterly*. Kingston. v. 39 (1932), pp. [512]-527.)

Relates the trial and conviction of eight members of the Communist Party of Canada. The trial was held November 2-13, 1931.

SCOTT, G. R. Shades of hammer and sickle. (In *Canadian comment*. Toronto. v. 6, no. 1 (Jan. 1937), pp. 9-10.)

Discusses the significance of a strong showing by the Communist Party in a Toronto civic election, relating, in general terms, to Communism in Canada.

SMITH, ALBERT EDWARD All my life; an autobiography. Toronto, Progress Books, 1949. 224 p.

STAROBIN, JOSEPH ROBERT Origins of the Canadian Communist Party. By Joseph R. Starobin. (In *The Canadian forum*. Toronto. v. 48, no. 575 (Dec. 1968), pp. 201-203.)

A review article of Soldiers of the International, a history of the Communist Party of Canada, 1919-1929, by W. Rodney. Toronto, University of Toronto Press, 1968.

STARR, MICHAEL 50 years of Communism. By Hon. Michael Starr. (In *Canada month*. Montreal. v. 7, no. 11 (Nov. 1967), pp. 12-13.)

STEIN, DAVID LEWIS The slow comeback of Canada's Communists. (In *Maclean's*. Toronto. v. 74, no. 15 July 29, 1961), pp. 7; 37-39.)

STEWART, HERBERT L. Communism: abused word. (In *Saturday night*. Toronto. v. 53, no. 30 (May 28, 1938), p. 3.)

Author comments on the listing of Communist organizations in the government's "Report on labor organization in Canada" and on the enforcement of Section 98 of the Criminal Code.

SULLIVAN, JOHN ALAN Here's how Communists rob and wreck Canadian labor unions. By Pat Sullivan. (In *New world*. Toronto. v. 8, no. 4 (June 1947), pp. 11-13.)

An interview.

——— Red sails on the Great Lakes. By J. A. (Pat) Sullivan. Toronto, Macmillan, 1955. ix, 189 p.

An account of the effort made by the Communist Party to control Canadian trade unions. The Author was a member of the Communist Party of Canada for eleven years and seeks "to show . . . that the Labour Progressive Party (Communist Party of Canada) is not a political party in the popular acceptance of that term". – Foreword.

THOMAS, MITCHELL Communism in Canada. (In *Maclean's*. Toronto. v. 44, no. 10 (May 15, 1931), pp. 7; 50; 53-56.)

TRACEY, HAL Difference of opinion. Are the Reds whistling in the dark? (In *Saturday night*. Toronto. v. 66, no. 34 (May 29, 1951), p. 10.)

Discusses the question: "Are the Communists losing their grip on Canadian trade unions?"

VANCE, CATHERINE Not by gods, but by people; the story of Bella Hall Gould. Toronto, Progress Books, 1968. 65 p.

Concerns Isabella Elizabeth Hall, a founding member of the Workers (Communist) Party of Canada in 1922.

WRIGHT, JAMES Why a Communist represents Montreal-Cartier. By Jim Wright. (In *Saturday night*. Toronto. v. 58, no. 51 (Aug. 28, 1943), pp. 14-15.)

Concerns Fred Rose.

PART II

GOVERNMENT AND POLITICAL INSTITUTIONS

GENERAL WORKS

AITCHISON, JAMES HERMISTON Le rôle fondamental de la collaboration interprovinciale. (In Sabourin, Louis (ed.) *Le système politique du Canada.* Ottawa, 1968. pp. [229]-242.)

ANGERS, FRANCOIS ALBERT Vers la République du Canada. [Montréal] Editions de l'Action nationale, 1948. 68 p.

ANGUS, HENRY FORBES Administration and democracy. (In Clark, R. M. (ed.) *Canadian issues.* [Toronto, c1961] pp. [xiii]-xx.)

ANTON, FRANK ROBERT Government supervised strike votes. A study prepared for the Department of Labour, Ottawa, under the University Research Program. Toronto, CCH Canadian [1961] xi, 190 p.

—— The role of government in the settlement of industrial disputes in Canada. With special reference to conciliation in Ontario and supervised strike voting in Alberta and British Columbia. [London, 1961-62?] 1 v.
Thesis (PH D) – University of London.

ARES, RICHARD La Confédération: pacte ou loi? (In *L'Action nationale.* Montréal. v. 34 (nov. 1949), pp. [194]-230; v. 34 (déc. 1949), pp. [243]-277.)
In two parts.

—— La Confédération; pacte ou loi? Montréal, Editions de l'Action nationale [1949] 77 p.

—— La Confédération: pacte ou loi? (In *Relations.* Montréal. [26. année] no 311 (déc. 1966), pp. 328-330.)

—— Les cultures de l'Etat. (In *L'Action nationale.* Montréal. v. 48 (mai/juin 1959), pp. [392]-401.)

—— Dossier sur le Pacte fédératif de 1867: La Confédération; pacte ou loi? Nouv. éd., entièrement refondue et mise à jour. Montréal, Bellarmin, 1967. 264 p.

—— Pour qui l'Etat? (In *Relations.* Montréal. 21. année, no 245 (mai 1961), pp. 116-118.)

—— Pour quoi l'Etat? (In *Relations.* Montréal. 21. année, no 247 (juil. 1961), pp. 175-179.)

AUBERT DE LA RIIE, P. Vers une réorganisation du nord canadien. (In *Canadian public administration.* Toronto. v. 9 (1966), pp. 376-389.)

BAIDEN, R. M. Government and the bond market. (In *Saturday night.* Toronto. v. 74, no. 3 (Jan. 31, 1959), pp. [16]-17; 32.)

BARBE, RAOUL P. Régime fiscal des entreprises publiques au Canada. (In *Canadian public administration.* Toronto. v. 10 (1967), pp. 147-160.)

BATES, STEWART Financial history of Canadian governments. A study prepared for the Royal Commission on Dominion-Provincial Relations by Stewart Bates. Ottawa, 1939. iv, 309 leaves.
Reproduced typescript.
Issued also in French.

—— Government forecasting in Canada. (In *The Canadian journal of economics and political science.* [Toronto] v. 12 (1946), pp. 361-378.)

"This paper was presented at the annual meeting of the Canadian Political Science Association in Toronto on May 24, 1946."

Examines the attempt on the part of the government "to develop a technique of forecasting suited to Canadian conditions and . . . to extend this as a basis for consideration of policy. This paper is a report on the progress of this forecasting unit . . .".

BECK, JAMES MURRAY The government of Nova Scotia. By J. Murray Beck. Toronto, University of Toronto Press, 1957. xii, 372 p. (Canadian government series, 8.)

Chapter 20: Nova Scotia in Canadian federation.

BELL, ANDREW BEAUCHAMP MAC INTOSH Canada and Dominion status. [Kingston, Ont., 1935] vi, 151 leaves.

Thesis (MA) – Queen's University.

BERTRAND, JEAN JACQUES La Confédération, en théorie . . . et en pratique. (In Congress on Canadian Affairs, 1st, Quebec, 1961. *Le Canada, expérience ratée . . . ou réussie?* [Québec] 1962. pp. 147-154.)

BONENFANT, JEAN CHARLES Les institutions politiques canadiennes. [Québec] Presses Universitaires Laval, 1954. 204 p. (Culture populaire, 9.)

BORDEN, ROBERT LAIRD The evolution of institutions of government in Canada. By R. L. Borden. (In Canadian Club of Vancouver. *Addresses.* Vancouver. (1906/08), pp. 92-97.)

Address delivered September 24, 1907.

BOURINOT, SIR JOHN GEORGE The Canadian Dominion and proposed Australian Commonwealth: a study in comparative politics. By J. G. Bourinot. (In Royal Society of Canada. *Proceedings and transactions.* Ottawa. ser. 2, v. 1 (1895), section 2, pp. 3-43.)

"Read May 15th, 1895."

"This paper is intended as a supplement to a series of papers on comparative politics . . .".

—— Canadian studies in comparative politics. By John George Bourinot. (In Royal Society of Canada. *Proceedings and transactions.* Montreal. [ser. 1] v. 8 (1890), section 2, pp. 3-36.)

"Read May 27, 1890."

—— Canadian studies in comparative politics. I. The English character of Canadian

institutions. II. Comparison between the political systems of Canada and the United States. III. Federal government in Switzerland compared with that in Canada. Montreal, Dawson Bros., 1890. 92 p.

—— Canadian studies in comparative politics: parliamentary compared with congressional government. By B. J. G. Bourinot. (In Royal Society of Canada, *Proceedings and transactions.* Ottawa [ser. 1] v. 11 (1893), section 2, pp. 77-108.)

"Read May 23, 1893."

"This paper is intended as a continuation or supplement of the series commenced under the title of 'Canadian studies in comparative politics' . . ."

—— English principles of Canadian government. By J. G. Bourinot (In *The Canadian magazine of politics, science, art and literature.* Toronto. v. 9 (1897), pp. [93]-101.)

—— Federal government in Canada. By John G. Bourinot. Baltimore, N. Murray, publication agent, Johns Hopkins University, 1889. 162 p. (Johns Hopkins University studies in historical and political science, 7th ser., 10-12.)

—— How Canada is governed; a short account of its executive, legislative, judicial and municipal institutions, with an historical outline of their origin and development. Toronto, Copp, Clark. 1895. xiv, 344 p.

—— How Canada is governed; a short account of its executive, legislative, judicial and municipal institutions, with an historical outline of their origin and development, 11th ed., rev. and edited by Francis H. Gisborne. Toronto, Copp, Clark [1918] xiv, 371 p.

—— Responsible government in Canada; its history and results. (In National Club of Toronto. *Maple leaves.* Toronto [1891] pp. [35]-83.)

BOVEY, WILFRID This democratic empire. By Lieut.-Col. Wilfrid Bovey. (In Empire Club of Canada. *Addresses.* Toronto. (1939/40), pp. 283-297.)

Address delivered February 8, 1940.

A lecture describing "specifically the nations which the Statute of Westminster mentions, the United Kingdom, the Dominion of Canada, the Commonwealth of Australia, the Dominion of New Zealand, the Union of South Africa, the Irish Free State and Newfoundland". – (p. 285)

BRADY, ALEXANDER Canada and the model of Westminster. (In Hamilton, W. B. (ed.) *The transfer of institutions*. Durham, N.C., 1964. pp. [59]-80.)

—— Democracy in the Dominions. A comparative study in institutions. Issued under the auspices of the Canadian Institute of International Affairs and the Royal Institute of International Affairs. 3d. ed. [Toronto] University of Toronto Press [c1958] 614 p.

Part one: Canada.

—— Democracy in the overseas Dominions. (In Martin, C. B. (ed.) *Canada in peace and war*. London, 1941. pp. 212-244.)

—— Federations: the Canadian and British West Indies. (In Duke University, Durham, N.C., Commonwealth-Studies Center. *Evolving Canadian federalism*. Durham, N.C., 1958. pp. [161]-180.)

—— The modern federation; some trends and problems. (In Ontario Advisory Committee on Confederation. *Background papers and reports*. [Toronto] 1967. v. 1, pp. [1]-24.)

Revised version of a paper prepared in 1966. Presented April 1967.

—— The state and economic life. (In Brown, G. W. (ed.) *Canada*. Berkeley, 1953 [c1950] pp. 353-371.)

Considers "the role of the state in the economic life of Canada".

BREWIN, FRANCIS ANDREW Faribault's and Fowlers's [!] Canada. Two leading Canadians look at what ails Canada, and propose a new fundamental law to cure those ills. By Andrew Brewin. (In *Commentator*. Toronto. v. 9, no. 5 (May 1965), pp. 5-7.)

A review article of *Ten to one; the Confederation wager*, by M. Faribault and R. M. Fowler. Toronto, McClelland and Stuart, 1965.

BROWNSTONE, M. The Canadian system of government in the face of modern demands. (In *Canadian public administration*. Toronto. v. 11 (1968), pp. [428]-439.)

BRUNET, MICHEL Les "Canadians" l'Etat fédéral et l'éducation des citoyens du Canada. (In *L'Action nationale*. Montréal. v. 47 (nov. 1957), pp. [273]-284.)

—— La science politique au service de l'union canadienne. (In *L'Action natio-*

nale. Montréal. v. 44 (déc. 1954), pp. 272-292.)

BRYCE, JAMES BRYCE, VISCOUNT Modern democracies. London, Macmillan, 1923. 2 v.

Canada: v. 1. chapters 33-37.

BURNS, RONALD M. The evolving structure of Canadian government; six lectures by R. M. Burns [Winnipeg] University of Manitoba [1966] 59 p.

Cover title.

Lectures delivered during the week beginning April 25, 1966.

Sponsored by the Division of Management Studies, Dept. of University Extension and Adult Education, University of Manitoba and the Manitoba Civil Service Commission.

BURON, EDMOND Où va le Canada? (In *Revue de l'Université d'Ottawa*. Ottawa. 2. année (1932), pp. [298]-315; [434]-452.)

A comparative analysis relating to Canadian sovereignty.

BUSSIERE, EUGENE La notion de gouvernement. [Québec] 1941. 1 v.

Thesis (MA) – Laval University.

BYRON, WILLIAM Ottawa makes a discovery. (In *MacLean's*. Toronto. v. 32, no. 1 (Jan. 1919), pp. [36]-38.)

Concerns the idea of advertising in government.

CADIEUX, MARCEL Démocratie canadienne. Par Marcel Cadieux et Paul Tremblay. (In *Revue trimestrielle canadienne*. Montréal. v. 29 (mars 1943), pp. [41]-56.)

CANADA. ADVISORY COMMISSION ON THE DEVELOPMENT OF GOVERNMENT IN THE NORTHWEST TERRITORIES Report of the Advisory Commission on the Development of Government in the Northwest Territories (1966) which examined and made recommendations upon the institutions of government of Canada's largest colonial territory: two excerpts. (In *Journal of Canadian studies*. Peterborough, Ont. v. 2, no. 1 (1967), pp. 40-53.)

CARDINAL, JEAN GUY Financial institutions. (In *Quebec in the Canada of tomorrow*. Toronto, 1968, pp. [FF-1]-FF-9.)

CARROTHERS, ALFRED WILLIAM ROOKE Canada; reluctant imperialist. By A. W. R. Carrothers. (In *Journal of Canadian studies*. Peterborough, Ont. v. 2, no. 1 (1967), pp. 11-23.)

The Author discusses the findings and his experiences while working on the Advisory Commission on the Development of Government in the Northwest Territories. The Report was issued in 1966.

CHALOULT, RENE   Vers l'indépendance. (In Le Canada français. Québec. v. 17, no. 10 (1930), pp. [678]-689.)
Discusses the evolution of the Canadian constitution and dominion status.

CHARTIER, EMILE   Au berceau de la Confédération. (In Revue canadienne. Montréal. nouv. sér., v. 22 (1918), pp. [166]-179.)
A critical review of La Confédération canadienne, par Lionel Groulx. Montréal, 1918. Discusses provisions in the B.N.A. Act relating to French-Canadian rights and the protection of minority rights in general.

CHAUVIN, FRANCIS X.   An independent state on the St. Lawrence. (In Saturday night. Toronto. v. 60, no. 24 (Feb. 17, 1945), pp. 6-7.)
"Analyses opinions submitted, in 1921-22, by a group of French Canadian intellectuals on the subject of Canadian independence and a French Catholic State on the St. Lawrence."

CLARKE, NELSON   For a new pact of Confederation. (In The Marxist quarterly. Toronto. no. 15 (autumn 1965), pp. 16-26.)

CLOKIE, HUGH MC DOWALL   Canadian government and politics. [New and rev. ed.] Toronto, Longmans, Green [1950] viii, 370 p.
First edition 1944.

—— Emergency powers and civil liberties. By H. McD. Clokie. (In The Canadian journal of economics and political science. [Toronto] v. 13 (1947), pp. 384-394.)
"This paper was presented at the annual meeting of the Canadian Political Science Association in Quebec, May 29, 1947."
A comparative analysis.

—— The presentation of civil liberties. By H. McD. Clokie. (In The Canadian journal of economics and political science. [Toronto] v. 13 (1947), pp. 208-232.)
Examines the constitutional principle of civil liberty.

CONFEDERATION OF TOMORROW CONFERENCE, TORONTO, 1967   Proceedings. [Foreword by John P. Robarts. Toronto, pref. 1968] 233, 22 p.
Spiral binding.

—— Theme papers. Etudes de base. 2d ed. Introd. by H. I. Macdonald. Toronto, introd. 1968] 50, 55 p.
English and French.
Spiral binding.
Contents: The goals of Canadians. – The role of the English and French languages in Canada. – The ways in which the federal system could be improved (forms of federalism). – The ways in which the federal system could be improved (institutions). – The machinery and structure of federal-provincial and inter-provincial relationships in Canada.

CONGRES DES RELATIONS INDUSTRIELLES DE L'UNIVERSITE LAVAL, 21ST, QUEBEC, 1966   Une politique globale de la main-d'œuvre. Québec, Presses l'Université Laval, 1966. 165 p.
Sponsored by the Département des relations industrielles, de l'Université Laval. Held April 18-19, 1966.
Partial contents: Mise en oeuvre d'une politique de main-d'oeuvre, par L. Bélanger. – Politique fédérale et politique provinciale de la main d'oeuvre, par P. F. Côté, Y. Dubé et M. Guay.

CORRY, JAMES ALEXANDER   Changes in the functions of government. (In Canadian Historical Association. Report of the annual meeting. Toronto. (1945), pp. [15]-24.)

—— Democratic government and politics. Toronto, University of Toronto Press, 1946. viii, 468 p. (Canadian government series, 11.)

—— Democratic government and politics. By J. A. Corry and J. E. Hodgetts. 3d ed., rev. Toronto, University of Toronto Press, 1960, c1959. vii, 691 p. (Canadian government series, 1.)
". . . a comparison of the structure and working of government in Britain, the United States and Canada . . . combined with an . . . analysis of the problem of democratic government under present-day conditions . . ." – Pref.
American ed. (New York, Oxford University Press, 1947) has title: Elements of democratic government.

—— L'expansion des services administratifs depuis la Confédération. Etude préparée pour la Commission royale des relations entre le Dominion et les provinces, par J. A. Corry. Ottawa, 1939. 179 leaves.
Reproduced typescript.
Issued also in English.

—— The growth of government activities in Canada 1914-1921. (In Canadian Historical Association. *Report of the annual meeting.* Toronto. (1940), pp. 63-73.)

—— The growth of government activities since Confederation. A study prepared for the Royal Commission on Dominion-Provincial Relations. By J. A. Corry. Ottawa, 1939. 174 leaves.

Reproduced typescript.

Issued also in French.

—— Law and policy. By J. A. Corry. With a foreword by F. C. Cronkite. [Toronto] Clarke, Irwin, 1959. v. 78 p. (The W. M. Martin lectures, 1957.)

Lectures delivered at the University of Saskatchewan under the auspices of the Law Society of Saskatchewan.

An historical and comparative analysis.

CORRY, JAMES ALEXANDER (ed.) Legal essays in honour of Arthur Maxon. Edited by J. A. Corry, F. C. Cronkite & E. F. Whitmore. Toronto, Published in co-operation with the University of Saskatchewan by the University of Toronto Press, 1953. xi, 262 p.

Partial contents: The jurisdiction of the Canadian Parliament in matters of labour legislation, by G. R. Schmitt. – Statutory powers, by J. A. Corry. – Section 91 and 92 of the British North America Act and the Privy Council, by W. R. Jackett. – Classification of laws and the British North America Act, by W. R. Lederman.

CREIGHTON, DONALD GRANT Federal relations in Canada since 1914. (In Martin, C. B. (ed.) *Canada in peace and war.* London, 1941. pp. 29-57.)

DAWSON, ROBERT MAC GREGOR (ed.) Constitutional issues in Canada, 1900-1931. London, Oxford University Press, 1933. xvi, 482 p.

Excerpts from official documents, newspapers, and periodical material.

—— Democratic government in Canada. Rev. by W. F. Dawson. Rev. ed. Toronto, University of Toronto Press [1965, c1963] 194 p.

First published, 1949.

—— The government of Canada. Toronto, University of Toronto Press, 1947. x, 662 p. (Canadian government series, 2.)

—— The government of Canada. 5th ed., rev. by Norman Ward. [Toronto] University of Toronto Press [c1970] xiv, 569 p. (Canadian government series, 2.)

—— The principle of official independence, with particular reference to the political history of Canada. With an introd. by Graham Wallas. London, P. S. King; Toronto, S. B. Gundy, 1922. xv, 268 p. (Studies in economics and political science, no. 64 in the series of monographs by writers connected with the London School of Economics and Political Science.)

"This work has been approved by the University of London as a thesis for the D SC (Econ.) degree." – Introd.

DE HAPSBOURG, C. L. La Confédération canadienne. [Québec, 1942] 1 v.

Thesis (MA) – Laval University.

DONNELLY, MURRAY SAMUEL The government of Manitoba. By M. S. Donnelly. [Toronto] University of Toronto Press [c1963] vii, 185 p. (Canadian government series, 14.)

Partial contents: chapt. 2. Responsible government. – chapt. 3. Provincial rights; the great issues. – chapt. 11. Financial relationships between Manitoba and the federal government.

EWART, JOHN SKRIVING Canada's political status. (In *The Canadian historical review.* Toronto. v. 9 (1928), pp. 194-205.)

A reply to the article Recent changes in Canada's constitutional status, by A. B. Keith. (In *The Canadian historical review.* Toronto. v. 9 (1928), pp. 102-116.)

FARIBAULT, MARCEL Dix pour un; ou, Le pari confédératif. Par Marcel Faribault et Robert M. Fowler. Montréal, Presses de l'Université de Montréal, 1965. 163 p.

—— Ten to one; the Confederation wager. [By] Marcel Faribault and Robert M. Fowler. Toronto, McClelland and Stewart 1965. 150 p.

FAUCHER, ALBERT L'expérience économique du Québec et la Confédération. Par Albert Faucher et Gilles Paquet. (In *Journal of Canadian studies.* Peterborough, Ont. v. 1, no. 3 (1966), pp. 16-30.)

The Federation of Canada, 1867-1917; four lectures delivered in the University of Toronto in March, 1917 to commemorate the fiftieth anniversary of the Federation, by George M. Wrong, Sir John Willison, Z. A. Lash and R. A. Falconer. Toronto, Published for the University of Toronto by the Oxford University Press, 1917. 144 p.

Contents: The creation of the federal system in Canada, by G. M. Wrong. – Some political leaders in the Canadian federation, by J. Willison. – The working of federal institutions in Canada, by Z. A. Lash. – The quality of Canadian life, by R. A. Falconer.

FENSTON, JOHN   Quo vadis Canada? [n.p., 1955] 76 leaves.
> Limited edition of 25 copies.
> Study of Canadian constitutional history, with an emphasis on the problems relating to Quebec.

FERGUSON, GEORGE VICTOR   How we govern ourselves. By G. V. Ferguson. Toronto, Ryerson Press [1939] 32 p. (Contemporary affairs, no. 1.)
> A description of the national political system for the general reader.

FILION, GERARD   A legitimate role for government in business. (In Litvak, I. A. (ed.) The nation keepers. New York, Toronto [c1967] pp. 57-64.)
> Argues that "government intervention in the industrial and commercial sectors is not only inevitable but necessary". – p. 63.

Financial problems of our federal system. (In Queen's quarterly. Kingston. v. 40 (1933), pp. [580]-598.)
> Prepared by members of the Department of Political and Economic Science and of the course in Commerce at Queen's University.

FITZGERALD, GERALD F.   Canada's final steps to the fullness of sovereign power. [Ottawa] 1943. 338 leaves.
> Thesis (PH D) – University of Ottawa.

FORSEY, EUGENE ALFRED   The legislatures and executives of the federation. By Eugene Forsey. (In Ontario Advisory Committee on Confederation. Background papers and reports. [Toronto] 1967. v. 1, pp. [159]-173.)
> Presented October 1966.

—— Republic of Canada? By Eugene Forsey. (In Public affairs. Halifax. v. 14, no. 2 (winter 1952), pp. [11]-17.)
> Discusses the seven reasons advanced by Louis St. Laurent for replacing the word "Dominion" by "Canada".

FOX, PAUL WESLEY   Canadian government. [Toronto, Canadian Scene, 1964] 101 p.
> Originated as a series of talks by the Author delivered in 1963 on the program The learning stage, presented over radio station CJBC, Toronto. Presented with the

co-operation of the Canadian Broadcasting Corporation, the Canadian Association for Adult Education, and the Citizenship Division, Dept. of the Provincial Secretary and Citizenship, Government of Ontario.
> First edition 1963.

—— Regionalism and Confederation. By Paul W. Fox. (In Ontario Advisory Committee on Confederation. Background papers and reports. [Toronto, 1970] v. 2, pp. 1-27.)

GARDNER, GERARD   La frontière Canada-Labrador. (In Revue trimestrielle canadienne. Montréal. v. 24 (sept. 1938), pp. [272]-289.)

GENEST, JEAN   Les anglo-canadiens et le gouvernement du Canada. (In L'Action nationale. Montréal. v. 49 (jan. 1960), pp. [335]-358.)

GIBSON, FREDERICK W.   How Canada is governed. (In Queen's quarterly. Kingston. v. 57 (1950), pp. [479]-498.)
> A review article of The government of Canada, by R. M. Dawson. Toronto, University of Toronto Press, 1947.

GORDON, HOWARD SCOTT   The Bank of Canada in a system of responsible government. By H. S. Gordon. (In The Canadian journal of economics and political science. [Toronto] v. 27 (1961), pp. 1-22.)
> "The purpose of this paper is to examine the status and functions of the Bank of Canada against the background of the principle of responsible government."

GOW, DONALD JOHN SUTTON   Canadian federal administrative and political institutions; a role analysis. [Kingston, Ont.] 1968. 1 v.
> Thesis (PH D) – Queen's University.

GREY, RODNEY Y.   Canadian federal institutions and economic policy, 1939-50. By R. Y. Grey. [London, Eng., 1953] 1 v.
> Thesis (PH D) – London School of Economics, University of London.

HANKIN, FRANCIS   Recovery by control. A diagnosis and analysis of the relations between business and government in Canada. By Francis Hankin and T. W. L. MacDermot. Toronto, Dent, 1933. ix, 360 p.

—— The relations between government and business in Canada. A Round Table discussion [with] Francis Hankin [and] A. D. P. Heeney. (In Liberal Summer Conference, 1st, Port Hope, Ont., 1933. The Liberal way. Toronto, 1933. pp. 77-82.)

HASSARD, ALBERT RICHARD Canadian constitutional history and law. Toronto, Carswell, 1900. xiv, 176 p.

HAWKINS, GORDON (ed.) Order and good government. Edited by Gordon Hawkins. [Toronto] Published for Canadian Institute on Public Affairs by University of Toronto Press [c1965] x, 155 p.

Papers presented at the 33d Couchiching Conference, Geneva Park, Ont. Conference sponsored by the Canadian Institute on Public Affairs in co-operation with the Canadian Broadcasting Corporation July 25—August 1, 1964.

Partial contents: A provincial perspective, by W. Lloyd. – Getting things done in Parliament, by E. D. Fulton and P. Newman. – Can MP's do a better job? by P. Jewett. – The role of the private member, by R. Kelson and G. Baldwin. – Parliamentary rules and procedures, by S. Knowles. – The expert, the politician and the public, by M. Sharp. – The lack of Conservative-Liberal differences in Canadian politics, by P. Newman. – The political party; its organization, candidates, and finances, by R. Bell and R. Stanbury. – Order, good government and the press, by C. Lynch, N. DePoe, C. Young. – Quebec and national unity, by M. Lamontagne.

HELLING, RUDOLF La conception de l'élite et de la démocratie au Canada anglais. (In Cité libre Montréal. no. 86 (avril—mai 1966), pp. 11-14.)

HOOD, WILLIAM C. Economic policy in our federal state. By Wm. C. Hood. (In Crépeau, P. A. (ed.) The future of Canadian federalism. [Toronto, c1965] pp. [58]-76.)

HOUGHAM, GEORGE MILLARD The development of Dominion status; Canada, 1931-1945. Toronto, 1948. 219 leaves.

Thesis (MA) – University of Toronto.

HUTCHINS, PHYLLIS M. The role of the state in labour-management relations: a preface to post-war labour policy. (In The Manitoba arts review. Winnipeg. v. 3, no. 4 (fall 1943), pp. 32-45.)

INNIS, HAROLD ADAMS Government ownership and the Canadian scene. (In Canadian problems as seen by twenty outstanding men of Canada. Toronto, 1933. pp. [69]-90.)

INSTITUT CANADIEN DES AFFAIRES PUBLIQUES, MONTREAL Le Canada face à l'avenir; un pays qui s'interroge. Travaux présentés à la onzième conférence annuelle de l'Institut canadien des affaires publiques (ICAP) organisée avec le concours de la Société Radio-Canada, et compte rendu des discussions. Montréal, Editions du Jour [c1964] 134 p. (Collection: Les Idées du jour, D15.)

Partial contents: Une nouvelle constitution, par P. Laporte. – Le fédéralisme coopératif, par J. L. Pépin.

—— Le peuple souverain. Rapport de la première conférence annuelle de l'Institut canadien des affaires publiques organisée avec le concours de la Société Radio-Canada, Alpine Inn, Ste-Marguerite, du 29 septembre au 2 octobre 1954. [Montréal, 1955] 52 p.

Partial contents: Le peuple souverain, par H. Beauve-Méry, J. L. Gagnon et G. Pelletier. – Les partis politiques sont-ils indispensables? par A. Laurendeau, E. Forsey et J. Bruchési. – La bureaucratie au pouvoir? par J. Boucher, F. Scott et M. Faribault. – Obstacles à la démocratie, par P. E. Trudeau, J. Marchand et F. Vézina.

—— Le rôle de l'Etat. Travaux présentés à la 9ème conférence annuelle de l'Institut canadien des affaires publiques (ICAP) Organisée avec le concours de la Société Radio-Canada, et compte rendu des délibérations. Ouvrage publié sous la direction de André Raynauld. Montréal, Editions du Jour [1963, c1962] 168 p. (Collection: Les Idées du jour, D10.)

IRVINE, WILLIAM Co-operative government. With a foreword by H. W. Wood. Ottawa, Mutual Press, 1929. viii, 246 p.

Presents an argument for the adoption of a system of government based on functional representation.

—— The need for science in government. By W. Irvine. (In Canadian Congress journal. Montreal. v. 3, no. 6 (June 1924), pp. 9-11; 13.)

JACKMAN, L. J. The Newfoundland-Labrador boundary. (In The Newfoundland quarterly. St. John's, Nfld. v. 53, no. 4—v. 55, no. 1 (Dec. 1954—Mar. 1956).)

In five parts.

No more published?

KEITH, ARTHUR BERRIEDALE The constitutional law of the British Dominions. By A. B. Keith. London, Macmillan, 1933. xxvi, 522 p.

—— The Dominions as sovereign states; their constitutions and governments. By

A. B. Keith. London, Macmillan, 1938. xiv, 789 p.

Part 2: The government of the Dominions.

—— Imperial unity and the Dominions. Oxford, Clarendon Press, 1916. 626 p.

Partial contents: Part 1. The limitations of the autonomy of the Dominions. A. The governor. B. The legislature. C. The judicial power. D. The amendment of the constitution.

—— Recent changes in Canada's constitutional status. By A. B. Keith. (In *The Canadian historical review*. Toronto. v. 9 (1928), pp. 102-116.)

For a reply, see Canada's political status, by J. S. Ewart. (In *The Canadian historical review*. Toronto. v. 9 (1928), pp. 194-205.

—— Responsible government in the Dominions. 2d ed., rewritten and revised to 1927. Oxford, Clarendon Press, 1928. 2 v. [lxiv, 1339 p.]

—— The sovereignty of the British Dominions. By A. B. Keith. London, Macmillan, 1929. xxvi, 524 p.

KONINCK, CHARLES DE La Confédération, rempart contre le grand Etat. Pour la Commission royale d'enquête sur les problèmes constitutionnels. [Québec, 1955?] 36 leaves.

At head of title: Annexe 1.

Mimeographed.

KRAUTER, JOSEPH FRANCIS Civil liberties and the Canadian minorities. [Urbana, 1968] 1 v.

Thesis (PH D) – University of Illinois.

LAMONTAGNE, MAURICE The role of government. (In Canadian Westinghouse Company, limited, Hamilton, Ont. *Canada's tomorrow*. Toronto, 1954. pp. 119-152.)

LANGFORD, GEORGE B. Educating a democracy. (In Empire Club of Canada. *Addresses*. Toronto. (1942/43), pp. 396-409.)

Address delivered March 11, 1943.

LANGIS, PIERRE PAUL Le Canada, monarchie constitutionnelle en union personnelle avec les autres membres du Commonwealth. (In *Revue trimestrielle canadienne*. Montréal. v. 27 (sept. 1941), pp. [299]-310.)

LANGSTONE, ROSA WILLETTS Responsible government in Canada. By Rosa W. Langstone. With a pref. by Sir Raymond Beazley. London, Toronto, Dent [1931] xi, 241 p.

LAPOINTE, ERNEST Le Statut de Westminster et l'évolution nationale du Canada. (In *Revue trimestrielle canadienne*. Montréal. v. 18 (mars 1932), pp. [1]-18.)

Address delivered in Montreal on January 16, 1932.

LASH, ZEBULON AITON The working of federal institutions in Canada. By Z. A. Lash. (In *The Federation of Canada, 1867-1917*. Toronto, 1917. pp. [77]-107.)

LASKIN, BORA Canadian constitutional law; cases, text and notes on distribution of legislative power. By the Honourable Mr. Justice Bora Laskin. 3d ed. Toronto, Carswell Co., 1966. xxxii, 1104 p.

First ed. 1951; 2d ed. 1960.

LAURENDEAU, ANDRE Le français et le fonctionnarisme fédéral. (In *L'Action nationale*. Montréal. v. 41 (fév. 1953), pp. [104]-112.)

LAURISTON, VICTOR Why not unite all nine provinces? One central government —that was Sir John A's original idea, says this writer. (In *Maclean's*. Toronto. v. 45, no. 6 (Mar. 15, 1932), pp. 10; 34.)

LAVIGNE, WILFRID L'orientation des dépenses publiques depuis la Confédération. (In *Revue trimestrielle canadienne*. Montréal. v. 16, no. 64 (déc. 1930), pp. [396]-424.)

LEDERMAN, WILLIAM RALPH Legislative power to implement treaty obligations in Canada. By W. R. Lederman. (In Aitchison, J. H. (ed.) *The political process in Canada*. [Toronto, c1963] pp. [171]-181.)

LEFROY, AUGUSTUS HENRY FRAZER The British versus the American system of national government. Being a paper read before the Toronto Branch of the Imperial Federation League on Thursday, December 18th, 1890. Toronto, Williamson, 1891. 42 p.

—— Canada's federal system; being a treatise on Canadian constitutional law under the British North America Act. By A. H. F. Lefroy. Toronto, Carswell Co., 1913. lxviii, 898 p.

"To describe this work as a second edition of the one published in 1898-9 under the name of The law of legislative power in Canada would be misleading. Although I have endeavoured to retain the principal features of that work, I have entirely rewritten it, and greatly altered the arrangement". – Pref.

—— The law of legislative power in Canada. By A. H. F. Lefroy. Toronto, Toronto Law Book and Pub. Co., 1897-98. lxx, 825 p.

LEGENDRE, NAPOLEON Notre constitution et nos institutions. (In *Revue de Montréal*. 2. année, & 2 (1878), pp. [92]-101; [149]-160; [201]-218.)

—— Notre constitution et nos institutions. Montréal, J. A. Plinquet, 1878. 42 p.

LEGER, JEAN MARC Considérations sur l'idée de République. (In *L'Action nationale*. Montréal. v. 34 (sept. 1949), pp. [6]-11.)

LEMIEUX, EDMOND De l'optimisme juridique au pessimisme politique. (In *L'Action nationale*. Montréal. v. 17 (juin 1941), pp. [473]-480.)
Compares the constitutions of the United States and Canada.

—— Une république fédérative et sociale. (In *L'Action nationale*. Montréal. v. 32 (oct. 1948), pp. [126]-132.)

LEMIEUX, RODOLPHE Les origines du droit franco-canadien. Montréal, Théoret, 1901. xxix, 483 p.

LE SUEUR, WILLIAM DAWSON Problems of government in Canada. By W. D. LeSueur. (In *Queen's quarterly*. Kingston. v. 2 (1894/95), pp. [198]-209.)
Examines the problems related to democratic political institutions.

LEVESQUE, ALBERT Le Statut de Westminster et la révolution politico-culturelle depuis 1931. (In *L'Action nationale*. Montréal. v. 49(fév. 1960), pp. [455]-475.)

—— L'unité fonctionnelle de la civilisation canadienne. (In *L'Action nationale*. Montréal. v. 46 (avril/mai 1957), pp. [587]-642.)

LEWIS, DAVID How much welfare does social responsibility demand? (In Litvak, I. A. (ed.) *The nation keepers*. New York, Toronto [c1967] pp. 65-75.)
Argues "that we abandon the traditional attitudes to government spending" . . . Favours the idea of government expansion in the area of social welfare.

LINGARD, CHARLES CECIL Territorial government in Canada; the autonomy question in the old North-West Territories. Toronto, University of Toronto Press, 1946. xi, 269 p.

LITVAK, ISAIAH A. (ed.) The nation keepers; Canadian business perspectives.

Foreword by Lester B. Pearson. New York, Toronto, McGraw-Hill [c1967] xiv, 255 p.
"The chief aim of this book is to supply an integrated perspective of the business environment . . . through an intensive examination of those components of the social, economic and political dimensions" having the most impact on Canadian business. – Pref.
Partial contents: Government and business, by A. A. Cumming. – The government and the economy, by T. C. Douglas. – A legitimate role for government in business, by G. Filion. – How much welfare does social responsibility demand?, by D. Lewis. – Canadian businessmen, reluctant politicians, by M. W. McCutcheon. – Canada and Quebec, can this marriage be saved, by D. Johnson. – Provincial powers and national goals, by J. Robarts.

LLOYD, WOODROW STANLEY The positive role of government. By W. S. Lloyd. (In *Canadian public administration*. Toronto. v. 5 (1962), pp. 402-407.)
This address was delivered to the Institute of Public Administration of Canada at the fourteenth annual conference, Regina, Saskatchewan, September 5-8, 1962.

—— The role of government in Canadian education. Toronto, W. J. Gage, 1959. 98 p. (The Quance lectures in Canadian education, 1959.)

LOGAN, HAROLD AMOS State intervention and assistance in collective bargaining; the Canadian experience 1943-1954. By H. A. Logan. [Toronto] University of Toronto Press, 1956. vii, 176 p. (Canadian studies in economics, 6.)

LOWER, ARTHUR REGINALD MARSDEN What this country needs is 10 new provinces. To that old cry "Canada has too many governments" this noted historian retorts, "Nonsense—our big provinces behave like imperial powers and should be carved up". By Arthur Lower. (In *Maclean's*. Toronto. v. 61, no. 19 [i.e. 20] (Oct. 15, 1948), pp. 7; 77-79.)

MC DOUGALL, DONALD J. Canada and Ireland; a contrast in constitutional development. By D. J. McDougall. (In Flenley, Ralph (ed.) *Essays in Canadian history*. Toronto, 1939. pp. 68-93.)

MAC FARLANE, RONALD OLIVER Canada: one country or nine provinces? By R. O. MacFarlane. (In *The Dalhousie review*. Halifax. v. 18 (1938/39), pp. [9]-16.)

Examines the nature of Canadian confederation.

MC GOUN, ARCH. Mr. Royal's pamphlet. By Arch. McGoun, Jr. (In *The Week.* Toronto. v. 11, no. 20 (Apr. 13, 1894), pp. 469-471; v. 11, no. 21 (Apr. 20, 1894), pp. 493-495.)
In two parts.
A review article of *A republic or a colony?* By J. Royal. Montreal, 1894.

MAC GUIGAN, MARK RUDOLPH The development of civil liberties in Canada. By Mark R. MacGuigan. (In *Queen's quarterly.* Kingston. v. 72 (1965), pp. [270]-288.)

MC INNIS, EDGAR WARDELL Two North American federations: a comparison. By Edgar McInnis. (In Flenley, Ralph (ed.) *Essays in Canadian history.* Toronto, 1939. pp. 94-118.)

MC KELVIE, B. A. General survey of taxation problems. (In Canadian Broadcasting Corporation. *The Canadian constitution.* Toronto. [c1938] pp. 59-68.)
"Discussed by the Constitutional Club, Vancouver, October 31, 1937."
Considers the problems of Canadian taxation in a constitutional framework.

MAC KINNON, FRANK The government of Prince Edward Island. Toronto, University of Toronto Press, 1951. xii, 385 p. (Canadian government series, 5.)
Chapter 14: The province and the Dominion.

MACKINTOSH, MARGARET Government intervention in labour disputes in Canada. (In *Queen's quarterly.* Kingston. v. 31 (1923/24), pp. 298-328.)
—— Government intervention in labour disputes in Canada. Kingston [Ont.] Jackson Press, 1924. 30 p. (Bulletin of the Departments of History and Political and Economic Science in Queen's University, no. 47.)
Cover title.

MC LEAN, JAMES A. Essays in the financial history of Canada. New York, Columbia College, 1894. 76 p.
Thesis (PH D) – Columbia University.
Partial contents: The financial basis of Confederation (pp. 59-76). Considers section 118 of the British North America Act.

MC LENNAN, DAVID ROSS Canadian government procurement. [Ottawa, 1952] 1 v.
Thesis (PH D) – University of Ottawa.

MC NAUGHT, KENNETH WILLIAM KIRKPATRICK National affairs. By Kenneth McNaught. (In *Saturday night.* Toronto. v. 80, no. 2 (Feb. 1965), pp. 8-9.)
Discusses the issue of whether Canada should be a monarchy or a republic.

MAGNAN, CHARLES JOSEPH Manuel de droit civique; notre constitutions et nos institutions. Par C. J. Magnan. Québec, Typ. de C. Darveau, 1895. 414 p.

MAHEUX, ARTHUR French Canadians and democracy. (In *University of Toronto quarterly.* [Toronto] v. 27 (1957/58), pp. 341-351.)

MALLORY, JAMES RUSSELL Changing techniques of Canadian government. By J. R. Mallory. (In *Public affairs.* Halifax, v. 7, no. 2 (winter 1944), pp. 112-117.)
—— The "compact" theory of Confederation. By J. R. Mallory. (In *The Dalhousie review.* Halifax. v. 21 (1941/42), pp. [342]-351.)
—— The proper role of the state, federally and provincially. By James R. Mallory. (In Congress on Canadian Affairs, 1st, Quebec, 1961. *Le Canada, expérience ratée ... ou réussie?* [Québec] 1962. pp. [89]-99.)
—— The structure of Canadian government. By J. R. Mallory. Toronto, Macmillan [c1971] xii, 418 p.

MANN, WILLIAM EDWARD (comp.) Canada; a sociological profile. [Toronto] Copp, Clark [c1968] xii, 522 p.
[Part] 9: Political institutions and behaviour.
A book of readings.

MARTIAL, JEAN ALBERT Government control of aviation in Canada. [Montreal, 1953] 1 v.
Thesis (LL M) – McGill University.

MARTIN, CHESTER BAILEY Foundations of Canadian nationhood. Toronto, University of Toronto Press, 1955. xx, 554 p.

MEIGHEN, ARTHUR The welfare state. By the Rt. Hon. Arthur Meighen. (In *Public affairs.* Halifax. v. 13, no. 2 (winter 1951). pp. [75]-85.)
A statement of general principle.

MHUN, HENRY La politique économique fédérale. (In Institut canadien des affaires publiques, Montreal, *Le rôle de l'Etat.* Montréal [c1962] pp. [35]-44.)

MIGNAULT, PIERRE BASILE Quelques aperçus sur le développement du principe de l'autonomie au Canada avant et depuis le "Statute of Westminster" de 1931. Par le juge P. B. Mignault. (In Royal Society of Canada. *Proceedings and transactions.* Ottawa. ser. 3, v. 26 (1932), section 1, pp. 45-64.)

"Lu à la réunion de mai 1932."

MOFFETT, SAMUEL ERASMUS The Americanization of Canada. [New York] 1907. 126 p.

Thesis (PH D) – Columbia University.

Partial contents: Chapt. 2. The progress of government.

Chapter 2 is a comparative examination of the American and Canadian forms of government.

MORGAN, HENRY JAMES Dr. Alpheus Todd and Canadian constitutional history. By Henry J. Morgan. (In *The Week.* Toronto. v. 10, no. 46 (Oct. 13, 1893), pp. 1095-1096.)

"Henry J. Morgan in Ottawa Citizen."

MORGAN, J. H. Dominion status. (In *The Dalhousie review.* Halifax. v. 9 (1929/30), pp. [131]-156.)

"The Rhodes lecture, delivered in University College, London, on 15th March last."

MORIN, WILFRID Nos droits minoritaires; les minorités françaises au Canada. Montréal, Editions Fides [1943] 431 p. (Philosophie et problèmes contemporains, 2.)

MUNRO, WILLIAM BENNETT American influence on Canadian government. Toronto, Macmillan, 1929. xi, 153 p. (The Marfleet lectures delivered at the University of Toronto, 1929.)

Contents: Constitutional analogies and contrasts. – Political parties and practical politics. – City government in Canada.

NANTEL, MARECHAL Nos institutions politiques et judiciaires. (In *Les Cahiers des dix.* Montréal. no. 11 (1946), pp. [191]-200.)

NEUENDORFF, GWENDOLINE Studies in the evolution of dominion status; The governor-generalship of Canada and The development of Canadian nationalism. By Gwen Neuendorff. With a foreword by Harold J. Laski. London, Allen & Unwin [1942] vi, 379 p.

"First published in 1942."

OLIVIE, FERNANDO Canadá; una monarquia americana. Madrid, Ediciones Cultura hispánica, 1957. 398 p.

OLLIVIER, MAURICE Le Canada, pays souverain? Le Statut de Westminster. Montréal, A. Lévesque [1935] 229 p. (Documents politiques.)

—— Méthodes législatives et formes de gouvernement. Parallèle entre l'Angleterre, les Etats Unis et le Canada. (In *Revue trimestrielle canadienne.* Montréal. v. 10 (sept. 1924), pp. [384]-390.)

—— Problems of Canadian sovereignty from the British North America Act, 1867 to the Statute of Westminster, 1931. Toronto, Canada Law Book Co., 1945. xi, 491 p.

—— Le Statut de Westminster. Etude de l'évolution politique au Canada. (In *Revue trimestrielle canadienne.* Montréal. v. 19 (mars 1933), pp. [12]-44.)

"Résumé d'une thèse de doctorat, soutenue devant la Faculté de droit de l'Université de Montréal, 18 février 1933."

ONTARIO ADVISORY COMMITTEE ON CONFEDERATION Background papers and reports. [v. 1. Pref. by John Robarts. Toronto] Queen's Printer of Ontario, 1967. 435 p.

Partial contents: The modern federation, by A. Brady. – The nature and problems of a Bill of Rights, by W. R. Lederman. – The process of constitutional amendment for Canada, by W. R. Lederman. – A Supreme Court in a bicultural society, by E. McWhinney. – The legislatures and executives of the federation, by E. Forsey. – Constitutional monarchy and the provinces, by E. Forsey. – Memorandum on the Associate States, by E. Forsey.

—— Background papers and reports. v. 2. [Pref. by John P. Robarts. Toronto, W. Kinmond, Queen's Printer and Publisher, 1970] xxiv, 369 p.

Partial contents: Regionalism and Confederation, by P. W. Fox. – Geo-politics and the Canadian union, by J. Conway. – The nature of a bicultural constitutionalism, by E. McWhinney. – Our present discontents, by E. Forsey. – What is wrong with the British North America Act? by C. R. Magone. – The distribution of legislative power, by A. Brady. – The provincial interest in broadcasting under the Canadian constitution, by R. G. Atkey. – Concerning a Bill of Rights for Canada and Ontario, by W. R. Lederman. – Thoughts on reform of the Supreme Court of Canada, by W. R. Lederman. – Second chambers in federal political systems, by R. L. Watts. – The Senate, by E. Forsey. – The national capital problem, by J. H. Perry.

ONTARIO WOODSWORTH MEMORIAL FOUNDATION Democratic planning; a symposium. Toronto, 1962. 36 p.

Papers by J. C. Weldon, G. W. Cadbury and M. K. Oliver presented at a public Study Conference on Economic Planning for Canadians, sponsored by the Metropolitan Toronto Committee for the New Democratic Party, October 1961.

Partial contents: Federal-provincial planning, by M. K. Oliver.

O'SULLIVAN, DENNIS AMBROSE Government in Canada; the principles and institutions of our federal and provincial constitutions. The B.N.A. Act, 1867, compared with the United States Constitution. With a sketch of the constitutional history of Canada. 2d ed., enl. and improved. Toronto, Carswell, 1887. xix, 344 p.

—— A manual of government in Canada; or, The principles and institutions of our federal and provincial constitutions. By D. A. O'Sullivan. Toronto, J. C. Stuart, 1879. xiii, 246 p.

OWEN, GEORGE ROBERT WHITLEY Freedom of opinion: a comparative study of public liberty in France and Canada. [Montreal] 1934. 1 v.
Thesis (MA) – McGill University.

PARENTEAU, ROLAND Economic planning; its requirements inside a federal system. (In Quebec in the Canada of tomorrow. Toronto, 1968 pp. [0-1]-0-8.)

PEARCE, HAYWOOD J. Problems occasioned by ministerial government within the federal state of Canada. (In The Canadian historical review. Toronto. v. 6 (1925), pp. 104-109.)

PERRY, JOHN HARVEY The scope of government enterprises. By J. Harvey Perry. (In Institute of Public Administration of Canada. Proceedings of the annual conference. Toronto. 8th (1956), pp. 139-149.)

Petit dossier sur le pacte fédératif. (In L'Action nationale. Montréal. v. 34 (sept. 1949), pp. [61]-67; v. 34 (oct. 1949), pp. [156]-160.)
In two parts.
"Bornons-nous à quelques textes que nous classerons en quatre catégories: le témoignage des juristes, l'opinion que les Pères de la Confédération entretenaient sur

leur œuvre, le jugement des politiques, enfin quelques extraits de la jurisprudence qui continuent de faire autorité."

PORRITT, EDWARD Evolution of the Dominion of Canada; its government and its politics. Yonkers-on-Hudson, N.Y., World Book Co., 1920 [c1918] xix, 540 p. maps. (Government handbooks.)

PORTER, JOHN A. Power and freedom in Canadian democracy. By John Porter. (In Oliver, M. K. (ed.) Social purpose for Canada. [Toronto, c1961], pp. [27]-56.)

RAND, IVAN CLEVELAND Canada and democracy. (Fredericton, N.B., University of New Brunswick, 1950). 11 p. (Sesquicentennial lectures, 1950.)
Delivered at the Law School, Saint John, N.B., March 15, 1950.

RAPSEY, KEITH H. An overdose of drugs. (In Canada month. Montreal. v. 8, no. 1 (Jan. 1968), pp. 24-25.)
Discusses the Keynesian theory of government intervention in the economy with reference to Canadian government application of that theory.

RATTRAY, WILLIAM JORDON Colonial self-government. By W. J. Rattray. (In Rose-Belford's Canadian monthly and national review. Toronto. v. 4 (1880), pp. 539-544.)
A review article of Parliamentary government in the British Colonies, by Alpheus Todd. Boston, 1880.

REA, KENNETH J. (ed.) Business and government in Canada; selected readings Edited by K. J. Rea and J. T. McLeod. Toronto, Methuen [c1969] xiv, 412 p.

RIDDELL, WILLIAM RENWICK The constitutional history of Canada. By the Honourable Mr. Justice Riddell. (In Canadian Club of Toronto. Addresses. Toronto. (1911/12), pp. 14-34.)
Address delivered November 6, 1911.

—— The constitutional history of Canada. By the Hon. W. R. Riddell. (In Canadian Club of Montreal. Addresses. [Montreal] (1911/12), pp. 85-107.)
Address delivered January 15, 1912.

ROBERTSON, R. G. The evolution of territorial government in Canada. (In Aitchison, J. H. (ed.) The political process in Canada. [Toronto, c1963] pp. [136]-152.)

ROGERS, NORMAN MC LEOD The compact theory of Confederation. By N. McL. Rogers. (In Canadian Political Science

Association. *Papers and proceedings of the annual meeting.* [Kingston, Ont.] v. 3 (1931), pp. [205]-230.)

—— The foundation of federal unity. (In *The Dalhousie review.* Halifax. v. 4 (1924/25), pp. [77]-85.)

ROWAT, DONALD CAMERON The problems of governing federal capitals. By Donald C. Rowat. (In *Canadian journal of political science.* Toronto. v. 1 (1968), pp. [345]-356.)
Examines "the proposal that Canada's capital should be governed as a federal district".

ROWELL, NEWTON WESLEY Canada; a nation; Canadian constitutional developments. Addresses delivered by the Hon. N. W. Rowell . . . at the American Bar Ass'n meeting, Minneapolis, 1923. Toronto, University of Toronto Press, 1923. 31 p.

ROYAL, JOSEPH La crise actuelle: Le Canada, république ou colonie. Montréal, E. Sénécal, 1894. 105 p.
Published in English under title: A republic or a colony? Some remarks on the present crisis.

—— A republic or a colony? Some remarks on the present crisis. Montreal, E. Sénécal, 1894. 108 p.
Published in French under title: La crise actuelle: Le Canada, république ou colonie.

RUSSELL, PETER H. A democratic approach to civil liberties. (In Vaughan, Frederick (ed.) *Contemporary issues in Canadian politics.* Scarborough, Ont. [c1970] pp. 83-105.)
"Reprinted with permission of the University of Toronto law journal."

—— Planning isn't always socialism. By Peter Russell. (In *The Canadian commentator.* Toronto. v. 6, no. 7/8 (July/Aug. 1962), pp. 21.)
A critical review of Ontario Woodsworth Memorial Foundation. *Democratic planning; a symposium.* (papers by J.C. Weldon, G. W. Cadbury and M. K. Oliver) Toronto, 1962. (36 p.)

SANDWELL, BERNARD KEBLE The Dominion and absolute sovereignty. By B. K. Sandwell. (In *Willisons monthly.* Toronto. v. 4, no. 2 (July 1928), pp. 60-61.)

—— From the editor's chair. Canada's government system mysterious but it works. By B. K. Sandwell. (In *Saturday night.* Toronto. v. 63, no. 19 (Feb. 14, 1948), p. [14].)
A review article of *The government of Canada,* by R. M. Dawson. Toronto, University of Toronto Press, 1947.

—— Mr. Forsey's queries. The B.N.A. Act and "Dominion". By B. K. Sandwell. (In *Saturday night.* Toronto. v. 67, no. 42 (July 26, 1952), pp. 5; 36.)
Cf. Republic of Canada? By E. A. Forsey. (In *Public affairs.* Halifax. v. 14, no. 2 (winter 1952), pp. [11]-17.)

—— Sovereignty in Canada. By B. K. Sandwell. (In *Queen's quarterly.* Kingston. v. 39 (1932), pp. [193]-209.)

SANTOS, C. R. Public administration as politics. (In *Canadian public administration.* Toronto. v. 12 (1969), pp. [213]-223.)

SCHINDELER, FREDERICK FERNAND Social science research and participatory democracy in Canada. By Fred Schindeler and C. Michael Lanphier. (In *Canadian public administration.* Toronto. v. 12 (1969), pp. [481]-498.)

SCOTT, FRANCIS REGINALD Freedom of speech in Canada. By F. R. Scott. (In Canadian Political Science Association. *Papers and proceedings of the annual meeting.* [Kingston, Ont.] v. 5 (1933), pp. [169]-189.)

SENECAL, JACQUES Eugene Forsey, P.-E. Trudeau and the question: "What is a nation?" (In *The Marxist quarterly.* Toronto. no. 7 (autumn 1963), pp. 21-26.)

SISSONS, CHARLES BRUCE The rights of minorities in a democracy. By C. B. Sissons. (In Royal Society of Canada. *Proceedings and transactions.* Ottawa. ser. 3, v. 48 (1954), section 2, pp. 99-106.)
Comparative and historical remarks.

SMITH, LAWRENCE B. Recent Canadian economic growth and the role of government. (In *Journal of Canadian studies.* Peterborough. v. 3, no. 1 (1968), pp. 45-50.)

STANLEY, GEORGE FRANCIS GILMAN Act or pact; another look at Confederation. (In Canadian Historical Association. *Report of the annual meeting.* [Ottawa] (1956), pp. [1]-25.)

—— Act or pact? Another look at Confederation. By G. F. G. Stanley. (In *Confederation; essays by D. G. Creighton* [*and others*] [Toronto, c1967] pp. [94]-118.)

"Reprinted from Canadian Historical Association, Report, 1956."

STEVENSON, MABEL MC LUHAN Our government; a book for Canadians. Toronto, G. J. McLeod [c1917] 178 p.

A handbook. This book "aims to state the elementary facts about the Canadian system of self-government". - Foreword.

STRAYER, BARRY L. One prairie province. The constitutional processes for prairie union. By B. L. Strayer. (In *Canadian public administration*. Toronto. v. 13 (1970), pp. [337]-343.)

". . . presented at a conference entitled 'One prairie province? A question for Canada', in Lethbridge, Alberta, May 10-13, 1970."

STURSBERG, PETER Badly needed: a reforum of federal government. (In *Commentator*. Toronto. v. 10, no. 10 (Oct. 1966), pp. 7-9.)

TAYLOR, MALCOLM GORDON The role of the medical profession in the formulation and execution of public policy. By Malcolm G. Taylor. (In *Canadian public administration*. Toronto. v. 3 (1960), pp. 233-255.)

Examines "the medical profession in its relation to government in Canada . . .".

"This article was based on a paper presented at the annual meeting of the Canadian Political Science Association in Saskatoon, June 5, 1959."

THOMAS, LEWIS HERBERT The constitutional development of the North West Territories, 1870-1888. [Saskatoon] 1941. 97 leaves.

Thesis (MA)-University of Saskatchewan.

THORBURN, HUGH GARNET Politics in New Brunswick By Hugh G. Thorburn. Toronto, University of Toronto Press, 1961. vi, 217 p. (Canadian government series, 10.)

Chapter 7: The federal representatives.

TODD, ALPHEUS Parliamentary government in the British colonies. Boston, Little, Brown, 1880. xii, 607 p.

Partial contents: Chapt. 4, pt. 2. c. Provincial government in Canada; 1. Dominion control in matters of legislation. 2. Dominion control over the Canadian provinces in matters of administration.

TOMIE, FREDERICK LEO A comparative study of committees in the legislative process of Canada and the United States. [Fredericton, N.B.] 1963. 1 v.

Thesis (MA) - University of New Brunswick.

TUPPER, SIR CHARLES HIBBERT Colonies and constitutional law. (In *The Dalhousie review*. Halifax. v. 2 (1922/23), pp. [438]-443.)

WALLACE, MARY ELISABETH The changing Canadian state; a study of the changing conception of the state as revealed in Canadian social legislation, 1867-1948. [New York, 1950] 399 leaves.

Thesis (PH D) - Columbia University.

—— The origin of the social welfare state in Canada, 1867-1900. By Elisabeth Wallace. (In *The Canadian journal of economics and political science*. Toronto. v. 16 (1950), pp. 383-393.)

WARD, NORMAN MC QUEEN The structure of government. By Norman Ward. (In Careless, J. M. S. (ed.) *The Canadians, 1867-1967*. Toronto, 1967. pp. 713-733.)

WELLS, DALTON COURTWRIGHT Taxing power in Canada. Being a thesis on the power of governing bodies in Canada to impose taxation. Toronto, 1928. 184 leaves.

Thesis (MA) - University of Toronto.

WHALEN, HUGH The peaceful coexistence of government and business. (In *Canadian public administration*. Toronto. v. 4 (1961), pp. 1-15.)

"This paper was presented to the twelfth annual conference of the Institute of Public Administration of Canada, at Banff, Alberta, September 14-17, 1960."

WOODLEY, CHARLES WILLIAM Administrafor development; the co-ordination of federal and territorial government activities in the Northwest Territories. [Kingston, Ont.] 1965. 1 v.

Thesis (MA) - Queen's University.

WRIGHT, C. P. To finance Padlock appeals. (In *The Canadian forum*. Toronto. v. 19, no. 225 (Oct. 1939), pp. 215-220.)

Details the three occasions when "the Dominion Government furnished full financial support to the prosecution of concrete actions on serious constitutional issues of the day". The constitutional issues were the Common Schools Act passed by the New Brunswick legislature in 1871 and the Canada Temperance Act passed by the federal Parliament in 1878 (direct aid was given while testing the Canada Temperance Act in 1879) and, thirdly, by a Dominion order-in-council issued October 26, 1881.

WRONG, GEORGE MC KINNON   The creation of the federal system in Canada. (In *The Federation of Canada, 1867-1917*. Toronto, 1917. pp. [1]-38.)

DOMINION–PROVINCIAL RELATIONS

AITCHISON, JAMES HERMISTON   The Rowell-Sirois report. By J. H. Aitchison. (In *The McMaster University quarterly*. Hamilton. v. 50, no. 3 (Mar. 1941), pp. 14-16; 20.)

Discusses, briefly, the proposals presented in the Report of the Royal Commission on Dominion-Provincial Relations. Ottawa, 1940.

ANGERS, FRANCOIS ALBERT   A quelle sauce veut-on nous manger? (In *L'Action nationale*. Montréal. v. 16 (déc. 1940), pp. [289]-306.)

A discussion of the Report of the Royal Commission on Dominion-Provincial Relations. Ottawa, 1940 (3 v.) The Rowell-Sirois report.

——— The associate state option. (In *Quebec in the Canada of tomorrow*. Toronto, 1968, pp. [L-1]-L-9.)

——— L'autonomie est-elle une formule négative? (In *L'Action nationale*. Montréal. v. 44 (fév. 1955), pp. [473]-489.)

At head of title: Notre enquête 1955 [no] 2.

Concerns federal-provincial relations.

——— La centralisation et les relations fédérales-provinciales. [Québec] Commission royale d'enquête sur les problèmes constitutionnels, 1956. 316 p.

At head of title: Annexe 11.

Mimeographed.

——— La Chambre de commerce et les relations fédérales-provinciales. (In *Relations*. Montréal. 10. année, no 115 (juil. 1950), pp. 190-193.)

——— Comment la centralisation progresse. (In *L'Action nationale*. Montréal. v. 40 (déc. 1952), pp. [191]-206.)

——— La conférence fédérale-provinciale de juillet. (In *L'Action nationale*. Montréal. v. 50 (sept. 1960), pp. [23]-40.)

The Dominion-provincial fiscal conference held July 25, 1960.

——— Essai sur la centralisation; analyse de principe politique et économique dans les perspectives [*sic*] canadiennes. Par François-Albert Angers, avec la collaboration de Pierre Harvey et Jacques Parizeau. Montréal, Presses de l'Ecole des hautes études commerciales, Editions de la Librairie Beauchemin [1960] 331 p.

——— Le fédéral et les universités. (In *L'Action nationale*. Montréal. v. 39 (jan./fév. 1952), pp. [7]-29.)

"Les arguments fallacieux du Rapport Massey, (II)".

Concerns the Report of the Royal Commission on National Development in the Arts, Letters and Sciences. Ottawa, 1951. (Commonly referred to as the Massey report.)

——— L'heure de la grande offensive centralisatrice. (In *L'Action nationale*. Montréal. v. 28 (sept. 1946), pp. [9]-21.)

An essay on federal-provincial relations.

——— L'intégration du fédéralisme. Par François Albert Angers et René Tremblay. (In Institut canadien des affaires publiques, Montréal. *Le fédéralisme*. [Montréal, 1955] pp. 35-44.)

——— L'intégration du fédéralisme. (In *La Nouvelle revue canadienne*. Ottawa. v. 3, no 5 (May/July 1956), pp. [275]-281.)

——— Nous avons le moyen de régler nos problèmes nous-mêmes. (In *L'Action nationale*. Montréal. v. 27 (mars 1946), pp. [204]-215.)

An essay on federal-provincial relations.

——— Octrois aux universités et position constitutionnelle du Québec. I. La législation provinciale de la dernière session. (In *L'Action nationale*. Montréal. v. 50 (nov. 1960), pp. [222]-232.)

——— Octrois aux universités et position constitutionnelle du Québec. II. La scène fédérale. (In *L'Action nationale*. Montréal. v. 50 (déc. 1960), pp. [330]-342.)

—— L'option des Etats associés. (In *Le Québec dans le Canada de demain*. Montréal [c1967] t. 1, pp. 133-140.)

—— Les propositions fédérales aux provinces et l'avenir des Canadiens français. (In *Revue de l'Université d'Ottawa*. [Ottawa] 17. année (1947), pp. [13]-33.)

—— Les propositions fédérales aux provinces et les droits des Canadiens français. (In *Culture*. Québec. v. 7 (1946), pp. [22]-33.)

—— La querelle des octrois universitaires. (In *L'Action nationale*. Montréal. v. 46 (jan./fév. 1957), pp. [368]-391.)

—— Rapatriement ou dépaysement? Editorial. Par Le Directeur. (In *L'Action nationale*. Montréal. v. 51 (fév. 1962), pp. [453]-465.)

—— Rien n'est réglé! (In *L'Action nationale*. Montréal. v. 45 (mai 1956), pp. [772]-784.)

Concerns federal-provincial relations.

—— Secours direct familial. (In *L'Action nationale*. Montréal. v. 25 (mai 1945), pp. [330]-353.)

—— Le séparatisme marque des points! Editorial. Par le Directeur. (In *L'Action nationale*. Montréal. v. 51 (mars 1962), pp. [549]-559.)

Concerns federal-provincial relations.

—— La situation ce soir . . . sur le front fédéral-provincial. (In *L'Action nationale*. Montréal. v. 29 (mars 1947), pp. [169]-187.)

ANGERS, PIERRE L'assistance financière de l'Etat à l'enseignement supérieur. (In *Relations*. Montréal. 17. année, no 198 (juin 1957), pp. 143-145.)

ARES, RICHARD L'aide fédérale à l'éducation. (In *Relations*. Montréal. 16. année, no 188 (août 1956), pp. 211-214; 16. année, no 189 (sept. 1956), pp. 236-238.)

In two parts.

—— La colossale entreprise de rebâtir un Canada à deux. La conférence constitutionnelle. (In *Relations*. Montréal. [28. année] no 325 (mars 1968), pp. 72-73.)

—— La conférence d'Ottawa. (In *Relations*. Montréal. 10. année, no 110 (fév. 1950), pp. 32-36.)

Concerns the Constitutional Conference of Federal and Provincial Governments held in Ottawa, January 10-12, 1950.

—— La conférence fédérale-provinciale de novembre 1957. (In *Relations*. Montréal. 18. année, no 205 (jan. 1958), pp. 2-5.)

—— Des subventions fédérales à l'enseignement primaire, pourquoi pas? (In *Relations*. Montréal, 17. année, no 195 (mars 1957), pp. 61-64.)

—— Le fédéralisme canadien après un siècle; bilan d'un siècle. (In *Le Québec dans le Canada de demain*. Montréal [c1967] t. 1, pp. [9]-19.)

—— Fédéralisme et centralisation. (In *L'Action nationale*. Montréal. v. 37 (jan. 1951), pp. [5]-14.)

Défense et illustration du fédéralisme, ptie 4.

—— "Le fédéralisme et la société canadienne-française" de Pierre Elliott Trudeau. (In *Relations*. Montréal. [27. année] no 322 (déc. 1967), pp. 318-320.)

A critique of *Le fédéralisme et la société canadienne-française*, par P. E. Trudeau. Montréal, Editions HMH, 1967.

—— Le fédéralisme et les subventions aux universités. (In *L'Action nationale*. Montréal. v. 46 (jan./fév. 1957), pp. [343]-354.)

—— Le fédéralisme, ses principes de base et sa valeur humaine. Montréal, Bellarmin, 1951. 32 p. (Institut social populaire, no. 441.)

—— Les octrois fédéraux aux universités. (In *Relations*. Montréal. 16. année, no 192 (déc. 1956), pp. 340-343.)

—— La prochaine conférence fédérale-provinciale. (In *Relations*. Montréal. [28. année] no 324 (fév. 1968), pp. 36-38.)

—— La Québec à la conférence d'Ottawa. (In *Relations*. Montréal. 10. année, no 109 (jan. 1950), pp. 9-12.)

Concerns the Constitutional Conference of Federal and Provincial Governments held at Ottawa, January 10-12, 1950.

—— Québec ou Canada français? Quatre événements récents presque simultanés: les Etats Généraux, les propos du général de Gaulle, la conférence de Toronto et le Rapport Laurendeau-Dunton, posent la question cruciale. (In *Relations*. Montréal. [28. année] no 323 (jan. 1968), pp. 8-10.)

ATKEY, RONALD G. The provincial interest in broadcasting under the Canadian constitution. (In Ontario Advisory Committee on Confederation. *Background papers and reports*. [Toronto, 1970] v. 2, pp. 189-255.)

BARBEAU, RAYMOND   Refus de la centralisation. (In *L'Action nationale*. Montréal. v. 50 (juin 1961), pp. [995]-1005.)

Review article of *Essai sur la centralisation*, par F. A. Angers. Montréal, 1960.

BARKWAY, MICHAEL   Conference or personal duel? (In *Saturday night*. Toronto. v. 65, no. 14 (Jan. 10, 1950), pp. 8; 12.)

Concerns the Dominion-Provincial Conference which met at Ottawa January 10-12, 1950.

The Bases of Confederation. (In *The Nation*. Toronto. v. 1, no. 2 (Apr. 9, 1874), p. 20.)

Discusses the need for a policy in order to define federal-provincial financial arrangements.

BECK, JAMES MURRAY   Canadian federalism in ferment. (In Leach, R. H. (ed.) *Contemporary Canada*. Durham, N.C., 1967. pp. [148]-176.)

——   New look in finance. The Dominion-provincial tussle. By J. M. Beck. (In *Queen's quarterly*. Kingston. v. 63 (1956), pp. [214]-227.)

——   The shaping of Canadian federalism; central authority or provincial right? Edited by J. M. Beck. Toronto, Copp Clark [c1971] xiv, 229 p. (Issues in Canadian history.)

A selection of readings.

BEECROFT, ERIC ARMOUR   Federalism and the written constitution. Toronto, 1927. 124 leaves.

Thesis (MA) – University of Toronto.

BELANGER, LAURENT   Mise en œuvre d'une politique de main-d'œuvre. (In Congrès des relations industrielles de l'Université Laval, 21st, Québec, 1966. *Une politique globale de la main-d'œuvre*. Québec, 1966. pp. 57-78.)

Suggests two systems of government organization in order to define and co-ordinate federal and provincial responsibilities in labour matters.

BELOFF, MAX   Reflections at the end of the Conference. By Max Beloff and Ivor Jennings. (In Hawkins, Gordon (ed.) *Concepts of federalism*. [Toronto] 1965. pp. 93-106.)

A summary of impressions gathered from the papers presented at the 34th Couchiching Conference held at Geneva Park, Ont., July 31—August 6, 1965. A comparative discussion of Canadian federalism.

BENOIT, AUGUSTE   La domination d'Ottawa d'après le rapport Tremblay. (In *Les Cahiers de Nouvelle-France*. Montréal. no 3 (juil./sept. 1957), pp. 226-229.)

——   Le rapport Tremblay met une base à la Cité. (In *Les Cahiers de Nouvelle-France*. Montréal. no 2 (avril/juin 1957), pp. 116-119.)

BERNARD, ANDRE C.   Parliamentary control of public finance in the province of Quebec. [Montreal, 1965] 1 v.

Thesis (MA) – McGill University.

BERNARD, L.   Federalism and public administration in Canada; study in constitutional law and practice. [London, 1963-64?] 1 v.

Thesis (PH D) – University of London.

BIDLAKE, GEORGE   The case of the Maritime provinces. (In *Saturday night*. Toronto. v. 38, no. 30 (June 2, 1923), p. 2.)

Concerns federal-provincial relations.

BIRCH, ANTHONY HAROLD   Federalism, finance and social legislation in Canada, Australia, and the United States. Oxford, Clarendon Press, 1955. xiv, 314 p.

Based on a thesis, University of London, 1951.

BLACK BEAVER   Inside story of the Sirois Conference. By Black beaver. (In *Saturday night*. Toronto. v. 56, no. 20 (Jan. 25, 1941), pp. 8-9.)

Relates to the Dominion-provincial constitutional conference held at Ottawa, January 14-15, 1941.

BLACK, EDWIN ROBERT   Canadian concepts of federalism. [Durham, N.C.] 1962 [c1963] xi, 305 leaves.

Thesis (PH D) – Duke University.

Abstracted in *Dissertation abstracts*, v. 24 (1963), no. 1, pp. 365-366.

——   A different perspective on Canadian federalism. By Edwin R. Black and Alan C. Cairns. [Vancouver, B.C., 1965?] 36 leaves.

——   A different perspective on Canadian federalism. By Edwin R. Black and Alan C. Cairns. (In *Canadian public administration*. Toronto. v. 9 (1966), pp. 27-44.)

——   Le fédéralisme canadien; une nouvelle perspective. Par Edwin R. Black et Alan C. Cairns. (In Sabourin, Louis (ed.) *Le système politique du Canada*. Ottawa, 1968. pp. [51]-76.)

——   Oil offshore troubles the waters. By

Edwin R. Black. (In *Queen's quarterly*. Kingston. v. 72 (1965), pp. [589]-603.)

Concerns the offshore oil dispute between British Columbia and the federal government.

BLUMENFELD, HANS The role of the federal government in urban affairs. (In *The Journal of liberal thought*. [Ottawa. v.] 2, no. 2 (spring 1966), pp. 35-44.)

BOND, LESLIE BERNARD The disallowance of provincial acts in the Dominion of Canada. Aurora, 1926-27. 103 leaves.

Thesis (MA) – University of Toronto.

BONENFANT, JEAN CHARLES The birth and development of the idea of special status for Quebec. (In *Quebec in the Canada of tomorrow*. [Toronto, 1968] pp. [D-1]-D-10.)

—— Le fédéralisme dans la constitution canadienne. (In Cours de formation national, 7ᵉ session, Montréal, 1961. *L'état du Québec*. Saint-Hyacinthe [Qué., 1962] pp. 19-36.)

—— Le fédéralisme et les peuples. (In *La Nouvelle revue canadienne*. Ottawa. v. 3, no 4 (mars/avril 1965), pp. 201-203.)

—— Genèse et développement de l'idée d'un statut particulier au Québec. (In *Le Québec dans le Canada de demain*. Montréal. [c1967] t. 1, pp. 50-57.)

BOOS, ALBERT WILLIAM The financial arrangements between the provinces and the Dominion. By A. W. Boos. Toronto, Macmillan Co. of Canada, publishers for the Dept. of Economics and Political Science, McGill University, 1930. 99 p. (McGill University economic studies, no. 12.)

"One of the National problems of Canada series."

BOURASSA, ROBERT Quebec's demands and the problem of sharing fiscal resources. (In *Quebec in the Canada of tomorrow*. [Toronto, 1968] pp. [P-1]-P-10.)

BOUVIER, EMILE Centralisation et unité nationale. Le rapport Marsh. (In *Relations*. Montréal. 3. année, no 33 (sept. 1943), pp. 231-235.)

—— Un nouveau fédéralisme s'impose-t-il au Canada? (In *Relations*. Montréal. 14. année, no 165 (sept. 1954), pp. 248-251.)

A review article of *Le fédéralisme canadien*, by M. Lamontagne. Québec, Presses Universitaires, 1954.

BOWIE, ROBERT RICHARDSON (ed.) Studies in federalism. Directed and edited by

Robert R. Bowie and Carl J. Friedrich. Boston, Little, Brown, 1954. xiii, 887 p.

Comparative analysis of the constitutions of Australia, Canada, Germany, Switzerland, and the United States.

BRADY, ALEXANDER Quebec and Canadian federalism. (In *The Canadian journal of economics and political science*. [Toronto] v. 25 (1959), pp. 259-270.)

Analyses the significance and recommendations of the Report of the Royal Commission of Inquiry on Constitutional Problems, issued in 1956. The Commission was appointed by the province of Quebec, under the chairmanship of Judge Thomas Tremblay (4 v.).

—— Quebec and Canadian federalism. (In Lederman, W. R. (ed.) *The courts and the Canadian constitution*. [Toronto, c1964] pp. [47]-62.)

Reprinted from *The Canadian journal of economics and political science*, v. 25 (1959), pp. 259-70.

Analyses the recommendation of Inquiry on Constitutional Problems. Quebec, 1956. Chairman, Judge Thomas Tremblay.

—— Report of the Royal Commission on Dominion-Provincial Relations. (In *The Canadian historical review*. Toronto. v. 21 (1940), pp. 245-253.)

Published Ottawa, King's Printer, 1940.

BRAIDWOOD, DARRELL THOMAS A survey of Dominion-provincial conferences, 1906-1941. [Vancouver] 1941. 127 leaves.

Thesis (MA) – University of British Columbia.

BRUNET, MICHEL Quand le gouvernement d'Ottawa acceptera-t-il de se soumettre à la constitution? (In *L'Action nationale*. Montréal. v. 46 (nov. 1956), pp. [191]-215.)

"L'aide fédérale aux universités et le problème des relations fédérales-provinciales."

—— Quand le gouvernement d'Ottawa acceptera-t-il de se soumettre à la constitution? (In *L'Action nationale*. Montréal. v. 46 (jan./fév. 1957), pp. [399]-422.)

Originally printed under the same title in *L'Action nationale*. Montréal, v. 46 (nov. 1956), pp. [191]-215.

BUCHANAN, E. C. Lobby and gallery. By E. C. B. (In *Saturday night*. Toronto. v. 42, no. 51 (Nov. 5, 1927), p. 4.)

Concerns the Dominion-Provincial Conference held November 3-10, 1927, and the method of amending the B.N.A. Act.

—— Lobby and gallery. By E. C. B. (In *Saturday night.* Toronto. v. 42, no. 52 (Nov. 12, 1927), p. 4.)

Discusses the Dominion-Provincial Conference held at Ottawa November 3-10, 1927.

—— National affairs. The Conference mouse. (In *Saturday night.* Toronto. v. 48, no. 12 (Jan. 28, 1933), p. 4.)

Concerns the federal-provincial conference held in January 1933.

BUCK, ARTHUR EUGENE Financing Canadian government. By A. E. Buck. Chicago, Public Administration Service, 1949. xi, 367 p.

This study is based on the primary assumption "that federal-provincial fiscal relationships are at the very core of government finance in Canada". – Pref.

BURCHILL, C. S. "Disallowance" in Alberta. Halifax. v. 18, no. 1 (Apr. 1938), p. [1]-8.)

BURNS, RONALD M. The machinery of federal-provincial relations. By R. M. Burns. (In *Canadian public administration.* Toronto. v. 8 (1965), pp. 527-534.)

—— Particular status; another view. By R. M. Burns. (In *Quebec in the Canada of tomorrow.* [Toronto, 1968] pp. [1-1]-1-17.)

—— The Royal Commission on Dominion-Provincial Relations; the Report in retrospect. (In Clark, R. M. (ed.) *Canadian issues.* Toronto, 1961. pp. [143]-157.)

Refers to the Rowell-Sirois report.

—— Some implications for federal-provincial relations. By R. M. Burns. (In *The Canadian forum.* Toronto. v. 47, no. 556 (May 1967), pp. 40-42.)

The Author examines the Report of the Royal Commission on Taxation. Ottawa, 1966 (7 v.)

CAMERON, C. D. W. The federal-provincial health program. (In Institute of Public Administration of Canada. *Proceedings of the annual conference.* Toronto. 8th (1956), pp. 11-17.)

CANADA. PRIME MINISTER'S OFFICE Federalism for the future; a statement of policy by the government of Canada. Le fédéralisme et l'avenir; déclaration de principe et exposé de la politique du Gouvernement du Canada. [Ottawa, Queen's Printer, 1968] 49 p.

Parallel texts, English and French.

Statement given at the Constitutional Conference, 1968, held in Ottawa, February 5, 6 and 7.

CANADA. ROYAL COMMISSION ON DOMINION-PROVINCIAL RELATIONS Report of the Royal Commission on Dominion-Provincial Relations. Ottawa, J. O. Patenaude, Printer to the King, 1940. 3 v.

Joseph Sirois, chairman.

Members of the Royal Commission: N. W. Rowell, Joseph Sirois, Thibaudeau Rinfret, John W. Dafoe, R. A. McKay, Henry F. Angus.

Commonly referred to as the Rowell-Sirois report.

Issued also in French.

Contents: Book I. Canada, 1867-1939. – Book II. Recommendations. – Book III. Documentation.

—— Appendix 1-8. Ottawa, J. O. Patenaude, Printer to the King, 1938-39 (18 v.).

—— The Rowell-Sirois report; an abridgement of Book I of the Royal Commission Report on Dominion-Provincial Relations. Edited and introduced by Donald V. Smiley. [Toronto] McClelland and Stewart [1965, c1963] 228 p. (Carleton library, no. 5.)

"The Report of the Royal Commission on Dominion-Provincial Relations was issued in three volumes by the King's Printer, Ottawa, in 1940. A photographic reproduction in one volume was published in 1954."

Membership of the Royal Commission: Hon. N. W. Rowell, Joseph Sirois, Hon. Thibaudeau Rinfret, John W. Dafoe, R. A. McKay, Henry F. Angus.

CANADA. ROYAL COMMISSION ON FINANCIAL ARRANGEMENTS BETWEEN THE DOMINION AND THE MARITIME PROVINCES Report. Ottawa, J. O. Patenaude, Printer to the King, 1935. 24 p.

Chairman: Sir Thomas White.

Popularly known as the White Commission.

CANADA. ROYAL COMMISSION ON MARITIME CLAIMS Report of the Royal Commission on Maritime Claims. The following is the complete report on Maritime province claims prepared and submitted to the government by the royal commission composed of Sir Andrew Rae Duncan, London, Eng., chairman; Judge W. B. Wallace of Nova Scotia and Professor Cyrus MacMillan of McGill University, Montreal.

(In *The Busy East of Canada*. Sackville, N.B. v. 17, no. 5 (Dec. 1926), pp. 4-33.)

Popularly known as the Duncan Report.

Canada—one or nine? (In *The Canadian forum*. Toronto. v. 20, no. 233 (June 1940), pp. 70-72.)

Discusses the Report of the Royal Commission on Dominion-Provincial Relations. Ottawa, 1940 (3 v.)

CANADIAN INSTITUTE ON ECONOMICS AND POLITICS Problems in Canadian unity; lectures given at the Canadian Institute on Economics and Politics, August 6 to 19, 1938. Edited by Violet Anderson. [Pref. by Sir Robert Falconer. Introduction by A. R. M. Lower] Toronto, T. Nelson [c1938] ix, 153 p.

Partial contents: The stresses and strains of Confederation, by G. F. Curtis. – One country or nine, by J. B. McGeachy. – The financial problem in Dominion-provincial relations, by W. A. McKague. – Some observations upon nationalism and provincialism in Canada, by F. H. Underhill.

Capitalization of the subsidies. (In *The Nation*. Toronto. v. 1, no. 10 (June 4, 1874), p. 116.)

Concerns the arrangement of subsidy accounts between the federal government and the provinces.

CAPLAN, NEIL Some factors affecting the resolution of a federal-provincial conflict. (In *Canadian journal of political science*. Toronto. v. 2 (1969), pp. [173]-186.)

Discusses "the offshore mineral rights dispute in Canada (which) has been . . . an open confrontation between governments since 1960".

CARDINAL, JEAN GUY Les institutions financières. (In *Québec dans le Canada de demain*. Montréal [1967] t. 2, pp. 117-124.)

Concerns federal-provincial relations.

CAREL, MAURICE Agriculture. Is it a federal or a provincial responsibility? (In *Quebec in the Canada of tomorrow*. [Toronto, 1968] pp. [EE-1]-EE-13.)

CARMAN, FRANCIS ASBURY Provincial rights —the people's wrongs. By F. A. Carman. (In *The Dalhousie review*. Halifax. v. 25 (1945/46), pp. [199]-206.)

An historical analysis concerning Dominion-provincial relations.

CARROTHERS, WILLIAM A. Problems of the Canadian federation. By W. A. Carrothers.

(In *The Canadian journal of economics and political science*. [Toronto] v. 1 (1935), pp. 26-40.)

Argues the case for "an economic inquiry into Dominion-provincial relations".

CAYGEON, ROBERT National affairs. Conference results. (In *Saturday night*. Toronto. v. 51, no. 7 (Dec. 21, 1935), p. 4.)

Discusses the eighth Dominion-Provincial Conference held at Ottawa, December 9-13, 1935.

CERIGO, S. G. La conférence fédérale-provinciale. Les dessous du "fédéralisme coopératif". (In *Cité libre*. Montréal. no. 63 (jan. 1964), pp. 4-12.)

Concerns the federal-provincial conference held at Ottawa November 26-29, 1963.

The Claim of Manitoba to her public lands. By J. D. C. (In *The Week*. Toronto. v. 2, no. 24 (May 14, 1885), pp. 374-375.)

A commentary on the article Provincial demands on the federal treasury, by Thorpe Mable (pseud.) (In *The Week*. Toronto. v. 2, (1885), pp. 212-213.)

CLEMENT, P. Les ententes fiscales entre le Québec et le gouvernement fédéral depuis 1940. [Québec, 1963] 1 v.

Thesis (MA) – Laval University.

CLEMENT, WILLIAM HENRY POPE The relations between the central and local governments of the United States and Canada compared. By W. H. P. Clement. (In *The Week*. Toronto. v. 13, no. 28 (June 5, 1896), pp. 663-666.)

CLOKIE, HUGH MC DOWALL Secession and federalism. By Hugh McD. Clokie. (In *The Manitoba arts review*. Winnipeg. v. 1, no. 2 (fall 1938), pp. 19-23.)

A comparative study.

COCKBURN, JAMES The power of disallowance and its national importance. By the Hon. James Cockburn, ex-Speaker of the House of Commons. (In *Rose-Belford's Canadian monthly and national review*. Toronto. v. 8 (1882), pp. 202-205.)

COHEN, JACOB L. Are we to be bottle-necked? By J. L. Cohen. (In *Saturday night*. Toronto. v. 56, no. 18 (Jan. 11, 1941), p. 6.)

"Is the whole question of recasting Canada's legislative setup to be slowed down to a walk? The author of this article, examining current criticism of the Rowell-Sirois Report, sees a very real danger of such a development."

—— Dominion has power to legislate for labor. By J. L. Cohen. (In *Saturday night.* Toronto. v. 62, no. 15 (Dec. 14, 1946), p. [22].)

"The author of this article . . . holds that the 1946 declarations of the Privy Council have the effect of restoring to the Dominion the power withheld from it by the decisions of 1896 and 1924 of legislating in the matter of labor relations, . . ."

COHEN, MAXWELL ABRAHAM Conference's big task is to find taxation plan. By Maxwell Cohen. (In *Saturday night.* Toronto. v. 60, no. 46 (July 21, 1945), p. 6.)

Concerns the Dominion-Provincial Conference on Reconstruction which opened in Ottawa, August 6, 1945.

—— The Dominion-provincial conference; some basic issues. Toronto, Ryerson [1945] 39 p.

Concerns the Dominion-Provincial Conference on Reconstruction held at Ottawa in 1945-46.

—— Dominion's proposals make 1945 sense. By Maxwell Cohen. (In *Saturday night.* Toronto. v. 60, no. 50 (Aug. 18, 1945), pp. 6-7.)

Concerns the Dominion-Provincial Conference on Reconstruction, with reference to the proposals made to the provinces by the federal government.

—— Premiers' conference has many problems. By Maxwell Cohen. (In *Saturday night.* Toronto. v. 60, no. 47 (July 28, 1945), p. [17].)

Concerns the Dominion-Provincial Conference on Reconstruction which opened in Ottawa, August 6, 1945.

COOK, GEORGE RAMSAY Provincial autonomy, minority rights and the compact theory, 1867-1921. By Ramsay Cook. [Ottawa, Queen's Printer for Canada, 1969] 81 p. (Studies of the Royal Commission on Bilingualism and Biculturalism, 4.)

CORRY, JAMES ALEXANDER Dominion-provincial relations. By J. A. Corry. (In *Public affairs.* Halifax. v. 6, no. 2 (special issue, 1942), pp. 101-105.)

—— Dominion-provincial relations. By J. A. Corry. (In *The Maritime advocate and busy East.* Sackville, N.B. v. 33, no. 12 (July 1943), pp. 23-24; 29-30.)

Reprinted from *Public affairs.*

—— The federal dilemma. By J. A. Corry. (In *The Canadian journal of economics*

and political science. [Toronto] v. 7 (1941), pp. 215-228.)

A comparative study of federalism.

COTE, PIERRE F. Politique fédérale et politique provinciale de la main d'œuvre. Par Pierre F. Côté, Yves Dubé et Marcel Guay. (In Congrès des relations industrielles de l'Université Laval, 21st, Quebec, 1966. *Une politique globale de la main-d'œuvre.* Québec, 1966. pp. 109-143.)

COURS DE FORMATION NATIONALE, 7e SESSION, MONTREAL, 1961 L'état du Québec; fédéralisme, autonomisme, souveraineté. Saint-Hyacinthe [Qué.] Editions Alerte [1962] 160 p.

"Documents relatifs à la septième session des Cours de formation nationale de la Fédération des Sociétés Saint-Jean-Baptiste du Québec, Montréal, 30 sept.-1er oct. 1961."

Partial contents: Le problème constitutionnel, par A. Leblanc. – Le fédéralisme dans la constitution canadienne, par J. C. Bonenfant. – Souveraineté et interdépendance dans un fédéralisme bi-culturel, par M. Lamontagne. – Le Canada français face à l'Acte de l'Amérique du Nord britannique, par F. A. Angers.

CRANE, DAVID Is authority shifting to the provinces? (In *Canada month.* Montreal. v. 3, no. 8 [i.e. 9] (Sept. 1963), pp. 7-8.)

CREPEAU, PAUL ANDRE (ed.) The future of Canadian federalism. L'avenir du fédéralisme canadien. Edited by P. A. Crépeau and C. B. Macpherson. [Toronto] University of Toronto Press [c1965] x, 188 p.

Papers and commentaries presented at the meeting of the Association of Canadian Law Teachers and the Canadian Political Science Association at Charlottetown, Prince Edward Island, in June 1964.

Text in English and French.

Contents: The five faces of federalism, by J. R. Mallory. – Federalism, nationalism and reason, by P. E. Trudeau. – Prospects for economic policy in a federal Canada, by J. Parizeau. – Economic policy in our federal state, by W. C. Hood. – The balanced interpretation of the federal distribution of legislative powers in Canada, by W. R. Lederman. – Les attitudes changeantes du Québec à l'entroit de la constitution de 1867, par J. Beetz. – Vers un nouvel équilibre constitutionnel au Canada, par J. Y. Morin. – Federalism, constitutionalism and legal change; legal implications of the "revolution" in Quebec, by E. McWhinney.

CROISAT, MAURICE Planification et fédéralisme. (In Canadian public administration. Toronto. v. 11 (1968), pp. [309]-321.)

CROWLE, HAROLD E. Concurrent powers may be solution. By H. E. Crowle. (In Saturday night. Toronto. v. 54, no. 39 (July 29, 1939), p. 3.)

Examines Dominion-provincial relations.

—— Concurrent powers should solve commerce impasse. By H. E. Crowle. (In Saturday night. Toronto. v. 54, no. 41 (Aug. 12, 1939), p. 2.)

Examines Dominion-provincial relations.

CURTIS, CLIFFORD AUSTIN War-time problems of local government. I. The Dominion-municipal relationship in the war organization, by C. A. Curtis. (In The Canadian journal of economics and political science. [Toronto] v. 9 (1943), pp. 394-404.)

Discusses the relationship between the Dominion government and municipal institutions.

Part two is The effect of war on municipal finance, by Carl H. Chatters.

CURTIS, GEORGE FREDERICK Nova Scotia's propositions to the Rowell Commission. By G. F. Curtis. (In Public affairs. Halifax. v. 1, no. 3 (Mar. 1938), pp. 114-118.)

DAGENAIS, ANDRE L'Etat libre du Saint-Laurent face à la nouvelle conjoncture politique. (In Les Cahiers de Nouvelle-France. Montréal. no 2 (avril/juin 1957), pp. 104-111.)

DAIGNAULT, RICHARD Dans le système parlementaire, à quoi servent les parlements? (In Le Magazine Maclean. Montréal. v. 5, no 10 (oct. 1965), pp. 6-7.)

Brief remarks.

DALE, PETER ALAN BERNARD The Fulton-Favreau formula; a study in Canadian federalism. [Montréal] 1967. 1 v.

Thesis (MA) – McGill University.

DANE, BARRY Provincial rights. (In The Week. Toronto. v. 1, no. 45 (Oct. 9, 1884), p. 713.)

Federal-provincial relations.

DANSEREAU, DOLLARD Centralisation ou décentralisation. (In Les Idées. Montréal. 1. année, v. 1 (1935), pp. [265]-272.)

DAVY, GEORGES Le fédéralisme et les peuples. Par Georges Davy et Jean-Charles Bonenfant. (In Institut canadien des affaires publiques, Montréal. Le fédéralisme. [Montréal, 1955] pp. 10-20.)

—— Le fédéralisme et les peuples. (In La Nouvelle revue canadienne. Ottawa. v. 3, no 4 (mars/avril 1956), pp. [193]-201.)

DEHEM, ROGER Planification économique et fédéralisme. Québec, Presses de l'Université Laval, 1968. 201 p.

"Etude faite originellement en 1965 pour le compte de la Commission royale d'enquête sur le bilinguisme et le biculturalisme au Canada."

DENIS, G. Coordination et contrôle dans les relations intergouvernementales au Canada. [Québec, 1964] 1 v.

Thesis (MA) – Laval University.

DESCHAMPS, JEAN Québec boude-t-il le progrès du Canada? (In L'Action nationale. Montréal. v. 44 (avril 1955), pp. [679]-684.)

At head of title: Notre enquête 1955 (4).

Concerns federal-provincial relations.

DION, GERMAIN Les relations fiscales fédérales-provinciales de 1942 à nos jours. [Ottawa] 1967. 1 v.

Thesis (MA) – University of Ottawa.

Disallowance and the province of Quebec. By D. C. R. (In The Week. Toronto. v. 4, no. 51 (Nov. 17, 1887), pp. 816-817.)

The Disputed boundaries. By C. L. (In The Week. Toronto. v. 1, no. 34 (July 24, 1884), pp. 534-535.)

Concerns the Ontario boundary dispute.

DOERN, AUDREY DIANE Erosion of federal power in Canada. [Ottawa] 1968. 1 v.

Thesis (MA) – Carleton University.

DOERN, G. BRUCE Vocational training and manpower policy. A case study in intergovernmental liaison. (In Canadian public administration. Toronto. v. 12 (1969), pp. [63]-71.)

DOMINION-PROVINCIAL CONFERENCE, OTTAWA, 1927 Precis of discussions; Dominion-Provincial Conference, November 3 to 10, 1927. Ottawa, F. A. Acland, Printer to the King, 1928. 38 p.

—— Sommaire des discussions; Conférence fédérale-provinciale, du 3 au 10 novembre 1927. Ottawa, F. A. Acland, Imprimeur du Roi, 1928. 38 p.

DOMINION-PROVINCIAL CONFERENCE, OTTAWA, 1935 Record of proceedings; Ottawa, December 9-13, 1935. Ottawa, J. O. Patenaude, Printer to the King, 1936. 74 p.

DOMINION-PROVINCIAL CONFERENCE, OTTAWA, 1941 Dominion-Provincial Conference. Plenary session, no. 1-2; Jan. 14-15, 1941. Ottawa, E. Cloutier, Printer to the King, 1941. 2 v.

Paged continuously.

Proceedings of the Conference.

Dominion-provincial conference: Mr. King is no Santa Claus. (In *Canadian comment*. Toronto. v. [1] (Jan. 1936), pp. 5-6.)

Summarizes the issues presented at the Dominion-Provincial Conference held at Ottawa, December 9-13, 1935.

DOMINION-PROVINCIAL CONFERENCE ON RECONSTRUCTION, OTTAWA, 1945-1946 Dominion and provincial submissions and plenary conference discussions. Ottawa, E. Cloutier, Printer to the King, 1946. xi, 624 (i.e. 670) p.

At head of title: Dominion-Provincial Conference (1945).

Includes proceedings of the conference, issued also separately with title: Plenary session . . . Dominion-Provincial Conference on Reconstruction.

Issued also in French under title: *Mémoires du dominion et des provinces et délibérations de la conférence plénière*. Ottawa, E. Cloutier, Imprimeur du Roi, 1946. (686 p.).

These conferences extended from August 1945 to May 1946.

DOUGLAS, R. A. An analysis of the provincial reception of the Fulton-Favreau formula. [London, Ont., 1967] 1 v.

Thesis (MA) – University of Western Ontario.

DRAYTON, SIR HENRY L. Our competing governments. The British North America Act has been misinterpreted but is still workable. It can be redrawn without interfering with provincial rights. By Sir Henry Drayton. (In *Canadian comment*. Toronto. v. 3, no. 9 (Sept. 1934), pp. [3]-4; 22-23.)

DUKE UNIVERSITY, DURHAM, N.C. COMMONWEALTH-STUDIES CENTER Evolving Canadian federalism. A. R. M. Lower, F. R. Scott, J. A. Corry, F. H. Soward and Alexander Brady. [Foreword by Paul H. Clyde. Introductory statement by B. U. Ratchford] Durham N.C., Duke University Press, 1958. xvi, 187 p. (Its Publications, 9.)

Papers delivered and discussed at a summer seminar of the Duke University Commonwealth-Studies Center in the summer of 1957.

Partial contents: Theories of Canadian federalism, by A. R. M. Lower. – French Canada and Canadian federalism, by F. R. Scott. – Constitutional trends and federalism, by J. A. Corry.

DUPRE J. STEFAN Tax powers versus spending responsibilities; an historical analysis of federal-provincial finance. By J. Stefan Dupré. (In University League for Social Reform. *The prospect for change*. Toronto [c1965] pp. 83-101.)

Studies the allocation of tax powers and spending responsibilities within the framework of a system based on the concept of federalism.

DUROCHER, RENE Maurice Duplessis et sa conception de l'autonomie provinciale au début de sa carrière politique. (In *Revue d'histoire de l'Amérique française*. Montréal. v. 23, no 1 (juin 1969), pp. 13-34.)

Federal-provincial relations are a central factor in this analysis.

An Eastern secessionist. Special correspondence of Willisons monthly. (In *Willisons monthly*. Toronto. v. 2, no. 9 (Feb. 1927), pp. 343-344.)

Discusses the points raised against the Duncan report in an article by W. Russell Maxwell published in the *Halifax Morning Chronicle*, January 1, 1927. Reference is to the Report of the Royal Commission on Maritime Claims. Ottawa, 1927. Sir Andrew Rae Duncan, chairman.

EAYRS, JAMES Canadian federalism and the United Nations. (In *The Canadian journal of economics and political science*. [Toronto] v. 16 (1950), pp. 172-183.)

Discusses how the existing Canadian constitution can obstruct effective international legislation.

"ECONOMIST" The deadlock in Dominion provincial finance. by "Economist". (In *Public affairs*. Halifax. v. 1, no. 1 (Aug. 1937), pp. [17]-18.)

EGGLESTON, WILFRID An arena for a clash of leaders. National conferences provide chance for 11 governments to argue meaning of Canada. (In *Saturday night*. Toronto. v. 65, no. 12 (Dec. 27, 1949), pp. 8-9.)

A historical survey of Dominion-provincial conferences.

—— Capital comment. Autonomy talk has limits. (In *Saturday night*. Toronto. v. 65, no. 15 (Jan. 17, 1950), p. 3.)

With reference to the Dominion-Provincial Conference held in January 1950.

—— Capital comment. Why the parley suceeded. (In *Saturday night*. Toronto. v. 65, no. 16 (Jan. 24, 1950), p. 3.)

With reference to the Dominion-Provincial Conference held at Ottawa, January 10-12, 1950.

—— Capital comment. Tax division still the key. (In *Saturday night*. Toronto. v. 65, no. 18 (Feb. 7, 1950), p. 3.)

". . . of all the debatable fields of power upon which the National Government and the provinces differ from time to time, the one which it was most important to settle satisfactorily was the field of taxation."

—— Capital comment. Delegation might be a benefit. (In *Saturday night*. Toronto. v. 66, no. 2 (Oct. 17, 1950), p. 3.)

Comments on a Supreme Court ruling on the distribution of powers between the federal and provincial governments.

—— Capital comment. New party will be different. (In *Saturday night*. Toronto. v. 66, no. 8 (Nov. 28, 1950), p. 3.)

Speculates on a federal-provincial conference which opened at Ottawa December 4, 1950.

—— Dominion-provincial subsidies and grants. A study prepared for the Royal Commission on Dominion-Provincial Relations by Wilfrid Eggleston and C. T. Kraft. Ottawa, 1939. iii, 200 leaves.

Reproduced typescript.

Issued also in French.

—— The Ottawa letter. Dominion-provincial cooperation will be essential in postwar. (In *Saturday night*. Toronto. v. 60, no. 23 (Feb. 10, 1945), p. 8.)

—— The Ottawa letter. Success of new conference will rest on vision and tolerance. (In *Saturday night*. Toronto. v. 60, no. 43 (June 30, 1945), p. 8.)

Refers to the Dominion-Provincial Conference on Reconstruction held August 1945 to May 1946.

—— The Ottawa letter. Conference to succeed will have to solve provincial revenues. (In *Saturday night*. Toronto. v. 60, no. 45 (July 14, 1945), p. 8.)

Concerns the Dominion-Provincial Conference on Reconstruction which opened in Ottawa, August 6, 1945.

—— The Ottawa letter. Can weaknesses be overcome by all governments' coopera-

tion. (In *Saturday night*. Toronto. v. 60, no. 47 (July 28, 1945), p. 8.)

Discusses the Dominion-Provincial Conference on Reconstruction which opened in Ottawa, August 6, 1945.

—— The Ottawa letter. In first exchange at Conference the Dominion was the winner. (In *Saturday night*. Toronto. v. 60, no. 49 (Aug. 11, 1945), p. 8.)

Concerns the Dominion-Provincial Conference on Reconstruction which opened in Ottawa, August 6, 1945.

—— The Ottawa letter. Most of the provinces fare very well under the Dominion offer. (In *Saturday night*. Toronto. v. 60, no. 50 (Aug. 18, 1945), p. 8.)

Concerns the Dominion-Provincial Conference on Reconstruction which opened in Ottawa, August 6, 1945.

—— The Ottawa letter. Provinces, having left tax field, find it impossible to return. (In *Saturday night*. Toronto. v. 61, no. 14 (Dec. 8, 1945), p. 8.)

Comments on Dominion-provincial relations on taxation.

—— The Ottawa letter. Ottawa and Ontario do not agree on way to provincial autonomy. (In *Saturday night*. Toronto. v. 61, no. 20 (Jan. 19, 1946), p. 8.)

—— The Ottawa letter. Ottawa's enormous obligations must be shared by provinces. (In *Saturday night*. Toronto. v. 61, no. 21 (Jan. 26, 1946), p. 8.)

Concerns Ontario's counter-proposals at a Dominion-provincial conference held at Ottawa in January 1946.

—— The Ottawa letter. Results of Premiers' conference secret but much speculation. (In *Saturday night*. Toronto. v. 61, no. 25 (Feb. 23, 1946), p. 8.)

Refers to a Dominion-provincial conference held at Ottawa in January 1946.

—— Ottawa letter. Obsolete federalism is core of Dominion-provincial problem. (In *Saturday night*. Toronto. v. 61, no. 33 (Apr. 20, 1946), p. 8.)

—— Ottawa letter. Ottawa conference at critical stage in tax deliberations. (In *Saturday night*. Toronto. v. 61, no. 35 (May 4, 1946), p. 8.)

Concerns the Dominion-Provincial Conference on Reconstruction held April 29 to May 3, 1946.

—— Ottawa letter. Failure of conference places all provinces in difficult position.

(In *Saturday night*. Toronto. v. 61, no. 36 (May 11, 1946), p. 8.)

Comments on the Dominion-Provincial Conference on Reconstruction held April 29—May 3, 1946.

—— Ottawa letter. Conference breakup leaves Ottawa facing momentous decision. (In *Saturday night*. Toronto. v. 61, no. 37 (May 18, 1946), p. 8.)

Refers to a Dominion-Provincial Conference on Reconstruction held April 29—May 3, 1946.

—— Ottawa letter. Possible federal tax cuts will reflect conference's failure. (In *Saturday night*. Toronto. v. 61, no. 39 (June 1, 1946), p. 8.)

Refers to a Dominion-Provincial Conference on Reconstruction held April 29—May 3, 1946.

—— Ottawa letter. Few signs of success in another Dominion-provincial meeting. (In *Saturday night*. Toronto. v. 62, no. 1 (Sept. 7, 1946), p. 8.)

—— Ottawa letter. Labor jurisdiction is a major Dominion-provincial problem. (In *Saturday night*. Toronto. v. 62, no. 8 (Oct. 26, 1946), p. 8.)

—— Ottawa letter. Process of decentralization is crux of current controversy. (In *Saturday night*. Toronto. v. 62, no. 14 (Dec. 7, 1946), p. 8.)

—— Ottawa letter. Dominion-provincial bargaining techniques remain the same. (In *Saturday night*. Toronto. v. 62, no. 17 (Dec. 28, 1946), p. 8.)

—— Ottawa letter. A rigid per capita formula for all provinces would be unjust. In *Saturday night*. Toronto. v. 62, no. 20 (Jan. 18, 1947), p. 8.)

—— Ottawa letter. Periodic angry outbursts keep up old provincial-federal friction. (In *Saturday night*. Toronto. v. 63, no. 23 (Mar. 13, 1948), p. 8.)

—— The road to nationhood; a chronicle of Dominion-Provincial relations. Toronto, Oxford University Press, 1946. xv, 337 p.

—— Rowell-Sirois report—the successful "failure". (In *Saturday night*. Toronto. v. 68, no. 14 (Jan. 10, 1953), p. 11.)

EWART, JOHN SKIRVING Some further comments on dominion-provincial relations. By John S. Ewart. (In Canadian Political Science Association. *Papers and proceed-ings of the annual meeting*. [Kingston, Ont.] v. 3 (1931), pp. [248]-258.)

FARIBAULT, MARCEL The Confederation's financial dilemma. (In Hawkins, Gordon (ed.) *Concepts of federalism*. [Toronto] 1965. pp. 36-45.)

Discusses federal-provincial fiscal problems in relation to the Canadian constitution.

FARQUHAR, GEORGE The problem of subsidies; the Maritime view. By G. Farquhar. (In Canadian Broadcasting Corporation. *The Canadian constitution*. Toronto [c1938] pp. 46-58.)

"Discussed by the Citadel Club, Halifax, October 24, 1937."

Defines and discusses subsidies as "the grants made by the Dominion to the Provinces . . . intended in 1867 to cover their costs of government."

FARQUHARSON, R. A. The provinces plead. Canada's seventy-year-old constitutional dilemma as the provinces see it. Necessity for compromise realized. (In *Maclean's*. Toronto. v. 50, no. 11 (June 1, 1937), pp. 18; 39-40.)

The Fathers of Confederation. (In *The Canadian forum*. Toronto. v. 17, no. 201 (Oct. 1937), pp. 226-228.)

An historical discussion of the problems confronting the Royal Commission investigating Dominion-provincial relations appointed by the Mackenzie King government August 14, 1937.

FAVREAU, GUY National leadership in Canadian federalism. (In Hawkins, Gordon, (ed.) *Concepts of federalism*. [Toronto] 1965. pp. 46-51.)

Discusses the rôle and attitude of the national government in meeting the problems of Canadian federalism.

FEDERAL-PROVINCIAL CONFERENCE, OTTAWA, 1963 Federal-Provincial Conference, 1963 . . . Proceedings [Ottawa] [R. Duhamel, Queen's Printer, 1964] 123 p.

Conference held November 26-29, 1963.

Federal subsidies. (In *Canadian comment*. Toronto. v. 4, no. 4 (Apr. 1935), pp. 10-11.)

FILION, GERARD Demain, il sera peut-être trop tard. (In *L'Action nationale*. Montréal. v. 46 (jan./fév. 1957), pp. [465]-471.)

Concerns federal aid to universities.

—— Québec, province différente. (In L'Action nationale. Montréal. v. 44 (mai 1955), pp. [763]-772.)
At head of title: Notre enquête 1955 (4).
Concerns federal-provincial relations.

Five just men. (In Canadian comment. Toronto. v. 6, no. 9 (Sept. 1937), pp. 4-5.)
Concerns the personel who conducted the Royal Commission on Dominion-provincial relations, appointed August 14, 1937: N. W. Rowell, J. W. Dafoe, T. Rinfret, H. F. Angus, R. A. MacKay.

FORGET, LUCIE Some aspects of federal-provincial fiscal relations. [Montreal, 1966] vii, 181 leaves.
Thesis (MA) – McGill University.

FORSEY, EUGENE ALFRED Are provinces to have Dominion status? By Eugene Forsey. (In Saturday night. Toronto. v. 63, no. 21 (Feb. 28, 1948), pp. [9]; [12].)

—— B.N.A. Act is no case for nine nations. By Eugene Forsey. (In Saturday night. Toronto. v. 63, no. 38 (June 26, 1948), pp. 18-19.)
Last of a series of articles "on the constitutional relations between the Dominion and the provinces . . .".

—— Concepts of federalism; some Canadian aspects. By Eugene Forsey. (In Hawkins, Gordon (ed.) Concepts of federalism. [Toronto] 1965, pp. 22-28.)
Argues that the essential problems of Canadian federalism are not concerned with problems of federalism but of Canadian dualism.

—— Constitutional monarchy and the provinces. By Eugene Forsey. (In Ontario Advisory Committee on Confederation. Background papers and reports. [Toronto] 1967. v. 1, pp. [175]-186.)
Presented October 1965.
Later reprinted under title: The monarchy in Canada (In Vaughan, F. (ed.) Contemporary issues in Canadian politics. Scarborough, Ont. [c1970] pp. 142-150.)

—— Disallowance; a contrast. By E. A. Forsey. (In The Canadian forum. Toronto. v. 18, no. 209 (June 1938), pp. 73-74.)
Discusses the Dominion government disallowance of three Alberta acts during the summer of 1937.

—— Disallowance of provincial acts, reservation of provincial bills, and refusal of assent by lieutenant-governors, 1937-47. By Eugene Forsey. (In The Canadian jour-

nal of economics and political science. [Toronto] v. 14 (1948), pp. 94-97.)

—— Disallowance of provincial acts, reservation of provincial bills, and refusal of assent by lieutenant-governors since 1867. By Eugene Forsey. (In The Canadian journal of economics and political science [Toronto] v. 4 (1938), pp. 47-59.)

—— Dominion status spurs Saskatchewan C.C.F. By Eugene Forsey. (In Saturday night. Toronto. v. 63, no. 29 (Apr. 24, 1948), p. [10].)
"This is the third of Mr. Forsey's series of articles on the more extreme claims for sovereign powers for the provinces which have been put forward recently by Canadian provincialists."

—— Memorandum on the Associate States. By Eugene Forsey. (In Ontario Advisory Committee on Confederation. Background papers and reports. Toronto, 1967, v. 1, pp. 187-192.)
Presented November 1966.

—— The monarchy in Canada. By Eugene Forsey. (In Vaughan, Frederick (ed.) Contemporary issues in Canadian politics. Scarborough, Ont. [c1970] pp. 142-150.)
Originally appeared under title: Constitutional monarchy and the provinces. (In Ontario Advisory Committee on Confederation. Background papers and reports. [Toronto] 1967. v. 1, [175]-186.)

—— Parliament's power to advise. By Eugene Forsey. (In The Canadian journal of economics and political science. [Toronto] v. 29 (1963), pp. 203-210.)
Considers, in an historical context, the parliamentary power of disallowance. The issue was raised on March 16, 1960, when Arnold Peters asked that Parliament give consideration to the disallowance of two Newfoundland acts passed in 1959.

—— Professor Hodgins' baker's dozen. By Eugene Forsey. (In The Canadian forum. Toronto. v. 44, no. 529 (Feb. 1965), pp. 253-255.)
A reply to A baker's dozen for the B 'n B, by B. W. Hodgins. (In The Canadian forum. Toronto. v. 44, no. 521 (1964), pp. 66-69.)
For a rejoinder see Dr. Forsey's rejection of the tacit agreement, by B. W. Hodgins. (In The Canadian forum. Toronto. v. 45, no. 534 (1965), pp. 89-90.)

—— Professor Morin's modest proposal. By Eugene Forsey. (In The Canadian forum. Toronto. v. 44, no. 524 (Sept. 1964), pp. [121]-125.)

Deals with Canadian federalism.

A searching answer to The need for a new Canadian federation, by J. Y. Morin (In *The Canadian forum.* Toronto. v. 44, no. 521 (1964), pp. 64-66.)

For a rejoinder see In defence of a modest proposal, by J. Y. Morin. (In *The Canadian forum.* Toronto. v. 44, no. 529 (1965), pp. 256-258.)

—— Should a legislature have plenary power? By Eugene Forsey. (In *Saturday night.* Toronto. v. 63, no. 32 (May 15, 1948), pp. 12-13.)

"Fourth of a series of articles . . . on the more extreme claims of some advocates of 'provincial rights'."

FOSTER, WALTER EDWARD   Justice for the Maritimes. By Hon. W. E. Foster, Premier of New Brunswick. (In *Maclean's.* Toronto. v. 34, no. 13 (July 1921), pp. 30-31.)

FOURNIER, JEAN PIERRE   The need for clarity. (In *The Canadian forum.* Toronto. v. 45, no. 541 (Feb. 1966), pp. 245-246.)

Sharp comments on Quebec-Ottawa relations and the evolving concept of special status.

"This comment was delivered on January 9 [1966] in the CBC's Capital report."

FOWLER, ROBERT MAC LAREN   Design for a new Dominion. "The Rowell-Sirois report is charged with significance for every individual Canadian living today and for his children and his grandchildren after him." Part. 1. By R. M. Fowler. (In *Maclean's.* Toronto. v. 53, no. 11 (June 1, 1940), pp. 8-9; 41; 43-45.)

Concerns the Report of the Royal Commission on Dominion-Provincial Relations. Ottawa, 1940. 3 v.

—— Design for a new Dominion. A behind-the-scenes story of the writing of the report which may become a charter of reconfederation. Part 2. By R. M. Fowler. (In *Maclean's.* Toronto. v. 53, no. 12 (June 15, 1940), pp. 15; 40-43.)

Concerns the Report of the Royal Commission on Dominion-Provincial Relations. Ottawa, 1940. 3 v.

—— Design for a new Dominion. A clear-cut explanation of the sweeping debt and taxation changes recommended by the Rowell-Sirois commission. Part 3. By R. M. Fowler. (In *Maclean's.* Toronto. v. 53, no. 14 (July 15, 1940), pp. 17; 24-26.)

Concerns the Report of the Royal Commission on Dominion-Provincial Relations. Ottawa, 1940. 3 v.

—— Design for a new Dominion. We should not wait for peace to implement the Rowell-Sirois Report. Adoption now would enhance our war effort by making government more efficient. Part 4. By R. M. Fowler. (In *Maclean's.* Toronto. v. 53, no. 18 (Sept. 15, 1940), pp. 20; 22; 24.)

FRASER, BLAIR   Backstage at Ottawa. Post mortem on a flop. By the Man with a Notebook. (In *Maclean's.* Toronto. v. 59, no. 11 (June 1, 1946), pp. 15; 81; 83.)

Discusses the breakdown of the 1946 Dominion-Provincial Conference.

—— Backstage at Ottawa. No garçon was Garson. By the Man with a Notebook. (In *Maclean's.* Toronto. v. 59, no. 23 (Dec. 1, 1946), pp. 75; 71.)

Concerns Premier Stuart Garson of Manitoba and the Dominion-Provincial Conference held in Ottawa during the spring of 1946.

—— Backstage at Ottawa. Misdeal! By the Man with a Notebook. (In *Maclean's.* Toronto. v. 60, no. 4 (Feb. 15, 1947), p. 15.)

Concerns federal-provincial financial relations.

—— Backstage at Ottawa. Will Ottawa open the cashbox? (In *Maclean's.* Toronto. v. 68, no. 20 (Oct. 1, 1955), pp. 9; 95.).

Concerns the allocation of federal funds to "have-not" provinces.

—— Backstage in Ottawa. If even a few provinces "opt out" of even a few national programs . . . (In *Maclean's.* Toronto. v. 77, no. 8 (Apr. 18. 1964), p. 4.)

—— Backstage in Ottawa. The lesson of the Quebec conference: we're moving still farther apart. (In *Maclean's.* Toronto. v. 77, no. 9 (May 2, 1964), pp. 1-2.)

Relates to the Federal-Provincial Conference held in Quebec City March 31—April 2, 1964.

—— Backstage in Ottawa. The truth about Quebec's sudden ambitions abroad. (In *Maclean's.* Toronto. v. 78, no. 11 (June 5, 1965), pp. 2-3.)

Discusses "the argument between Ottawa and Quebec about a province's right to negotiate with a foreign power".

—— Confederation, 1946. Here's plain talk on what the Dominion-provincial conferences mean to you and why we must make Confederation work. (In *Maclean's*. Toronto. v. 59, no. 6 (Mar. 15, 1946), pp. 10; 49-51; 53.)

FULTON, EDMUND DAVIE   Some financial aspects of Canadian federalism. By E. Davie Fulton. (In Hawkins, Gordon (ed.) *Concepts of federalism*. [Toronto] 1965. pp. 29-35.)

Presents "a viewpoint based on a working experience in the field of federal-provincial relations".

GAGNON, R.   Les sources du Rapport Tremblay en ce qui concerne les relations fédérales-provinciales. [Québec, 1961] 1 v.

Thesis (MA) – Laval University.

GALLANT, EDGAR   The machinery of federal-provincial relations. (In *Canadian public administration*. Toronto. v. 8 (1965), pp. 515-526.)

GARANT, PATRICE   Special status and public administration. (In *Quebec in the Canada of tomorrow*. [Toronto, 1968] pp. [T-1]-T-14.)

——   Le statut particulier et l'administration publique. (In *Le Québec dans le Canada de demain*. Montréal [1967] t. 2, pp. [9]-21.)

GARRY   Disallowance in Manitoba. By Garry. (In *The Week*. Toronto. v. 4, no. 11 (Feb. 10, 1887), pp. [167]-168.)

GAUTHIER, FRANCOISE   Centralisation ou décentralisation? Les constraintes de la politique économique. Montréal, Bellarmin, 1967. 94 p. (Cahiers de l'Institut social populaire, no. 8.)

GAUTIER, CHARLES   Canadiens français et services fédéraux. (In *L'Action nationale*. Montréal. v. 1 (juin 1933), pp. [343]-347.)

GERIN-LAJOIE, PAUL   Canadian federalism and the future. (In Hawkins, Gordon (ed.) *Concepts of federalism*. [Toronto] 1965. pp. 62-68.)

——   La Commission Tremblay. (In *Relations*. Montréal. 13. année, no 153 (sept. 1953), pp. 234-237.)

——   En marge de l'enquête provinciale sur les problèmes constitutionnels (I). Origines de nos problèmes constitutionnels et fiscaux actuels. (In *Relations*. Montréal. 13. année, no 149 (mai 1953), pp. 118-120.)

——   En marge de l'enquête provinciale sur les problèmes constitutionnels (II).

Les recommandations de la Commission Sirois et les accords fiscaux. (In *Relations*. Montréal. 13. année, no 159 (juin 1953), pp. 149-152.)

——   En marge de l'enquête provinciale sur les problèmes constitutionnels (III). Critique des accords fiscaux actuels. (In *Relations*. Montréal. 13. année, no 151 (juil 1953), pp. 183-185.)

——   En marge de l'enquête provinciale sur les problèmes constitutionnels – IV. Impasse au bifurcation dans l'histoire du Canada. (In *Relations*. Montréal. 13. année, no 152 (août 1953), pp. 208-211.)

——   Federal-provincial conference. Are we facing a constitutional deadlock? (In *Saturday night*. Toronto. v. 66, no. 48 (Sept. 4, 1951), pp. 12; [24].)

GETTYS, CORA LUELLA   The administration of Canadian conditional grants; a study in Dominion-provincial relationships. By Luella Gettys. Chicago, Published for the Committee on Public Administration of the Social Science Research Council by Public Administration Service, 1938. xiii, 193 p. (Committee on Public Administration. Social Science Research Council. Studies in Administration, v. 3.)

GILLIS, DUNCAN HUGH   The determinants of Canadian federalism. By D. H. Gillis. [London, Eng., 1948] 1 v.

Thesis (PH D) – London School of Economics, University of London.

GOUIN, SIR LOMER   Question actuelle. Le remaniement des subsides fédéraux en faveur des provinces. Développement d'un discours prononcé par l'Hon. M. Lomer Gouin à Montréal, mai 1903. Montréal, Beauchemin, 1903. 166 p.

GREY, RODNEY   Federal-provincial financing. (In *Queen's quarterly*. Kingston. v. 58 (1951), pp. [101]-112.)

Examines the changes occurring in federal-provincial financial relations.

GRUBE, GEORGE MAXIMILIAN ANTONY   Some weaknesses of the Sirois report. By G. M. A. Grube. (In *The Canadian forum*. Toronto. v. 20, no. 241 (Feb. 1941), pp. 334-336.)

Comments on the Report of the Royal Commission on Dominion-Provincial Relations. Ottawa, 1940. (3 v.).

HAIGHT, DAVID E.   Sharing of functions in Canadian federalism. By D. E. Haight. [Chicago, 1962] 216 leaves.

Thesis (PH D) – University of Chicago.

HANSON, ERIC J.   Federal-provincial implications of the Carter report. By E. J. Hanson. Don Mills, Ont., CCH Canadian
[c1967] 36 p.

Discussion of the Report of the Royal
Commission on Taxation. Ottawa, 1966
[i.e. 1966-67] (7 v.).

HAWKINS, GORDON (ed.)   Concepts of federalism. Edited by Gordon Hawkins. [To-
ronto] Canadian Institute on Public Affairs, 1965. x, 118 p.

Papers presented at the 34th Couchiching
Conference, Geneva Park, Ont. Conference
sponsored by the Canadian Institute on
Public Affairs and the Canadian Broadcasting Corporation held July 31 — August 6,
1965.

Partial contents: Concepts of federalism,
by I. Jennings. – Canada's needs; a new
consensus, by M. Sauvé. – Concepts of
federalism; some Canadian aspects, by E.
Forsey. – Some financial aspects of Canadian
federalism, by E. D. Fulton. – The Confederation's financial dilemma, by M. Faribault. – National leadership in Canadian
federalism, by G. Favreau. – The years of
the last chance, by D. Johnson. – Canadian
federalism and the future, by P. Gérin-
Lajoie. – Needed changes in the Canadian
constitution, by W. L. Morton. – Reflections
at the end of the Conference, by M. Beloff
and I. Jennings.

HEIGHINGTON, WILFRID   Constitution critics—what they sometimes forget. Provincial autonomy has given Canada better
government than if established privileges
had been invaded. By Wilfrid Heighington, KC, MPP. (In Canadian comment.
Toronto. v. 3, no. 12 (Dec. 1934), pp. [3]-
4; 26.)

HIGGINS, LARRATT T.   Behind the B.C. power
disputes II. How chaos came to the Columbia. By Larratt Higgins. (In Saturday
night. Toronto. v. 77, no. 11 (May 26,
1962), pp. [25]-[27].)

Includes references to the dispute between British Columbia and the federal
government over the terms of the Columbia
River Treaty signed January 17, 1961.

Part I is by J. A. Irving.

—— Power play in the Rockies. How Ottawa can cope with Bennett. By L. T. Higgins. (In Saturday night. Toronto. v. 76,
no. 19 (Sept. 16, 1961), pp. 15-16.)

Discusses the dispute between British
Columbia and the federal government over
the issue of Columbia River power.

HODGINS, BRUCE W.   A baker's dozen for
the B 'n B. (In The Canadian forum. Toronto. v. 44, no. 521 (June 1964), pp. 66-
69.)

The Author submits thirteen proposals
in an attempt to resolve the problems confronting the "body politic" of Canada. The
recommendations are based on a federal
concept of the country.

For a rejoinder see Professor Hodgins'
baker's dozen, by Eugene Forsey. (In The
Canadian forum. Toronto. v. 44, no. 529
(1965), pp. 253-255.)

—— Dr. Forsey's rejection of the tacit
agreement. A reply by Bruce W. Hodgins.
(In The Canadian forum. Toronto. v. 45,
no. 534 (July 1965), pp. 89-90.)

A reply to Professor Hodgins' baker's
dozen, by Eugene Forsey. (In The Canadian forum. Toronto. v. 44, no. 529 (1965),
pp. 253-255.)

HOROWITZ, GAD   Le statut particulier,
formule libératrice pour les deux commu-
nautés. (In Le Québec dans le Canada de
demain. Montréal [c1967] t. 1, pp. 88-92.)

HOWLEY, MICHAEL FRANCIS, ABP.   The Labrador boundary question. By the Most
Rev. Archbishop Howley. (In Royal Society of Canada. Proceedings and transactions. Ottawa. ser. 3, v. 1 (1907), section 2, pp. 291-305.)

HROMNYSKY, ROMAN   The western Canadian regional governments and the federal
system, 1900-1930. [Vancouver] 1965. 1 v.

Thesis (MA) – University of British
Columbia.

HURLEY, JAMES ROSS   Federalism, co-ordinate status and the Canadian situation.
(In Queen's quarterly. Kingston. v. 73
(1966), pp. [147]-166.)

INNIS, HAROLD ADAMS   The Rowell-Sirois
report. By H. A. Innis. (In The Canadian
journal of economics and political science.
Toronto. v. 6 (1940), pp. 562-571.)

A detailed review of the Report of the
Royal Commission on Dominion-Provincial
Relations. Ottawa, 1940. (3 v.).

INSTITUT CANADIEN DES AFFAIRES PUBLIQUES,
MONTREAL   Le fédéralisme. Rapport de la
deuxième conférence annuelle de l'Insti-
tut canadien des affaires publiques. Or-
ganisée avec le concours de la Société
Radio-Canada. Ste Adèle Lodge, Ste-
Adèle, P.Q., du 21 au 25 septembre 1955
[Montréal, 1955] 64 p.

Partial contents: Le fédéralisme et les peuples, par G. Davy et J. C. Bonenfant. – L'intégration du fédéralisme, par F. A. Angers et R. Tremblay. – Le fédéralisme, formule d'avenir? par J. Perrault et J. M. Nadeau.

Inter-Dominion and provincial finances. By C. L. (In *The Week*. Toronto. v. 1, no. 21 (April 24, 1884), pp. 327-328.)

IRVING, JOHN ALLAN   Behind the B.C. power disputes 1. Bennett's design for B.C. progress. By John A. Irving. (In *Saturday night*. Toronto. v. 77, no. 11 (May 26, 1962), pp. 18-24.)
Discusses the dispute between British Columbia and the federal government over the issue of Columbia River power.
Part 2 is by Larratt Higgins.

IRWIN, WILLIAM ARTHUR   Crisis in Alberta! By W. A. Irwin. (In *Maclean's*. Toronto. v. 50, no. 23 (Dec. 1, 1937), pp. 10-11, 48-50; v. 50, no. 24 (Dec. 15, 1937), pp. 15, 45-47.)
In two parts.
Concerns the Social Credit Party in Alberta and its relations to the federal government.

JACKSON, JAMES A.   The disallowance of Manitoba railway legislation in the 1880's: railway policy as a factor in the relations of Manitoba with the Dominion, 1878-1888. [Winnipeg] 1945. 136 leaves.
Thesis (MA) – University of Manitoba.

JENNINGS, F. X.   New Brunswick case before Rowell Commission. (In *Public affairs*. Halifax. v. 2, no. 1 (Aug. 1938), pp. 3-5.)

JENNINGS, SIR WILLIAM IVOR   Concepts of federalism. (In Hawkins, Gordon (ed.) *Concepts of federalism*. [Toronto] 1965. pp. 1-5.)
A general comparative and reflective statement on federalism.

JOHNSON, A. W.   The dynamics of federalism in Canada. (In *Canadian journal of political science*. Toronto. v. 1 (1968), pp. [18]-39.)
"A paper presented to the annual meeting of the Canadian Political Science Association at Ottawa on 8 June 1967."

JOHNSON, DANIEL   Canada and Quebec: can this marriage be saved? (In Litvak, I. A. (ed.) *The nation keepers*. New York, Toronto [c1967] pp. 181-204.)
Excerpts from the Author's *Egalité ou indépendance*. Montréal, c1965.

—— Egalité ou indépendance. Suivi des extraits de sa dernière conférence de presse sur les relations franco-québécoises. [Préf. par Paul Gros d'Aillon. Paris.] Editions J. Didier [1968] 126 p. (Forum)
"La première édition québecoise de ce livre fut publiée au printemps de 1965". – Pref.

JOHNSTON, RICHARD E.   The effect of judicial review on federal-state relations in Australia, Canada and the United States. Baton Rouge, Louisiana State University Press [c1969] xviii, 320 p.

JONES, ROBERT LESLIE   The Ontario-Manitoba boundary dispute. [Kingston, Ont.] 1928. 78 leaves.
Thesis (MA) – Queen's University.
The undetermined boundary between Canada and the lands of the Hudson's Bay Co. became a Dominion-provincial matter with the purchase of 1869-70. Cf. *Canadian graduate theses in the humanities and social sciences, 1921-1946*. Ottawa, 1951 (p. 57).

KEAR, ALLEN R.   Cooperative federalism; study of the federal-provincial continuing committee on fiscal and economic matters. By A. R. Kear. (In *Canadian public administration*. Toronto. v. 6 (1963), pp. 43-56.)

KEATE, STUART   The smile of the tiger. Why Bennett took over B.C. power. (In *Saturday night*. Toronto. v. 76, no. 19 (Sept. 16, 1961), pp. 11-14.)
Discusses the dispute between British Columbia and the federal government over the issue of Columbia River power.

KEIRSTEAD, BURTON SEELY   The Sirois report, an evaluation. By B. S. Keirstead. (In *Public affairs*. Halifax. v. 4, no. 1 (Aug. 1940), pp. [1]-7.)
Refers to the Report of the Royal Commission on Dominion-Provincial Relations. Ottawa, 1940 (3 v.).

KEIRSTEAD, WILFRED CURRIER   The bases of the federal subsidies. By W. C. Keirstead. (In Canadian Political Science Association. *Papers and proceedings of the annual meeting*. [Kingston, Ont.] v. 6 (1934), pp. [134]-161.)

—— The report of the White Commission. By W. C. Keirstead. (In *The Canadian journal of economics and political science*. [Toronto] v. 1 (1935), pp. 368-378.)
Commissioners: Sir Thomas White, chair-

man, Edward Walter Nesbitt and J. A. Mathieson.

The White Commission was appointed by the federal government in September 1934, on the request of the premiers of the Maritime provinces, to examine the financial arrangements between the provinces and the federal government. Official title: Royal Commission on Financial Arrangements between the Dominion and the Maritime Provinces. Report. Ottawa, Printer to the King, 1935. (24 p.)

KENNEDY, WILLIAM PAUL MC CLURE   The nature of Canadian federalism. (In *The Canadian historical review*. Toronto. v. 2 1921), pp. 106-125.)

KINTZINGER, HELEN JEANNETTE   American influence on Canadian federalism. [Iowa City, Iowa, 1927] ii, 165 leaves.

Thesis (MA) – University of Iowa.

KOOPS, W.   Federalisme de Canadese variëteit. Gravenhage, M. Nijhoff, 1955. xvi, 155 p.

KRAFT, CALVIN THEODORE   The financial relationship between the provinces and the Dominion of Canada. By C. T. Kraft. [Cambridge, Mass., 1937] 1 v.

Thesis (PH D) – Harvard University.

LAMONTAGNE, MAURICE   Le fédéralisme canadien; évolution et problèmes. Québec, Presses universitaires Laval, 1954. x, 298 p.

—— Quebec and national unity. By Hon. Maurice Lamontagne. (In Hawkins, Gordon (ed.) *Order and good government*. [Toronto, c1965] pp. 148-151.)

Brief remarks concerning federalism.

—— Souveraineté et interdépendance dans un fédéralisme bi-culturel. (In Cours de formation nationale, 7ᵉ session, Montréal, 1961. *L'état du Québec*. Saint-Hyacinthe [Qué., 1962] pp. 37-51.)

LAPOINTE, P. M.   Notes de la rédaction. La formule Fulton-Favreau place le Canada français dans un statut d'infériorité. (In *Le Magazine Maclean*. Montréal. v. 5, no 5 (mai 1965), p. 4.)

LAPORTE, PIERRE   Centralisation et unité nationale. (In *L'Action nationale*. Montréal. v. 45 (sept. [i.e. nov.] 1955), pp. [257]-262.)

At head of title: Notre enquête 1955 (4).

LASKIN, BORA   The provinces and international agreements. By Mr. Justice Bora Laskin. (In Vaughan, Frederick (ed.)

Contemporary issues in Canadian politics. Scarborough, Ont. [c1970] pp. 118-127.)

"Reprinted from Background papers and reports, Ontario Advisory Commission on Confederation, Toronto, Queen's Printer, 1967."

Involves discussion of the distribution of power between federal and provincial government in the Canadian constitution.

LAURENDEAU, ANDRE   André Laurendeau commente l'actualité politique. Mon hypothèse est la suivante: la Confédération vaut mieux que la séparation, pourvu qu'elle soit refaite. (In *Le Magazine Maclean*. Montréal. v. 2, no 3 (mars 1962), p. 5.)

—— En marge de la première rencontre d'Ottawa. (In *L'Action nationale*. Montréal. v. 35 (fév. 1950), pp. [156]-164.)

Comments on the Federal-Provincial Conference held at Ottawa, January 10-12, 1950.

—— Indépendance? Non: un Québec fort dans un fédéralisme neuf. (In *Le Magazine Maclean*. Montréal. v. 1, no 7 (sept. 1961), p. 3.)

—— Pas une moitié de solution. (In *L'Action nationale*. Montréal. v. 46 (jan./fév. 1957), pp. [392]-398.)

Concerns federal aid to universities.

LEACH, RICHARD H.   Interprovincial co-operation: neglected aspect of Canadian federalism. (In *Canadian public administration*. Toronto. v. 2 (1959), pp. 83-99.)

LEBEL, A.   Les relations financières fédérales-provinciales. Québec, 1961 1 v.

Thesis (MA) – Laval University.

LEDERMAN, WILLIAM RALPH   The balanced interpretation of the federal distribution of legislative powers in Canada. By W. R. Lederman. (In Crépeau, P. A. (ed.) *The future of Canadian federalism*. [Toronto, c1965), pp. [91]-112.)

—— The concurrent operation of federal and provincial laws in Canada. By W. R. Lederman. (In Lederman, W. R. (ed.) *The courts and the Canadian constitution*. [Toronto, c1964], pp. [200]-219.)

Reprinted from *The McGill law journal*, v. 9 (1962-63), p. 185-99.

Concerns the "federal distribution of legislative powers and responsibilities in Canada".

—— The limitations of co-operative federalism. By W. R. Lederman. (In Vaughan,

Frederick (ed.) *Contemporary issues in Canadian politics.* Scarborough, Ont. c1970. pp. 23-38.)

Reprinted from *The Canadian bar review,* vol. 45, 1967.

LEENEY, P. F.   Dominion-provincial conferences; a response capability of the Canadian political system [Ottawa, 1969] 1 v.

Thesis (MA) – Carleton University.

LEGAULT, GAETAN   La centralisation est-elle inévitable? (In *L'Action nationale.* Montréal. v. 44 (oct. 1954), pp. [104]-114; v. 44 (oct. [i.e. nov.] 1954) pp. [212]-220; v. 44 (déc. 1954), pp. [303]-313; v. 44 (déc. 1954 [i.e. jan. 1955]), pp. [378]-399.)

In four parts.

——   Ottawa est-il centralisateur? (In *L'Action nationale.* Montréal. v. 44 (juin 1955), pp. [896]-903.)

At head of title: Notre enquête 1955.

LEGER, JEAN MARC   Co-operative federalism or the new face of centralization. By J. M. L. (In *The Canadian forum.* Toronto. v. 43, no. 513 (Oct. 1963), pp. 155-156.)

"This strongly worded attack on 'co-operative federalism' is reprinted from Le Devoir of September 3 [1963]."

LEMIEUX, EDMOND   Défense de l'autonomie provinciale: un bilan. (In *L'Action nationale.* Montréal. v. 11 (mars 1938), pp. [245]-249.)

Concerns federal-provincial relations.

LEVESQUE, RENE   Le rôle de l'Etat, sur les plans fédérals et provincials. (In Congress on Canadian Affairs, 1st, Quebec, 1961. *Le Canada, expérience ratée . . . ou réussie?* [Québec] 1962. pp. [101]-115.)

LEVY, DAVID   Quebec, separate status or separate state? (In *Saturday night.* Toronto. v. 79, no. 6 (June 1964), pp. 13-16.)

LIGUE D'ACTION NATIONALE   Manifeste de la Ligue d'Action nationale sur la conférence fédérale-provinciale. (In *L'Action nationale.* Montréal. v. 27 (avril 1946), pp. [288]-300.)

LINGARD, CHARLES CECIL   Economic forces behind the demand for provincial status in the old North West Territories. (In *The Canadian historical review.* Toronto. v. 21 (1940), pp. 254-267.)

LIPSETT, R. W.   National affairs. Nine happy provinces. (In *Saturday night.* Toronto. v. 49, no. 12 (Jan. 27, 1934), p. 4.)

Comments on a Dominion-provincial conference held at Ottawa.

LITTLE, DALTON J.   Ottawa conference tackles economic ills. Are provincial codes doomed? — Will measures indicated by provincial premiers in session with Dominion government serve as chart to economic recovery? (In *Saturday night.* Toronto. v. 51, no. 7 (Dec. 21, 1935), pp. 17; 19; 24.)

Refers to the Dominion-Provincial Conference held December 9-13, 1935.

LLOYD, WOODROW   A provincial perspective. (In Hawkins, Gordon (ed.) *Order and good government.* Toronto. c1965 pp. 31-39.)

Discusses "the necessity for co-ordination between provincial governments in a horizontal sense and between the provinces and the federal government in a vertical sense."

LOUGHEED, WILLIAM FOSTER   Regional governmental administration and the Rowell-Sirois report. By W. F. Lougheed. (In *The Manitoba arts review.* Winnipeg. v. 2, no. 2 (winter 1940), pp. 35-42.)

LOWER, ARTHUR REGINALD MARSDEN   Theories of Canadian federalism — yesterday and today. (In Duke University, Durham, N.C. Commonwealth-Studies Center. *Evolving Canadian federalism.* Durham, N.C., 1958. pp. [3]-53.)

MABLE, THORPE   Provincial demands on the federal treasury. By Thorpe Mable [pseud.] (In *The Week.* Toronto. v. 2, no. 14 (Mar. 5, 1885), pp. 212-213.)

For a commentary on the article cited above see The claim of Manitoba to her public lands, by J. D. C. (In *The Week.* Toronto. v. 2 (May 14, 1885), pp. 374-375.)

MC CURDY, FLEMING BLANCHARD   How Nova Scotia suffers under federal policies. By Hon. F. B. McCurdy. (In *The Busy East of Canada.* Sackville, N.B. v. 23, no.6 (Jan. 1933), pp. 9-12; 18.)

Text of an address delivered before the Maritime Confederation Rights League in Saint John, N.B., on December 22, 1932.

MAC FARLANE, RONALD OLIVER   Provinces versus Dominion. By R. O. MacFarlane. (In *Queen's quarterly.* Kingston. v. 42 (1935), pp. [203]-214.)

The Author poses the question as to whether Canada is one nation or a collection of nine provinces.

MC GEACHY, JAMES BURNS One country or nine? Ten thousand pages of Rowell Commission evidence boils down to this. By J. B. McGeachy. (In *Maclean's*. Toronto. v. 51, no. 18 (Sept. 15, 1938), pp. 11; 44-45.)

—— One country or nine; the demands made by the provinces before the Rowell Commission. By J. B. McGeachy. (In Canadian Institute on Economics and Politics. *Problems in Canadian unity*. Toronto [c1938] pp. 34-42.)

MC INNIS, T. A. Completing Confederation in Saskatchewan. (In *Saturday night*. Toronto. v. 45, no. 29 (May 31, 1930), p. 3.)

March 24, 1930: "the signing of the preliminary agreement by the representatives of the Saskatchewan Government, by which the long standing differences between the Saskatchewan and federal government were removed."

MC KAGUE, WILLIAM ALLISON Federal division of power is challenged. Business organizations want simpler taxes, spenders want bigger taxes, but both agree on centralization — planned economy is incompatible with true federation. By W. McKague. (In *Saturday night*. Toronto. v. 53, no. 14 (Feb. 5, 1938), pp. [17]; 24.)

—— The financial problem in Dominion-provincial relations. By W. A. McKague. (In Canadian Institute on Economics and Politics. *Problems in Canadian unity*. Toronto [c1938] pp. 43-49.)

—— Provincialism — a problem or a privilege? Is an obstacle to the centralization of economic power in Canada. Citizens have right to local self-government along lines guaranteed by Act of the Confederation. By W. A. McKague. (In *Saturday night*. Toronto. v. 53, no. 41 (Aug. 13, 1938), pp. [17]; 21.)

—— Shift in government powers? Will Rowell Commission result in undue centralization of power and creation of irresponsible bureaucracy? By W. A. McKague. (In *Saturday night*. Toronto. v. 53, no. 6 (Dec. 11, 1937), pp. [25]; 27; 30.)

MAC KENZIE, NORMAN ARCHIBALD MAC RAE The federal problem and the B.N.A. Original intention of Fathers of Confederation was a strong centralized government. Modern convention of provincial rights a bar to effective action in dealing with economic problems. By Norman A. M.

MacKenzie. (In *Saturday night*. Toronto. v. 49, no. 3 (Nov. 25, 1933), p. 2.)

Part of a paper delivered before the Conservative Summer School at Newmarket, Ont. It was published in "Canadian problems as seen by twenty outstanding men of Canada". Toronto, 1933.

—— The federal problem and the British North America Act. (In *Canadian problems as seen by twenty outstanding men of Canada*. Toronto, 1933. pp. [247]-257.)

MAC KINNON, FRANK Communications between P.E.I. and the mainland. (In *The Dalhousie review*. Halifax. v. 29 (1949/50), pp. [182]-190.)

Reviews, historically, the relations between the provincial government in Charlottetown and the federal government in Ottawa.

—— The Royal Assent in Prince Edward Island: disallowance of provincial acts, reservation of provincial bills and the giving and withholding of assent by lieutenant-governors. (In *The Canadian journal of economics and political science*. Toronto. v. 15 (1949), pp. 216-220.)

MC LEOD, THOMAS H. Federal-provincial relations, 1958. [Pt.] I, by Thomas H. McLeod; [pt.] II, by J. Harvey Perry; [pt.] III, by Roland Parenteau. (In *Canadian public administration*. Toronto. v. 1, no. 3 (1958), pp. 1-25.)

MC NAIR, JOHN B. Address. By John B. McNair, Premier of New Brunswick. (In *The Maritime advocate and busy East*. Sackville, N.B. v. 36, no. 4 (Nov. 1945), pp. 11-14; 30.)

Delivered at the Dominion-Provincial Conference, August 6, 1945, in Ottawa.

MAC NUTT, WILLIAM STEWART The Atlantic revolution; a commentary on the Atlantic Premiers' Conference at Halifax, on May 8th, 1957. By W. S. MacNutt. (In *The Atlantic advocate*. Fredericton, N.B. v. 47, no. 9 (June 1957), pp. 11-13.)

Considers the relations between the Maritime provinces and the federal government in Ottawa.

MACPHAIL, SIR ANDREW The Dominion and the provinces. (In *The University magazine*. Montreal. v. 12 (1913), pp. [550]-567.)

MC QUEEN, R. Economic aspects of federalism; a prairie view. (In *The Canadian*

journal of economics and political science.
Toronto. v. 1 (1935), pp. 352-367.)

Poses, in part, the "general problem of
the British North America Act as applied
to the Prairie Provinces".

MC WHINNEY, EDWARD Federalism, constitutionalism, and legal change. Legal implications of the "revolution" in Quebec.
(In Crépeau, P. A. (ed.) *The future of
Canadian federalism.* [Toronto, c1965]
pp. [157]-168.)

—— The nature of a bicultural constitutionalism. (In Ontario Advisory Committee on Confederation. *Background
papers and reports.* [Toronto, 1970] v. 2,
pp. 50-59.)

MALLORY, JAMES RUSSELL Disallowance and
the national interest: the Alberta Social
Credit legislation of 1937. By J. R. Mallory (In *The Canadian journal of economics and political science.* Toronto. v. 14
(1948), pp. 342-357.)

"This paper was presented at the annual
meeting of the Canadian Political Science
Association in Vancouver, June 18, 1948."

Considers the issue of federal-provincial
relations raised over disallowance of Social
Credit government legislation August 17,
1937: the Credit of Alberta Regulation Act,
the Bank Employees Civil Rights Act and
the Judicature Act Amendment Act.

—— The five faces of federalism. (In Crépeau, P. A. (ed.) *The future of Canadian
federalism.* [Toronto, c1965] pp. [3]-15.)

—— The lieutenant-governor as a Dominion officer: the reservation of the three
Alberta bills in 1937. By J. R. Mallory. (In
*The Canadian journal of economics and
political science.* [Toronto] v. 14 (1948),
pp. 502-507.)

—— The lieutenant-governor's discretionary powers: the reservation of Bill 56. By
J. R. Mallory. (In *The Canadian journal
of economics and political science.* Toronto. v. 27 (1961), pp. 518-522.)

Discusses the constitutional issue of the
royal veto raised on April 8, 1961, by
the Lieutenant-Governor of Saskatchewan,
Frank L. Bastedo, in his indication that he
intended to reserve Bill 56: An Act to Provide for the Alteration of Certain Mineral
Contracts.

MARION, SERAPHIN Le pacte fédératif et les
minorités françaises au Canada. (In *Cahiers des dix.* Montréal. no. 29 (1964), pp.
89-113.

Maritime rights. Special correspondence of
Willisons monthly. (In *Willisons monthly.* Toronto. v. 1, no. 12 (May 1926), pp.
462-463.)

Concerns the Report of the Royal Com-
mission on Maritime Claims. Ottawa, F. A.
Acland, Printer to the King, 1927. Sir
Andrew Rae Duncan, chairman.

MARTYN, HOWE Stresses and conflicts in
Canada's economy. Problems before the
Rowell Commission. If Canadians desire
a united Canada, they must determine on
a national policy. Service performed by
Rowell Commission will be mainly fact-
finding and educational. (In *Saturday
night.* Toronto. v. 53, no. 1 (Nov. 6, 1937),
pp. [33]; 37.)

MAXWELL, JAMES ACKLEY The adjustment
of federal-provincial financial relations. By
J. A. Maxwell. (In *The Canadian journal
of economics and political science.* Toronto. v. 2 (1936), pp. 374-389.)

—— Aspects of Canadian federalism. By
J. A. Maxwell. (In *The Dalhousie review.*
Halifax. v. 16 (1936/37), pp. [275]-284.)

—— Better terms. By J. A. Maxwell. (In
Queen's quarterly. Kingston. v. 40 (1933),
pp. [125]-139.)

Examines "the federal subsidy system,
one feature of federal-provincial relations
requiring reform".

—— Federal subsidies to provincial gov-
ernments. By J. A. Maxwell. (In *The
Canadian forum.* Toronto. v. 13, no. 154
(July 1933), pp. 373-374.)

—— Federal subsidies to the provincial
governments in Canada. By J. A. Maxwell. Cambridge, Mass., Harvard University Press, 1937. xi, 284 p. (Harvard economic studies, v. 56.)

—— Financial relations between Manitoba
and the Dominion, 1870-86. By J. A. Maxwell. (In *The Canadian historical review.*
Toronto. v. 15 (1934), pp. 376-389.)

Substantial discussion on political relations.

—— Provincial conference and better
terms. By J. A. Maxwell. (In Canadian
Political Science Association. *Papers and
proceedings of the annual meeting.*
[Kingston, Ont.] v. 6 (1934), pp. [162]-
174.)

—— Recent developments in Dominion-
provincial fiscal relations in Canada. By
J. A. Maxwell. New York, National Bu-

reau of Economic Research, 1948. vi, 56 p. (Occasional paper, 25.)

MEEK, EDWARD Representative government and federalism. (In *The Canadian magazine of politics, science, art and literature.* Toronto. v. 6 (1895/96), pp. [561-568.)

MEEKISON, J. PETER (ed.) Canadian federalism; myth or reality. Edited by J. Peter Meekison, Toronto, Methuen [c1968] xv, 432 p.

Merrily we Rowell along. (In *The Canadian forum.* Toronto. v. 18, no. 209 (June 1938), pp. 72-73.)

Considers federal-provincial relations in a discussion of the Ontario brief submitted by Mitchell Hepburn to the Rowell-Sirois Commission.

MILLIGAN, FRANK ARCHIBALD Reservation of Manitoba bills and refusal of assent by Lieutenant-Governor Cauchon, 1877-82. By Frank Milligan. (In *The Canadian journal of economics and political science.* [Toronto] v. 14 (1948), pp. 247-248.)

MINVILLE, ESDRAS Les universités en face des octrois fédéraux. (In *L'Action nationale.* Montréal. v. 46 (déc. 1956), pp. [272]-283.)

—— Les universités en face des octrois fédéraux. (In *L'Action nationale.* Montréal. v. 46 (jan./fév. 1957), pp. [355]-367.)

Originally printed under the same title in *L'Action nationale*, Montréal, v. 46 (déc. 1956), pp. [272]-283.

MORIN, JACQUES YVAN The concept of special status; yesterday and today. (In *Quebec in the Canada of tomorrow.* Toronto, 1968. pp. [C-1]-C-20.)

A comparative study.

—— In defence of a modest proposal (a reply to Dr. Forsey). (In *The Canadian forum.* Toronto. v. 44, no. 529 (Feb. 1965), pp. 256-258.)

A reply to Professor Morin's modest proposal, by Eugene Forsey. (In *The Canadian forum.* Toronto. v. 44, no. 524 (1964), pp. [121]-125.)

Discussion centres on the ideas expressed in an article The need for a new Canadian federation, by J. Y. Morin. (In *The Canadian forum.* Toronto. v. 44, no. 521 (1964), pp. 64-66.)

—— The need for a new Canadian federation. (In *The Canadian forum.* Toronto. v. 44, no. 521 (June 1964), pp. 64-66.)

"An address to the University of Toronto Law Forum delivered on February 17, 1964 . . ."

For a rejoinder see Professor Morin's modest proposal, by Eugene Forsey. (In *The Canadian forum.* Toronto. v. 44, no. 524 (1964), pp. [121]-125.)

—— Les relations fédérales-provinciales. (In Sabourin, Louis (éd.) *Le système politique du Canada.* Ottawa, 1968. pp. [77]-85.)

—— The treaty-making power of Quebec. (In Vaughan, Frederick (ed.) *Contemporary issues in Canadian politics.* Scarborough, Ont. [c1970] pp. 128-138.)

Reprinted from *The Canadian bar review*, vol. 45, 1967.

The topic is placed in the context of federal-provincial relations and the Canadian constitution.

—— La voie du statut particulier: l'idée du statut particulier hier et aujourd'hui. (In *Le Québec dans le Canada de demain.* Montréal [c1967] t. 1, pp. 39-49.)

MORRIS, NEWTON OSWALD Recent federal-provincial fiscal arrangements; an evaluation. [Ottawa, 1962] 1 v.

Thesis (MA) – Carleton University.

MORRISON, JOHN CLAPHAM Oliver Mowat and the development of provincial rights in Ontario; a study in Dominion-Provincial relations, 1867-1896. [Toronto] Ontario Dept. of Public Records and Archives, 1961. 308 p. (In Ontario. Dept. of Public Records and Archives. *Three history theses.* [Toronto, 1961.)

Thesis (MA) – University of Toronto, 1947.

NADEAU, JEAN MARIE Le fédéralisme, formule d'avenir? (In *La Nouvelle revue canadienne.* Ottawa. v. 3, no 5 (May/July 1956), pp. [289]-294.)

NEWCOMER, J. Federalism and the Canadian party system. [Kent, 1960] 1 v.

Thesis (MA) – Ohio State University, Kent.

NEWMAN, PETER CHARLES Can Ottawa afford the provinces? A look at the economic pressures that made Confederation — and could destroy it. By Peter C. Newman. (In *Maclean's.* Toronto. v. 77, no. 3 (Feb. 8, 1964), p. 34.)

—— Portrait of a nation at the bargaining table. A new deal for Canadians. By Peter

C. Newman. (In *Maclean's*. Toronto. v. 77, no. 3 (Feb. 8, 1964), pp. 9; 33-36.)

Concerns federal-provincial relations.

—— Portrait of a nation at the bargaining table. Ten strong men and what they want. (In *Maclean's*. Toronto. v. 77, no. 3 (Feb. 8, 1964), pp. 10-13.)

Concerns W. A. C. Bennett, E. C. Manning, Woodrow Lloyd, Duff Roblin, John Robarts, Jean Lesage, Louis Robichaud, Robert Stanfield, Walter Shaw, Joey Smallwood.

The issue is Dominion-provincial relations.

NICOLET, JEAN   Le duel fédéral-provincial. (In *L'Action nationale*. Montréal. v. 26 (oct. 1945), pp. [118]-124.)

Discusses the Federal-Provincial Conference on Finance held at Ottawa in August 1945.

O'HEARN, D. P.   Could Ontario operate under Ottawa offer? (In *Saturday night*. Toronto. v. 62, no. 15 (Dec. 14, 1946), pp. 26-27.)

Refers to the negotiating of a tax agreement between the Ontario government of George Drew and the federal government.

O'LEARY, MICHAEL GRATTAN   They marched up the Hill. Canada's ten premiers — "All the king's men" have marched up Capital Hill to debate the Sirois report. Question: Will they put Canada together again? By M. Grattan O'Leary. (In *Maclean's*. Toronto. v. 54, no. 2 (Jan. 15, 1941), pp. 8; 42.)

OLIVER, MICHAEL KELWAY   Federal-provincial planning. (In Ontario Woodsworth Memorial Foundation. *Democratic planning; a symposium*. Toronto, 1962. pp. 29-36.)

PARENTEAU, ROLAND   Les gouvernements provinciaux seraient-ils des "gouvernements inférieurs"? (In *L'Action nationale*. Montréal. v. 45 (sept. [i.e. oct.] 1955), pp. [112]-120.)

At head of title: Notre enquête 1955 (4). Concerns federal-provincial relations.

PATTERSON, JAMES T.   Federalism in crisis. A comparative study of Canada and the United States in the depression of the 1930's. (In Hoar, Victor (comp.) *The great depression*. [Toronto, c1969] pp. 1-30.)

PATTULLO, THOMAS DUFFERIN   Dominion-provincial relations. By Thomas D. Pat-

tullo. (In Empire Club of Canada. *Adresses. Toronto*. (1946/47), pp. 98-108.)

Address delivered November 21, 1946.

—— Provinces must keep their income tax field. By T. D. Pattullo. (In *Saturday night*. Toronto. v. 59, no. 17 (Jan. 1, 1944), p. 5.)

PEARSON, NORMAN   A national minimum of civilised life. (In *The Journal of liberal thought*. Ottawa, v. 1, no. 1 (summer 1965), pp. 53-60.)

Concerns "the allocation of powers as between federal and provincial governments according to their interpretation of the British North America Act".

PELLETIER, GERARD   Préparer le dossier. (In *Le Québec dans le Canada de demain*. Montréal [c1967] t. 1, pp. 125-132.)

Concerns special status for Quebec.

—— Preparing the case. (In *Quebec in the Canada of tomorrow*. [Toronto, 1968] pp. [K-1]-K-10.)

Discusses the issue of special status for Quebec within the Canadian federation.

PEPIN, JEAN LUC   Cooperative federalism. (In *The Canadian forum*. Toronto. v. 44, no. 527 (Dec. 1964), pp. 206-210.)

"A speech by the federal MP for Drummond-Arthabaska and Parliamentary secretary to the Minister of Trade and Commerce at the Conférence de l'Institut canadien des affaires publiques, September 12, 1964."

—— Le fédéralisme coopératif. (In Institut canadien des affaires publiques, Montréal. *Le Canada face à l'avenir*. Montréal [c1964] pp. [113]-124.)

—— Quebec and federalism. By Jean Luc Pépin and René Lévesque. (In Glendon College Forum, Toronto, 1967. *Quebec: year eight*. [Toronto, c1968] pp. 39-67.)

PERLIN, ALBERT B.   A decade of Confederation. A Newfoundland editor's assessment. (In *The Atlantic advocate*. Fredericton, N.B. v. 49, no. 8 (Apr. 1959), pp. 17-27.)

Examines the nature and development of the relationship between Newfoundland and the federal government in Ottawa.

PERRAULT, ANTONIO   L'expérience canadienne du fédéralisme. (In *L'Action nationale*. Montréal. v. 30 (nov. 1947), pp. [189]-210.)

PERRAULT, JACQUES   Le fédéralisme, formule d'avenir? Par Jacques Perrault et Jean Marie Nadeau. (In Institut canadien des affaires publiques, Montréal. *Le fédéralisme.* [Montréal, 1955] pp. 45-[54].)

—— Le fédéralisme, formule d'avenir? (In *La Nouvelle revue canadienne.* Ottawa. v. 3, no. 5 (May/July 1956), pp. [285]-288.)

PERRY, JOHN HARVEY The historical background and development of federal-provincial financial relations. By J. Harvey Perry. (In *Canadian public administration.* Toronto. v. 5 (1962), pp. 23-27.)

"This paper was presented to the thirteenth annual conference of the Institute of Public Administration of Canada, September 6 to 9, 1961, Ste. Foy, Québec."

—— What price provincial autonomy? By J. Harvey Perry. (In *The Canadian journal of economics and political science.* Toronto. v. 21 (1955), pp. 432-445.)

"This paper was presented at the annual meeting of the Canadian Political Science Association in Toronto, June 1, 1955."

Examines federal-provincial finance in the context of the Canadian political federation.

PIGEON, LOUIS PHILIPPE The meaning of provincial autonomy. (In Lederman, W. R. (ed.) *The courts and the Canadian constitution.* [Toronto, c1964] pp. [35]-46.)

Reprinted from *The Canadian bar review,* v. 29 (1951), pp. 1126-35.

Considers the autonomist idea as it relates to the Canadian federation.

PLANTE, ALBERT Aide fédérale à l'éducation et minorités. (In *Relations.* Montréal. 14. année, no 157 (jan. 1954), pp. 4-6.)

PRENTIS, MARGARET Fiscal problems. Background to difficulties at Dominion-provincial conferences. (In *Canadian commentator.* Toronto. v. 4, no. 9 (Sept. 1960), pp. 10-11.)

Comments generally on problems relating to Dominion-provincial conferences in the period after 1948.

PRICE, VINCENT W. Who owns water powers, Dominion or provinces? Discussion of important questions arising from conflict between Dominion's powers to make laws regarding navigation and shipping "for the general advantage of Canada as a whole" and ownership of streams by provinces . . . (In *Saturday night.* Toronto. v. 42, no. 35 (July 16, 1927), pp. [13]; 20.)

Prohibition and licence. By D. C. R. (In *The Week.* Toronto. v. 5, no. 5 (Dec. 29, 1887), pp. [67]-68.)

Discusses the need for clarification as to "the respective rights of the Federal Parliament and the Provincial Legislatures with regard to the regulation and restriction of the liquor traffic".

Prohibition and the Duncan report. Special correspondence of Willisons monthly. (In *Willisons monthly.* Toronto. v. 2, no. 8 (Jan. 1927), pp. 299-300.)

Discusses the Report of the Royal Commission on Maritime Claims. Ottawa, 1927.

PROSS, AUGUST PAUL Dominion-provincial relations in the field of highway regulations. [Kingston, Ont.] 1963. ix, 174 leaves.

Thesis (MA) – Queen's University.

PROULX, PIERRE PAUL Une politique de main-d'œuvre. (In *Le Québec dans le Canada de demain.* Montréal [c1967] t. 2, pp. 96-105.)

Concerns federal-provincial relations.

Provincial demands on the federal treasury. (In *The Nation.* Toronto. v. 3, no. 19 (May 12, 1876), p. 219.)

QUEBEC (PROVINCE) ROYAL COMMISSION OF INQUIRY ON CONSTITUTIONAL PROBLEMS Report. [Québec] 1956 [i.e. 1957] 4 v. in 5.

Thomas Tremblay, chairman.

Bibliography: v. 4, p. [381]-409.

Le Québec dans le Canada de demain. [Introd. de Claude Ryan] Montréal, Editions du Jour [1967] 2 v. (Editions du Jour, 62-63.)

At head of title: Le Devoir.

First published as a supplement to *Le Devoir* of Montreal, June 30, 1967.

Partial contents: t. 1. Avenir constitutionnel et statut particulier: Le fédéralisme canadien après un siècle, par R. Arès. – Une nouvelle constitution, par M. Faribault. – Genèse et développement de l'idée d'un statut particulier au Québec, par J. C. Bonenfant. – Le contenu possible d'un statut particulier pour le Québec, par C. Ryan. – Les deux voies possible de l'égalité pour le Canada français, par D. Smiley. – Le statut particulier, par G. Horowitz. – Il faut modifier la constitution et reconnaître un statut particulier au Québec, par A. Brewin. – L'option des Etats associés, par F. A. Angers. – La main-d'oeuvre, par P. P. Proulx. – Les institutions financières, J. G.

Cardinal. t. 2. Vers un meilleur partage des pouvoirs: Le statut particulier et l'administration publique, par P. Garant. – La Cour suprême et la constitution, par J. Brossard. – L'extension de la capitale nationale en territoire québécois, par P. Sauriol. – Mariage et divorce dans l'ordre constitutionnel canadien, par A. Morel. – La politique économique doit-elle relever de Québec ou d'Ottawa, par O. E. Thur. – Le Comité parlementaire de la constitution, par J. J. Bertrand. – Préparer le dossier, par G. Pelletier.

Quebec, in the Canada of tomorrow. Translated from Le Devoir; special supplement – June 30, 1967. [Foreword by H. Ian Macdonald. Toronto] Ontario Advisory Committee on Confederation 1968. 1 v. (various pagings)

Translation of Le Québec dans le Canada de demain.

Reproduced from typescript.

Partial contents: Balance sheet of a century, by R. Arès. – A new constitution, by M. Faribault. – The birth and development of the idea of special status for Quebec, by J. C. Bonenfant. – The possible contents of special status for Quebec, by C. Ryan. – Two possible paths to equality for French Canada, by D. Smiley. – The necessity of modifying the constitution and recognizing a special status for Quebec, by A. Brewin. – Particular status, by R. M. Burns. – Preparing the case, by G. Pelletier. – The associate state option, by F. A. Angers. – Should our economic policy be determined by Quebec or by Ottawa? by O. E. Thur. – Economic planning, by R. Parenteau. – Quebec's demands and the problem of sharing fiscal resources, by R. Bourassa. – The parliamentary committee on the constitution, by J. J. Bertrand. – The Department of Intergovernmental Affairs, by C. Morin. – Special status and public administration, by P. Garant. – The Supreme Court and the constitution, by J. Brossard. – The extension of the national capital into Quebec territory, by P. Sauriol. – Marriage and divorce in the Canadian constitution, by A. Morel. – Constitutional implications of a housing policy, by P. Sauriol. – A manpower policy, by P. P. Proulx. – Agriculture, by M. Carel. – Financial institutions, by J. G. Cardinal. – Forty-eight years of licensing, by B. Benoist. – The concept of special status, by J. Y. Morin.

Le Rapport Tremblay. Montréal, Bellarmin, 1956. 32 p. (Institut social populaire. Publication no. 484.)

Concerns the Report of the Royal Commission of Inquiry on Constitutional Problems. Quebec [1957] (4. v. in 5).

REINKE, CARL Implementing the Sirois report. (In The Canadian spokesman. Ottawa. v. 1, no. 1 (Jan. 1941), pp. [40]-46.)

Discusses the recommendations of the Report of the Royal Commission on Dominion-Provincial Relations. Ottawa, 1940. (3 v.)

RITCHIE, DAVID LAKIE A beginning—now forward. By D. L. Ritchie. (In The New age. Montreal. v. 2, no. 32 (Aug. 15, 1940), p. 6.)

Concerns federal-provincial relations over legislation, with reference to unemployment insurance legislation.

—— Canada at the crossroads. By D. L. Ritchie. (In The New age. Montreal. v. 3, no. 3 (Jan. 23, 1941), pp. 6; 11.)

Concerns the Report of the Royal Commission on Dominion-Provincial Relations. Ottawa, 1940 (The Rowell-Sirois report).

RIVARD, ANTOINE Un engagement formel! (In L'Action nationale. Montréal. v. 40 (nov. 1952), pp. [101]-117.)

A thesis presented on the subject of federal-provincial relations.

ROBARTS, JOHN PARMENTER Provincial powers and national goals. (In Litvak, I. A. (ed.) The nation keepers. New York, Toronto [c1967] pp. 216-228.)

RODGERS, RAYMOND Ottawa letter. Federal-provincial tax squabble. (In Saturday night. Toronto. v. 76, no. 5 (Mar. 4, 1961), pp. [26]-27.)

ROGERS, NORMAN MC LEOD A crisis of federal finance. By Norman McL. Rogers. (In The Canadian forum. Toronto. v. 15, no. 170 (Nov. 1934), pp. 50-54.)

"It is the purpose of this article to direct attention to . . . the revision of the financial arrangements between the Dominion and the provinces."

—— Federal-provincial relations. A Round Table discussion [with] N. McL. Rogers: R. A. MacKay. (In Liberal Summer Conference, 1st, Port Hope, Ont., 1933. The Liberal way. Toronto, 1933. pp. 113-119.)

—— The genesis of provincial rights. (In The Canadian historical review. Toronto. v. 14 (1933), pp. 9-23.)

—— One path of reform. By Norman McL. Rogers. (In *The Canadian forum.* Toronto. v. 15, no. 171 (Dec. 1934), pp. 97-100.)

"It is the purpose of this article to direct attention to one matter which is deserving of careful preliminary investigation, namely, the revision of the financial arrangements between the Dominion and the provinces."

—— The political principles of federalism. By Norman McL. Rogers. (In *The Canadian journal of economics and political science.* Toronto. v. 1 (1935), pp. 337-347.)

A comparative study.

ROWAT, DONALD CAMERON   Recent developments in Canadian federalism. By D. C. Rowat. (In *The Canadian journal of economics and political science.* [Toronto] v. 18 (1952), pp. 1-16.)

Discusses the significant changes affecting the Canadian constitution since World War II: the revision of federal-provincial financial arrangements, the final interpretation of the constitution residing with the Supreme Court of Canada, the method of amending the constitution.

ROY, MICHEL   René Lévesque's very special kind of federalism. (In *Saturday night.* Toronto. v. 84, no. 1 (Jan. 1969), pp. 30-32.)

ROYAL, JOSEPH   L'équilibre inter-provincial. (In *Revue canadienne.* Montréal. nouv. sér. [t. 17] (1881), pp. [42]-56.)

Traces the constitutional development and controversy over federal-provincial relations.

RUMILLY, ROBERT   L'autonomie provinciale. Montréal, Editions de l'Arbre [1948] 302 p.

RUSSELL, ALEXANDER WILLIAM   The twilight of federalism; a comparative study of recent developments in Canadian and Australian federalism. [Winnipeg] 1961. 1 v.

Thesis (MA) – University of Manitoba.

RYAN, CLAUDE   Le contenu possible d'un statut particulier pour le Québec. (In *Le Québec dans le Canada de demain.* Montréal [c1967] t. 1, pp. 58-75.)

—— The enigma of French Canada. (In *Saturday night.* Toronto. v. 82, no. 1 (Jan. 1967), pp. 21-24.)

Onward to the centennial, 1.

Considers the position of Quebec within the Canadian confederation.

—— The possible contents of special status for Quebec. (In *Quebec in the Canada of tomorrow.* Toronto, 1968. pp. [E-1]-E-18.)

—— The possible contents of special status for Quebec. (In Vaughan, Frederick (ed.) *Contemporary issues in Canadian politics.* Scarborough, Ont. [c1970] pp. 39-47.)

"Reprinted . . . from 'Quebec in the Canada of tomorrow'. Translated from Le Devoir (special supplement) Montreal, 1967."

Also available in *Quebec in the Canada of tomorrow.* Toronto, 1968. pp. [E-1]-E-18.]

Attempts to "classify proposals" aimed at a revision of the Canadian constitution.

SABOURIN, LOUIS   Perspectives d'avenir du système politique canadien. (In his *Le système politique du Canada.* Ottawa, 1968. pp. [413]-422.)

Discusses, in the main, the principle of federalism in Canada.

SALYZYN, VLADIMIR   Federal-provincial tax sharing schemes. (In *Canadian public administration.* Toronto. v. 10 (1967), pp. 161-166.)

SANDWELL, BERNARD KEBLE   Does Alberta want to leave us? By B. K. Sandwell. (In *Saturday night.* Toronto. v. 51, no. 46 (Sept. 19, 1936), p. 3.)

Discusses the question of whether the enactments of the Alberta Legislature of 1936 concerning property and civil rights should be disallowed.

—— Eleven juggling governments. By B. K. Sandwell. (In *Saturday night.* Toronto. v. 66, no. 33 (May 22, 1951), p. 7.)

—— Federal disallowance. By B. K. Sandwell. (In *Queen's quarterly.* Kingston. v. 44 (1937), pp. [542]-548.)

—— From the editor's chair. This alliance of provinces is outside the constitution. By B. K. Sandwell. (In *Saturday night.* Toronto. v. 61, no. 20 (Jan. 19, 1946), p. 11.)

Comments on George Drew's scheme for provincial autonomy.

—— From the editor's chair. Dominion government given freer hand by conference's failure. By B. K. Sandwell. (In *Saturday night.* Toronto. v. 61, no. 36 (May 11, 1946), p. 11.)

Comments on the Dominion-Provincial Conference on Reconstruction held April 29—May 3, 1946.

—— From the editor's chair. Freedom of the air and the rights of the provinces. By B. K. Sandwell. (In *Saturday night*. Toronto. v. 61, no. 39 (June 1, 1946), pp. 18-19.)

—— From the editor's chair. A help to the study of the Dominion-provincial impasse. By B. K. Sandwell. (In *Saturday night*. Toronto. v. 62, no. 24 (Feb. 15, 1947), p. 11.)

Discusses *The road to nationhood*, by W. Eggleston, Toronto, Oxford University Press, 1946.

—— From the editor's chair. Who decides what matters are not in provincial jurisdiction? By B. K. Sandwell. (In *Saturday night*. Toronto. v. 64, no. 51 (Sept. 27, 1949), p. 16.)

—— From week to week. The dismemberment of Canada. By B. K. Sandwell. (In *Saturday night*. Toronto. v. 53, no. 50 (Oct. 15, 1938), p. 3.)

Concerns the Royal Commission on Dominion-Provincial Relations, and the illness of N. W. Rowell.

—— From week to week. Can we centralize power? By B. K. Sandwell. (In *Saturday night*. Toronto. v. 55, no. 34 (June 22, 1940), p. 3.)

—— From week to week. Well it were done quickly. By B. K. Sandwell. (In *Saturday night*. Toronto. v. 55, no. 41 (Aug. 10, 1940), p. 3.)

Concerns the Report of the Royal Commission on Dominion-Provincial Relations. Ottawa, 1940. (The Rowell-Sirois report).

—— [From] week to week. Back to Confederation. By B. K. Sandwell. (In *Saturday night*. Toronto. v. 56, no. 10 (Nov. 16, 1940), p. 6.)

Comments on Mackenzie King's announcement of a Dominion-provincial conference to consider the ". . . implementation of the main recommendations of the Sirois Commission . . .".

—— [From] week to week. All honorable men. By B. K. Sandwell. (In *Saturday night*. Toronto. v. 56, no. 20 (Jan. 25, 1941), p. 16.)

"Introductory portion of an address delivered to the Canadian Club and Women's Canadian Club of Montreal . . .".

Deals with the necessity of amending the constitution. Refers to Ontario walking out of the Dominion-provincial conference held January 14-15, 1941.

—— The provinces and the supremacy of the treaty power. By B. K. Sandwell. (In *Queen's quarterly*. Kingston. v. 37. (1930), pp. [543]-556.)

Examines the federal principle involved in federal-provincial relations.

SAUNDERS, ROBERT An approach to the financial relations of the Dominion of Canada and the provinces. (In *The Newfoundland quarterly*. St. John's, Nfld. v. 58, no. 2 (June 1959), pp. 6-7; 39-40.)

"This article is a reprint of one, by the same title and exactly the same content . . . published in the Newfoundland quarterly . . . [in] 1950."

SAUNDERS, STANLEY ALEXANDER Rowell-Sirois Commission. By S. A. Saunders. (In *Saturday night*. Toronto. v. 55, no. 13 (Jan. 27, 1940), pp. 4; 9.)

Concerns the Report of the Royal Commission on Dominion-Provincial Relations. Ottawa, 1940.

—— The Rowell-Sirois Commission. By S. A. Saunders and Eleanor Back. Toronto, Ryerson Press [1940-45] 2 v.

Contents: pt. 1. A summary of the Report. – pt. 2. A criticism of the Report.

SAURIOL, PAUL L'extension de la capitale nationale en territoire québécois. (In *Le Québec dans le Canada de demain*. Montréal [1967] t. 2, pp. 43-51.)

"Le Devoir, 15 juillet 1967."

—— The extension of the national capital into Quebec territory. (In *Quebec in the Canada of tomorrow*. [Toronto, 1968] pp. [X-1]-X-11.)

SAUVE, MAURICE Politique d'aménagement et collaboration intergouvernementale. Par l'honorable Maurice Sauvé. (In *Institut canadien des affaires publiques*. Montréal, 1966. *Disparités régionales d'une société opulente*. Montréal [1966] pp. [121-]-130.)

SAYWELL, JOHN TUPPER The end of the federal power? By John Saywell. (In *The Canadian forum*. Toronto. v. 41, no. 485 (June 1961), pp. 57-58.)

An analysis of the power of reservation and the office of lieutenant-governor, with reference to the decision taken by Lieutenant-Governor Bastedo of Saskatchewan to reserve Bill 56 in 1961.

—— Reservation revisited: Alberta, 1937. By John T. Saywell. (In *The Canadian*

journal of economics and political science.
[Toronto] v. 27 (1961), pp. 367-372.)

Discusses Lieutenant-Governor John Campbell Bowen's disallowance in August 1937 of three controversial bills passed by the Social Credit government.

The School question in Alberta. Special correspondence of Willisons monthly. (In *Willisons monthly.* Toronto. v. 2, no. 2 (July 1926), pp. 66-68.)

Relates to the passing of resources legislation and section 17 of the Alberta Autonomy Act.

SCOTT, ANTHONY DALTON Crossroads of Confederation. By Anthony Scott. (In *The Canadian forum.* Toronto. v. 35, no. 413 (June 1955), pp. 56-58.)

A discussion of federal-provincial financial relations.

—— Government policy and the public lands. By Anthony D. Scott. (In Clark, R. M. (ed.) *Canadian issues.* [Toronto, c1961] pp. [158]-168.)

Examines Dominion-provincial relations regarding provincial natural resources.

SCOTT, FRANCIS REGINALD Civil liberties & Canadian federalism. By F. R. Scott. [Toronto] Published in co-operation with Carleton University by University of Toronto Press [1961, c1959] 58 p. (Alan B. Plaunt memorial lectures, 1959.)

—— The development of Canadian federalism. By F. R. Scott. (In Canadian Political Science Association. *Papers and proceedings of the annual meeting.* [Kingston, Ont.] v. 3 (1931), pp. [231]-247.)

—— Federal jurisdiction over labour relations; a new look. By F. R. Scott (In *Relations industrielles.* Québec. v. 15, no. 1 (1960), pp. 31-53.)

Summary in French: Juridiction fédérale dans le domaine du travail; pour un réaménagement (pp. 48-53).

—— French-Canada and Canadian federalism. (In Duke University, Durham, N.C. Commonwealth-Studies Center. *Evolving Canadian federalism.* Durham, N.C., 1958. pp. [54]-91.)

—— The Royal Commission on Dominion-Provincial Relations. By F. R. Scott. (In *University of Toronto quarterly.* [Toronto] v. 7 (1937/38), pp. 141-151.)

—— Social planning and Canadian federalism. By F. R. Scott. (In Oliver, M. K.

(ed.) *Social purpose for Canada.* [Toronto, c1961] pp. [394-407.)

—— The special nature of Canadian federalism. By F. R. Scott. (In *The Canadian journal of economics and political science.* [Toronto] v. 13 (1947), pp. 13-25.)

Discusses the process of decentralization as part of the constitutional change in Canada after the Second World War.

SELLERS, WARREN Dominion-provincial relations. (In *Saturday night.* Toronto. v. 55, no. 29 (May 18, 1940), p. 13.)

Discusses the Report of the Royal Commission on Dominion-Provincial Relations. Ottawa, 1940. (The Rowell-Sirois report).

SHARMAN, GEORGE CAMPBELL The intergovernmental delegation of legislative power in Canada. [Kingston, 1970] iv, 107 leaves.

Thesis (MA) – Queen's University.

Sharping up their claws. (In *Canadian comment.* Toronto. v. 4, no. 12 (Dec. 1935), pp. 7-8.)

Concerns Dominion-provincial relations. Considers the issues before the Conference of Provincial Premiers held in Ottawa December 9-13, 1935.

SHUMIATCHER, MORRIS C. Disallowance: the constitution's atomic bomb. (In *The Canadian forum.* Toronto. v. 25, no. 298 (Nov. 1945), pp. 179-181.)

A discussion of the power of disallowance, especially relating to the issue raised between the federal government and the CCF government in Saskatchewan over provincial legislation passed in 1944.

SILCOX, CLARIS EDWIN Canadian federalism. By C. E. Silcox. (In *Canadian commentator.* Toronto. v. 3, no. 7/8 (July/Aug. 1959), pp. 4-6.)

A comparative study illustrating the unique features of the Canadian federal system.

SIMEON, RICHARD EDMUND BARRINGTON Federalism and policy-making; federal-provincial negotiation in Canada. [New Haven, Conn., 1968, c1969] iii, 448 leaves.

Thesis (PH D) – Yale University.

The Sirois report — a discussion of some aspects. The Sirois Commission as historians, by Frank H. Underhill. Conservation, by Robert F. Legget. A British Columbia view, by Dorothy G. Steeves. (In *The Canadian forum.* Toronto. v. 20, no. 238 (Nov. 1940), pp. 233-239.)

Concerns the Report of the Royal Commission on Dominion-Provincial Relations. Ottawa, 1940 (3 v.).

The Sirois report — further discussion. What the Sirois report proposes. Education, by Eric Wiseman. (In *The Canadian forum.* Toronto. v. 20, no. 239 (Dec. 1940), pp. 261-266.)

Concerns the Report of the Royal Commission on Dominion-Provincial Relations. Ottawa, 1940 (3 v.).

SMILEY, DONALD VICTOR   Canadian federalism and the resolution of federal-provincial conflict. By Donald V. Smiley. (In Vaughan, Frederick (ed.) *Contemporary issues in Canadian politics.* Scarborough, Ont. [c1970] pp. 48-66.)

—— Federalism, nationalism and the scope of public activity in Canada. (In University League for Social Reform. *Nationalism in Canada.* Toronto. [1966] pp. 95-111.)

—— Public administration and Canadian federalism. (In *Canadian public administration.* Toronto. v. 7 (1964), pp. 371-388.)

—— The Rowell-Sirois report, provincial autonomy, and post-war Canadian federalism. By D. V. Smiley. (In *The Canadian journal of economics and political science.* [Toronto] v. 28 (1962), pp. 54-69.)

"This paper was presented at the annual meeting of the Canadian Political Science Association in Montreal on June 9, 1961."

Analyses the "perspective" of provincial autonomy in the fields of health, welfare and education, presented in the Report of the Royal Commission on Dominion-Provincial Relations, Ottawa, 1940 (3 v.).

—— The two themes of Canadian federalism. By Donald V. Smiley. (In *The Canadian journal of economics and political science.* [Toronto] v. 31 (1965), pp. [80]-97.)

"This essay is an attempt to view Canadian federalism as both an economic and a cultural device and to analyse the past and present interrelationship of the two sets of factors."

SMITH, HERBERT ARTHUR   Federalism in North America; a comparative study of institutions in the United States and Canada. Boston, Chipman Law Pub. Co., 1923. vii, 328 p.

SOCIETE SAINT-JEAN-BAPTISTE DE MONTREAL   Le fédéralisme; l'Acte de l'Amérique du Nord britannique et les Canadiens français. Mémoire ... au Comité parlementaire de la Constitution du Gouvernement du Québec. [Montréal, 1964] 125 p.

—— New constitution for Canada. A proposal for a new sovereign status for Quebec, associated with English Canada, comes from the St-Jean-Baptiste Society in Montreal. (In *Commentator.* Toronto. v. 8, no. 9 (Sept. 1964), pp. 10-11.)

"This proposal is contained in a brief submitted to Quebec's Legislative Committee on the Constitution."

STANBURY, ROBERT   The federal role in education. (In *Queen's quarterly.* Kingston. v. 74 (1967), pp. [363]-379.)

"An address to the Education Finance Conference, Canadian Teachers' Federation at Winnipeg, Man., February 9, 1967."

STEVENSON, JOHN A.   Ottawa letter. No fireworks but Quebec watched. (In *Saturday night.* Toronto. v. 68, no. 23 (Mar. 14, 1953), pp. 14-15.)

Concerns federal-provincial arrangements on taxation, with special reference to Quebec.

—— Ottawa letter. A study of unemployment relief. (In *Saturday night.* Toronto. v. 70, no. 31 (May 14, 1955), pp. 13-14.)

Comments on a federal-provincial conference April 26-27, 1955.

—— Ottawa letter. Age and bargaining power. (In *Saturday night.* Toronto. v. 70, no. 43 (Oct. 29, 1955), pp. 22-23.)

Comments on a federal-provincial conference held in October 1955.

STURSBERG, PETER   Ottawa letter. (In *Saturday night.* Toronto. v. 79, no. 7 (July 1964), pp. 7-9.)

Describes meetings held by René Lévesque and Arthur Laing to discuss the transfer of Eskimos living in Quebec from federal to provincial jurisdiction.

THATCHER, MAX B.   The political island of Quebec; a study in federalism. [Evanston, Ill., 1953] vi, 644 leaves.

Thesis (PH D) – Northwestern University.

Attempts to determine the significance of Quebec's position, without the Canadian confederation, through an analysis of the nature of the social, economic, constitutional and political development of French Canada. (Abstracted in Dissertation abstracts, v. 13 (1953), no. 6, p. 1241).

THUR, OTTO E. La politique économique doit-elle relever de Québec ou d'Ottawa. (In Le Québec dans le Canada de demain. Montréal [c1967] t. 1, pp. 144-160.)

—— Should be our economic policy be determined by Quebec or by Ottawa? (In Quebec in the Canada of tomorrow. [Toronto, 1968] pp. [N-1] N-20.)

Federal-provincial relations.

TODD, ARDYN ROBBINS The federal-provincial conference and co-operative federalism. [Wolfville, N.S.] 1966. 1 v.

Thesis (BA Honours) – Acadia University.

Concerns the federal-provincial conference held in Ottawa November 26-29, 1963.

TRABOULSEE, ANTHONY Prince Edward Island's case before the Rowell Commission. (In Public affairs. Halifax. v. 2 (1938), pp. 60-63.)

—— Prince Edward Island's case before the Rowell Commission. (In The Maritime advocate and busy East. Sackville, N.B. v. 29, no. 10 (May 1939), pp. 13-14.)

TREMBLAY, ANDRE Les compétences législatives au Canada et les pouvoirs provinciaux en matière de propriété et de droits civils. Ottawa, Editions de l'Université d'Ottawa, 1967. 350 p. (Travaux de la faculté de droit de l'Université d'Ottawa. Collection des monographies, t. 3.)

Thesis (PH D) – University of Ottawa, 1967.

TREMBLAY, RENE L'intégration du fédéralisme. (In La Nouvelle revue canadienne. Ottawa. v. 3, no 5 (May/July 1956), pp. 282-284.)

TREPANIER, VICTOR Une question de vie ou de mort pour les droits provinciaux. Plaidoyer autonomiste pour les nationalistes, les indépendants et les vrais libéraux. [Québec, 1953?] 89 p.

At head of title: L'élection du 10 août.

TRUDEAU, PIERRE ELLIOTT Federalism and the French Canadians. With an introd. by John T. Saywell. Toronto, Macmillan, 1968. xxvi, 212 p.

Translation of Le fédéralisme et la société canadienne-française.

First published in French: Montréal, Editions HMH, 1967.

—— Federalism, nationalism and reason. (In Crépeau, P. A. (ed.) The future of Canadian federalism. [Toronto, c1965] pp. [16]-35.)

—— Le fédéralisme et la société canadienne-française. Montréal, Editions HMH,

1967. xiii, 227 p. (Collection Constantes, v. 10.)

—— Les octrois fédéraux aux universités. (In Cité libre. Montréal. no. 16 (1957), pp. [9]-31.)

—— Les octrois fédéraux aux universités. (In L'Action nationale. Montréal. v. 46 (jan./fév. 1957), pp. [436]-464.)

—— The practice and theory of federalism. By P. E. Trudeau. (In Oliver, M. K. (ed.) Social purpose for Canada. [Toronto, c1961] pp. [371]-393.)

—— The practice and theory of federalism. (In Vaughan, Frederick (ed.) Contemporary issues in Canadian politics. Scarborough, Ont. [c1970] pp. 2-21.)

Reprinted from Oliver, M. K. (ed.) Social purpose for Canada. Toronto, University of Toronto Press, 1961. p. [371]-393.

TUCK, RAPHAEL Social security: an administrative solution to the Dominion-provincial problem. (In The Canadian journal of economics and political science. [Toronto] v. 13 (1947), pp. 256-275.)

"This article is an attempt to evolve an administrative technique for Dominion-provincial co-operation in the social services . . . within the framework or confines of the existing British North America Act of 1867."

UNDERHILL, FRANK HAWKINS Dominion-provincial relations. By Frank H. Underhill. (In Co-operative Commonwealth Federation (Ontario). Planning for freedom. 2d ed. [Toronto] 1944. pp. 149-161.)

Lecture delivered February 21, 1944.

An Urgent need. (In Canadian illustrated news. Montreal. v. 1, no. 14 (Feb. 5, 1870), p. 210.)

Concerns the constitution of a Court of Appeal, especially to define Dominion-provincial relations.

VAN GOGH, LUCY Our State Rights doctrine. (In Saturday night. Toronto. v. 57, no. 17 (Jan. 3, 1942), p. 10.)

"A criticism of Dr. A. P. Paterson's recently stated theory of . . . the State Rights doctrine of Canada in its most extreme form . . .".

VANIER, ANATOLE Un nouveau craquement. (In L'Action française. Montréal. v. 9 (mai 1923), pp. [285]-290.)

Discusses the tendency toward separatism within the Canadian confederation.

—— Québec et le fédéral; Québec et les minorités françaises. (In *L'Action nationale*. Montréal. v. 10 (nov. 1937), pp. [155]-167.)

At head of title: Pour une politique nationale.

VIGEANT, PIERRE Autonomisme et électoralisme. (In *L'Action nationale*. Montréal. v. 33 (mars/avril 1949), pp. [188]-196.)

Examines the issue of federal-provincial relations.

WADE, FREDERICK COATE The disallowance policy. By F. C. W. (In *The Week*. Toronto. v. 4, no. 42 (Sept. 15, 1887), pp. [671]-673.)

WAINES, W. J. Dominion-provincial financial arrangements: an examination of objectives. (In *The Canadian journal of economics and political science*. [Toronto] v. 19 (1953), pp. 304-315.)

"This paper was presented at the annual meeting of the Canadian Political Science Association in London, June 3, 1953."

—— The problem of subsidies; a Western view. (In Canadian Broadcasting Corporation. *The Canadian constitution*. [Toronto] [c1938] pp. 35-45.)

"Discussed by the Kelsey Club, Winnipeg, October 17, 1937."

Considers the provisions of the British North America Act in its financial aspects with reference to the federal-provincial distribution of powers involving the spending of money and the raising of revenue.

WAKEMAN, ALBERT C. The trend towards centralization in Canada. (In *Saturday night*. Toronto. v. 56, no. 41 (June 21, 1941), pp. [34]-35.)

WALLACE, DONALD B. Canada—a nation or a name. (In *Canadian magazine*. Toronto. v. 90, no. 6 (Dec. 1938), pp. 16-17; 63-64.)

A discussion of the Report of the Royal Commission on Dominion-Provincial Relations. Ottawa, 1940. (3 v.)

WALTON, FREDERICK PARKER Marriage law in Canada. By F. P. Walton. (In *The University magazine*. Montreal. v. 12 (1913), pp. [271]-287.)

Includes discussion of the issue over the distribution of legislative powers between the federal and provincial governments.

WARD, JUDITH BARBARA Federal-provincial relations within the Liberal Party of British Columbia. [Vancouver, 1966] 1 v.

Thesis (MA) – University of British Columbia.

WEISS, DAVID Quebec's welfare renaissance. (In *Viewpoints*. Montreal. v. 1, no. 2 (1966), pp. 10-17.)

Discusses federal-provincial relations in evaluating the impact of the Report of the Study Committee on Public Assistance (Boucher report) published in Quebec in June 1963.

WESTMASCOTT, MARTIN WILLIAM Concepts of federalism, 1864-1964; some aspects compared. [Ottawa] 1966. 1 v.

Thesis (MA) – Carleton University.

WESTON, WILLIAM Can Dominion-Provincial probe produce anything practical? (In *Saturday night*. Toronto. v. 54, no. 6 (Dec. 10, 1938), pp. [15]; 19.)

Concerns the Royal Commission on Dominion-Provincial Relations, appointed August 14, 1937.

What the Sirois report proposes. (In *The Canadian forum*. Toronto. v. 20, no. 239 (Dec. 1940), pp. 263-265.)

A brief statement of the main recommendations of the Report of the Royal Commission on Dominion-Provincial Relations. Ottawa, 1940. (3 v.)

WHITELEY, A. A. In defence of provincial rights. (In *The Canadian forum*. Toronto. v. 12, no. 142 (July 1932), pp. 370-371.)

Presents a case against the increasing of federal powers in Canada.

WHITING, FRANCES JOAN Federal-provincial tax rental agreements; an assessment. [Winnipeg] 1954. 207 leaves.

Thesis (MA) – University of Manitoba.

WOODLEY, CHARLES WILLIAM Administration for development; the co-ordination of federal and territorial government activities in the North West Territories. [Kingston, 1965] xii, 299 leaves.

Thesis (MA) – Queen's University.

WOODLEY, E. C. Federalism, American and Canadian; a survey and comparison. (In *Culture*. Québec. v. 6 (1945), pp. [413]-421.)

WOODS, HARRY DOUGLAS The Sirois report before the Ottawa Conference. By H. D. Woods. (In *Public affairs*. Halifax. v. 4, no. 3 (Mar. 1941), pp. 117-123.)

Report of the Royal Commission on Dominion-Provincial Relations was discussed during a conference on Dominion-provincial relations held at Ottawa January 14-15, 1941.

YEOMANS, D. R. Decentralization of authority. (In *Canadian public administration*. Toronto. v. 12 (1969), pp. [9]-25.)

YOUNG, MC GREGOR Disallowance of provincial statutes. (In *The University*

monthly. Toronto. v. 10, no. 5 (Mar. 1910), pp. 275-287.)

Cites historical examples.

ZASLOW, MORRIS The Ontario boundary question. (In Ontario Historical Society. *Profiles of a province*. Toronto, 1967. pp. 107-113.)

THE CONSTITUTION

ADAMSON, AGAR CAWTHRA The Fulton-Favreau formula, 1960-1966. [Kingston, Ont.] 1967. vi, 363 leaves.

Thesis (MA) – Queen's University.

AIKIN, JAMES ALEX. Rewriting the national constitution. By J. Alex. Aikin. (In *The Canadian forum*. Toronto. v. 15, no. 174 (Mar. 1935), pp. 207-211.)

ALEXANDER, E. R. Amendment to the constitution of Canada—alternatives to the Fulton and Favreau bills. By E. R. Alexander. (In *The Journal of liberal thought*. Ottawa. [v.] 1, no. 1 (summer 1965), pp. 91-99.)

"This article is based on an address to Canadian Law Teachers' Association meeting in Vancouver, June 1965. A larger treatment of this subject by author, appeared in the Canadian Bar Review June 1965."

ANGERS, FRANCOIS ALBERT Le Canada français face à l'Acte de l'Amérique du Nord britannique. (In Cours de formation nationale, 7e session, Montréal, 1961. *L'état du Québec*. Saint-Hyacinthe [Qué., 1962] pp. 53-102.)

—— Constitution canadienne et droits de l'homme; éditorial. Par Le Directeur. (In *L'Action nationale*. Montréal. v. 50 (oct. 1960), pp. [109]-122.)

—— Le problème fiscal et la constitution. (In *L'Action nationale*. Montréal v. 35 (jan. 1950), pp. [9]-34.)

—— La sécurité sociale et les problèmes constitutionnels. [Québec] Commission royale d'enquête sur les problèmes constitutionnels, 1955. 2 v.

At head of title: Annexe 3.
Mimeographed.

ANGUS, HENRY FORBES The Canadian constitution and the United Nations Charter.

By H. F. Angus. (In *The Canadian journal of economics and political science*. [Toronto] v. 12 (1946), pp. 127-135.)

Discusses the power to negotiate and implement treaties and its relation to the federal nature of the Canadian constitution.

ARES, RICHARD Après la conférence de Québec. (In *Relations*. Montréal. 10. année, no 119 (nov. 1950), pp. 321-324.)

Concerns the conference on the constitution held in Quebec September 25, 1950.

—— La constitution. (In Sabourin, Louis (éd.) *Le système politique du Canada*. Ottawa, 1968. pp. [35]-50.)

—— "Constitutional amendment in Canada." (In *Relations*. Montréal. 10. année, no 120 (déc. 1950), pp. 351-353.)

Reviews *Constitutional amendment in Canada*, by P. Gérin-Lajoie. Toronto, University of Toronto Press, 1950.

—— La formule du rapatriement de la constitution. (In *Relations*. Montréal. 22. année, no 253 (jan. 1962), pp. 6-9.)

—— Le rapatriement de la constitution. (In *Relations*. Montréal. 9. année, no 108 (déc. 1949), pp. 316-319.)

ARMOUR, EDWARD DOUGLAS Dicey on the constitution of Canada. (In *The Week*. Toronto. v. 3, no. 6 (Jan. 7, 1886), pp. [83]-84).

Refers to A. V. Dicey.

BALCER, LEON The repatriation of our constitution. An address by the Honourable Leon Balcer. (In Empire Club of Canada. *Addresses*. Toronto. (1964/65), pp. [47-53].)

Address delivered October 22, 1964.

BANKS, RIDEAU Revise B.N.A. [Act] gently. (In *Saturday night*. Toronto. v. 52, no. 34 (June 26, 1937), p. 4.)

BARR, G. H. Why Canada requires a new constitution. (In *Saturday night*. Toronto. v. 59, no. 43 (July 1, 1944), p. 14.)

BEAUCHESNE, ARTHUR Les constitutions des Dominions. (In *Revue de l'Université d'Ottawa*. [Ottawa] 1. année (1931), pp. [162]-176.)
A comparative analysis.

BEETZ, JEAN Les attitudes changeantes du Québec à l'endroit de la constitution de 1867. (In Crépeau, P. A. (ed.) *The future of Canadian federalism*. [Toronto, c1965] pp. [113]-138.)

BENOIST, BERNARD Forty-eight years of licensing; or, The constitutional foundations of broadcasting. (In *Quebec in the Canada of tomorrow*. Toronto, 1968. pp. [HH-1]-HH-11.)

BERTRAND, JEAN JACQUES Le Comité parlementaire de la constitution. (In *Le Québec dans le Canada de demain*. Montréal [c1967] t. 1, pp. 184-191.)
This committee was formed by the Legislative Assembly of Quebec on June 7, 1963, to review the Canadian constitution.

—— The Parliamentary Committee on the constitution. (In *Quebec in the Canada of tomorrow*. [Toronto, 1968] pp. [R-1]-R-11.)

BISSONNETTE, BERNARD Essai sur la constitution du Canada. Préf. de Louis Baudouin. Montréal. Editions de Jour [1963] 199 p.

BONENFANT, JEAN CHARLES La genèse de la loi de 1867 concernant l'Amérique du nord britannique. (In *Culture*. Québec. v. 9 (1948), pp. [3]-17.)

BORDEN, SIR ROBERT LAIRD Canadian constitutional studies. [Toronto] University of Toronto Press, 1922. 163 p. (The Marfleet lectures, University of Toronto, October, 1921.)

BOURINOT, SIR JOHN GEORGE The law of the Canadian constitution. By J. Geo. Bourinot. (In *The Week*. Toronto. v. 10, no. 11 (Feb. 10, 1893), pp. 251-253.)

BOUTILIER, HELEN R. The constitutional development of the North West Territories, 1870-1905. [Vancouver] 1932. 214 leaves.
Thesis (MA) – University of British Columbia.
Points out that the acquisition of the North West created a "colonial problem" within Canada.

BRADY, ALEXANDER Constitutional amendment and the federation. (In *The Canadian journal of economics and political science*. [Toronto] v. 29 (1963), pp. 486-494.)
"This paper was presented at the annual meeting of the Canadian Political Science Association in Quebec, June 7, 1963."

BREWIN, FRANCIS ANDREW Il faut modifier la constitution et reconnaître un statut particulier au Québec. By Andrew Brewin. (In *Le Québec dans le Canada de demain*. Montréal [c1967] t. 1, pp. 94-103.)

—— The necessity of modifying the constitution and recognizing a special status for Quebec. By Andrew Brewin. (In *Quebec in the Canada of tomorrow*. [Toronto, 1968] pp. [H-1]-H-11.)

BROWN, JOHN C. Should the constitution be amended? (In *The Canadian magazine of politics, science, art and literature*. Toronto. v. 19 (1902), pp. 117-120.)

BROWNE, GERALD PETER The Judicial Committee and the British North America Act. An analysis of the interpretative scheme for the distribution of legislative powers. By G. P. Browne. [Toronto] University of Toronto Press [1967] xvii, 246 p.
Revision of Author's thesis, Oxford, 1963.

BUCHANAN, DONALD W. National affairs. Two views of B.N.A. Act. (In *Saturday night*. Toronto. v. 50, no. 6 (Dec. 15, 1934), p. 4.)
Considers the interpretation advanced by Charles Cahan and Henry H. Stevens.

CAHAN, CHARLES HAZLITT The British North America Act, 1867. By Hon. C. H. Cahan. (In Canadian Club of Toronto. *Addresses*. Toronto. (1937/38), pp. 73-98.)
Address delivered November 15, 1937.

—— Limitations of the constitution. With special relation to the Canadian naval question. By C. H. Cahan. (In *The Canadian courier*. Toronto. v. 14, no. 23 (Nov. 8, 1913), p. 6.)

CAMERON, EDWARD ROBERT The Canadian constitution, as interpreted by the Judicial Committee of the Privy Council in its judgments. Together with a collection of all the decisions of the Judicial Committee which deal therewith. Winnipeg, Butterworth, 1915-30. 2 v.

Vol. 2 has imprint: Toronto, The Carswell Co., 1930.

Vol. 2 "contains all the constitutional decisions reported in the Appeal cases 1916 to 1929". Cf. Foreword.

CANADA. CONSTITUTION   Actes de l'Amérique du Nord britannique, et statuts connexes . . . 1867-1962. Préparés et annotés par Maurice Ollivier. [Ottawa, R. Duhamel, Imprimeur de la Reine, 1962] 675 p.

—— British North America Act and amendments (together with other acts and orders in Council relating to the constitution of Canada and of its provinces) 1867-1943 (with prefix containing text of Quebec resolutions, 1864 and London resolutions, 1866) Ottawa, E. Cloutier, Printer to the King, 1943. 357 p.
"Selected and annotated by Dr. Maurice Ollivier". – Note.

—— The British North America Act (as amended) with notes on certain provisions of the Act by Eugene Forsey. (In *Canada month*. Montreal. v. 4, no. 4 (Apr. 1964), pp. 21-32.)
Issued as an insert.

—— British North America acts and selected statutes, 1867-1962. Prepared and annotated by Maurice Ollivier. [Ottawa, R. Duhamel, Queen's Printer, 1962] 662 p.

—— A consolidation of the British North America acts, 1867 to 1952. Prepared by Elmer A. Driedger. [Consolidated as of January 1, 1957. Ottawa, 1956] iv, 50 p.
"[Includes] the substance of the law contained in the series of enactments known as the British North America acts, and other enactments modifying the provisions of the original British North America Act, 1867."

—— A consolidation of the British North America acts, 1867 to 1960. Prepared by Elmer A. Driedger. [Consolidated as of Jan. 1, 1964. Ottawa, R. Duhamel, Queen's Printer, 1964] iv, 50 p.
"[Includes] the substance of the law contained in the series of enactments known as the British North America Acts, and other enactments modifying the provisions of the original British North America Act, 1867."

—— A consolidation of the British North America acts, 1867 to 1964. Prepared by Elmer A. Driedger. [Consolidated as of August 1, 1965. Ottawa, R. Duhamel, Queen's Printer, 1965] iv, 50 p.

CANADA. DEPT. OF JUSTICE   The amendment of the constitution of Canada. Honourable Guy Favreau, Minister of Justice. [Introd. by Lester B. Pearson. Ottawa, R. Duhamel, Queen's Printer, 1965] viii, 129 p.

Canada's constitution; an important State paper. (In *The Week*. Toronto. v. 7, no. 37 (Aug. 15, 1890), pp. 587-588.)
The Author of the State paper was J. A. Chapleau, Secretary of State.

The Canadian and the American constitution. By J. H. B. (In *The Week*. Toronto. v. 6, no. 18 (Apr. 5, 1889), p. 281.)

CANADIAN BROADCASTING CORPORATION   The Canadian constitution. A series of broadcast discussions sponsored by the Canadian Broadcasting Corporation. Toronto, T. Nelson [c1938] vii, 179 p.
". . . three discussion clubs participated: the Constitutional Club of Vancouver, the Citadel Club of Halifax and the Kelsey Club of Winnipeg" commencing September 26, 1937, and ending January 12, 1938. – Prefatory note.
Contents: The constitution approached historically, by R. O. MacFarlane. – Comparative treatment, by F. H. Soward. – The nature of the problem, by G. F. Curtis. – The problem of subsidies; a western view, by W. J. Waines. – The problem of subsidies; the maritime view, by G. Farquhar. – General survey of taxation problems, by B. A. McKelvie. – Social legislation, the western view, by M. Hyman. – Social legislation, the maritime view, by E. E. Kelley. – Marketing problems, by D. Steeves. – Treaty-making powers, by S. E. Smith. – Appeals to the Privy Council, by C. J. Burchell. – Uniformity of legislation, by L. J. Ladner. – Methods of amendment, by R. F. Mc-Williams. – Methods of amendment, by J. E. Rutledge.

CARMAN, FRANCIS ASBURY   "Social security" and B.N.A. Act. By F. A. Carman. (In *The Dalhousie review*. Halifax. v. 23 (1943/44), pp. [23]-28.)

CASS-BEGGS, DAVID NORMAN   How might one administer a Canadian power grid? By D. Cass-Beggs. (In *Canadian public administration*. Toronto. v. 7 (1964), pp. 333-342.)
A discussion of the constitutional factors involved in the "federal government's owning, constructing and operating multi-purpose water projects anywhere in Canada."

CHAUSSE, FERNAND Que devons-nous à la Confédération? (In *Revue trimestrielle canadienne.* Montréal. v. 21 (déc. 1935), pp. [417]-432.)

An historical examination of the British North America Act.

CHAUVIN, FRANCIS X. The constitution, an obstacle to unity. (In *Saturday night.* Toronto. v. 60, no. 34 (Apr. 28, 1945), pp. 24-25.)

Considers a revision of the British North America Act.

CHEFFINS, RONALD I. The constitutional process in Canada. [Foreword by Paul W. Fox] Toronto, McGraw-Hill [c1969] x, 179 p. (McGraw-Hill series in Canadian politics.)

CLARK, GORDON MORTIMER Constitutions of Canada. Toronto, 1900. 79 leaves.

Thesis (MA) – University of Toronto.

CLAXTON, BROOKE Social reform and the constitution. (In *The Canadian journal of economics and political science.* [Toronto] v. 1 (1935), pp. 409-435.)

"The paper was prepared for presentation at the annual meeting of the Canadian Political Science Association on May 30, 1935."

CLEMENT, WILLIAM HENRY POPE The law of the Canadian constitution. By the Hon. W. H. P. Clement. 3d ed. Toronto. Carswell Co., 1916. xxix, 1099 p.

CLOKIE, HUGH MC DOWALL Basic problems of the Canadian constitution. By H. McD. Clokie. (In *The Canadian journal of economics and political science.* [Toronto] v. 8 (1942), pp. 1-32.)

—— Constitutional revision. By H. McD. Clokie. (In *The Manitoba arts review.* Winnipeg. v. 3, no. 5 [i.e. 4, no. 1] (spring 1944), pp. 21-29.)

COHEN, MAXWELL ABRAHAM Economic controls and Canada's constitution. By Maxwell Cohen. (In *Saturday night.* Toronto. v. 57, no. 28 (Mar. 21, 1942), pp. 10-11.)

The Constitution of Canada. (In *The Week.* Toronto. v. 7, no. 20 (Apr. 18, 1890), pp. 311-312.)

CONSTITUTIONAL CONFERENCE OF FEDERAL AND PROVINCIAL GOVERNMENTS, OTTAWA, 1950 Proceedings. January 10-12, 1950, Ottawa, E. Cloutier, King's Printer, 1950, 128 p.

Published also in French.

COOK, GEORGE RAMSAY A triumph of federalism. By Ramsay Cook. (In *The Canadian forum.* Toronto. v. 47, no. 566 (Mar. 1968), pp. [265]-266.)

Part 1 of Constitutional Conference, two views. Part 2 is Constitution without tiers? by Abraham Rotstein, pp. 266-268.

An analysis of the Constitutional Conference held February 5-7, 1968.

CORRY, JAMES ALEXANDER The constitution and the problems of peace. (In Anderson, Violet (ed.) *This is the peace.* Toronto [1945] pp. 80-95.)

—— Constitutional trends and federalism. By J. A. Corry. (In Duke University, Durham, N.C. Commonwealth-Studies Center. *Evolving Canadian federalism.* Durham, N.C., 1958. pp. [92]-125.)

—— Constitutional trends and federalism. By J. A. Corry. (In Clark, R. M. (ed.) *Canadian issues.* Toronto, 1961. pp. [3]-22.)

—— Decisions of the judicial committee, 1930-9. By J. A. Corry. (In *The Canadian journal of economics and political science.* [Toronto] v. 5 (1939), pp. 509-512.)

A review article of *Canadian constitutional decisions of the Judicial Committee of the Privy Council, 1930 to 1939,* edited and annotated by C. P. Plaxton. Ottawa, King's Printer, 1939.

Part 2 of Recent government publications on the B.N.A. Act. Part 1 is The O'Connor report, by F. C. Cronkite, pp. 504-509.

COWELL, DAVID ARTHUR Devising an amendment formula for Canada; the development of the Fulton-Favreau formula. [Georgetown, D.C.] c1969. 326 leaves.

Thesis (PH D) – Georgetown University, 1968.

CRONKITE, FREDERICK CLINTON The O'Connor report. By F. C. Cronkite. (In *The Canadian journal of economics and political science.* [Toronto] v. 5 (1939), pp. 504-509.)

Part 1 of Recent government publications on the B.N.A. Act. Part 2 is Decisions of the Judicial Committee, 1930-9, by J. A. Corry, pp. 509-512.

A review article of this Report which deals with the distribution of powers provided in the British North America Act.

The Report was directed by W. F. O'Connor under the official title: Report pursuant to resolution of the Senate to the

Honourable the Speaker by the Parliamentary Counsel relating to the enactment of the British North America Act, 1867, any lack of consonance between its terms and judicial construction of them and cognate matters. Ottawa, King's Printer, 1939.

CRONYN, HUME   The weak spot in our Canadian constitution; an address. (In Empire Club of Canada. *Addresses.* Toronto. (1925), pp. 295-309.)

Address delivered October 28, 1925.

CROWLE, HAROLD E.   Canada's constitution must be remodelled. (In *Saturday night.* Toronto. v. 60, no. 48 (Aug. 4, 1945), pp. 14-15.)

—— Proposed adjustments to the Constitution. (In *Saturday night.* Toronto. v. 61, no. 6 (Oct. 13, 1945), pp. 16-[17].)

—— A simple plan for amending the constitution. (In *Saturday night.* Toronto. v. 52, no. 28 (May 15, 1937), p. 2.)

CURTIS, GEORGE FREDERICK   The nature of the problem. By G. F. Curtis. (In Canadian Broadcasting Corporation. *The Canadian constitution.* Toronto [c1938] pp. 25-34.)

"Discussed by the Citadel Club, Halifax, October 10, 1937."

Considers the nature of the Canadian constitutional problem, i.e. its adaptability to contemporary conditions.

DAFOE, JOHN WESLEY   Revising the constitution. By John W. Dafoe. (In *Queen's quarterly.* Kingston. v. 37 (1930), pp. [1]-17.)

DANSEREAU, DOLLARD   La constitution canadienne est-elle illogique? (In *L'Action nationale.* Montréal. v. 4 (nov. 1934), pp. [177]-184.)

DAWSON, ROBERT MAC GREGOR   The federal constitution. (In Brown, G. W. (ed.) *Canada.* Berkeley, 1953 [c1950] pp. 281-296.)

DE CELLES, ALFRED DUCLOS   Les constitutions du Canada. Montréal, Beauchemin, 1918. 76 p.

—— Les constitutions du Canada — étude politique. Par A. D. DeCelles. (In Royal Society of Canada. *Proceedings and transactions.* Ottawa. ser. 2, v. 6 (1900), section 1, pp. 3-22.)

"Lu le 29 mai 1900."

DEXTER, GRANT   Commerce and the Canadian constitution. (In *Queen's quarterly.* Kingston. v. 39 (1932), pp. [250]-260.)

Considers the effect of the question of constitutional reform upon business.

—— The constitutional impasse. A layman's explanation of how our "constitutional straitjacket" is harassing business, wasting the taxpayer's money and impeding social progress. (In *Maclean's.* Toronto. v. 44, no. 6 (Mar. 15, 1931), pp. 5; 65-67.)

DORION, NOEL   La constitution canadienne. Montréal, Bellarmin, 1955. 31 p. (Institut social populaire, no. 480.)

—— La fiscalité canadienne à la constitution. Par Noël Dorion, MP. (In *L'Action nationale.* Montréal. v. 48 (sept./oct. 1958), pp. [16]-30.)

"Premier discours prononcé à la Chambre des Communes par Me Dorion . . . ."

DOUGLAS, BENSON T.   Fundamental freedoms and the Canadian constitution. [Halifax, N.S., 1955] 1 v.

Thesis (LL M) – Dalhousie University.

DOUPE, JACK H.   The Act they want to scrap. By J. H. D. [i.e. Jack H. Doupe?] (In *Canada month.* Montreal. v. 4, no. 4 (Apr. 1964), p. 20.)

An introduction to the text of the British North America Act, with notes by Eugene Forsey, which was published as an insert for the April 1964 issue of *Canada month.*

DOUTRE, JOSEPH   Constitution of Canada: the British North America Act, 1867; its interpretation. To which is added the Quebec resolution of 1864, and the Constitution of the United States. Montreal, J. Lovell, 1880. vi, 414 p.

EGERTON, HUGH EDWARD   Canadian constitutional development, shown by selected speeches and explanatory notes by H. E. Egerton and W. L. Grant. London, J. Murray, 1907. xxii, 472 p.

—— Federations and unions within the British Empire. Oxford, Clarendon Press. 1911. 302 p.

"The British North America Act, 1867": pp. [121]-168.

An analysis of the British North America Act: pp. 17-40.

EGGLESTON, WILFRID   Amending the Canadian constitution. (In *Queen's quarterly.* Kingston. v. 56 (1949), pp. [576]-585.)

—— Capital comment. Amending the constitution. (In *Saturday night.* Toronto. v. 65, no. 47 (Aug. 29, 1950), p. 3.)

—— Capital comment. The conference at Quebec City. (In *Saturday night.* Toronto. v. 65, no. 51 (Oct. 3, 1950), p. 3.)

Refers to the constitutional conference held at Quebec City September 25, 1950.

—— Ottawa letter. "Compact" theory of amending B.N.A. Act historically weak. (In *Saturday night.* Toronto. v. 61, no. 41 (June 15, 1946), p. 8.)

—— Ottawa letter. Federal machinery for amending constitution needs overhaul. (In *Saturday night.* Toronto. v. 61, no. 45 (July 13, 1946), p. 8.)

—— Ottawa view. Constitutional remake. We have to find acceptable means of creating amending machinery. (In *Saturday night.* Toronto. v. 64, no. 52 (Oct. 4, 1949), p. 4.)

FARIBAULT, MARCEL A new constitution. (In *Quebec in the Canada of tomorrow.* [Toronto, 1968] pp. [B-1]-B-23.)

—— Une nouvelle constitution: nécessité et critères. (In *Le Québec dans le Canada de demain* Montréal [c1967] t. 1, pp. 20-38.)

—— Quebec and the Canadian constitution. (In *Seminar on French Canada* [Montreal, 1963] pp. 98-109.)

—— La révision constitutionnelle; premiers fondements. Montréal, Fides [c1970] 223 p. (Bibliothèque économique et sociale.)

—— Vers une nouvelle constitution. Montréal, Fides [c1967] 249 p. (Bibliothèque économique et sociale.)

FITZGERALD, GERALD F. The compact theory, and the consent of the provinces to amendments. (In *Revue de l'Université d'Ottawa.* [Ottawa] 13. année (1943), pp. [456]-465.)

Examines legal amendment to the British North America Act.

FLAHERTY, J. FRANCIS Will post-war period see B.N.A. Act overhauled? By Francis Flaherty. (In *Saturday night.* Toronto. v. 59, no. 28 (Mar. 18, 1944), p. 12.)

FORSEY, EUGENE ALFRED The British North America Act and biculturalism. By Eugene Forsey. (In *Queen's quarterly.* Kingston. v. 71 (1964), pp. [141]-149.)

FOWLER, ROBERT MAC LAREN The question of the constitution. By R. M. Fowler. (In Lower, A. R. M. (ed.) *War and reconstruction.* Toronto [c1942] pp. 60-68.)

FRASER, BLAIR Backstage at Ottawa. Britain wants home rule, too. By the Man with the Notebook. (In *Maclean's.* Toronto. v. 59, no. 22 (Nov. 15, 1946), pp. 15; 71.)

Discusses the amendment to the B.N.A. Act by an act of Parliament.

—— Backstage at Ottawa. Orphans, greenhorns and the B.N.A. Act. By the Man with a Notebook. (In *Maclean's.* Toronto. v. 62, no. 20 (Oct. 15, 1949), pp. 14; 70-71.)

FULTON, EDMUND DAVIE Commentary and viewpoint [on the Canadian constitution]. (In Hawkins, Gordon (ed.) *Concepts of federalism.* [Toronto] 1965. pp. 69-77.)

Discusses proposed changes to the Canadian constitution and the Constitution Amending Formula (the Fulton-Favreau formula) drawn up at conferences held during 1960-61.

GARANT, PATRICE A propos de la réforme constitutionnelle. La montée des francophones et l'établissement de structures de coordination. (In *Culture.* Québec. v. 29 (1968), pp. [230]-239.)

GASCON, WILFRID Le texte qui manque dans la constitution. Par W. Gascon. (In *Les Annales; lettres, histoire, sciences, arts.* Ottawa. [v.] 2, no. 6-7 (juin-juil. 1923), pp. 4-5.)

Comparative comments on the provision for minority rights in the Canadian constitution.

GERIN-LAJOIE, PAUL Constitutional amendment in Canada. Toronto, University of Toronto Press, 1950. xliii, 340 p. (Canadian government series, 3.)

Includes the Statute of Westminster, 1931, and the British North America (no. 2) Act, 1949.

—— Réflexions sur la constitution canadienne. Montréal, Bellarmin, 1952. 32 p. (Institut social populaire, no. 455.)

GIBSON, R. DALE Fulton's folly. Patriating the constitution. (In *Canadian dimension.* Winnipeg. v. 2, no. 2 (Jan./Feb. 1965), pp. 8-9.)

Refers to Davie Fulton and his proposed amendment to the Canadian constitution.

GODEFROY, LOUIS Note sur la constitution du Canada. (In *Culture.* Québec. v. 3 (1942), pp. [460]-466.)

GOUIN, LEON MERCIER Esquisse de droit constitutionnel. (In *Revue trimestrielle canadienne.* Montréal. v. 4 (mai 1918), pp. [69]-76.)

GRAY, V. EVAN Just how to amend our constitution. The electors, not government, is the ultimate political sovereign. Here is a working plan for a proper constitutional method (In *Saturday night.* Toronto. v. 65, no. 48 (Sept. 12, 1950), pp. 10; 38.)

GT. BRIT. PRIVY COUNCIL. JUDICIAL COMMITTEE Decisions relating to the British North America Act, 1867, and the Canadian Constitution, 1867-1954. Arranged by Richard A. Olmsted. Ottawa, E. Cloutier, Queen's printer, 1954. 3 v.

GROULX, LIONEL ADOLPHE La constitution fédérative de 1867; origine, teneur, modifications, portée. Par Lionel Groulx. (In *Revue canadienne.* Montréal. nouv. sér., v. 14 (1914), pp. [385]-398.)

The latter part of the article comments on the post-1867 federal system.

—— Nos luttes constitutionnelles. Montréal, Le Devoir, 1915-16. 5 pts.

Contents: no. 1. La constitution de l'Angleterre. Le Canada politique en 1791. – no. 2. La question des subsides. – no. 3. La responsabilité ministérielle. – no. 4. La liberté scolaire. – no. 5. Les droits du français.

HEAVYSEGE, M. ROSS By what method shall B.N.A. Act be revised? (In *Saturday night.* Toronto. v. 59, no. 13 (Dec. 4, 1943), pp. 10-11.)

HOPKINS, EDWARD RUSSELL Confederation at the crossroads; the Canadian constitution. Toronto, McClelland and Stewart [c1968] 423 p.

HOUSTON, WILLIAM (ed.) Documents illustrative of the Canadian constitution. Edited, with notes and appendixes. Toronto, Carswell, 1891. xxii, 338 p.

Cover title: Constitutional documents of Canada.

Reprinted: Freeport, N.Y., Books for Libraries Press, 1970.

HUME, J. A. Fully autonomous Canada with new constitution. (In *Saturday night.* Toronto. v. 64, no. 46 (Aug. 23, 1949), p. 8.)

"J. A. Hume . . . discusses the changes which have already been made in the British North America Act, and outlines the problems which may arise in the drafting of a new constitution to meet modern conditions."

JACKETT, WILBURN ROY Sections 91 and 92 of the British North America Act and the

Privy Council. By W. R. Jackett. (In Corry, J. A. (ed.) *Legal essays in honour of Arthur Moxon.* [Toronto] 1953. pp. 156-182.)

JENNINGS, SIR WILLIAM IVOR Constitutional laws of the Commonwealth. By Sir Ivor Jennings. [3d ed.] Vol. I. The monarchies. Oxford, Clarendon Press, 1957. xxiv, 496 p.

First published 1938 under title: *Constitutional laws of the British Empire.*

No more published?

"The Dominion constitution of Canada": pp. [185]-264.

KENNEDY, HUGH What we owe to the Canadian constitution. By Hon. Hugh Kennedy, Chief Justice, Irish Free State. (In Canadian Club of Toronto. *Addresses.* Toronto. (1928/29), pp. 25-40.)

Address delivered September 5, 1928.

KENNEDY, WILLIAM PAUL MC CLURE The constitution of Canada; an introduction to its development and law. By W. P. M. Kennedy. London, Toronto, Oxford University Press, 1922. xx, 519 p.

—— The constitution of Canada, 1534-1937; an introduction to its development, law and custom. By W. P. M. Kennedy. 2d ed. London, Toronto, Oxford University Press [1938] xxvii, 628 p.

KENNEDY, WILLIAM PAUL MC CLURE (ed.) Documents of the Canadian constitution, 1759-1915. Selected and edited by W. P. M. Kennedy. Toronto, Oxford University Press, 1918. xxxii, 707 p.

KENNEDY, WILLIAM PAUL MC CLURE Some aspects of Canadian and Australian federal constitutional law. Ithaca, N.Y., Cornell University, 1930. 13 p.

—— Some aspects of the theories and workings of constitutional law: the Fred Morgan Kirby lectures delivered at Lafayette College, 1931. New York, Macmillan, 1932. xiv, 142 p.

KENNEDY, WILLIAM PAUL MC CLURE (ed.) Statutes, treaties and documents of the Canadian constitution, 1713-1929. 2d ed., rev. and enl. Oxford, Oxford University Press, 1930. xxviii, 752 p.

Running title: Constitutional documents of Canada.

KENNEDY, WILLIAM PAUL MC CLURE The terms of the British North America Act. By W. P. M. Kennedy. (In Flenley, Ralph (ed.) *Essays in Canadian history.* Toronto, 1939. pp. 121-131.)

LA FOREST, GERARD VINCENT JOSEPH The allocation of taxing power under the Canadian constitution. Toronto, Canadian Tax Foundation, c1967. 185 p. (Canadian tax papers, no. 46.)

"... prepared in partial fulfilment of the requirements for the degree of Doctor of the Science of Law at the Yale Law School". – Pref.

—— Natural resources and public property under the Canadian constitution. [Toronto] University of Toronto Press [c1969] xiv, 230 p.

"The study ... is largely confined to the provisions of the B.N.A. acts dealing specifically with natural resources and public property and the position of the federal and provincial authorities under these." – Introd.

LANGIS, PIERRE PAUL Le mouvement revisionniste. Avant la conférence fédérale-provinciale. (In Relations. Montréal. 5. année, no 56 (août 1945), pp. 207-209.)

Refers to revising the Canadian constitution.

LA PIERRE, LAURIER JOSEPH LUCIEN My constitution for Canada. By Laurier L. La-Pierre. (In Canadian dimension. Winnipeg. v. 5, no. 5 (June/July 1968), pp. 20-23.)

LAPORTE, PIERRE Une nouvelle constitution. (In Institut canadien des affaires publiques, Montréal. Le Canada face à l'avenir. Montréal [c1964] pp. [108]-112.)

LAURENT, EDOUARD Quelle est la nature de l'acte de 1867? [Québec, Editions du "Cap diamant", 1942] 36 p. (Cahiers de l'Ecole des sciences sociales politiques et économiques de Laval, [v. 1] no. 8.)

"Ce cahier est publié en collaboration avec la Société canadienne de l'enseignement postscolaire."

LAWSON, W. J. The Canadian constitution. A study of the written and unwritten features of our system of government. Ottawa, Queen's Printer, 1960. 29 p.

—— La constitution canadienne. Ottawa, Imprimeur de la Reine, 1953. 39 p.

LEBLANC, ALBERT Le problème constitutionnel. (In Cours de formation national, 7ᵉ session, Montréal, 1961. L'état du Québec. Saint-Hyacinthe [Qué., 1962] pp. 11-18.)

LEDERMAN, WILLIAM RALPH Classification of laws and the British North America

Act. By W. R. Lederman. (In Corry, J. A. (ed.) Legal essays in honour of Arthur Moxon. [Toronto] 1953. pp. 183-207.)

This analysis undertakes "to criticize and restate the accepted doctrine for interpretation of the B.N.A. Act."

—— Classification of laws and the British North America Act. By W. R. Lederman. (In his The courts and the Canadian constitution. [Toronto, c1964] pp. [177]-199.)

Reprinted from Corry, J. A. (ed.) Legal essays in honour of Arthur Moxon. Toronto, University of Toronto Press, 1953. (pp. 183-207).

—— The process of constitutional amendment for Canada. By W. R. Lederman. (In Ontario Advisory Committee on Confederation. Background papers and reports. [Toronto] 1967. v. 1. pp. [75]-87.)

"This paper also appears in the McGill law journal, vol. 12, no. 4, 1966." Presented January, 1967.

LEFROY, AUGUSTUS HENRY FRAZER Leading cases in Canadian constitutional law. Toronto, Carswell, 1914. xxi, 116 p.

Second ed. published 1920.

—— Points of special interest in Canada's federal constitution. By A. H. F. Lefroy. (In Canadian Political Science Association. Papers and proceedings of the annual meeting. [Kingston, Ont.] v. 1 (1913), pp. [90]-97.)

—— A short treatise on Canadian constitutional law, by A. H. F. Lefroy. With an historical introd. by W. P. M. Kennedy. London, Sweet and Maxwell; Toronto, Carswell Co., 1918. xlviii, 322 p.

LERY, LOUIS C. de Notre constitution en marche. (In Relations. Montréal. 6. année, no 64 (avril 1946), pp. 103-105.)

—— Où trouver notre constitution? (In Relations. Montréal. 6. année, no 63 (mars 1946), pp. 68-70.)

LEVESQUE, ALBERT A quoi bon importer une constitution moribonde? (In Nouvelle-France. Montréal. no 14 (juil./sept. 1960), pp. 98-104.)

—— Le problème constitutionnel. (In Nouvelle-France. Montréal. no 15 (nov./déc. 1960), pp. 198-201.)

LIPPSETT, R. W. National affairs. Revolt from B.N.A. Act. (In Saturday night. Toronto. v. 49, no. 6 (Dec. 16, 1933), p. 4.)

LIVINGSTON, WILLIAM S. Federalism and constitutional change. Oxford, Clarendon Press, 1956. x, 380 p.

Partial contents: The amendment of the Canadian constitution (pp. [16]-109).

LORANGER, THOMAS JEAN JACQUES Letters upon the interpretation of the federal constitution known as the British North America Act, 1867. By the Honourable Mr. Justice T. J. J. Loranger. First letter. Translation. Quebec, Printed at the Morning Chronicle Office, 1884. vii, 63 p.

Translation of Lettres sur l'interprétation de la constitution fédérale. . . . Première lettre. Québec, Impr. A. Côté et Cie, 1883, (126 p.)

—— Lettres sur l'interprétation de la constitution fédérale; dite l'Acte de l'Amérique britannique du Nord, 1867, par T. J. J. Loranger. Première lettre. Québec, Impr. A. Coté, 1883. 61 p.

LYON, J. NOEL (ed.) Canadian constitutional law in a modern perspective. Edited by J. Noel Lyon and Ronald G. Atkey. [Toronto] University of Toronto Press [c1970] liv, 1351 p.

MC ARTHUR, DUNCAN Revision of the constitution. By D. McArthur. (In Queen's quarterly. Kingston. v. 41 (1934), pp. 124-128.)

Considers "the composition of the Senate and the distribution of sovereign powers between the Dominion and the provinces".

MC CAIG, JAMES The origin and growth of the Canadian constitution. Toronto, 1897. 39 leaves.

Thesis (MA) – University of Toronto.

MAC DONALD, VINCENT CHRISTOPHER Our constitution seventy years after. By Dean Vincent C. MacDonald. (In Saturday night. Toronto. v. 52, no. 41 (Aug. 14, 1937), p. 2.)

Based on an address delivered in Halifax to the annual Conference of the Canadian Passenger Association and the Canadian Travellers' Association on June 17, 1937.

MAC FARLANE, RONALD OLIVER The constitution approached historically. By R. O. MacFarlane. (In Canadian Broadcasting Corporation. The Canadian constitution. Toronto [c1938] pp. 1-13.)

"Discussed by the Kelsey Club, Winnipeg, September 26, 1937."

MC GREGOR, DONALD ANDERSON Methods of amendment. By D. A. McGregor. (In

Canadian Broadcasting Corporation. The Canadian constitution. Toronto [c1938] pp. 164-173.)

"Discussed by the Constitutional Club, Vancouver, January 2, 1938."

Considers the amending of the British North America Act.

MAC GUIGAN, MARK RUDOLPH What price an all-Canadian constitution? By Mark R. MacGuigan. (In Commentator. Toronto. v. 8, no. 10 (Oct. 1964), pp. 14-16.)

Discusses the proposals introduced by Davie Fulton to secure the patriation of the Canadian constitution.

MC WILLIAMS, ROLAND FAIRBAIRN Methods of amendment. By R. F. McWilliams. (In Canadian Broadcasting Corporation. The Canadian constitution. Toronto [c1938] pp. 138-152.)

"Discussed by the Kelsey Club, Winnipeg, December 19, 1937."

Concerns the amending of the British North America Act.

MAGONE, CLIFFORD RICHARD What is wrong with the British North America Act? By C. R. Magone. (In Ontario Advisory Committee on Confederation. Background papers and reports. [Toronto, 1970] v. 2, pp. 85-91.)

MALLORY, JAMES RUSSELL Constitutional amendment in Canada. By J. R. Mallory. (In The Canadian journal of economics and political science. [Toronto] v. 17 (1951), pp. 389-394.)

A review article of Constitutional amendment in Canada, by Paul Gérin-Lajoie. Toronto, University of Toronto Press, 1950.

—— Constitutional amendment now. By J. R. Mallory. (In The Dalhousie review. Halifax. v. 23 (1943/44), pp. [29]-35.)

MARTIN, CHESTER BAILEY Responsible government and its corollaries in the Canadian constitution. By Chester Martin. (In Royal Society of Canada. Proceedings and transactions. Ottawa. ser. 3, v. 17 (1923), section 2, pp. 41-56.)

"Read May meeting, 1923."

MEEK, EDWARD The Canadian constitution; its fictions and realities. (In The Canadian magazine of politics, science, art and literature. Toronto. v. 3 (1894), pp. [425]-435.)

MILLAR, LILLIAN D. Nothing must hinder B.N.A. Act revision. (In Saturday night.

Toronto. v. 60, no. 43 (June 30, 1945), pp. 12-13.)

MOREL, ANDRE Mariage et divorce dans l'ordre constitutionnel canadien. (In Le Québec dans le Canada de demain. Montréal [1967] t. 2, pp. 59-68.)

—— Marriage and divorce in the Canadian constitution. (In Quebec in the Canada of tomorrow. [Toronto, 1968] pp. [X-1]-X-11.)

MORIN, JACQUES YVAN Quebec and constitutional arbitration; between Scylla and Charybdis. (In Vaughan, Frederick (ed.) Contemporary issues in Canadian politics. Scarborough, Ont. [c1970] pp. 256-269.)

Reprinted from The Canadian bar review, vol. 45, no. 3 (1967). Translation of Le Québec et l'arbitage constitutionnel; de Charybde en Scylla.

Considers "the creation of a constitutional court that would be consistent with the existence of the two Canadian nations".

—— Le rapatriement de la constitution. (In Cité libre. Montréal. no 72 (déc. 1964), pp. 9-12.)

—— Vers un nouvel équilibre constitutionnel au Canada. (In Crépeau, P. A. (ed.) The future of Canadian federalism. [Toronto, c1965] pp. [141]-168.)

MORTON, WILLIAM LEWIS Needed changes in the Canadian constitution. By W. L. Morton. (In Hawkins, Gordon (ed.) Concepts of federalism. [Toronto] 1965. pp. 82-92.)

Presents an historical consideration of the problems involved with amendment to the British North America Act.

MUNRO, JOSEPH EDWIN CRAWFORD The constitution of Canada. By J. E. C. Munro. Cambridge, University Press, 1889. xxxvi, 356 p.

O'HEARN, PETER JOSEPH THOMAS Peace, order and good government; a new constitution for Canada. Toronto, Macmillan, 1964. 325 p.

"Notes" (chiefly bibliographical): p. 289-317.

O'LEARY, MICHAEL GRATTAN Backstage at Ottawa. By a Politician with a Notebook. (In Maclean's. Toronto. v. 50, no. 5 (Mar. 1, 1937), pp. 14; 52-53.)

Discusses revising the British North America Act, etc.

—— Our constitutional tangle. By M. Grattan O'Leary. (In Maclean's. Toronto.

v. 50, no. 6 (Mar. 15, 1937), pp. 11; 63-64.)

OLLIVIER, MAURICE L'avenir constitutionnel du Canada. [Montréal] A. Lévesque [1935] 181 p. (Documents politiques.)

O'NEIL, PIERRE C. Ottawa constitutional conference: Who speaks for Quebec? (In Commentator. Toronto. v. 12, no. 3 (Mar. 1968), pp. 14-16.)

Comments on the constitutional conference held in Ottawa, February 5-7, 1968.

PARKINSON, JOSEPH F. Does the B.N.A. Act need revision? By J. F. Parkinson. (In Canadian comment. Toronto. v. 3, no. 3 (Mar. 1934), pp. [5]-6; 32.)

PEARSON, LESTER BOWLES [On constitutional change] Document. (In Journal of Canadian studies. Peterborough, Ont. v. 2, no. 4 (1967), pp. 52-56.)

". . . the text of Prime Minister Lester B. Pearson's address to the Conference on the economics of Canadian unity, Banff, Alberta, October 15, 1967."

Title taken from table of contents.

PELLAND, LEO La réforme de la constitution. III. Le droit civil des provinces. (In L'Action nationale. Montréal. v. 7 (mai 1936), pp. [259]-274.)

Section I, Questions préalables, and section II, Les questions financières, are by Léopold Richer (v. 7, pp. [67]-87, [131]-153) and Anatole Vanier (v. 7, pp. [195]-208), respectively.

PEPIN, GILLES Les tribunaux administratifs et la constitution; étude des articles 96 à 101 de l'A.A.N.B. Montréal, Presses de l'Université de Montréal, 1969. xviii, 426 p. (Collection: Institut de recherche en droit public.)

"Etude commanditée par le Comité parlementaire de la Constitution".

"This study was submitted to the Parliamentary Committee on the Constitution under the title: Les difficultés constitutionnelles suscitées par la création de tribunaux administratifs québécois.

PERRAULT, ANTONIO Déceptions et griefs. (In L'Actions français. Montréal. v. 17 (mai/juin 1927), pp. [385]-402.)

Criticizes the interpretation of the Canadian constitution of 1867.

PERRAULT, JACQUES La "Couronne" et la constitution canadienne. (In L'Action nationale. Montréal. v. 32 (oct. 1948), pp. [113]-125.)

PILKINGTON, WILFRED   A critique of the Canadian constitution. [Edmonton] 1942. 163 leaves.

Thesis (MA) – University of Alberta.

PLAXTON, CHARLES PERCY (ed.)   Canadian constitutional decisions of the Judicial Committee of the Privy Council, 1930 to 1939. Edited and annotated by Charles Percy Plaxton. Ottawa, J. O. Patenaude, Printer to the King, 1939. lxxi, 457 p.

"Compiled and edited for the Department of Justice by Charles Percy Plaxton, KC, acting Deputy Minister." – Foreword.

POPE, SIR JOSEPH (ed.)   Confederation. Being a series of hitherto unpublished documents bearing on the British North America Act. Edited by Joseph Pope. Toronto, Carswell Co., 1895. viii, 324 p.

Partial contents: Various drafts of the British North America bill. – The British North America Act. – Appendices.

PORTER, DANA   What's wrong with Canada's constitution. An address by Hon. Dana Porter, Attorney-General of Ontario. (In Empire Club of Canada. Addresses. Toronto. (1951/52), pp. 25-38.)

Address delivered October 4, 1951.

PRITCHARD, H. L.   Eleventh hour now strikes for better B.N.A. Act. (In Saturday night. Toronto. v. 64, no. 27 (Apr. 12, 1949), pp. [11]; [18].)

Revision of constitution will strengthen Canada. By V. E. G. (In Saturday night. Toronto. v. 59, no. 34 (Apr. 29, 1944), p. 21.)

RICHER, LEOPOLD   La réforme de la constitution. I. Questions préalables. (In L'Action nationale. Montréal. v. 7 (fév. 1936), pp. [6]-87; v. 7 (mars 1936), pp. [131]-153.)

In four parts.

Section 2, Les questions financières, and Section 3, Le droit civil des provinces, are by Anatole Vanier (pp. [195]-208) and Léo Pelland (pp. [259]-274) respectively.

RIDDELL, WILLIAM RENWICK   The Canadian and American constitutions; a comparison. (In The Canadian magazine of politics, science, art and literature. Toronto. v. 35 (1910), pp. 108-114.)

—— The Canadian constitution in form and in fact, by the Honourable William Renwick Riddell. New York, Columbia University Press, 1923. 77 p. (Columbia University lectures. George Blumenthal Foundation, 1923.)

"Four lectures delivered . . . at Columbia University . . . April and May, 1923". – Pref.

—— The constitution of Canada in its history and practical working. New Haven, Yale University Press; Toronto, Oxford University Press, 1917. xi, 170 p. (Yale lectures on the responsibility of citizenship.)

Four lectures delivered in the Dodge Foundation. Cf. Pref.

—— Some origins of "The British North America Act, 1867". (In Royal Society of Canada. Proceedings and transactions. Ottawa. ser. 3, v. 11 (1917), section 2, pp. 71-97.)

"Read May meeting, 1917."

—— Some remarks on the constitutions of Canada and the United States. By the Hon. W. R. Riddell. (In Empire Club of Canada. Addresses. Toronto. (1909/10), pp. 188-199.)

Address delivered March 17, 1910.

ROGERS, NORMAN MC LEOD   The constitutional impasse. By Norman McL. Rogers. (In Queen's quarterly. Kingston. v. [1 (1934), pp. [475]-486.)

Discusses the procedures for constitutional revision.

—— The dead hand. By Norman McL. Rogers. (In The Canadian forum. Toronto. v. 14, no. 167 (Aug. 1934), pp. 421-423.)

Discusses "the growing strength of the movement for constitutional revision".

—— Government by the dead. By Norman McL. Rogers. (In The Canadian forum. Toronto. v. 12, no. 134 (Nov. 1931), pp. 46-49.)

A discussion of constitutional problems.

—— Our incredible constitution. By Norman McL. Rogers. (In The Canadian forum. Toronto. v. 13, no. 150 (Mar. 1933), pp. 210-212.)

ROSS, SIR GEORGE WILLIAM   The making of the Canadian constitution. Address by the Hon. G. W. Ross before the Women's Canadian Club, Montreal, January 21st, 1908. Lady Drummond, President of the Club presiding. [Montreal? 1908?] 14, [2] p.

—— The place of the King in the British constitution. By the Hon. Sir George W. Ross. (In Empire Club of Canada. Addresses. (1909/10), pp. 257-275.)

Address delivered May 23, 1910.

Includes references to Canada.

ROTSTEIN, ABRAHAM   Constitution without tiers? (In *The Canadian forum*. Toronto. v. 47, no. 566 (Mar. 1968), pp. 266-268.)
Part 2 of Constitutional Conference, two views. Part 1 is A triumph of federalism, by Ramsay Cook, pp. [265]-266.
An analysis of the Constitutional Conference held February 5-7, 1968.

RUSSELL, PETER H. (ed.)   Leading constitutional decisions; cases on the British North America Act. Edited and with an introd. by Peter H. Russell. Toronto, McClelland and Stewart [c1965] xxviii, 234 p. (The Carleton library, no. 23.)
"This collection is confined to cases which are concerned to the division of legislative power . . .".

RUTLEDGE, JAMES EDWARD   Methods of amendment. By J. E. Rutledge. (In Canadian Broadcasting Corporation. *The Canadian constitution*. Toronto. [c1938] pp. 153-163.)
"Discussed by the Citadel Club of Halifax, December 26, 1937."
Discusses the amending of the British North America Act.

SANDWELL, BERNARD KEBLE   Abolition of Canada's sovereignty. Decision of recent interprovincial conference on amendments to B.N.A. Act fraught with danger. By Bernard K. Sandwell. (In *Saturday night*. Toronto. v. 46, no. 25 (May 2, 1931), pp. 2-3.)

—— Canada at testing point. Making of a really great constitution requires high confidence on part of all citizens in fellow citizens' justice. By B. K. Sandwell. (In *Saturday night*. Toronto. v. 66, no. 8 (Nov. 28, 1950), p. 7.)

—— Constitutional change in Canada. By B. K. Sandwell. (In *Queen's quarterly*. Kingston. v. 50 (1943), pp. [414]-418.)

—— The editor's chair. B.N.A. Act must be changed. By B. K. Sandwell. (In *Saturday night*. Toronto. v. 58, no. 46 (July 24, 1943), p. 15.)

—— From week to week. Freeing the B.N.A. Act. By B. K. Sandwell. (In *Saturday night*. Toronto. v. 54, no. 23 (Apr. 8, 1939), p. 3.)

—— From week to week. Reviving the B.N.A. Act. By B. K. Sandwell. (In *Saturday night*. Toronto. v. 54, no. 24 (Apr. 15, 1939), p. 3.)

—— A salute for the constitution. A protest against irreverence, for the work of the Fathers and a plea for veneration of the document that makes us what we are. By B. K. Sandwell. (In *Maclean's*. Toronto. v. 44, no. 17 (Sept. 1, 1931), pp. 9; 34; 36.)

—— Trade and commerce. By B. K. Sandwell. (In *Saturday night*. Toronto. v. 53, no. 13 (Jan. 29, 1938), p. 3.)
"The supreme example of what has happened to the British North America Act at the hands of interpreters determined to give it a provincial construction is the interpretation assigned to Section 91, subsection 2, and to Section 92, subsection 13, respectively."

—— Why our own constitution? Growth of demand for Canadian control of B.N.A. Act is rapid since West Australia case showed U.K. would not intervene. By B. K. Sandwell. (In *Saturday night*. Toronto. v. 66, no. 4 (Oct. 31, 1950), p. 7.)

—— The Willisian constitution. By B. K. Sandwell. (In *Saturday night*. Toronto. v. 66, no. 45 (Aug. 14, 1951), p. 7.)
Discusses an article written by John Willis in the March 1951 issue of *The Canadian Bar review*, concerning the Canadian constitution.

SAURIOL, PAUL   Constitutional implications of a housing policy. (In *Quebec in the Canada of tomorrow*. [Toronto, 1968] pp. [BB-1]-BB-11.)

SCOTT, FRANCIS REGINALD   The Canadian constitution and human rights. By Frank R. Scott. Four radio talks as heard on CBC University of The Air [in March and April, 1959] Toronto, Canadian Broadcasting Corporation [1959] 52 p.
Contents: The historical tradition. – The constitution of 1867 and human rights. – The growth of freedom concepts in Canada since 1867. – A bill of rights for all Canadians.

—— The constitution and the post-war world. By F. R. Scott. (In Brady, Alexander (ed.) *Canada after the war*. Toronto, 1943. pp. 60-87.)
Considers Canadian wartime legislation and states a case for a general revision of the B.N.A. Act to meet the needs, especially in the area of social services, of postwar reconstruction in Canada.

—— Constitutional adaptations to changing functions of government. By F. R. Scott. (In *The Canadian journal of eco-*

nomics and political science. [Toronto] v. 11 (1945), pp. 329-341.)

Discusses the constitutional changes needed to meet the expanding role of political institutions.

—— Our changing constitution. By F. R. Scott. (In Royal Society of Canada. *Proceedings and transactions.* Ottawa. ser. 3, v. 55 (1961), section 2, pp. 83-95.)

—— Our changing constitution. By F. R. Scott. (In Lederman, W. R. (ed.) *The courts and the Canadian constitution.* [Toronto, c1964] pp. [19]-34.)

Reprinted from *Proceedings of the Royal Society of Canada.* 3d series, v. 55 (1961), pp. 83-95.

SCOTT, WALTER SAMUEL The Canadian constitution, historically explained by annotated statutes, original documents and leading cases. Toronto, Carswell, 1918. vl, 289 p.

SIFTON, SIR CLIFFORD Some Canadian constitutional problems. (In *The Canadian historical review.* Toronto. v. 3 (1922), pp. 3-23.)

SILCOX, CLARIS EDWIN Are family allowances unconstitutional? (In *Saturday night.* Toronto. v. 60, no. 5 (Oct. 7, 1944), pp. 10-11.)

SISSONS, CHARLES BRUCE Section 93. By C. B. Sissons. (In Royal Society of Canada. *Proceedings and transactions.* Ottawa. ser. 3, v. 55 (1961), section 2, pp. 1-7.)

"The purpose of this paper is to present a closer study of those rights presumed to exist in respect to denominational schools as embodied in Section 93 of the British North America Act."

SKELTON, OSCAR DOUGLAS The world's most rigid constitution. By O. D. Skelton. (In *The Canadian courier.* Toronto. v. 14, no. 5 (July 15, 1913), p. 16.)

Comments on the British North America Act.

SMITH, C. B. Let Britain amend the B.N.A. Act. (In *Canadian comment.* Toronto. v. 5, no. 4 (Apr. 1936), p. 6.)

SMITH, DOLAND BLAIR The removal of the imperial limitations from the Canadian constitution. [Vancouver] 1925. 80 leaves.

Thesis (MA) – University of British Columbia.

SMITH, SIDNEY EARLE Treaty-making powers. (In Canadian Broadcasting Corpora-

tion. *The Canadian constitution.* Toronto [c1938] pp. 102-114.)

"Discussed by the Kelsey Club, Winnipeg, November 28, 1937."

SMITH, THURLOW BRADBROOKE Nationality and the British North America Act. [Halifax, 1955] 235 leaves.

Thesis (MA) – Dalhousie University.

"A study of the influence of minority groups on our constitution at its formation, with special reference to written constitutional guarantees which they received and their subsequent judicial interpretation."

SOWARD, FREDERICK HUBERT Comparative treatment. By F. H. Soward. (In Canadian Broadcasting Corporation. *The Canadian constitution.* Toronto [c1938] pp. 14-24.)

"Discussed by the Constitutional Club, Vancouver, October 3, 1937."

A comparative discussion relating to the federal constitutions of Canada, Australia and the United States.

STANLEY, GEORGE FRANCIS GILMAN A short history of the Canadian constitution. By George F. G. Stanley. Toronto, Ryerson Press, 1969. ix, 230 p.

STRAYER, BARRY L. The flexibility of the B.N.A. Act. (In University League for Social Reform. *Agenda 1970.* [Toronto, c1968] pp. [197]-216.)

TEECE, RICHARD CLIVE A comparison between the federal constitution of Canada and Australia. Sydney, W. E. Smith, 1902. iv, 71 p. (Beauchamp prize essay, University of Sydney, 1902.)

THOMPSON, BRAM Canada's distorted constitution. (In *Willisons monthly.* Toronto. v. 2, no. 7 (Dec. 1926), pp. 264-267.)

UNDERHILL, FRANK HAWKINS The B.N.A. Act. By F. H. U. (In *The Canadian forum.* Toronto. v. 14, no. 162 (Mar. 1934), pp. 205-207.)

VANIER, ANATOLE La réforme de la constitution. II. Les questions financières. (In *L'Action nationale.* Montréal. v. 7 (avril 1936), pp. [195]-208.)

Section I, Questions préalables, is by Léopold Richer. (v. 4, pp. [67]-87, [131]-153).

VARCOE, FREDERICK PERCY The constitution of Canada. [2d ed.] Toronto, Carswell, 1965. xvi, 314 p.

First ed. (Toronto, Carswell, 1954) has title: *The distribution of legislative power in Canada.*

—— The distribution of legislative power in Canada. Toronto, Carswell, 1954. xiv, 270 p.

WALSH, SAM French Canada and the constitution. (In *The Marxist quarterly*. Toronto. no. 7 (autumn 1963), pp. 37-45.)

WATKINS, ERNEST Canada's constitution. Proposed retirement of judges stretched our umbilical cord. (In *Canadian commentator*. Toronto. v. 4, no. 9 (Sept. 1960), pp. 2-4.)

—— Political Canada. A sovereign state? (In *Canada month*. Montreal. v. 3, no. 11 (Nov. 1963), p. 38.)

Concerns amending the British North America Act.

WILLIS, JOHN The war and the constitution. (In *Public affairs*. Halifax. v. 3, no. 4 (June 1940), pp. 193-195.)

World War II, 1939-1945.

WILLS, HAROLD A. Constitution headliner.

(In *Saturday night*. Toronto. v. 52, no. 30 (May 29, 1937), p. [1].)

Comments on the annual meeting of the Canadian Political Science Association and Canada's constitutional problems.

—— Does B.N.A. Act hinder economic action? Canadian constitution provides for growth but not change. Necessity of centralized control with regard to industry. A new division of power between Dominion and provinces need not affect minority safeguards. (In *Saturday night*. Toronto. v. 48, no. 42 (Aug. 26, 1933), p. 2.)

Written constitutions. (In *The Week*. Toronto. v. 12, no. 27 (May 31, 1895), pp. 629-630.)

ZASLOW, MORRIS Recent constitutional developments in Canada's northern territories. (In *Canadian public administration*. Toronto. v. 10 (1967), pp. 167-180.)

GOVERNMENT ORGANIZATION AND ADMINISTRATION

ANDERSON, STANLEY V. Canadian ombudsman proposals. Berkeley, Institute of Governmental Studies, University of California, 1966. xi, 168 p.

Mimeographed.

ANGERS, FRANCOIS ALBERT Des chiffres édifiants! (In *L'Action nationale*. Montréal. v. 19 (juil. 1942), pp. [421]-430.)

A compilation of statistics analysing important positions held in the federal government by French Canadians.

ARMSTRONG, ROBERT Some aspects of policy determination in the development of the collective bargaining legislation in the Public Service of Canada. (In *Canadian public administration*. Toronto. v. 11 (1968), pp. [485]-493.)

ASHLEY, CHARLES ALLAN Canadian crown corporations; some aspects of their administration and control. By C. A. Ashley and R. G. H. Smails. Toronto, Macmillan, 1965. x, 360 p.

—— "Glassco Commission": the final report. By C. A. Ashley. (In *The Canadian forum*. Toronto. v. 43, no. 512 (Sept. 1963), p. 132.)

Comments on the Report of the Royal

Commission on Government Organization. Ottawa, Queen's Printer, 1962-63 (5 v.).

—— The "Glassco" Commission's first report. By C. A. Ashley. (In *The Canadian forum*. Toronto. v. 42, no. 501 (Oct. 1962), pp. 153-155.)

Comments on the Report of the Royal Commission on Government Organization. Ottawa, Queen's Printer, 1962-63 (5 v.).

—— The Glassco reports: second volume. By C. A. Ashley. (In *The Canadian forum*. Toronto. v. 42, no. 505 (Feb. 1963), pp. 254-256.)

Comments on the Report of the Royal Commission on Government Organization. Ottawa, Queen's Printer, 1962-63 (5 v.).

—— Glassco III. By C. A. Ashley. (In *The Canadian forum*. Toronto. v. 43, no. 507 (Apr. 1963), pp. 11-12.)

Comments on the Report of the Royal Commission on Government Organization. Ottawa, Queen's Printer, 1962-63 (5 v.).

BALLS, HERBERT R. Issue control and pre-audit for authority; the functions of the Comptroller of the Treasury. (In *Canadian public administration*. Toronto. v. 3 (1960), pp. 118-133.)

—— The Public Accounts; their purpose: an administrative view. (In *Canadian public administration*. Toronto. v. 7 (1964), pp. 422-441.)

"I propose first to review briefly and in summary form the history of the Public Accounts in the United Kingdom and Canada . . . ." – The Author (p. 422).

BARKWAY, MICHAEL How Ottawa figures your taxes. Nation's fiscal policy isn't born anew with each budget. Study on trend of the Canadian economy goes on all year. (In *Saturday night*. Toronto. v. 67, no. 23 (Mar. 15, 1952), pp. 16; 26.)

—— Ottawa view. No civil service ivory tower. (In *Saturday night*. Toronto. v. 68, no. 1 (Oct. 11, 1952), pp. 4; 9.)

—— A sharp look at the bureaucrats. If you find a civil servant doing something useless, don't blame him; blame his minister. (In *Saturday night*. Toronto. v. 66, no. 13 (Jan. 2, 1951), pp. 10; 36.)

BAUER, WILLIAM EDWARD The Department of the Interior and Dominion lands, 1873-1891; a study in administration. [Kingston, Ont., 1953] vii, 153 leaves.

Thesis (MA) – Queen's University.

BIELER, JEAN HENRI The role of the deputy minister: I. By J. H. Bieler. (In *Canadian public administration*. Toronto. v. 4 (1961), pp. 353-356.)

"This paper was presented to the thirteenth annual conference of the Institute of Public Administration of Canada at Ste. Foy, Québec, September 6 to 9, 1961."

Part II is by R. M. Burns.

BLAKE, GORDON Customs administration in Canada; an essay in tariff technology. [Toronto] University of Toronto Press, 1957. 193 p. (Canadian studies in economics, no. 9.)

Includes analysis with historical and political implications.

—— The customs administration in Canadian historical development. (In *The Canadian journal of economics and political science*. [Toronto] v. 22 (1956), pp. 497-508.)

"This paper was presented at the annual meeting of the Canadian Political Science Association in Montreal, June 6, 1956."

BORDEN, SIR ROBERT LAIRD Problem of an efficient civil service. By the Right Honourable Sir Robert Borden. (In The Canadian Historical Association. *Report of the annual meeting*. Ottawa. (1931), pp. 5-34.)

An historical account of civil service reform.

BREBNER, JOHN BARTLET Canada must improve permanent government. By J. B. Brebner. (In *Saturday night*. Toronto. v. 51, no. 4 (Nov. 30, 1935), p. 2.)

Concerns the permanent civil service.

BRIDGES, EDWARD ETTINGDENE BRIDGES, BARON The relationship between ministers and the permanent departmental head. The relationship between governments and government-controlled corporations. [Toronto] Institute of Public Administration of Canada [1964] 31 p.; 32 p. (The W. Clifford Clark memorial lectures, 1964.)

Cover title.

French and English; French text inverted.

BUCHANAN, E. C. National affairs. (In *Saturday night*. Toronto. v. 47, no. 17 (Mar. 5, 1932), p. 4.)

Concerns the civil service and the debates in the House of Commons on "civil service subjects".

BURNS, RONALD M. The role of the deputy minister: II. By R. M. Burns. (In *Canadian public administration*. Toronto. v. 4 (1961), pp. 357-362.)

"This paper was presented to the thirteenth annual conference of the Institute of Public Administration of Canada at Ste. Foy, Québec, September 6 to 9, 1961."

Part I is by J. H. Bieler.

CAIDEN, GERALD ELLIOT A comparative study of the federal civil service of Canada and the Commonwealth public service of Australia. [London, 1958-59?] 1 v.

Thesis (PH D) – University of London.

—— The federal civil service of Canada. [London, 1960] 470 p.

Mimeographed.

CALDWELL, GEORGE HAROLD Unity of command. A comparison of the top level organization structures of the government of Canada and of large scale private enterprises. [Ottawa] 1963. 1 v.

Thesis (MA) – Carleton University.

—— Unity of command. A comparison of the top level organization structures of the government of Canada and of large scale private enterprise. By G. H. Caldwell. (In *Canadian public administration*. Toronto. v. 7 (1964), pp. 510-545.)

CALLARD, KEITH B. Administrative training in Canadian governments. (In Institute of Public Administration of Canada. *Proceedings of the annual conference.* Toronto. 9th (1957), pp. 47-56.)

CANADA. CIVIL SERVICE COMMISSION Personnel administration in the public service; a review of civil service legislation. [Ottawa, Queen's Printer, 1959] 160 p.

On cover: Report of the Civil Service Commission of Canada, Ottawa, December 1958.
Commissioners: A. D. P. Heeney, Chairman of the Civil Service Commission, R. E. Addison and Paul Pelletier.

CANADA. ROYAL COMMISSION ON CIVIL SERVICE, 1892 Report of the Royal commissioners appointed to enquire into certain matters relating to the civil service of Canada, 1892. Printed by order of Parliament. Ottawa, Printed by S. E. Dawson, Printer to the Queen, 1892. xcv, 733 p. ([Parliament, 1891-1892. Sessional papers] no. 16c.)

Commissioners: Geo. Hague, G. W. Burbidge, E. J. Barbeau, J. M. Courtney.

CANADA. ROYAL COMMISSION ON GOVERNMENT ORGANIZATION [Report] Ottawa, Queen's Printer [1962-63] 5 v.

Commissioners: John Grant Glassco, chairman; Robert Watson Seller and F. Eugene Therrier.

CARLYLE, GRANT MORTON A businessman looks at government and business. By G. M. Carlyle. (In *Canadian public administration.* Toronto. v. 4 (1961), pp. 16-25.)

"This paper was presented to the twelfth annual conference of the Institute of Public Administration of Canada at Banff, Alberta, September 14-17, 1960."

CARR, D. W. The legislative-administrative structure in Canada; its significance for agricultural resource development. (In *Canadian public administration.* Toronto. v. 5 (1962), pp. 156-171.)

CARTER, F. A. G. Organizing for northern administration: a practical problem in decentralization. By F. A. G. Carter and R. A. J. Phillips. (In *Canadian public administration.* Toronto. v. 5 (1962), pp. 104-116.)

CASEY, GEORGE ELLIOTT Civil service reform. By G. E. Casey. (In *The Canadian monthly and national review.* Toronto. v. 11 (1877), pp. 83-91.)

CASS-BEGGS, DAVID NORMAN Government and business. [n.p., 1960] 23 leaves.

Cover title.
"Presentation made to the 12th Annual Conference – Institute of Public Administration of Canada, Banff School of Fine Arts, Banff, Alberta—September 14-17, 1960."

CATHERWOOD, ROBERT Some problems of personnel in public employment with special reference to the new Canada Civil Service Act. (In Canadian Club of Ottawa. *Addresses.* Ottawa. (1918/19), pp. 167-173.)

CHALMERS, FLOYD SHERMAN The rising cost of government. By Floyd S. Chalmers. (In *Maclean's.* Toronto. v. 44, no. 23 (Dec. 1, 1931), pp. 10-11; 44-46.)

Civil service discontent: the cause and remedy. By C. W. S. (In *The Canadian nation.* Ottawa, v. 1, no. 9 (Sept. 20, 1919), pp. 8-10.)

CLARK, WILLIAM CLIFFORD Financial administration of the Government of Canada. By W. C. Clark. (In *The Canadian journal of economics and political science.* [Toronto] v. 4 (1938), pp. 391-419.)

CLOKIE, HUGH MC DOWALL The machinery of government. (In Brown, G. W. (ed.) *Canada.* Berkeley, 1953 [c1950] pp. 297-313.)

CLOUTIER, SYLVAIN Le statut de la fonction publique du Canada, son histoire. (In *Canadian public administration.* Toronto. v. 10 (1967), pp. 550-513.)

COATS, ROBERT HAMILTON Beginnings in Canadian statistics. By R. H. Coats. (In *The Canadian historical review.* Toronto. v. 27 (1946), pp. 109-130.)

—— The place of statistics in national administration—function and organization of statistics—scope and method of the Dominion Bureau of Statistics. By R. H. Coats. (In Royal Society of Canada. *Proceedings and transactions.* Ottawa. ser. 3, v. 23 (1929), section 2, pp. 81-93.)

"Read May meeting, 1929."

COGHLAN, FRANCIS A. James Bryce and the establishment of the Department of External Affairs. By F. A. Coghlan. (In Canadian Historical Association. *Historical papers.* [Ottawa] (1968), pp. [84]-93.)

COKE, J. Efforts to control marketing by government boards or organizations acting with government support. (In Canadian Political Science Association. *Papers and proceedings of the annual meeting.* [Kingston, Ont.] v. 5 (1933), pp. [90]-105.)

COLE, TAYLOR   The Canadian bureaucracy; a study of Canadian civil servants and other public employees, 1939-1947. Durham, N.C., Duke University Press, 1949. ix, 292 p. (Duke University publications.)

———   The Canadian bureaucracy and federalism, 1947-1965. Denver, University of Denver [1966] 35 p. (Social Science Foundation and Graduate School of International Studies, University of Denver. Monograph series in world affairs, v. 3, monograph no. 3.)

COLQUHOUN, ARTHUR HUGH URQUHART   Civil service reform. By A. H. U. Colquhoun. (In *The Canadian magazine of politics, science, art and literature.* Toronto. v. 7 (1896), pp. 569-571.)

CONSEIL DE LA VIE FRANCAISE EN AMERIQUE   Les Canadiens français dans le fonctionnairisme fédéral. Mémoire au premier ministre du Canada. Québec, Editions Ferland, 1960. 27 p.
Text in French and English.

COOPER, JOHN ALEXANDER   Civil service reform. By John A. Cooper. (In Canadian Club of Fort William. *Annual.* [Fort William] (1910), pp. 5-12.)
Address delivered March 8, 1909.

COPPS, EDWIN   Ottawa letter. The energetic Energy Board. (In *Saturday night.* Toronto. v. 75, no. 3 (Feb. 6, 1960), pp. 21-22.)
Concerns the personnel and work of the National Energy Board appointed by the Diefenbaker government.

COTE, ERNEST ADOLPHE   The public services in a bicultural community. By E. A. Côté. (In *Canadian public administration.* Toronto. v. 11 (1968), pp. [280]-290.)
"This paper was presented at the 1967 annual conference of the Institute of Public Administration of Canada."

COURTNEY, JOHN MORTIMER   The Finance Department of Canada. By J. M. Courtney. (In Canadian Club of Toronto. *Addresses.* Toronto. (1906/07), pp. [13]-20.)
Address delivered November 19, 1906.

COUTTS, WALTER BARRY   An external viewpoint on the shape of the Public Accounts. By W. B. Coutts. (In *Canadian public administration.* Toronto. v. 7 (1964), pp. 442-450.)

CRAICK, WILLIAM ARNOT   The railroad pass and the deadhead. By W. A. Craick. (In *MacLean's magazine.* Toronto. v. 22, no. 5 (Sept. 1911), pp. [180]-186.)
Discusses the distribution and holding of free railroad passes: the life pass; the annual pass, held by officials and members of Parliament; the trip pass. The Dominion Railway Act provided the issuing of free passes.

CURRIE, ARCHIBALD WILLIAM   The Post Office since 1867. By A. W. Currie. (In *The Canadian journal of economics and political science.* Toronto. v. 24 (1958), pp. 241-250.)

CURRIE, SIR ARTHUR WILLIAM   Canada needs a super-civil service. By Sir Arthur W. Currie. (In *Maclean's.* Toronto. v. 37, no. 21 (Nov. 1, 1924), pp. 11-12; 57-58.)

Customs administrations of Canada and the United States in contrast. Special correspondence of Willisons monthly. (In *Willisons monthly.* Toronto. v. 1, no. 4 (Sept. 1925), pp. 154-157.)

DALTON, WILLIAM J.   Advisory board and responsible government in Canada. [Ottawa, 1960. 1 v.
Thesis (PH D) – University of Ottawa.

DAVID, LAURENT OLIVIER   Les démissions. Par L.-O. David. (In *L'Opinion publique.* Montréal. v. 10, no. 31 (31 juil. 1879), p. [361].)
Concerns unjust firings in the civil service.

DAWSON, HELEN JONES   Relations between farm organizations and the civil service in Canada and Great Britain. (In *Canadian public administration.* Toronto. v. 10 (1967), pp. 450-470.)

DAWSON, ROBERT MAC GREGOR   The Canadian civil service. By R. MacGregor Dawson. (In *The Canadian journal of economics and political science.* [Toronto] v. 2 (1936), pp. 288-300.)

———   The Canadian civil service, 1867-1880. (In *The Canadian historical review.* Toronto. v. 7 (1926), pp. 34-45.)

———   The civil service of Canada. London, Oxford University Press, 1929. 266 p.

———   The functions of a civil service. By R. MacG. Dawson. (In *The Dalhousie review.* Halifax. v. 7 (1927/28), pp. [512]-522.)

———   The Select Committee on the Civil Service, 1938. By R. MacGregor Dawson.

(In *The Canadian journal of economics and political science.* [Toronto] v. 5 (1939), pp. 179-194.)

DES ROCHES, JACQUES M. The creation of new administrative structures: the federal Department of Industry. By J. M. Des Roches. (In *Canadian public administration.* Toronto. v. 8 (1965), pp. 285-291.)

—— The evolution of the organization of federal government in Canada. (In *Canadian public administration.* Toronto. v. 5 (1962), pp. 408-427.)

DEUTSCH, ANTAL Thirty per cent and all that ... (In *Queen's quarterly.* Kingston. v. 73 (1966), pp. [496]-502.)
Concerns collective bargaining in the civil service.

DEUTSCH, JOHN J. The public service in a changing society. (In *Canadian public administration.* Toronto. v. 11 (1969), pp. 1-8.)
"The W. Clifford Clark memorial lecture, 1967."

—— Le service public dans une société en évolution. (In *Canadian public administration.* Toronto. v. 11 (1968), pp. 9-17.)
"W. Clifford Clark memorial lecture, 1967."

DRAYTON, SIR HENRY LUMLEY Should our governments economize? By Sir Henry L. Drayton. (In *Canadian comment.* Toronto. v. 3, no. 8 (Aug. 1934), pp. [3]-4.)
"The first of a series of articles on the need for economy in Canadian governments."

DUNN, SAMUEL O. Government versus private management of the railways. (In Canadian Club of Montreal. *Addresses.* [Montreal] (1916/17), pp. [95-110].)
Address delivered November 27, 1916.

DWIVEDI, ONKAR PRASAD Civil servants of Canada; a study of their rights. [Ottawa, Ont.] 1964. 1 v.
Thesis (MA) – Carleton University.

—— A code of conduct for civil servants. By O. P. Dwivedi. (In *The Dalhousie review.* Halifax. v. 44, no. 4 (winter 1964/65), pp. [452]-458.)

—— Political rights of Canada's public servants. By O. P. Dwivedi and J. P. Kyba. (In Vaughan, Frederick (ed.) *Contemporary issues in Canadian politics.* Scarborough, Ont. [c1970] pp. 230-239.)
Discusses the revised Civil Service Act of

1961 and the Public Service Employment Act of 1967.

DYMOND, W. R. The role of the union in the public service as opposed to its role in private business. (In Institute of Public Administration of Canada. *Proceedings of the annual conference.* Toronto. 5th (1953), pp. 55-64.)

EARL, C. GORDON Functions and administration of the Canadian Wheat Board. (In Institute of Public Administration of Canada. *Proceedings of the annual conference.* Toronto. 3d (1951), pp. 417-433.)

EAYRS, JAMES The origins of Canada's Department of External Affairs. (In *The Canadian journal of economics and political science.* [Toronto] v. 25 (1959), pp. 109-128.)

EGGLESTON, WILFRID Ottawa letter. Quebec fears of centralization fired by English bureaucracy. (In *Saturday night.* Toronto. v. 61, no. 46 (July 20, 1946), p. 8.)
Includes a list of top-ranking members of the permanent civil service chiefs of public corporations, and other similar bodies.

EMRYS, TREVOR Ottawa report. The turn against decentralization. (In *Canadian dimension.* Winnipeg. v. 2, no. 1 (Nov./Dec. 1964), p. 7.)

FAVREAU, GUY Les corporations de la couronne. (In Institut canadien des affaires publiques, Montréal. *Le rôle de l'Etat.* Montréal [c1963, c1962] pp. [71]-89.)

FLAHERTY, J. FRANCIS Ottawa letter. Why so few French Canadians in civil service? Committee asks. By Frank Flaherty. (In *Saturday night.* Toronto. v. 62, no. 46 (July 19, 1947), p. 8.)

FLORENDEAU Nos employés publics. (In *La Revue moderne.* Montréal. 1. année, no 3 (15 jan. 1920), pp. 8-13.)

FRANKEL, SAUL JACOB Staff relations in the Canadian federal civil service. Montreal, 1958. 1 v.
Thesis (PH D) – McGill University.

—— Staff relations in the Canadian federal public service: experience with joint consultation. By S. J. Frankel. (In *The Canadian journal of economics and political science.* [Toronto] v. 22 (1956), pp. 509-522.)
"This paper was presented at the annual meeting of the Canadian Political Science Association in Montreal, June 7, 1956."

—— Staff relations in the civil service; the Canadian experience. Montreal, McGill University Press, 1962. ix, 331 p.

Partial contents: Part 1. The federal government.

The study "refers to persons employed in government departments operating under direct ministerial control" . . . The investigation attempts to "provide an interesting case history in constitutional development". – Introd.

—— Staff relations in the civil service: who represents the government? By S. J. Frankel. (In *The Canadian journal of economics and political science*. [Toronto] v. 25 (1959), pp. 11-22.)

—— The state as employer and the civil service. By S. J. Frankel. (In *Relations industrielles*. Québec. v. 18 (1963), pp. [318]-333.)

Summary in French: L'Etat employeur et la fonction publique (p. 332-333).

FRASER, BLAIR Backstage at Ottawa. Can a civil servant say what he thinks? By the Man with a Notebook. (In *Maclean's*. Toronto. v. 59, no. 1 (Jan. 1, 1946), pp. 15; 48-49.)

—— Backstage at Ottawa. How much can a civil servant tip? (In *Maclean's*. Toronto. v. 67, no. 12 (June 15, 1954), pp. 6; 87.)

—— Backstage at Ottawa. Will we get better postal service? (In *Maclean's*. Toronto. v. 67, no. 16 (Aug. 15, 1954), pp. 5; 59.)

—— Backstage at Ottawa. How dead is the spoils system in the civil service? (In *Maclean's*. Toronto. v. 72, no. 6 (Mar. 14, 1959), p. 2.)

—— Backstage at Ottawa. The law they can't repeal. (In *Maclean's*. Toronto. v. 73, no. 4 (Feb. 13, 1960), p. 2.)

Discusses efficiency in government in the light of Parkinson's law.

—— Do civil servants earn their salaries? (In *Maclean's*. Toronto. v. 66, no. 2 (Jan. 15, 1953), pp. 23; 47-50.)

FRASER, ELLIOTT C. Administration of the Canadian income tax law. (In *The Canadian journal of economics and political science*. Toronto. v. 4 (1938), pp. 377-390.)

GADSBY, HENRY FRANKLIN Funny but not vulgar. By H. F. Gadsby. (In *Saturday night*. Toronto. v. 32, no. 39 (July 12, 1919), p. 4.)

Concerns classification in the civil service.

GAGNON, ANATOLE Success in administrative employment in the government service. [Ottawa, 1950]. xii, 131 leaves.

Thesis (MA) – University of Ottawa.

GAUTIER, CHARLES Le bilinguisme dans les services fédéraux. (In *L'Action française*. Montréal. v. 13 (mars 1925), pp. [130]-145.)

GOLDBERG, S. A. Some recent developments in the Dominion Bureau of Statistics. (In *The Canadian journal of economics and political science*. [Toronto] v. 21 (1955), pp. 52-63.)

GORDON, WALTER LOCKHART Government organization and methods units vs external management consultants. By Walter L. Gordon and A. W. Johnson. (In Institute of Public Administration of Canada. *Proceedings of the annual conference*. Toronto. 4th (1952), pp. 27-41.)

GRANT, MAUDE Government needs undersecretaries. (In *Saturday night*. Toronto. v. 57, no. 13 (Dec. 6, 1941), p. 10.)

Argues that "a serious omission in government in Canada is the failure here to train young men in the work of parliamentary and cabinet government, responsible to the people".

GRANT, WILLIAM LAWSON The civil service of Canada. By W. L. Grant. (In *The University of Toronto quarterly*. [Toronto] v. 3 (1933/34), pp. 428-438.)

—— The civil service of Canada. By W. L. Grant. (In *The Canadian forum*. Toronto. v. 15, no. 173 (Feb. 1935), pp. 171-172.)

The Author died in Toronto February 3, 1935.

GRENON, JEAN YVES Secrétaire d'ambassade. (In *L'Action nationale*. Montréal. v. 50 (jan. 1961), pp. [420]-433.)

Discusses the Canadian diplomatic service.

GREY, RODNEY Bureaucracy and Ottawa. (In *Queen's quarterly*. Kingston. v. 57 (1950), pp. [88]-98.)

Reviews the function and problems of the public service of Canada.

—— Ottawa has personnel trouble. The great increase in the number of civil servants has created an administrative headache. (In *Saturday night.* Toronto. v. 65, no. 5 (Nov. 8, 1949), p. 13.)

HEENEY, ARNOLD DANFORD PATRICK   Civil service reform, 1958. By A. D. P. Heeney. (In *The Canadian journal of economics and political science.* [Toronto] v. 25 (1959), pp. 1-10.)

"A revised version of a paper delivered at the annual meeting of the Canadian Political Science Association in Edmonton, June 6, 1958."

—— Some aspects of administrative reform in the public service. By A. D. P. Heeney. (In *Canadian public administration.* Toronto. v. 9 (1966), pp. 221-225.)

—— Traditions and trends in Canada's public service. (In Empire Club of Canada. *Addresses.* Toronto. (1957/58), pp. 173-181.)

Address delivered January 30, 1958.

HICKS, HENRY DAVIES   Civil servants and politicians; a defence of politicians. (In *Canadian public administration.* Toronto. v. 6 (1963), pp. 261-273.)

"A paper presented to a meeting of the Halifax Regional Group, the Institute of Public Administration of Canada, on November 22, 1960."

HODGETTS, JOHN EDWIN   Administration and politics: the case of the Canadian Broadcasting Corporation. By J. E. Hodgetts. (In *The Canadian journal of economics and political science.* [Toronto] v. 12 (1946), pp. 454-469.)

"This paper was presented at the annual meeting of the Canadian Political Science Association of Toronto, May 24, 1946."

—— Canadian public administration; a book of readings. Edited by J. E. Hodgetts and D. C. Corbett. Toronto, Macmillan, 1960. xii, 575 p.

—— Challenge and response; a retrospective view of the public service of Canada. By J. E. Hodgetts. (In *Canadian public administration.* Toronto. v. 7 (1964), pp. 409-421.)

—— The changing nature of the public service. By J. E. Hodgetts. (In Vaughan, Frederick (ed.) *Contemporary issues in Canadian politics.* Scarborough, Ont. [c1970] pp. 200-209.)

Discusses the nature of the Canadian public service; its development and changing function.

—— The civil service and policy formation. By J. E. Hodgetts. (In *The Canadian journal of economics and political science.* Toronto. v. 23 (1957), pp. 467-479.)

"This paper was presented at the annual meeting of the Canadian Political Science Association in Ottawa, June 13, 1957."

—— The civil service and policy formation. By J. E. Hodgetts. (In Kruhlak, O. M. (comp.) *The Canadian political process.* Toronto, [c1970] pp. 466-478.)

Reprinted from *Canadian journal of economics and political science.* Toronto. v. 23 (1957), pp. 467-479.

—— General manager and master mind are roles of a deputy minister. By J. E. Hodgetts. (In *Saturday night.* Toronto. v. 64, no. 10 (Dec. 11, 1948), pp. 6-7.)

—— Public power and ivory power. By J. E. Hodgetts. (In University League for Social Reform. *Agenda 1970.* [Toronto, c1968] pp. [256]-280.)

Discusses government use of expertise in the initiating and formulating of government policies.

HUGHES, SAMUEL HARVEY SHIRECLIFFE   The public official: Parliament, the public and press. By S. H. S. Hughes. (In *Canadian public administration.* Toronto. v. 3 (1960), pp. 289-298.)

"This paper was presented to the twelfth annual conference of the Institute of Public Administration of Canada, at Banff, Alberta, September 14-17, 1960."

—— Some aspects of the public service. By Hon. S. H. S. Hughes, Chairman, Civil Service Commission of Canada. (In Empire Club of Canada. *Addresses.* Toronto. (1959/60), pp. 302-315.)

Address delivered April 28, 1960.

The Invisible government. (In *The Canadian forum.* Toronto. v. 15, no. 172 (Jan. 1935), p. 142.)

A brief sketch of the Canadian civil service.

JAMES, MUNGO   Ottawa letter. Where bureaucrats hold the purse. (In *Saturday night.* Toronto. v. 81, no. 10 (Oct. 1966), p. 18; 20; 22.)

Concerns the power held by the Treasury Board officials over public spending. Considers attempts to reform this situation.

JEWETT, PAULINE MAE   Advisory committees in Canadian government. Kingston, Ont. 1945. 86 leaves.

Thesis (MA) – Queen's University.

—— The Wartime Prices and Trade Board; a case study in Canadian public administration. [Cambridge, Mass., 1950] 1 v.
Thesis (PH D) – Radcliffe.

JOHANSON, H.   Towards an aggregate analysis of public service. (In *Canadian public administration*. Toronto. v. 9 (1966), pp. 367-375.)

JOHNSON, A. W.   Efficiency in government and business. (In *Canadian public administration*. Toronto. v. 6 (1963), pp. 245-260.)

—— The role of the deputy minister: III. (In *Canadian public administration*. Toronto. v. 4 (1961), pp. 363-373.)
"This paper was presented to the thirteenth annual conference of the Institute of Public Administration of Canada at Ste. Foy, Québec, September 6 to 9, 1961."

KEENLEYSIDE, HUGH LLEWELLYN   The Department of External Affairs. By H. L. Keenleyside. (In *Queen's quarterly*. Kingston. v. 44 (1937), pp. [483]-495.)
Traces the historical development and describes the function of the Department.

KEMP, HERBERT DOUGLAS   The Department of the Interior in the West, 1873-1883; an examination of some hitherto neglected aspects of the work of the outside service. [Winnipeg, 1950] 159 leaves.
Thesis (MA) – University of Manitoba.

KEMP, HUBERT RICHMOND   Price control in Canada. By H. R. Kemp. (In *Public affairs*. Halifax. v. 3, no. 4 (June 1940), pp. 181-185.)
Concerns the powers and function of the Wartime Prices and Trade Board.

KERNAGHAN, WILLIAM DAVID KENNETH   Bureaucracy in Canadian government; selected readings. Edited by W. D. K. Kernaghan. Toronto, Methuen [c1969] viii, 190 p.

KEYFITZ, N.   Robert Coats and the organization of statistics. By N. Keyfitz and H. F. Greenway. (In *The Canadian journal of economics and political science*. [Toronto] v. 27 (1961), pp. 313-322.)
Considers the career of Robert Coats, appointed first Dominion Statistician in 1915, who was instrumental in the formation of the Dominion Bureau of Statistics.

KRAUSE, ROBERT   The Auditor-General and responsible government. [Windsor, Ont., 1967] 1 v.
Thesis (MA) – University of Windsor.

KRISTJANSON, BALDUR H.   Some thoughts on planning at the federal level. (In *Canadian public administration*. Toronto. v. 8 (1965), pp. 143-151.)
"Paper delivered at meeting of the Saskatchewan Regional Group of the Institute of Public Administration of Canada."

KWAVNICK, D.   French Canadians and the civil service of Canada. (In *Canadian public administration*. Toronto. v. 11 (1968), pp. 97-112.)

LABERGE, E. P.   L'administration fédérale. Par E. P. Laberge. (In Sabourin, Louis (ed.) *Le système politique du Canada*. Ottawa, 1968. p. [153]-163. fold. diagr.)
"Le gouvernment du Canada . . . février 1967": fold. diagram inserted between p. 156-157.

LEMIEUX, J. R.   Esquisse de la Gendarmerie royale du Canada. (In *Canadian public administration*. Toronto. v. 5 (1962), pp. 186-193.)
"Etude d'abord présentée en treizième d'administration publique du Canada, du 6 au 9 septembre, 1961. Ste. Foy, Québec."

LEMIEUX, RODOLPHE   Development of the postal service in Canada. By Hon. Rodolphe Lemieux. (In Canadian Club of Montreal. *Addresses*. [Montreal] (1911/12), pp. 75-83.)
Address delivered January 8, 1912.

LESAGE, JEAN   L'administration publique et le bien commun. (In *Canadian public administration*. Toronto. v. 4 (1961), pp. 345-351.)

LEVESQUE, ALBERT   L'état de la législation linguistique dans l'enseignement et l'administration au Canada, 1957. (In *L'Action nationale*. Montréal. v. 47 (mai/juin 1958), pp. [531]-548.)

LLAMBIAS, HENRY JOHN   The need for an ombudsman system in Canada. [Ottawa, Ont.] 1964. 1 v.
Thesis (PH D) – Carleton University.

LUSSIER, ROLAND   L'organisation d'un système de selection dans une entreprise gouvernementale. [Montréal, 1954] 1 v.
Thesis (L PH) – University of Montreal.

LYNGSETH, D. M.   The use of organization and methods in Canadian government. (In *Canadian public administration*. Toronto. v. 5 (1962), pp. 428-492.)
"A thesis submitted to Carleton University in partial fulfilment of the requirements for the degree of Master of Arts in Public Administration, August, 1962."

MC CREADY, JOHN E. BLAKNEY Civil service as it was. By J. E. B. McCready. (In *The Canadian magazine of politics, science, art and literature.* Toronto. v. 29 (1907), pp. 408-412.)

"Personal reminiscences of a time when the 'axe' hung over every man subject to the spoils system."

MC DONALD, G. P. A. Labour, manpower and government reorganization. By G. P. A. McDonald. (In *Canadian public administration.* Toronto. v. 10 (1967), pp. 471-[498].)

Appendix I-VI (diagrams): pp. [496-498]. Discusses the creation of a Department of Manpower and Immigration announced December 17, 1965.

THE MACE Shaking up the Service. By the Mace. (In *Saturday night.* Toronto. [v. 36, no. 3] (Nov. 13, 1920), p. 4.)

Concerns the civil service.

MAC INNES, T. R. L. History of Indian administration in Canada. (In *The Canadian journal of economics and political science.* [Toronto] v. 12 (1946), pp. 387-394.)

"This paper was presented at the annual meeting of the Canadian Political Science Association in Toronto, May 24, 1946."

Traces the historical development of the administration of Indian affairs by the Canadian government.

MACLEAN, RODERICK DUNCAN An examination of the role of the Comptroller of the Treasury. [Kingston, 1963] 1. v.

Thesis (MA) – Queen's University.

—— An examination of the role of the Comptroller of the Treasury. (In *Canadian public administration.* Toronto. v. 7 (1964), pp. 1-133.)

"A thesis presented to the faculty of the School of Graduate Studies, Queen's University, in partial fulfilment of the requirements for the degree Master of Arts, September, 1962."

MC LEOD, THOMAS H. Administrative and constitutional problems peculiar to Crown corporations. (In Institute of Public Administration of Canada. *Proceedings of the annual conference.* Toronto. 8th (1956), pp. 153-160.)

—— Glassco commission report. By T. H. McLeod. (In *Canadian public administration.* Toronto. v. 6 (1963), pp. 386-406.)

A discussion of the Report of the Royal Commission on Government Organization. Ottawa [1962-63] (5 v.).

"This paper was presented to the fifteenth annual conference of the Institute of Public Administration of Canada, September 4-7, 1963, Ottawa, Ontario."

MAGOR, ROBERT J. Business looks at government. "Sound government regulations are the only means by which unfair competition can be checked." (In *Maclean's.* Toronto. v. 48, no. 22 (Nov. 15, 1935), p. 26.)

MAGRATH, CHARLES ALEXANDER The civil service. By C. A. Magrath. (In *The University magazine.* Montreal. v. 12 (1913), pp. [247]-255.)

MALLORY, JAMES RUSSELL The minister's office staff; an unreformed part of the public service. By J. R. Mallory. (In *Canadian public administration.* Toronto. v. 10 (1967), pp. 25-34.)

MARCH, ROMAN ROBERT The Canadian Department of External Affairs; growth and organization, 1944-1958. [Ottawa, 1958] 152 leaves.

Thesis (MA) – Carleton University.

MARSH, D'ARCY Democracy at work: the machinery of Parliament Hill and the civil service. Toronto, Macmillan, 1938. 100 p. (Canadian Broadcasting Corporation publications, no. 3.)

MARSHALL, HERBERT Dominion Bureau of Statistics. (In Institute of Public Administration of Canada. *Proceedings of the annual conference.* Toronto. 8th (1956), pp. 239-248.)

—— The role of the Dominion Bureau of Statistics in the post-war world. (In *The Canadian journal of economics and political science.* [Toronto] v. 19 (1953), pp. 281-290.)

"Presidential address delivered at London, June 4, 1953, at the joint meeting of the Canadian Historical Association and the Canadian Political Science Association."

MARSHALL, J. T. The application of computers in the government of Canada. (In *Canadian public administration.* Toronto. v. 6 (1963), pp. 148-155.)

MENZIES, MERRILL WARREN The Canadian Wheat Board; a study in the development of Canadian agricultural policy. [Saskatoon, 1949] 1 v.

Thesis (MA)–University of Saskatchewan.

MEREDITH, EDMUND ALLEN The public service of the Dominion. Considered with reference to the present scale of prices and wages. By E. A. Meredith. (In *The Canadian monthly and national review*. Toronto. v. 3 (1873), pp. [1]-12.)

MINEHAN, LANCELOT Civil service reform. By Rev. Father L. Minehan. (In Empire Club of Canada. *Addresses*. Toronto. (1906/07), pp. 71-76.)

At head of title: Empire Club speeches.
Address presented November 8, 1906.

MONTAGUE, J. TAIT Manpower as department? (In *The Canadian forum*. Toronto. v. 45, no. 541 (Feb. 1966), pp. [241]-242.)

General comments on the creation of a federal Department of Manpower.

MORIN, CLAUDE The Department of Intergovernmental Affairs. (In *Quebec in the Canada of tomorrow*. [Toronto, 1968] pp. S-1-[S-9].)

Discusses the rôle of this provincial department in federal-provincial relations.

MURRAY, W. W. Anomalies of Ottawa. (In *Maclean's*. Toronto. v. 43, no. 5 (Mar. 1, 1930), pp. 14; 36; 38.)

Depicts inadequate government facilities.

NEWMAN, CHRISTINA (MC CALL) The Establishments that govern us. By Christina Newman. (In *Saturday night*. Toronto. v. 83, no. 5 (May 1968), pp. 23-26.)

The New Establishments, 1.
Analyses the power and function of the federal bureaucracy.

NICHOLLS, G. V. V. Safeguards in the exercise of governmental discretion. (In *Canadian public administration*. Toronto. v. 7 (1964), pp. 500-509.)

Concerns administrative tribunals.
"A paper delivered to the Institute of Public Administration of Canada, Halifax chapter, on March 12, 1964."

NICHOLSON, BYRON The Solicitor-General of Canada. (In *The Canadian magazine of politics, science, art and literature*. Toronto. v. 10 (1897/98), pp. 315-321.)

NORTH, NICHOLAS Canada counts noses. (In *Maclean's*. Toronto. v. 34, no. 10 (May 15, 1921), pp. 9; 53-55.)

The sixth Dominion census and "the first census taken in Canada under the jurisdiction of the Department of Trade and Commerce".

O'LEARY, MICHAEL GRATTAN Ottawa's orgy of extravagance. By Grattan O'Leary. (In *Maclean's*. Toronto. v. 37, no. 2 (Jan. 15, 1924), pp. 9-11; v. 37, no. 3 (Feb. 1, 1924), pp. 11-13; v. 37, no. 4 (Feb. 15, 1924), pp. 19-21, 46; v. 37, no. 5 (Mar. 1, 1924), pp. 14-15, 55.)

Concerns inefficiency in the public service. "O'Leary makes nine suggestions which make for efficiency and a lower tax rate."
In a series of four articles.

—— Where our Government is housed. By Grattan O'Leary. (In *Maclean's*. Toronto. v. 37, no. 6 (Mar. 15, 1924), pp. 26; 41.)

"Our scattered federal government is housed in thirty-eight different buildings on twenty-five different streets."

PAUL, R. DICKERSON Ottawa letter. No collective bargaining. (In *Saturday night*. Toronto. v. 75, no. 16 (Aug. 6, 1960), p. 26; 28.)

Discusses the revising of the Civil Service Act, taking into account the recommendations of the "Heeney report", i.e. the Report of the Civil Service Commission on Personnel Administration in the Public Service, 1958.

PAYNE, J. L. The civil servant. (In *The University magazine*. Montreal. v. 6 (1907), pp. [507]-513.)

PELLETIER, PAUL The Heeney report. (In Institute of Public Administration of Canada. *Proceedings of the annual conference*. Toronto. 11th (1959), pp. 63-74.)

Discusses the report of the Civil Service Commission entitled: Personnel administration in the public service; a review of civil service legislation. Ottawa, 1959. 160 p. (A. D. P. Heeney, chairman.)

PHELAN, V. C. The servants of the state. (In *Saturday night*. Toronto. v. 52, no. 1 (Nov. 7, 1936), p. 19.)

Concerns the Canadian civil service.

PHILLIPS, ALAN The government girl. (In *Maclean's*. Toronto. v. 66, no. 2 (Jan. 15, 1953), pp. 24-25; 38-42.)

Discusses women in the civil service.

Political partisanship in the civil service. By G. B. (In *The Week*. Toronto. v. 13, no. 47 (Oct. 16, 1896), pp. 1115-1116.)

PORTER, JOHN A. Higher public servants and the bureaucratic elite in Canada. By John Porter. (In *The Canadian journal of economics and political science.* Toronto. v. 24 (1958), pp. 483-501.)

Appendix (pp. 497-501): The selection of the bureaucratic elite.

The Author presents data on the careers and social background of top personnel of the Canadian federal public service.

POZNANSKA, ALICE   La commission Glassco. Un rapport dont on n'a pas assez parlé. (In *Cité libre.* Montréal. no. 62 (déc. 1963), pp. 13-18.)

An essay on the Report of the Royal Commission on Government Organization. Ottawa, 1962-63. 5 v.

PRIVES, MOSHE Z.   Career and promotion in the federal civil service of Canada. By M. Z. Prives. (In *Canadian public administration.* Toronto. v. 3 (1960), pp. 179-190.)

—— Career in civil service; Canada, Great Britain and the United States. [Montreal, 1958] 229 leaves.

Thesis (PH D) – McGill University.

RAINE, NORMAN REILLY   Guarding the nation's health. (In *Maclean's.* Toronto. v. 40, no. 5 (Mar. 1, 1927), pp. 14-15; 42; 44-46.)

An essay on the Department of Health.

—— Help wanted. The welfare of every man who works is the Department of Labor's special concern. (In *Maclean's.* Toronto. v. 41, no. 6 (Mar. 15, 1928), pp. 17-18; 62.)

Describes the function of the Department of Labour.

—— Treasury of the nation. (In *Maclean's.* Toronto. v. 40, no. 3 (Feb. 1, 1927), pp. 8-9; 32-34; 38.)

Concerns the Department of Finance.

READE, JOHN COLLINGWOOD   Necessity for reform in federal civil service. (In *Saturday night.* Toronto. v. 51, no. 10 (Jan. 11, 1936), p. 2.)

ROBERTSON, GORDON   Administration for development in northern Canada; the growth and evolution of government. (In *Canadian public administration.* Toronto. v. 3 (1960), pp. 354-362.)

"This paper was presented to the twelfth annual conference of the Institute of Public Administration of Canada, at Banff, Alberta, September 14-17, 1960."

ROWAT, DONALD CAMERON   An ombudsman scheme for Canada. By Donald C. Rowat. (In *The Canadian journal of eco-*

nomics and political science. Toronto. v. 28 (1962), pp. 543-556.)

"A revised version of the paper presented under the title of 'The nordic public defenders' at the annual meeting of the Canadian Political Science Association in Hamilton, June 9, 1962."

SANDWELL, A. H.   Does Canada need an air ministry? By Flight Com. A. H. Sandwell. (In *Saturday night.* Toronto. v. 55, no. 18 (Mar. 2, 1940), p. 3.)

SAYN-WITTGENSTEIN, L.   Forestry, from branch to department. (In *Canadian public administration.* Toronto. v. 6 (1963), pp. 434-452.)

"Part of a thesis submitted to Carleton University in 1962 in partial fulfilment of the requirements for the degree of Master of Arts in Public Administration."

SCANLON, THOMAS JOSEPH   Promoting the government of Canada. A study of the information, explanation and promotional activities of the federal government departments. [Kingston, Ont.] 1964. ix, 166 leaves.

Thesis (MA) – Queen's University.

SCOTT, DUNCAN CAMPBELL   The administration of Indian affairs in Canada. By D. C. Scott. Toronto, Canadian Institute of International Affairs, 1931. 29 p.

Prepared for the fourth bi-annual conference held by the Institute of Pacific Relations at Hangchow from Oct. 18 to Nov. 3, 1931.

Analyses the position of Indians under the Canadian government.

SCOTT, FRANCIS REGINALD   Canada, Quebec and bilingualism. By F. R. Scott. (In *Queen's quarterly.* Kingston. v. 54 (1947), pp. [1]-7.)

Comments on government use of the two official languages of Canada.

SHARP, MITCHELL WILLIAM   Measurements of efficiency in government and business. By M. W. Sharp. (In *Canadian public administration.* Toronto. v. 3 (1960), pp. 150-156.)

"This paper was prepared for oral delivery to a Senior Management Course for Federal Government officials."

SHORTT, ADAM   The Canadian civil service. (In Canadian Club of Toronto. *Addresses.* Toronto. (1908/09), pp. 125-133.)

Address delivered March 29, 1909.

—— The taking of the civil service out of politics. (In Canadian Club of Winnipeg.

Report. Winnipeg. 8th (1911/12), pp. 23-26.)

Summary and excerpts of an address delivered January 25, 1912.

SMITH, DOROTHY BLAKEY   The parliament buildings; a postscript to Parkinson. (In *Canadian public administration.* Toronto. v. 6 (1963), pp. 453-462.)

"This paper was presented to a meeting of the Victoria Regional Group, Institute of Public Administration of Canada in May, 1962."

STEAD, GORDON WILSON   The Treasury Board of Canada. By G. W. Stead. (In Institute of Public Administration of Canada. *Proceedings of the annual conference.* Toronto. 7th (1955), pp. 79-96.)

STEELE, GRANVILLE GEORGE ERNEST   The Treasury Board as a control agency. By G. G. E. Steele. (In *Canadian public administration.* Toronto. v. 4 (1961), pp. 197-205.)

"This paper was presented to the Civil Service Commission Senior Officers' Course in Government Administration, Arnprior, Ontario, September, 1960."

STEEVES, DOROTHY   Marketing problems. (In Canadian Broadcasting Corporation. *The Canadian constitution.* Toronto [c1938] pp. 90-101.)

"Discussed by the Constitutional Club of Vancouver, November 21, 1937."

Concerns government regulation and control of the marketing of natural products in Canada.

STEVENSON, JOHN A.   Ottawa letter. Deflated honors and inflated payrolls. (In *Saturday night.* Toronto. v. 70, no. 15 (Jan. 15, 1955), p. 11.)

Concerns the civil service.

STRICK, J. C.   Quantitative analysis & political responsibility. By J. C. Strick and W. L. White. (In *The Canadian forum.* Toronto. v. 47, no. 561 (Oct. 1967), pp. 155-157.)

Considers the recommendations put forth by the Report of the Royal Commission on Government Organization. Ottawa, 1962-63. (5 v.)

STURSBERG, PETER   Postmark Ottawa. (In *The Canadian Saturday night.* Toronto. v. 77, no. 17 (Oct. 1962), pp. 26-27.)

Comments on the Report of the Royal Commission on Government Organization,

Ottawa, 1962-63, popularly known as the Glassco report.

SYLVESTRE, GUY   Canada's first legation. (In *Queen's quarterly.* Kingston. v. 59 (1952), pp. [53]-62.)

Concerns Vincent Massey as first Canadian ambassador to the United States, and reviews the development of the Canadian diplomatic service.

THORBURN, HUGH GARNET   An ombudsman for Canada? By Hugh Thorburn. (In *The Canadian forum.* Toronto. v. 40, no. 473 (June 1960), p. 53.)

TUNNOCH, G. V.   The Bureau of Government Organization. Improvement by order-in-council, committee, and anomaly. (In *Canadian public administration.* Toronto. v. 8 (1965), pp. 558-568.)

——   The Glassco commission; did it cost more than it was worth? (In *Canadian public administration.* Toronto. v. 7 (1964), pp. 389-397.)

Discusses the Report of the Royal Commission on Government Organization. Ottawa [1962-63] (5 v.)

VAISON, ROBERT A.   Collective bargaining in the federal public service. The achievement of a milestone in personnel relations. (In *Canadian public administration.* Toronto. v. 12 (1969), pp. [108]-122.)

VAN BLARICOM, GEORGE B.   The protectors of Royalty in Canada. By G. B. Van Blaricom. (In *The Busy man's magazine.* Toronto. v. 18, no. 6 (Oct. 1909), pp. 19-26.)

Concerns the Dominion Police Force of Canada.

VEITCH, W. F.   Administrative research in government. (In Institute of Public Administration of Canada. *Proceedings of the annual conference.* Toronto. 8th (1956), pp. 223-235.)

WARD, WILLIAM PETER   The administration of justice in the North-West Territories, 1870-1887. [Edmonton, Alta.] 1966. 1 v.

Thesis (MA) – University of Alberta.

WHITE, WALTER LE ROY   Policy, politics and the Treasury Board in Canadian government. By W. L. White and J. C. Strick. Don Mills, Ont., Science Research Associates (Canada) [1970] v, 157 p.

——   The Treasury Board and Parliament. By Walter L. White and John C. Strick.

(In *Canadian public administration.* Toronto. v. 10 (1967), pp. 209-222.)

—— The Treasury Board in Canada. [Ann Arbor, 1965] v, 253 leaves.
Thesis (PH D) – University of Michigan.

—— The Treasury Board in 19th century Canada. By W. L. White. (In *Queen's quarterly.* Kingston. v. 74 (1967), pp. [492]-505.)

WILLISON, SIR JOHN STEPHEN Civil service reform. By J. S. Willison. (In Canadian Club of Toronto. *Addresses.* Toronto. (1906/07), pp. 139-152.)
Address delivered April 29, 1907.

—— Civil service reform in Canada. By J. S. Willison. (In Empire Club of Canada. *Addresses.* Toronto. (1907/08), pp. 126-131.)
At head of title: Empire Club speeches.
Address presented December 5, 1907.

WILLMS, ABRAHAM MARTIN The administration of research on administration in the government of Canada. By A. M. Willms. (In *Canadian public administration.* Toronto. v. 10 (1967), pp. 405-416.)

—— Organization in Canadian government administration. By A. M. Willms. Ottawa, School of Public Administration, Carleton University, 1965. 157 p.
Cover title.

WILLMS, ABRAHAM MARTIN (ed.) Public administration in Canada: selected readings. Edited by A. M. Willms and W. D. K. Kernaghan. Toronto, Methuen [c1968] xi, 473 p.
"The primary purpose of this book is to examine the institutions and processes of public administration in Canada . . .".

WILSON, VINCENT SEYMOUR Staffing in the Canadian federal bureaucracy. With specific reference to its historical determinants and the socio-cultural variables affecting recruitment and job mobility in the senior echelons. [Kingston] 1970 [c1971] ix, 375 leaves.
Thesis (PH D) – Queen's University, 1971.

WRIGHT, ARTHUR R. An examination of the role of the Board of Transport Commissioners for Canada as a regulatory tribunal. (In *Canadian public administration.* Toronto. v. 6 (1963), pp. 349-385.)
"Part of a thesis submitted to Carleton University in partial fulfilment of the requirements for the degree of Master of Arts in Public Administration."

WRONG, GEORGE MC KINNON Civil service reform. An address by Prof. G. M. Wrong. (In Empire Club of Canada. *Addresses.* Toronto. (1917/18), pp. 131-139.)
Address delivered February 28, 1918.

THE EXECUTIVE

BANKS, MARGARET AMELIA Privy Council, cabinet and ministry in Britain and Canada: a story of confusion. By Margaret A. Banks. (In *The Canadian journal of economics and political science.* [Toronto] v. 31 (1965), pp. [193]-205.)
Describes, historically, the attempt to clarify the relationship between Privy Council, cabinet, and ministry.

BARBE, RAOUL P. Les sociétés de la couronne. Par Raoul Barbe. (In Sabourin, Louis (ed.) *Le système politique du Canada.* Ottawa, 1968. pp. [165]-183.)

BEAUCHAMP, JEAN JOSEPH The jurisprudence of the Privy Council. Containing a digest of all the decisions of the Privy Council since the publication of the first volume in 1891. Montreal, Wilson et Lafleur, 1909. xiv, 452 p.

BRADEN, MICHAEL H. A distinctive Canada requires a continuing monarchy. (In *Canada month.* Montreal. v. 7, no. 4 (Apr. 1967), pp. 12-15.)
Discusses the role of constitutional monarchy in Canada. Argues for its continuation.

BROWNE, GERALD PETER The Judicial Committee of the Privy Council and the distribution of legislative power in the British North America Act, 1867. [Vancouver] 1953. iii, 145 leaves.
Thesis (MA) – University of British Columbia.

—— The Judicial Committee of the Privy Council and the distribution of legislative powers in the British North America Act, 1867. [Oxford, 1963] 1 v.
Thesis – Oxford.

BURCHELL, CHARLES J. Appeals to the Privy Council. By C. J. Burchell. (In Canadian Broadcasting Corporation. *The Canadian constitution.* Toronto [c1938] pp. 115-126.)

"Discussed by the Citadel Club, Halifax, December 5, 1937."

Concerns "appeals from Canadian courts to the Privy Council in England, particularly in constitutional cases".

CLARK, E. R. The Privy Council and the constitution. By E. R. Clark. (In *The Dalhousie review.* Halifax. v. 19 (1939/40), pp. [65]-75.)

CLARK, JOHN MURRAY The judicial committee of the Privy Council. By J. M. Clark. (In Empire Club of Canada. *Addresses.* Toronto. (1908/09), pp. 142-157.)

At head of title: Empire Club speeches.

Address presented March 1, 1909.

COOPER, JOHN ALEXANDER The Canadian premier and the United States president. (In *The Canadian magazine of politics, science, art and literature.* Toronto. v. 2 (1893/94), pp. [415]-421.)

CULLINGHAM, GORDON V. Canada: unconscious republic? (In *The Canadian forum.* Toronto. v. 32, no. 383 (Dec. 1952), pp. 198-199.)

Examines the assumption that the Governor-General is regarded as the Canadian head of state.

DAWSON, ROBERT MAC GREGOR The cabinet —position and personnel. By R. MacGregor Dawson. (In *The Canadian journal of economics and political science.* [Toronto] v. 12 (1946), pp. 261-281.)

"The presidential address delivered at the annual meeting of the Canadian Political Science Association, May 24, 1946."

—— The cabinet position and personnel. By R. MacGregor Dawson. (In Kruhlak, O. M. (comp.) *The Canadian political process.* Toronto [c1970] pp. 345-366.)

Reprinted from *Canadian journal of economics and political science.* Toronto. v. 12 (1946), pp. 261-281.

—— The independence of the Lieutenant-Governor. By R. MacG. Dawson. (In *The Dalhousie review.* Halifax. v. 2 (1922/23), pp. [230]-246.)

DEACON, C. F. The governor-generalship; a rejoinder. (In *The Canadian magazine of politics, science, art and literature.* Toronto. v. 28 (1906/07), pp. 499-500.)

"Contending that election would not improve the system, with a general defence of the present system."

A rejoinder to The governor-generalship, by W. D. Lighthall. (In *The Canadian magazine of politics, science, art and literature.* Toronto. v. 28 (1906/07), pp. 372-374.)

EGGLESTON, WILFRID The cabinet and pressure groups. (In Institute of Public Administration of Canada. *Proceedings of the annual conference.* Toronto. 5th (1953), pp. 157-167.)

EVATT, HERBERT VERE The king and his dominion governors; a study of the reserve powers of the Crown in Great Britain and the Dominion. By the Honourable Mr. Justice Herbert Vere Evatt. London, Oxford University Press, 1936. xvi, 324 p.

EWART, JOHN SKIRVING The governor-generalship. By John S. Ewart. (In *The Canadian forum.* Toronto. v. 8, no. 91 (Apr. 1928), pp. 598-599.)

—— Judicial appeals to the Privy Council. 1. The case for discontinuing appeals. By John S. Ewart. (In *Queen's quarterly.* Kingston. v. 37 (1930), pp. [456]-473.)

Part 2, The case for appeals (p. [474]-489) is by George H. Sedgewick.

EWART, T. SEATON The royal prerogative and war. By T. S. Ewart. (In *The Canadian forum.* Toronto. v. 18, no. 213 (Oct. 1938), pp. 203-204.)

Discusses the confused interpretation of Canada's constitutional right to remain independent of a war involving Great Britain.

FORSEY, EUGENE ALFRED Le cabinet fédéral. Par Eugene Forsey. (In Sabourin, Louis (éd.) *Le système politique du Canada.* Ottawa, 1968. pp. [103]-116.)

—— La constitution du Canada et la couronne. Par Eugene Forsey. (In *Relations.* Montréal. 3. année, no 31 (juil. 1943), pp. 186-188.)

Translated from the English.

—— The Crown and Canada's constitution. By Eugene Forsey. (In *Saturday night.* Toronto. v. 58, no. 37 (May 22, 1943), pp. 6-7; v. 58, no. 38 (May 29, 1943), pp. 9-10.)

In two parts.

—— The Crown and the constitution. By Eugene Forsey. (In *The Dalhousie review.* Halifax. v. 23 (1953/54), pp. [31]-49.)

A comparative and historical analysis with emphasis on the constitutional issue raised between Lord Byng and Mackenzie King in 1926.

—— Lieutenant-governors are not ambassadors. By Eugene Forsey. (In *Saturday night*. Toronto. v. 63, no. 24 (Mar. 20, 1948), pp. [12-13].)

Second of a series of articles on claims for sovereign powers for the provinces. Concerns the appointment of lieutenant-governors.

—— Meetings of the Queen's Privy Council for Canada, 1867-1882. By Eugene Forsey. (In *The Canadian journal of economics and political science*. [Toronto] v. 32 (1966), pp. [489]-498.)

—— Oaths of ministers without portfolio. By Eugene Forsey. (In *The Canadian journal of economics and political science*. [Toronto] v. 14 (1948), pp. 246-247.)

Includes discussion of the crisis in the cabinet of Sir Mackenzie Bowell in January 1896.

—— The royal power of dissolution of Parliament in the British Commonwealth. [Montreal] 1941. 1 v.

Thesis (PH D) – McGill University.

Includes an analysis of the Canadian constitutional issue of 1926.

—— The Royal power of dissolution of Parliament in the British Commonwealth. By Eugene A. Forsey. With a foreword by Sir John A. R. Marriott. Toronto, Oxford University Press, 1943. xix, 316 p.

On cover: Dissolution of Parliament.

Substantial attention is given to an analysis of the King-Byng constitutional crisis of 1926.

—— The Royal power of dissolution of Parliament in the British Commonwealth. By Eugene A. Forsey. Toronto, Oxford University Press [1968] xxviii, 324 p. (Oxford in Canada paperback, OCP-16.)

First published 1943.

Substantial attention is given to an analysis of the King-Byng constitutional issue of 1926.

—— The royal prerogative of dissolution of Parliament. By Eugene A. Forsey. (In Canadian Political Science Association. *Papers and proceedings of the annual meeting*. [Kingston, Ont.] v. 2 (1930), pp. [81]-94.)

Contains an analysis of the King-Byng constitutional crisis of 1926.

A "Free Press" view of Crown and dissolution. (In *Saturday night*. Toronto. v. 58, no. 45 (July 17, 1943), p. 11.)

"Reprinted from Winnipeg Free Press" of June 29.

For a rejoinder see B. K. Sandwell. From the editor's chair. What the "Free Press" is rescuing. (In *Saturday night*. Toronto. v. 58, no. 45. p. 9.)

The Functions of a governor-general. By a political onlooker. (In *The Canadian magazine of politics, science, art and literature*. Toronto. v. 15 (1900), pp. 167-170.)

HALLIDAY, W. E. D. The executive of the government of Canada. (In *Canadian public administration*. Toronto. v. 2 (1959), pp. 229-241.)

HAMILTON, CHARLES FREDERICK The person and the idea. By C. Frederick Hamilton. (In *The University magazine*. Montreal. v. 9 (1910), pp. [115]-124.)

Concerns "the procedure of appointing a representative of the Crown in Canada".

HEENEY, ARNOLD DANFORD PATRICK Cabinet government in Canada: some recent developments in the machinery of the central executive. By A. D. P. Heeney. (In *The Canadian journal of economics and political science*. [Toronto] v. 12 (1946), pp. 282-301.)

Appendix A: Functions of the Prime Minister; Appendix B: War-time cabinet committees.

HISTORICUS Concerning the prerogative. By Historicus. (In *The Canadian magazine of politics, science, art and literature*. Toronto. v. 29 (1907), pp. 118-122.)

"A review of the King's authority, privileges and limitations, particularly with respect to Colonial application."

HODGETTS, JOHN EDWIN Parliament and the powers of the cabinet. By J. E. Hodgetts. (In *Queen's quarterly*. Kingston. v. 52 (1945), pp. [465]-477.)

Considers the statement made by J. L. Ilsley, Minister of Finance, concerning the source of cabinet authority and the right of a cabinet minister to withhold information.

HODGINS, THOMAS The prerogative of the Crown in colonial legislation. (In Rose-Belford's *Canadian monthly and national review*. Toronto. v. 5 (1880), pp. 385-397.)

HUMPHREY, JOHN P.   The Privy Council is a legislative body. (In *The Canadian forum*. Toronto. v. 19, no. 230 (Mar. 1940), pp. 383-385.)

IRVING, R. G.   A study of certain prerogative powers of the Canadian governor-generalship under Lord Dufferin, 1872-78. [London, 1964-65?] 1 v.
Thesis (B LITT) – Oxford.

LAMBERTON, HENRY RICHARD   The evolution of the governor-generalship of the Dominion of Canada. [Minneapolis] 1936. ii, 165 leaves.
Thesis (MA) – University of Minnesota.

LEMIRE, P.   Le ministère du Travail; sa législation, ses implications administratives. [Québec, 1964] 1 v.
Thesis (MA) – Laval University.

LERY, LOUIS C. DE   L'appel au Conseil privé. (In *Relations*. Montréal. 7. année, no 76 (avril 1947), pp. 102-104.)

LIGHTHALL, WILLIAM DOUW   The governor-generalship. By W. D. Lighthall. (In *The Canadian magazine of politics, science, art and literature*. Toronto. v. 28 (1906/07), pp. 372-374.)
"An outspoken criticism of the Governor-General's function in Canada, and a plea for a radical change."
For a rejoinder see The governor-generalship, by C. F. Deacon. (In *The Canadian magazine of politics, science, art and literature*. Toronto. v. 28 (1906/07), pp. 499-500.)

MC GRATH, SIR PATRICK THOMAS   A layman's view of the Privy Council. By Sir Patrick McGrath. (In *The Dalhousie review*. Halifax. v. 7 (1927/28), pp. [291]-301.)

MAC KENZIE, NORMAN ARCHIBALD MAC RAE   The Privy Council and the treaty power. By Norman MacKenzie. (In *Saturday night*. Toronto. v. 52, no. 23 (Apr. 10, 1937), p. 2.)

MC KEOUGH, WILLIAM DARCY   The relationship of ministers and civil servants. By the Honourable W. Darcy McKeough. (In *Canadian public administration*. Toronto. v. 12 (1969), pp. [1]-8.)

MAC PHERSON, M. A.   The relationship between the senior public servant and the minister of the crown. (In Institute of Public Administration of Canada. *Proceedings of the annual conference*. Toronto. 5th (1953), pp. 143-151.)

MALLORY, JAMES RUSSELL   The appointment of the governor-general: responsible government, autonomy, and the royal prerogative. By J. R. Mallory. (In *The Canadian journal of economics and political science*. Toronto. v. 26 (1960), pp. 96-107.)
Discusses the constitutional complexities involved in the appointment of John Buchan (Lord Tweedsmuir) as Governor-General of Canada in 1935.

—— La couronne. Par J. R. Mallory. (In Sabourin, Louis (ed.) *Le système politique du Canada*. Ottawa, 1968. pp. [80]-101.)

MASSEY, VINCENT   The crown in Canada. (In his *Confederation on the march*. Toronto, 1965. pp. [65]-81.)
"An address delivered at ... the Canadian Club of Toronto, February 8, 1965."

MIGNAULT, PIERRE BASILE   L'appel au Conseil Privé. Par P. B. Mignault. (In Royal Society of Canada. *Proceedings and transactions*. Ottawa. ser. 3, v. 30 (1936), section 1, pp. 11-28.)

MILLIGAN, FRANK ARCHIBALD   The lieutenant-governorship in Manitoba, 1870-1882. [Winnipeg, 1948] 1 v.
Thesis (MA) – University of Manitoba.

PHILLIPS, LESTER HENRY   The Governor-General of Canada. [Ann Arbor, 1936] 158 leaves.
Thesis (MA) – University of Michigan.

PIERSON, COEN GALLATIN   Canada and the Privy Council. London, Stevens [c1960] xii, 119 p.
Also published Toronto, Carswell, 1960.

POWER, LAWRENCE GEOFFREY   The prerogative of dissolution. With special reference to its limitations. By Senator L. G. Power. (In *The Canadian magazine of politics, science, art and literature*. Toronto. v. 6 (1895/96), pp. [493]-502.)

The Privy Council of Canada. (In *The Dominion illustrated*. Montreal. v. 3, no. 72 (Nov. 16, 1889), p. 307.)

REDFORD, ROBERT W.   The powers of the Governor-General. (In *Saturday night*. Toronto. v. 74, no. 9 (Apr. 25, 1959), pp. 12-[13]; 45-46.)

RIDDELL, WILLIAM RENWICK   Appeals to the Privy Council. By the Honourable William Renwick Riddell. (In Empire Club of Canada. *Addresses*. Toronto. (1927), pp. 57-85.)

Address delivered March 17, 1927.

SAGE, WALTER NOBLE The position of the Lieutenant-Governor in British Columbia in the years following Confederation. By W. N. Sage. (In Flenley, Ralph (ed.) *Essays in Canadian history*. Toronto, 1939. pp. 178-203.)

SANDWELL, BERNARD KEBLE The Crown in Great Britain and Canada. By B. K. Sandwell. (In *Saturday night*. Toronto. v. 51, no. 22 (Apr. 4, 1936), p. 2.)

Discusses "the exercise by the Crown of a restraining influence upon the legislative tendencies of radical Parliaments".

—— From the editor's chair. The Crown in moments of crisis. By B. K. Sandwell. (In *Saturday night*. Toronto. v. 58, no. 31 (Apr. 10, 1943), p. 14.)

Discusses the function of the Crown in Canada.

—— From the editor's chair. What the "Free Press" is rescuing. By B. K. Sandwell. (In *Saturday night*. Toronto. v. 58, no. 45 (July 17, 1943), p. 9.)

"A reply to an editorial article in the Winnipeg Free Press", reprinted in *Saturday night* under title: A "Free Press" view of Crown and dissolution.

—— From the editor's chair. Canadian Governor General can't properly represent the King. By B. K. Sandwell. (In *Saturday night*. Toronto. v. 60, no. 49 (Aug. 11, 1945), p. 11.)

—— From week to week. Of royal governors. By B. K. Sandwell. (In *Saturday night*. Toronto. v. 54, no. 40 (Aug. 5, 1939), p. 3.)

Comments on the views expressed by Ward Price concerning the office of Governor-General.

—— Our governor general. By B. K. Sandwell. (In *Queen's quarterly*. Kingston. v. 59 (1952), pp. [84]-91.)

SAYWELL, JOHN TUPPER The office of the lieutenant-governor; a study in Canadian government and politics. [Cambridge, Mass.] 1956. 1 v.

Thesis (PH D) – Harvard University.

—— The office of lieutenant-governor; a study in Canadian government and politics. By John T. Saywell. Toronto, University of Toronto Press, 1957. xii, 302 p. (Canadian government series, 9.)

SCOTT, FRANCIS REGINALD The Privy Council and minority rights. By F. R. Scott. (In *Queen's quarterly*. Kingston. v. 37 (1930), pp. [668]-678.)

SEDGEWICK, GEORGE H. Judicial appeals to the Privy Council. II. The case for appeals. (In *Queen's quarterly*. Kingston. v. 37 (1930), pp. [474]-489.)

Part 1, The case for discontinuing appeals (pp. [456]-473) is by John S. Ewart.

Article is followed by Mr. Ewart's reply pp. [490]-494).

STRAYER, BARRY L. Crown immunity and the power of judicial review. By B. L. Strayer. (In Lang, O. E. (ed.) *Contemporary problems of public law in Canada*. [Toronto, c1968] pp. [71]-89.)

Examines "the extent and manner of modification of Crown immunity in Canada, and its relationship to the needs of Canadian federalism".

STUCHEN, PHILIP SIDNEY Canadian appeals to the judicial committee of the Privy Council; a historical review. [Kingston, Ont.] 1934. 144 leaves.

Thesis (MA) – Queen's University.

TELLIER, PAUL M. Pour une réforme des cabinets de ministres fédéraux. (In *Canadian public administration*. Toronto. v. 11 (1968), pp. [414]-427.)

TENNANT, PAUL R. French Canadian representation in the Canadian cabinet; an overview. [Chicago] 1970. 326 leaves.

Thesis (PH D) – University of Chicago.

WARD, NORMAN MC QUEEN The monarchy in society. By Norman Ward. (In *The Dalhousie review*. Halifax. v. 39 (1950/51), p. [346]-351.)

Considers the social nature of the position held by the lieutenant-governor in Canadian society.

Royal Commissions

BENNETT, GORDON LLOYD An administrator looks behind the scenes of a royal commission. [Ottawa, 1964] 198 leaves.

Thesis (MA) – Carleton University.

BRADY, ALEXANDER Royal commissions in the Dominion: a note on current political practice. By A. Brady. (In *University of Toronto quarterly*. [Toronto] v. 8 (1938/39), pp. 284-292.)

COURTNEY, JOHN CHILDS Canadian royal commissions of inquiry, 1946 to 1962; an investigation of an executive instrument of inquiry. [Durham, N.C., 1964] viii, 207 leaves.

Thesis (PH D) – Duke University.

Abstracted in *Dissertation abstracts*, v. 25 (1964), no. 5, pp. 3092-3093.

—— In defence of royal commissions. By John C. Courtney. (In *Canadian public administration*. Toronto. v. 12 (1969), pp. [198]-212.)

DOERN, G. BRUCE The role of royal commissions in the general policy process and in federal-provincial relations. (In *Canadian public administration*. Toronto. v. 10 (1967), pp. 417-433.)

FOWKE, VERNON CLIFFORD Royal commissions and Canadian agricultural policy. By V. C. Fowke. (In *The Canadian journal of economics and political science*. Toronto. v. 14 (1948), pp. 163-175.)

HANSON, HUGH R. Inside royal commissions. (In *Canadian public administration*. Toronto. v. 12 (1969), pp. [356]-364.)

HODGETTS, JOHN EDWIN The role of royal commissions in Canadian government. By J. E. Hodgetts. (In Institute of Public Administration of Canada. *Proceedings of the annual conference*. Toronto. 3d (1951), pp. 351-367.)

—— Royal commissions of inquiry in Canada; a study in investigative technique. Toronto, 1940. 274 leaves.

Thesis (MA) – University of Toronto.

—— Should Canada be de-commissioned? A commoner's view of royal commissions. By J. E. Hodgetts. (In *Queen's quarterly*. Kingston. v. 70 (1963), pp. [475]-490.)

LADANY, THOMAS A. The royal commission and its use by the government of Canada in the 1960's. [Ottawa] 1970. 132 leaves.

Thesis (MA) – Carleton University.

MAGILL, ROBERT Private business and royal commissions. (In *The Dalhousie review*. Halifax. v. 1 (1921/22), pp. [233]-242.)

PALTIEL, KHAYYAM ZEV Les commissions royales d'enquête. (In Sabourin, Louis (ed.) *Le système politique du Canada*. Ottawa, 1968. pp. [379]-388.)

SELLAR, WATSON A century of commissions of inquiry. (In *Canadian bar review*. Toronto. v. 35 (1947), pp. 1-28.)

STURSBERG, PETER Canada and its royal commissions. (In *Saturday night*. Toronto. v. 76, no. 2 (Jan. 21, 1961), pp. 12-13.)

WALLS, C. E. S. Royal commissions; their influence on public policy. (In *Canadian public administration*. Toronto. v. 12 (1969), pp. [365]-371.)

PARLIAMENT

GENERAL WORKS

AMOURS, R. D. La peine capitale et le Parlement canadien. [Québec, 1964] 1 v.

Thesis (MA) – Laval University.

ARMOUR, EDWARD DOUGLAS The Canadian legislatures and their relative powers. By E. Douglas Armour. (In *The Week*. Toronto. v. 1, no. 40 (Sept. 4, 1884), pp. 631-632.)

A review article of *Parliamentary procedure and practice*, by J. G. Bourinot. Montreal, 1884.

As volume of government business grows is Canada's Parliament really outdated? By D. L. C. (In *Canada month*. Montreal. v. 3, no. 7 [i.e. 8] (Aug. 1963), pp. 8-9.)

BARBE, RAOUL P. Le contrôle parlementaire des entreprises publiques au Canada. (In *Canadian public administration*. Toronto. v. 12 (1969), pp. [463]-480.)

BARKWAY, MICHAEL Ottawa view. Parliament and public opinion. (In *Saturday night*. Toronto. v. 68, no. 9 (Dec. 6, 1952), pp. 4; 8.)

BEAUCHESNE, ARTHUR My stand: legislatures are not parliaments! (In *Saturday night*. Toronto. v. 59, no. 12 (Nov. 27, 1943), pp. 16-17.)

First of two articles.

—— My stand: legislatures are not parliaments! (In *Saturday night*. Toronto. v. 59, no. 14 (Dec. 11, 1943), pp. 24-25.)

Second of two articles. "This article deals mainly with the claim of these bodies to the power of declaring and defining the privilege and immunities of themselves and their members. . . ."

BECK, JAMES MURRAY The argument for abolishing closure. By J. M. Beck. (In *Canadian commentator*. v. 2, no. 3 (Mar. 1958), pp. 9-10.)

—— The Canadian Parliament and divorce. By J. Murray Beck. (In *The Canadian journal of economics and political science*. [Toronto] v. 23 (1957), pp. 297-312.)

BLAIR, RONALD What happens to Parliament? (In University League for Social Reform. *Agenda 1970*. [Toronto, c1968] pp. [217]-240.)

Assesses the institution of Parliament by dealing with constitutional evolution in nineteenth-century Great Britain and the application of British constitutional development to Canada. Relates parliamentary government to the political party system.

BOND, FRANKLIN Hansard is enlivened by biting repartee. (In *Saturday night*. Toronto. v. 61, no. 30 (Mar. 30, 1946), p. 16.)

BORDEN, SIR ROBERT LAIRD Recent developments in parliamentary institutions. By R. L. Borden. (In Empire Club of Canada. *Addresses*. Toronto. (1905/06), pp. 62-72.)

At head of title: Empire Club speeches.
Address presented November 22, 1905.

BRADY, ALEXANDER The distribution of legislative power. (In Ontario Advisory Committee on Confederation. *Background papers and reports*. [Toronto, 1970] v. 2, pp. 92-114.)

BREBNER, JOHN BARTLET Patronage and parliamentary government. (In Canadian Historical Association. *Report of the annual meeting*. Toronto. (1938), pp. 22-30.)

BROWER, EDWARD JULIEN Parliamentary committees in the federal government. Toronto, 1950. 342 leaves.

Thesis (MA) – University of Toronto.

BUSING, THOMAS HERBERT Some aspects of parliamentary reform. [Ottawa] 1966. 1 v.

Thesis (MA) – Carleton University.

CLEMENT, WILLIAM HENRY POPE Has the Parliament of Canada constituent powers? By W. H. P. Clement. (In *The Week*. Toronto. v. 10, no. 45 (Oct. 6, 1893), pp. 1062-1063; v. 10, no. 47 (Oct. 20, 1893), pp. 1110-1111.)

In two parts.

COLBY, CHARLES CARROLL Parliamentary government in Canada. A lecture read before the law school of Bishop's College, Sherbrooke. Montreal, Dawson Bros., 1886. 57 p.

A Liberal-Conservative member of the House of Commons for the constituency of Stanstead, Que., 1867-1891.

DAWSON, WILLIAM FOSTER La procédure parlementaire. Par W. F. Dawson. (In Sabourin, Louis (ed.) *Le système politique du Canada*. Ottawa, 1968. pp. [141]-152.)

DEACHMAN, ROBERT JOHN Parliament and the future. By R. J. Deachman. (In *Saturday night*. Toronto. v. 58, no. 10 (Nov. 14, 1942), p. 6.)

"It is not the platform that makes the party . . . . It is the fighting power and energy of individual members in the legislative body."

—— Parliament must talk less and think more. By R. J. Deachman. (In *Saturday night*. Toronto. v. 62, no. 33 (Apr. 19, 1947), p. 21.)

". . . a former MP, makes concrete suggestions to improve the quality of debate and the dispatch of the nation's business by its legislators."

DEUTSCH, JOHN J. Parliament and the civil service. Can the complex be controlled? (In *Queen's quarterly*. Kingston. v. 63 (1956), pp. [565]-573.)

DIEFENBAKER, JOHN GEORGE The role of the Opposition. By John Diefenbaker. (In *Canada month*. Montreal. v. 3, no. 12 (Dec. 1963), pp. 21-22.)

—— The role of the Opposition in Parliament. An address by John G. Diefenbaker, member for Lake Centre, Sask. (In Empire Club of Canada. *Addresses*. Toronto. (1949/50), pp. 67-74.)

Address delivered October 27, 1949.

DUNN, OSCAR A propos de rapports parlementaires. (In *L'Opinion publique*. Montréal. v. 5, no. 20 (14 mai 1874), p. [229].)

Concerns official reporting of parliamentary debates.

EAYRS, JAMES The legislature: foreign policy, legislative-executive relations and the parliamentary system. (In Kruhlak, O. M. (comp.) *The Canadian political process*. Toronto [c1970] pp. 447-465.)

Reprinted from the author's *The art of the possible*. Toronto, 1961 (pp. 103-123).

EGGLESTON, WILFRID Leaves from a pressman's log. Parliament and the Press Gallery. (In *Queen's quarterly*. Kingston. v. 63 (1956), pp. [548]-564.)

The Author served as a member of the Press Gallery from 1929 to 1947.

—— The Ottawa letter. Parliament also operating with hand tools in a machine age. (In *Saturday night*. Toronto. v. 60, no. 25 (Feb. 24, 1945), p. 8.)

Concerns "streamlining" methods for hiring MPs, civil servants, etc.

—— Ottawa letter. Parliament has new high degree of sensitivity to problems. (In *Saturday night*. Toronto. v. 61, no. 30 (Mar. 30, 1946), p. 8.)

Comments on Parliament "as an institution."

—— Ottawa letter. Parliament needs an overhauling to deal with agenda on time. (In *Saturday night*. Toronto. v. 62, no. 39 (May 31, 1947), p. 8.)

—— Ottawa letter. No tampering with Hansard record under pressure from members. (In *Saturday night*. Toronto. v. 63, no. 21 (Feb. 28, 1948), p. 8.)

Comments on the deletion of material from *Hansard*, during an exchange between members during a debate on the Address from the Throne.

ELDON, DONALD Toward a well informed Parliament. The uses of research. (In *Queen's quarterly*. Kingston. v. 63 (1956), pp. [509]-524.)

FAUCHER DE SAINT-MAURICE, NARCISSE HENRI EDOUARD Procédure parlementaire, avec décisions des orateurs, jugements, règlements, etc., du Conseil législatif et de l'Assemblée législative (1867-1885) Texte français et anglais. Montréal, 1885. 787 p.

FISHER, DOUGLAS MASON Parliamentary committees in the 24th parliament. By D. M. Fisher. (In *Waterloo review*. Waterloo, Ont. v. 2, no. 2 (winter 1960), pp. 61-78.)

FLEMING, SIR SANDFORD An appeal to the Canadian Institute on the Rectification of Parliament. Together with the conditions on which the Council of the Institute offers to award one thousand dollars for prize essays. Toronto, Copp, Clark, 1892. 176 p.

FORSEY, EUGENE ALFRED Extension of the life of legislatures. By Eugene Forsey. (In *The Canadian journal of economics and political science*. Toronto. v. 26 (1960), pp. 604-616.)

Examines the constitutionality of the right of federal parliaments and provincial legislatures to prolong their existence in office.

FRASER, BLAIR Backstage at Ottawa. Will new rules hog-tie the opposition? (In *Maclean's*. Toronto. v. 67, no. 21 (Nov. 1, 1954), pp. 6; 66.)

Concerns new procedural rules "to lay down rigid limits for all regular debates".

—— Backstage in Ottawa. The timid bid to change the rules so Parliament can get on with the job. (In *Maclean's*. Toronto. v. 77, no. 12 (June 20, 1964), pp. 1-2.)

FRASER, THOMAS M. The golden words of Parliament. By T. M. Fraser. (In *Saturday night*. Toronto. v. 38, no. 10 [i.e. 8] (Dec. 23, 1922), p. 3.)

Comments on the decline of oratory in Parliament.

—— Taking down our members. By T. M. Fraser. (In *Maclean's*. Toronto. v. 35, no. 5 (Mar. 1, 1922), pp. 16; 47-48.)

Discusses the official reporting of the Canadian Parliament, i.e. Hansard: its historical development, nature and function.

FULTON, EDMUND DAVIE Getting things done in Parliament. By E. Davie Fulton. (In Hawkins, Gordon (ed.) *Order and good government*. [Toronto, c1965] pp. 43-50.)

—— The purpose of Parliament. By E. Davie Fulton, Progressive Conservative Member for Kamloops, B.C. (In Empire Club of Canada. *Addresses*. Toronto. (1956/57), pp. 320-335.)

Address delivered April 11, 1957.

GADSBY, HENRY FRANKLIN The message bearers. By H. F. Gadsby. (In *Saturday night*. Toronto. v. 30, no. 19 (Feb. 17, 1917), p. 4.)

Discusses function of the parliamentary message-bearer.

—— Putting the "pep" in Parliament. By H. F. Gadsby. (In *MacLean's magazine*. Toronto. v. 30, no. 8 (June 1917), pp. [36]-38; 58-62.)

GILMOR, R. PAUL The Canadian Broadcasting Corporation and parliamentary responsibility. [Windsor, Ont.] 1963. 1 v.

Thesis (MA) – University of Windsor.

GORDON, WALTER LOCKHART The need to streamline our parliamentary procedures. By Walter Gordon. (In *The Journal of liberal thought*. Ottawa. [v.] 3, no. 1 (winter 1966/67), pp. 161-166.)

"Notes for remarks by the Honorable Walter L. Gordon to the Osgoode Hall Legal and Literary Society, Toronto, Monday, March 20, 1967."

GUTHRIE, HUGH Parliamentary government. By Hon. Hugh Guthrie. (In Club canadien de Québec. *Problèmes de l'heure*. Québec, 1935. pp. 99-105.)

"From the Quebec Chronicle-Telegraph, November, 1933."

HAMBLETON, GEORGE The Parliament of Canada. [Rev.] Toronto, Ryerson Press [1961] viii, 124. p.

First published in 1951.

HARRIS, WALTER EDWARD A more business-like Parliament. Recent procedural reforms. By Walter E. Harris. (In *Queen's quarterly*. Kingston. v. 63 (1956), pp. [540]-547.)

HOCKIN, THOMAS ALEXANDER The loyal opposition in Canada; an introduction to its ideal roles and their practical implementation for representative and responsible government. [Cambridge, Mass.] 1966. xi, 446 leaves.

Thesis (PH D) – Harvard University.

HOLLAND, GEORGE CLARKE Black Rod— origin and history of this quaint office in Canada and a sketch of those who have held the post. (In *Saturday night*. Toronto. v. 37, no. 27 (May 6, 1922), pp. 2; 12.)

—— The reporting service of Parliament. An historical review of how the record of debates has been handled over a long period of years. (In *Saturday night*. Toronto. [v. 37, no. 7] (Dec. 17, 1921), pp. 2-3.)

HOPKINS, EDWARD RUSSELL How Parliament works; an examination of the functioning of the Parliament of Canada. By E. Russell Hopkins. [Ottawa, Queen's Printer, 1966] 50 p.

"Reprinted from Current Affairs, no. 2 in the Citizenship series, Bureau of Current Affairs, Department of National Defence, Ottawa, Canada 1953, revised 1957. Reprinted 1963 and 1966". – Verso of title-page.

—— Saving Parliament's time. Some needed reforms. By E. R. Hopkins. (In *Queen's quarterly*. Kingston. v. 61 (1954), pp. [516]-528.)

Proposes concrete procedural reforms to speed parliamentary business.

JEWETT, PAULINE MAE The reform of Parliament. By Pauline Jewett. (In *Journal of Canadian studies*. Peterborough, Ont. v. 1, no. 3 (1966), pp. 11-16.)

—— Run for Parliament and you invite exhaustion, frustration. An ex-MP tells why people do it. By Pauline Jewett. (In *Maclean's*. Toronto. v. 81, no. 8 (Aug. 1968), pp. 8; 56.)

KEAR, ALLEN R. The parliamentary secretary in Britain and in Canada; a comparative study.

Thesis (MA) – Queen's University.

KING, T. W. Once again Parliament. A glimpse behind the drop curtain at the Government opera. (In *The Canadian courier*. Toronto. v. 10 [i.e. 8] No. 24 [i.e. 25] (Nov. 19, 1910), pp. 12-13.)

Brief remarks on the institution of Parliament.

KNOWLES, STANLEY HOWARD Parliamentary rules and procedures. By Stanley Knowles. (In Hawkins, Gordon (ed.) *Order and good government*. [Toronto, c1965] pp. 69-75.)

—— The role of the Opposition in Parliament. (In Empire Club of Canada. *Addresses*. Toronto. (1956/57), pp. 290-301.)

Address delivered March 21, 1957.

—— The role of the Opposition in Parliament. [Toronto, Ont. Woodsworth Memorial Foundation, 1957] 11 p.

Cover title.

Text of an address delivered to the Empire Club of Canada, Toronto, March 21, 1957.

—— Some thoughts on parliamentary procedure. Safeguarding basic rights. By Stanley Knowles. (In *Queen's quarterly*. Kingston. v. 63 (1956), pp. [525]-527.)

KORNBERG, ALLAN Some differences in role perception among Canadian legislators. [Ann Arbor] University of Michigan, 1964. x, 274 leaves.

Thesis (PH D) – University of Michigan. Abstracted in *Dissertation abstracts*, v. 25 (1965), no. 10, pp. 6040-6041.

LAJOIE, ANDREE Le pouvoir déclaratoire du parlement. Augmentation discrétionnaire de la compétence fédérale du Canada.

Montréal, Presses de l'Université de Montréal, 1969. 164 p. (Collection: Institut de recherche en droit public.)

"Etude commanditée par le Comité parlementaire de la Constitution". – Verso of title-page.

LANDON, FRED The Dominion Parliament. (In *The Canadian magazine of politics, science, art and literature*. Toronto. v. 60 (1922/23), pp. 287-292.)

LAWRENCE, MARGARET Democratic symbolism. (In *Saturday night*. Toronto. v. 53, no. 14 (Feb. 5, 1938), p. [1].)

Comments on the ceremonies during the opening of Parliament.

LEGGO, WILLIAM Are legislatures parliaments! (In Rose-Belford's *Canadian monthly and national review*. Toronto. v. 3 (1879), pp. 345-358.)

A review article of *Are legislatures parliaments? A study and review*, by Fennings Taylor. Montreal, Lovell, 1879.

LERY, LOUIS C. DE Le divorce au Parlement. (In *Relations*. Montréal. 20. année, no 230 (fév. 1960), pp. 34-36.)

Discusses the report of the British Royal Commission on Marriage and Divorce, 1951-55, relating it to the Canadian situation.

LEWIS, JOHN The business of legislation. (In *The University magazine*. Montreal. v. 6 (1907), pp. [299]-307.)

LLOYD, TREVOR OWEN The reform of parliamentary proceedings. By Trevor Lloyd. (In University League for Social Reform. *The prospect of change*. Toronto [c1965] pp. 23-39.)

MACDONNELL, J. M. Parliament and the purse. Current procedure and problems. (In *Queen's quarterly*. Kingston. v. 63 (1956), pp. [528]-539.)

THE MACE Making Hansard popular. By the Mace. (In *Saturday night*. Toronto. v. 39, no. 35 (July 19, 1924), p. 4.)

MC GEACHY, JAMES BURNS Our Parliament; its organization and work. By J. B. McGeachy of the Globe and Mail, Toronto. (In Empire Club of Canada. *Addresses*. Toronto. (1954/55), pp. 151-160.)

Address delivered January 20, 1955.

MAC KAY, DOUGLAS Embalmers of oratory. (In *Maclean's*. Toronto. v. 40, no. 6 (Mar. 15, 1927), p. 10.)

". . . four million words a year . . . and Hansard has to record every one of them."

MAC LEOD, NORMAN M. The handwriting on Parliament's wall. (In Empire Club of Canada. *Addresses*. Toronto. (1937/38), pp. 357-375.)

Address delivered April 21, 1938.

Contends that there is a "progressive weakening" of the "democratic national legislature of this Dominion".

MALLORY, JAMES RUSSELL The courts and the sovereignty of the Canadian Parliament. By J. R. Mallory. In *The Canadian journal of economics and political science*. [Toronto] v. 10 (1944), pp. 165-178.)

—— Delegated legislation in Canada: recent changes in machinery. By J. R. Mallory. (In *The Canadian journal of economics and political science*. [Toronto] v. 19 (1953), pp. 462-471.)

Examines the necessity to create machinery in order "that bureaucratic legislation may receive the same debate, critcism and review as ordinary legislation".

—— The uses of legislative committees. By J. R. Mallory. (In *Canadian public administration*. Toronto. v. 6 (1963), pp. 1-14.)

"This paper was presented to the fourteenth annual conference of the Institute of Public Administration of Canada, September 5 to 8, 1962, Regina, Saskatchewan."

MOORE, WILLIAM HENRY Parliament and economic control. (In *The University of Toronto quarterly*. [Toronto] v. 4 (1934/35), pp. 315-326.)

MUNRO, J. K. Conversation vs. closure. (In *Maclean's*. Toronto. v. 34, no. 9 (May 1, 1921), pp. 28-29.)

—— Parliament is death on precedents. (In *Maclean's*. Toronto. v. 34, no. 11 (June 1, 1921), pp. 20-21; 40.)

NASEER, SYED MOHAMED Parliament and the public corporations in Canada; a study in public ownership and accountability. [Montreal, 1962] 1 v.

Thesis (MA) – McGill University.

NEWMAN, PETER CHARLES What is wrong with Parliament? An address by Peter C. Newman. (In Empire Club of Canada. *Addresses*. [Don Mills, Ont.] (1963/64), pp. [108]-117.)

Address delivered November 21, 1963.

NIELSEN, ERIK The duty of the Opposition. [In *Commentator*. Toronto. v. 10, no. 5 (May 1966), pp. 12-13; 15.)

"Erik Nielsen, QC, is the PC member of Parliament for the Yukon."

NIELSEN, RICHARD Let's *see* our politicians at work. (In *Maclean's*. Toronto. v. 81, no. 9 (Sept. 1968), pp. 36-37.)

Argues the point for television as an asset in public affairs and for televised coverage of Parliament.

O'LEARY, MICHAEL GRATTAN The decline of oratory in Parliament. By M. Grattan O'Leary. (In *The Dalhousie review*. Halifax. v. 2 (1922/23), pp. [161]-164.)

—— What's wrong with Parliament? By M. Grattan O'Leary. (In *Maclean's*. Toronto. v. 52, no. 1 (Jan. 1, 1939), pp. 7; 24.)

OLLIVIER, MAURICE Le Parlement et la confection des lois. (In *Revue de l'Université d'Ottawa*. [Ottawa] 16. année (1946), pp. [71]-84.)

An historical and comparative analysis.

OXLEY, JAMES MACDONALD Official reporting in Parliament. (In *The Week*. Toronto. v. 1, no. 7 (Jan. 17, 1884), pp. 100-101.)

PENDRITH, ROBERT Whigs, Tories and bomb plots. (In *Canadian life*. Toronto. v. 1, no. 3 (winter 1949/50), pp. 5; 33.)

Compares briefly the procedure of a British and Canadian parliamentary session.

POULIOT, JEAN FRANCOIS My fight with Parliament. (In *New world*. Toronto. v. 7, no. 5 (July 1946), p. 18.)

Contends that "the main issue is the return of responsible government".

RICHER, LEOPOLD Le Parlement et les parlementaires. (In *L'Action nationale*. Montréal. v. 15 (jan. 1940), pp. [15]-25.)

"Extrait de la préface de Silhouettes du monde politique."

The Rights of Parliament. (In *The Week*. Toronto. v. 10, no. 11 (Feb. 10, 1893), pp. 245-246.)

Concerns the presentation of documents to Parliament.

ROBERTSON, R. G. The Canadian Parliament and cabinet in the face of modern demands. (In *Canadian public administration*. Toronto. v. 11 (1968), pp. [272]-279.)

"This paper was presented at the 1967 annual conference of the Institute of Public Administration of Canada."

—— The Canadian Parliament and cabinet in the face of modern demands. (In

Vaughan, Frederick (ed.) *Contemporary issues in Canadian politics*. Scarborough, Ont. [c1970] p. 151-158.)

Reprinted from *Canadian public administration*, Toronto, v. 11, no. 3 (1968).

ROBINETTE, JOHN J. Radio legislation. Can it be enacted by the Dominion Parliament? (In *The Canadian forum*. Toronto. v. 11, no. 128 (May 1931), pp. 294-295.)

SANDWELL, BERNARD KEBLE From the editor's chair. Hansard is not only readable but it also has its humors. By B. K. Sandwell. (In *Saturday night*. Toronto. v. 59, no. 26 (Mar. 4, 1944), p. 15.)

—— That "supreme" Parliament. If a limited legislature is not parliamentary then Canada has already abandoned the parliamentary constitution. By B. K. Sandwell. (In *Saturday night*. Toronto. v. 66, no. 21 (Feb. 27, 1951), p. 7.)

SCHMITT, GILBERT R. The jurisdiction of the Canadian Parliament in matters of labour legislation. (In Corry, J. A. (ed.) *Legal essays in honour of Arthur Moxon*. [Toronto] 1953. pp. 49-66.)

SEGAL, NORTON HART The parliamentary question in Canada. [Montreal] 1965. 1 v.
Thesis (MA) – McGill University.

SMITH, BROCK AUSTIN The legislative role of parliamentary committees in Canada. A case study of the Special Joint Committee of the Senate and the House of Commons on employer-employee relations in the public service of Canada. [Montreal] 1969. 109 leaves.
Thesis (MA) – McGill University.
Half-title: The Public Service Committee, 1966-67; a case study.

SMITH, DENIS President and Parliament; the transformation of parliamentary government in Canada. (In Kruhlak, O. M. (comp.) *The Canadian political process*. Toronto [c1970] pp. 367-382.)

"This paper was presented to the Priorities for Canada Conference, Niagara Falls, Ontario, October 10, 1969."

SMITH, IRVING NORMAN Hansard—the story of the making of Hansard—official record of the debates in Canada's Houses of Parliament. By I. Norman Smith. (In *Maclean's*. Toronto. v. 53, no. 17 (Sept. 1, 1940), pp. 8; 28-29.)

STEVENSON, JOHN A. Dreary politics. The last session at Ottawa underlines need for some streamlining. By J. A. Stevenson. (In

Canadian commentator. Toronto. v. 4, no. 9 (Sept. 1960), pp. 4-5.)

Presents the third session of the 24th parliament as an illustrative example to advocate efficiency in parliamentary procedures.

—— Ottawa letter. Parliamentary pay and allowances. (In *Saturday night.* Toronto. v. 69, no. 16 (Jan. 23, 1954), p. 12.)

—— Ottawa letter. Manners and morals. (In *Saturday night.* Toronto. v. 73, no. 19 (Sept. 13, 1958), pp. 6-7.)

Comments on parliamentary deportment.

STEWART, JOHN BENJAMIN Parliament and executive in wartime Canada, 1939-1945. [New York, 1954] 275 leaves.

Thesis (PH D) – Columbia University.

STURSBERG, PETER Postmark Ottawa. (In *The Canadian Saturday night.* Toronto. v. 78, no. 1 (Jan. 1963), pp. 7-8.)

Discusses parliamentary reform.

TAYLOR, FENNINGS Are legislatures parliaments? A study and review. Montreal, J. Lovell, 1879. 208 p.

TODD, ALFRED Traité sur les formalités à suivre pour obtenir ou contester la passation de bills privés dans le Parlement du Canada; et ordres permanents des deux Chambres à cet égard. 4. éd. Ottawa, Hunter Rose et Lemieux, 1869. vii, 165 p.

"L'édition actuelle de cet ouvrage fut alors preparée sous l'autorité de l'Assemblée Législative, pour l'usage de la Législature de Québec". - Préf.

—— A treatise on the proceedings to be adopted in conducting or opposing private bills in the Parliament of Canada. And the standing orders of both Houses in relation thereto. 3d ed., embracing the latest changes in the practice. Ottawa, J. Durie, 1868. iv, 159 p.

TOOMBS, WILBERT NELSON An analysis of parliamentary debates on federal financial participation in education in Canada, 1867-1960. [Edmonton, Alta.] 1966. 1 v.

Thesis (PH D) – University of Alberta.

TUCK, RAPHAEL The dangers of dissolution of Parliament. (In *Public affairs.* Halifax. v. 9, no. 4 (Sept. 1946), pp. 215-219.)

Discusses a proposal "suggested by the Progressive Conservative Party that the term of the Canadian Parliament be fixed in duration".

UNDERHILL, FRANK HAWKINS Parliament and the constitution. (In League for So-

cial Reconstruction. Research Committee. *Social planning for Canada.* Toronto [c1935] pp. 489-511.)

Author identified in *On Canada; essays in honour of Frank H. Underhill.* Edited by N. Penlington. [Toronto] University of Toronto Press, 1971 ("Bibliography": p. 134).

WALKER, HARRY W. Parliamentary procedure. By H. W. Walker (In *Queen's quarterly.* Kingston. v. 58 (1951), pp. [228]-236.)

—— Question time in Parliament. (In *Queen's quarterly.* Kingston. v. 59 (1952), pp. [64]-71.)

Argues for a reform of the question-and-answer procedures.

WARD, NORMAN MC QUEEN Confederation and responsible government. By Norman Ward. (In *The Canadian journal of economics and political science.* Toronto. v. 24 (1958), pp. 44-56.)

Examines the legislative aspects of government financial control. Considers, primarily, the function of Parliament.

WATSON, SAMUEL JAMES The powers of Canadian parliaments. By S. J. Watson. (In Rose-Belford's *Canadian monthly and national review.* Toronto. v. 3 (1879), pp. [561]-571.)

—— The powers of Canadian parliaments. By S. J. Watson. Toronto, C. B. Robinson, printer, 1880. xii, 160 p.

WAYLING, THOMAS Hansard is as Hansard does—all for $3.00. (In *Saturday night.* Toronto. v. 59, no. 34 (Apr. 29, 1944), pp. 16-17.)

"Here is an account of how the Hansard reporters work and why it is that reports are so accurate."

WEIR, WILLIAM GILBERT Minding parliament's business. The party whip. By W. G. Weir. (In *Queen's quarterly.* Kingston. v. 63 (1956), pp. [503]-508.)

WHITTAKER, G. C. The Ottawa letter. Parliament's servants have no sinecures. (In *Saturday night.* Toronto. v. 57, no. 44 (July 1942), p. 10.)

Concerns the inefficiencies related to the parliamentary machinery of government.

WILSON, KENNETH R. Backstage at Ottawa. By the Man with a Notebook. (In *Maclean's.* Toronto. v. 55, no. 17 (Sept. 1, 1942), pp. 15; 34.)

Discusses improving the procedure of parliamentary debate.

WOODSWORTH, JAMES SHAVER Canada's parliamentary machine. How the wheels go 'round. By J. S. Woodsworth. (In *Canadian Congress journal*. Montreal. v. 6, no. 3 (Mar. 1927), pp. 9-12.)

"Diagram showing the interlocking of the various departments and affiliations of the Federal Government and the several provinces": p. 11.

—— Parliament as a social welfare agency. By J. S. Woodsworth. (In *Canadian Congress journal*. Montreal. v. 7, no. 9 (Sept. 1928), pp. 25-27.)

YOUNG, E. C. Parliament can't get on without Hansard. (In *Saturday night*. Toronto. v. 61, no. 14 (Dec. 8, 1945), pp. 24-25.)

The Senate

ACHINTRE, AUGUSTE Semaine politique. Par A. Achintre. (In *L'Opinion publique*. Montréal. v. 6, no. 10 (11 mars 1875), pp. 118-119.)

Concerns the motion by David Mills for the reorganization of the Senate, and other matters.

ALBINSKI, HENRY S. The Canadian Senate; politics and the constitution. (In Kruhlak, O. M. *The Canadian political process*. Toronto [c1970] pp. 398-418.)

Reprinted from *American political science review*, Washington, D.C., v. 57 (1963), pp. 378-391.

BELDING, A. M. The Fathers and the Senate. (In *Saturday night*. Toronto. v. 49, no. 49 (Oct. 13, 1934), p. 12.)

Refers to the concept and function of the Senate as viewed by the Fathers of Confederation.

BONENFANT, JEAN CHARLES Le Sénat. (In Sabourin, Louis (ed.) *Le système politique du Canada*. Ottawa, 1968. pp. [131]-139.)

BRIGGS, ELSWORTH DONALD The Senate: reform or reconstruction? By E. D. Briggs. (In *Queen's quarterly*. Kingston. v. 75 (1968), pp. [91]-104.)

CAMPBELL, EDWIN COLIN Role perceptions of Canadian senators. [Edmonton, Alta.] 1966. 1 v.

Thesis (MA) – University of Alberta.

CANADA. PRIME MINISTER'S OFFICE The future of the Senate. By the Government of Canada. (In Vaughan, Frederick (ed.) *Contemporary issues in Canadian politics*. Scarborough, Ont. [c1970] pp. 196-198.)

"Included in the Constitution and the people of Canada, published by the Government of Canada on the occasion of the second meeting of the Constitutional Conference, February, 1969."

CARMAN, FRANCIS ASBURY The Maritime grievance and Senate reform. (In *MacLean's magazine*. Toronto. v. 21, no. 6 (Apr. 1911), pp. [52]-55.)

CHAUVIN, GUY The Senate of Canada. With particular reference to the Diefenbaker years. [Halifax, N.S.] 1966. 1 v.

Thesis (MA) – Dalhousie University.

CONSEIL DE LA VIE FRANCAISE EN AMERIQUE La représentation canadienne-française au Sénat canadien. Québec, Editions Ferland, 1966. 27 p.

Added title page in English: *French-Canadian representation in the Canadian Senate*. Text in English and French.

The Constitution of the Senate. (In *The Nation*. Toronto. v. 1, no. 3 (Apr. 16, 1874), p. 35.)

Argues for a Senate selected by means of indirect election.

CROWTHER, KEITH F. The Senate of Canada, 1867-1884. [Kingston, Ont.] 1925. 97 leaves.

Thesis (MA) – Queen's University.

DAVID, LAURENT OLIVIER Réforme du Sénat. (In his *Au soir de la vie*. Montréal, 1924. pp. [235]-239.)

—— Le sénat, sa mission et ses œuvres. (In his *Au soir de la vie*. Montréal, 1924. pp. [219]-226.)

DAVIS, THOMAS OSBORNE The Senate and Senate reform. By Hon. T. Osborne Davis. (In *The Canadian courier*. Toronto. v. 3, no. 15 (Mar. 14, 1908), pp. 10-11.)

The Debate on the reform of the Senate. (In *The Nation*. Toronto. v. 2, no. 10 (Mar. 12, 1875), pp. 115-117.)

A Doomed Senate. (In *The Nation*. Toronto. v. 2, no. 9 (Mar. 5, 1875), p. 102.)

Discusses the scheme for a reformed Senate presented by David Mills.

EGGLESTON, WILFRID Capital comment. Senate asks "Commons reform". (In *Saturday night*. Toronto. v. 65, no. 35 (June 6, 1950), p. 3.)

—— Capital comment. Senate reform again to fare. (In *Saturday night*. Toronto v. 66, no. 21 (Feb. 27, 1951), p. 3.)

—— Capital comment. Ways to reform the Senate. (In *Saturday night*. Toronto. v. 66, no. 24 (Mar. 20, 1951), p. 3.)

—— Capital comment. A senator deals with critics. (In *Saturday night*. Toronto. v. 66, no. 43 (July 31, 1951), p. 3.)
Senator Thomas Farquhar answers a broadcast commentary criticizing the Senate and its function.

—— The Ottawa letter. Despite criticism, the Senate is useful and can be more so. (In *Saturday night*. Toronto. v. 61, no. 10 (Nov. 10, 1945), p. 8.)

—— Ottawa letter. How to insure adequate opposition in gradually one-sided Senate? (In *Saturday night*. Toronto. v. 63, no. 26 (Apr. 3, 1948), p. 8.)
Comments on the predominantly Liberal Party membership of the Senate.

FLAHERTY, J. FRANCIS Ottawa letter. Provincial government selections proposed as reform for Senate. By Frank Flaherty. (In *Saturday night*. Toronto. v. 62, no. 49 (Aug. 9, 1947), p. 8.)

—— The Senate could take a hand in control. By Francis Flaherty. (In *Saturday night*. Toronto. v. 60, no. 26 (Mar. 3, 1945), p. 11.)
Conceives the Senate as performing an investigating function in conjunction with the House of Commons.

FORSEY, EUGENE ALFRED Appointment of extra senators under Section 26 of the British North America Act. By Eugene Forsey. (In *The Canadian journal of economics and political science*. [Toronto] v. 12 (1946), pp. 159-167.)
Illustrates the discussion with several historical examples from governing administrations commencing with the government of Alexander Mackenzie, which took office November 7, 1873.

—— A bi-national Second Chamber? By Eugene Forsey. (In *The Canadian forum*. Toronto. v. 44, no. 526 (Nov. 1964), pp. [169]-171.)
A reply to A bi-national Second Chamber, by Trevor Lloyd. (In *The Canadian forum*. Toronto. v. 44, no. 521 (1964), pp. 69-70.)

—— The Senate. By Eugene Forsey. (In Ontario Advisory Committee on Confederation. *Background papers and reports*. [Toronto, 1970] v. 2, pp. 356-363.)

FRASER, BLAIR Here is the new Senate chosen by ten well known Canadians. And Blair Fraser tells this is why we need it. (In *Maclean's*. Toronto. v. 67, no. 8 (Apr. 15, 1954), pp. [12]-13; 107-111.)

GADSBY, HENRY FRANKLIN Over the Speaker's chair. By H. F. Gadsby. (In *Saturday night*. Toronto. v. 28, no. 28 (Apr. 24, 1915), p. 4.)
Concerns the Senate.

—— The Senate reborn. By H. F. Gadsby. (In *Saturday night*. Toronto. v. 32, no. 40 (July 19, 1919), pp. 4; 10.)
A historical discussion of the Senate.

—— Shall we slay the Senate? By H. F. Gadsby. (In *MacLean's magazine*. Toronto. v. 30, no. 6 (Apr. 1917), pp. [29]-31; 77-80.)

GELINAS, AIME Le "Globe" et le Sénat. Par A. Gélinas. (In *L'Opinion publique*. Montréal. v. 11, no. 24 (10 juin 1880), pp. [277]-278.)
Discusses the sudden change in the *Globe's* position concerning the Senate.

—— Le Sénat. Par A. Gélinas. (In *L'Opinion publique*. Montréal. v. 10, no. 11 (13 mars 1879), p. [121].)

GRAY, JAMES HENRY In defence of the Senate. By James H. Gray. (In *The Canadian forum*. Toronto. v. 15, no. 169 (Oct. 1934), pp. 18-19.)

HAGUE, GEORGE The rationale of a second parliamentary Chamber. (In Royal Society of Canada. *Proceedings and transactions*. Ottawa. ser. 2, v. 4 (1898), section 2, pp. 43-51.)
"Communicated by Sir John Bourinot and read May 26th, 1898."

HANNAY, ARTHUR BURNS Canadian Senate a national asset. By Arthur Hannay. (In *Maclean's*. Toronto. v. 38, no. 8 (Apr. 15, 1925), pp. 26; 49; 52.)

—— National affairs—the valuable work of our Upper Chamber. By A. B. Hannay. (In *MacLean's magazine*. Toronto. v. 28, no. 2 (Dec. 1914), pp. [5]-8; 119.)

HOLLAND, GEORGE CLARKE The House impregnable. (In *The Canadian magazine of politics, science, art and literature*. Toronto. v. 43 (1914), pp. 50-54.)
Concerns the Senate of Canada.

—— The Red Chamber; an appreciation of the Canadian Senate. By George Clarke Holland, Official reporter of the Senate. (In *The Canadian magazine of politics, science, art and literature*. Toronto. v. 37 (1911), pp. 156-164.)

HOYT, WILLIAM LLOYD The composition of the Canadian Senate, 1935-51. [Wolfville, N.S., 1952] 123 leaves.
Thesis (MA) – Acadia University.

IRVINE, WILLIAM   Re-organizing the Senate. By Wm. Irvine. (In *Canadian Congress journal*. Montreal. v. 4, no. 1 (Jan. 1925), pp. 39-40.)

JONCAS, PIERRE   Introduction au problème de la représentation des intérêts au Sénat canadien. [Québec, 1958] 1 v.
Thesis (MA) – Laval University.

KETTLE, JOHN   The Senate. (In *Canada month*. Montreal. v. 5, no. 1 (Jan. 1965), pp. 11-15.)

KUNZ, FRANK ANDREW   The modern Senate of Canada, 1925-1963; a re-appraisal. By F. A. Kunz. Toronto, University of Toronto Press [c1965] xii, 395 p. (Canadian government series, 15.)

—— Second chambers; a comparative study with special reference to the Senate of Canada. [Montreal] 1961. 1 v.
Thesis (MA) – McGill University.

—— The Senate and contemporary politics, 1925-1961; a re-appraisal [Montreal] 1963. 1 v.
Thesis (PH D) – McGill University.

LANDRY, PHILIPPE   La représentation de la race française au Sénat. Par P. Landry. (In *L'Action française*. Montréal. 1. année (mars 1917), pp. [65]-73.)

LEDERLE, JOHN W.   Party forms in the Senate. (In *Queen's quarterly*. Kingston. v. 57 (1950), pp. [21]-32.)

LERY, LOUIS C. DE   Le divorce au Sénat. (In *Relations*. Montréal. 16. année, no 187 (juil. 1956), pp. 195-197.)

LLOYD, TREVOR OWEN   A bi-national Second Chamber. By Trevor Lloyd. (In *The Canadian forum*. Toronto. v. 44, no. 521 (June 1964), pp. 69-70.)
The Author argues "that Canada should have a Second Chamber elected on a basis of equal representation for French-Canada and English-Canada . . ."
For a rejoinder see A bi-national Second Chamber? by Eugene Forsey. (In *The Canadian forum*. Toronto. v. 44, no. 526 (1964), pp. [169]-171.)

LYON, PEYTON VAUGHN   A new idea for Senate reform. Give the provinces more power and say in the Canadian Senate as is done in West Germany. . . . By Peyton V. Lyon. (In *The Canadian commentator*. Toronto. v. 6, no. 7-8 (July-Aug. 1962), pp. 24-25.)

MC CONNELL, HOWARD   Constitutional reform. A comprehensive review of Senates,

past and present. (In *Saturday night*. Toronto. v. 36 no. 6 (Dec. 4, 1920), p. 2; v. 36, no. 7 (Dec. 11, 1920), p. 2.)
In two parts.

THE MACE   The empty cupboard. By the Mace. (In *Saturday night*. Toronto. v. 39, no. 24 (May 3, 1924), p. 4.)
Comments on the lack of work for the Senate.

—— No outsiders need apply. By the Mace. (In *Saturday night*. Toronto. v. 36, no. 7 (Dec. 11, 1920), p. 4.)
Concerns selection of members to the Senate.

—— Something for the Senate's stocking. By the Mace. (In *Saturday night*. Toronto. v. 40, no. 5 (Dec. 20, 1924), p. 4.)
Concerns Senate reform.

—— Women for the Senate. By the Mace. (In *Saturday night*. Toronto. v. 38, no. 32 (June 16, 1923), p. 4.)
Concerns a proposal for women Senators.

MAC GREGOR, IAN   A history of Senate reform in Canada, 1867-1957. [Kingston, Ont.] 1957. 299 leaves.
Thesis (MA) – Queen's University.

MAC KAY, ROBERT ALEXANDER   Here's how to reform the Senate. By R. A. MacKay. (In *Commentator*. Toronto. v. 7, no. 5 (May 1963), pp. 2-3.)

—— To end or mend the Senate. By R. H. [*sic*] MacKay. (In *Queen's quarterly*. Kingston. v. 71 (1964), pp. [287]-296.)

—— The unreformed Senate of Canada. With an introd. by George M. Wrong. London, Oxford University Press, 1926. xvi, 284 p.
Thesis (PH D) – Princeton University, 1924.

—— The unreformed Senate of Canada. Rev. ed. Toronto, McClelland and Stewart [c1963] 216 p. (The Carleton library, no. 6.)
First ed. published: London, Oxford University Press, 1926.
Published also as thesis (PH D) Princeton University, 1924.

MEIGHEN, ARTHUR   The Canadian Senate. (In *Queen's quarterly*. Kingston. v. 44 (1937), pp. [152]-163.)
"This article has been revised by the author for Queen's quarterly from a speech delivered by him before the Canadian Club, Montreal."

MENARD, C.   Le Bill C-72; tarif douanier et le Sénat canadien. [Québec, 1962] 1 v.

Thesis (MA) – Laval University.

MORIN, JACQUES YVAN   Un nouveau rôle pour un Sénat moribond. (In Cité libre. Montréal. no. 68 (juin-juil. 1964), pp. 3-7.)

MOWAT, HERBERT MACDONALD   Mend, not end, the Senate. By H. M. Mowat. (In Queen's quarterly. Kingston. v. 15 (1907/08), pp. [42]-47.)

"Schedule of senatorial districts [and] Present representation": p. 47.

A New Senate . . . Maclean's presents nominations for an entirely new Senate, chosen from all walks of life by a special panel of non-partisan contributions representing all the provinces. (In Maclean's. Toronto. v. 67, no. 8 (Apr. 15, 1954), pp. 11; 112-116.)

NICOLET, JEAN   Le Sénat est-il intouchable? (In L'Action nationale. Montréal. v. 27 (fév. 1946), pp. 127-131.)

The Nominated Chamber. (In The Nation. v. 1, no. 32 (Nov. 5, 1874), p. 380.)

An historical and comparative analysis of the Senate.

O'LEARY, MICHAEL GRATTAN   What of the Senate? The pros and cons of the movement for reform of the Dominion's Upper Chamber. By M. Grattan O'Leary. (In Maclean's. Toronto. v. 41, no. 1 (Jan. 1, 1928), pp. 14-15; 40-41.)

PEPIN, JEAN LUC   Relance d'un éternel problème: réforme ou abolition du Sénat. (In Le Magazine Maclean. Montréal. v. 1, no. 6 (août 1961), p. 2.)

POWER, LAWRENCE GEOFFREY   The Second Chamber. By Senator L. G. Power. (In The Canadian magazine of politics, science, art and literature. Toronto. v. 56 (1920/21), pp. 544-545.)

RICHARDSON, BURTON TAYLOR   Ottawa view. Again, Senate reform. May become completely one-party House; the Carnegie proposal. By B. T. Richardson. (In Saturday night. Toronto. v. 64, no. 42 (July 26, 1949), p. 4.)

RODGERS, RAYMOND   Ottawa letter. Senate stance: fact and fiction. (In Saturday night. Toronto. v. 76, no. 16 (Aug. 5, 1961), pp. 23-24.)

ROEBUCK, ARTHUR WENTWORTH   Tinkering with Senate of doubtful value. By A. W.

Roebuck. (In Saturday night. Toronto. v. 69, no. 21 (Feb. 27, 1954), pp. 7-8.)

—— What should be done with the Canadian Senate? An exchange of views by the Honourable Arthur Roebuck, a member of the Senate of Canada and B. T. Richardson, Editor of the Toronto Telegram. (In Empire Club of Canada. Addresses. Toronto. (1958/59), pp. 261-273.)

Address delivered March 12, 1959.

ROSS, SIR GEORGE WILLIAM   The Senate of Canada; its constitution, powers and duties. Historically considered by Sir George Ross. Toronto, Copp, Clark Co. [1914] xvi, 124 p.

—— Senate reform. By Hon. Geo. W. Ross. (In Canadian Club of Toronto. Addresses. Toronto. (1907/08), pp. 161-165.)

Address delivered April 21, 1908.

—— Senate reform according to the constitution. (In The Canadian magazine of politics, science, art and literature. Toronto. v. 37 (1911), pp. 231-235.)

SANDWELL, BERNARD KEBLE   From week to week. Ottawa's House of Lords. By B. K. Sandwell. (In Saturday night. Toronto. v. 53, no. 45 (Sept. 10, 1938), p. 3.)

Concerns the Senate.

The Senate's "veto". (In The Nation. Toronto. v. 1, no. 8 (May 21, 1874), p. 92.)

Discusses the principle of senatorial independent judgment, citing the issue over a measure passed by the House of Commons to transfer the electoral riding of Tuckersmith.

SHAW, HUGH   Should the Senate be reformed? (In New world. Toronto. v. 7, no. 4 (June 1946), pp. 9-11.)

SILCOX, CLARIS EDWIN   What to do with the Senate. The Senate should not only represent provincial interests, and perform its review function; in a modernized democracy it should also represent Management and Labor, Educators, Consumers, etc. (In Canadian commentator. Toronto. v. 1, no. 8 (Aug. 1957), p. 3.)

The second of two articles on the Senate.

—— Why we have a Senate. (In Canadian commentator. Toronto. v. 1, no. 7 (July 1957), p. 13.)

First of two articles on the Senate.

SIMON, PETER S.   Reform of the Senate. To give senators the business business practices proposed. (In Canadian commentator. Toronto. v. 4, no. 11 (Nov. 1960), pp. 13-15.)

SMITH, GOLDWIN   Reform of the Senate. (In *The Canadian magazine of politics, science, art, and literature.* Toronto. v. 30 (1907/08), pp. 491-493.)

SOULSBY, E. J.   Another suggestion for Senate reformers. (In *The Canadian forum.* Toronto. v. 7, no. 73 (Oct. 1926), pp. 397-398.)

—— The Senate; a suggestion. (In *The Canadian forum.* Toronto. v. 6, no. 65 (Feb. 1926), pp. 141-142.)

STEVENSON, JOHN A.   All the parties should advocate early reform of the Senate. (In *Saturday night.* Toronto. v. 64, no. 8 (Nov. 27, 1948), pp. 6-7.)

—— Ottawa letter. Much reluctance on reform. (In *Saturday night.* Toronto. v. 69, no. 37 (June 19, 1954), pp. 12-13.)
Concerns reform of the Senate.

—— Ottawa letter. Senators fail to view with alarm. (In *Saturday night.* Toronto. v. 70, no. 33 (June 11, 1955), p. 13.)
Comments on the reaction to a bill introduced by W. D. Euler dealing with the filling of vacancies in the Senate.

—— Ottawa letter. Some new blood but no reform. (In *Saturday night.* Toronto. v. 70, no. 38 (Aug. 20, 1955), pp. 11-12.)
Concerns the Senate.

STURSBERG, PETER   Ottawa letter. The curious ways of senators. (In *Saturday night.* Toronto. v. 77, no. 6 (Mar. 17, 1962), pp. 29-30.)
Discussion on the Senate, prompted by the resignation of John Thomas Haig.

TANGUAY, F.   Le bicaméralisme et son application au Sénat canadien. Ottawa, 1952. 1 v.
Thesis (MA) – University of Ottawa.

TURNER, JOHN NAPIER   The Senate of Canada—political conundrum. By John N. Turner. (In Clark, R. M. (ed.) *Canadian issues.* Toronto. [c1961] pp. [57]-80.)

WARD, NORMAN MCQUEEN   Senatorial scoreboard, haste and leisure. By Norman Ward. (In *Saturday night.* Toronto. v. 69, no. 35 (June 5, 1954), pp. 7-8.)

WATTS, R. L.   Second chambers in federal political systems. (In Ontario Advisory Committee on Confederation. *Background papers and reports.* [Toronto, 1970] v. 2, pp. 315-355.)

WHITE, J. FRANCIS   Unrest in the Senate. By J. F. White. (In *The Canadian forum.*

Toronto. v. 7, no. 80 (May 1927), pp. 230-231.)

WILES, LAURA MARION   The Senate of Canada, 1950-1954. [Kingston, Ont., 1955] 101 leaves.
Thesis (MA) – Queen's University.

The House of Commons

Representation

ARCHAMBAULT, JEAN BAPTISTE   Réformes electorales. (In *La Revue canadienne.* Montréal. t. 49 (1905), pp. [161]-178.)

ARCHIBALD, EDITH JESSIE (MORTIMER)   That franchise question. From a woman's standpoint. By Edith J. Archibald. (In *The Lake magazine.* [Toronto] v. 1, no. 7 (Feb. 1893), pp. [403]-408.)
A reply to the article Woman suffrage, by J. W. Longley. (In *The Lake magazine.* [Toronto] v. 1, no. 4 (Nov. 1892), pp. [193]-199.)

The Ballot and the new election law. (In *The Nation.* Toronto. v. 2, no. 3 (Jan. 22, 1875), pp. 32-33.)

The Ballot bill. (In *The Nation.* Toronto. v. 1, no. 5 (Apr. 30, 1874), pp. 58.)
Comments briefly on the ballot clauses of the Election Bill.

BIGGAR, OLIVER MOWAT   Electoral reform. A Round Table discussion [with] O. M. Biggar [and] The Hon. A. Knatchbull-Hugessen. (In Liberal Summer Conference, 1st, Port Hope, Ont., 1933. *The Liberal way.* Toronto, 1933. pp. 121-125.)

BOURINOT, SIR JOHN GEORGE   The referendum. By J. G. Bourinot. (In *The Week.* Toronto. v. 10, no. 13 (Feb. 24, 1893), pp. 295-296.)

The Change in representation. (In *The Busy East of Canada.* Sackville, N.B. v. 6, no. 2 (Sept. 1915), p. 11.)
Brief discussion on the effects of redistribution based on the census taken during 1911.

COLQUHOUN, ARTHUR HUGH URQUHART   University MP's in Canada. By A. H. U. Colquhoun. (In *The McGill University magazine.* Montreal. v. 1 (1902), pp. [206]-208.)
Presents a proposal for university representation in the Canadian Parliament.

Compulsory voting. (In *The Nation.* Toronto. v. 1, no. 10 (June 4, 1874), pp. 117-118.)

Discusses the principle of compulsory voting.

Compulsory voting. (In *Canadian illustrated news*. Montreal. v. 10, no. 24 (Dec. 12, 1874), p. 370.)

A Compulsory voting bill. (In *The Nation*. Toronto. v. 1, no. 36 (Dec. 3, 1874), p. 428.)

Discusses, in general terms, a bill introduced by Mr. Bethune in the Ontario legislature.

The Compulsory voting bill. (In *The Nation*. Toronto. v. 1, no. 38 (Dec. 17, 1874), p. 454.)

A brief analysis as to "the effect which the operation of compulsory voting might produce on separate constituencies". Considers the effect of abstentions from voting in the 1874 general elections.

DE CELLES, ALFRED DUCLOS La Chambre est morte, vive la Chambre! Par A.-D. De-Celles. (In *L'Opinion publique*. Montréal. v. 12, no. 45 (10 nov. 1881), p. [527].)

Refers to the abolition by Quebec's Legislative Assembly of "le double mandat" which allowed a person to hold, simultaneously, a seat in the federal Parliament and in the provincial Legislature.

DEXTER, GRANT The battle of the ballots. By A. G. Dexter. (In *Maclean's*. Toronto. v. 43, no. 14 (July 15, 1930), pp. 3-4; 45.)

"A description of the electoral machinery which will enable five million voters to record their verdict on July 28."

Relates to the federal election held July 28, 1930.

DODWELL, CHARLES EDWARD WILLOUGHBY The case for a restricted franchise. By C. E. W. Dodwell. (In *Saturday night*. Toronto. v. 37, no. 30 (May 27, 1922), p. 3.)

—— The case for a restricted franchise. By C. E. W. Dodwell. (In *The Dalhousie review*. Halifax. v. 2 (1922/23), pp. [79]-88.)

DUNCAN, J. L. The referendum. (In *The University monthly*. Toronto. v. 10, no. 6 (Apr. 1910), pp. 338-348.)

A comparative study.

DUNN, OSCAR Le cens d'éligibilité. (In *L'Opinion publique*. Montréal. v. 4, no. 45 (6 nov. 1873), pp. [531]-532.)

Discusses the property qualifications required to stand for Parliament. Relates to the electoral bill initiated by Sir John A. Macdonald in 1873.

—— La loi électorale. (In *L'Opinion publique*. Montréal. v. 5, no. 45 (5 nov. 1874), p. [541].)

—— La loi électorale. (In his *Dix ans de journalisme*. Montréal, 1876. pp. [197]-227.)

—— Le scrutin secret. (In *L'Opinion publique*. Montréal. v. 4, no. 46 (13 nov. 1873), pp. [543]-544.)

Comments on the principle of the secret ballot, which was adopted by Parliament during the winter session of 1872/73.

—— Le serment. (In *L'Opinion publique*. Montréal. v. 5, no. 46 (12 nov. 1874), p. [553].)

Discusses the practice of false oath-taking by voters during parliamentary elections.

Effective voting. (In *The Week*. Toronto. v. 11, no. 9 (Jan. 26, 1894), pp. 197-198.)

EGGLESTON, WILFRID The Ottawa letter. Redistribution of seats certain but how and when are questions. (In *Saturday night*. Toronto. v. 61, no. 27 (Mar. 9, 1946), p. 8.)

—— Ottawa letter. Electoral reform problem grows with the number of parties. (In *Saturday night*. Toronto. v. 62, no. 11 (Nov. 16, 1946), p. 8.)

The Election Bills. (In *The Nation*. Toronto. v. 1, no. 5 (Apr. 30, 1874), p. 56.)

Concludes that "the chief points of the measure effect a vast improvement on the old law".

Electoral reform. By a voter. (In *Saturday night*. Toronto. v. 53, no. 23 (Apr. 9, 1938), pp. [1]; 2.)

FERLAND, POTHIER Mémoire relatif à la loi électorale et à l'administration électorale. [Montréal, 1963] 33 p.

Mimeographed.

The Franchise for farmers' sons. (In *The Nation*. Toronto. v. 1, no. 31 (Oct. 29, 1874), p. 368.)

FRASER, BLAIR Backstage at Ottawa. When bribery was smart. (In *Maclean's*. Toronto. v. 66, no. 17 (Sept. 1, 1953), pp. 6; 62.)

A historical discussion of voting procedures during elections.

GAGNE, WALLACE DONALD GEORGE Class voting in Canada. [Rochester, N.Y.?, 1969, i.e. 1970] vii, 142 leaves.

Thesis (PH D) - University of Rochester.

GELINAS, AIME A propos de politique. Par A. G. (In L'Opinion publique. Montréal. v. 8, no. 9 (1 mars 1877), p. [97].)

Criticizes the election system in Canada.

GLASHAN, JOHN GALL Proportional representation in Canada. [Vancouver] 1951. 89 leaves.

Thesis (MA) – University of British Columbia.

GOOD, WILLIAM CHARLES Proportional representation desirable. By W. C. Good. (In The Canadian forum. Toronto. v. 7, no. 83 (Aug. 1927), pp. 334-336.)

The above is a rejoinder to the article "P.R.": some objections and an alternative, by E. J. Soulsby. (In The Canadian forum. Toronto, v. 7, no. 79 (1927), pp. 202-204.)

For a reply see Ears to the ground, by E. J. Soulsby (In The Canadian forum. Toronto. v. 8, no. 85 (Oct. 1927), pp. 397-399.)

Government by the people. (In The Week. Toronto. v. 10, no. 38 (Aug. 18, 1893), pp. 893-894.)

Refers to an article Referendum and plebiscite, by G. W. Ross. (In The Canadian magazine of politics, science, art and literature. Toronto. v. 1, no. 6 (1893), pp. [445]-450.)

HAHN, HARLAN Voting in Canadian communities. A taxonomy of referendum issues. (In Canadian journal of political science. Toronto. v. 1 (1968), pp. [462]-469.)

HAMBLETON, GEORGE Our unrepresentative Parliament. (In The Dalhousie review. Halifax. v. 29, 1949/50), pp. [434]-438.)

Concerns the issue of disparity between the popular vote and number of candidates returned, citing the results of the 1945 and 1949 general elections.

HILL, HAMNETT PINHEY Proportional representation. By Hamnett P. Hill, MLA. (In Canadian Club of Ottawa. The Canadian Club year book. Ottawa (1919/20), pp. 199-206.)

A comparative analysis.

HOOPER, RONALD Proportional representation; the machinery through which to obtain it. (In The Canadian nation. Ottawa. v. 1, no. 10 (Oct. 4, 1919), pp. 12-14.)

—— What is meant by "P.R." and the "alternative vote". (In Canadian Congress journal. Ottawa. v. 1, no. 4 (Apr. 1922), pp. 181-185.)

Concerns the question of proportional representation.

HUMPHREYS, JOHN H. A national Parliament—a new basis of representation. (In Canadian Club of Montreal. Addresses. [Montreal] (1915/16), pp. 141-149.)

Address delivered February 21, 1916.

An historical and comparative analysis presented by the General Secretary of the Proportional Representation Society.

KERR, ESTELLE M. Where women vote in Canada. (In The Canadian courier. Toronto. v. 11, no. 24 (May 11, 1912), pp. 15; 22.)

KOCH, ERIC Transferable vote would amend electoral system. (In Saturday night. Toronto. v. 60, no. 4 (Sept. 30, 1944), pp. 14-15.)

KORNBERG, ALLAN The recruitment of candidates for the Canadian House of Commons. By Allan Kornberg and Hal H. Winsborough. (In Kruhlak, O. M. (comp.) The Canadian political process. Toronto [c1970] pp. 224-244.)

Reprinted from American political science review, Washington, D.C., v. 62 (1968), pp. 1242-1257.

LAING, LIONEL H. The nature of Canada's parliamentary representation. (In The Canadian journal of economics and political science. Toronto. v. 12 (1946), pp. 509-516.)

Analyses the background of members of the parliament elected in June 1945 using data provided by the Canadian parliamentary guide.

LEATHES, SONIA Votes for women. (In The University magazine. Montreal. v. 13 (1914), pp. [68]-78.)

LEFEBVRE, GEORGINA Le suffrage féminin. (In Le Terroir. Québec. v. 3, no. 1 (mai 1922), pp. [7]-18.)

"Conférence faite par Mademoiselle Georgina Lefebvre (Ginevra), le 23 novembre 1921, à l'Hôtel-de-Ville, à une séance de la Société des arts, sciences et lettres."

LEFROY, AUGUSTUS HENRY FRAZER Should Canadian women have the parliamentary vote? By A. H. F. Lefroy. (In Queen's quarterly. Kingston. v. 21 (1913/14), pp. [91]-96.)

LONGLEY, JAMES WILBERFORCE Woman suffrage. By Hon. J. W. Longley, Attorney General of Nova Scotia. (In The Lake magazine. [Toronto] v. 1, no. 4 (Nov. 1892), pp. [193]-199.)

Presents arguments against extending the franchise to women.

For rejoinders see the articles Woman suffrage; a reply, by Katharine M. M'Kenzie (In *The Lake magazine.* [Toronto] v. 1, no. 6 (Jan. 1893), pp. [327]-331) and That franchise question by Edith I. Archibald (In *The Lake magazine.* [Toronto] v. 1, no. 7 (Feb. 1893), pp. [403]-408.)

LUGRIN, N. DE BERTRAND   The Orientals and the franchise. (In *Canadian courier.* Toronto. v. 25, no. 21 (July 15, 1920), p. 11.)

LUKE, EDITH M.   Woman suffrage in Canada. (In *The Canadian magazine of politics, science, art and literature.* Toronto. v. 5 (1895), pp. [328]-336.)

MC CULLY, LAURA ELIZABETH   The woman suffrage movement in Canada. Illustrated with photographs. By Laura E. McCully. (In *Canada-West.* London, Ont. v. 5, no. 6 (Apr. 1909), pp. 371-375.)

MC ILWRAITH, MARY   Misrepresentative government. A plea for proportional representation to end the distortion in seats in the House of Commons which our present electoral system produces. (In *Commentator.* Toronto. v. 7, no. 3 (Mar. 1963), pp. 7-9.)

M'KENZIE, KATHARINE M'LAGAN   Woman suffrage; a reply. (In *The Lake magazine.* [Toronto] v. 1, no. 6 (Jan. 1893), pp. [327]-331.)

A reply to the article Woman suffrage, by J. W. Longley. (In *The Lake magazine.* [Toronto] v. 1, no. 4 (Nov. 1892), pp. [193]-199.)

MACNAGHTEN, R. E.   A plea for woman suffrage in Canada. (In *The Canadian magazine of politics, science, art and literature.* Toronto. v. 29 (1907), pp. 146-152.)

MAGURN, ARNOTT JAMES   Redistribution in the Commons. By Arnott J. Magurn. (In *The Canadian magazine of politics, science, art and literature.* Toronto. v. 43 (1914), pp. 183-186.)

MATHEWS, JEHU   Personal representation and the representation of minorities. (In *The Canadian monthly and national review.* Toronto. v. 12 (1878), pp. [437]-446; [549]-559; v. 13 (1878), pp. 148-157.)
In three parts.

THE MONOCLE MAN   Woman suffrage and conscription. By the Monocle Man. (In *The [Canadian] courier.* Toronto. v. 20, no. 19 (Oct. 7, 1916), p. 12.)

MORIN, FERNAND   L'exercice du droit de vote et la protection des actionnaires minoritaires dans les compagnies ontariennes et québecoises. Toronto, 1960. 97 leaves.

Thesis (LL M) – University of Toronto.

MORTON, WILLIAM LEWIS   The extension of the franchise in Canada; a study in democratic nationalism. (In Canadian Historical Association. *Report of the annual meeting.* Toronto. (1943), pp. 72-81.)

MOUSSEAU, JOSEPH ALFRED   Lois électorales. Par J. A. Mousseau. (In *L'Opinion publique.* Montréal. v. 2, no. 30 (27 juil. 1871), p. 365.)

—— Réforme électorale. Par J. A. Mousseau. (In *L'Opinion publique.* Montréal. v. 2, no. 32 (19 août 1871), p. 389.)

NICOLET, JEAN   Réformes électorales. (In *L'Action nationale.* Montréal. v. 27 (jan. 1946), pp. [58]-64.)

PELLETIER, GEORGES   Le droit de suffrage. Montréal, L'Ecole sociale populaire, 1942. 29 p. (L'Ecole sociale populaire. Publication no. 345.)

PERRY, ANNE ANDERSON   Is women's suffrage a fizzle? Has the woman voter sacrificed the interests of her sex to mere party allegiance? (In *Maclean's.* Toronto. v. 41, no. 3 (Feb. 1, 1928), pp. 6-7; 58-59; 63.)

QUALTER, TERENCE H.   Seats and votes. An application of the cube law to the Canadian electoral system. (In *Canadian journal of political science.* Toronto. v. 1 (1968), pp. [336]-344.)

RANDALL-JONES, A. R.   "Prop. Rep." and its drawbacks. (In *Saturday night.* Toronto. v. 45, no. 24 (Apr. 26, 1930), p. 2.)

Discusses the idea of proportional representation.

Representation of minorities. (In *The Nation.* Toronto. v. 1, no. 30 (Oct. 22, 1874), p. 356.)

ROSS, SIR GEORGE WILLIAM   Referendum and plebiscite. By Hon. G. W. Ross, Minister of Education, Ontario. (In *The Canadian magazine of politics, science, art and literature.* Toronto. v. 1 (1893), pp. [445]-450.)

A comparative analysis.

For comments on the above, see Government by the people. (In *The Week.* Toronto. v. 10, no. 38 (Aug. 18, 1883), pp. 893-894.)

—— Responsible government vs. referendum. By Sir George W. Ross. (In *The Canadian courier*. Toronto. v. 9, no. 5 (Dec. 31, 1910), p. 10.)

SANDWELL, BERNARD KEBLE From week to week. Disfranchised minorities. By B. K. Sandwell. (In *Saturday night*. Toronto. v. 55, no. 24 (Apr. 13, 1940), p. 3.)
Concerns proportional representation.

—— Problem of non-voting voters. Why not leave constituencies memberless where majority of electors fail to go to the polls? By Bernard K. Sandwell. (In *Saturday night*. Toronto. v. 47, no. 9 (Jan. 9, 1932), p. 15.)

SCHINDELER, FREDERICK FERNAND One man one vote: one vote one value. By Fred Schindeler. (In *Journal of Canadian studies*. Peterborough. v. 3, no. 1 (1968), pp. 13-20.)

Secret voting. (In *The Nation*. Toronto. v. 1, no. 6 (May 7, 1874), pp. 69-70.)
A comparative discussion of voting by ballot.

SKELTON, ISABEL Canadian women and the suffrage. (In *The Canadian magazine of politics, science, art and literature*. Toronto. v. 41 (1913), pp. 162-165.)

SKELTON, OSCAR DOUGLAS Proportional representation. By O. D. Skelton. (In *Queen's quarterly*. Kingston. v. 27 (1919/20), pp. 329-330.)

—— The referendum. By O. D. Skelton. (In *The University magazine*. Montreal. v. 12 (1913), pp. [197]-214.)
A comparative analysis.

SOULSBY, E. J. Ears to the ground. A reply to Mr. W. C. Good. (In *The Canadian forum*. Toronto. v. 8, no. 85 (Oct. 1927), pp. 397-399.)
The above is an answer to Proportional representation desirable, by W. C. Good. (In *The Canadian forum*. Toronto. v. 7, no. 83 (1927), pp. 334-336.)

—— "P.R.": some objections and an alternative. (In *The Canadian forum*. Toronto. v. 7, no. 79 (Apr. 1927), pp. 202-204.)
A discussion of proportional representation.
For a rejoinder to the above, see Proportional representation desirable, by W. C. Good. (In *The Canadian forum*. Toronto. v. 7, no. 83 (1927), pp. 334-336.)

STURSBERG, PETER Ottawa letter. Liquor, bribery and old-time democracy. (In *Saturday night*. Toronto. v. 77, no. 13 (June 23, 1962), pp. 8-10.)
A retrospective discussion of voting procedures and electioneering practices.

—— Ottawa letter. No rep by pop till '67. (In *Saturday night*. Toronto. v. 78, no. 9 (Oct. 1953), pp. 7-8.)
Concerns redistribution of parliamentary seats.

TAYLOR, FENNINGS Notes on the ballot. (In *The Canadian monthly and national review*. Toronto. v. 3 (1873), pp. 488-497.)

VAUGHAN, WALTER Woman suffrage today. (In *The University magazine*. Montreal. v. 15 (1916), pp. [575]-587.)
A comparative analysis.

Le Vote des femmes. (In *L'Opinion publique*. Montréal. v. 14, no. 20 (17 mai 1883), p. [229].)

WALLIS, ARTHUR FREDERICK A cheap and simple franchise. By Arthur F. Wallis. (In *The Lake magazine*. [Toronto] v. 1, no. 1 (Aug. 1892), pp. [21]-27.)
Advocates manhood suffrage.

WARD, NORMAN MC QUEEN The basis of representation in the House of Commons. By Norman Ward.
"This paper was presented at the annual meeting of the Canadian Political Science Association in Halifax, June 9, 1949."

—— The Canadian House of Commons: representation. Toronto, 1949. 383 leaves.
Thesis (PH D) – University of Toronto.

—— The Canadian House of Commons: representation. By Norman Ward. Toronto, University of Toronto Press, 1950. xii, 307 p. (Canadian government series, 4.)

—— A century of constituencies. By Norman Ward. (In *Canadian public administration*. Toronto. v. 10 (1967), pp. 105-122.)
Reviews the parliamentary debates held over the issue of redistribution during the 1960s.

—— A century of constituencies. By Norman Ward. (In Vaughan, Frederick (ed.) *Contemporary issues in Canadian politics*. Scarborough, Ont. [c1970] pp. 166-176.)
Reprinted from *Canadian public administration*, Toronto, v. 10, no. 1 (1967), pp. 105-122.

—— Parliamentary representation in Canada. By Norman Ward. (In *The Canadian journal of economics and political science.* [Toronto] v. 13 (1947), pp. 447-464.)

A statistical analysis of the federal parliaments from 1867 to 1945.

—— The redistribution of 1952. By Norman Ward. (In *The Canadian journal of economics and political science.* [Toronto] v. 19 (1953), pp. 341-360.)

"This paper was presented at the annual meeting of the Canadian Political Science Association in London, on June 3, 1953."

Examines the "unique" features of the redistribution of federal constituencies in 1952.

—— Voting in Canadian two-member constituencies. By Norman Ward. (In *Public affairs.* Halifax. v. 9, no. 4 (Sept. 1946), pp. [220]-223.)

Provides a table: Election returns federal two member constituencies. 1887-1945. (p. 221).

—— Voting in Canadian two-member contituencies. By Norman Ward. (In Courtney, J. C. (ed.) *Voting in Canada.* Scarborough, Ont., c1967 pp. 125-129.)

"Reprinted from Public affairs, IX (September) 1946."

Function and Personnel

AITCHISON, JAMES HERMISTON   The speakership of the Canadian House of Commons. By J. H. Aitchison. (In Clark, R. M. (ed.) *Canadian issues.* Toronto, 1961. pp. [23]-56.)

ALLMAND, WARREN   MP's and public pressure. By Warren Allmand, MP. (In *Canada month.* Montreal. v. 7, no. 5 (May 1967), pp. 22-23.)

The author is Liberal MP for Montreal Notre Dame de Grâce.

ARCHAMBAULT, JOSEPH   La publication de la traduction des discours prononcés en français. (In *L'Action française.* Montréal. v. 4 (juil. 1920) pp. [333]-336.)

"Discours de M. Joseph Archambault, député du comté de Chambly-Verchères, Chambre des communes, Ottawa, mercredi, 24 mars, 1920."

ARMSTRONG, ROBERT   The Standing Committee on Public Accounts, 1946-59. [Montreal, 1960] 1 v.

Thesis (MA) – McGill University.

BALDWIN, GERALD WILLIAM   Your member in Parliament needs more power over spending. By G. W. Baldwin, MP. (In

Canada month. Montreal. v. 8, no. 1 (Jan. 1968), pp. 30-32.)

BALLS, HERBERT R.   The Public Accounts Committee. (In *Canadian public administration.* Toronto. v. 6 (1963), pp. 15-34.)

"This was presented to the fourteenth annual conference of the Institute of Public Administration of Canada, September 5 to 8, 1962, Regina, Saskatchewan."

BANKS, RIDEAU   Ottawa letter. How to get good MP's. (In *Saturday night.* Toronto. v. 53, no. 25 (Apr. 23, 1938), p. 4.)

Concerns the electoral reform bills.

BARKWAY, MICHAEL   Does Parliament talk too much? How can our Commons make better use of the sessions? Are Committees the answer? (In *Saturday night.* Toronto. v. 65, no. 16 (Jan. 24, 1950), p. 8.)

—— How does your MP rate? Parliament is the assurance that the ordinary people will always have the last word. (In *Saturday night.* Toronto. v. 65, no. 1 (Oct. 11, 1949), pp. 12; 18.)

—— A more efficient assembly. Can the Commons straighten itself out? (In *Saturday night.* Toronto. v. 66, no. 39 (July 3, 1951), pp. 11; 15.)

BEAUDOIN, LOUIS RENE   Mr. Speaker. By the Hon. L. René Beaudoin, the Speaker of the House of Commons, Ottawa. (In *Empire Club of Canada. Addresses.* Toronto. (1956/57), pp. 34-50.)

Address delivered October 25, 1956.

BERTRAND, JEAN JACQUES   Le député; législateur ou patroneux. (In *Institut canadien des affaires publiques,* Montréal. *Nos hommes politiques.* Montréal. [c1964] pp. [33]-41.)

BIRD, JOHN   Making work for idle MP's. (In *Canadian commentator.* Toronto. v. 2, no. 6 (June 1958), p. 3.)

Discusses the work load and work patterns of members of Parliament.

BOURINOT, SIR JOHN GEORGE   The House of Commons in session. By J. G. Bourinot. (In *The Canadian monthly and national review.* Toronto. v. 11 (1877), pp. 279-287.)

A description and explanation of parliamentary procedure.

—— Mr. Speaker. By J. G. Bourinot. (In *The Canadian monthly and national review.* Toronto. v. 13 (1878), pp. 129-136.)

CAMPBELL, M. S. Filibusters in the Canadian House of Commons. [Wolfville, N.S., 1952] 1 v.
Thesis (MA) – Acadia University.

CANADA, PARLIAMENT. HOUSE OF COMMONS Décisions des orateurs de la Chambre des communes du Canada, 1867-1900. Par L. G. Desjardins. Decisions of the Speakers of the House of Commons of Canada, 1867-1900. By L. G. Desjardins. [Quebec? pref. 1901] 415 p.
French and English on opposite pages.

—— Decision of the Speakers of the House of Commons of Canada, 1867-1900. By L. G. Desjardins. Quebec, 1901. 207 p.

CAWTHORNE, GRAHAM The loneliest parliamentarian. The Speaker of the Commons sits above the party battle, yet he is always accessible to members who want advice. (In Saturday night. Toronto. v. 67, no. 50 (Sept. 20, 1952), pp. 13; 25.)

CHOUIMARD, L. Quelques aspects de la représentation parliamentaire canadienne durant la période qui s'étend de 1949 à 1962. [Québec, 1964] 1 v.
Thesis (MA) – Laval University.

COPPS, EDWIN Ottawa letter. Speak up to Mr. Speaker. (In Saturday night. Toronto. v. 75, no. 14 (July 9, 1960), pp. [29]-30.)
Discusses the invitation issued by Roland Michener to the Parliamentary Press Gallery to advance suggestions for implementing more efficient parliamentary procedures.

CORRY, JAMES ALEXANDER Adaptation of parliamentary processes to the modern state. By J. A. Corry. (In The Canadian journal of economics and political science. Toronto. v. 20 (1954), pp. 1-9.)
Discusses problems facing the Canadian House of Commons as a result of expanding responsibilities.

COX, GEORGE OLUWOLE VALLANCOURT Questions in the Canadian House of Commons. [Fredericton, N.B.] 1962. 1 v.
Thesis (MA) – University of New Brunswick.

CRAICK, WILLIAM ARNOT Mr. Speaker: a glimpse of the man and the office from the human interest side. By W. A. Craick. (In MacLean's magazine. Toronto. v. 28, no. 5 (Mar. 1915), pp. [31]-34; 81-82.)
Describes the function of the Speaker.

DAVID, LAURENT OLIVIER La Chambre. Par L.-O. David. (In L'Opinion publique.

Montréal. v. 9, no. 8 (21 fév. 1878), pp. 86, 88; v. 9, no. 10 (7 mars 1878), p. 110.)
In two parts.
Gives information on the various officials serving in the House of Commons and Senate: who they are, their salaries, etc.

DAWSON, WILLIAM FOSTER The development of procedure in the House of Commons of Canada. London [1957-58?] 1 v.
Thesis (D PHIL) – Oxford.

—— The development of the standing orders of the House of Commons of Canada. [Kingston, Ont., 1953] 149 leaves.
Thesis (MA) – Queen's University.

—— Parliamentary privilege in the Canadian House of Commons. By W. F. Dawson. (In The Canadian journal of economics and political science. [Toronto] v. 25 (1959), pp. 462-470.)
"This paper was presented at the annual meeting of the Canadian Political Science Association in Saskatoon, June 5, 1959."

—— Procedure in the Canadian House of Commons. [Toronto] University of Toronto Press [1962] x, 271 p. (Canadian government series, 12.)

DEACHMAN, ROBERT JOHN Our MP's should not be treated meanly. By R. J. Deachman. (In Saturday night. Toronto. v. 61, no. 19 (Jan. 12, 1946), p. 19.)
Defends a $2,000 salary raise for Members of Parliament.

DEXTER, GRANT What does an MP do? By A. G. Dexter. (In Maclean's. Toronto. v. 42, no. 6 (Mar. 15, 1929), pp. 16; 49-50; 52.)

DEXTER, SUSAN Smile! There's a camera in the House. (In Maclean's. Toronto. v. 80, no. 4 (Apr. 1967), pp. 4b; 4d; 108a-108b.)
Considers whether proceedings of the House of Commons ought to be televised.

EGGLESTON, WILFRID Capital comment. A changing House of Commons. (In Saturday night. Toronto. v. 66, no. 17 (Jan. 30, 1951), p. 3.)

FALARDEAU, JEAN CHARLES Mort ou résurrection du député? (In Institut canadien des affaires publiques, Montreal. Nos hommes politiques. Montréal [c1964] pp. [115]-119.)

FARQUHARSON, R. A. Are we starving our MP's? (In Saturday night. Toronto. v. 68, no. 7 (Nov. 22, 1952), pp. [1]; 19-21.)

FISHER, DOUGLAS MASON How good or bad is your MP? By Douglas Fisher. (In Mac-

clean's. Toronto. v. 79, no. 3 (Feb. 5, 1966), pp. 17-19; 31-32.)

FRANCIS, ANNE   Underpaid, overworked, and—unobtainable. (In *The Canadian. commentator.* Toronto. v. 6, no. 1 (Jan. 1962), pp. 1-2; 16; [25].)

Describes the routine and the problems confronting a conscientious member of Parliament.

FRASER, BLAIR   Backstage at Ottawa. Time for an independent Speaker. (In *Maclean's.* Toronto. v. 69, no. 15 (July 21, 1956), pp. 8; 45.)

——   Backstage at Ottawa. A back-bencher's revolt? Inadequate salaries, slow promotions. (In *Maclean's.* Toronto. v. 72, no. 12 (June 6, 1959), p. 2.)

Douglas Fisher of the CCF raised the question of inadequate salaries.

——   Backstage at Ottawa. The backbenchers' unemployment problem. They're able, anxious and bored stiff. (In *Maclean's.* Toronto, v. 73, no. 5 (Feb. 27, 1960), p. 2.)

HAMBLETON, GEORGE   Our unregenerate Commons. (In *The Dalhousie review.* Halifax. v. 8 (1928/29), pp. [316]-320.)

HARDY, REGINALD   Parliamentary leg-pullers. When MP's clown party lines drop. (In *Saturday night.* Toronto. v. 67, no. 3 Oct. 27, 1951), pp. [11]; 32-33.)

HOCKIN, THOMAS ALEXANDER   The standing committees of Canada's House of Commons since 1966. (In Kruhlak, O. M. (comp.) *The Canadian political process.* Toronto [c1970] pp. 383-397.)

Is the House of Commons too big? (In *The Canadian courier.* Toronto. v. 15, no. 15 (Mar. 14, 1914), pp. 10-11.)

Records some of the responses from members of Parliament to a circular letter sent out by the *Canadian courier.*

JEWETT, PAULINE MAE   Can MP's do a better job? By Pauline Jewett. (In Hawkins, Gordon (ed.) *Order and good government.* [Toronto, c1965] pp. 54-61.)

——   How can the greatest number of Canadians participate in day-to-day politics and influence MP's? A plan for new independent parties within parties—outside Parliament. By Pauline Jewett. (In *Maclean's.* Toronto. v. 81, no. 11 (Nov. 1968), p. 14.)

——   What every new MP should know—from a writer who learned the hard way: as an MP. By Pauline Jewett. (In *Mac-*

lean's. Toronto. v. 81, no. 10 (Oct. 1968), p. [11].)

JUVET, C. S.   The 1960 Estimates Committee; spur to economy and efficiency? (In *Canadian public administration.* Toronto. v. 7 (1964), pp. 479-499.)

KELSON, ROBERT N.   The role of the private member. (In Hawkins, Gordon (ed.) *Order and good government.* [Toronto, c1965] pp. 62-68.)

KETTLE, JOHN   Mr. Speaker. (In *Canada month.* Montreal. v. 8, no. 6 (June 1968), pp. 12-15.)

A *Canada month* profile.

Considers the argument for a permanent Speaker in the House of Commons. Presents the case for Lucien Lamoureux to "become the first permanent Speaker in the Commonwealth".

KING, TOM   How the MP's earn their salt. (In *Canada month.* London, Ont. v. 20, no. 6 (Oct. 1916), pp. 347-349.)

Describes the nature and function of Parliament.

LEGGET, ROBERT FERGUSON   The professions and Parliament. By Robert F. Legget. (In *The Canadian forum.* Toronto. v. 15, no. 173 (Feb. 1935), pp. 180-182.)

An analysis of the professional qualifications of the personnel of Parliament.

LEVESQUE, RENE   Ce que font les députés. (In Institut canadien des affaires publiques, Montreal. *Nos hommes politiques.* Montréal [c1964] pp. [55]-58.)

MC CREADY, JOHN E. BLAKENEY   The Commons of Canada. By J. E. B. McCready. (In *Stewart's quarterly.* St. John, N.B. v. 4, no. 1 (Apr. 1870), pp. 59-67.)

MACDONALD, DONALD STOVEL   Change in the House of Commons; new rules. By the Honourable Donald S. Macdonald. (In *Canadian public administration.* Toronto. v. 13 (1970), pp. [30]-39.)

——   Changements à la Chambre des Communes; les nouveaux règlements. Par l'honorable Donald S. Macdonald. (In *Canadian public administration.* Toronto. v. 13 (1970), pp. [40]-50.)

MALLORY, JAMES RUSSELL   The financial administration of the House of Commons. By J. R. Mallory. (In *The Canadian journal of economics and political science.* Toronto. v. 23 (1957), pp. 108-113.)

Discusses the customary practice which grants the House of Commons responsibility for its own internal financial administration.

THE MEMBER FOR CANADA MP's, good, bad, indifferent. By the Member for Canada. (In *The Canadian courier*. Toronto. v. 19, no. 12 (Feb. 19, 1916), pp. 10-11; 18.)

MICHENER, DANIEL ROLAND The House of Commons from the Speaker's chair. By the Honourable D. Roland Michener, Speaker of the House of Commons in the 23rd parliament. (In Empire Club of Canada. *Addresses*. Toronto. (1957/58), pp. 300-311.)

Address delivered April 17, 1958.

THE MONOCLE MAN Can we do without members of Parliament? By the Monocle Man. (In *The Canadian courier*. Toronto. v. 19, no. 13 (Feb. 26, 1916), p. 10.)

O'LEARY, DILLON Parliamentary business drowned in talk. If the business of the country is to be transacted, the Canadian Commons' talkathons must be limited by closure or guillotine. (In *Commentator*. Toronto. v. 8, no. 7/8 (July/Aug. 1964), pp. 7-8.)

PAGE, DONALD Streamlining the procedures of the Canadian House of Commons, 1963-1966. (In *The Canadian journal of economics and political science*. [Toronto] v. 33 (1967), pp. [27]-49.)

"This paper was originally prepared under the direction of Professor J. E. Hodgetts as part of doctoral studies at the University of Toronto."

PEPIN, JEAN LUC Les conditions d'une restauration des Communes. (In *Le Magazine Maclean*. Montréal. v. 1, no. 2 (avril 1961), p. 2.)

PERRAULT, JACQUES La Chambre se forme en comité. (In *L'Action nationale*. Montréal. v. 19 (juil. 1942), pp. [414]-420.)

POWER, CHARLES GAVAN Career politician. The changing role of the MP. By C. G. Power. (In *Queen's quarterly*. Kingston. v. 63 (1956), pp. [478]-490.)

ROBERTS, JOHN Methods of giving MP's independence and power. (In *The Globe and mail*. Toronto. (Nov. 21, 1970), p. 7.)

"Mr. Roberts is Liberal member of Parliament for York Simcoe".

RODGERS, RAYMOND Ottawa letter. Pity the poor private member. (In *Saturday night*. Toronto. v. 75, no. 26 (Dec. 24, 1960), pp. 29-30.)

ROE, J. SYDNEY Mr. Speaker. (In *Saturday night*. Toronto. [v. 30, no. 49] (Sept. 22, 1917), p. 4.)

Discusses various Speakers of the House of Commons.

SANDWELL, BERNARD KEBLE The electors' hired man. By B. K. Sandwell. (In *Queen's quarterly*. Kingston. v. 46 (1939), pp. [170]-175.)

Comments on the "hired man" theory which considers Members of Parliament as employed by their constituencies.

—— From the editor's chair. Let's make the parliamentary hired man work for his money. By B. K. Sandwell. (In *Saturday night*. Toronto. v. 61, no. 17 (Dec. 29, 1945), p. 10.)

Comments on the $2,000 increase in salaries to members of Parliament.

SEGSWORTH, R. V. A comparative study of participation in the Canadian House of Commons. [Ottawa, 1969] 1 v.

Thesis (MA) – Carleton University.

SINGH, SANT PARKASH The Canadian Committee on Estimates. [Montreal, 1962] 1 v.

Thesis (MA) – McGill University.

SMILEY, DONALD VICTOR A comparative study of party discipline in the House of Commons of the United States and Canada and in the Congress of the United States. [Evanston, Ill., 1954] 252 leaves.

Thesis (PH D) – Northwestern University.

SMITH, DENIS The Speaker. (In *The Canadian forum*. Toronto. v. 43, no. 507 (Apr. 1963), pp. 4-5.)

A proposal for an independent Speakership.

—— The speakership of the Canadian House of Commons; some proposals. (In Vaughan, Frederick (ed.) *Contemporary issues in Canadian politics*. Scarborough, Ont. c1970. pp. 177-192.)

"A paper prepared for the House of Commons Special Committee on Procedure and Organization, April, 1965."

STEVENSON, JOHN A. Ottawa letter. A limit of $606 on members' speeches. (In *Saturday night*. Toronto. v. 70, no. 20 (Feb. 19, 1955), p. 9.)

Comments on imposing a time limit on speeches in the House of Commons.

A Symposium of MP's. How can the Commons improve procedure? (In *Saturday night*. Toronto. v. 67, no. 34 (May 31, 1952), pp. 10; 27.)

Four Members of Parliament give their views. They are: Hughes Cleaver (L. Halton, Ont.), Donald Fleming (PC, Toronto-Eglinton), Stanley Knowles (CCF, Winnipeg–N. Centre), and Walter Harris L., Grey-Bruce).

THOMAS, PAUL GRIFFITH   A study of the Canadian House of Commons Committee on Broadcasting, 1958-67. By Paul G. Thomas. [Winnipeg] 1968. iv, 229 leaves. Thesis (MA) – University of Manitoba.

TREMBLAY, JEAN NOEL   Ce que font les députés. (In Institut canadien des affaires publiques, Montreal. *Nos hommes politiques.* Montréal [c1964] pp. [43]-51.)

TROYER, WARNER   Our impecunious MP's. (In *Saturday night.* Toronto. v. 78, no. 8 (Sept. 1963), p. 28.)

WARD, NORMAN MC QUEEN   Best Commons attenders live farthest away. By Norman Ward. (In *Saturday night.* Toronto. v. 64, no. 36 (June 14, 1949), p. [13].)

—— La Chambre des communes. Par Norman Ward. (In Sabourin, Louis (ed.) *Le système politique du Canada.* Ottawa, 1968. pp. [117]-130.)

—— The Committee on Estimates. By Norman Ward. (In *Canadian public administration* Toronto. v. 6 (1963), pp. 35-42.) "This paper was presented to the fourteenth annual conference of Canada, September 5 to 8, 1962, Regina, Saskatchewan."

—— The formative years of the House of Commons, 1867-91. By Norman Ward. (In *The Canadian journal of economics and political science.* Toronto. v. 18 (1952), pp. 431-451.) Traces the development of the function and organization of the House of Commons and its institutions: the Speakership, the Hansard, the Library, etc.

—— Giveaway program in the Commons. By Norman Ward. (In *Saturday night.* Toronto. v. 72, no. 6 (Mar. 16, 1957), pp. 9-10.) "When orders and regulations having the force of law steadily grow in number, Parliament cannot avoid a decline in relative importance. It has failed to adopt proper methods of scrutiny."

—— Parliament now bilingual at last. By Norman Ward. (In *Saturday night.* Toronto. v. 74, no. 2 (Jan. 17, 1959), pp. 12-[13]; 38.) Written on the occasion when, on January 15, 1959, a simultaneous translation system was introduced in the House of Commons. Traces the development of translation services for use in Parliament.

—— The public purse; a study in Canadian democracy. By Norman Ward. Toronto, University of Toronto Press. c1962. viii, 334 p. (Canadian government series, 11.) Concerns parliamentary control over public expenditures, with emphasis on the House of Commons.

—— Stop MP's absenteeism by better pay methods. By N. Ward. (In *Saturday night.* Toronto. v. 63, no. 48 (Sept. 4, 1948), p. 27.)

WATKINS, ERNEST   Political Canada. A new House. (In *Canada month.* Montreal. v. 4 [i.e. 5] no. 3 (Mar. 1965), pp. 19-20.) Advances a proposal for a reconstructed House of Commons.

WHITTAKER, G. C.   The Ottawa letter. CBC report is a plaunt document. (In *Saturday night.* Toronto. v. 57, no. 47 (Aug. 1, 1942), p. 8.) Concerns a House of Commons inquiry into the operations of the Canadian Broadcasting Corporation.

LEGISLATION AND THE JUDICIARY

ABBOTT, HENRY   A treatise on the railway law of Canada. By Harry Abbott. Montreal, C. Theoret, 1896. 648 p.

ACHINTRE, AUGUSTE   Nos gravures. La Cour Suprême. Par A. Achintre. (In *L'Opinion publique.* Montréal. v. 6, no. 42 (21 oct. 1875), pp. 496-497.) Brief factual biographical sketches and

portraits of members appointed to the Supreme Court of Canada created in 1875: Hon. William Buell Richards, Chief Justice Hon. Jean-Thomas Taschereau, Hon. Samuel Henry Strong, Hon. William Johnston Ritchie, Hon. William A. Henry, and Hon. T. Fournier.

—— Semaine politique. Par A. Achintre.

(In *L'Opinion publique*. Montréal. v. 6, no. 14 (8 avril 1875), pp. 166-167.)

Discusses the bill creating a Supreme Court in Canada.

L'ACTION FRANCAISE Nos lois françaises. (In *L'Action française*. Montréal. v. 17 (avril 1927), pp. [195]-210.)

At head of title: La doctrine de l'Action française.

Relates to the Canadian constitution.

ANDERSON, J. E. The Drug bill; aspects of the policy process [Kingston? 1970] 16, 2 leaves. (In Canadian Political Science Association. *Papers presented at the annual meeting*. Kingston. 42d (1970), v. 2 [pt.] 17.)

Reproduced typescript.

ANGUS, HENRY FORBES A contribution to international ill-will. (The Immigration Act and the Chinese Immigration Act and certain orders-in-council.) By H. F. Angus. (In *The Dalhousie review*. Halifax. v. 13 (1933/34), pp. [23]-33.)

APPELLANT The Supreme Court of Canada. By Appellant. (In *Willisons monthly*. Toronto. v. 2, no. 12 (May 1927), pp. 470-473.)

BALLS, HERBERT R. The development of government expenditure control: the issue and audit phases. (In *The Canadian journal of economics and political science*. Toronto. v. 10 (1944), pp. 464-475.)

Discusses the Consolidated Revenue and Audit Act of 1931 which "is the statutory embodiment of the principles underlying the control which the Parliament of Canada exercises over the receipt and issue of moneys from the Consolidated Revenue Fund".

BASTEDO, SAMUEL TOVEL Government annuities. By S. T. Bastedo. (In *Queen's quarterly*. Kingston. v. 18 (1910/11), pp. [87]-99.)

"Address delivered to the Employers' Association in Toronto."

Concerns the Canadian Government Annuities Act of 1908.

BEAUDOIN, GERALD A. Le système judiciaire canadien. (In Sabourin, Louis (ed.) *Le système politique du Canada*. Ottawa, 1968. pp. [351]-377.)

BECK, JAMES MURRAY One Bill of Rights or two? By J. M. Beck. (In *The Dalhousie review*. Halifax. v. 39 (1959/60), pp. [31]-42.)

One is a legislative Bill of Rights; the second, a bill of rights by judicial decision.

BELLAMY, DAVID The Small Business Loans Act; a case study in pressure group activity. [Kingston, 1964] 1 v.

Thesis (MA) – Queen's University.

BLAIR, D. G. Combines; the continuing dilemma. (In Lang, O. E. (ed.) *Contemporary problems of public law in Canada*. [Toronto, c1968] pp. [127]-163.)

Considers the nature and application of Canadian combines legislation.

BROSSARD, JACQUES La Cour suprême et la constitution. (In *Le Québec dans le Canada de demain*. Montréal [c1967] t. 2, pp. 22-29.)

—— La Cour suprême et la constitution; le forum constitutionnel au Canada. Montréal, Presses de l'Université de Montréal, 1968. 427 p. (Collection: Institut de recherche en droit public.)

"Etude commanditée par le Comité parlementaire de la Constitution". – Verso of title page.

—— The Supreme Court and the constitution. (In *Quebec in the Canada of tomorrow*. [Toronto, 1968] pp. [U-1]-U-11.)

BROWN, JOHN CLIVE LLOYD The decision to amend the Department of Labour Act, 1957. [Toronto, 1963] 64 leaves.

Thesis (MA) – University of Toronto.

BURCHILL, C. S. The origins of Canadian irrigation law. (In *The Canadian historical review*. Toronto. v. 29 (1948), pp. 353-362.)

BURNS, C. A. Canada's highest tribunal. Strong and representative men who constitute the Supreme Court. (In *Saturday night*. Toronto. v. 44, no. 29 (June 1, 1929), p. 2.)

CANADA. DEPT. OF JUSTICE Correspondence, reports of the ministers of justice, and Orders in Council upon the subject of Dominion and provincial legislation, 1867-1920. Compiled under the direction of the Honourable, the Minister of Justice, by W. E. Hodgins of the Department of Justice. Ottawa, Government Print. Bureau, 1896-1922. 2 v.

Vol. 1. 1867-1895; vol. 2. 1896-1920.

Vol. 2. has title: Correspondence, reports of the Minister of Justice, and Orders in Council upon the subject of provincial legislation. Compiled by Francis H. Gisborne, parliamentary counsel, and Arthur A.

Fraser, assistant to the parliamentary counsel. Ottawa, F. A. Acland, Printer to the King, 1922.

Binder's title: v. 1. Dominion and provincial legislation, 1867-1895; v. 2. Provincial legislation, 1896-1920.

Vol. 2 also issued in parts.

CANADA. LAWS, STATUTES, ETC. Canadian emergency control legislation: The Defence Production Act, The Emergency Powers Act. Statutes of 1951. Toronto, CCH Canadian [1951] 29 p. (Incl. cover) Cover title.

CAYGEON, ROBERT National affairs. Uses of judicial probes. (In *Saturday night*. Toronto. v. 51, no. 15 (Feb. 15, 1936), p. 4.)

CLOKIE, HUGH MC DOWALL Judicial review, federalism, and the Canadian constitution. By H. McD. Clokie. (In *The Canadian journal of economics and political science*. [Toronto] v. 8 (1942), pp. 537-556.)

"This paper was read at the annual meeting of the Canadian Political Science Association in May, 1942."

CORRY, JAMES ALEXANDER Statutory powers. By J. A. Corry. (In his *Legal essays in honour of Arthur Moxon*. [Toronto] 1953. pp. 127-155.)

Discusses the confused judicial and legislative aspects in determining the nature and application of a statutory power.

COTTERILL, MURRAY Who wants to handle the labor laws? (In *Saturday night*. Toronto. v. 61, no. 45 (July 13, 1946), pp. 22-23.)

Argues that the federal government should have control over labour relations and wages.

CRAICK, WILLIAM ARNOT Canada's Supreme Court at work. The personnel, problems and peculiarities of the country's highest tribunal. By W. A. Craick. (In *MacLean's magazine*. Toronto. v. 27, no. 5 (Mar. 1914), pp. [13]-16; 137-138.)

CRONKITE, FREDERICK CLINTON Political theories and conventions: their incorporation into the positive law. By F. C. Cronkite. (In *The Canadian journal of economics and political science*. Toronto. v. 5 (1939), pp. 403-416.)

Discusses the concept and application of constitutional law interpreted as positive law in Canadian courts.

CROWLE, HAROLD E. The Bank of Canada. Advantages and disadvantages of private

and public control of central banks. Where Canada stands. (In *Saturday night*. Toronto. v. 49, no. 45 (Sept. 15, 1934), pp. [17]; 24.)

With reference to the Bank of Canada Act.

CURRIER, JAMES EVERETT WILSON (comp.) A concordance of the Railway Act. Revised statutes of Canada, 1906, chap. 37. 2d ed. Prepared and compiled by J. E. W. Currier of the Department of Railways and Canals. Ottawa. [Printed by the Rolla L. Crain Co.] 1907. 153 p.

DAVISON, JAMES FORRESTER The problem of the Lemieux Act. By J. F. Davison. (In *The Dalhousie review*. Halifax. v. 5 (1925/26), pp. [54]-64.)

Concerns the Industrial Disputes Investigation Act.

DRIEDGER, ELMER A. The Canadian Bill of Rights. By E. A. Driedger. (In Lang, O. E. (ed.) *Contemporary problems of public law in Canada*. [Toronto, c1968) pp. [31]-48.)

ELLIOTT, C. FRASER The administration of the Canadian Income Tax Law. (In *The Canadian journal of economics and political science*. Toronto. v. 4 (1938), pp. 377-390.)

FORSEY, EUGENE ALFRED Removal of Superior Court judges. By Eugene Forsey. (In *Commentator*. Toronto. v. 10, no. 2 (Feb. 1966), pp. 17-19.)

GRANT, J. A. C. Judicial review in Canada; procedural aspects. (In Kruhlak, O. M. (comp.) *The Canadian political process*. Toronto [c1970] pp. 419-441.)

Reprinted from *The Canadian bar review*. Toronto. v. 42 (1964), pp. 195-224.

GRAY, GRATTAN Seven wise men. With Privy Council appeals ended. Ottawa's seven men in scarlet will be second in power only to Parliament. (In *Maclean's*. Toronto. v. 62, no. 6 (Mar. 15, 1949), pp. 8-9; 65-67.)

Concerns Chief Justice T. Rinfret and Justices Estey, Rand, Kerwin, Taschereau, Kellock, and Locke.

HARVEY, ALAN BURNSIDE Tendencies in legislation. By A. B. Harvey. (In *Queen's quarterly*. Kingston. v. 38 (1931), pp. [711]-723.)

Considers certain trends in contemporary legislation and the effect upon the common law.

HAYDON, ANDREW The relations between legislation and morality. (In *Queen's quarterly*. Kingston. v. 7 (1899/1900), pp. [1]-20.)

Discusses specific aspects of contemporary Canadian legislation, citing regulations governing the traffic in liquor and the Lord's Day Act.

HUMPHREY, JOHN P. Judicial control over administrative action with special reference to the province of Quebec. (In *The Canadian journal of economics and political science*. [Toronto] v. 5 (1939), pp. 417-431.)

Considers the form of judicial or legislative controls advisable to meet the problems of increased state intervention as a function of power by the executive branch of the government.

HYMAN, MARCUS Social legislation; the Western view. (In Canadian Broadcasting Corporation. *The Canadian constitution*. Toronto [c1938] pp. 69-80.)

"Discussed by the Kelsey Club, Winnipeg, November 1, 1937."

Discusses social legislation, with reference to the constitution.

KELLEY, E. E. Social legislation, the Maritime view. (In Canadian Broadcasting Corporation. *The Canadian constitution*. Toronto [c1938] pp. 81-89.)

"Discussed by the Citadel Club, Halifax, November 14, 1937."

Considers Canadian legislation, with reference to social security.

KERNAGHAN, WILLIAM DAVID KENNETH Civil liberties and a constitutional bill of rights. By Kenneth Kernaghan. (In Vaughan, Frederick (ed.) *Contemporary issues in Canadian politics*. Scarborough, Ont. [c1970] pp. 68-82.)

Central to this inquiry "is an account of the events and personalities associated with the movement toward the enactment in 1960 of the Canadian Bill of Rights and toward the current proposal for a Canadian charter of human rights".

LADNER, LEON J. Uniformity of legislation. (In Canadian Broadcasting Corporation. *The Canadian constitution*. Toronto. [c1938] pp. 127-137.)

"Discussed by the Constitutional Club, Vancouver, December 12, 1937."

LAING, LIONEL HASSELL Merchant shipping legislation and admiralty jurisdiction in Canada. [Cambridge, Mass., 1935] 1 v.

Thesis (PH D) – Harvard University.

LALONDE, MARC Les journaux et la loi au Canada. (In *Cité libre*. Montréal. no. 86 (avril/mai 1966), pp. 15-21; no. 87 (juin 1966), pp. 20-28; nos. 88/89 (juil./août 1966), pp. 19-26.)

In three parts.

LANG, OTTO EMIL (ed.) Contemporary problems of public law in Canada; essays in honour of Dean F. C. Cronkite. Edited by O. E. Lang. [Toronto] Published for the College of Law, University of Saskatchewan by University of Toronto Press [c1968] 171 p.

Partial contents: The Canadian Bill of Rights, by E. A. Driedger. – Freedom of the press, by E. A. Tollefson. – Crown immunity and the power of judicial review, by B. L. Strayer. – Combines, by D. G. Blair.

LASKIN, BORA Peace, order and good government; re-examined. (In Lederman, W. R. (ed.) *The courts and the Canadian constitution*. Toronto, c1964. pp. 66-104.)

". . . a re-examination of the judicially determined content of the introduction clause of section 91 of the British North America Act."

Reprinted from *The Canadian bar review*, v. 25 (1947), pp. 1054-87.

—— The Supreme Court of Canada; a final court of and for Canadians. (In Lederman, W. R. (ed.) *The courts and the Canadian constitution*. [Toronto, c1964] pp. [125]-151.)

Reprinted from *The Canadian bar review*, v. 29 (1951), pp. 1038-1042.

LEDERMAN, WILLIAM RALPH Concerning a Bill of Rights for Canada and Ontario. By W. R. Lederman. (In Ontario Advisory Committee on Confederation. *Background papers and reports*. [Toronto, 1970] v. 2, pp. 273-293.)

LEDERMAN, WILLIAM RALPH (ed.) The courts and the Canadian constitution. A selection of essays edited and with an introd. by W. R. Lederman. [Toronto] McClelland and Stewart [c1964] 248 p. (The Carleton library, no. 16.)

Partial contents: Our changing constitution, by F. R. Scott. – The meaning of provincial autonomy, by L. P. Pigeon. – Quebec and Canadian federalism, by A. Brady. – Peace, order and good government; reexamined, by B. Laskin. – The establishment of the Supreme Court of Canada, by F. MacKinnon. – The Supreme Court of Canada; a final court of and for Canadians, by B. Laskin. – Legislative power and the Supreme Court in the fifties, by V. C. Mac-Donald. – Classification of laws and the British North America Act, by W. R. Lederman. – The concurrent operation of federal and provincial laws in Canada, by W. R. Lederman. – The nature, use and effect of reference cases in Canadian constitutonal law, by G. Rubin.

LEDERMAN, WILLIAM RALPH   The nature and problems of a Bill of Rights. By W. R. Lederman. (In Ontario Advisory Committee on Confederation. *Background papers and reports.* [Toronto] 1967. v. 1, pp. [25]-36.)
"This paper was originally published in the Canadian bar review, vol. 37, March, 1959." Presented November, 1966.

——   Thoughts on reform of the Supreme Court of Canada. By W. R. Lederman. (In Ontario Advisory Committee on Confederation. *Background papers and reports.* [Toronto, 1970] v. 2, pp. 294-314.)
"First published in the Alberta law review, January 1970 (volume 8, no. 1)."

LORENTSEN, EDITH   Fifty years of labour legislation in Canada. By Edith Lorentsen and Evelyn Woolner. (In *The Labour gazette.* Ottawa. v. 50, no. 9 (Sept. 1950), pp. [1412]-1459.)

LOWER, ARTHUR REGINALD MARSDEN   The Bill of Rights. The War Measures Act "an iniquitous piece of legislation". By A. R. M. Lower. (In *Canadian commentator.* Toronto. v. 3, no. 3 (Mar. 1959), pp. 2-3.)

MACBETH, MADGE HAMILTON (LYONS)   The seven justices of the red robes. A quick sketch of Canada's Supreme Court. By Madge Macbeth and Leslie T. White. (In *Maclean's.* Toronto. v. 49, no. 7 (Apr. 1, 1936), pp. 26; 44; 46-47.)

MAC DONALD, VINCENT CHRISTOPHER   Legislative power and the Supreme Court in the fifties. Lectures delivered at the Osgoode Hall Law School, March 1960. Toronto, Butterworths, 1961. 28 p.
Contents: pt. 1. Scope of lectures. – pt. 2. The validity of statutes. – pt. 3. The Court; its method, functions and future.

——   Legislative power and the Supreme Court in the fifties. (In Lederman, W. R. (ed.) *The courts and the Canadian constitution.* [Toronto, c1964] pp. [152]-176.)
Originally published under the above title. Toronto, Butterworths, 1961. (28 p.)

Includes discussion on "matters related to the function of the Court as a constitutional exposition, and to its methods of adjudication".

MACDONNELL, GEORGE MILNES   The relations of legislation and morality. By G. M. Macdonnell. (In *Queen's quarterly.* Kingston. v. 7 (1899/1900), pp. [299]-309.)

MC GREGOR, FRED A.   Canada's method of industrial peace. (In *The McMaster University monthly.* Toronto. v. 21, no. 2 (Nov. 1911), pp. 58-64.)
Discusses the aims and methods of the Industrial Disputes Investigation Act, popularly known as the Lemieux Act, passed in 1907.

MAC KINNON, FRANK   The establishment of the Supreme Court of Canada. (In *The Canadian historical review.* Toronto. v. 27 (1946), pp. 258-274.)

——   The establishment of the Supreme Court of Canada. (In Lederman, W. R. (ed.) *The courts and the Canadian constitution.* [Toronto, c1964] pp. [106]-124.)
Reprinted from *The Canadian historical review,* v. 27 (1946), pp. [106]-124.

MC WHINNEY, EDWARD   The Canadian Supreme Court and constitutional reviews. (In Vaughan, Frederick (ed.) *Contemporary issues in Canadian politics.* Scarborough, Ont. [c1970] pp. 242-255.)
Reprinted from *The Canadian bar review,* vol. 45, 1967.

——   A Supreme Court in a bicultural society; the future role of the Canadian Supreme Court. (In Ontario Advisory Committee on Confederation. *Background papers and reports.* [Toronto] 1967. v. 1, pp. [89]-99.)
Presented June, 1965.

MIGNAULT, PIERRE BASILE   Le droit civil canadien. Basé sur les "Répétitions écrites sur le code civil" de Frédéric Mourlon, avec revue de la jurisprudence de nos tribunaux. Montréal, Whiteford & Théoret, 1895-1916. 9 v.
Vol. 6 published by C. Théoret; v. 7-9 by Wilson and Lafleur.

——   Indépendance des juges. Par l'honorable juge P. B. Mignault. (In Royal Society of Canada. *Proceedings and transactions.* Ottawa. ser. 3, v. 21 (1927), section 1, pp. 29-50.)
"Lu à la réunion de mai 1927."
A comparative analysis.

MOSS, JOHN HENRY   Copyright in Canada. By John H. Moss. (In *The University magazine*. Montreal. v. 13 (1914), pp. [194]-211.)

Traces the Canadian historical background up to the passage of the British Copyright Act of 1911.

NORMANDIN, A. B.   La législation et l'administration des eaux. (In *Revue trimestrielle canadienne*. Montréal. v. 15 (juin 1929), pp. [187]-197.)

NORRIS, LEONARD   The Statute of Westminster. By L. Norris. (In Okanagan Historical Society. *Report*. Vernon, B.C. 10th (1943), pp. 5-8.)

NORRIS, T. G.   The Natural Products Marketing Act, 1934. I. Constitutional validity, by T. G. Norris. II. Notes on the administration of the Act, by W. C. Hopper. (In *The Canadian journal of economics and political science*. [Toronto] v. 1, no. 3 (Aug. 1935), pp. 465-481.)

OLLIVIER, MAURICE   Structure juridique de l'Etat canadien. (In *Revue de l'Université d'Ottawa*. [Ottawa] 18. année (1948), pp. [280]-293.)

PAGNELO, S.   Lettres sur la réforme judiciaire. Montréal, J. Chapleau, 1880. iv, 241 p.

PECK, S. R.   Scalogram analysis of the Supreme Court of Canada. (In Vaughan, Frederick (ed.) *Contemporary issues in Canadian politics*. Scarborough, Ont. [c1970] pp. 270-286.)

Reprinted from *The Canadian bar review*, vol. 45, 1967.

PERRAULT, ANTONIO   Le bilinguisme fédéral; aspect juridique. (In *L'Action française*. Montréal. v. 13 (fév. 1925), pp. [66]-94.)

—— La Cour suprême du Canada. (In *Relations*. Montréal. 13. année, no. 145 (jan. 1953), pp. 18-20.)

—— Termes juridiques. (In *L'Action française*. Montréal. v. 6 (sept. 1921), pp. [557]-560.)

ROACH, EDISON LAWRENCE   The Civil Service Act, 1961. [Ottawa, Ont.] 1964. 1 v. Thesis (MA) – Carleton University.

ROSENBLUTH, G.   Canadian anti-combines administration, 1952-1960. By G. Rosenbluth and H. G. Thorburn. (In *The Canadian journal of economics and political science*. [Toronto] v. 27 (1961), pp. 498-508.)

"A paper given at the meeting of the Canadian Political Science Association in Montreal on June 10, 1961."

Examines the revisions to the Combines Investigation Act in 1952 and 1960, and reviews the administration of the Act between 1952 and 1960 in relation to certain concepts about the process of government in Canada.

RUBIN, GERALD   The nature, use and effect of reference cases in Canadian constitutional law. (In Lederman, W. R. (ed.) *The courts and the Canadian constitution*. [Toronto, c1964] pp. [220]-248.)

Reprinted from *The McGill law journal*, v. 6 (1959/60), pp. 168-190.

Discusses federal reference legislation.

RYAN, STUART   Charting our liberties. The proposed Canadian Bill of Rights. (In *Queen's quarterly*. Kingston. v. 66 (1959), pp. [389]-404.)

". . . appraises the proposed legislation in the context of our traditional liberties."

SANDWELL, BERNARD KEBLE   A Canadian Bill of Rights. By B. K. Sandwell. (In *Queen's quarterly*. Kingston. v. 58 (1951), pp. [264]-273.)

—— The Canadian Copyright Act. By B. K. Sandwell. (In *Queen's quarterly*. Kingston. v. 29 (1921/22), pp. 182-188.)

—— The copyright situation. By B. K. Sandwell. (In *Queen's quarterly*. Kingston. v. 38 (1931), pp. [335]-347.)

—— Supreme Court and the constitution. By B. K. Sandwell. (In *Saturday night*. Toronto. v. 67, no. 46 (Aug. 23, 1952), p. 10.)

—— The Supreme Court: liberty's safeguard. By B. K. Sandwell. (In *Saturday night*. Toronto. v. 67, no. 45 (Aug. 16, 1952), p. [9].)

SCHMEISER, DOUGLAS A.   Civil liberties in Canada. By D. A. Schmeiser. [London] Oxford University Press, 1964. xviii, 302 p.

"This work is written primarily from a legal point of view." But the issues of civil rights have been presented "in their legal and constitutional setting, with some reference to their historical development". - Pref.

Note: Chapt. 4. Denominational education (pp. [125]-195).

SKEOCH, LAWRENCE ALEXANDER   Combines legislation. An examination of proposed amendments. By L. A. Skeoch. (In *Queen's quarterly*. Kingston. v. 66 (1959), pp. [87]-96.)

SMAILS, REGINALD GEORGE HAMPDEN The Dominion Companies Act, 1934: an appraisal. By R. G. H. Smails. (In *The Canadian journal of economics and political science*. [Toronto] v. 1 (1935), pp. 52-63.)

Considers the problems relating to the clarification of jurisdiction over companies.

SMILEY, DONALD VICTOR The case against the Canadian Charter of Human Rights. (In *Canadian journal of political science*. Toronto. v. 2 (1969), pp. [277]-291.)

Presidential address to the Canadian Political Science Association at York University, June 4, 1969.

STEWART, BRYCE M. The Employment and Social Insurance Bill. (In *The Canadian journal of economics and political science*. Toronto. v. 1 (1935), pp. 436-464.)

Legislation was passed in 1935.

TARNOPOLSKY, WALTER SURMA The Canadian Bill of Rights. [London, 1962-63?] 1 v.

Thesis (LL M) – University of London.

—— The Canadian Bill of Rights. Toronto, Carswell, 1966. xxix, 246 p.

THOMPSON, BRAM Canada's national status. Canada's constitution, 1867. Subversive enactments of Parliament of Canada. Canada's constitution now a hotchpotch. Regina, The University Press, 1928. 20 p.

A legal argument demonstrating that the Dominion Land Act of 1872 and the Acts establishing Manitoba, Alberta and Saskatchewan are subversions of the British North America Act, 1867. (CHR. v. 9, no. 2. (1928), p. 187).

TOLLEFSON, EDWIN ARCHER Freedom of the press. By E. A. Tollefson. (In Lang, O. E. (ed.) *Contemporary problems of public law in Canada*. [Toronto, c1968] pp. [49]-70.)

Discusses government jurisdiction over the press, with special reference to the Alberta Press Bill (1937) which was disallowed by the Lieutenant-Governor of Alberta and referred to the Supreme Court of Canada.

TRUDEAU, PIERRE ELLIOTT Canadian Charter of Human Rights. (In Vaughan, Frederick (ed.) *Contemporary issues in Canadian politics*. Scarborough, Ont. [c1970] pp. 106-117.)

Reprinted from *A Canadian Charter of Human Rights*, by P. E. Trudeau. Ottawa, Queen's Printer, 1968.

WESTON, WILLIAM Rule by law or by administration? B. C. Supreme Court says that Legislature cannot endow administrative department with lawmaking power. Will judgment be upheld? Far-reaching effects. (In *Saturday night*. Toronto. v. 52, no. 32 (June 12, 1937), pp. [21]; 28.)

Concerns the ruling in 1937 by Justice A. M. Manson "that the Lieutenant-Governor-in-Council can administer the law, but can not make it." Refers to the validity of the Provincial Natural Products Marketing Act of 1934, as amended in 1936.

WICKSTEED, RICHARD J. The judicial committee. (In *The Canadian magazine of politics, science, art and literature*. Toronto. v. 8 (1896/97), pp. 273-274.)

WILLIS, JOHN Uniformity of legislation in Canada. (In *Public affairs*. Halifax. v. 5, no. 4 (summer 1942), pp. [169]-173.)

Discusses the work of the Conference of Commissioners on Uniformity of Legislation in Canada.

WILSON, A. D. Canadian housing legislation. (In *Canadian public administration*. Toronto. v. 2 (1959), pp. 214-228.)

Considers the development of public housing as a political subject gaining the recognized interest of government.

GUIDE TO SOURCES

GENERAL WORKS, OUTLINES, GUIDES, ETC.

BAIN, JAMES Canadian public documents. (In *The Canadian magazine of politics, science, art and literature.* Toronto. v. 25 (1905), pp. 125-127.)

The Librarian of the Toronto Public Library (1883-1908) describes the problems involved obtaining official government publications and lists suggested remedies for the situation.

BEAULIEU, ANDRE Guide d'histoire du Canada. Par André Beaulieu, Jean Hamelin et Benoît Bernier. Québec, Presses de l'Université Laval, 1969. xvi, 540 p. (Les Cahiers de l'Institut d'histoire, 13.)

". . . avec la collaboration de Luc-André Biron, Jean Dosmond, Jean-Pierre Gagnon, Serge Gagnon, Yves Tessier."

A revised and augmented edition of *Guide de l'étudiant en histoire du Canada,* par Jean Hamelin et André Beaulieu. (Québec, Presses de l'Université Laval, 1965.)

BLISS, JOHN WILLIAM MICHAEL (ed.) Canadian history in documents, 1763-1966. Edited by J. M. Bliss. Toronto, Ryerson Press [1966] xiv, 397 p. (Ryerson paperbacks, 11.)

"Documentary sources": pp. 385-390.

The editor intends this collection of documentary material primarily for the use of "senior high school students and university students taking introductory courses in Canadian history". Emphasis is on political and constitutional themes, but includes material on western expansion during the Laurier era and early-twentieth-century Canadian society.

BROWN, ROBERT CRAIG (ed.) Confederation to 1949. Edited by R. C. Brown and M. E. Prang. Scarborough, Ont., Prentice-Hall of Canada [c1966] xvi, 334 p. (Canadian historical documents series, v. 3.)

BURPEE, LAWRENCE JOHNSTONE Co-operation in historical research. (In *The University magazine.* Montreal. v. 7 (1908), pp. [360]-370.)

—— Only Canada has no National Library. By Lawrence J. Burpee. (In *Saturday night.* Toronto. v. 58, no. 50 (Aug. 21, 1943), p. 14.)

Describes this as "a project which has been agitated for more than thirty years" and as having the support in particular of Sir Wilfrid Laurier.

CANADA. DEPT. OF THE INTERIOR Electoral atlas of the Dominion of Canada. According to the Redistribution Act of 1914 and the Amending Act of 1915. Honorable Louis Coderre, Secretary of State. J. G. Foley, Clk. of the Crown in Chancery. Prepared under the direction of J. E. Chalifour, Chief Geographer, Department of the Interior. [Ottawa] 1915. 230 col. maps.

CANADIAN HISTORICAL ASSOCIATION Historical papers. Communications historiques. 1966- [Ottawa] v.

Continues the association's Report of the annual meeting.

Title varies: 1966-67, Historical papers

presented at the annual meeting. (Added title page in French.)

—— Report of the annual meeting. 1915-65. [Ottawa, etc.] 51 v.

Title varies slightly.

Reports for 1915-21 issued by the Association under an earlier name: Historic Landmarks Association of Canada.

English and French.

Some issues have added title page in French.

Continued by its Historical papers presented at the annual meeting.

Includes list of affiliated societies and organizations.

Indexes: 1922-51. 1 v.

CHERWINSKI, W. J. C. The Left in Canadian history, 1911-1969; bibliographical note. By W. J. C. Cherwinski. (In *Journal of Canadian studies*. Peterborough, Ont. v. 4, no. 4 (1969), pp. 51-60.)

Contributions to Canadian economics. v. 1-7; 1928-34. Toronto, University of Toronto Press [etc.] 7 v. illus., maps. (University of Toronto studies. History and economics.)

Bibliography of current publications on Canadian economics included in each volume.

Superseded by the Canadian journal of economics and political science in 1935.

Index to v. 1-7 in the Canadian journal of economics and political science, v. 1, pp. 131-135.

DOUGHTY, SIR ARTHUR GEORGE The preservation of historical documents in Canada. By A. G. Doughty. (In Royal Society of Canada. *Proceedings and transactions.* Ottawa. ser. 3, v. 18 (1924), section 2, pp. 63-73.)

"Read May meeting, 1914 [i.e. 1924]."

FISK, HARVEY EDWARD The Dominion of Canada: its growth and achievement; its relation to the British Empire; its form of government; its natural and developed resources; its home and foreign trade; its national finances; its banking and currency system, and its railroads and its shipping. By Harvey E. Fisk. New York, Bankers Trust Co., 1920. 174 p. diagr., map.

". . . the Bankers Trust Company has been led to prepare this book in order that the company, its stockholders, clients and friends might have at hand for ready reference reliable data about Canada." – To the reader.

The Gallup poll results. Toronto, Canadian Institute of Public Opinion. no.

Continued by Public opinion news service.

The Gallup report. Dec. 20, 1967- . Toronto, Canadian Institute of Public Opinion. no.

Continues the Public opinion news service.

HAMELIN, JEAN Guide de l'étudiant en histoire du Canada. Par Jean Hamelin et André Beaulieu. Préf. de Marcel Trudel. Québec, Presses de l'Université Laval, 1965] iv, 274 leaves.

Later edition: Guide d'histoire du Canada, par André Beaulieu, Jean Hamelin et Benoît Bernier. Québec, Presses de l'Université Laval, 1969.

HOPKINS, JOHN CASTELL A chronology of Canadian history from Confederation in 1867 up to the end of 1900. An appendix to the Canadian annual review of public affairs, 1905. [Toronto, Canadian Annual Review of Public Affairs, 1905] xxxvii p.

KENNEDY, WILLIAM PAUL MC CLURE Annual survey of the literature of constitutional and administrative law. By W. P. M. Kennedy. (In *The Canadian historical review.* Toronto. v. 14 (1933), pp. 305-317.)

—— Annual survey of the literature of constitutional and administrative law. By W. P. M. Kennedy. (In *The Canadian historical review.* Toronto. v. 15 (1934), pp. 298-305.)

—— Annual survey of the literature of constitutional and administrative law. By W. P. M. Kennedy. (In *The Canadian historical review.* Toronto. v. 17 (1936), pp. 320-331.)

KERR, DONALD GORDON GRADY A historical atlas of Canada. Editor: D. G. G. Kerr; cartography: preparation by C.C.J. Bond, drawing by Ellsworth M. Walsh assisted by Edward Banks and Roy Petticrew. 2d ed. Don Mills, Ont., Nelson [1966] ix, 120 p. illus. (part col.) col. maps.

First edition published in 1960; third edition in 1975.

KERR, WILFRED BRENTON Historical literature on Canada's participation in the Great War. By W. B. Kerr. (In *The Canadian historical review.* Toronto. v. 14 (1933), pp. 412-436.)

Bibliography: pp. 428-436.

—— Supplementary list of historical literature relating to Canada's part in the Great War. By W. B. Kerr. (In *The Canadian Historical review*. Toronto. v. 15 (1934), pp. 181-190.)

LAMB, WILLIAM KAYE   Seventy-five years of Canadian bibliography. By W. Kaye Lamb. (In Royal Society of Canada. *Proceedings and transactions*. Ottawa. ser. 3, v. 51 (1957), section 2, pp. 1-11.)

Evaluates the works cited in the essay.

LAWRENCE, BERTHA   A survey of the materials to be found in the Provincial Legislative Library, Alberta, for the study of Canadian history and more particularly that of Western Canada. [Edmonton] 1936. 419 leaves.

Thesis (MA) – University of Alberta.

Abstracts are given of many of the titles.

The Legal news. Edited by James Kirby. v. 1-20; Jan. 5, 1878–Dec. 15, 1897. Montreal, R. White [etc.] 20 v.

Weekly, 1878-91; semimonthly, 1892-97.

Consists of table of cases, reported, noted and digested.

LITERARY AND HISTORICAL SOCIETY OF QUEBEC   Historical documents. ser. 1– Quebec. [etc.] Telegraph Print. Co. [etc.] 1838- v. illus. (part fold.)

Ceased publication with ser. 10 (1927). Cf. Union list of serials.

Title varies: ser. 1 issued without title; ser. 2 and 4, Manuscripts relating to the early history of Canada; [ser. 6] Manuscripts.

MILES, HENRY HOPPER   Canadian archives. By Henry H. Miles. (In *Stewart's quarterly*. St. John, N.B. v. 5, no. 1 (Apr. 1871), pp. 9-20.)

MOREL, ANDRE   Canada français. [Bruxelles, Editions de l'Institut de sociologie, Université libre de Bruxelles] 1963. 43 p. (Introduction bibliographique à l'histoire du droit et à l'ethnologie juridique, publiée sous la direction de John Gilissen [no] F/11).

Public opinion news service.   -Dec. 16, 1967. Toronto, Canadian Institute of Public Opinion. no.

Continues the Gallup poll results.

Continued by the Gallup report.

REID, JOHN HOTCHKISS STEWART (ed.)   A source-book of Canadian history. Selected documents and personal papers by J. H. Stewart Reid, Kenneth McNaught and

Harry S. Crowe. [Rev. ed. with index] Toronto, Longmans, Green, [c1964] xvi, 485 p.

First published Toronto, Longmans, Green [1959].

Review of historical publications relating to Canada. v. 1-22; 1896-1917/18. Toronto, University of Toronto Press [etc.] 1897-1919. 22 v. (University of Toronto studies.)

The 1st volume (1896) includes important publications of 1895.

G. M. Wrong, editor (with H. H. Langton, 1897-1910, 1913-17/18; W. S. Wallace, 1911-1917/18).

Publisher varies: 1896, W. Briggs; 1897-1903, the Librarian of the University of Toronto; 1904-08, Morang; 1913-16, Glasgow, Brook for University of Toronto.

Superseded by the Canadian historical review.

—— Index, vols. I-X. By H. H. Langton. Toronto, Morang, 1907. 202 p. (University of Toronto studies.)

—— Index, vols. XI-XX. By Laura Mason. [Toronto] University of Toronto, published by the Librarian, 1918. 218 p. (University of Toronto studies.)

RYDER, DOROTHY E. (ed.)   Canadian reference sources; a selective guide. Ottawa, Canadian Library Association, 1973. x, 185 p.

Supplement published in 1975.

SAGE, WALTER NOBLE   Where stands Canadian history. By Walter N. Sage. (In Canadian Historical Association. *Report of the annual meeting*. Toronto. (1945), pp. 5-14.)

Presidential address.

A review of Canadian historical literature.

SMITH, IRVING NORMAN   Library of Parliament. By I. Norman Smith. (In *Maclean's*. Toronto. v. 53, no. 8 (Apr. 15, 1940), pp. 18-19; 45-47.)

Contains general information about Canadian historical figures, e.g. Mackenzie King, Sir John A. Macdonald, etc.

STORY, NORAH   The Oxford companion to Canadian history and literature. Toronto, Oxford University Press, 1967. xi, 935 p. maps.

TALMAN, JAMES JOHN (ed.)   Basic documents in Canadian history. By James J.

Talman. Princeton, N.J., Toronto, Van Nostrand Co. [c1959] 189 p. (An Anvil original, no. 40.)

"The purpose of this volume is to provide a selection of documents to illustrate the development of Canada. . . ."

TROTTER, REGINALD GEORGE Canadian history; a syllabus and guide to reading. New and enl. ed. Toronto, Macmillan, 1934. xiv, 193 p.

URQUHART, MALCOLM CHARLES (ed.) Historical statistics of Canada. By M. C. Urquhart and K. A. H. Buckley. Cambridge [Eng.] University Press, 1965. xv, 672 p.

"Sponsored by Canadian Political Science Association and Social Science Research Council of Canada."

Covers the period 1867-1960.

WALLACE, WILLIAM STEWART The bibliography of "Canadiana". (In *The University magazine*. Montreal. v. 11 (1912), pp. [284]-288.)

BIBLIOGRAPHIES, LISTS, INDEXES, CATALOGUES, ETC.

America, history and life. v. 1- July 1964- Santa Barbara, Calif., Published by the Clio Press for the American Bibliographical Center. v.

"A guide to periodical literature."

Abstracts periodical articles, etc., on the history of the United States and Canada. The Canadian material divides into general history, discovery period to the proclamation of 1763, 1763 to Confederation, Dominion of Canada, 1867-1945, Canada 1945 to the present and regional or local history.

Atlantic Provinces checklist. v. 1-9; 1957-65. Halifax, Atlantic Provinces Library Association in cooperation with Atlantic Provinces Economic Council. 9 v.

"A guide to current information in books, pamphlets, government publications, magazine articles and documentary films relating to the four Atlantic Provinces . . ." (varies slightly).

"Compiled and edited by members of the Atlantic Provinces Library Association."

Bibliography of publications by Henry F. Angus. (In Clark, R. M. (ed.) *Canadian issues*. [Toronto c1961] pp. [367]-371.)

BOULT, REYNALD A bibliography of Canadian law. Prepared for the International Committee for Social Sciences Documentation under the auspices of the International Association of Legal Science. With the support of the Canadian Association of Comparative Law and the Canadian and Foreign Law Research Centre. Montreal, Wilson and Lafleur, 1966. xii, 393 p.

Text partly in French, partly in English. Added title page in French.

BRAULT, LUCIEN Francis-J. Audet et son œuvre; bio-bibliographie. Avec préf. de Victor Morin. Ottawa [Hull, L'Impr. Leclerc] 1940. 92 p. port.

"Cet ouvrage a été tiré à 250 exemplaires."

BURPEE, LAWRENCE JOHNSTONE A Canadian bibliography of the year 1901. By Lawrence J. Burpee. (In Royal Society of Canada. *Proceedings and transactions*. Ottawa. ser 2, v. 8 (1902), section 2, pp. 233-344.)

"Read May 27, 1902."

—— Index and dictionary of Canadian history. Edited by Lawrence J. Burpee and Arthur G. Doughty. Ed. de luxe. Toronto, Morang, 1911. xvi, 446 p. fold front., fold. map. (The Makers of Canada.)

"Analytical index to the entire series of twenty volumes", which constitutes the Makers of Canada series. A bibliographical index.

—— List of papers contributed to section two of the Royal Society of Canada— 1882-1924. By Lawrence J. Burpee. (In Royal Society of Canada. *Proceedings and transactions*. Ottawa. ser. 3, v. 19 (1925), section 2, pp. 9-17.)

"Read May meeting, 1925."

CANADA. PUBLIC ARCHIVES Catalogue of pamphlets in the Public Archives of Canada . . . with index. Prepared by Magdalen Casey. Ottawa, F. A. Acland, Printer to the King, 1931-32. 2 v. (Publications of the Public Archives of Canada, no. 13.)

Added title page in French; introd. in English and French.

"Published by the authority of the Secretary of State under the direction of the Dominion Archivist."

"In 1903 the Department of Public Archives published a first list of pamphlets . . . In 1916 Mr. Norman Fee prepared a new catalogue . . . up to the time of Confederation . . . It is now necessary to revise the old catalogue . . . to include pamphlets published after 1867". – Introd.

Contents: [v. 1] 1493-1877. – [v.] 2 1878-1931.

—— Preliminary inventory. Manuscript group 26; Prime Ministers' papers. [Ottawa] 1958. 28 p.

At head of title: Public Archives of Canada. Manuscript Division.

—— Preliminary inventory. Manuscript group 28; records of post-Confederation corporate bodies. [Ottawa] 1960. 38 p.

At head of title: Public Archives of Canada. Manuscript Division.

—— Preliminary inventory. Manuscript group 29; nineteenth century post-Confederation manuscripts, 1867-1900. [Ottawa] 1962. 48 p.

At head of title: Public Archives of Canada. Manuscript Division.

—— Preliminary inventory. Manuscript group 30; twentieth century manuscripts. [Ottawa, Queen's Printer] 1966. v, 87 p.

Issued by the Manuscript Division of the Public Archives.

—— Preliminary inventory. Record groups, no. 14: Record of Parliament, 1775-1915; no. 15: Department of the Interior; no. 16: Department of National Revenue. [Ottawa] 1957. 30 p. diagr.

At head of title: Public Archives of Canada. Manuscript Division.

CANADA. SUPREME COURT Index to the Supreme Court of Canada reports, 1876-1950 (volumes 1 to 64 and 1923 to 1950). By John Southall and Gerald D. Sanagan. Toronto, Butterworth, 1952. 2 v. (vi, 900 p.)

—— Cumulative supplement. 3d. Comprising all cases reported during the years 1951-1962. By Gerald D. Sanagan. Toronto, Butterworth, 1963. 89 p.

Canadian book-prices current. v. 1-3; 1950/ 55–1959/62. Toronto, McClelland and Stewart [1957-1964] 3 v.

Vols. 1 and 2 compiled by Robert M. Hamilton; vol. 3 compiled by Rita Butterfield, assisted by Robert M. Hamilton.

Includes books, pamphlets, periodicals and broadsides. Excludes books published since 1945.

Provides useful and accurate publishing data.

Vol. 3 (1959/1962) is the last vol. published to date.

Canadian books in print. Catalogue des livres canadiens en librairie. 1967- [Toronto] Published by University of Toronto Press for the Canadian Books in Print Committee. v.

Vols. for 1967-68 published by Canadian Books in Print Committee.

Issued in parts: Author, Title and Publisher index.

The Canadian catalogue of books published in Canada, about Canada, as well as those written by Canadians with imprint 1921-1949. With cumulated author index. [2d] consolidated English language reprint ed. [Toronto] Toronto Public Libraries, 1967. 1 v. (various pagings).

Reprint ed. of the English sections of the Canadian catalogue, published annually 1921/22 to 1949.

First ed. 1959, in 2 v.

"The Canadian Catalogue was published yearly from 1921-22 to 1949, and in 1950 was succeeded by an annual record of Canadian publishing produced under the authority of the Canadian Bibliographic Centre of the National Library, Ottawa. The first year, the original title was retained. . . . From 1951 on, the publication became Canadiana and was published by the National Library, Ottawa". – Introd. note.

CANADIAN HISTORICAL ASSOCIATION. REPORT OF THE ANNUAL MEETING (INDEXES) Index to the Annual report, 1922-1951. Ottawa, Canadian Historical Association, 1952. 43 p.

Cover title.

Title page in French.

Bilingual.

The Index lists authors and subjects separately. cf. [Introd.] R. A. Preston.

Prepared by Mrs. Janet Craig.

—— Index to Annual report, 1952-1966 and Historical papers, 1967-1968. Index du Rapport annuel 1952-1966 et Communications historiques, 1967-1968. Ottawa, Canadian Historical Association, 1969. vi, 28 p.

Prepared by Miss Grace Maurice.

Contents: Table of Contents. – Author index. – Subject index.

THE CANADIAN HISTORICAL REVIEW. (INDEX-ES) Index. Volumes I-X, 1920-1929. By Julia Jarvis and Alison Ewart. [Preface by W. S. Wallace. Toronto] University of Toronto Press, 1930. 284 p. (University of Toronto studies.)

"Miss Jarvis has compiled the author index, and Miss Ewart the subject index". – Pref.

—— Index. Volumes XI-XX, 1930-1939. Compiled by the Editorial Department of the University of Toronto Press under the direction of Alison Hewitt. [Preface by George W. Brown] Toronto, University of Toronto Press, 1944. vi, 432 p. (University of Toronto studies.)

—— The Canadian historical review index. Volumes XXI-XXX, 1940-1949. Compiled by the Editorial Department of the University of Toronto Press. [Toronto] University of Toronto Press [c1959] 404 p.

Author and subject index.

". . . fifth in a series of decennial indexes which were begun in 1907 for the annual Review of historical publications relating to Canada, and which have been continued for its successor, the Canadian historical review. The first two were for volumes I-XX of the annual Review, which was founded by Professor George M. Wrong in 1896. The third Index covered the first ten years of the present quarterly Review, which was established in 1920, and the fourth brought the work down to the end of 1939". – Editorial note.

CANADIAN HISTORICAL REVIEW. (INDEXES) The Canadian historical review index. Volumes XXXI-LI, 1950-70. [Toronto] University of Toronto Press [c1974]. 219 p.

CANADIAN JOURNAL OF ECONOMICS AND PO-LITICAL SCIENCE. (INDEXES) Decennial index to the Canadian journal of economics and political science. The journal of the Canadian Political Science Association. Volumes I-X (1935-1944) [Toronto] University of Toronto Press, 1945. 64 p.

"This index was prepared by Mrs. K. W. Klawe with the assistance of the Editorial Department of the University of Toronto Press.

An index to Contributions to Canadian economics and the Proceedings of the Canadian Political Science Association, forerunners of the Canadian journal of economics

and political science was published in the first number of this Journal."

—— Decennial index. Volumes XI-XX (1945-1954) [Toronto] Canadian Political Science Association [Printed by University of Toronto Press] 1955. 53 p.

"This index was prepared by Mrs. Stanley Ward."

—— Decennial index. Volumes XXI-XXX (1955-1964) [Toronto] Canadian Political Science Association [Printed by University of Toronto Press] 1965. 61 p.

THE CANADIAN MAGAZINE OF POLITICS, SCI-ENCE, ART AND LITERATURE. (INDEXES) A comprehensive index of the first twenty-five volumes of the Canadian magazine, March, 1893-October, 1905. Toronto, Ontario Pub. Co., 1907. 55 p.

Arranged in two parts, listing articles and authors.

CANADIAN TAX FOUNDATION Index of Canadian Tax Foundation publications, 1945-1971. [Toronto, c1976]. vi, 236 p.

Canadiana. 1950/51– Ottawa, National Library of Canada, 1953 [v. 1, 1962] -

Issued monthly (semimonthly Jan.-Nov. 1951) with annual cumulations.

Issues for 1951-52 published by the Canadian Bibliographic Centre; which became the National Library in 1953.

Supersedes Canadian catalogue of books published in Canada, about Canada, as well as those written by Canadians, compiled 1921-49, by the Toronto Public Libraries.

CARSWELL COMPANY, LIMITED, TORONTO Catalogue of Canadian publications, including historical and general books, statutes and other government imprints, pamphlets, magazines and miscellaneous books. Toronto, Carswell Co., 1900. 71 p.

Catalogue de l'édition au Canada français. 1958– [Montréal] v.

Title varies: 1958-62, Catalogue collectif de l'édition canadienne.

Issued 1958-65 by the Association des éditeurs canadiens (1958 under the association's former name: Société des éditeurs canadiens); 1966/67- by the Conseil supérieur du livre.

"Publié . . . avec le concours du Ministère des affaires culturelles du Québec."

CONTRIBUTIONS TO CANADIAN ECONOMICS. (INDEXES) Index to "Contributions to Canadian economics", v. 1-7, and to "The Papers and proceedings of the Canadian

Political Science Association", v. 1-6. (In *The Canadian journal of economics and political science*. Toronto. v. 1, no. 1 (Feb. 1935), pp. 131-135.)

LE DEVOIR, MONTREAL. (INDEXES) Index. v. [1]-6; 1966-71. [Québec] Centre de documentation, Bibliothèque Université Laval. 6 v. in 9.

Issued monthly and annually.

Continued by Index de l'actualité, vue à travers la presse écrite.

DIONNE, NARCISSE EUTROPE Inventaire chronologique, par N. E. Dionne. Québec, 1905-09. 4 v.

Title varies.

Index to v. 1 issued separately with special title-page: Table des noms et des matières. Inventaire chronologique des livres . . . etc. pub. en langue française dans la province de Québec . . . 1764-1906.

Published by the Royal Society of Canada. Also issued in the Proceedings and transactions of the Society, 2d ser., v. 10-12, 14; 1904-06, 1908.

Partial contents: t. 1. Inventaire chronologique des livres, brochures, journaux et revues publiés en langue française dans la province de Québec depuis l'établissement de l'imprimerie au Canada jusqu'à nos jours, 1764-1905. – t. 3. Inventaire chronologique des livres, brochures, journaux et revues publiés en langue anglaise dans la province de Québec, 1764-1906.

—— Inventaire chronologique des livres, brochures, journaux et revues publiés en diverses langues dans et hors la province de Québec. Premier supplément, par N.-E. Dionne . . . 1904-1912. Québec, 1912. 76 p.

—— Travaux historiques publiés depuis trente ans. Par le Dr. N.-E. Dionne. Québec, Typ. Laflamme & Proulx, 1909. 27 p. port.

At head of title: 1879-1909.

GAGNON, PHILEAS Essai de bibliographie canadienne; inventaire d'une bibliothèque comprenant imprimés, manuscrits, estampes, etc., relatifs à l'histoire du Canada et des pays adjacents, avec des notes bibliographiques. Québec, L'Auteur, 1895-1913. 2 v. facsims., port.

Volume 2: Collection Gagnon, depuis 1895 à 1909 inclusivement, d'après les notes bibliographiques et le catalogue de l'auteur. Préf. de l'échevin Victor Morin. Pub. par la cité de Montréal sous la direction de Frédéric Villeneuve, bibliothécaire en chef. Montréal [Impr. "La Patrie"] 1913.

The collection was acquired by the city of Montreal in 1909 as a nucleus for the public library.

HAIGHT, WILLET RICKETSON Canadian catalogue of books 1791-1897; 1791-1895 and the two annual supplements for 1896 and 1897. London, H. Pordes, 1958. 130, 48, 57, [19] p.

Facsimile reprint of Canadian catalogue of books and two annual supplements first published Toronto, Haight, 1896, 1898 and 1904.

HARVARD UNIVERSITY. LIBRARY Canadian history and literature; classification schedule, classified listing by call number, alphabetical listing by author or title, chronological listing. Cambridge [Mass.] Distributed by the Harvard University Press, 1968. 411 p. (Its Widener Library shelf-list, 20.)

Includes material published about Canada to 1967.

JOHNSON, DANIEL Index to Supreme Court cases, 1923-1950. All decisions of the Supreme Court of Canada published in Canada law reports from 1923 to 1950 inclusive. With relevant annotations regarding appeals to the Privy Council. By Daniel Johnson and Reginald D. Tormey. Montreal, Wilson et Lafleur [1951] viii, 1315 p.

KINGSTON, ONT. QUEEN'S UNIVERSITY. LIBRARY A note on the manuscript collection in the Douglas Library, Queen's University. By E. C. Kyte, librarian. Kingston, 1943. 26 p.

Letters in Canada. 1935– (In *The University of Toronto quarterly*. [Toronto] v. 5- (1935/36-).)

LIBOIRON, ALBERT A. (comp.) Federalism and intergovernmental relations in Australia, Canada, the United States and other countries; a bibliography. Compiled by Albert A. Liboiron. Kingston, Ont., Institute of Intergovernmental Relations, Queen's University, 1967. vi, 231 leaves.

Mimeographed.

LOCHHEAD, DOUGLAS GRANT Bibliography of Canadian bibliographies. 2d ed., rev. and enl. Compiled by Douglas Lochhead. Index compiled by Peter E. Greig. [Toronto] Published in association with the Bibliographical Society of Canada by University of Toronto Press [1972] xiv, 312 p.

Added title page: Bibliographie des bibliographies canadiennes.

Rev. and enl. edition of Bibliography of Canadian bibliographies, compiled by Raymond Tanghe, first published 1960, the three supplements embracing the years 1961-65, and new information to June 1970.
Pref. and introd. also in French.

LOWTHER, BARBARA J. A bibliography of British Columbia; laying the foundations 1849-1899. By Barbara J. Lowther, with the assistance of Muriel Laing. [Victoria, B.C., University of Victoria, c1968] xii, 328 p.
"Prepared under the auspices of the Social Sciences Research Centre, University of Victoria."

MACLEAN'S. (INDEXES) An index to Maclean's magazine, 1914-1937. Compiled by Peter Mitchell. Ottawa, Canadian Library Association, 1965. 140 p. (Canadian Library Association. Occasional paper no. 47.)
Cover title.

NEW BRUNSWICK MUSEUM, ST. JOHN. DEPT. OF CANADIAN HISTORY. ARCHIVES DIVISION Inventory of manuscripts. [Saint John, N.B.] 1967. 154 p.
Cover title.

Ouvrages publiés sur Laurier; liste partielle (In Le Bulletin des recherches historiques. Lévis. v. 40, no. 6 (juin 1934), pp. 383-384.)

PEEL, BRUCE BRADEN (comp.) A bibliography of the Prairie Provinces to 1953 with biographical index. 2d ed. [Toronto] University of Toronto Press [c1973] xxviii, 780 p.
First ed. published 1956.

QUEBEC (PROVINCE) ROYAL COMMISSION OF INQUIRY ON CONSTITUTIONAL PROBLEMS Table analytique des mémoires et autres documents consultés par la commission. [Par le] Secrétariat de la commission. [n.p.] 1956. xiii, 209 (i.e. 211) p.
At head of title: Annexe 10.

Recent publications relating to Canada. 1920- (In The Canadian historical review. [Toronto] v. 1- (1920-).)

ROYAL COMMONWEALTH SOCIETY. LIBRARY Subject catalogue of the Library of the Royal Empire Society, formerly Royal Colonial Institute. By Evans Lewin. [London, Royal Empire Society] 1930-37. 4 v.
Includes not only books and pamphlets, but also articles in reviews and journals, papers read before learned and other societies, etc.

Partial contents: v. 3. The Dominion of Canada and its provinces, the Dominion of Newfoundland, the West Indies, and colonial America.

—— Biography catalogue of the Library of the Royal Commonwealth Society. By Donald H. Simpson, librarian. London, Royal Commonwealth Society, 1961. xxiii, 511 p.

—— Subject catalogue of the Royal Commonwealth Society, London. Boston, G. K. Hall, 1971. 7 v.
"The Subject catalogue . . . was published . . . in 1930-37, and was reprinted with new introductions in 1967. The Biography catalogue appeared in 1961. . . . The present publication supplements these volumes by reproducing all the cards added between the date of their publication and March 1971." – Introd.
Partial contents: v. 5. The Americas.

TANGHE, RAYMOND Bibliography of Canadian bibliographies. Toronto, Published in association with the Bibliographical Society of Canada by University of Toronto Press, 1960. 206 p.
Added title page: Bibliographie des bibliographies canadiennes.
Annotations are in English or French according to the language of the titles listed.

—— Supplement, 1960/61-1964/65. Toronto, Bibliographical Society of Canada, 1962-66. 3 v.
Cover title.
Biennial.

THOMSON, INGA Bibliography of J. W. Dafoe, 1866-1944. Compiled by Inga Thomson and Marcella Dafoe. (In The Canadian journal of economics and political science. Toronto. v. 10 (1944), pp. 213-215.)
Presented as an incomplete bibliography. Lists books, articles and addresses.

TOD, DOROTHEA DOUGLAS A check list of Canadian imprints, 1900-1925. Catalogue d'ouvrages imprimés au Canada. Compiled by Dorothea D. Tod & Audrey Cordingley. Prelim. checking ed. Ottawa, Canadian Bibliographic Centre, Public Archives of Canada, 1950. 370 leaves.
Cover title.
Text in English and French.

TORONTO. PUBLIC LIBRARIES Guide to the manuscript collection in the Toronto Public Libraries. [Enl. ed., prepared by Don-

alda Putnam and Edith Firth. Toronto]
1954. iv, 116 p.

First ed. published in 1940 under title:
Preliminary guide to the manuscript collection in the Toronto Public Libraries.

"The manuscript collection of the Toronto Public Libraries consists mainly of
. . . Upper Canadian historical manuscripts.
. . . There are several large sets of personal
papers and many single pieces, including
diaries, account-books, letter-books and
single documents" some of which are relevant to the post-Confederation period.

—— Preliminary guide to the manuscript
collection in the Toronto Public Libraries,
Prepared by Florence B. Murray and Elsie
McLeod Murray, under the direction of
Charles R. Sanderson. [Toronto] 1940. iv,
60 p.

"Comprised largely of Canadian, and
more particularly of Upper Canadian historical manuscripts, although it contains
some British and American items. . . . Only
. . . manuscripts antedating 1900 have been
included." – Prefatory note.

Later edition published in 1954 under
title: Guide to the manuscript collection in
the Toronto Public Libraries.

TROTTER, REGINALD GEORGE The bibliography of Canadian constitutional history.
By Reginald G. Trotter. (In Bibliographical Society of America. *Papers.* Chicago.
v. 22, pt. 1 (1928), pp. 1-12.)

Running title: Canadian constitutional
history.

Union list of manuscripts in Canadian repositories. Catalogue collectif des manuscrits des archives canadiennes. Director:
W. Kaye Lamb. Editor: Robert S. Gordon.
Editorial team: Barry E. Hyman [and
others] Ottawa [Queen's Printer] 1968.
x, 734 p.

On cover: Joint project of the Public
Archives of Canada and the Humanities
Research Council of Canada.

English and French.

Revised ed., in 2 vols., published in 1975.

U.S. LIBRARY OF CONGRESS. DIVISION OF BIBLIOGRAPHY List of references on reciprocity. Compiled under the direction of the
Chief Bibliographer. 1st ed.: Appleton
Prentiss Clark Griffin; 2d ed., with additions: H. H. B. Meyer. Washington, Gov.
Print. Off., 1910. 137 p.

"Reciprocity with Canada and Newfoundland occupies thirty-one pages. A
chronological arrangement by class of publication . . . enables the history of the
movement to be seen. The first debate on
the subject in the American House of Representatives was reported in January 1849.
The latest magazine article quoted was published in October 1910". – Review of historical publications relating to Canada, v.
15, p. 136.

WALLACE, WILLIAM STEWART The Ryerson
imprint; a check-list of the books and pamphlets published by the Ryerson Press
since the foundation of the House in 1829.
Toronto, Ryerson Press [1954] 141 p.

WARD, JANE (comp.) The published works
of H. A. Innis. Prepared by Jane Ward.
(In *The Canadian journal of economics
and political science.* [Toronto] v. 19
(1953), pp. 233-244.)

A listing of books, articles, addresses,
etc., arranged in chronological order.

WATTERS, REGINALD EYRE A checklist of
Canadian literature and background materials, 1628-1960. In two parts: first, a comprehensive list of the books which constitute Canadian literature written in English; and second, a selective list of other
books by Canadian authors which reveal
the backgrounds of that literature. 2d ed.,
rev. and enl. [Toronto] University of Toronto Press [1972] xxiv, 1085 p.

First edition published in 1959.

Includes non-fiction background material.

WINKS, ROBIN WILLIAM EVERT Canada. By
Robin W. Winks. (In his *The historiography of the British Empire-Commonwealth;
trends, interpretations and resources.* Durham, N.C., Duke University Press, 1966.
pp. 69-136.)

A bibliographical essay reviewing historical writings in Canada.

—— Recent trends and new literature in
Canadian history. By Robin W. Winks.
Washington, Service Center for Teachers
of History [1959] 56 p. (Service Center
for Teachers of History. Publication no.
19.)

An expanded version of this bibliographical essay was later published under the title
"Canada". (In Winks, R. W. *The historiography of the British Empire-Commonwealth.* Durham, N.C., Duke University
Press, 1966. pp. 69-136.)

Writings on American history. 1902–
[Washington, etc., Govt. Print. Off., etc.]
1904- v.

1902-35 include material on Canada.

Vols. for 1909-11 reprinted from the *Annual report* of the American Historical Association; 1918-29 issued as supplement to the report; 1930-31, 1935- issued as v. 2 of the report; 1932, as v. 3 and 1933-34 as the complete report.

No bibliographies issued for 1904-05.

DICTIONARIES, ENCYCLOPEDIAS, HANDBOOKS, DIRECTORIES, ETC.

ADAM, GRAEME MERCER (ed.) Prominent men of Canada; a collection of persons distinguished in professional and political life, and in the commerce and industry of Canada. Edited by G. Mercer Adam. Toronto, Canadian Biographical Pub. Co., 1892. 476 p. plate, ports.

AUDET, FRANCOIS JOSEPH Canadian historical dates and events, 1492-1915. By Francis J. Audet. Ottawa, Printed by G. Beauregard, 1917. 239 p.

—— Gouverneurs, lieutenants-gouverneurs et administrateurs de la province de Québec, des Bas et Haut Canadas, du Canada sous l'union et de la puissance du Canada, 1763-1908. Par Francis J. Audet. [Ottawa, Imprimé pour la Société royale du Canada, 1909] 85-124 p. facsims. (On cover: Des mémoires de la Société royale du Canada. vol. II, sec. I. 3. sér. 1908-1909.)

Biographies canadiennes-françaises. 1.- année; 1920- Montréal, Editions biographiques canadiennes-françaises [etc.] v. illus., ports.

Compilers: 1. année (1920), J. A. Fortier. - 2.-14. année (1922-42), Raphaël Ouimet. - 15-20. année (1948-65), J.A. Fortin.

BOURINOT, SIR JOHN GEORGE Bourinot's Rules of order. A manual on the practices and usages of the House of Commons of Canada, and on procedure at public assemblies, including meetings of shareholders and directors of companies, political conventions, and other gatherings. Rev. by J. Gordon Dubroy. 2d ed. [Toronto] McClelland and Stewart [c1963] xii, 116 p.

—— A Canadian manual on the procedure at meetings of municipal councils, shareholders and directors of companies, synods, conventions, societies and public bodies generally, with an introductory review of the rules and usages of Parliament that govern public assemblies in Canada. Toronto, Carswell Co., 1894. viii, 444 p.

—— A manual of the constitutional history of Canada from the earliest period to the year 1888, including the British North America Act, 1867 and a digest of judicial decisions on questions of legislative jurisdiction. Montreal, Dawson Bros., 1888. xii, 238 p.

"This treatise is in a large measure a revised republication of certain chapters of the author's large book on Parliamentary practice and procedure in Canada". – Prefatory note.

—— A manual of the constitutional history of Canada from the earliest period to 1901; including the British North America Act of 1867, a digest of judicial decisions on important questions of legislative jurisdiction, and observations on the working of parliamentary government. New ed., rev. and enl. Toronto, Copp, Clark Co., 1901. xii, 246 p.

—— Parliamentary procedure and practice, with an introductory account of the origin and growth of parliamentary institutions in the Dominion of Canada. Montreal, Dawson Bros., 1884. xv, 785 p.

—— Parliamentary procedure and practice; with a review of the origin, growth and operation of parliamentary institutions in the Dominion of Canada, and an appendix, containing the British North America Act of 1867, and amending acts. 2d ed., rev. and enl. Montreal, Dawson Bros., 1892. xx, 929 p.

—— Parliamentary procedure and practice in the Dominion of Canada. With historical introd. and an appendix. 3d ed. Edited by Thomas Barnard Flint. Toronto, Canada Law Book Co., 1903. xviii, 892 p.

—— Parliamentary procedure and practice in the Dominion of Canada. 4th ed. Edited by Thomas Barnard Flint. Toronto, Canada Law Book Co., 1916. xx, 693 p.

BURPEE, LAWRENCE JOHNSTONE (ed.) The Oxford encyclopaedia of Canadian history, by Lawrence J. Burpee. London, Toronto, Oxford University Press, 1926. vi, 699 p. front., maps. (The Makers of Canada series. Anniversary ed. [v. 12].)

"A far more comprehensive work than" his Index and dictionary of Canadian history, 1911. Cf. Introd.

CAMPEAU, FABIEN RENE EDOUARD Illustrated guide to the Senate and House of Commons of Canada, containing the portraits and autographs of . . . the Governor General, the members of the Cabinet . . . and the members and officers of the Senate and House of Commons . . . with the autographs and political biography of members of both Houses . . . Published by F. R. E. Campeau, Ottawa. [v. 1-3] Ottawa, Printed by A. Bureau [etc.] 1875-85. 3 v. fold. diagr., ports.

Title varies: 1875, Illustrated guide to the House of Commons; 1879. Illustrated guide to the House of Commons and Senate.

Published also in French.

CANADA. BUREAU OF STATISTICS Canada, 1930- . The official handbook of present conditions and recent progress. [Ottawa, Queen's Printer] v. illus.

Subtitle varies.

Issued also in French.

Issue for 1967 has title: Canada one hundred, 1867-1967.

—— Canada, 1930- . Un manuel des conditions actuelles et des progrès récents de la puissance. [Ottawa, F. A. Acland, imprimeur] v. illus.

Issued also in English, 1930-

CANADA. PARLIAMENT. HOUSE OF COMMONS Rules and forms of the House of Commons of Canada, with annotations, and an extensive index; a compendium of Canadian parliamentary practice. Prepared for the use of members of Parliament by Arthur Beauchesne. Toronto, Canada Law Book Co., 1922. 313 p.

—— Rules and forms of the House of Commons of Canada, with annotations, comments and precedents; a compendium of Canadian parliamentary practice. Prepared for the use of members of Parliament by Arthur Beauchesne. 3d ed. Toronto, Canada Law Book Co., 1943. lviii, 899 p.

—— Rules and forms, with annotations, comments and precedents; a compendium of Canadian parliamentary practice. Prepared for the use of members of Parlia-

ment by Arthur Beauchesne. 4th ed. Toronto, Carswell Co., 1958. xviii, 567 p.

Includes legislation.

—— Index, by Maurice Ollivier. Ottawa, R. Duhamel, Queen's Printer, 1961. 37 p.

CANADA. PARLIAMENT. SENATE Canada. Forms of proceeding of the Senate of Canada. Ottawa, F. A. Acland, Printer to the King, 1932. 58 p.

—— Canada. Rules of the Senate of Canada. Printed by order of the Senate. Ottawa, F. A. Acland, Printer to the King, 1932. xii, 77 p.

—— Rules, orders and forms of proceeding of the Senate of Canada. Ottawa, Printed by MacLean, Roger, 1876. 160 p.

—— Rules, orders and forms of proceeding of the Senate of Canada. Compiled and rev. under direction of special committee, by Alexander R. Soutter. Ottawa, Government Print. Bureau, 1896. x, 222 p.

—— Senate manual. Printed by order of the Senate. Ottawa, S. E. Dawson [Printer to the King] 1907. xii, 292 p.

At head of title: Canada.

On cover: Rules, orders and forms of proceeding of the Senate of Canada.

CANADA. PRIVY COUNCIL Guide to Canadian ministries since Confederation, July 1, 1867–January 1, 1957. Ottawa, Public Archives of Canada, 1957. 103 p. ports.

CANADA. PUBLIC ARCHIVES The Canadian directory of Parliament, 1867-1967. Edited by J. K. Johnson. Ottawa [Queen's Printer] 1968. viii, 731 p.

Contains "political-biographical information. . . . The biographical sketches and the three appendices . . . constitute a record of the parliamentary careers of the more than 3100 men and women who have held office in the Canadian Senate and House of Commons during Canada's first one hundred years". – Introd.

Appendix III: List of parliaments and general elections (pp. 725-731).

—— Political figures, 1867-1948. [Ottawa, Queen's Printer] 1960. 64 p. (Its Preliminary inventory. Manuscript group no. 27.)

—— Répertoire des ministères canadiens depuis la confédération; 1er juillet 1867– 1er janvier 1957. Ottawa, 1958. 103 p. ports.

"Ce travail est en majeure partie l'oeuvre de . . . M. R. Mackenzie."

The Canadian album. Men of Canada; or, Success by example in religion, patriotism, business, law, medicine, education and agriculture; containing portraits of some of Canada's chief business men, statesmen, farmers, men of the learned professions, and others. Also, an authentic sketch of their lives. Edited by Rev. Wm. Cochrane. Brantford, Ont., Bradley, Garretson, 1891-96. 5 v. illus., ports.

> Vol. 5 has title: The Canadian album. Encyclopedic Canada . . . Edited by J. Castell Hopkins.

Canadian almanac & directory. [1st]- year; 1848- . Toronto, Copp, Clark [etc.] v. maps (part fold.)

> Title varies: 1848-50, Scobie & Balfour's Canadian almanac, and repository of useful knowledge. – 1851-54, Scobie's Canadian almanac. – 1855-56, Maclear & Co.'s Canadian almanac. – 1857-94, The Canadian almanac. – 1895-1926, The Canadian almanac and miscellaneous directory. – 1927-47, The Canadian almanac and legal and court directory.

> Publisher varies: 1848-50, Scobie & Balfour. – 1851-54, H. Scobie. – 1855-61, Maclear. – 1862-69, W. C. Chewett.

The Canadian biographical dictionary and portrait gallery of eminent and self-made men. Toronto, American Biographical Pub. Co., 1880-81. 2 v. ports.

> Contents: v. 1. Ontario. – v. 2. Quebec and Maritime provinces.

THE CANADIAN HISTORICAL REVIEW Canadian historical societies. (In *The Canadian historical review*. Toronto. v. 12 (1931), pp. 356-363.)

> ". . . a list of Canadian historical societies with short notes indicating the scope and nature of their activities."

CANADIAN NEWSPAPER SERVICE, LTD. "National reference book" (illustrated) containing data on Canadian business personalities and the firms they represent. [Montreal] v. ports.

> Title varies: -4th ed., "Reference book"; biographical reference data and other general information; 5th-7th eds., National reference book on Canadian men and women; 8th-9th eds., National reference book on Canadian personalities; 10th ed., National reference book on Canadian business personalities.

The Canadian Parliament; biographical sketches and photo-engravures of the sen-ators and members of the House of Commons of Canada. Being the tenth Parliament, elected November 3, 1904. Montreal, Perrault Print. Co., 1906. 255 p. illus. (chiefly ports.)

The Canadian parliamentary companion. 1862-97. Ottawa [etc.] J. Durie [etc.] v.

> Title varies: 1877-82, The Canadian parliamentary companion and annual register.

> Editors: 1862-76, H. J. Morgan. – 1877-82, C. H. Mackintosh. – 1883-97, J. A. Gemmill.

> Superseded by the Canadian parliamentary guide.

The Canadian parliamentary guide. 1898/99- Ottawa [etc.] v.

> Not published 1911, 1913.

> Supersedes the Canadian parliamentary companion.

> Title varies: 1898/99– , The parliamentary guide and work of general reference. – 19 –1908, The Canadian parliamentary guide and work of general reference.

> Editors: 1898/99–192 , A. J. Magurn. – 19 –25, E. J. Chambers. – 1926-45, A. L. Normandin. – 1946– , P. G. Normandin.

The Canadian who's who. A biographical dictionary of notable living men and women. v. 1- 1910- . Toronto, Who's Who Canadian Publications [etc.] v.

> "With which is incorporated 'Canadian men and women of the time.'"

> Subtitle varies.

> Editors: v. 2 (1936/37) – v. 3 (1938/39), Sir C. G. D. Roberts and A. L. Tunnell.

> Kept up to date by supplements with title: Who's who biographical service, Canada.

> Occupation index, with title: Who's what in Canadian who's who, accompanies v. 11-

CHARLESWORTH, HECTOR WILLOUGHBY (ed.) A cyclopaedia of Canadian biography. Brief biographies of persons distinguished in the professional, military and political life, and the commerce and industry of Canada, in the twentieth century. Edited by Hector Charlesworth. Toronto, Hunter-Rose Co., 1919. xii, 303 p. ports. [National biographical series, 3.)

> "A cyclopaedia of Canadian biography. . . . Ed. by Geo. Maclean Rose", 1886-88, forms vol. 1 and 2 of the series.

COTÉ, NARCISSE OMER (ed.) Political appointments, parliaments and the judicial bench in the Dominion of Canada, 1867 to 1895. Edited by N. Omer Coté. Ottawa, Thorburn, 1896. xii, 468 p.

—— Supplement: 1896 to 1903. Ottawa, Paynter & Abbott, printers, 1903. 470-632 p.

COTE, NARCISSE OMER Political appointments, parliaments and the judicial bench in the Dominion of Canada, 1896 to 1917; being a continuation up to the 30th June, 1917, of the first volume published in 1896, which covered the period from the 1st July, 1867, to the 31st December 1895; the two volumes forming a complete record for the first half century of the Canadian Confederation, 1867 to 1917. By N. Omer Coté. Ottawa, Printed by Lowe-Martin Co., 1917. viii, 384 p.

COWAN, JOHN Canada's governors-general, 1867-1952. With a foreword by R. C. Wallace. Toronto, York Pub. Co. [c1952] xxvi, 210 p. illus., ports.

Biographical sketches, with extracts from public addresses.

—— Canada's governors-general, Lord Monck to General Vanier. With a foreword by J. Keiller MacKay. [Centennial ed.] Toronto, York Pub. Co. [pref. 1965] xxvi, 260 p. illus., ports.

First published Toronto, York Pub. Co., 1952 under title: Canada's governors-general, 1867-1952.

DENMAN, NORRIS How to organize an election. [Montréal] Editions du jour [c1962] 138 p. illus. (Editions du jour. [Publications] A1.)

Handbook for federal, provincial and municipal elections.

DENT, JOHN CHARLES The Canadian portrait gallery. By John Charles Dent, assisted by a staff of contributors. Toronto, J. B. Magurn, 1880-81. 4 v. col. port.

Dictionary of Canadian biography. [Toronto] University of Toronto Press [1966-] v.

First general editor: George W. Brown.
Added title page in English and French.
Published also in French.
Includes bibliographies.
This monumental work is in progress.

Dictionnaire biographique du Canada. [Québec] Les Presses de l'Université Laval [1965-] v.

First general editor: George W. Brown.
Added title page in French and English.
Published also in English.
Includes bibliographies.

Directory [of] historical societies and agencies in the United States and Canada. 1956- . Nashville, Tenn. [etc.] American Association for State and Local History. v. illus.

Biennial.
Title varies slightly.

Encyclopedia Canadiana. [Editor-in-chief: John E. Robbins. Centennial ed.] Toronto, Grolier of Canada [c1966] 10 v. illus. (part col.)

Encyclopedia of Canada. General editor: W. Stewart Wallace. Toronto, University Associates of Canada, 1935-37. 6 v. illus.

—— Newfoundland supplement. Editor: Robert H. Blackburn. Toronto, University Associates of Canada, 1949. 104 p. illus. (part col.)

An Encyclopaedia of Canadian biography. Containing brief sketches and steel engravings of Canada's prominent men. Montreal, Canadian Press Syndicate, 1904-07. 3 v. ports.

ERMATINGER, CHARLES OAKES Canadian franchise and election laws. A manual for the use of revising officers, municipal officers, candidates, agents and electors. With supplement containing the amending acts of 1886, by C. O. Ermatinger. Toronto, Carswell, 1886. xxiii, 423 p.

Author was "one of Her Majesty's Counsel and member for East Elgin in the Legislature of Ontario".

EVANS, GWYNNETH (comp.) Women in federal politics; a bio-bibliography. Les femmes au fédéral; une bio-bibliographie. Compiled by Gwynneth Evans. Editor: Marion C. Wilson. Ottawa [National Library] 1975. 80 p.

Consists of short biographical sketches of each woman senator and member of Parliament.

GARLAND, NICHOLAS SURREY ZACCHEUS Parliamentary directory and statistical guide, compiled for the use of Parliament. By N. Surrey Garland. 1st ed., corr. to 1st March, 1885. Ottawa, A. S. Woodburn, 1885. ix, 247 p. col. illus., plans.

At head of title: Sixth session, third parliament.

GEOFFRION, LOUIS PHILIPPE Notre vocabulaire parlementaire; son origine, son caractère, ses conditions d'existence, son perfectionnement. Québec, Impr. de l'Action sociale, 1918. 16 p.

"Conférence faite à la séance publique de la Société du parler français le 14 mars 1918."

HOPKINS, JOHN CASTELL (ed.) Canada; an encyclopaedia of the country. The Canadian dominion considered in its historic relations, its natural resources, its material progress and its national development, by a corps of eminent writers and specialists. Edited by J. Castell Hopkins. Toronto, Linscott Pub. Co. [1898-1900] 6 v. illus.

—— Index, topical and personal. Toronto, Linscott Pub. Co. [1900] 188 p.

HUEY, JOHN ALEXANDER (comp.) The wardens, councillors, parliamentary representatives, judicial officers, and county officials of the county of Lambton for 100 years from 1849 to 1949. [Sarnia, Ont., Lambton] County Council, 1950. 111 p. illus. ports.

Cover title.

JOHNSON, GEORGE Alphabet of first things in Canada; a ready reference book of Canadian events. 3d ed. Ottawa, Printed by the Mortimer Co., 1897. 212 p.

LE JEUNE, LOUIS MARIE Dictionnaire général de biographie, histoire, littérature, agriculture, commerce, industrie et des arts, sciences, mœurs, coutumes, institutions politiques et religieuses du Canada . . . [Ottawa] Université d'Ottawa [1931] 2 v. illus.

LEMIEUX, LOUIS JOSEPH The governors-general of Canada, 1608-1931. Published and copyrighted by L. J. Lemieux. [London, Printed by Lake & Bell, 1931] xiv, 325 p. plates, ports.

MC CORD, FREDERICK AUGUSTUS Hand-book of Canadian dates. By Fred A. McCord. Montreal, Dawson Bros., 1888. 102 p.

"Whenever possible recourse has been had to original sources of information". - Pref.

McGraw-Hill directory and almanac of Canada, 1966-71. Toronto, McGraw-Hill Co. of Canada, 1966-71. 6 v.

Annual.

Superseded by Corpus directory and almanac of Canada.

MIGNAULT, PIERRE BASILE Manuel de droit parlementaire; ou, Cours élémentaire de droit constitutionnel, précédé d'une esquisse historique du régime parlementaire en Angleterre et au Canada. Par P. B. Mignault. Montréal, A. Périard, 1889. xxi, 476 p.

MORGAN, HENRY JAMES (ed.) The Canadian men and women of the time; a handbook of Canadian biography of living characters. 2d ed. Toronto, W. Briggs, 1912. xx, 1218 p. 2 ports.

First edition published in 1898.

—— Types of Canadian women and of women who are or have been connected with Canada. Vol. 1. Toronto, W. Briggs, 1903. 382 p. ports.

No more published.

MORICE, ADRIEN GABRIEL Dictionnaire historique des Canadiens et des Métis français de l'Ouest. Par A.-G. Morice. Québec, Chez l'auteur, 1908. xl, 329 p.

National encyclopedia of Canadian biography. Jesse Edgar Middleton [and] W. Scott Downs, directing editors. Toronto, Dominion Pub. Co., 1935-37. 2 v. ports.

O'SULLIVAN, DENNIS AMBROSE A manual of government in Canada; or, The principles and institutions of our federal and provincial constitutions. By D. A. O'Sullivan. Toronto, J. C. Stuart, 1879. xiii, 246 p.

Parliamentary representation of Missisquoi from the beginning of Parliaments in Canada. (In Missisquoi County Historical Society. Report. St. John's, Que. 2d (1907), pp. [29]-30.)

Consists of a listing.

PAUL ARTHUR AND ASSOCIATES, LIMITED Twenty-fourth parliament of Canada. Vingt-quatrième parlement du Canada. Ottawa, 1960 [c1959] 40 p. (chiefly illus., ports.)

"Published by authority of the Speakers of the Senate and of the House of Commons."

Text in English and French.

Includes photographs of members of the House of Commons, Senators, and officers of the House of Commons and Senate.

Limited ed.

QUAIN, REDMOND Manual of departments and agencies of the Government of Canada. By Redmond Quain, J. Hamilton Quain and Redmond Quain, Jr. Toronto, Butterworth, 1956. xi, 313 p. diagrs. (1 fold.)

Half-title and title on spine: The Quain manual.

RAYMOND GENEST INC. The enumerator's guide, applicable to federal elections (Canada) Montreal [1968] 25, 25 p.

French and English bound back to back. French title: Le guide de l'énumérateur.

ROSE, GEORGE MACLEAN (ed.) A cyclopaedia of Canadian biography; being chiefly men of the time. A collection of persons distinguished in professional and political life; leaders in the commerce and industry of Canada, and successful pioneers. Toronto, Rose Pub. Co., 1886-88. 2 v. (Rose's national biographical series, 1-2.)
Cover title: Representative Canadians.

SCARROW, HOWARD ALBERT Canada votes. A handbook of federal and provincial election data. New Orleans, Hauser Press [c1962] x, 238 p. diagrs. (A Galleon book.)
Commentary and statistical background for federal elections, 1878-1958, and provincial elections, 1920-1960.

A Standard dictionary of Canadian biography; the Canadian who was who. Editors: Charles G. D. Roberts and Arthur L. Tunnell. Library edition. Toronto, Trans-Canada Press, 1934-38. 2 v.
Contents: v. 1. 1875-1933. – v. 2. 1875-1937.

TAYLOR, JAMES P. The cardinal facts of Canadian history. Carefully gathered from the most trustworthy sources. Toronto, Hunter, Rose Co., Printers, 1899. 228 p. front.

"The British North America Act, 1867": pp. [193]-222.

WALLACE, WILLIAM STEWART (ed.) The dictionary of Canadian biography. Toronto, Macmillan, 1926. iv, 433 p.
"No living person . . . included". – Pref.

—— The dictionary of Canadian biography. By W. Stewart Wallace. 2d ed., rev. and enl. Toronto, Macmillan, 1945. 2 v.
"No living person . . . included." – Pref. to 1st ed.

—— The Macmillan dictionary of Canadian biography. By W. Stewart Wallace. [Pref. by W. S. Wallace] 3d ed., rev. and enl. London, Toronto, Macmillan [1963] 822 p.
Previous editions (1926, 1945) published under title: The dictionary of Canadian biography.
The aim of the third edition is to include all significant Canadian personalities who died before 1961.

Who's who in Canada; an illustrated biographical record of men and women of the time. 1912- . Toronto, International Press [etc.] v. ports.
Biennial.
Title varies: 1912-21, who's who and why (subtitle varies).

ANNUALS, YEARBOOKS, ETC.

CANADA. BUREAU OF STATISTICS Canada year book. Official statistical annual of the resources, history, institutions, and social and economic conditions of Canada. 1905- . Ottawa, 1906- . v. illus.
Annual.
Issued also in French, 1905-
Title varies: 1905-1911, The Canada year book . . . Second series; 1912-1921, The Canada year book; 1922/23 – The Canada year book; the official statistical annual of the resources, history. . . . Subtitle varies: 1905-1916/17, issued by the Census and Statistics Office; 1918- by the Bureau of Statistics.
Continues the Statistical year book of Canada. (Canada. Dept. of Agriculture).

CANADA. DEPT. OF AGRICULTURE The statistical year-book of Canada . . . 1886-1904.

[First-] twentieth year of issue. Ottawa, 1886-1905. 20 v. fold. diagrs., fold. maps.
Published by the Dept. of Agriculture.
1885-1888 have title: Statistical abstract and record.
Continued by the Canada year book. (Canada. Bureau of Statistics).

Canada 1867 and 1967; a century of change. The Statesman's year-book for the year 1868, edited by Frederick Martin, and for the year 1967-68, edited by S. H. Steinberg. With a pref. by Harold Macmillan. London, Macmillan, 1967. 1 v. (various pagings)
Extracts from the Statesman's year-book.

Canadian annual review. 1960- . [Toronto] University of Toronto Press [1961]- v.
Edited by John T. Saywell, 1960-

English or French.

Supersedes The Canadian annual review of public affairs, issued for the years 1901-38.

The Canadian annual review of public affairs. 1901-1937/38. Toronto, Canadian Review Co. [etc., 1902-1940] 35 v. illus.

Edited by J. Castell Hopkins, 1901-1922.

The volume for 1901 was originally published by G. N. Morang as Morang's Annual register of Canadian affairs, 1901.

Each issue includes a Canadian obituary record and a record of Canadian books of the year.

Superseded by Canadian annual review, 1960-

CANADIAN TAX FOUNDATION The national finances. An analysis of the revenues and expenditures of the government of Canada. 1st- 1954/55- Toronto. v. illus. Annual.

Data is gathered from the Estimates, House of Commons and Senate Debates, departmental reports and statements to the press, etc.

The Dominion annual register and review for the 12th-20th year of the Canadian union, 1878-86. Edited by Henry James Morgan. Montreal, E. Sénécal, printers [etc.] 1879-87. 8 v.

The years 1880 and 1881 were published in one volume.

Imprint varies: 1878, Montreal, Dawson Bros. – 1879, Ottawa, MacLean, Roger. – 1880/81, Montreal, J. Lovell. – 1882-85, Toronto, Hunter, Rose.

The Year book and almanac of Canada . . . Being an annual statistical abstract of the Dominion and a register of legislation and of public men in British North America. 1867- . Montreal [etc.] Maclean, Roger [etc.] 1866- . v. diagrs. (part fold.) maps (part fold., part col.)

Title varies: 1867, Year-book and almanac of British North America.

Publisher varies: 1867, Lowe & Chamberlin. – 1868-71, J. Lowe. – 1872-73, Ottawa, J. Bailiff. – 1874, Ottawa, Robertson, Roger.

Editors: 1867-70, A. Harvey. – 1871, J. Lowe.

NEWSPAPERS AND PERIODICALS

American newspapers, 1821-1936; a union list of files available in the United States and Canada. Edited by Winifred Gregory under the auspices of the Bibliographical Society of America. New York, H. W. Wilson Co., 1937. 791 p.

Running title: Union list of newspapers.

Committee: James Thayer Gerould, Harry Miller Lydenberg, Henry Spaulding Parsons.

"The arrangement is alphabetical by state or province and city". – Introd.

——— An alphabetical index to the titles. Arranged by Avis G. Clarke. Oxford, Mass., 1958. 1036 leaves.

Typescript (carbon copy).

BEAULIEU, ANDRE (comp.) Les journaux du Québec de 1764 à 1964. Par André Beaulieu et Jean Hamelin. Préf. de Jean-Charles Bonenfant. Québec, Presses de l'Université Laval, 1965. xxvi, 329 p. (Les Cahiers de l'Institut d'histoire, 6.)

CANADIAN LIBRARY ASSOCIATION. MICROFILM COMMITTEE Canadian newspapers on

microfilm; catalogue. Compiled under the supervision of Sheila A. Egoff. Ottawa, Canadian Library Association, 1959-
v. (loose-leaf)

Kept up to date by loose-leaf supplements and revised sheets.

The Canadian newspaper directory. [1st]-16th ed.; 1892-1923. Montreal, A. McKim. 16 v.

"A complete list of the newspapers and periodicals published in the Dominion of Canada and Newfoundland, with full particulars."

Continued by McKim's directory of Canadian publications. Known commonly as McKim's directory.

Canadian periodical index. v. 1-5; 1928-32. Windsor, Ont., Public Library. 5 v.

Superseded by the Canadian periodical index (1938-47) and the Canadian index to periodicals and documentary films (1948-).

——— First annual cumulation. 1931. Windsor, Ont., Public Library, 1932. 1 v.

Cumulated from quarterly issues. Includes the final issue of 1930.

Canadian periodical index. 1938-47. Toronto, Ontario Dept. of Education, Public Libraries Branch, 1939-49. 10 v.

Supersedes Canadian periodical index (1928-32).

1938-46 have subtitle: A cumulation of the quarterly indexes published in the Ontario Library Review, compiled by the Circulation Department of the University of Toronto Library, under the direction of May L. Newton, MA (1946 by May L. Newton and M. Roxalyn Finch).

Superseded by Canadian index to periodicals and documentary films (1948-).

Canadian periodical index. v. 1- . Jan. 1948- . Ottawa, Canadian Library Association. v.

Monthly, with an annual cumulation; twelve-year cumulation for 1948-59.

Supersedes Canadian periodical index issued 1938-47.

Title varies: 1948-63, Canadian index to periodicals and documentary films (varies slightly).

Some vols. have added title or t.p. in French.

Vol. for 1951 published by the Canadian Library Association in cooperation with the Canadian Bibliographic Centre; 1952-67 by the Association with the National Library of Canada.

Canadian periodical index; an author and subject index. January 1938–December 1947. May L. Newton: editor; 1947 editor: Dorothy Davidson. Cumulation editor: Betty Jean Faurschou. Ottawa, Canadian Library Association: Association canadienne des bibliothèques, 1966 [c1962] 3 v.

Cumulation of the annual volumes.

This "10 year cumulation has been sponsored by the Council of the Canadian Library Association—Association canadienne des bibliothèques—as part of its 1967 Centennial programme and to mark the 120th anniversary of the first periodical index". – Pref.

CENTRAL PRESS AGENCY, LTD. Directory of Canadian newspapers for 1900. Being a catalogue of all newspapers and periodicals published in Canada and Newfoundland, with customs tariff and law relating to newspaper postage. Toronto, Central Press Agency, 1900. 12 v, 13-290 p. (pp. 189-290, advertisements).

COLQUHOUN, ARTHUR HUGH URQUHART A century of Canadian magazines. By Arthur H. U. Colquhoun. (In The Canadian magazine of politics, science, art and literature. Toronto. v. 17 (1901), pp. 141-149.)

"A list of Canadian magazines": p. 149.

DAFOE, JOHN WESLEY Early Winnipeg newspapers. By J. W. Dafoe. (In Historical and Scientific Society of Manitoba. Papers. Winnipeg. ser. 3, no. 3 (1947), pp.14-24.)

ELLIOTT, ROBBINS L. (comp.) The Canadian labour press from 1867: a chronological annotated directory. By Robbins L. Elliott. (In The Canadian journal of economics and political science. [Toronto] v. 14 (1948), pp. 220-245.)

Lists 239 labour publications.

HARPER, JOHN RUSSELL Historical directory of New Brunswick newspapers and periodicals. Foreword by Desmond Pacey. Fredericton, University of New Brunswick [c1961] xxii, 121 p. fold. facsim.

A Joint catalogue of the serials in the libraries of the city of Toronto. Edited by Robert H. Blackburn. 5th ed. [Toronto] University of Toronto Press, 1953. 602 p.

Includes new titles and changes up to beginning of 1952.

First ed. published in 1898 under title: A Joint catalogue of the periodicals, publications, and transactions of societies and other books published at intervals to be found in the various libraries of the city of Toronto.

KINGSTON, ONT. QUEEN'S UNIVERSITY. LIBRARY Catalogue of Canadian newspapers in the Douglas Library, Queen's University. [Compiled by Lorraine C. Ellison, Peter E. Greig and William F. E. Morley] Kingston [Ont.] Douglas Library, Queen's University, 1969 xxi [i.e. xvi] leaves, 196 p. (Douglas Library occasional papers, no. 1.)

Reproduced from typewritten copy.

LUNN, JEAN Bibliography of the history of the Canadian press. (In The Canadian historical review. Toronto. v. 22 (1941), pp. 416-433.)

MAC DONALD, MARY CHRISTINE Historical directory of Saskatchewan newspapers, 1878-1950. Compiled by Christine Mac-

Donald. Saskatoon, Office of the Saskatchewan Archives, University of Saskatchewan, 1951. iii leaves, 114 p.

> Lists 493 papers.
>
> Mimeographed.

MC DOUGALL, ROBERT LAW   A study of Canadian periodical literature of the nineteenth century. Toronto, 1950. 415 leaves.

> Thesis (PH D) – University of Toronto.
>
> Includes studies of the *Canadian journal of science, literature and history* and *The Canadian monthly and national review*.

McKim's directory of Canadian publications. 17th-35th ed.; 1924-42. Montreal, A. McKim. 19 v. illus.

> Continues the Canadian newspaper directory.
>
> On spine: The Canadian newspaper directory.
>
> "A complete list of the newspapers and periodicals published in the Dominion of Canada and Newfoundland. With full particulars."

N. W. Ayer & Son's directory, newspapers and periodicals. 1880-   . Philadelphia. v. maps.

> "A guide to publications printed and published in the United States and its Territories, the Dominion of Canada, Bermuda, the Republics of Panama and the Philippines; descriptions of the states, provinces, cities and towns in which they are published; classified lists; 70 maps." (Subtitle varies slightly).
>
> Title varies: 1880-1929, N. W. Ayer & Son's American newspaper annual and directory (varies slightly).
>
> Absorbed Rowell's American newspaper directory in 1910 and assumed its numbering, 42d-   year.
>
> Continued by Ayer directory of publications.

New serial titles. A union list of serials commencing publication after December 31, 1949. 1950/60-   . Washington, Library of Congress. v.

> "Prepared under the sponsorship of the Joint Committee on the Union List of Serials."
>
> Supplement to the Union list of serials, 3d edition.
>
> Monthly, with annual cumulations which are in turn cumulated over five- or ten-year periods.

OTTAWA. NATIONAL LIBRARY   Periodicals in the social sciences and humanities currently received by Canadian libraries. Inventaire des périodiques de sciences sociales et d'humanités que possèdent les bibliothèques canadiennes. [Ottawa, Queen's Printer] 1968. 2 v. (xiii, 1836 p.)

> Compiled by the Bibliography Division of the Reference Branch of the Library.

SEVERANCE, HENRY ORMAL   A guide to the current periodicals and serials of the United States and Canada. 5th ed., 1931. Compiled by Henry Ormal Severance. Ann Arbor, Mich., G. Wahr, 1931. 432 p.

> First published in 1907.

TETU, HORACE   Journaux et revues de Québec par ordre chronologique, 3. éd. Québec, 1883. 26 p.

> "Tirage: 125 exemplaires."

TOD, DOROTHEA DOUGLAS   A bibliography of Canadian literary periodicals, 1789-1900. Part I. English-Canadian, compiled by Dorothea D. Tod. Part II. French-Canadian, compiled by Audrey Cordingley. Presented by W. S. Wallace. (In Royal Society of Canada. *Proceedings and transactions*. Ottawa. ser. 3, v. 26 (1932), section 2, pp. 87-96.)

> The term "literary" is given a loose interpretation: many periodicals listed are of a general nature.

Ulrich's international periodicals directory. A classified guide to current periodicals, foreign and domestic [1st]-   [1932]-   New York, R. R. Bowker Co.   v.

> Title varies: 1932-38, Periodicals directory.
>
> – 1943-63, Ulrich's periodicals directory.
>
> Subtitle varies slightly.
>
> Editors: 1932-47, Carolyn F. Ulrich. – 1951-65/66, Eileen C. Graves.
>
> Issued 1965/66–1967/68 in 2 vols.: v. 1, Scientific, technical & medical; v. 2, Arts, humanities, business & social sciences: 1969/70-   in parts.

Union list of serials in libraries of the United States and Canada. 3d ed. Edited by Edna Brown Titus. New York, H. W. Wilson Co., 1965. 5 v. (4649 p.)

> "Under the sponsorship of the Joint Committee on the Union List of Serials with the co-operation of the Library of Congress."
>
> Coverage after Jan. 1, 1950, continued by New serial titles, issued monthly by the Library of Congress.

U. S. LIBRARY OF CONGRESS. UNION CATALOG DIVISION   Newspapers on microfilm. [1st]-   ed. Washington [etc.] Library of Congress [etc.] 1948-   . v.

"Compiled under the direction of George A. Schwegmann, Jr., chief".

Supplements accompany some vols.

Wood (T. F.) and Company. T. F. Wood & Co.'s Canadian newspaper directory, con-taining accurate lists of all the newspapers and periodicals published in the Dominion of Canada and province of Newfoundland. Montreal, Wood, 1876. 79 p.

No more published.

GOVERNMENT DOCUMENTS

ADAM, MARGARET ISABELLA (comp.) Guide to the principal parliamentary papers relating to the Dominions, 1812-1911. Prepared by Margaret I. Adam, John Ewing and James Munro. Edinburgh, Oliver and Boyd, 1913. viii, 190 p.

Contents: Parliamentary papers relating to: Canada; Newfoundland; . . . ; Emigration and colonisation; Dominions (miscellaneous) – Colonial secretaries, 1812-1911. – Index.

BURPEE, LAWRENCE JOHNSTONE Check-list of Canadian public documents. (In Bibliographical Society of America. *Papers*. Chicago. v. 8, no. 1-2. (1914), pp. 51-56.)

CANADA The Canada gazette. [v. 1]-v. 28, no. 26; Oct. 2, 1841-June 26, 1869. Ottawa [etc.] 28 v.

The official organ of the government of the Province of Canada. It was issued weekly by the Queen's Printer in Kingston, Montreal, Toronto or Ottawa, the place of publication depending usually on where the seat of government was located.

Issues for Oct. 2, 1841—Dec. 31, 1852, have no vol. numbering, called no. 1-604.

English or French.

Superseded by the Canada gazette, 1867-

—— The Canada gazette. La gazette du Canada. v. 1- . July 1, 1867- . Ottawa. v.

The official organ of the Government through which the people of Canada are acquainted with governmental activities. Includes proclamations and all government notices, such as appointments, bankruptcy notices, etc.

Issued by the Queen's or King's Printer. English or French.

Beginning Jan. 1947 published in 2 pts.: 1. General. 2. Statutory orders and regulations. (English and French in separate vols.)

Supersedes the Canada gazette, 1841-69.

Supplements issued to some of the numbers.

CANADA. BUREAU OF STATISTICS DBS catalogue. Catalogue du BFS. [Ottawa, Queen's Printer] v.

Vols. for issued in 2 pts.: Part 1: Publications; Part 2: Data files and unpublished information.

Kept up to date by supplements.

CANADA. BUREAU OF STATISTICS. LIBRARY Historical catalogue of Dominion Bureau of Statistics publications, 1918-1960. Catalogue rétrospectif des publications du Bureau fédéral de la statistique. Ottawa, DBS Library, Canada Year Book Division, Dominion Bureau of Statistics, 1966 [i.e. 1967] xiv, 298 p.

"DBS Cat. No. 11-504".

CANADA. CHIEF ELECTORAL OFFICE By-elections held...; report of the Chief Electoral Officer. Elections partielles tenues . . . ; rapport du Directeur général des élections. 1906- . Ottawa, Queen's Printer. v.

Title varies.

Reports cover only those years during which by-elections, or, since 1951, Northwest Territories elections, were held. Prior to 1920 issued by the Clerk of the Crown in Chancery.

Report for 1904 in the Return of the 10th general election; 1916, not printed. Found also in Sessional papers, 1906-1924; in Annual departmental reports, 1925-55.

Issued in English and French.

Cf. Higgins, M. *Canadian government publications*. Chicago, 1935.

—— General election; report of the Chief Electoral Officer. Election générale; rapport du Directeur général des élections. 1868- . Ottawa, Queen's Printer. v.

Irregular; only general election years are covered by reports.

Prior to 1920 issued by the Clerk of the Crown in Chancery.

Issued also in Sessional papers, 1868-1924; in Annual departmental reports, 1925-53.

Usually issued in French and English.

Cf. Higgins, M. Canadian government publications. Chicago, 1935.

CANADA. DEPT. OF LABOUR Report on labour organization in Canada. 1911-Ottawa, 1912- . v.

Issued also in French.

Issued by the Department of Labour, 1911-

Title varies slightly.

"The rise and fall of the many labour parties . . . is catalogued in the annual reports". – Young, W. D. Anatomy of a party. Toronto, 1969. (p. 23, footnote).

CANADA. DEPT. OF PUBLIC PRINTING AND STATIONERY Canadian government publications. Publications du gouvernement canadien. Catalogue. 1895- Ottawa, Queen's Printer. v.

Beginning in 1953 issued daily with monthly and annual cumulations.

Title varies: 1896-1927, Price list of government publications. – 1928-39, Catalogue of official publications of the Parliament and Government of Canada. – 1943-48, Government publications; annual catalogue. (Other slight variations).

Issued 19 -27 by the Department's Stationery Division; 1928-39 by its Division of Documents.

Supplements accompany most issues.

Catalogue for 1953 and 1954 each issued in 2 v., listing separately publications in English and publications in French.

—— Canadian government publications. Sectional catalogue. Ottawa, Queen's Printer. v.

Departmental publications.

CANADA. PUBLIC ARCHIVES A guide to the documents in the Manuscript Room at the Public Archives of Canada. Vol. I. Prepared by David W. Parker. Ottawa, Government Print. Bureau, 1914. 318 p. (Publications of the Archives of Canada, no. 10.)

Published by authority of the Secretary of State under the direction of the Archives.

The Canadian abridgment. Statutes of Canada judicially considered, including index of regulations in force. 1856-1953. By Leonard G. Wrinch. Toronto, Burroughs (Eastern) 1953. 633 p.

—— First permanent cumulative supplement. 1954-1958. Edited by Anne Brown. Toronto, Burroughs (Eastern) 1959. 496 p.

—— Supplement from 1958 to . Edited by Anne Brown. Toronto, Burroughs (Eastern) 1961- . 1 v. (loose-leaf)

On spine: Supplement B.

CARSWELL COMPANY, LTD. Check list of the statutes of the Dominion of Canada, the provinces, the earlier legislatures and Newfoundland. [Toronto, 1909?] 52 p.

Caption title.

EWART, JOHN SKIRVING Ewart's index of the statutes. Being an alphabetical index of all the public statutes passed by the legislatures of the late province of Canada, the Dominion of Canada, and the province of Ontario, subsequent to consolidation and down to and inclusive of the year 1873; and of the province of Quebec down to and inclusive of the year 1872. By John S. Ewart. 2d ed. Toronto, R. Carswell, 1874. 191 p.

—— Ewart's index of the statutes. Being an alphabetical index of all the public statutes passed by the Parliament of the Dominion of Canada from 1874 to 1878 inclusive. By the Legislative Assembly of Ontario from 1874 to the revised statutes. And by the Legislative Assembly of Quebec from 1873 to 1876 inclusive. And of all Orders in Council, and other matter which have been published with the statutes. By John S. Ewart. Toronto, Rowsell & Hutchison, 1878. 99 p.

"The present edition of the Index of the Statutes is intended as a supplement to the edition of 1874." – Pref.

HENDERSON, GEORGE FLETCHER Federal royal commissions in Canada, 1867-1966; a checklist. [Toronto] University of Toronto Press [c1967] xvi, 212 p.

HIGGINS, MARION VILLIERS Canadian government publications; a manual for librarians. With an introd. by Gerhard R. Lomer. Chicago, American Library Association, 1935. ix, 582 p.

LAND, REGINALD BRIAN A description and guide to the use of Canadian government publications.. By Brian Land. (In Fox, P. W. (ed.) Politics: Canada; culture and process. 3d ed. Toronto. [c1970] pp. 501-512.)

Also appears (In Fox, P. W. (ed.) Politics:

Canada; recent readings. Toronto [1963, c1962] pp. [335]-344; Fox, P. W. (ed.) *Politics: Canada; problems in Canadian government.* 2d ed. Toronto [c1966] pp. 384-396.)

MURRAY, FLORENCE B.   Canadian government document catalogs and check-lists. (In *The Library quarterly.* Chicago. v. 6 (1936), pp. 237-262.)

Organization of the Government of Canada. June 1958-   . Ottawa, Queen's Printer. v. illus.

　　1958-63 issued by the Dept. of Public Printing and Stationery.

　　Also in French ed.

　　Vols. for July 1965-   are loose-leaf, to be kept up to date by revisions.

PREMONT, JACQUES   Publicité des documents officiels. (In *Canadian public administra-*

tion. Toronto. v. 11 (1968), pp. [449]-453.)

STEWART, A. MC NAUGHTON   Index to Dominion and provincial statutes from the earliest period down to and including the year 1900. Montreal, J. Lovell, 1901. 589 p.

STEWART, SHEILA I. (comp.)   Statutes, orders, and official statements relating to Canadian war-time economic controls. By Sheila I. Stewart. (In *The Canadian journal of economics and political science.* [Toronto] v. 13 (1947), pp. 99-114.)

　　Consists of a lengthy bibliography listing federal statutes, orders-in-council and administrative regulations issued under the authority of the War Measures Act of 1914, and in effect in Canada through the period 1939-1947.

THESES

ASSOCIATION OF SPECIAL LIBRARIES AND INFORMATION BUREAUX (ASLIB)   Index to theses accepted for higher degrees in the universities of Great Britain and Ireland. v. 1-   . 1950/51-   . London. v.

　　Annual.

CANADA. PUBLIC ARCHIVES   Register of postgraduate dissertations in progress in history and related subjects. Répertoire des thèses en cours portant sur des sujets d'histoire et autres sujets connexes. no. 1-1966-   [Ottawa] Canadian Historical Association. v.

　　Formerly included in the *Canadian historical review* (1927-1965).

CANADIAN POLITICAL SCIENCE ASSOCIATION   Theses in Canadian political studies, completed and in progress. Thèses canadiennes en sciences politiques, complétées et en cours de rédaction. Kingston, Ont., Dept. of Political Studies, Queen's University, 1970-   . 71 p.

　　Lists more than 1400 titles for the period 1919-1970.

　　To be updated by annual supplements.

Dissertation abstracts. Abstracts of dissertations available on microfilm or as xerographic reproductions. v. 1-29; 1938-June

1969. Ann Arbor, Mich., University Microfilms. 29 v. in

　　Title varies: 1938-51, Microfilm abstracts. Subtitle varies.

　　Compiled for the Association of Research Libraries.

　　Vols. for July 1966—June 1969 issued in two parts: A, The humanities and social sciences; B, The sciences and engineering.

　　Continued by Dissertation abstracts international.

　　Indexes: Vols. 1-29, 1938—June 1969. 9 v.

Graduate theses in Canadian history and related subjects. (In *The Canadian historical review.* Toronto. v. 8-46 (1927-65.)

　　Superseded by the Register of post-graduate dissertations in progress in history and related subjects [compiled by the Public Archives of Canada].

Historical research for university degrees in the United Kingdom; list no. [1]-   1931/32-   . London, 1933-   . v.

　　Issued by the Institute of Historical Research, University of London.

　　Formerly included in the periodical History (as section: University research), later in the Bulletin of the Institute of Historical Research, v. 7-9.

Vols. for 1931/32–1965/66 issued as "Theses supplement no. 1-27 to the Bulletin of the Institute of Historical Research, but constitute List no. 1-27."

Beginning with no. 19 issued in 2 parts: Theses completed, and Theses in progress (no. 28-   ) called Part 1 and Part 2 respectively).

HUMANITIES RESEARCH COUNCIL OF CANADA Canadian graduate theses in the humanities and social sciences, 1921-1946. Thèses des gradués canadiens dans les humanités et les sciences sociales. [Ottawa, E. Cloutier, Printer to the King, 1951] 194 p.

Text in English and French.

Compiled by a joint committee of the Humanities Research Council of Canada and the Canadian Social Science Research Council.

Masters abstracts. Abstracts of selected masters theses on microfilm. v. 1-   1962- Ann Arbor, Mich., University Microfilms. v.

Indexes: Vols. 1-5, 1962-67. 1 v.

MILLS, JUDITH EILEEN (comp.) University of Toronto doctoral theses, 1897-1967. A bibliography compiled by Judy Mills and Irene Dombra. [Toronto] Published for University of Toronto Library by University of Toronto Press [c1968] xi, 186 p.

OTTAWA. NATIONAL LIBRARY Canadian theses. Thèses canadiennes. 1952-   . Ottawa.   v.

This is a listing of completed theses.

—— Canadian theses. Thèses canadiennes, 1947-1960. Ottawa, 1973. 2 v.

A listing of completed theses.

SASKATCHEWAN. UNIVERSITY University of Saskatchewan postgraduate theses, 1912-1966. Saskatoon, 1967. iii, 93 p.

A DESCRIPTIVE LIST
OF PERIODICALS
EXAMINED

Acadiensis; a quarterly devoted to the interests of the maritime provinces of Canada. v. 1-8; Jan. 1901-Oct. 1908. [St. John, N.B.] 8 v. illus., ports.

> Edited by D. R. Jack.

L'Action canadienne-française; revue mensuelle. v. 19-20; jan.-déc. 1928. Montréal. 2 v.

> Continues *L'Action française*.
>
> Includes a supplementary issue published Mar. 1929.
>
> Vols. 19-20 also called 12. année.
>
> Published Jan.-Sept. 1928 by the Ligue d'action canadienne-française; Oct.-Dec. 1928, by the Librairie d'action canadienne-française.
>
> Superseded by *L'Action nationale*.

L'Action française; revue mensuelle. v. [1]-18; jan. 1917-déc. 1927. Montréal, Ligue d'action française [etc.] 18 v.

> Vols. 1-18 also called 1.-11. année.
>
> Published 1917-21 by the society under its earlier name: Ligue des droits des Français.
>
> Edited by Lionel Groulx and others.
>
> Continued by *L'Action canadienne-française*.

L'Action nationale. v. 1-   ; jan. 1933-   . Montréal, Ligue d'action nationale. v.   .

> Supersedes *L'Action canadienne-française*.
>
> Vols. 1-46 also called 1.-23. année.
>
> Editors: 1933-34, Harry Bernard; 1934-37, Arthur Laurendeau; 1937-42, André Laurendeau; 1943-46, F. A. Angers, with others; 1946-47, Guy Frégault; 1947-48, Dominique Beaudin; 1948-54, André Laurendeau; 1954-

59, Pierre Laporte; 1959-67, F. A. Angers; 1967- Jean Genest.

Alberta historical review. v. 1-   . Apr. 1953-   . Edmonton, Calgary; Historical Society of Alberta.   v. illus., ports.

> Indexes: Vols. 1-5, 1953-57, in v. 5.
>   Vols. 1-15, 1953-67, in v. 15.

Amérique française. v. 1-   nov. 1941- Montréal.   v. illus., ports.

> Vols. 1-3, 5-6 called 1.-3., 5.-6. année; vols. for Oct. 1944-Jan. 1946 are unnumbered, but constitute v. 4-5, no. 1; vols. 7-9 called new ser., v. 1-3.
>
> Indexes: Vols. 7-13, 1948/49-1955, in v. 13.

Les Annales; lettres, histoire, sciences, arts. 1.-4. année, no. 3; jan. 1922-mai 1925. Ottawa, Institut canadien-français. 4 v.

Arts review. v. [14]-17, no. 1; 1962-Jan. 1965. Winnipeg, Varsity Arts Student Body Council of the University of Manitoba [etc.] 4 v.

> Continues the *Manitoba arts review*.
>
> Title varies: 1962-63, *The University of Manitoba arts review*.

Asticou. cahier no 1-   . 24 juin 1968-   . Hull, Que., Société historique de l'ouest du Québec. no   . illus., ports.

The Atlantic advocate. v. 47-   Sept. 1956-   . Fredericton, N.B., University Press of New Brunswick. v.   illus., ports.

> Continues the *Maritime advocate and busy East*. . .
>
> Incorporates the *Atlantic guardian*, Apr. 1958.

Atlantic guardian; the magazine of New-foundland. v. 1-14; Jan. 1945-Dec. 1957, St. John's, Nfld. [etc.] Guardian Ltd. [etc.] 14 v. illus., ports.

> Publication suspended Nov. 1952-Apr. 1953.
> Subtitle varies.
> Edited by E. Young.
> Published in Montreal, 1945-June 1951.
> Absorbed by the *Atlantic advocate* Apr. 1958.
> Indexes: Vols. 1-10, 1945-53, in v. 11.

BC *studies.* no. 1- ; winter 1968/69- Vancouver. no. . illus.

> Editors: 1968/69- Margaret Prang and Walter Young.
> Indexes: No. 1-12, 1968-72, with no. 12.

British Columbia Historical Association *Report and proceedings.* 1st-4th; 1922/23-1925/29. Victoria, B.C. 4 no. illus., ports.

> Report year irregular.
> Title varies slightly.
> Superseded by *British Columbia historical quarterly.*

The British Columbia historical quarterly. v. 1-21; Jan. 1937-1957/58. Victoria, B.C. 21 v. illus., ports.

> Supersedes Report and proceedings of the British Columbia Historical Association.
> "Published by the Archives of British Columbia in co-operation with the British Columbia Historical Association."
> Editors: 1937-46, W. K. Lamb; 1947-57/58, W. E. Ireland.

Le Bulletin des recherches historiques; revue d'archéologie, d'histoire, de biographie, de bibliographie, de numismatique, etc., etc. v. 1- jan. 1895- . Lévis [Qué.] v. illus., ports.

> Publication suspended after v. 70, no. 2 (Apr. 1968).
> Title-pages read: Recherches historiques...
> On cover, 1895-Feb. 1923: Organe de la Société des études historiques; Mar. 1923-Dec. 1948: Organe du Bureau des archives de la province de Québec.
> Editors: 1895-1948, P. G. Roy; 1949-68, Antoine Roy.
> Indexes: Vols. 1-10, 1895-1904, in v. 10.
>> Vols. 1-31, 1895-1925. 4 v. (issued as Archives de la province de Québec. [v. 11])

The Busy man's Canada; the national magazine of progress and development. Toronto. v. illus., ports.

Published 1911-1914. Cf. Union list of serials.
> Subtitle varies.

The Busy man's magazine. v. 1-21, no. 4; 1896-Feb. 1911. Toronto [etc.] v.

> Title varies: -Nov. 1905, *The Business magazine* ("formerly 'Business' ")
> Continued by *Maclean's.*

The Bystander; a . . . review of current events, Canadian and general. v. 1-3, Jan. 1880-Oct. 1883; new ser., Oct. 1889-Sept. 1890. Toronto, Hunter, Rose. 4 v.

> Written and published by Goldwin Smith.
> Monthly, Jan. 1880-June 1881; quarterly, Jan.-Oct. 1883; monthly, Oct. 1889-Sept. 1890.
> Publication suspended, July 1881-Dec. 1882.

Cahiers de Cité libre. no 1-5, sept./oct. 1966-juin 1967; nouv. sér. automne 1967- Montréal. v.

> No. 1- also called 17.- année, in continuation of *Cité Libre,* which it supersedes.
> Vol. numbering irregular.
> Each no. in new ser. has also a distinctive title.
> Supplements accompany some issues.

Les Cahiers de Nouvelle-France; revue trimestrielle du Canada français. no 1-12; jan./mars 1957-jan./mars 1960. Montréal, Associés de Neuve-France. 12 no.

> Continued by *Nouvelle-France,* 1960-64.

Les Cahiers des Dix. no 1- . Montréal, 1936- . v. illus., ports.

> Publication of Les Dix.

Le Canada-français; revue publiée sous la direction d'un comité de professeurs de l'Université Laval. v. 1-4; 1888-91. Québec, Imp. de L.-J. Demers. 4 v.

> "Religion, philosophie, histoire, beaux-arts, sciences et lettres."
> Includes supplement: *Collection de documents inédits sur le Canada et l'Amérique.*
> Indexes: Vols. 1-4, 1888-91, in v. 4.

Le Canada français. v. 1-33; sept. 1918-juin 1946. Québec. 33 v.

> Formed by the union of *Parler français* and *La Nouvelle-France.*
> "Publication de l'Université Laval; organe de la Société du parler français au Canada."
> "Deuxième série du Parler français."
> Superseded by *La Revue de l'Université Laval...*
> Indexes: Vols. 1-4, 1918-20, in v. 4.

Canada month; a magazine for freedom. v. 1- Oct. 1961- . Montreal, Canada Week. v. illus., ports.

Vol. 1, no. 1 preceded by a number dated July 1, 1961, called Forerunner issue.

Subtitle varies.

Edited, in turn, by D. E. Woodward, John Kettle and J. H. Doupe.

Canada monthly. v. 7, no. 2-v. 24; Dec. 1909-Sept. 28, 1918. London [Ont.] Vanderhoof, Scott [etc.] 18 v. illus., ports.

Continues Canada-West.

Canada-West. v. 1-7, no. 1; Nov. 1906-Nov. 1909. London [Ont.] Vanderhoof-Gunn Co. 7 v. illus., ports.

Continued by *Canada monthly.*

The Canadian; a magazine of business & national affairs. Mar.-July 1962. Toronto. 1 v. illus., ports.

Preceded by a number, published in 1961, called Preview issue.

Edited by Arthur Lowe.

Aug. 1962 merged with *Saturday night* to form the *Canadian Saturday night.*

Canadian Catholic Historical Association *Report.* 1933/34-1965. [Ottawa] 32 v.

Continued by the association's *Study sessions...*

Includes the reports of the association's English and French sections, the latter issued in French with title: Rapport [de] la Société canadienne d'histoire de l'Eglise catholique.

Indexes: 1933/34-1958. 1 v.

Canadian Catholic Historical Association *Study sessions.* 1966- [Ottawa] v.

Continues the association's *Report.*

Vols. for 1966- called 33rd-

Includes the study sessions of the association's English and French sections, the latter issued in French with title: Sessions d'étude.

Canadian Club of Fort William *Annual.* 1908-10. [Fort William, Ont.] 2 v. ports.

No more published?

Canadian Club of Hamilton *Addresses.* 1912/13-1914/15. Hamilton, Ont. 3 v. illus., ports.

No more published?

Canadian Club of Montreal *Addresses.* 1911/12-1918/19. [Montreal] 8 v. illus.

No more published?

Canadian Club of Ottawa *The Canadian Club year book.* 1903/09-1923/24. [Ottawa] 15 v. in 14. ports.

Title varies: 1903/09-1918/19, 1920/21, *Addresses.*

No more published?

Canadian Club of Toronto *Addresses.* 1903/04-1938/39. Toronto, Warwick Bros. & Rutter. 36 v.

Cover title: Proceedings.

Issues for 1929/30-1938/39 also called v. 27-36.

No more published?

Canadian Club of Vancouver *Addresses and proceedings.* 1906/08-1912/13. [Vancouver] 4 v. ports.

Title varies: 1906/08, Addresses (cover title: Proceedings)

No more published?

Canadian Club of Winnipeg. *Annual report.* [1st]-14th; 1904/05-1917/18. [Winnipeg] 14 v. illus., ports.

Title varies slightly.

No more published?

Canadian comment. v. 1, no. 2-v. 7, no. 5; Feb. 1932-May 1938. Toronto, Current Publications. 7 v. illus., ports.

Cover title.

Caption title: Feb.-Dec. 1932, Canadian comment on this changing world; Jan. 1933-May 1938, Canadian comment on current events.

Vol. 1, no. 1 not published. Cf. May 1932 issue.

Canadian commentator. v. 1-5, no. 11; Jan. 1957-Nov. 1961. Toronto, W. H. Baxter. 5 v.

Editors: 1957-61, Marcus Long; 1961, P. W. Fox.

Continued by the *Commentator.*

Canadian courier. v. 1-26, no. 1; Dec. 1, 1906-Oct. 15, 1920. Toronto, Courier Press. 25 v. illus., ports.

Title varies: Sept. 16, 1916-Mar. 31, 1917, *The Courier.*

Edited by J. A. Cooper.

Canadian dimension. v. 1- [1963]- Winnipeg. v. illus., ports.

Editor: 1963- C. W. Gonick.

No. 1/2 issued without date.

The Canadian forum; an independent journal of opinion and the arts. v. 1- (no. 1-); Oct. 1920- Toronto. v. illus.

Supersedes the *Rebel.*

Subtitle varies.

Canadian Historical Association *Historical papers.* Communications historiques. 1966- [Ottawa] v.

Continues the association's Report of the annual meeting.

"A selection from the papers presented at the ... annual meeting ..."

Title varies: 1966-67, Historical papers presented at the annual meeting. (Added title page in French.)

Canadian Historical Association   *Report of the annual meeting.* 1915-65. [Ottawa, etc.] 51 v. illus.

Title varies slightly.

Reports for 1915-21 issued by the association under its earlier name: Historic Landmarks Association of Canada.

English and French.

Some issues have added title page in French.

Continued by the association's *Historical papers.*

Indexes: 1922-51. 1 v.

The Canadian historical review. v. 1-Mar. 1920-   . Toronto, University of Toronto Press.   v. illus.

Supersedes Review of historical publications relating to Canada.

Editors: 1920-29, W.S. Wallace with others; 1930-48, G. W. Brown and others; 1949-58, J. M. S. Careless with others; 1958-63, J. T. Saywell (1963, with Ramsay Cook); 1964-68, Ramsay Cook (1965-67, with R. Craig Brown; 1968, with R. Craig Brown and Michael Cross); 1969-   R. Craig Brown with Michael Cross.

Includes section: Recent publications relating to Canada.

Indexes: Vols. 1-10, 1920-29. 1 v.
Vols. 11-20, 1930-39. 1 v.
Vols. 21-30, 1940-49. 1 v.
Vols. 31-51, 1950-70 1. v.

Canadian illustrated news. v. 1-28; Oct. 30, 1869-Dec. 29, 1883. Montreal, Burland Lithographic Co. [etc.] 28 v. illus., ports.

Founded and for some years published by G. E. Desbarats.

Some vols. accompanied by unnumbered supplements.

The Canadian journal of economics and political science; the journal of the Canadian Political Science Association. v. 1-33; Feb. 1935-Nov. 1967. [Toronto] University of Toronto Press. 33 v. illus.

Supersedes *Contributions to Canadian economics* and *Papers and proceedings* of the Canadian Political Science Association.

"Index to 'Contributions to Canadian economics' (volumes I-VII) and to 'The Papers and proceedings of the Canadian Political Science Association' (volumes I-VI": v. 1, pp. 131-135.

Superseded by the *Canadian journal of political science* and the *Canadian journal of economics.*

Indexes: Vols. 1-10, 1935-44. 1 v.
Vols. 11-20, 1945-54. 1 v.
Vols. 21-30, 1955-64. 1 v.

Canadian journal of political science. Revue canadienne de science politique. v. 1-Mar. 1968-   . Toronto, University of Toronto Press.   v.

Supersedes in part the *Canadian journal of economics and political science.*

Issued jointly by the Canadian Political Science Association and Société canadienne de science politique.

Vols. 2- contain indexes cumulative from v. 1.

The Canadian Liberal monthly. v. 1-5, no. 8; Sept. 1913-Apr. 1918. Ottawa, Central Information Office of the Canadian Liberal Party. 5 v. illus.

The Canadian Liberal monthly, although "published in the interests of Liberalism, its appeal is not to partisans, but rather to all persons, irrespective of party, who desire a fair understanding of public questions and honest, efficient and progressive government in Canada". – v. 1, no. 1, p. 2.

Canadian life. v. 1-2, no. 3; Mar./Apr. 1949-May/June 1952. Toronto, Advance Pub. Co. 2 v. illus., ports.

The Canadian magazine. v. 1-91, no. 4; Mar. 1893-Apr. 1939. Toronto, Canadian Magazines, [etc.] 91 v. illus., ports.

Title varies: 1893-Jan. 1925, *The Canadian magazine of politics, science, art and literature* (cover title, Aug. 1895-Jan. 1925: *The Canadian magazine*); Feb. 1925-July 1937, *The Canadian magazine* (varies); Aug. 1937-1939, *Canadian* (running title: *The Canadian magazine*).

Oct. 1931 not published.

Absorbed *Massey's magazine* in July 1897.

Indexes: Vols. 1-25, 1893-Oct. 1905. 1 v.

The Canadian monthly and national review. v. 1-13; Jan. 1872-June 1878. Toronto, Adam, Stevenson [etc.] 13 v. illus.

Founded by G. Mercer Adam, with the cooperation of Goldwin Smith and others.

United with *Belford's monthly magazine* to form *Rose-Belford's Canadian monthly and national review.*

A supplement entitled "Annals of Canada", compiled by William White, was issued with the *Canadian monthly* from Mar. 1875 to May 1878.

The Canadian nation; a national journal devoted to constructive Canadian thought.

v. 1, no. 1-26; Mar. 15, 1919-May 15, 1920. Ottawa [etc.] 26 no.

    Edited by D. M. LeBourdais.

    Nos. 1-7 published in Calgary.

    No more published?

The Canadian nation. v. 1-2, no. 2; Feb. 1928-May/June 1929. Ottawa, Association of Canadian Clubs. 2 v. illus.

    Issues for Feb.-Apr. 1928 have no numbering, but constitute v. 1, no. 1-2.

Canadian Political Science Association *Papers and proceedings of the annual meeting.* v. [1]-6; 1913-34. Montreal [etc.] 6 v. illus.

    No meetings held between 1913-1930.

    Title varies slightly.

    Superseded by the *Canadian journal of economics and political science.*

    Index to v. 1-6 in the *Canadian journal of economics and political science,* v. 1, pp. 131-135.

Canadian public administration. Administration publique du Canada. v. 1-   Mar. 1958- . Toronto. v.

    "Journal of the Institute of Public Administration of Canada".

    Indexes: Vols. 1-15, 1958-72. 1 v.

The Canadian spokesman; the magazine on national affairs. v. 1, no. 1-4; Jan.-May 1941. Ottawa, J. S. Connolley. 4 no. ports.

Canadiana; a collection of Canadian notes published monthly. v. 1-2; Jan. 1889-Dec. 1890. Montreal, Gazette Print. Co. 2 v. illus.

    Edited by W. J. White.

Chatelaine. v. 1-   Mar. 1928-   Toronto, Maclean-Hunter [etc.]   v. illus., ports.

    Absorbed *Canadian home journal* in Sept. 1958.

Cité libre. [1.]-16. année (no 1-88/89); juin 1950-juil./août 1966. Montréal. 16 v.

    1950-53 (nos. 1-8) also called v. 1-3.

    Edited by P. E. Trudeau, Gérard Pelletier, and others.

    Superseded by *Cahiers de Cité libre.*

Commentator. v. 5, no. 12-v. 15 no. 10; Dec. 1961-Oct. 1971. Toronto, W. H. Baxter. 10 v. illus., ports.

    Continues the *Canadian commentator.*

    Cover title, Dec. 1961-Sept. 1962: *The Canadian commentator.*

    Editors: 1961-64, P. W. Fox; 1964-71, John Gellner; 1971, Gordon Donaldson.

Culture; revue trimestrielle, sciences religieuses et profanes au Canada. v. 1-31; mars 1940-déc. 1970. Québec, Association des recherches sur les sciences religieuses et profanes au Canada. 31 v.

    Vol. 1 also called v. 5 in continuation of the numbering of *Nos cahiers,* which it supersedes.

    English and French.

    Indexes: Vols. 1-31, 1940-70, with v. 31.

Dalhousie review. v. 1-   Apr. 1921-Halifax, N.S., Dalhousie University Press [etc.] v.

    Published 1921-spring 1966 by Review Pub. Co.

The Dominion illustrated monthly. v. 1-7, July 7, 1888-Dec. 26, 1891; [ser. 2] v. 1-3, Feb. 1892-95. Montreal, Sabiston Lithographic and Pub. Co. [etc.] 10 v. illus., ports.

    Title varies: 1888-91, *The Dominion illustrated,* a Canadian pictorial weekly.

    Founded and for some years published by G. E. Desbarats.

    Contains a wide selection of portraits of political and other public personalities.

The Dominion review. v. 1-4; Mar. 1896-Dec. 1899. Toronto. 4 v.

Elgin Historical Society *Publications.* no. [1]-   St. Thomas, Ont., 1895-   . v. illus., ports.

    Nos. 1-4 published by the society under its earlier name: Elgin Historical and Scientific Institute.

    Each no. has distinctive title; some nos. published without series title.

Empire Club of Canada *Addresses.* 1903/04-   Toronto.   v. ports.

    Title varies: 1903/04-1910/11, *Empire Club speeches.*

    Title varies slightly.

    Indexes: 1903/04-1953, in 1952/53.

               1903/04-1964, in 1963/64.

Essex Historical Society *Papers and addresses.* v. 1-3. Windsor, Ont. 1913-21. 3 v. illus., ports.

The Grand Manan historian. no. 1-   May 1934-   . Grand Manan, N.B. Grand Manan Historical Society.   no. illus., ports.

    Some nos. have also distinctive title.

Histoire sociale. Social history. v. 1-   avril 1968-   [Ottawa] Editions de l'Université d'Ottawa.

    Issued jointly by the Université d'Ottawa and Carleton University.

Historic Kingston. no. 1-   1952-   Kingston, Ont., Kingston Historical Society. v. illus., ports.

"Being the Transactions of the Kingston Historical Society."

Historical and Scientific Society of Manitoba *Papers.* ser. 3, no. [1]-   1944/45- Winnipeg.   v. illus., ports.

Continues the society's *Transactions.*

Title varies: 1964/65-1965/66, *Transactions.*

Cover title: 1966/67-   *Transactions.*

Some issues accompanied by supplements.

Historical and Scientific Society of Manitoba *Transactions.* no. 1-72, Oct. 10, 1882-Nov. 1906; new ser., no. 1-5, Nov. 24, 1926-July 1930. Winnipeg. 77 no. illus.

Title varies: no. 1-2, 4-5, *Publication.*

A general title page was issued for Transaction no. 1-34 and Annual reports for the years 1880 to 1888 with title: *Transactions and proceedings.*

No. 7-11 are numbered no. 1-5 "season 1883-4"; new ser., no. 1-2 issued without vol. numbering.

Transaction no. 1-19, 23 published by the society under its earlier name: Manitoba Scientific and Historical Society.

Continued by the society's *Papers.*

Horizons; the Marxist quarterly. no. 19-28; autumn 1966-winter 1969. Toronto, Progress Books. 10 no.

Continues the *Marxist quarterly.*

English and French.

Edited by Stanley B. Ryerson.

Index to no. 19-27 includes that to no. 11-18 of the journal under its earlier title.

Huron Institute   *Papers and records.* v. 1-3. Collingwood, Ont., 1909-39. 3 v. illus., ports.

No more published?

Les Idées. v. 1-9, no 6; jan. 1935-juin 1939. Montréal, Editions du Totem. 9 v.

Vols. 1-9 also called 1.-5. année.

Edited by Albert Pelletier.

Institut canadien de Montréal   *Annuaire.* 1866-69. Montréal, Impr. L. Perrault [etc.] 4 no.

Institut canadien de Québec   *Annuaire.* no 1-13; 1874-89. Québec, Impr. générale A. Côté. 13 no. in 12.

Institute of Public Administration of Canada *Proceedings of the annual conference.* 1st-11th; 1949-59. Toronto. 11 v.

Jack Canuck; a weekly review of what the people think, say and do. v. 1-   July 29, 1911-   Toronto, R. Rogers.   v. illus.

Subtitle varies slightly.

Journal of Canadian studies. Revue d'études canadiennes. v. 1-   May 1966- Peterborough, Ont., Trent University. v.

Kent Historical Society   *Papers and addresses.* v. [1]-   Chatham, Ont., 1914- v. illus., ports.

Publication suspended 1925-50.

Vols. for 1914-24 have no vol. numbering but constitute v. 1-6.

La Kermesse; revue hebdomadaire. no. 1-11/12; 23 sept. 1892-27 mars 1893. Québec, Impr. L. Brousseau. 12 nos. in 10.

Concerned primarily with literature and history of Quebec.

Kingston, Ont. Queen's University   *Bulletin of the departments of History and Political and Economic Science.* no. 1-59; Oct. 1911-May 1930. Kingston. 59 no.

Each no. has also distinctive title.

The Lake magazine. v. 1, no. 1-9; Aug. 1892-Apr. 1893. Toronto, Lake Pub. Co. 9 no. illus., ports.

No more published?

Lennox and Addington Historical Society *Papers and records.* v. 1-13. Napanee, Ont., 1909-28. 13 v. illus., ports.

Some vols. have also distinctive title.

London and Middlesex Historical Society *Transactions.* pt. [1]-15; 1902/07-1937. [London, Ont.] 1908-37. 15 v. illus., ports.

Title varies: 1902/07, *Programs;* 1908/09, *Papers.*

No more published?

McGill University   *Economic studies.* no. 1-17. Montreal, Published by the Packet-Times Press [etc.] Orillia, for the Dept. of Economics and Political Science, McGill University [1925-30] 17 no. illus.

Cover title, no. 1-4: McGill University publication series XV.

Each no. has also distinctive title.

McGill University   *Publications.* Series VI: History and economics. no. 1-17. Montreal, 1910-31 [no. 1, 1921] 17 no. illus., ports.

No. 2 issued without series title or number.

Each no. has also distinctive title.

Le Maclean. v. 1-   mars 1961-   . Montréal, Maclean-Hunter.   v. illus., ports.

Title varies: 1961-avril 1971, *Le Magazine Maclean.*

Maclean's; Canada's national magazine. v. 21, no. 5- Mar. 1911- . Toronto, Maclean-Hunter [etc.] v. illus., ports.

Continues the *Busy man's magazine*.

Title varies: 1911-Mar. 1, 1921, *MacLean's magazine*.

Indexes: Vols. 27-50, 1914-37. 1 v.

The McMaster University monthly. v. 1-39; June 1891-May 1930. Toronto. 39 v. illus., ports.

Superseded by the *McMaster silhouette*, the *Marmor*, and the *McMaster monthly* (later the *Muse*).

The Manitoba arts review. v. 1-[13]; spring 1938-1958/59. [Winnipeg] Varsity Arts Council of the Faculty of Arts of the University of Manitoba [etc.] 13 v.

Publication suspended between winter 1948/49 and winter 1952.

Continued by *Arts review*.

Indexes: vol. 1-4, 1938-45, in v. 4.

The Manitoban; a monthly magazine and review of current events. v. 1-2, no. 10; Dec. 1891-Oct. 1893. Winnipeg. 2 v. illus., ports.

No more published?

The Maritime advocate and busy East Sackville, N.B., Busy East Press. v. illus., ports.

Published 1910-Mar. 1956. Cf. Union list of serials.

Title varies: 1910-July 1933, *Busy East of Canada*.

Continued by the *Atlantic advocate*.

The Marxist quarterly. no. 1-18; spring 1962-summer 1966. Toronto, Progress Books. 18 no. illus.

Edited by Stanley B. Ryerson.

Continued by *Horizons*.

Indexes: No. 1-10, 1962-64, in no. 10.

Index to no. 11-18 included with that to no. 19-27 of the journal under its later title.

Massey's magazine. v. 1-3; Jan. 1896-June 1897. Toronto, Massey Press. 3 v. illus., ports.

Edited by F. W. Falls.

Merged into the *Canadian magazine*.

Mer douce; the Algonquin Historical Society magazine. no. 1-14; May 1921-June 1924. Toronto. 14 no. illus., ports.

Issues for May 1921-Oct./Nov. 1922 called v. 1, no. 1-v. 2, no. 2.

Subtitle varies.

Published May 1921-Jan./Mar. 1922 by the society under its earlier name: Georgian Bay Historical Society.

No more published?

Missisquoi County Historical Society Report. 1st- [1899/1905]- [Bedford, Que., etc.] 1906- v. illus., ports.

Title varies: 4th (1908/09), 6th-7th (1960-61), *Annual report*; 8th (1965) *Historical report*; 9th (1967)- have distinctive titles only and are called v. 9-

Publication suspended between the issue of the fifth report in 1913 and the sixth in 1960.

Le Monde illustré. 1.-24. année, [no 24]; 10 mai 1884-12 oct. 1907. Montréal. 24 v. illus., ports.

Title varies: Apr. 19, 1892-June 15, 1907, *Album universel*. (At head of title in smaller type, Le Monde illustré.)

Beginning with Apr. 24, 1886, includes supplement entitled "Feuilleton du Monde illustré", called later "Feuilleton de l'Album universel".

Includes portraits of Canadian politicians.

Le Mouvement catholique; revue hebdomadaire du mouvement catholique dans le monde entier. v. 1-5; jan. 1898-juin 1900/ , Trois Rivières, Qué. 5 v.

The Muse. v. 40-69, Nov. 1930-1960; [1961]- Hamilton, Ont., Board of Publications, McMaster University [etc.] v. illus.

Supersedes in part the *McMaster University monthly* and continues its vol. numbering.

Title varies: Nov. 1930-Mar. 1935, *The McMaster monthly*; Nov. 1935-Apr. 1938, *The Quarterly*, McMaster University; Nov. 1938-Apr. 1942, *The McMaster University quarterly*; Dec. 1942-Dec. 1944, *The Muse*, McMaster University (cover title: The McMaster University Muse); Feb. 1945-Apr. 1946, *The McMaster University muse*; Nov. 1946-spring 1953, *The McMaster muse* (cover title: Nov. 1949- , Muse).

The Nation. v. 1-3, no. 39; Apr. 2, 1874-Sept. 29, 1876. Toronto. 3 v.

Edited by E. L. Godkin.

Organ of the Canada First movement.

The National monthly and Canadian home. v. 3-11, no. 3; Oct. 1905-Apr. 1906. Toronto. 6 no. illus., ports.

Formed by the union of the *National monthly of Canada* and *Canadian home*.

Continues the vol. numbering of *Canadian home*.

Vol. 3, no. 2-v. 10, no. 1 omitted in numbering.

The National monthly of Canada. v. 1-7, no. 3; June 1902-Sept. 1905. Toronto. 7 v. illus., ports.

United with the *Canadian home* to form the *National monthly and Canadian home.*

The New age; a family journal of social and economic progress. v. 1-3, no. 10; Sept. 21, 1939-June 1941. Montreal, New Age Associates. 3 v. illus.

New Brunswick Historical Society *Collections.* no. 1- . St. John, N.B., 1894-v. illus., ports.

Publication suspended 1931-54.
No. 1-3 called v. 1.

The New Brunswick magazine. v. 1-5, no. 1; July 1898-Feb. 1905. St. John, N.B. 5 v. illus., ports.

Publication suspended Jan. 1900-Aug. 1904.
Founded by W. K. Reynolds.

New Dominion monthly. Oct. 1867-Jan. 1879. Montreal, J. Dougall. v. illus., ports.

Vols. for Oct. 1867-June 1869 called v. 1-4, no. 3.

New frontier. v. 1-2, no. 5; Apr. 1936-Oct. 1937. Toronto. 2 v. illus.

Editors: Margaret Gould, Dorothy Livesay, William Lawson, J. F. White (with Leo Kennedy, Apr.-June 1936).

New frontiers. v. 1-5, no. 2; winter 1952-summer 1956. Toronto. 5 v. illus.

Edited by Margaret Fairley.
Indexes: Vols. 1-4, 1952-55, with v. 4.

New world. v. 1-9, no. 1; Mar. 1940-Feb./Mar. 1948. Toronto, Anglo-Canadian Publishers. 9 v. illus., ports.

Title varies: 1940-Jan. 1944, *New world illustrated* (cover title: Nov. 1942-Jan. 1944, New world).
Published 1940-Feb. 1943 in Montreal.
Edited by J. K. Thomas, published by E. P. Taylor.
Merged into *New liberty.*

Newfoundland quarterly. v. 1- July 1901-. St. John's, Nfld., Creative Printers and Publishers [etc.] v. illus., ports.

Suspended during 1952.
Title varies: Nov. 1966-June 1970, *The New Newfoundland quarterly* (cover title: Nov. 1966-winter 1970/71).
Published 1901-51 by J. J. Evans, 1953-spring 1965 by L. W. Jones.
Issues for Nov. 1966- include "Aspects",

the official organ of the Newfoundland Historical Society.

Niagara Historical Society *Records of Niagara.* no. 1- Niagara-on-the-Lake, Ont. [etc.] 1896- v. illus., ports.

Title varies: 1896, *Transactions;* no. 2-37 (1897-1925) [Publications].
No. 16 not numbered.
The second editions of no. 1, 7 and 10 issued as no. 12, 21 and 19 respectively.
Some nos. have also distinctive title.

La Nouvelle-France; revue mensuelle. v. 1, no. 1-15; 1 août 1881-1 juil. 1882. Québec. 15 no.

Preceded by a number called "numéro-spécimen" dated May 1, 1881.
Subtitle varies.
Edited by Jacques Auger.

La Nouvelle-France; revue des intérêts religieux et nationaux du Canada français. t. 1-17; jan. 1902-juin 1918. Québec. 17 v. illus.

United with *Parler français* to form *Le Canada français,* 1918-46.

Nouvelle-France; revue trimestrielle du Canada français. no. 13-23/24; avril/juin 1960-64. Montréal, Associés de Neuve-France. no.

Continues *Les Cahiers de Nouvelle-France.*
Title in masthead: La Revue Nouvelle-France.
No more published?

La Nouvelle relève. v. [1]-6, no 5; sept. 1941-sept. 1948. Montréal. 6 v.

Supersedes *La Relève.*

La Nouvelle revue canadienne. v. 1-3, no. 5; fév./mars 1951-May/July 1956. Ottawa. 3 v.

Vol. 3, no. 3-5 in English and French.
Vol. 3, no. 4-5 have title: NRC; La Nouvelle revue canadienne, National review of Canada.
Indexes: Vols. 1-3, no. 3, 1951-Apr./May 1954 (1 v.)
No more published?

Nova Francia; revue d'histoire du Canada. v. 1-7, no. 2; 24 juin 1925-juil./déc. 1932. Paris. 7 v. illus., ports.

"Organe de la Société d'histoire du Canada."

Nova Scotia Historical Society *Collections.* v. 1- 1878- . Halifax, 1879-v. illus., ports.

Title varies: 1878 and 1882/83, *Report and*

collections of the Nova Scotia Historical Society.

Indexes: Vols. 1-32, 1878-1959, in v. 33.

Okanagan Historical Society *Annual report*. 1st- 1926- Vernon, B.C. v. illus., ports.

Title varies slightly.

Reports for 1926-31 issued by the society under its earlier name: Okanagan Historical and Natural History Society.

Edited by Margaret A. Ormsby and others.

The Onlooker; a literary journal of independent critical opinion on public affairs. v. 1-2, no. 4; Apr. 1920-June 1922. Toronto. 2 v.

Subtitle varies.

Edited by James Cobourg Hodgins.

Consists of running comments on contemporary political affairs in Canada and abroad. Articles are, for the most part, unsigned.

No more published?

Ontario Historical Society *Papers and records*. v. 1-38. Toronto, 1899-1946. 38 v. illus., ports.

Vol. 4, pt. 2 never issued.

Continued by *Ontario history*.

Indexes: Vols. 1-20, 1899-1923, in v. 20.

Vols. 1-32, 1899-1937, in v. 32.

Vols. 33-43, 1939-51, in v. 42.

Ontario history. v. 39- 1947- . Toronto, Ontario Historical Society. v. illus., ports.

Continues the society's *Papers and records*.

Annual, 1947-48; quarterly, 1949-

Issues for 1947-June 1962 have added title: *Papers & records*.

Absorbed the society's *News letter* in 1949.

Index: Vols. 1-64, 1899-1972. 1 v.

L'Opinion publique; journal hebdomadaire illustré. v. 1-14; 1 jan. 1870-27 déc. 1883. Montréal, Cie lithographique-Burland [etc.] 14 v. illus., ports.

Subtitle varies slightly. ·

Editors: 1870-73, L. O. David, J. A. Mousseau; 1873-74, Oscar Dunn; 1875, A. Achintre; 1876, G. E. Desbarats.

Our generation. v. 1- autumn 1961- Montreal. v. illus.

Title varies: 1961-Apr. 1965, *Our generation against nuclear war*.

Vol. 1-5, no. 1 issued by the Student Union for Peace Action (v. 1-3, no. 2, under its earlier name: Combined Universities Campaign for Nuclear Disarmament).

The Outlook. v. 1-14; Apr. 20, 1948-Mar. 1962. Toronto, Responsible Enterprise. 14 v. illus.

Published by Gladstone Murray.

Parti pris. v. [1]-5, no. 8/9; oct. 1963-été 1968. Montréal. 5 v. illus., ports.

Concentrates on politics in the province of Quebec.

Le Pays laurentien; revue mensuelle. 1.-3. année; jan. 1916-déc. 1918. Montréal, G. Malchelosse. 3 v. illus., ports.

Editors: 1916, Pierre Heribert; 1917-18, Gérard Malchelosse and Emile Coderre.

Superseded by *Revue nationale* (Montreal, 1919-32).

The Prince Edward Island magazine. v. 1- . Mar. 1899- . Charlottetown, P.E.I., A. Irwin. v. illus., ports.

Ceased publication 1905? cf. Union list of serials.

Includes Mar. 1904- . The Educational outlook.

Public affairs. v. 1-15, no. 3; Aug. 1937-spring 1953. Halifax, N.S., Institute of Public Affairs, Dalhousie University. 15 v.

Official journal of the Union of Nova Scotia Municipalities, Union of New Brunswick Municipalities and Maritime Bureau of Industrial Relations, 1938-48.

Quebec (City) Université Laval. Faculté des sciences sociales *Cahiers*. v. [1]-5. Québec, 1941-49. 5 v.

Each no. has also distinctive title.

Vols. for 1941-43 issued by the Faculty under an earlier name: Ecole des sciences sociales, politiques et économiques de Laval.

Vols. for 1945-49 issued by the Faculty's Service extérieur d'éducation sociale.

Some nos. issued in cooperation with Société canadienne d'enseignement postscolaire.

Superseded by *Culture populaire*, issued by the Centre de culture populaire, Université Laval.

Queen's quarterly. v. 1- July 1893- Kingston, Ont., Queen's University. v. illus.

Indexes: Vols. 1-60, 1893-1953. 1 v.

Vols. 61-75, 1954-68. 1 v.

The Rebel. v. 1-4, no. 6; Feb. 1917-Mar. 1920. Toronto. 4 v. illus.

"Published by members of the University of Toronto."

Superseded by the *Canadian forum*.

Recherches sociographiques. v. 1- jan./ mars 1960- . Québec, Presses de l'Université Laval. v. illus.

Published by the Département de sociologie et d'anthropologie (called 1960, Départment de sociologie) of the Université Laval (1960-61 in collaboration with Centre de recherches sociales).

Indexes: Vols. 1-5, 1960-64. 1 v.

Relations. 1.- année; jan. 1941- Montréal. v.

Supersedes *L'Ordre nouveau.*

"Publié par un groupe de membres de la Compagnie de Jésus."

Published 1941-49 by Ecole sociale populaire (later Institut sociale populaire).

Indexes: Vols. 1-10, 1941-50, with v. 11.

Le Réveil; journal hebdomadaire. v. 1, no. 1-31; 27 mai-23 déc. 1876. Montréal, A. Buies. 31 no.

Edited by Arthur Buies.

Published May 27-Sept. 16 in Quebec.

Review of historical publications relating to Canada. v. 1-22; 1896-1917/18. Toronto, University of Toronto Press [etc.] 1897-1919. 22 v. (University of Toronto studies)

G. M. Wrong, editor (with H. H. Langton, 1897-1910, 1913-18; W. S. Wallace, 1911-18).

Published by W. Briggs, 1897; the librarian of the University of Toronto, 1898-1903; Morang, 1904-09.

Superseded by the *Canadian historical review.*

Indexes: Vols. 1-10, 1895-1905. 1 v.

Vols. 11-20, 1906-1915. 1 v.

La Revue acadienne; publication historique et littéraire. 1.-2. année, no 3; jan. 1917-mai/juin 1918. Montréal. 2 v. illus., ports.

Edited by E. D. Aucoin.

Revue canadienne. t. 1-53; 1864-1907; nouv. sér. v. 1-27, 1908-22. Montréal. 80 v. in illus.

Vols. 17-23 (1881-87) also called new ser., v. 1-7; v. 24-28 (1888-92), ser. 3, v. 1-4.

Vols. 29-53 also called 29.-43. année.

Vols. 27 (1891) and 28 (1892) incorrectly called v. 26 and 27.

Title varies slightly.

Indexes: Vols. 1-16, 1864-79, with v. 16.

Vols. 1-53, 1864-1907. 1 v.

Revue d'histoire de l'Amérique française. v. 1- juin 1947- - Montréal, Institut d'histoire de l'Amérique française. v.

Editors: 1947-67, Lionel Groulx; 1967- Rosario Bilodeau.

Indexes: Vols. 1-10, 1947-57, in v. 10.

Vols. 11-20, 1957-67. 1 v.

Revue d'histoire de la Gaspésie. v. 1- jan./mars 1963- . Gaspé, Société historique de la Gaspésie. v. illus., ports.

English and French.

Revue de l'Université d'Ottawa. 1.- année; 1931- [Ottawa] v. illus.

Contributions in French and English.

Indexes: Vols. 1-10, 1931-40. 1 v.

Vols. 11-20, 1941-50. 1 v.

Vols.21-30, 1951-60. 1 v.

Vols. 31-40, 1961-70. 1 v.

La Revue de l'Université de Sherbrooke. v. 1-5; nov. 1960-juin 1965. Sherbrooke, Que. 5 v. illus.

English and French.

La Revue de l'Université Laval, v. 1-21, no. 4; sept. 1946-déc. 1966. Québec. 21 v.

Supersedes *Le Canada français,* 1918-46.

"Publication de l'Université Laval et de la Société du parler français au Canada."

Indexes: Vols. 1-18, 1946-63. 1 v.

Revue de Montréal. t. 1-5, no. 1; fév. 1877-81. Montréal. 5 v.

Vols. 1-5 also called 1.-5. année.

La Revue franco-américaine. t. 1-10; avril 1908-avril 1913. Montréal [etc.] 10 v. illus., ports.

Vols. 1-10 also called 1.-5. année.

Vols. 1-6 published in Quebec.

Accompanied by supplement "L'illustration".

La Revue moderne. 1.-42. année, no 2; 15 nov. 1919-juin 1960. Montréal. 42 v. illus., ports.

Publication suspended Dec. 1938-Apr. 1939.

Superseded by *Châtelaine* (Montreal, 1960-).

La Revue nationale; magazine mensuel illustré. v. 1-3; fév. 1895-mars 1896. Montréal, J.-D. Chartrand. 3 v. illus., ports.

La Revue nationale. Montréal. v.

Issued 1919-32. Cf. Union list of serials.

Supersedes *Le Pays laurentien.*

"Organe de la Société Saint-Jean-Baptiste de Montréal."

La Revue socialiste; pour l'indépendance absolue du Québec et la libération prolétarienne-nationale des Canadiens français. no 1- printemps 1959- Montréal. no. illus.

Editors: 1959- Raoul Roy.

Revue trimestrielle canadienne. v. 1-40 (no 1-160); mai 1915-hiver 1954. Montréal. 40 v. illus.

Published by the Association des diplômés de polytechnique (called May 1915-Sept. 1942, Association des anciens élèves) of the Ecole polytechnique, Université de Montréal.

Vols. 1-40 also called 1.-40. année.

Continued by *L'Ingénieur*.

Rose-Belford's Canadian monthly and national review. v. 1-8; July 1878-June 1882. Toronto, Rose-Belford Pub. Co. 8 v. illus.

Formed by the union of *Canadian monthly* and *National review* and *Belford's monthly magazine*.

Editors: 1878-79, George Stewart, Jr.; 1879-82, G. M. Adam.

Royal Society of Canada *Proceedings and transactions. Délibérations et mémoires.* v. 1-12, 1882/83-1894; ser. 2, v. 1-12, 1895-1906; ser. 3, v. 1-56, 1907-62; ser. 4, v. 1- , 1963- . Ottawa, [etc.] v. illus., ports.

Added t.p. in French, 1882/83-1968: Mémoires et comptes rendus de la Société royale du Canada.

Some vols. accompanied by supplements.

Indexes: General index.

Vols. 1-12, 1882-94, in v. 12.

Vols. 1-ser. 2, v. 12, 1882-1906. 1 v.

Vols. 1-ser. 3, v. 36, 1882-1943, Transactions, Sections 1-2. 1 v.

Author index.

Ser. 3, v. 1-35, 1907-41, Transactions, Sections 1-5. 1 v.

Saguenayensia; revue de la Société historique du Saguenay. v. 1- jan./fév. 1959- . Chicoutimi. v. illus., ports.

Supersedes the Society's Bulletin.

Editor: 1959- Victor Tremblay.

Indexes: Vols. 1-8, 1959-66, in v. 9.

Saskatchewan history. v. 1- winter 1948- . Saskatoon. v. illus., ports.

"Published . . . under the auspices of the Saskatchewan Archives Board."

Edited by Hilda Neatby, L. H. Thomas, and others.

Saturday night. v. 1- Dec. 3, 1887- Toronto. v. illus., ports.

Title varies: 1887-July 15, 1911, *Toronto Saturday night;* Aug. 1962-June/July 1963, *The Canadian Saturday night.*

Absorbed the *Canadian* in Aug. 1962.

Editors: 1887-1906, Edmund E. Sheppard; 1906-09, Joseph T. Clark; 1909-26, Frederick Paul; 1926-32, Hector Charlesworth; 1932-51, B. K. Sandwell.

The Saturday reader. v. 1-4 (no. 1-104) Sept. 9, 1865-Aug. 31, 1867. Montreal, R.Worthington [etc.] 4 v. illus., ports.

Sept-jours. [1.]- année; 17 sept. 1966- Montréal. v. illus., ports.

Sample issue, called no. 0, issued in June 1966.

Simcoe County Pioneer and Historical Society *Pioneer papers.* no. 1-6. Barrie [Ont.] 1908-17. 6 no. illus., ports.

Société historique acadienne *Cahier.* 1.- 1961- . Moncton, N.B. v. illus.

No. 12- also called v. 2, no. 2.

Indexes: No. 1-20, 1961-68, in no. 20.

Société historique de la Chaudière *Publication.* no. 1- . Ste-Marie de Beauce (St. Joseph de Beauce) 1948- . v. illus.

Each no. has also distinctive title.

Société historique de la Côte-du-Sud *Bulletin.* no [1]- [1949?] Sainte-Anne-de-la-Pocatière, Que. no. illus.

First issue unnumbered, undated and lacks title.

Issued to 1953 by the society under its earlier name: Société historique de Kamouraska.

Société historique de Montréal *Mémoires.* [1.]-12. livr. Montréal, 1859-1921. 12 v.

Title varies: 1859, *Mémoires et documents relatifs à l'histoire du Canada;* 2.-3. livr. (1859-60), *Mémoires et documents.*

Nos. 4-12 have also distinctive titles.

No more published?

Contains material on pre-Confederation only.

Société historique de Québec *Cahiers d'histoire.* no 1- Québec, 1947- no. illus., ports.

No. 1 issued by the Society under an earlier name: Société d'histoire régionale de Québec.

Each no. has also distinctive title.

Société historique de Saint-Boniface *Bulletin.* v. 1-5, fasc. 3; 1911-15. St. Boniface, Man. [etc.] 5 v. illus., ports.

Vol. 5, pt. 2 dated 1916.

English and French.

Société historique du Nouvel-Ontario *Documents historiques.* no. 1- Sudbury, Ont., 1942- . no. illus., ports.

Each no. has also distinctive title.

Indexes: No. 1-35, 1942-58, in no. 36.

Société Saint Jean Baptiste de Québec   *Annales*. v. [1]-4; 1880-1902. Québec, 1881-1903. 4 v. illus.

> Title varies: 1880-89: *Fête nationale des Canadiens-Français.*
>
> Compiled by H. J. J. B. Chouinard.

The Statesman; a national weekly journal of progressive thought. no. 3; July 27, 1918-Jan. 15, 1921. Toronto. 4 v.

> Edited by Lindsay Crawford.

Stewart's quarterly; an original magazine. v. 1-5; Apr. 1867-Jan. 1872. St. John, N.B., Printed by H. Chubb. 5 v.

> Caption title: 1867-Jan. 1870, *Stewart's literary quarterly magazine.*
>
> Cover title: Apr. 1869-Jan. 1870, *Stewart's quarterly magazine.*
>
> Edited by George Stewart.

The Tamarack review. issue 1-   autumn 1956-   . Toronto.   no. illus.

> Indexes: No. 1-20, autumn 1956-summer 1961, in no. 21.
>
> No. 21-41, autumn 1961-autumn 1966, in no. 42.

Le Terroir; revue mensuelle illustrée. v. 1-20; juil. 1918-mars 1946. Québec.   v. illus., ports.

> "Organe de la Société des arts, sciences et lettres de Québec."
>
> Subtitle varies slightly.
>
> No more published?

Thunder Bay Historical Society   *Papers*. 1908/09-1927/28. [Fort William, Ont.] 17 v. illus., ports.

> Title varies: 1909/10, *Reports of officers and papers.*
>
> Includes the society's annual report.

The University magazine. v. 1-19, no. 2; Dec. 1901-Apr. 1920. Montreal [etc.] 19 v. illus., ports.

> Title varies: 1901-06: *The McGill University magazine.*
>
> Issued Oct. 1907-20 by a committee for McGill University, Toronto University, and Dalhousie College.
>
> Editor, 1907-20, Andrew Macphail.

The University of Toronto monthly. v. 1-48, no. 3; July 1900-Dec. 1947. [Toronto] Alumni Federation of the University of Toronto [etc.] 48 v. illus., ports.

> Title varies: Nov. 1907-Nov. 1918, *The University monthly.*
>
> Errors in numbering.
>
> Issued July 1900-Dec. 1921 by the Society under the name: University of Toronto Alumni Association.
>
> Incorporated in the *Varsity graduate.*
>
> Supplements accompany some numbers.

The University of Toronto quarterly. v. 1-3, no. 2; Mar. 1895-Dec. 1896. Toronto. 3 v. illus.

University of Toronto quarterly. v. 1-Oct. 1931-   [Toronto] University of Toronto Press.   v. illus.

The University of Windsor review; a publication of the University of Windsor. [v. 1]-   spring 1965-   . Windsor, Ont. v. illus.

University quarterly review; occupied with subjects of current thought. 1st-2d quarter; Feb.-June 1890. Toronto. 2 v.

La Vie canadienne. t. 1-2, no. 10; 11 juil. 1918-25 mai 1919. Québec. 2 v.

Waterloo Historical Society   *Annual volume*. 1st-   [1912/13]-   Kitchener, Ont., 1913-   . v. illus., ports.

> Title varies: 1912/13-56, *Annual report*; 1966-   issued without title.

The Waterloo review. no. 1-6; spring 1958-winter 1961. [Waterloo, Ont., etc.] 6 no.

> No. 1-4 issued as v. 1, no. 1-2, v. 2, no. 1-2.
>
> Title varies slightly.
>
> Absorbed by *Alphabet.*

The Week; a Canadian journal of politics, literature, science and arts. v. 1-13, no. 52; Dec. 6, 1883-Nov. 20, 1896. Toronto. 13 v.

> Subtitle varies.
>
> Edited, 1883-Feb. 1884, by C. G. D. Roberts.

Welland County Historical Society   *Papers and records*. v. 1-5. Welland [Ont. 1924]-38. 5 v. illus., ports.

> Title varies: 1924, *Publication.*
>
> Vols. 1 and 4 have also distinctive titles.
>
> No more published?

Wellington County Historical Society   *Records*. v. 1-3; 1932-34. [Guelph, Ont.] 1933-   . 3 v. illus., ports.

> No more published?

Wentworth Historical Society   *Papers and records*. v. 1-11; 1892-1924. Hamilton [Ont.] 11 v. illus., ports.

> Title varies: 1892, 1902-08, *Journal and transactions*; 1899, *Transactions.*

Western Ontario historical notes. v. 1-Dec. 1942-   . London, Ont., Library, University of Western Ontario.   v. illus., ports.

Western Ontario history nuggets. no. 1-London, Ont., Lawson Memorial Library,

University of Western Ontario [1943]-
. no. illus., ports.
> Reproduced from typewritten copy.
> Each no. has also distinctive title.

Willisons monthly; a national magazine devoted to the discussion of public affairs affecting Canada and the Empire. v. 1-5, no. 3 (no. 1-51); June 1925-Sept. 1929. Toronto [etc.] Willisons. 5 v. illus., ports.
> Edited by Sir John Willison, June 1925-May 1927.
>> Published in Sarnia, Ont., Jan.-Sept. 1929.
>> Merged into *Canadian forum*.

A special feature is the section "From month to month" edited by Sir John Willison until his death in May 1927.

Women's Canadian Historical Society of Ottawa *Transactions*. v. 1-   1901-
[Ottawa]   v. illus.
> Publication suspended 1929-53.

Women's Canadian Historical Society of Toronto *Annual report and transactions*. no. 1-28; 1896-1933/34. [Toronto]   v. illus., ports.
> Previous to 1919/20 *Reports* and *Transactions* issued separately.

AUTHOR INDEX

Numbers supplied are column numbers.
Numbers following the colon are item numbers within
the column, counting 1 (one) as the first full entry
in the column.

SUBJECT INDEX

Numbers supplied are column numbers.
Numbers following the colon are item numbers within
the column, counting 1 (one) as the first full entry
in the column.

sible government, 151:9
Elections, federal; (1935),
718:4; (1962), 464:5; (1963),
489:3; (1965), 490:1
British North America Act,
809:10; 869:5; 883:5; 904:1;
927-954; amendment of,
405:3; 411:6; 419:2; 442:2;
470:6; amending formula,
see Fulton-Favreau formula;
distribution of powers, see
Distribution of powers;
financial provisions, see
Dominion-provincial rela-
tions, finance; repatriation
of, see Constitution
Broadcasting, 77:5; 98:2-3; 116:3;
333:3; 340:1; 442:8; 791:10;
870:11; 929:4; 1027:1; 1028:6.
See also Radio; Television;
Canadian Broadcasting
Corporation; Media
Broder, Andrew, 534:7
Brodeur, Louis Philippe, 686:9;
706:9
Brooks, Alfred Johnson, 602:5
Brown, George, 152:6; 638:7-
10; 639:6-7; 646:4; 647:6;
650:1; 653:1; oratory of,
150:8; and "big push" letter
(1872), 644:1; 646:3; 647:2;
648:8; 651:1; and labour,
126:4; and Macdonald, 149:5;
and Ontario South by-elec-
tion (1876), 144:6; and
reciprocity, 638:5; 648:7
Brown, Gordon, 138:6
Bruce, Alex D., 259:11
Bruce, Herbert Alexander
("Bruce Report"), see Canadian Medical Service Overseas, Report on
Bruce, John, 153:9
Brunet, Michel, 32:12
Bryce, James Bryce, viscount,
24:4; 958:10. See also
External Affairs, Dept. of
Bryce, Robert, 34:7
Buchanan, William Francis
Asbury, 716:2
Buck, Tim, 830:2; 832:3; 835:10;
836:1. See also Communist
Party
Budget, 119:5; 323:1; (1878),
654:10; (1885), 181:9-10;
(1909), 657:8; (1923/24),
716:9; (1928), 268:8; 291:10;
(1934), 565:6; (1936), 748:7;
(1939), 728:3; (1940), 722:9;
728:4; 744:4; 745:3; (1945),
725:3; 744:3; (1947), 346:2;
358:5; 730:5; (1948), 727:1-2;
(1949), 412:1; (1950), 405:1;
(1953), 401:1; (1958), 619:5;

621:5; (1961), 618:10-11;
621:1. See also Economic
policy; Fiscal policy
Burnaby-Coquitlam, B.C., 94:1;
464:2; 819:7
Burns, Patrick, 301:8; 333:2
Burton, Edgar G., 44:4
Business, 87:9; 92:2; 202:5;
316:4; 309:4; 419:10; 437:6;
816:1; 1030:1; 1039:1; and
government, 111:1; 320:2;
321:8; 323:4; 488:8; 849:3;
850:8-9; 862:6; 866:6; 957:5;
958:1; 974:6. See also Banking; Budget; Combines;
Economic policy; Finance;
Fiscal policy; Price controls;
Price spreads; Tariff
By-elections, 104:3; 231:8;
365:4; 373:5. See individual
listing under province and
constituency
Byng of Vimy, Julian
Hedworth George Byng,
viscount, 293:8. See also
Constitutional issue of 1926
Byng of Vimy, Marie Evelyn
Byng, viscountess, 283:5;
288:5
The Bystander, Toronto, 49:9;
and Canada Temperance
Act, 169:8. See also Smith,
Goldwin

C.C.F., see Co-operative Commonwealth Federation
C.P.R., see Canadian Pacific
Railway
Cabinet, 849:6; 861:6; 980:6;
982:3, 5; 986:5; (1867),
131:10; 138:7; 513:3; (1878),
172:3; (1896), 222:3; (1911),
207:8; 543:7; (1921), 272:9;
(1935), 314:11; (1948),
425:8; and Civil Service,
983:9-10; discretionary
powers, 982:7; function of,
72:8; 118:4; French Cana-
dians in, 986:6; leadership
in, 89:9; Minister, 80:5; 292:4;
329:8; 454:3; and ministry,
977:7; oaths, 981:2; position
of, 979:6-7; and pressure
groups, 980:1; and Privy
Council, 977:7; secretary to,
732:9; representative nature,
92:4; and war, 377:1. See also
Prime Minister
Cahan, Charles Hazlitt, 581:6
Calder, James Alexander,
558:11; 559:1
Cameron, John, 655:5
Cameron, Malcolm Colin,
135:7; 647:5

Camp, Dalton, 617:4; 627:9
Campaign funds, 57:3-4; 87:7;
99:2; 100:4-5; 109:2; 116:1;
253:7; 308:8; 323:8; 326:1;
338:6
Campbell, Sir Alexander,
497:2; 506:5; 518:6; 526:6
Canada and the Canadian
question (1891), 177:9. See
also Smith, Goldwin
Canada as a republic, see
Republic
Canada Council, 761:6
Canada First, 46:10; 124:1;
125:1; 126:5; 128:9; 131:7;
132:1-2; 134:5; 135:1; 137:5;
169:10; 170:1; 175:7; 178:1-2
Canada revue, 170:2
Canada Temperance Act
(1878), 152:2; 169:8; 187:8, 10;
726:5. See also Prohibition
Canada under the administra-
tion of the Earl of Dufferin
(1878), 146:3; 149:10
Canadian-American relations,
68:9; 465:9; 625:5
Canadian Army Medical
Corps, 230:2
Canadian Broadcasting Corpo-
ration, 365:10; 434:6; 479:9;
748:1; 761:5; 775:3; 791:10;
965:5; 992:9; 1028:6. See also
Media; Radio; Television
Canadian Club, 62:3; 89:1;
175:5; 209:7; 213:4; 226:7
Canadian Congress of
Labour, 830:1. See also
Labour; Trade unions
Canadian Council of Agri-
culture, 235:9. See also
Agriculture; Farmers
Canadian Federation of Agri-
culture, 65:6; 96:8. See also
Agriculture; Farmers
Canadian Forum, 100:6
Canadian High Commissioner
to London, 510:7
Canadian Institute of Public
Opinion, see Public opinion
surveys
Canadian Labour Congress,
437:3; 455:9; 489:2; and
C.C.F., 794:8; 800:5; 807:1;
811:3. See also Labour;
Trade unions
Canadian Manufacturers'
Association, 59:1-3
Canadian Medical Service
Overseas, Report on, 230:2
Canadian National Railways,
108:10; 315:1; 337:3; 341:4;
389:3. See also Railways
Canadian Northern Railway,